EQ

EQ

Encyclopaedia of the Qurʾān

VOLUME THREE

J–O

Jane Dammen McAuliffe, *General Editor*

Brill, Leiden–Boston

2003

ISBN 90 04 12354 7

Printed in The Netherlands on acid-free paper.

ABBREVIATIONS

AI = *Annales islamologiques*
AIUON = *Annali dell' Istituto Universitario Orientale di Napoli*
AO = *Acta orientalia*
AO-H = *Acta orientalia (Academiae Scientiarum Hungaricae)*
Arabica = *Arabica. Revue d'études arabes*
ARW = *Archiv für Religionswissenschaft*
AUU = *Acta Universitatis Upsaliensis*
BASOR = *Bulletin of the American Schools of Oriental Research*
BEO = *Bulletin d'études orientales de l'Institut Français de Damas*
BGA = *Bibliotheca geographorum arabicorum*
BIFAO = *Bulletin de l'Institut Français d'Archéologie Orientale du Caire*
BO = *Bibliotheca orientalis*
BSA = *Budapest studies in Arabic*
BSOAS = *Bulletin of the School of Oriental and African Studies*
Der Islam = *Der Islam. Zeitschrift für Geschichte und Kultur des islamischen Orients*
EI[1] = *Encyclopaedia of Islam,* 1st ed., Leiden 1913-38
EI[2] = *Encyclopaedia of Islam,* new ed., Leiden 1954-2002
ER = *Encyclopedia of religion,* ed. M. Eliade, New York 1986
ERE = *Encyclopaedia of religion and ethics*
GMS = *Gibb memorial series*
HO = *Handbuch der Orientalistik*
IA = *Islâm ansiklopedisi*
IBLA = *Revue de l'Institut des Belles Lettres Arabes, Tunis*
IC = *Islamic culture*
IJMES = *International journal of Middle East studies*
IOS = *Israel oriental studies*
IQ = *The Islamic quarterly*
Iran = *Iran. Journal of the British Institute of Persian Studies*
JA = *Journal asiatique*
JAL = *Journal of Arabic literature*
JAOS = *Journal of the American Oriental Society*
JE = *Jewish encyclopaedia*
JESHO = *Journal of the economic and social history of the Orient*
JIS = *Journal of Islamic studies*
JNES = *Journal of Near Eastern studies*
JRAS = *Journal of the Royal Asiatic Society*
JSAI = *Jerusalem studies in Arabic and Islam*
JSS = *Journal of Semitic studies*
MFOB = *Mélanges de la Faculté Orientale de l'Université St. Joseph de Beyrouth*
MIDEO = *Mélanges de l'Institut Dominicain d'études orientales du Caire*
MO = *Le monde oriental*
MSOS = *Mitteilungen des Seminars für orientalische Sprachen, westasiatische Studien*
Muséon = *Le Muséon. Revue des études orientales*
MW = *The Muslim world*
OC = *Oriens christianus*

OLZ = *Orientalistische Literaturzeitung*
Orientalia = *Orientalia. Commentarii periodici Pontificii Instituti Biblici*
Qanṭara = *al-Qanṭara. Revista de estudios arabes*
QSA = *Quaderni de studi arabi*
RCEA = *Répertoire chronologique d'épigraphie arabe*
REI = *Revue des études islamiques*
REJ = *Revue des études juives*
REMMM = *Revue du monde musulman et de la Méditerranée*
RHR = *Revue de l'histoire des religions*
RIMA = *Revue de l'Institut des Manuscrits Arabes*
RMM = *Revue du monde musulman*
RO = *Rocznik Orientalistyczny*
ROC = *Revue de l'orient chrétien*
RSO = *Rivista degli studi orientali*
SIr = *Studia iranica*
SI = *Studia islamica*
WI = *Die Welt des Islams*
WKAS = *Wörterbuch der klassischen arabischen Sprache*
WO = *Welt des Orients*
WZKM = *Wiener Zeitschrift für die Kunde des Morgenlandes*
ZAL = *Zeitschrift für arabische Linguistik*
ZDMG = *Zeitschrift der Deutschen Morgenländischen Gesellschaft*
ZGAIW = *Zeitschrift für Geschichte der arabisch-islamischen Wissenschaften*
ZS = *Zeitschrift für Semitistik*

AUTHORS OF ARTICLES

VOLUME III

Khaled M. Abou El Fadl, University of California at Los Angeles
Nasr Hamid Abu Zayd, University of Leiden
Charles J. Adams, McGill University (emeritus)
Ilai Alon, Tel Aviv University
Ludwig Ammann, Freiburg im Breisgau
Talal Asad, The Graduate Center, CUNY
Michael L. Bates, The American Numismatic Society, New York
Daniel Beaumont, University of Rochester, NY
Sheila Blair, Boston College
Khalid Y. Blankinship, Temple University, Philadelphia
Jonathan M. Bloom, Boston College
Issa J. Boullata, McGill University, Montreal
William M. Brinner, University of California, Berkeley
Jonathan E. Brockopp, Bard College, Annandale, NY
Ronald P. Buckley, University of Manchester
Heribert Busse, Muhlheim/Main
Simonetta Calderini, University of Surrey Roehampton
Jacqueline Chabbi, University of Paris
William R. Darrow, Williams College, Williamstown, MA
Jean-Louis Déclais, Centre Diocésain, Oran
François Déroche, École Pratique des Hautes Études, Paris
Jamal Elias, Amherst College, Amherst, MA
Mohammad Fadel, Augusta, GA
Reuven Firestone, Hebrew Union College, Los Angeles
Ersilia Francesca, Università degli Studi di Napoli "L'Orientale"
Patrick D. Gaffney, University of Notre Dame
Avner Giladi, University of Haifa
Claude Gilliot, University of Aix-en-Provence
Shalom L. Goldman, Emory University
Matthew S. Gordon, Miami University, Oxford, OH
William A. Graham, Harvard University
Frank Griffel, Yale University
Sidney H. Griffith, The Catholic University of America
Denis Gril, University of Aix-en-Provence
Sebastian Günther, University of Toronto
Wael B. Hallaq, McGill University

Isaac Hasson, Hebrew University, Jerusalem
Gerald R. Hawting, University of London
Peter Heath, American University of Beirut
Charles Hirschkind, University of Wisconsin
Shiu-Sian Angel Hsu, Santa Ana, CA
Alice C. Hunsberger, Asia Society, New York
Anthony Hearle Johns, Australian National University
Alan Jones, University of Oxford
Wadad Kadi (al-Qadi), University of Chicago
Marion H. Katz, Mount Holyoke College, South Hadley, MA
Meir-Jacob Kister, Hebrew University, Jerusalem
Ernst Axel Knauf, University of Bern
Alexander D. Knysh, University of Michigan
Kathryn Kueny, Lawrence University, Appleton, WI
Arzina R. Lalani, Institute of Ismaili Studies, London
Ella Landau-Tasseron, Hebrew University, Jerusalem
Pierre Larcher, University of Aix-en-Provence
Joseph Lowry, University of Pennsylvania
Gabriele Mandel Khan, Milan, Italy
Roxanne D. Marcotte, The University of Queensland, Australia
Manuela Marin, University of Madrid
Louise Marlow, Wellesley College, Wellesley, MA
Keith Massey, Jessup, MD
Ingrid Mattson, Hartford Seminary, Hartford, CT
Christopher Melchert, University of Oxford
Mustansir Mir, Youngstown State University, Youngstown, OH
Ebrahim Moosa, Duke University
Harald Motzki, University of Nijmegen
Ian R. Netton, University of Leeds
Angelika Neuwirth, Free University, Berlin
Irmeli Perho, The Royal Library, Copenhagen
Daniel C. Peterson, Brigham Young University
Wim Raven, University of Frankfurt
G. John Renard, St. Louis University
Efim A. Rezvan, Russian Academy of Sciences, St. Petersburg
Andrew Rippin, University of Victoria
Neal S. Robinson, University of Wales
Uri Rubin, Tel-Aviv University
Said S. Said, University of Durham
Sabine Schmidtke, Free University, Berlin
Cornelia Schöck, University of Freiburg im Breisgau
Marco Schöller, University of Köln
Stuart D. Sears, American University in Cairo
Michael A. Sells, Haverford College, Haverford, PA
Irfan Shahid, Georgetown University
Priscilla P. Soucek, New York University
Barbara Stowasser, Georgetown University
Roberto Tottoli, Università degli Studi di Napoli "L'Orientale"
Gérard Troupeau, École Pratique des Hautes Études, Paris
Daniel M. Varisco, Hofstra University
David Waines, Lancaster University
Paul E. Walker, University of Chicago
Gisela Webb, Seton Hall University
Lutz Wiederhold, University Library, Halle
A.H. Mathias Zahniser, Asbury Theological Seminary, Wilmore, KY
Muhammad Qasim Zaman, Brown University

SHORT TITLES

Abbott, *Studies II*
N. Abbott, *Studies in Arabic literary papyri. II. Qurʾānic commentary and tradition*, Chicago 1967

ʿAbd al-Bāqī
Muḥammad Fuʾād ʿAbd al-Bāqī, *al-Muʿjam al-mufahras li-alfāẓ al-Qurʾān al-karīm*, Cairo 1945

ʿAbd al-Jabbār, *Mutashābih*
ʿAbd al-Jabbār b. Aḥmad al-Asadābādī al-Qāḍī al-Hamadhānī, *Mutashābih al-Qurʾān*, ed. ʿAdnān M. Zarzūr, 2 vols., Cairo 1969

ʿAbd al-Jabbār, *Tanzīh*
ʿAbd al-Jabbār b. Aḥmad al-Asadābādī al-Qāḍī al-Hamadhānī, *Tanzīh al-Qurʾān ʿan al-maṭāʿin*, Beirut 1966

ʿAbd al-Raḥmān, *ʿAṣrī*
ʿĀʾisha ʿAbd al-Raḥmān, *al-Qurʾān wa-l-tafsīr al-ʿaṣrī*, Cairo 1970

ʿAbd al-Raḥmān, *Tafsīr*
ʿĀʾisha ʿAbd al-Raḥmān, *al-Tafsīr al-bayānī lil-Qurʾān al-karīm*, 3rd ed., Cairo 1968

ʿAbd al-Razzāq, *Muṣannaf*
ʿAbd al-Razzāq b. Hammām al-Ṣanʿānī, *al-Muṣannaf*, ed. Ḥabīb al-Raḥmān al-Aʿẓamī, 11 vols., Beirut 1390/1970; 2nd ed. Johannesburg 1983; ed. Muḥammad Sālim Samāra, 4 vols. (with indices of ḥadīth), Beirut 1408/1988

ʿAbd al-Razzāq, *Tafsīr*
ʿAbd al-Razzāq b. Hammām al-Ṣanʿānī, *al-Tafsīr*, ed. Muṣṭafā Muslim Muḥammad, 3 vols. in 4, Riyadh 1410/1989; ed. ʿAbd al-Muʿṭī Amīn Qalʿajī, 2 vols., Beirut 1411/1991; ed. Maḥmūd Muḥammad ʿAbduh, 3 vols., Beirut 1419/1999

Abū Dāwūd
Abū Dāwūd Sulaymān b. al-Ashʿath al-Sijistānī, *Sunan*, ed. Muḥammad Muḥyī l-Dīn ʿAbd al-Ḥamīd, 4 vols., Cairo 1339/1920; ed. Kamāl Yūsuf al-Ḥūt, 2 vols., Beirut 1988

Abū l-Futūḥ Rāzī, *Rawḥ*
Abū l-Futūḥ Ḥusayn b. ʿAlī Rāzī, *Rawḥ al-jinān wa-rūḥ al-janān*, 12 vols., Tehran 1282-7/1962-5; 5 vols., Qumm n.d.

Abū Ḥayyān, *Baḥr*
Abū Ḥayyān al-Gharnāṭī, *Tafsīr al-baḥr al-muḥīṭ*, 8 vols., Cairo 1328-9/1911; repr. Beirut 1983; ed. ʿĀdil Aḥmad ʿAbd al-Mawjūd and ʿAlī Muḥammad Muʿawwaḍ, 8 vols., Beirut 1993

Abū l-Layth al-Samarqandī, *Tafsīr*
Abū l-Layth Naṣr b. Muḥammad b. Aḥmad al-Samarqandī, *Baḥr al-ʿulūm*, ed. ʿAbd al-Raḥīm Aḥmad al-Zaqqa, 3 vols., Baghdad 1985-6; ed. ʿAlī Muḥammad Muʿawwaḍ et al., 3 vols., Beirut 1413/1993

Abū Shāma, *Murshid*
ʿAbd al-Raḥmān b. Ismāʿīl Abū Shāma, *Kitāb al-Murshid al-wajīz ilā ʿulūm tataʿallaq bi-l-kitāb al-ʿazīz,* ed. Ṭayyar Altikulaç, Istanbul 1968

Abū ʿUbayd, *Faḍāʾil*
Abū ʿUbayd al-Qāsim b. Sallām, *Faḍāʾil al-Qurʾān,* ed. Wahbī Sulaymān Khāwajī, Beirut 1411/1991

Abū ʿUbayd, *Gharīb*
Abū ʿUbayd al-Qāsim b. Sallām, *Gharīb al-ḥadīth,* ed. Muḥammad ʿAbd al-Muʿīd Khān, 4 vols., Hyderabad 1384-7/1964-7; 2 vols., Beirut 1406/1986; ed. Ḥusayn Muḥammad M. Sharaf et al., 4 vols., Cairo 1404-15/1984-94; ed. Masʿūd Ḥijāzī et al., Cairo 1419/1999

Abū ʿUbayd, *Nāsikh*
Abū ʿUbayd al-Qāsim b. Sallām, *Kitāb al-Nāsikh wa-l-mansūkh,* ed. J. Burton, Cambridge 1987

Abū ʿUbayda, *Majāz*
Abū ʿUbayda Maʿmar b. al-Muthannā al-Taymī, *Majāz al-Qurʾān,* ed. F. Sezgin, 2 vols., Cairo 1954-62

Akhfash, *Maʿānī*
Abū l-Ḥasan Saʿīd b. Masʿada al-Akhfash al-Awsaṭ, *Maʿānī l-Qurʾān,* ed. Fāʾiz Fāris al-Ḥamad, 2nd ed., 2 vols., Kuwait 1981; ed. ʿAbd al-Amīr Muḥammad Amīn al-Ward, Beirut 1405/1985; ed. Hudā Maḥmūd Qurrāʿa, Cairo 1990

Allard, *Analyse*
M. Allard, *Analyse conceptuelle du Coran sur cartes perforées,* Paris 1963

Ālūsī, *Rūḥ*
Maḥmūd b. ʿAbdallāh al-Ālūsī, *Rūḥ al-maʿānī fī tafsīr al-Qurʾān al-ʿaẓīm wa-l-sabʿ al-mathānī,* 30 vols. in 15, Cairo 1345/1926; repr. Beirut n.d.

ʿĀmilī, *Aʿyān*
Muḥsin al-Amīn al-ʿĀmilī, *Aʿyān al-shīʿa,* 56 parts, Damascus 1935-63; 11 vols., Beirut 1986

Anbārī, *Bayān*
Abū l-Barakāt ʿAbd al-Raḥmān b. Muḥammad b. al-Anbārī, *al-Bayān fī gharīb iʿrāb al-Qurʾān,* ed. Ṭāhā ʿAbd al-Ḥamīd and Muṣṭafā al-Saqqā, 2 vols., Cairo 1969-70

Anbārī, *Nuzha*
Abū l-Barakāt ʿAbd al-Raḥmān b. Muḥammad al-Anbārī, *Nuzhat al-alibbāʾ fī ṭabaqāt al-udabāʾ,* Cairo 1294; Stockholm 1963; ed. Ibrāhīm al-Sāmarrāʾī, Baghdad 1970

Arberry
A.J. Arberry, *The Koran interpreted,* London 1955

Arkoun, *Lectures*
M. Arkoun, *Lectures du Coran,* Paris 1982

ʿAyyāshī, *Tafsīr*
Muḥammad b. Masʿūd al-ʿAyyāshī, *Tafsīr,* 2 vols., Tehran 1380/1961

Baghawī, *Maʿālim*
al-Ḥusayn b. Masʿūd al-Shāfiʿī al-Baghawī, *Tafsīr al-Baghawī al-musammā bi-Maʿālim al-tanzīl,* ed. Khālid ʿAbd al-Raḥmān al-ʿAkk and Marwān Sawār, 4 vols., Beirut 1983

Baghdādī, *Farq*
Abū Manṣūr ʿAbd al-Qāhir b. Ṭāhir al-Baghdādī, *al-Farq bayna l-firāq,* ed. Muḥammad Badr, Cairo 1328/1910; ed. Muḥammad Muḥyī l-Dīn ʿAbd al-Ḥamīd, Cairo n.d.

Baghdādī, *Taʾrīkh Baghdād*
Abū Bakr Aḥmad b. ʿAlī al-Khaṭīb al-Baghdādī, *Taʾrīkh Baghdād,* 14 vols., Cairo 1349/1931

Baḥrānī, *Burhān*
Hāshim b. Sulaymān al-Baḥrānī, *Kitāb al-Burhān fī tafsīr al-Qurʾān,* ed. Maḥmūd b. Jaʿfar al-Mūsawī al-Zarandī et al., 4 vols., Tehran 1375/1995; repr. Beirut 1403/1983

Baljon, *Modern*
I.M.S. Baljon, *Modern Muslim Koran interpretation (1880-1960),* Leiden 1961, 1968

Bāqillānī, *Iʿjāz*
al-Qāḍī Abū Bakr Muḥammad b. al-Ṭayyib al-Bāqillānī, *Iʿjāz al-Qurʾān,* ed. al-Sayyid Aḥmad Ṣaqr, Cairo 1954

Bāqillānī, *Intiṣār*
al-Qāḍī Abū Bakr Muḥammad b. al-Ṭayyib al-Bāqillānī, *Nukat al-intiṣār li-naql al-Qurʾān,* ed. Muḥammad Zaghlūl Salām, Alexandria 1971

Bayḍāwī, *Anwār*
ʿAbdallāh b. ʿUmar al-Bayḍāwī, *Anwār al-tanzīl wa-asrār al-taʾwīl,* ed. H.O. Fleischer, 2 vols., Leipzig 1846; Beirut 1988

Beeston, *CHAL*
A.F.L. Beeston et al., eds., *The Cambridge history of Arabic literature,* 4 vols. to date, Cambridge 1983-

Bell, *Commentary*
R. Bell, *A commentary on the Qurʾān,* ed. C.E. Bosworth and M.E.J. Richardson, 2 vols., Manchester 1991

Bell, *Qurʾān*
R. Bell, *The Qurʾān. Translated, with a critical re-arrangement of the sūras,* 2 vols., Edinburgh 1939; repr. 1960

Beltz, *Mythen*
W. Beltz, *Die Mythen des Koran. Der Schlüssel zum Islam,* Düsseldorf 1980

Bergsträsser, *Verneinungs*
G. Bergsträsser, *Verneinungs- und Fragepartikeln und Verwandtes im Ḳurʾān,* Leipzig 1914

Biqāʿī, *Naẓm*
Burhān al-Dīn Ibrāhīm b. ʿUmar al-Biqāʿī, *Naẓm al-durar fī tanāsub al-āyāt wa-l-suwar,* 22 vols., Hyderabad 1969-84; repr. Cairo 1992

Birkeland, *Lord*
H. Birkeland, *The Lord guideth. Studies on primitive Islam,* Oslo 1956

Birkeland, *Opposition*
H. Birkeland, *Old Muslim opposition against interpretation of the Koran,* Oslo 1955

Blachère
R. Blachère, *Le Coran. Traduit de l'arabe,* Paris 1966

Blachère, *Introduction*
R. Blachère, *Introduction au Coran,* Paris 1947

Bobzin, *Koran*
H. Bobzin, *Der Koran. Eine Einführung,* Munich 1999

Bobzin, *Reformation*
H. Bobzin, *Der Koran im Zeitalter der Reformation. Studien zur Frühgeschichte der Arabistik und Islamkunde in Europa,* Beirut/Stuttgart 1995

Bouman, *Conflit*
J. Bouman, *Le conflit autour du Coran et la solution d'al-Bāqillānī,* Amsterdam 1959

Bouman, *Gott und Mensch*
J. Bouman, *Gott und Mensch im Koran. Eine Strukturform religiöser Anthropologie anhand des Beispiels Allāh und Muḥammad,* Darmstadt 1977

Böwering, *Mystical*
G. Böwering, *The mystical vision of existence in classical Islam. The qurʾānic hermeneutics of the Ṣūfī Sahl at-Tustarī (d. 283/896),* Berlin 1980

Brockelmann, *GAL*
C. Brockelmann, *Geschichte der arabischen Litteratur,* 2nd ed., 2 vols. and 3 vols. suppl., Leiden 1943-9; with new introduction, Leiden 1996

Buhl, *Das Leben*
F. Buhl, *Das Leben Muhammeds,* trans. H.H. Schaeder, Leipzig 1930; 1931 (3rd ed.)

Bukhārī, *Ṣaḥīḥ*
Abū ʿAbdallāh Muḥammad b. Ismāʿīl al-Bukhārī, *Kitāb al-Jāmiʿ al-ṣaḥīḥ,* ed. L. Krehl and T.W. Juynboll, 4 vols., Leiden 1862-1908; 9 vols., Cairo 1958

Burton, *Collection*
J. Burton, *The collection of the Qurʾān,* Cambridge 1977

Chabbi, *Seigneur*
J. Chabbi, *Le seigneur des tribus. L'islam de Mahomet,* Paris 1997

Creswell, *EMA*
K.A.C. Creswell, *Early Muslim architecture,* 2 vols., Oxford 1932-40; 2nd ed., London 1969

Dāmaghānī, *Wujūh*
al-Ḥusayn b. Muḥammad al-Dāmaghānī, *al-Wujūh wa-l-naẓāʾir li-alfāẓ Kitāb Allāh al-ʿazīz,* ed. Muḥammad Ḥasan Abū l-ʿAẓm al-Zafītī, 3 vols., Cairo 1412-16/

1992-5; ed. ʿAbd al-ʿAzīz Sayyid al-Ahl (as *Qāmūs al-Qurʾān*), Beirut 1970

Damīrī, *Ḥayāt*
Muḥammad b. Mūsā al-Damīrī, *Ḥayāt al-ḥayawān al-kubrā*, 2 vols., Cairo 1956

Dānī, *Muqniʿ*
Abū ʿAmr ʿUthmān b. Saʿīd al-Dānī, *al-Muqniʿ fī rasm maṣāḥif al-amṣār maʿa Kitāb al-Naqṭ = Orthographie und Punktierung des Koran*, ed. O. Pretzl, Leipzig/Istanbul 1932; ed. Muḥammad al-Ṣadīq Qamḥawī, Cairo n.d.

Dānī, *Naqṭ*
Abū ʿAmr ʿUthmān b. Saʿīd al-Dānī, *al-Muḥkam fī naqṭ al-maṣāḥif*, ed. ʿIzzat Ḥasan, Damascus 1379/1960

Dānī, *Taysīr*
Abū ʿAmr ʿUthmān b. Saʿīd al-Dānī, *Kitāb al-Taysīr fī l-qirāʾāt al-sabʿ = Das Lehrbuch der sieben Koranlesungen*, ed. O. Pretzl, Leipzig/Istanbul 1930

Dāraquṭnī, *Muʾtalif*
Abū l-Ḥasan ʿAlī b. ʿUmar al-Dāraquṭnī, *al-Muʾtalif wa-l-mukhtalif*, ed. Muwaffaq b. ʿAbdallāh b. ʿAbd al-Qādir, 5 vols., Beirut 1986

Dārimī, *Sunan*
ʿAbdallāh b. ʿAbd al-Rāḥmān al-Dārimī, *Sunan*, Cairo 1966

Darwaza, *Tafsīr*
Muḥammad ʿIzzat Darwaza, *al-Tafsir al-ḥadīth*, 12 vols., Cairo 1381-3/1962-4

Dāwūdī, *Ṭabaqāt*
Muḥammad b. ʿAlī al-Dāwūdī, *Ṭabaqāt al-mufassirīn*, ed. ʿAlī Muḥammad ʿUmar, 2 vols., Beirut 1983

Dhahabī, *Mufassirūn*
Muḥammad Ḥusayn al-Dhahabī, *al-Tafsīr wa-l-mufassirūn*, 2 vols., Cairo 1976

Dhahabī, *Qurrāʾ*
Shams al-Dīn Muḥammad b. Aḥmad al-Dhahabī, *Maʿrifat al-qurrāʾ al-kibār ʿalā l-ṭabaqāt wa-l-aʿṣār*, ed. Sayyid Jad al-Ḥaqq, n.p. 1969

Dhahabī, *Siyar*
Shams al-Dīn Muḥammad b. Aḥmad al-Dhahabī, *Siyar aʿlām al-nubalāʾ*, ed. Shuʿayb al-Arnaʾūṭ et al., 25 vols., Beirut 1981-8

Dhahabī, *Tadhkira*
Shams al-Dīn Muḥammad b. Aḥmad al-Dhahabī, *Tadhkirat al-ḥuffāẓ*, 4 vols., Hyderabad 1375/1955

Dhahabī, *Taʾrīkh*
Shams al-Dīn Muḥammad b. Aḥmad al-Dhahabī, *Taʾrīkh al-Islām*, ed. ʿUmar ʿAbd al-Salām Tadmurī, 52 vols. to date, Beirut 1989-; 4 vols. (years 601-640), ed. Bashshār ʿAwwād Maʿrūf et al., Beirut 1408/1988

van Ess, *TG*
J. van Ess, *Theologie und Gesellschaft im 2. und 3. Jahrhundert Hidschra. Eine Geschichte des religiösen Denkens im frühen Islam*, 6 vols., Berlin/New York 1991-7

Fārisī, *Ḥujja*
Abū ʿAlī al-Ḥasan b. ʿAlī al-Fārisī, *al-Ḥujja lil-qurrāʾ al-sabʿa*, ed. Badr al-Dīn al-Qahwajī et al., 4 vols., Damascus 1985-91

Farrāʾ, *Maʿānī*
Abū Zakariyyāʾ Yaḥyā b. Ziyād al-Farrāʾ, *Maʿānī l-Qurʾān*, ed. Aḥmad Yūsuf Najātī and Muḥammad ʿAlī l-Najjār, 3 vols., Cairo 1955-72

Fīrūzābādī, *Baṣāʾir*
Majd al-Dīn Muḥammad b. Yaʿqūb al-Fīrūzābādī *Baṣāʾir dhawī l-tamyīz fī laṭāʾif al-kitāb al-ʿazīz*, ed. Muḥammad ʿAlī l-Najjār, 4 vols., Cairo 1964; repr. Beirut n.d.

GAP
W. Fischer and H. Gätje, eds., *Grundriss der arabischen Philologie*, 3 vols., Wiesbaden 1982-92

Gardet and Anawati, *Introduction*
L. Gardet and M.M. Anawati, *Introduction à la théologie musulmane*, Paris 1948, 3rd ed., 1981

Gilliot, *Elt*
C. Gilliot, *Exégèse, langue, et théologie en Islam. L'exégèse coranique de Ṭabarī (m. 310/923)*, Paris 1990

Gimaret, *Jubbāʾī*
D. Gimaret, *Une lecture muʿtazilite du Coran. Le tafsīr d'Abū ʿAlī al-Djubbāʾī (m. 303/915) partiellement reconstitué à partir de ses citateurs,* Louvain/Paris 1994
Goldziher, *GS*
I. Goldziher, *Gesammelte Schriften,* ed. J. Desomogyi, 6 vols., Hildesheim 1967-73
Goldziher, *MS*
I. Goldziher, *Muhammedanische Studien,* 2 vols., Halle 1888-90; trans., C.R. Barber and S.M. Stern, *Muslim studies,* London 1967-72
Goldziher, *Richtungen*
I. Goldziher, *Die Richtungen der islamischen Koranauslegung,* Leiden 1920; repr. 1970
Graham, *Beyond*
W.A. Graham, *Beyond the written word. Oral aspects of scripture in the history of religion,* Cambridge and New York 1989
Grimme, *Mohammed, I-II*
H. Grimme, *Mohammed. I, Das Leben nach den Quellen. II, Einleitung in den Koran. System der koranischen Theologie,* Münster 1892-5
Grünbaum, *Beiträge*
M. Grünbaum, *Neue Beiträge zur semitischen Sagenkunde,* Leiden 1893
Ḥājjī Khalīfa, *Kashf*
Muṣṭafā ʿAbdallāh Ḥājjī Khalīfa, *Kashf al-ẓunūn,* ed. and trans. G. Flügel, 7 vols., Leipzig 1835-58; ed. Şerefettin Yaltkaya and Kilisli Rifat Bilge, 2 vols., Istanbul 1941-3; repr. Beirut 1992-3
Hawting, *Idolatry*
G.R. Hawting, *The idea of idolatry and the emergence of Islam. From polemic to history,* Cambridge 1999
Hawting and Shareef, *Approaches*
G.R. Hawting and A.A. Shareef (eds.), *Approaches to the Qurʾān,* London 1993
Ḥawwā, *Tafsīr*
Saʿīd Ḥawwā, *al-Asās fī l-tafsīr,* 11 vols., Cairo 1405/1985
Horovitz, *KU*
J. Horovitz, *Koranische Untersuchungen,* Berlin/Leipzig 1926
Hūd b. Muḥakkam, *Tafsīr*
Hūd b. Muḥakkam/Muḥkim al-Huwwārī, *Tafsīr,* ed. Balḥājj Saʿīd Sharīfī, 4 vols., Beirut 1990
Ibn ʿAbbās, *Gharīb*
ʿAbdallāh b. ʿAbbās (attributed to), *Gharīb al-Qurʾān,* ed. Muḥammad ʿAbd al-Raḥīm, Beirut 1993
Ibn Abī l-Iṣbaʿ, *Badīʿ*
Ibn Abī l-Iṣbaʿ al-Miṣrī, *Badīʿ al-Qurʾān,* ed. Ḥifnī Muḥammad Sharaf, Cairo n.d.
Ibn Abī Uṣaybiʿa, *ʿUyūn*
Aḥmad b. al-Qāsim b. Abī Uṣaybiʿa, *ʿUyūn al-anbāʾ fī ṭabaqāt al-aṭibbāʾ,* ed. A. Müller, 2 vols., Cairo 1299/1882; 3 vols., Beirut 1957
Ibn al-Anbārī, *Īḍāḥ*
Abū Bakr Muḥammad b. al-Qāsim b. al-Anbārī, *Īḍāḥ al-waqf wa-l-ibtidāʾ fī Kitāb Allāh,* ed. Muḥyī l-Dīn ʿAbd al-Raḥmān Ramaḍān, 2 vols., Damascus 1391/1971
Ibn al-ʿArabī, *Aḥkām*
Muḥammad b. ʿAbdallāh Abū Bakr b. al-ʿArabī, *Aḥkām al-Qurʾān,* 2nd ed., Cairo 1392/1972
Ibn al-ʿArabī, *Tafsīr*
Muḥammad b. ʿAbdallāh Abū Bakr b. al-ʿArabī, *Tafsīr al-Qurʾān,* 2 vols., Beirut 1968 (see Qāshānī)
Ibn ʿAsākir, *Taʾrīkh*
ʿAlī b. al-Ḥasan b. ʿAsākir, *Taʾrīkh madīnat Dimashq,* abridged ed. ʿAbd al-Qādir Bardān and Aḥmad ʿUbayd, 7 vols., Damascus 1329-51/1911-31; facsimile ed., 19 vols., Amman n.d.; 29 vols., Damascus 1404-8/1984-8; ed. Muḥyī l-Dīn ʿUmar b. Gharāma al-ʿAmrāwī, 80 vols., Beirut 1995-2000
Ibn ʿĀshūr, *Tafsīr*
Muḥammad al-Ṭāhir b. ʿĀshūr, *al-Tafsīr al-taḥrīrī wa-l-tanwīrī,* 30 vols., Tunis 1984
Ibn ʿAskar, *Takmīl*
Muḥammad b. ʿAlī al-Ghassānī b. ʿAskar, *al-Takmīl wa-l-itmām li-Kitāb al-Taʿrīf wa-l-iʿlām,* ed. Ḥasan Ismāʿīl Marwa, Beirut/Damascus 1418/1997 (see Suhaylī)

Ibn al-Athīr, *Kāmil*
'Izz al-Dīn 'Alī b. al-Athīr, *al-Kāmil fī l-ta'rīkh,* ed. C.J. Tornberg, 14 vols., Leiden 1851-76; corrected repr. 13 vols., Beirut 1385-7/1965-7
Ibn al-Athīr, *Nihāya*
Majd al-Dīn al-Mubārak b. al-Athīr, *al-Nihāya fī gharīb al-ḥadīth wa-l-athar,* ed. Ṭāhir Aḥmad al-Zāwī and Maḥmūd al-Ṭanāḥī, 5 vols., Cairo 1963-6
Ibn 'Aṭiyya, *Muḥarrar*
Abū Muḥammad 'Abd al-Ḥaqq b. Ghālib b. 'Aṭiyya al-Gharnāṭī, *al-Muḥarrar al-wajīz,* ed. 'Abd al-Salām 'Abd al-Shāfī Muḥammad, 5 vols., Beirut 1413/1993
Ibn Ḍurays, *Faḍā'il*
Muḥammad b. Ayyūb b. Ḍurays, *Faḍā'il al-Qur'ān,* ed. Ghazwa Budayr, Damascus 1988
Ibn Ḥajar, *Tahdhīb*
Ibn Ḥajar al-'Asqalānī, *Tahdhīb al-tahdhīb,* 12 vols., Hyderabad 1325-7/1907-9; Beirut 1968
Ibn Ḥanbal, *Musnad*
Aḥmad b. Ḥanbal, *Musnad,* ed. Muḥammad al-Zuhrī al-Ghamrāwī, 6 vols., Cairo 1313/1895; repr. Beirut 1978; ed. Aḥmad Muḥammad Shākir et al., 20 vols., Cairo 1416/1995
Ibn Ḥazm, *Milal*
'Alī b. Aḥmad b. Sa'īd b. Ḥazm, *al-Fiṣal fī l-milal wa-l-ahwā' wa-l-niḥal,* ed. Muḥammad Ibrāhīm Naṣr and 'Abd al-Raḥmān 'Umayra, 5 vols., Beirut 1995
Ibn al-'Imād, *Shadharāt*
'Abd al-Ḥayy b. Aḥmad b. al-'Imād, *Shadharāt al-dhahab fī akhbār man dhahab,* 8 vols., Cairo 1350-1/1931-2; repr. Beirut n.d.
Ibn Isḥāq, *Sīra*
Muḥammad b. Isḥāq, *Sīrat rasūl Allāh* (recension of 'Abd al-Malik b. Hishām), ed. F. Wüstenfeld, Göttingen 1858-60; repr. Beirut n.d.; ed. Muṣṭafā al-Ṣaqqā et al., 4 vols. in 2, 2nd ed., Cairo 1955
Ibn Isḥāq-Guillaume
Muḥammad b. Isḥāq, *The life of Muhammad. A translation of Ibn Isḥāq's* Sīrat rasūl Allāh, trans. A. Guillaume, Oxford 1955; repr. Karachi 1967
Ibn al-Jawzī, *Funūn*
Abū l-Faraj 'Abd al-Raḥmān b. 'Alī b. al-Jawzī, *Funūn al-afnān fī 'ajā'ib 'ulūm al-Qur'ān,* ed. Rashīd 'Abd al-Raḥmān al-'Ubaydī, Baghdad 1408/1988
Ibn al-Jawzī, *Muntaẓam*
Abū l-Faraj 'Abd al-Raḥmān b. 'Alī b. al-Jawzī, *al-Muntaẓam fī ta'rīkh al-mulūk wa-l-umam,* ed. Muḥammad and Muṣṭafā 'Abd al-Qādir 'Aṭā, 19 vols., Beirut 1412/1922; ed. Suhayl Zakkār, 11 vols. in 13, Beirut 1995-6
Ibn al-Jawzī, *Nuzha*
Abū l-Faraj 'Abd al-Raḥmān b. 'Alī b. al-Jawzī, *Nuzhat al-a'yun al-nawāẓir fī 'ilm al-wujūh wa-l-naẓā'ir,* ed. Muḥammad 'Abd al-Karīm Kāẓim al-Rāḍī, Beirut 1404/1984
Ibn al-Jawzī, *Zād*
Abū l-Faraj 'Abd al-Raḥmān b. Alī b. al-Jawzī, *Zād al-masīr fī 'ilm al-tafsīr,* intr. Muḥammad Zuhayr al-Shāwīsh, 9 vols., Damascus 1384-5/1964-5; annot. Aḥmad Shams al-Dīn, 8 vols., Beirut 1414/1994
Ibn al-Jazarī, *Ghāya*
Shams al-Dīn Abū l-Khayr Muḥammad b. Muḥammad b. al-Jazarī, *Ghāyat al-nihāya fī ṭabaqāt al-qurrā' = Das biographische Lexikon der Koranleser,* 3 vols. in 2, ed. G. Bergsträsser and O. Pretzl, Leipzig/Cairo 1933-5
Ibn al-Jazarī, *Munjid*
Shams al-Dīn Abū l-Khayr Muḥammad b. Muḥammad b. al-Jazarī, *Munjid al-muqri'īn wa-murshid al-ṭālibīn,* ed. Muḥammad Ḥabīb Allāh al-Shanqīṭī et al., Cairo 1350/1931; Beirut 1980
Ibn al-Jazarī, *Nashr*
Shams al-Dīn Abū l-Khayr Muḥammad b. Muḥammad b. al-Jazarī, *Kitāb al-Nashr fī l-qirā'āt al-'ashr,* ed. 'Alī Muḥammad al-Ḍabbā', 2 vols., Cairo 1940; repr. Beirut n.d.
Ibn Jinnī, *Muḥtasab*
Abū l-Fatḥ 'Uthmān b. Jinnī, *al-Muḥtasab fī*

tabyīn wujūh shawādhdh al-qirāʾāt wa-l-īḍāḥ ʿanhā, 2 vols., ed. ʿAlī al-Najdī Nāṣif et al., Cairo 1386-9/1966-9; repr. 1994
Ibn Kathīr, *Bidāya*
ʿImād al-Dīn Ismāʿīl b. ʿUmar b. Kathīr, *al-Bidāya wa-l-nihāya,* 14 vols., Beirut/ Riyadh 1966; repr. Beirut 1988
Ibn Kathīr, *Faḍāʾil*
ʿImād al-Dīn Ismāʿīl b. ʿUmar b. Kathīr, *Faḍāʾil al-Qurʾān,* Beirut 1979
Ibn Kathīr, *Tafsīr*
ʿImād al-Dīn Ismāʿīl b. ʿUmar b. Kathīr, *Tafsīr al-Qurʾān al-ʿaẓīm,* ed. ʿAbd al-ʿAzīz Ghunaym et al., 8 vols., Cairo 1390/1971; 4 vols., Cairo n.d.; repr. Beirut 1980
Ibn Khālawayh, *Ḥujja*
Abū ʿAbdallāh al-Ḥusayn b. Aḥmad b. Khālawayh, *al-Ḥujja fī l-qirāʾāt al-sabʿ,* ed. ʿAbd al-ʿĀl Salīm Mukarram, Beirut 1971
Ibn Khālawayh, *Iʿrāb*
Abū ʿAbdallāh al-Ḥusayn b. Aḥmad b. Khālawayh, *Iʿrāb thalāthīn sūra min al-Qurʾān al-karīm,* Baghdad 1967
Ibn Khālawayh, *Iʿrāb al-qirāʾāt*
Abū ʿAbdallāh al-Ḥusayn b. Aḥmad b. Khālawayh, *Iʿrāb al-qirāʾāt al-sabʿ wa-ʿilaluhā,* ed. ʿAbd al-Raḥmān b. Sulaymān al-Uthaymīn, 2 vols., Cairo 1413/1992
Ibn Khaldūn, *ʿIbar*
ʿAbd al-Raḥmān b. Khaldūn, *Kitāb al-ʿIbar,* ed. Naṣr al-Ḥūrīnī, 7 vols., Būlāq 1284/ 1867
Ibn Khaldūn-Rosenthal
ʿAbd al-Raḥmān b. Khaldūn, *The Muqaddimah,* trans. F. Rosenthal, 3 vols., New York 1958; 2nd rev. ed., Princeton 1967
Ibn Khallikān, *Wafayāt*
Shams al-Dīn b. Khallikān, *Wafayāt al-aʿyān wa-anbāʾ abnāʾ al-zamān,* ed. F. Wüstenfeld, 4 vols., Göttingen 1835-50; ed. Iḥsān ʿAbbās, 8 vols., Beirut 1968-72; trans. M. De Slane, *Ibn Khallikān's biographical dictionary,* 4 vols., Paris 1842-71; repr. New York 1961
Ibn Māja
Muḥammad b. Yazīd b. Māja, *Sunan,* ed. Muḥammad Fuʾād ʿAbd al-Bāqī, 2 vols., Cairo 1952-3
Ibn Mujāhid, *Sabʿa*
Abū Bakr Aḥmad b. Mūsā b. Mujāhid, *Kitāb al-Sabʿa fī l-qirāʾāt,* ed. Shawqī Ḍayf, Cairo 1979
Ibn al-Nadīm, *Fihrist*
Muḥammad b. Isḥāq b. al-Nadīm, *Kitāb al-Fihrist,* ed. G. Flügel, 2 vols., Leipzig 1871-2; ed. Riḍā Tajaddud, Tehran 1971; 2nd ed., Beirut 1988
Ibn al-Nadīm-Dodge
Muḥammad b. Isḥāq b. al-Nadīm, *The Fihrist of al-Nadīm,* trans. B. Dodge, 2 vols., New York/London 1970
Ibn al-Naqīb, *Muqaddima*
Abū ʿAbdallāh Muḥammad b. Sulaymān al-Naqīb, *Muqaddimat al-tafsīr fī ʿulūm al-bayān wa-l-maʿānī wa-l-badīʿ wa-iʿjāz al-Qurʾān,* ed. Zakariyyāʾ Saʿīd ʿAlī, Cairo 1415/1995
Ibn Qayyim al-Jawziyya, *Tibyān*
Muḥammad b. Abī Bakr b. Qayyim al-Jawziyya, *al-Tibyān fī aqsām al-Qurʾān,* Beirut 1982
Ibn al-Qifṭī, *Ḥukamāʾ*
Abū l-Ḥasan ʿAlī b. Yūsuf b. al-Qifṭī, *Taʾrīkh al-ḥukamāʾ,* ed. J. Lippert, Leipzig 1903; repr. Baghdad 1967
Ibn Qutayba, *Gharīb*
Abū Muḥammad ʿAbdallāh b. Muslim al-Dīnawarī b. Qutayba, *Tafsīr gharīb al-Qurʾān,* ed. al-Sayyid Aḥmad Ṣaqr, Cairo 1958; Beirut 1978
Ibn Qutayba, *al-Shiʿr*
Abū Muḥammad ʿAbdallāh b. Muslim al-Dīnawarī b. Qutayba, *Kitāb al-Shiʿr wa-l-shuʿarāʾ,* ed. M.J. de Goeje, Leiden 1900
Ibn Qutayba, *Taʾwīl*
Abū Muḥammad ʿAbdallāh b. Muslim al-Dīnawarī b. Qutayba, *Taʾwīl mushkil al-Qurʾān,* ed. al-Sayyid Aḥmad Ṣaqr, Cairo 1954; Cairo 1973; Medina 1981
Ibn Qutayba-Lecomte
G. Lecomte, *Le traité des divergences du hadīt d'Ibn Qutayba,* Damascus 1962

Ibn Sa'd, *Ṭabaqāt*
Muḥammad b. Sa'd, *al-Ṭabaqāt al-kubrā,* ed. H. Sachau et al., 9 vols., Leiden 1905-40; ed. Iḥsān 'Abbās, 9 vols., Beirut 1957-8

Ibn Taymiyya, *Daqā'iq*
Taqī l-Dīn Aḥmad b. 'Abd al-Ḥalīm b. Taymiyya, *Daqā'iq al-tafsīr. al-Jāmi' li-tafsīr al-Imām Ibn Taymiyya,* ed. Muḥammad al-Sayyid al-Julaynid, 6 vols. in 3, Jedda/Beirut/Damascus 1986

Ibn Taymiyya, *Muqaddima*
Taqī l-Dīn Aḥmad b. 'Abd al-Ḥalīm b. Taymiyya, *Muqaddima fī uṣūl al-tafsīr,* Beirut 1392/1972; Riyadh 1382/1962

Ibn Wahb, *al-Jāmi'*
'Abdallāh b. Wahb, *al-Ǧāmi'. Die Koranswissenschaften,* ed. M. Muranyi, Wiesbaden 1992

Ibyārī, *Mawsū'a*
Ibrāhīm al-Ibyārī and 'Abd al-Ṣabūr Marzūq, *al-Mawsū'a al-qur'āniyya,* 6 vols., Cairo 1388/1969; 11 vols., Cairo 1405/1984

Ihsanoglu, *Translations*
E. İhsanoğlu (ed.), *World bibliography of translations of the meanings of the holy Qur'ān. Printed translations* 1515-1980, Istanbul 1406/1986

Iṣfahānī, *Aghānī*
Abū l-Faraj al-Iṣfahānī, *Kitāb al-Aghānī,* 21 vols. in 7, Cairo 1323/1905; 25 vols., Beirut 1955-62

Iṣfahānī, *Muqaddima*
Abū l-Ḥasan al-'Āmilī al-Iṣfahānī, *Muqaddimat tafsīr mir'āt al-anwār wa-mishkāt al-asrār,* ed. Maḥmūd b. Ja'far al-Mūsawī al-Zarandī, Tehran 1374/1954

Iṣlāḥī, *Tadabbur*
Amīn Aḥsan Iṣlāḥī, *Tadabbur-i Qur'ān,* 8 vols., Lahore 1967-80

'Iyāḍ b. Mūsā, *Shifā'*
al-Qāḍī Abū l-Faḍl 'Iyāḍ b. Mūsā, *al-Shifā' bi-ta'rīf ḥuqūq al-muṣṭafā,* 2 vols. in 1, Damascus 1978; ed. Muḥammad Amīn Qara et al., Amman 1407/1986

Izutsu, *Concepts*
Toshihiko Izutsu, *Ethico-religious concepts in the Qur'ān,* Montreal 1966

Izutsu, *God*
Toshihiko Izutsu, *God and man in the Koran,* New York 1964; repr. 1980

Jāḥiẓ, *Bayān*
'Amr b. Baḥr al-Jāḥiẓ, *al-Bayān wa-l-tabyīn,* ed. 'Abd al-Salām Muḥammad Hārūn, 4 vols., Cairo 1948-50; repr. Beirut n.d.

Jalālayn
Jalāl al-Dīn Muḥammad b. Aḥmad al-Maḥallī and Jalāl al-Dīn al-Suyūṭī, *Tafsīr al-Jalālayn,* Damascus 1385/1965

Jansen, *Egypt*
J.J.G. Jansen, *The interpretation of the Koran in modern Egypt,* Leiden 1974, 1980

Jaṣṣāṣ, *Aḥkām*
Abū Bakr Aḥmad b. 'Abdallāh al-Jaṣṣās al-Rāzī, *Aḥkām al-Qur'ān,* 3 vols., Istanbul 1335-8/1916-19

Jawālīqī, *Mu'arrab*
Abū Manṣūr Mawhūb b. Aḥmad al-Jawālīqī, *al-Mu'arrab min al-kalām al-'ajamī 'alā ḥurūf al-mu'jam,* ed. Aḥmad Muḥammad Shākir, Cairo 1361/1942

Jeffery, *For. vocab.*
A. Jeffery, *Foreign vocabulary of the Qur'ān,* Baroda 1938

Jeffery, *Materials*
A. Jeffery, *Materials for the history of the text of the Qur'ān. The Kitāb al-Maṣāḥif of Ibn Abī Dāwūd together with a collection of the variant readings from the codices of Ibn Mas'ūd, etc.,* Leiden 1937

Jeffery, *Muqaddimas*
A. Jeffery, *Two muqaddimas to the Qur'ānic sciences. The muqaddima to the* Kitab al-Mabani *and the muqaddima of Ibn 'Atiyya to his* Tafsir, Cairo 1954

Jurjānī, *Asrār*
'Abd al-Qāhir al-Jurjāni, *Asrār al-balāgha,* ed. H. Ritter, Istanbul 1954

Jurjānī, *Dalā'il*
'Abd al-Qāhir al-Jurjānī, *Dalā'il i'jāz al-*

Qur'ān, Cairo 1372; ed. Maḥmūd Muḥammad Shākir, Cairo 1404/1984

Justi, *Namenbuch*
F. Justi, *Iranisches Namenbuch*, Marburg 1895

Kaḥḥāla, *Mu'jam*
'Umar Riḍā Kaḥḥāla, *Mu'jam al-mu'allifīn*, 15 vols. in 8, Beirut n.d.; Damascus 1957-61

Kaḥḥāla, *Nisā'*
'Umar Riḍā Kaḥḥāla, *A'lām al-nisā' fī 'ālamay al-'Arab wa-l-Islām*, 5 vols., Damascus 1379/1959

Kāshānī, *Minhaj*
Mullā Fatḥ Allāh Kāshānī, *Minhaj al-ṣādiqīn fī ilzām al-mukhālifīn*, 10 vols., Tehran 1347[solar]/1969

Kāshānī, *Ṣāfī*
Mullā Muḥsin Fayd Kāshānī, *al-Ṣāfī fī tafsīr kalām Allāh al-wāfī*, ed. Ḥusayn al-A'lamī, 5 vols., Beirut 1399/1979

Khāzin, *Lubāb*
'Alā' al-Dīn al-Khāzin, *Lubāb al-ta'wīl fī ma'ānī l-tanzīl*, Cairo 1381/1961

Khwānsārī, *Rawdāt*
Muḥammad Bāqir al-Mūsawī al-Khwānsārī, *Rawdāt al-jannāt*, ed. Asad Allāh Ismā'īlīyān, 8 vols., Tehran 1392/1972

Kisā'ī, *Mutashābih*
'Alī b. Ḥamza al-Kisā'ī, *Kitāb Mutashābih al-Qur'ān*, ed. Ṣabīḥ al-Tamīmī, Tripoli 1994

Kisā'ī, *Qiṣaṣ*
Muḥammad b. 'Abdallāh al-Kisā'ī, *Vita prophetarum auctore Muḥammed ben 'Abdallāh al-Kisā'ī*, ed. I. Eisenberg, 2 vols., Leiden 1922-3

Kulaynī, *Kāfī*
Abū Ja'far Muḥammad b. Ya'qūb al-Kulayn, *Rawḍat al-kāfī*, ed. 'Alī Akbar al-Ghifārī, Najaf 1395/1966; repr. Beirut n.d.

Kutubī, *Fawāt*
Ibn Shākir al-Kutubī, *Fawāt al-wafayāt*, 2 vols., Cairo 1299/1882; ed. Iḥsān 'Abbās, 5 vols., Beirut 1973-4

Lane
E.W. Lane, *An Arabic-English lexicon*, 1 vol. in 8 parts., London 1863-93; New York 1955-6; repr. 2 vols., Cambridge 1984

Lecker, *Muslims*
M. Lecker, *Muslims, Jews and pagans. Studies on early Islamic Medina*, Leiden 1995

Le Strange, *Lands*
G. Le Strange, *The lands of the eastern caliphate*, 2nd ed., Cambridge 1930

Lisān al-'Arab
Muḥammad b. al-Mukarram b. Manẓūr, *Lisān al-'Arab*, 15 vols., Beirut 1955-6; ed. 'Alī Shīrī, 18 vols., Beirut 1988

Lüling, *Ur-Qur'ān*
G. Lüling, *Über den Ur-Qur'ān. Ansätze zur Rekonstruktion der vorislamisch-christlicher Strophenlieder im Qur'ān*, Erlangen 1972; 2nd ed. 1993

Makkī, *Ibāna*
Makkī b. Abī Ṭālib al-Qaysī, *Kitāb al-Ibāna 'an ma'ānī l-qirā'āt*, ed. Muḥyī l-Dīn Ramaḍān, Damascus 1979

Makkī, *Kashf*
Makkī b. Abī Ṭālib al-Qaysī, *al-Kashf 'an wujūh al-qirā'āt al-sab' wa-'ilalihā wa-ḥujajihā*, ed. Muḥyī l-Dīn Ramaḍān, 2 vols., Damascus 1974

Makkī, *Mushkil*
Makkī b. Abī Ṭālib al-Qaysī, *Mushkil i'rāb al-Qur'ān*, ed. Yāsīn M. al-Sawwās, Damascus 1974

Mālik, *Muwaṭṭa'*
Mālik b. Anas, *al-Muwaṭṭa'*, ed. Muḥammad Fu'ād 'Abd al-Bāqī, Cairo 1952-3; Beirut 1985; ed. 'Abd al-Majīd Turkī, Beirut 1994

Mas'ūdī, *Murūj*
Abū 'Alī b. al-Ḥusayn al-Mas'ūdī, *Murūj al-dhahab*, ed. C. Barbier de Meynard and Pavet de Courteille, 9 vols., Paris 1861-77; ed. and trans. Ch. Pellat, *Les prairies d'or*, 7 vols. text and 4 vols. translation, Paris-Beirut 1962-89; ed. Qāsim al-Shamā'ī al-Rifā'ī, 4 vols., Beirut 1989

Māturīdī, *Ta'wīlāt*
Abū Manṣūr Muḥammad b. Muḥammad al-Māturīdī, *Ta'wīlāt ahl al-sunna*, ed. Ibrāhīm and al-Sayyid ʿAwadayn, Cairo 1391/1971; ed. Jāsim Muḥammad al-Jubūrī, Baghdad 1404/1983
Māwardī, *Nukat*
ʿAlī b. Muḥammad al-Māwardī, *al-Nukat wa-l-ʿuyūn fī l-tafsīr*, ed. al-Sayyid b. ʿAbd al-Maqṣūd b. ʿAbd al-Raḥīm, 6 vols., Beirut 1412/1992
McAuliffe, *Qur'ānic*
J.D. McAuliffe, *Qur'ānic Christians. An analysis of classical and modern exegesis*, Cambridge 1991
Mir, *Dictionary*
M. Mir, *Dictionary of Qur'ānic terms and concepts*, New York 1987
Mir, *Verbal*
M. Mir, *Verbal idioms of the Qur'ān*, Ann Arbor, MI 1989
Mufaḍḍaliyyāt
al-Mufaḍḍal b. Muḥammad al-Ḍabbī, *al-Mufaḍḍaliyyāt*, ed. Aḥmad Muḥammad Shākir and ʿAbd al-Salām Muḥammad Hārūn, Cairo 1942
Muir, *Mahomet*
W. Muir, *The life of Mahomet. With introductory chapters on the original sources of the biography of Mahomet, I-IV*, London 1858-61
Mujāhid, *Tafsīr*
Abū l-Ḥajjāj Mujāhid b. Jabr, *al-Tafsīr*, ed. ʿAbd al-Raḥmān b. Ṭāhir b. Muḥammad al-Suwartī, Qatar 1976; ed. Muḥammad ʿAbd al-Salām Abū l-Nīl, Cairo 1989
Mukarram, *Muʿjam al-qirā'āt*
ʿAbd al-Āl Salīm Mukarram, *Muʿjam al-qirā'āt al-qur'āniyya*, 8 vols. to date, Kuwait 1982-
Muqātil, *Ashbāh*
Abū l-Ḥasan Muqātil b. Sulaymān al-Balkhī, *al-Ashbāh wa-l-naẓā'ir fī l-Qur'ān al-karīm*, ed. ʿAbdallāh Maḥmūd Shiḥāta, Cairo 1975
Muqātil, *Khams mi'a*
Abū l-Ḥasan Muqātil b. Sulaymān al-Balkhī, *Tafsīr al-khams mi'at āya min al-Qur'ān*, ed. I. Goldfeld, Shfaram 1980
Muqātil, *Tafsīr*
Abū l-Ḥasan Muqātil b. Sulaymān al-Balkhī, *al-Tafsīr*, ed. ʿAbdallāh Maḥmūd Shiḥāta, 5 vols., Cairo 1980-7
Muslim, *Ṣaḥīḥ*
Muslim b. al-Ḥajjāj, *Ṣaḥīḥ*, ed. Muḥammad Fu'ād ʿAbd al-Bāqī, 5 vols., Cairo 1955-6
Nāfiʿ, *Masā'il*
Masā'il al-Imām ʿan as'ilat Nāfiʿ b. al-Azraq wa-ajwibat ʿAbd Allāh b. ʿAbbas, ed. ʿAbd al-Raḥmān ʿUmayra, Cairo 1413/1994
Nagel, *Einschübe*
T. Nagel, *Medinensische Einschübe in mekkanischen Suren*, Göttingen 1995
Nagel, *Koran*
T. Nagel, *Der Koran. Einführung-Texte-Erläuterungen*, Munich 1983
Naḥḥās, *Iʿrāb*
Abū Jaʿfar Aḥmad b. Muḥammad al-Naḥḥās, *Iʿrāb al-Qur'ān*, ed. Zuhayr Ghāzī Zāhid, 2nd ed., 5 vols., Beirut 1985, 1988
Nasafī, *Tafsīr*
ʿAbdallāh b. Aḥmad b. Maḥmūd al-Nasafī, *Madārik al-tanzil wa-ḥaqā'iq al-ta'wīl*, ed. Zakariyyā' ʿUmayrāt, 2 vols. Beirut 1415/1995
Nasā'ī, *Faḍā'il*
Aḥmad b. Shuʿayb al-Nasā'ī, *Faḍā'il al-Qur'ān*, ed. Samīr al-Khūlī, Beirut 1985
Nasā'ī, *Sunan*
Aḥmad b. Shuʿayb al-Nasā'ī, *al-Sunan al-kubrā*, ed. ʿAbd al-Ghaffār Sulaymān al-Bundārī and al-Sayyid Kisrawī Ḥasan, 6 vols., Beirut 1411/1991
Nawawī, *Sharḥ*
Abū Zakariyyā' Yaḥyā b. Sharaf al-Nawawī, *Sharḥ Ṣaḥīḥ Muslim*, 18 vols. in 9, Cairo 1349/1929-30; ed. Khalīl Muḥammad Shīḥā, 19 vols. in 10, Beirut 1995
Neuwirth, *Studien*
A. Neuwirth, *Studien zur Komposition der mekkanischen Suren*, Berlin 1981
Nīsābūrī, *Tafsīr*
Abū l-Qāsim al-Ḥasan b. Muḥammad b.

Ḥabīb al-Nīsābūrī, *Tafsīr gharāʾib al-Qurʾān wa-raghāʾib al-furqān,* on the margin of Ṭabarī, *Jāmiʿ al-bayān,* 30 vols., Cairo 1323-9/1905-11; repr. Beirut 1392/1972; ed. Ibrāhīm ʿAṭwa ʿAwaḍ, 13 vols., Cairo 1962-4

Nöldeke, *GQ*
T. Nöldeke, *Geschichte des Qorāns,* new edition by F. Schwally, G. Bergsträsser and O. Pretzl, 3 vols., Leipzig 1909-38

Nwyia, *Exégèse*
P. Nwyia, *Exégèse coranique et langage mystique. Nouvel essai sur le lexique technique des mystiques musulmans,* Beirut 1970

Paret, *Kommentar*
R. Paret, *Der Koran. Kommentar und Konkordanz,* Stuttgart 1971; 1977; Kohlhammer 1980

Paret, *Koran*
R. Paret, *Der Koran. Übersetzung,* Stuttgart 1962

Paret (ed.), *Koran*
R. Paret (ed.) *Der Koran,* Darmstadt 1975

Penrice, *Dictionary*
J. Penrice, *A dictionary and glossary of the Koran,* London 1873; repr. 1971

Pickthall, *Koran*
M.M. Pickthall, *The meaning of the glorious Koran,* London 1930; New York 1976

Qāshānī, *Taʾwīl*
ʿAbd al-Razzāq al-Qāshānī, *Taʾwīl al-Qurʾān,* 2 vols., Beirut 1968 (see Ibn al-ʿArabī)

Qāsimī, *Tafsīr*
Muḥammad Jamāl al-Dīn al-Qāsimī, *Maḥāsin al-taʾwīl,* 18 vols., Cairo 1957-70

Qasṭallānī, *Laṭāʾif*
Aḥmad b. Muḥammad b. Abī Bakr al-Qasṭallānī, *Laṭāʾif al-ishārāt li-funūn al-qirāʾāt,* ed. ʿĀmir al-Sayyid ʿUthmān and ʿAbd al-Ṣabūr Shāhīn, Cairo 1972

Qasṭallānī, *Mawāhib*
Aḥmad b. Muḥammad b. Abī Bakr al-Qasṭallānī, *al-Mawāhib al-laduniyya bi-l-minaḥ al-muḥammadiyya,* ed. Ṣāliḥ Aḥmad al-Shāmī, 4 vols., Beirut/Damascus/Amman 1412/1991

Qummī, *Tafsīr*
Abū l-Ḥasan ʿAlī b. Ibrāhīm al-Qummī, *Tafsīr,* ed. Ṭayyib al-Mūsāwī al-Jazāʾirī, 2 vols., Najaf 1387/1967; Beirut 1991

Qurṭubī, *Jāmiʿ*
Abū ʿAbdallāh Muḥammad b. Aḥmad al-Qurṭubī, *al-Jāmiʿ li-aḥkām al-Qurʾān,* ed. Aḥmad ʿAbd al-ʿAlīm al-Bardūnī et al., 20 vols., Cairo 1952-67; Beirut 1965-7

Qushayrī, *Laṭāʾif*
Abū l-Qāsim ʿAbd al-Karīm b. Hawāzin al-Qushayrī, *Laṭāʾif al-ishārāt,* ed. Ibrāḥim Basyūnī, 6 vols., Cairo 1968-71

Quṭb, *Ẓilāl*
Sayyid Quṭb Ibrāhīm Ḥusayn Shādhilī, *Fī ẓilāl al-Qurʾān,* 6 vols., Beirut 1393-4/1973-4; rev. 11th ed., Cairo 1993

al-Rāghib al-Iṣfahānī, *Mufradāt*
Abū l-Qāsim al-Ḥusayn al-Rāghib al-Iṣfahānī, *Muʿjam mufradāt alfāẓ al-Qurʾān,* Beirut 1392/1972

Rashīd Riḍā, *Manār*
Muḥammad Rashīd Riḍā and Muḥammad ʿAbduh, *Tafsīr al-Qurʾān al-ḥakīm al-shahīr bi-Tafsīr al-Manār,* 12 vols., Beirut n.d.

Rāzī, *Tafsīr*
Fakhr al-Dīn al-Rāzī, *al-Tafsīr al-kabīr (Mafātīḥ al-ghayb),* ed. Muḥammad Muḥyī l-Dīn ʿAbd al-Ḥamīd, 32 vols. in 16, Cairo 1352/1933; Tehran n.d.; Beirut 1981

Rippin, *Approaches*
Andrew Rippin (ed.), *Approaches to the history of the interpretation of the Qurʾān,* Oxford 1988

Rummānī et al., *Rasāʾil*
ʿAlī b. ʿĪsā al-Rummānī, Ḥamd b. Muḥammad al-Khaṭṭābī and ʿAbd al-Qāhir al-Jurjānī, *Thalāth rasāʾil fī iʿjāz al-Qurʾān,* ed. Muḥammad Khalaf Allāh Aḥmad and Muḥammad Zaghlūl Sallām, Cairo 1976

Rūzbihān al-Baqlī, *ʿArāʾis*
Rūzbihān b. Abī Naṣr al-Baqlī, *ʿArāʾis al-bayān fī ḥaqāʾiq al-Qurʾān,* 2 vols., Cawnpore 1301/1884

Ṣābūnī, *Tafsīr*
Muḥammad ʿAlī Ṣābūnī, *Ṣafwat al-tafāsīr. Tafsīr lil-Qurʾān al-karīm,* 3 vols., Beirut 1981
Ṣafadī, *Wāfī*
Khalīl b. Aybak al-Ṣafadī, *al-Wāfī bi-l-wafayāt. Das biographische Lexikon des Ṣalāḥaddīn Ḫalīl ibn Aibak aṣ-Ṣafadī,* ed. H. Ritter et al., 24 vols. to date, Wiesbaden-Beirut-Damascus 1962-
Sakhāwī, *Jamāl*
ʿAlam al-Dīn ʿAlī b. Muḥammad al-Sakhāwī, *Jamāl al-qurrāʾ wa-kamāl al-iqrāʾ,* ed. ʿAlī Ḥusayn al-Bawwāb, 2 vols., Mecca 1408/1987
Ṣaliḥī, *Subul*
Shams al-Dīn Muḥammad b. Yūsuf al-Ṣāliḥī, *Subul al-hudā wa-l-rashād,* ed. ʿĀdil Aḥmad ʿAbd al-Mawjūd and ʿAlī Muḥammad Muʿawwad, 12 vols., Beirut 1414/1993
Samʿānī, *Ansāb*
ʿAbd al-Karīm b. Muḥammad al-Samʿānī, *Kitāb al-Ansāb,* facsimile ed., D.S. Margoliouth, Leiden 1912; ed. Muḥammad ʿAbd al-Muʿīd Khān et al., 13 vols., Hyderabad 1382-1402/1962-82
Schawāhid-Indices
A. Fischer and E. Bräunlich (eds.), *Indices der Reimwörter und der Dichter der in den arabischen Schawāhid-Kommentaren und in verwandten Werken erläuterten Belegverse,* Leipzig 1934-45
Schwarzbaum, *Legends*
H. Schwarzbaum, *Biblical and extra-biblical legends in Islamic folk-literature,* Wallford-Hessen 1982
Sezgin, GAS
F. Sezgin, *Geschichte des arabischen Schrifttums,* 9 vols., Leiden 1967-84
Shāfiʿī, *Aḥkām*
Muḥammad b. Idrīs al-Shāfiʿī, *Aḥkām al-Qurʾān,* 2 vols. in 1, Beirut 1980
Shāfiʿī, *Mufassirān*
Muḥammad Shāfiʿī, *Mufassirān-i shīʿah,* Shiraz 1349[solar]/1970
Shahrastānī, *Milal*
Abū l-Fatḥ Muḥammad al-Shahrastānī, *al-Milal wa-l-niḥal,* ed. W. Cureton, 2 vols., London 1846; ed. Muḥammad Fatḥ Allāh Badrān, 2 vols., Cairo 1947-55; ed. Fahmī Muḥammad, Beirut 1992
Shawkānī, *Tafsīr*
Abū ʿAbdallāh Muḥammad b. ʿAlī al-Shawkānī, *Fatḥ al-qadīr al-jāmiʿ bayna fannay l-riwāya wa-l-dirāya fī ʿilm al-tafsīr,* 5 vols., Cairo 1349/1930; repr. Beirut 1973
Sibṭ Ibn al-Jawzī, *Mirʾāt*
Shams al-Dīn Abū l-Muẓaffar Yūsuf b. Qizoğlu Sibṭ Ibn al-Jawzī, *Mirʾāt al-zamān fī taʾrīkh al-aʿyān,* ed. Iḥsān ʿAbbās, Beirut 1405/1985
Speyer, *Erzählungen*
Heinrich Speyer, *Die biblischen Erzählungen im Qoran,* Gräfenhainich 1931; repr. Hildesheim 1961
Sprenger, *Moḥammad*
A. Sprenger, *Das Leben und die Lehre des Mohammad,* 3 vols., 2nd ed., Berlin 1869
Storey, PL
C.A. Storey, *Persian literature. A bio-bibliographical survey,* 2 vols. in 5, London 1927
Sufyān al-Thawrī, *Tafsīr*
Abū ʿAbdallāh Sufyān al-Thawrī, *al-Tafsīr,* ed. Imtiyāz ʿAlī ʿArshī, Beirut 1403/1983
Suhaylī, *Taʿrīf*
Abū l-Qāsim ʿAbd al-Raḥmān b. ʿAbdallāh al-Suhaylī, *al-Taʿrīf wa-l-iʿlām fī mā ubhima fī l-Qurʾān min al-asmāʾ wa-l-aʿlām,* ed. ʿAbdallāh Muḥammad ʿAlī al-Naqrāṭ, Tripoli 1401/1992
Sulamī, *Ziyādāt*
Abū ʿAbd al-Raḥmān Muḥammad b. al-Ḥusayn al-Sulamī, *Ziyādāt ḥaqāʾiq al-tafsīr,* ed. G. Böwering, Beirut 1995
Suyūṭī, *Durr*
Jalāl al-Dīn al-Suyūṭī, *al-Durr al-manthūr fī l-tafsīr bi-l-maʾthūr,* 6 vols., Beirut 1990
Suyūṭī, *Ḥuffāẓ*
Jalāl al-Dīn al-Suyūṭī, *Ṭabaqāt al-ḥuffāẓ,* ed. ʿAlī Muḥammad ʿUmar, Cairo 1973

Suyūṭī, *Itqān*
Jalāl al-Dīn al-Suyūṭī, *al-Itqān fī ʿulūm al-Qurʾān,* ed. Muḥammad Abū l-Faḍl Ibrāhīm, 4 vols. in 2, Cairo 1967
Suyūṭī, *Khaṣāʾiṣ*
Jalāl al-Dīn al-Suyūṭī, *al-Khaṣāʾiṣ al-kubrā,* Hyderabad 1320/1902; repr. Beirut n.d.
Suyūṭī, *Mufḥamāt*
Jalāl al-Dīn al-Suyūṭī, *al-Mufḥamāt al-aqrān fī mubhamāt al-Qurʾān,* ed. Muṣṭafā Dīb al-Bughā, Damascus and Beirut 1403/1982
Suyūṭī, *Muhadhdhab*
Jalāl al-Dīn al-Suyūṭī, *al-Muhadhdhab fī mā waqaʿa fī l-Qurʾān min al-muʿarrab,* ed. al-Tihāmī al-Rājī al-Hāshimī, Rabat n.d.; in *Rasāʾil fī l-fiqh wa-l-lugha,* ed. ʿAbdallāh al-Jubūrī, Beirut 1982, pp. 179-235
Suyūṭī, *Ṭabaqāt*
Jalāl al-Dīn al-Suyūṭī, *Ṭabaqāt al-mufassirīn,* ed. ʿAlī Muḥammad ʿUmar, Cairo 1976
Suyūṭī, *Taḥbīr*
Jalāl al-Dīn al-Suyūṭī, *al-Taḥbīr fī ʿilm al-tafsīr,* ed. Fatḥī ʿAbd al-Qādir Farīd, Cairo 1406/1986
Suyūṭī, *Tanāsuq*
Jalāl al-Dīn al-Suyūṭī, *Tanāsuq al-durar fī tanāsub al-suwar,* ed. ʿAbd al-Qādir Aḥmad ʿAṭā, Beirut 1406/1986
Ṭabarānī, *Awsaṭ*
Abū l-Qāsim Sulaymān b. Aḥmad al-Ṭabarānī, *al-Muʿjam al-awsaṭ,* ed. Ṭāriq b. ʿAwaḍ Allāh b. Muḥammad and ʿAbd al-Muḥsin Ibrāhīm al-Ḥusaynī, 10 vols., Cairo 1415/1995
Ṭabarānī, *Kabīr*
Abū l-Qāsim Sulaymān b. Aḥmad al-Ṭabarānī, *al-Muʿjam al-kabīr,* ed. Ḥamdī ʿAbd al-Majīd al-Salafī, vols. i-xii, xvii-xx and xxii-xxv, Baghdad 1398-1404/1977-83; Mosul 1401/1983
Ṭabarī, *Tafsīr*
Abū Jaʿfar Muḥammad b. Jarīr al-Ṭabarī, *Jāmiʿ al-bayān ʿan taʾwīl āy al-Qurʾān* [up to Q 14:27], ed. Maḥmūd Muḥammad Shākir and Aḥmad Muḥammad Shākir, 16 vols., Cairo 1954-68; 2nd ed. for some vols., Cairo 1969; ed. Aḥmad Saʿīd ʿAlī et al., 30 vols., Cairo 1373-77/1954-7; repr. Beirut 1984
Ṭabarī, *Taʾrīkh*
Abū Jaʿfar Muḥammad b. Jarīr al-Ṭabarī, *Taʾrīkh al-rusul wa-l-mulūk,* ed. M.J. de Goeje et al., 15 vols., Leiden 1879-1901; ed. Muḥammad Abū l-Faḍl Ibrāhīm, 10 vols., Cairo 1960-9
Ṭabarsī, *Majmaʿ*
Abū ʿAlī l-Faḍl b. al-Ḥasan al-Ṭabarsī, *Majmaʿ al-bayān fī tafsīr al-Qurʾān,* intr. Muḥsin al-Amīn al-Ḥusaynī al-ʿĀmilī, 30 vols. in 6, Beirut 1380/1961
Ṭabāṭabāʾī, *Mīzān*
Muḥammad Ḥusayn Ṭabāṭabāʾī, *al-Mīzān fī tafsīr al-Qurʾān,* 20 vols., Beirut 1393-4/1973-4; vol. xxi, Beirut 1985
Tāj al-ʿarūs
Muḥibb al-Dīn al-Sayyid Muḥammad Murtaḍā al-Zabīdī, *Sharḥ al-qāmūs al-musammā Tāj al-ʿarūs min jawāhir al-Qāmūs,* 10 vols., Cairo 1306-7; ed. ʿAbd al-Sattār Aḥmad Faraj et al., 40 vols., Kuwait 1965-2001
Thaʿālibī, *Iʿjāz*
ʿAbd al-Malik b. Muḥammad al-Thaʿālibī, *al-Iʿjāz wa-l-ījāz,* ed. Iskandar Āṣāt, Constantinople 1897; Beirut 1983
Thaʿālibī, *Iqtibās*
ʿAbd al-Malik b. Muḥammad al-Thaʿālibī, *al-Iqtibās min al-Qurʾān al-karīm,* ed. Ibtisām Marhūn al-Ṣaffār and Mujāhid Muṣṭafā Bahjat, 2 vols. in 1, Cairo 1412/1992
Thaʿālibī, *Yatīma*
ʿAbd al-Malik b. Muḥammad al-Thaʿālibī, *Yatīmat al-dahr fī maḥāsin ahl al-ʿaṣr,* 4 vols., Damascus 1304/1886-7; ed. Muḥammad Muḥyī l-Dīn ʿAbd al-Ḥamīd, 4 vols., Cairo 1375-7/1956-8
Thaʿlabī, *Qiṣaṣ*
Aḥmad b. Muḥammad b. Ibrāhīm al-Thaʿlabī, *Qiṣaṣ al-anbiyāʾ al-musammā bi-ʿArāʾis al-majālis,* Cairo 1322; repr. Beirut 1980

Tha'labī-Goldfeld
I. Goldfeld, *Qur'ānic commentary in the eastern Islamic tradition of the first four centuries of the hijra. An annotated edition of the preface to al-Tha'labī's "Kitāb al-Kashf wa-l-bayān 'an Tafsīr al-Qur'ān,"* Acre 1984

Tirmidhī, *Ṣaḥīḥ*
Abū 'Īsā Muḥammad b. 'Īsā al-Tirmidhī, *al-Jāmi' al-ṣaḥīḥ*, ed. Aḥmad Muḥammad Shākir et al., 5 vols., Cairo 1937-65

Ṭūsī, *Fihrist*
Muḥammad b. al-Ḥasan al-Ṭūsī, *al-Fihrist*, Najaf 1356/1937; Beirut 1983

Ṭūsī, *Tibyān*
Muḥammad b. al-Ḥasan al-Ṭūsī, *al-Tibyān fī tafsīr al-Qur'ān*, intr. Āghā Buzurk al-Ṭihrānī, 10 vols., Najaf 1376-83/1957-63

Tustarī, *Tafsīr*
Sahl b. 'Abdallāh al-Tustarī, *Tafsīr al-Qur'ān al-'aẓīm*, Cairo 1329/1911

'Ukbarī, *Tibyān*
Abū l-Baqā' 'Abdallāh b. al-Ḥusayn al-'Ukbarī, *al-Tibyān fī i'rāb al-Qur'ān*, ed. 'Alī Muḥammad al-Bajāwī, 2 vols., Cairo 1396/1976

Wagtendonk, *Fasting*
K. Wagtendonk, *Fasting in the Koran*, Leiden 1968

Wāḥidī, *Asbāb*
Abū l-Ḥasan 'Alī b. Aḥmad al-Nīsābūrī al-Wāḥidī, *Asbāb al-nuzūl*, Cairo 1968

Wāḥidī, *Wasīṭ*
Abū l-Ḥasan 'Alī b. Aḥmad al-Nīsābūrī al-Wāḥidī, *al-Wasīṭ fī tafsīr al-Qur'ān*, ed. 'Ādil Aḥmad 'Abd al-Mawjūd et al., 4 vols., Beirut 1415/1994

Wansbrough, *QS*
J. Wansbrough, *Quranic studies. Sources and methods of scriptural interpretation*, Oxford 1977

Wāqidī, *Maghāzī*
Muḥammad b. 'Umar al-Wāqidī, *Kitāb al-Maghāzī*, ed. M. Jones, 3 vols., London 1966

Watt-Bell, *Introduction*
W.M. Watt, *Bell's introduction to the Qur'ān*, Edinburgh 1970, 1991

Wensinck, *Concordance*
A.J. Wensinck et al., *Concordance et indices de la tradition musulmane*, 8 vols., Leiden 1936-79; repr. 8 vols. in 4, 1992

Wensinck, *Handbook*
A.J. Wensinck, *A handbook of early Muhammadan tradition*, Leiden 1927

Wild, *Text*
S. Wild (ed.), *The Qur'ān as text*, Leiden 1996

Yaḥyā b. Sallām, *Tafsīr*
Yaḥyā b. Sallām al-Baṣrī, *al-Taṣārīf. Tafsīr al-Qur'ān mimmā shtabahat asmā'uhu wa-taṣarrafat ma'ānīhi*, ed. Hind Shalabī, Tunis 1979

Ya'qūbī, *Buldān*
Aḥmad b. Abī Ya'qūb b. Wāḍiḥ al-Ya'qūbī, *Kitāb al-Buldān*, ed. M.J. de Goeje, Leiden 1892, 1967

Ya'qūbī, *Ta'rīkh*
Aḥmad b. Abī Ya'qūb b. Wāḍiḥ al-Ya'qūbī, *Ibn Wādhih qui dicitur al-Ja'qubi historiae*, ed. M.T. Houtsma, 2 vols., Leiden 1883; repr. 1969

Yāqūt, *Buldān*
Yāqūt b. 'Abdallāh al-Ḥamawī, *Mu'jam al-buldān*, ed. F. Wüstenfeld, 6 vols., Leipzig 1863-6; 5 vols., Beirut 1374-6/1955-7; ed. Farīd 'Abd al-'Azīz al-Jundī, 7 vols., Beirut 1990

Yāqūt, *Irshād*
Yāqūt b. 'Abdallāh al-Ḥamawī, *Irshād al-arīb ilā ma'rifat al-adīb. Mu'jam al-udabā'*, ed. D.S. Margoliouth, 7 vols., London and Leiden 1923-6; ed. Iḥsān 'Abbās, 7 vols., Beirut 1993

Zajjāj, *Ma'ānī*
Abū Isḥāq Ibrāhīm b. Muḥammad b. al-Sarī l-Zajjāj, *Ma'ānī l-Qur'ān wa-i'rābuhu*, ed. 'Abd al-Jalīl 'Abduh Shalabī, 5 vols., Beirut 1408/1988

Zamakhsharī, *Asās*
Maḥmūd b. 'Umar al-Zamakhsharī, *Asās al-balāgha*, Beirut 1979

Zamakhsharī, *Kashshāf*
Maḥmūd b. 'Umar al-Zamakhsharī, *al-*

Kashshāf ʿan ḥaqāʾiq ghawāmiḍ al-tanzīl wa-ʿuyūn al-aqāwīl fī wujūh al-taʾwīl, 4 vols., Beirut 1366/1947; ed. Muḥammad ʿAbd al-Salām Shāhīn, 4 vols., Beirut 1995

Zambaur, *Manuel*
E. de Zambaur, *Manuel de généalogie et de chronologie pour l'histoire de l'Islam,* Hanover 1927; repr. Bad Pyrmont 1955

Zarkashī, *Burhān*
Badr al-Dīn al-Zarkashī, *al-Burhān fī ʿulūm al-Qurʾān,* ed. Muḥammad Abū l-Faḍl Ibrāhīm, 4 vols., Cairo 1957; Beirut 1972; ed. Yūsuf ʿAbd al-Raḥmān al-Marʿashlī et al., 4 vols., Beirut 1994

Zayd b. ʿAlī, *Musnad*
Zayd b. ʿAlī Zayn al-ʿĀbidīn, *Musnad,* ed. Bakr b. Muḥammad ʿĀshūr, 1328/1910; Beirut 1983

Ziriklī, *Aʿlām*
Khayr al-Dīn al-Ziriklī, *al-Aʿlām. Qāmūs tarājim li-ashhar al-rijāl wa-l-nisāʾ min al-ʿArab wa-l-mustaʿribīn wa-l-mustashriqīn,* 10 vols., Damascus 1373-8/1954-9; 8 vols., Beirut 1979

Zubaydī, *Ṭabaqāt*
Abū Bakr Muḥammad b. al-Ḥasan al-Zubaydī, *Ṭabaqāt al-naḥwiyyīn wa-l-lughawiyyīn,* ed. Muḥammad Abū l-Faḍl Ibrāhīm, Cairo 1373/1954

Zubayrī, *Nasab*
Muṣʿab al-Zubayrī, *Nasab Quraysh,* ed. E. Lévi-Provençal, Cairo 1953

Zurqānī, *Sharḥ*
Muḥammad b. ʿAbd al-Bāqī al-Miṣrī al-Mālik, *Sharḥ al-mawāhib al-laduniyya,* ed. Muḥammad ʿAbd al-ʿAzīz al-Khālidī, 12 vols., Beirut 1417/1996

J

Jacob

Biblical patriarch, son of Isaac (q.v.), mentioned sixteen times by name in the Qurʾān and probably referred to by the name Isrāʾīl another two times (see ISRAEL). The form of the name in Arabic, Yaʿqūb, may have come directly from the Hebrew or may have been filtered through Syriac (Jeffery, *For. vocab.*, 291; see FOREIGN VOCABULARY); the name was apparently used in pre-Islamic times in Arabia (Horovitz, Jewish proper names, 152; id., *KU*, 152-3; see PRE-ISLAMIC ARABIA AND THE QURʾĀN). Most frequently, Jacob is mentioned simply within the list of patriarchs along with Abraham (q.v.) and Isaac, following Jewish tradition (Q 6:84; 11:71; 12:38; 19:49; 21:72; 29:27; 38:45), with Ishmael (q.v.) added on occasion (Q 2:136, 140; 3:84; 4:163; and perhaps 2:132). The narrative of the life of Jacob in the Qurʾān is primarily limited to his role in the Joseph (q.v.) story in which he orders his sons not to all go through a single gate into the city (Q 12:67; see Shapiro, *Haggadischen Elemente*, i, 55-6) and in which he becomes blind due to his sorrow (over Joseph, cf. Q 12:84). His sight, however, is restored when his face (q.v.) is touched by the shirt of Joseph (Q 12:93, 96; see VISION AND BLINDNESS; CLOTHING). Jacob's last words (*Gen* 49) are also echoed in Q 2:133, "… when he said to his sons, 'What will you serve after me?' They said, 'We will serve your God and the God of your fathers Abraham, Ishmael and Isaac, one God; to him we surrender' " (see POLYTHEISM AND ATHEISM; MONOTHEISM).

The observation that the Qurʾān appears to consider Jacob a brother of Isaac rather than his son (although on other occasions, it is clear that this type of confusion has not taken place, e.g. Q 2:132, "Abraham charged his sons with this and Jacob likewise") has become a motif in polemical literature. Based on passages "We gave him Isaac and Jacob" (Q 6:84; 19:49; 21:72; 29:27) and "We gave her the glad tidings of Isaac and, after Isaac, Jacob" (Q 11:71), the charge has been laid that there was a misunderstanding of the relationship between Jacob and Isaac. It is clear, however, that later Muslims were not the least bit confused on the issue, all recognizing that the relationship between the two as related in the Bible was accurate (Geiger, *Judaism and Islam*, 108-9; Speyer, *Erzählungen*, 170-1).

The biblical renaming of Jacob as Israel (thus providing the personal dimension of the idea of the "Children of Israel" [q.v.] as well as the territorial and tribal; see *Gen*

32:28) is likely reflected in the use of "Israel" in Q 3:93, "All food was lawful to the Children of Israel save what Israel forbade for himself (see FORBIDDEN; LAWFUL AND UNLAWFUL)" — which probably refers to the account of Genesis 32:33 — and in Q 19:58, "of those we bore with Noah (q.v.), and of the seed of Abraham and Israel." No further elaboration of this name change and its significance in genealogical terms can be noted in the Qurʾān.

When the story of Jacob is retold in the "stories of the prophets" literature *(qiṣaṣ al-anbiyāʾ),* the account of Jacob and Esau receives a good deal of attention even though it is unmentioned in the Qurʾān itself (e.g. Ṭabarī, *Taʾrīkh,* i, 354-60). The etymology of the name of Jacob is retold in these accounts as an etiological narrative that works as well in Arabic as it does in Hebrew: Jacob held on to Esau's heel (*ʿaqb* in Arabic) when the twins were being born, although the etymology of Esau as derived from "refusing," *ʿaṣā,* does not produce a fully meaningful narrative within the picture of their birth (cf. *Gen* 25:25-6; Ginzberg, *Legends,* i, 315; v, 274).

Andrew Rippin

Bibliography
Primary: Kisāʾī, *Qiṣaṣ,* 163-7; Ṭabarī, *The history of al-Ṭabarī. ii. Prophets and patriarchs,* trans. W.M. Brinner, Albany, NY 1987, 134-9, 148-50, 167-84; id., *Taʾrīkh,* ed. De Goeje, i, 354-60, 372-4, 393-413; Thaʿlabī, *Qiṣaṣ,* 88-90.
Secondary: A. Geiger, *Was hat Mohammed aus dem Judentume aufgenommen?* Bonn 1838 (Eng. trans. *Judaism and Islam,* Madras 1898); L. Ginzberg, *The legends of the Jews,* 7 vols., Philadelphia 1909-36; Horovitz, Jewish proper names in the Koran, in *Hebrew Union College annual* 2 (1925), 152; id., *KU;* I. Shapiro, *Die haggadischen Elemente im erzählenden Teil des Korans,* Berlin 1907; Speyer, *Erzählungen.*

Jahannam see HELL AND HELLFIRE

Jāhiliyya see AGE OF IGNORANCE

Jail see PRISONERS

Jālūt see GOLIATH

Jealousy see ENVY

Jerusalem

The holy city sacred to Judaism, Christianity and Islam, Jerusalem (Īliyāʾ, *bayt al-maqdis,* Ūrīshalayim, al-Quds) is not mentioned by name in the Qurʾān. As Islam is, however, deeply rooted in Judaism and Christianity (see JEWS AND JUDAISM; CHRISTIANS AND CHRISTIANITY), many stories with a biblical background are undoubtedly situated in Jerusalem and some of these stories have been included in the holy book of the Muslims (see NARRATIVES). Further, one must bear in mind that the designation *bayt al-maqdis* (lit. "house of the holy," from Heb. *Bēt ha-miqdāsh,* the Temple), has three meanings: first, the Jewish Temple and its successor, the Temple Mount *(al-ḥaram al-sharīf)* with the Dome of the Rock and the Aqṣā Mosque (q.v.); second, the city of Jerusalem; third, the holy land *(al-arḍ al-muqaddasa)* as a whole.

Based on relevant passages in the Qurʾān, Muslim tradition created an image of Jerusalem that combined Jewish and Christian elements with specifically Islamic ones. The main sources to be consulted in presenting this image are the vast corpus of Qurʾān commentaries (*tafsīr,* see EXEGESIS OF THE QURʾĀN: CLASSICAL AND MEDIEVAL; EXEGESIS OF THE QURʾĀN: EARLY MODERN AND CONTEMPORARY) and the *faḍāʾil al-Quds* ("Virtues of Jerusalem") literature. By its very nature, the literary genre of *faḍāʾil al-Quds* is an expression of local pride, which explains why the authors active in this field found more material in the Qurʾān in favor of Jerusalem than did the qurʾānic commentators *(mufassirūn)*. Likewise, they claimed exclusiveness for Jerusalem in passages for which the *mufassirūn* offered a variety of interpretations.

There are a number of instances in which there is general agreement — in both commentary *(tafsīr)* and *faḍāʾil*-literature — that certain qurʾānic passages allude to Jerusalem, rather than other places. This applies, for instance, to the identification of "the farthest mosque" *(al-masjid al-aqṣā)* in Q 17:1 with al-Ḥaram al-Sharīf in Jerusalem, which is said to have been the destination of Muḥammad's "night journey" *(isrāʾ)* and the scene of his ascension (q.v.; *miʿrāj*). It is the site of the Jewish Temple, which was destroyed by the Romans in the year 70 C.E. and reconstructed by the Muslims during the caliphate of ʿUmar b. al-Khaṭṭāb (r. 13-23/634-44). There is, however, disagreement as to whether Muḥammad prayed in the sanctuary or not. Had he done so, it would have been incumbent on Muslims also to visit Jerusalem when on the pilgrimage (q.v.; *ḥajj*) to Mecca (q.v.). Therefore, some theologians denied the idea of Muḥammad's praying in the sanctuary. According to others, however, confirmation of the belief in one God *(tawḥīd)* was revealed in Jerusalem when Muḥammad prayed with the prophets, his predecessors in office, in the sanctuary (see PROPHETS AND PROPHETHOOD). General agreement likewise exists regarding the interpretation of Q 2:142-50, where the change of the direction of prayer *(qibla*, q.v.) is discussed. It has been accepted that the direction of prayer was Jerusalem before it was changed to the Kaʿba (q.v.) in Mecca.

The setting of many biblical stories incorporated in the Qurʾān is Jerusalem or the holy land, although the name is not explicitly mentioned. Jewish and Christian traditions — both apocryphal and canonical — such as those about the location of the last judgment (q.v.) in Jerusalem, have been adopted by Muslims. Q 50:41, "And listen for the day when the caller will call out from a place quite near *(min makānin qarībin)*," is said to refer to Jerusalem, the "place quite near" being the holy rock *(al-ṣakhra)* in the al-Ḥaram al-Sharīf. The angel Isrāfīl, standing on the holy rock, will call the dead to rise from their graves (see DEATH AND THE DEAD; RESURRECTION). It is a place appropriate for the purpose because it is next to heaven (see HEAVEN AND SKY). There is, on the other hand, an interpretation offered by al-Zamakhsharī (d. 538/1144; *Kashshāf*, ad loc.) according to which "a place quite near" means the feet of the dead or the roots of their hair.

Many other identifications of places are not as unequivocal as those just mentioned. There are numerous cases in which, in accordance with the generally accepted exegetical tendency to amass traditional interpretations, one or more sites in addition to Jerusalem have been proposed; in other words, these places compete with Jerusalem. Sometimes such competing sites are situated in the holy land, including Syria (q.v.) and Jordan. A rivalry on a higher level, however, is that between Jerusalem and the holy cities of Mecca and Medina (q.v.) or between the holy land and the rest of the world (see COSMOLOGY). The latter is present in the interpretation of Q 7:137, "And we made a people, considered weak, inheritors of land *(arḍ)* in both east and west — land whereupon we sent down our blessings (see BLESSING; OPPRESSED ON EARTH, THE)." The blessed land is Syria or, according to another interpretation, the whole world, because God conferred the kingdom of the world upon

David (q.v.) and Solomon (q.v.). Q 21:105, "Before this we wrote in the Psalms (q.v.; *al-zabūr*) after the message *(al-dhikr):* My servants, the righteous, shall inherit the earth," is, according to Speyer (*Erzählungen*, 285), the only word-for-word citation of the Bible (*Ps* 37:19; *Matt* 5:5; see SCRIPTURE AND THE QURʾĀN). Although it undoubtedly refers to the holy land, other interpretations have been offered: It means paradise (q.v.), which is to be granted to the believers (see BELIEF AND UNBELIEF), but also this world, the universal kingdom of Islam (q.v.). The inheritance will come at the end of times, when Jesus (q.v.) descends from heaven to fight the unbelievers, subjecting the whole world to Islamic rule. The decisive battle will be fought in Jerusalem (see APOCALYPSE).

More often, Jerusalem competes with Mecca, as both are cities, and the holy land with the Ḥijāz. Q 17:60, "We granted the vision which we showed you," has been explained in two ways: It is the vision Muḥammad had after his return from the night journey *(isrāʾ)*. When the Quraysh (q.v.) called him a liar (see LIE; OPPOSITION TO MUḤAMMAD; INSANITY), the Prophet had a vision of *bayt al-maqdis*, which enabled him to answer questions that the Meccans were asking in order to examine the veracity of his story. Another interpretation is that Muḥammad had a vision of the forthcoming conquest of Mecca at al-Ḥudaybiya (q.v.), when the Quraysh prevented him from entering Mecca to offer sacrifices at the Kaʿba (see EXPEDITIONS AND BATTLES). Q 2:114, "And who is more unjust (see JUSTICE AND INJUSTICE) than he who forbids that in places for the worship of God, God's name should be celebrated, whose zeal is to ruin them?" possibly refers to the destruction of the Temple either by Nebuchadnezzar or Titus. It has been interpreted, however, as referring to Mecca and the Kaʿba, when the heathens, before Muḥammad's emigration (q.v.; *hijra*), prevented him from worshiping at the Kaʿba. Another interpretation says that this happened at al-Ḥudaybiya. The olive tree *(zaytūn)* mentioned in Q 95:1, by which an oath (see OATHS) is sworn, has been explained both as meaning what it is, a valuable plant, and as denoting the hill on which *bayt al-maqdis* stands.

The rivalry between Jerusalem and Mecca is also apparent in the question about whether it was Isaac (q.v.) or Ishmael (q.v.) whom Abraham (q.v.) was ordered to slaughter as a sacrifice (q.v.). The story is recounted in Q 37:99-111, but the narrative leaves open the identity of the potential victim. If it was Isaac, Jerusalem would be the place of the sacrifice; otherwise, it would be Mecca or nearby Minā. Conversely, the account of the building of the Kaʿba in Q 2:125 is in favor of Ishmael, for he assisted his father, which proves his presence in Mecca.

Another example of Jerusalem's rivalry with Mecca may be found with the interpretation of the parable of the divine light (q.v.) in Q 24:35-6. It could be an allusion to candles lit in churches and monasteries (Paret, *Kommentar*, 360; see CHURCH; MONASTICISM AND MONKS), but another interpretation exists: the houses *(buyūt)* mentioned in Q 24:36, in which the light is lit, are four structures, all erected by prophets. These four are: the Kaʿba, built by Abraham and Ishmael, *bayt al-maqdis* built by David and Solomon, *masjid al-Madīna*, and *masjid qubāʾ*, both built by Muḥammad; each can be deemed to be a "mosque (q.v.) founded on piety" (Q 9:108). Here, Jerusalem is put on a par with the holy places in the Ḥijāz. Al-Rāzī (d. 606/1210; *Tafsīr*, xxiv, 3, ad Q 24:36), however, cites another interpretation in the name of al-Ḥasan al-Baṣrī, who identifies the houses, without explaining the plural, with *bayt al-maqdis* because it is illuminated by ten thousand candles.

Jerusalem competes not only with Mecca,

but also with the other world: *al-sāhira* mentioned in Q 79:14 is said to be the surface of the earth to which the dead will ascend on the day of resurrection. Some commentators define it geographically as the plain to the north of Jerusalem on which humankind will gather during the day of judgment. According to others, it is a plain destined for the gathering of the unbelievers, causing such fright as to prevent people from slumbering. Another exegetical tradition explains *al-sāhira* as the new earth *(al-arḍ al-jadīda),* which will replace this earth when the world comes to an end; and, finally, according to yet another understanding, it is hell (*jahannam,* see HELL AND HELLFIRE).

Also understood to have both eschatological and this-worldly connotations is the wall mentioned in Q 57:13: "A wall will be put up between them, with a gate therein, within it will be mercy (q.v.), and without it, all alongside, will be punishment (see REWARD AND PUNISHMENT)." The wall is understood to be the eastern wall of the al-Ḥaram al-Sharīf, above Wādī Jahannam (the Kedron Valley), the gate is Bāb al-Raḥma, the Gate of Mercy, one of the two entrances of the Golden Gate. According to some commentators, though, it is the partition between paradise and hell, a kind of purgatory, the gate where the elect will enter paradise (see BARZAKH; BARRIER). On the day of resurrection those raised from the dead will rush to a goal-post *(nuṣub),* mentioned in Q 70:43. This is understood by some to be the holy rock in Jerusalem, but by others to be a signpost *(ʿalam)* to which the believers — or an idol to which the polytheists (see IDOLS AND IMAGES; POLYTHEISM AND ATHEISM) — will rush on the day of judgment.

Rivalry exists on the local level between Jerusalem and other towns of Palestine and Syria. The town *(al-qarya)* mentioned in Q 2:58, whose gate the Israelites were ordered to enter with humility, is identified in the exegetical literature as Jerusalem or Jericho. When Jericho is mentioned, the remark is added that it is located not far from Jerusalem. But according to some commentators, it is the gate of Cairo or Egypt *(Miṣr).* Another example: "The one who passed by a town, all in ruins to its roofs" (Q 2:259) was either ʿUzayr (identified with Ezra, q.v.) or Jeremiah (who bewailed the destruction of Jerusalem) or the legendary al-Khiḍr (see KHAḌIR/KHIḌR). There are three proposals about the name of the town: first, Sābūr on the Tigris, situated between Wāsiṭ and al-Madāʾin; second, Jerusalem; and third, the town of "those who abandoned their homes, though they were thousands, for fear of death," mentioned in Q 2:243. There are various explanations of the holy land *(al-arḍ al-muqaddasa)* mentioned in Q 5:21: It is said to be Jericho, Jordan (al-Urdunn), and Palestine, or Ṭūr (Mt. Sinai; see SINAI) and its surroundings. According to others it is al-Shām (Syria or Damascus), or simply Jericho. Equally various are the locations given for the *rabwa* (lit. great or high place) in Q 23:50, where Mary (q.v.), the mother of Jesus, found shelter with her son: the Ghūṭa (plain) of Damascus, Jerusalem, Ramla, or Egypt, the latter apparently a reminiscence of the flight of Joseph, Mary and Jesus to Egypt (q.v.) as told in the Gospels (q.v.).

The Shīʿī viewpoint (see SHĪʿISM AND THE QURʾĀN) is especially evident in the various interpretations, found in both Sunnī and Shīʿī authors, of Muḥammad's vision mentioned in Q 17:60. Al-Māwardī (d. 450/1058; *Nukat,* iii, 253) and al-Ṭabarsī (d. 548/1154; *Majmaʿ,* xv, 66-7), following al-Ṭabarī (d. 310/923; *Tafsīr,* xv, 110-3), give three interpretations of this vision: the first explains it as Muḥammad's vision during the *isrāʾ;* the second, as a vision while Muḥammad was sleeping (according to Ibn ʿAbbās, Muḥammad sees himself entering Mecca; see DREAMS AND SLEEP;

FORETELLING; VISIONS); and the third, also as a vision while sleeping (according to Sahl b. Saʿd, the vision is of people like donkeys climbing on the pulpits *[manābir]*). While al-Ṭabarī expresses a preference for the first explanation, al-Māwardī gives no such opinion. Shīʿī exegetes, such as al-Ṭabarsī and al-Ṭabāṭabāʾī (d. 1982; *Mukhtaṣar al-Mīzān*), stress that this passage has nothing to do with Jerusalem, nor with Mecca, but maintain that it refers to future events, the misdeeds of the Umayyads who deprived the ʿAlids of their legitimate claim to the caliphate (see CALIPH; POLITICS AND THE QURʾĀN): Muḥammad saw them climbing on his pulpit, behaving like apes.

Modern commentators such as Rashīd Riḍā *(Manār),* al-Mawdūdī *(Tafhīm),* al-Zuḥaylī *(Tafsīr)* and Tuʿaylib *(Fatḥ),* present the traditional interpretations on many of the verses already discussed. After making their own positions clear, however, they provide events and places in the context of the life of Muḥammad and the history of early Islam in Arabia rather than locating these in Jerusalem. To mention but a few examples: Those who, according to Q 2:114, prevented the pious from visiting the sanctuaries, and even tried to ruin them, were not Nebuchadnezzar or Titus, but the heathens in Mecca before the emigration *(hijra)*. Rashīd Riḍā derives the protection of synagogues and churches as practiced in Islam from Q 2:114 (see RELIGIOUS PLURALISM AND THE QURʾĀN). That Muḥammad prayed inside the sanctuary of *bayt al-maqdis* during his night journey is not contested in principle in modern *tafsīr;* it is no longer considered an issue of heated debate. The land promised to the pious in Q 21:105 is paradise, the wall with the gate in Q 57:13 will be put up in the other world, and *al-sāhira* in Q 79:14 belongs to the world to come or remains geographically undefined. Generally modern *tafsīr* prefers theological interpretation and the discussion of problems pertaining to the religious law *(sharīʿa)* to a consideration of problems in the history of the holy places and their basis in biblical lore (see LAW AND THE QURʾĀN; HISTORY AND THE QURʾĀN; THEOLOGY AND THE QURʾĀN).

Finally, the close relation between Jerusalem and the Qurʾān found expression in the enumeration of merits earned by those who recite certain sūras (see RECITATION OF THE QURʾĀN): The person who recites Q 29 "The Spider" (Sūrat al-ʿAnkabūt) will receive for each verse the same recompense as those who conquered Jerusalem, and those who recite Q 5 "The Table Spread" (Sūrat al-Māʾida; see TABLE) and Q 30 "The Romans" (Sūrat al-Rūm; see BYZANTINES) will be compensated for each verse as those who visit Jerusalem (Fīrūzābādī, *Baṣāʾir,* i, 364, 369). See also SACRED PRECINCTS.

Heribert Busse

Bibliography

Primary (In addition to the commentaries on the passages cited above found in the works of *tafsīr* from Muqātil b. Sulaymān down to modern authors): Fazārī, Burhān al-Dīn b. al-Firkā, *Bāʿith al-nufūs ilā ziyārat al-Quds al-maḥrūs,* trans. Ch.D. Matthews, *Palestine. Mohammedan holy land,* New Haven 1949, 1-41; Fīrūzābādī, *Baṣāʾir;* Maqdisī, Abū l-Maʿālī al-Musharraf b. al-Murajjā, *Faḍāʾil bayt al-maqdis wa-l-Khalīl wa-faḍāʾil al-Shām,* ed. O. Livne-Kafri, Shfaram 1995; Maqdisī, Muḥammad b. ʿAbd al-Wāḥid, *Faḍāʾil bayt al-maqdis,* ed. M.M. al-Ḥāfiẓ, Damascus 1985, 8, 11, 20, 24, 28; Maqdisī, Shihāb al-Dīn Abū Maḥmūd b. Tamīm, *Muthīr al-gharām ilā ziyārat al-Quds wa-l-Shām,* ed. A. al-Khuṭaymī, Beirut 1994; Māwardī, *Nukat;* Mawdūdī, *Tafhīm al-Qurʾān,* 6 vols., Lahore 1949-72; Eng. trans. *The meaning of the Qurʾān,* Lahore 1967; Rashīd Riḍā, *Manār;* Rāzī, *Tafsīr,* ed. M. Muḥyī l-Dīn, Cairo 1933-62; Suyūṭī, Shams al-Dīn Abū ʿAlī Muḥammad b. Aḥmad, *Itḥāf al-akhiṣṣāʾ bi-faḍāʾil al-masjid al-aqṣā,* ed. A. Ramaḍān Aḥmad, Cairo 1984; Ṭabarī, *Tafsīr,* ed. Shākir; Ṭabarsī, *Majmaʿ;* Ṭabāṭabāʾī, *Mukhtaṣar al-Mīzān;* Tuʿaylib, ʿAbd al-Munʿim Aḥmad, *Fatḥ al-raḥmān fī tafsīr al-Qurʾān,* 7 vols.,

Cairo 1995; ʿUlaymī, Mujīr al-Dīn Abū l-Yaman ʿAbd al-Raḥmān b. Muḥammad, *al-Uns al-jalīl bi-tārīkh al-Quds wa-l-Khalīl,* Amman 1973, i, 226-7; Wāsiṭī, Muḥammad b. Aḥmad, *Faḍāʾil al-bayt al-muqaddas,* ed. I. Hasson, Jerusalem 1979; Zamakhsharī, *Kashshāf;* al-Zuḥaylī, Wahba, *al-Tafsīr al-wajīz wa-maʿahu asbāb al-nuzūl wa-qawāʿid al-tartīl ʿalā hāmish al-Qurʾān al-karīm,* Damascus 1995.
Secondary: H. Busse, Bāb Ḥiṭṭa. Qurʾān 2:58 and the entry into Jerusalem, in *JSAI* 22 (1998), 1-17; id., Jerusalem in the story of Muḥammad's night journey and ascension, in *JSAI* 14 (1991), 1-40; C. Gilliot, Coran 17, *Isrāʾ,* 1, dans la recherche occidentale. De la critique des traditions du Coran comme texte, in M.A. Amir-Moezzi (ed.), *Le voyage intiatique en terre d'Islam. Ascensions célestes et itinéraires spirituels,* Paris 1996, 1-26; I. Hasson, The Muslim view of Jerusalem. The Qurʾān and ḥadīth, in J. Prawer and H. Ben-Shammai (eds.), *The history of Jerusalem. The early Muslim period.* 638-1099, New York 1996, 349-85; A. Kaplony, *The Haram of Jerusalem 324-1099. Temple, Friday Mosque, area of spiritual power,* Stuttgart 2002; A. Neuwirth, From the Sacred Mosque to the Remote Temple. Sūrat al-Isrāʾ between text and commentary, in J.D. McAuliffe, B.D. Walfish and J.W. Goering (eds.), *With reverence for the word. Medieval scriptural exegesis in Judaism, Christianity and Islam,* New York 2003, 376-407; Paret, *Kommentar;* Speyer, *Erzählungen.*

Jest

see LAUGHTER; MOCKERY

Jesus

The first-century Jewish teacher and wonder worker believed by Christians to be the Son of God, he is named in the Qurʾān as one of the prophets before Muḥammad who came with a scripture (see BOOK; CHRISTIANS AND CHRISTIANITY; PROPHETS AND PROPHETHOOD). The qurʾānic form of Jesus' name is ʿĪsā. It is attested twenty-five times, often in the form ʿĪsā b. Maryam, Jesus son of Mary. The Qurʾān asserts that he was a prophet and gives him the unique title "the Messiah" (see ANOINTING). It affirms his virginal conception (see MARY; HOLY SPIRIT); cites miracles which he performed by divine permission (see MIRACLE); and states that God raised him into his presence. It probably also alludes to his future return. It denies, however, that he was divine (as noted, one of his qurʾānic identifications is as the "son of Mary"; see below for further discussion of this title) and attaches no significance to the cross. As traditionally interpreted by Muslims, it also denies that he was crucified (see CRUCIFIXION).

Inventory of the qurʾānic Jesus material

The relevant passages are listed here in chronological order in accordance with Nöldeke's classification (see CHRONOLOGY AND THE QURʾĀN). For the sake of comparison, the order implied by the headings of the standard Egyptian edition of the Qurʾān is also given (see Robinson, *Discovering,* 72-96). For example N 58/E 44 indicates that according to Nöldeke the sūra in question was the fifty-eighth revealed but that it was the forty-fourth according to the standard Egyptian edition: Q 19:16-40, 88-95 (N 58/E 44); Q 43:57-65, 81-2 (N 61/E 109); Q 23:50 (N 64/E 74); Q 21:91-93 (N 65/E 73); Q 42:13-14 (N 83/E 86); Q 6:83-90 (N 89/E 55); Q 2:87, 135-141, 252-253 (N 91/E 87); Q 3:42-64, 81-85 (N 97/E 89); Q 33:7-8 (N 103/E 90); Q 4:156-159, 163-165, 171-172 (N 100/E 92); Q 57:26-27 (N 99/E 94); Q 66:10-12 (N 109/E 107); Q 61:6, 14 (N 98/E 109); Q 5:17-18, 46-47, 72-78, 109-118 (N 114/E 112); Q 9:30-31 (N 113/E 113).

There is widespread agreement that the first six passages cited above (i.e. those down to and including Q 6:83-90) were revealed in Mecca and the others in Medina. The chronological order, however, is only approximate and some of the earlier sūras have almost certainly been revised. The dating of the passages in Q 19 is particularly problematic. There is a tradition that the Muslims who emigrated to

Abyssinia (q.v.) recited part of this sūra to the Negus (Ibn Isḥāq-Guillaume, 150-3) which would make it quite early (see EMIGRATION). In any case, the reference in Q 19:17 to an angel (q.v.), 'our spirit,' appearing in visible form strongly suggests that the sūra is Meccan. Moreover, Q 43:57 implies that the Prophet's audience had already heard an extensive revelation about "the son of Mary" and Q 23:50 probably alludes to a specific element in this particular version of his story (cf. Q 19:22-6). Q 19:34-40, however, which has a different rhyme from the rest of the sūra (see FORM AND STRUCTURE OF THE QUR'ĀN), was almost certainly added later and the references to "the book" (Q 19:12, 16, 30, etc.) are probably late Meccan or early Medinan.

The name ʿĪsā, its origin and significance

The name "Jesus" (ʿĪsā) occurs twenty-five times: nine times by itself (Q 2:136; 3:52, 55, 59, 84; 4:163; 6:85; 42:13; 43:63) and sixteen times in conjunction with one or more other names or titles (Q 2:87, 253; 3:45; 4:157, 171; 5:46, 78, 110, 112, 114, 116; 19:34; 33:7; 57:27; 61:6, 14). It was probably absent from the original version of Q 19:16-40 and it is not found in sūras 23 or 61, but it is attested in the other twelve sūras listed above.

The qur'ānic spelling of Jesus' name is strikingly different from any currently used by Christians. The English form "Jesus" is derived from the Latin *Iesus* which in turn is based on the Greek *Iēsous*. It is generally held, however, that because Jesus was a Palestinian Jew, his original name must have been Hebrew and that the Greek *Iēsous* represents the Hebrew *Yēshūaʿ* which is an abbreviated form of *Yᵉhōshūaʿ* (or *Yᵉhōshuaʿ*). The original meaning of *Yᵉhōshūaʿ* was "Yahweh helps" but it was popularly understood to mean, "Yahweh saves." When the New Testament was translated from Greek into Syriac, *Iēsous* was rendered *Yēshūʿ*, although Syriac-speaking Nestorian Christians called him *Ishuʿ*. After the rise of Islam, the gospels (q.v.) were eventually translated from Syriac into Arabic and *Yeshūʿ* was rendered *Yasūʿ*, which is what Arab Christians call Jesus to this day.

The grounds for thinking that Jesus' original name was *Yeshuaʿ* are: 1) The Hebrew scriptures mention several people called *Yᵉhōshūaʿ*, *Yᵉhōshuaʿ* or *Yēshūaʿ*, including Moses' successor Joshua son of Nūn whose name is spelled in all three ways. In the Septuagint, these names are almost invariably rendered as *Iēsous* (Brown et al., *Hebrew and English lexicon*, 221). 2) By the first century, only the short form *Yēshūaʿ* was in use. 3) The New Testament refers to Moses' successor, Joshua, in Acts 7:45 and Hebrews 4:8, and in both instances it gives his name in Greek as *Iēsous*. 4) According to Matthew 1:21, an angel told Joseph in a dream that Mary would have a son, and added "Thou shalt call his name Jesus for it is he who shall save his people from their sins." As there is no play-on-words in the Greek, Matthew's readers were presumably familiar with the original Hebrew name and its etymology.

Western scholars, because of their conviction that Jesus' authentic Hebrew name is *Yēshūaʿ*, have been puzzled by the Qur'ān's reference to him as ʿĪsā. They have offered a number of explanations for this apparent anomaly. One suggestion is that *y-sh-ʿ*, the Hebrew consonants of *Yēshūaʿ*, have been reversed for some cryptic reason to give *ʿ-s-y*, the Arabic consonants of ʿĪsā. Those who favor this view note that in ancient Mesopotamia certain divine names were written in one way and pronounced in another; for example EN-ZU was read ZU-EN (Michaud, *Jésus*, 15). Scarcely more plausible is the suggestion that the Jews called Jesus "Esau" (Hebrew *ʿEsaw*) out of hatred and that

Muḥammad learned this name from them not realizing that it was an insult (see JEWS AND JUDAISM; POLEMIC AND POLEMICAL LANGUAGE). Admittedly, in Arabic Esau is usually written *ʿĪsū* and this might have been changed into *ʿĪsā* in order to assimilate it to other qurʾānic names ending in *-ā*. There is no evidence, however, that the Jews have ever called Jesus Esau. Moreover, the Qurʾān criticizes them for insulting Jesus' mother (Q 4:156), and Muḥammad's many Christian acquaintances would surely have corrected him if he had unwittingly adopted a Jewish insult against Jesus himself. A third suggestion is that Jesus' name has been altered deliberately to assimilate it to Mūsā (Moses, q.v.), with whom he is sometimes paired. There may be other examples of this phenomenon in the Qurʾān, for instance, Saul (q.v.) and Goliath (q.v.) are called Ṭālūt and Jālūt, Aaron (q.v.) and Korah (q.v.) are called Hārūn and Qārūn. A fourth suggestion is that, already before the rise of Islam, Christians in Arabia may have coined the name ʿĪsā from one of the Syriac forms *Yeshūʿ* or *Ishūʿ*. Arabic often employs an initial *ʿayn* in words borrowed from Aramaic or Syriac and the dropping of the final Hebrew *ʿayin* is evidenced in the form *Yisho* of the "köktürkish" Manichaean fragments from Turfan (Jefferey, *For. vocab.*, 220; see FOREIGN VOCABULARY). Although there is no irrefutable evidence that the name ʿĪsā was in use in pre-Islamic times (see PRE-ISLAMIC ARABIA AND THE QURʾĀN), there was a monastery in Syria which may have been known as the *ʿĪsāniyya* as early as 571 C.E. (Mingana, Syriac influence, 84; see SYRIAC AND THE QURʾĀN; MONASTICISM AND MONKS).

While many Muslim scholars entertain the possibility that the qurʾānic form of Jesus' name reflects the usage of certain Christians in Muḥammad's milieu, others maintain that ʿĪsā was, in fact, the original form of Jesus' name. Sarwat Anis al-Assiouty (*Jésus*, 110-19) champions this view. Among the arguments which he adduces, the following merit consideration:

1) If Jesus' original name had been *Yēshūaʿ*, the final *ʿayin* would have been retained in Aramaic sources which mention him. In the Talmud, however, he is called *Yēshū*.

2) In Matthew 1:21, the angel states that it is Jesus himself, not Yahweh, who will save his people. Thus, far from supporting the derivation of *Iesous* from *Yeshuaʿ*, this biblical verse militates against it.

3) Josephus used the Greek name *Iēsous* to denote three people mentioned in the Bible whose Hebrew names were not *Yēshūaʿ*, *Yᵉhōshūaʿ* or *Yᵉhōshuaʿ*. They were Saul's son *Yishwī* (Anglicized as "Ishvi" in the RSV of I Samuel 14:49), the Levite *Abīshūaʿ* (mentioned in I Chronicles 6:4, etc.) and *Yishwah* the son of Asher (Anglicized as "Ishva" in the RSV of Genesis 46:17).

4) Around the middle of the second century, Justin Martyr penned his famous *Dialogue with Trypho the Jew*. Justin, a Christian who wrote in Greek and knew no Hebrew, argued at length that the Old Testament story of Joshua should be interpreted typologically as referring to Jesus. Under his influence, most Christians subsequently assumed that Jesus' Hebrew name must have been the same as Joshua's.

5) Jesus' name should be derived ultimately from the Hebrew verb *ʿāsā*, "to do," which also means "to bring about" in the sense of effecting a deliverance. This etymology would make better sense of Matthew 1:21 than the assumption that his Hebrew name was *Yēshūaʿ*. Moreover, in the first centuries of the Christian era, Nabatean pilgrims inscribed the name *ʿs* on rocks in the region of Sinai, and the name is also found in inscriptions in southern Arabia and the region between Syria

(q.v.) and Jordan (see ARCHAEOLOGY AND THE QUR'ĀN).

None of al-Assiouty's arguments is decisive and some of them are unsound. The Talmudic *Yēshū* may be a deliberate deformation of Jesus' name to ensure that his memory would be blotted out. Matthew 1:21 should be read in conjunction with Matthew 1:23, where Jesus is identified as Emmanuel, "God with us"; from the evangelist's viewpoint, therefore, it would have been entirely appropriate for his name to mean "Yahweh saves." Although Josephus furnishes important evidence for the wide variety of Hebrew names represented in Greek by *Iēsous,* it is noteworthy that none of these names begins with an *ʿayin.* Justin Martyr elaborated the Joshua/Jesus typology but he did not invent it; it was already implicit in Hebrews 4:8. It is true that the Hebrew verb *ʿāsā,* "to do," can mean "to bring about" in the sense of effecting a deliverance. In biblical passages where it has this latter meaning, however, the subject is invariably Yahweh (Brown et al., *Hebrew and English lexicon,* 795). Moreover, as the verb is not Aramaic and is not certainly found in south Semitic languages (ibid., 793) it is not relevant to the interpretation of the pre-Islamic inscriptions which the author mentions.

According to al-Rāghib al-Iṣfahānī (fl. fifth/eleventh cent.), some authorities took ʿĪsā to be an Arabic name and derived it from *ʿays,* "a stallion's urine" (Jefferey, *For. vocab.,* 219). As urine was used to bleach clothes, this bizarre suggestion probably arose among interpreters who were familiar with the tradition that Jesus' disciples were fullers. The *Lisān al-ʿArab* mentions two other Arabic derivations: from *ʿayas,* "a reddish whiteness," or from *ʿaws,* the verbal noun of *ʿawasa,* "to roam about." The former should perhaps be explained in the light of the ḥadīth (SEE ḤADĪTH AND THE QUR'ĀN) in which the Prophet describes Jesus as "ruddy *(aḥmar)* as if he had just come from the bath." The latter is probably linked with attempts to derive Jesus' title *al-Masīḥ* from *masaḥa,* "to pace" or "to survey." Ṭabāṭabāʾī (d. 1982) favors a tradition which derives *ʿĪsa* from *yaʿīsh,* "he lives," because the name of Zechariah's (q.v.) son, Yaḥyā (John; see JOHN THE BAPTIST), likewise has this meaning, and because in Q 3 the two births are announced in similar fashion. Nevertheless, several classical philologists thought that ʿĪsā was a Hebrew or Syriac name that had been Arabicized and this view was endorsed by a number of classical commentators (for a recent analysis in which a misreading of the unpointed Arabic is suggested, see Bellamy, Textual criticism, 6; see ARABIC LANGUAGE; ARABIC SCRIPT; COLLECTION OF THE QUR'ĀN).

By way of conclusion, it is worth summarizing the salient features of the debate about the origins of the qurʾānic form of Jesus' name. It is not certain that Jesus' original name was *Yēshūaʿ.* The view that it was, and that it connoted that he was the Savior, cannot be traced back to earlier than around 80 C.E., the time when Hebrews and Matthew were written. In any case, ʿĪsā, the qurʾānic form of his name, has no such connotations. The attempts to derive that form from an Arabic root are, however, far-fetched and show, if anything, that it had no obvious associations for the native speaker of Arabic. It is just possible that ʿĪsā was actually Jesus' original name, although it seems more likely that it is an Arabicized form of the name current among Syriac-speaking Christians as was recognized by a number of classical authorities. This Arabicized form may be pre-Islamic but there is no compelling evidence that it is. Nor are there grounds for thinking that its purpose is polemical.

References to Jesus as "the son of Mary" and "the Messiah"

The expression "the son of Mary" is attested twenty-three times. By itself, it occurs in only two Meccan verses: Q 43:57 and Q 23:50. In the other instances, which are all Medinan, it is invariably preceded by "Jesus," "the Messiah" or "the Messiah Jesus."

An Arabic name *(ism)* is often followed by a familial attribution *(nasab),* "the son of X." Moreover, the *nasab* may also be employed in isolation. Thus as regards its position, form and employment, "the son of Mary" resembles a *nasab*. In a *nasab,* however, X is normally the name of the person's father. Very occasionally, one encounters a *nasab* in which X denotes the person's mother; for example, "the son of the Byzantine woman," "the son of the blue-eyed woman," or "the son of the daughter of al-Aʿazz" (Schimmel, *Islamic names,* 9). Note, however, that in these examples X is not the mother's name but a *nasab* indicating her place of origin, a nickname drawing attention to one of her distinguishing features or her own *nasab*. This last type of *nasab* is employed when the maternal family is more distinguished than the paternal line: for instance the Aʿazz in the above-mentioned example was a vizier.

Because there is no exact parallel to the expression "the son of Mary," its origin and significance are disputed. It is attested only once in the New Testament, in Mark 6:3, where Jesus' townsfolk say, "Is not this the carpenter the son of Mary?" Some interpreters think this biblical passage merely implies that Mary was a widow whereas others detect an insult: a hint that Jesus was perhaps illegitimate. Neither explanation suits the qurʾānic context because Joseph is not mentioned in the Qurʾān, and among the Arabs an illegitimate child was called Ibn Abīhi, "son of his father." Nor need it be supposed that the Qurʾān imitated the usage of the Ethiopic church (*pace* Bishop, The son of Mary) for it is unlikely that Ethiopian Christians called Jesus "the son of Mary" (Parrinder, *Jesus,* 25-6) and although the Qurʾān contains a number of Ethiopic loan words they occur mostly in Medinan sūras. In the opinion of the present writer, during the Meccan period the expression was used merely for ease of reference. Bearing in mind that in the earliest reference to Jesus (Q 19:16-33) the principal character was Mary, with Jesus figuring as her unnamed child, the brief allusions to Jesus as Mary's son in the subsequent revelations concerning Jesus (those in Q 43 and 23) are entirely understandable. In the Medinan period, however, many of the revelations about Jesus were concerned with countering Christian claims about him. Hence, the expression "the son of Mary" took on polemical overtones; it was an implicit reminder that Jesus is not the son of God as the Christians allege (also, some suggest implausibly a reflection of Trinitarian doctrines with Mary as the mother of God; see TRINITY). The classical commentators do not distinguish between the Meccan and Medinan usage. They interpret the expression as a counter-thrust to Christian claims but also regard it as an honorific title because of the high status that the Qurʾān ascribes to Mary (see WOMEN AND THE QURʾĀN; GENDER).

The term "the Messiah" (al-Masīḥ) is attested eleven times and is found only in Medinan revelations. It occurs by itself three times; followed by "the son of Mary" five times; and followed by "Jesus the son of Mary" three times. There can be little doubt that it is derived ultimately from the Hebrew *Māshīaḥ,* which means "anointed" or "Messiah." In ancient Israel, kings and priests were consecrated by anointing their heads with oil. After the Babylonian exile, there arose in some circles expectations of a future ideal Davidic ruler, God's anointed par excellence, an eschatological figure who would usher in an age of peace. Whereas the Jews maintain that this Messiah is yet to come, Christians claim that Jesus had this God-given role and that he was wrongly killed but will return in glory. In the Greek New Testament, *Messias,* the Hellenized transliteration of the Hebrew word, occurs only twice (John 1:41; 4:25). The New Testament writers showed a marked preference for the literal Greek translation *Christos,* "Christ." According to one tradition, Jesus was instituted as the Messiah when God anointed *(echrisen)* him with the Holy Spirit at his baptism (Acts 10:38; cf. Luke 1:15-22; 4:17-21). He is, however, frequently referred to as *Iēsous Christos,* "Jesus Christ," or *Christos Iēsous,* "Christ Jesus," almost as if *Christos* were an additional name rather than a title.

Arabic lexicographers regarded al-Masīḥ as a *laqab,* or nickname, and attempted to give it an Arabic etymology. Al-Fīrūzabādī (d. 817/1415) claimed to have heard no less than fifty-six explanations of this sort (Lane, 2714). Only those most frequently encountered in the classical commentaries will be mentioned here. It was widely held that it was derived from the verb *masaḥa,* which occurs five times in the Qurʾān: four times in instructions on performing ablutions by "wiping" various parts of the body with water (Q 5:6) or clean earth (Q 4:43; 5:6; see CLEANLINESS AND ABLUTION; RITUAL PURITY) and once in a reference to Solomon's (q.v.) "stroking" his horses (Q 38:33). Most of those who took this line thought that *masīḥ* was an adjective with the force of a passive participle and meant "touched" or "anointed." They variously suggested that Jesus was given this nickname because he was touched by Gabriel's (q.v.) wing at birth to protect him from Satan (see DEVIL); because he was anointed with oil, as were all the prophets; or because he was anointed with God's blessing (q.v.; cf. Q 19:31). Others held that *masīḥ* was an adjective with the force of an active participle. They claimed that he was given the nickname because he laid hands on the sick and healed them (see ILLNESS AND HEALTH); or because he washed men from their faults and sins (see SIN, MAJOR AND MINOR). This last explanation was generally frowned on because the Qurʾān insists on individual responsibility and denies that a person can count on anyone but God to save him (Q 2:286; 6:70; see FORGIVENESS; INTERCESSION; FREEDOM AND PREDESTINATION; SALVATION). Finally, there were those who maintained that although *masīḥ* had the force of an active participle it was derived not from *masaḥa* but from *sāḥa,* a verb meaning to travel about in the cause of religion (Q 9:2; see JOURNEY) and hence to be devout (Q 9:112; 66:5; see also FASTING). They alleged that Jesus received this nickname because of his itinerant lifestyle (see further Arnaldez, *Jésus fils de Marie,* 84-7).

The explanation why the lexicographers exercised such ingenuity in trying to account for the qurʾānic term, and why they put forward such diverse explanations, is that a *laqab* may be bestowed for a whole range of reasons. There are *laqab*s that are honorific titles but there are others that merely indicate a person's trade or physical characteristics so as to help identify him. Despite the *prima facie* plausibility of the etymologies mentioned above, however, it should be noted that those which seem to indicate qualities that Jesus shared with other prophets do not do justice to the fact that he alone is called al-Masīḥ in the Qurʾān. It seems likely that the first hearers of the revelations would have been aware that al-Masīḥ was a dignified title which the Christians held was uniquely applicable to Jesus. Nevertheless, the qurʾānic title does not have precisely the same connotations as "Messiah" or "Christ" in the New Testament. Several of the New Testament writers stressed that Jesus was the Davidic Messiah, and two of them furnished genealogies tracing his "descent" from David through Joseph, despite the fact that they apparently believed in the virginal conception (Matthew 1:1-16, Luke 3:23-8). In the Qurʾān, on the other hand, the link between Jesus and David (q.v.) is tenuous (Q 5:78); Mary's betrothal to Joseph is not mentioned; and what is stressed is Jesus' descent from Adam (see ADAM AND EVE) via Noah (q.v.), Abraham (q.v.), ʿImrān (q.v.) and Mary (Q 3:33-45).

Jesus' conception and infancy and the description of him as "word" and "spirit"

In Q 19 God recounts that, while Mary was in seclusion, he sent his spirit to her in the form of a man who announced that, despite being a virgin, she would conceive a boy-child by divine decree (Q 19:16-21); that she conceived and withdrew to a remote place where her labor pains drove her in despair to the trunk of a palm tree (Q 19:22-3; see DATE PALM); that after she had given birth, her baby told her to refresh herself from the ripe dates and a stream which God had miraculously provided (Q 19:24-6); and that when she returned to her people he spoke up in her defense (Q 19:27-33). Q 3 includes a similar account of the annunciation (Q 3:42-7), although here God's agent is described as "the angels." Q 3 and 5 both allude to Jesus' speaking in the cradle (Q 3:46; 5:110).

In the biblical version of the annunciation, God's agent is named as Gabriel rather than the spirit (q.v.; Luke 1:26). Some Christians, however, may have regarded them as identical on the basis of Tatian's gospel harmony, the *Diatesseron,* in which Luke's account of the annunciation is followed immediately by Matthew's report of how Mary was found to be with child by the Holy Spirit. The miracle of the palm tree and the stream is mentioned in the Latin *Gospel of pseudo-Matthew;* and, according to the *Arabic infancy gospel* Jesus spoke while still a child in the cradle. Although these two apocryphal writings post-date the rise of Islam, Christians in Muḥammad's audience were probably familiar with the episodes to which they refer. The Qurʾān's reference to Mary's labor pains, on the other hand, may have been intended to counter the Christian belief in Jesus' divinity and Mary's perpetual virginity.

Most commentators identify the spirit who was sent to Mary as Gabriel, on the grounds that both designations appear to be used interchangeably elsewhere for the revelatory angel (Q 2:97; 16:102; 26:193; see REVELATION AND INSPIRATION). Gerock (*Versuch,* 36-46) claims that the Qurʾān regards Gabriel as Jesus' father. This interpretation can be ruled out because the Qurʾān defends Mary against the charge of unchastity (Q 4:156; see CHASTITY), although some of the classical commentators suggest that the effect of Gabriel's sudden appearance in human form was to arouse Mary's desire, as in an erotic dream, and thereby facilitate the descent of the maternal fluid into her womb (Robinson, *Christ,* 161, 187).

In Q 23:50, God states that he set the son of Mary and his mother as a sign (see SIGNS) and that he sheltered them on a hilltop "where there was both a cool place and a spring" *(dhāti qarārin wa-maʿīnin).* The suggestion made by some Christian authors that this is an allusion to the assumption of Mary which allegedly took place on a hill in Ephesus, is wide of the mark. The verse seems rather to refer back to the circumstances surrounding Jesus' birth, which were mentioned in Q 19 where Mary was instructed to drink from a stream that appeared miraculously (Q 19:24-6; see SPRINGS AND FOUNTAINS). There is even a verbal echo of the infant Jesus' words to her, "refresh yourself," literally "cool your eye" (*qarrī 'aynan*, Q 19:26). Other verses in Q 23 deny that God has taken a son (Q 23:91) and warn against appealing to another deity beside him (Q 23:117). It is clear therefore that neither Jesus nor Mary is to be regarded as a divine being. Together, however, they constitute a "sign:" probably a reference to the virginal conception, which, like the miraculous creation (q.v.) of the first man, points to God's power to raise the dead (compare Q 23:12-6; see DEATH AND THE DEAD; BIOLOGY AS THE CREATION AND STAGES OF LIFE).

Q 21:91-3 alludes to Mary and her son without naming them. Here, too, they are said to constitute a sign. The only new element is God's statement that she "guarded her chastity (*farjahā*, literally, her opening) so we breathed into her *(fīhā)* of our spirit" (Q 21:91). An almost identical statement occurs in Q 66:12, the only difference being that there God says that he breathed "into it" *(fīhi)*, "it" presumably being Mary's *farj*. In both instances, the probable reference is to God's creating life in her womb without her having sexual intercourse. Similar language is used elsewhere to describe how he gave life to the first man (Q 15:29; 32:9; 38:72). Some of the classical commentators, however, assumed that "our spirit" in Q 21:91 and 66:12 denoted Gabriel, as in Q 19:17. They therefore reasoned that Mary literally "guarded her opening" from Gabriel on the specific occasion of the annunciation and debated whether the reference was to her vulva (the usual meaning of *farj*) or to an aperture in her clothing. They cited reports alleging that she conceived after he blew up her skirt, down the neck of her chemise, into her sleeve or into her mouth (Robinson, Fakhr al-Dīn, 15).

There are two Medinan verses which clearly state that Jesus is God's word (see WORD OF GOD), namely Q 3:45 and Q 4:171. Moreover, it is sometimes held that Q 3:39 and 19:34 (a Medinan passage in Q 19) also imply this. As the context of these verses is Jesus' conception, birth and infancy, it is appropriate to discuss them at this point. Christian apologists often argue that they echo the teaching of John's Gospel, which states that God's divine Word *(logos)*, which was with him in the beginning and through whom he created all things, became flesh in Jesus Christ (John 1:1-18). We shall see, however, that although the Qur'ān calls Jesus "a word from God" it does not endorse the orthodox Christian view that he was the incarnation of a pre-existent divine hypostasis.

Q 3:39 recalls that the angels announced to Zechariah the good news (q.v.) of the forthcoming birth of John, who would "confirm the truth of a word from God." Arabic does not distinguish between upper and lower case letters, but as *kalima* lacks the definite article it should probably be rendered "word" rather than "Word." The classical commentators generally assumed that the "word" in question was Jesus. They cited a number of traditions in support of this, including one from Ibn 'Abbās, which relates how John bowed down in reverence before Jesus when they were both babes in their mothers' wombs. Although some of the early philologists argued that in this context *kalima* denotes a "book" or "scripture," the traditional interpretation is preferable in view of Q 3:45, which recalls how the angels told Mary: "God announces to you good news of a word from him; his name will be the Messiah Jesus son of Mary...." Here *kalima* clearly refers to Jesus and, as the annunciation to Mary is the structural homologue of the earlier annunciation to Zechariah, it seems likely that *kalima* refers to Jesus there as well. Nevertheless, it should be noted that, whereas *kalima* is a feminine noun, the pronominal suffix attached to "name" is masculine. Thus the name "the Messiah Jesus son of Mary" is attributed to the male person indicated by the word, rather than to the word itself. Elsewhere in the Qurʾān *kalima* usually denotes a divine decree, and this seems also to be the case here. The classical commentators argued convincingly that Jesus is called a "word" primarily because, as was also the case with Adam, God brought him into existence merely by uttering the command "Be!" as is stated a few verses later in Q 3:59 (see COSMOLOGY).

Q 4:171 is more overtly polemical. The People of the Book (q.v.) are ordered not to exaggerate in their religion and to speak nothing except the truth about God. The Messiah Jesus son of Mary was only God's envoy (see MESSENGER) and "his word which he cast unto Mary" and a spirit from him. Here, Jesus and the "word" are even more closely associated because the verb "cast" is followed by the redundant feminine object pronoun. Nevertheless, as there is no suggestion that Jesus was God's sole envoy and, as "spirit" is indefinite, "his word" should probably be construed as "a word of his," without any implication of uniqueness. In any case, the polemical context and the insistence that Jesus is *only* an envoy, word and spirit, should caution Christian apologists from interpreting *kalima* in the light of orthodox Christian *logos* theology.

Q 19:34 contains the word *qawl*, which can mean either "word" or "statement." Two of the seven readers (see READINGS OF THE QURʾĀN), ʿĀṣim in Kūfa and Ibn ʿĀmir in Damascus, vocalized the crucial expression as *qawla l-ḥaqqi*, giving *qawl* an accusative ending. This is the reading found in Flügel's text and in the standard Egyptian edition of the Qurʾān, which are the basis of most English translations. If it is accepted, the expression introduces an exclamation and the verse should be rendered: "That is Jesus son of Mary — statement of the truth concerning which they are in doubt!" In which case, "statement of the truth" simply refers to the previous story and has no bearing on the qurʾānic teaching about Jesus as a word from God. The other five readers, however, favored *qawlu l-ḥaqqi*, with *qawl* in the nominative. This reading, which may well be the more original, can be construed in two ways: either as the predicate of a sentence whose subject has been omitted, namely "[It is] a statement of the truth" or as a nominal phrase in apposition to Jesus, namely "Word of Truth." In view of the fact that this verse is part of a highly polemical Medinan addition to the sūra and that the next verse denies that God has taken a son, the former interpretation seems the more probable.

The understanding of Jesus as God's word in the minimalist sense that he was brought into existence by God's command is in line with the teaching of the Nestorian Christians (O'Shaugnessy, *Word*, 24) as is the Qurʾān's stress on the similarity of the virginal conception and the creation of Adam (Robinson, *Christ*, 156-7). The statement that he was both a word and a "spirit" *(rūḥ)* from God (Q 4:171) is more difficult to interpret in view of the range of meanings ascribed to spirit in the Qurʾān. It may, however, reflect a thought-world akin to that of Psalm 33:6, where God's creative word and breath (Hebrew *rūach*) are treated as synonyms because an utterance is invariably accompanied by outbreathing.

His status and mission

The Qurʾān emphatically denies that Jesus was God, a subsidiary deity or the son of God (e.g. Q 5:17, 72, 116; 9:30; see POLYTHEISM AND ATHEISM). He was merely a "servant" (q.v.) of God (Q 4:172; 19:30; 43:59) and was required to pray and to pay alms (*zakāt*, Q 19:31; see ALMSGIVING; PRAYER). He and his mother needed to eat food (Q 5:75; see FOOD AND DRINK) and God could destroy them both if he wished (Q 5:17). He was nonetheless a "mercy (q.v.) from God" (Q 19:21), a "prophet" (*nabī*, Q 19:30) and an "envoy" (*rasūl*, Q 3:49, 53; 4:171; 5:75, 61:6), "eminent" in this world and the hereafter (see ESCHATOLOGY) and "one of those brought near" (Q 3:45).

Although Jesus was a sign for humanity as a whole (Q 19:21), his specific mission was to the Children of Israel (q.v.; e.g. Q 3:49; 43:59). God taught him the Torah (q.v.) and the Gospel (Q 3:48; 5:110) and supported him with the Holy Spirit (Q 2:87, 253; 5:110) — possibly an allusion to his baptism (q.v.) but most commentators assume that the reference is to Gabriel. Jesus attested the truth of what was in the Torah (Q 3:50; 5:46; 61:6); made lawful some of the things that were forbidden to the Children of Israel in his day (Q 3:50; see LAWFUL AND UNLAWFUL; FORBIDDEN); clarified some of the things that they disagreed about (Q 43:63); and urged them to worship God alone (e.g. Q 5:117). Like David before him, he cursed those of his people who disbelieved (Q 5:78).

He is credited with a number of miracles including creating birds from clay; healing a blind person and a leper; raising the dead; and telling the Children of Israel what they ate and what they stored in their houses (Q 3:49; 5:110). The miracle of the birds is mentioned in the apocryphal *Infancy Gospel of Thomas*, and the healings and resuscitations correspond to those narrated in the canonical gospels. From the qurʾānic perspective, however, none of these miracles implies that he possessed divine status or supernatural power; they were simply God-given signs of the authenticity of his mission, "clear proofs" which the unbelievers nevertheless dismissed as sorcery (Q 5:110; 61:6; see PROOF; BELIEF AND UNBELIEF).

A further miracle attributed to Jesus is that, at the request of his disciples, he asked God to send down "a table (q.v.) spread with food" (Q 5:112-5). The Arabic word translated by this phrase is *māʾida*. The lexicographers derived it from the verb *māda*, "to feed," but it is probably an Ethiopic loanword for it resembles the term used by Abyssinian Christians to denote the eucharistic table. Moreover, as Jesus speaks of the table as a "festival" for his disciples, there can be little doubt that the episode describes the institution of the Eucharist at the Last Supper; but, in accordance with traditional Christian typology, it appears to have conflated the Last Supper with the gospel feeding miracles and the Hebrew Bible story of how God sent down manna to the Israelites in the wilderness. Although the Qurʾān seems at this point to acknowledge the legitimacy of a specifically Christian ritual that originated with Jesus, the next verse makes clear that Jesus did not instruct people to worship him and his mother (Q 5:116). Moreover, the ritual is not linked with Jesus' atoning death. On the contrary, as God punishes whom he wills and forgives whom he wills, there can be no question of the participants enjoying a special status or gaining immunity from punishment (Q 5:18, 115; see REWARD AND PUNISHMENT).

The Qurʾān recognizes that God granted special favors to some of the envoys who preceded Muḥammad, in the case of Jesus by supporting him with the Holy Spirit and enabling him to perform miracles

(Q 2:253). Moreover, it singles out Noah, Abraham, Moses and Jesus as prophets with whom God established a strong covenant (q.v.; Q 33:7; compare 42:13). It urges the Muslims, however, to believe in all of God's envoys and not make a distinction between them (Q 2:136, 285; 3:84; 4:152) because they all taught essentially the same religion. Thus Jesus' name also figures in more extensive lists of messengers (Q 4:163; 6:84-6).

From the qurʾānic perspective, like the other envoys, Jesus was a precursor of Muḥammad. This is underscored in three ways. First, Jesus and Muḥammad are depicted as having had similar experiences. For instance, both were sent as a "mercy," both needed to eat food, both had "helpers" (*anṣār*, see APOSTLE; EMIGRANTS AND HELPERS) and both were suspected of sorcery (Robinson, *Christ*, 36-8; see INSANITY; SOOTHSAYERS; MAGIC). Second, God informs Muḥammad that he has inspired him in the same way as he inspired his predecessors including Jesus (Q 4:163; 42:13). Third, Jesus is said to have foretold the coming of an envoy called Aḥmad (Q 61:6), the heavenly name of Muḥammad.

The plot to kill him, his exaltation and future descent

According to Islamic tradition, when the Jews sought to kill Jesus, God outwitted them by projecting his likeness onto someone else whom they mistakenly crucified. Meanwhile, he caused Jesus to ascend to the second or third heaven (see HEAVEN AND SKY), where he is still alive. Jesus will return to kill the Antichrist (q.v.), and after a forty-year reign of peace he will eventually die and be buried in Medina (see APOCALYPSE). On the day of resurrection (q.v.), he will be a witness against the unbelieving People of the Book. It is questionable whether the qurʾānic data provides sufficiently solid foundations to bear the weight of this construction.

In Q 19 the child Jesus speaks of the day of his birth, the day he will die, and the day he will be raised alive (Q 19:33). From the similar statement about John (Q 19:15), and from subsequent verses that deal with eschatology (Q 19:37-9, 66), it has been inferred that Jesus will be raised alive at the general resurrection. There is not the slightest hint, however, that his death also lies in the future. On the contrary, given only this sūra, the assumption would be that it already lay in the past like John's.

Q 43 includes the cryptic assertion that "he" or "it" (the pronominal suffix *-hu* could mean either) is "knowledge for the hour" (Q 43:61). The classical commentators mention three traditional interpretations: (i) Jesus' future descent is a portent which will signal that the hour is approaching, (ii) the Qurʾān imparts knowledge concerning the resurrection and judgment (see LAST JUDGMENT), and (iii) Jesus' raising of the dead by divine permission brings knowledge that God has the power to raise the dead (Robinson, *Christ*, 90-3). Instead of *ʿilm*, "knowledge," Ibn ʿAbbās (d. ca. 67/686), Qatāda (d. ca. 117/735), and al-Ḍaḥḥāk (d. 115/723) allegedly read *ʿalam*, "sign, distinguishing mark," which would strengthen the case for the first interpretation, whereas Ubayy (see COMPANIONS OF THE PROPHET) allegedly read *dhikr*, "reminder," which would seem to lend weight to the second (see EXEGESIS OF THE QURʾĀN: CLASSICAL AND MEDIEVAL). As Jesus is the subject of verse 59 and verse 63, it is probably he, rather than the Qurʾān, who is the subject of verse 61. Additionally, in view of the predominant concern with eschatology in verses 65-78, it seems likely that verse 61 alludes to Jesus' future descent rather than to his miraculous raising of the dead. Nevertheless, there is nothing to indicate that his future descent requires him to have been spared death on the cross.

Q 3 contains two consecutive verses which have a bearing on this topic. First there is a reference to Jesus' unbelieving opponents, "And they plotted and God plotted, and God is the best of plotters" (Q 3:54). This is followed by a statement about what God said to him, "When God said, 'Jesus, I am going to receive you and raise you to myself...'" (Q 3:55). Muslim commentators usually assume that both verses refer to the same incident, namely the Jews' plot against Jesus' life and God's counter-plot to rescue him by having them crucify a look-alike substitute. Although there may be a close link between the two verses, the staccato nature of much qur'ānic narrative should be a caution against supposing that this is necessarily the case. Therefore each verse will be considered in turn.

The verb *makara*, "to plot, plan or scheme," and its derivatives, occur in thirteen sūras spanning Nöldeke's second and third Meccan periods, and in Q 8 and 3 which are Medinan. When human beings are the subject of this verb, they are usually unbelievers who plot against specific envoys of God including Noah (Q 71:22), Ṣāliḥ (q.v.; Q 27:50), Moses (Q 40:45), and Muḥammad (Q 8:30; 13:42), or against God's signs (Q 10:21) thereby hindering others from believing (Q 34:33). When God is the subject of the verb, the reference is invariably to his counter-plot, but the emphasis may be on his rescue of the envoy (Q 8:30; see PROTECTION), the immediate punishment of the unbelievers (Q 7:99, 27:50 f.; see CHASTISEMENT AND PUNISHMENT; PUNISHMENT STORIES), the recording of their misdeeds (Q 10:21; see RECORD OF HUMAN ACTIONS) or their eventual punishment in the hereafter (Q 13:42). Hence, in Q 3:54 the unbelievers' plot could have been an attempt on Jesus' life — either the final plot to kill him or one which took place earlier in his ministry (see Q 5:110, compare Luke 4:30 and John 8:59) — or an attempt to subvert his message. God's counter-plot could have entailed his rescue of Jesus, but it might equally well have been his punishment of the Jews by destroying Jerusalem (q.v.), or his preservation of Jesus' monotheistic teaching. It is true that Noah, Ṣāliḥ and Moses were all rescued by God and that the Qur'ān warns against thinking that he would fail his envoys (Q 14:47), which seems to strengthen the case for thinking that Q 3:54 implies that Jesus was delivered from death. On the other hand, the same sūra explicitly mentions the possibility of Muḥammad dying or being killed (Q 3:144) and states that the Muslims who were killed at Uḥud (see EXPEDITIONS AND BATTLES; FIGHTING; JIHĀD) are not dead but "alive with their lord" (Q 3:169). Thus Jesus' death, ostensibly at the hands of his enemies, cannot be ruled out on the basis of Q 3:54.

The interpretation of Q 3:55 hinges on the meaning of the present participle of the verb *tawaffā* (Robinson, *Christ*, 117-26), which was rendered above as "going to receive." The finite verb is attested twenty-two times and the imperative three times. When God is the subject it can mean to receive souls in their sleep (q.v.; Q 6:60; 39:42) but it more frequently means "cause to die." As this latter meaning is attested in Q 3:193 and as the Qur'ān uses the verb in other sūras when speaking about Muḥammad's death (Q 10:46; 13:40; 40:77), there is a *prima facie* case for construing God's words to Jesus to mean that he was going to cause him to die and raise him into his presence. Most of the classical commentators, however, took them to mean that he would cause Jesus to sleep and to ascend in that condition or that he would snatch him alive from the earth. The minority, who conceded that the participle does mean "cause to die," nevertheless denied that Jesus was crucified. Some of them argued that the order of the verbs is inverted for stylistic reasons and that, although God has already caused Jesus to ascend, his death still lies in the future. Others held that God caused him to die a normal death, while his substitute was being crucified, and that he then caused him to ascend.

In Q 4, the Jews are criticized for boasting that they killed Jesus (Q 4:157-9). The interpretation of this passage poses a number of problems (Robinson, *Christ*, 78-89, 106-11, 127-41). First, there is the statement, "They did not kill him or crucify him." Traditionally, Muslim interpreters have held that this is a categorical denial of Jesus' death by crucifixion. It may simply mean, however, that although the Jews thought that they had killed Jesus, Muslims should not think of him as dead because, from the qurʾānic perspective, he is alive with God like the martyrs of Uḥud (Q 3:169, see above; see MARTYR).

The second problem centers on the clause *wa-lākin shubbiha lahum* (Q 4:157). Most of the classical commentators understood it to mean "but he [i.e. the person whom they killed] was made to resemble [Jesus] for them." In support of this they cited traditional accounts of how God projected Jesus' likeness (Arabic *shibh*) onto someone else. These accounts, however, are unreliable for they differ over the identity of the person in question, some saying that he was a loyal disciple of Jesus who volunteered to die in his place, others that he was Judas Iscariot or one of the men sent to arrest Jesus. The non-standard interpretation that regards the verb as impersonal and construes the clause as "but it was made to seem like that to them" avoids the need to identify any person onto whom Jesus' identity was projected.

A third problem is posed by the words "God raised him to himself" (Q 4:158). The verb is *rafaʿa* (compare the use of the participle *rāfiʿ* in the similar context in Q 3:55). The classical commentators invariably took it to mean that God caused Jesus to ascend bodily into the second or third heaven where Muḥammad allegedly saw him on the night of the *miʿrāj* (see ASCENSION). It is arguable, however, that it is simply a graphic way of saying that God honored him, for elsewhere the same verb is used to denote God's raising envoys in rank (e.g. Q 2:253), his exalting Muḥammad's reputation (Q 94:4) and the ascent of good works into his presence (Q 35:10; see GOOD DEEDS).

The final problem is the ambiguity of the words "his death" in Q 4:159. The classical commentators mentioned two principal interpretations: either it refers to the death of each individual Jew and Christian, because immediately before their death they will recognize the truth about Jesus, or it refers to Jesus' death, because he is still alive and all the People of the Book will believe in him when he descends to kill the Antichrist. A good case can be made for the former interpretation on syntactical grounds, for the whole sentence constitutes an oath used as a threat (see LANGUAGE AND STYLE OF THE QURʾĀN). Moreover, the reading "their death," which is attributed to Ubayy, supports this interpretation. Owing to the influence of the ḥadīths about Jesus' future descent, however, the view that the verse referred to Jesus' death gained widespread support.

The assertion that Jesus will be a witness against the People of the Book (Q 4:159) is unproblematic and accords with the qurʾānic teaching that God will raise a witness against every community (Q 16:89).

In Q 5:117, Jesus says to God, "I was a witness over them while I dwelt among them, and when you received me you were the watcher over them." The word rendered 'you received' is the first person plural perfect of *tawaffā*, a verb whose meaning was discussed earlier in connection with Q 3:55. It most probably refers here to Jesus' death or rapture before his exaltation, which already lies in the past. As the statement occurs, however, in a conversation that will take place on the last day, it is just conceivable that it refers to Jesus' future death after his descent to kill the Antichrist.

From the above analysis, it should be obvious that the qurʾānic teaching about Jesus' death is not entirely clear-cut. Three things, however, may be said with certainty. First, the Qurʾān attaches no salvific importance to his death. Second, it does not mention his resurrection on the third day and has no need of it as proof of God's power to raise the dead. Third, although the Jews thought that they had killed Jesus, from God's viewpoint they did not kill or crucify him. Beyond this is the realm of speculation. The classical commentators generally began with the questionable premise that Q 4:157-9 contains an unambiguous denial of Jesus' death by crucifixion. They found confirmation of this in the existence of traditional reports about a look-alike substitute and ḥadīths about Jesus' future descent. Then they interpreted the other qurʾānic references to Jesus' death in the light of their understanding of this one passage. If, however, the other passages are examined without presupposition and Q 4:157-9 is then interpreted in the light of them, it can be read as a denial of the ultimate reality of Jesus' death rather than a categorical denial that he died. The traditional reports about the crucifixion of a look-alike substitute probably originated in circles in contact with Gnostic Christians. They may also owe something to early Shīʿī speculation about the fate of the Imāms (see IMĀM; SHĪʿISM AND THE QURʾĀN).

Neal Robinson

Bibliography

Primary (in addition to the classical commentaries on the verses mentioned above): Ibn Isḥāq-Guillaume.

Secondary: ʿAbd al-Tafahum (= K. Cragg), The Qurʾān and Holy Communion, in *MW* 40 (1959), 239-48; G.C. Anawati, ʿĪsā, in *EI²*, iv, 81-6; T. Andrae, *Der Ursprung des Islams und das Christentum*, Uppsala 1926; R. Arnaldez, *Jésus dans la pensée musulmane*, Paris 1988; id., *Jésus fils de Marie prophète de l'Islam*, Paris 1980; S.A. al-Assiouty, *Jésus le non-Juif*, Paris 1987; M.M. Ayoub, *The Qurʾān and its interpreters. ii. The House of ʿImrān*, Albany 1992; id., Towards an Islamic Christology. I: An image of Jesus in early Shii Muslim literature, in *MW* 66 (1976), 163-88; II: The death of Jesus, reality or delusion, in *MW* 70 (1980), 91-121; R. Bell, *The origin of Islam in its Christian environment*, London 1926; J. Bellamy, Textual criticism of the Koran, in *JAOS* 121 (2001), 1-6; E.E.F. Bishop, The son of Mary, in *MW* 24 (1934), 236-45; J. Bowman, The debt of Islam to monophysite Syrian Christianity, in *Nederlands Theologisch Tijdschrift* 19 (1964-5), 177-201; F. Brown, S.R. Driver and C.A. Briggs, *A Hebrew and English lexicon of the Old Testament*, Oxford 1907 (repr. with corrections 1966); K. Cragg, *Jesus and the Muslim. An exploration*, London 1985; E.E. Elder, The crucifixion in the Qurʾān, in *MW* 13 (1923), 242-58; G.F. Gerock, *Versuch einer Darstellung der Christologie des Koran*, Hamburg 1839; E. Gräf, Zu den christlichen Einflüssen im Koran, in J.F. Thiel (ed.), *al-Bahit. Festschrift J. Henninger zum 70. Geburtstag am 12. Mai 1976*, Bonn 1976, 114-44; H. Grégoire, Mahomet et le Monophysisme, in *Mélanges Charles Diehl. i. Histoire*, Paris 1930, 107-19; J. Hämeen-Anttila, *Jeesus. Allahin Profeetta*, Helsinki 1998; M. Hayek, *Le Christ de l'Islam*, Paris 1959; id., L'origine des termes ʿĪsā al-Masīḥ (Jesus Christ) dans le Coran, in *L'orient chrétien* 7 (1962), 223-54, 365-82; E. Hennecke, *New Testament apocrypha*, 2 vols., London 1963, i; J. Henninger, *Spuren christlicher Glaubenswahrheiten im Koran*, Schöneck 1951; Jefferey, *For. vocab.*; Lane; G. Lüling, *Über den Ur-Qurʾān. Ansätze zur Rekonstruktion vorislamischer christlicher Strophenlieder im Qurʾān*, Erlangen 1974; D.B. MacDonald, The development of the idea of the Spirit in Islam, in *MW* 22 (1932), 25-42; M.M. Manneval, *La christologie du Coran,* Toulouse 1867; L. Massignon, Le Christ dans les Évangiles selon Ghazālī, in *REI* (1932), 523-36; McAuliffe, *Qurʾānic,* esp. 129-59 (chap. 4); H. Michaud, *Jésus selon le Coran,* Neuchâtel 1960; A. Mingana, Syriac influence on the style of the Kurʾan, in *Bulletin of the John Rylands Library,* 1927, 77-98; J. Nurbakhsh, *Jesus in the eyes of the Sufis,* London 1983; Th.J. O'Shaughnessy, *Word of God in the Qurʾān,* Rome 1984; G. Parrinder, *Jesus in the Qurʾān,* London 1965; H. Räisänen, *Das Koranische Jesusbild,* Helsinki 1971; id., The portrait of Jesus in the Qurʾān. Reflections of a biblical scholar, in *MW* 70 (1980), 122-33; G. Risse, *Gott ist Christus, der Sohn der Maria: Ein Studie zum Christusbild im Koran,* Bonn 1989; N. Robinson, ʿAbd al-Razzāq al-Qāshānī's comments on Sura 19, in *Islamochristiana* 17 (1991), 21-33; id., *Christ in Islam and Christianity,* Albany 1991; id., Christian and Muslim perspectives on Jesus in the Qurʾān, in A. Linzey and P. Wexler (eds.), *Fundamentalism and tolerance. An agenda for theology and society,* London 1991, 92-105, 171-2; id., Covenant, communal boundaries and forgiveness in Sūrat al-Māʾida, in *Journal of qurʾanic studies* (forthcoming); id., Creating birds from clay. A miracle of Jesus in the Qurʾān and in classical Muslim exegesis, in *MW* 79 (1989), 1-13; id., *Discovering the Qurʾān. A contemporary approach to a veiled text,* London 1996; id., Fakhr al-Dīn al-Rāzī and the virginal conception, in *Islamochristiana* 14 (1988), 1-16; id., Hands outstretched. Towards a re-reading of Sūrat al-Māʾida, in *Journal of qurʾanic studies* 3 (2001), 1-19; id., Jesus and Mary in the Qurʾān. Some neglected affinities, in *Religion* 20 (1990), 161-75; id., The qurʾānic Jesus, the Jesus of history, and the myth of God incarnate, in V.S. Sugirtharaja, *Frances Young Festschrift* (forthcoming); id., The structure and interpretation of Sūrat al-Muʾminūn, in *Journal of qurʾanic studies* 2 (2000), 89-106; J. Robson, *Christ in Islam,* London 1929; M.P. Roncaglia, Éléments Ébionites et Elkésaïtes dans le Coran, in *Proche orient chrétien* 21 (1971), 101-25; *RSV* = *The Bible, revised standard version,* London 1952; E. Sayous, *Jésus-Christ d'après Mahomet,* Paris and Leipzig 1880; C. Schedl, *Muhammad und Jesus,* Vienna 1978; A. Schimmel, *Islamic names,* Edinburgh 1989; id., *Jesus und Maria in der Islamischen Mystik,* Munich 1996; O.H. Schumann, *Der Christus der Muslime,* Gütersloh 1975; J.S. Trimingham, *Christianity among the Arabs in pre-Islamic times,* London 1979; R.C. Zaehner, *At sundry times,* London 1958; A.H.M. Zahniser, The forms of tawaffā in the Qurʾān. A contribution to Christian-Muslim dialogue, in *MW* 79 (1989), 14-24; S.M. Zwemer, *The Moslem Christ,* Edinburgh 1912.

Jewels and Gems see METALS AND MINERALS

Jews and Judaism

Terminology

The Arabic term denoting "Jews" is *yahūd,* which occurs seven times in the Qurʾān. The form *hūd* also denotes the same and appears in this sense three times. The singular, *yahūdī,* occurs once. From *yahūd/hūd* was derived the secondary verb *hāda,* which means "to be a Jew/Jewish." "Those who were Jews" *(hādū)* is mentioned ten times. This verb appears once with the complementary *ilā* (Q 7:156), in which case it denotes "to return to." It is put into the mouth of Moses (q.v.), who says to God: "We have returned *(hudnā)* to you." Obviously, this is a play on *yahūd,* on behalf of whom Moses is speaking here (see Paret, *Kommentar,* ad Q 7:156). Outside the Qurʾān the transitive *hawwada* is used in the sense of "he made him a Jew." The form *yahūdiyya,* which denotes "Judaism," or "the Jewish religion," is also non-qurʾānic (cf. Lane, s.v. *h-w-d*). In addition to *yahūd* and its derivatives, the Qurʾān addresses the Jews as "Children of Israel" (q.v.), which alludes to their ancestral origin. Sometimes the Christians (see CHRISTIANS AND CHRISTIANITY), too, are included in this designation. The Jews are called by this appellation to imply that the fate of the old Children of Israel is continued through their descendants. Apart from the ethnic designations, the Qurʾān addresses the Jews as "People of the Book" (q.v.). This is a religious evaluation of them, and refers to the fact that they had prophets sent to them with revealed scriptures (see BOOK; PROPHETS AND PROPHETHOOD). The Jews are not the only community with a revealed book. Q 6:156 mentions two parties to whom the book was revealed before the Muslims, and they stand for the Jews and the Christians respectively.

Jews as believers

The image of the qurʾānic Jews is far from uniform (which, as an aside, is true concerning almost any other qurʾānic theme), and the attitude towards them is ambivalent. On the one hand, they are recognized as true believers, while on the other, they are rejected as infidels (see BELIEF AND UNBELIEF; FAITH). As for their image as believers, the passage stating this in the most explicit way is Q 2:62: "Those who have believed and those who have been Jews, and the Christians and the Sabians (q.v.; Ṣābiʾūn), whoever believes in God and in the last day (see LAST JUDGMENT) and does good (see GOOD DEEDS), their reward (see REWARD AND PUNISHMENT) awaits them with their lord (q.v.), and no fear (q.v.) shall be on them, neither shall they sorrow." A divine reward is promised here to the Jews as well as to the other monotheistic communities, provided they remain monotheists believing in God and the last judgment. The same statement is repeated almost verbatim in Q 5:69, but in Q 22:17 a significant change is noticeable. The monotheistic communities are not alone, the Persians (*majūs*, lit. Magians) and the Arab polytheists (*mushrikūn*, see POLYTHEISM AND ATHEISM; IDOLATRY AND IDOLATERS) being mentioned, too. Concerning all of them it is stated that "God will decide between them on the day of resurrection (q.v.)..." No automatic reward is mentioned here, which renders the message to the non-Muslim monotheists more reserved in comparison with the former passages.

Other passages, however, recognize Jews as believers only on the condition that they believe in the concrete Islamic message as represented in the Qurʾān. Jews who did accept the Islamic message are mentioned in several qurʾānic passages, in which, however, they are always an exceptional minority among a majority of sinful Jews. Q 4:162, for instance, refers to "those (of the Jews) who are "firmly rooted in knowledge (see KNOWLEDGE AND LEARNING)," and identifies them as those who believe in the Qurʾān as well as in the scriptures revealed to previous prophets. They are mentioned in contrast to the evil-doing Jews who take usury (q.v.), whom the Qurʾān denounces in the previous verse (see EVIL DEEDS). The same applies to Q 4:46, in which a minority of believers is mentioned among a majority of Jews refusing to obey the qurʾānic Prophet.

Passages employing the appellation "People of the Book" reveal similar nuances. In some verses, the People of the Book are recognized as believers on the mere basis of their monotheism. Most explicit is Q 3:64: "Say: O People of the Book, come to a word (which is) fair between us and you, (to wit) that we serve no one but God, that we associate nothing with him, and that none of us take others as lords beside God." As observed by W.M. Watt (*Muhammad at Medina*, 201), this passage offers the People of the Book a common framework of faith on the basis of monotheism and nothing else. The People of the Book are referred to in Q 16:43 as the people of the "reminder" (*dhikr*, another term for a revealed scripture) and, in this case, they are treated as authoritative experts on prophetic matters. The skeptic listeners of the qurʾānic Prophet are invited to consult them and learn that God indeed may send a mortal messenger (q.v.) as he did in the past. Even the qurʾānic Prophet himself is requested in Q 10:94 to consult "those who have read the book" before him, if he is in doubt concerning his own prophetic revelation. As potential partners in a common system of monotheistic faith, the dietary laws of the People of the Book were proclaimed acceptable (see FOOD AND DRINK; LAWFUL AND UNLAWFUL; FORBIDDEN), and in one qurʾānic passage (Q 5:5), the Muslims were given permission to eat their food as well as to marry women from among them (see MARRIAGE AND DIVORCE). The Islamic fasting (q.v.) days were also introduced with reference to the fast of the previous communities (Q 2:183). Their places of worship (q.v.), too, are treated favorably in Q 22:40, which seems to refer to synagogues and churches, as well as to mosques (see CHURCH; MOSQUE; SACRED PRECINCTS). The verse states that God has protected them from being pulled down.

But other qurʾānic passages using the label "People of the Book" distinguish between the believers and non-believers among them, the believers being those accepting the qurʾānic message. For example, in Q 3:199 it is stated that "Among the People of the Book are some who believe in God and in what has been sent down to you (i.e. to the qurʾānic Prophet), and in what has been sent down to them, humbling themselves to God..." These believers are again an exceptional minority. This is indicated in Q 3:110, which says that some of the People of the Book are believers, "but most of them are ungodly" (*al-fāsiqūn*, see HYPOCRITES AND HYPOCRISY). The believers among the People of the Book are described in Q 5:66 as a "just nation" *(umma muqtaṣida)* among a majority of evil-doers.

Other passages provide vivid descriptions of the piety (q.v.) of the believers among the People of the Book and of their admiration for the qurʾānic revelation. In Q 3:113-4 they are described as an "upright community, reciting the signs of God (i.e. the Qurʾān; see RECITATION OF THE QURʾĀN) at the drawing on of night, prostrating themselves (see BOWING AND PROSTRATION), believing in God and the last day... and strive with one another in hastening to good deeds." In Q 17:107-9 we read: "Those who were given the knowledge before it (i.e. before the Qurʾān), when it (i.e. the Qurʾān) is recited to them, fall down upon their faces prostrating... and they fall down upon their faces weeping, and it increases them in humility" (see VIRTUES AND VICES). Elsewhere it is asserted that these believers will be rewarded twice over, thanks to their belief in their own revealed scriptures as well as in the Qurʾān (Q 28:52-4).

Jews as sinners

But the Qurʾān is engaged mainly in dealing with the sinners among the Jews and the attack on them is shaped according to models that one encounters in the New Testament. In the latter, the Jews are already accused of having persecuted and murdered their own prophets (Matthew 5:12, 23:30-1; Luke 11:47). The prophets whom they killed are said to have foretold the coming of Jesus (Acts 7:52) and the Jews are said to have persecuted Jesus himself, plotting to kill him (John 7:1; 18:12; Acts 9:29). They are also described as stirring up the gentiles against Jesus' apostles (see APOSTLE) and as conspiring to kill them, too (Acts 13:50; 14:2; 20:3; 26:2). The Jews are further accused of not keeping the Torah (q.v.), which had been given to them (Acts 7:53). The conviction of the Jews that they were God's chosen people is also refuted and it is stressed that God is not only of the Jews but also of the gentiles (Romans 3:29). On the other hand, a group of Jews who believed in the message of the apostles is also mentioned (Acts 14:1).

All these elements recur in the qurʾānic attack on the Jews. To begin with, the Jewish arrogance (q.v.) stemming from the conviction that the people of Israel (q.v.)

were God's chosen nation, is reproved in various ways. In Q 2:111, the Jews, as well as the Christians, are challenged to prove their claim that only they will enter paradise (q.v.). In Q 5:18 the qur'ānic Prophet is requested to refute the idea that the Jews and the Christians were no less than "the sons of God and his beloved ones." The qur'ānic Prophet is requested to tell them that if this were so, God would not have punished them as he did. The arrogant Jews seem also to be referred to in Q 4:49, which speaks about people who consider themselves pure, while only God decides whom to purify. Elsewhere (Q 62:6) it is maintained that if the Jews are really God's favorites, to the exclusion of other people, then they had better die soon. This is a sarcastic response to their unfounded conviction that paradise is in store for them (see also Q 2:94). The same arrogance is attributed to them in verses dubbing them "People of the Book." In these verses they are said to have believed that they would only spend a few days in hell (Q 2:79-80; 3:23-4; see HELL AND HELLFIRE). The Qur'ān replies that they have no monopoly on God's mercy (q.v.) and that God extends it to whom he wills (Q 57:29).

The Jews have lost their right to be considered a chosen people mainly because of their insubordination (see DISOBEDIENCE) and disbelief. The Qur'ān imputes to them the blame of persecuting and killing their own prophets (Q 3:181, 183), a sin that is usually mentioned with allusion to the Children of Israel (Q 2:61, 87, 91; 4:155; 5:70). The Christians, too, share some of the blame because they have rejected the prophets sent to the Jews. This is implied in Q 2:113 where the Jews and the Christians reject each other's religion as a false one. This they do in spite of the fact that they read "the book" which testifies to the relevance of all prophets sent by God. Likewise, in Q 4:151, the Qur'ān condemns unbelievers *(kāfirūn)* who have only believed in some prophets while rejecting others. It seems that the rift between Jews and Christians is also referred to in Q 23:53 (cf. Q 15:90-1), which condemns those who divide their religion into sects (*zubur*, see RELIGIOUS PLURALISM AND THE QUR'ĀN; PARTIES AND FACTIONS). Apart from persecuting the prophets, the Jews are blamed for failing to keep the laws of their own Torah. In Q 62:5, those who have been given the Torah but do not act upon its stipulations are likened to an ass carrying books. The Torah, it is said elsewhere, contains guidance and light (q.v.) by which the prophets and the rabbis judged the Jews, but those who do not judge by what God has revealed are unbelievers (Q 5:44; see JUDGMENT; SCHOLAR). Elsewhere they are said to have believed only in parts of the book and to have disbelieved in its other parts (Q 2:85). The Christians, too, are suspected of ignoring their own law as is implied in Q 5:68, in which the People of the Book are warned against failing to observe the Torah and the Gospel (q.v.; *Injīl*). In fact, a party of the People of the Book is accused of deliberate rejection of the scriptures given to them by their prophets. They have cast them behind their backs, yet they expect to be praised for their assumed devotion to the Torah (Q 2:101; 3:187-8). But the Jews, or rather the People of the Book, were also offered a chance to be forgiven, on condition that they started observing the Torah and the Gospel and all of God's revealed scriptures. If they had, God would have blessed them with an abundance of food (Q 5:65-6).

The Qur'ān is also aware of the wrath of God, which resulted in various hardships that the Jews suffered in the course of their history (see TRIAL; PUNISHMENT STORIES). Their rigid dietary laws, for example, which the Qur'ān adopts in a passage mentioned above, are interpreted elsewhere in the Qurʾān as a punishment from God inflicted on the Jews for oppressing the poor and for taking usury (Q 4:160-1; cf. 6:146; 16:118). The Qurʾān further claims that these restrictions were not yet prescribed in the Torah, in which all kinds of food were still permitted except for that which Israel (see JACOB) prohibited (Q 3:93). Apart from the dietary restrictions, the state of internal friction and discord, which divided the Jews into sects, was also seen as a sign of God's vengeance (Q 5:64; see CORRUPTION; ANGER). The key term conveying the idea of God's anger with the Jews is *ghaḍab*, "wrath." It occurs in a passage (Q 2:90) dealing with the Children of Israel, in which it is stated that they "were laden with wrath upon wrath" for their disbelief. In another verse (Q 5:60), which is addressed to the People of the Book, allusion is made to those whom God has cursed and with whom he has been angry *(ghaḍiba)* and turned into apes and pigs. Transformation into apes recurs elsewhere in the Qurʾān as a punishment inflicted on the Children of Israel for violating the Sabbath (q.v.; Q 2:65; cf. 7:166; see CHATISEMENT AND PUNISHMENT).

The Jewish anti-Islamic sins

In the qurʾānic purview, the sins committed by the Jews with respect to their own scriptures continued into Islamic times, bearing grave anti-Islamic implications. These come out in passages imputing to the Jews the distortion *(taḥrīf)* of the original text of their own sacred scriptures (Q 4:46; 5:13, 41-3; cf. Q 2:75; see SCRIPTURE AND THE QURʾĀN). This seems to be treated indirectly also in Q 2:79, which denounces those "who write the book with their own hands and then they say, 'This is of God,' in order to sell it at a small price..." (see SELLING AND BUYING). It is probably implied here that the Jews sold the believers forged copies of their scriptures (see FORGERY). In one verse (Q 3:78), the act of perversion is oral, performed by people who "twist" the book with their tongues, making the false claim that this is the true form of the book. In this context, the Jews are also accused of playing with (Hebrew?) words that bear a mischievous sense (Q 4:46; cf. Q 2:104). All this is designed to mislead and offend the Muslims and their Prophet. The distortion of the Torah goes hand in hand with the Jewish sin of rejecting those rulings of the qurʾānic Prophet that corresponded to their own laws. After having made him a judge, they refuse to follow his verdict, and the Qurʾān blames them for preferring the legal advice of others (Q 5:41-3; see LAW AND THE QURʾĀN). The Jews are also said to have plotted to conceal from the Muslim believers what God revealed to them, so as not to give the believers arguments which they might use against them (Q 2:76; cf. Q 4:37; 2:42; see DEBATE AND DISPUTATION). The sin of concealment is imputed mainly to the People of the Book (Q 2:146; 3:71). They are said to have made their scriptures into separate writings *(qarāṭīs)*, much of which they concealed (Q 6:91). The message of the qurʾānic Prophet reintroduces those parts of the previous scriptures that the People of the Book attempted to conceal (Q 5:15). The Qurʾān promises the sinners guilty of concealment a severe curse (q.v.) from God (Q 2:159), which is the fire (q.v.) of hell (Q 2:174). When accusing the Jews of concealing the Torah, the Qurʾān apparently refers to those parts in their scriptures that foretold the emergence of Muḥammad (q.v.). This is supported by qurʾānic verses asserting that the description of the Islamic Prophet was recorded in the Torah and the Gospel as the "gentile" (*ummī*, see ILLITERACY) Prophet (Q 7:157) and that Jesus (q.v.) knew him as Aḥmad (Q 61:6).

The Jews, or rather the People of the Book, are also accused of rejecting the authenticity of the Qurʾān as the true Word of God (q.v.). On one occasion, they demand that the Prophet produce a book from heaven (Q 4:153; see HEAVENLY BOOK) and they seem to have in mind the written Torah of Moses. Their demand seems to be designed to annoy the Prophet who only receives sporadic oral revelations (see REVELATION AND INSPIRATION; ORALITY; ORALITY AND WRITING IN ARABIA). It implies that the People of the Book do not believe him to be a true prophet. In some other passages, their conduct is the result of sheer envy (q.v.). They are jealous of the believers who have been blessed with God's bounty as this emanates from the Qurʾān that has been given to them (see BLESSING; GRACE). Their rejection of the Islamic scripture out of jealousy has turned them into unbelievers *(kāfirūn)* in the eyes of the Qurʾān (Q 2:89-90, 105). Their frustration is described most vividly in Q 3:119, according to which, whenever the People of the Book meet the believers, they pretend to believe in the Qurʾān, but when they are alone they bite their nails in rage at the believers. Moreover, the jealous People of the Book are said to have tried to make the believers revert to unbelief (Q 2:109; see also Q 3:69, 99-100; 4:54; 5:59). They conspire to achieve this by pretending to believe in the Qurʾān in the morning and by disbelieving in it in the evening (Q 3:72), i.e. they attempt to convey the impression that they only stopped believing in the Qurʾān after having examined it carefully, and not out of spite. The rejection of the Qurʾān by the Jews seems also to be treated in Q 2:97-8. Here, the "enemies of Gabriel" (q.v.) are attacked and tagged as unbelievers *(kāfirūn)*. Implicit here is the idea that the Jews rejected the Qurʾān because it was brought to Muḥammad by the angel Gabriel, whom the Jews considered their enemy. The Qurʾān asserts that Gabriel brought down the Qurʾān by God's will and that whoever is an enemy to any of God's angels (see ANGEL) will be punished by God as an unbeliever. The main polemical argument used in response to the Jewish rejection of the Qurʾān revolves around the idea that this scripture confirms the message of the previous scriptures. This means that the People of the Book must believe in it as well as in their own scriptures. They cannot believe only in some of God's holy books and reject the others (e.g. Q 2:89-91).

The Jews are not just unbelievers but also idolaters. In Q 9:30-1 they are accused of believing that Ezra (q.v.; ʿUzayr) was the son of God, just as the Christians held that the Messiah was the son of God. The Qurʾān reacts to both tenets by asserting that one must associate nothing with God. This implies that the Jews and the Christians are associators *(mushrikūn)*, i.e. they associate idols with God in a polytheistic form of worship. Moreover, in Q 4:51, "those who have been given part of the book," who are probably the Jews, are said to have believed in the Jibt and the Ṭāghūt (cf. Q 5:60), which may imply a kind of idol worship (see IDOLS AND IMAGES).

The gravest aspect of the Jewish anti-Islamic sin is the hostility towards the Muslim believers. In this respect, the Qurʾān differentiates between them and the Christians. This comes out in Q 5:82, which states that the Jews as well as the associators *(alladhīna ashrakū)* are the strongest in enmity against the believers, while the Christians, particularly priests and monks, are the closest in love to the believers (see MONASTICISM AND MONKS). But in Q 3:186, the enemies of the Muslims are identified by the more comprehensive label "People of the Book" and here again they are coupled with the *mushrikūn*. Together they cause the believers to "hear much annoying talk" *(la-tasmaʿunna)*. Another aspect of the hostility attributed to the People of the Book is revealed in Q 3:75 in which some of them claim that they have no moral obligations with respect to the "gentiles" *(ummiyyīn)*, and therefore do not pay their financial debts (see DEBT) back to them. (See also POLEMIC AND POLEMICAL LANGUAGE.)

The dissociation from the Jews

Another aspect of the image of the Jews as enemies of the believers is revealed in passages in which a tendency to dissociate from them, as well as from the Christians, is noticed. To begin with, in Q 5:51, the believers are warned against taking the Jews and the Christians for friends (*awliyāʾ*, see CLIENTS AND CLIENTAGE; FRIENDS AND FRIENDSHIP). It is stressed that the Jews and the Christians are each other's friends, and whoever associates with them becomes one of them. In Q 5:57, a similar injunction is given concerning the People of the Book. It is added that they, as well as the unbelievers *(kuffār)*, have taken the religion of the believers for a mockery (q.v.) and a joke, and this is why the believers should not be friendly with them. The People of the Book are dealt with also in Q 42:15, where the qurʾānic Prophet is warned against following their evil inclinations (*ahwāʾ*, see GOOD AND EVIL). Instead of following them, he is directed elsewhere to adhere to the law *(sharīʿa)* that God has given him (Q 45:18). The law is based on what God has revealed to him, i.e. the Qurʾān, and since it confirms the scriptures revealed previously to the Jews and the Christians, the qurʾānic Prophet is requested to judge between the People of the Book according to it. But in so doing he must beware of their evil inclinations and be cautious of them, lest they seduce him from part of what God has revealed to him (Q 5:49).

Other passages draw a sharper distinction between the alternative recommended law and what is defined as the "evil inclination" of the People of the Book. Some of these passages deal with the issue of the direction of prayer (*qibla*, q.v.). In Q 2:145 it is stated that the People of the Book and the Muslims reject each other's *qibla*, and the qurʾānic Prophet is warned not to follow the evil inclinations of the former. Another verse, Q 2:142, indicates that the conflict over the *qibla* started when the Muslims abandoned their original *qibla*, i.e. the one to which the People of the Book were accustomed, and adopted another one, which caused the "foolish people" to wonder what made the believers change their former *qibla*. The final *qibla* sanctioned by the Qurʾān is the one directed towards the sacred mosque (in Mecca). Thus, the alternative *qibla* is Mecca (q.v.), which most probably was designed to replace the Jewish *qibla* of Jerusalem (q.v.), although the latter is never mentioned explicitly in the Qurʾān.

A more dogmatic definition of the recommended substitute for the "evil inclinations" of the Jews and the Christians is provided in Q 2:120. Here, the Jews and the Christians wish for the qurʾānic Prophet to embrace their respective religions, but God tells him to proclaim instead his adherence to the "right course" or "guidance" *(hudā)* of God. The same is repeated in Q 2:135 but the recommended substitute is defined here more concretely as the religion *(milla)* of Abraham (q.v.). The latter is said to have been a *ḥanīf* (q.v.), i.e. a non-Jewish and a non-Christian monotheist. The particularistic insistence on Abraham's non-Jewish and non-Christian identity comes out in explicit statements as, for example, in Q 2:140, where Abraham as well as Ishmael (q.v.), Isaac (q.v.), Jacob and the Tribes (i.e. Jacob's sons) are said to have been neither Jews nor Christians (Q 2:140).

Elsewhere, the non-Jewish/non-Christian identity is linked to Abraham through the assertion that the Torah and the Gospel were only revealed after him (Q 3:65). This statement is addressed to the People of the Book, most likely with the intention of refuting their own aspirations concerning Abraham, whose religious heritage they were probably claiming to have preserved. In other words, the image of Abraham has been appropriated from the Jews and the Christians and was turned into the prototype of the non-Jewish and non-Christian model of Islam. This is also the context of Q 3:67-8, which asserts that the people nearest to Abraham are the Muslim believers.

The punishment of the Jews

The response to the Jewish rejection of the Islamic message as described in the Qurʾān consists not only in various dogmatic maneuvers but also in military pressure (see JIHĀD; FIGHTING). The latter course is hinted at in Q 29:46, in which the qurʾānic Prophet is advised to dispute with the People of the Book in a fair manner, "except those of them who act unjustly." This implies that the evildoers among the People of the Book deserve harsh measures, perhaps even war (q.v.). Other passages give up the hope of ever convincing the Jews and elaborate on the punishment that they deserve for their unbelief. According to some verses, the punishment awaits the Jews in the indefinite future. This is implied, for example, in Q 3:20, which says that if the People of the Book turn their backs on the qurʾānic Prophet, he can do nothing but deliver his message, a verse which is taken to mean that it is God's business to deal with such people in his own time. This idea is even clearer in Q 2:109, in which the believers are urged to pardon and forgive (see FORGIVENESS) the People of the Book until God brings his command (concerning them).

But the Jewish-Muslim relationship as described in yet other verses is explicitly warlike. In one passage (Q 5:64), the military option seems to have been taken up by the Jews themselves. It is stated here that whenever they light the fire of war, God puts it out. In Q 2:85, which is addressed to the Children of Israel, allusion is made to certain hostile acts they carry out against some unidentified groups. Yet in other passages, the Jews are the party that comes under the Islamic military pressure and their military weaknesses are exposed. In Q 59:14, for example, it is observed that the People of the Book never fight the believers in one solid formation but only in sporadic groups, hiding behind the walls of their fortresses. They are divided among themselves and fight each other strongly. The People of the Book have suffered actual defeat, which is mentioned in Q 59:1-4. Here, they are described as being driven out of their houses, although they thought that their fortresses would defend them against God. In Q 59:11-12, the expulsion of the unbelieving People of the Book is mentioned yet again, this time with reference to the hypocrites *(munāfiqūn),* who have not kept their promise to help the People of the Book. A similar pattern of military defeat recurs in Q 33:26-7, which says that God has brought down the People of the Book from their fortresses and cast fear into their hearts (see HEART). The believers have slain some of them and taken others captive (see CAPTIVES). God bequeathed upon the believers their lands and possessions (see BOOTY; EXPEDITIONS AND BATTLES).

Apart from the military defeat of the People of the Book, the Qurʾān also refers very briefly to their social status under Islamic domination (see SOCIAL RELA-

TIONS; SOCIAL INTERACTIONS; COMMUNITY AND SOCIETY IN THE QURʾĀN). They must be killed unless they pay tribute (the *jizya,* see TAXATION; POLL TAX) but even then, they remain socially inferior to the believers (Q 9:29).

The qurʾānic Jews and the life of Muḥammad
The concrete relationship between the qurʾānic Jews and the life of Muḥammad is provided in the realm of the biography of Muḥammad (the *sīra,* see SĪRA AND THE QURʾĀN). One of the earliest biographies of Muḥammad is that of Ibn Isḥāq (d. 150/768), of which the best-known version is that of Ibn Hishām (d. 218/833). Ibn Isḥāq's compilation served as a model to later historiographers who quoted large portions of his accounts. His compilation contains numerous allusions to qurʾānic verses about the Jews. Most of them appear in the chapters about Muḥammad's stay in Medina (q.v.) and are associated with the history of the Jewish tribes of that city, namely, Qaynuqāʿ (q.v.), Naḍīr (q.v.) and Qurayẓa (q.v.). These tribes based their military power on fortresses built of stone, within which they lived, and thanks to which they retained predominance over their Arab neighbors. The arrival of the Jews in Medina is described in the sources as a prolonged process containing waves of refugees from Syria (q.v.) following the Babylonian and the Roman conquests of that area. Some traditions provide the Jews with a priestly pedigree originating in Moses' brother, Aaron (q.v.), but other traditions trace their origins to certain ancient Arab clans who are said to have converted to Judaism (see TRIBES AND CLANS).

Ibn Isḥāq incorporates Q 2:85 within a description of some pre-Islamic alliances formed between the Jewish tribes and the Arab inhabitants of Medina, the Aws and the Khazraj. The qurʾānic verse is addressed to the Children of Israel, accusing them of slaying their people and of turning a party from among them out of their homes, unlawfully going against their own. Ibn Isḥāq has associated this verse with the military clashes that broke out between the various Jewish/Arab alliances in pre-Islamic Medina (Ibn Isḥāq, *Sīra,* ii, 188-9). The first Jewish tribe defeated by Muḥammad was Qaynuqāʿ. Ibn Isḥāq adduces Q 3:12, which addresses "those who disbelieve," in reference to the fate of this tribe: they are told that they shall be vanquished and driven to hell together. Although this verse does not mention the Jews in particular, Ibn Isḥāq has nevertheless applied it to them, to illustrate God's wrath with the arrogant Jews of Qaynuqāʿ (Ibn Isḥāq, *Sīra,* ii, 201). Q 5:51, which does mention the Jews and warns the believers against taking them as friends, appears in Ibn Isḥāq (*Sīra,* iii, 52-3) within an account about a Muslim who dissolved his alliance with the Qaynuqāʿ out of fidelity to Muḥammad. The story implies that the Qurʾān encourages believers to sever their former pacts with the Jews. The tribe of Naḍīr was next to be attacked by the Muslim warriors and Ibn Isḥāq associates large portions of Q 59 (Sūrat al-Ḥashr, "The Gathering") with them. He asserts that most of this sūra was revealed in connection with the defeat of this Jewish tribe (*Sīra,* iii, 202-4; see OCCASIONS OF REVELATION). Another qurʾānic passage, Q 5:11, was connected with Naḍīr's plot to assassinate Muḥammad when he came to their premises in order to discuss a problem of blood money (q.v.; Ibn Isḥāq, *Sīra,* ii, 211-12). The verse itself bears no direct relation to the Jews, merely stating that God stopped some people from "stretching forth their hands" against the believers. By applying the verse to the Jews, Ibn Isḥāq betrays yet again his desire to illustrate

God's dismay with the Jewish anti-Islamic hostility by recourse to as many qurʾānic verses as possible. For the massacre of the tribe of Qurayẓa (q.v.), Ibn Isḥāq alludes to Q 33:26, which mentions the People of the Book whom God drove down from their fortresses. The Qurʾān says that they backed the unbelievers and that the believers killed some of them and took another part captive. The Qurʾān goes on to say that God made the believers heirs to the land and dwellings of the defeated People of the Book as well as to "a land that you have not yet trodden" (Q 33:27). The latter is taken by Ibn Isḥāq to be a forecast of the Islamic conquest of the Jewish settlement in Khaybar (Ibn Isḥāq, *Sīra*, iii, 261-2). In other exegetical compilations (*tafsīr*, see EXEGESIS OF THE QURʾĀN: CLASSICAL AND MEDIEVAL), additional verses have been connected to the affair of Qurayẓa. Most noteworthy is Q 8:55-8, in which instructions are given for treating "those with whom you make an agreement, then they break their agreement every time" (see BREAKING TRUSTS AND CONTRACTS; CONTRACTS AND ALLIANCES).

Apart from the military clash between Muḥammad and the Jews of Medina, Ibn Isḥāq (*Sīra*, ii, 160-221) dedicates a lengthy chapter to the polemical discourse between the two parties, and here, too, numerous qurʾānic allusions are provided. In his introduction to this chapter, Ibn Isḥāq observes that the Jewish rabbis showed hostility to Muḥammad because God chose his apostle from the Arabs (q.v.). The rabbis were joined by hypocrites *(munāfiqūn)* from the Aws and the Khazraj who clung to the polytheism of their fathers. The Jewish rabbis used to annoy the Prophet with questions and introduced confusion so as to confound the truth (q.v.) with falsity (see LIE). The Qurʾān was revealed with reference to these questions of theirs. Further on, Ibn Isḥāq provides specific accounts with names of hostile Jews, about whom the various qurʾānic passages were allegedly revealed. These accounts impute to them the stereotyped qurʾānic sins of arrogance, jealousy, mockery, distortion of scriptures, etc. (see SIN, MAJOR AND MINOR).

In connection with the sin of concealing parts of scripture, as imputed to the Jews in Q 2:76, Ibn Isḥāq's traditions (see ḤADĪTH AND THE QURʾĀN) assert that the Jews concealed God's command to believe in Muḥammad's prophethood (*Sīra*, ii, 185; see PROPHETS AND PROPHETHOOD). As for the qurʾānic allegation that the Jews did not judge "by what God revealed," i.e. that they falsified the laws of the revealed Torah (Q 5:41-3), Ibn Isḥāq has recorded a tradition dealing with the issue of the penalty of death by stoning (q.v.; *rajm*), which adulterers must incur (see ADULTERY AND FORNICATION; BOUNDARIES AND PRECEPTS). The Jews reportedly rejected this law while Muḥammad endorsed it. They also concealed the fact that this law was written in their own Torah. They did so out of jealousy so as not to admit that Muḥammad was a genuine prophet, well guided in the divine laws (Ibn Isḥāq, *Sīra*, ii, 213-14). The sin of ignoring the evidence of their own Torah is imputed to the Jews also in Ibn Isḥāq's report about the religion of Abraham. The report alludes to Q 3:23, which mentions the invitation to the book of God given to those who have received a portion of the scripture *(a-lam tara ilā lladhīna ūtū naṣīban mina l-kitāb yudʿawna ilā kitābi llāh),* that it might judge between them. The verse goes on to say that a party of them turned down the offer. Tradition relates that the verse was revealed following a debate that took place in a Jewish school *(bayt al-midrās)* between a number of Jews and Muḥammad. Muḥammad announced that his religion was that of Abraham but the Jews claimed that Abraham was Jewish. When, however, Muḥammad asked them to let the Torah judge between them, they refused (Ibn Isḥāq, *Sīra,* ii, 201). The Jewish conviction that they were genuine holders of Abraham's religious legacy comes out also in a tradition about the changing of the *qibla* from Jerusalem to Mecca, which alludes to Q 2:142. The tradition identifies the "fools" of this verse (see IGNORANCE) with a delegation of Jews who came to Muḥammad claiming that following the true religion of Abraham means reverting to the *qibla* of Jerusalem (Ibn Isḥāq, *Sīra,* ii, 198-9). Another tradition makes it even clearer that both parties, Muslims and Jews, claimed to be holding the true religion of Abraham and accused each other of distorting it. The tradition says that in this context, Q 5:68 was revealed. It tells the People of the Book that they follow no good until they keep the Torah and the gospel (Ibn Isḥāq; *Sīra,* ii, 217). Thus it is clear that in Ibn Isḥāq's presentation, the idea of the religion of Abraham is not regarded as a newly introduced concept but merely as an old Jewish idea that acquired a new non-Jewish Islamic interpretation. This interpretation was considered closer to the genuine message of the Torah than the Jewish one.

Among the passages quoted in Ibn Isḥāq's reports about the Jewish-Islamic polemics, some make no direct reference to Jews. For example, Q 3:7 mentions "those in whose hearts there is perversity *(zaygh),*" equating them with those who follow those parts of the Qurʾān that are ambiguous (q.v.; *mutashābihāt*). They do so in order to mislead, and impose (their own) interpretation upon, the Muslims. Ibn Isḥāq identifies the perverts with some Jews of Medina and says that they used to examine the mysterious letters that open some of the qurʾānic chapters, trying to figure out what their numerical value meant (see MYSTERIOUS LETTERS; NUMEROLOGY). When they failed, they expressed their doubts concerning Muḥammad's prophethood (Ibn Isḥāq, *Sīra,* ii, 194-5). Another similar case is that of Q 2:6-7, in which anonymous unbelievers *(alladhīna kafarū)* are condemned. It is said about them that "God has set a seal upon their hearts and upon their hearing and there is a covering over their eyes (q.v.), and there is a great punishment for them" (see HEARING AND DEAFNESS; SEEING AND HEARING; VISION AND BLINDNESS). Ibn Isḥāq (*Sīra,* ii, 178) identifies these doomed unbelievers as the Jewish rabbis. He says that these rabbis are also referred to in Q 2:14, which speaks about devils (*shayāṭīn,* see DEVIL), with whom some unbelievers conspire against the Muslims. While the "devils" are the Jews, the unbelievers, according to Ibn Isḥāq (*Sīra,* ii, 179), are the hypocrites *(munāfiqūn).* Q 2:170 refers to some stubborn people who refuse to become Muslims and insist on following the faith of their fathers. Here, too, according to Ibn Isḥāq (*Sīra,* ii, 200-1), the Qurʾān alludes to certain Jews whose names he specifies. Q 7:187 mentions some anonymous people inquiring when the "hour" shall come (see APOCALYPSE) and, again, Ibn Isḥāq (*Sīra,* ii, 218) says that they were the Jews and provides a list of their names. Even Q 112, which declares the undefined unity of God, without reference to any unbelievers, was revealed, according to Ibn Isḥāq (*Sīra,* ii, 220-1), in response to irritating questions posed to Muḥammad by certain Jews.

In various exegetical sources, other verses have been associated with the Jewish-Islamic conflict. For example, Q 58:8 condemns people who "hold secret counsels for sin" and greet the qurʾānic Prophet in a depraved manner. This was interpreted as referring to the Jews who reportedly greeted Muḥammad by saying *al-sām ʿalayka* ("destruction be upon you"), instead of *al-salām ʿalayka* ("peace be upon you").

On the other hand, Ibn Isḥāq is also aware of some Medinan Jews who converted to Islam and his report about them alludes to Q 3:113, which mentions an "upright" party among the People of the Book. He provides a list of their names — the best known of which being that of ʿAbdallāh b. Salām — and describes the dismay of the rabbis at their conversion to Islam (Ibn Isḥāq, *Sīra*, ii, 206). Ibn Salām's name recurs in later exegetical compilations *(tafsīr)* in association with other verses mentioning believers among the Jews or the People of the Book (Q 4:46, 162; 5:66; 10:94; 28:52-4). Ibn Salām is occasionally contrasted with Kaʿb b. al-Ashraf, a Jewish archenemy of the Prophet (of the tribe of Naḍīr), who was assassinated at the behest of Muḥammad. Ibn al-Ashraf's name, too, was read into the Qurʾān and it occurs, for example, in the commentaries on Q 3:75. That verse speaks of two types of people belonging to the People of the Book: those who pay back their debts to the believers in full and those who do not. Ibn Salām is mentioned as one of the former and Ibn al-Ashraf as one of the latter. Ibn al-Ashraf also figures in the exegesis of Q 3:186, in which the believers are said to have been hearing "much annoying talk" from the People of the Book. The commentators say that the verse refers to Ibn al-Ashraf who used to compose satirical anti-Islamic poetry (see POETRY AND POETS). His name is also included in the exegesis of Q 3:78, which speaks about those who "twist" the book, i.e. the Qurʾān, with their tongues. Q 4:51-2 mentions people whom God has cursed because they told the unbelievers that the latter's faith was better than the Islamic one. The exegetes say that the passage refers to Ibn al-Ashraf, who supported the Quraysh and their idols and reviled Muḥammad's religion (q.v.). The Prophet's doomed "enemy" *(shāniʾ)* of Q 108:3 is also identified with him (see ENEMIES; OPPOSITION TO MUḤAMMAD).

It may be noted in passing that some of the qurʾānic verses that refer to believers among the People of the Book did not remain confined to the Jewish sphere and appear also in a specific Christian context. For example, Q 28:54, which states that the believers among the People of the Book shall be granted their reward twice, was interpreted as referring to Ibn Salām as well as to Salmān al-Fārisī. The latter changed his faith from Christianity to Islam and became a celebrated Companion of the Prophet (see COMPANIONS OF THE PROPHET). The verse is also said to refer to believers among the Christians of Abyssinia (q.v.) who joined Muḥammad's warriors in Medina (Suyūṭī, *Durr*, v, 131-3; see EMIGRANTS AND HELPERS). This verse also inspired a ḥadīth that is attributed to the Prophet, which says that whoever embraces Islam from among the "people of the two books," will be rewarded twice and whoever embraces Islam from among the associators *(mushrikūn)*, will be rewarded once (Ibn Ḥanbal, *Musnad*, v, 259). The same verse was eventually worked into the Prophet's letter to the Byzantine emperor (see BYZANTINES). The letter promises him a double reward in return for his conversion to Islam. The same letter contains also the verbatim wording of Q 3:64, which extends an invitation to the People of the Book to join the Muslims in a common monotheistic faith (e.g. Bukhārī, *Ṣaḥīḥ*, iv, 57 [56:102]).

Qurʾānic Jews and the Islamic community

The sinful Jews of the Qurʾān were eventually turned into a model of evil of which the entire Islamic community must beware. This emerges from the exegesis of qurʾānic passages that denounce people who became divided by inner conflicts and dissension (e.g. Q 3:105; 6:159). The verses instruct the qurʾānic Prophet to dissociate from them and the commentators have identified them with the Jews, as well as the Christians. It was thus implied that the Islamic community should be cautious not to follow the Jewish and Christian precedent of discord. Such warning was intended mainly against heretical groups, like the Khārijīs (q.v.) and the Qadarīs who were accused of introducing Jewish models of schism into Islamic society, although the introduction of Jewish ideas is most commonly associated with the Shīʿīs, especially ʿAbdallāh b. Sabaʾ and al-Mukhtār (d. 67/687; see SHĪʿISM AND THE QURʾĀN). Verses dealing with the fate of unbelievers in hell (e.g. Q 18:103-6) were likewise interpreted as referring to the Jews with the same anti-heretical aim in mind (for details see Rubin, *Between Bible and Qurʾān,* 160-3, 208-12). In addition to those verses about the wrath *(ghaḍab)* of God in which the Jews are mentioned explicitly, various qurʾānic allusions to anonymous groups who have come under God's wrath were also interpreted as referring to the Jews (e.g. Q 1:7; 60:13). The punishment of transformation into apes and pigs, which the qurʾānic People of the Book incurred as a result of God's wrath, reappears in traditions about Jews of Islamic times. In some of these traditions, the Prophet himself is involved and he is said to have addressed them as "brothers of apes and pigs." Some traditions have applied the same punishment to certain heretical Islamic groups such as the Qadarīs (Rubin, *Between Bible and Qurʾān,* 213-32; see HERESY).

Numerous qurʾānic passages associated with the Jews emerge also in the discussions of their status as *ahl al-dhimma,* "people under protection" (i.e. of the Islamic community, the *umma,* see PROTECTION). Especially noteworthy is the qurʾānic passage that contains the term *dhimma* (Q 9:7-15). It deals with associators *(mushrikūn),* concerning whom the Qurʾān says that their protection remains valid as long as they remain loyal to the believers (see LOYALTY). If they break their oaths (see OATHS AND PROMISES) and revile the Islamic religion, then the believers must fight them. Muslim scholars applied this passage to the obligation of loyalty with which the Jewish and Christian *dhimmīs* must treat their Muslim protectors (Ibn Qayyim, *Dhimma,* iii, 1379 f.). Q 9:28 is also noteworthy. It proclaims that the *mushrikūn* are impure *(najas,* see PURITY AND IMPURITY) and therefore they should not approach the "sacred mosque." Muslim scholars took this statement as the scriptural basis for the injunction (usually attributed to the Prophet himself) to prevent Jews and Christians from entering the Arabian peninsula (Ibn Qayyim, *Dhimma,* i, 370-408).

Qurʾānic Jews and modern scholarship

Modern scholars have usually taken the qurʾānic treatment of the Jews as a point of departure for their historical analysis of Muḥammad's relations with the Jews of Medina. In so doing, they have followed the traditional Islamic approach, which sees in the Qurʾān an authentic collection of Muḥammad's prophecies. The scholars have adopted a historiographical narrative (see HISTORY AND THE QURʾĀN) about a so-called "break" between Muḥammad and the Jews of Medina, usually dated to shortly before the battle of Badr (q.v.) in March 624 C.E. The scholars defined Muḥammad's policy until the break as dedicated to attempts at gaining the support of the Jews. An extra-qurʾānic document known as the Constitution of Medina (recorded in Ibn Isḥāq, *Sīra,* ii, 147-50), which is relatively favorable to the Jews, was dated to this stage. The reason for the "break" with the Jews, according to the scholars, was the Jewish reluctance to respond to Muḥammad's appeal. Consequently, the Prophet changed his attitude towards them and embarked on a military offensive against them. This narrative runs parallel to the supposed evolution of the idea of holy war (*jihād,* q.v.). The scholars have built into this narrative of escalating conflict the various qur'ānic verses about the Jews. Broadly speaking, verses relatively tolerant of the Jews were marked by the scholars as early Medinan (see CHRONOLOGY AND THE QUR'ĀN), assuming that they were revealed before the break. The break is reflected in qur'ānic passages about the military clash with the People of the Book, as well as in the verses about the new *qibla* and the non-Jewish/non-Christian identity of Abraham. In view of doubts raised more recently by some scholars, however, who suggested that the Qur'ān gained its final shape much later than in the days of Muḥammad and perhaps not even in Arabia (cf. Wansbrough, *QS;* see POST-ENLIGHTENMENT ACADEMIC STUDY OF THE QUR'ĀN), the historicity of the supposed relations between Muḥammad and the Jews is no longer self-evident. One cannot rule out the possibility that at least some components of the narrative of the "break" with the Jews stem from post-conquest conditions that were projected back into Muḥammad's time.

Uri Rubin

Bibliography
Primary: Bukhārī, *Ṣaḥīḥ,* 9 vols., Cairo 1958; Ibn Ḥanbal, *Musnad,* 6 vols., repr. Beirut 1978; Ibn Isḥāq, *Sīra,* ed. Muṣṭafā al-Saqqā et al., repr. Beirut 1971; Ibn Qayyim al-Jawziyya, *Aḥkām ahl al-dhimma,* ed. Y. al-Bakrī and Sh. al-ʿĀrūrī, Riyadh 1997; Suyūṭī, *Durr.*
Secondary: C. Adang, *Muslim writers on Judaism and the Hebrew Bible. From Ibn Rabban to Ibn Ḥazm,* Leiden 1996; A. Barakat, *Muhammad and the Jews,* New Delhi 1979; R.S. Faizer, Muhammad and the Medinan Jews. A comparison of the texts of Ibn Ishaq's *Kitāb Sīrat rasūl Allāh* with al-Waqidi's *Kitāb al-Maghāzī,* in IJMES 28 (1996), 463-89; M. Gil, The origin of the Jews of Yathrib, in JSAI 4 (1984), 203-24; S.D. Goitein, *Jews and Arabs. Their contacts through the ages,* New York 1974; G.R. Hawting, al-Mukhtār b. Abī ʿUbayd, in EI², vii, 521-4; M.G.S. Hodgson, ʿAbd Allāh b. Sabaʾ, in EI², i, 51; R.S. Humphreys, *Islamic history. A framework for inquiry,* Minneapolis 1988 (especially 255-83), Princeton 1991 (rev. ed.); M.J. Kister, The massacre of the Banū Qurayẓa, in JSAI 8 (1986), 61-96; Lane; M. Lecker, *Jews and Arabs in pre- and early Islamic Arabia,* Aldershot 1998; id., *Muslims, Jews and pagans. Studies on early Islamic Medina,* Leiden 1995; B. Lewis, *The Jews of Islam,* Princeton 1984; A. Noth, Abgrenzungsprobleme zwischen Muslimen und nicht-Muslimen. Die "Bedingungen ʿUmars *(al-shurūṭ al-ʿumariyya)*" unter einem anderen Aspect gelesen, in JSAI 9 (1987), 290-315; Paret, *Kommentar;* U. Rubin, *Between Bible and Qur'ān. The Children of Israel and the Islamic self-image,* Princeton 1999; id., The constitution of Medina. Some notes, in SI 62 (1985), 5-23; id., Qur'ān and *tafsīr.* The case of *ʿan yadin,* in *Der Islam* 70 (1993), 133-44; M. Schöller, *Exegetisches Denken und Prophetenbiographie: eine quellenkritische Analyse der Sira-Überlieferung zu Muhammads Konflikt mit den Juden,* Wiesbaden 1998; id., *Sīra* and *tafsīr.* Muḥammad al-Kalbī on the Jews of Medina, in H. Motzki (ed.), *The biography of Muḥammad. The issue of the sources,* Leiden 2000, 18-48; R.B. Serjeant, The *Sunnah Jāmiʿah,* pacts with the Yathrib Jews, and the *Taḥrīm* of Yathrib. Analysis and translation of the documents comprised in the so-called "Constitution of Medina," in BSOAS 41 (1978), 1-42; G. Vajda, Juifs et musulmans selon le *ḥadīt,* in JA 229 (1937), 57-127; Wansbrough, *QS;* S.M. Wasserstrom, *Between Muslim and Jew. The problem of symbiosis under early Islam,* Princeton 1995; W.M. Watt, *Muhammad at Medina,* Oxford 1956 (especially 192-220); A.J. Wensinck, *Muhammad and the Jews of Medina,* trans. and ed. W. Behn, Freiburg im Breisgrau 1975.

Jibrīl see GABRIEL

Jibt

A word of uncertain etymology, the noun *jibt* occurs only once in the Qur'ān, but is also used in poetry and prophetic traditions from the early Islamic centuries (see POETRY AND POETS; ḤADĪTH AND THE

QURʾĀN). Generally, *jibt* has three possible meanings: it is used to describe any false object of belief or worship (see IDOLS AND IMAGES), an individual who exceeds all bounds of propriety (see MODERATION) or a state of oppression (q.v.) and injustice (*Lisān al-ʿArab,* ii, 164; *Tāj al-ʿarūs,* iii, 32; see JUSTICE AND INJUSTICE). It is mentioned in Q 4:51 in the context of condemning those People of the Book (q.v.) who gave credence to the unbelievers (see BELIEF AND UNBELIEF) and attempted to incite them against Muslims.

Some early authorities asserted that the word passed into Arabic from the language of the Ḥabasha (i.e. Ethiopic: that of the former inhabitants of today's Sudan and Ethiopia; see ABYSSINIA; FOREIGN VOCABULARY; cf. Jeffery, *For. vocab.,* 99-100; Suyūṭī, *Muhadhdhab,* 204), where, reportedly, it meant "sorcery" or "a demon" (see MAGIC; DEVIL). Other authorities maintained that the word was derived from the Arabic term *jibsun,* meaning "a person of ill repute and character" (Māwardī, *Nukat,* i, 494-5; ʿAbd al-Raḥīm, *Tafsīr,* i, 284). In the Qurʾān and in numerous theological works, *jibt* is most often correlated with the word *ṭāghūt (al-jibt wa-l-ṭāghūt),* an expression that means divination (q.v.), sorcery or idol worship (see IDOLATRY AND IDOLATERS). Some commentators on the Qurʾān (see EXEGESIS OF THE QURʾĀN: CLASSICAL AND MEDIEVAL) claimed that *jibt* and *ṭāghūt* were the names of two idols worshipped by the Quraysh (q.v.) in Mecca (q.v.; Qurṭubī, *Jāmiʿ,* v, 248-9; Qāsimī, *Tafsīr,* iii, 172). Others claimed that *jibt* referred to a specific person named Ḥuyayy b. Akhṭab while *ṭāghūt* referred to Kaʿb b. al-Ashraf, two Jewish leaders who, after the battle of Uḥud (see EXPEDITIONS AND BATTLES), went to Mecca in order to conspire with the Quraysh to destroy the Muslims in Medina (q.v.; Ṭabarī, *Tafsīr,* viii, esp. 461-5, 469-70 [ad Q 4:51]; Ibn Kathīr, *Tafsīr,* ad loc.; see JEWS AND JUDAISM; OPPOSITION TO MUḤAMMAD). Still other authorities maintained that *jibt* means sorcery or divination while *ṭāghūt* means a sorcerer or diviner (Zamakhsharī, *Kashshāf,* i, 274; Ibn ʿĀdil, *Lubāb,* vi, 420-2). The influential premodern jurist and theologian, Fakhr al-Dīn al-Rāzī (d. 606/1210; *Tafsīr,* v, 103-4), asserted that the expression has come to describe any condition of extreme evil (see GOOD AND EVIL) and corruption (q.v.).

Khaled M. Abdu El Fadl

Bibliography
Primary: M. ʿAbd al-Raḥīm, *Tafsīr al-Ḥasan al-Baṣrī,* 2 vols., Cairo n.d.; Ibn ʿĀdil, Abū Ḥafṣ ʿUmar b. ʿAlī, *al-Lubāb fī ʿulūm al-kitāb,* ed. ʿĀ.A. ʿAbd al-Mawjūd and ʿA.M. Muʿawwaḍ, 20 vols., Beirut 1998; Ibn Kathīr, *Tafsīr; Lisān al-ʿArab,* Beirut 1997²; Māwardī, *Nukat;* Qāsimī, *Tafsīr,* Beirut 1997; Qurṭubī, *Jāmiʿ;* Rāzī, *Tafsīr,* 32 vols. in 16, Beirut 1990; Ṭabarī, *Tafsīr,* ed. Shākir; *Tāj al-ʿarūs,* Beirut 1994; Zamakhsharī, *Kashshāf,* 4 vols., Beirut n.d.
Secondary: T. Fahd, *Le panthéon de l'arabie centrale à la vielle de l'hégire,* Paris 1968, 240 n. 2 (on *jibt* and *ṭāghūt*); G. Hawting, *The idea of idolatry and the emergence of Islam,* London 1999, 56-7; T. Nöldeke, *Neue Beiträge zur semitischen Sprachwissenschaft,* Strassburg 1910, 47-8 (for an Ethiopic origin of *jibt; ṭāghūt* is disussed on p. 48); Paret, *Kommentar,* 96 (discussion of an Ethiopic origin of *jibt*).

Jihād

Struggle, or striving, but often understood both within the Muslim tradition and beyond it as warfare against infidels (see FIGHTING; WAR; BELIEF AND UNBELIEF). The term *jihād* derives from the root *j-h-d,* denoting effort, exhaustion, exertion, strain. Derivatives of this root occur in forty-one qurʾānic verses. Five of these contain the phrase *jahd aymānihim,* meaning "[to swear] the strongest oath," which is irrelevant to the present discussion (see OATHS), and not all the remaining verses refer to warfare.

Since the concept of jihād is related to warfare, discussions of the subject often contain explicit or implicit value-judgments and apologetics. In fact, the subjects of jihād and warfare in Islam are always treated as one. There are, however, two reasons to discuss them separately. First, jihād is a concept much broader than warfare. Secondly, the doctrine of warfare can be derived from the Qurʾān without resorting to the term jihād at all. Therefore, in this article the derivatives of the root *j-h-d* in the Qurʾān will be discussed first, followed by a survey of the doctrine of warfare as expressed in the Qurʾān.

The root j-h-d *and its derivatives in the Qurʾān*

The root *j-h-d* does not have bellicose connotations in pre-Islamic usage (see PRE-ISLAMIC ARABIA AND THE QURʾĀN). Judging by linguistic criteria alone (see LANGUAGE AND STYLE OF THE QURʾĀN), without having recourse to qurʾānic exegesis (see EXEGESIS OF THE QURʾĀN: CLASSICAL AND MEDIEVAL), only ten out of the thirty-six relevant qurʾānic references can be unequivocally interpreted as signifying warfare. The rest are unspecified, some of them clearly denoting efforts or struggles other than fighting. The following guidelines help determine whether or not the term *j-h-d* in a given verse refers to warfare:

(a) when the term is juxtaposed with a military idiom, such as "shirkers" (*mukhallafūn, qāʿidūn,* Q 4:95; 9:81, 86) or "go on raids" (*infirū,* Q 9:41; see EXPEDITIONS AND BATTLES). Verses in which *j-h-d* is connected to "asking leave/finding excuses" *(istiʾdhān)* also seem to be dealing with warfare (Q 9:44; cf. 9:86, which combines both "ask leave" and "shirkers");

(b) when the content of the verse discloses its military significance (Q 5:54, where there is a linkage between harshness towards unbelievers, fearlessness and *j-h-d;* Q 60:1, where "enemies" [q.v.] and departing for jihād are mentioned);

(c) when the context of the verse indicates a military significance. Textual context is difficult to use because of the methods of assembling the text to which the history of the collection of the Qurʾān (q.v.) attests. As indicated in this history, verses that were revealed on different occasions (see OCCASIONS OF REVELATION; CHRONOLOGY AND THE QURʾĀN) were placed in sequence. Sometimes, fully contradictory verses were placed together, apparently because they deal with the same topic (e.g. Q 2:190-3; 8:72-5). Occasionally, however, the continuity between sequential verses is clear and the textual context may be used to clarify the warlike intention of a verse (Q 9:41, the context being 9:38-41; Q 9:44, the context being 9:44-6; these two verses also fall under category (a) above; Q 9:88, the context being 9:87-92);

(d) when *j-h-d* in the third form is followed by a direct object. It denotes, literally, two parties, each trying to exhaust the other, hence the notion of combat (Q 9:73 = 66:9; but cf. Q 25:52, *wa-jāhidhum bihi jihādan kabīran,* where the Prophet is instructed to combat by peaceful means, namely, by the Qurʾān; see DEBATE AND DISPUTATION).

In sum, there are only ten places in the Qurʾān where *j-h-d* definitely denotes warfare. To these may be added four verses that establish the status of "those who believed, emigrated (see EMIGRATION) and exerted themselves" (*inna lladhīna āmanū wa-hājarū wa-jāhadū,* Q 8:72, 74; 9:20; cf. 8:75). Since warfare is strongly advocated in the Qurʾān, it stands to reason that references to the high status of the "strugglers" *(mujāhidūn)* are, in fact, references to warriors. It is clear, however, that in these verses the reference is to the Emigrants (*muhājirūn*, see EMIGRANTS AND HELPERS). It may be pointed out that sometimes *j-h-d* occurs as the counterpart of *hijra*, "emigration," presumably the Muslims' emigration to Medina (q.v.; Q 2:218; 8:72-5; 9:20; 16:110, cf. 9:24). Strangely, there is no qurʾānic reference to the military contribution or warlike attributes of the Helpers (*anṣār*, i.e. those Medinans who helped the émigrés; such references do, however, abound in the historical and ḥadīth literature; see ḤADĪTH AND THE QURʾĀN).

There is one case where *j-h-d* is applied to an impious struggle, namely, the struggle of disbelieving parents (q.v.) to prevent their offspring (see CHILDREN; FAMILY) from adhering to the true religion (q.v.; Q 29:8).

But in many verses it is not possible to determine the kind of effort indicated by *j-h-d*. There are many commentators who leave the terms unspecified in these instances, whereas others interpret also these ambiguous cases as warfare against infidels (see commentaries to Q 2:218; 3:142; 5:35; 9:16, 19, 20, 24; 16:110; 29:6, 69; 47:31; 61:11). Still others understand the doubtful cases in one or more of the following ways: (a) combat against one's own desires and weaknesses (see SIN, MAJOR AND MINOR), (b) perseverance in observing the religious law (see LAW AND THE QURʾĀN), (c) seeking religious knowledge (*ṭalab al-ʿilm*, see KNOWLEDGE AND LEARNING), (d) observance of the sunna (q.v.), (e) obedience (q.v.) to God and summoning people to worship him, and so on (see e.g. Khāzin, *Lubāb*, v, 200; Ibn Abī Ḥātim, *Tafsīr*, ix, 3084). All these meanings, however, are never explicit in the Qurʾān. Also, the phrases denoting the "greater" jihād (i.e. one's personal struggle to be a better Muslim) that are common in later literature, namely, "struggle of the self" (*jihād al-nafs*) or "struggle with the devil" (*jihād al-shayṭān*, see DEVIL), do not occur in the Qurʾān (see THEOLOGY AND THE QURʾĀN; ETHICS AND THE QURʾĀN; GOOD AND EVIL).

The qurʾānic concept of jihād was not originally connected with antagonism between the believers and other people. The semantic field of the root *j-h-d* as well as its use in the Qurʾān suggest another provenance. It may be an expression of the ancient and ubiquitous notion that the believers must prove to the deity their worthiness for divine reward (see REWARD AND PUNISHMENT; MARTYRS). This proof is achieved by enduring various kinds of hardships and self-mortification. Fasting and pilgrimage belong to this category as do celibacy and poverty. Conversely, hardships that befall the believers are understood as divine tests designed to provide the believers with opportunities to prove themselves worthy (see TRIAL). These ancient religious ideas found expression in the Qurʾān. God announces many times that he subjects the believers to tests and he reprimands those who are not able, or not willing, to endure (e.g. Q 2:155-6, 214; 3:142; 4:48; 47:4; see TRUST AND PATIENCE; JOY AND MISERY; PUNISHMENT STORIES). In Islam, in addition to giving the believers the opportunity to prove themselves, the tests also help establish the distinction between the true believers on the one hand, and the pretenders and the unbelievers on the other (see HYPOCRITES AND HYPOCRISY). The tests also help determine the relative status of the members of the community (see COMMUNITY AND SOCIETY IN THE QURʾĀN). One of the means of testing is jihād. In this capacity jihād may mean participation in warfare, but also any other effort made in connection with adherence to the true religion (see Q 3:142; 9:16; 47:31; cf. Q 9:24, 44, 88. Only Q 9:44 and 9:88 certainly refer to warfare, judging by the context. See also Q 4:76-7, 95-6; 9:90-4; 29:10-1; 47:20; 49:14-5; 57:10, 25.).

Sometimes not jihād but death (see DEATH AND THE DEAD) or battle *(qitāl)* "in the way of God" are explicitly mentioned as a test (Q 3:166-7; 47:4; cf. 3:154-5; 4:66; 33:11, 23-4).

Very little of the peaceful sense of *j-h-d* remained in Muslim culture and the understanding of jihād as war became predominant. Nevertheless, there are verses in the Qurʾān that attest to other significations. The best example is Q 22:78. By linguistic and contextual criteria, the phrase "exert yourself in the way of God as is his right" *(wa-jāhidū fī llāhi ḥaqqa jihādihi)* clearly does not refer to warfare, but to other forms of effort made by way of obedience to God. The verse is part of the doctrine of the "religion of Abraham" *(millat Ibrāhīm),* which regards the patriarch as the first, original Muslim (see Q 2:125-36; see ABRAHAM; ḤANĪF). Q 22:78 instructs Muslims to perform the religious duties originally prescribed to Abraham. While asking the believers to exert themselves and to do their utmost to this end *(jāhidū),* the verse points out that the requirement should not be deemed too much to ask, since God "has laid no hardship on you in your religion." The theme of war is not touched upon at all in this verse. In the same vein, Q 49:15 deals with definitions of belief and the phrase "those who strive" *(alladhīna… jāhadū)* apparently refers not to warriors but to those who perform all the divine ordinances (cf. Bayḍāwī, *Anwār,* ii, 277). Yet many commentators (including al-Ṭabarī, d. 310/923) insist that in these two cases the term refers to participation in warfare.

The warlike meaning of jihād thus predominates, to the extent that *q-t-l,* "kill," was sometimes glossed by *j-h-d* (e.g. Bayḍāwī, *Anwār,* i, 105, ad Q 2:190). This predominance is perhaps to be explained by the fact that in this sense of "war," jihād was given a legal definition, legal categories and regulations, aspects which were discussed at length by the jurists (who often, however, used the term *siyar* instead of jihād). Also the parallelism between the qurʾānic phrases jihād "in the way of God" *(fī sabīli llāh)* and *qitāl* "in the way of God" may have contributed to the equation of *j-h-d* with terms of warfare. In fact the phrase "in the way of God" itself came to mean "warfare against infidels," although it is not necessarily so in the Qurʾān (see e.g. "emigration in the way of God" in Q 4:100; 16:41; 22:58; 24:23).

The doctrine of warfare in the Qurʾān

Islam is a system of beliefs, ritual and law (see FAITH; RITUAL AND THE QURʾĀN) and its legal system covers all spheres of life, including warfare. Many rulings and attitudes relating to warfare are scattered throughout the Qurʾān, mainly in the Medinan sūras. Yet, derivatives of the root *j-h-d* are absent from the majority of these verses. Forms of the root *q-t-l* are used forty-four times in relation to warfare (although derivatives of this root are also used in other contexts). In addition, there are many verses relating to this subject in which neither *j-h-d* nor *q-t-l* occur.

The qurʾānic rulings and attitudes regarding warfare are often ambiguous and contradictory so that there is no one coherent doctrine of warfare in the Qurʾān, especially when the text is read without reference to its exegetical tradition. These contradictions and ambiguities resulted from historical developments and were later amplified by differences of opinion among exegetes. The Prophet led a dynamic career, having been at war for years with various enemies and under changing circumstances. Such variations and developments are doubtlessly reflected in qurʾānic verses and account for some of the contradictions. The course of these developments, however, is not clear, for the same reasons that obstruct a decisive reconstruction of the Prophet's biography (see SĪRA AND THE QURʾĀN; MUḤAMMAD). In addition, differences of opinion eventually arose due to the various possibilities of interpretations. The language of the Qurʾān is often obscure and, even when not so, many terms, phrases and sentences have more than one possible meaning or implication. For example, the sentence "we have our endeavors *(aʿmāl)*, you have yours" (Q 2:139; 42:15; cf. 10:41; 109:6) may be interpreted in several ways: (a) it enjoins tolerance towards other religions (see RELIGIOUS PLURALISM AND THE QURʾĀN), (b) it merely states a fact, (c) it constitutes a threat, or (d) it employs "endeavors" but means "reward for the endeavors," in which case it is also merely a statement of a fact, not an implied imperative. The first of these interpretations contradicts the qurʾānic order to initiate war against the infidels (Q 2:191, 193, 244; 8:39; 9:5, 29, 36 etc.; see e.g. Ibn al-Jawzī, *Nawāsikh,* 175-6, 440; Ṭabarī, *Tafsīr,* xi, 118-9). Another example is Q 2:190 (cf. 2:194). It contains the seemingly clear phrase "fight in the way of God those who fight you and do not trespass" (see BOUNDARIES AND PRECEPTS). This may be taken either as prescribing defensive war or as an instruction to refrain from harming non-combatants (see e.g. Jaṣṣāṣ, *Aḥkām,* i, 257). The former contradicts the above-mentioned qurʾānic order to initiate war. These are only two of a multitude of examples.

Commentators developed special techniques to deal with qurʾānic contradictions, chief among them abrogation (q.v.; *naskh*) and specification (*ʿāmm wa-khāṣṣ,* literally "general versus specific"). Abrogation seeks to replace the rulings of certain verses by others, on the grounds that the latter were revealed to the Prophet later than the former. Specification is designed to restrict or ban certain injunctions and prohibitions. This is done by establishing that the verse in question only applies to a definite group or to a specific event in the past. In contrast to abrogation, specification often occurs without the use of the technical terms *ʿāmm* and *khāṣṣ*.

A rarely applied, but very significant device, is the assignation of differing qurʾānic rules to different situations. Whereas the techniques of abrogation and specification aim at distilling one absolutely binding rule out of a number of possibilities, the technique of assignation leaves open a number of options and allows the authorities the power to decide which of the mutually-exclusive qurʾānic rules applies in a given situation. There are other exegetical devices used in order to resolve contradictions, such as denying linguistically possible implications (e.g. for Q 2:62), "supplementing" verses (*taqdīr,* e.g. for Q 10:41) and assigning appropriate contents to qurʾānic words (e.g. equating the term *silm/salm,* "peace," with Islam, for Q 2:208 and 8:61, see Ṭabarī, *Tafsīr,* ii, 322-5; x, 34).

The verses relating to warfare may be classified under the following headings: (a) the order to fight, (b) exhortations (q.v.), (c) the purpose of warfare, (d) conscription, (e) permission to retreat, (f) the treatment of prisoners (q.v.; see also HOSTAGES; CAPTIVES), and (g) booty (q.v.). There are also miscellaneous practical and tactical instructions. The first topic is covered by a large number of verses, whereas the rest are confined to a few verses each.

The order to fight involves the issue of attitudes towards the other. Muslim scholars considered more than one hundred verses as relevant to this topic. Even an address to the Prophet such as "you are merely a warner" (q.v.; Q 11:12) was sometimes understood as an implicit instruction to leave the infidels alone. Thus the verses expressing attitudes towards the infidels include explicit or implicit instructions to the Prophet, or to the Muslims, which may be defined as follows: (a) to be patient and to stay aloof from the infidels (Q 2:139; 3:20, 111; 4:80-1; 5:99, 105; 6:66, 69, 70, 104; 7:180, 199; 10:99, 108-9; 11:121-2; 13:40; 15:3, 94-5; 16:82; 17:54; 19:84; 20:130; 22:68; 23:54; 24:54; 25:43; 27:92; 29:50; 30:60; 31:23; 32:30; 33:48; 34:25; 35:23; 37:174; 38:70; 39:15; 40:55, 77; 42:6, 48; 43:83; 44:59; 46:35; 50:45; 51:54; 52:31, 45, 48; 53:29; 54:6; 68:44, 48; 70:5, 42; 73:10-1; 74:11; 76:24; 88:22), (b) to forgive them or treat them kindly (Q 2:109; 5:13; 15:85; 43:89; 45:14; 60:8-9; 64:14; see FORGIVENESS; MERCY), (c) to tolerate them (Q 2:62, 256; 5:69, but cf. 3:19; 5:82; see TOLERANCE AND COMPULSION), (d) to preach or argue with them peaceably (Q 3:64; 4:63; 16:64, 125; 29:46; 41:34; see INVITATION), and (e) to fight them under certain restrictions (Q 2:190, 191-4, 217; 4:91; 9:36, 123; 16:126; 22:39-40). There are also qurʾānic references to treaties with infidels and to peace (Q 2:208; 4:90; 8:61; cf. Q 3:28; 47:35; see CONTRACTS AND ALLIANCES). All these are in conflict with the clear orders to fight, expressed in Q 9:5 and 9:29 (cf. Q 2:244). Q 9:5 instructs the Muslims to fight the idolaters *(mushrikūn)* until they are converted to Islam and is known as "the sword verse" (*āyat al-sayf,* see POLYTHEISM AND ATHEISM). Q 9:29 orders Muslims to fight the People of the Book (q.v.) until they consent to pay tribute (*jizya,* see POLL TAX), thereby recognizing the superiority of Islam. It is known as "the *jizya* verse" (*āyat al-jizya,* occasionally also as "the sword verse"). The Qurʾān does not lay down rules for cases of Muslim defeat, although there is a long passage discussing such an occurrence (Q 3:139-75, see also 4:104; see VICTORY).

A broad consensus among medieval exegetes and jurists exists on the issue of waging war. The simplest and earliest solution of the problem of contradictions in the Qurʾān was to consider Q 9:5 and 9:29 as abrogating all the other statements. Scholars seem sometimes to have deliberately expanded the list of the abrogated verses, including in it material that is irrelevant to the issue of waging war (e.g. Q 2:83, see Ibn al-Bārzī, *Nāsikh,* 23; Ibn al-Jawzī, *Muṣaffā,* 14; id., *Nawāsikh,* 156-8; Bayḍāwī, *Anwār,* i, 70; Ṭabarī, *Tafsīr,* i, 311; other examples: Q 3:111; 4:63; 16:126; 23:96; 25:63; 28:55; 38:88; 39:3). The number of verses abrogated by Q 9:5 and 9:29 is sometimes said to exceed 120 (Ibn al-Bārzī, *Nāsikh,* 22-3 and passim; also Powers, Exegetical genre, 138). Several verses are considered as both abrogating and abrogated, in turn, by others. The Muslim tradition, followed by modern scholars (see POST-ENLIGHTENMENT ACADEMIC STUDY OF THE QURʾĀN), associated various verses with developments in the career of the Prophet. It is related that, in the beginning, God instructed the Prophet to avoid the infidels and to forgive them. The Prophet was actually forbidden to wage war while in Mecca (q.v.). After the emigration to Medina *(hijra)* the Muslims were first permitted to fight in retaliation for the injustice (see JUSTICE AND INJUSTICE) done them by the Meccans (Q 22:39-40). Then came the order to fight the infidels generally, yet certain restrictions were prescribed. Eventually all restrictions were removed and all treaties with infidels were repudiated by Q 9:1-14, and the ultimate divine orders were expressed in Q 9:5 and 9:29. (There are many versions of this scheme, see ʿAbdallāh b. Wahb, *Jāmiʿ,* fol. 15b; Abū ʿUbayd, *Nāsikh,* 190-7; Bayḍāwī, *Anwār,* i, 634; Khāzin, *Lubāb,* i, 168; Shāfiʿī, *Tafsīr,* 166-73; Jaṣṣāṣ, *Aḥkām,* i, 256-63; cf. Ibn al-Jawzī, *Nawāsikh,* 230.) This evolutionary explanation relies on the technique of abrogation to account for the contradictory statements in the Qurʾān. Although details are disputed, this explanation is not a post-qurʾānic development constructed retrospectively (see Firestone, *Jihād,* esp. chaps. 3-4). In addition to its obvious rationality, this evolution is attested in the Qurʾān itself (Q 4:77). Many exegetes, however, avoided the technique of abrogation for theological and methodological reasons, but achieved the same result by other means (e.g. Ibn al-Jawzī, *Nawāsikh*). Thus, in spite of differences of opinions regarding the interpretation of the verses and the relations between them, the broad consensus on the main issue remained: whether by abrogation, specification or other techniques, the order to fight unconditionally (Q 9:5 and 9:29) prevailed. Some commentators, however, argued that the verses allowing peace (Q 4:90; 8:61) were neither abrogated nor specified, but remained in force. By the assignation technique, peace is allowed when it is in the best interest of the Muslims (e.g. in times of Muslim weakness, see e.g. Jaṣṣāṣ, *Aḥkām,* ii, 220; iii, 69-70). In fact this was the position adopted by the four major schools of law (see Peters, *Jihād,* 32-7).

Exhortations to battle occur many times in the Qurʾān and the Prophet is told to urge his followers to fight (Q 4:84; 8:65). In addition to the verses that contain various instructions, there are those that promise reward to warriors and reprimand shirkers, threatening them with God's wrath (Q 2:154; 3:195; 4:74, 104; 9:38-9, 88-9, 111; 22:58-9; 33:23-4; 61:10-3; see also Q 3:139-75, which encourages the Muslims after a defeat). The verses that establish the distinction between true believers and hypocrites (see above) may also serve the same end.

In a few verses, the cause or purpose of Muslim warfare is mentioned as self-defense, and retaliation for aggression, for the expulsion from Mecca and for the violation of treaties (Q 2:217; 4:84, 91; 5:33; 9:12-3; 22:39-40; 60:9, cf. 4:89). In one case, defense of weak brethren is adduced (Q 4:75; see BROTHER AND BROTHERHOOD). On the basis of the "sword verse" (Q 9:5) and the "*jizya* verse" (Q 9:29) it is clear that the purpose of fighting the idolaters is to convert them to Islam, whereas the purpose of fighting the People of the Book is to dominate them. Many commentators interpret Q 2:193 and 8:39 ("fight them until there is no *fitna*") as an instruction to convert all the polytheists to Islam by force if need be (e.g. Khāzin, *Lubāb,* ii, 183; Jaṣṣāṣ, *Aḥkām,* i, 260). It appears, however, that *fitna* (see DISSENSION; PARTIES AND FACTIONS) originally did not mean polytheism, but referred to attempts by infidels to entice Muslims away from Islam. Such attempts are mentioned in many qurʾānic verses (e.g. Q 3:149; 14:30; 17:73-4; for Q 2:193 see e.g. Ṭabarī, *Tafsīr,* ii, 254; see APOSTASY). Thus the purpose of war in Q 2:193 and 8:39 would be not conversion of infidels, but the preservation of the Muslim community. Conversion as the purpose of Muslim warfare is also implied by some interpretations of Q 2:192 and 48:16. In later literature the formulation of the purpose of war is "that God's word reign supreme" *(li-takūna kalimatu llāhi hiya l-ʿulyā),* but in the Qurʾān this phrase is not associated with warfare (Q 9:40; cf. 9:33 = 61:9; 48:28).

The verses relevant to conscription are Q 2:216; 4:71; 9:39-41, 90-3, 120, 122; cf. Q 48:17. The verses implying that only a part of the community is required to participate in warfare prevail over those that stipulate or imply general conscription (see ʿAbdallāh b. Wahb, *Jāmiʿ,* fol. 16a-b; Ibn al-Jawzī, *Nawāsikh,* 438; Bayḍāwī, *Anwār,* i, 405; Shāfiʿī, *Tafsīr,* 140-1, 145, 148; Zuhrī, *Nāsikh,* 28-9; see also Paret, *Kommentar,*

215-6; id., Sure 9, 122). In post-qurʾānic legal idiom it is stated that warfare *(jihād)* is a collective duty *(farḍ ʿalā l-kifāya)*.

Permission to retreat occurs three times. In Q 8:15-6 retreat is forbidden unless it is intended to be temporary and is done for tactical reasons. These verses are considered by some scholars to have been abrogated by Q 8:65, which permits retreat only if the enemies outnumber the Muslims by more than ten times. This rule was, in turn, replaced by Q 8:66, which reduces the proportion to two to one (Bayḍāwī, *Anwār,* i, 361; Ṭabarī, *Tafsīr,* ix, 200-3; Ibn al-Jawzī, *Nawāsikh,* 415-8; Abū ʿUbayd, *Nāsikh,* 192-3). This issue is sometimes discussed in relation to Q 2:195 as well.

The taking of prisoners is forbidden in Q 8:67 (see also Q 8:70-1). This verse is considered as abrogated by Q 47:4, which allows the Muslims to take prisoners, to free them for no compensation at all or to do so in exchange for ransom (Qurṭubī, *Aḥkām,* iv, 2884-7; vii, 6047-9; Jaṣṣāṣ, *Aḥkām,* iii, 71-4; Abū ʿUbayd, *Nāsikh,* 209-16; Ṭabarī, *Tafsīr,* x, 42-4). Nowhere in the Qurʾān is there a reference to the permissibility (or otherwise) of executing prisoners. There is, however, disagreement among commentators regarding the apparent contradiction between Q 47:4 and the categorical order to kill the idolaters in Q 9:5 (Ibn al-Jawzī, *Nawāsikh,* 425-7; Ṭabarī, *Tafsīr,* x, 80-1; xxvi, 40-3; Qurṭubī, *Aḥkām,* vii, 6047-8; Jaṣṣāṣ, *Aḥkām,* iii, 390-2). Booty is discussed in Q 4:94; 8:1, 41, 68-9; 59:6-8 and other practical matters relating to war occur in Q 2:239; 4:101-3; 8:56-8, 60; 61:4.

In the legal literature qurʾānic verses are sometimes cited which appear to be irrelevant to the discussions. Thus Q 48:24-5 were adduced in the discussion of non-discriminating weapons (ballista, *manjanīq,* e.g. Ibn Abī Zayd, *Kitāb al-Jihād,* 70-1). Q 59:5 was used in the discussion of the permissibility to destroy the enemy's property (e.g. Ṭabarī, *Tafsīr,* xxviii, 32). Q 6:137 was adduced as proof that no enemy-children should be killed (e.g. Shāfiʿī, *Tafsīr,* 121).

Finally, the origins of the notion of the sacredness of Islamic warfare should be mentioned. Although jihād and warfare are disparate concepts, only partly overlapping, both are endowed with sanctity. The sanctity of jihād was discussed above. The sacredness of warfare derives, first, from the causative link between warfare on the one hand, and divine command and divine decree on the other. Another source is the association of warfare with divine reward and punishment. The roles of warring as a divine test and as a pledge that the believers give to God (Q 33:15, 23) add another dimension to the sacredness of warfare. Finally, God's direct intervention in the military exploits of his community sanctifies these exploits (Q 3:13, 123-7; 8:7-12, 17-19, 26; 9:14, 25-6, 40; 33:9-10, 25-7; 48:20-4; see BADR).

Ella Landau-Tasseron

Bibliography

Primary: ʿAbdallāh b. Wahb, *al-Jāmiʿ, die Koranwissenschaften,* ed. M. Muranyi, Wiesbaden 1992; Abū ʿUbayd, *al-Nāsikh wa-l-mansūkh fī l-Qurʾān al-ʿazīz,* ed. M. al-Mudayfir, Riyadh 1997; Bayḍāwī, *Anwār;* Ibn Abī Ḥātim, ʿAbd al-Raḥmān b. Muḥammad, *Tafsīr al-Qurʾān al-ʿaẓīm,* ed. A.M. al-Ṭayyib, 9 vols., Mecca 1997; Ibn al-Bārzī, Hibat Allāh b. ʿAbd al-Raḥīm, *Nāsikh al-Qurʾān al-ʿazīz wa-mansūkhuhu,* ed. Ḥ.Ṣ. al-Ḍāmin, Beirut 1989; Ibn al-Jawzī, *al-Muṣaffā bi-akuff ahl al-rusūkh min ʿilm al-nāsikh wa-l-mansūkh,* ed. Ḥ.Ṣ. al-Ḍāmin, Beirut 1989; id., *Nawāsikh al-Qurʾān,* ed. Ḥ.S. Asad al-Dārānī, Damascus 1990; Ibn Shihāb al-Zuhrī, *al-Nāsikh wa-l-mansūkh,* ed. Ḥ.Ṣ. al-Ḍāmin, Beirut 1988; Jaṣṣāṣ, *Aḥkām;* Khāzin, *Lubāb,* 7 vols., Cairo 1957; Qurṭubī, *Jāmiʿ,* 8 vols., Cairo n.d.; al-Shāfiʿī, Muḥammad b. Idrīs, *Tafsīr,* comp. and ed. M. b. Sayyid al-Shūrā, Beirut 1995; Ṭabarī, *Tafsīr,* 30 pts. in 12 vols., Cairo 1954-7.

Secondary: T.J. Arnold, *The preaching of Islam. A history of the propagation of the Muslim faith,* London 1913²; H. Busse, The Arab conquest in revelation and politics, in *IOS* 10 (1980), 14-20; R. Firestone, *Jihād. The origin of holy war in Islam,* New York 1999; M.K. Haykal, *al-Jihād wa-l-qitāl fī l-siyāsati l-sharʿiyya,* Beirut 1996; A.A. Jannatī, Defense and jihad in the Qurʾān, in *al-Tawḥīd* 1 (1984), 39-54; M.J. Kister, *ʿAn yadin* (Qurʾān IX/29). An attempt at interpretation, in *Arabica* 11 (1964), 272-8; A. Morabia, *Le Ǧihād dans l'Islam médiéval. Le "combat sacré" des origines au XIIᵉ siècle,* Paris 1986; M. Muṭahhari, Jihad in the Qurʾān, in M. Abedi and G. Legenhausen (eds.), *Jihād and shahādat. Struggle and martyrdom in Islam,* Houston 1986, 81-124; A. Noth, *Heiliger Krieg und heiliger Kampf in Islam und Christentum,* Bonn 1966; H.T. Obbink, *De heilige oorlog volgens den Koran,* Leiden 1901; Paret, *Kommentar;* id., Sure 9, 122, in *WI* 2 (1953), 232-6; R. Peters, *Islam and colonialism. The doctrine of jihad in modern history,* The Hague 1976; D. Powers, The exegetical genre *nāsikh al-Qurʾān wa-mansūkhuhu,* in Rippin, *Approaches,* 117-38; ʿAbdallāh b. Aḥmad al-Qādirī, *al-Jihād fī sabīli llāh. Ḥaqīqatuhu wa-ghāyatuhu,* Jeddah 1992; U. Rubin, *Barāʾa.* A study of some qurʾānic passages, in *JSAI* 5 (1984), 13-32; A. Sachedina, The development of jihād in Islamic revelation and history, in J.T. Johnson and J. Kelsay (eds.), *Cross, crescent and sword,* New York 1990, 35-50; A. Schleifer, Jihād and traditional Islamic consciousness, in *IQ* 27 (1983), 173-203; id., Understanding *jihād.* Definition and methodology, in *IQ* 27 (1983), 118-31; F. Schwally, Der heilige Krieg des Islam in religionsgeschichtlicher und staatsrechtlicher Beleuchtung, in *Internationale Monatsschrift für Wissenschaft, Kunst und Technik* 6 (1916), 689-714; W.M. Watt, Islamic conceptions of the holy war, in T.P. Murphy (ed.), *The holy war,* Columbus, OH 1976, 141-56; A.L. Wismar, *A study in tolerance as practiced by Muḥammad and his immediate successors,* New York 1966.

Jinn

A category of created beings believed to possess powers for evil and good. Although their existence is never doubted, the jinn (Eng. "genie") are presented in the Qurʾān as figures whose effective role has been considerably curtailed in comparison to that accorded to them by various forms of pre-Islamic religion.

Unlike their rivals, the *rabb* and the *rabba,* the "lords" and "ladies," supernatural protectors and "allies" *(awliyāʾ)* of the tribes (see TRIBES AND CLANS) that God, in the fullness of his lordship, succeeds in making disappear (Q 53:23, "They are but names which you have named"), the jinn survive at the heart of the new religion. The Qurʾān limits itself to denying them the greater part of their powers — those, at any rate, that they could have claimed from the lord of the Qurʾān. In particular, they are shorn of their primordial function relative to humankind, that of uncovering the secrets (q.v.) of destiny *(ghayb),* thereby possessing knowledge of the future and of the world of the invisible (see HIDDEN AND THE HIDDEN; DESTINY; FATE). In the account of the death of Solomon (q.v.; Q 34:14), the jinn, having failed to grasp that the king is dead, continue to serve him in humility and abasement — thus demonstrating their ignorance of the *ghayb.* But the very fact that the Qurʾān dispossesses them, allows, at the same time, for recognition of their former role as mediators between the invisible world and humankind. The Qurʾān finds itself in the surprising position of having to come to terms with the jinn, i.e. subjecting them to its God, so powerful is the image they conjure up in popular imagination and local beliefs. In doing this, the text of the Qurʾān permits us to confirm part of what has been suggested concerning the way in which the desert Arabs (see ARABS; BEDOUIN; PRE-ISLAMIC ARABIA AND THE QURʾĀN) of the sixth century C.E. viewed their relationship to the jinn.

Regarded as having lost their faculty of familiarity with the invisible, the jinn were also seen as having lost their "power" or "faculty of action" (*sulṭān,* e.g. Q 55:33). *Sulṭān* is the exclusive preserve of the God of the Qurʾān, who dispenses it to whomsoever he wishes (Q 14:11; 59:6; etc.; see POWER AND IMPOTENCE). He never delegates complete mastery to anyone, however, since omnipotence remains one of his exclusive properties (see GOD AND HIS ATTRIBUTES). One should consider this assertion about the reduction of the jinn's powers in the light of the qur'ānic denial of the powers attributed to magic (q.v.; *siḥr*). The qur'ānic allusions to magic seem to demand the presence of an initiator (himself human and dependent on a supernatural being) who "teaches" *(yuʿallimu)* it, that is — in this context — gives "guidelines" (*aʿlām;* cf. Q 2:102; 20:71). The people of Mecca called Muḥammad the "lying sorcerer" (*sāḥir kadhdhāb,* Q 38:4); he is denounced as "bewitched" (*masḥūr,* Q 17:47); he is said to be "possessed by jinn" (*majnūn,* Q 15:6; see INSANITY; LIE). In another passage it is the "satans, devils" (*shayāṭīn,* the equivalent of the jinn in the Qur'ān — see below) who "teach magic to men" (*yuʿallimūna l-nāsa l-siḥar,* Q 2:102). Nonetheless, a pervasive sentiment that the jinn still need to be appeased can be seen in the persistent ritual sacrifices to the jinn, which have been more or less openly admitted until very recently among the desert shepherds. This demonstrates that the powers denied the jinn are nevertheless understood to remain vital despite the passage of centuries (e.g. the sacrifice of the tent reported by Jaussen, *Coutumes,* 339; Wellhausen, *Reste,* 151 also quotes the slightly earlier observations made by Doughty in *Travels,* ii, 629).

Ethnographic research indicates that, despite the qur'ānic statements to the contrary, people continue to believe in the quietly disconcerting presence of these beings, who haunt the spaces to which people do not belong but through which they are nevertheless constrained to pass whenever going from place to place. Their vague hordes appear to be contained, rather than reduced to impotence, in those territories which belong to them and where humans are at constant risk of encountering them. An acknowledgment of divine omnipotence coexists in uneasy tension, within the minds of many Muslims, with the fear that the jinn remain as dangerous and as unpredictable to access as ever.

The jinn most often figure in the Qur'ān in the form of a collectivity. The other name applied to them is *shayāṭīn,* "satans, devils" (associated with the Eng. "demons"), a name whose semantic evolution from classical Greek is worthy of particular attention (see FOREIGN VOCABULARY). The equivalence between the terms jinn and *shayṭān,* already familiar in pre-Islamic Arabia, is confirmed in the Qur'ān with reference to the supernatural beings who are said to be in Solomon's service. They are indicated — indiscriminately — by both these terms: in Q 27:17, 39 and 34:12, 14 it is the jinn who serve Solomon; but in Q 21:82 and 38:37 they are called *shayāṭīn.* Parallel to the use of their designation in the plural, the "satans" come to acquire the status of a proper name, "the Satan" *(al-shayṭān),* a rebel against God (Q 17:27; 19:44) and an enemy *(ʿaduww)* of people (e.g. Q 17:53, and numerous other places in the Qur'ān; see DEVIL).

As regards Iblīs, the qur'ānic *diabolos* (lit. the Gk. term means "he who divides [by calumny]"; this is the Septuagint's translation of the Heb. *sāṭān* [derived from *Job* 1, "the adversary" or "the accuser" — in fact, he who proposes to put the just person to "the test"]), his qur'ānic attestations are far less significant than either the singular or the plural occurrences of *shayṭān.* Iblīs is of immediate interest in the context of the jinn, however, because he is identified as one of them in Q 18:50. Iblīs enters the qur'ānic discourse in the context of a particular narrative, that of his refusal to prostrate himself before Adam (see BOWING AND PROSTRATION; ADAM AND EVE). A.J. Wensinck (Iblīs) sees an origin of this account in the *Life of Adam and Eve* (Kautsch, *Apokryphen,* § 15; also in Riessler, *Altjüdisches Schrifttum*). It should be noted, though, that the more ancient "Vie Grecque d'Adam et

Ève," presented in Dupont-Sommer and Philonenko *(La Bible),* does not contain the passage in question; in the Latin version, however, the "devil" *(der Teufel)* does reject any obligation to prostrate himself before Adam and refuses to obey the command of the archangel Michael (q.v.). The incident is placed after the account of the fall of man from the garden of Eden. In the account contained in the Qurʾān, the order to prostrate comes directly from God without the archangel's (see ANGEL) intervention. Iblīs incurs divine wrath (see ANGER) upon his refusal and sees, at his own request, his punishment "deferred" *(inẓār* or *taʾkhīr).* He is appointed the "great tempter" (*mughawwī* or *mughwī,* see TRIAL) of humankind until the resurrection (q.v.). In several passages in the Qurʾān this sequence is placed before the account of the fall *(hubūṭ)* of Adam, which is told only subsequently (see FALL OF MAN; GARDEN). This is a reversal of the order of the pseudo-epigraphical texts noted above, in which the fall precedes the devil's confrontation with God. Finally, it should be noted that the qurʾānic tempter of Adam in the garden of paradise (q.v.) is always called *shayṭān* and never Iblīs.

Does the juxtaposition of the two texts (that of the refusal on the part of Iblīs and that of the fall of Adam) imply a continuity of the account or its re-working in the canonical text? The question should at least be asked. In several cases, passages dealing with Iblīs are followed by the account of the fall (Q 2:34; 7:11; 15:31, 32; 17:61; 20:116; 26:95; 34:20; 38:74, 75). It is only in the single verse of Q 18:50 that Iblīs is designated expressly as a jinn. In the other passages he is depicted as a rebellious angel without, however, any explicit mention of his angelic nature; in fact, the text essentially states the following: the angels *(malāʾika)* prostrated themselves except Iblīs *(illā Iblīs)* who refused. In Q 38:76, Iblīs, of whom it has just been said (Q 38:73-4) that he alone among the angels refused, justifies his disobedience (q.v.) saying that he was created from *nār* (the usual translation, but not necessarily appropriate here, is "fire"), and therefore he should not have to prostrate himself before a creature "of clay" (q.v.; *ṭīn*). Does this mean that it justifies his status as a jinn? According to local traditions, the *nār* from which the jinn are created (see below) most certainly does not correspond to "fire" (q.v.), while in the ancient tradition of the Near East — and, *a fortiori,* in the Bible — angelic nature is clearly "igneous" (cf. the Seraphim, etc.; if this meaning prevails, then Iblīs could well be identified as an "angel," in the Near Eastern sense of the term).

The Qurʾān says nothing about the material from which the angels are created. The Islamic tradition regards them as being made from *nūr,* the "cold light of the night," that of the moon (q.v.), which is also the light of guidance and of knowledge (see KNOWLEDGE AND LEARNING), precisely the opposite of *nār,* which is diurnal and solar. As opposed to the jinn, who are incontestably figures from local beliefs, angels (*malak,* pl. *malāʾika,* lit. "envoys," from the root *l-ʾ-k*) are not a local construct: they are attested in Ethiopic and Hebrew, as well as in inscriptions from northeastern Arabia. Although there may have been particular, local understandings of "angels," the qurʾānic discourse on the subject is highly polemical. Perhaps, therefore, the qurʾānic "angels" should not be taken as referring to a local religion, as has sometimes been said in connection with a cult of the "daughters of Allāh" — alleged to be the angels (see below).

Despite the single occurrence in which Iblīs, the "devil" of the Qurʾān, is designated a jinn — could this be an interpolation? — he would seem, thanks to his specific narrative insertion (i.e. his refusal to prostrate to Adam; his corrupting mission is also biblical), to have origins clearly distinct from those of the local jinn/*shayṭān*. It is only at a later date, in the post-qurʾānic Islamic tradition, that he is finally completely assimilated into *al-shayṭān*, the "Satan" of the Qurʾān as the prototype of all beings hostile to humankind. The two diabolical representations live on in Islamic tradition, enacting a complex destiny often in combination, or encounter, with other negative figures such as various sorts of dragons derived from the ancient Near Eastern traditions. The adventures ascribed to them subsequently have little to do with their itinerary as stated in the Qurʾān.

Even if the jinn of the Qurʾān are shown as deprived of part of their powers because they no longer manage to uncover the secrets of heaven, they can nonetheless raise themselves up to heaven's gates (cf. Q 15:18; 37:10; 72:8-9; see HEAVEN AND SKY). The account of the heavenly ascension of the jinn is obviously not commanded by God — unlike the routes taken by the angels, which, just like those taken by men, must be marked with signposts (e.g. Q 15:14; see also the term *sabab*, pl. *asbāb*, used to designate the obligatory routes for both men and angels at Q 18:84-5, 89, 92; 40:36-7; it should be noted that, for the angels, the *ʿurūj* is specifically a movement of "descending and reascending" at Q 15:14; 32:5; 34:2; 57:4; 70:4). But Islamic tradition has continued to recognize the jinn's ability to move in all spaces without needing to follow a trail. This mobility probably corresponds to an ancient local belief that has remained deeply embedded, namely that of the notion — vital in the society of sixth and seventh century Arabia — of movement from place to place and the concept of a route.

Can it therefore be said that the representation of the jinn contained in the Qurʾān is essentially defensive and, in some ways, in continuity with the past? The Qurʾān confirms the division of the earth into two territories — that of humankind and that of the jinn. The formula contained in the Qurʾān, *al-ins wa-l-jinn*, "the humans and the jinn" (also, *al-jinn wa-l-ins*), is clearly dominant in the statements the Qurʾān makes concerning the jinn for there are twenty examples of this conjunction of jinn and humanity (using the collective noun *jinn:* Q 6:112, 128, 130; 7:38, 179; 17:88; 27:17; 41:25, 29; 46:18; 51:56; 55:33; 72:5, 6; using the singular *jānn* employed as a collective noun: Q 55:39, 56, 74; using the plural form *al-jinna wa-l-nās*, "jinn and people [or tribes]": Q 11:119; 32:13; 114:6). The God of the Qurʾān is presented as master of the two spaces. But the ancient representation of the co-existence of this fundamentally bipartite division of the earth (q.v.) remains intact.

With regard to *shayāṭīn al-insi wa-l-jinni* at Q 6:112, "satanic men and jinn," it could be asked to what the "satanization" here evoked corresponds. Since the verse probably belongs to the Medinan period (see CHRONOLOGY AND THE QURʾĀN) it can doubtless be compared to the various passages denouncing an "alliance" *(walāʾ)* between humans and the "demons" *(shayāṭīn)*, a designation that should be regarded as another name for the jinn: the infidels adopt these "demons" as allies (Q 7:27, 30; cf. 17:27), but the alliance will in no case benefit them (Q 2:16; see CONTRACTS AND ALLIANCES; CLIENTS AND CLIENTAGE). There is also a series of occurrences where the alliance is with "the Satan," the term being used as a proper name. He is as much a betrayer of the cause of humankind as are the "demons," and will lead people to their damnation (see REWARD AND PUNISHMENT): Q 25:29 reflects this theme, that of *khadhūl*, the "abandonment" of humanity by its pseudo-ally, the Satan (see ENEMIES). The same theme is to be found in Q 25:18 with the earlier deities designated periphrastically as "that which is adored apart from God" (see POLYTHEISM AND ATHEISM). These passages correspond to the evolution of the demonology proper to the Qurʾān, which ends up individualizing the satanic figure in a symbolic role that seems to condense together all the negative aspects of the "demons," variously named. Like an unavoidable figure of the anti-god he seems to remain capable of trapping humans (e.g. Q 27:24 or 58:19).

The theme of demonization and the accusation of pacts with the jinn apply specifically to the Medinan enemies of Muḥammad (see MEDINA; OPPOSITION TO MUḤAMMAD), the "impious" (*kāfirūn,* the ancient "ingrates" of tribal Arabia, "those who fail to recognize a benefit received"; see BELIEF AND UNBELIEF; GRATITUDE AND INGRATITUDE; BLESSING), the "hypocrites" (*munāfiqūn,* formerly used of "cowards," and, as noted by Watt, also the term used to designate Muḥammad's political enemies in Medina; see HYPOCRITES AND HYPOCRISY), or however they are named. It is a technique of qurʾānic polemical discourse (see POLEMIC AND POLEMICAL LANGUAGE) typical of the Medinan era, corresponding to conflict situations in which the religious argument often comes to the aid of the political (see POLITICS AND THE QURʾĀN; LANGUAGE AND STYLE OF THE QURʾĀN). This is in contrast to the Meccan period, in which Muḥammad is accused by his own of being "possessed by the jinn." The antithetical relationship between the jinn as negative allies and God as the only positive ally (*walī,* e.g. Q 4:45) lends itself to conjecture about a "cult" alleged to be devoted to the jinn. In particular, some qurʾānic passages that discuss the jinn utilize terminology similar to that concerning the "service" rendered to God: i.e. *ʿibādat al-jinn* (there is also a passage on the "service" devoted to Satan, Q 36:60). But, just like people, the jinn must adore God alone (Q 51:56). Just like humans they are subjected to the last judgment (q.v.; Q 37:158). Like the "people of the tribes" *(nās),* a number of them are destined for hell (q.v.; Q 11:119; for further references to the infernal destiny of the jinn, see Q 6:128; 7:38, 179; 32:13; 55:39).

In the Qurʾān, the theme of the nations that were destroyed because of their rebellion is also applied to the jinn (see PUNISHMENT STORIES). One passage (Q 6:130) attributes to the jinn, after the fashion of humans, "envoys from among you *(minkum)*… who warned you" (see MESSENGER; WARNER), but this passage seems to have its origins in a form of rhetorical symmetry and nothing more is known about it (see FORM AND STRUCTURE OF THE QURʾĀN; RHETORIC OF THE QURʾĀN). The disappearance of the "nations" *(umam)* of the jinn is also associated — without providing any further detail — with that of the human "nations" that have disappeared (Q 41:25; 46:18; cf. Q 7:38, where disappearance is associated with "hell" *(nār)*; see GENERATIONS). This is probably an extrapolation of the Qurʾān's discourse, bringing the punishment of the impious, of the deniers and of those who fail to recognize the "signs" (q.v.; *āyāt*) of God to its logical conclusion. The jinn of the Qurʾān again lose ground with reference to their previous status. They are reduced to sharing the eschatological destiny of humankind (see ESCHATOLOGY).

In this type of passage it is impossible to distinguish that which has its origins in beliefs and practices evident in seventh-century Arabia from that which belongs to the Qurʾān's polemical discourse and the controversy pursued with enemies in an attempt to confuse them by the force of words (cf. Q 2:14, where the hypocrites are with their "demons"; in Q 6:121, it is these demons who push "their minions", i.e. Muḥammad's adversaries, to "controversy" or "disputation," *mujādala,* see DEBATE AND DISPUTATION).

It is also no easy task to uncover the reality of the belief that is being fought over in the tangled Meccan passages about a "cult of angels" *(ʿibādat al-malāʾika)* — which seems to become confused with a cult of the jinn (Q 34:41; cf. also the "invocation," *ʿawdh,* addressed to the jinn in Q 72:6) — and about the representation of angels as "daughters" *(banāt)* of God (Q 6:100; 16:57; 37:149, 153; 43:16; 52:39). In Q 37:150-2 it is a question of a belief in the fact that the lord is said to have procreated angels of the female gender (q.v.), while in verse 158 of the same sūra, a form of "kinship" *(nasab)* is alleged between God and the jinn. In Q 6:100, the jinn are said to be "associates" *(shurakāʾ)* of God while the "daughters of God" are once again evoked. It appears that in this polemic, pseudo-angelized figures are being reduced to jinn, the pseudo-angelized figures who, in the final analysis, would seem to be the tribes' local protecting goddesses who are to disappear slowly but surely under a variety of disguises (see the remarks made by Wellhausen [*Reste,* 24] regarding the term "daughter of God," which he compares to the representation of the *Beney Elohim*). In all likelihood it is also a way of reducing them to a minor, subordinate role by declaring that, just like humans, they are "created beings." And yet their nature is stated to be different from that of humankind. The Qurʾān says that they are made from *nār.* The usual translation, "fire," probably makes no sense in the context. The image conjured up is that of a representation of wreaths of smoke and mirages of "the burning air of the solar day" and not that of flames. This metaphorical transposition could also be recognized in the numerous qurʾānic uses of the concept of *nār* (regarding the nature of the jinn, see Q 15:27, "created from the fire of *al-samūm*"; and Q 55:15, *min mārijin min nārin,* a difficult formulation which would make the jinn "unformed beings created from the reverberated heat" and not, as in some translations — such as that of Kazimirski — beings created from a "pure fire without smoke"; see, for an attempt at a more precise explanation of the two passages, Chabbi, *Seigneur,* 190 f.).

But this difference in nature that the Qurʾān is constrained to admit, can only permit the jinn to retain powers that enable them to outclass humans. Thus, although the jinn are no longer able to hear what heaven says about destiny, they are nonetheless still represented as being perfectly capable of rising up to heaven without divine assistance. The divine guard at the gates of heaven requires all of its powers, launching against them "fiery traces" *(shihāb),* to throw them back to earth and prevent them from collecting the secrets of the future (Q 37:10; 72:8-9). A further valiant deed could have been credited to a jinn of Solomon's court who is said to be *ʿifrīt* (q.v.), "very skillful and crafty." He suggested to his master that, in an instant, he could bring him the throne of the queen of Sheba (see BILQĪS); but the jinn does not have the time to demonstrate his powers (which are manifestly seen as effective) since his place is taken by a more suitable member of the king's retinue — one who "knew the scripture" — who accomplished the mission "in the twinkling of an eye" (Q 27:39-40).

In fact, therefore, the approach taken by the Qurʾān to the jinn seems to be paradoxical. A final quotation will demonstrate another way in which the Qurʾān treats them: their persistent power can be perceived as a constant theme when the Qurʾān itself appeals to their testimony (see WITNESSING AND TESTIFYING) in order to convince men who refuse to believe. These are the "believing jinn," called to aid in attesting to the pre-eminence of a *qurʾān* (a verbal noun designating "the message faithfully transmitted" and not yet Qurʾān as a proper noun) that they have heard by chance and that they call "marvelous" (*ʿajab*, Q 72:1; see MARVELS; MIRACLE). If the jinn themselves are convinced, how could humans not be convinced? The reasoning must have been seen as incontestable.

A non-Arabic origin of the word *jinn* is not immediately traceable, even though it is cognate to the root *j-n-n*, present in most of the ancient Semitic languages, albeit as a designation of a garden or a cultivated place with trees (the Hebrew *gan;* this latter meaning is retained in Arabic, wherein the triliteral root *j-n-n* is used to designate a "cover" of vegetation). On the other hand, the Ethiopic *gānen* has the meaning of "demon, evil spirit." Sometimes this Ethiopic term is said to be of Syriac origin (Leslau, *Dictionary*, 198), from the root *g-n-n*, "recover, reside in, descend upon" (this is used of the Holy Ghost, see Payne Smith, *Dictionary*, 73; see HOLY SPIRIT). But Syriac (see SYRIAC AND THE QURʾĀN) does not appear to provide the negative meaning "possessed," a meaning well-attested in Arabic and Ethiopic. It is probable, therefore, that this latter meaning of *jinn* is a development specific to Arabic, which passed into Ethiopic. At any rate, the term *jinn*, with its derivatives *jānn, jinna, jinnī* (in the masculine, the feminine and the collective, respectively), is fully attested in the Arabic of the era of the Qurʾān. The representation and perception of the permanent encounter with, and the otherness of, these metamorphic beings lend support to their imaginary existence in the minds of people. The Qurʾān strives to turn to its God's advantage the fear inspired by the jinn and to annihilate the powers attributed to them by the pastoral and nomadic societies of western Arabia. Nevertheless, these strange creatures have continued to exist in a particularly intense manner in a wide variety of disguises in the collective imaginings of Islamic societies. They encountered and merged with other supernatural beings already long resident in the territories conquered by Islam. Some of these retained their original names such as, for instance, the *div* in Iran. Others would lose their identity, at least in appearance, and be assimilated with the figures, most surely negative, that can be definitively identified as jinn.

Jacqueline Chabbi

Bibliography
A. Caquot, Anges et démons en Israël, in *Sources Orientales VIII. Génies anges et démons*, Paris 1971, 115-51; J. Chabbi, *Le Seigneur des tribus. L'islam de Mahomet*, Paris 1997, 185-232; Ch.M. Doughty, *Travels in Arabia deserta*, Cambridge 1888, New York 1979; A. Dupont-Sommer and M. Philonenko, *La Bible. Écrits intertestamentaires*, Paris 1987; P.A. Eichler, *Die Dschinn, Teufel und Engel im Koran*, Leipzig 1928; T. Fahd, Anges, démons et djinns en Islam, in *Sources Orientales VIII. Génies anges et démons*, Paris 1971, 155-213 (with important bibliography); A. Jaussen, *Coutumes des Arabes au pays de Moab*, Paris 1907, 1947; Jeffery, *For. vocab.;* E. Kautsch, *Apokryphen und Pseudepigraphen des Alten Testaments*, Tübingen 1900-21; W. Leslau, *Comparative dictionary of Geʿez*, Wiesbaden 1987; J. Payne Smith, *Compendious Syriac dictionary*, Oxford 1903; P. Riessler, *Altjüdisches Schrifttum ausserhalb der Bibel*, Augsburg 1928; W.M. Watt, *Muhammad at Medina*, London 1956; A.T. Welch, Allah and other supernatural beings. The emergence of the qurʾānic doctine of tawḥid, in *JAAR* 47 (1980), 733-58; J. Wellhausen, *Reste arabischen Heidentums*, Berlin 1887, 1927, 1961³, 148-59 (chap.

Geister und Gespenster; Wellhausen often depends on the observations made by Doughty in *Travels in Arabia deserta*); A.J. Wensinck/L. Gardet, Iblīs, in *EI*[2], iii, 668-9.

Jizya see POLL TAX; TAXATION

Job

One of the prophetic figures preceding Muḥammad common to the Jewish, Christian and Islamic traditions (see PROPHETS AND PROPHETHOOD). Job (Ayyūb) is mentioned in only four pericopes: Q 6:83-7 and 4:163 set him in the company of the prophets while Q 38:41-2 and Q 21:83-4 allude to his distinctive vocation and charisma.

In Q 6:83-90, together with Abraham (q.v.), Isaac (q.v.), Jacob (q.v.), Noah (q.v.), David (q.v.), Solomon (q.v.), Joseph (q.v.), Moses (q.v.) and Aaron (q.v.), Zechariah (q.v.), John (see JOHN THE BAPTIST), Jesus (q.v.), Elias (see ELIJAH), Ishmael (q.v.), Elisha (q.v.), Jonah (q.v.) and Lot (q.v.), he is included among those God has guided, chosen and preferred to ordinary humankind (see ELECTION), to whom he has given scripture (see BOOK; SCRIPTURE AND THE QUR'ĀN), authority (q.v.), prophethood and whose example is to be followed. In Q 4:163, Job is named among those to whom a revelation (see REVELATION AND INSPIRATION) has been given so that humans will not be able to claim ignorance (q.v.) of God's will. The names given include those mentioned in the pericope cited above — omitting Joseph, Zechariah, John, Elias, Elisha and Lot, but adding "the tribes" (*al-asbāṭ*, see CHILDREN OF ISRAEL; TRIBES AND CLANS), and two general categories subsuming all the other prophets, those mentioned to Muḥammad, and those not mentioned to him.

As for Job's special character, Q 38:41-2 presents Job calling to his lord, "Satan (see DEVIL) has indeed touched me with hardship and pain (see TRIAL)." God responds to his cry, "Scuff [the earth] with your foot. Here is [water] a place to cleanse yourself, [it is] cooling, it is drink." Job obeys. A spring appears in which he bathes and from which he drinks. His kin and "the like of them with them" are restored to him as an act of divine mercy (q.v.). God then (Q 38:44) commands him to strike "her" (the ellipsed pronoun in *fa-ḍrib bihi* has no explicit referent) with a sprig of leaves in order to keep an oath he has made (see OATHS). The pericope ends with a formula of praise — "How excellent a servant! Constantly was he turned [to God]" *(niʿma l-ʿabdu innahu awwāb)* — which, in Q 38:30, celebrates the virtues of Solomon, the only other prophet to be honored with this formula. Q 21:83-4 likewise tells of Job's call to his lord, God's hearing of him, removal of the hurt upon him, restoration of what he had lost, and his praise of God as "most merciful of the merciful."

Both of the pericopes that indicate Job's special character are allusive, but the exegetical tradition (see EXEGESIS OF THE QUR'ĀN: CLASSICAL AND MEDIEVAL), as summarized by al-Ṭabarī (d. 310/923; *Tafsīr*, ad loc.), supplies an inter-text in the light of which they may be understood. Job cried out because God had allowed Satan to put him to the test by destroying his livestock, slaying his kin, and afflicting him with a painful disease (see ILLNESS AND HEALTH). Because he remained faithful while put to the test, God heard his cry, healed him with a miraculous spring, and restored to him two-fold both his kin, and the property taken from him. The person to be struck with a sprig in Q 38:44 refers to his wife. She alone, during his illness, had not deserted him. But she was tempted by Satan, to whom she had urged Job to sacrifice a kid in order to be healed. Job swore an oath (see OATHS) that if cured, he would punish her with a hundred lashes. Because of her faithfulness, God alleviated this punishment, telling Job to strike her once with a sprig of one hundred leaves.

In the light of this inter-text, the status and role of Job in the divine economy of prophetic guidance is clear. These two pericopes present Job's distinctive charisma, that of patience in enduring undeserved suffering without challenging God to explain his wisdom (q.v.) in putting him to the test (see TRUST AND PATIENCE). The story of Job in the Qurʾān then is understood primarily as a reward narrative (see BLESSING), with an emphasis different from that of the story of Job in the Bible.

A.H. Johns

Bibliography

Primary: Ibn Kathīr, *Bidāya*, i, 220-5; Kisāʾī, *Qiṣaṣ;* id., *The tales of the prophets of al-Kisaʾi*, trans. W.M. Thackston, Jr., Boston 1978, 192-204; Ṭabarī, *The history of al-Ṭabarī. ii. Prophets and patriarchs*, trans. W.M. Brinner, Albany 1987, 140-3; id., *Tafsīr;* id., *Taʾrīkh*, ed. de Goeje, i, 361-5; al-Ṭarafī, Abū ʿAbdallāh Muḥammad b. Aḥmad b. Muṭarraf al-Kinānī, *Storie dei profeti*, trans. R. Tottoli, Genoa 1997, 166-79; Thaʿlabī, *Qiṣaṣ*, Beirut n.d.

Secondary: J.-L. Déclais, *Les premiers musulmans face à la tradition biblique. Trois récits sur Job*, Paris 1996 (contains a translation of Ṭabarī's commentary on Q 21:83-4); J.-F. le Grain, Variations musulmanes sur le thème de Job, in *Bulletin d'études orientales* 37-8 (1985-6), 51-114; A. Jeffery, Ayyūb, in *EI*², i, 795-6; A.H. Johns, Narrative, intertext and allusion in the qurʾānic presentation of Job, in *Journal of qurʾanic studies* 1 (1999), 1-25; id., Three stories of a prophet. Al-Ṭabarī's treatment of Job in Sūrat al-Anbiyāʾ 83-4, in *Journal of qurʾanic studies* 3 (2001), 39-61; 4 (2002), 49-60; D.B. Macdonald, Some external evidence on the original form of the legend of Job, in *American journal of Semitic languages and literatures* 14 (1898), 137-64 (includes a translation of al-Thaʿlabī's section on Job); R. Tottoli, *Biblical prophets in the Qurʾān and Muslim literature*, Richmond, Surrey 2002.

John the Baptist

The New Testament herald of Jesus (q.v.) who also figures in the Qurʾān (see SCRIPTURE AND THE QURʾĀN). John the Baptist, son of Zechariah (q.v.), called in Arabic Yaḥyā b. Zakariyyā, is mentioned by name five times in the Qurʾān. In Q 3:39, John is described as noble, chaste and a prophet who will "witness the truth (q.v.) of a word from God," that is, Jesus (see PROPHETS AND PROPHETHOOD; WORD OF GOD; WITNESSING AND TESTIFYING). Q 6:85 speaks of John along with Zechariah, Jesus and Elias (see ELIJAH) as being of the "righteous." Q 19:7 announces the forthcoming birth of John to Zechariah (see GOOD NEWS) with the remark that this name was being used for the first time (or that this was the first prophet by that name; cf. *Luke* 1:59-63). Q 19:12 conveys the command to John to be a prophet with a book (q.v.; usually taken by Muslim exegetes [see EXEGESIS OF THE QURʾĀN: CLASSICAL AND MEDIEVAL] to mean that John confirms the Torah [q.v.], not that he brought a new scripture). Q 21:90 explains that John's birth was a response to Zechariah's prayer, and the curing of his wife's barrenness. The spelling of the name Yaḥyā for Yoḥanan is known from pre-Islamic times and is probably derived from Christian Arabic usage (see CHRISTIANS AND CHRISTIANITY). Muslim exegetes frequently trace the name to a root sense of "to quicken" or "to make alive" and connect this to the barrenness of John's mother and to his people's absence of faith, themes that are present in the Qurʾān.

Although the qurʾānic details of the story of John are few, extended discussions concerning him have arisen throughout Muslim history. For example, the idea that John was "chaste" *(ḥaṣūr)* provoked a good deal of debate (see ABSTINENCE; ASCETICISM).

In their discussions of Q 3:39, some exegetes understood this word to be intended in its sexual sense of being incapable of coitus ("he had a penis no bigger than this piece of straw," Ṭabarī, *Tafsīr,* vi, 377, a prophetic ḥadīth on the authority of Saʿīd b. al-Musayyab) or of abstaining from it. Other exegetes rejected that view, for it would suggest some sort of imperfection on the part of the prophet, and argued that the word means only that John was free from impure actions and thoughts, and that it does not preclude John's having been married (see MARRIAGE AND DIVORCE) and fathering children (q.v.).

The Muslim rendering of the birth, life and death of John have, in general, been elaborated on the basis of the Christian accounts. John, it is said, was born six months prior to Jesus. He became a prophet, traveled to Palestine, met and baptized Jesus in the Jordan river and departed with twelve disciples to teach the people (see APOSTLE; BAPTISM). At the instigation of Salome, Herod had John put to death prior to Jesus' death and ascension. Many of the accounts, however, have become confused and place John's life in the era of Nebuchadnezzar. This is especially evident in stories related to John's death (which is not mentioned in the Qurʾān). The Israelite king Josiah, it is said, killed John, the son of Zechariah, and Nebuchadnezzar attacked Jerusalem (q.v.) as a result. In these accounts, the king's action is motivated by his desire to marry his own niece, an action of which John disapproved. The conspiracy of the girl's mother then led to the death of John (cf. the story of Salome, *Matt* 14:1-11; *Mark* 6:16-29). Nebuchadnezzar invaded in order to solve problems that arose as a result of John's death (or God simply inspired him to do so). The source of this chronological confusion is likely found in the name Zechariah (a name which had already occasioned confusion within the biblical tradition) with a conflation taking place of the author of the biblical book of Zechariah, the Zechariah of Isaiah 8, the prophet Zechariah of 2 Chronicles 24:22 (who was killed by King Joash), and Zakariyyā, the father of John. Al-Ṭabarī (d. 310/923), in recounting these traditions, indicates that he is well aware that many regard these stories as false and based on a historical error, there being 461 years between the lives of Nebuchadnezzar and John the Baptist.

Andrew Rippin

Bibliography

Primary: Ibn Kathīr, *Tafsīr,* 4 vols., Cairo n.d.; Kisāʾī, *Qiṣaṣ;* Muqātil, *Tafsīr;* Ṭabarī, *Tafsīr,* ed. Shākir; id., *Taʾrīkh,* ed. de Goeje; al-Ṭarafī, Abū ʿAbdallāh Muḥammad b. Aḥmad, *Storie dei profeti,* Ital. trans. R. Tottoli, Genova 1997, 27, 297, 300-3, 312, 346; Thaʿlabī, *Qiṣaṣ.*

Secondary: M.M. Ayoub, *The Qurʾān and its interpreters. ii. The House of ʿImrān,* Albany 1992, 109-12 (on the meaning of John as "chaste"); E. Beck, *Das christliche Mönchtum im Koran,* Helsinki 1946; J.C.L. Gibson, John the Baptist in Muslim writings, in *MW* 45 (1955), 334-45; Horovitz, *KU;* Jeffery, *For. vocab.;* G. Parrinder, *Jesus in the Qurʾān,* London 1965, chap. 5; H. Schützinger, Die arabische Legende von Nebukadnezar und Johannes dem Täufer, in *Der Islam* 40 (1965), 113-40; D. Sidersky, *Les origines des légendes musulmanes dans le Coran et dans les vies des prophètes,* Paris 1933, 139-40; R. Tottoli, *Biblical prophets in the Qurʾān and Muslim literature,* Richmond, Surrey 2002; id., *Le* Qiṣaṣ al-anbiyāʾ *di Ṭarafī,* Ph.D. thesis, Naples 1996, 487-8 (notes to paragraphs 426-31; includes list of Arabic sources parallel to al-Ṭabarī).

Jonah

One of the prophets mentioned in both the Bible and the Qurʾān (see PROPHETS AND PROPHETHOOD). Jonah (Yūnus b. Mittai, Heb. Jōnā ben Amittai) is named five times in the Qurʾān: Q 4:163 lists him together with Abraham (q.v.), Jesus (q.v.) and other prophets who have received revelations (see REVELATION AND INSPIRATION); as rightly-guided he is cited together with Zechariah (q.v.), Jesus and other prophets in Q 6:85-86; his people *(qawm Yūnus)* were, according to Q 10:98, the only ones who escaped divine punishment because they had repented (see PUNISHMENT STORIES; REPENTANCE AND PENANCE).

As told in the Qurʾān, the story of Jonah resembles in many details the account narrated in the biblical book of Jonah. Jonah, also called Dhū l-Nūn ("the man of the whale"), rebelled against God's mission, ran away in wrath, was swallowed by the fish, praised God, confessed his sin in the belly of the fish, and was thrown ashore (Q 21:87-8). This and the rest of the story is told in Q 37:139-48: When he was saved, he found shade under a tree, and was sent "to a hundred thousand or more." In Q 68:48-50, Muḥammad is admonished to wait with patience (see TRUST AND PATIENCE) for the command of the lord, and not to behave like "the man of the fish" *(ṣāḥib al-ḥūt)*, who went away without God's permission.

Muslim tradition as expressed in qurʾānic commentary (*tafsīr*, see EXEGESIS OF THE QURʾĀN: CLASSICAL AND MEDIEVAL) and the "tales of the prophets" *(qiṣaṣ al-anbiyāʾ)* embellished the short account given in the Qurʾān with many details, continuing Jewish and Christian teachings (see SCRIPTURE AND THE QURʾĀN; MYTHS AND LEGENDS IN THE QURʾĀN). There are two different versions of the story, one following in broad lines the biblical account, while the other has a somewhat different sequence of events. The first relates that Jonah delivered his message in Nineveh and went away in wrath when people did not follow him and divine punishment did not arrive promptly. He went on board a ship, was swallowed by the fish, cast ashore, and returned to Nineveh. Upon his arrival, he found that in his absence the inhabitants had repented and punishment had been suspended. So he settled there. According to other accounts, he took to wandering about as an ascetic, accompanied by the king of Nineveh who had renounced the throne, ceding it to a shepherd who had assisted Jonah on his way back to the city.

A full account of Jonah's biography has been provided by al-Kisāʾī (*Qiṣaṣ*, 296-301; Eng. trans. in id., *Tales*, 321-6). Jonah was born when his mother Ṣadaqa was far beyond the age of childbearing. In his early life he practiced asceticism (q.v.); then he married Anak, the daughter of Zakariyyā b. Yūḥannā, a rich merchant of Ramla. When he was called to prophethood he went to Nineveh, accompanied by his wife and two sons. He lost them as he crossed the Tigris. Jonah was rebuked while preaching in Nineveh and he left the city because of imminent punishment, watched the city from a nearby hill, went on board a ship, was swallowed by the fish and cast ashore, and was reunited with his family on his way back to Nineveh. Finding the inhabitants in a state of happiness he spent the rest of his life there.

The story of Jonah posed theological problems for Muslims, as it had for Jews and Christians. Jews took offence at the sending of an Israelite prophet to the pagans, whereas Christians saw in him the model of evangelization to the heathens. This is mirrored in Muslim tradition in a story with an obviously Jewish or Judeo-Christian background (see JEWS AND JUDAISM; CHRISTIANS AND CHRISTIANITY): King Hezekiah, on the advice of Isaiah (q.v.), ordered Jonah to bring back the tribes in exile who had been abducted by the king of Nineveh. Angry at the king,

Jonah went away, was swallowed by the fish, repented of his disobedience (q.v.), was cast ashore and then went to Nineveh to accomplish his mission. The inhabitants first rebuked him, but finally they let the Israelites go.

Another problem was Jonah's anger. He was angry because God had postponed punishment for Nineveh (*Jon* 4:1). This is likewise told in Q 21:87: "When he departed in wrath *(idh dhahaba mughāḍiban)*." Yet, this is rather vague, leaving open the reason for Jonah's emotional reaction (cf. e.g. Schwarzbaum, *Biblical and extra-biblical legends*, 112). As Muslims did not consider it acceptable for a prophet to show such an attitude toward God's orders (see OBEDIENCE), they offered alternative explanations: He was enraged at King Hezekiah who had ordered him to go to Nineveh on the advice of a prophet but, evidently, without any divine instruction. Another solution was to declare the obstinacy of the people of Nineveh as the cause of Jonah's wrath (see INSOLENCE AND OBSTINACY). A third explanation was his being angry at the urgency of his mission: The angel Gabriel (q.v.), who brought the orders, did not allow him any time for preparation, not even to put on his sandals. Jonah therefore went away in anger, seeking refuge on board a ship. His refusal to transmit the message was a grave offence, indeed. Another offence was his departure — without God's permission — from Nineveh because the punishment of its inhabitants was not forthcoming. In Q 68:48, Muḥammad is cautioned against making such an emigration (q.v.; *hijra*) without waiting for divine permission. Jonah repented in the belly of the fish, confessing that he was a sinner: "I was indeed wrong (*innī kuntu mina l-ẓālimīn*, Q 21:87)."

Another question with theological implications is the doubt (see UNCERTAINTY) Jonah had about God's omnipotence (see POWER AND IMPOTENCE; FREEDOM AND PREDESTINATION). Q 21:87, *fa-ẓanna an lan naqdira ʿalayhi*, may be translated "He imagined that we had no power over him." Two answers were found to avoid the accusation of unbelief (see BELIEF AND UNBELIEF): One was that Jonah did not expect imprisonment in the narrow belly of the fish, *qadara* meaning "to measure the size," not only "to have power." Another solution was to provide the phrase with a question mark. On the other hand, being swallowed by a fish was not the proper punishment of one who questioned God's omnipotence. God, however, granted Jonah a loan *(salaf)* because he had displayed piety (q.v.) and devotion before he was disobedient. God, therefore, was not ready to leave him to the devil (q.v.), and instead punished him by locking him up in the belly of the fish for some time. "Had it not been that he glorified God" *(fa-law lā annahu kāna min al-musabbiḥīn)* before he refused to obey God's orders "he would certainly have remained inside the fish till the day of resurrection" (q.v.; Q 37:143 f.). His imprisonment in the belly of the fish was not a punishment *(ʿuqūba)*, but a correction (*taʾdīb*, see CHASTISEMENT AND PUNISHMENT; REWARD AND PUNISHMENT).

Because Jonah was impatient, he does not belong to the prophets of "inflexible purpose" (*ūlū l-ʿazm*, Q 46:35) praised for their patience. He was saved because he prayed when he was in distress (see PRAYER). Therefore, he is a model for the pious Muslim in case of need. He is likewise a model for the penitent. His mother conceived him, according to al-Kisāʾī (*Qiṣaṣ*, 296; *Tales*, 321), on the eve, i.e. the day before ʿĀshūrā, the Jewish Day of Atonement. This means that Jonah was destined for atonement. In Jewish life, the eve of the Day of Atonement had taken on the character of a festival (see FASTING; FESTIVALS AND COMMEMORATIVE DAYS). It was a Friday, as al-Kisāʾī adds, and it was on that day that the punishment of Nineveh was cancelled (cf. Rāzī, *Tafsīr,* ad Q 10:98). It can parenthetically be remarked that the book of Jonah is read in synagogues during the Day of Atonement afternoon service.

The church fathers explained Jonah's sojourn of three days in the belly of the fish and his salvation as a prefiguration of the death and resurrection of Jesus. The length of his sojourn in the fish is, however, not mentioned in the Qur'ān. Muslim tradition narrates three days, though other figures have also been proposed, ranging from one day to one month or forty days.

Heribert Busse

Bibliography
Primary (In addition to the commentaries on the above-mentioned passages found in works of *tafsīr* from Muqātil b. Sulaymān down to modern authors): Biqāʿī, *Naẓm,* vi, 343-45, ad Q 37:139-48 (contains a full Arabic translation of the biblical book of Jonah); Ibn Kathīr, *Qiṣaṣ al-anbiyā',* ed. S. al-Laḥḥām, Beirut 1988, 293-302 (this part of Ibn Kathīr's *"Qiṣaṣ"* is taken from his *Bidāya,* i, 231-7); Kisāʾī, *Qiṣaṣ,* 296-301; id., *The tales of the prophets of al-Kisa'i,* trans. W.M. Thackston, Jr., Boston 1978, 321-6; Mirkhond (Mīr Khwānd), *The Rauzat-us-safa. Or, Garden of purity,* 2 pts. in 5 vols., trans. E. Rehatsek, London 1891-4, pt. I vol. ii, 112-20; Rāzī, *Tafsīr;* Ṭabarī, *The history of al-Ṭabarī. iv. The ancient kingdoms,* trans. M. Perlmann, Albany 1987, 160-6; id., *Ta'rīkh,* ed. de Goeje, i, 782-9; Talmud, *Megillah* 31a; al-Ṭarafī, Abū ʿAbdallāh Muḥammad b. Aḥmad, *Storie dei profeti,* trans. R. Tottoli, Genoa 1997, 125-35; Thaʿlabī, *Qiṣaṣ,* 366-70.
Secondary: C. Castillo Castillo, Jonas en la leyenda musulmana. Estudio comparado, in *Qanṭara* 4 (1983), 89-100; H. Schwarzbaum, *Biblical and extra-biblical legends in Islamic folk-literature,* Walldorf-Hessen 1982; Speyer, *Erzählungen,* 407-10.

Joseph

The son of Jacob (q.v.; Yaʿqūb), whose story is told in Sūrat Yūsuf ("Joseph"), the twelfth sūra of the Qur'ān. This sūra is devoted to the story of Joseph (Yūsuf) and, as such, it is the Qur'ān's longest sustained narrative of one character's life. The sūra's 111 verses *(āyāt)* relate events in Joseph's life ranging from his youthful conversations with his father Jacob and his brothers (see BENJAMIN; BROTHER AND BROTHERHOOD), conversations that lead to Joseph's exile and imprisonment, to the resolution of the family's conflicts through divine guidance and inspiration (see REVELATION AND INSPIRATION). Q 12:3 announces that "the best of stories" *(aḥsan al-qaṣaṣ),* is to be related (see NARRATIVES). Qur'ān commentaries differ as to whether this is a direct reference to the story at hand or a more general statement on the nature of qur'ānic narrative. Those commentators who see Joseph's as the best of all stories give a multiplicity of reasons for its superiority (see MYTHS AND LEGENDS IN THE QUR'ĀN). "It is the most beautiful because of the lessons concealed in it, on account of Joseph's generosity, and its wealth of matter — in which prophets (see PROPHETS AND PROPHETHOOD), angels (see ANGEL), devils (see DEVIL), jinn (q.v.), men, animals, birds (see COSMOLOGY; ANIMAL LIFE), rulers (see KINGS AND RULERS; COMMUNITY AND SOCIETY IN THE QUR'ĀN), and subjects play a part" (Thaʿlabī, *Qiṣaṣ,* ad loc.).

Throughout the sūra, there are interjections that exhort the believers to see the hand of God in human affairs and to recognize the power of true prophecy (Q 12:7, 56-7). Joseph can thus be seen as exemplifying the basic paradigm of the Qur'ān: he is a prophet *(nabī)* who is derided and exiled, but is eventually vindicated and rises to prominence. As such, he serves as a model for the life of Muḥammad and many of the qur'ānic commentaries (*tafāsīr,* see EXEGESIS OF THE QUR'ĀN: CLASSICAL AND MEDIEVAL) see this as a central theme and function of the sūra (see also OPPOSITION TO MUḤAMMAD). This interpretation is strengthened by the "occasions of revelation" (q.v.; *asbāb al-nuzūl*) tradition, which places the circumstance of Sūrat Yūsuf's revelation at the point where Muḥammad is challenged by skeptics who doubt his knowledge of the narratives of the Children of Israel (q.v.; *banū Isrāʾīl,* Bayḍāwī, *Anwār*). The sūra is one response to this challenge, and is thus greatly detailed and includes information not known from earlier tellings of the stories of Jacob's family.

In his commentary on the opening of the sūra, "These are the signs of the manifest book" (Q 12:1), al-Bayḍāwī offers an alternative reading to the simple meaning of the text. He explains it thus: "This is the sūra which makes plain to the Jews that which they asked... it is recorded that their learned men said to the chiefs of the polytheists, 'Ask Muḥammad why Jacob's family moved from Syria (q.v.) to Egypt (q.v.), and about the story of Joseph,' whereupon this sūra was revealed." On one occasion Muḥammad is asked for even greater detail, whereupon he reveals the names of the stars (see PLANETS AND STARS) that Joseph saw in his dream (cf. Zamakhsharī, *Kashshāf;* see JEWS AND JUDAISM).

Dreams (see DREAMS AND SLEEP) are central to this narrative. Joseph's dream of ascension to power, an ambition so bitterly resented by his brothers, is featured in Q 12:4-7. The king of Egypt's (see PHARAOH) dreams trouble him, they are "a jumble of dreams" *(aḍghāthu aḥlāmin),* and only Joseph can offer the true interpretation (Q 12:43-9). Here one can see the compression of narrative at work in the sūra. While in the Joseph narratives of the Hebrew Bible, both dream episodes — those of Joseph and those of the Pharaoh — have two dreams each, the Qurʾān tells of only one dream for each figure. The essence of their messages is conveyed through the manner in which these dreams are written and their expressed interpretations (see SCRIPTURE AND THE QURʾĀN).

The two dream episodes are separated by that section of the narrative that has received the most exegetical and literary attention (both in Islamic and Western culture): the episode in which his master's wife attempts to seduce Joseph (Q 12:23-31). The reasons for Joseph's rejection of the unnamed older woman are not directly stated. Rather, it is related that he was led away from temptation when he saw the "proof of his lord" (*burhān rabbihi,* Q 12:24), variously interpreted as an image of the master of the house or as an image of his father Jacob. Other interpretations understand the interruption as a "call" of divine origin telling Joseph not to sin or as the actual appearance on the wall of qurʾānic verses warning against sin (see SIN, MAJOR AND MINOR; ADULTERY AND FORNICATION; SEX AND SEXUALITY).

Joseph's adventure with his master's wife and his subsequent encounter with "the women of the city" lead him to prison, a prison from which he is freed after he interprets the king's dream. The Qurʾān here emphasizes Joseph's innocence and sets the stage for the second half of the narrative to unfold. This latter half of Sūrat Yūsuf is focused on the dramatic encounters between Joseph and his family. Shuttling between their father Jacob and their brother Joseph, the brothers (who remain unnamed), seek a resolution of the family conflict. Before the brothers and their father enter Egypt together (Q 12:100) the conflict is resolved. Joseph assures his brothers that they will not be blamed and Jacob is told that his children are forgiven. As the narrative closes, the sūra exhorts the reader/listener to see the actions of God at work in this story, actions which are made manifest only through God's messengers (see MESSENGER).

Joseph's name appears in two sūras other than Sūrat Yūsuf. In a list of earlier prophetic figures, Joseph's name appears between those of Job (Ayyūb) and Moses (Mūsā; Q 6:84). On this same theme of Joseph as one of the earlier messengers — and thus a predecessor of, and model for, Muḥammad — see Q 40:34, where it is stated that "Joseph brought you the clear signs (q.v.) before, yet you continued in doubt (q.v.) concerning what he brought you until, when he perished, you said 'God will never send forth a messenger after him'."

Neither Joseph's death nor burial is mentioned in the Qurʾān, but they do figure in Islamic legends. Al-Ṭabarī (d. 310/923) relates a tradition that Joseph lived to the age of 120. He also cites the biblical tradition that tells of Joseph's death at an earlier age, "In the Torah (q.v.) it is said that he lived one hundred and ten years, and that Ephraim and Manasseh were born to him." The use of Joseph's coffin to ensure Egypt's fertility also appears in Islamic folklore. In his commentary on Sūrat Yūsuf, al-Bayḍāwī (d. ca. 685/1286) says, "... the Egyptians disputed about Joseph's burial place until they were on the verge of fighting, so they decided to place him in a marble sarcophagus and bury him in the Nile in such a way that the water would pass over him and thereafter reach all of Egypt. Then the Egyptians would all be on an equal footing in regard to him." From Egypt, Joseph's bones are carried to Syria (al-Shām). There are contending Islamic traditions as to Joseph's final burial place. One tradition places it in the Ḥaram al-Khalīl in Hebron (cf. Yāqūt, *Buldān*, ii, 498-9). Another situates it in the village of Balata (Yāqūt, *Buldān*, i, 710; al-Harawī, *Guide*, 61), near Nablus. As this brief overview demonstrates, the commentarial and folkloric traditions concerning Sūrat Yūsuf are particularly rich. While earlier Western scholarship focused on comparisons between this sūra and the Hebrew Bible's Joseph narratives, the more recent scholarship focuses on the literary qualities of the sūra and on the relevance of this narrative to the life of Muḥammad.

S. Goldman

Bibliography
Primary: Bayḍāwī, *Anwār;* al-Harawī al-Mawṣilī, Tāqī l-Dīn, *Guide des lieux de pèlerinage,* trans. J. Sourdel-Thomine, Damascus 1957, 61; Kisāʾī, *Qiṣaṣ;* trans. W.M. Thackston, *The tales of the prophets of al-Kisaʾi,* Boston 1978, 178-80; Ṭabarī, *Tafsīr;* Thaʿlabī, *Qiṣaṣ;* Yāqūt, *Buldān,* ed. Wüstenfeld; Zamakhsharī, *Kashshāf.*
Secondary: A.F.L. Beeston, *Baidawi's commentary on surah 12 of the Qurʾān,* Oxford 1963; S. Goldman, *The wiles of women, the wiles of men. Joseph and Potiphar's wife in ancient Near Eastern, Jewish, and Islamic folklore,* New York 1995; A.H. Johns, "She desired him and he desired her" (Qurʾān 12:24). ʿAbd al-Raʾūf's treatment of an episode of the Joseph story in *Tarjumān al-Mustafīd,* in *Archipel* 57 (1999), 109-34; M. Mir, The qurʾānic story of Joseph. Plot, themes and characters, in *MW* 76 (1986), 1-15; A.-L. de Prémare, *Joseph et Muhammad. Le chapitre 12 du Coran,* Aix-en-Provence 1989; Speyer, *Erzählungen,* 187-224; R. Tottoli, *I profeti biblici nella tradizione islamica,* Brescia 1999, 52-7; M.R. Waldman, New approaches to "biblical" materials in the Qurʾān, in W.M. Brinner and S.D. Ricks (eds.), *Papers presented at the Institute for Islamic-Judaic Studies. Center for Judaic Studies, University of Denver,* Atlanta 1986 (*Studies in Islamic and Judaic traditions* 110 [1986]), 47-63; B.M. Wheeler, *Prophets in the Qurʾān,* London 2002, 127-45 (for the translation of some exegetical texts).

Journey

Voyage, usually of some length, from one place to another. Terms to be translated as "journey, trip, travel," occur throughout the Qurʾān. Perhaps the most obvious, and most frequent, are derivatives of *s-f-r, s-y-r,* and *ḍ-r-b (fī).* Of this set, eight (Q 2:184, 185, 283; 4:43; 5:6 *[s-f-r];* 4:101; 5:106; 73:20 *[ḍ-r-b]*) concern legal prescriptions brought into play by the act of travel (see LAW AND THE QURʾĀN). For example, Q 2:184-5, "[fast; see FASTING] for a given number of days, but if any among you is ill (see ILLNESS AND HEALTH) or on a journey *(ʿalā safarin),* [fast] on an equal number of other days." (Commentary on this passage appears limited; see Ayoub, *Qurʾān,* 193-5.) Q 2:283 addresses pledges of trust (see OATHS; CONTRACTS AND ALLIANCES); Q 5:106 finding sound witnesses (in executing bequests; see INHERITANCE; WITNESSING AND TESTIFYING); and Q 4:43 and 5:6 allowing travelers alternate forms of ritual cleansing (see CLEANLINESS AND ABLUTION) prior to prayer (q.v.). Q 4:101, "when you travel through the world *(wa-idhā ḍarabtum fī l-arḍ),* you occur no sin (see SIN, MAJOR AND MINOR) if you shorten the prayer," speaks to risks for the traveler in hostile territory. The last of the set, Q 73:20, recognizes the traveler's need to curtail reading of the Qurʾān (see RECITATION OF THE QURʾĀN; RITUAL AND THE QURʾĀN) when circumstances require it.

A second category reflects, more generally, movement in the name of God or, more properly, "upon the path of God" (*fī sabīli llāhi,* cf. Q 2:190, 218, 262, 273; 5:54; 22:9; 24:22; see PATH OR WAY). Q 9:41, on the arduous nature of service to God, is an example; so, too, is Q 4:94, in which the believer is told to display vigilance and humility when venturing into the world. Q 9:111 refers to those who "wander" in such manner; the term *sāʾiḥ,* here used in the plural, is understood by Arabic lexicographers to refer to ascetics (see ASCETICISM), specifically those devoted to fasting (see *Lisān al-ʿArab*). A final category appears to denote simply instances of movement from place to place: i.e. Q 3:156 *(ḍ-r-b),* which refers to the travel of unbelievers (see BELIEF AND UNBELIEF). Nearly all of the derivatives of *s-y-r* fall into this category, such as Q 12:109, "do they not travel through the world?" Two references to Moses (q.v.), Q 18:62 and Q 28:29, speak of his travel; and Q 34:18 *(al-sayr)* and Q 34:19 *(asfārinā),* in reference to the people of Sabaʾ (see SHEBA), treat distances or stages of journey.

A further term, *riḥla,* in Q 106:2, proved unsettling to the exegetes. It is one of four uses of derivatives of *r-ḥ-l;* the remaining three, Q 12:62, 70, 75, treat the saddlebags *(raḥl,* pl. *riḥāl)* of Joseph's (q.v.) brothers (see BROTHER AND BROTHERHOOD). The term *riḥla* occurs in Q 106 (Sūrat Quraysh — known also as Sūrat Īlāf) ostensibly in reference to the pair of journeys taken by the Quraysh (q.v.) at set points of the year, one in the cold, the second in the hot season (see SEASONS). Al-Ṭabarī (d. 310/923; *Tafsīr,* ad loc) indicates that many of the early commentators (see EXEGESIS OF THE QURʾĀN: CLASSICAL AND MEDIEVAL) understood that the Quraysh, for reasons of commerce ("they were merchants"; see SELLING AND BUYING; CARAVAN), underwent a winter *riḥla* to Yemen (q.v.; usually, the view is, because of the favorable weather) and a summer *riḥla* to Syria (q.v.). While his apparent preference lies with this reading, al-Ṭabarī cites an alternate view, that both journeys were confined to the Ḥijāz (see GEOGRAPHY; PRE-ISLAMIC ARABIA AND THE QURʾĀN). Later commentators would occasionally relate these journeys to the performance of the lesser and greater pilgrimages (*ʿumra* and *ḥajj,* respectively; see PILGRIMAGE). In sum, and particularly in later commentaries, the exegetes are uncertain as to the meaning of the term other than as a reference to journeys of some kind undertaken by the Quraysh. Further questions surrounding *riḥla* are treated by, among others, P. Crone (*Meccan trade,* 204-14) and F.E. Peters (*Muhammad,* 88-92). The first such problem concerns the relationship of Sūrat Quraysh to Sūrat al-Fīl ("The Elephant"; Q 106 and Q 105 respectively). Some early exegetes treat the two as a single sūra; al-Ṭabarī (*Tafsīr,* xxx, 197-8), however, weighs in against this view (see I. Shahīd, Two sūras, for a modern counterview). Closely related problems arise in reference to *īlāf,* about which the commentaries are in frequent disagreement — both with regard to the reading (see READINGS OF THE QURʾĀN; ORTHOGRAPHY; ARABIC SCRIPT) and the interpretation. If the frequently expressed view is correct, that it refers to arrangements permitted by God and executed by the Quraysh in order to create the proper conditions for safe passage, or, simply, the order created by God that allowed the Quraysh to survive, even thrive (see BLESSING; GRACE; MERCY), one is still left with the question regarding the nature of these journeys.

Riḥla takes on, beginning with the early Islamic tradition, the notion of travel as an act of piety (q.v.) and scholarship (see KNOWLEDGE AND LEARNING). In a well-known ḥadīth (see ḤADĪTH AND THE QURʾĀN), the Prophet urges believers to seek "knowledge, wisdom" *(ʿilm)* even as far as China, if need be. Drawing, if indirectly, on this impulse, and joining it frequently to participation in the pilgrimage *(ḥajj),* Muslim authors crafted a genre of travel literature (see TRIPS AND VOYAGES). Premier examples of the genre are the works of Ibn Jubayr (d. 614/1217) and Ibn Baṭṭūṭa (d. 770/1377). I.R. Netton (Riḥla) provides a useful initial bibliography.

Matthew S. Gordon

Bibliography
Primary: Dārimī, *Sunan,* Cairo 2000, i, 133-6; Ṭabarī, *Tafsīr,* Beirut 1972; Ṭabarsī, *Majmaʿ,* Sidon 1365/1937, ix, 544-5.
Secondary: M.M. Ayoub, *The Qurʾān and its interpreters,* vol. i, Albany 1984; P. Crone, *Meccan trade and the rise of Islam,* Princeton 1987; I.R. Netton, Riḥla, in *EI²*, viii, 528; F.E. Peters, *Muhammad and the origins of Islam,* Albany 1994; I. Shahīd, Two qurʾānic sūras. *Al-Fīl* and *Qurayš,* in W. al-Qāḍī (ed.), *Studia arabica et islamica,* Beirut 1981, 429-36.

Joy and Misery

The state of happiness and that of wretchedness, respectively. References to joy and misery are frequent in the Qurʾān, are expressed either directly or by implication, and pertain both to this world and the next (see ESCHATOLOGY). Pleasures of this world are neither condemned nor forbidden (q.v.; see also ASCETICISM; ABSTINENCE; WEALTH; POVERTY AND THE POOR; LAWFUL AND UNLAWFUL), but believers are to be mindful about the source of these pleasures (see GRATITUDE AND INGRATITUDE). Current wretchedness is not a sure sign of divine favor or disfavor (see BLESSING; GRACE; CURSE; REWARD AND PUNISHMENT; TRIAL): the true believer, however, is to assist those who are less fortunate (see ETHICS AND THE QURʾĀN; COMMUNITY AND SOCIETY IN THE QURʾĀN). While the joys and miseries of the present life are not absent from the qurʾānic discourse, it is the states of joy and misery experienced in the next life upon which the Qurʾān places its strongest emphasis (see REWARD AND PUNISHMENT).

Among the most recurrent themes is the relative worthlessness of the joys of this world in comparison with those of the hereafter, as in Q 57:20, "The present life is but the joy of delusion." The word rendered here as "joy" is *matāʿ,* which also occurs in the following passages: "Surely, this present life is but a passing enjoyment *(matāʿ)* and the hereafter is the abode [in which] to settle" (Q 40:39); "And those things you have been given are only a provision *(matāʿ)* of this life and its adornment, and whatever is with God is better and more lasting" (Q 28:60; also 13:26 and 42:36); and "The enjoyment *(matāʿ)* of this world is but little, and the hereafter is better for the one who is pious" (Q 4:77; cf. 9:38). Equally significant is the contrast between the pleasures, delights, and enjoyments of this world and the punishment to be visited upon those who do not submit to God (see REWARD AND PUNISHMENT; HELL AND HELLFIRE; FIRE). The forgers of lies against God are promised "a little enjoyment *(matāʿ),* and for them is a painful chastisement" (Q 16:117; see CHASTISEMENT AND PUNISHMENT) or "A brief enjoyment. Then their abode is hell" (Q 3:197). Of like import are passages that emphasize accountability to God at the end of life. People who become rebellious after God has rescued them from the terrors of the sea are told, "O people, your rebellion (q.v.) is against yourselves — only a *matāʿ* of this world's life. Then to us is your return" (Q 10:23).

For the most part, words from the root *m-t-ʿ* have reference to material things rather than to the spiritual joys of the hereafter: they designate things that are useful, of benefit, that bring satisfaction, that meet needs or that inspire delight and pleasure. Such is the meaning of those verses that speak of a provision *(matāʿ)* for this world, as in Q 3:14: "Fair seeming to people is made the love of desires, of women, of sons (see CHILDREN), of hoarded treasures of gold (q.v.) and silver and branded horses and cattle and tilth (see ANIMAL LIFE; AGRICULTURE AND VEGETATION). This is the provision *(matāʿ)* of the life of this world." More basically, *matāʿ* indicates the necessities of life, those things which are required to sustain existence and which afford pleasure. There is mention of a " 'goodly provision' for you for a certain time" (Q 11:3), also of an "abode and provision for you for a time" (Q 7:24) and of "an enjoyment *(matāʿ)* for you and your cattle" (Q 79:33; 80:32). Firewood is both a reminder of God as provider of all things and a boon *(matāʿ)* to wayfarers in the desert (q.v.; Q 56:73) and the produce of the sea is characterized as a "provision for you and for the travelers" (Q 5:96; see HUNTING AND FISHING). Muslims are also warned of the desire of the unbelievers (see BELIEF AND UNBELIEF) that they be heedless of their weapons and their possessions (Q 4:102; see INSTRUMENTS; FIGHTING; EXPEDITIONS AND BATTLES). The material meaning is clear in such passages as that in which Muslims are commanded: "When you ask them [the Prophet's wives; see WIVES OF THE PROPHET] for something *(matāʿ)* ask them from behind a veil" (q.v.; Q 33:53).

The concept of *matāʿ* as material goods or possessions also appears in the story of Joseph (q.v.). Joseph's brothers fabricate an explanation for the disappearance of their young sibling by telling their father that they had left Joseph behind to mind their baggage *(matāʿ)* while they ran races and that he had been eaten by a wolf (Q 12:17). Later, when Joseph's brothers return to their father from their trip to buy corn in Egypt and open their things *(amtāʿ),* they find that their money has been returned to them (Q 12:65). In the same story, again, Joseph asserts (in reference to the king's missing drinking cup; see CUPS AND VESSELS) that he will hold responsible only him in whose possession the goods *(matāʿ)* are found (Q 12:79).

The essentially material nature of *matāʿ* is underlined also by the commands to make honorable provision for divorced women (Q 2:241; see MARRIAGE AND DIVORCE). The affluent man should do so according to his means and the person in more straitened circumstances according to his, in agreement with established custom (Q 2:236). Those who die should also leave a bequest to surviving wives that will offer provision for a period of one year without their being turned out (Q 2:240; see INHERITANCE).

Another set of meanings relating to joy is expressed in forms of the root *f-r-ḥ* which means "to be happy, delighted, cheerful," etc. The noun *farḥa,* signifying "joy," does not appear as such in the Qurʾān, but there are frequent occurrences of other words from this root that point to the experience of joy. One such is the verb "to rejoice." Uses of this verb may be divided into those which indicate positive causes for rejoicing and those which refer to negative causes. One affirmative reason to rejoice is the mercy (q.v.) of God: "and when we cause men to taste mercy they rejoice in it" (Q 30:36; 42:48); also "Say: let them rejoice in the grace and mercy of God. It is better than what they hoard" (Q 10:58). A major source of joy is the revelation (see REVELATION AND INSPIRATION): "Rejoice in what was sent down to you" (Q 13:36) and "on that day the faithful will rejoice in God's help" (Q 30:4, 5). God, indeed, controls all things for both good and ill "so that you do not grieve for what has escaped you nor rejoice in what he has given you" (Q 57:23; see FREEDOM AND PREDESTINATION). God both amplifies and diminishes the provision for men, and "they rejoice in this present life" (Q 13:26). Addressing those who refused to participate with the Muslims in battle, the Qurʾān says that those lost are not killed or dead, but are alive and have sustenance "rejoicing in the grace God has bestowed on them" (Q 3:170). Even mundane physical events are reason to rejoice as sailors do when they encounter a fair wind (Q 10:22; see AIR AND WIND).

Rejoicing can occur, however, for reasons that are not in themselves good. When this happens, the joy expressed is often equivalent to boasting (see BOAST), pride (q.v.), haughtiness, arrogance (q.v.) or ingratitude (see GRATITUDE AND INGRATITUDE). For instance, at the time of the emigration (q.v.; *hijra*) to Medina (q.v.), "those who were left behind rejoiced in tarrying" (Q 9:81). The present sent by the Queen of Sheba (see BILQĪS) to King Solomon (q.v.) earned him a rebuke, as he exulted in the gift instead of recognizing that what God had given was better (Q 27:36). Pride and arrogance were also involved in the case of Qārūn, biblical Korah (q.v.), the wealthy Jew whose people warned him: "Do not boast *(lā tafraḥ),* God does not love boasters *(fariḥīn)*" (Q 28:76). The fate of previous peoples shows their haughtiness and its consequences; when messengers came to them with clear arguments "they exulted in the knowledge they already had" (Q 40:83; see PROOF; KNOWLEDGE AND LEARNING) and what they had formerly mocked came to pass (see MOCKERY). When the unbelievers rejected what had been said to them but, nonetheless, experienced much good, "they rejoiced in what had been given them" (Q 6:44), but God seized them suddenly. When the fortunes of a man change for the good after his having suffered, he may become ungrateful: "Certainly, he is exultant, boastful" (Q 11:10). As for the unbelievers, "If something good happens to you, it grieves them, and if something bad happens to you, they take joy in it" (Q 3:120; see GOOD AND EVIL). In a nearly identical verse the unbelievers also take credit for the hardship that may afflict the believers, "and they turn away rejoicing" (Q 9:50). Pride in what they have is likewise characteristic of the various groups into which the Muslim community is divided, "each party rejoicing in what it has" (Q 23:53; 30:32; see PARTIES AND FACTIONS). Finally, it is made clear that rejoicing or exulting in the wrong things has serious consequences: "And do not think that those who exult in what they have done... are free from punishment" (Q 3:188). They will, indeed, endure the torments of hell because they "exulted in the land unjustly" (Q 40:75).

Quite similar in usage and meaning are some words from the root *b-sh-r,* meaning "to be joyous or to rejoice in good tidings." The Prophet is described in the Qurʾān as a *bashīr* or bearer of good news (q.v.). Q 3:169 and 170 show that *faraḥ* and *b-sh-r* are synonymous terms in their meaning of rejoicing. Those who were killed in battle are joyous *(fariḥīn)* in what God has given them of his grace and rejoice *(yastabshirūna)* for those who have not yet joined them that they have neither fear (q.v.) nor grief. They rejoice *(yastabshirūna)* in God's favor and his grace (Q 3:171). Physical events are also a source of joy as, for example, when the rain falls (Q 30:48; see WATER; NATURE AS SIGNS). Of more spiritual import is revelation, which, as it comes, strengthens the faith (q.v.) of the believers, "and they are joyful" *(yastabshirūna,* Q 9:124). There is none more faithful to a promise than God (see OATHS; CONTRACTS AND ALLIANCES; BREAKING TRUSTS AND CONTRACTS); the believers are commanded "rejoice, therefore, in the bargain you have made" (Q 9:111). In the story of Lot (q.v.) there is an example of rejoicing in evil (Q 15:67) when the townspeople come to him demanding the messengers whom Lot has accepted as his guests. On the last and terrible day of judgment (see LAST JUDGMENT) there will be some faces that are bright, "laughing, joyous" (Q 80:39), while others will be covered with dust in gloom and darkness (q.v.). The unbelievers seek intercession (q.v.) with other than God though it is useless for them to do so. "When God alone is mentioned, the hearts (see HEART) of those who believe not in the hereafter shrink *(ashma'azzat),* and when those besides him are mentioned, lo! they are joyful" (Q 39:45).

Joy is also indicated by the word *naʿīm* from the root, *n-ʿ-m,* which means "to be happy, to be glad, to delight, to take pleasure in something, or to enjoy something." *Naʿīm* may be translated as "bliss," for it points to a particularly intense sense of joy, in fact, to the very pinnacle of delight and pleasurable feeling that humans may experience. In all seventeen of its occurrences in the Qurʾān, *naʿīm* is associated either with paradise (q.v.) or with the fate of the righteous on the day of judgment, as in Q 102:8: "On that day you will certainly be questioned about true bliss." There shall be judgment for the evildoers (see EVIL DEEDS) and rewards for the righteous of whom "you know in their faces the radiance of bliss" (Q 83:24); "Surely, the righteous are in bliss" (Q 82:13; 83:22). The concept figures most often in descriptions of paradise which refer to gardens of bliss or gardens of delight (e.g. Q 10:9; 22:56; see GARDEN) where the righteous may dwell eternally (see ETERNITY). "And when you look there, you see bliss and a great kingdom" (Q 76:20). There are closely related words from the same root that also point to things which give joy. *Niʿma,* meaning "blessing (q.v.), favor, or grace (q.v.)" and used in connection with God's beneficence to man, is found fifty times in the Qurʾān. There are also eighteen occurrences of verbs from the same root, all conveying the idea of blessing.

Another set of words that refers to joy comes from the root *s-r-r,* "to make happy, to gladden," yielding also the nouns happiness and gladness. For example, when Moses (q.v.) commanded his people to sacrifice a cow, he replied to their request for a description of it, saying that it was "a golden cow, bright in color, gladdening the beholders" (Q 2:69; see CALF OF GOLD). More significant is the use of the passive participle *(masrūran)* in connection with the judgment day. One who is given his book behind his back, although "he used to live among his people joyfully" will taste perdition and enter into burning fire (Q 84:10-3). In contrast, he who is judged righteous "will return to his people joyfully" (Q 84:9). God "will ward off the evil of that day from them and give them radiance and gladness" (Q 76:11). Again the theme of judgment day is the context for the use of another term signifying joy, namely *fākih* (of the root *f-k-h*). The word is evidenced twice in predictions of the coming judgment, "The inhabitants of paradise today are busy in their rejoicing" (Q 36:55) and "The dutiful will surely be in gardens and in bliss, rejoicing because of what their lord has given them" (Q 52:17, 18). In Q 11:105 another term for happiness, *saʿīd*, is used in an eschatological context (cf. also Q 11:108): the state of contentment of those assigned a heavenly reward is explicitly contrasted with the misery of those who are consigned to the fire of hell (Q 11:106).

The Qurʾān speaks with great frequency of the reward, recompense or wage prepared for those who believe and are righteous (see JUSTICE AND INJUSTICE). The references are far too numerous to be detailed here, but they may be explored by reference to terms from such roots as *ʿ-dh-b*, *ʿ-q-b*, *th-w-b*, *j-z-y*, and *kh-r-j*. Reward and punishment are, indeed, among the very central themes of the qurʾānic message. As one of its consequences reward surely brings joy to those who receive it, since that reward is nothing less than an eternity in paradise, the ultimate joy to which the qurʾānic revelation urges humankind to aspire.

As with the understanding of joy, the concept of misery also has a double aspect, one related to worldly life and the other to the hereafter. In mundane terms, misery is a consequence of poverty and deprivation (see POVERTY AND THE POOR; DESPAIR; OPPRESSED ON EARTH, THE). The pursuit of righteousness requires choosing the uphill road, one element of which is to feed "the poor man *(miskīn)* lying in the dust" (Q 90:16). In addition to the eschatological sense that is found in Q 11:105-6 (mentioned above), derivatives of *sh-q-y* carry the sense of unprosperous (Q 20:2, 123; 19:48 and others), of adversity (Q 23:106), and of wretchedness (Q 87:11). The Qurʾān exhibits a humanitarian concern for the deprived, especially in the chapters generally held to belong to the first parts of the revelation. Among the actions that define a pious Muslim is the giving of wealth (q.v.) to "the near of kin (see KINSHIP), and the orphans (q.v.) and the needy and the wayfarer" (Q 2:177; see HOSPITALITY AND COURTESY; JOURNEY). In short, it takes notice of the misery of poverty and distress. Endurance in times of distress and affliction are another mark of the pious believer. In accord with its broad insistence upon God's sovereignty the Qurʾān underlines that it is he who delivered Noah (q.v.) and his people from their great distress and, indeed, is the deliverer from every distress (Q 6:64; 21:76; 37:76, 115). There is also mention of God's seizing people with misery and hardship (Q 2:214; 6:42; 7:94; see TRIAL; PUNISHMENT STORIES). All of these references have to do with poverty and the pain that accompanies it.

Undoubtedly, however, the greatest misery is otherworldly, that of hell, the place for which all are destined who do not heed the message of God. Some of the most graphic passages of the Qurʾān are devoted to descriptions of the miseries to be endured in hell. Its inhabitants will be roasted (Q 38:56), and will be made to suffer a blazing fire in which they must dwell forever. They will be paraded about Jahannam (hell) hobbling on their knees (Q 19:68). As for the unbeliever, "Hell is before him, and he is given oozing pus to drink (see FOOD AND DRINK); he drinks it little by little and is not able to swallow it; and death comes to him from every side; yet he does not die" (Q 14:16-7). "And whenever they try to escape from it, from anguish, they are turned back" (Q 22:22). The torments of hell are a recompense, wage or reward for the evil of the evildoers and for the denials of those who disbelieved. By their deeds they have earned a mighty chastisement, a painful punishment. The promise of eternal misery to come is one of the most persistent and compelling of all qurʾānic themes.

Charles J. Adams

Bibliography
Primary: Dāmaghānī, *Wujūh*, ii, 221-2 (for *matāʿ*); ii, 112-3 (for *farḥ*); Yaḥyā b. Sallām, *al-Taṣārīf. Tafsīr al-Qurʾān mimmā shtabahat asmāʾuhu wa-taṣarrafat maʿānīhi*, ed. Hind Shiblī, Tunis 1979, 243-4 (for *farḥ*).
Secondary: W. Graham, 'The winds to herald his mercy' and other 'signs for those of certain faith.' Nature as token of God's sovereignty and grace in the Qurʾān, in S. Lee, W. Proudfoot and A. Blackwell (eds.), *Faithful imagining. Essays in honor of Richard R. Niebuhr*, Atlanta 1995, 19-38; Hanna E. Kassis, *A concordance of the Qurʾān*, Berkeley 1983.

Judgment

Opinion or decision; pronouncement of such. Judgment is an integral part of the whole qurʾānic ethos and is intrinsically linked to creation (q.v.) itself, which is not just a random act but teleological and divinely ordained (see COSMOLOGY; FATE; FREEDOM AND PREDESTINATION). God, who is the sole source of creation and sustenance (q.v.; see also BLESSING; FOOD AND DRINK), is also the lord (q.v.) of the day of judgment (see LAST JUDGMENT). Consequently, the concept of God's final "judgment," which eventually became one of the tenets of faith (q.v.; *aqāʾid*, see also CREEDS), is found throughout the Qurʾān, with subsequent expansion and refinement by the exegetical tradition (see EXEGESIS OF THE QURʾĀN: CLASSICAL AND MEDIEVAL). But judgment is not the prerogative of God alone. The Qurʾān, which acknowledges that in the course of their daily lives, humans, too, pass judgment, sets forth general (and, in certain cases, specific) guidelines by which humans should judge (see ARBITRATION).

The Qurʾān contains no unique term for judgment, human or divine. Rather, a range of vocabulary is employed to convey the concept: *ḥukm, qaḍāʾ, dīn, ḥisāb, raʾy, rashad/rushd* and others. Among these, *ḥukm* — a verbal noun of the verb *ḥakama* (from the triliteral root *ḥ-k-m)* meaning "to judge, give verdict or provide decision" — and its cognates occurs most comprehensively. One derivative, *ḥakam* (pl. *ḥukkām)*, was historically associated with pre-Islamic judges or, rather, arbitrators (see PRE-ISLAMIC ARABIA AND THE QURʾĀN), a meaning apparent in the Qurʾān in the prescription of appointing an arbitrator *(ḥakam)* from each family in case of domestic disputes between husband and wife (Q 4:35; see FAMILY; MARRIAGE AND DIVORCE; LAW AND THE QURʾĀN). Wisdom (q.v.; *ḥikma*) and authority (q.v.; *ḥukm*) are also derived from the root letters *ḥ-k-m*. The correlation between judgment and wisdom is demonstrated in the description of God as both "the judge" *(al-ḥākim* and *al-ḥakam)* and "the wise" (*al-ḥakīm;* cf. Gimaret, *Noms divins*, 74, 347-9; see GOD AND HIS ATTRIBUTES). God is also described in the Qurʾān as "the best of judges" (*khayr al-ḥākimīn*, Q 7:87; 10:109; 12:80; cf. Gimaret, *Noms divins*, 74, 347-9) and "the most just of judges" (*aḥkam al-ḥākimīn*, Q 11:45 and 95:8; see JUSTICE AND INJUSTICE).

The term *ḥukm* occurs in the early Meccan verses (see CHRONOLOGY AND THE QURʾĀN) where human judgment of the pagans is contrasted to the divine judgment (Q 5:50; see POLYTHEISM AND ATHEISM; IDOLATRY AND IDOLATERS). *Ḥukm* is also mentioned in the Qurʾān with regard to Muḥammad's prophetic authority to judge individuals (see PROPHETS AND

PROPHETHOOD). Moses (q.v.), David (q.v.), Jesus (q.v.) and others are mentioned in this context, together with the Torah (q.v.; Q 5:44) and the Gospel (q.v.; Q 5:47). In this respect, though, special emphasis is placed upon Muḥammad, and the Qurʾān is called the "Arabic code/judgment" (*ḥukm ʿarabī,* Q 13:37). Muḥammad was, in fact, invited to Medina (q.v.) because of his personal authority as a judge or arbiter in tribal disputes (see EMIGRATION; POLITICS AND THE QURʾĀN; TRIBES AND CLANS).

Derivatives of another triliteral root, *q-ḍ-y,* are also employed for judgment or decision in the Qurʾān; the verb *(qāḍa)* occurs frequently, referring primarily to an act of God, indicating his absolute power (cf. Q 6:58; 39:75; see Dāmaghānī, *Wujūh,* ii, 138; cf. Abū l-Baqāʾ, *al-Kulliyyāt,* 705a; see POWER AND IMPOTENCE). The judicial decision *(qāḍaʾ)* is generally considered as part of judgment *(ḥukm),* since whenever someone gives a verdict or a decree, judgment is invariably passed (cf. *Tāj al-ʿarūs,* s.v.). But in the Qurʾān, the verb *ḥakama* and its cognates usually relate to the Prophet's judicial activities (e.g. Q 4:105), while the verb *qaḍā,* from which the word for "judge" *(qāḍī)* is derived, mainly refers (with the exception of Q 10:71 and 20:72) not to the judgment of a judge, but to a sovereign ordinance of either God or the Prophet. Both verbs occur simultaneously in Q 4:65: "But no, by your lord, they can have no real faith until they make you a judge *(yuḥakkimūka)* in all disputes between them and thereafter find no resistance within their souls of what you decide *(qaḍayta),* but accept them with total conviction." The first verb *(yuḥakkimūka)* refers to the arbitrating aspect of the Prophet's activity, while the second *(qaḍayta)* emphasizes the authoritative character of his decision, raising it to a level of belief (*īmān,* see BELIEF AND UNBELIEF). While al-Zamakhsharī (d. 538/1144; *Kashshāf,* ad loc.) and al-Bayḍāwī (d. prob. 716/1316-7; *Tafsīr,* ad loc.) only stress the emphatic *lām* in the verse, al-Ṭabarī (d. 310/923; *Tafsīr,* ad loc.) includes a reference to peoples' sincerity of belief as dependent upon whether God or the Prophet were appointed as judges in their affairs and their not feeling any uneasiness about the ensuing decisions. Al-Qummī (d. 328/939; *Tafsīr,* ad loc.), on the other hand, designates *yuḥakkimūka* as referring to ʿAlī (see ʿALĪ B. ABĪ ṬĀLIB) and the second verb *(qaḍayta)* to the Prophet's decision regarding ʿAlī's imāmate (*walāya;* see CLIENTS AND CLIENTAGE; FRIENDS AND FRIENDSHIP).

Muḥammad had been sent by God to teach humans how to act, what to do and what to avoid in order to be judged favorably in the reckoning on the day of judgment (see GOOD DEEDS; EVIL DEEDS; LAWFUL AND UNLAWFUL). In Islam, therefore, law is an all-embracing body of religious commandments (q.v.) and prohibitions (see FORBIDDEN; PROHIBITED DEGREES); it consists not only of a legal system, but also of rules governing worship (q.v.) and ritual (see RITUAL AND THE QURʾĀN). There is a recurrent insistence on the merits of forgiveness (q.v.) in the Qurʾān, with words such as *ʿafā, ṣafaḥa, ghafara* in Q 2:109; 3:134; 23:96; 42:37, 40, 43; 64:14, etc. (see also MERCY). Although a life (q.v.) for a life and an eye (q.v.) for an eye is ordained in the Qurʾān (see RETALIATION; BLOOD MONEY), there is a qualification pertaining to the action of those who voluntarily overlook the injustice done to them, a response which is regarded as atonement (q.v.) for their own actions.

Ethics (see ETHICS AND THE QURʾĀN) is an integral part of law, and the Qurʾān includes many ethical injunctions such as to judge with justice (Q 4:58; 5:42; 6:152), not to offer bribes (Q 2:188), to give true evidence (Q 4:135; 5:8; see LIE; WITNESSING AND TESTIFYING) and to give full weight and measure (Q 17:35; 55:7-9; 83:1-3; see WEIGHTS AND MEASURES). Transactions and contracts are to be committed to writing and fulfilled, especially in relation to returning a trust or deposit *(amāna)* to its owner (e.g. Q 2:283; see BREAKING TRUSTS AND CONTRACTS; CONTRACTS AND ALLIANCES; SELLING AND BUYING). Judging others wrongly is abhorred in the Qurʾān as is judging others on the basis of suspicions (q.v.; *ẓann*). A different aspect of judgment is portrayed in Q 49:11-12, where believers are asked not to laugh (see LAUGHTER), label, defame or be sarcastic to others (see MOCKERY) as, in God's view, it is possible that those whom they judge are actually better than themselves. Explicit warning is given not to enquire curiously into the affairs of others as well as not to blame, set up one against the other, talk about each other or backbite (see GOSSIP), the last-mentioned of which is equated with eating the flesh of one's dead brother (see BROTHER AND BROTHERHOOD).

Dīn is another expression for judgment in the Qurʾān, although its etymology lends itself to two additional meanings: custom (see SUNNA) and religion (q.v.). Whatever their differences in origin and meaning, these meanings are conceptually related. Thus, *dayn,* which means debt (q.v.) due at a fixed time, semantically connects to *dīn* as custom or usage, which, in its turn, gives the idea of God-given direction (see ASTRAY; PATH OR WAY). Judging involves guiding someone in the right direction, often through rebuke and retribution. Arabic philologists often derive *dīn* from *dāna lahu* meaning to submit to the obligations imposed by God (for *dīn* in the sense of obedience [q.v.], see Jeffery, *For. vocab.,* 131-3; Izutsu, *God,* 219-29). "The judge" *(al-dayyān)* is one of God's names, which people also applied to ʿAlī b. Abī Ṭālib as the sage of the community (cf. *Lisān al-ʿArab,* s.v.; for *al-dayyān* as an attribute of God, cf. also Gimaret, *Noms divins,* 350-1).

Al-Bāqillānī (d. 403/1013; *Kitāb al-Tamhīd,* 345) distinguishes several possible meanings of *dīn,* including judgment in the sense of retribution, in the sense of decision *(ḥukm),* as well as of doctrine *(madhhab)* and the religion of truth (q.v.; *dīn al-ḥaqq*). The sense of judgment and retribution occurs frequently in the early sūras of the Meccan period: four times independently, and twelve as part of the expression "the day of judgment" *(yawm al-dīn).* This is synonymous with "the day of reckoning" (*yawm al-ḥisāb,* Q 40:27; 14:41; cf. 37:20, 26, 53), "the day of resurrection" *(yawm al-qiyāma),* the "return" *(maʿād)* and "the hour" (*al-sāʿa,* see ESCHATOLOGY; APOCALYPSE). Many other names are given in the Qurʾān; as many as 1,700 verses refer to the resurrection (q.v.; cf. *Rasāʾil Ikhwān al-Ṣafāʾ,* iii, 286-7, which cites numerous names for the final day, such as *yawm al-faṣl, yawm al-tanādī, yawm al-āzifa*).

Eschatological judgment in the Qurʾān is inevitable (Q 3:9) and God is swift in dealing with the account *(ḥisāb).* In Q 75:26-8 there is reference to an initial judgment occurring immediately after death, while other passages in Q 56 (Sūrat al-Wāqiʿa, "The Event"), speak of the inevitable event, alluding to the hour of judgment *(al-sāʿa),* when each soul will be evaluated according to what it has earned (see GOOD AND EVIL; RECORD OF HUMAN ACTIONS). At the final resurrection the whole present order gives way to a new one as portrayed in Q 14:48 (see DEATH AND THE DEAD). The rendering of accounts — required from all people — is to be given to God alone (Q 13:40; 26:113). God is "prompt in demanding an account" (Q 2:202, 3:19 and 199) of each person's actions, which will have been inscribed on a "roll." The day of judgment is described as the day when the world will be rolled up like a scroll and nothing on the scales of God's judgment will be overlooked: an atom's weight of good will be manifest and so will an atom's weight of evil. If the good deeds outweigh the bad, people will receive their accounts in their right hands and receive their reward, while those whose deeds are unfavorable will receive them in their left hands and be punished (see REWARD AND PUNISHMENT).

"The Heights" (Q 7, Sūrat al-Aʿrāf) mentions those on the heights who hear and address the people of paradise (q.v.; Q 7:46-7; see PEOPLE OF THE HEIGHTS). It is only the sanctified, who, having perfected themselves, will enter paradise. Those who are not perfect will enter an intermediary state as they undergo final purification. "The Event" (Q 56, Sūrat al-Wāqiʿa) seeks to judge three types of souls: the companions of the left, the companions of the right and those that are foremost *(al-sābiqūn),* to be equated with those who are brought close to God's throne (*al-muqarrabūn,* see THRONE OF GOD). Clearly, there seems to be a fundamental difference of degree, between which some Shīʿa and the Ṣūfīs did not hesitate to distinguish (see ṢŪFISM AND THE QURʾĀN): those who achieve salvation (q.v.) and those who attain beatitude. In their view, salvation is the reward for the exoteric religion, while the aim of the esoteric path is the beatific vision (see FACE OF GOD; SEEING AND HEARING; VISION AND BLINDNESS; VISIONS).

Judgment invariably involves an evaluation of right or wrong, true or false and good or bad (see PAIRS AND PAIRING). Philosophically, it involves the rational faculty as observed by the authors of the *Rasʾāil Ikhwān al-Ṣafāʾ,* who regard "judgment on things as a product of the intellect (q.v.)." In the Qurʾān, this meaning is apparent in the word *raʾy,* used in numerous verses (e.g. Q 6:40) in which God asks people about their thoughts at the time when the wrath (see ANGER) of God will befall them and when the hour of judgment is near. *Raʾy* can be used in a variety of ways: seeing physically with one's eyes, considering or perceiving things with one's heart (q.v.) and even sensing things through one's beliefs (cf. *Lisān al-ʿArab,* s.v.; see KNOWLEDGE AND LEARNING). It can also connote a belief about something or someone and for wrong belief, God's judgment falls upon people as punishment (cf. *Tāj al-ʿarūs,* s.v.; see CHASTISEMENT AND PUNISHMENT). In the debates of the fourth/tenth century among the various legal schools, the *ahl al-raʾy* were those who were accused by the *ahl al-ḥadīth* of practicing analogical deduction *(qiyās)* by giving judgments according to their opinions, as they could not find an appropriate prophetic tradition to support their arguments (see ḤADĪTH AND THE QURʾĀN; TRADITIONAL DISCIPLINES OF QURʾĀNIC STUDY).

Another qurʾānic lexeme used in connection with judgment is *rashad/rushd.* In Q 4:6, God speaks of giving orphans (q.v.) their wealth when they attain "sound judgment" (*rushd,* see MATURITY). People differ with regard to the meaning of *rushd:* among the interpretations of the passage that he discusses, al-Ṭabarī (*Tafsīr,* iv, 252) relates that some consider it to be soundness of intellect and righteousness in religion. Al-Zamakhsharī (*Kashshāf,* i, 501) also mentions several traditions: Abū Ḥanīfa (d. 150/767) explained that *rushd* was informed guidance on all aspects of good actions, while Ibn ʿAbbās (d. 68/686-8) maintained that it was righteousness in using intellect and preserving wealth (q.v.), whereas Mālik b. Anas (d. 179/796) and al-Shāfiʿī (d. 204/820) held that it was righteousness in religion.

The notion of judgment raises the issue

of intercessory disputation on behalf of the soul (q.v.; Q 4:109), which invariably involves matters of repentance (*tawba*, see REPENTANCE AND PENANCE), intercession (q.v.; *shafāʿa*) and compassion *(raḥma)*. Not all Sunnī schools accept the possibility of prophetic intercession *(shafāʿa)*, and those who do argue about whether it applies only to Muḥammad or to all prophets. The Shīʿa, on the other hand, accept this doctrine without question and also extend it to the Imāms (see IMĀM; SHĪʿISM AND THE QURʾĀN). Although Q 4:64 elucidates the concept of intercession *(shafāʿa)*, mentioning the Prophet's role, other verses, such as Q 16:111, speak of the "day that every soul shall come debating on its own behalf."

In conclusion, it may be said that although the final, eschatological judgment dominates the qurʾānic discourse, the concept is not absent from discussions of the present world, in which humans are called to judge fairly, and by what is best.

Arzina R. Lalani

Bibliography
Primary: Abū l-Baqāʾ al-Kaffawī, Ayyūb b. Mūsā, *al-Kulliyyāt*, ed. ʿA. Darwīsh and M. al-Miṣrī, Beirut 1998; ʿAlī b. Muḥammad al-Walīd, *Tāj al-ʿaqāʾid wa-maʿdan al-fawāʾid*, Beirut 1967; Bāqillānī, *Kitāb al-Tamhīd*, ed. R.J. McCarthy, Beirut 1957; Bayḍāwī, *Anwār; Dāmaghānī*, *Wujūh; Lisān al-ʿArab*, Beirut 1955-6; al-Nuʿmān, Abū Ḥanīfa (al-Qāḍī), *Taʾwīl al-daʿāʾim*, ed. M.H. al-Aʿẓamī, Cairo 1968-72; Qummī, *Tafsīr*, 2 vols., Beirut 1968; *Rasāʾil Ikhwān al-Ṣafāʾ*, ed. Kh. Ziriklī, 4 vols., Cairo 1928; Ṭabarī, *Tafsīr*, ed. ʿAlī; *Tāj al-ʿarūs*, 10 vols., Cairo 1306-7; Zamakhsharī, *Kashshāf*, 4 vols., Beirut n.d.
Secondary: M.M. Bar-Asher, *Scripture and exegesis in early Imāmī Shiism*, Jerusalem 1999; D. Gimaret, *Les noms divins en Islam*, Paris 1988; Izutsu, *God;* Jeffery, *For. vocab.;* M. Khadduri, *The Islamic concept of justice*, Baltimore 1984; Lane; J.D. McAuliffe, 'Debate with them in a better way.' The construction of a qurʾānic commonplace, in A. Neuwirth et al. (eds.), *Myths, historical archetypes and symbolic figures in Arabic literature*, Beirut 1999, 163-88; J. Schacht, *An introduction to Islamic law*, Oxford 1974.

Jūdī

Mount (Jabal) Jūdī, also written Djūdī (modern Turkish, Cudi), the name of a mountain mass and its highest point in SE Turkey, near the borders of Iraq (q.v.) and Syria (q.v.). Mount Jūdī is attested once in the Qurʾān, at Q 11:44, as al-Jūdī, the site where Noah's (q.v.) ark (q.v.) rested on dry land after the flood (see MYTHS AND LEGENDS IN THE QURʾĀN; SCRIPTURE AND THE QURʾĀN; GEOGRAPHY). There has been considerable disagreement about the actual site to which this story refers. Largely due to western Christian misinterpretation of the Hebrew *"hārê Arārāṭ,"* literally "*mountains* of Ararat" (*Gen* 8:4), as *Mount* Ararat (q.v.), the passage has been interpreted as referring to a single mountain since about the tenth century. Thus, the tallest mountain near the present-day border of Turkey with Armenia, once known as Masik, came to be named Mount Ararat and is generally identified today as the site of the ark's landing. In the Hebrew scriptures the name Ararat was actually the Hebrew rendition of Urarṭu, the name of the ancient kingdom that covered the territory of eastern Turkey, and included both mountains, today's Ararat and Jabal Jūdī. This extensive mountainous area has been known variously as Qardū in Aramaic and Syriac texts; Gordyene by Greek, Roman, and later Christian writers; and Kordukh in Armenian. The Jewish-Aramaic *Targum Onkelos*, possibly based on an earlier Babylonian tradition, translates the Hebrew of Genesis 8:4 as "ṭurē Qardū" ("mountains of Qardū") and later rabbinic sources have generally described Qardū as the mountains where the ark rested (cf. Ṭabarī, *History*, 366 n. 1137). The variant forms of this name led some scholars to connect Qardū wrongly with Kurd and Kurdistan, despite the difference between K and Q.

According to Yāqūt (*Muʿjam*, ii, 144-5),

Jūdī in the Qurʾān seems to have denoted a mountain in Arabia, a designation possibly based on earlier Arabian traditions (see PRE-ISLAMIC ARABIA AND THE QURʾĀN). The transfer of the designated locale from Arabia to upper Mesopotamia and the territory of Urarṭu must have taken place early during the Arab invasion of that region. Today, the areas around both Mount Ararat and Jabal Jūdī are filled with memorials and legends referring to the flood and the life of Noah (q.v.) and his family after they left the ark. This holds true about a particular structure, once a monastery, on the supposed site of Noah's worship of God after the flood. According to Le Strange, from the village of Jazīrat Ibn ʿUmar, Jūdī was visible to the east, with the "Mosque of Noah" on its summit and Qaryat Thamānīn ("the village of eighty") at the mountain's foot (*Lands*, 94). The village's name refers to one of several traditions about how many humans survived the flood in the ark, which vary between seven survivors (Noah, his three sons and their spouses) and eighty, including seventy-three descendants of Seth, son of Adam. This village is supposedly where Noah himself settled after the flood and although all the survivors except for Noah and his immediate descendants perished, all of today's humanity is descended from those seven or eight. Because of the qurʾānic reference to al-Jūdī and to its early identification with Noah, the mountain and its surrounding area became a pilgrimage site for Muslims, Jews and eastern Christians.

William M. Brinner

Bibliography
Primary: Ṭabarī, *The history of al-Ṭabarī. i. From the creation to the flood*, trans. F. Rosenthal, Albany 1989; al-Thaʿlabī, ʿAbd al-Malik b. Muḥammad, *ʿArāʾis al-majālis*, Cairo 1900, 42; Yāqūt, *Buldān*, ed. Wüstenfeld, i, 932 (Thamānīn); ii, 144-5 (Jūdī).
Secondary: Th. Bois, Kurds, Kurdistan, in *EI²*, v, 447-9; L. Ginzberg, *Legends of the Jews*, 7 vols., Philadelphia 1955, v, 186, n. 48 (to i, 165, in the story of Noah); G. Le Strange, *The lands of the eastern Caliphate*, Cambridge 1905; M. Streck, Djūdī, in *EI²*, ii, 573-4.

Jug see CUPS AND VESSELS

Jugular Vein see ARTERY AND VEIN

Justice and Injustice

Equitable action according to God's will; action that transgresses God's bounds. One of the key dichotomies in the Qurʾān, it separates divine from human action, moral from immoral behavior (see ETHICS AND THE QURʾĀN). The Qurʾān uses several different words and metaphors to convey this moral balance. *ʿAdl* and *qisṭ* can be used to speak of justice as equitable action but justice can also be defined as correct or truthful action, in which case *ṣidq* or *ḥaqq* may be used. Metaphors (see METAPHOR) such as the balance (*mīzān*, see WEIGHTS AND MEASURES; INSTRUMENTS), inheritance (q.v.) shares *(naṣīb)* and even brotherhood (see BROTHER AND BROTHERHOOD) can describe the underlying principles of justice. The usual word for injustice in the Qurʾān is *ẓulm*, which has the sense of stepping beyond the boundaries of right action (see BOUNDARIES AND PRECEPTS), specifically, a *ẓālim* is one who does wrong to others or to himself. But human injustice can also be expressed in the larger sense of sinning, opposing God, or ascribing partners to God, for which there are many terms, such as *faḥshāʾ* and *baghy* (see SIN, MAJOR AND MINOR; POLYTHEISM AND ATHEISM; DISOBEDIENCE).

In post-qurʾānic Arabic, *ʿadl* became the technical term for justice and the Muʿtazilī theologians were known as *ahlu l-ʿadl wa-l-tawḥīd,* "the people of justice and unity," for their defense of the doctrine of God's essential justice (see MUʿTAZILĪS; THEOLOGY AND THE QURʾĀN). The Qurʾān also uses the term *ʿadl* but relatively rarely (only fourteen times in the sense of justice or equity) and in a much broader fashion. While God's words are described as *ʿadl* in Q 6:115, more common is the use of *ʿadl* or its verbal derivatives to mean equal treatment of wives or disputants (Q 4:3, 58, 129; 5:8; 42:15; 49:9; see WOMEN AND THE QURʾĀN; FAMILY; DEBATE AND DISPUTATION; SOCIAL INTERACTIONS). The qurʾānic range is demonstrated by the use of three synonyms for *ʿadl: qisṭ,* "equity," in the case of just witnesses (Q 5:8; cf. 4:135), *ṣidq,* "truthfulness," in Q 6:115 and *iḥsān,* "good deeds" (q.v.), in Q 16:90. Nowhere in the Qurʾān is God called *al-ʿadl,* although this is often listed as one of his most beautiful names (see GOD AND HIS ATTRIBUTES).

As for the many other qurʾānic terms that may denote justice, most continue the metaphor of symmetry and balance such as the *mīzān* (pl. *mawāzīn),* the "scales of justice," in which good deeds are weighed on the last day (Q 7:8-9; 23:102-3; 101:6-7; see LAST JUDGMENT). But scholars have argued that the idea of justice must be extended to include other metaphors; for instance, Khadduri (*Islamic conception,* 7) sees an abstract principle of equal rights in the declaration that the believers are brothers (Q 49:10). Further, Rahbar (*God of justice,* 231-2) points out that *ḥaqq,* "truth or reality," may also be translated as "justice." So, Q 16:3 *(khalaqa l-samāwāti wa-l-arḍa bi-l-ḥaqq)* should be interpreted as "He created the heavens and the earth with justice." Two of these metaphors are connected in Q 7:8, which reads, "The weighing on that day is just *(wa-l-waznu yawmaʾidhin al-ḥaqq).*" But here Arberry and Rahbar both translate *ḥaqq* as "true" even though al-Bayḍāwī *(Anwār)* and the Jalālayn gloss it as *ʿadl;* al-Qurṭubī *(Jāmiʿ)* regards the whole phrase as a metaphor for justice. The fact that the Arabic could support both readings indicates that the technical differentiation of *ʿadl* and *ḥaqq* is a post-qurʾānic development. Wagner (*La justice,* 13-4) has argued that the absence of a technical term for justice in the Qurʾān allows for a conception of justice which transcends human language.

A similar semantic range is found for injustice. *Jawr,* the technical word for injustice in classical theology, is not found in the Qurʾān; rather, several words are used to convey the sense of injustice. For example, Q 16:90 lists three terms as having a meaning opposite to *ʿadl:* "Surely God bids to justice *(ʿadl),* good deeds and giving to relatives; and he forbids indecency *(al-faḥshāʾ),* disobedience *(al-munkar)* and insolence *(al-baghy).*" Of these words, the first two are mentioned in dozens of other places in the Qurʾān. The last, while less common, is also listed as an antonym to *ʿadl* in Q 49:9. Another word indicative of injustice is *ṭāghūt* (in fourteen places this word, as well as other derivatives of *ṭ-gh-y,* are connected with unbelief, *kufr;* see e.g. Q 2:257; 5:64; see BELIEF AND UNBELIEF; INSOLENCE AND OBSTINACY; IDOLS AND IMAGES); *haḍm* is also placed in apposition to *ẓulm* in Q 20:112.

Ẓulm is most usually a general word for sin or transgression and so is found as a synonym for *zūr,* "falsehood" (see LIE), in Q 25:4 and for *mujrim,* "sinner," in Q 7:40-1 (see also Q 11:116). The transgressor *(ẓālim,* pl. *ẓālimūn)* is referred to over one hundred times. For example, in Q 2:35 Adam and Eve (q.v.) are warned that they will be among the *ẓālimūn* if they transgress God's command not to touch the tree; theft (q.v.; Q 5:38-9; 12:75) and lying (e.g. Q 6:21) also make one a *ẓālim* (Izutsu, *Concepts,* 164-72). But while *ʿadl* is never used in explicit reference to God, *ẓulm* is; in fact, Q 20:112 demonstrates a technical usage of *ẓulm* to refer to God's actions, which are explicitly not unjust (also Q 3:108; 6:131; 11:117). Furthermore, the emphatic form *ẓallām* is only used as a negative description of God; it is found in five exhortations that declare that God is not unjust (e.g. Q 3:182). The common qurʾānic phrase "those who wronged themselves" (*anfusahum yaẓlimūn* in Q 2:57 and nine other places; *ẓalamū anfusahum* in Q 3:117 and five other places; see also *ẓālimun li-nafsihi* in Q 18:35; 35:32; 37:113) almost always refers to ancient peoples who were punished, or will be damned to hell, because they did not recognize God's prophets (see GENERATIONS; PROPHETS AND PROPHETHOOD; PUNISHMENT STORIES; HELL AND HELLFIRE). *Ẓalama nafsahu* in Q 2:231 and 65:1, however, refers to those who do not follow proper divorce proceedings (see MARRIAGE AND DIVORCE). In terms of God, therefore, injustice may be seen as the diametrical opposite of justice but in terms of human behavior, injustice is not a lack of justice as much as it is an active resistance of God's guidance. Q 65:1 specifies: "the one who transgresses the bounds of God has wronged himself" (*wa-man yataʿadda ḥudūda llāhi fa-qad ẓalama nafsahu*).

Interestingly, the very words for just actions also share Arabic roots with metaphors for injustice. So Q 6:150 defines the unbelievers as those who make something else equivalent to their lord (*wa-hum bi-rabbihim yaʿdilūn*, see also Q 6:1, 70). *ʿAdala ʿan* means "to deviate from the right course," and so Lane (v, 1972) understands Q 27:60 as "they are a people who deviate" (*qawmun yaʿdilūn*). Attempts to reconcile these divergent usages in the Qurʾān are attributed to very early sources (see, for instance, the explanation of ʿAbd al-Mālik b. Marwān [d. 86/705] in *Lisān al-ʿArab*, xi, 431-2; partial trans. in Khadduri, *Islamic conception*, 7-8). The *qāsiṭūn* also deviate from the right course in Q 72:14-5, where they are placed in opposition to the *muslimūn*.

Moving from semantics to the broad teachings of the Qurʾān, one can isolate three fields of moral action in terms of justice and injustice: human-human relations; human-divine relations; and God's own activity. As for the first category, specific areas addressed by the Qurʾān include both public and private affairs, such as fair measures in the market (Q 6:152; see MARKETS), fair testimony (Q 4:135; 5:8, 95, 106; 65:2; see WITNESSING AND TESTIFYING; CONTRACTS AND ALLIANCES), just recording of debts (Q 2:282; see DEBT), impartial judgments (Q 4:58; see JUDGMENT) and just treatment of co-wives (Q 4:3, 129; see CONCUBINES) and orphans (q.v.; Q 4:3, 10; 6:152). There are also general injunctions to act and speak in a just manner (Q 5:8; 6:152; 16:90; 49:9). These injunctions are cited extensively in books of Islamic law and works on ethics (see LAW AND THE QURʾĀN). The existence of these exhortations is itself qurʾānic recognition that human beings are unjust to one another, particularly when they are in positions of power (see POWER AND IMPOTENCE; OPPRESSION). Q 4:10 specifically refers to those who consume the assets of orphans unjustly (*ẓulman*) and Q 4:129 simply states: "You will not be able to be equitable (*taʿdilū*) among [your] wives."

God's justice in relationship to his creatures has already been mentioned in metaphors of the scales of justice and the many qurʾānic references to his judgment on the last day. But God also created the heavens (see HEAVEN AND SKY) and the earth (q.v.) with justice (Q 6:73 and eleven other places; see CREATION; COSMOLOGY), and his words of revelation continue that work of justice (Q 6:115; see REVELATION AND INSPIRATION; WORD OF GOD). In fact, God is intimately involved in all human actions "for God in the qurʾānic conception interferes in the minutest details of human affairs" (Izutsu, *Concepts,* 166; see FREEDOM AND PREDESTINATION). Acts among humans, therefore, are not merely in terms of human justice but rather they are to occur within God's bounds *(ḥudūdu llāh).* Further, when speaking of divorce in Q 2:231 and 65:1, the Qurʾān uses language otherwise reserved for judgment day ("he wronged himself," *ẓalama nafsahu*) to describe those who would transgress God's rules.

The third category, God's own characterization as just, is dealt with primarily in terms of his right to judge humankind. The defense of this right is expressed in an account of history repeated throughout the Qurʾān. Not only did God create the heavens and the earth, he asked the souls (see SOUL) of all humankind to testify: "Am I not your lord?" (Q 7:172), thereby establishing his right to judge them, should they begin worshipping idols (SEE IDOLS AND IMAGES). According to the Qurʾān, human beings forgot that covenant (q.v.) and went astray (q.v.), despite the many prophets and warners (see WARNER) sent to remind them. In going astray, of course, they wronged themselves (*ẓalamū anfusahum,* see above). And as for the many peoples whom God destroyed for their wickedness, he would never have done so unjustly (*bi-ẓulm,* Q 6:131 and 11:117). As mentioned above, God's scales for weighing good deeds are just and he will not begrudge anyone *(lā yaẓlimu)* the weight of an ant (Q 4:40). The Qurʾān specifically complains about those who prefer the judgment *(ḥukm)* of the Age of Ignorance (q.v.) to the judgment of God (Q 5:50). The qurʾānic exhortation that believers render justice and be just in their actions, therefore, is part of their acceptance of this cosmology of justice.

Although, as noted above, the Qurʾān does not call God *al-ʿadl,* this epithet is found in lists of God's most beautiful names. In his treatise on these names, al-Ghazālī (d. 505/1111) finds an elegant connection among the various qurʾānic images of justice and God's creative act. In allusion to Q 82:6-7 which reads: "your generous lord who created you and shaped you and wrought you in symmetry (*ʿadalaka,* see BIOLOGY AS THE CREATION AND STAGES OF LIFE)," he writes: "By creating these [bodily] members he is generous, and by placing them in their particular placement he is just.... He suspended the hands and arms from the shoulders, and had he suspended them from the head or the loins or the knees, the imbalance resulting from that would be evident.... What you should know, in short, is that nothing has been created except in the placement intended for it" (Ghazālī, *Names,* 93-4). By focusing on God's intended placement as evidence of his justice, al-Ghazālī both displays his orthodox theology (God's actions define justice, not the reverse) and also the lexical opposition of justice to injustice *(ẓulm),* literally "that which is out of place."

Al-Ghazālī's attempt to reconcile qurʾānic conceptions of justice and injustice is the product of centuries of theological speculation. Already in the years immediately following Muḥammad's death, Muslims witnessed vast examples of human injustice during the civil wars *(fitan)* that tore apart the early Muslim community. Questions naturally arose as to God's role in acts of human injustice. The Khārijīs (q.v.) argued that the grave sinner *(fāsiq)* was no longer a Muslim and must be combated with the sword in this world, while others said that God alone would punish the grave sinner at judgment day. These debates continued to ask whether human and divine acts are separate from one another. Muʿtazilīs began to argue that God was essentially just and therefore bound to do the better, while human beings could commit injustices by acting against God's will. Others understood God's action and human action to be intimately connected, with nothing occurring outside of God's will. As a result, qurʾānic interpreters derived two distinctive notions of justice from the Qurʾān: Muʿtazilīs like al-Zamakhsharī (d. 538/1144) found that "God's justice implies 'human free will'" and their opponents, like al-Bayḍāwī (d. 716/1316-7), maintained "that God's justice lies in his dealing as possessor and Lord, and in making decisions according to his will" (Ibrahim, Concept, 14). Al-Bayḍāwī's position thus closely mirrors that of the Ashʿarīs, who held that God's actions were by definition just.

Islamic law also offers interpretations of qurʾānic justice but does so largely by maintaining a separation between divine and human justice. The classical legal handbooks were organized into two major categories, beginning with duties owed to God *(ʿibādāt),* followed by duties owed to other human beings *(muʿāmalāt).* Such a categorization may have developed from a pseudo-Aristotelian conception of justice (Heffening, Aufbau, 107). Books of legal theory dealt primarily with questions of procedure and interpretation and only rarely with the relationship between divine and human justice. The qurʾānic conception of divine justice as invading all aspects of human interaction played, however, a key role in defining court procedure. At least in theory, the Islamic judge was only to render justice on the basis of the apparent evidence, and was not responsible for the actual truth of a case, since ultimately the plaintiffs were responsible to God (Heffening, Aufbau, 107). This also explains the wide use of oaths (q.v.) in the Islamic court to ascertain the truth of a matter (following the qurʾānic precedent in Q 24:4-9; see BREAKING TRUSTS AND CONTRACTS; CHASTITY). Yet unlike court function in Judaism, court punishments in Islam are not in lieu of eternal punishment. Rather, God reserves the right to exact further justice on the last day (see Q 5:37; 24:19). The legal principles of *istiḥsān* and *maṣlaḥa* have been used by medieval and modern reformers to argue that general qurʾānic injunctions to promote justice may override specific qurʾānic laws. The principle of *istiḥsān* is sometimes based on Q 39:55, "follow the best *(aḥsana)* of that which has been sent down to you" (see also Q 39:18). Likewise, the virtue of equity (*inṣāf,* a word not found in the Qurʾān) in Islamic ethical treatises may be seen as a continuation of principles of equity and justice in the Qurʾān.

The movement from the injustice of the Age of Ignorance *(jāhiliyya)* to the justice of the Muslim community, described in the Qurʾān, has become one of the central teachings of the Islamic religion. This movement is not merely a historical event, played out in the revelation of the Qurʾān to the Prophet but it is also the practical theology of the Qāḍī's court, the motivating force of proselytizers (see INVITATION) and the explanation of God's continued action in this world. This movement will be complete on the last day, when each soul will be rewarded for what it has earned, and there will be no injustice (Q 40:17).

Jonathan E. Brockopp

Bibliography
Primary: Bayḍāwī, *Anwār;* al-Ghazālī, Abū Ḥāmid Muḥammad, *The ninety-nine beautiful names of God,* trans. D. Burrell and N. Daher, Cambridge 1995; Ibn Miskawayh, *The refinement of character,* trans. C.K. Zurayk, Beirut 1968; id., *Tahdhīb al-akhlāq,* ed. C.K. Zurayk, Beirut 1966; *Jalālayn; Lisān al-ʿArab;* Qurṭubī, *Jāmiʿ.*
Secondary: M. Arkoun, Inṣāf, in *EI²,* iii, 1236-7; S. Burkhalter, Completion in continuity. Cosmogony and ethics in Islam, in R. Lovin and F. Reynolds (eds.), *Cosmogony and ethical order,* Chicago 1985, 225-50; van Ess, *TG,* i; L. Gardet, Fāsiḳ, in *EI²,* ii, 833-4; W. Hallaq, *A history of*

Islamic legal theories. An introduction to Sunnī uṣūl al-fiqh, Cambridge 1997; W. Heffening, Zum Aufbau der islamischen Rechtswerke, in W. Heffening and W. Kirfel (eds.), *Studien Geschichte und Kultur des nahen und fernen Ostens. Paul Kahle zum 60. Geburtstag,* Leiden 1935, 101-18; L. Ibrahim, The concept of divine justice according to al-Zamakhsharī and al-Bayḍāwī, in *Hamdard islamicus* 3 (1980), 3-17; Izutsu, *Concepts;* M. Khadduri, *The Islamic conception of justice,* Baltimore 1984; Lane; R. Paret, Istiḥsān and Istiṣlāḥ, in *EI²*, iv, 255-9; D. Rahbar, *God of justice. A study in the ethical doctrine of the Qurʾān,* Leiden 1960; É. Tyan, ʿAdl, in *EI²*, i, 209-10; id., *Histoire de l'organisation judiciaire en pays d'Islam,* Leiden 1960²; G. Wagner, *La justice dans l'ancien testament et le Coran aux niveaux des mariages et des échanges de biens,* Neuchâtel 1977; W.M. Watt, *The formative period of Islamic thought,* Edinburgh 1973; A.J. Wensinck, *The Muslim creed,* Cambridge 1932.

K

Kaʿba

A cube shaped building situated inside the Great Mosque *(al-masjid al-ḥarām)* at Mecca. Although the term *kaʿba* is attested only twice in the Qurʾān (Q 5:95, 97), there are other qurʾānic expressions that have traditionally been understood as designations for this structure (i.e. certain instances of *al-bayt* [lit. "the house," see HOUSE, DOMESTIC AND DIVINE]; as well as of *masjid* [see MOSQUE]). In Islamic tradition, it is often referred to as "the house (or sanctuary) of God" *(bayt Allāh),* and for the vast majority of Muslims it is the most sacred spot on earth. The name Kaʿba is generally explained as indicating its "cubic" or "quadrangular" *(murabbaʿ)* form.

Description

Its ground plan is an irregular oblong, the size of which has been variously stated: a reliable approximation is 40 feet (12 meters) long, 33 feet (10 m.) wide and 50 feet (15 m.) high. Its four corners are aligned approximately north (the "Iraqi" corner), east, south (the "Yemeni" corner) and west. Built into its eastern corner is a large black stone, known as *al-ḥajar al-aswad* or *al-rukn,* which is the object of special veneration when worshippers make the ritual sevenfold circumambulation *(ṭawāf)* around the outside of the Kaʿba (see WORSHIP).

The building has one door, situated towards the eastern end of the northeastern wall and raised about six feet (2 m.) above ground level. It is accessible from steps that are wheeled into place but worship takes place around and outside the Kaʿba. Entry inside, although highly prized, is not a required act, and access to the interior is limited. Adjacent to the northwestern wall is a semi-circular area known as *al-ḥijr,* demarcated by a low wall (sometimes referred to as *al-ḥaṭīm*) that does not quite touch the wall of the Kaʿba. The building is normally enclosed in an ornately decorated covering cloth known as the *kiswa,* which is renewed annually.

The Kaʿba in Islamic practice

The Kaʿba is the focus of the *ḥajj* (major pilgrimage) and the *ʿumra* (minor pilgrimage), in that each begins and ends with the ceremony of circumambulation (see PILGRIMAGE). The *ḥajj,* however, involves the performance of rituals at a distance from the Kaʿba, outside Mecca itself, and the law places a greater importance on some of those rituals — such as the "standing" *(wuqūf)* at ʿArafa (see ʿARAFĀT) and the slaughtering of animals at Minā — than it does upon the circumambulation of the Kaʿba. To miss the *wuqūf* is usually counted as invalidating the *ḥajj,* while the day of slaughtering (10th of Dhū l-Ḥijja; see CALENDAR) is often identified with "the great day of the *ḥajj*" (Q 9:3; see SLAUGHTER). Wellhausen proposed that Muḥammad linked pre-Islamic *ḥajj* ceremonies that had nothing to do with Mecca (q.v.) and the Kaʿba, with those of the *ʿumra,* which were performed in Mecca around the Kaʿba, in order to give the Islamic *ḥajj* a greater association with Mecca.

Muslims must face towards the Kaʿba when performing the obligatory prayers (*ṣalāt,* see PRAYER) and certain other rituals such as the slaughter of animals for consumption or as religious offerings (see CONSECRATION OF ANIMALS; SACRIFICE). The dead are buried facing towards it (see DEATH AND THE DEAD). In other words, the Kaʿba marks the *qibla* (q.v.), the sacred direction that distinguishes Islam from other monotheistic religions. It figures large in traditions about pre-Islamic Arabia (the *jāhiliyya,* see AGE OF IGNORANCE) and the life of the Prophet (see SĪRA AND THE QURʾĀN), and ʿAlī (see ʿALĪ B. ABĪ ṬĀLIB) is sometimes reported to have been born inside it. It features only to a limited extent in Muslim eschatology (q.v.), which centers much more on Jerusalem (q.v.).

The Kaʿba and the Qurʾān

The expression *al-kaʿba* occurs only twice in the Qurʾān (Q 5:95, 97) and commentators naturally identify each as references to the Kaʿba at Mecca. In addition there are many other passages which are understood as alluding to it, using the term *al-bayt* (house or sanctuary), sometimes qualified by an adjective such as "sacred" *(ḥarām),* "ancient" *(ʿatīq)* or "visited" (? *maʿmūr,* Q 52:4).

Q 5:95 occurs in regulations which prohibit the *muḥrim* (a person who has entered the sacral state of *iḥrām* that is obligatory for anyone making *ḥajj* or *ʿumra*) from killing game (see RITUAL PURITY; HUNTING AND FISHING). It lays down that, if a *muḥrim* does intentionally kill a wild animal, he must provide as compensation *(jazāʾ),* from among the animals of the pasture *(al-naʿam),* an equivalent to the animal killed, "as an offering to reach the Kaʿba" *(hadyan bāligha l-kaʿbati).* Q 5:97 tells us that God has made the Kaʿba, the sacred house *(al-kaʿba al-bayt al-ḥarām),* a support (? *qiyām;* commentators debate the precise meaning) for the people, together with the sacred month (see MONTHS), the (animal) offerings *(al-hady)* and the garlands (*al-qalāʾid;* which are placed on the necks of the offerings).

Some of the passages in which "the house" *(al-bayt)* is understood to mean the Kaʿba associate it with Abraham (q.v.) and, slightly less consistently, Ishmael (q.v.). Q 2:125 alludes to God's making "the house" a place of meeting (? *mathāba*) and sanctuary *(amn),* and commanding that Abraham's "standing place" *(maqām Ibrāhīm)* should be a place of prayer. It goes on to refer to God's ordering Abraham and Ishmael, "Purify my house for those who circumambulate, make retreat, bow and prostrate [there]" (*an ṭahhirā baytiya lil-ṭāʾifīna wa-l-ʿākifīna wa-l-rukkaʿi l-sujūdi,* see BOWING AND PROSTRATION). That list of those for whom it is to be purified is repeated with a slight variant in Q 22:26 which recalls that God "prepared"(? *bawwaʾa*) for Abraham the place of the house and commanded him to purify "my house for those who circumambulate, stand, bow and prostrate [there]." Q 2:127 alludes to Abraham and Ishmael "raising the foundations" of the house *(wa-idh yarfaʿu Ibrāhīmu l-qawāʿida mina l-bayti wa-Ismāʿīlu).* These verses are understood as referring to the building or rebuilding of the Kaʿba by

Abraham and Ishmael at God's command (see further below) and Q 3:96, which says that the first house established for humankind was that at Bakka *(inna awwala baytin wuḍiʿa lil-nāsi la-lladhī bi-Bakkata),* is also frequently interpreted as a reference to the origins of the Kaʿba.

Other qurʾānic references to the house associate it with *ḥajj, ʿumra* and animal offerings. Q 3:97 (following the immediately preceding mention of the "first house" at Bakka) states that in it are clear signs — the standing place of Abraham, that those who enter it have security, and that those of humankind who are able have the duty to God of the *ḥajj* of the house *(ḥajju l-bayti).* Q 2:158 assures those who make the *ḥajj* of the house, or *ʿumra,* that there is no harm if they circumambulate al-Ṣafā and al-Marwa (see ṢAFĀ AND MARWA), which are among the signs (q.v.) of God *(inna l-Ṣafā wa-l-Marwata min shaʿāʾiri llāhi).* Al-Ṣafā and al-Marwa are the names given to two small hills outside the "sacred mosque" *(al-masjid al-ḥarām)* in Mecca. Circumambulation of them, or rather passage between them (usually called *saʿy*), is part of the ritual required both for the *ḥajj* and the *ʿumra,* and the commentators explain in various ways why it might have been thought that making *ṭawāf* of them involved "harm."

Q 5:2 includes among a number of things which must not be profaned "those going to the sacred house, seeking merit and pleasure from their lord" *(yabtaghūna faḍlan min rabbihim wa-riḍwānan).* Q 22:29, following a brief setting out of the duty of *ḥajj* in connection with the slaughter and consumption of animals, says that after the food has been eaten those taking part should end their (ritual) dishevelment, fulfil their vows and make circumambulation of the ancient house *(bi-l-bayti l-ʿatīqi).* Q 22:33 indicates that the animals which are to be offered may be used until a certain time, after which they are to be brought to the ancient house (for slaughter).

Q 8:35 makes it clear that those who "disbelieve" also worship at the house, although their prayer *(ṣalāt)* is merely whistling and handclapping *(mukāʾan wa-taṣdiyatan,* see BELIEF AND UNBELIEF; MOCKERY). Q 106:3 urges that Quraysh (q.v.) should worship "the lord of this house" in gratitude for what he has done for them. In Q 52:4 there is an oath, "by the visited (?) house!" *(wa-l-bayti l-maʿmūri,* see OATHS). Sometimes this is understood not as referring to the Kaʿba itself but to its prototype in the highest heaven (see HEAVEN AND SKY), constantly circumambulated by angels (see ANGEL) beneath the throne of God (q.v.).

The frequent qurʾānic expression *al-masjid al-ḥarām* (Q 2:144, 149, 150, 191, 196, 217; 5:2; 8:34; 9:7, 19, 28; 17:1; 22:25; 48:25, 27) also sometimes seems to have the general sense of "sanctuary," just like *bayt,* and in commentary is occasionally equated with the Kaʿba. The most obvious example concerns the so-called *qibla* verses (Q 2:144, 149, 150) in which God orders the believers to turn their faces towards *al-masjid al-ḥarām.* These verses are understood as the revelation that specifies the *qibla* for Muslims. Some commentators argue that the precise direction of the *qibla* is the Kaʿba, or even a particular point of the Kaʿba, and this leads them to read *al-masjid al-ḥarām* here as equivalent to the Kaʿba.

Historically, the mosque containing the Kaʿba in Mecca, known as *al-masjid al-ḥarām,* is reported to have been built only after the death of the Prophet. The traditional scholars assert, however, that in pre-Islamic times the area around the Kaʿba was known as *al-masjid al-ḥarām* even though there was no building so-called. In this way they avoid the apparent anachronism involved in accepting that all of the Qurʾān had been revealed before the death of the Prophet and that its references to *al-masjid al-ḥarām* apply to the same entity that bears that name in Islam, while yet agreeing that the mosque in Mecca post-dates the death of the Prophet.

The Kaʿba in Muslim tradition
Commentary on the above verses is concerned to relate them on the one hand to a large number of traditional stories concerned with the origins of the Meccan Kaʿba and the activity of Abraham in connection with it; and on the other with legal discussions of the *ḥajj*, the *ʿumra* and the rites associated with them (see LAW AND THE QURʾĀN). Thus, the discussions in works of commentary draw on, and are themselves reflected in, many other genres of Islamic literature — stories of the prophets (see PROPHETS AND PROPHETHOOD), law books, local histories of Mecca, traditional biographical material on Muḥammad, and others.

As for its origins and pre-Islamic history, several reports say that the Kaʿba existed before the creation of the world as a sort of froth on the primordial waters from which God made the world. It was the place of worship for Adam (see ADAM AND EVE) after his expulsion from paradise (q.v.; see also FALL OF MAN; GARDEN), compensating him for his loss and allowing him to imitate on earth the circumambulation of the angels around the divine throne in heaven. *Bakka* in Q 3:96 is interpreted as a name of Mecca, various explanations of it being adduced. This "first house" was destroyed in the flood God had sent to punish the people of Noah (q.v.), although its "foundations" (*qawāʿid*, Q 2:127) remained.

Subsequently, in the time of Abraham, God commanded him to go to Mecca to rebuild it. Ishmael was already in Mecca, having previously been taken and left there together with his mother Hagar by Abraham. The father and son then fulfilled God's command. The black stone was revealed to them by an angel and placed in the wall where it is today. It was, say some reports, originally white but it become black because of the sins of the people of the Age of Ignorance *(jāhiliyya)* or, alternatively, as a consequence of the many fires which afflicted the Kaʿba. When the walls became too high for Abraham to reach, he stood on a stone which is often identified as the *maqām Ibrāhīm* ("standing place of Abraham") referred to in Q 2:125. After the building was finished that stone was placed outside the Kaʿba and, although it was subsequently moved around, it is still there near the Kaʿba today. Having completed the work, Abraham then summoned all of humankind, including the generations still unborn, to come to fulfil there the rituals which he himself had been shown by the angel Gabriel (q.v.). Some see the *maqām Ibrāhīm* as a stone on which Abraham stood to deliver this summons.

Prominent in these and other reports about the Kaʿba is the idea of the navel of the earth. The Kaʿba or *bayt* is described as the central point from which the earth was spread out. It is the point of the earth that is directly beneath the divine throne in the highest heaven, and each of the seven heavens has its analogue. Similarly, it stands above the center of the seven spheres beneath the earth. If any one of these *bayt*s were to fall, they would all fall one upon another down to the lowest earth *(ilā tukhūm al-arḍ al-suflā)*. In reports of this type the distinction between the *bayt* and the town of Mecca is often blurred so that Mecca, which is situated in fact in a valley, is sometimes referred to as a hill or mountain *(jabal Makka)*, in accordance with the concept of the navel as a protrusion above the surrounding area. (For further material on this concept, see the article of Wensinck given in the bibliography.)

Having been instituted by Abraham as a

center of monotheism, the Kaʿba was then, over time, corrupted and it came to be the center of the polytheism (see POLYTHEISM AND ATHEISM) and idolatry (*shirk*, see IDOLATRY AND IDOLATERS), which dominated central Arabia in the centuries before the sending of the prophet Muḥammad (see PRE-ISLAMIC ARABIA AND THE QURʾĀN). Some remnants of Abrahamic monotheism survived but idols (see IDOLS AND IMAGES) were installed and worshipped in and around the Kaʿba. Muḥammad's preaching and activities eventually achieved the defeat of Arab paganism and the restoration of the Kaʿba as the sanctuary of the one, true God. It is against this background that the references to the futile *ṣalāt* of the unbelievers at the *bayt* (Q 8:35) and the call for Quraysh to worship "the lord of this house" (Q 106:3) are understood.

Issues involving the law discussed in connection with the qurʾānic verses cited above include whether *ʿumra* has the same obligatory status as *ḥajj* (Q 2:158; 3:97), the nature of the compensation to be offered by the *muḥrim* who has intentionally killed a wild animal (Q 5:95), the precise point of the *qibla* (Q 2:144) and the status of the *ṭawāf* or *saʿy* between al-Ṣafā and al-Marwa (Q 2:158).

A non-traditional perspective

The unanimous traditional view is that the qurʾānic passages discussed above all originated with reference to the Kaʿba at Mecca and that the Meccan Kaʿba before Islam had the same central importance that it afterwards received in Islam. Qurʾānic commentary reflects those two presuppositions (see EXEGESIS OF THE QURʾĀN: CLASSICAL AND MEDIEVAL). The qurʾānic text itself seems neither to substantiate nor disprove them. It may be noted, however, that the expression *al-masjid al-ḥarām* as the name of the place of worship in contention between the believers and unbelievers is much more common and more prominent in the Qurʾān than is *al-kaʿba*, and the traditional identification of *al-masjid al-ḥarām* as a pre-Islamic name for the area around the Meccan Kaʿba may be an attempt at harmonization. It is notable, too, that the sanctuary *(bayt)* associated in the text with Abraham is not explicitly identified there as *al-kaʿba*, apart from the reference in Q 5:97 to *al-kaʿba al-bayt al-ḥarām*, which could incorporate a gloss. The identification of the *bayt* with the Meccan Kaʿba is mainly a product of the literary tradition rather than of the Qurʾān itself. Muslim tradition itself suggests that there were other *kaʿba*s besides the Meccan one and some evidence from outside Muslim tradition suggests a link between the word *kaʿba* and a stele or bethel connected with the worship of Dusares in Nabataean Petra (Ryckmans, Dhu 'l-Sharā; see GEOGRAPHY). There are some grounds, therefore, for hesitation in face of the traditional understandings of the qurʾānic passages. How far one is prepared to question them will largely depend on one's views about the origins of the qurʾānic text and of the Muslim sanctuary at Mecca.

Gerald R. Hawting

Bibliography
Primary: al-Azraqī, Abū l-Walīd Aḥmad b. Muḥammad, *Akhbār Makka*, ed. R. Malḥas, Beirut 1969; al-Fāsī, Abū l-Ṭayyib Muḥammad b. Aḥmad, *Shifāʾ al-gharām bi-akhbār al-balad al-ḥarām*, ed. ʿA. Tadmurī, 2 vols., Beirut 1985; Ibn Isḥāq, *Sīra;* Ibn Isḥāq-Guillaume; Ibn al-Kalbī, *Kitāb al-Aṣnām*, text and German translation in R. Klinke-Rosenberger, *Das Götzenbuch*, Leipzig 1941; Eng. trans. N.A. Faris, *The book of idols*, Princeton 1952; Ṭabarī, *Tafsīr* (on the verses referred to in the article); al-Ṭabarī, Muḥibb al-Dīn, *al-Qirā*, ed. M. al-Saqqā, Cairo 1970².
Secondary: T. Fahd, *Le panthéon de l'Arabie centrale à la veille de l'hégire*, Paris 1968, esp. 203-36; M. Gaudefroy-Demombynes, *Le pèlerinage à la*

Mekke, Paris 1923; G.E. von Grunebaum, *Muhammadan festivals,* New York 1951, chapter 2; G.R. Hawting, The origins of the Muslim sanctuary at Mecca, in G.H.A. Juynboll (ed.), *Studies in the first century of Islamic society,* Carbondale and Edwardsville 1982; J.H. Mordtmann, Dusares bei Epiphanius, in ZDMG 29 (1876), 99-106; U. Rubin, The Kaʿba. Aspects of its ritual functions, in JSAI 8 (1986), 97-131; G. Ryckmans, Dhu 'l-Sharā, in EI[2], ii, 246-7; J. Wellhausen, *Reste arabischen Heidentums,* Berlin 1897[2]; A.J. Wensinck, The ideas of western Semites concerning the navel of the earth, in *Verhandelingen der Koninklijke Akademie van Wetenschappen te Amsterdam, Afdeeling Letterkunde, Nieuwe Reeks,* deel 17 (1916), no. 1, repr. in *Studies of A.J. Wensinck,* New York 1978; A.J. Wensinck/ J. Jomier, Kaʿba, in EI[2], iv, 317-22; A.J. Wensinck/ D. King, Ḳibla, in EI[2], v, 82-8.

Kāhin see SOOTHSAYERS

Kalām see WORD OF GOD; THEOLOGY AND THE QURʾĀN; SPEECH

Keys see INSTRUMENTS; HIDDEN AND THE HIDDEN

Khadīja

Khadīja bint al-Khuwaylid of the clan of Asad of the tribe of Quraysh (q.v.) was the Prophet's first wife, mother of all his children except one, and the first to believe in his mission. Inasmuch as she died three years before the emigration (q.v.; *hijra*) to Medina, and the revelations specifically addressed to the members of the Prophet's household (see FAMILY OF THE PROPHET; PEOPLE OF THE HOUSE; REVELATION AND INSPIRATION; OCCASIONS OF REVELATION) were vouchsafed in Medina (q.v.), Khadīja's name appears rarely in the exegetical literature (see EXEGESIS OF THE QURʾĀN: CLASSICAL AND MEDIEVAL). Her role in the genres of biographies of Muḥammad (*sīra,* see SĪRA AND THE QURʾĀN) and "stories of the prophets" (*qiṣaṣ al-anbiyāʾ,* see PROPHETS AND PROPHETHOOD) works, as well as in popular piety, however, has been immense.

Khadīja was an aristocratic, wealthy Meccan merchant woman who in two previous marriages had given birth to two sons and a daughter. As a widow, she obtained Muḥammad's services as steward of her merchandise in a Syrian trading venture, during which a young boy of her household named Maysara is said to have witnessed several miracles that foretold Muḥammad's rise to prophethood. The venture was a commercial success and, impressed by Muḥammad's good character and trustworthiness, Khadīja offered him marriage. Traditional sources indicate that the marriage proposal was extended by Muḥammad and his uncle Ḥamza b. ʿAbd al-Muṭṭalib (q.v.) to Khadīja's father Khuwaylid b. Asad (Ibn Isḥāq-Guillaume, 82-3) or it was her uncle ʿAmr b. Asad who married her to the Prophet (Ibn Saʿd, i, 132-3). Most traditions place Muḥammad's age at that time at twenty-five and Khadīja's at forty. She bore her husband at least five children: four daughters (Zaynab, Umm Kulthūm, Fāṭima, Ruqayya) and one or possibly two sons (al-Qāsim, ʿAbdallāh; who, however, may be the same, while al-Ṭāhir and al-Ṭayyib are generally taken to be epithets of ʿAbdallāh; Ibn Isḥāq-Guillaume, 82-3). Khadīja's material, emotional, and spiritual support were crucial to the success of Muḥammad's mission. The exegetical literature on the Qurʾān generally links Q 93:8, "did he not find you needy and enrich you" with their marriage (see POVERTY AND THE POOR). Khadīja reported Muḥammad's first miraculous experiences and especially his call to prophethood to her Christian cousin Waraqa b. Nawfal who likened the event to Moses' (q.v.) receiving of the law (Ibn Isḥāq-Guillaume, 83, 107; see TORAH; COMMANDMENTS; there is also speculation that this Waraqa may have furnished Muḥammad with details of Christian belief; cf. Sprenger, *Leben,* i, 124-34; see INFORMANTS; CHRISTIANS AND CHRISTIANITY). According to many traditions (see ḤADĪTH AND THE QURʾĀN), she was the first to believe in God, his apostle (see MESSENGER), and the truth of the message, meaning that she was the Prophet's first follower and, after Muḥammad himself, the second Muslim. According to others his cousin ʿAlī b. Abī Ṭālib (q.v.) was the second Muslim and Khadīja the third (see FAITH; BELIEF AND UNBELIEF; COMPANIONS OF THE PROPHET). During her lifetime, she remained the Prophet's only wife (see WIVES OF THE PROPHET; MARRIAGE AND DIVORCE) and his mainstay in the battles against his Meccan enemies (Ibn Isḥāq-Guillaume, 111-14; see OPPOSITION TO MUḤAMMAD).

Khadīja's rank among God's chosen women, indeed her cosmological importance, is established in the exegetical literature on Q 66:11-2 and 3:42 (see WOMEN AND THE QURʾĀN). In the context of Q 66:11-2, she is placed in association with Pharaoh's (q.v.) wife (Āsya) and Mary (q.v.) the daughter of ʿImrān (q.v.; the mother of Jesus, q.v.), both examples to those who believe, because of her great service to the Prophet's mission. Regarding Q 3:42, the angels' words to Mary that God had chosen her above the women of the worlds, Khadīja's name appears prominently in the exegetical debate on Mary's ranking both among the qurʾānic women figures and also in relation to three selected elite women of the Prophet's household, i.e. Khadīja herself, Muḥammad's later wife ʿĀʾisha (see ʿĀʾISHA BINT ABĪ BAKR), and his and Khadīja's daughter Fāṭima (q.v.). Here, the larger number of traditions recorded in exegetical *(tafsīr)* and *qiṣaṣ al-anbiyāʾ* literature establish on the authority of the Prophet that Mary and Fāṭima, Khadīja and Āsya are the best women of the world and the ruling females in heaven (see HEAVEN AND SKY). While the traditions on ʿĀʾisha's inclusion in this group are fewer in number, many hagiographic accounts affirm that Mary and Āsya, Khadīja and ʿĀʾisha will all be Muḥammad's consorts in paradise (q.v.), where Khadīja's heavenly mansion is located between the houses of Mary and Āsya (Ṭabarī, *Tafsīr,* vi, 393-400; Rāzī, *Tafsīr,* viii, 45-6; Bayḍāwī, *Anwār,* i, 155; Ibn Kathīr, *Qiṣaṣ,* ii, 375-83.)

Barbara Freyer Stowasser

Bibliography
Primary: Bayḍāwī, *Anwār;* Ibn Isḥāq-Guillaume; Ibn Kathīr, *Qiṣaṣ al-anbiyāʾ,* Cairo 1968; Ibn Saʿd, *Ṭabaqāt,* Beirut 1957-8, i, 131-4, 156-7; viii, 14-9; Rāzī, *Tafsīr,* ed. M. Muḥyī l-Dīn; Ṭabarī, *Tafsīr,* ed. Shākir.
Secondary: Syed A.A. Razwy, *Khadija-tul-Kubra,* Elmhurst 1990; A. Sprenger, *Das Leben und die Lehre des Moḥammad,* 3 vols., Berlin 1869², i, 81, 124-34 (on Waraqa b. Nawfal); B. Freyer Stowasser, *Women in the Qurʾān, traditions, and interpretation,* New York 1994 (index); W.M. Watt, *Muḥammad at Mecca,* Oxford 1953; id., *Muḥammad at Medina,* Oxford 1956 (indices).

Khaḍir/Khiḍr

Islamic tradition identifies as al-Khaḍir (or Khiḍr), an otherwise unnamed "servant (q.v.) of God" who appears in Sūrat al-Kahf ("The Cave"; Q 18:60-82), in connection with Moses' (q.v.) quest for the "confluence of the two seas" (see BARRIER; NATURE AS SIGNS). Interpretations run a wide gamut. Al-Zamakhsharī (d. 538/1144; *Kashshāf,* ii, 703) asserts that Khiḍr lived from the time of Dhū l-Qarnayn (see ALEXANDER) to that of Moses; Sayyid Quṭb (d. 1966; *Ẓilāl,* iv, 2276-82) sets that tradition aside, calling him only "the righteous servant." Moses and an unnamed companion (traditionally, Joshua son of Nūn) set out carrying a fish for food; mysteriously coming to life, the fish escapes into the sea. According to a ḥadīth cited by many exegetes (e.g. Ibn al-Jawzī, *Zād,* v, 119; see ḤADĪTH AND THE QURʾĀN) to explain the context of the journey, Moses rises to address the Children of Israel (q.v.) and someone asks him who is the most learned among them. When Moses answers that he himself is, God reveals that one yet more learned awaits Moses at the confluence of the two seas. Al-Ṭabarī (d. 310/923; *Tafsīr,* viii, 251) adds that Khiḍr is also the most beloved and most firmly decisive.

The qurʾānic account, enhanced with certain exegetical details, continues as follows: God then tells Moses that he will meet this most learned servant at the place where his fish escapes. But Joshua fails to tell Moses that he has lost the fish so the two must retrace their steps to the spot where Khiḍr awaits. Moses asks Khiḍr to teach him what he knows, but Khiḍr warns that Moses will not have the patience to bear with him. Moses insists he will be a good student, agreeing not to question Khiḍr's actions. The travelers embark on a ship, which Khiḍr proceeds to scuttle (see SHIPS). Moses inquires how he could do such a thing, and Khiḍr warns the Prophet. Later as they walk along the shore, Khiḍr spots some boys playing and kills one of them summarily. Moses again confronts Khiḍr. Further along they come to a town whose inhabitants refuse to feed the hungry travelers. Nevertheless, Khiḍr repairs a portion of a wall on the point of collapsing. Again Moses takes exception, and that is the last straw: Khiḍr decides to explain his actions, but from then on Moses is on his own. Khiḍr had scuttled the boat to prevent a wicked king from commandeering it for evil purposes; he had killed the boy lest the child grieve his good parents by a wayward life; and he had rebuilt the wall so that the treasure that lay beneath would be safe until the two orphaned sons of the wall's owner could reach their majority and thus claim their inheritance (see ORPHANS; GUARDIANSHIP; INHERITANCE).

Exegetes discuss such questions as the origin of the guide's name, the identity of the seas, the nature of Khiḍr's learning, and his spiritual status. He got the name Khiḍr, "green," because, according to a ḥadīth cited by several exegetes (e.g. Qurṭubī, *Jāmiʿ,* xi, 12; Ibn Kathīr, *Tafsīr,* iii, 105), whenever he prayed, everything around him waxed verdant. Exegetes generally agree that Khiḍr's divinely infused knowledge was esoteric, whereas that of Moses was more exoteric (e.g. Abū Ḥayyān, *Baḥr,* vi, 139; see KNOWLEDGE AND LEARNING). Al-Ṭabarī (*Tafsīr,* viii, 251) among others suggests the two seas were the Persian in the east and the Greek in the west (see GEOGRAPHY). But of equal importance is the metaphorical view that Moses and Khiḍr were themselves the two "seas" since they both possessed oceans of knowledge, albeit of different kinds (Abū Ḥayyān, *Baḥr,* vi, 136; Zamakhsharī, *Kashshāf,* ii, 703; see METAPHOR). Many interpreters call Khiḍr a prophet, arguing that only prophetic revelation *(waḥy)* could account for his bizarre actions and that a ranking prophet like Moses would surely follow only a figure of greater stature (see PROPHETS AND PROPHETHOOD; REVELATION AND INSPIRATION). Various exegetes gloss "mercy" (q.v.; Q 18:65) as *waḥy* or *nubūwwa* (Zamakhsharī, *Kashshāf,* ii, 705; Nasafī, *Tafsīr,* iii, 34). Ibn al-ʿArabī (d. 543/1148; *Aḥkām,* iii, 241) notes that the conditions Khiḍr imposed on Moses are understandable in that all Muslims must accept certain conditions in following the prophets. Muḥyī al-Dīn b. al-ʿArabī (d. 638/1240;

Fuṣūṣ, 202-5) parallels Khiḍr's actions with events in Moses' life: the scuttling of the ship with the infant Moses' rescue from the Nile, Khiḍr's murder of the boy with Moses' killing the Copt, and Khiḍr's not asking recompense for rebuilding the crumbling wall with Moses' drawing water at Midian (q.v.) without remuneration.

Khiḍr also appears in the various major versions of the "stories of the prophets" *(qiṣaṣ al-anbiyā᾿)* genre. These accounts have a sort of "midrashic" quality, spinning a narrative to fill in the gaps in the scriptural text (Kisā᾿ī), sometimes speculating on such details as the precise location of events and identities of individuals in the stories (Thaʿlabī). An extra-qur᾿ānic aspect of the Khiḍr legend is the story of his search for the water (q.v.) of life (q.v.), so that Khiḍr comes to share the immortality of Jesus (q.v.), Idrīs (q.v.) and Ilyās (see ELIJAH). Khiḍr's arrival at the spring (see SPRINGS AND FOUNTAINS) is naturally associated with his power to affect the spiritual "greening" of humankind. Ibn Kathīr (d. 774/1373; *Qiṣaṣ,* 342) intertwines Khiḍr's story with that of Ilyās and calls the two "brothers" (see BROTHER AND BROTHERHOOD).

The early exegete Muqātil b. Sulaymān (d. 150/767) explains Khiḍr's link with Ilyās etymologically. As the one person with greater knowledge than Moses, Khiḍr's learning was "expansive, all inclusive," from *wasaʿa,* "to be wide," which Muqātil claims is from the same root (see ARABIC LANGUAGE) as the name Ilyās. Muqātil has Moses find Khiḍr dressed in wool, whereupon Khiḍr recognizes Moses as prophet of Israel (q.v.). According to Muqātil, Khiḍr's knowledge exceeds that of Moses because God has given diverse gifts to various prophets — not, as others have said, because Khiḍr was a saint and therefore superior to a prophet in esoteric knowledge (Muqātil, *Tafsīr,* ii, 592-9). An editor later attached a ḥadīth to Muqātil's commentary, according to which Khiḍr is a *walī* (saint) whose knowledge comes through virtue (see ṢŪFISM AND THE QUR᾿ĀN). Moses asks Khiḍr how he came to be gifted with immortality (see DEATH AND THE DEAD; ETERNITY), endowed with the ability to read hearts (see HEART) and see with God's eye (see ANTHROPOMORPHISM). Khiḍr responds that it is because he has obeyed God perfectly and neither fears nor hopes in any but God (Nwyia, *Exégèse,* 88-90; see FEAR; OBEDIENCE; HOPE). Al-Sarrāj (d. 378/988; *Lumaʿ,* 422-4) corrects the mistaken notion that *wilāya* (sainthood) is superior to *risāla* (being a messenger of God), a misinterpretation of Q 18:64 f. Moses' illumination far outstrips any that Khiḍr could have sustained.

Khiḍr's ongoing spiritual function becomes an important issue for certain Ṣūfī orders in particular, who regarded Khiḍr as an initiating *shaykh.* Muḥyī al-Dīn b. al-ʿArabī says he first met Khiḍr in Seville and received the Ṣūfī patched frock *(khirqa)* from him and calls him the fourth pillar along with Jesus, Idrīs, and Ilyās in the celestial hierarchy of initiation (Addas, *Red sulphur,* 62-5, 116-7, 144-5). Muḥammad b. ʿAbdallāh b. al-ʿArabī (d. 543/1148) observes that "anyone who wants to know without doubt that power and aid belong only to God must sail the sea," taking the ship Khiḍr scuttled as a symbol of spiritual poverty (*Aḥkām,* iii, 242; see POVERTY AND THE POOR). Jalāl al-Dīn al-Rūmī (d. 672/1273; *Dīwān,* poems 2521:10, 408:1-2) takes the metaphor further, identifying the ship as the body of the Ṣūfī that must be broken and purified by Khiḍr's love. Finally, Abū Ḥayyān (d. 745/1344; *Baḥr,* vi, 139) suggests the purpose of the whole story is guidance and incentive to travel on the search for knowledge (see JOURNEY), and instruction on the etiquette of the quest.

John Renard

Bibliography
Primary: Abū Ḥayyān, *Baḥr,* Beirut 1993, vi, 133-48; Ibn al-ʿArabī, *Aḥkām,* iii, 236-42; Ibn al-ʿArabī, Muḥyī al-Dīn, *The bezels of wisdom,* trans. R.W.J. Austin, New York 1980, 256-60 (trans. of *Fuṣūṣ al-ḥikam*); id., *Fuṣūṣ al-ḥikam,* ed. A. ʿAfīfī, Cairo 1946, 202-13, 302-5 (ʿAfīfī's commentary); Ibn al-Jawzī, *Zād,* Beirut 1994, v, 119-35; Ibn Kathīr, *Qiṣaṣ al-anbiyāʾ,* Beirut 1997, 336-50; id., *Tafsīr,* Beirut 1996, iii, 96-105; Jalāl al-Dīn Rūmī, *Kulliyāt-i dīvān-i shams,* ed. B. Furuzanfar, Tehran 1970; Kisāʾī, *Qiṣaṣ,* 230-3; id., *The tales of the prophets of al-Kisaʾi,* trans. W.M. Thackston, Boston 1978, 247-50; Muqātil, *Tafsīr;* Nasafī, *Tafsīr,* Beirut 1996, iii, 33-9; Niẓām al-Dīn Awliyāʾ, *Morals for the heart,* trans. B. Lawrence, Mahwah, NJ 1992; Qurṭubī, *Jāmiʿ,* 21 vols., Beirut 1996[5], xi, 8-31; Quṭb, *Ẓilāl,* iv, 2276-82; al-Sarrāj, Abū Naṣr ʿAbdallāh b. ʿAlī, *Kitāb al-Lumaʿ,* ed. R.A. Nicholson, London 1963; Ṭabarī, *Tafsīr,* 12 vols., Beirut 1992, viii, 251-70; Thaʿlabī, *Qiṣaṣ,* 192-204; Zamakhsharī, *Kashshāf,* ii, 702-14.
Secondary: C. Addas, *Quest for the red sulphur,* Cambridge 1993; I. Friedlaender, *Die Chadirlegende und der Alexanderroman,* Leipzig 1913; Nwyia, *Exégèse;* J. Renard, *All the king's falcons. Rumi on prophets and revelation,* New York 1994; A.J. Wensinck, al-Khaḍir, in EI[2], iv, 902-5 (EI[1], iv, 861-5).

Khalīl

see ABRAHAM; FRIENDS AND FRIENDSHIP

Khārijīs

The strongest opposition party in early Islam, their name (Ar. *khārijī,* pl. *khawārij*) is derived from the Arabic triliteral root *kh-r-j,* which has as its basic meaning "to go out," "to take the field against someone" and "to rise in revolt" (Ṭabarī, *Taʾrīkh,* ii, 32; trans. Morony, 37; see FIGHTING; JIHĀD). In the case in point, it means "to secede from the community." Although forms of *kh-r-j* appear numerous times in the Qurʾān with varied meanings, the group in question took its name from the usage in Q 9:46, where the root *kh-r-j,* denoting "to go out to combat," is opposed to the verb *qaʿada,* which denotes people who held back from the war (q.v.; see EXPEDITIONS AND BATTLES). The earliest Khārijīs were those who withdrew from ʿAlī b. Abī Ṭālib's (q.v.) army when he agreed to the arbitration (q.v.) at the battle of Ṣiffīn in 37/657 (see POLITICS AND THE QURʾĀN). Another name given to these first Khārijīs is al-Shurāt (lit. "the vendors") — meaning those who have sold their soul for the cause of God. This appears to have been the name they themselves used, and it has also been extended to their descendants (cf. Levi Della Vida, Khāridjites; Higgins, *Qurʾānic exchange*).

Early traditions state that a breeding-ground for the Khārijīs could be found among the Qurʾān readers (see RECITERS OF THE QURʾĀN), who displayed extreme piety (q.v.) and asceticism (q.v.). The earliest Khārijīs, just like the Arabs (q.v.) of Kūfa and Baṣra, were all bedouins (see BEDOUIN), who had migrated to the garrison cities (see CITY). In this respect there is little distinguishing information to provide other than that they were much less concerned with the system of genealogy based on kinship (q.v.). As a consequence of this stance, their doctrines had enormous appeal for minority groups within the newly emerging Islamic community (see HERESY; THEOLOGY AND THE QURʾĀN).

The earliest of ʿAlī's opponents were called Ḥarūrīs, from Ḥarūrāʾ, the place in which some twelve thousand men had gathered, those who, in protest against the arbitration, had seceded as ʿAlī entered Kūfa in Rabīʿ I 37/Aug.-Sept. 658, after the conclusion of the arbitration agreement. Also among them were many who had initially accepted the arbitration but now acknowledged their mistake and no longer recognized ʿAlī as their leader. Their oath of allegiance was to God on the basis of "ordering what is good and prohibiting what is reprehensible" (on this concept, see M. Cook, *Commanding right;* see also GOOD AND EVIL; LAWFUL AND UNLAW-

FUL; ETHICS AND THE QUR'ĀN; VIRTUES AND VICES, COMMANDING AND FORBIDDING). The Ḥarūrīs were initially secessionists, not rebels. They wished to secede from the community to protect their principles. They were also called Muḥakkima from their motto "No judgment (q.v.) but God's" *(lā ḥukma illā li-llāh)*. They accused those who supported the arbitration of having acted contemptibly toward God by appointing human arbitrators. People who shouted *"lā ḥukma illā li-llāh"* at the battle of Ṣiffīn most likely meant that ʿUthmān (q.v.) had broken God's law as revealed in the Qurʾān (see LAW AND THE QURʾĀN) and was therefore worthy of death, and not that the question between ʿAlī and Muʿāwiya should be left to the "arbitrament of war" (Watt, Kharijite thought, 217-8). They also held that Muʿāwiya was a rebel and that according to Q 49:9, rebels are outlaws who should be fought until they repent (see REBELLION; REPENTANCE AND PENANCE). Arbitration was thus a mistake because no one had the right to substitute a human decision for God's clear pronouncement (Barradī, *Jawāhir*, 120).

The rupture among ʿAlī's followers proved serious since it brought a wider dogmatic schism to the fore. The Khārijīs objected to the concept of personal alliance to the imām (q.v.). In their view, allegiance should be bound not to a particular person (see COMMUNITY AND SOCIETY IN THE QURʾĀN), but to the Qurʾān and the sunna (q.v.) of the Prophet, Abū Bakr (q.v.) and ʿUmar (q.v.). They denied that the right to the imāmate should be based on close kinship with Muḥammad (see SHĪʿISM AND THE QURʾĀN), for that was irrelevant in their eyes. These differences found military expression when the Khārijīs from Kūfa and Baṣra assembled in Nahrawān. After calling for a resumption of the war with Muʿāwiya, who had been acknowledged by some as caliph (q.v.) before the end of Dhū l-Qaʿda 37/April-May 658 (Hinds, Muʿawiya, 265), ʿAlī invited them to join him and to fight their common enemy. Faced with their refusal, ʿAlī decided to deal with it before carrying out his campaign to Syria (q.v.). The Khārijīs fought desperately but they were outnumbered by ʿAlī's followers and the battle turned into a one-sided massacre. The battle of Nahrawān (9 Ṣafar 38/17 July 658) set the seal on the division between Shīʿa (q.v.) and Khārijīs, and made the Khārijīs' split with the community irreparable.

Khārijī revolts

During the Umayyad period, several Khārijī revolts broke out in various Muslim lands, causing the caliphate to suffer material damage as well as a blow to its pride. Large sections of territory were removed from its administration. The Azāriqa, one of the main branches of the Khārijīs, threatened Baṣra, while other Khārijī groups who emerged from the region of Mawṣil (i.e. the high Tigris country between Mārdīn and Niṣībīn) endangered Kūfa (cf. Levi Della Vida, Khāridjites, 1075-6). The chief persecutors of the Khārijīs were the governors of Iraq, Ziyād b. Abīhi (d. 53/673) and his son ʿUbayd Allāh, who became governor there in the year 55/674. They proceeded against the Khārijīs with harsh measures and killed and imprisoned many of them. As the Umayyad caliphate began to collapse, the Khārijīs turned into a revolutionary movement. The small numbers of troops, which had previously characterized the Khārijī armies, swelled to powerful masses. During this late Umayyad period, the revolts of the Ibāḍīs, a moderate branch of the Khārijīs (who spread to the Maghrib, the Ḥaḍramawt and ʿUmān) constituted a greater menace to the caliphate than did the Azāriqī uprisings (cf. Lewicki, al-Ibāḍiyya, 650). After occupying the Ḥaḍramawt and Ṣanʿāʾ, the capital of southern Arabia, in 129/746-47, the Ibāḍi army, under the command of Abū Ḥamza, took Mecca (q.v.) and Medina (q.v.). Abū Ḥamza was a skilled soldier, but also a scholar and a preacher who gave sermons from the Prophet's pulpit (see MOSQUE) that have been preserved in the Arabic chronicles (Darjīnī, *Ṭabaqāt*, ii, 266-72). The Ibāḍīs were defeated and, for the most part, massacred in the middle of Jumādā I 130/January 748. The Umayyad army reconquered Medina and then Mecca but were forced to conclude a peace treaty with the Ibāḍīs of the Ḥaḍramawt.

The Khārijī revolts continued after the ascension of the ʿAbbāsids. The Ibāḍīs and the Ṣufrites, another moderate branch of Khārijism, succeeded in establishing their rule in the Maghrib. Again in ʿUmān, the Ibāḍīs had some success in a revolt about 132/750. Towards the second half of the second/eighth century they rose up again and recommenced their activities in the region creating an imāmate, which continued to exist almost without interruption for over 1200 years. There were revolts in other regions that were successful for some years and then died down. In various districts around Mawṣil, in northern Iraq, sixteen revolts have been recorded in the years between the middle of the second/eighth and the middle of the fourth/tenth century; Sijistān and southern Khurāsān also witnessed Khārijī revolts.

Khārijī sects

The weakness of the Khārijī movement lay in its incapacity to preserve both religious and political unity. A number of schisms *(iftirāq)* resulting from dogmatic disputes as well as from political crises culminated in the formation of several theological and political subdivisions *(firqa)*. Some of the Khārijīs adopted political quietism and moderation, while others took to activism and extremism. The extremists followed Nāfiʿ b. al-Azraq or Ḥanẓala b. Bayhas. The Azāriqa (who met a violent end in Ṭabarīstan in 78-9/698-9) upheld the *istiʿrāḍ* (the indiscriminate killing of the non-Khārijī Muslims, including their children), submitted new recruits to a severe inquisition, disregarded the practice of the dissimulation (q.v.; *taqiyya*) of one's real belief, considered unbelief a grave sin and insisted on the eternal punishment for the grave sinner (see BELIEF AND UNBELIEF; SIN, MAJOR AND MINOR; ETERNITY). The Bayhasiyya were as fierce as the Azāriqa in that they approved of the killing of non-Khārijī Muslims and the taking of their goods (see BOOTY). The followers of Najda b. ʿĀmir represented a milder tendency. The Najadāt permitted dissimulation *(taqiyya)* and quietism, as they did not expect everyone to join with them in the fight against the unbelievers. Another branch of the Khārijīs were the ʿAjārida, who stem from ʿAbd al-Karīm b. ʿAjarrad. They insisted on the supremacy of divine law and on the upright conduct of individuals.

The most moderate branch of the Khārijīs — and today the only survivors — were the Ibāḍīs. They appeared in Baṣra in 65/684-5, when ʿAbdallāh b. Ibāḍ broke away from the Khārijī extremists over which attitude was to be adopted towards other Muslims and joined a group of quietists who had gathered around Abū Bilāl Mirdās b. Udayya al-Tamīmī. During the first half of the second/eighth century, Ibāḍism began to undergo a profound change: from being part of the Khārijī sect, it became an autonomous movement with a defined membership, doctrine and organized missionary activities. At present, Ibāḍīs form the main part of the population in the oases of Mzāb in Algeria, of Zawāra and Jebel Naffūsa in Tripolitania, on the island of Jerba in Tunisia and in

ʿUmān, while small groups are also found on the island of Zanzibar. Another moderate branch of the Khārijīs were the Ṣufriyya, whose teachings spread among the remote Berber tribes of the western Maghrib.

Khārijī doctrine

The Khārijīs made important contributions to Islamic thought, and to the formation of Islamic culture. A considerable amount of historical and theological material has been preserved by the Ibāḍīs (for a discussion of Ibāḍī exegesis of the Qurʾān, see Gilliot, Le commentaire coranique de Hūd b. Muḥakkam), but apart from this Ibāḍī material, the only source for the Khārijī thought is the Sunnī historical and heresiographical tradition. The religion of the Khārijīs had as its aim paradise (q.v.). They did not think of victory (q.v.) on earth (q.v.). They wished to save their souls (see SOUL) by fighting the impious with a total lack of consideration for themselves and others (see SALVATION). The core of the theological teaching of the Khārijīs was the conception of a righteous God who demands righteousness from his subjects (see JUSTICE AND INJUSTICE). Indeed, the earliest Khārijite propositions attempted to place the believer in a direct relationship to God. Khārijism attached great importance to religious principles that stressed the responsibility of the individual, such as the obligation of "promoting good and preventing evil" and the conception of the relationship between works and faith (q.v.). Anyone who committed a capital sin, failed to obey the divine law (see OBEDIENCE) or introduced innovations (see INNOVATION) was an infidel and was to be combated as long as he remained dissident. Moreover, if there were no repentance, the transgressor would be condemned to eternal punishment in hell (see REWARD AND PUNISHMENT; HELL AND HELLFIRE). This doctrine was used to support the Khārijī view that the killers of ʿUthmān could be justified in their act, and, for the Azāriqa, it became the theological basis for their action.

The obvious corollary of the doctrine of human responsibility was the doctrine of divine decree (*qadar*, see FREEDOM AND PREDESTINATION). Al-Ashʿarī (d. 324/935-6; *Maqālāt*, 93, 96, 104, 116) mentions some Khārijī groups that agreed with the Muʿtazila (see MUʿTAZILĪS) in affirming human free will, but the general attitude of the Khārijīs supported the doctrine of predestination. The debate on *qadar* emerged in the Ibāḍī community during the imāmate of Abū ʿUbayda (first half of the second/eighth century), who was conscious of the danger to the community of carrying rational argument and disputation too far (see DEBATE AND DISPUTATION). He fiercely opposed ʿAbdallāh b. Yazīd al-Fazārī for his rigidly rational reasoning and expelled Ḥamza al-Kūfī (cf. van Ess, *TG*, ii, 203-4) and ʿAṭiyya (cf. van Ess, *TG*, iv, 204), suspected to be followers of Ghaylān al-Dimashqī (cf. van Ess, *TG*, i, 73-5). According to Abū ʿUbayda, God is all-powerful and all-knowing (see GOD AND HIS ATTRIBUTES); he knows people's acts but he does not determine them. Thus the individual is responsible for his or her actions and will be judged for them (Darjīnī, *Ṭabaqāt*, ii, 233; Shammākhī, *Siyar*, 84-5; see LAST JUDGMENT; RECORD OF HUMAN ACTIONS). The Khārijī theological doctrine shared a number of features with Muʿtazilī theology as a result of a parallel development, since the center of Ibāḍism was still Baṣra at the time when the founders of Muʿtazilism were active there (Moreno, *Note*, 312-3). Khārijīs and Muʿtazilīs used the same arguments, often borrowed from each other, to substantiate their doctrines. In general, the dogma of the Khārijīs resembled certain main points made by the Muʿtazilīs, as in the case of the doctrine of anti-anthropomorphism (see ANTHROPOMORPHISM) and the theory of the createdness of the Qurʾān (q.v.). This latter doctrine was well established among the early Ibāḍīs in the Maghrib, as shown by a treatise in which the Rustamid imām Abū al-Yaqẓān (r. 241-81/855-94) quotes early Ibāḍī scholars (Cremonesi, *Un antico documento,* 148 f.) on the matter. In ʿUmān, the doctrine was first introduced only at the beginning of the third/ninth century, though it was opposed until the sixth/twelfth century.

The question of the imāmate was central for the Khārijī movement, together with the related question of membership in the community, which depended on the acceptance of its specific doctrines. It was on this latter question that the movement split into various sects over minor differences. The Khārijīs were not anarchists: they upheld the necessity of an imām, but rejected imāms such as ʿUthmān, ʿAlī and Muʿāwiya, insisting upon the personal qualities of the imām and his duty to enjoin good and forbid evil. They held that the limitation of the imāmate to the Quraysh (q.v.) was not valid: the most meritorious Muslim should be elected whatever his ethnic origins might be. In other words, for the Khārijīs, personal merits overruled considerations of descent. In their view, leadership stems from personal excellence, and the confidence that the community placed in its imām constitutes his authority (q.v.). When an imām commits major sins, his followers should not immediately dissociate themselves from him *(al-barāʾa ʿanhu),* but call him to formal repentance (cf. Rubinacci, Barāʾa, 1027-8). If he repents, and does not continue in his errors, then he retains his imāmate; if he does not, then it is the duty of his followers to dissociate themselves from him and, if necessary, fight him. The Khārijīs supported the principle that any Muslim could be elevated to the supreme dignity of the imāmate, even if he were "an Abyssinian slave whose nose has been cut off" (Shahrastānī, *Milal,* 87; see ABYSSINIA; SLAVES AND SLAVERY). The Ibāḍī sources state that the imām must be male, an adult in full possession of his faculties and so on (see MATURITY; KINGS AND RULERS), but they do not regard a slave as eligible for the caliphate (Wilkinson, Ibadi Imāma, 538). The formulation of "even an Abyssinian slave" causes misunderstanding. It actually means that the Khārijīs held any qualified Muslim, even one of slavish origin, eligible to the imāmate — provided that he was of irreproachable character. Originally this "black slave" tradition was not a Khārijī statement nor was it concerned with the qualification of the imāmate. It expressed Sunnī quietism, which maintained that rulers must be obeyed however illegitimate they may be (Crone, 'Even an Ethiopian slave,' 60-1).

It should be added that the Ibāḍīs were also eminent jurists (see TRADITIONAL DISCIPLINES OF QURʾĀNIC STUDY). The Ibāḍī school is one of the oldest surviving schools of law. Its foundation was attributed to Jābir b. Zayd (d. ca. 100/718-9). The first jurists of the movement were trained at his "circle" *(ḥalqa):* Abū Nūḥ Ṣāliḥ al-Dahhān, Ḥayyān al-Aʿraj, Ḍumām b. al-Sāʾib, Jaʿfar b. al-Sammāk, and Abū ʿUbayda al-Tamīmī propagated the doctrine learnt from Jābir in secret meetings *(majālis),* at which the members of the sect discussed questions of law and dogma. The first Ibāḍīs lived in places where Islamic law began to develop, namely in Baṣra and Kūfa, but also in the Ḥijāz, in close contact with the learned experts of the time with whom they exchanged opinions and teachings. Al-Ḥasan al-Baṣrī (d. 110/728) and Ibn ʿAbbās (d. 68/686-8) were teachers as well as personal friends of Jābir, and the first Ibāḍīs recognized the authority of the Sunnī traditionists (see ḤADĪTH AND THE QURʾĀN) who were among Jābir's pupils: Qatāda b. Diʿāma, ʿAmr b. Harim, ʿAmr b. Dīnār, Tamīm b. Ḥuwayṣ, and ʿUmāra b. Ḥayyān.

Some scholars have argued that the Ibāḍīs derived their law from the orthodox schools, introducing only such superficial modifications as were required by their own political and dogmatic tenets (Schacht, *Origins*, 260 f.). Recent studies on the Ibāḍī *madhhab* show, however, that from the beginning the Ibāḍīs took a line detached from Sunnī schools and thus contributed to the general development of Islamic jurisprudence (Ennami, *Studies in Ibāḍism*, chap. iv; Wilkinson, The early development, 125-44; Francesca, The formation; id., *Teoria e practica*, esp. chaps. 1-3).

Ersilia Francesca

Bibliography

Primary: al-Ashʿarī, Abū l-Ḥasan, ʿAlī b. ʿIsmāʿīl, *Maqālāt al-islāmiyyīn*, ed. H. Ritter, Istanbul 1929; Baghdādī, *Farq*, Cairo 1328/1910; Balādhurī, Aḥmad b. Yaḥyā b. Jābir, *Ansāb al-ashrāf*, ed. W. Ahlwardt, Greifswald 1883; al-Barrādī, Abū al-Faḍl *Kitāb al-Jawāhir*, lithograph, Cairo 1302/1884-5; P. Crone and F. Zimmermann (eds.), *The Epistle of Sālim ibn Dhakwān*, Oxford 2001; al-Darjīnī, Abū l-Abbās Aḥmad b. Saʿīd, *Kitāb Ṭabaqāt al-mashāyikh bi-l-Maghrib*, ed. I. Ṭallāy, 2 vols., Constantine 1394/1974; Ibn Ḥazm, *Milal*, 5 vols., Cairo 1317-21; Ibn Sallām, *Kitāb Ibn Sallām. Eine ibaditisch-magribinische Geschichte des Islams aus dem 3./9. Jahrhundert*, ed. W. Schwartz and S. b. Yaʿqūq, Wiesbaden 1986; al-Jayṭālī, Abū Ṭāhir Ismāʿīl, *Qawāʿid al-Islām*, 2 vols., Ghārdāya 1976; I. Kāshif (ed.), *[al-]Siyar wa-l-jawābāt li-ʿulamāʾ wa-aʾimmat ʿUmān*, 2 vols., Oman 1989; Masʿūdī, *Murūj*, ed. C. Pellat, al-Mubarrad, Abū l-ʿAbbās Muḥammad b. Yazīd, *Kāmil*, ed. W. Wright, 3 vols., Leipzig 1974-92, trans. O. Rescher, *Die Kharidschitenkapitel aus dem Kāmil*, Stuttgart 1922; Shahrastānī, *Milal*, ed. W. Cureton; al-Shammākhī, Abū l-ʿAbbās Aḥmad b. Saʿīd, *Kitāb al-Siyar*, lithograph, Cairo 1301/1883; Ṭabarī, *Taʾrīkh;* id., *The history of al-Ṭabarī. xviii. Between civil wars. The caliphate of Muʿawiyah*, trans. M. Morony, Albany 1987; al-Warjlānī, Abū Zakariyyāʾ Yaḥyā b. Abī Bakr, *Kitāb Siyar al aʾimma wa-akhbārihim*, ed. I. al-ʿArabī, Alger 1399/1979; trans. E. Masqueray, *La chronique d'Abou Zakaria*, Alger 1878, trans. R. Le Tourneau, La chronique d'Abū Zakariyyāʾ al-Warānī, in *Revue africaine* 104 (1960), 99-176, 322-90; 105 (1961), 117-76, 323-74; al-Wisyānī, Sālim b. ʿAbd al-Sallām, *Kitāb al-Siyar*, ms. Z. Smogorzewski, Cracow 00277, fol. 1-189.

Secondary: R. Brünnow, *Die Charidschiten unter den ersten Omayyaden. Ein Beitrag zur Geschichte der ersten islamischen Jahrhunderts*, Leiden 1884; L. Caetani, *Annali dell'Islām*, 10 vols., Milan 1905-26, ix, 541-56; x, 76-151; 168-95; M. Cook, *Commanding right and forbidding wrong in Islamic thought*, Cambridge, UK 2000; V. Cremonesi, Un antico documento ibāḍita sul Corano creato, in *Studi maghrebini* 1 (1966), 133-61; P. Crone, 'Even an Ethiopian slave.' The transformation of a Sunnī tradition, in BSOAS 57 (1994), 59-67; P. Cuperly, *Introduction à l'étude de l'Ibadisme et de sa théologie*, Alger 1984; H. Djaït, *La grande discorde. Religion et politique dans l'Islam des origines*, Paris 1989; A. Kh. Ennami, *Studies in Ibāḍism*, Beirut 1972-3; van Ess, TG (esp. i, 404-16 for the Khārijīs in Kūfa; ii, 186-233 for the Ibāḍīs in Baṣra; ii, 460-6 for the Khārijīs in Wāsiṭ; ii, 572-84 for the Khārijīs in Iran; ii, 590-600 for the Khārijīs in Khorasān; ii, 601-4 for the Ibāḍīs in Khurāsān; ii, 613-24 for the Khārijīs in middle and southern Iran; ii, 618-24 for the later Khārijīs; ii, 655-6 for the Khārijīs in Mecca; ii, 656-9 for the Ibāḍīs in Mecca); E. Francesca, The formation and early development of the Ibāḍī madhhab, in JSAI 28 (2003); id., *Teoria e pratica del commercio nell'Islam medievale. I contratti di vendita e di commenda nel diritto ibāḍita*, Rome 2002; F. Gabrieli, Sulle origini del movimento ḫārigita, in *Rendiconti. Atti della Accademia Nazionale dei Lincei* 7 (1941-2), 110-7; C. Gilliot, Le commentaire coranique de Hūd b. Muḥakkam, in *Arabica* 44 (1997), 179-23; M. Guidi, Sui Ḫārigiti, in RSO 21 (1994), 1-14; A.C. Higgins, *The qurʾānic exchange of the self in the poetry of Shurāt (Khārijī) political identity (37-132 A.H./657-750 A.D.)*, Ph.D. diss., Chicago 2001; M. Hinds, Muʿāwiya I, in EI², vii, 263-8; N. Koribaa, *Les Kharidjites. Démocrates de l'Islam*, Paris 1991; G. Levi Della Vida, Khāridjites, in EI², iv, 1106-9; T. Lewicki, al-Ibāḍiyya, in EI², iii, 648-66; K. Lewinstein, The Azāriqa in Islamic heresiography, in *BSOAS* 54 (1991), 251-68; W. Madelung, The Shiite and Khārijite contribution to pre-Ashʿarite *kalām*, in P. Morewedge (ed.), *Islamic philosophical theology*, Albany, N.Y. 1979, 120-39; id., *The succession to Muḥammad. A study of the early caliphate*, Cambridge 1997; id. and K. Lewinstein, Ṣufriyya, in *EI²*, ix, 766-9; M. Moreno, Note di teologia ibāḍita, in *AIUON* 3 (1949), 299-313; ʿĀ.Y. Muʿammar, *al-Ibāḍiyya bayna l-firaq al-islāmiyya*, Ghārdāya 1987; ʿA. Najjār, *al-Ibāḍiyya wa-madā ṣilatihā bi-l-khawārij*, Cairo 1993; C.A. Nallino, Rapporti tra la dogmatica Muʿtazilita e quella degli Ibāḍiti dell'Africa settentrionale, in *RSO* 7 (1916-8), 455-60; U. Rebstock, *Die Ibāḍiten im Maġreb (2./8.-4./10. Jh.). Die Geschichte einer Berberbewegung im Gewand des Islams*, Berlin 1983; R. Rubinacci, ʿAdjārida, in *EI²*, i, 213; id., Azārika, in *EI²*, i, 833-4; id., Barāʾa, in *EI²*, i, 1026-8; id., Nadjadāt, in *EI²*, vii, 860-1; E.A. Salem, *Political theory and institutions of the Khawaridj*, Baltimore 1959; J. Schacht, *The origins of Muhammadan jurisprudence*, Oxford 1950; W. Schwartz, *Die Anfänge der Ibaditen in Nordafrika — der Beitrag einer islamischen Minderheit zur Ausbreitung des Islams*, Wiesbaden 1983; W. Thomson, Khārijitism and the Khārijites, in W.G. Shellabear (ed.), *The Macdonald presentation volume*, London 1933, 371-89; L. Veccia Vaglieri, Il conflitto ʿAlī-Muʿāwiya e la secessione khārigita riesaminati alla luce di fonti ibāḍite, in *AIUON* 4 (1952), 1-94; id., Ḥarūrāʾ, in *EI²*, iii, 242-3; id., Sulle denominazione Hawāziǧ, in *RSO* 26 (1951), 41-6; id., Traduzione di passi riguardanti il conflitto ʿAlī-Muʿāwiya e la secessione khārigita, in *AIUON* 5 (1953), 1-98; id., Le vicende del ḫārigismo in epoca abbaside, in *RSO* 24 (1949), 31-44; W.M. Watt, Kharijite thought in the Umayyad period, in *Der Islam* 36 (1961), 215-32; J. Wellhausen, *Die religiöspolitischen Oppositionsparteien im alten Islam*, Berlin 1901; J. Wilkinson, The early development of the Ibāḍī movement in Basra, in G.H.A. Juynboll, *Studies on the first century of Islamic society*, Carbondale 1982, 125-44; id., The Ibāḍī imāma, in *BSOAS* 39 (1976), 535-51.

Khaybar see EXPEDITIONS AND BATTLES

Kifl, Dhū al- see DHŪ L-KIFL; EZEKIEL; ELIJAH

Kindness see MERCY

King, Kingdom see KINGS AND RULERS

Kings and Rulers

Royal male sovereigns and other political leaders. The Arabic term *malik*, "king," appears thirteen times in the Qurʾān (its plural form *mulūk* appears twice), and is derived from the root *m-l-k*, which connotes possession (q.v.), having power or dominion over someone or something (see POWER AND IMPOTENCE), or capacity, the ability to obtain something.

Other qurʾānic terms relevant to this subject include *mulk*, "dominion, power or kingdom," and *malakūt*, "dominion or kingdom." The former, which is attested many times in the Qurʾān, may be associated either with God or with human beings, while the latter, which appears only four times, is used exclusively in divine contexts, as in Q 6:75 when God shows Abraham (q.v.) "the kingdom of the heavens and the earth" (*malakūta l-samāwāti wa-l-arḍ*, see HEAVEN AND SKY; EARTH) or Q 36:83: "Glory be to him in whose hand is dominion *(malakūt)* over all things." The term *khalīfa* (derived from the root *kh-l-f*, which connotes succession or deputyship; see CALIPH), is attested twice in the Qurʾān, and in its application to David (q.v.) in Q 38:26, this term, too, strongly suggests rulership (Lewis, *Political language*, 44; see also Paret, Signification coranique; al-Qāḍī, The term "khalīfa"). The term *imām* (q.v.; pl. *aʾimma*), a title which, like *khalīfa*, was greatly preferred by many Muslim political thinkers to *malik* in the early centuries of the Islamic period, also appears in the Qurʾān, where it connotes leadership, and has sometimes been interpreted in a political sense (see POLITICS AND THE QURʾĀN; also, although attested in the Qurʾān, the term *sulṭān* never appears there in the sense of governmental power, a sense that was to become prevalent in later centuries).

Although the words *malik* and *mulk* are used in the Qurʾān in both human and divine contexts, the scripture and its traditional interpreters (see EXEGESIS OF THE QURʾĀN: CLASSICAL AND MEDIEVAL) distinguish between true, eternal sovereignty (q.v.), that of God, and the temporal power that God grants briefly to whom he wishes (see ETERNITY). Commentators on the verse Q 3:26, where God is addressed as "the possessor of sovereignty, [you] who give sovereignty to whom you wish, and take sovereignty away from whom you wish, and exalt whom you wish and humble whom you wish" *(mālika l-mulki tuʾtī l-mulka man tashāʾu wa-tanziʿu l-mulka mimman tashāʾu wa-tuʿizzu man tashāʾu wa-tudhillu man tashāʾ),* draw a specific contrast between divine and human sovereignty. For al-Ṭabarī (d. 310/923), the verse emphasizes God's total control over the disposition of temporal power. "All that is in your hands and at your behest; no one in your creation (q.v.) can do anything about it," al-Ṭabarī writes (*Tafsīr,* vi, 301). As an illustration of God's ability to elevate and depose kings in ways that human beings would never consider possible, al-Ṭabarī (followed by several later commentators) cites the ḥadīth according to which Muḥammad purportedly promised his people that they would eventually gain sovereignty over the Persian and Byzantine empires (Ṭabarī, *Tafsīr,* vi, 299-301; see also Rāzī, *Tafsīr,* viii, 4; see BYZANTINES; ḤADĪTH AND THE QURʾĀN).

Q 3:26 is significant in Muʿtazilī theology, since some Muʿtazilīs (q.v.), as a consequence of their emphasis on divine justice (see JUSTICE AND INJUSTICE), rejected the idea that God could bestow kingship on an unbeliever (see BELIEF AND UNBELIEF; for a discussion of this issue, see Ṭūsī, *Tibyān,* ii, 430-1; Zamakhsharī, *Kashshāf,* i, 350; and further Māwardī, *Nukat,* i, 381-2). While al-Ṭabarī gives precedence to interpretations of Q 3:26 that understand the verse as referring to temporal power, he and later commentators also record alternative opinions, including the view according to which *mulk* should be understood here in the sense of prophethood (Ṭabarī, *Tafsīr,* vi, 300; Ṭūsī, *Tibyān,* ii, 429; see PROPHETS AND PROPHETHOOD). In his treatment of this view, Fakhr al-Dīn al-Rāzī (d. 606/1210) explains: "Prophethood is the highest rank of sovereignty, because the scholars (see SCHOLAR; KNOWLEDGE AND LEARNING) have a great deal of command over the interior aspects of people, and tyrants (see OPPRESSION) have command over the external aspects of people, whereas the commands of prophets are effective on the interior and exterior aspects" (Rāzī, *Tafsīr,* viii, 5; see also AUTHORITY and OBEDIENCE for discussion of another verse with theological overtones that had ramifications on later Islamic political history, namely Q 4:59, in which the believers are instructed to obey God, the messenger [q.v.] and "those of you who are in authority *[ūlī l-amr minkum]*").

In reference to God, the term *malik* is invested with sacrality: in Q 20:114, God is called "the true king" *(al-maliku l-ḥaqq;* see also Q 25:26, *al-mulku yawmaʾidhin al-ḥaqq)* and he is twice described as "the holy king" (*al-maliku l-quddūs;* the latter term is generally interpreted as meaning "pure, devoid of any impurity or deficiency"; see Bayḍāwī, *Anwār,* ii, 326, ad Q 59:23 and Ṭūsī, *Tibyān,* x, 3-4, ad Q 62:1). In Q 114:2, God is "the king of humankind" *(maliki l-nās).* In contrast to its use as a divine appellation, the term *malik,* when applied to earthly monarchs, often carries negative connotations in the Qurʾān. For example, in Q 27:34, the Queen of Sheba (q.v.)

remarks, "When kings enter a town, they ruin it and make the grandest of its people wretched." God may grant sovereignty to those whom he favors, such as David, Solomon (q.v.) and Joseph (q.v.; it is noteworthy, however, that the Qurʾān does not attach the title of "king" to any of these figures); and Saul (q.v.; of whom the term "king" is used). In order to fulfil the divine purpose, God may also confer kingship on negative characters, such as Pharaoh (q.v.; who is described as "the king" in Q 12:43, 50, 54, 72, 76), and the unnamed "king who confiscates every good ship (see SHIPS)" mentioned in Q 18:79 (on his possible identity, see Bayḍāwī, *Anwār*, i, 570-1; see also KHAḌIR/KHIḌR). As a woman, the Queen of Sheba — known to Islamic tradition as Bilqīs (q.v.) — of whom the term "queen" is not used in the Qurʾān but who is described as "a woman who rules over them" (*imraʾatan tamlikuhum*, Q 27:23), stands in a category of her own: for all her splendor, she is as an unbeliever and a woman subservient to Solomon (see WOMEN AND THE QURʾĀN).

God's sovereignty, unlike that of earthly kings, is absolute. He is repeatedly described as possessing "sovereignty over the heavens and the earth" *(lillāhi mulku l-samāwāti wa-l-arḍi).* In many instances, the phrase is interpreted as a reference to God's creative power: at Q 24:42, al-Bayḍāwī (d. 685/1286 or 692/1293) glosses the qurʾānic text with the explication "for he is the creator of them both, and of the essences, accidents and actions within them" (*Anwār*, ii, 26; see COSMOLOGY; THEOLOGY AND THE QURʾĀN). Sometimes the description of God as possessing sovereignty over the heavens and the earth is meant to correct the errors of other religious groups, who may have failed to recognize that "God is powerful without qualification" (*qādir ʿalā l-iṭlāq;* Bayḍāwī, *Anwār*, i, 252, ad Q 5:17; see PARTIES AND FACTIONS). God's possession of sovereignty may also be presented as a challenge to the unbelievers and their gods (see IDOLS AND IMAGES; IDOLATRY AND IDOLATERS). Q 38:10 asks: "Or do they possess sovereignty over the heavens and the earth and what lies between them?" Q 4:53-4, a passage interpreted as a reference to the Jews (see JEWS AND JUDAISM), asks: "Or do they possess a portion of the sovereignty? If they did, they would not give the people so much as the speck on a date stone. Or are they jealous of the people for what God has given them of his bounty (see BLESSING; GRACE)? For we gave the family of Abraham the book (q.v.) and wisdom (q.v.), and we gave them great sovereignty." (See the interpretations of these verses in Ṭūsī, *Tibyān*, iii, 228; al-Bayḍāwī, *Anwār*, i, 213-4.)

The qurʾānic notion of God's sovereignty is also linked to the assertion of his uniqueness (see GOD AND HIS ATTRIBUTES). Twice the Qurʾān states, "He has no partner in sovereignty" (*lam yakun lahu sharīkun fī l-mulk*, Q 17:111; 25:2; in the former verse, *mulk* is interpreted by Bayḍāwī, *Anwār*, i, 554, simply as "divinity"). On the day of judgment (see LAST JUDGMENT), sovereignty will be God's (Q 22:56). Sovereignty is also among the phenomena that will be seen by those in paradise (q.v.): "And when you see, you shall see felicity and great sovereignty" (*wa-idha raʾayta thamma raʾayta naʿīman wa-mulkan kabīran*, Q 76:20; cf. the ḥadīth recounted in Bayḍāwī, *Anwār*, ii, 376).

On the earthly plane, kingship is depicted as a great but treacherous bounty that human beings, even those who receive divine favor, are naturally inclined to covet. For instance, Satan (see DEVIL) tempts Adam (see ADAM AND EVE; FALL OF MAN) with the prospect of imperishable sovereignty: "O Adam! Shall I show you to the tree of immortality (see ETERNITY) and sovereignty that never declines?" (Q 20:120, *yā Ādamu hal adulluka ʿalā shajarati l-khuldi wa-mulkin lā yablā*). Joseph addresses God with gratitude (see GRATITUDE AND INGRATITUDE) for the sovereignty he has received from him (Q 12:101; see Quṭb, *Ẓilāl*, iv, 2029-30) and Solomon prays for kingship (Q 38:35). Those whom God leads astray (q.v.; see also FREEDOM AND PREDESTINATION) seem almost intoxicated by the power of kingship. In Q 2:258, for example, Nimrod (q.v.) argues with Abraham about the latter's God on the grounds that Nimrod himself received kingship. (For the reason given above in connection with Q 3:26, Muʿtazilī commentators also paid close attention to Q 2:258; see Zamakhsharī, *Kashshāf*, i, 304-5, where two explanations are given: that God gave Nimrod the wealth [q.v.], servants and followers that allowed him to become victorious [see VICTORY], but did not make him victorious directly; or, that God made Nimrod a king as a test for his servants [see SLAVES AND SLAVERY].) Similarly, Pharaoh boasts of his claim to the kingship (kingdom) of Egypt (q.v.; Q 43:51). In his commentary on this passage, Sayyid Quṭb (d. 1966) contrasts Pharaoh's kingdom of Egypt with the divine sovereignty over the heavens and the earth, and notes how the masses, whose eyes are dazzled by the accoutrements of Pharaoh's sovereignty, fail to perceive, in their hearts (see HEART), the insignificance of these royal trappings (*Ẓilāl*, v, 3193; for a Ṣūfī interpretation of the qurʾānic Pharaoh, see Böwering, *Mystical*, 190-2; see ṢŪFISM AND THE QURʾĀN).

However powerful kings may appear to be on earth, the Qurʾān makes clear that their authority in no way detracts from the overwhelming totality of God's power. The Qurʾān strongly implies the contingency and the brevity of human, worldly kingship (e.g. Q 40:29, "O my people! Today the kingdom is yours, who are triumphant in the earth; but who will come to our aid in the face of God's strength when it reaches us?"). Worldly power is invariably presented as part of God's creation, utterly contingent on him and at his disposal. This subordination of earthly rulership to divine power is often emphasized in the exegetical literature. For example, the Persian Shīʿī commentator Abū l-Futūḥ Rāzī (d. 525/1131 or later; see SHIʿISM AND THE QURʾĀN), in his discussion of Q 67:1, "Praise be to the one by whose hand is sovereignty, and he is powerful over all things" *(tabāraka lladhī bi-yadihi l-mulku wa-huwa ʿalā kulli shayʾin qadīrun)*, interprets the phrase *bi-yadihi l-mulk* as follows: "Kingship *(pād-shāhī)*... is by his command *(amr)* and power *(qudrat)*, with 'hand' (q.v.) connoting strength and power, implying the sense of the administration and execution of affairs; the meaning is that sovereignty is his creation and at his disposal, such that he can bring it into existence and non-existence, increase it or decrease it, or modify it in various ways according to his wishes" (Abū l-Futūḥ Rāzī, *Rawḥ*, xi, 208; a similar view is given by Ṭūsī, *Tibyān*, x, 57, who describes God as *mālik al-mulūk*, "the possessor of kings"; see also Rāzī, *Tafsīr*, viii, 4, ad Q 3:26).

The Children of Israel (q.v.) are said to have received special divine attention, for they were at times favored with both prophethood and kingship. Moses proclaims: "O my people! Remember God's favor to you, how he made prophets among you and made you kings, and gave you that which he did not give to any [other] of his creatures" (*yā qawmi ʾdhkurū niʿmata llāhi ʿalaykum idh jaʿala fīkum anbiyāʾa wa-jaʿalakum mulūkan wa-ātākum mā lam yuʾti aḥadan min al-ʿālamīn*, Q 5:20; for the exegetical treatment of this verse, see below). David and Solomon both combine their service as prophets with the possession of *mulk*. Of David, Q 38:20 states, "We made his kingdom strong and gave him the wisdom and clear speech" *(wa shadadnā mulkahu wa-ātaynāhu l-ḥikmata wa-faṣla l-khiṭāb);* similarly Q 2:251, "God gave him [David] the kingdom and the wisdom *(al-mulka wa-l-ḥikma)* and instructed him as to his will." Q 38:26 describes David also as a deputy or successor on earth *(yā Dā'ūdu innā ja'alnāka khalīfatan fī l-arḍ),* a phrase for which al-Bayḍāwī (*Anwār,* ii, 186) records two interpretations: that it refers to kingship *(mulk)* on earth, or that it portrays David as a successor to earlier prophets. A reference to Solomon's kingdom appears in Q 2:102 and an extensive treatment of Solomon's career is given in Q 27. In Q 38:35 he prays to God for forgiveness (q.v.), and also for sovereignty (for the role of Solomon as "the proof of God for kings" in Ṣūfī tradition, see Böwering, *Mystical,* 64). While neither David nor Solomon is designated a king in the Qur'ān, their examples, and especially the proof-text Q 38:26, are routinely cited in discussions of the excellence of kingship and its divine origins in later Islamic mirror literature.

A somewhat more ambiguous case is that of Saul, known in the Qur'ān as Ṭālūt. The Israelites are told by their prophet (who is nameless in the qur'ānic account) that, in response to their request, God has sent them Saul as their king; yet the people reject Saul. Q 2:247: "Their prophet said to them: 'God has sent you Ṭālūt as a king *(malik).*' They said: 'How is it that he should have sovereignty over us, when we are more worthy of kingship than he is? For he has not been given an abundance of wealth.' He said: 'God has chosen him over you, and has increased him largely in wisdom and stature. God gives his sovereignty to whom he wishes.'" The commentators account for the Israelites' rejection of Saul by noting that he was poor, a shepherd, water carrier or tanner, and that he came from Benjamin's (q.v.) stock, among whom neither prophethood nor kingship had appeared (Ṭabarī, *Tafsīr,* v, 306 f.; Rāzī, *Tafsīr,* vi, 184-5; Bayḍāwī, *Anwār,* i, 127-8). The prophet (on whose identity see Bayḍāwī, *Anwār,* i, 127) went on to tell them that the ark (q.v.; *tābūt*) would come to them as a sign of Saul's kingdom (Q 2:248).

The exegetical literature reflects an apparent intent in some circles to minimize any possibly positive qur'ānic emphasis on temporal kingship and this is most readily apparent in connection with the qur'ānic passages that treat the singular combination of prophethood and kingship enjoyed on occasion by the Israelites. In Q 5:20 (cited above), for example, Moses reminds his people of God's favor to them, in that he made prophets among them and made them kings. Al-Ṭabarī, followed by al-Ṭūsī (d. 460/1067) and others, records a number of interpretations, several of which suggest that the text indicates not that the Israelites were kings, but that they were masters — of themselves, their womenfolk (see GENDER), their possessions, and so on (Ṭabarī, *Tafsīr,* x, 160-3; Ṭūsī, *Tibyān,* iii, 481; Bayḍāwī, *Anwār,* i, 253: "God delivered them out of slavery in Egypt and made them masters *[mālikūn]* of their persons and their affairs, and so God called them 'kings'"). Similarly, in his commentary on Q 27:15, "And we gave knowledge to David and Solomon, and they said: 'Praise be to God, who has favored us over many of his believing servants!'" *(alladhī faḍḍalanā 'alā kathīrin min 'ibādihi l-mu'minīn),* al-Bayḍāwī (d. prob. 716/1316-7; *Anwār,* ii, 64-5) explicitly subordinates kingship to knowledge when he writes: "In this is a proof of the excellence of knowledge and the nobility of those who possess it, in that they [David and Solomon] gave thanks for knowledge and made it the basis of excellence, and they did not consider the kingship that they had also been given, though [that kingship] had not been given to anyone else." When, in the following verse (Q 27:16), the Qur'ān states that Solomon inherited from David, al-Bayḍāwī (*Anwār,* ii, 65) describes his inheritance as "prophethood, or knowledge, or kingship" (see also Māwardī, *Nukat,* iv, 198).

The term *imām (*pl. *aʾimma)* suggests a person (or, in other contexts, a book, or a pattern) to be followed and in some instances in the Qurʾān the word may include the idea of political leadership. Perhaps most strikingly, God appoints Abraham as an *imām* (Q 2:124: *qāla innī jāʿiluka lil-nāsi imāman).* For al-Ṭabarī (*Tafsīr,* iii, 18) this means that God intended that Abraham should be followed. Al-Māwardī (d. 450/1058) follows al-Ṭabarī's interpretation and notes its particular relevance to prayer (q.v.; *Nukat,* i, 185; for a fuller treatment of the verse's meaning from a Shīʿī perspective, see Ṭūsī, *Tibyān,* i, 446, where the exegete records views according to which God by this verse made the imāmate incumbent on Abraham; on the Shīʿī view that Abraham combined the functions of prophethood and the imāmate, see Momen, *Introduction,* 147, and for Shīʿī readings of the Qurʾān on the subject of the historical imāms, see Momen, *Introduction,* 151-3).

In two cases, the term *aʾimma* is followed by the phrase "who guide by our command" *(aʾimmatan yahdūna bi-amrinā)* — Q 21:73: "And we made them leaders who guide by our command, and we inspired them to do good deeds (q.v.), maintain prayer and almsgiving (q.v.), and they were worshippers (see WORSHIP) of us" and Q 32:24: "And we made among them [the Children of Israel] leaders who guide by our command" — which some commentators took to mean moral leaders, "leaders in goodness," while others understood it as a reference to prophets (Māwardī, *Nukat,* iv, 366). In Q 28:5, the Qurʾān states that God wished to make the oppressed (*alladhīna stuḍʿifū fī l-arḍ,* see OPPRESSED ON EARTH; JOY AND MISERY) into leaders (*aʾimma,* Māwardī, *Nukat,* iv, 234; Bayḍāwī, *Anwār,* ii, 77). In Q 9:12, the term *imām,* in the sense of a human leader, appears in a negative context: the reference there to "the leaders of unbelief" *(aʾimmata l-kufr)* is interpreted variously as referring to the leaders of the polytheists (see POLYTHEISM AND ATHEISM), the leaders of Quraysh (q.v.) or those who intended to oust the Prophet (Māwardī, *Nukat,* ii, 345; Ṭūsī, *Tibyān,* v, 214; see OPPOSITION TO MUḤAMMAD).

Louise Marlow

Bibliography

Primary: Abū l-Futūḥ Rāzī, *Rawḥ,* 12 vols.; Bayḍāwī, *Anwār;* Māwardī, *Nukat;* Quṭb, *Ẓilāl;* Rāzī, *Tafsīr,* ed. ʿA. Muḥammad, Cairo 1938; Ṭabarī, *Tafsīr,* ed. Shākir; Ṭūsī, *Tibyān;* Zamakhsharī, *Kashshāf,* Beirut 1947.

Secondary: A. Ayalon, Malik, in *EI²,* vi, 261-2; A. al-Azmeh, *Muslim kingship,* London 1997; Böwering, *Mystical;* B. Lewis, *The political language of Islam,* Chicago 1988; Mir, *Dictionary;* M. Momen, *An introduction to Shīʿī Islam,* New Haven 1985; Paret, *Koran;* id., Signification coranique de *ḫalīfa* et d'autres dérivés de la racine *ḫalafa,* in *SI* 31 (1970), 211-17; Penrice, *Dictionary;* M. Plessner, Mulk, in *EI²,* vii, 546-7; W. al-Qāḍī, The term "khalīfa" in early exegetical literature, in *WI* 28 (1988), 392-411; F. Rahman, *Major themes of the Qurʾān,* Minneapolis 1980; 1989.

Kinship

Relationship by blood or marriage. Although there is no single term that corresponds precisely to the English term "kinship," the Qurʾān contains a variety of what might be identified as "kinship terms": *qurbā* (near relative); *arḥām* (close kin, maternal kin); *ʿashīra* (clan, tribe; see TRIBES AND CLANS); *zawj* (husband); *zawja* (wife); *imraʾa* (wife, woman); *ṣāḥiba* (wife, companion, friend; the masc. sing., *ṣāḥib,* is also attested in the Qurʾān, but does not have the familial connotation of the feminine form); *akh* (brother, friend; see BROTHER AND BROTHERHOOD; FRIENDS AND FRIENDSHIP); *ḥamīm* (solicitous relative, close friend); *ṣihr* (affine, relation through marriage); *nasab* (lineage, kindred, attribution) and many others.

In "the legal verses" *(āyāt al-aḥkām),* those that contain stipulations on a variety of matters, the Qurʾān also employs terms to set forth rules for marriage, divorce (see MARRIAGE AND DIVORCE) and inheritance *(mīrāth, turāth),* which are foundational to the *sharīʿa* (see LAW AND THE QURʾĀN). (In the case of marriage and divorce, the qurʾānic text contains primarily verbal forms: "to marry," *zawwaja, aḥṣana, nakaḥa,* etc., "to divorce," *ṭallaqa, ẓāhara, ṭalaqa;* the nominal forms that are prominent in the discourse of the *sharīʿa,* such as *nikāḥ, ṭalāq,* etc., are not as prevalent in the Qurʾān; but cf. for *nikāḥ* Q 2:235, 237; 24:33; for *ṭalāq* Q 2:227, 229; and, as the name of a sūra, Q 65, "Sūrat al-Ṭalāq.") As with all interpretations, the English glosses given here depend on particular judgments regarding "comparable" work done by words in two discourses.

The terms selected at random and cited above are among those used in the Qurʾān to urge or discourage certain kinds of behavior. Some are also used to specify particular rights and duties. But neither in the matter of moral exhortation and prohibition (see ETHICS AND THE QURʾĀN; SOCIAL INTERACTIONS; PROHIBITED DEGREES), nor in that of defining succession to property rights, are the people concerned necessarily connected by "biological links." For example, those who look after the affairs of orphans (q.v.) are urged to regard them as "brothers" (Q 2:220); qurʾānic inheritance rules affect people related by affinity *(muṣāhara);* and various kinship terms can convey the sense of "friendship," "solicitude," etc., which raises the question of how so-called primary meanings are to be determined.

There is an explicit assumption held by scholars since the nineteenth century that the people of the Ḥijāz (see GEOGRAPHY), among whom the Qurʾān was revealed, lived in a society that was essentially organized in "kinship" terms (see PRE-ISLAMIC ARABIA AND THE QURʾĀN). This assumption has serious implications for assessing the political, legal and moral reforms initiated by the Qurʾān (see POLITICS AND THE QURʾĀN; COMMUNITY AND SOCIETY IN THE QURʾĀN). One of the first to talk about pre-Islamic and early Islamic "tribal" society in detail was Smith (*Kinship and marriage,* 1885), a major figure in the history of both orientalist and anthropological thought. The idea of "kinship" as the organizing principle of "early" societies had been a continuous part of evolutionary social thinking since before his time. It has been increasingly problematized, however, in contemporary anthropology (see Needham, *Rethinking kinship*). Most recently, Schneider *(Critique)* has demonstrated the questionable character of assumptions about "kinship organization." Although they frequently draw on anthropology when discussing the society whose members first listened to the Qurʾān (see ORALITY; REVELATION AND INSPIRATION), orientalists do not appear to have taken these important developments in anthropological theory into account.

The nineteenth-century belief that the seventh-century Ḥijāz was a "kinship-based society" allowed orientalists to interpret and explain references to "kinship" in the Qurʾān as a continuation of or break from pre-Islamic (*jāhilī,* see AGE OF IGNORANCE) principles and values. Thus Smith maintains that kinship among pre-Islamic Arabs signified the blood shared by all the members of a tribe, the common substance that defined each individual's responsibility for — among other things — exacting vengeance in the name of the tribe (see RETALIATION; BLOOD MONEY). Many others have echoed this view — even a century after Smith, including Bashīr *(Tawāzun al-naqāʾiḍ),* Donner *(Early Islamic conquests)* and Crone (Tribes and states).

Smith argues that since all amicable social relations were conceived in terms of "common blood," the extensions of such relations had to be sealed by blood-rites. "The commingling of blood by which two men became brothers or two kins (sic) allies, and the fiction of adoption [see CHILDREN] by which a new tribesman was feigned to be the veritable son of a member of the tribe, are both evidences of the highest value that the Arabs were incapable of conceiving any absolute social obligation or social unity which was not based on kinship; for a legal fiction is always adopted to reconcile an act with a principle too firmly established to be simply ignored" (Smith, *Kinship and marriage,* 51). Smith does not notice the double meaning he gives to "kinship" here — the one being a "biological" link and the other a "cultural representation" of the latter — just as he fails to notice that the existence of rites of friendship and adoption in the Age of Ignorance *(jāhiliyya)* indicates that an absolute obligation could be extended to those who did not share "common blood" (see CLIENTS AND CLIENTAGE). The point is that what he calls "a legal fiction" is not a statement that refers to imagined kinship but what Austin *(How to do)* called a "performative act."

The notion of kinship, as expressed in a variety of terms (*qarāba, nasab, ʿashīra, qawm, ḥayy,* etc.), is not simply an instance of "culture hitching a ride on nature" (Crone, Tribes and states, 355), i.e. of rights and duties attributed to biological facts. As a notion, kinship articulates distinctive ideas of social relations, morality and cosmology (q.v.), through which certain cultural facts can be constructed. Marriages as well as adoption create jural relations with mutual rights and obligations between persons who do not share "common blood." These relationships are not confused with "blood relationships." Marriage, for example, is a voluntary contract that is best seen as articulating one aspect of the total set of gender relations (see Rivière, Marriage; see GENDER) — and that is precisely how it is envisaged in the Qurʾān, often in explicit contrast to the Age of Ignorance. The relationship between blood brothers in the Age of Ignorance was apparently free of the rights and obligations that were legally ascribed to kinship roles. (The Qurʾān, of course, rejects legal adoption — see Q 33:4, 37 — as it rejects rites involving human blood.) This means that "blood brotherhood" (like friendship) in the Age of Ignorance was based on what Levi-Strauss calls metaphor (similitude) as against metonymy (consubstantiation). When the Qurʾān repudiates the attribution of *nasab* between God and jinn (q.v.) it is both "similitude" and "consubstantiation" that are being denied (Q 37:158-9; see METAPHOR; SIMILES; GOD AND HIS ATTRIBUTES; FAITH; POLYTHEISM AND ATHEISM).

Crone agrees with conventional historians (including Watt, *Muhammad at Mecca; Muhammad at Medina,* whom she attacks) that Mecca was "a tribal" society — a society based on "kinship." "In social terms," she observes, "the protection [q.v.] that Muhammad is said to have enjoyed from his own kin, first as an orphan and next as a prophet, would indicate the tribal system to have been intact" (Crone, *Meccan trade,* 233). Her argument, however, is not logically necessary. Yet Crone's insistence that "the tribal system" was "intact" does raise interesting questions about the relationship of her "model" to her "data," because it is not entirely clear how someone who denies the credibility of all traditional Islamic sources relating to Meccan society at the time of the Prophet is able to make such an assertion. The answer would appear to lie in her resort to the writings of nineteenth-century European travelers and twentieth-century ethnographers (cf. Crone, *Meccan trade,* 236) — a style of historical inference adopted by other orientalists (e.g. Donner, *Early Islamic conquests*), even when they have not, as the radical skeptics have, dismissed all early Islamic sources (see Donner, *Narratives,* for a sober survey). Contemporary ethnographic studies of tribes — pastoral as well as agricultural — are useful for thinking about early historical periods, not because one can extrapolate from present social arrangements, which are extremely diverse, to distant historical ones, but because they can sensitize one to problems that need to be addressed when speculating about Islamic history (see HISTORY AND THE QURʾĀN). The idea that contemporary "tribes" are living fossils of ancient ways of social life belongs to a theory of social evolution that anthropologists have long ago demolished and abandoned.

The resort to the modern ethnography of tribes for purposes of historical reconstruction also plays a crucial part in Powers' *(Studies)* revisionist account of the origins of the Islamic law of inheritance. When Smith reconstructed pre-Islamic Arabian society he represented the Islamic rules of inheritance as a modification of pre-Islamic *(jāhilī)* ones. Smith's thesis eventually became the established orientalist view. It is this view that Powers has challenged on the basis of a re-reading of the inheritance verses (especially Q 4:12, 176), to which arguments about the syntax of a qurʾānic sentence and the meaning of the word *kalāla* are central (*kalāla* has been understood to mean "someone who has no parents or children, and therefore no direct heirs"; Powers translates it as "daughter-in-law"; see INHERITANCE; GRAMMAR AND THE QURʾĀN). Powers' thesis is that the received Islamic system of inheritance *(ʿilm al-farāʾiḍ)* is quite different not only from the pre-Islamic one but also from the proto-Islamic system of the Qurʾān that gave a far greater scope to the principle of testamentary bequests than the *sharīʿa* allows. In evolutionary terms, the shift from the pre-Islamic system to the proto-Islamic one represents a double progress, (a) from the constraints of kinship to the freedom of contract (see CONTRACTS AND ALLIANCES; BREAKING TRUSTS AND CONTRACTS) and (b) from the principle of inheritance by seniority (brother to brother) to the principle of generational inheritance (father to son). Powers sums this up as "a transition from nomadism to sedentary life and from tribalism to individualism" (*Studies,* 210). The *ʿilm al-farāʾiḍ* is therefore seen as a backward move, a clumsy compromise in the interests of power.

According to Powers, the proto-Islamic system was distorted for political reasons by the Prophet's immediate successors who imposed the orthodox reading on the relevant verses (see READINGS OF THE QURʾĀN; COLLECTION OF THE QURʾĀN). The idea that the Prophet's most trusted Companions (see COMPANIONS OF THE PROPHET) and oldest converts would engage in a conspiracy against him concerning the proper meaning of a divine verse which inaugurated a new legal dispensation, one that was presumably in force during the Prophet's lifetime, seems, according to Powers' critics, far-fetched. (For this and other critical points relating to Arabic syntax and the etymology of *kalāla,* see Ziadeh, Review of Powers; see also ARABIC

LANGUAGE; LANGUAGE AND STYLE OF THE QURʾĀN.) Some Muslim modernists (e.g. Arkoun, *Min al-ijtihād*), however, have received Powers' re-interpretation of the "kinship" *kalāla* with enthusiasm because it supports their desire to challenge what they see as the ideological manipulation of the qurʾānic text by jurists and theologians determined to impose traditional authority (q.v.) on all believers and to prevent the use of critical reason by the individual (see ISLAM; CONTEMPORARY CRITICAL PRACTICES AND THE QURʾĀN).

So what does "kinship" mean in the Qurʾān? Certainly not "common blood," a Western idiom, because the Arabic for "blood" *(damm)* is never used in the Qurʾān to denote that which relatives share in common (see BLOOD AND BLOOD CLOT; BIOLOGY AS THE CREATION AND STAGES OF LIFE). From a Muslim exegetical perspective, signification must be sought in the connection between believer and text. For pious Muslims qurʾānic meanings are not mechanically determined by grammatical and lexical criteria or by some objective context (see OCCASIONS OF REVELATION). Far from being a simple injunction, piety (q.v.) and fear (q.v.) of God *(birr wa-taqwā)* on the part of attentive Muslims is understood to be a presupposition for arriving at the meanings of the Qurʾān, because the divine recitation evokes and confirms what is already in the heart (q.v.) of the faithful man or woman (see BELIEF AND UNBELIEF; RECITATION OF THE QURʾĀN).

A number of themes emerge through the qurʾānic use of "kinship" terms. To begin with, any similitude and common substance between God and humans is strongly rejected (e.g. Q 5:18, and most famously in Sūrat al-Ikhlāṣ, "Sincere Devotion," Q 112; see ANTHROPOMORPHISM). God cannot be likened or compared to anything — particularly as everything is of his creation (q.v.). The Qurʾān does, however, recognize friendship between God and humans, but friendship in this case transcends the absence of similitude: for it was God who chose to make Abraham (q.v.) his friend *(khalīl)* because the latter had given his entire being to him (Q 4:125; see ḤANĪF). The faithful, on the other hand, are bound by their common faith and the union of their hearts, which makes them brothers to one another (Q 3:103; 49:10). God has endowed human beings in this world with bonds of descent and affinity *(nasaban wa-ṣihran)* — that is to say, with enduring relations that are inherited as well as voluntarily undertaken (Q 25:54). Thus one owes obedience (q.v.) to one's parents (q.v.) — and especially to one's mother (Q 31:14): parents are to be welcomed and honored, just as the prophet Joseph (q.v.) welcomed his mother and his father (Q 12:99-100). Indeed obedience to parents is a virtue (see VIRTUES AND VICES, COMMANDING AND FORBIDDING) even if they happen to be non-Muslims (Q 40:8), so long as this does not involve disobedience (q.v.) to God (Q 58:22). (See, for example, the widely used textbook on the prescribed relations between parents and children in Islam, Ṣāliḥ, *ʿAlāqāt al-ābāʾ*, 15-41.) But on the day of judgment (see LAST JUDGMENT) one stands alone before God surveying one's completed life (Q 23:101). All inherited and created bonds of life are there dissolved. One flees from all one's kin — including one's parents, brothers, spouse *(ṣāḥiba)*, and children (Q 80:33-7). On that day any sense of kinship as common substance is proven meaningless. Only similitude links us together. Hence one must temper worldly attachments of every kind.

As understood by the faithful Muslim, the qurʾānic language of kinship articulates ways of behaving in this world in full consciousness of God, rather than representing the traces of a secular society in the process of evolving from tribalism to individualism. See also FAMILY.

Talal Asad

Bibliography
M. Arkoun, *Min al-ijtihād ilā naqd al-ʿaql al-islāmī*, Beirut 1993; J.L. Austin, *How to do things with words*, Oxford 1962; S. Bashīr, *Tawāzun al-naqāʾiḍ. Muḥāḍarāt fī l-jāhiliyya wa-ṣadri l-islām*, Jerusalem 1978; G.-H. Bousquet and F. Peltier, *Les successions agnatiques mitigées. Étude comparée du régime successoral en droit germanique et en droit musulman*, Paris 1935; P. Crone, *Meccan trade and the rise of Islam*, Princeton 1987; id., Tribes and states in the Middle East, in *JRAS* Series 3 vol. 3 (1993), 353-76; F.M. Donner, *The early Islamic conquests*, Princeton 1981; id., *Narratives of Islamic origin. The beginnings of Islamic historical writing*, Princeton 1998; R. Needham (ed.), *Rethinking kinship and marriage*, London 1971; D.S. Powers, *Studies in Qurʾān and ḥadīth*, Berkeley 1986; P.G. Rivière, Marriage. A reassessment, in R. Needham, *Rethinking kinship and marriage*, London 1971, 57-74; F. Rosenthal, Nasab, in *EI*², vii, 967-8; S.I. Ṣāliḥ, *ʿAlāqāt al-ābāʾ bi-l-abnāʾ fī l-sharīʿati l-islāmiyya*, Jeddah 1981, repr. 1984; D.M. Schneider, *A critique of the study of kinship*, Ann Arbor 1984; W.R. Smith, *Kinship and marriage in early Arabia*, Cambridge 1885; W.M. Watt, *Muhammad at Mecca*, Oxford 1953; id., *Muhammad at Medina*, Oxford 1956; Watt-Bell, *Introduction;* F.J. Ziadeh, Review of Powers' *Studies in Qurʾān and ḥadīth* (1986), in *JAOS* 108 (1988), 487-8.

Kitāb see BOOK; PEOPLE OF THE BOOK; SCRIPTURE AND THE QURʾĀN

Knife see INSTRUMENTS

Knowledge and Learning

Cognitive understanding and its acquisition. Concepts of knowledge and learning appear frequently in nearly all types of Islamic discourse. They are commonly subsumed under a variety of Arabic words such as *ʿilm, maʿrifa, fiqh, ḥikma* and *shuʿūr*, and the verbs and verbal derivatives of each, many of which find representation in the Qurʾān itself, at least in form if not in meaning.

The problem of defining knowledge and explaining its relationship to faith (q.v.) on the one hand, and to action and works on the other (see GOOD DEEDS; EVIL DEEDS; ETHICS AND THE QURʾĀN), became, for example, the subject of intense debate and eventual elaboration involving precision and technical complexity. One example is the great concern of the experts about establishing that human knowledge is contingent and temporally produced whereas that of God is not, although he somehow, despite the paradox, comprehends and is the author of what humans think (see INTELLECT; FREEDOM AND PREDESTINATION). For both philosophy *(falsafa)* and theology *(kalām)* a precise understanding of the nature of knowledge *(ʿilm)* is, in fact, for this and many other reasons an essential first premise to all subsequent reasoning (see PHILOSOPHY AND THE QURʾĀN; THEOLOGY AND THE QURʾĀN). A major category of Islamic literature took up the theme of the enumeration of the sciences *(iḥṣāʾ al-ʿulūm)*, that is, of laying out schematically all knowledge and explaining its value, ranks, and the relationship of one kind to the others. Religious scholars in Islam are "those who know" *(ʿulamāʾ*, sing. *ʿālim)*. The search for knowledge *(ṭalab al-ʿilm)* is a duty for all Muslims, but especially for those who aspire to attain the status of a learned authority (q.v.). Seeking knowledge implies both finding and studying with a teacher and traveling to distant lands (even to China). Ṣūfī mystics (see ṢŪFISM AND THE QURʾĀN) sought to separate the process of knowing through intuitive perception *(dhawq)* and presence from discursive learning and rational or intellectual reasoning — an effort that has led to an impressively sophisticated body of writings, both by the Ṣūfīs and by those who would deny their approach. Even earlier Muslims debated, as yet another example, the extent to which knowledge is confined to, or conveyed exclusively within, a natural language and its grammar (see GRAMMAR AND THE QURʾĀN; ARABIC LANGUAGE; LANGUAGE, CONCEPT OF). For example, is what can be known in Arabic — the language of the Islamic revelation — different from Greek science and philosophy in part because of its linguistic home? Or does there exist a universal logic of thought that transcends (and is therefore superior to) particular expressions in use in a given culture? The ḥadīth (see ḤADĪTH AND THE QURʾĀN), as yet one more category, already include numerous admonitions about the value of knowledge, its reward and the duty to seek it, to gather and preserve it, to journey abroad in search of it. In it teachers are accorded high honor; Muḥammad was a teacher; the angel Gabriel (q.v.) also (see TEACHING).

All these examples merely hint at the enormous importance of knowledge and learning in the Islamic world over time and place from the earliest period of post-qurʾānic Islam to the present (see TEACHING AND PREACHING THE QURʾĀN). Every facet of Islamic thought was and continues to be affected by it. But it is doubtful that these concepts of knowledge or of learning and the characteristic value placed on them in Islam generally, come from the Qurʾān itself or find an echo there. It is, of course, always possible, and often done, to interpret the sacred text to draw on its amazing flexibility and thus yield almost any meaning from its words (see EXEGESIS OF THE QURʾĀN: CLASSICAL AND MEDIEVAL; EXEGESIS OF THE QURʾĀN: EARLY MODERN AND CONTEMPORARY). Nevertheless, given the original context for the Qurʾān, claiming as it does to represent the very words of God and not those of humans except secondarily, the perspective from which it speaks is not that of the community of Muslims. It does not reflect their later need to acquire or preserve knowledge.

In the world of the Qurʾān God alone knows (see GOD AND HIS ATTRIBUTES); truth (q.v.) is his. In it either humans do not know, even though they may think they know, or God causes a select few of them to possess a limited degree of knowledge and truth (see IGNORANCE; IMPECCABILITY). They know what he lets them know. This starkly different view of knowledge is perhaps best approached by observing a common theme in later Islamic thought of how to know God and, almost as important, how to express and verbally explain knowing God. One aspect of the problem is that God is infinite and no finite creature can know an infinite (see ANTHROPOMORPHISM). Knowing a thing implies comprehending the thing as it really and truly is. But that is impossible in relation to the infinite, unlimited, inexhaustible God. God cannot be known by humans; they will merely come to "acknowledge" him or "be aware" of him. Some authors make a distinction here between "knowing" (the verb *ʿalima*) and "recognizing" (the verb *ʿarafa*).

But, even so, is there any correspondence at all between the knowledge that God has and what knowledge the human possesses, acquires, or comes to know? Obviously, God himself does not learn, but does he teach? An important theme in Islamic writings concerns the relative worth of study and effort versus the spontaneous acquisition of inspired enlightenment (see REVELATION AND INSPIRATION; PROPHETS AND PROPHETHOOD). Should the seeker of knowledge — here the exact meaning of knowledge can vary — read books and take instruction, or avoid both and prepare for the infusion of knowledge by grace through pious practice and exercise (see PIETY)?

In the Qurʾān the fact that God is all-knowing *(ʿalīm),* knows what humans do not, and knows the unseen *(ʿālim al-ghayb, ʿallām al-ghayb)* is stressed constantly (see HIDDEN AND THE HIDDEN). The term all-knowing *(ʿalīm)* appears literally again and again, often in combination with all-wise (*ḥakīm,* see WISDOM; JUDGMENT) but also with all-hearing (*samīʿ,* see HEARING AND DEAFNESS; SEEING AND HEARING). One phrase states clearly that "over and above every person who has knowledge is the all-knowing" (Q 12:76). In fact, every qurʾānic instance (thirteen in all) of the term "knower" (*ʿālim* [sing.]), which is the same word as that used later for the learned scholar, is followed by "unseen" *(ghayb)* and therefore refers unambiguously to God. It is true that there are references (five) to "those with knowledge" in the plural *(ʿālimūn, ʿulamāʾ)* and several expressions for humans "who know, understand, are aware" *(ūlū l-albāb,* for example, or *al-rāsikhūn fī l-ʿilm).* Nevertheless, God's preponderance and omniscience is overwhelming, so much so as to bring into question what it means to assert that humans, even the prophets, know.

A further issue is how they come to know whatever it is that they know. Strictly within the Qurʾān, the terms for knowing and knowledge (*ʿilm, maʿrifa, fiqh, shuʿūr* and the various forms they take) seem to suggest not a degree or quantity, but an absolute, in which the known object is simply the truth — what truly is — in its ultimate reality and not some fact of ordinary perception. Common human knowledge in its mundane form lacks value in comparison. Thus, to have knowledge or to come to have knowledge implies becoming aware of the true nature of the universe as God's creation (q.v.) and of his role in it. In most cases, qurʾānic references to those who know or do not know indicate only whether or not the person or persons understands this truth and do not indicate an acquired or accumulated degree of learning. Those who have knowledge *(al-ʿulamāʾ)* are simply those who truly fear (q.v.) God (Q 35:28). Q 3:66 (among others) refers to those who argue about a matter about which they have no knowledge; only God knows what they think they know.

The opposites of knowledge are ignorance *(jahl),* which is not having guidance (*hudā,* as in Q 6:35; see ASTRAY; ERROR), supposition or conjecture (Q 53:28) and the following of personal whims in the absence of knowledge (as in Q 6:119 and 30:29), all of which denote a failure, often willful, to perceive and acknowledge the truth. Even the expressions for those who possess understanding *(ūlū l-albāb),* who are firmly grounded in knowledge *(al-rāsikhūn fī l-ʿilm)* or who come to know that which they formerly knew not *(mā lam yaʿlam, mā lam takun taʿlam),* indicate, not learning in the normal sense of that word, but having such knowledge, that is, of being wise in matters of religion (q.v.) and the affairs of God.

Given that knowledge does not depend on study and learning, it is fair to ask if the Qurʾān contains a concept of instruction as in either the teaching by God of humans or humans of other humans, leading some to become more learned than others. There are in fact several verses that, in accordance with the Qurʾān's fertile elasticity, can be construed in this manner. Most use the second — that is, transitive — form of the verb "to know" *(ʿalima),* thus to "teach" *(ʿallama).* Important examples include "he taught Adam the names of all things" (Q 2:31; see ADAM AND EVE); "we have no knowledge except that which you taught us" (Q 2:32); "the most merciful taught the Qurʾān; he created man and taught him the explanation *(al-bayān)*" (Q 55:1-4); "Lord... you have taught me [Joseph] the interpretation of events" (Q 12:101; see JOSEPH; DREAMS AND SLEEP; FORETELLING; DIVINATION; PORTENTS); and "we have been taught the language of the birds" (27:16; see ANIMAL LIFE). It is easy to see how these cases can be, as they have been, understood as proof that God acts as the teacher of humankind, at least of the prophets. In a closely parallel example, however, God instead "brings" or "bestows" *(ātā)* knowledge: "we have brought to David (q.v.) and Solomon (q.v.) knowledge" (Q 27:15); the sense is rather of God's *causing* the recipient to know something, not by instruction but by instantaneous revelation. "God revealed *(anzala)* to you the book (q.v.), and wisdom and caused you to know that which you previously knew not" (Q 4:113). This latter sense fits better the tone of the Qurʾān and of the power of God as expressed in it generally (see POWER AND IMPOTENCE). The slow accumulation of items of knowledge applies solely to humans learning from other humans. It involves a temporal and sequential process quite different from that of God. Accordingly, therefore, the first of these verses reads: "he caused Adam to have knowledge of the names of all things" and thus it does not imply a process of learning or that, despite his knowledge, Adam was "learned."

The cryptic words of Q 96:4-5, "he it is who taught by the pen; taught humankind *(al-insān)* what it knew not" suggest, however, the opposite since they indicate, if taken literally, a form of instruction that by its very nature must be sequentially ordered. The commentators note, however, that the verse may rather be read such that God taught the *use of* the pen, that is, writing itself. Nevertheless, the more common interpretation is that he taught *by means of* the pen and therefore quite possibly these verses point to some type of book learning (see BOOK; WRITING AND WRITING MATERIALS). A few isolated verses also mention learning or instruction in a situation involving humans imparting (or purportedly imparting) knowledge from one to the other. Two of these (Q 44:14 and 16:103), however, cite false imputations that Muḥammad had been taught what he knew by another man (a foreigner; see INFORMANTS; STRANGERS AND FOREIGNERS). One more verse (Q 2:102) speaks of a kind of sorcery or magic (q.v.) taught by devils (see DEVIL) for evil purposes, such as a spell to separate a man and his wife (see MARRIAGE AND DIVORCE; JINN).

Yet another verse (Q 9:122) contains a verb form that usually denotes quite clearly "to study" *(tafaqqaha)* and is there joined with the word "religion" *(li-yatafaqqahū fī l-dīn)*, in a phrase that would translate "that they may study (or become learned in) religion." The verse as a whole cautions the Muslims not to go to war (q.v.) altogether but to leave behind a contingent when the rest go out. But according to a widely accepted interpretation (credited by the commentary tradition to Ibn ʿAbbās [d. 68/686-8]), it applies specifically to a time when the Prophet was then actively receiving revelations and other instructions from God and, if none of the Muslims were to stay with him at home, none would come to know those aspects of the religion imparted to him in that interval. Subsequently, they could neither transmit it accurately to those not present nor insure its later preservation. And yet another view is that it is the party that goes out to war (not those who remain behind) that gains a deeper understanding and appreciation of religion — witnessing in this case how, by God's support, a few Muslims can defeat a much larger force of unbelievers (see EXPEDITIONS AND BATTLES) — and brings that truth back with them to share with the others (see FIGHTING; JIHĀD). Both interpretations are related, for example, by Fakhr al-Dīn al-Rāzī (d. 606/1210; *Tafsīr,* xvi, 225-7), among others. Thus, despite the use of this quite suggestive verb, given the context of the passage as a whole, the "study of religion" which is what some authorities would later have it imply, is not necessarily what was involved in this particular situation.

Paul E. Walker

Bibliography
Primary (in addition to the standard commentaries on the verses cited above): al-Ghazālī, Abū Ḥāmid Muḥammad, *The book of knowledge. Being a translation with notes of the* Kitāb al-ʿIlm *of al-Ghazālī's* Iḥyāʾ ʿulūm al-dīn, trans. N.A. Fāris, Lahore 1962, 1970² (rev. ed.); Rāzī, *Tafsīr,* ed. M. Muḥyī l-Dīn.
Secondary: ʿAbd al-Bāqī; R. Arnaldez, Maʿrifa, in *EI²*, vi, 568-71; [Ed.], ʿIlm, in *EI²*, iii, 1133-4; F. Rosenthal, *Knowledge triumphant. The concept of knowledge in medieval Islam,* Leiden 1970; Wensinck, *Concordance* (s.v. ʿilm); id., *Handbook* (s.v. knowledge).

Korah

A figure living at the time of Moses (q.v.) who is mentioned both in the Bible and the Qurʾān. He is described in Q 28:76-82 and briefly mentioned in two other verses. Korah (Ar. Qārūn) is introduced as one of the people of Moses, yet one who treated them unjustly (Q 28:76-82; see JUSTICE AND INJUSTICE; OPPRESSION). God accorded him such enormous treasures that "its very keys *(mafātiḥahu)* were too heavy a burden for a company of men" (Q 28:76) to carry. When people urged him to use his wealth (q.v.) for God's purposes and, with the world to come in mind (see ESCHATOLOGY), he would answer that the only reason he possessed his wealth was because of his knowledge (see KNOWLEDGE AND LEARNING). Finally, when Korah "went forth unto his people in his adornment" (Q 28:79) and his people argued about his fortune, God decreed his death, making the earth swallow him and his house (see PUNISHMENT STORIES; CHASTISEMENT AND PUNISHMENT). Two other verses mention the name of Korah. In the first of these (Q 29:39) he, along with Pharaoh (q.v.) and Hāmān (q.v.), arrogantly (see ARROGANCE) opposes the signs (q.v.) brought by Moses, while in the other he, along with Pharaoh and Hāmān, accuses Moses of being a lying sorcerer (Q 40:24; see SOOTHSAYERS; MAGIC; LIE; INSANITY).

As well as containing some elements that are similar to the biblical story of Korah (cf. *Num* 16; see SCRIPTURE AND THE QURʾĀN; MYTHS AND LEGENDS IN THE QURʾĀN), the Qurʾān mainly stresses the fact, which had already been highlighted in rabbinical literature, of his great wealth. A saying of Muḥammad, which reflects qurʾānic content, mentions his name along with those of Hāmān and Pharaoh as examples of people destined to go to hell (q.v.; Ibn Ḥanbal, *Musnad,* ii, 169). Exegetical traditions usually recount that Korah was Moses' cousin or, according to Muḥammad b. Isḥāq (d. 150/767), his uncle (Ṭabarī, *Tafsīr,* xx, 105; see EXEGESIS OF THE QURʾĀN: CLASSICAL AND MEDIEVAL). He was so handsome or his voice, while reciting the Torah (q.v.), was so beautiful that he was named the Enlightened *(al-munawwar).* His appearance among his people is described with a wealth of detail, from his luxurious dress to the magnificence of his escort, consisting of three hundred maids, four thousand riding beasts with purple saddles or with seventy thousand or more soldiers. The keys of his treasures were the leather keys of his storehouses; they were no larger than a finger and so heavy that only forty men or forty camels or sixty mules could carry them.

Korah, envious of the prophethood of Moses and of the sacerdotal privileges of Aaron (q.v.; Abū l-Layth al-Samarqandī, *Tafsīr,* ii, 525; see PROPHETS AND PROPHETHOOD), planned to get rid of Moses when the duty of the alms tax was revealed (see ALMSGIVING). He paid a woman to accuse Moses of adultery (see ADULTERY AND FORNICATION) but the woman, when examined by Moses, retracted her accusation and unmasked Korah's plan. Moses ordered the earth to seize Korah and, in spite of his pleas, he and his house were completely swallowed up (Muqātil, *Tafsīr,* iii, 357). Other traditions state that every day Korah sinks deeper into the earth by the height of a man and that he will continue sinking at this rate until the day of resurrection (q.v.). It is also said, however, that while sinking in the earth, one day Korah heard Jonah's (q.v.) voice in the belly of the whale and that he felt sorry when he learned of Moses' and Aaron's death; as a reward for this, God relieved him of the punishment (Majlisī, *Biḥār,* xiii, 253; see REWARD AND PUNISHMENT). Some other reports tell of Korah's knowledge of alchemy and they are usually linked to the qur'ānic statement about his knowledge. Some traditions specify that he was able to change lead and copper into silver and gold (q.v.) or that Korah learned the art of alchemy from his wife, who was Moses' sister (Kisāʾī, *Qiṣaṣ,* 229; see MEDICINE AND THE QURʾĀN; METALS AND MINERALS).

The origin of the Arabic form of the name of Korah *(Qārūn)* is unknown but seems to parallel the form of other names such as Aaron (*Hārūn,* Horovitz, *KU,* 131).

Roberto Tottoli

Bibliography

Primary: ʿAbd al-Razzāq, *Tafsīr,* ii, 93-4; Abū l-Layth al-Samarqandī, *Tafsīr,* ii, 525-8; Ibn Ḥanbal, *Musnad,* Cairo 1895, ii, 169; Ibn al-Jawzī, *Zād,* Damascus 1953-4, vi, 239-45; Khāzin, *Lubāb,* v, 181-5; Kisāʾī, *Qiṣaṣ,* 229-30; al-Majlisī, Muḥammad Bāqir, *Biḥār al-anwār,* Beirut 1983, xiii, 249-58; Māwardī, *Nukat,* iv, 264-71; Mujāhid, *Tafsīr,* ed. Abū l-Nīl, 532-3; Muqātil, *Tafsīr,* iii, 355-8; Qummī, *Tafsīr,* Beirut 1991, ii, 144-6; Rāzī, *Tafsīr,* xxv, 12-8; Sibṭ Ibn al-Jawzī, *Mirʾāt,* 449-52; Suyūṭī, *Durr,* 8 vols., Cairo 1983, vi, 436-43; Ṭabarī, *Tafsīr,* Cairo 1968, xx, 105-22; id., *Taʾrīkh,* ed. de Goeje, i, 517-27; Thaʿlabī, *Qiṣaṣ,* 188-92; id., *al-Tabṣira,* Beirut 1970, i, 251-4.

Secondary: A. Geiger, *Was hat Mohammed aus dem Judenthume aufgenommen?* Leipzig 1902, 153; Horovitz, *KU,* 131; Jeffery, *For. vocab.,* 231-2; D.B. Macdonald, Ḳārūn, in *EI²*, iv, 673; D. Sidersky, *Les origines des légendes musulmanes dans le Coran et dans les vies des prophètes,* Paris 1933, 95-97; Speyer, *Erzählungen,* 342-4.

L

Labor see MANUAL LABOR; BIRTH

Lactation

Production of milk for nursing a child; the act of nursing a child. Q 2:233, 4:23 and 65:6, all dating (according to Bell) from the Medinan period (see CHRONOLOGY AND THE QURʾĀN), lay the foundations of an Islamic "ethics of breastfeeding" (the Arabic terms for which utilize derivatives of the triliteral root *r-ḍ-ʿ*). In the Medinan sūra Q 22:2, nurses *(kull murḍiʿa)* and nurslings *(mā arḍaʿat)* are mentioned in an eschatological context (see ESCHATOLOGY); the qurʾānic story of Moses' (q.v.) infancy (the Medinan Q 28:7, 12) includes references to nursing and wet nurses *(marāḍiʿ)*; and, finally, weaning *(fiṣāl)* is described as part of the stages of life (the Medinan Q 46:15; cf. the Meccan Q 31:14; see BIOLOGY AS THE CREATION AND STAGES OF LIFE).

That breastfeeding is a maternal instinct is implied in Q 22:2 and, even more strongly, in Q 28:7-12. In Q 22:2, nursing mothers, who due to grief and anxiety neglect their own nurslings, are listed among the signs of the dramatic displacement that will shake the universe on the day of judgment (see LAST JUDGMENT; APOCALYPSE). Moreover, in Q 28:7-12, the love and care of Moses' mother for her nursling find emphatic expression. Q 28:12 shows that the Arabs (q.v.) of the early seventh century were aware that infants sometimes reject the milk (q.v.) of women other than their own mothers (see CHILDREN; PRE-ISLAMIC ARABIA AND THE QURʾĀN).

Q 2:233 calls upon the nurslings' fathers to "provide reputably for their [e.g. their repudiated, lactating wives] food and clothing" during "two full years" (cf. Q 31:14: *wa-fiṣāluhu fī ʿāmayni*) unless both father and mother "by mutual agreement and consultation desire [weaning] (earlier)" (see PARENTS; FAMILY). This could be read as an effort to protect repudiated (see MARRIAGE AND DIVORCE) women who were nursing — and their nurslings — in a society which was becoming sedentary (see GEOGRAPHY; CITY) and experiencing increasing individualism as well as a transition from a matrilineal to a patrilineal family structure (Bianquis, Family, 614; Watt, *Muhammad,* 272-89; see PATRIARCHY; GENDER; WOMEN AND THE QURʾĀN). Wet-nursing (q.v.), in this context of the separation of the parents, is sanctioned by the same verse. Q 65:6 explicitly refers, moreover, to the repudiated (divorced) wife who is being paid to nurse her own infant.

Q 4:23 mentions milk mothers and milk sisters among those with whom a man may not have sexual relations (see PROHIBITED DEGREES; SEX AND SEXUALITY). It thus adds a unique element to a long Semitic tradition of prohibitions of marriage by extending the range of incest beyond its definition in Judaism and Christianity (Héritier, *Deux soeurs,* 87-91; see also FOSTERAGE; SCRIPTURE AND THE QURʾĀN; JEWS AND JUDAISM; CHRISTIANS AND CHRISTIANITY). According to Watt, the principle that milk-relationship is on the same level as blood-relationship may be seen as a concession to matrilineal groups which, practicing forms of polyandry, avoided undue endogamy by making certain degrees of milk-relationship a barrier to marriage (Watt, *Muhammad,* 281; cf. Schacht/Burton and Chelhod, Raḍāʿ, 362; see also KINSHIP; BLOOD AND BLOOD CLOT).

Islamic rules concerning lactation, as formulated in works of qurʾānic exegesis, ḥadīth and *fiqh,* are based on the normative verses among the above-mentioned. These were interpreted against a background of circumstances and needs that sometimes differed from those of the early Muslim community (see COMMUNITY AND SOCIETY IN THE QURʾĀN). One example would be the growing importance of hired wet-nursing among urban higher social groups of the Muslim world in the high Middle Ages. Thus, Ibn al-ʿArabī (d. 543/1148; *Aḥkām,* 202-6) refers to no less than fifteen legal questions, the answers to which are based on Q 2:233. Such questions include, for instance, whether breastfeeding is a mother's right or duty and, assuming it is her duty, whether or not noble women are exempted from fulfilling it. Ibn al-ʿArabī further concludes that a mother's right to the custody of her child (*ḥaḍāna,* not mentioned in the Qurʾān) is based on Q 2:233 since the functions of — and therefore the right to — lactation *(raḍāʿ)* and *ḥaḍāna* cannot be separated (cf. Ilkiyā al-Harrāsī, *Aḥkām,* i/ii, 187).

Ḥadīth and qurʾānic commentaries, postulating a connection between the mother's milk and her husband's semen, explain Q 4:23 (explicitly referring to milk mother and milk sisters only) as intended to duplicate for milk relationships the list of those blood relatives with whom a Muslim man is forbidden to contract marriage (Giladi, *Infants,* 24-7).

Avner Giladi

Bibliography
Primary: al-Harrāsī, ʿImād al-Dīn ʿAlī b. Muḥammad b. ʿAlī Ilkiyā Abū l-Ḥasan al-Ṭabarī, *Aḥkām al-Qurʾān,* 4 vols., Beirut 1983; Ibn al-ʿArabī, *Aḥkām,* Cairo 1957.
Secondary: Th. Bianquis, The family in Arab Islam, in A. Burguière et al. (eds.), *A history of the family,* 2 vols., Cambridge 1996, i, 601-47; A. Giladi, *Infants, parents and wet nurses. Medieval Islamic views on breastfeeding and their social implications,* Leiden 1999; F. Heritier, *Les deux soeurs et leur mère,* Paris 1994; J. Schacht/J. Burton and J. Chelhod, Raḍāʿ, in *EI²,* viii, 361-2; M.W. Watt, *Muhammad at Medina,* Oxford 1956.

Ladder see ASCENSION

Lamp

Manufactured light-giving object. The most common reference to a lamp (Ar. *miṣbāḥ* and *sirāj*) in the Qurʾān is a metaphoric use (see METAPHOR) of the word *sirāj* to designate the sun (q.v.): "And we built over you seven firmaments (see HEAVEN AND SKY) and made a splendid light *(sirājan wahhājan)*" (Q 78:12-3; cf. Dāmaghānī,

Wujūh, i, 442); "And he made the moon (q.v.) a light among them and he made the sun a lamp *(al-shamsa sirājan)*" (Q 71:16); and "Blessed is he who made constellations (see PLANETS AND STARS) in the sky and made in it a lamp *(sirājan)* and a light-giving moon" (Q 25:61). On one occasion (Q 33:46), however, the prophet Muḥammad is referred to as a light-giving lamp (*sirājan munīran,* see NAMES OF THE PROPHET).

The most celebrated reference to a lamp *(miṣbāḥ)* is in Q 24:35, commonly know as the "Light Verse" (*āyat al-nūr;* cf. Dāmaghānī, *Wujūh,* ii, 231; see LIGHT; MATERIAL CULTURE AND THE QUR'ĀN).

Jamal J. Elias

Bibliography (see also Bibliography of LIGHT)
Dāmaghānī, *Wujūh,* ed. Zafītī.

Land see GEOGRAPHY; CREATION

Language, Concept of

The uniquely human faculty of (primarily) verbal expression. In the Qur'ān, the concept of language is expressed by the word *lisān* (lit. tongue). The other common term for language, *lugha,* which is well-attested in classical and modern standard Arabic (see ARABIC LANGUAGE), does not appear in the Qur'ān; one encounters only the related words *laghw* and *lāghiya,* which express exclusively the connotation of "vain utterance."

There are twenty-five occurrences of the word *lisān* in the Qur'ān, fifteen in the singular and ten in the plural (*alsina;* the other plural, *alsun,* is not attested in the Qur'ān; cf. 'Abd al-Bāqī). In all of its occurrences in the plural, *lisān* actually refers to the tongue as the organ of speech, a meaning found in six of its occurrences in the singular. While *lisān* designates the tongue as the organ of speech, speech (q.v.) itself and the act of speaking are designated by the verb *qāla* and its derivatives as, for example, in Q 20:27-8: "Unloose the knot upon my tongue that they might understand my words" *(wa-uḥlul 'uqdatan min lisānī yafqahū qawlī).* The common metonymy — one encounters it in more than one language — of the tongue, the organ of speech, being used to mean the language articulated by means of that organ, appears in the nine remaining occurrences of *lisān* in the singular.

As to other important developments, the most interesting is surely Q 14:4: "And we have sent no messenger (q.v.) save with the tongue of his people that he might make all clear to them" *(wa-mā arsalnā min rasūlin illā bi-lisāni qawmihi li-yubayyina lahum).* The first part of this sentence is a restrictive clause offered as the premise to an argument whose conclusion constitutes a well known theological thesis: namely, that the Arabic of the Qur'ān is itself the very language of Muḥammad, that is to say, a hypothetical "dialect of Quraysh (q.v.)," hypothetical in the sense that it is not documented in an independent manner (see DIALECTS).

The second part of Q 14:4 is based on a common conception of language as an articulation of thought *(tabyīn).* Thus, efficacy in preaching (see also Q 19:97 and 44:58, *yassarnāhu bi-lisānika,* "now we have made it easy by your tongue"; see PROPHETS AND PROPHETHOOD; WARNER; GOOD NEWS) is linked to a language viewed either as a commonly-spoken vernacular or as a hypothetically-constructed linguistic vehicle. According to the theological thesis mentioned above, the qur'ānic language is indeed the vernacular of Quraysh. But for many Arabists, the Arabic of the Qurʾān is very close, if not identical, to the pre-Islamic poetic *koiné,* itself a hypothetical construct (see POETS AND POETRY; LANGUAGE AND STYLE OF THE QURʾĀN; FORM AND STRUCTURE OF THE QURʾĀN). Some other linguists turn towards a third hypothesis: the late homogenization of both language forms (for a general overview, see Jones, Language). The use of the second verbal form, *bayyana,* with an explicit object in Q 14:4 (see Ṭabarī, *Tafsīr,* xvi, 616, for an example of classical commentary on this passage) suggests that *mubīn,* as an active participle of the fourth verbal form, *abāna* (see GRAMMAR AND THE QURʾĀN), may be similarly understood. See, for example, Q 26:195, where *lisān ʿarabī mubīn,* "a clear Arabic tongue," can be understood as "an Arabic tongue that makes [all things] clear" (Ṭabarī, *Tafsīr,* xix, 112, for this signification). But the opposition found in Q 16:103 between a *lisān* qualified simply as *aʿjamī* and a *lisān* with the double qualification of *ʿarabī* and *mubīn* makes one understand the former qualifier as the antonym of the two latter ones. In other words, its possible translation as "barbarous" conveys the dual sense of non-Arabic *(ʿajamī)* and unclear *(aʿjam).* For the exegetes' debates on the meaning of *aʿjamī,* see Wansbrough (*QS,* 98-9), who includes this notion of *ʿarabī* and *mubīn* as functional equivalents.

In the juxtaposition of terms found in Q 16:103, one notes a furtive slip from an objective state, the communicative function of any language, to a subjective state, the clarity bestowed only on Arabic. It is this shift of signification that supported the theological logo-centrism of the medieval period (for example, see Shāfiʿī, *Risāla,* 34-55; also Gilliot, *Elt,* chapters 3 and 4) and provided justification for the linguistic nationalism of the modern era *(qawmiyya* < *qawm)* and what the American linguist Ferguson has described as "myths about Arabic." See also ILLITERACY; INIMITABILITY; FOREIGN VOCABULARY; ARABS; ARABIC SCRIPT.

Pierre Larcher

Bibliography

Primary: al-Shāfiʿī, Muḥammad b. Idrīs, *al-Risāla,* ed. A.M. Shākir, Cairo 1939; Ṭabarī, *Tafsīr,* ed. Shākir.

Secondary: ʿAbd al-Bāqī; C.A. Ferguson, Myths about Arabic, in R.S. Harrell (ed.), *Languages and linguistics monograph series,* Georgetown 1959, 75-82 (repr. in R.K. Belnap and N. Haeri [eds.], *Structuralist studies in Arabic linguistics. Charles A. Ferguson's papers 1954-1994,* Leiden 1997, 250-6); Gilliot, *Elt;* A. Jones, The language of the Qurʾān, in K. Dévényi, T. Iványi and A. Shivtiel (eds.), *Proceedings of the Colloquium on Arabic lexicology and lexicography* (C.A.L.L.), Budapest 1993, 29-48; Wansbrough, *QS.*

Language and Style of the Qurʾān

The semantic field of "language" includes several triliteral Arabic roots: *l-s-n* (Dāmaghānī, *Wujūh,* ii, 200-1; see H. Jenssen, Arabic language, 132; see also LANGUAGE, CONCEPT OF), *k-l-m* (Yaḥyā b. Sallām, *Taṣārīf,* 303-5; Dāmaghānī, *Wujūh,* ii, 186-7), *q-w-l, l-ḥ-n* (Khan, *Die exegetischen Teile,* 276, on Q 47: 30: "the burden of their talk," *laḥn al-qawl;* Fück, *ʿArabīya,* 133; Fr. trans. 202; Ullmann, *Wa-ḫairu,* 21-2). It should be noted that *lugha* in the sense of manner of speaking (Fr. *parler,* Ger. *Redeweise*) is totally absent from the Qurʾān — although the root *l-gh-w* is attested, but with the meanings of "vain conversation" (Q 23:3), "to talk idly" (Q 41:26), "idle talk" (Q 19:62; see GOSSIP), or to be "unintentional" in an oath (Q 2:225; 5:89; Dāmaghānī, *Wujūh,* ii, 198; Ibn al-Jawzī, *Nuzha,* 531-2; see OATHS).

The Qurʾān asserts of itself: "this is plain/clear Arabic tongue/speech/

language *(lisānun ʿarabiyyun mubīnun)*" (Q 16:103), or that it is "in plain/clear Arabic tongue/speech/language" (Q 26:195). In any case, this was the meaning of these verses according to the exegetes (see EXEGESIS OF THE QURĀN: CLASSICAL AND MEDIEVAL), and most translations have followed their lead, which, as will be discussed below, is problematic. It should be noted that, in Arabic — as in English — the concept of "language" is multivalent, including both an oral and a written manifestation. As will be discussed below, the interplay between these two aspects of language in the formation of the qurʾānic corpus is only imperfectly understood, a situation that leads to contested explanations for certain features of the qurʾānic language (for more on this subject, see ORALITY).

Various general positions on the language and style of the Qurʾān

There are many opposing points of view on the language and style of the Qurʾān, as will appear through a selection of quotations taken from both Muslim and non-Muslim scholars (for reactions of Muslims through the ages, see below). The Muslim translator of the Qurʾān, M. Pickthall (d. 1935), a British convert to Islam, described the Qurʾān as an "inimitable symphony, the very sounds of which move men to tears and ecstasy" (Pickthall, vii). An earlier (non-Muslim) English translator of the Qurʾān, G. Sale (d. 1736) thought that: "The style of the Korân is generally beautiful and fluent, especially where it imitates the prophetic manner and scripture phrases. It is concise and often obscure, adorned with bold figures after the eastern taste, enlivened with florid and sententious expressions, and in many places, especially when the majesty and attributes of God are described (see GOD AND HIS ATTRIBUTES), sublime and magnificent" (*Preliminary discourse*, 66). For the Austrian J. von Hammer-Purgstall (d. 1856): "The Koran is not only the law book of Islam (see LAW AND THE QURʾĀN), but also a masterpiece of Arabic poetic art (see POETRY AND POETS). Only the high magic of the language could give to the speech of Abdallah's son the stamp of the speech (q.v.) of God" (Die letzten vierzig Suren, 25). For F.J. Steingass (d. 1903), the Qurʾān is: "[...] A work, then, which calls forth so powerful and seemingly incompatible emotions even in the distant reader — distant as to time, and still more so as to mental development — a work which not only conquers the repugnance with which he may begin its perusal, but changes this adverse feeling into astonishment and admiration" (Hughes/Steingass, Qurʾān, 526-7). Another translator of the Qurʾān, J. Berque (d. 1995), has tried to find a "diplomatic" solution in the face of the peculiar language and style of the Qurʾān, speaking of its "interlacing structure," "symphonic effects" and "inordinating junctions" (*jonctions démesurantes*, Berque, *Langages*, 200-7; cf. id., *Coran*, 740: "a triangular speech"; id., *Relire*, 33-4), showing with these unusual qualifications the difficulty he had in expressing a consistently positive judgment, such as, "It is not necessary to be a Muslim to be sensitive to the remarkable beauty of this text, to its fullness and universal value" (id., *Relire*, 129).

On the other hand, R. Bell (d. 1952) remarked that, for a long time, occidental scholars called attention to "the grammatical unevennesses and interruption of sense which occur in the Qurʾān" (Bell, *Commentary*, i, xx). Indeed the qurʾānic scholar and Semitist Th. Nöldeke (d. 1930) had already qualified the qurʾānic language as: "drawling, dull and prosaic" (Nöldeke, *Geschichte*, 107, on the sūras of the third Meccan period; cf. id., *De origine*, 55; id., *GQ*, i, 143, n. 2, written by Schwally: "Muḥammad was at the very most a middle-size stylist"). For this German scholar, "while many parts of the Koran undoubtedly have considerable rhetorical power, even over an unbelieving reader, the book, aesthetically considered, is by no means a first-rate performance" (Nöldeke, Koran, 34). In Strassburg, he also wrote that "the sound linguistic sense of the Arabs (q.v.) almost entirely preserved them from imitating the oddnesses and weaknesses of the qurʾānic language" (Nöldeke, Sprache, 22; Fr. trans. *Remarques*, 34). J. Barth (d. 1914) was struck by "the disruptions of the relations" in the sūras (*Störungen der Zusammenhänge;* Studien, 113). The Iraqi English Semitist A. Mingana (d. 1937) thought that the style of the Qurʾān "suffers from the disabilities that always characterize a first attempt in a new literary language which is under the influence of an older and more fixed literature" (Syriac influence, 78; this older literature being for him Syriac; see SYRIAC AND THE QURʾĀN). For the specialist in Arabic literature and Ṣūfism (see ṢŪFISM AND THE QURʾĀN), R.A. Nicholson (d. 1945), "The preposterous arrangment of the Koran [...] is mainly responsible for the opinion held by European readers that it is obscure, tiresome, uninteresting; a farrago of long-winded narratives (q.v.) and prosaic exhortations (q.v.), quite unworthy to be named in the same breath with the Prophetical Books of the Old Testament" (*Literary history,* 161; see FORM AND STRUCTURE OF THE QURʾĀN; SCRIPTURE AND THE QURʾĀN).

Other intellectuals waver between reactions of disgust and attraction in reading the Qurʾān. In this category may be placed J.W. Goethe (d. 1832): "The Koran repeats itself from sura to sura [...] with all sort of amplifications, unbridled tautologies and repetitions which constitute the body of this sacred book, which, each time we turn to it, is repugnant, but it soon attracts, astounds, and in the end enforces reverence [...]. The style of the Koran, in accordance with its contents and aim is stern, grand, terrible, here and there truly sublime" (Goethe, *Noten,* 33-5).

In fact, there are two conceptions of the Qurʾān. The first is theological and is proper to the world of Islam. It is a matter of beliefs, and because beliefs in the Islamic areas are obligatory, of dogmas (see BELIEF AND UNBELIEF; CREEDS). The other conception is anthropological, and because of the reason just mentioned, it is represented only outside of the world of Islam, although not only by non-Muslims: some Muslims, admittedly very few (and usually not living in Muslim countries), also maintain this conception of the Qurʾān. For those who subscribe to the first conception, the Qurʾān is the eternal speech of God (see WORD OF GOD; ETERNITY; CREATEDNESS OF THE QURʾĀN); for those who maintain the second position, the Qurʾān is a text which has a history. The same conceptual dichotomy is to be found concerning the language and the style of the Qurʾān. To remove any doubt and misunderstanding on this issue we will try to deal with each of these conceptions independently, setting apart the Islamic theological thesis from the hypotheses of the Arabists.

The theological thesis on the language of the Qurʾān

For clarity of exposition, we shall first introduce this thesis in a general and theoretical way, followed by a more detailed development of some points contained therein.

The general formulation of the theological thesis

By "theological thesis" is meant the position which imposed itself definitively in Islam around the fourth/tenth century, but which had already existed from the end of the second/eighth and the beginning of the third/ninth centuries, although not in such a formalized, theoretical format. It begins with the assertion: The language of the Qurʾān is Arabic. But which Arabic (see DIALECTS)? This question found an answer in Islamic theology, wherein a special way of interpreting the qurʾānic text itself follows the qurʾānic statement: "And we never sent a messenger (q.v.) save with the language/tongue of his folk, that he might make [the message] clear for them" (*li-yubayyina lahum,* Q 14:4). The exegetes conclude from this verse that the language of the Qurʾān is that of Muḥammad and his Companions (see COMPANIONS OF THE PROPHET), understood as the dialect of Ḥijāz (see PRE-ISLAMIC ARABIA AND THE QURʾĀN), and more particularly of the Quraysh (q.v.). To that first identification, qurʾānic Arabic = the Ḥijāzī dialect or the dialect of the Quraysh *(al-lugha al-ḥijāziyya, lughat Quraysh),* they added a second one: the language of the Quraysh = *al-lugha al-fuṣḥā.* This last expression is the Arabic denomination of what the Arabists themselves call "classical Arabic."

That identification originates less in the qurʾānic text than in an Islamic conception of the Qurʾān, as it appears in the work of the philologist and jurist Ibn Fāris (d. 395/1004). In the Qurʾān itself *lugha,* with the meaning of language, or the feminine comparative *fuṣḥā* do not occur, but only the masculine of this last form: "My brother Aaron (q.v.) is more eloquent than me in speech [or, "speaks better than me"; *afṣaḥu minnī lisānan*]" (Q 28:34). This verse shows, however, that the *faṣāḥa* 1) is above all, a quality of the one who speaks, 2) that there are degrees in it, and 3) that it is only metonymically transferred from the locutor to the language, in this case by the means of a specification (in Arabic grammar *tamyīz;* here *lisānan* indicates eloquence "concerning" language).

We find an echo of the qurʾānic formulation in the following affirmation of a scholar of Rayy quoted by Ibn Fāris with a chain of authority (see ḤADĪTH AND THE QURʾĀN), Ismāʿīl b. Abī ʿUbayd Allāh Muʿāwiya b. ʿUbayd Allāh al-Ashʿarī (d. first half third/ninth cent.), whose father was the vizier and secretary of the caliph al-Mahdī: "The Qurayshites are the most refined of the Arabs by their tongues and the purest by their language *(afṣaḥ al-ʿarab alsinatan wa aṣfāhum lughatan).*" To that affirmation no justification is given, save a dogmatical one: "The reason is that God... has chosen and elected (see ELECTION) them among all the Arabs *(dhālika anna llāha... khtārahum min jamīʿ al-ʿarab wa-ṣṭafāhum),* and among them he has chosen the prophet of mercy (q.v.), Muḥammad" (Ibn Fāris, *al-Ṣāḥibī,* 52; Rabin, *West-Arabian,* 22-3).

The metonymy is again seen at work in the book of the grammarian Ibn Jinnī (d. 392/1002; *Khaṣāʾiṣ,* i, 260; see GRAMMAR AND THE QURʾĀN) saying of the language of the Ḥijāz: "it is the purest and the oldest *(al-lugha al-fuṣḥā al-qudmā).*" Here, it is true, a third idea appears, linking superority to precedence or antiquity. It is already in Sībawayhi (d. 177/793 or 180/796; *Kitāb,* ed. Derenbourg, ii, 37, l. 15; ed. Būlāq, ii, 40; ed. Hārūn, iii, 278): "the Ḥijāzī is the first and oldest language" (*wa-l-ḥijāziyya hiya l-lugha l-ūlā l-qudmā;* Levin, Sībawayhi's attitude, 215-6, and n. 61). Of course, this declaration could be a later interpolation. It is the qualification of a philologist, the counterpart of the concept of "the corruption of language" *(fasād al-lugha):* to say that language is subject to corruption is to aknowledge but also to condemn linguistic change, which is diachronic. Traditionally the linguistic superiority of the Quraysh has been seen as the consequence of their being at greatest remove from the non-Arabic speaking areas: "Therefore, the dialect [or, better, "manner of speaking," Fr. *parler,* Ger. *Redeweise*] of the Quraysh was the most correct and purest Arabic dialect *(afṣaḥa l-lughāti l-ʿarabiyyati wa-asfaḥa),* because the Quraysh were on all sides far removed from the lands of the non-Arabs" (Ibn Khaldūn, *ʿIbar,* 1072; Eng. trans. Ibn Khaldūn-Rosenthal, iii, 343). But Ibn Fāris himself (*al-Ṣāḥibī,* 52) considers this superiority to be the product of the selection of the best elements of the different Arabic dialects, a selection made possible by the fact that Mecca (q.v.) was the center of an inter-tribal pilgrimage (q.v.; we shall see the interpretation given by Kahle to this conception).

The Qurʾān on its own language and style. Does the Qurʾān really say it is in "a clear Arabic tongue"?
As the Qurʾān is a very self-referential text (Wild, *Mensch,* 33), it has often been said that it was "somewhat self-conscious with respect to its language" (Jenssen, Arabic language, 132), providing commentary on its own language, style, and perhaps arrangement. Support for this view is drawn, first of all, from the apparent qurʾānic qualification of itself as being "plain/clear Arabic tongue/speech/language."

It would appear, however, that most of the occurrences of *lisān* in the Qurʾān refer to "tongue" as a vocal organ (Wansbrough, *QS,* 99; see also LANGUAGE, CONCEPT OF), like Q 39:28: "A lecture in Arabic, containing no crookedness (*ghayra dhī ʿiwajin,* without distortion)"; and in this case it can be related to a topos of prophetical communication (see PROPHETS AND PROPHETHOOD; REVELATION AND INSPIRATION), reflecting the speech difficulties associated with the calling of Moses (q.v.; Exodus 4:10-7): "O my lord, I am not eloquent, neither heretofore, nor since you have spoken unto your servant, but I am slow of speech, and of a slow tongue" (verse 10). The Qurʾān, too, knows this story, as evidenced by Q 20:27, wherein Moses says: "And loose a knot from my tongue" (cf. also Q 28:34, "My brother Aaron is more eloquent than me in speech *[afṣaḥu minnī lisānan],*" which is a reversal of Exodus 4:14-5: "Is not Aaron thy brother? I know that he can speak well [...]. And thou shalt speak unto him, and put words in his mouth and I will be with thy mouth [or: I will help you speak], and with his mouth."). Such is the case also for Q 19:97: "And we make it [this scripture] easy for your tongue *(yassarnāhu bi-lisānika).*" It should be noted that the same expression in Q 44:58 has been translated by Pickthall, with no apparent reason for translating the two passages differently, as: "[...] easy in thy language." This theme becomes a refrain in Q 54:17, 22, 40: "And in truth we have made the Qurʾān easy to remember" (see MEMORY). Such texts "could support the hypothesis that linguistic allusions in the Qurʾān are not to the Arabic language but rather, to the task of prophetical communication" (Wansbrough, *QS,* ibid.; cf. Robinson, *Discovering,* 158-9).

The Qurʾān says not only that it is in Arabic or Arabic tongue/speech/language *(lisān),* but it seems also to declare that it is in a plain/clear *(mubīn)* tongue/speech/language: "We have revealed it, a lecture *(qurʾānan)* in Arabic" (Q 12:2; 20:113); "We revealed it, a decisive utterance *(ḥukman)* in Arabic" (Q 13:37); "a lecture in Arabic" (Q 39:28; 41:3; 42:7; 43:3); "this is a confirming scripture in the Arabic language" *(lisānan ʿarabiyyan)* (Q 46:12); "in plain Arabic speech" *(bi-lisānin ʿarabiyyin mubīnin)* (Q 26:195; cf. 16:103; see Rippin, Foreign vocabulary, 226).

The reasons why the Qurʾān insists on the quality and value of its own language seem to be polemical and apologetic (see POLEMIC AND POLEMICAL LANGUAGE). The argument for its Arabic character, first of all, should be put in relation with Q 14:4: "We never sent a messenger save with the language/tongue of his folk *(bi-lisāni qawmihi),* that he might make [the message] clear for them." This declaration, by stressing the language of this messenger (Muḥammad) and this folk (the Arabs), can be understood as a declaration of the ethnocentric nature of this prophetic mission, but also as a divine proof of its universality (Wansbrough, *QS*, 52-3, 98), challenging another sacred language, Hebrew (op. cit. 81), perhaps also Syriac, or more generally Aramaic (see INFORMANTS).

But in stressing that it is in Arabic, the Qurʾān answers also to accusations which were adressed to Muḥammad during the Meccan period (see OPPOSITION TO MUḤAMMAD): "And we know well what they say: Only a man teaches him. The speech of whom they falsely hint *(yulḥidūna ilayhi)* is outlandish *(aʿjamī),* and this is clear Arabic speech" (Q 16:103). The commentators explain *yulḥidūna* (Kūfan reading: *yalḥadūna;* Ṭabarī, *Tafsīr,* xiv, 180; see READINGS OF THE QURʾĀN) by "to incline to, to become fond of" (Muqātil, *Tafsīr,* ii, 487; Farrāʾ, *Maʿānī,* ii, 113), which is the meaning of the Arabic *laḥada*. But these explanations seem not to be convincing. Indeed, it has been shown elsewhere that the linguistic and social context to which this verse refers could be a Syriac one: the Arabic root *l-ḥ-d,* being probably an adaptation of the Syriac *lʿez,* "to speak enigmatically," "to allude to," like the Arabic root *l-gh-z* (Luxenberg, *Lesart,* 87-91; Gilliot, Coran, § 6; see also INFORMANTS).

The contrast of *aʿjamī,* often understood as barbarous or outlandish, with *ʿarabī*/Arabic, becomes very significant, if we consider Q 41:44: "And if we had appointed it a lecture in a foreign tongue *(qurʾānan aʿjamiyyan)* they would assuredly have said: If only its verses (q.v.) were expounded *(fuṣṣilat)* [so that we might understand]? What! A foreign tongue and an Arab *(aʿjamiyyun wa-ʿarabiyyun)?*" (or, in the rendition of Arberry: "If We had made it a barbarous Koran [...] Why are its signs (q.v.) not distinguished? What, barbarous and Arabic?"). *Fuṣṣilat* was undertood by an early exegete, al-Suddī (d. 128/745), as "clarified" *(buyyinat,* Ṭabarī, *Tafsīr,* xxiv, 127; Thaʿlabī, *Tafsīr,* not quoting al-Suddī: "whose verses are clear; they reach us so that we understand it. We are a people of Arabs, we have nothing to do with non-Arabs *[ʿajamiyya]*"; cf. Muqātil, *Tafsīr,* iii, 746: "Why are its verses not expounded clearly in Arabic?").

The expression "In plain/clear Arabic speech/tongue *(bi-lisānin ʿarabiyyin mubīnin)*" (Q 26:195; cf. 16:103) still needs more reflection, because the translation given here is — like most translations of the phrase — misleading from the point of view of morphology, and consequently of semantics. *Mubīn* is the active participle of the causative-factitive *abāna,* which can be understood as: "making [things] clear." Such an understanding of that expression is suggested by Q 14:4, which utilizes the causative factitive *bayyana:* "And we never sent a messenger save with the language/tongue of his folk, that he might *make* [the message] *clear* for them *(li-yubayyina lahum).*"

But the adjectival opposition found in Q 16:103 between *aʿjamī* on the one hand, and *ʿarabī* and *mubīn,* on the other, was understood by the exegetes as "barbarous," i.e. non-Arabic *(ʿajamī)* and indistinct *(aʿjamī),* in contradistinction with clear/pure Arabic (Wansbrough, *QS,* 98-9; see LANGUAGE, CONCEPT OF; for the opposing traditional view, variously expressed, i.e. "in clear Arabic/pure tongue," see Widengren, *Apostle,* 151-2, in relation to the question of a pre-Islamic Arabic translation of the Bible; Horovitz, *KU,* 75).

The consequence, according to the theologians, is that the Qurʾān must be in a "smooth, soft, and plain/distinct speech *(sahl, layyin, wāḍiḥ)*": "In the Qurʾān there is no unusual/obscure *(gharīb)* sound-complex *(ḥarf)* from the manner of speaking *(lugha)* of the Quraysh, save three, because the speech *(kalām)* of the Quraysh is smooth, soft, and plain/distinct, and the speech of the [other] Arabs is uncivilized *(waḥshī)*, unusual/obscure" (Abū l-ʿIzz Wāsiṭī, d. 521/1127, *al-Irshād fī l-qirāʾāt al-ʿashr,* quoted by Suyūṭī, *Itqān*, chap. 37, ed. Ibrāhīm, ii, 124). This dogma of the alleged superiority of the Ḥijāzī dialect did not have, in reality, great consequences in choosing among the various readings of the Qurʾān. In fact, "the home dialect of the Prophet has not occupied a particular place" in the qurʾānic readings (Beck, ʿArabiyya, 182), but, rather, the grammarians and exegetes tried to preserve a certain scientific autonomy in this respect (Gilliot, Précellence, 100; id., *Elt*, 135-64; 171-84). Some contemporary Muslim scholars have, for this reason, accused them of "distorting" the qurʾānic readings, e.g. the book entitled "Defence of the readings transmitted via different channels against the exegete al-Ṭabarī" (Anṣārī, *Difāʿ ʿan al-qirāʾāt al-mutawātira*...).

The superiority of the Arabic language and the excellence of the Arabic of the Qurʾān

The Muslim scholars of religious sciences (see TRADITIONAL DISCIPLINES OF QURʾĀNIC STUDY) and the ancient Arab philologists have spared no effort in enhancing the alleged superiority of the Arabic language over other languages: "Of all tongues, that of the Arabs is the richest and the most extensive in ways of expression *(madhhaban)*. Do we know any man except a prophet who apprehended all of it?" (Shāfiʿī [d. 204/820], *Risāla*, 42, no. 138/[modified] Eng. trans., 88; Fr. trans., 69; Ibn Fāris, *al-Ṣāḥibī*, 40-7; Goldziher, Sprachgelehrsamkeit, iii, 207-11). The Kūfan exegete, grammarian and jurist, al-Farrāʾ (d. 207/822), explains the superiority of the speech of the Quraysh in a particular way, namely as based upon the pilgrimage and their outstanding taste and capacity of selection: "[His fictive interlocutor saying] Sagacity and beauty came to them merely because the Arabs were accustomed to come to the sanctuary for *ḥajj* and *ʿumra*, both their women and men. The women made the circuit round the House unveiled and performed the ceremonies with uncovered faces. So they selected them by sight and thought after of dignity and beauty. By this they gained superiority besides those qualities by which they were particularly distinguished. [al-Farrāʾ answers] We said: In the same way they were accustomed to hear from the tribes of the Arabs their dialects; so they could choose from every dialect that which was the best in it. So their speech became elegant and nothing of the more vulgar forms of speech was mixed up with it" (a text of al-Farrāʾ in Kahle, *Geniza*, 345; Eng. trans. Kahle, Arabic readers, 70). In a word, the Quraysh through their sagacity in choice were prepared to become the "chosen people of God" in language, that is Arabic.

The Muʿtazilite theologian and man of letters, al-Jāḥiẓ (d. 255/867; see MUʿTAZILĪS) is no less explicit on this subject, using the example of poetry whose "excellence is limited to the Arabs and to those who speak the tongue of the Arabs, and it is impossible that [Arabic] poetry should be translated and it cannot be conveyed [into another language]." He explains that, in translation, the meter, the rhyme, the rhythm, arrangement *(naẓm)* and verse would be destroyed. Of course, everybody, including al-Jāḥiẓ, is familiar with the difficulty of translating poetry. But for this theologian only the Arabs have poetry in the sense of the Arabic term *qaṣīda* (odes) and accord with its norms; his primary point is the superiority of the Arabic language as a presupposition for the excellence of the qurʾānic Arabic (Jāḥiẓ, *Ḥayawān,* i, 74-5; Gilliot, *Elt,* 86). We could, of course, continue to quote a number of philologists, exegetes and theologians on this matter drawn from all periods of Islamic history up to the present day; but these samples are sufficient to provide an insight into the essential features of this apologetic discourse.

The "Challenge Verses"

In the religious *imaginaire* on the language of the Qurʾān, the Challenge Verses (*āyāt al-taḥaddī:* Q 2:23; 10:38; 11:13; 17:88; 52:33-4; see Wansbrough, *QS,* 79-82; Gilliot, *Elt,* 84-6; Radscheit, *Herausforderung;* van Ess, *TG,* iv, 607-8; see also PROVOCATION; INIMITABILITY) have also played a major role in the elaboration of a conception of a *lingua sacra*. These verses continue to be an important theme of Muslim apologetics, although they might be better explained in the context of Jewish polemics. The objection of the adversaries of Muḥammad here seems to have had nothing to do with language, and the answer of the Qurʾān, "then bring a sūra like unto it," also appears not to refer to language (see SŪRAS). Three of these verses are a response to the accusation of forgery (q.v.) against Muḥammad: "He has invented it" (*iftarāhu,* Q 10:38; 11:13; *taqawwalahu,* Q 52:33). The framework indicates a "'rabbinical' test of prophethood" (Wansbrough, *QS,* 79): "Verily, though humankind and the jinn (q.v.) should assemble to produce the like of this Qurʾān, they could not..." (Q 17: 88). The audience was not at all impressed by the product given by Muḥammad, which they did not find particularly coherent — in any case, not as coherent as the other revealed books (Muqātil, *Tafsīr,* iii, 234; Ṭabarī, *Tafsīr,* xix, 10, ad Q 25:32; van Ess, *TG,* iv, 608; see BOOK): "Why is the Qurʾān not revealed unto him all at once? [It is revealed] thus that we may strengthen your heart (q.v.) therewith; and we have arranged it in right order" (*wa-rattalnāhu tartīlan;* Arberry: "better in exposition," Q 25:32).

But the same verbal noun *(nomen verbi), tartīl,* is problematic (Paret, *Kommentar,* 492). Several interpretations have been given by ancient exegetes: to proceed in a leisurely manner, pronounce distinctly, to recite part after part (Ṭabarī, *Tafsīr,* xxix, 126-7, ad Q 73:4; Lane, *Lexicon,* i, 1028). Besides, it can be understood elsewhere as recitation or cantilation: "and chant the Qurʾān in measure" (*wa-rattili l-qurʾāna tartīlan,* Q 73:4; Arberry: "and chant the Koran very distinctly"; Andrae, *Ursprung,* 192: "and recite the Koran in equal sections"). But this last passage has been also understood as "and make the Qurʾān distinct," perhaps alluding to Muḥammad "at the labour in composition" (Bell, *Origin,* 97; id., *Commentary,* ii, 444). It could also refer to the style of the Qurʾān: "the sense of the word [in Q 25:32] is not exactly known, but it is likely to refer to the rhyme, the existence of which cannot be denied" (Mingana, Qurʾān, 545 b).

The adversaries of Muḥammad — but not only they — in fact, most of the Quraysh were not particularly impressed by the language or the content of his predication: "muddled dreams (see DREAMS AND SLEEP); nay, he has but invented it; nay, he is but a poet. Let him bring us a portent even as those of old [i.e. messengers] were sent [with portents]" (Q 21:5; Blachère, *Histoire,* ii, 232). Despite the original auditors' apparent skepticism as to the excellence of the qurʾānic language, Muslim exegetes, philologists, jurists and theologians (see THEOLOGY AND THE QURʾĀN) opened the door to an elaboration of sacral representations and mythical constructions on the pre-eminence of the Arabic language and the supposed superiority and inimitability of the qurʾānic language, sentiments which were not present *expressis verbis* in the Qurʾān.

The foreign words

But Q 41:44 became also a *locus classicus* in qurʾānic exegesis in the debate over the occurrence of foreign words in the Qurʾān (in addition to Rippin, Foreign vocabulary, 226, see Ibn al-Jawzī, *Funūn,* 186-93) and, with Q 16:103, on the informants of Muḥammad (see Madigan, *Self-image,* 199-200; see also INFORMANTS). Some ancient exegetes had general pronouncements on the issue: according to the Kūfan companion of Ibn Masʿūd, Abū Maysara al-Hamdānī (d. 63/682): "There are [expressions] in the Qurʾān from every language *(lisān)*" (Ibn Abī Shayba, *Muṣannaf,* [*Kitāb* 22. *Faḍāʾil al-Qurʾān, bāb* 7], vi, 121, no. 29953; Ṭabarī, *Tafsīr,* i, 14, no. 6/Eng. trans. *Commentary,* i, 13; Suyūṭī, *Itqān,* chap. 38, ed. Ibrāhīm, ii, 126; id, *Muhadhdhab,* 194, ed. al-Hāshimī, 60-1). The same words are also attributed to the Khurasānī exegete al-Ḍaḥḥāk b. Muzāḥim (d. 105/723; Ibn Abī Shayba, ibid., no. 29952; Suyūṭī, *Muhadhdhab,* 194, ed. al-Hāshimī, 61). Or, according to another Kūfan, Saʿīd b. Jubayr (d. 95/714): "There is no language *(lugha)* on the earth which God has not revealed in the Qurʾān. And he [Ibn Jubayr or somebody else in the chain] said: the name of Jibrīl (Gabriel, q.v.) is the servant/man *(ʿabd)* of God, and the name of Mikāʾīl (Michael, q.v.) is the small servant/man of God" (see for this etymology Ṭabarī, *Tafsīr,* ii, 389-92, ad Q 2:97: *jabr* means *ʿabd,* servant/man). Wansbrough (followed, unfortunately, by Gilliot, *Elt,* 103), writes that the tradition of Ibn Jubayr was transmitted by Muqātil (*QS,* 218). It is indeed in Muqātil (*Tafsīr,* ii, 606), but it was added with a chain of authority by one of the transmitters of this book, ʿAbdallāh b. Thābit al-Tawwazī (d. 308/920; Gilliot, Muqātil, 41; see ḤADĪTH AND THE QURʾĀN). Or, according to Wahb b. Munabbih (d. 110/728): "There are only a few languages which are not represented in some way in the Qurʾān" (Suyūṭī, *Itqān,* chap. 38, ed. Ibrāhīm, ii, 135; id., *Muhadhdhab,* 213, ed. al-Hāshimī, 106-7; id., *Durr,* i, 335, l. 16-7, ad Q 2: 260, quoted from the qurʾānic commentary of Abū Bakr b. al-Mundhir, d. 318/930). But the tradition of Ibn Jubayr is also presented as one of the occasions of the revelation (q.v.) of the verse under discussion, Q 41:44 (Ṭabarī, *Tafsīr,* xxiv, 127; Thaʿlabī, *Tafsīr,* ad Q 41:44), because of the word *aʿjamī,* linked by ancient exegetes to the theme of the informants (Muqātil, *Tafsīr,* iii, 745-6; Thaʿlabī, *Tafsīr,* quoting Muqātil; see Gilliot, Informants, 513). That which "is not of the speech of the Arabs" was not, however, to everybody's taste, and some ancient philologists who had extreme arabophile sentiments had hard opinions on this issue and condemned others: "some knowledgeable *(naḥārīr)* [philologists] sometimes introduce non-Arabic words as pure Arabic out of their desire to mislead people and make them fail" (al-Khalīl b. Aḥmad, d. 175/791, *Kitāb al-ʿAyn,* i, 53, quoted by Talmon, *Arabic grammar,* 122).

All this entirely contradicts the quasi-dogma of the "purity" of the Arabic of the Qurʾān, but a theologian can always find a solution to a seeming contradiction, namely by transforming its object into a quality or a "miracle" (q.v.): "Other books were revealed only in the language of the nation to whom they were adressed, while the Qurʾān contains words from all Arabic dialects, and from Greek, Persian, and Ethiopic besides" (Ibn al-Naqīb, d. 698/1298, in Suyūṭī, *Itqān,* chap. 38, ed. Ibrāhīm, ii, 127; Gilliot, *Elt,* 101; Rabin, *West-Arabian,* 19). It is possible that a tradition attributed to Muḥammad and transmitted from Ibn Masʿūd had an influence here on the theological representation of the superiority of the Qurʾān over the other revealed books: "The first book was revealed from a single door, in a single manner (*ḥarf,* or, "genre, sound-complex"; this last, in other contexts, according to Rabin, *West-Arabian,* 9), but the Qurʾān was revealed in seven manners…" (Ṭabarī, *Tafsīr,* ed. Shākir, i, 68, no. 67; Gilliot, Les sept "lectures." II, 56; id., Langue, 91-2).

The problems of qurʾānic grammar

Up until the present day, special books have been written by Muslims on this issue, particularly with the aim of finding a solution to the following problem: "What the grammarians forbid, although it occurs in the Qurʾān" (Ḥassūn, *al-Naḥw l-qurʾānī,* 12-114; Anṣārī, *Naẓariyya;* see also GRAMMAR AND THE QURʾĀN), or related issues, like "The defence of the Qurʾān against the grammarians and the Orientalists" (Anṣārī, *al-Difāʿ ʿan al-Qurʾān…*).

The mythical narratives on the superiority of Arabic

Interpretrations of the passages of the Qurʾān that understand the language in a sacral and theological orientation, combined with ethnocentric Arab conceptions, have contributed to the elaboration of a hierarchy of languages, at the summit of which stands Arabic. Even if these ideas existed before, they were only systematically collected during the second half of the second/eighth and the third/ninth centuries. The constitution of an empire and the construction of a mythical conception of a common "perfect" language go together.

We find a statement about this hierarchy by the Cordoban jurist and historian ʿAbd al-Malik b. Ḥabīb (d. 238/852), for whom the languages of the "prophets" were Arabic, Syriac and Hebrew: All the sons of Israel (q.v.; i.e. Jacob, q.v.) spoke Hebrew (see also CHILDREN OF ISRAEL); the first whom God allowed to speak it was Isaac (q.v.). Syriac was the language of five prophets: Idrīs (q.v.), Noah (q.v.), Abraham (q.v.), Lot (q.v.) and Jonah (q.v.). Twelve of them spoke Arabic: Adam (see ADAM AND EVE), Seth, Hūd (q.v.), Ṣāliḥ (q.v.), Ishmael (q.v.), Shuʿayb (q.v.), al-Khiḍr (see KHAḌIR/KHIḌR), "the three in Sūrat Yā Sīn" (Q 36:14), Jonah, Khālid b. Sinān al-ʿAbsī, and Muḥammad. According to ʿAbd al-Malik b. Ḥabīb, Adam first spoke Arabic, but later this language was distorted and changed into Syriac (ʿAbd al-Malik b. Ḥabīb, *Taʾrīkh,* 27-8; Suyūṭī, *Muzhir,* i, 30-1/Eng. trans. Czapkiewicz, *Views,* 66-7; Goldziher, *Grammar,* 44-5; Loucel, Origine. IV, 167-8).

This last opinion is supported by a tradition attributed to an individual often cited on such matters, the cousin and Companion of Muḥammad (who was ca. 10 years old when Muḥammad died), namely Ibn ʿAbbās (d. 69/688): "His [i.e. Adam's] language in paradise (q.v.) was Arabic, but when he disobeyed his lord (q.v.), God deprived him of Arabic, and he spoke Syriac. God, however, restored him to his grace *(tāba ʿalayhi),* and he gave him back Arabic" (Ibn ʿAsākir, *Taʾrīkh,* vii, 407; Suyūṭī, *Muzhir,* i, 30; Loucel, Origine. IV, 167). It has been said that Adam "spoke 700,000 languages, of which the best was Arabic" (Thaʿlabī, *Tafsīr,* ad Q 55:4, from an anonymous source; Goldziher, *Grammar,* 45, quoting Baghawī, *Maʿālim,* presently still only in manuscript form; but the figure "700" in Baghawī, *Maʿālim,* iv, 266 has to be corrected!). The exegetes *(ahl al-taʾwīl)* explain the diversity of languages in the following way: God taught all the languages to Adam, but when his sons were scattered, each of them spoke one language, then each group that issued from them spoke its own language (Wāḥidī, *Wasīṭ,* i, 116; Nīsābūrī, *Tafsīr,* i, 220; Abū Ḥayyān, *Baḥr,* i, 145, ad Q 2:31).

These endeavors of the Muslim exegetes and theologians express a mimetic concurrence with trends found among the Jews (see JEWS AND JUDAISM) and the Syrians; for the latter, however, Adam spoke Syriac/Aramaic (Grünbaum, *Beiträge*, 63). Other sources refer to seventy two, seventy or eighty languages in the world (Goldziher, *Grammar*, 45-6; Loucel, Origine. IV, 169-70: only for 72).

The influence of the theological representations appears in the desperate attempts of the jurists to give sense to a set of contradictory, or disparate, ideas or facts: at the beginning there was a single language which God taught to Adam (see KNOWLEDGE AND LEARNING), and it was, of course, the best one, Arabic (because the Qurʾān is in Arabic); there are several languages; the Arabic of the Qurʾān is the best Arabic; the Prophet was an Arab, and he belonged to the tribe of Quraysh (see TRIBES AND CLANS). One of the solutions found, with recourse to legends and argumentation, was the following: at the beginning God taught a single language to humankind; the other languages were taught only later to the offspring of Noah, after the flood (according to Abū Manṣūr ʿAbd al-Qāhir al-Baghdādī, d. 429/1037); according to Ibn ʿAbbās, the first to speak Arabic was Ishmael, which is interpreted as "pure Arabic," meaning the Arabic of the Quraysh, "because the Arabic of Qaḥṭān and Ḥimyar [South Arabic] was spoken before Ishmael" (Zarkashī, *Baḥr*, ii, 16; Suyūṭī, *Muzhir*, i, 27, quoting him; Goldziher, *Grammar*, 44).

These mythical narratives on language which are quoted in different genres of literature (exegesis, historiography, *adab*, etc.), and, even up to the present, appear in popular books, play a major role in the linguistic *imaginaire* of the Muslims. They are as important as the arguments of the scholars, who, moreover, also quote them to confirm their line of argument and to establish it definitively in the minds of their readers (for the origin of speech according to the grammarian Ibn Jinnī, see Versteegh, *Arabic linguistic tradition*, 100-14; on al-Suyūṭī's [d. 911/1505] presentation, see A. Czapkiewicz, *Views*, 64-6).

The "creation" of a Prophet against his competitors (poets, soothsayers, orators, story-tellers, etc.)

The strategy of Muḥammad and of the first generations of Muslim scholars concerning poetry and poets had a reason other than the traditional tribal defense of honor (q.v.; *ʿirḍ;* Nahshalī, *Mumtiʿ*, 220-7: How the Arabs protected themselves and defended their honor with poetry; Jacob, *Beduinenleben*, 176-8; Farès, *Honneur*, passim), even if Muḥammad saw himself more and more as a supra-tribal chief and was concerned to defend his own reputation. This other reason was a linguistically theological one.

Not only had the Qurʾān to be sharply distinguished from poetry (Hirschberg, *Jüdische und christliche Lehren*, 27-32; Gilliot, Poète, 378-9, § 111, 116) and the rhymed prose (q.v.; *sajʿ*) of the Arab soothsayers (q.v.), but its superiority to poetry had to be demonstrated, an idea which was not obvious. Before the Arab poets, diviners (see DIVINATION; FORETELLING) and orators, Muḥammad had to "create" himself with the help of his supporters and to be "created" by the first generations of Muslim scholars. *The* Prophet whose language was excellent, "the most Arab of the Arabs," is depicted as, after his birth, having been placed in the care of another in order to be nursed (see LACTATION; WET-NURSING; FOSTERAGE) and brought up in clans whose Arabic was the "purest" (see also SĪRA AND THE QURʾĀN). According to the Companion Abū Saʿīd al-Khudrī, Muḥammad is supposed to have said: "I am the Prophet who does not lie (q.v), I am the son of ʿAbd al-Muṭṭalib, I am the one who speaks the best Arabic (or "the most Arab of the Arabs," *aʿrab al-ʿArab*). The Quraysh has procreated me, I grew up in the tribe of Saʿd b. Bakr [his nurse Ḥalīma was of that clan]! [So you should not ask] from where this my manner of speaking comes *(fa-annā ya'tīnī l-laḥnu)*" (Ṭabarānī, *Kabīr,* vi, 35-6, no. 5437; Ibn al-Sarrāj al-Shantarīnī, *Tanbīh,* 121-2; Gilliot, Poète, 385). Or: "Of you, I am the one whose Arabic is the best *(anā aʿrabukum),* I am from the Quraysh, my language is that of the Saʿd b. Bakr" (Ibn Saʿd, *Ṭabaqāt,* i, 113; cf. Suyūṭī, *Khaṣā'iṣ,* i, 63); "I am of the Arabs whose language is the most pure and understandable *(anā afṣaḥ al-ʿArab).*" This long translation is the nearest to the meaning of *faṣīḥ* at this time: whose Arabic is *"rein, verständlich,"* in opposition to the foreign languages, but also to the Arabic of the Arabs of the "frontiers" (Vollers, in his review of Nöldeke *[Zur Grammatik],* 126). Or: "I am the most eloquent creature" (Suyūṭī, *Muzhir,* i, 209-13; Wansbrough, *QS,* 93-4). Or, more expressly in relation to the Qur'ān: "Love the Arabs for three reasons, because I am Arab, the Qur'ān is Arabic, and the speech of the people of paradise is Arabic" (Ibn al-Anbārī, *Īḍāḥ,* i, 21; Kahle, Qur'ān, 174, no. 28; 173, no. 22; cf. Muqātil b. Sulaymān declaring: "The speech *[kalām]* of the inhabitants of the sky is Arabic"; Ibn al-Sarrāj al-Shantarīnī, *Tanbīh,* 77. This declaration was included in a tradition attributed to Muḥammad which continues: "and their language when they are standing before God in the last judgment [q.v.]"; Kahle, Qur'ān, 173-4, no. 25).

It should be noticed that these declarations of (or sayings attributed to) Muḥammad on the best language pertain to the categories of the pride (q.v.; *fakhr*) of the ancient Arabs and their poetry, and that they can be extended to other fields, for instance in that other saying of Muḥammad transmitted from the Companion Anas b. Mālik: "I was made superior to people with four qualities: generosity (see GIFT-GIVING), bravery (see COURAGE), frequency of sexual intercourse *(kathrat al-jimāʿ),* great violence *(shiddat al-baṭsh)*" (Abū Bakr al-Ismāʿīlī, *Muʿjam,* ii, 621-2, no. 251; Ibn ʿAsākir, *Ta'rīkh,* viii, 69-70). These traditional tribal values of the ancient Arabs, and above all the quality of the language, were transformed into proofs of prophecy.

This was and still is a necessary presupposition to persuade the Arabs and the non-Arab Muslims of the so-called superiority and inimitability of the qur'ānic language, style and content (Gilliot, *Elt,* 73-93, but also chaps. four and five). Through lack of written Arabic texts at their disposal (see ORALITY AND WRITING IN ARABIA), they could only lean on the "thesaurus of the Arabs" *(dīwān al-ʿArab),* poetry, according to a celebrated declaration attributed again to Ibn ʿAbbās (Ibn al-Anbārī, *Īḍāḥ,* i, 99-101, no. 118, 120; taken up by Suyūṭī, *Itqān,* chap. 36, 281, ed. Ibrāhīm, ii, 67; Wansbrough, *QS,* 217; Gilliot, Poète, 374-5; cf. Goldziher, *Richtungen,* 70). This ancient poetry became a benediction from the divine favor (see BLESSING; GRACE) because the "best language," Arabic, was destined to prepare the coming of a still "more excellent" language, tongue and speech, the language of the Qur'ān (Abū Ḥātim al-Rāzī, *Zīna,* i, 92), the *lingua linguarum, scilicet Verbum Dei!*

But these scholars were conscious that the poet had been a dangerous competitor to the Prophet of Islam and to the text he presented as revelation (Gilliot, Poète, 331-2; 380-8). Indeed, according to the Baṣran philologist, also a specialist in ancient poetry and qur'ānic readings, Abū ʿAmr b. al-ʿAlā' (d. 154/771), in a statement transmitted by his pupil, the Baṣran philologist al-Aṣmaʿī (d. 213/828): "The poets occupied, among the Arabs (bedouins, see BEDOUIN) during the Age of Ignorance (q.v.), the rank occupied by prophets in the nations [which have received a revelation];

then the sedentaries entered in relation with them *(khālaṭahum)* and were taken on by poetry *(iktasabū bi-l-shiʿri)*, and the poets lost their rank. And after that came Islam and the revelation of the Qurʾān, and poetry became vilified and qualified as falsehood *(bi-tahjīn al-shiʿr wa-takdhībihi)*. As a consequence, the poets lost their rank even further. At last they used flattery and fawning *(al-malaq wa-l-taḍarruʿ)*, and people disdained them" (Abū Ḥātim al-Rāzī, *Zīna*, i, 95; cf. Nahshalī, *Mumtiʿ*, 25). This ideological break between the "Age of Ignorance" — in another epistemological context the "savage thought" of C. Levi-Strauss — and Islam will lead Muslim scholars to a paradox: on the one hand, pre-Islamic poets and poetry are disparaged, but on the other hand their language, although it is, from their point of view, less sublime than the language of the Qurʾān, is extraordinarily praised because the verses of these poets are considered to be the best, sometimes the only evidence that can be quoted as support *(shawāhid)* for argumentation in the sciences of language (Baghdādī, *Khizāna*, i, 5-17/Fr. trans. Gilliot, Citations, 297-316). A certain nostalgia may be seen behind the laudatory break which al-Aṣmaʿī traces between "savage thought" on the one hand and "culture" — here, Islam — on the other when he declares: "Poetry is harsh *(nakid)*; therefore it is strong and easy in evil (see GOOD AND EVIL), but if it is used in good, it becomes weak. For instance, Hassān b. Thābit was one of the best poets *(fuḥūl al-shuʿarāʾ)* in the Age of Ignorance, but when Islam came, his poetry was dropped *(saqaṭa shiʿruhu)*" (Ibn al-Athīr, *Usd*, ii, 6, l. 17-18; Goldziher, Alte und neue Poesie, 136; with some difference in Ibn Qutayba, *al-Shiʿr*, 170, l. 9-11). But al-Aṣmaʿī, like the other philologists, collectors of poetry, jurists, exegetes, etc., is "at the borders of the orality (q.v.) to which he wishes to put an end [...]. The *ʿālim* [scholar] establishes a civilization of literacy and of its ways of thinking. As the builder of a culture he wants to control the relations between written science and knowledge which is orally transmitted" (Bencheikh, *Essai*, II).

But before poetry came to be controlled by philologists who were also jurists and specialists in the Qurʾān, traditions were employed to create a "united" language, or, better, the imaginary model of such a language, which had to be, more or less, in accordance with the "qurʾānic model." These prophetic, or alleged prophetic, traditions had to be recalled, produced, or coined, against or in favor of poetry, giving a certain status to poets and poetry, so that they would not be competitors to the Prophet and to the book he had delivered. Ancient poetry was necessary to explain, justify and enhance the alleged preeminence of the qurʾānic language; but it had also to be put in its "proper place," so that the Qurʾān should not be compared with human productions.

The philologists and theologians, in arranging and harmonizing the different and even contradictory traditions which circulated about the Arabic of the Qurʾān, the "eloquence" of the Prophet and of the Arabs — traditions whose enormous numbers, variety, contradictions and repetitions make the reader's head swim, so that one is tempted simply to believe them and stick to the reasoning of the theologians — have established the enduring conception of a *lingua sacra*. Not only believers, but also many Orientalists in their presentations of the Arabic and qurʾānic language have been influenced by the power of this conviction.

The hypotheses of the Arabists

A gulf lies between the theological thesis and the approach of a linguist, as it already appears in the following declaration of one of the founders of the Arabists' school, F.L. Fleischer (d. 1888): "The question for us is not: What is the purest, the most beautiful and correct Arabic, but what is Arabic in general?" (Über arabische Lexicographie, 5).

What constitutes the strength of the theological thesis for believers is precisely what represents its weakness for the critical scholar: It is based only on the qur'ānic text and upon conviction, without any verification of another nature. The extant (and scanty) epigraphic material (see EPIGRAPHY AND THE QUR'ĀN) that evidences a language close to classical Arabic, insofar as its graphemes and the hazards of deciphering them allow, comes exclusively from northern Arabia (see ARABIC SCRIPT; ORTHOGRAPHY). More precisely, it is from areas that were under the control of the Ghassān and the Lakhm, considered to be Arabs whose "linguistic habit was not perfect *(fa-lam takun lughatuhum tāmmat al-malaka)*" "because they had contact with non-Arabs *(bi-mukhālaṭat al-aʿājim)*" (Ibn Khaldūn, *ʿIbar,* 1072/Eng. trans. Ibn Khaldūn-Rosenthal, iii, 343).

Moreover, from the data preserved by the Arab grammarians and compiled by Rabin (*West-Arabian*, passim), it appears that pre-Islamic Arabic was heterogenous, but that a regional east-west differentiation could be seen in it (for a detailed list of the features, above all morphological and syntactic, see Blachère, *Histoire,* i, 70-5; Versteegh, *Arabic,* 41-6). Now, what the Arabs call *al-lugha al-fuṣḥā* and the Arabists term classical Arabic coincides with neither eastern nor western Arabic, although — taken as a whole — it is closer to the eastern sphere.

The different arabist hypotheses have their origin in the contradiction between the theological thesis and these data. These hypotheses can be reduced to two: one weak, the other strong. Moreover, they have in common the presupposition of a diglossic situation in ancient Arabia: i.e. the coexistence of, on the one hand, the various dialects of the Arab tribes, and, on the other, a common language (which, among other things, was the vehicle of poetry, and for that reason, has been termed poetic *koiné*). Poetic *koiné* pertains to the ancient Arabic linguistic type, whereas the dialects should be, if not entirely at least partly, of the neo-Arabic type. The difference between both is the presence of *iʿrāb* (case and mood endings) in the common language, its absence in the dialects.

But the Arabists do not agree on the origin of this *koiné*. For some — who think in terms of the Greek *koiné,* the basis of which is Attic Greek — it has a geographic origin: according to this hypothesis, this shared language began as an inter-tribal or super-tribal language, at the point of encounter of the two dialectical areas of Arabia, that is to say in central or north-eastern Arabia. For others — who consider it along the lines of the Homeric Greek model — it is a *Kunstsprache,* an artificial language of great antiquity, without any connection to the linguistic reality. The Arabists also do not agree on the interpretation of *iʿrāb*. For some, it is syntactic, even if they recognize that its functionality is weak, not to say non-existent (see the debate between Blau, Synthetic Character, and Corriente, Functional yield; id., Again on the functional yield). For others it is linked to the constraints of prosody and rhyme in an oral-formulaic poetry (Zwettler, Classical Arabic poetry).

In this context, the weak hypothesis is that of the majority of Arabists. For them the qur'ānic Arabic is, save for some "Ḥijāzī" peculiarities, basically the same as the Arabic of pre-Islamic poetry; hence the qualification of "poetic and qur'ānic *koiné,*" sometimes given to that language, and which is considered to be the basis of classical Arabic (Blachère, *Histoire,* i, 82: "*koïnè* coranico-poétique").

The strong hypothesis is originally that of Vollers (d. 1909). He concludes that the Qurʾān was first delivered by Muḥammad in the vernacular of Mecca (q.v.), a west Arabian speech missing, among other features, the *iʿrāb* (Vollers, *Volkssprache,* 169; Zwettler, *Oral tradition,* 117-8, with discussion of this thesis; Versteegh, *Arabic,* 40-1), before it was later rewritten in the common language of poetry (Vollers, *Volkssprache,* 175-85). For Vollers this language, though it is the basis of the literary classical language, is primarily an eastern Arabic speech, fitted, among other features, with *iʿrāb*. More than the question of the *iʿrāb,* that of the "glottal stop" (*hamza,* Vollers, *Volkssprache,* 83-97) best summarizes the hypothesis of Vollers. It is said that the inhabitants of the Ḥijāz were characterized by the loss of the glottal stop *(takhfīf al-hamza),* contrary to the other Arabs who used the glottal stop *(taḥqīq al-hamza)*. And we know that the qurʾānic orthography attests the addition of the *hamza,* a mark of the realization of the glottal stop.

The hypothesis of Vollers was taken up again by P.E. Kahle (d. 1964), but in a modified form (he does not maintain that the Qurʾān was rewritten). He admits, without any further explanatory discussion, that the consonantal ductus (see CODICES OF THE QURʾĀN; COLLECTION OF THE QURʾĀN; MUṢḤAF), traditionally attributed to the caliph ʿUthmān (q.v.) represents the Arabic spoken in Mecca (Kahle, *Geniza,* 142), but for him the "readings" *(qirāʾāt, variae lectiones)* of that ductus express the influence of the poetic language. He based his hypothesis on a great number of traditions, more than 120, quoted in the *Tamhīd fī maʿrifat al-tajwīd* of al-Ḥasan b. Muḥammad al-Mālikī (d. 438/1046), in which people are exhorted to recite the Qurʾān, respecting the *iʿrāb* (Kahle, Qurʾān, 171-9). Since Kahle's contributions appeared, older works containing the traditions upon which he based his theory have been made available (e.g. Abū ʿUbayd, *Faḍāʾil,* 208-10, and passim; Ibn Abī Shayba, *Muṣannaf, [Kitāb 22. Faḍāʾil al-Qurʾān, bāb 1],* vi, 117-8, nos. 29903-19).

As Kahle remarks: "The recommendation to read the Koran with these vocalic endings presupposes that they were often not read" (*Geniza,* 145 n. 1). As some of these traditions were also known by the grammarian al-Farrāʾ (d. 207/822; Kahle, *Geniza,* 345-6 [Ar. text], 143-6 [Eng. trans.]; we should also add that some of the traditions were also known by Abū ʿUbayd al-Qāsim b. Sallām [d. 224/838] and by Ibn Abī Shayba [d. 235/849]), this reveals the existence of a problem in the second/eighth century.

Two interpretations of that issue are possible. The first, a minimalist understanding, is that there was a slackening in the recitation of the Qurʾān (q.v.) because of the non-Arab converts: in this case, these traditions are a call to order, reprimands, to stop a prevalent "lax reading" and to enforce an "exact reading" (Kahle, *Geniza,* 147). But the other possibility is that the grammarians and readers *(qurrāʾ, qaraʾa)* want to enforce on the community a reading and recitation consonant with an ideal Arabic that they have just established by the means of a large collection of data gathered from the bedouins and from poetry. Kahle inclines to this second interpretation, putting forward the concept he encountered in al-Farrāʾ (and which is also to be found in Ibn Fāris; see the translation of the text of al-Farrāʾ above), who presents the Arabic of the Ḥijāz, and thus of the Qurʾān, as a selection from the best of the various dialects (Kahle, Qurʾān, 179-82; id., *Geniza,* 145-6; id., Arabic readers, 69-70). To him the presentation of al-Farrāʾ is an acknowledgment of the influence of poetic language on that of the Qurʾān, although he "antedated the influence of Bedouin poetry to an earlier period" (Kahle, *Geniza,* 146). Indeed, when it is released from its subjective elements, such a conception amounts to saying that the qurʾānic language borrows features from different dialects (Fr. *parlers*), in other words that it is an inter-language.

Whereas the hypothesis of Vollers caused a scandal in Muslim circles and prompted a debate among the Arabists (Geyer, Review; and notably Nöldeke, Einige Bemerkungen; id., Der Koran und die ʿArabīja), it seems that the hypothesis of Kahle has not really garnered much attention, with the notable exception of J. Fück (d. 1974), who rejected it (Fück, *ʿArabīya,* 3-4, n. 4/Fr. trans., 4-5, n. 4; see also Rabin, Beginnings, 25-9).

Now, however, things are changing with the progress in Arabic studies of sociolinguistics and of the history of linguistics. The Arabists today have gone beyond the diglossic representation of Arabic and are in favor of a polyglossic conception of Arabic and of a continuum, even of an inherent variation. In doing so they take up again, in some way, the conception that the most ancient Arab grammarians, notably Sībawayhi, had of Arabic. These last did not understand the *lughāt* ("dialects") as discrete varieties, but only as variants, good or bad, of one and the same language. In this context, the various "readings" *(qirāʾāt)* of the Qurʾān can be seen as the reflection of this linguistic variation. J. Owens has shown recently that the practice of the "major assimilation" (*al-idghām al-kabīr,* i.e. a consonantal assimilation between words) traditionally linked with the reader Abū ʿAmr (d. 154/770), did not imply linguistically the loss of the inflexional ending, but only the absence of short vowels, inflexional or not, at the ending. This means that "[Voller's] assumption that there was a koranic variant without case ending receives plausible support from the koranic reading tradition itself" (Owens, Idġām al-kabīr, 504).

Lastly, it should be noticed that none of the hypotheses of the Arabists challenges the following two assertions of the Muslim tradition: 1) the Qurʾān transmits the predication of the one Muḥammad, and 2) there exists an ʿUthmānic codex. This discussion of qurʾānic language would be enlarged if, on the one hand, the hypothesis of Wansbrough *(QS)* — i.e. that there was a slower elaboration of the qurʾānic text than is traditionally supposed — were taken into consideration, and, on the other, if, besides the "small variation" (different readings of the same ductus), the "great variation" (the existence of a non-ʿUthmānic codex) were also taken into account (Gilliot, Coran, § 29; id. Reconstruction, § 15).

From language to style

The link between qurʾānic language and the linguistic style of the Qurʾān itself is the notion of *bayān,* and it is not by chance that the founder of Bābism (see BAHĀʾĪS), ʿAlī Muḥammad (d. 1850) wrote a book intended to replace the Qurʾān, entitled *al-Bayān* (Bausani, Bāb). *Bayān,* a verbal noun *(nomen verbi:* distinctness; Fr. *le fait d'être distinct),* occurs only three times in the Qurʾān (Q 55:4; 75:19; 3:138; Bell, *Commentary,* ii, 329; Paret, *Kommentar,* 465; Blachère, ii, 74-5), e.g. Q 55:3-4: "He has created man. He has taught him utterance" (*al-bayāna;* or, "the capacity of clear exposition"; Arberry: "the Explanation"; Blachère: "l'Exposé"). Moreover, *tibyān* (exposition, explanation) occurs once (Q 16:89), and the active participle *(nomen agentis), mubīn,* twice qualifies the "Arabic tongue" (*lisān ʿarabī,* Q 16:103; 26:195; see LANGUAGE, CONCEPT OF). But twelve times *mubīn* qualifies "book" (*kitāb,* Q 5:15; 6:59; 10:61; 11:6; 12:1; 15:1; 26:2; 27:1, 75; 28:2; 34:3; 44:2), seven times it modifies *balāgh* (Q 5:92; 16:35, 82; 24:54; 29:18; 36:17; 64:12), and twice *qur'ān* (Q 15:1; 36:29). In this context, *mubīn* can be interpreted as the active participle *(nomen agentis)* of the fourth (causative) verbal form, *abāna,* used with an implicit object, simply a synonym of the second verbal form, *bayyana,* meaning "making [things] distinct/clear." But *abāna* can also be seen as an implicitly reflexive causative, and in this case *mubīn* is interpreted as "showing [itself] distinct/clear," as suggested by the explicit reflexive in Q 37:117: "*al-kitāb al-mustabīn*" (the clear scripture). The high number of the occurrences of the root *b-y-n* and its derivatives indicates that *bayān* is a characteristic of speech.

Developed at length by Shāfiʿī (d. 204/820), the idea is that the Qur'ān says things clearly; jurist that he was, he demonstrates this theory beginning with the legal obligations (see BOUNDARIES AND PRECEPTS; LAW AND THE QUR'ĀN; AMBIGUOUS; ABROGATION). But this is said with the underlying conviction that the Qur'ān expresses itself clearly because it is in Arabic (we should remember here that "Qur'ān" is qualified six times as "Arabic"; Shāfiʿī, *Risāla,* 20-40/Eng. trans. 67-80/Fr. trans. 53-68; Yahia, *Contribution,* 361-410; 368-71: on Jāḥiẓ; cf. Bāqillānī, *Intiṣār,* 256-71; Gilliot, *Elt,* 73; id., Parcours, 92-6). The central character of *bayān* in matters of style is attested by the fact that the phrase *ʿilm al-bayān* (see von Grunebaum, Bayān) competes with *ʿilm al-balāgha* for denoting Arabic rhetoric (which is not an oratorical art, but the art of all manners of speaking: poetical, oratorical, epistolary, etc.). But, for the most part — as opposed to *ʿilm al-maʿānī* — it designates the part of *ʿilm al-balāgha* which deals with the expression of the *maʿnā* i.e. the *latẓ,* in other words, stylistics. It should be noticed that the dogma of the inimitability of the Qur'ān was linked with the theme (almost an article of faith) of the "eloquency" *(balāgha)* of Muḥammad, which is in accordance with the theological representations on the "purity" of the language of Quraysh, and naturally the consummate "purity" of the language of the "chosen/purified *(al-muṣṭafā)*" one, Muḥammad, their kinsman, as seen above (see Rāfiʿī [d. 1937], "The inimitability of the Qur'ān and the prophetic eloquence" [in Arabic; *Iʿjāz al-Qur'ān wa-l-balāgha al-nabawiyya*], 277-342; on this book, see Boullata, Rhetorical interpretation, 148).

The theological thesis on the style of the Qur'ān

The theological thesis about the style of the Qur'ān, however, goes far beyond the proclamation of the alleged clarity of the qur'ānic discourse, this clarity itself being linked to the language in which it is formulated. Its core is certainly the dogma of the *iʿjāz al-Qur'ān* (van Ess, *TG,* iv, 609-11; see also INIMITABILITY). Two points should be emphasized here. First, the dogma of the Qur'ān's inimitability is to the style of the Qur'ān what the equation "language of the Qur'ān = the speech of the Quraysh = *al-lugha al-fuṣḥā*" is to its language; i.e. it, too, is the result of the intersection of a textual element (the so-called Challenge Verses) and of the Islamic conception of the Qur'ān as the speech of God *(kalām Allāh)*. Secondly, the "inimitability" is bound to the stylistic order through the clear theological affirmation of the Muʿtazilite theologian and philologist al-Rummānī (d. 384/994) on the *balāgha* of the Qur'ān: "Its highest [rank is such that it] incapacitates *(muʿjiz)* [anyone who attempts to reach it]; it is the *balāgha* of the Qur'ān" (*Nukat,* in Rummānī et al., *Rasā'il,* 75). From this point of view, most books on Islamic rhetoric function as the "maidservant of theology" *(rhetorica ancilla theologiae),* as illustrated by the title of the book by the great rhetorician ʿAbd al-Qāhir al-Jurjānī (d. 471/1078): "The proofs of the inimitability [of the Qur'ān]" (*Dalāʾil al-iʿjāz;* Abu Deeb, *al-Jurjānī;* Boullata, Rhetorical interpretation, 146-7).

The literary structure and arrangement or construction (*naẓm,* a root which does not occur in the Qur'ān; see Abu Deeb, *Al-Jurjānī,* 24-38; for Fakhr al-Dīn al-Rāzī: Lagarde, *Index,* no. 2564; Gilliot, Parcours, 100-6) of the Qur'ān is far from being self-evident. For this reason, Muslim scholars have not only dealt with this theme, but have composed works entitled *Naẓm al-Qurʾān* (for this genre and a list of such books, see Audebert, *L'inimitabilité,* 58-9, 193-4; see also LITERARY STRUCTURES OF THE QUR'ĀN). But the theological debate concerning the core of its "inimitability" and the question of its createdness or uncreatedness also played a role in the genesis of this genre (van Ess, *TG,* iv, 112; many Arabic studies on this theme have been published: e.g. on Zamakhsharī: Jundī, *al-Naẓm al-qurʾānī*). Eventually, entire qur'ānic commentaries came to contain this word in their title, e.g. the Karrāmite of Nīshāpūr, al-ʿĀṣimī (Abū Muḥammad Aḥmad b. Muḥammad b. ʿAlī, d. 450/1058), composed the *Kitāb al-Mabānī li-naẓm al-maʿānī,* whose introduction has been published (Jeffery, *Muqaddimas,* 5-20; for the identification of the author, see Gilliot, Théologie musulmane, 182-3). This genre was also related to the principle of correspondence (*munāsaba;* see Suyūṭī, *Itqān,* chap. 62, ed. Ibrāhīm, iii, 369-89 *[Munāsabat al-āyāt wa-l-suwar];* id., *Muʿtarak,* i, 54-74; id., *Taḥbīr,* 371-7; for Fakhr al-Dīn al-Rāzī: Lagarde, *Index,* no. 2479; Gilliot, Parcours, 106-9) between the sūras and between the verses (see also al-Suyūṭī's special book entitled "The symmetry of the pearls. On the correspondence of the sūras," which he seems to have compiled from his larger book "The secrets of revelation" *[Asrār al-tanzīl];* see Suyūṭī, *Tanāsuq,* 53-4). The qur'ānic commentary of Burhān al-Dīn Abū l-Ḥasan Ibrāhīm al-Biqāʿī (d. 885/1480) combines in his title the words "arrangement/construction" and "correspondence" *(naẓm, tanāsub):* "The string of pearls. On the correspondence of the verses and sūras" *(Naẓm al-durar fī tanāsub al-āyāt wa-l-suwar).*

Generally speaking, all of the elements of style to be found in all great literature are seen as unique and almost special to the Qur'ān because of the dogma of its inimitability. Even its weaknesses are viewed as wonderful, if not miraculous (see the introduction of Ṭabarī, *Tafsīr,* ed. Shākir, i, 8-12/Eng. trans. in *Commentary,* i, 8-12; Gilliot, *Elt,* 73-8).

The positions of the Arabists on the style of the Qurʾān

Some positions until recently

Read with eyes other than those of faith, qur'ānic style is generally not assessed as being particularly clear, and "much of the text... is... far from being as *mubīn* ("clear") as the Qur'ān claims to be!" (Puin, Observations, 107; cf. Hirschfeld, *New researches,* 6-7). Moreover, it does not arouse the general non-Muslim audience to such a degree of "enthusiam" (Sfar, *Coran,* 117-8, 100-1) as that of the Muslims who are alleged to have fallen down dead upon hearing its recitation (Wiesmüller, *Die vom Koran getöten;* cf. Kermani, *Gott ist schön,* chap. 4, "Das Wunder," 233-314; id., Aesthetic reception).

To understand this reaction of the non-believer, the Qur'ān should first be characterized as "speech" (Fr. *discours*) as opposed to such comparable "texts," i.e. the Hebrew Bible and the Gospels (q.v.; see also TORAH). To proceed so, it is possible to refer to a noteworthy opposition found within the Arabic linguistic tradition, that of two types of speech *(kalām),* the *khabar* and the *inshāʾ,* which is equivalent to the Austinian categories of "constative," as opposed to "performative utterances" (Austin, *How to do things with words*). According to these categories, the Hebrew Bible and the Gospels present themselves as *khabar*s (narratives on the creation [q.v.] of the world, the history of the Jewish people, the life of Jesus), even if these texts, whether considered as historical or mythic, are also edifying. On the other hand, the Qurʾān presents itself as non-narrative speech (*inshāʾ*; cf. the traditional appellation: paranesis): the narratives (q.v.) it contains, often incomplete, are a type of argumentation by example (see NATURE AS SIGNS; MYTHS AND LEGENDS IN THE QURʾĀN).

The lack of a narrative thread and the repetitions in the Qurʾān, when they do not provoke a negative reaction, compel the specialist to search for another organizational schema of the text, beyond that which is immediately apparent. The need for an alternative pattern behind the ordering of the text appears above all in the problem of the structure of the sūras. Of course, the ancient Muslim scholars, being experts in the Arabic language, were well aware of the organizational infelicities in the qurʾānic text, but as men of faith they had to underscore the "miraculous" organization *(naẓm)* of the entire text, and to find rhetorical devices to resolve each problematic issue, e.g. the *iqtiṣāṣ*, the "refrain" (Fr. *reprise*), when the passage was too allusive, incomplete or even truncated. In this case of the "refrain," the exegete had to refer to another verse in the same sūra or in another, from which the truncated passage is supposed to have been "taken" *(maʾkhūdh min)*, or where it is "told accurately" (Ibn Fāris, *al-Ṣāḥibī*, 239; Suyūṭī, *Itqān*, ed. Ibrāhīm, iii, 302), e.g. "and we gave him his reward in the world, and lo! in the hereafter (see ESCHATOLOGY) he verily is among the righteous" (Q 29:27), has to be understood [as taken] from "But whoso comes unto him a believer, having done good works (see GOOD DEEDS), for such are the good stations" (Q 20:75; see REWARD AND PUNISHMENT). This phenomenon could perhaps be related to a variety of the *enthymema*.

For reasons which have been put forth above, it is sacrilegious in a Muslim milieu to compare the Qurʾān to poetry, but it is evident that the language of the Qurʾān can be studied by a linguist in the same way as poetic language. The poetics of Jakobson (Closing statements), is one example of how the expertise of a linguist may be applied to the Qurʾān, especially from the point of view of "parallelism," a central concept of that poetics.

In view of the position it has taken with respect to the Qurʾān, the religious thought of Islam has tended to impose a conception that became more radical over time. According to this conception, the Qurʾān is an original work that owes nothing to an external influence, be it local or foreign. The polemics against the orators (*khaṭīb*s) and soothsayers (*kāhin*s), as well as those against the appearance of loanwords in the Qurʾān and those surrounding the meaning of the adjective *ummī* (q.v.), as it is applied to Muḥammad in the Qurʾān (Q 7:157, 158; "illiterate" messenger as opposed to messenger "of the community"; see ILLITERACY), should be interpreted in this context. Concerning this last-mentioned debate, A. Jones maintains that "[T]he notion that *ummī* means 'illiterate' is neither early nor accurate. It can only mean 'of the *umma*'" (Oral, 58, n. 5). Contrary to the theological views concerning the style of the Qurʾān, Jones has shown, despite the scarcity of preserved materials, that the qurʾānic style owes much to previous Arabic styles. These previous styles can be summarized in the following four categories: the style of the soothsayer (Jones, Language, 33-7: *kāhin* utterances), of the orator (Jones, Language, 38-41: *khaṭīb* utterances), of the story-teller (Jones, Language, 41-2: *qāṣṣ*), of the "written documentary style" in the Medinan material (Jones, Language, 42-4: a comparison between a part of the Constitution of Medina and Q 2:158, 196). In support of this thesis of Jones, the following declaration attributed to Muḥammad can be quoted: "This poetry is rhymed expression of the speech of the Arabs *(sajʿ min kalām al-ʿArab)*. Thanks to it, what the beggar asks for is given to him, anger is tamed, and people convene in their assemblies of deliberation *(nādīhim)*" (Subkī, *Ṭabaqāt,* i, 224; Goldziher, Higâʾ-Poesie, 59). Jones would argue that Muḥammad knew well the efficacy of rhymed prose, and for that reason he used it in the Qurʾān.

Finally, Jones provides two very helpful visual representations of the registers of Arabic at the rise of Islam (Jones, Oral, 57). Although practically nothing survives of these registers, he sketches the relationships between — and among — the literary prose registers, on the one hand (poets, soothsayers and preachers), and the dialects of the people, on the other. These charts are useful for conceptualizing the place of the Qurʾān within the linguistic streams of pre-Islamic Arabia (see also ORALITY AND WRITING IN ARABIA).

The question of the rhymed prose *(sajʿ)* in the Qurʾān still needs further research, because, as noticed a long time ago, Semitic literature has a great liking for it, and, as seen above, Muḥammad knew its effects very well: it "strikes the minds through its allusions, echoes, assonances and rhymes" (Grünbaum, Beiträge, 186). Later Muslim rhetoricians distinguished three or four types of rhymed prose in the Qurʾān: 1) *al-muṭarraf* (touched at the extremity), words having a different prosodic measure *(wazn)* at the end of the elements of the phrase, but similar final letters: Q 71:13-4 *(waqāran* vs. *aṭwāran)*; 2) *al-mutawāzī* (parallel), with similar prosodic measure, i.e. the same number of letters, and the same final letters *(al-wazn wa-l-warī)*: Q 88:13-4 *(marfūʿa* vs. *mawḍūʿa)*; 3) *al-muwāzana* (cadence), final words with similar prosodic measure, but different endings: Q 88:15-6 *(masfūfa* vs. *mabthūtha)*; 4) *al-mumāthala* (similarity), wherein all the words have corresponding prosodic measure in each member, but different endings: Q 37:117-8 (Ibn Abī l-Iṣbaʿ, *Badīʿ,* 108-9; Rāzī, *Nihāya,* 142-3; Ibn al-Naqīb, *Muqaddima,* 471-5; Nuwayrī, *Nihāya,* vii, 103-5; Garcin de Tassy, *Rhétorique,* 154-8; Mehren, *Rhetorik,* 167-8). In the best examples of the genre, each of the members (here *fawāṣil,* pl. of *fāṣila,* "dividers") have the same measure: Q 56:28-9, "*fī sidrin makhḍūdin/wa-ṭalḥin manḍūdin* (Among thornless lote-trees/And clustered plantains)." The second or third member can, however, be a little longer than the previous one (Q 69:30-3). But for the same rhetoricians, the contrary is not permitted, save when the difference is tiny (Q 105:1-2). For them the most beautiful rhymed prose is that whose members have only a few words, from two to ten; if otherwise, it is considered to be "drawling," as Q 8:43-4 (Mehren, *Rhetorik,* 166-7; on the dividers in the Qurʾān, from the traditional Muslim point of view, see Ḥasnāwī, *al-Fāṣila fī l-Qurʾān*).

There are still other valuable points of view and theses on the style of the Qurʾān which have not been presented here (for some discussion of these, see INIMITABILITY). Some examples are the discussions on the literary features and rhetorical devices (see Ṣammūd, *al-Tafkīr al-balāghī,* 33-46, and passim; see also LITERATURE AND THE QURʾĀN; LITERARY STRUCTURES OF THE QURʾĀN), and especially the interesting studies of A. Neuwirth on the relationship between liturgy and canonization of the text, "the structurally definable verse groups," contextuality, etc. (Neuwirth,

Einige Bermerkungen; id., Vom Rezitationstext/Fr. trans. Du texte de récitation; see also her article FORM AND STRUCTURE OF THE QUR'ĀN).

The ancient Christian or Syriac connection

Some scholars (unfortunately, too few) have drawn attention to the importance of the Aramaic or Syriac substratum in the formation of the Qur'ān, basing their hypotheses on the fact that Syro-Aramaic or Syriac was the language of written communication in the Near East from the 2nd to the 7th centuries C.E. and was also a liturgical language. The stylistic idiosyncrasies of the Qur'ān did not escape Th. Nöldeke (Nöldeke, Sprache/Fr. trans. *Remarques critiques*). In addition to his observations on the Syriac loanwords in the Qur'ān, which others, prior to him, had noted, A. Mingana noticed that the qur'ānic style "suffers from the disabilities that always characterize a first attempt in a new literary language which is under the influence of an older and more fixed literature," and that "its author had to contend with immense difficulties" (Mingana, Syriac influence, 78). But his observations led him to a hypothesis that is the opposite of the "credo" of Nöldeke which, until today, has been prevalent among most western scholars of Islam. This "credo" of Nöldeke is that, in spite of its "drawling, dull and prosaic" style (Nöldeke, *Geschichte,* 107), the Arabic of the Qur'ān is "classical Arabic." In his research, Mingana observed and emphasized the Syriac influences on the phraseology of the Qur'ān, and placed them under six distinct headings: proper names, religious terms, common words, orthography, construction of sentences and foreign historical references (see also FOREIGN VOCABULARY). Unfortunately, his remarks, although referred to by some scholars, were not taken into general account for two reasons: First, Mingana, too occupied with other works on Syriac, had no time to develop his hypothesis further. (His argument was further undermined by the fact that the material he had gathered in his article was not very important.) Secondly, the "dogma" of the Islamicists *(Islamwissenchaftler, islamologues)* on the "classicism" of the qur'ānic Arabic continued and still continues to impose itself as self-evident proof, in spite of numerous objections to their own thesis expressed by the supporters of the alleged *al-'arabiyya al-fuṣḥā* of the Qur'ān.

Without being particularly influenced by Mingana's article and having other concerns than this scholar, the German liberal Protestant theologian and Semitist G. Lüling wrote an important study which has also been overlooked and ignored (Ger. *totgeschwiegen*) by Islamicists and Arabists. This study, *Über den Ur-Qur'ān* ("On the primitive Qur'ān"), has recently been translated into English under the title *A challenge to Islam for reformation*, with the suggestive subtitle, "The rediscovery and reliable reconstruction of a comprehensive pre-Islamic Christian hymnal hidden in the Koran under earliest Islamic reinterpretation." The point of departure is not the Qur'ān, but Lüling's own scholarly orientation defined as promoting an "emphasis directed at self-criticism against the falsification of Christianity by its Hellenization resulting in the dogma of the trinity [sic, with a lowercase "t"] [...], as well as against the falsification of the history of Judaism" (*Challenge,* lxiii, a passage not present in the German original). The theses of Lüling on the Qur'ān are as follows: 1) About one-third of the present-day qur'ānic text contains as a hidden groundlayer an originally pre-Islamic Christian text. 2) The transmitted qur'ānic text contains four different layers, given here chronologically: the oldest, the texts of a pre-Islamic Christian strophic hymnody;

the texts of the new Islamic interpretation; historically parallel to the second layer is the original purely Islamic material, which is to be attributed to Muḥammad (about two-thirds of the whole Qur'ān); and, finally, the texts of the post-Muḥammadan editors of the Qur'ān. 3) The transmitted Islamic qur'ānic text is the result of several successive editorial revisions. 4) The presence of the successive layers in the qur'ānic text can be confirmed by material in Muslim tradition (Gilliot, Deux études, 22-4; Ibn Rawandi, Pre-Islamic Christian strophic, 655-68). Of course, the theses of Lüling should be discussed, and not simply ignored, as has been the case until now (for more details on this work, see the reviews of Rodinson, Gilliot and Ibn Rawandi. For a second book of Lüling, *Die Wiederentdeckung des Propheten Muhammad,* see the reviews of Gilliot and Ibn Rawandi).

Recently, another Semitist scholar, Ch. Luxenberg, has taken up Mingana's thesis in his work on the Syriac influence on the Qur'ān and outlined the heuristic clearly. Beginning with those passages that are unclear to western commentators, the method runs as follows: First, check if there is a plausible explanation in qur'ānic exegesis, above all that of al-Ṭabarī (d. 310/923), possibly overlooked by western scholars. If this does not resolve the problem, then check whether a classical Arabic dictionary, primarily Ibn Manẓūr's (d. 711/1311) *Lisān al-ʿArab,* records a meaning unknown to Ṭabarī and his earlier sources. If this turns up nothing, check if the Arabic expression has a homonymous root in Syriac, with a different meaning that fits the context. In many cases, Luxenberg found that the Syriac word with its meaning makes more sense than the Arabic term employed by the Qur'ān. It is to be noted that these first steps of the heuristic do not alter the consonantal text of the Cairene edition of the Qur'ān. If, however, these steps do not avail, he recommends changing one or more diacritical marks to see if that results in an Arabic expression that makes more sense. Luxenberg found that many instances of problematic lexemes may be shown to be misreadings of one consonant for another. If this method does not produce results, then the investigator should change one or several diacritical points and then check if there is a homonymous Syriac root with a plausible meaning. If there is still no solution, he checks to see if the Arabic is a calque of a Syriac expression. Calques may be of two kinds: morphological and semantic. A morphological calque is a borrowing that preserves the structure of the source word but uses the morphemes of the target language. A semantic calque assigns the borrowed meaning to a word that did not have the meaning previously, but which is otherwise synonymous with the source word (Luxenberg, *Lesart,* 10-15; Phenix and Horn, Review, § 12-4; Gilliot, Langue, § 4).

Of course, Luxenberg's work must be discussed by Semitists and Islamicists, and poses other complicated problems, e.g. on the history of the redaction of the Qur'ān. But some of his theses do appear convincing, at least to the present writers. For instance, Q 108 (Sūrat al-Kawthar), a text which has little meaning for a normal reader, and which is also a *crux interpretum* for the Islamic exegetes, has been convincingly deciphered by Luxenberg. Behind it can be found the well-known passage of 1 Peter 5:8-9: "Be sensible, watch, because your adversary the devil (q.v.) walks about seeking someone he may devour, whom you should firmly resist in the faith" (Luxenberg, *Lesart,* 269-76). We could mention also Luxenberg's treament of Q 96 (op. cit., 276-85). But his dealing with Q 44:54 and Q 52:20, concerning the supposed "virgins of paradise" (houris, q.v.) has already struck a number of those who have read this book. Instead of these mythic creatures "whom neither man nor jinn (q.v.) has deflowered before them" (Q 55:56; Bell, *Commentary,* ii, 551), or "whom neither man nor jinni will have touched before them" (Pickthall), are the grapes/fruits of paradise "that neither man nor jinn have defiled before them": "Darin [befinden sich] herabhängende [pflückreife] Früchte, die weder Mensch noch Genius vor ihnen je bepfleckt hat" (Luxenberg, *Lesart,* 248-51; also discussed in the following reviews of Luxenberg's work: Nabielek, Weintrauben statt Jungfrauen, 72; Gilliot, Langue, § 4; Phenix and Horn, Review, § 30-4).

In support of the thesis of Luxenberg we could refer to the informants (q.v.) of Muḥammad in Mecca, some of whom, according to the Islamic tradition, read the scripture or books, or knew Jewish or Christian scriptures. There is also the fact that the secretary of Muḥammad, Zayd b. Thābit, certainly knew Aramaic or Syriac before Muḥammad's emigration (q.v.) to Yathrib (Medina, q.v.). In a well-known Muslim tradition, with many versions, Muḥammad asks Zayd b. Thābit to learn the Hebrew and/or Aramaic/Syriac script (see Lecker, Zayd b. Thābit, 267; Gilliot, Coran, § 9-12). The hypothesis has been expressed according to which these traditions proceed to a situation reversal: the Jew Zayd b. Thābit already knew Hebrew and/or Aramaic/Syriac script; this, however, was embarrassing for Muḥammad or for the first or second generation of Muslims because it could be deduced, as in the case of the informants of Muḥammad, that the Prophet had borrowed religious knowledge from his secretary, and consequently from the Jewish or Christian scriptures. So the origin of Zayd's literary knowledge (see LITERACY) may have come from an initiative, on the part of Muḥammad, to suppress these allegations (Gilliot, Langue, § 4). But the following text of the Muʿtazilite theologian of Baghdād, Abū l-Qāsim al-Balkhī (al-Kaʿbī, d. 319/931), which seems a confirmation of our hypothesis of a reversal of the actual situation, has recently become available:

I [Kaʿbī], concerning that issue, asked people well-versed in the science of the life of the Prophet (*ahl al-ʿilm bi-l-sīra,* see SĪRA AND THE QURʾĀN), among whom were Ibn Abī l-Zinād, Muḥammad b. Ṣāliḥ (d. 252/866) and ʿAbdallāh b. Jaʿfar (probably Ibn al-Ward, d. 351/962) who impugned that firmly, saying: How could somebody have taught writing to Zayd, who had learned it before the messenger of God came to [Medina]? Indeed, there were more people who could write in Medina than in Mecca. In reality when Islam came to Mecca, there were already about ten who could read, and when it was the turn of Medina, there were already twenty in it, among whom was Zayd b. Thābit, who wrote Arabic and Hebrew [...]" (Abū l-Qāsim al-Balkhī [al-Kaʿbī], *Qābūl al-akhbār,* i, 202; Gilliot, Coran, § 12).

Without his realizing it, Luxenberg's work falls within the tradition and genre of the readings *(qirāʾāt)* of the Qurʾān. It becomes still more obvious if we distinguish between "the small variation" (various readings of the same ductus) and "the great variation" (variations of the ductus, i.e. non-"ʿUthmānic" codices), on the one hand, and "a greater variation" (an Arabic/Aramaic transliteration of the ductus), on the other hand. The method of Luxenberg applied to passages of the Qurʾān which are particularly obscure cannot be brushed aside by the mere repetition of the Nöldeke/Spitaler thesis, or, as some would say, dogma (see Spitaler, Review of Fück, *ʿArabīya*). It must be examined seriously. From a linguistic point of view the undertaking of Luxenberg is one of the most interesting. It will provoke in some Islamic circles the same emotion as did the hypothesis of Vollers formerly, because it amounts to seeing in the Qurʾān a kind of palimpsest. Such hypotheses, and the reactions they generate, push scholarship on the language and style of the Qurʾān continually to examine and question its acknowledged (and implicit) premises.

Claude Gilliot and Pierre Larcher

Bibliography

Primary: ʿAbd al-Mālik b. Ḥabīb, Abū Marwān al-Qurṭubī, *Kitāb al-Taʾrīkh. La Historia,* ed. J. Aguadé, Madrid 1991; Abū Bakr al-Ismāʿīlī, *Kitāb al-Muʿjam fī asāmī shuyūkh Abī Bakr al-Ismāʿīlī,* ed. Z.M. Manṣūr, 3 vols. in 2, Medina 1990; Abū Ḥātim al-Rāzī, A. b. Ḥamdān, *Kitāb al-Zīna fī l-kalimāt al-islāmiyya al-ʿarabiyya,* Foreword by Ibrāhīm Anīs, ed. Ī. al-Hamdānī, 2 vols. in 1, Cairo 1957-8; 3 vols. in 1, n.p. n.d. (i-ii unchanged; iii, ed. ʿA. Sallūm al-Samarrāʾī; on sects absent from the first ed.); Abū Ḥayyān, *Baḥr,* 8 vols., Cairo 1911; Abū l-Qāsim al-Balkhī (al-Kaʿbī), *Qābūl al-akhbār,* ed. M. Abū ʿAmr al-Ḥusayn b. ʿUmar b. ʿAbd al-Raḥīm, 2 vols., Beirut 2000; Abū ʿUbayd, *Faḍāʾil,* ed. Khāwajī; Baghawī, *Maʿālim;* Baghdādī, ʿAbd al-Qādir, *Khizānat al-adab wa-lubb lubāb lisān al-ʿarab,* ed. ʿA.M. Hārūn, 13 vols., Cairo 1967-86, i, 5-17; Fr. trans. in Gilliot, Citations, 297-316; Bāqillānī, *Nukat al-intiṣār li-naql al-Qurʾān,* ed. M. Zaghlūl Sallām, Alexandria 1971; Dāmaghānī, *Wujūh,* ed. Zafītī, 2 vols.; Farrāʾ, *Maʿānī;* Ibn Abī Shayba, Abū Bakr ʿAbdallāh b. Muḥammad, *al-Muṣannaf fī l-aḥādīth wa-l-āthār,* 9 vols., text revised by M.ʿA. Shāhīn, Beirut 1995; Ibn Abī l-Iṣbaʿ, *Badīʿ;* Ibn al-Anbārī, *Īḍāḥ,* i, 4-110; Ibn ʿAsākir, *Taʾrīkh,* ed. al-ʿAmrawī, 80 vols., Beirut 1995-2000; Ibn al-Athīr, ʿIzz al-Dīn Abū l-Ḥasan ʿAlī b. Muḥammad, *Usd al-ghāba fī maʿrifat al-ṣaḥāba,* ed. M. Fāyid et al., 7 vols., Cairo 1970[2]; Ibn Fāris, Abū l-Ḥusayn Aḥmad, *al-Ṣāḥibī fī fiqh al-lugha,* ed. M. El-Chouémi, Beirut 1964, 31-83; Ibn al-Jawzī, *Funūn;* id., *Nuzha;* Ibn Jinnī, *al-Khaṣāʾiṣ,* ed. M.ʿA. al-Najjār, 3 vols., Cairo 1952-6; Ibn Khaldūn, *ʿIbar,* 7 vols., Beirut 1967, vol. i; Ibn Khaldūn-Rosenthal; Ibn al-Naqīb, *Muqaddima;* Ibn Qutayba, *al-Shiʿr;* Ibn Saʿd, *Ṭabaqāt,* ed. I. ʿAbbās; Ibn al-Sarrāj al-Shantarīnī, Abū Bakr Muḥammad b. ʿAbd al-Malik, *Tanbīh al-albāb ʿalā faḍāʾil al-iʿrāb,* ed. M. al-ʿAwfī, Cairo 1989; Jāḥiẓ, *Kitāb al-Ḥayawān,* ed. ʿA.M. Hārūn, 7 vols., Cairo 1938-45, Beirut 1969[3] (based on 2nd rev. ed.); Jurjānī, *Dalāʾil,* ed. M.M. Shākir, Cairo 1984; *Lisān al-ʿArab;* Muqātil, *Tafsīr;* Nahshalī al-Qayrawānī, ʿAbd al-Karīm, *al-Mumtiʿ fī ʿilm al-shiʿr wa-ʿamalihi,* ed. M. al-Kaʿbī, Tunis 1978; Nīsābūrī, *Tafsīr,* on the margin of Ṭabarī, *Tafsīr,* 30 vols., Cairo 1905-11; Nuwayrī, Shihāb al-Dīn Aḥmad b. ʿAbd al-Wahhāb, *Nihāyat al-arab fī funūn al-adab,* 27 vols., Cairo 1964-85; Rāzī, *Nihāyat al-ījāz wa-dirāyat al-iʿjāz,* ed. Bakrī Shaykh Amīn, Beirut 1985; Rummānī et al., *Rasāʾil;* Shāfiʿī, Muḥammad b. Idrīs, *al-Risāla,* ed. A.M. Shākir, Cairo 1940; Eng. trans. M. Khadduri, *Islamic jurisprudence. Shāfiʿī's Risāla,* Baltimore 1961; Fr. trans L. Souami, *La Risâla,* Arles 1997; Sībawayhi, Abū Bishr ʿAmr b. ʿUthmān b. Qanbar, *al-Kitāb,* ed. H. Derenbourg [*Le Livre de Sībawaihi.* Traité de grammaire arabe], 2 vols., Paris 1881-9; 2 vols., Būlāq (Cairo) 1898-9; ed. ʿA. Hārūn, 5 vols., Cairo 1966-77; Subkī, Tāj al-Dīn ʿAbd al-Wahhāb, *Ṭabaqāt al-shāfiʿiyya al-kubrā,* ed. M.M. al-Ṭanāḥī and ʿA. al-Ḥulw, 10 vols., Cairo 1964-76, i, 220-314 (on poetry); Suyūṭī, Jalāl al-Dīn, *al-Akhbār al-marwiyya bi-sabab waḍʿ al-ʿarabiyya,* in ʿA. al-Jubūrī (ed.), *Rasāʾil fī l-fiqh wa-l-lugha,* Beirut 1982, 147-75 [see also Czapkiewicz below]; id., *Durr;* id., *Itqān,* ed. A. Sprenger et al., Calcutta 1852-4, repr. Osnabrück 1980; ed. M. Abū l-Faḍl Ibrāhīm, Cairo 1974 (1967[1], different pagination); id., *Khaṣāʾiṣ,* i, 63 (chap. on the tongue of Muḥammad, a miraculous sign); id., *Muhadhdhab,* in ʿA. al-Jubūrī (ed.), *Rasāʾil fī l-fiqh wa-l-lugha,* Beirut 1982, 179-235 (good ed.); ed. Ṭ. al-Rājī al-Hāshimī (poor ed.); id., *Muʿtarak al-aqrān fī iʿjāz al-Qurʾān,* ed. ʿA.M. al-Bijāwī, 3 vols., Cairo 1969-72; id., *al-Muzhir fī ʿulūm al-lugha wa-anwāʿihā,* ed. A. Jādd al-Mawlā et al., 2 vols., Cairo 1958, i, 7-103 (chap. 1); i, 184-213 (chap. 9); id., *Taḥbīr;* id., *Tanāsuq;* Ṭabarānī, *Kabīr;* Ṭabarī, *Tafsīr,* ed. Shākir (from the beginning to Q 14:27); ed. Aḥmad Saʿīd ʿAlī et al. (used here from Q 14:28 to the end); Eng. trans. J. Cooper, *The commentary on the Qurʾān.* Vol. 1, gen. eds. W.F. Madelung and A. Jones, New York 1987-; Thaʿlabī, Abū Isḥāq Aḥmad b. Muḥammad, *al-Kashf wa-l-bayān ʿan tafsīr al-Qurʾān,* ms. Istanbul, Ahmet III 76. From sūra 5 to the end of the Qurʾān, part 4 (ad Q 41:44); Wāḥidī, *Wasīṭ;* Yaḥyā b. Sallām, *al-Taṣārīf. Tafsīr al-Qurʾān mimmā shtabahat asmāʾuhu wa-taṣarrafat maʿānīhi,* ed. H. Shiblī, Tunis 1979; Zarkashī, Badr al-Dīn Muḥammad b. Bahādur, *al-Baḥr al-muḥīṭ fī uṣūl al-fiqh,* ed. ʿA.ʿA. al-ʿĀnī, 6 vols., Kuwait 1989.

Secondary: K. Abu Deeb, *Al-Jurjānī's theory of poetic imagery,* Warminster 1979; T. Andrae, *Der Ursprung des Islams und das Christentum,* Uppsala

1926; A.M. al-Anṣārī, *Difāʿ ʿan al-qirāʾāt al-mutawātira fī muwājahat al-Ṭabarī al-mufassir,* Cairo 1978; id., *al-Difāʿ ʿan al-Qurʾān ḍidd al-naḥwiyyīn wa-l-mustashriqīn,* Cairo 1973; id., *Naẓariyyat al-naḥw al-qurʾānī,* Cairo 1984; Arberry; C.-F. Audebert, *al-Ḫaṭṭābī et l'inimitabilité du Coran,* Damascus 1982 (trans. of al-Khaṭṭābī, *Bayān iʿjāz al-Qurʾān*); J.L. Austin, *How to do things with words,* Oxford 1962; J. Barth, Studien zur Kritik und Exegese des Qorāns, in *Der Islam* 6 (1915-6), 113-48; A. Bausani, Bāb, in *EI²*, i, 833-5; E. Beck, ʿArabiyya, sunna und ʿāmma in der Koranlesung des zweiten Jahrhundert, in *Orientalia* 15 (1946), 180-224; Bell; id., *Commentary;* id., *The origin of Islam in its Christian environment,* London 1926; J.E. Bencheikh, *Poétique arabe. Précédée de Essai sur un discours critique,* Paris 1989², I-XXXII; J. Berque, *Le Coran. Essai de traduction de l'arabe, annoté et suivi d'une étude exégétique,* Paris 1990; id., *Langages arabes du présent,* Paris 1974; id., *Relire le Coran,* Paris 1993; Blachère; id., *Histoire de la littérature arabe. Des origines à la fin du XVᵉ siècle de J.-C,* 3 vols., Paris 1952-66, ii, 195-236; J. Blau, On the problem of the synthetic character of the classical Arabic as against Judaeo-Arabic (middle Arabic), in *The Jewish quarterly review [N.S.]* 63 (1972), 29-38; repr. in id., *Studies in middle Arabic and its Judaeo-Arabic variety,* Jerusalem 1988, 260-9; I.J. Boullata (ed.), *Literary structures of religious meaning in the Qurʾān,* Richmond, Surrey 2000; id., The rhetorical interpretation of the Qurʾān. *Iʿjāz* and related topics, in Rippin, *Approaches,* 139-57; J. Bouman, *Le conflit autour du Coran et la solution d'al-Bāqillānī,* Amsterdam 1959; J. Burton, Linguistic errors in the Qurʾān, in *JSS* 33 (1988), 181-96; F. Corriente, Again on the functional yield of some synthetic devices in Arabic and Semitic morphology (A reply to J. Blau), in *The Jewish quarterly review [N.S.]* 64 (1973-74), 154-63; id., On the functional yield of some synthetic devices in Arabic and Semitic morphology, in *The Jewish quarterly review [N.S.]* 62 (1971), 20-50; A. Czapkiewicz, *The views of the medieval Arab philologists on language and its origin in the light of as-Suyûtî's "al-Muzhir,"* Cracow 1988 (partial Eng. trans. of *al-Muzhir,* with notes and Ar. text; Suyūṭī's sources are discussed on pp. 25-39); van Ess, *TG;* B. Farès, *L'honneur chez les Arabes avant l'Islam,* Paris 1932; F.L. Fleischer, Über arabische Lexicographie und Ṯaʿālibī's Fiḳh al-luġa, in *Berichten über die Verhandlungen der Königlich Sächsischen Gesellschaft der Wissenschaften zu Leipzig. Philologische-historische Klasse* (1854), 1-14; repr. in H.L. Fleischer, *Kleinere Schriften,* 3 vols., Osnabrück 1968, iii, 152-66; J. Fück, *ʿArabīya. Untersuchungen zur Arabischen Sprach-und Stilgeschichte,* Berlin 1950; Fr. trans. Ch. Denizeau, *ʿArabīya. Recherches sur l'histoire de la langue et du style arabe,* Paris 1955; Review: A. Spitaler, in *BO* 10 (1953), 144-50; J.H. Garcin de Tassy, *Rhétorique et prosodie des langues de l'Orient musulman,* Paris 1873, repr. Amsterdam 1970; R.E. Geyer, Review of Vollers, *Volkssprache,* in *Göttingische gelehrte Anzeigen* 171 (1909), 10-55; id., Zur Strophik des Qurâns, in *WZKM* 22 (1908), 265-286; Eng. trans. The strophic structure of the Koran, in Ibn Warraq (ed. and trans.), *What the Koran really says. Language, text, and commentary,* Amherst 2002, 625-46; C. Gilliot, Les citations probantes *(šawāhid)* en langue, in *Arabica* 43 (1996), 297-356; id., Le Coran. Fruit d'un travail collectif? in D. DeSmet, G. de Callatay and J. van Reeth (eds.), *Al-kitāb. La sacralité du texte dans le monde de l'Islam. Actes du Symposium International tenu à Leuven et Louvain-la-Neuve du 29 may au 1 juin* 2002, Brussels 2003 (forthcoming), § 6, 23 and passim; id., Deux études (see under Lüling); id., *Elt,* 73-203; id., Informants, in *EQ,* ii, 512-8; id., Langue (see below under Luxenberg); id., Muqātil, grand exégète, traditionniste et théologien maudit, in *JA* 27 (1991), 39-92; id., Parcours exégétiques. De Ṭabarī à Rāzī (sourate 55), in *Études Arabes/Analyses-Théorie* 1 (1983), 67-116; id., Poète ou prophète? Les traditions concernant la poésie et les poètes attribuées au prophète de l'islam et aux premières générations musulmanes, in F. Sanagustin (ed.), *Paroles, signes, mythes. Mélanges offerts à Jamal Eddine Bencheikh,* Damascus 2001, 331-96; id., Précellence = Langue et Coran selon Tabari. La précellence du Coran, in *SI* 68 (1988), 79-106; id., Une reconstruction critique du Coran, in M. Kropp (ed.), *Results of contemporary research on the Qurʾān. The question of a historio-critical text of the Qurʾān,* Beirut 2003 (forthcoming); id., Les sept "lectures." Corps social et écriture révélée. I, in *SI* 61 (1985), 5-25; II, in *SI* 63 (1986), 49-62; id., La théologie musulmane en Asie Centrale et au Khorasan, in *Arabica* 49 (2002), 135-203; J.W. Goethe, *Noten und Abhandlungen zum West-östlichen Divan,* in G. von Loeper et al. (eds.), *Goethes Werke,* 55 vols. (in 63), Weimar 1887-1918, vii, 33-5; I. Goldziher, Alte und neue Poesie im Urtheile der arabischen Kritiker, in id. (ed.), *Abhandlungen zur arabischen Philologie,* Leiden 1896, 122-76; id., Beiträge zur Geschichte der Sprachgelehrsamkeit bei den Arabern. III. Abu-l-Husein ibn Fâris, in *Sitzungsberichte der Kais. Akademie der Wissenschafteen in Wien philosophische-historrische Classe* 73 (1873), 511-52; repr. J. Desomogyi (ed.), *Gesammelte Schriften,* Hildesheim 1964, 187-228; id., *On the history of grammar among the Arabs,* trans. and ed. K. Dévényi and T. Iványi, Amsterdam/Philadelphia 1994; id., *Richtungen;* id., Ueber die Vorgeschichte des Higâʾ-Poesie, in id. (ed.), *Abhandlugen zur arabischen Philologie,* Leiden 1896,

1-105; Grünbaum, *Beiträge;* id., Beiträge zur vergleichenden Mythologie der Hagada, in ZDMG 31 (1877), 183-359; G. von Grunebaum, Bayān, in EI², i, 1114-6; J. von Hammer-Purgstall, Die letzten vierzig Suren des Koran als eine Probe einer gereimten Übersetzung, in *Fundgruben des Orients* 2 (1811), 25-47; M. al-Ḥasnāwī, *al-Fāṣila fī l-Qurʾān,* Aleppo 1977(?); Kh. b. al-Ḥassūn, *al-Naḥw al-qurʾānī,* Amman 2002; N. al-Ḥimṣī, *Fikrat al-iʿjāz* (from early times to the present), Beirut 1980²; J.W. Hirschberg, *Jüdische und christliche Lehren im vor- und frühislamischen Arabien. Ein Beitrag zur Enstehungsgeschichte des Islams,* Krakow 1939; H. Hirschfeld, *New researches into the composition and exegesis of the Qoran,* London 1902; Horovitz, KU; T. Hughes/F.J. Steingass, Qurʾān, in T.P. Hughes, *A dictionary of Islam,* Lahore 1885; reprint New Delhi 1976, 483-530 (article Qurʾān, revised and supplemented by F.J. Steingass); Ibn Rawandi, On pre-Islamic Christian strophic poetical texts in the Koran. A critical look at the work of Günter Lüling, in Ibn Warraq (ed. and trans.), *What the Koran really says. Language, text, and commentary,* Amherst 2002, 653-710; Ibn Warraq (ed. and trans.), *What the Koran really says. Language, text, and commentary,* Amherst 2002; G. Jacob, *Altarabisches Beduinenleben. Nach den Quellen geschildert,* Berlin 1897²; repr. Hildesheim 1967; R. Jakobson, Closing statements. Linguistics and poetics, in T.A. Sebeok (ed.), *Style in language,* New York 1960, 350-77; Jeffery, *Muqaddimas;* H. Jenssen, Arabic language, in EQ, i, 127-35; A. Jones, The language of the Qurʾān, in *The Arabist* 6-7 (1994), 29-48; id., Narrative technique in the Qurʾān and in early poetry, in JAL 25 (1994), 185-91 (also in *The Arabist* 8 [1994], 45-54); id., The oral and the written. Some thoughts about the qurʾanic text, in *The Arabist* 17 (1996), 57-66; D. al-Jundī, *al-Naẓm al-qurʾānī fī Kashshāf al-Ẓamakhsharī,* Cairo 1969; P.E. Kahle, The Arabic readers of the Koran, in JNES 8 (1949), 65-71; repr. in Ibn Warraq (ed. and trans.), *What the Koran really says. Language, text, and commentary,* Amherst 2002, 201-10; id., *The Cairo Geniza,* Oxford 1959², 141-9, 345-6 (ed. of a text of al-Farrāʾ); id., The Qurʾān and the ʿarabīya, in S. Loewinger and J. Somogyi (eds.), *Ignace Goldziher memorial volume,* Budapest 1948, 163-8; N. Kermani, The aesthetic reception of the Qurʾān as reflected in early Muslim history, in I.J. Boullata (ed.), *Literary structures of religious meaning in the Qurʾān,* Richmond, Surrey 2000, 205-76; id., *Gott ist schön. Das Ästhetische Erleben des Koran,* Münich 1999; review of C. Gilliot, in *Arabica* 47 (2000), 571-4; M. Khan, *Die exegetischen Teile des* Kitāb al-ʿAyn. *Zur ältesten philologischen Koranexegese,* Berlin 1994; L. Kopf, Religious influences on medieval Arabic philology, in SI 5 (1956), 33-59; repr. in L. Kopf, *Studies in Arabic and Hebrew lexicography,* ed. M.H. Goshen-Gottstein, Jerusalem 1976, 19-45; M. Lagarde, *Index du Grand Commentaire de Faḫr al-Dīn al-Rāzī,* Leiden 1996; C. de Landberg, *La langue arabe et ses dialectes,* Leiden 1905; Lane, *An Arabic-English lexicon,* 2 vols. (repr.); P. Larcher, Coran et théorie linguistique de l'énonciation, in *Arabica* 47 (2000), 441-56; M. Lecker, *Jews and Arabs in pre- and early Islamic Arabia,* Aldershot 1999; id., Zayd b. Thābit. 'A Jew with two sidelocks.' Judaism and literacy in pre-Islamic Medina (Yathrib), in JNES 56 (1997), 259-73; A. Levin, Sîbawayhi's attitude to the spoken language, in JSAI 17 (1994), 204-43; repr. in id., *Arabic linguistic thought and dialectology,* Jerusalem 1998, chap. 12; H. Loucel, L'origine du language d'après les grammairiens arabes, in *Arabica* 10 (1963), 188-208, 253-81; 11 (1964), 57-72, 151-87; G. Lüling, *Über den Ur-Qurʾān. Ansätze zur Rekonstruktion vorislamischer christlicher Strophenlieder im Qurʾān,* Erlangen 1974 (1993²); Eng. trans. *A challenge to Islam for reformation,* Dehli 2003 [Reviews: M. Rodinson in *Der Islam* 54 (1977), 321-25, and C. Gilliot, Deux études sur le Coran, in *Arabica* 30 (1983), 16-37]; id., *Die Wiederentdeckung des Propheten Muhammad. Eine Kritik am 'christlichen' Abendland,* Erlangen 1981; C. Luxenberg, *Die syro-aramäische Lesart des Koran. Ein Beitrag zur Entschlüsselung der Koran-sprache,* Berlin 2000 [Reviews: Gilliot, Langue = Langue et Coran. Une lecture syro-araméenne du Coran, forthcoming in *Arabica* 50 (2003), § 4 [quoted here according to §]; R. Nabielek, Weintrauben statt Jungfrauen. Zu einer neuen Lesart des Korans, in *Informationsprojekt Naher und Mittlerer Osten* 23-4 (Berlin 2000), 66-72; R.R. Phenix and C.B. Horn, in *Hugoye. Journal of Syriac studies* 6 (January 2003) on http://syrcom.cua.edu/Hugoye]; D. Madigan, *The Qurʾān's self-image. Writing and authority in Islam's scripture,* Princeton 2001; R.C. Martin, Structural analysis and the Qurʾān. Newer approaches to the study of Islamic texts, in *Journal of the American Academy of Religion (Thematic Studies)* 47 (1979), 665-83; id., Understanding the Qurʾān in text and context, in *History of religions* 21 (1982), 361-84; A.F. Mehren, *Die Rhetorik der Araber,* Copenhagen/Vienna 1853; A. Mingana, Qurʾān, in ERE, x, 538-50; id., Syriac influence on the style of the Kuran, in *Bulletin of the John Rylands Library* 11 (1927), 77-98; repr. in Ibn Warraq (ed. and trans.), *What the Koran really says. Language, text, and commentary,* Amherst 2002, 171-92; E. Mittwoch, Die Berliner arabische Handschrift Ahlwardt No 683 (eine angebliche Schrift des Ibn ʿAbbās), in T.W. Arnold and R.A. Nicholson (eds.), *A volume of oriental studies presented to Edward G. Brown,* Cambridge 1922, 339-44; D.H. Müller, *Die Propheten in ihrer ursprünglichen Form. Die Grund-*

gesetze der ursemitischen Poesie erschlossen und nachgewiesen in Bibel, Keilinschriften und Koran und in ihren Wirkungen erkannt in den Chören der griechischen Tragödie, 2 vols. in 1, Vienna 1896; F.R. Müller, *Untersuchungen zur reimprosa im Koran,* Bonn 1969; A. Neuwirth, Einige Bermerkungen zum besonderen sprachlichen und literarischen Charakter des Koran, in ZDMG *Supplement* [XIX Deutscher Orientalistentag, Freiburg im Breisgau, vom 28. September bis 4. Oktober 1975] 3 (1977), 736-9; Eng. trans. Some notes on the distinctive linguistic and literary character of the Qurʾān, in A. Rippin (ed.), *The Qurʾan. Style and content,* Aldershot 2001, 253-7; id., Form and structure of the Qurʾān, in *EQ,* ii, 245-66; id., Vom Rezitationstext über die Liturgie zum Kanon. Zu Entstehung und Wiederauflösung der Surenkomposition im Verlauf der Entwicklung eines islamischen Kultus, in Wild, *Text,* 69-105; Fr. trans. Du texte de récitation au canon en passant par la liturgie. A propos de la genèse de la composition des sourates et de sa redissolution au cours du développement du culte islamique, in *Arabica* 47 (2000), 194-229; R.A. Nicholson, *A literary history of the Arabs,* Cambridge 1930; Th. Nöldeke, *Beiträge zur semitischen Sprachwissenschaft,* Strassburg 1904; id., Einige Bemerkungen über die Sprache der alten Araber, in *Zeitschrift für Assyriologie* 12 (1897), 171-87; repr. (with some differences) Das klassische Arabisch und die arabischen Dialekte, in id., *Beiträge zur semitischen Sprachwissenschaft,* Strassburg 1904, 1-14; id., *GQ* (single vol. refs *[Geschichte]* are to the Göttingen ed. of 1860); id., The Koran, in J. Suntherland Black (trans.), *Sketches from eastern history,* London 1892, repr. Beirut 1963, 21-59; id., Der Koran und die ʿArabīja, in id., *Neue Beiträge zur semitischen Sprachwissenschaft,* Strassburg 1910, 1-5; id., *Neue Beiträge zur semitischen Sprachwissenschaft,* Strassburg 1910; id., *De origine et compositione surarum qoranicarum ipsiusque Qorani,* Göttingen 1856; id., Zur Sprache des Korāns, in id., *Neue Beiträge zur semitischen Sprachwissenschaft,* Strassburg 1910, 1-30; Fr. trans. G.-H. Bousquet, *Remarques critiques sur le style et la syntaxe du Coran,* Paris 1953, conclusion; J. Owens, *Idġām al-kabīr* and the history of the Arabic language, in W. Arnold and H. Bobzin (eds.) *"Sprich doch (mit deinen Knechten) Aramäisch, wir verstehen es!" 60 Beiträge zur Semitistik für Otto Jastrow zum 60. Geburtstag,* Wiesbaden 2002, 503-20; Paret, *Kommentar;* id., The Qurʾān. I, in Beeston, *CHAL,* i, 186-227 (196-205); Pickthall; G.R. Puin, Observations on early qurʾānic manuscripts in Ṣanʿāʾ, in Wild, *Text,* 107-11; C. Rabin, *Ancient West-Arabian,* London 1951; id., The beginnings of classical Arabic, in *SI* 4 (1955), 19-37; M. Radscheit, *Die koranische Herausforderung. Die taḥaddī-Verse im Rahmen der Polemikpassagen des Korans,* Berlin 1996; M.Ṣ. al-Rāfiʿī, *Iʿjāz al-Qurʾān wa-l-balāgha al-nabawiyya,* Cairo 1922[2]; repr. *Majmūʿat M.Ṣ. al-Rāfiʿī,* Beirut n.d.; E.A. Rezvan, The Qurʾān and its world. V, in *Manuscripta orientalia* 4 (1998), 26-39; A. Rippin, Foreign vocabulary, in *EQ,* ii, 226-37; N. Robinson, *Discovering the Qurʾān. A contemporary approach to a veiled text,* London 1996; G. Sale, *The preliminary discourse to the Koran* [extract from *The Koran commonly called Alcoran of Mohammed:* translated, to which is prefixed a preliminary discourse, London 1734], with an Introduction by Sir Edward Denison Ross, London n.d. (ca. 1940?); Ḥ. Ṣammūd, *al-Tafkīr al-balāghī ʿinda l-ʿarab,* Tunis 1981; M. Sfar, *Le Coran est-il authentique?* Paris 2000; M. Sister, Metaphern und Vergleiche im Koran, in *Mitteilungen des Seminars für Orientalisch Sprachen zu Berlin,* 2. Abt. *Westasiatische Studien* 34 (1931), 103-54; R. Talmon, *Arabic grammar in its formative age. Kitāb al-ʿAyn and its attribution to Ḫalīl b. Aḥmad,* Leiden 1997; M. Ullmann, *Wa-ḫairu l-ḥadīṯi mā kāna laḥnan,* Munich 1979; K. Versteegh, *The Arabic language,* Edinburgh 2001 (1997[1]); id., *The Arabic linguistic tradition,* London 1997; K. Vollers, review of Th. Nöldeke, *Zur Grammatik des classischen Arabisch,* Vienna 1896, in *Zeischrift für Assyriologie* 12 (1897), 125-39; id., *Volkssprache und Schriftsprache im alten Arabien,* Strassburg 1906, repr. Amsterdam 1981; Wansbrough, *QS;* Watt-Bell, *Introduction,* 69-85; G. Weil, *Historisch-kritische Einleitung in den Koran. Zweite verbesserte Auflage,* Bielefeld 1878 (Bielefeld 1844[1]); G. Widengren, *Muhammad, the apostle of God, and his ascension,* Uppsala 1955; B. Wiesmüller, *Die vom Koran getöten. Aṯ-Ṯaʿlabī's Qatlā al-Qurʾān nach der Istanbuler und den Leidener Handschriften,* Köln 1996; S. Wild, *Mensch, Prophet und Gott im Koran. Muslimische Exegeten des 20. Jahrhunderts und das Menschenbild der Moderne,* Münster 2001; J. Willmet, *Lexicon linguae Arabicae in Coranum, Haririum et vitam Timuri,* Rotterdam/London 1784 (see Rezvan, Qurʾān, 26); M.M. Yahia, *La contribution de l'Imam aš-Šāfiʿī à la méthodologie juridique de l'islam sunnite,* Thèse de doctorat, Paris 2003; M. Zwettler, Classical Arabic poetry between folk and oral literature, in *JAOS* 96 (1976), 198-212; id., A Mantic manifesto. The sūra of "The Poets" and the qurʾānic foundations of prophetic authority, in J.L. Kugel (ed.), *Poetry and prophecy,* Ithaca 1990, 75-119; id., *The oral tradition of classical Arabic poetry,* Columbus, OH 1978, 97-188.

Last Day

see ESCHATOLOGY; APOCALYPSE; LAST JUDGMENT

Last Judgment

God's final assessment of humankind. The subject of the last judgment *(yawm al-dīn, yawm al-qiyāma)* is one of the most important themes in the Qurʾān. It appears in many forms, especially in the first Meccan sūras (see CHRONOLOGY AND THE QURʾĀN), which are dominated by the idea of the nearing day of resurrection (*yawm al-qiyāma,* see RESURRECTION) when all creatures, including jinn (q.v.) and animals (see ANIMAL LIFE), must be judged (see JUDGMENT).

Belief in the last judgment, with the concomitant belief in paradise (q.v.; *al-janna*) for those who performed good deeds (q.v.) and in hell (*jahannam,* see HELL AND HELLFIRE) for those who did not believe in God and did evil (see GOOD AND EVIL; EVIL DEEDS), became one of "the pillars of faith" (*arkān al-īmān,* cf. Q 4:136; see FAITH; BELIEF AND UNBELIEF), as these were called by later Muslim sources. Many sūras indicate that those who trust in God and in the day of resurrection are considered to be believers (Q 2:62, 126, 177; 3:114; 4:162; 5:69; 9:18) and those who refute these tenets are unbelievers, or those who have gone "astray" (q.v.; Q 4:136), and Muslims must fight them (Q 9:29; see JIHĀD; FIGHTING; WAR). The ḥadīth literature adds material to emphasize the importance, in Islam, of belief in the resurrection (*al-qiyāma,* al-Bayhaqī, *Shuʿab al-īmān,* ii, 5-72; see ḤADĪTH AND THE QURʾĀN).

Certain Western researchers suppose (Seale, Arab's concern, 90-1) that Muḥammad tried, at the beginning of his prophecy, to convince his audience that there was going to be a day of resurrection. Considering their reaction (Q 75:3-4; 79:10-1) to this concept, Muḥammad then warned them that there was going to be a day of judgment (Q 44:40). This line of thinking also maintains that the Meccans' refutation of Muḥammad's doctrine of resurrection and a day of reckoning — and their tendency to ridicule these issues — may explain the abundance of references to these themes in the Qurʾān, as well as the conflation of *yawm al-qiyāma* and *yawm al-dīn.* There is reason to believe that such qurʾānic abundance, supported by a flux of interpretations and ḥadīths elaborating the details of the last judgment, may have led P. Casanova to the following explanation for Muḥammad's failure to designate a successor: namely, Muḥammad was convinced that the end of the world was so close at hand that he himself would witness it, and, consequently, there was no need for him to name a successor (Casanova, *Mohammed,* 12; for a critical view, see Watt-Bell, *Introduction,* 53-4; see CALIPH).

Qurʾānic appellations of the day of the last judgment

The most frequently occurring terms that refer to the last judgment in the Meccan sūras are, as mentioned above, "day of resurrection" (*yawm al-qiyāma,* seventy times in Meccan and Medinan sūras) and "day of judgment" (*yawm al-dīn,* thirteen times: Q 1:4; 15:35; 26:82; 37:20; 38:78; 51:12; 56:56; 70:26; 74:46; 82:15, 17, 18; 83:11; and four times without *yawm,* Q 51:6; 82:9; 95:7; 107:1). In the Medinan sūras, the dominant terms are "the last day" (*al-yawm al-ākhir,* twenty-six times: Q 2:8, 62, 126, 177, 228, 232, 264; 3:114; 4:38, 39, 59, 136, 162; 5:69; 9:18, 19, 29, 44, 45, 99; 24:2; 29:36; 33:21; 58:22; 60:6; 65:2) and *al-ākhira* (115 times). This last term, however, is mostly used for "the life to come," "the last dwelling." Some exegetes explain this term as "the mansion of the last hour" (*dār al-sāʿa al-ākhira,* Nasafī, *Tafsīr,* ad Q 6:32) or "the upraising, resurrection, paradise, hell, reckoning and balance" (… *al-ākhira… ay al-baʿth wa-l-qiyāma wa-l-janna wa-l-nār wa-l-ḥisāb wa-l-mīzān,* Ibn Kathīr, *Tafsīr,* ad Q 2:4).

The "day of resurrection" *(yawm al-qiyāma)* is also termed *al-yawm al-ākhir,* "since it is the last day and there is no day after it" (Ṭabarī, *Tafsīr,* i, 271).

Many terms or locutions appear in the Qurʾān that are explained by the majority of exegetes as synonymous with *yawm al-dīn.* The following are the most important of these designations: "the hour" (*al-sāʿa,* thirty-five times: Q 6:31, 40; 7:187; 12:107; 15:85; 16:77; 18:21, 36; 19:75; 20:15; 21:49; 22:1, 7, 55; 25:11; 30:12, 14, 55; 31:34; 33:63; 34:3; 40:46; 41:47, 50; 42:17, 18; 43:61, 66, 85; 45:27, 32 ; 47:18; 54:1, 46; 79:42); "dreadful day" (*yawm ʿaẓīm,* Q 6:15; 10:15); "the day of anguish" (*yawm al-ḥasra,* Q 19:39); "barren day" (*yawm ʿaqīm,* Q 22:55; "since after it there will be no night," cf. Ṭabarī, *Tafsīr,* i, 272); "the day of the upraising" (*yawm al-baʿth,* Q 30:56); "the day of decision" (*yawm al-faṣl,* Q 37:21; 44:40; 77:13, 14, 38; 78:17); "the day of reckoning" (*yawm al-ḥisāb,* Q 38:16, 26, 53; 40:27; see WEIGHTS AND MEASURES) and "the day when the reckoning will be established" (*yawma yaqūmu l-ḥisābu,* Q 14:41); "the day of encounter" (*yawm al-talāq,* Q 40:15); "the day of the imminent" (*yawm al-āzifa,* Q 40:18) and "the imminent" (*al-āzifa,* Q 53:57); "the day of invocation" (*yawm al-tanādi,* Q 40:32); "the day of gathering" (*yawm al-jamʿ,* Q 42:7; 64:9); "the day of the threat" (*yawm al-waʿīd,* Q 50:20); "the day of eternity" (*yawm al-khulūd,* Q 50:34; see ETERNITY); "the day of coming forth" (*yawm al-khurūj,* Q 50:42); "the terror" (*al-wāqiʿa,* Q 56:1; 69:15); "the day of mutual fraud" (*yawm al-taghābun,* Q 64:9; see LIE; HONESTY; MARKETS); "the indubitable" (*al-ḥāqqa,* Q 69:1, 2, 3; see TRUTH); "the clatterer" (*al-qāriʿa,* Q 69:4; 101:1, 2, 3); "the great catastrophe" (*al-ṭāmma al-kubrā,* Q 79:34); "the blast" (*al-ṣākhkha,* Q 80:33); "the promised day" (*al-yawm al-mawʿūd,* Q 85:2) and "the enveloper" (*al-ghāshiya,* Q 88:1).

Exegetes add some expressions which are said to refer to the day of the last judgment: "[fear] a day when no soul (q.v.) shall avail another" (*yawman lā tajzī nafsun ʿan nafsin shayʾan,* Q 2:123); "the day when some faces (see FACE) are whitened, and some faces blackened" (*yawma tabyaḍḍu wujūhun wa-taswaddu wujūhun,* Q 3:106); "a day wherein shall be neither bargaining nor befriending" (*yawmun lā bayʿun fīhi wa-lā khilālun,* Q 14:31; see FRIENDS AND FRIENDSHIP); "the day when their excuses shall not profit the evildoers" (*yawma lā yanfaʿu al-ẓālimīna maʿdhiratuhum,* Q 40:52), or "a day when no soul shall possess aught to succor another soul" (*yawma lā tamliku nafsun li-nafsin shayʾan,* Q 82:19). This list is far from exhaustive. Al-Ghazālī (d. 505/1111), for example, gives more than one hundred names or epithets designating *yawm al-qiyāma* (Ghazālī, *Iḥyāʾ,* vi, 161; Fīrūzābādī, *Baṣāʾir,* v, 416-21; Ibn Kathīr, *Ashrāṭ al-sāʿa,* 83-4, citing ʿAbd al-Ḥaqq al-Ishbīlī's *Kitāb al-ʿĀqiba;* ʿAwājī; *al-Ḥayāt al-ākhira,* i, 45-55.

Creating a comprehensive vision

The qurʾānic material on the last judgment is very rich and colorful but the allusions in the holy book do not provide a comprehensive picture of all of its details. As the various phases of the day of resurrection (*yawm al-qiyāma*) are mentioned in different sūras, sometimes clearly, sometimes metaphorically (see METAPHOR), but generally without an arranged description of these phases, there was a need to reconstruct the qurʾānic vision of this theme in order to provide a complete picture. Such a task was performed by a number of Muslim authors, who drew upon one or more of the following categories to assist them in their efforts at elaborating upon the qurʾānic material: exegetical literature (*tafsīr,* see EXEGESIS OF THE QURʾĀN: CLASSICAL AND MEDIEVAL), ḥadīth, prophetic biography (*sīra,* see SĪRA AND THE QUR'ĀN), ascetic literature (*zuhd,* see ASCETICISM), the "tales of the prophets" *(qiṣaṣ al-anbiyā'),* material of Jewish and Christian origin *(isrā'īliyyāt),* and Ṣūfī writings (see ṢŪFISM AND THE QUR'ĀN). These genres contributed to the evolution of a new branch in the Muslim religious literature dealing with the day of resurrection *(yawm al-qiyāma),* including its preliminary signs (*ashrāṭ al-sā'a,* cf. Q 47:18), detailed descriptions of its events, the last judgment, the intercession (q.v.) of the prophets (see PROPHETS AND PROPHETHOOD) and then the reward or punishment (see REWARD AND PUNISHMENT) of each human being according to his or her behavior on earth. This branch is generally known as *aḥwāl yawm al-qiyāma* ("dreads of the day of resurrection"). One of the oldest treatises dedicated to this topic is the *Kitāb al-Aḥwāl* of Ibn Abī al-Dunyā (d. 281/894; see also TRADITIONAL DISCIPLINES OF QUR'ĀNIC STUDY).

Time of the last judgment

The Qur'ān has a variety of allusions to the time of the day of judgment: (a) nobody, including the Prophet, can anticipate when it is expected to happen: only God knows its exact date (Q 7:187; 31:34; 33:63; 41:47; 43:85; 79:42-4); (b) "the hour" *(al-sā'a)* may be very close (Q 21:1; 33:63; 42:17; 54:1; 70:6-7; it is "as a twinkling of the eye or even nearer," *ka-lamḥi l-baṣari aw huwa aqrabu,* Q 16:77; cf. 54:50); (c) it will occur suddenly (*baghtatan,* Q 6:31; 7:187; 12:107; 22:55; 43:66; 47:18). Ibn Kathīr (d. 774/1373) gives a very detailed list of qur'ānic verses and traditions on this matter (*Ashrāṭ al-sā'a,* 26-35; Wensinck, *Handbook,* s.v. *s-w-'*).

Signs of the hour

A number of preliminary "signs of the hour" *(ashrāṭ al-sā'a)* are enumerated in the Qur'ān. On many occasions, and more especially in the Meccan sūras, the Qur'ān denotes signs that will presage and foretell the last judgment (see APOCALYPSE). Most of these signs are natural catastrophes and some of them appear collectively in Q 81:1-14: the sun (q.v.) will be darkened, the stars (see PLANETS AND STARS) will be thrown down, the mountains will be set moving, the pregnant camels (see CAMEL) will be neglected, the savage beasts will be mustered (see ANIMAL LIFE), the seas will be set boiling (or will overflow), the souls will be coupled (with their bodies), the buried female infant will be asked for what sin she was slain (see INFANTICIDE), the scrolls (q.v.; of deeds, good and bad) will be unrolled (see RECORD OF HUMAN ACTION), heaven will be stripped away, hell will be set blazing and paradise (see GARDEN) will be brought near. The mountains (will fly) like "tufts of carded wool" (Q 101:5) and graves will be overturned (Q 100:9; see DEATH AND THE DEAD; COSMOLOGY).

Later Islamic literary genres add other signs like the rising of the sun from the west; the appearance of the Antichrist (q.v.; *al-masīḥ al-dajjāl,* or simply *al-dajjāl*); the descent from heaven of the Messiah 'Īsā b. Maryam (see JESUS; some reports attest that *al-mahdī al-muntaẓar* is 'Īsā b. Maryam; Dānī, *Sunan,* v, 1075-80) who will fight the Antichrist, break the crosses (of the Christians; see CHRISTIANS AND CHRISTIANITY) and exterminate the pigs (*yaksiru* or *yaduqqu l-ṣalīb wa-yaqtulu l-khinzīr;* Dānī, *Sunan,* 239-40, 242; Sibṭ Ibn al-Jawzī, *Mir'āt,* i, 582-5; Ṣāliḥ, *Qiyāma,* i, 71-5; see JEWS AND JUDAISM; POLEMIC AND POLEMICAL LANGUAGE); the appearance of the *dābba* (the reptile or the beast of burden) mentioned in Q 27:82 ('Abd al-Razzāq, *Tafsīr,* ii, 84; Muslim, *Ṣaḥīḥ, K. al-Fitan,* n. 2901; Nu'aym b. Ḥammād, *Kitāb al-Fitan,* 401-5). Three countries (in the east, the west and Arabia; see GEOGRAPHY) will sink, and a fire from 'Adan will drive humankind to the gathering place *(al-maḥshar)*. Gog and Magog (q.v.; Yaʾjūj and Maʾjūj) will attack the entire world, but will be eliminated near Jerusalem (q.v.; Nasāʾī, *Sunan,* vi, 424 ad Q 27:82 gives a list of ten signs including the qurʾānic ones; Gardet, *Les grands problèmes,* 262, n. 6). The literature of apocalyptic portents (*fitan* and *malāḥim,* Fahd, Djafr; id., Malḥama; Bashear, Apocalyptic materials, and the literature cited there; id., Muslim apocalypses) abounds in prophecies about wars predicting the last judgment. As an aside, modern Aḥmadī (see AḤMADIYYA) *tafsīr* regards *al-dajjāl* as representing the missionary activities of the western Christian peoples, and Yaʾjūj and Maʾjūj as representing their materialistic and political authorities (*Tafsīr Sūrat al-Kahf,* 105).

The resurrection

In Q 39:67-75, there is a detailed description of the events of the resurrection (*al-qiyāma, al-baʿth, al-maʿād* or *al-nushūr;* cf. Izutsu, *God,* 90-4). The entire earth will be grasped by God's hand (q.v.) and the heavens will be rolled up in his right hand. The trumpet *(al-ṣūr)* shall be blown and all creatures, including angels (see ANGEL), will die, except those whom God wills. Then, it shall be blown again and they will be standing and looking on: "And the earth (q.v.) shall shine with the light of its lord (q.v.), and the book (q.v.) shall be set in place, and the prophets and witnesses (*al-shuhadāʾ,* see MARTYR; WITNESSING AND TESTIFYING) shall be brought, and justly the issue be decided between them, and they not wronged. Every soul shall be paid in full for what it has wrought; and God knows very well what they do. Then the unbelievers shall be driven in companies into hell until, when they have come forth, then its gates will be opened… It shall be said, 'Enter the gates of hell, do dwell therein forever!'… Then those that feared their lord shall be driven in companies into paradise, until, when they have come forth, and its gates are opened, and its keepers will say to them: '… enter in, to dwell forever'… And you shall see the angels encircling about the throne (see THRONE OF GOD) proclaiming the praise of their lord (see LAUDATION; GLORIFICATION OF GOD); and justly the issue shall be decided between them…."

Such a description raises some questions in Islamic theology (the question of anthropomorphism [q.v.; *tajsīm*]: God's hand, his right hand; the questions of God's justice that arise if the identity of believers and unbelievers is known; see FREEDOM AND PREDESTINATION; JUSTICE AND INJUSTICE; THEOLOGY AND THE QURʾĀN) and provokes discussions in the eschatological literature, particularly about the identity of the creatures who will be exempted from dying after the first blow of the trumpet: the angel/angels Gabriel (q.v.; Jibrīl), Michael (q.v.; Mīkāʾīl), Isrāfīl, "the angel of death" *(malak al-mawt),* or God's throne-bearers and the fair females (*al-ḥūr al-ʿīn,* cf. Q 44:54; 52:20; 55:72; 56:22; Nasafī, *Tafsīr,* iv, 66; see HOURIS), or the martyrs (*al-shuhadāʾ,* cf. Q 3:169: *qutilū fī sabīli llāhi;* see PATH OR WAY), or the prophets (possibly Moses [q.v.; Mūsā]?) or the immortal boys (*wildānun mukhalladūna,* Q 56:17; 76:19); and the interval of time between the two trumpet-calls (forty days, weeks, months or years; cf. Qurṭubī, *Tadhkira,* i, 194-201). Since the ordering of events at this stage of the judgment day is not consistent and is sometimes even contradictory, many authors tried to arrange them (Ibn Kathīr, *Nihāya,* i, 270-373; ʿAwājī, *al-Ḥayāt al-ākhira*). Following these sources, an attempt of arrangement of these supposed events is presented below.

(a) "The blowing of the trumpet" *(al-nafkh fī l-ṣūr)*. This is attested ten times in the Qurʾān (also *nuqira fī l-nāqūr; nāqūr* is attested once, at Q 74:8; *al-nāqūr = al-ṣūr;* Fīrūzābādī, *Baṣāʾir,* v, 113). In the Qurʾān, the identity of the blower is not revealed. In all the verses dealing with *al-nafkh fī l-ṣūr,* the verb appears in the passive tense. Traditions relate that the archangel Isrāfīl is appointed to this task (Ibn al-Jawzī, *Tabṣira,* ii, 309-11). He will stand at the eastern or western gate of Jerusalem (Īliyāʾ; Suyūṭī, *Durr,* v, 339) or at "the rock of Jerusalem" (*ṣakhrat bayt al-maqdis,* Ṭabarī, *Tafsīr,* xvi, 183) and blow. After the first blowing, generally called *nafkhat al-ṣaʿq,* "whosoever is in the heavens and whosoever is in the earth shall swoon *(ṣaʿiqa),* save those whom God wills" (Q 39:68). The exegetes explain the verb *ṣaʿiqa* in this context as "to die" (*māta, Lisān al-ʿArab,* s.v. *ṣ-ʿ-q;* Nasafī, *Tafsīr,* iv, 66; this meaning is peculiar to the usage of the tribes of ʿUmān, cf. Ibn ʿAbbās [attr.], *al-Lughāt fī l-Qurʾān,* 17). There were also discussions concerning the number of times the trumpet was blown. Most exegetes mention two, the blowing of the "swooning" *(nafkhat al-ṣaʿq)* and that of the resurrection *(nafkhat al-baʿth).* Some, drawing upon Q 27:87-8, add a third blowing, "the terrifying" (*nafkhat al-fazaʿ,* ʿAwājī, *al-Ḥayāt al-ākhira,* i, 189-97). There are also traditions attributed to Muḥammad that he will be the first to be resurrected, but will be surprised to see Moses holding God's throne (Bukhārī, *Ṣaḥīḥ,* vi, 451; Muslim, *Ṣaḥīḥ,* iv, 1844).

(b) The returning to life. It should be noted here that some believe that *al-baʿth,* the "returning to life," understood as the "resurrection of the souls and bodies" (Ibn Kathīr, *Tafsīr,* iii, 206), means the "corporal rising" from the graves (*al-maʿād al-jismānī,* Safārīnī, *Mukhtaṣar,* 387).

(c) "The gathering" *(al-ḥashr).* Creatures, including humankind, jinn and animals, will be gathered (Q 6:38; 42:29; 81:5). Relying on Q 7:29 and 21:104, the exegetes explain that humankind will be gathered "barefoot, naked and uncircumcised" (*ḥufātan ʿurātan ghurlan,* see CLOTHING; CIRCUMCISION). The unbelievers will be gathered to hell prone on their faces (*yuḥsharūna ʿalā wujūhihim,* Q 25:34; cf. 17:97). Al-Bukhārī (d. 256/870; *Ṣaḥīḥ,* vi, 137) reports that Muḥammad replied to somebody who did not understand this situation, saying: "Will not the one who made the person walk on his feet in this world (see CREATION), be able to make him walk on his face on the day of resurrection?"

(d) "The standing" before God *(al-qiyām, al-wuqūf).* All creatures, including angels and jinn, have to stand (cf. Q 78:38). The unbelievers will stand in the blazing sun, finding no shade anywhere (Q 56:42-3; 77:29-31; see HOT AND COLD).

(e) "The survey" (*al-ʿarḍ,* Q 11:18; cf. 18:48; 69:18). This term is likened in many sources to "a king surveying his army or his subjects." Al-Rāzī (d. 606/1210) rejects this interpretation and prefers to interpret *al-ʿarḍ* as "the settling of accounts with, and the interrogation" (*al-muḥāsaba wa-l-musāʾala,* Rāzī, *Tafsīr,* xxx, 110).

(f) The personal books *(kutub)* or sheets *(ṣuḥuf, ṣaḥāʾif al-aʿmāl)* containing all the acts of each person will be laid open (Q 17:13; 52:2-3; 81:10). The one "who is given his book in his right hand" will enter paradise, but "whosoever is given his book in his left hand" will roast in hell (Q 69:19-37). Some are given their books behind their backs; they will invoke their own destruction (Q 84:10-1). In some cases, God will change the evil into good deeds (Q 25:70).

(g) The balances of justice *(al-mawāzīna al-qisṭa)* will be set up (Q 21:47). "Whosoever's scales [of good deeds] are heavy, they are the prosperous [by entering paradise] and whosoever's scales are light, they have lost their souls [by entering hell]" (Q 7:8-9; 23:102-3; cf. 101:6-9).

(h) The creatures will bear witness against

themselves (Q 6:130). Their hands, legs, ears, eyes, tongues and skins will testify against them (Q 24:24; 36:65; 41:22; 75:14). The prophets will submit testimony against their peoples (Q 5:109). Jesus will be a witness against the misguided among the People of the Book (q.v., *ahl al-kitāb*) — the Jews who believed that they had already crucified him and the Christians who believed that he is the son of God (Q 4:159).

(i) "The investigation" *(al-musāʾala)*. God will interrogate the messengers (see MESSENGER) and the peoples to whom they were sent (Q 7:6). The messengers will be interrogated about the response they received from people to their message (Q 5:109). The investigation will also include angels (Q 34:40-1).

(j) The intercession *(shafāʿa)* in favor of somebody will not be accepted that day except from the one to whom God has given permission (see Q 2:254; 7:53; 10:3; 20:109; 21:28; 74:48). The exegetes make a connection between *al-kawthar* (Q 108:1), a river in paradise and *al-ḥawḍ*, Muḥammad's private basin outside or inside paradise, from which believers will be invited to drink. Traditions stress the superiority of Muḥammad to all other prophets since he alone has been given this privilege (ʿAwājī, *al-Ḥayāt al-ākhira*, i, 277-530). P. Casanova (*Mohammed*, 19-20) hypothesized that the first Muslim generation believed that Muḥammad, the last prophet, had to preside over the last judgment and to serve as their advocate in the presence of God. Shīʿī literature states that later the *shafāʿa* was bestowed on the Prophet's descendants, the imāms (Bar-Asher, *Scripture and exegesis*, 180-9; see IMĀM; SHĪʿISM AND THE QURʾĀN).

(k) A bridge *(ṣirāṭ)* will be set up above and across hell (Q 37:22-3) from one end to the other. Ḥadīth literature adds very rich descriptions of this bridge and the manner in which different kinds of people will cross it. The sinners will slope downward into hell and the believers will enter paradise.

Some details cited above led the exegetes and other Muslim scholars to accept the doctrine of predestination since the identity of sinners and believers is known before doomsday (Q 74:31). But it is at the day of judgment *(yawm al-dīn)* that the fate (q.v.) of each creature is made explicit.

Explanation of some eschatological terms

Some terms dealing with the last judgment raised problems, which the exegetes and lexicographers tried to solve. One of the early Meccan sūras, Q 75, is called *al-Qiyāma* ("The Resurrection") because the word appears in its first verse. This term is generally explained by the lexicographers as *yawm al-baʿth, yaqūmu fīhi l-khalqu bayna yaday al-ḥayy al-qayyūm*, "the day of returning to life, when all the creatures will rise before the ever-living, the one who sustains (see GOD AND HIS ATTRIBUTES)." It seems that this word, *qiyāma*, is not Arabic. Ibn Manẓūr (d. 711/1311) cites in the *Lisān al-ʿArab* an anonymous tradition that suggests that *qiyāma* is a borrowing from the Syriac/Aramaic *qiyamathā*. Al-Suyūṭī (d. 911/1505) repeats this assertion when he speaks about *al-qayyūm* (*Itqān*, 172). The "first judgment" or *al-qiyāma al-ṣughrā* is supposed to be *ʿadhāb al-qabr*, "the torment of the grave," also termed the punishment of *al-barzakh* (purgatory; see BARZAKH), which includes the interrogation of the two angels, Munkar and Nakīr. Many utterances attributed to Muḥammad and cited in the canonical corpus ascribe to the Jews the first allusions to *ʿadhāb al-qabr* (Nawawī, *Sharḥ*, v, 85-6).

In Arabic, the root *d-y-n (dīn)* poses some difficulties since it has three different etymologies and, in consequence, different connotations: (1) religion; (2) custom, usage *(al-ʿāda wa-l-shaʾn)*; (3) punishment, reward *(al-jazāʾ wa-l-mukāfaʾa*; cf. *Lisān al-ʿArab)* or judgment (*Ibn ʿAbbās… al-dīn: yawm ḥisāb al-khalāʾiq wa-huwa yawm al-qiyāma;* cf. Rāzī, *Tafsīr,* i, 29). This last connotation forms the basis of interpretations like the one — attributed to Qatāda (d. ca. 117/735) — that explains *yawm al-dīn* in Q 1:4 as "the day on which God will judge humankind according to their acts" (*yawm yadīnu llāhu l-ʿibāda bi-aʿmālihim,* ʿAbd al-Razzāq, *Tafsīr,* i, 37). The dominant meaning of *dīn* in Arabic is, however, "religion, religious law, custom" (Gardet, Dīn; id., *L'Islam,* 29-32). It seems that the sense "judgment" and "custom" is borrowed from the Hebraeo-Aramaic usage, which has its roots in Akkadian (*dīnum,* "judgment," *dayyānum,* "judge"). On the basis of this root, the meaning of "sentence" is presumed. The title *dayyānum* was given in Akkadian to a judge, king or god. The *dināti,* "laws," served as direction or guidance for the judges to pass sentence on each case (*Encyclopaedia biblica,* s.v. mishpaṭ). In view of this etymology, it seems that M. Gaudefroy-Demombynes (*Mahomet,* 449-58, especially 454-5) was correct when he translated *yawm al-dīn* as "the day when God gives a direction to each human being." See also LAW AND THE QURʾĀN.

The place of the last judgment

The Qurʾān does not identify explicitly the place of the last judgment. The Companions of the Prophet (q.v.; *ṣaḥāba*), his Followers *(tābiʿūn)* and later exegetes tried to find hints which could help to identify the precise location. For example, Q 57:13 was explained as referring to Jerusalem (Wāsiṭī, *Faḍāʾil,* 14-6, no. 14-7) and Q 50:41 to the rock of Jerusalem (ibid., 88-9, no. 143-5). The need for a satisfactory answer caused the Muslims to search the traditions of Judaism and Christianity, since both allotted Jerusalem a dominant role in eschatology (q.v.) and considered it as the scene of the envisioned end of days (Prawer, Christian attitudes, 314-25). In this context, it is worth remembering that, at the beginning of the second/eighth century, Jerusalem was generally recognized in Muslim circles as the third holy place in Islam (Kister, You shall only set; Neuwirth, Sacred mosque). Later, there emerged traditions of Jewish or Christian origin where the connection was made between verses of the Qurʾān pertaining to the end of days and Jerusalem: "Nawf al-Bikālī [the nephew of Kaʿb al-Aḥbār] reported to the caliph ʿAbd al-Malik (r. 65-85/685-705) that in a verse of the Bible, God said to Jerusalem *(bayt al-maqdis):* 'There are within you six things: my residence, my judgment place, my gathering place, my paradise, my hell and my balance *(inna fī kitābi llāhi l-munazzal anna llāha yaqūlu: fīka sittu khiṣālin, fīka maqāmī wa-ḥisābī wa-maḥsharī wa-jannatī wa-nārī wa-mīzānī)*'" (Wāsiṭī, *Faḍāʾil,* 23).

The Umayyad regime openly encouraged this view because it gave them legitimization to move the Muslim center of worship from Medina (q.v.), the city of the Prophet, to Syria (q.v.), which includes Jerusalem: Muʿāwiya b. Abī Sufyān (d. 60/680), the first Umayyad caliph, propagated the use of the term "land of ingathering and resurrection on judgment day" *(arḍ al-maḥshar wa-l-manshar)* with regard to Jerusalem (Wāsiṭī, *Faḍāʾil,* introduction, 20). At that time, the Muslims did not see any harm in absorbing Jewish and Christian traditions (Kister, Ḥaddithū ʿan banī isrāʾīl), particularly if the traditions reinforced the words of the Qurʾān or explained unclear matters (see AMBIGUOUS; DIFFICULT PASSAGES). One of the oldest sources to preserve such material is the *Tafsīr* of Muqātil b. Sulaymān (d. 150/768; here it should be noted that ʿAbdallāh M. Shaḥāta, the editor of the *Tafsīr,* chose to transfer from the text to the footnotes these and other traditions extolling Jerusalem, since "most of them are *isrāʾīliyyāt*" [Muqātil, *Tafsīr,* ii, 513-5], in spite of the fact that they were included in the body of the text of three out of the four manuscripts which he had consulted for his edition). Here are some examples of such traditions: "God will set his seat on the day of the resurrection upon the land of Jerusalem"; "Jesus is destined to descend from heaven in the land of Jerusalem"; "God will destroy Gog and Magog in Jerusalem"; "The gathering of the dead and their resurrection will be in the land of Jerusalem"; "The *sirāṭ* (the narrow bridge over Gehenna) goes forth from the land of Jerusalem to the garden of Eden and hell" (see the English translation of these traditions in the appendix of Hasson, The Muslim view of Jerusalem). But this tendency of the early Islamic tradition to absorb Jewish and Christian material brought forth a reaction. The most vigorous representative of this reaction is Ibn Taymiyya (d. 728/1328), who attacked all the traditions connecting the resurrection day with Jerusalem (see his *Qāʿida*).

The last judgment in some previous religions

The Qurʾān supposes that, in genuine Judaism and Christianity, the belief in *al-ākhira,* the resurrection and punishment or reward, formed a basic part of the message of Moses (Mūsā) and Jesus (ʿĪsā, Q 12:101; 19:33; 20:14-6; 40:42-3). The Muslims think that the Jews, after "having perverted words from their meanings" (Q 2:75; 4:46; 5:13, 41; see FORGERY), removed the concept of the resurrection from the Bible (ʿAwājī, *al-Ḥayāt al-ākhira,* i, 116-23). Muslim tradition connects the punishment after death in the grave *(ʿadhāb al-qabr)* to a Jewish source (Nawawī, *Sharḥ,* v, 85-6). It is therefore worth reviewing similar ideas in previous religions and in Islam.

Most of the signs of the hour *(ashrāṭ al-sāʿa)* appear in the Hebrew Bible and in rabbinic literature; these are known as *ḥevlei mashiyyaḥ,* "the tribulations preceding the coming of the Messiah" (Grossman, Jerusalem, 295-303). Some examples of the similarities between the qurʾānic and biblical descriptions of these events are: the vision of the dry bones in Ezekiel 37; Yaʾjūj and Maʾjūj (Q 21:96) — the biblical Gog and Magog — "will swiftly swarm from every mound"; "signs of the hour" abound in *Isa* 24; and *Isa* 27:1, but especially 27:13, "... the great trumpet shall be blown, and they shall come which were ready to perish in the land of Assyria, and the outcasts in the land of Egypt, and shall worship the lord in the holy mount of Jerusalem," bring to mind *al-ṣūr* or *al-nāqūr,* particularly in view of the Muslim explanation that *al-ṣūr* is a horn (Tirmidhī, *Ṣaḥīḥ,* iv, 620; Abū Dāwūd, ii, 537), the traditional Jewish *shofar.* The traditions explaining that the gathering and the last judgment must be in Jerusalem have their origin, perhaps, in this verse and in the *midrashim,* the homiletic interpretations of the scriptures. The blowing of the trumpet, the day of the lord, "a day of darkness and of gloominess," the earth which shall quake, the heavens which shall tremble, and the sun and the moon which shall be dark are mentioned in Joel 2. The gathering of all the heathen will be in the valley of Jehoshaphat: "for there will I sit to judge all the heathen round about" (*Joel* 4:12; see also *Amos* 5:18-20; *Zeph* 1; *Isa* 66:16, 24). To explain the prevalence of such imagery, H. Gressmann (*Ursprung*) claimed one century ago that there circulated, among many ancient peoples in the epoch of the prophets of Israel, prophecies about disasters (earthquakes, fires and volcanoes...) which would destroy the world and about a paradise with rivers of milk, honey and fresh water.

In the Book of Daniel 12:2, which retained a Persian influence and was very popular in the first century of Islam since many Muslims wanted to know the exact date of the last judgment, there appears the idea of the resurrection and of everlasting life for some and everlasting shame and contempt for others. S. Shaked and W. Sundermann (Eschatology) very clearly show Zoroastrian and Manichean influences on eschatological material within Second Temple Judaism, Christianity and, later, on Islam. M. Gaudefroy-Demombynes (*Mahomet*, 405) claimed that, in the period of the emigration (q.v.; *hijra*) to Medina, the qurʾānic verses stopped reporting about the punishment of sinners on earth and began to mention the last judgment. While a similar sequence has been suggested for the Hebrew Bible, there is no consensus on this matter among scholars of the Qurʾān.

In the New Testament, the Revelation of John contains many elements of the resurrection, but they do not resemble the qurʾānic scheme. Gibb (*Mohammedanism*, 26-7) is certain that the doctrine of the last judgment in the Qurʾān was derived from Christian sources, especially from the writings of the Syriac Christian Fathers and monks (see SYRIAC AND THE QURʾĀN; MONASTICISM AND MONKS). Tor Andrae, who devoted considerable attention to possible Christian antecedents (see esp. *Der Ursprung des Islams und das Cristentum*), finds expression of the idea that nobody can determine the date of the last hour in Mark 13:32. Only God knows about that day or hour. Finally, many last judgment scenes appear, with some modifications, in early Christian apocalypses (Maier, Staging the gaze). Although the "beast" in *Hermas vision* 4, which represents a coming persecution, or the "leviathan" in Isaiah 27:1, which represents evil powers, are reminiscent of the *dābba* in Q 27:82 which became one of the "signs of the hour" *(ashrāṭ al-sāʿa)*, Annemarie Schimmel correctly asserts that "the Koranic descriptions of Judgment and Hell do not reach the fantastic descriptions of, for example, Christian apocalyptic writing."

Isaac Hasson

Bibliography

Primary: ʿAbd al-Razzāq, *Tafsīr*, ed. M.M. Muḥammad, ii, 84; Abū Dāwūd; Barzanjī, Muḥammad b. Rasūl al-Ḥusaynī, *al-Ishāʿa li-ashrāṭ al-sāʿa*, Jeddah 1997 (rich in *fitan* traditions); al-Bastawī, ʿAbd al-ʿAlīm ʿA.ʿA, *Aḥādīth al-mahdī al-ḍaʿīfa wa-l-mawḍūʿa*, Beirut 1999; id., *al-Mahdī al-muntaẓar fī ḍawʾ al-aḥādīth wa-l-āthār al-ṣaḥīḥa*, Beirut 1999; al-Bayhaqī, Abū Bakr Aḥmad b. al-Ḥusayn, *al-Jāmiʿ li-shuʿab al-īmān*, ed. ʿA.ʿA. Ḥāmid, 10 vols. (incomplete), Bombay 1986-90 (esp. ii, 5-335 and iii, 7-304); Bukhārī, *Ṣaḥīḥ*, 9 vols., Cairo 1958; Dānī, *al-Sunan al-wārida fī l-fitan wa-ghawāʾilihā wa-l-sāʿati wa-ashrāṭihā*, ed. Riḍāʾ Allāh al-Mubārakfūrī, 6 vols. in 3, Riyadh 1995 (esp. vols. iv-vi); Fīrūzābādī, *Baṣāʾir*, ed. ʿA. al-ʿAlīm al-Ṭaḥāwī, Beirut n.d.; al-Ghazālī, Abū Ḥāmid Muḥammad, *Iḥyāʾ ʿulūm al-dīn*, ed. Dār al-Khayr, 6 vols. in 5, n.p. n.d., vi, 153-202 *(Fī ahwāl al-mayyi min waqt nafkhat al-ṣūr);* Ibn ʿAbbās (attr.), *al-Lughāt fī l-Qurʾān*, ed. Ṣ. al-Dīn al-Munajjid, Beirut 1978; Ibn al-Jawzī, *al-Tabṣira*, Beirut 1986; Ibn Kathīr, *Ashrāṭ al-sāʿa wa-umūr al-ākhira*, Beirut 1998 (abr. ed. of Ibn Kathīr, *Nihāya* by M. b. Aḥmad Kanʿān); id., *al-Nihāya fī l-fitan wa-l-malāḥim*, ed. M.A. ʿAbd al-ʿAzīz, Cairo 1986; id., *Tafsīr*; Ibn Khuzayma, Abū Bakr Muḥammad b. Isḥāq, *al-Tawḥīd wa-ithbāt ṣifāt al-rabb*, ed. M.Kh. Harrās, Beirut 1983, 70-4; 95-100; 149-61; 167-97; 231-68, and 374-6; Ibn Taymiyya, *Qāʿida fī ziyārat bayt al-maqdis*, ed. Ch. Mathews, in JAOS 66 (1939), 7-17; *Lisān al-ʿArab;* Muqātil, *Tafsīr;* Muslim, *Ṣaḥīḥ;* Nasafī, *Tafsīr*; Nasāʾī, *Sunan;* Nawawī, *Sharḥ;* Nuʿaym b. Ḥammād al-Khuzāʿī, *Kitāb al-Fitan*, ed. S. Zakkār, Beirut 1993; Qurṭubī, *al-Tadhkira fī ahwāl al-mawtā wa-umūr al-ākhira*, ed. A. Ḥijāzī al-Saqqā, Cairo 1980; Rāzī, *Tafsīr*, ed. Asʿad M. al-Ṭayyib, Mecca 1997; al-Saffārīnī, Shams al-Dīn Abū ʿAlī Muḥammad b. Aḥmad, *Mukhtaṣar lawāmiʿ al-anwār al-bahiyya*, Damascus 1931, 387; Ṣibṭ Ibn al-Jawzī, *Mirʾāt;* Suyūṭī, *Durr;* id., *Itqān;* Ṭabarī, *Tafsīr; Tafsīr sūrat al-kahf*, ed. Faḍl Ilāhī Bashīr, Haifa 1979; Tirmidhī, *Ṣaḥīḥ;* al-Tirmidhī, Muḥammad b. ʿAlī al-Ḥakīm, *al-Amthāl min al-kitāb wa-l-sunna*, ed. M. ʿAbd al-Qādir ʿAṭā, Beirut 1989, 42, 180-4; al-Wāsiṭī, Abū Bakr Muḥammad b. Aḥmad, *Faḍāʾil al-bayt al-muqaddas*, ed. I. Hasson, Jerusalem 1979, traditions no. 14-7, 26, 28, 35, 39, 55, 65, 71, 81, 85-6, 89, 100, 108, 114-5, 118, 126, 142-5, 150-3 and 165.

Secondary: T. Andrae, *Der Ursprung des Islams und das Cristentum,* Uppsala 1926; Fr. trans. J. Roche, *Les origines de l'Islam et le Christianisme,* Paris 1955; Gh. b. ʿA. ʿAwāji, *al-Ḥayāt al-ākhira mā bayna al-baʿth ilā dukhūl al-janna aw al-nār,* Cairo 1997; M.M. Bar-Asher, *Scripture and exegesis in early Imāmī Shiism,* Leiden/Jerusalem 1999, 180-9; S. Bashear, Apocalyptic and other materials on early Muslim-Byzantine wars. A review of Arabic sources, in *JRAS* 3/1 (1991), 173-207; id., Muslim apocalypses and the Hour. A case-study in traditional reinterpretation, in *IOS* 13 (1993), 75-99; B. Carra de Vaux, Barzakh, in *EI*^{2}, i, 1071-2; P. Casanova, *Mohammed et la fin du monde. Étude critique sur l'Islam primitif,* Paris 1911-24; M. Cook, *Muhammad,* Oxford 1983; R. Eklund, *Life between death and resurrection according to Islam,* Uppsala 1941; Ṣ. El-Ṣāleḥ, *La vie future selon le Coran,* Paris 1971; *Encyclopaedia biblica,* 8 vols., Jerusalem 1950-82; T. Fahd, Djafr, in *EI*^{2}, ii, 375-7; id., Malḥama, in *EI*^{2}, vi, 247; D. Galloway, The resurrection and judgment in the Qurʾān, in *MW* 12 (1922), 348-72; L. Gardet, Dīn, in *EI*^{2}, ii, 293-6; id., *Les grands problèmes de la théologie musulmane. Dieu et la destinée de l'homme,* Paris 1967; id., *L'Islam, religion et communauté,* Paris 1970, 95-107; id., Ḳiyāma, in *EI*^{2}, v, 235-8; M. Gaudefroy-Demombynes, *Mahomet,* Paris 1969, 401-47; A. Geiger, *Judaism and Islam,* trans. F.M. Young, New York 1970, 45-64; H.A.R. Gibb, *Mohammedanism,* Oxford 1969; P. Gignoux, Les doctrines eschatologiques de Narsai, in *L'orient syrien* 11 (1966), 321-52, 461-88; 12 (1967), 23-54; H. Gressmann, *Ursprung der israelitisch-jüdischen Eschatologie,* Göttingen 1905; A. Grossman, Jerusalem in Jewish apocalyptic literature, in J. Prawer and H. Ben Shammai (eds.), *The history of Jerusalem. The early Muslim period.* 638-1099, New York 1996, 295-310; G.E. von Grunebaum, *Classical Islam. A history. 600-1258,* London 1970, 28-30, 33; I. Hasson, The Muslim view of Jerusalem. The Qurʾān and ḥadīth, in J. Prawer and H. Ben Shammai (eds.), *The history of Jerusalem. The early Muslim period. 638-1099,* New York 1996, 349-85; Izutsu, *God,* 90-4; 220-2; M.M. Khān and M.T. al-Hilālī, *Interpretation of the meanings of the noble Qurʾān,* Medina 1994^4; M.J. Kister, *Ḥaddithū ʿan banī isrāʾīla wa-lā ḥaraja.* A study of an early tradition, in *IOS* 2 (1972), 215-39; id., You shall only set out for three mosques. A study of an early tradition, in *Muséon* 82 (1969), 173-96; H.O. Maier, Staging the gaze. Early Christian apocalypses and narrative self-representation, in *Harvard theological review* 90 (1997), 131-54; A. Neuwirth, From the sacred mosque to the remote temple. Sūrat al-Isrāʾ between text and commentary, in J.D. McAuliffe, B. Walfish and J. Goering (eds.), *With reverence for the word. Medieval scriptural exegesis in Judaism, Christianity and Islam,* Oxford 2003, 376-407; T. O'Shaughnessy, *Muḥammad's thoughts on death. A thematic study of the qurʾanic data,* Leiden 1969 (important concerning Syriac Christian sources); J. Prawer, Christian attitudes towards Jerusalem in the early Middle Ages, in J. Prawer and H. Ben Shammai (eds.), *The history of Jerusalem. The early Muslim period. 638-1099,* New York 1996, 311-48; Y. Rāgib, Faux morts et enterrés vifs dans l'espace musulman, in *SI* 57 (1983), 5-30 (especially 28-30); M.A. Ṣāliḥ, *al-Qiyāma, mashāhiduhā wa-ʿiẓātuhā fī l-sunna l-nabawiyya,* Beirut 1994; A. Schimmel, *Islam. An introduction,* New York 1992, 12-4, 73-89; M.S. Seale, An Arab's concern with life after death, in id., *Qurʾān and Bible. Studies in interpretation and dialogue,* London 1978, 90-8; S. Shaked and W. Sundermann, Eschatology, in *Encyclopaedia Iranica,* viii, 1998, 565-75; Watt-Bell, *Introduction;* Wensinck, *Handbook;* id./A.S. Tritton, ʿAdhāb al-ḳabr, in *EI*^{2}, i, 186-7.

Laudation

The act or instance of praising or extolling, the object of such praise often being God. More precisely, laudation *(ḥamd)* in the qurʾānic context refers to the specific formulaic phrase "praise belongs to God" *(al-ḥamdu li-llāh),* which occurs twenty-four times in the Qurʾān. Perhaps the most significant instance of this formulaic phrase appears in the opening chapter of the Qurʾān (see FĀTIḤA), directly following the *basmala* (q.v.). Here (i.e. Q 1:2), in the very first line of the Qurʾān, the phrase is assertive (*inshāʾī,* see FORM AND STRUCTURE OF THE QURʾĀN; LANGUAGE AND STYLE OF THE QURʾĀN) in its use, as the one uttering it creates a verbal expression of the actual praise (q.v.) he directs toward God. Given its prominent position in the text, this instance of lauding God becomes an essential and vital act for those who believe, a trial (q.v.) and test for those who submit (see FAITH; BELIEF AND UNBELIEF). In addition to this formulaic phrase, there are several rhetorical variations of *ḥamd* that also point to the act of commending one's lord (q.v.), which occur in twenty-one other qurʾānic verses.

According to al-Ṭabarī (d. 310/923; *Tafsīr*, i, 136), the phrase "praise belongs to God" means that gratitude belongs entirely to God alone for all the generous gifts he has bestowed upon his servants (see GRATITUDE AND INGRATITUDE; GIFT-GIVING; SERVANT). Praise may not be directed to anything that might be worshipped besides him nor to anything he has created (see CREATION; WORSHIP). Not only the praising of the speaker, but all possible praising belongs to God alone. Only God has the power to give his creation the sustenance, nourishment and the means through which one can achieve eternal salvation (q.v.; see also ETERNITY; BLESSING; GRACE). No one has the right to claim or demand what God freely gives; for this reason alone all praise belongs to him. In the revelatory proclamation (see REVELATION AND INSPIRATION), all praiseworthiness proceeds from him and to him it must return.

The exegetical literature (see EXEGESIS OF THE QURʾĀN: CLASSICAL AND MEDIEVAL) debates the rather intricate relationship between *ḥamd*, "praise," *shukr*, "gratitude," and other forms of exaltation (for *subḥāna llāhi*, see GLORIFICATION OF GOD). Some traditions suggest that by giving praise to God one is thanking him for all he has given; others say praise means expressing one's subservience *(al-istikhdhāʾ)* or one's commendation *(thanāʾ)* to him. Others assert a more qualitative difference between praising and thanking: when one praises God one praises him for his most beautiful names and attributes (see GOD AND HIS ATTRIBUTES), but when one thanks him, one is thanking him for his munificence and favors. However that debate is decided, God orders his servants to extol him in terms befitting him. Praise belongs to him for all things, both beneficial and painful (see also GOOD AND EVIL).

Kathryn Kueny

Bibliography
Primary: Ṭabarī, *Tafsīr*, ed. Shākir.
Secondary: A. Giese and A.K. Reinhart, Shukr, in *EI²*, ix, 496-8; H.E. Kassis, *A concordance of the Qurʾān*, London 1983; Lane; D.B. MacDonald, Ḥamdala, in *EI²*, iii, 122-3; Pickthall.

Laughter

Sound and/or facial expressions generally indicative of merriment. Laughter does not figure prominently in the Qurʾān: verb forms and participles derived from *ḍ-ḥ-k* occur just ten times compared to a stunning 179 appearances of its synonymous Hebrew cognates *s-ʾ-ḥ-q/ṣ-ḥ-q* in the Hebrew Bible. *B-s-m* for smiling appears just once and never the onomatopoetic *q-h-q-h* for strong laughter (an Arabic root form which, incidentally, more or less reverses and doubles the western Semitic onomatopoetic **-ḥ-q* from which the various triliterals for laughter seem to be derived). Laughter in the Qurʾān usually expresses disbelief in God and his messages/messengers (Q 11:71; 43:47; 53:60; see BELIEF AND UNBELIEF; MESSENGER). This is also apparent when the unbelievers laugh at and mock the believers (Q 23:110; 83:29). Laughter is thus closely linked with the subject of mockery (q.v.). Only once does it express harmless amusement (Q 27:19) and twice joy (Q 9:82; 80:39; see JOY AND MISERY). But while the joyful laughter of hypocrites (see HYPOCRITES AND HYPOCRISY) who stay behind instead of fighting (q.v.) for God's cause (see JIHĀD; PATH OR WAY) signals a sinful disobedience (q.v.) that equals disbelief, the laughing faces of those who achieved paradise (q.v.) are the reward of dutiful belief (see REWARD AND PUNISHMENT).

The references to laughter predominantly reflect the initial experience of Muḥammad as well as any other prophet (as attested by similar references to laughter and mockery in the Hebrew Bible; see PROPHETS AND PROPHETHOOD): their message is derided. The qurʾānic message counters this derision with eschatological threats (see ESCHATOLOGY). The last judgment (q.v.) will bring a reversal of fate (q.v.) and those who laughed sinfully will cry (Q 9:82; see WEEPING) and be laughed at by the believers (Q 83:34; for a similar threat of reversal in the New Testament, see *Luke* 6:25; for a corresponding prediction regarding mockery in the Qurʾān, see Q 9:79).

To explicate these overriding assessments, several verses and exegetical statements merit more detailed comments. First of all, the Qurʾān never categorically condemns laughter as such. Pellat's (Seriousness, 354) interpretation of Q 9:82 is clearly mistaken: the laughing hypocrites will be punished with prolonged crying for staying behind, not simply for laughing. The only verse to suggest that crying might generally be more appropriate than laughing is Q 53:57-62: "The approaching (hour) is imminent. None but God can avert it. Do you wonder at this news and laugh and will you not weep? You are raising your heads proudly [or, amusing yourselves: *wa-antum sāmidūna*]. Prostrate yourselves before God and worship!" Here (Q 53:60), it may be argued, it is not just the surprised laughter of disbelief in the last judgment that is inappropriate, but laughter in general, as opposed to crying (Ammann, *Vorbild und Vernunft*, 78). This can be interpreted as recommending a serious and more specifically pious attitude towards life instead of godless frivolity (see PIETY). But it remains open to debate whether, first, the recommendation holds true beyond the very moment of speaking or the limited period during which the revelation expected the end of the world to happen at any moment (see APOCALYPSE; REVELATION AND INSPIRATION); and, second, whether weeping should be limited to times of prayer (in the moderate sense of "There is a time for weeping and a time for laughing," *Eccles* 3:4) or cultivated as much as possible. The latter, rather extreme literalist view — that weeping should be cultivated as much as possible — was taken by the ascetic "weepers" *(bakkāʾ)*, those mystics who denounced laughter and shed many tears during their devotional exercises (Meier, Bakkāʾ; see ṢŪFISM AND THE QURʾĀN; PRAYER). The minimalist view — that at least prayer is certainly not a time for laughing — found acceptance in several law schools (ʿAbd al-Razzāq, *Muṣannaf*, i, nos. 3760-8 and 3770-8; Ibn Abī Shayba, *Muṣannaf*, i, 387 f.; see LAW AND THE QURʾĀN).

The eschatological contempt for this world betrayed by Q 53:60 and best attested by its dismissal as mere play and amusement in Q 6:32 flourished in pious circles and especially among early ascetics who provided numerous dicta against laughter (Ammann, *Vorbild und Vernunft*, 74 f.), some of which found their way into ḥadīth collections and qurʾānic exegesis (see ASCETICISM; ḤADĪTH AND THE QURʾĀN; EXEGESIS OF THE QURʾĀN: CLASSICAL AND MEDIEVAL). Thus, the "small" and "big" (i.e. sin) of Q 18:49 could be interpreted as laughter, or as smiling and laughing, respectively (Ṭabarī, *Tafsīr*, ad Q 18:49; see SIN, MAJOR AND MINOR). But if such arbitrary embellishments are discounted, the one instance of qurʾānic reserve against laughter that is open to exegetical generalization is a far cry from the Bible's unconditional loathing (*Eccles* 7:6; *James* 4:9; *Sir* 21:20; *Eccles* 2:2; *Eph* 5:4; and, most instructive by comparison, *Luke* 6:25).

Q 53:60 is remarkable for another aspect that often goes unnoticed: it reflects the popular conception already attested in pre-Islamic Arabian poetry (see POETRY AND POETS; PRE-ISLAMIC ARABIA AND THE QUR'ĀN) that laughter is caused by surprise *(taʿajjub)*. Much later medical and philosophical theories of laughter based on this conception seem to be indebted to theological debates rather than Greek authors (Ammann, *Vorbild und Vernunft*, 14-9; see THEOLOGY AND THE QUR'ĀN; MEDICINE AND THE QUR'ĀN; PHILOSOPHY AND THE QUR'ĀN). The debates were triggered by two verses. In Q 11:71-4, God's messengers reassure a frightened Abraham (q.v.); his wife Sara laughs, is told that she will give birth to Isaac (q.v.; Isḥāq) and Jacob (q.v.; Yaʿqūb) and, being old, she wonders at this strange thing *(shay' ʿajīb)*. Her surprise, in turn, is called into question by the messengers: "Do you wonder *(taʿjabīna)* at God's command?" This is one of the rare examples where doubt (q.v.) in a prophetic message is noted, but not condemned as sinful. The chronology of the biblical version of the story (*Gen* 18:10-5), in which Sara laughs *after* she hears the lord's announcement, makes clear the reason for Sara's laughter: she is surprised at the idea of giving birth at her age. But Muslim commentators, beginning with Muḥammad's cousin Ibn ʿAbbās (d. 68/686-8), were faced with a text that has Sara laughing *before* she even knows what to laugh at. There were three solutions to this problem (Ammann, *Vorbild und Vernunft*, 19 f.; Ṭabarī, *Tafsīr* and Ṭabarsī, *Majmaʿ*, ad Q 11:71): some exegetes restored the Bible's sequence and meaning, others identified an earlier reason for surprised or joyful laughter, while a third group claimed that *ḍaḥikat* here actually means *ḥāḍat* — she menstruated (see MENSTRUATION). The last opinion is not supported by sound philological evidence and seems particularly ill-advised since there is no reason for surprise if Sara had already menstruated before she is told she will give birth, but it has been duly cited by lexicographers ever since its initial proposal. The etymological message of the biblical story — Isaac (Isḥāq) takes his name from his parents' laughter — is clear in Hebrew, but not in Arabic, and thus escaped Muslim commentators. The loss of this detail need not be greatly regretted since the value of this folk etymology has been doubted anyway: the name Isḥāq is probably of theophoric origin and expressed the wish that God should either laugh, that is, welcome the new-born or grown-up bearer of the name, or make him laugh, that is, happy.

This leads to Q 53:36-44, which contains the only theological statement about laughter in the Qur'ān (Q 53:43-4). It portrays God as the creator or ultimate cause of laughter and weeping: "Was it not prophesied to him what is [said] in the scrolls (q.v.) of Moses (q.v.; Mūsā) and Abraham [...] that God is the end [of all], and that it is he who causes to laugh and to weep *(aḍḥaka wa-abkā)*, and that it is he who causes to die and to live *(amāta wa-aḥyā)?*" It is in the context of God's primordial and eschatological roles of creator and terminator that God is credited with causing woman and man to laugh and to weep (see CREATION; FREEDOM AND PREDESTINATION). The verses, in fact, summarize how human destiny (q.v.) must be interpreted from the point of view of salvation history (see HISTORY AND THE QUR'ĀN; SALVATION). The joy and grief expressed by laughter and tears, corresponding, in the final analysis, to life (q.v.) and death (see DEATH AND THE DEAD), are both sent by God. The exact wording conspicuously reverses the internal sequence of the two pairs: laugh — weep, die — live (see PAIRS AND PAIRING). There is more to this than just the formal exigency of rhymed prose (q.v.; *sajʿ*). Ending on a note of hope (q.v.), the final *aḥyā* suggests that the creator both causes people to live in this world and revives them in the hereafter, that is, finally raises them from the dead. This may mean that at least believers have more reason to laugh than to weep, and it certainly invalidates the maximalist reading of the end of Q 53:60-2 (mentioned above), which would like to rule out laughter completely. For Muslim commentators, the theological question posed by this verse was whether God literally creates human laughter and weeping or only the reasons for it, such as joy and grief. The latter explanation was promoted by Muʿtazilīs (q.v.) bent on defending free will against the determinist causative phrasing of the verse. But there was one concession: irresistible laughter is God-sent laughter; thus the involuntary act is interpreted as willed by God (Ammann, *Vorbild und Vernunft*, 21 f.; Ṭabarī, *Tafsīr;* Ṭabarsī, *Majmaʿ;* Rāzī, *Tafsīr* ad Q 53:43).

In the Qurʾān (as opposed to the biblical portrayal), God is never portrayed as laughing, but in several ḥadīths he is (see Gimaret, *Dieu à l'image de l'homme*, 265-79). This portrayal also sparked theological objections, this time against the implied anthropomorphism (q.v.). One of the more fascinating arguments jointly refutes God's laughter and surprise by pointing out that only someone who originally did not know could wonder and laugh at something — whereas God is all-knowing (see GOD AND HIS ATTRIBUTES). Surprise and laughter here and elsewhere are both seen as prerogatives of humans and linked with their rational faculties (Ammann, *Vorbild und Vernunft*, 42 f. and 26 f.; Lecomte, *Traité des divergences*, 235 f.; Zamakhsharī, *Kashshāf*, ad Q 37:12; see INTELLECT).

The perplexing *fa-tabassama ḍāḥikan min qawlihā* of Q 27:19 is probably best understood as "he [Solomon] smiled amused at her [the ant's] word" (Ammann, *Vorbild und Vernunft*, 9 f.; see SOLOMON; ANIMAL LIFE). But it may also reflect a long-standing rule of Near Eastern etiquette attested by Christian, Persian and also pre-Islamic Arabic sources (see e.g. the verse by Aws b. Ḥajar about women who "laugh but smilingly," *mā yaḍḥakna illā tabassuman*). This rule of cultured laughter subdued to a mere smile was later attributed to the Prophet (Ammann, *Vorbild und Vernunft*, 88-109 and 47-61). There is no reason to believe that the ḥadīth in question was not fabricated. But it constitutes a respectable compromise between the Prophet's well-attested loud laughter in some instances and his ominous warning that "If you knew what I know, you would laugh little and weep much!" (Ammann, *Vorbild und Vernunft*, 48 and 65-68).

Ludwig Ammann

Bibliography
Primary: ʿAbd al-Razzāq, *Muṣannaf;* Ibn Abū Shayba, Abū Bakr ʿAbdallāh b. Muḥammad, *Kitāb al-Muṣannaf fī l-ḥadīth wa-l-āthār,* Bombay 1979-83; Rāzī, *Tafsīr;* Ṭabarī, *Tafsīr;* Ṭabarsī, *Majmaʿ;* Zamakhsharī, *Kashshāf.*
Secondary: L. Ammann, *Vorbild und Vernunft. Die Regelung von Lachen und Scherzen im mittelalterlichen Islam,* Hildesheim 1993 (full bibli.); R. Bartelmus, Śāḥaq/ṣāḥaq, in H.-J. Fabry and H. Ringgren, *Theologisches Wörterbuch zum Alten Testament,* 8 vols., Stuttgart 1973-95, vii, 730-45; D. Gimaret, *Dieu à l'image de l'homme,* Paris 1997; G. Lecomte, *Le traité des divergences du ḥadīth d'Ibn Qutayba (mort en 276/889),* Damascus 1962; F. Meier, Bakkāʾ, in *EI²*, i, 959-61; Ch. Pellat, al-Djidd wa 'l-hazl, in *EI²*, ii, 536-7; id., Seriousness and humour in early Islam, in *Islamic studies* 2 (1962), 353-63; S.P. Stetkevych, Sarah and the hyena. Laughter, menstruation and the genesis of a double entendre, in *History of religions* 35 (1996), 11-41.

Law and the Qurʾān

The Qurʾān has a curious function in Islamic law. It is doubtless considered the first and foremost of the four major sources of the law (i.e. the *sharīʿa*). Yet in substantive legal terms and in comparison with the full corpus of the *sharīʿa*, the Qurʾān provides a relatively minor body of legal subject matter, although a few of the most central rulings that govern the life of Muslim society and the individual (see COMMUNITY AND SOCIETY IN THE QUR'ĀN; ETHICS AND THE QUR'ĀN) are explicitly stated in it, or derived from one or another of its verses. The centrality of the Qur'ān in the *sharīʿa* stems more from theological and intellectual considerations of the law and less from its ability to provide substantive legal subject matter (see THEOLOGY AND THE QUR'ĀN).

The early legal history of the text

While it is true that the Qur'ān is primarily a book of religious and moral prescriptions, there is no doubt that it encompasses pieces of legislation strictly defined. In propounding his message, the Prophet wished to break away from pre-Islamic Arabian values and institutions, but only insofar as he needed to establish, once and for all, the foundations of the new religion (see ISLAM; PRE-ISLAMIC ARABIA AND THE QUR'ĀN). Pragmatically, he could not have done away with all the social practices and institutions that had prevailed prior and up to his time. Among the multitude of exhortations (q.v.) and prescriptions found in the Qur'ān, there are a good number of legal and quasi-legal stipulations. Thus legislation was introduced in select matters of ritual (see RITUAL AND THE QUR'ĀN), alms-tax (see ALMSGIVING; TAXATION), property (q.v.) and treatment of orphans (q.v.), inheritance (q.v.), usury (q.v.), consumption of alcohol (see INTOXICATION; WINE), marriage, separation, divorce (see MARRIAGE AND DIVORCE), sexual intercourse (see SEX AND SEXUALITY), adultery (see ADULTERY AND FORNICATION), theft (q.v.) and homicide (see MURDER; BLOODSHED).

Medieval Muslim jurists and modern scholars seem to agree that the Qur'ān contains some five hundred verses with explicitly legal content. In comparison with the body of qur'ānic material as a whole, the legal verses appear rather exiguous, conveying the impression that the Qur'ān's preoccupation with legal matters is nothing more than incidental. At the same time, it has frequently been noted by Islamicists that the Qur'ān often repeats itself both literally and thematically. If we accept this to be the case, it would mean that the relative size of the legal subject matter, where repetition rarely occurs, is larger than previously thought. And if we consider the fact that the average length of the legal verse is twice or even thrice that of the average non-legal verse, it is not difficult to argue that the Qur'ān contains no less legal material than does the Torah, which is commonly known as "The Law" (Goitein, The birth-hour, 24). Therefore, while qur'ānic law constitutes a relatively minor part of the *sharīʿa,* the Qur'ān, in and by itself, is no less legalistic than the Torah.

The law of the Torah, Gospel and Qur'ān

This affirmation of significant legal content in the Qur'ān is crucial since it goes against conventional wisdom, which asserts that the Qur'ān acquired legal importance for early Muslims only toward the end of the first century A.H. (ca. 720 C.E.). Even in Mecca (q.v.), the Prophet already thought of the community he aimed to create in terms of a political and social unit (see POLITICS AND THE QUR'ĀN; SOCIAL RELATIONS). This explains his success in organizing the Arab and Jewish tribes (see TRIBES AND CLANS; JEWS AND JUDAISM; ARABS) in a body politic immediately after arriving in Medina (q.v.). The constitution that he drafted in this city betrays a mind very familiar with formulaic legal documents, a fact that is hardly surprising in light of the legal thrust of the Qur'ān and the role he had played as an arbitration judge (*ḥakam,* see JUSTICE AND INJUSTICE; MUḤAMMAD). In Medina, he continued to play this role for some time, relying in his decisions, so it seems, on customary law and tribal practices hitherto prevailing. But from the Qurʾān we learn that at a certain point of time after his arrival in Medina the Prophet came to think of his message as one that carried with it the law of God, just as did the Torah (q.v.) and the Gospel (q.v.). Sūra 5, revealed at Medina, marshals a list of commands, admonitions and explicit prohibitions concerning a great variety of issues, from eating swine meat to theft (see FOOD AND DRINK; LAWFUL AND UNLAWFUL; PROHIBITED DEGREES; BOUNDARIES AND PRECEPTS). References to the Jews and Christians (see CHRISTIANS AND CHRISTIANITY), and their respective scriptures recur throughout. In Q 5:43 God asks, with a sense of astonishment, why the Jews resort to Muḥammad in his capacity as a judge "when they have the Torah which contains the judgment (q.v.) of God." The Qurʾān continues: "We have revealed the Torah in which there is guidance and light (q.v.), by which the prophets who surrendered [to God] judged the Jews, and the rabbis and priests judged by such of God's scriptures (see BOOK) as they were bidden to observe" (Q 5:44). In Q 5:46, the Qurʾān addresses the Christians, saying in effect that God sent Jesus (q.v.) to confirm the prophethood (see PROPHETS AND PROPHETHOOD) of Moses (q.v.), and the Gospel to reassert the "guidance and advice" revealed in the Torah. "So let the people of the Gospel judge by that which God had revealed therein, for whosoever judged not by that which God revealed: such are sinners" (Q 5:47).

This is sufficient to show that the Prophet not only considered the Jews and Christians as possessing their own divine law but also as bound by the application of this law. If the Jews and Christians each have their own law, then what about Muslims? The Qurʾān here does not shirk from giving an explicit answer: "We have revealed unto you the book (viz. the Qurʾān) with the truth, confirming whatever scripture was before it... so judge between them by that which God had revealed, and do not follow their desires away from the truth... *for we have made for each of you* (i.e. Muslims, Christians and Jews) *a law and a normative way to follow.* If God had willed, he would have made all of you one community" (Q 5:48). But God did not wish to do so, and he thus created three communities with three sets of laws, so that each community could follow *its own* law. And like the Christians and Jews, the Prophet is again commanded (repeatedly throughout the Qurʾān) to judge by what God revealed to him, for "who is better than God in judgment?" (Q 5:49-50).

Sūra 5, or at least verses 42-50 therein, seems to have been precipitated by an incident in which certain Jewish tribes resorted to the Prophet to adjudicate among them. It is unlikely that such an event would have taken place any later than 5 A.H., since the repeated references to rabbis implies a context of time when there remained a substantial Jewish presence in Medina, which could not have been the case after this date. Be that as it may, the incident seems to have marked a turning point in the career of the Prophet, and from that point on he began to think of his religion as one that should afford the Muslim community a set of laws separate from those of other religions. This may also account for the fact that it is in Medina that the overwhelming bulk of qurʾānic legislation occurred (see CHRONOLOGY AND THE QURʾĀN; OCCASIONS OF REVELATION).

Muḥammad and the caliphs and the law

Although the Qurʾān did not provide Muslims with an all-encompassing system of law, the evidence suggests that the Prophet was strongly inclined to move in that direction. This inclination finds eloquent testimony in the stand of the Qur'ān on the matter of the consumption of date- and grape-wine. In the Meccan phase, wines were obviously permitted: "From date-palm and grapes you derive alcoholic drinks, and from them you make good livelihood *(rizqan ḥasanan)*. Lo! therein is indeed a portent for people who have sense" (Q 16:67). In Medina, the position of the Qur'ān changes, expressing a growing distrust toward alcoholic beverages. "They ask you (viz. Muḥammad) about wine *(khamr)* and gambling (q.v.; *maysir*). Say: 'In both there is sin (see SIN, MAJOR AND MINOR), and utility for people'" (Q 2:219). The sense of aversion increases further: "O you who believe (see BELIEF AND UNBELIEF), do not come to pray when you are drunken, till you know what you utter" (Q 4:43). Here, one observes a provisional prohibition against the consumption of alcohol only at times when Muslims intended to pray (see PRAYER). Finally, a categorical command is revealed in Q 5:90-1, whereby Muslims are to avoid alcohol, games of chance (see DIVINATION; FORETELLING) and idols altogether (see IDOLS AND IMAGES; IDOLATRY AND IDOLATERS). It is interesting that the final, decisive stand on alcohol occurs in sūra 5 which, as we have seen, marks a turning point in the legislative outlook of the Prophet.

This turning point, however, should not be seen as constituting an entirely clean break from the previous practices of the Prophet, for he already played the role of a judge, both as a traditional arbitrator as well as a prophet. The turning point only marked the beginning of a new process whereby all events affecting the nascent Muslim community had therefore to be adjudicated according to God's law, whose agent was none other than the Prophet. This is clearly attested to not only in the Qur'ān but also in the so-called Constitution of Medina, a document whose authenticity can hardly be contested.

That all matters should have been subject to the divine and prophetic decree must not be taken to mean that all the old problems encountered by the Prophet were given new solutions. Although a historical record of this early period is lacking in credibility (see HISTORY AND THE QUR'ĀN; ḤADĪTH AND THE QUR'ĀN), we may assert that, with the exception of what may be called the qur'ānic legal reform, the Prophet generally followed existing pre-Islamic Arab practices. Indeed, one might argue that while these practices constituted the bulk of prevalent norms, the qur'ānic legislation constituted nothing more than a supplement. It was not until later that pre-Islamic Arab practices were Islamicized by their inclusion under the rubric of prophetic sunna (q.v.).

Before the prophetic sunna came to play an important role in the law, and even while the conquests were underway and Medina was still the capital, there were mainly two sets of laws on the basis of which the leaders of the nascent Muslim community modeled their conduct, namely, pre-Islamic Arab customary law and the Qur'ān. The former was by and large the only "system" of law known to the conquerors, while the latter contained and symbolized the mission in whose name these conquerors were fighting (q.v.; see also EXPEDITIONS AND BATTLES). The importance of the Qur'ān and its injunctions for the early Muslims can hardly be overstated. Early Monophysite sources inform us that when Abū Bakr, the first caliph (q.v.; d. 13/634), deployed his armies to conquer Syria (q.v.), he addressed his generals with the following words: "When you enter the land, kill neither old man nor child.... Establish a covenant with every city and people who receives you, give them your assurances and let them live according to their laws.... Those who do not receive you, you are to fight, conducting yourselves carefully in accordance with the ordinances and upright laws transmitted to you from God, at the hands of our Prophet" (Brock, Syriac views, 12, 200; see WAR). It is interesting to observe that in this passage the reference to the Qurʾān is unambiguous, although one is not entirely sure whether or not the "upright laws" might refer in part to legal ordinances other than those laid down in the Qurʾān. But even more interesting is the contrast drawn between the laws of the conquered nations and the law transmitted from God through the Prophet. Abū Bakr's orders to allow the mainly Christian inhabitants of Syria to regulate their affairs by their own laws is rather reminiscent of the Qurʾān's discourse in sūra 5, where each religion was to apply to itself its own set of laws. Here, Abū Bakr was implicitly and, later in the passage, explicitly adhering to the Qurʾān's letter and spirit, and in a sense to the personal stand adopted by the Prophet on this issue which is inextricably connected with the very act of revelation (see REVELATION AND INSPIRATION).

The early caliphs, including the Umayyads, considered themselves the deputies of God on earth, and thus seem to have felt free to dispense justice in accordance with the Qurʾān. Abū Bakr, in consonance with the wishes expressed in his speech to the army of Syria, seems to have adhered, as a rule, to the prescriptions of the Qurʾān. Among other things, he enforced the prohibition on alcohol and fixed the penalty for its violation at forty lashes (see CHASTISEMENT AND PUNISHMENT). While enforcing the law in this case indicates the centrality of the qurʾānic injunctions, it also demonstrates that beyond the very fact of the qurʾānic prohibition (see FORBIDDEN) there was little juristic experience or guidance to go by. For this punishment, deemed to have been fixed arbitrarily, was soon altered by ʿUmar and ʿAlī (see ʿALĪ B. ABĪ ṬĀLIB) to eighty lashes, the reasoning being, so it seems, that intoxication was deemed analogous to the offense of falsely accusing a person of committing adultery *(qadhf)*, for which the Qurʾān fixed the penalty of eighty lashes. ʿUmar was not only the first to impose the new penalty for inebriation but he is also reported to have forcefully insisted on strict adherence to the Qurʾān in matters of ritual, which became an integral part of the law.

The increasing importance of the Qurʾān as a religious and legal text manifested itself in the need to collect the scattered material of the book and thence to establish a vulgate (see COLLECTION OF THE QURʾĀN; CODICES OF THE QURʾĀN). ʿUthmān (q.v.), who followed in the steps of his two predecessors in enforcing the rulings of the Qurʾān, took it upon himself to discharge this task. The collection of the Qurʾān must have had a primary legal significance, for it defined the subject matter of the text and thus gave the legally-minded a *textus receptus* on which to draw. The monumental event of establishing a vulgate signified the beginning of what may be described as the textual attention accorded the Qurʾān (see TRADITIONAL DISCIPLINES OF QURʾĀNIC STUDY; FORM AND STRUCTURE OF THE QURʾĀN; LANGUAGE AND STYLE OF THE QURʾĀN; GRAMMAR AND THE QURʾĀN). This attention reached its zenith only centuries later, but the decades that followed the event determined the direction of what was to come.

During the ensuing decades, Muslim men of learning turned their attention to the explicit legal contents of the Qurʾān. The paucity of credible sources from this period does not allow us to form a comprehensive picture of the developments in qurʾānic studies. The scope of activities that took place in connection with the development of the theory of abrogation (q.v.), however, may give us some clues as to the extent to which the Qur'ān played a role in elaborating Islamic jurisprudence.

Origins of the theory of abrogation

The rudimentary beginnings of the theory of abrogation seem to have arisen in response to the need for reconciling what appeared to the early Muslims to be seeming contradictions within the body of legal verses in the Qur'ān. The most immediate concern for these Muslims was neither theology nor dogma (see FAITH; CREEDS), for these were matters that acquired significance only later. Rather, their primary interest lay in how they might realize or manifest obedience (q.v.) to their God, a duty that was explicitly stressed in the Qur'ān. In other words, Islam meant, even as early as the middle of the first century, adherence to the will of God as articulated in his book. Thus it was felt necessary to determine what the stand of the Qur'ān was with regard to particular issues. Where there was more than one qur'ānic decree pertinent to a single matter, such a determination was no easy task. And to solve such difficulties, it was essential to determine which verses might be deemed to repeal others in the text of the Qur'ān.

The Companions of the Prophet (q.v.) are reported to have provided the impetus to such discussions. But the Muslim sources make relatively few references to the activities of the Companions in this field. It was the generation of the Successors that became most closely associated with discussions on abrogation, and with controversies about the status of particular verses (see EXEGESIS OF THE QUR'ĀN: CLASSICAL AND MEDIEVAL). The names of Ibrāhīm al-Nakhaʿī (d. 95/713), Muslim b. Yasār (d. 101/719), Mujāhid b. Jabr (d. 104/722), and al-Ḥasan al-Baṣrī (d. 110/728) were among the most prominent in such discussions. Qatāda b. Diʿāma al-Sadūsī (d. 117/735) and the renowned Ibn Shihāb al-Zuhrī (d. 124/742) also left writings that attest to the birth of the theory of abrogation, which by their time had already been articulated in writing. Though their original works were likely subjected to revision by later writers, the core of their thought has proven difficult to dismiss as inauthentic. Even if this core is reduced to a minimum, it nonetheless manifests an awareness on the part of these scholars of the legal thrust of the qur'ānic text. For it is clear that the treatises were exclusively concerned with the ramifications of those verses that had direct bearing on legal issues.

The theory of abrogation appears to have developed in a context in which some qur'ānic prescriptions contradicted the actual reality and practices of the community, thus giving rise to the need for interpreting away, or canceling out, the effect of those verses seen to be discordant with other verses more in line with certain practices. Whatever the case may have been, the very nature of this theory points up the fact that whatever contradiction or problem needed to be settled, it had to be settled within the purview of qur'ānic authority. This accords with the assertion that the Umayyad caliphs not only saw themselves as the deputies of God on earth, and thus the instruments for carrying out God's justice as embodied in the Qur'ān, but also as the propounders of the law in its (then) widest sense. In addition to fiscal laws and rules of war, they regularly concerned themselves with establishing and enforcing rules regarding marriage, divorce, succession, manumission (see SLAVES AND SLAVERY), pre-emption, blood money (q.v.), ritual and other matters. The promulgation of these rules could only have been carried out in the name of the lord on whose behalf these caliphs claimed to serve as deputies.

The Qurʾān in legal theory

With the evolution of the doctrine of abrogation and other aspects of qurʾānic legal studies, legal theory *(uṣūl al-fiqh)* began to emerge during the second/eighth and third/ninth centuries. In this theory, the Qurʾān occupied a central role as the first source of the law, and this because, logically and ontologically, everything else either depends on or derives from it. Just as consensus and the inferential method of juridical *qiyās* were justified by means of prophetic sunna, this sunna, together with its derivatives, were justified by the Qurʾān. The explicit commands to obey the Prophet and to emulate his behavior ensured that the apostolic example (see MESSENGER) became a source of law which supplements, in substantive terms, the qurʾānic legal content, and guarantees, in theoretical terms, the authoritativeness *(ḥujjiyya)* of other legal sources subsidiary to it. The chain of authority thus begins with God's book in which his attribute of speech (q.v.; see also GOD AND HIS ATTRIBUTES; WORD OF GOD) not only manifests itself but is also made identical with the law.

Qurʾānic authority

The Qurʾān also guarantees the authoritativeness of the legal sources in epistemological terms. Metaphysically, God's existence is assumed to be apodictically demonstrated, which entails the certainty that the Qurʾān is an embodiment of God's speech. That the Qurʾān is known with certainty to embody one of the most essential of God's attributes does not necessarily entail the conclusion that its subject matter, as known to the post-apostolic community, is certain. It is after all acknowledged as conceivable that its contents, or portions thereof, may have been forgotten or distorted, just as the Christians and Jews are said to have corrupted their own scriptures (see CORRUPTION; FORGERY). As a safeguard against such distortions and omissions, or perhaps in defense of qurʾānic authenticity, among other things, legal theory developed the doctrine of multiple, recurrent transmission, known as *tawātur*. According to this doctrine, three conditions must be met for the *tawātur* transmission to take place. First, the channels of transmission must be sufficiently numerous as to preclude any possibility of error (q.v.) or collaboration on a forgery. Second, the very first class of transmitters had to have received sensory knowledge (see SEEING AND HEARING) of what the Prophet declared to be revelation. Third, these two conditions must be met at each stage of transmission beginning with the first class and ending with the present community.

The recurrent mode of transmission yields necessary, certain knowledge, so that the mind, upon receiving reported information of this type, need not even exercise its faculty of reasoning and reflection. Upon hearing recurrent transmissions of the verses, the mind has no choice but to admit the contents of the verses *a priori* as true and genuine. Unlike acquired knowledge, which occurs to the mind only after it conducts inferential operations, necessary knowledge is lodged in the mind spontaneously (see KNOWLEDGE AND LEARNING). Thus, upon hearing a verse, or for that matter any report, from a single transmitter, one is presumed to have gained probable knowledge of its contents and its authenticity. In order to reach a level of necessary knowledge, the verse must be transmitted a sufficient number of times and each time by a different transmitter. Thus, the Qurʾān's expansive assimilation in the Muslim community, in both synchronic and diachronic terms, guarantees the certainty of its contents in the sense that its language is passed down through generations of Muslims in complete and accurate fashion (see TRUTH).

But does this guarantee certitude in construing the signification of its language? Qur'ānic legal language, the jurists admitted, suffers in many instances from ambiguity — a situation that gave rise to the taxonomy known as *muḥkam/mutashābih* (clear/ambiguous). According to this taxonomy, the Qur'ān contains univocal and equivocal language, the former having the epistemological status of certainty because it is capable of but one interpretation yielding a single, unquestionable meaning. The latter, however, is merely probable since it lends itself to be construed in more than one way. Thus, in theory, the qur'ānic language distinguishes itself from prophetic ḥadīth in that while it includes both *muḥkam* and *mutashābih* — a problem which also pervades the ḥadīth — its transmission is deemed to be ever certain, whereas the ḥadīth's transmission is considered to be often, if not dominantly, suspect (see ḤADĪTH AND THE QUR'ĀN).

Fashioned thus, the theoretical discourse was agenda-laden. In order to exclude probability from the mode of qur'ānic transmission, the text was to be defined by the very terms of the transmission that guaranteed its certainty. In other words, instead of including in the qur'ānic text material that could be defined as probable, the *textus receptus* was limited to that body of material that was considered to have undergone *tawātur* transmission. The admittedly insignificant material that boasted only probabilistic status, such as Ibn Mas'ūd's (d. 32/652-3) recension, was *a priori* excluded from the *textus receptus*. Dubious recensions were to be treated as equivalent to prophetic ḥadīths, the justification being that such Companions as Ibn Mas'ūd may have thought that the material they had heard from the Prophet was qur'ānic when in fact it was from the sunna.

Be that as it may, the qur'ānic text presented the jurist with no problem insofar as transmission and authenticity were concerned. Rather, the difficulty was with hermeneutics; i.e. how to interpret the qur'ānic language in the ultimate task of constructing legal norms. The aim of linguistic interpretation is to determine whether, for instance, a word is ambiguous, univocal, general, particular, constituting a trope, a command, etc. Each word is analyzed in light of one or more of these categories, one of the first being the category of tropes. The great majority of legal theorists maintain that most words in the Arabic language are used in their real sense and that metaphorical language is limited. Some jurists, however, such as Abū Isḥāq al-Isfarā'īnī (d. 418/1027), are reported to have taken the position that tropes do not occur in the Arabic language, the implication being that the Qur'ān is free of metaphors (see METAPHOR). A few others admit the existence of metaphors in the language but reject the claim that the Qur'ān contains any such words. The majority, however, hold the position that the Qur'ān does contain metaphors, and in support of this they adduce, among others, Q 19:4: "And the head has flared up with grey hair." It is obvious that the head itself does not "flare up" and that the metaphor issues from the substitution of fire (q.v.) for hair.

Words used in their real meanings are said to be either clear *(mubayyan, mufassar)* or ambiguous *(mujmal)*. The latter category encompasses all expressions the denotations of which are so general and imprecise that the hearer would be expected to understand neither the intention of the speaker nor the point being made. The ambiguity stems from the fact that the referent in the case of such words includes several attributes or different genera. In Q 17:33: "And he who is killed wrongfully, we have given power *(sulṭān)* to his heir," the term "power" (see POWER AND IMPOTENCE) is utterly ambiguous, since it could refer to a variety of genera, such as retaliation (q.v.), right to blood money, or even the right to pardon the murderer. This ambiguity explains why *mujmal* words tend to prevent texts containing them from having binding legal effect, for the ruling or the subject of that ruling derived from them would not be sufficiently clear as to enable Muslim jurists to understand what exactly is being commanded. It is only when such words are brought out of the realm of ambiguity into that of clarity by means of other clear "speech" that the legal effects of *mujmal* texts become binding.

Ambiguity is the result not only of the use of vague language, as evidenced in the aforementioned verse, but also of homonymous nouns that designate more than one object. An example illustrating the difficulty is the Arabic word *ʿayn,* which equally refers to an eye (see EYES), to the spring (see SPRINGS AND FOUNTAINS) from which water issues, and to a distinguished person of noble lineage. Furthermore, ambiguity may accrue to an otherwise clear expression by virtue of the fact that it is associated with an ambiguous statement. For instance, Q 5:1: "The beast of cattle is made lawful unto you (for food)" is, as it stands, fairly clear. Immediately thereafter, however, the verse continues with the statement: "except for that which is unannounced for you," thus rendering the earlier statement ambiguous, since what is unannounced cannot be known without further documentation.

Univocal language in the texts of revelation is known as *naṣṣ,* since its meaning is so clear as to engender certitude in the mind. When we hear the word "four" we automatically know that it is neither three nor five, nor any other number. To know what "four" means we have no need for other language to explain the denotation of the word. It is self-sufficiently clear. Against those few who maintained that the *naṣṣ* rarely occurs in connection with legal matters, the majority of jurists argue that univocal language is quite abundant in the texts.

Equivocal words

Words whose signification is not readily obvious are of two types, the first of which includes those whose meaning is so general *(ʿāmm)* that they need to be particularized if they are to yield any legal effects. The second type includes words with two or more possible meanings, one of which — the *ẓāhir* — is deemed, by virtue of supporting evidence, superior to the others. Words that equally include two or more individuals of the genus to which they refer are deemed general *(ʿāmm).* Thus all plurals accompanied by a definite article are general terms, e.g. *al-muslimūn,* "the Muslims." Some jurists considered words of this kind to belong to the category of the general even when not accompanied by a definite article. In addition to its function of defining words, this article serves, in the Arabic language, to render words applicable to all members of a class. Accordingly, when the article is attached to singular nouns, these nouns will refer to the generality of individuals within a certain class. *Al-insān* or *al-muslim* thus refers not to a particular individual but, respectively, to human beings or to Muslims generally. Yet another group of words considered to be general is that of the interrogative particles, classified in Arabic as nouns.

A general word in the Qurʾān may be particularized only by means of relevant words or statements provided by the revealed texts. By relevant is meant words or statements that apply to the same genus denoted by the general word. Particularization *(takhṣīṣ)* thus means exclusion from the general of a part that was subsumed under that general. For example, while in Q 2:238, which reads "Perform prayers, as well as the midmost prayer (see NOON)," the midmost prayer is specified, it cannot be said to have been particularized. Particularization would have applied if the verse had been revealed as saying "Perform prayers except for the midmost one."

A classic example of particularization occurs in Q 5:3, "Forbidden unto you (for food) is carrion," which was particularized by a prophetic report allowing the consumption, among others, of dead fish (see HUNTING AND FISHING). This example also makes clear that such reports, including solitary ones, can, at least according to some jurists, particularize the Qur'ān. Similarly, the Qur'ān can, as one can expect, particularize the sunna. Indeed, the vast majority of jurists held that statements in one of the two sources could particularize statements in the other.

There are at least two other types of particularization that apply to two different texts. The first type of particularization takes place when a proviso or a condition *(sharṭ)* is attached to, or brought to bear upon, a general statement. Q 3:97, for example, reads: "And pilgrimage (q.v.) to the house (see KAʿBA; HOUSE, DOMESTIC AND DIVINE) is a duty unto God for mankind, for him who can find a way thither." It is plain here that the obligation to go on pilgrimage is waived in the case of those who have no means to perform it. The second type, on the other hand, is particularization by means of introducing into the general statement, not a condition, but a quality *(ṣifa)*. This is known as the qualification *(taqyīd)* of an unrestricted *(muṭlaq)* word or statement. For instance, in cases where a man swears not to resume a normal marital relationship with his wife *(ẓihār)*, but later does, the penalty fixed in the Qur'ān is "freeing a slave" (Q 58:3). But the penalty for accidental homicide is "freeing a believing slave" (Q 4:92). The attribute "believing" has qualified, or particularized, the word "slave."

When a qualifying attribute is to be found nowhere in the texts, the unrestricted expression must be taken to refer to the general category subsumed under that expression. And when a qualified word appears without an object to qualify, the word must be taken to apply only to that case which is subject to the qualification. Some difficulties arise, however, concerning the extent to which the principle of qualification should be applied when an unrestricted word meets with a qualifying attribute. In Q 58:4, it is stipulated that the penalty for *ẓihār* is either "fasting (q.v.) for two successive months (q.v.)" or "feeding sixty needy persons." Unlike the general command to feed sixty persons, fasting here is qualified by the requirement that it be successive. Since these are two different types of penance (see REPENTANCE AND PENANCE), one relating to feeding, the other to fasting, the qualification applicable to the latter must not be extended to the former. But when the two penances (or rulings) are of the same nature, the attribute must be taken to qualify the unrestricted word or sentence. For instance, Q 2:282: "have witnesses (attest to the sale) when you sell one to another" is qualified by an earlier passage in the same verse stipulating "call to witness, from among you, two witnesses, and if two men are not available, then a man and two women" (see WITNESSING AND TESTIFYING; GENDER).

In this case, both the qualified and the unrestricted rulings are one and the same, and they pertain to a single case, namely, concluding a contract of sale (see SELLING

AND BUYING). But what would the interpretative attitude be in a situation where the qualified and unrestricted rulings are identical but the cases which give rise to them are different? Such is the case with *ẓihār* and accidental homicide. The penalty for the former is "freeing a slave" whereas for the latter it is "freeing a believing slave" (Q 58:3, 4:92). In such an event, the latter must be considered to qualify the former, a consideration said to be grounded in reasoning, not in the actual language of the texts. That is to say, in the contract of sale God made it clear in the language *(lafẓ)* of the Qurʾān that a witness of a certain sort is meant, but in *ẓihār* and accidental homicide there is no provision of specific language to this effect; the jurist merely reasons, on the basis of the text, that this was God's intention.

We have said that equivocal words are classifiable into two broad categories, one encompassing general terms *(ʿāmm)*, together with those that may be called unrestricted *(mufaṣṣal)*, and the other including words that are capable of more than one interpretation. Through a process of interpretation, technically known as *taʾwīl*, one of the meanings, the *ẓāhir*, is deemed by the interpreter to be the most likely among the candidates, because it presents evidence that is absent in the case of the other possible meanings. An example of this sort of evidence would be language that takes the imperative *(amr)* or prohibitive *(nahy)* form, to mention the two most significant linguistic types in legal hermeneutics.

The jurists are unanimous in their view that revelation is intended to lay down a system of obligation and that the imperative and the prohibitive forms (whose prototypes, respectively, are "Do" and "Do not do") constitute the backbone of that system's deontology. Without coming to grips with the hermeneutical ramifications of these two forms, obedience to God can never be achieved. For it is chiefly through these that God chose to express the greatest part of his revelation.

Commands and prohibitions

Perhaps the most important question with regard to the imperative form was its legal effect. When someone commands another by saying "Do this," should this be construed as falling only within the legal value of the obligatory *(wājib)* or also within that of the recommended *(mandūb)* or the indifferent *(mubāḥ)?* The Qurʾān states "Hold the prayer" (Q 2:43), a phrase that was unanimously understood to convey an obligation. At the same time, the Qurʾān stipulates "Write (your slaves a contract of emancipation) if you are aware of any good in them" (Q 24:33), language which was construed as a recommendation. Furthermore, in Q 5:2, the statement "When you have left the sacred precinct, then go hunting" was taken to indicate that hunting outside the Kaʿba is an act to which the law is indifferent.

Adducing such texts as proof, a minority among the jurists held that the imperative form in qurʾānic language is a homonym, equally capable of indicating obligation, recommendation and indifference. Others maintained that it signifies only recommendation. The majority of jurists, however, rejected these positions and held the imperative to be an instrument for decreeing only obligatory acts. Whenever the imperative is construed as inducing a legal value other than obligation, this construal would have to be based on evidence extraneous to the imperative form in question. Conversely, whenever the imperative form stands apart from any contextual evidence *(qarīna)*, it must be presumed to convey an obligation.

Once adopted by the majority, the position that the imperative form, in the absence of contextual evidence, indicates obligation was given added support by arguments developed by a number of leading jurists. The chief argument (drawn, as would be expected, from both the Qurʾān and the sunna) is that when God commanded Muslims to perform certain acts, he meant them as obligations that can only be violated on pain of punishment: "When it is said unto them: Bow down, they bow not down! Woe unto the repudiators on that day" (Q 77:48-9).

A corollary of the determination of linguistic signification is that the jurist needs to reconcile conflicting texts relevant to a particular case whose solution is pending. He must first attempt to harmonize them so that each may be brought to bear upon a solution to the case. But should the texts prove to be so contradictory as to be incapable of harmonization, the jurist must resort to the theory of abrogation *(naskh)* with a view to determining which of the two texts repeals the other. Thus, abrogation involves the replacement of one text, which would have otherwise had a legal effect, by another one embodying a legal value contradictory to the first.

Elaboration of the theory of abrogation

The juridical justification for the theory of abrogation derives from the common idea, sanctioned by consensus, that the religion of Islam abrogated many, and sometimes all, of the laws upheld by the earlier religions (see SCRIPTURE AND THE QURʾĀN; RELIGIOUS PLURALISM AND THE QURʾĀN). It is a fundamental creed, furthermore, that Islam not only deems these religions legitimate but also considers itself to be the bearer of their legacy. That the Prophet repealed his predecessors' laws therefore goes to prove that abrogation is a valid hermeneutical instrument, one which is specifically approved in Q 2:106: "Such of our revelation as we abrogate or cause to be forgotten, we bring (in place) one better or the like thereof," and Q 16:101: "When we put a revelation in place of another, and God knows best what he reveals, they say: 'Lo, you are but inventing. Most of them know not.'" These verses were taken to show that abrogation is applicable to revelation within Islam.

It must be stressed that the wide majority of jurists espoused the view that it is not the texts themselves which are actually abrogated, but rather the legal rulings comprised in these texts. The text *qua* text is not subject to repeal, for to argue that God revealed conflicting and even contradictory statements would entail that one of the statements is false, which would in turn lead to the highly objectionable conclusion that God has revealed an untruth.

Why there should be, in the first place, conflicting and even contradictory rulings is not a question in which the jurists were very interested. That such rulings existed, however, was undeniable and that they should be made to abrogate one another was deemed a necessity. The criteria that determined which text abrogates another mainly revolved around the chronology of qurʾānic revelation and the diachronic sequence of the Prophet's career. Certain later texts simply abrogated earlier ones.

But is it possible that behind abrogation there are latent divine considerations at work mitigating the severity of the repealed rulings? Only a minority of jurists appears to have maintained that since God is merciful and compassionate he aimed at reducing hardships for his creatures (see MERCY). Abrogating a lenient ruling by a less lenient or a harsher one would run counter to his attribute as a merciful God. Besides, God himself had pronounced that "He desires for you ease, and he desires no hardship" (Q 2:185). Accordingly, repealing a ruling by a harsher one would contravene his own pronouncement. Their opponents, however, rejected this argument. They maintained that to say that God cannot repeal a ruling by another which involves added hardship would be tantamount to saying that he cannot, or does not, impose hardships in his law, and this is plainly false. Furthermore, this argument would lead to the absurd conclusion that he cannot cause someone to be ill after having been healthy or blind after having enjoyed perfect vision (see ILLNESS AND HEALTH; VISION AND BLINDNESS). They reject the aforementioned qurʾānic verse (Q 2:185) as an invalid argument since it bears exclusively upon hardships involved in a quite specific and limited context, namely, the fast of Ramaḍān (q.v.). They likewise reject their opponents' interpretation of the qurʾānic verse 2:106, which states that God abrogates a verse only to introduce in its place another that is either similar to, or better than it. What is "better," they argue, is not necessarily that which is more lenient and more agreeable but rather that which is ultimately more rewarding in this life and in the hereafter (see REWARD AND PUNISHMENT; ESCHATOLOGY). And since the reward is greater, it may well be that the abrogating text comprises a less lenient ruling than that which was abrogated.

Criteria for abrogation

If God's motives for abrogation cannot be determined, then these motives cannot serve to establish which of the two conflicting legal rulings should repeal the other. The criteria of abrogation must thus rest elsewhere. The first, and most convincing criterion may be found in an explicit statement in the abrogating text, stating, for instance, that it was revealed specifically in order to repeal another. The second is the chronological order of revelation, namely, that a later text, in point of time, repeals an earlier one. The difficulty that arises here is to determine the chronology of texts. The first obvious evidence is one that appears in the text itself, as with the previous criterion. But such explicit statements are admittedly difficult to come by. Most conflicting texts therefore have to be dated by external evidence.

The third criterion is consensus. Should the community, represented by its scholars, agree to adopt one ruling in preference to another, then the latter is deemed abrogated since the community cannot agree on an error. The very fact of abandoning one ruling in favor of another is tantamount to abrogating the disfavored ruling. A number of jurists, however, rejected consensus as having the capability to abrogate, their argument being that any consensus must be based on the revealed texts, and if these texts contain no evidence of abrogation in the first place, then consensus as a sanctioning instrument cannot decide in such a matter. To put it differently, since consensus cannot go beyond the evidence of the texts, it is the texts and only the texts that determine whether or not one ruling can abrogate another. If a ruling subject to consensus happened to abrogate another conflicting ruling, the abrogation would be based on evidence existing in the texts, not on consensus.

If consensus is rejected as incapable on its own of abrogating a ruling, it is because of a cardinal principle in the theory of abrogation which stipulates that derivative principles cannot be employed to abrogate all or any part of the source from which they are derived. This explains why consensus and juridical inference *(qiyās),* both based on the Qurʾān and the sunna, were deemed by the great majority of jurists, and in fact by mainstream Sunnism, to lack the power to repeal either prophetic reports or qurʾānic verses.

The other cardinal principle, to which resort is quite often made in jurisprudential arguments, is that an epistemologically inferior text cannot repeal a superior one. Thus a text whose truth or authenticity is only presumed (= probable: *ẓannī*) can by no means abrogate another text qualified as certain *(qaṭʿ, yaqīn)*. On the other hand, texts which are considered of equal epistemological value or of the same species may repeal one another. This principle seems to represent an extension of Q 2:106 which speaks of abrogating verses and replacing them by similar or better ones. Hence, it is a universal principle that, like the Qur'ān, concurrent prophetic reports *(mutawātir)* may abrogate one another. The same rule applies in fact to solitary reports *(āḥād)*. Furthermore, according to the logic of this principle, an epistemologically superior text can abrogate an inferior one. Thus the Qur'ān and the concurrent sunna may abrogate solitary reports, but not vice versa.

Within the Qur'ān and the sunna, moreover, a text expressing a pronouncement *(qawl)* may repeal another text of the same species, just as a text embodying a deed *(fiʿl)* may repeal another text of the same kind. Moreover, in conformity with the principle that a superior text may repeal an inferior one, the abrogation of a "deed-text" by a "pronouncement-text" is deemed valid. For the latter is equal to the former in that it represents a statement relative to a particular ruling, but it differs from the former in one important respect: namely, that a "pronouncement-text" transcends itself and is semantically brought to bear upon other situations, whereas the "deed-text" is confined to the very situation which gave rise to it in the first place. A "deed-text" bespeaks an action that has taken place; it is simply a statement of an event. A "pronouncement-text," on the other hand, may include a command or a generalization that could have ramifications extending beyond the context in which it was uttered. Q 6:135 and 155, taken to be "pronouncement-texts," enjoin Muslims to follow the Prophet. So does Q 33:21: "Verily, in the messenger of God you have a good example *(uswatun)*."

Since one qur'ānic verse can repeal another, it was commonly held that a verse may abrogate a prophetic report, particularly because the Qur'ān is deemed to be of a more distinguished stature. In justification of this view, some jurists further argued that since the Qur'ān is accepted as capable of particularizing the sunna, it can just as easily abrogate it. Other jurists, while adopting the position that the Qur'ān can repeal the sunna, rejected the argument from particularization. Particularization, they held, represents an imperfect analogy with abrogation — the latter entails a total replacement of one legal text by another, whereas the former does not involve abrogation, but merely delimits the scope of a text so as to render it less ambiguous.

Qur'ān and sunna

The qur'ānic abrogation of the sunna has also historical precedent to recommend it. One such precedent was the Prophet's peace treaty with the Qurayshīs (see QURAYSH) of Mecca (q.v.) whereby he agreed to return to Mecca all those who converted to Islam as well as those who wished to join his camp. But just before sending back a group of women who had adopted Islam as a religion, Q 60:10 was revealed, ordering Muslims not to continue with their plans, thereby abrogating the Prophet's practice as expressed in the treaty. Another instance of qur'ānic abrogation is found in verses Q 2:144 and 2:150, which command Muslims to pray in the direction of Mecca instead of Jerusalem (q.v.), the direction which the Prophet had earlier decreed to be valid (see QIBLA).

More controversial was the question of

whether the sunna can repeal the Qurʾān. Those who espoused the view that the Qurʾān may not be abrogated by the sunna advanced Q 2:106 which, as we have seen, states that if God repeals a verse, he does so only to replace it by another which is either similar to, or better than it. The sunna, they maintained, is neither equal to, or better than the Qurʾān, and thus no report can repeal a qurʾānic verse. On the basis of the same verse they furthermore argued that abrogation rests with God alone, and that this precludes the Prophet from having the capacity to abrogate.

On the other hand, the proponents of the doctrine that the sunna can abrogate the Qurʾān rejected the view that the Prophet did not possess this capacity, for while it is true that he could act alone, he did speak on behalf of God when he undertook to abrogate a verse. The central argument of the proponents of this view, however, revolved around epistemology: both the Qurʾān and the concurrent reports yield certitude, and being of equal epistemological status, they can abrogate each other. Opponents of this argument rejected it on the grounds that consensus also leads to certainty but lacks the power to repeal. Moreover, they maintained, the epistemological equivalence of the two sources does not necessarily mean that there exists a mutuality of abrogation. Both solitary reports and *qiyās,* for instance, lead to probable knowledge, and yet the former may serve to abrogate, whereas the latter may not. The reason for this is that these reports in particular, and the sunna in general, constitute the principal source *(aṣl)* from which the authority for *qiyās* is derived. A derivative can by no means repeal its own source and since, it was argued, the Qurʾān is the source of the sunna as well as superior to it, the sunna can never repeal the Qurʾān.

Another disagreement with far-reaching consequences arose concerning the ability of solitary reports to repeal the Qurʾān and the concurrent sunna. One group of jurists, espousing the view that solitary reports can abrogate the Qurʾān and concurrent sunna, maintained that their position was defensible not only by rational argument but that such abrogation had taken place at the time of the Prophet. Rationally, the mere notion that a certain solitary report can substitute for a particular concurrent sunna or a qurʾānic verse is sufficient proof that this sunna or verse lacks the certitude that is otherwise associated with it. Since certainty is lacking, the solitary report would not be epistemologically inferior to the Qurʾān and the concurrent sunna, and therefore capable of abrogating the latter. It was further argued that solitary reports had been commonly accepted as capable of particularizing the concurrent sunna and the Qurʾān, and that if they had the power to particularize, they must have the power to repeal. But the most convincing argument in support of this position was perhaps that which drew on the dynamics of revelation at the time of the Prophet. A classical case in point is Q 2:180, which decrees that "It is prescribed for you, when death approaches one of you, if he has wealth, that he bequeath unto parents and near relatives (see FAMILY; KINSHIP) in kindness." This verse, some jurists maintained, was abrogated by the solitary report "No bequest in favor of an heir." Since parents and near relatives are considered by the Qurʾān as heirs, Q 2:180 was considered repealed, this constituting clear evidence that solitary reports can repeal the Qurʾān and, *a fortiori,* the concurrent sunna.

The opponents of this doctrine rejected any argument which arrogated to solitary reports an epistemological status equal to that of the Qurʾān and the concurrent sunna. The very possibility, they argued, of casting doubt on the certainty generated by these texts is *a priori* precluded. As they saw it, solitary reports, being presumptive to the core, can by no means repeal the Qur᾿ān or concurrent reports. Furthermore, any attempt at equating particularization with abrogation is nullified by the fact that particularization involves the substitution of partial textual evidence for other evidence by bringing two texts to bear, conjointly, upon the solution of a given legal problem. Abrogation, in contrast, and by definition, entails the complete substitution of one text for another, the latter becoming devoid of any legal effect. The example of *qiyās* served to bolster this argument: this method of legal inference is commonly accepted as capable of particularizing the Qur᾿ān and the sunna but it cannot, by universal agreement, repeal these sources. Finally, opponents of this doctrine dismissed the occurrence of abrogation on the basis of a solitary report in the case of bequests as an instance of faulty hermeneutics. The solitary report "No bequest in favor of an heir" did not, they insisted, abrogate the aforementioned qur᾿ānic verse. Rather, the verse was abrogated by Q 4:11 which stipulates that parents, depending on the number and the degree of relation of other heirs, must receive fixed shares of the estate after all debts have been settled and the bequest allocated to its beneficiary. The specification that the parents' shares are determined *subsequent* to the allocation of the bequest is ample proof that it is this verse which repealed Q 2:180, and not the solitary report. If anything, these jurists argued, this report served only to confirm the qur᾿ānic abrogation, a fact made clear in the first part of the report — a part usually omitted by those who used it to support their case for the abrogation of qur᾿ānic verses by solitary reports. In its entirety, the report reads as follows: "God has given each one his due right; therefore, no bequest to an heir." The attribution of the injunction to God, it is argued, is eloquent confirmation that the Prophet acknowledged and merely endorsed the abrogation of Q 2:180 by Q 4:11.

The Qur᾿ān in later legal discourse

The preceding outline represents the mainstream juristic discourse on the Qur᾿ān, discourse which was to dominate legal theory until the nineteenth century. Nonetheless, there were a number of theoretical attempts to formulate different legal concepts of the Qur᾿ān's function in law. The most notable and influential of these was al-Shāṭibī's (d. 790/1388) singular and creative doctrine.

Al-Shāṭibī's holistic theory

Going beyond the conventional, atomistic view of the Qur᾿ān, al-Shāṭibī presents us with a unique theory in which the text is seen as an integral whole, where one verse or part cannot be properly understood without reference not only to other parts but also to the particular and general circumstances in which the text was revealed *(asbāb al-nuzūl)*. Without such a referential approach, the meaning of the verses and the intention of God behind revealing them will not be intelligible to the human mind. All this, however, presupposes full knowledge of the linguistic conventions prevalent among the Arabs during the time of revelation (see ARABIC LANGUAGE; LANGUAGE, CONCEPT OF). God addressed the Arabs in a language they understood with reference to a reality that was specifically theirs, and since both language and reality may — and al-Shāṭibī implies that they do — differ from later usages and realities, the jurist must thoroughly ground himself in the linguistic and historic context of the Qur᾿ān's revelation.

Thus adequate knowledge of the Arabic

language and of the circumstances of revelation, coupled with a holistic reading of the text, can guarantee what al-Shāṭibī deems a reasonable, moderate, and middle-of-the-road interpretation. To be properly understood, a qur᾿ānic verse must be viewed in light of the verses that preceded it in time. Passages in the text revealed later must therefore be explained in terms of the earlier ones just as the entire Medinan revelation must be viewed in light of the Qur᾿ān's Meccan phase. And within each of the phases (Medinan and Meccan), the latter verses are to be interpreted only after full consideration is given to what was revealed earlier. An example of this general principle is the Meccan sūra, Sūrat al-An῾ām (Q 6, "The Cattle"), which embodied a holistic structure of the universal principles *(uṣūl kulliyya)* of the law. Setting aside any part of it will lead to blighting the entire legal system. When the Prophet migrated to Medina (see EMIGRATION), Q 2, Sūrat al-Baqara ("The Cow"), was revealed in order to explicate the general principles of the law. Though some of these details appeared elsewhere, here are found specific laws of ritual, diet, crime, commercial transactions (see BREAKING TRUSTS AND CONTRACTS), marriage, etc. The universal principles established in Q 2 concerning the preservation of one's religion, life, mind, offspring and property are all confirmed in the sūra. Thus what was revealed in Medina subsequent to Sūrat al-Baqara must be viewed in its light. The significance of chronology here can hardly be exaggerated.

That the later sūras and verses explain what was revealed prior to them in time leads to a certain hierarchy in the Qur᾿ān, with the very early sūras being the most comprehensive. Even if a Medinan verse appears general in scope, there must always be a more general verse revealed earlier, the later verses always supplementing the earlier ones. The Meccan revelation thus constitutes the ultimate reference, particularly those parts of it revealed at the outset of the Prophet's career. These latter lay down the most general and universal principles, namely, the protection of the right to religion, life, thought, progeny and property. Later revelation, particularly the Medinan, may complement these principles, but they primarily provide explanations and details relative to these universals.

Whether or not the Qur᾿ān contains all the details of the law, God perfected for Muslims their religion by the time the last verse of the text was revealed. Citing Q 5:3, "Today I have perfected your religion for you," al-Shāṭibī argues that the Qur᾿ān contains all the basic elements of faith, spiritual and practical. It treated of all things and, conversely, nothing that is essential in religion and life stands outside its compass.

The logical consequence of this argument represents no less than a complete relegation of the prophetic sunna to a secondary status and al-Shāṭibī, to be sure, does reach this very conclusion. But though the Qur᾿ān lays down the foundations of the law and religion, no rulings should be extracted from it without consulting the sunna because the latter, just like the Medinan revelation, provides explanation of and detailed annotation to the Qur᾿ān. Nevertheless, al-Shāṭibī affirms the completeness and self-sufficiency of the latter and, in consequence, rejects the view that the sunna offers any substantive addition to the Qur᾿ān.

Al-Shāṭibī's position here is no doubt novel, signaling a total departure from the conventional view propounded in legal theory. He asserts that in the jurisprudent's reasoning about individual legal cases, the Qur᾿ān merits attention before the sunna.

The latter's demotion to second place here is the result of the higher degree of certitude the Qur᾿ān enjoys. While both sources *as a whole* are certain, the individual verses possess a degree of certitude higher than that enjoyed by individual prophetic reports.

The traditional doctrine of legal theory affirms that when the Qur᾿ān is ambiguous on a particular matter, or when it fails to address a given problem with exactitude and clarity, the sunna intervenes to determine the specific intent of the divine lawgiver. A case in point is the qur᾿ānic injunction to cut off the thief's hand. The sunna delimited the qur᾿ānic instruction by decreeing that the punishment can only be imposed when theft is accompanied by breaking and entering and when the value of the stolen goods exceeds a certain prescribed amount. In the same vein, the general qur᾿ānic permission for matrimony was narrowed down by the sunna in the form of a ban on marriage with the maternal or paternal aunt of one's wife. Al-Shāṭibī does accept the authority of the sunna in such cases, but only insofar as it complements the Qur᾿ān. The sunna, in his view, merely brings out and articulates the intention of the Qur᾿ān. If a jurist establishes the exact meaning of a verse, we cannot say, al-Shāṭibī analogically argues, that the ruling based on that verse stems from the authority of the jurist himself. He, like the sunna, functions only as an interpreter of what is ultimately the very word of God.

Al-Shāṭibī on competing evidence in legal cases

When the jurist is presented with two different or contradictory pieces of evidence, both of which enjoy the same degree of certainty — thus precluding the possibility of one superseding the other — the common practice was to choose the evidence that was more suitable to the particular case at hand, even though it might not be qur᾿ānic. Al-Shāṭibī sees no problem with doing so because the evidence in the sunna represents, in the final analysis, an explanation or reformulation of a general qur᾿ānic text. Put differently, the evidential competition is not between the Qur᾿ān and the sunna, but, ultimately, between two different or seemingly contradictory statements within the Qur᾿ān. The latter, al-Shāṭibī reaffirms, contains the essence of the *sharī῾a,* while anything else represents, so to speak, footnotes to the self-sufficient book. Here al-Shāṭibī's hypothetical interlocutor replies by citing a number of qur᾿ānic verses (such as Q 4:59, 5:92, 59:7) to the effect that the Prophet must be obeyed and that his sunna constitutes a source of authority equal to that of the Qur᾿ān. The specific directive to bow to the Prophet's authority clearly indicates that he did introduce injunctions unspecified in the Qur᾿ān. Several prophetic reports to the same effect are then cited, condemning those who make the Qur᾿ān their sole reference.

But al-Shāṭibī does not see how this evidence refutes his position. When the sunna clarifies a verse pertaining to a particular legal ruling, the same ruling ultimately remains grounded in the Qur᾿ān, not the sunna. Both God and the Prophet presumably bestow on it a certain authority. Distinguishing between the two sanctioning authorities does not entail differentiating between two different rulings. In other words, when the Qur᾿ān calls, as it does, upon believers to obey God and the Prophet, it is understood that the Prophet's authority derives, in the final analysis, from that of God. And since no distinction is being made between two different rulings belonging to a single case, then there is no proof that the sunna contains material that falls outside the compass of the Qur᾿ān.

A major role which the sunna plays vis-à-vis the Qurʾān is to privilege one verse over another in deciding a particular case of law. For instance, the Qurʾān generally permitted the consumption of good food and forbade that of putrid victuals without, however, defining the status of many specific types. The sunna then intervened to decide each kind in accordance with the principles regulated in the Qurʾān, by subsuming certain foods under one legal norm or the other. In this way, the meat of donkeys and certain predatory animals came to be prohibited. Similarly, God forbade the ingestion of inebriants but permitted non-alcoholic beverages. The rationale behind this prohibition was the effect of alcohol on the mind in distracting the Muslim from worshipping his lord, let alone its negative social effects. The sunna interfered here by determining to which of the two categories date-wine and semi-intoxicating beverages belong. On the basis of qurʾānic data, the sunna furthermore articulated the classic dictum that any beverage which inebriates when consumed in large quantities is prohibited even in small quantities.

Al-Shāṭibī on the subsidiarity of the sunna

But all this does not change the fact that the roots of the sunna ultimately lay in the book. Indeed, the sunna may contain some legal subject matter which is found neither in a terse statement of the Qurʾān nor even in its more ambiguous or indirect passages (see DIFFICULT PASSAGES). Yet, its subject matter still has its origins in the Qurʾān. It is al-Shāṭibī's fundamental assumption that each qurʾānic verse or statement possesses multifaceted meanings, some direct and others oblique. While a verse may exist in its own particular context and may appear to have an immediate, obvious meaning, this very verse may, at the same time, manifest another meaning that is identical to those found in other verses. Put differently, a group of verses may have one theme in common which happens to be subsidiary to the main meaning in each verse. The inductive corroboration of one verse by the others lends the common theme a certain authority that would reach the degree of certitude. But whereas this theme remains hidden in the linguistic terrains of the Qurʾān, the sunna reveals it in the form of a prophetic report. The result of one such case of corroboration is the well-known and all-important prophetic report "No injury and counter injury in Islam."

The Qurʾān, however, does provide what al-Shāṭibī characterizes as the most important foundation of the law, namely, the principles that aim to serve the interests of people, be they those of the individual or the community. For, after all, the entire enterprise of the *sharīʿa* was instituted in the interests of Muslims whether these pertain to life in this world or in the hereafter. In order to safeguard these interests, the *sharīʿa* seeks to implement the principles of public welfare. The sunna, in the detail it lends to particular cases, is none other than an extension and detailed elaboration of the all-embracing qurʾānic principles.

By relegating the sunna to a status subsidiary to the Qurʾān and by hierarchically and chronologically structuring qurʾānic material, al-Shāṭibī was aiming at achieving a particular result. He was of the opinion that Meccan revelation, with all its characteristic universality, is general and simple in nature, intended for an unlettered audience (see ILLITERACY). It is addressed to the community at large, to the legal expert and layman alike. Every Muslim, hailing from any walk of life, can comprehend it and can thus heed its injunctions without any intermediary. The Medinan revelation, on the other hand, came down to explicate, in some technical detail, the universal principles laid down earlier. Hence, only the legal experts are equipped to deal with and understand the Medinan text. The complexity of its subject matter simply precludes the layman from confronting it directly.

The universality and generality of the Meccan revelation in effect means that it is devoid of mitigation and juridical license. The Medinan texts were thus revealed in order to modify and qualify the rigor that was communicated at an earlier point in time. Al-Shāṭibī reminds us at this stage that the Ṣūfīs set aside the Medinan licenses and adhered solely to the stringent demands of the Meccan sūras (see ṢŪFISM AND THE QUR'ĀN). He strongly insinuates that the Ṣūfīs attempted to impose their view of the law upon the general public of laymen. By insisting on the intellectual simplicity of the Meccan revelation, al-Shāṭibī was in effect arguing that laymen should be left alone to understand and comply with this revelation. He seems to say that if the Ṣūfīs choose to subject themselves to rigorous piety (q.v.), so be it. But it is not within their legitimate right to impose their will and perception of the law on the community of laymen. In these terms, he addresses himself equally to the jurisconsults who, he advises, must not make evident to the public any of their practices that are unusually strict. It is, therefore, for the purpose of achieving this end that al-Shāṭibī recast the traditional, mainstream qur'ānic methodology in a new form.

The Qur'ān in modern legal reform

It is to be stressed that of all traditional sources and legal elements, the Qur'ān alone survives largely intact in modern thinking with respect to the sources of law. The prophetic ḥadīth is being largely and progressively marginalized; consensus is being radically reformulated and recast to fit western principles of parliamentary democracy; *qiyās* has been largely abandoned; public interest *(maṣlaḥa, istiṣlāḥ)* and juristic preference *(istiḥsān)* are still being invoked, but they too are being laden with modern notions which would render them unrecognizable to a traditional jurist.

While it is true, however, that the Qur'ān survives intact in the sense that no change has been effected in the perception of its contents and authority (see CONTEMPORARY CRITICAL PRACTICES AND THE QUR'ĀN; EXEGESIS OF THE QUR'ĀN: EARLY MODERN AND CONTEMPORARY), it has, as have all the other sources, been stripped of the traditional interpretive tools that were employed in exploiting its positive legal repertoire. Thus, such notions as the ambiguous, univocal and metaphorical are no longer deemed pertinent for the modern legal interpretation of the text.

Much of the law of personal status in the Muslim world today still derives from the *sharīʿa,* although certain changes and modifications in this law have taken place. The Qur'ān afforded a good deal of subject matter in the construction of family law, a fact which explains why the reformers have been reluctant to affect fundamental reform in a legal sphere that has been for centuries so close to the heart of Muslims.

But the fact remains that the modern law of Muslim states has no theoretical, religious or intellectual backing. Realizing the total collapse of traditional legal theory, *uṣūl al-fiqh,* a number of twentieth-century Muslim intellectuals have attempted to formulate a theoretical substitute for the traditional methodology of the law. The great majority of reformers have been unsuccessful in their quest to construct a new theoretical function for the Qur'ān. To varying degrees, they have intentionally or otherwise abandoned the traditional theoretical apparatus and yet at the same time have failed to locate a theoretical substitute that is direly needed. Many have reduced the law to a fairly narrow utilitarian concept, thereby relegating revelation to a position subservient to utilitarian imperatives. One of the most notable reformers, and one in whose theory the Qur'ān plays a major role, is the Pakistani scholar and intellectual Fazlur Rahman (d. 1988).

Rahman's method

Rahman takes strong exception to the traditional theory and its authors, blaming them for a fragmented view of the revealed sources, especially the Qur'ān. In his opinion, both the traditional legal theorists and the exegetes treated the Qur'ān verse by verse, and the sunna, report by report. The lack of cross-reference to the textual sources was thus responsible for the absence of an effective *Weltanschauung* that is cohesive and meaningful for life as a whole. A central ingredient in the task of understanding the qur'ānic message as a unity is to analyze it against a background, and that background is the Arabian society in which Islam first arose. Thus a thorough understanding of the Meccan social, economic and tribal institutions becomes necessary in order to understand the import of revelation for the purpose of universalizing it beyond the context of the Prophet's career.

In an attempt to explain the significance of understanding the Qur'ān as a whole and within a situational context, Rahman takes the case of alcoholic beverages, declared prohibited by the traditional jurists. As we have already seen, the Qur'ān initially considered alcohol among the blessings of God, along with milk (q.v.) and honey (q.v.; Q 16:66-9). Later, when Muslims moved to Medina, some Companions urged the Prophet to ban alcohol. Consequently, Q 2:219 was revealed, stipulating a qualified prohibition of wine. Thereafter, on two successive occasions (Q 4:43, 5:90-1), wine was finally banned categorically.

From this gradual prohibition of alcohol, the jurists concluded that the last verse, Q 5:90-1, abrogated those which preceded it, and in an attempt to rationalize this abrogation they resorted to what Rahman terms the "law of gradation," according to which the Qur'ān sought to wean Muslims from certain ingrained habits in a piecemeal fashion, instead of commanding a sudden prohibition. Hence, it was necessary to support this law of gradation by other considerations in order to make the contradiction between the various verses intelligible. In the Meccan period, the Muslims were a small minority, constituting an informal community, not a society. It appears, Rahman says, that alcohol consumption in the midst of this community was in no way a common practice. But when the more prominent Meccans converted to Islam at a later stage, there were many who were in the habit of drinking alcohol. The evolution of this minority into a community and then into an informal state coincided with the growing problem of alcohol consumption; hence the final qur'ānic prohibition imposed on all inebriating substances.

It is thus necessary to draw from the isolated verses, which are particular and fragmented in nature, a general principle that embodies the rationale behind a certain ruling. The failure of the traditional jurists to elicit such principles, Rahman argues, has led to chaos. A telling example of this failure may be found in the case of polygamous marriage. In Q 4:2, the Qur'ān alludes to, and forbids, the guardians' abuse and unlawful seizure of the property of orphaned children with whom they were entrusted. In Q 4:127, the Qur'ān says that these guardians should marry the orphaned girls when they come of age rather than return their property to them. Accordingly, in Q 4:3 the Qur'ān says that if the guardians cannot do justice to the orphan's property and if they insist on marrying them, then they may marry up to four, provided that they treat them justly. If they cannot afford them such a treatment, then they must marry only one. On the other hand, Q 4:129 stipulates that it is impossible to do justice among a plurality of wives. Like the case of alcohol, the Qur'ān is seemingly contradictory here: while it permits marriage to four wives if they can be treated with justice, it declares that justice can never be done in a polygamous marriage. But it must not be forgotten, Rahman asserts, that the whole qur'ānic discussion occurred within the limited context of orphaned women, not unconditionally. The traditional jurists deemed the permission to marry up to four wives as carrying a legal force, whereas the demand to do justice to them was considered to be a mere recommendation, devoid of any binding effect. With this interpretation, the traditional jurists turned the issue of polygamy right on its head, taking a specific verse to be binding and the general principle to be a recommendation. In "eliciting general principles of different order from the Qur'ān... the most general becomes the most basic and the most deserving of implementation, while the specific rulings will be subsumed under them" (Rahman, Interpreting the Qur'ān, 49). In accordance with this principle, Rahman argues, the justice verse in polygamous marriages should have been accorded a status superior to that of the specific verse giving permission to marry up to four wives. The priority given to the justice verse in this case is further supported by the recurrent and persistent qur'ānic theme of the need to do justice.

Rahman's "double movement theory"

The task of eliciting general principles from specific rulings in the Qur'ān and the sunna must be undertaken, then, with full consideration of the sociological forces that produced these rulings. Inasmuch as the Qur'ān gives, be it directly or obliquely, the reasons for certain ethical and legal rulings, an understanding of these reasons becomes essential for drawing general principles. The multifaceted ingredients making up the revealed texts, along with those ingredients making up the background of revelation, must therefore "be brought together to yield a unified and comprehensive socio-moral theory squarely based upon the Qur'ān and its *sunna* counterparts" (Rahman, Towards reformulating, 221). But it may be objected that the process of eliciting general principles in this manner is excessively subjective. In refuting this claim, Rahman invokes the fact that the Qur'ān speaks of its own purposes and objectives, a fact that should contribute to minimizing subjectivity. Furthermore, whatever difference of opinion results from the existing subjectivity should be of great value, provided that each opinion is seriously and carefully considered.

This process of eliciting general principles represents the first step towards implementing a new methodology of the law. This methodology consists of two movements of juristic thought, one proceeding from the particular to the general (i.e. eliciting general principles from specific cases), the other from the general to the particular. Hence the designation of Rahman's methodology as "the double movement theory." In the second movement, the general principles elicited from the revealed sources are brought to bear upon the present conditions of Muslim society. This presupposes a thorough understanding of these conditions, equal in magnitude to that required to understand the revealed texts against their background. But since the present situation can never be identical to the prophetic past, and since it could differ from it "in certain important respects," it is required that "we apply those general principles of the Qurʾān (as well as those of the sunna) to the current situation espousing that which is worthy of espousing and rejecting that which must be rejected" (Rahman, Interpreting the Qurʾān, 49). Just what the criteria are for rejecting certain "important respects" and not others is a crucial question that Rahman does not seem to answer decisively. For if these respects are important and yet are capable of being neutralized, then there is no guarantee that essential qurʾānic and sunnaic elements or even principles will not be set aside.

The weakness of Rahman's methodology also lies in the not altogether clear mechanics of the second movement, that is, the application of the systematic principles derived from the revealed texts and their contexts to present-day situations. Furthermore, the relatively few cases which he repeatedly cites in his writings on the subject do not represent the full spectrum of cases in the law, with the result that his methodology may be considered incapable of providing a scope comprehensive enough to afford modern Muslims the methodological means of solving problems different in nature than those he so frequently cites. What of those cases for which a textual statement is available but no information as to the context of its revelation? Or, still, how do modern Muslims address fundamental problems facing their societies when no applicable qurʾānic or sunnaic text can be located? That Rahman does not seem to provide answers for such questions may be a function of his interest in elaborating a methodology confined in outlook to the revealed texts rather than a methodology of law proper.

Wael Hallaq

Bibliography

Primary: al-ʿAbbādī, Aḥmad b. Qāsim, *Sharḥ ʿalā Sharḥ al-Maḥallī ʿalā l-waraqāt,* printed on the margins of al-Shawkānī's *Irshād al-fuḥūl,* Surabaya n.d.; Abū ʿUbayd al-Qāsim b. Sallām, *Kitāb al-Nāsikh wa-l-mansūkh,* ed. J. Burton, Suffolk 1987; al-Āmidī, Abū l-Ḥasan ʿAlī Sayf al-Dīn, *al-Iḥkām fī uṣūl al-aḥkām,* 3 vols., Cairo 1968; al-Bājī, Abū l-Walīd b. Khalaf, *Iḥkām al-fuṣūl fī aḥkām al-uṣūl,* Beirut 1986; Bayḍāwī, *Minhāj al-wuṣūl ilā ʿilm al-uṣūl,* printed with Jamāl al-Dīn al-Asnawī, *Nihāyat al-sūl fī sharḥ minhāj al-wuṣūl ilā ʿilm al-uṣūl lil-Bayḍāwī,* 3 vols., Cairo 1317/1899; al-Bayhaqī, Abū Bakr Aḥmad b. al-Ḥusayn, *Aḥkām al-Qurʾān,* 2 vols., Beirut 1975; al-Bukhārī, ʿAlāʾ al-Dīn, *Kashf al-asrār,* 4 vols., Istanbul 1890, repr. Beirut 1974; Ibn al-Farrāʾ, Abū Yaʿlā l-Baghdādī, *al-ʿUdda fī uṣūl al-fiqh,* ed. A. Mubārakī, 3 vols., Beirut 1980; Muḥammad Ibn Ḥazm, *Muʿjam al-fiqh,* 2 vols., Damascus 1966; Mullā Khusraw, Muḥammad b. ʿAlī, *Mirqāt al-wuṣūl ilā ʿilm al-uṣūl,* Cairo 1902; Muqātil, *Khams miʾa;* al-Shāṭibī, Abū Isḥāq Ibrāhīm, *al-Muwāfaqāt fī uṣūl al-aḥkām,* ed. M. Muḥyī l-Dīn ʿAbd al-Ḥamīd, 4 vols., Cairo 1970; Shuʿla, Muḥammad b. Aḥmad (Abū ʿAbdallāh Shuʿla l-Mūṣilī Ibn al-Muwaqqiʿ), *Ṣafwat al-rāsikh fī ʿilm al-mansūkh wa-l-nāsikh,* ed. R. ʿAbd al-Tawwāb, Cairo 1995; al-Ṭūfī, Najm al-Dīn Sulaymān, *Sharḥ mukhtaṣar al-rawḍa,* ed. ʿA. al-Turkī, 3 vols., Beirut 1987.

Secondary: M.M. Bravmann, *The spiritual background of early Islam,* Leiden 1972; S.P. Brock, Syriac views of emergent Islam, in G.H.A. Juynboll (ed.), *Studies on the first century of Islamic society,* Carbondale, IL 1982, 9-21; J. Burton, *The sources of Islamic law. Islamic theories of abrogation,* Edinburgh 1990; P. Crone and M. Hinds, *God's caliph. Religious authority in the first centuries of Islam,* Cambridge 1986; S.D. Goitein, The birth-hour of Muslim law, in *MW* 50 (1960), 23-9; Y. Goldfeld, The development of theory on qurʾānic exegesis in Islamic scholarship, in *SI* 67 (1988), 6-27; W.B. Hallaq, *A history of Islamic legal theories,* Cambridge 1997; id., The primacy of the Qurʾān in Shāṭibī's legal theory, in id. and D. Little (eds.), *Islamic studies presented to Charles J. Adams,* Leiden 1991, 69-90 (repr. in id., *Law and legal theory in classical and medieval Islam,* Aldershot 1995, XI); F. Rahman, Divine revelation and holy Prophet, in *Pakistan times,* 25 August 1968, 2-5; id., Interpreting the Qurʾān, in *Inquiry* 3 (May 1986), 45-9; id., *Major themes of the Qurʾān,* Minneapolis 1980; id., Some key ethical concepts of the Qurʾān, in *Journal of religious ethics* 11 (1983), 170-85; id., Towards reformulating the methodology of Islamic law, in *New York University journal of international law and politics* 12 (1979),

210-2; A. Rippin, Al-Zuhrī, *naskh al-Qurʾān* and the problem of early *tafsīr* texts, in BSOAS 47 (1984), 22-43; R. Roberts, *The social laws of the Qorân*, London 1925, repr. London 1990 (Eng. trans. of *Familienrecht im Qorân*); M. Sharūr, *al-Kitāb wa-l-Qurʾān. Qirāʾa muʿāṣira*, Cairo 1992; B. Weiss, *The search for God's law. Islamic jurisprudence in the writings of Sayf al-Dīn al-Amidī*, Salt Lake City 1992.

Lawful and Unlawful

That which is legally authorized, and that which is not. Among its various legislative pronouncements, the Qurʾān declares certain objects and actions lawful or unlawful. The words *ḥalāl*, "lawful, allowed, permitted," and *ḥarām*, "unlawful, forbidden, prohibited," and cognate terms from the triliteral roots *ḥ-l-l* and *ḥ-r-m*, respectively, most often designate these two categories and are of relatively frequent occurrence. Qurʾānic declarations of lawfulness or unlawfulness are limited to a relatively few areas of the law as later elaborated by Muslim jurists: for the most part, ritual, family law and dietary matters (see RITUAL AND THE QURʾĀN; FAMILY; MARRIAGE AND DIVORCE; FOOD AND DRINK). On the other hand, the lawful/unlawful rubric also has non-legislative functions in the Qurʾān. Although the seemingly primary categories of *ḥalāl* and *ḥarām* were largely eclipsed by jurisprudential rubrics that were developed subsequently, the terms retained significance in ascetic thought (see ASCETICISM) and have recently become prominent in popular handbooks of religious law.

Vocabulary

Apart from denoting lawfulness, the root *ḥ-l-l* indicates an exit from the ritual state connected with the pilgrimage (q.v.) and re-entry into the profane state (*idhā ḥalaltum*, Q 5:2; see RITUAL PURITY). In this sense, too, it is the antonym of *ḥ-r-m* (see below). Concretely, it refers to dissolution (e.g. Q 66:2, metaphorically, of an oath; see BREAKING TRUSTS AND CONTRACTS; OATHS) and also alighting (e.g. Q 20:86, again metaphorically, of God's wrath; see ANGER). The most common means for indicating lawfulness in the Qurʾān is to use the causative verb *aḥalla*, "to make lawful," usually with God as the subject (e.g. Q 7:157, "He makes the good things lawful for them") but it is sometimes passive (e.g. Q 5:1, concerning certain livestock; see ANIMAL LIFE; BOUNTY). In one instance it occurs in the first person plural, in an address to Muḥammad (Q 33:50; see FORM AND STRUCTURE OF THE QURʾĀN; LANGUAGE AND STYLE OF THE QURʾĀN). Very occasionally, people are made the subject of this verb, to suggest that they wrongly deem something lawful (e.g. Q 9:37, though words derived from *ḥ-r-m* are more common in such accusations; see below). Finally, it should be noted that the intransitive verb *ḥalla*, "to be lawful," occasionally appears in the negative, to indicate that something is not lawful (e.g. Q 2:230, providing that one's wife ceases to be lawful, i.e. available for sexual intercourse, after divorce). The Qurʾān also employs the adjectives *ḥill* and *ḥalāl* to indicate lawfulness (e.g. in Q 5:5 and Q 8:69, respectively, concerning certain foods).

Words derived from the root *ḥ-r-m* not only connote God's making something unlawful but also frequently express the idea of sacredness (see SANCTITY AND THE SACRED), e.g. *al-shahr al-ḥarām*, "the sacred month" (Q 2:194; see MONTHS); *al-ḥaram*, "the sacred precinct," where the Kaʿba (q.v.) is located (Q 28:57); *ḥurum*, persons in the ritual state associated with pilgrimage (e.g. Q 5:1); and *ḥurumāt*, certain sacred ordinances or institutions (Q 2:194; 22:30). The *ḥ-r-m*-derived counterpart to *aḥalla* is the causative verb *ḥarrama*, "to make unlawful," and, as in the case of the former, God is frequently its subject (e.g. Q 2:173, concerning foods). The Qurʾān does not employ an intransitive verb derived from *ḥ-r-m,* making do instead with the passive of *ḥarrama* (e.g. Q 5:3, also concerning foods) and the related passive participle (e.g. Q 6:145, again concerning foods; the corresponding participial form from *aḥalla* is not found in the Qurʾān). A number of passages use *ḥarrama* in the first person plural and in most of these God recounts how he had previously made certain things, especially foods, unlawful for the Jews (Q 4:160; 6:146; 16:118; 28:12; see JEWS AND JUDAISM). The counterpart of the adjective *ḥalāl* is *ḥarām,* though they only appear together twice (Q 10:59; 16:116). There is no *ḥ-r-m*-derived equivalent to the form *ḥill* but in Q 21:95 the Kūfan tradition of variant readings (see READINGS OF THE QURʾĀN) substitutes the word *ḥirm* for *ḥarām* (see Jeffery, *Materials,* e.g. 62, codex of Ibn Masʿūd). Later legal theorists paired *ḥill* with the non-qurʾānic term *ḥurma* (e.g. Fakhr al-Dīn al-Rāzī [d. 606/1210], *Maḥṣūl,* i, 15).

Especially in regard to dietary rules, *ḥalāl* and *ḥarām* parallel to a degree the Levitical categories of clean and unclean, respectively. As noted, though, *ḥalāl* and *ḥarām* also connote profaneness and sacredness, respectively, suggesting a potentially puzzling link between what is sacred and what is unclean. Possibly, a pre-qurʾānic connection existed between sacredness and ritual-related restrictions *(ḥarām)* on the one hand and the profane state and a general lack of restrictions *(ḥalāl)* on the other. Thus, the objects of qurʾānic prohibitions would have been assimilated to a category of ritually mandated restrictions rather than ritual impurity (see Heninger, Pureté). However that may be, the qurʾānic terms are paralleled to some extent by the Hebrew pair *mūtar* and *asūr,* meaning permitted ("loosened," semantically equivalent to *ḥ-l-l*) and forbidden (q.v.; Wansbrough, *QS,* 174).

Certain other terms in the Qurʾān also connote lawfulness and unlawfulness. A number of passages use the word *junāḥ,* "sin," in variants of the phrase "It is not a sin for you to…" as an indirect means of describing lawful activities (e.g. Q 2:198, permitting commercial activity while in the ritual state required of pilgrims; see MARKETS; SELLING AND BUYING; SIN, MAJOR AND MINOR). Rhetorically, passages employing *junāḥ* often imply that the activity in question might have been thought unlawful and hence required clarification. Commentators (see EXEGESIS OF THE QURʾĀN: CLASSICAL AND MEDIEVAL) gloss the word *ḥijr* as meaning *ḥarām* in two passages. In Q 6:138, unnamed persons declare certain produce and livestock *ḥijr,* which means, according to the commentators, that it was declared *ḥarām,* "off-limits, or sacrosanct," in connection with a pagan rite (e.g. Ṭabarī, *Tafsīr,* xii, 139-40). In Q 25:22, the phrase *ḥijr mahjūr* appears in the following sentence: "On the day they see the angels (see ANGEL), there will be no glad tidings then for the wrongdoers, and they will say *ḥijran mahjūran.*" Some commentators attribute the phrase in question to the angels and gloss it as meaning *ḥarām muḥarram,* that is, either paradise (q.v.) or the glad tidings (see GOOD NEWS) will be "strictly forbidden" to the wrongdoers (e.g. Bayḍāwī, *Anwār,* ii, 37). The phrase *ḥijr mahjūr* also appears in Q 25:53, where it seems to refer concretely to physical separation (e.g. Bayḍāwī, *Anwār,* ii, 43), and the word *ḥijr* appears alone in Q 89:5, where it is traditionally understood to mean "intelligence" (e.g. Bayḍāwī, *Anwār,* ii, 401; see INTELLECT; KNOWLEDGE AND LEARNING). The word *suḥt* appears at Q 5:42 and twice at Q 5:62-3, always in the phrase "eaters/eating of *suḥt*" *(akkālūna lil-suḥti, aklihimu l-suḥta),* an apparently derogatory reference to the Jews. The commentators took *suḥt* to refer either generally to unlawful gain or specifically to bribes accepted by Jewish judges (e.g. Ṭabarī, *Tafsīr,* x, 318-24, 447-8), thus connecting it with the remainder of Q 5:42, in which the Prophet is given permission to adjudicate Jewish legal matters. In Leviticus 22:25, a Hebrew cognate, *mashḥat,* refers to inherent "corruption" or "mutilation" which renders certain ritual offerings unfit (see CONSECRATION OF ANIMALS; CORRUPTION) but the more usual sense of the biblical Hebrew cognate is "destruction," which is how a related Arabic word is used at Q 20:61. According to Jeffery (*For. vocab.,* 165-6), *suḥt* means "unlawful" in a technical sense. He notes an interesting parallel with the Talmud (Shabb. 140b, discussing the principle of *bal tashḥīt* derived from *Deut* 20:19) but opts for a Syriac origin of the word (*sūḥtā,* "depravity, corruption"). The remainder of this discussion deals only with words derived from the roots *ḥ-l-l* and *ḥ-r-m.*

What is lawful and unlawful?

As noted above, qurʾānic declarations of lawfulness and unlawfulness pertain mostly to ritual, dietary law and family law. For example, Q 5:96 declares the hunting of land animals while in the ritual state for the pilgrimage to have been outlawed *(ḥurrima)* but fishing and eating the catch lawful (*uḥilla,* see HUNTING AND FISHING). In regard to dietary matters, the most prominent and oft-repeated rule provides that God has made unlawful *(ḥarrama)* carrion (q.v.), blood, swine flesh and what is consecrated to other than God (Q 2:173; 16:115; and with slight variations at Q 5:3 and 6:145). The largest number of rules that use this rubric concern family law. Q 4:22-4, for example, details which women have been made unlawful *(ḥurrimat)* to marry and which lawful *(uḥilla).* A noteworthy principle of Islamic commercial law at Q 2:275 provides that God made lawful *(aḥalla)* sales transactions and forbade *(ḥarrama)* usury (q.v.).

In contrast to the many overtly legislative passages which pronounce on lawfulness and unlawfulness, other passages employ the lawful/unlawful rubric to suggest that the Muslims are, perhaps, subject to fewer legal restrictions than previous communities. Several such passages use words derived from the roots *ḥ-l-l* and *ṭ-y-b* to suggest that God has begun to expand the category of the lawful, as in Q 5:5: "Today the good things *(al-ṭayyibāt)* have been made lawful for you *(uḥilla lakum)*" (see also Q 2:172-3 [with *ḥ-r-m*]; 5:4, 88; 7:157; 16:114). Other passages contain an implicit or explicit charge that certain human beings have mistakenly declared things lawful or unlawful (mostly the latter). These fall into three main groups: those in which people are enjoined not to outlaw what God has provided (Q 5:87; 6:140; 7:32; 10:59); those which generally complain that people have wrongly forbidden or made lawful unspecified things (Q 6:148; 9:29; 16:35, 116; 66:1); and those in which people are accused of wrongly outlawing (or permitting) certain specified things, mostly in connection with pagan practices (see generally Q 6:138-50; 9:37; see IDOLATRY AND IDOLATERS).

Finally, several passages use the lawful/unlawful rubric to suggest that the Jews labored under a more burdensome law than the Muslims, either because the former created unnecessary rules (Q 3:93) or because God wished to punish them (Q 4:160; 6:146; 16:118). The process of repealing this more onerous law imposed on the Jews apparently begins with Jesus (q.v.), who says in Q 3:50 that he has come as a confirmation of the Torah (q.v.), to make lawful *(li-uḥilla)* some of the things which had previously been forbidden (*ḥurrima,* compare *Matt* 5:17-9, in which Jesus denies that he has come to relax the Law).

Post-qurʾānic developments

Early commentators, such as Ibn ʿAbbās (d. 68/687) and Muḥammad al-Kalbī (d. 146/763) are said to have recognized declarations of lawfulness and unlawfulness *(ḥalāl wa-ḥarām)* as one among several fundamental modes of qurʾānic discourse (Versteegh, *Arabic grammar,* 64, 106; see also Wansbrough, *QS,* 149, 173-4; see LITERARY STRUCTURES OF THE QURʾĀN). Exegetes and legal theorists, however, soon moved beyond this basic qurʾānic distinction. The commentator and grammarian al-Farrāʾ (d. 207/822), for example, differentiates between qurʾānic prohibitions (sing. *nahy*) which aim merely to inculcate proper etiquette *(adab)* and those which function to outlaw something (*nahy muḥarrim;* Kinberg, *Lexicon,* 863). This move marks the extraction of an abstracted and generalized concept of unlawfulness (and implicitly lawfulness), inferable from a text's language and capable of being applied and elaborated outside the confines of those qurʾānic passages that used the root *ḥ-r-m (*or *ḥ-l-l).* Al-Shāfiʿī (d. 204/820), for example, applied this same *adab/taḥrīm* distinction to prophetic ḥadīth (Shāfiʿī, *Risāla,* par. 926-60; see ḤADĪTH AND THE QURʾĀN).

Scrutiny of the variously formulated legislative provisions in revealed texts, and speculation on their potentially disparate legal consequences, led jurists to a theory of gradations of legal obligation. More precisely, legal theorists developed a classificatory scheme of moral evaluations *(aḥkām,* sing. *ḥukm)* to which all human acts could be assigned: mandatory *(wājib),* recommended *(mandūb),* merely permitted *(mubāḥ),* disapproved *(makrūh),* and forbidden *(ḥarām* or *maḥẓūr).* In a sense, the first four categories could be considered refinements of what is *ḥalāl* (Jackson, *Islamic law,* 118) but it is really only the outer categories of mandatory and forbidden that have the force of rules (Weiss, *The spirit,* 18-9), and they do not parallel the categories of *ḥalāl* and *ḥarām* (*ḥalāl*/lawful being a broader and different sort of category than *wājib*/ mandatory). This graded scale eclipsed the fundamental qurʾānic binary of *ḥalāl/ ḥarām,* which came to be applied only in much more limited fashion to certain things (e.g. wine [q.v.; see also INTOXICANTS]) and persons (e.g. potential spouses; Schacht, *Introduction,* 121 n. 2; see PROHIBITED DEGREES). Contrasting with these developments in speculative legal hermeneutics, there emerged a pietistic tendency to view the world as fundamentally divisible into realms of lawfulness and unlawfulness. This "scrupulosity" (for a good example of which, see Cooperson's description of Aḥmad b. Ḥanbal [d. 241/ 845], *Arabic biography,* 112-8) may, perhaps, be considered a concern with ritual purity in the widest possible sense, but is in any event connected with the rise to prominence of the traditionists, part of whose "programme" was "to identify the categories 'forbidden' and 'invalid' " (Schacht, *Introduction,* 46). The great theologian al-Ghazālī (d. 505/1111) may be said to have reconciled to some extent the legal-hermeneutical and ethical-ascetic uses of the lawful/unlawful rubric in Book xiv of his *Iḥyāʾ ʿulūm al-dīn* (Revivification of the religious sciences), the *Kitāb al-ḥalāl wa-l-ḥarām* ("Book of the lawful and the unlawful," Fr. trans. R. Morelon, *Le livre du licite et de l'illicite*). Al-Ghazālī criticizes the view that the world has become so corrupted that one is no longer in a position to observe the distinction between *ḥalāl* and *ḥarām.* He insists, rather, that scrupulosity *(waraʿ),* an even stricter standard than *ḥarām,* is still possible. Practicing *waraʿ*

requires that one avoid not only what is *ḥarām* but also many things (and actions) which, though technically *ḥalāl,* possess the quality of *shubha,* "dubiousness" (for the more usual technical legal meaning of which, see Rowson, Shubha). Al-Ghazālī's technically accomplished analysis represents an interesting application of speculative modes of juridical thinking to an anti-theoretical, pietistic concern (see THEOLOGY AND THE QUR'ĀN).

In recent times, a number of popular books giving practical guidance on the application of Islamic law in everyday life take the categories of lawful and unlawful as their organizing principle. A prominent such work is *al-Ḥalāl wa-l-ḥarām fī l-Islām* (Eng. trans. *The lawful and the prohibited in Islam*) by Yūsuf al-Qaraḍāwī (b. 1926). In the introduction, al-Qaraḍāwī says that he is the first to author a work devoted entirely to the topic of *ḥalāl* and *ḥarām.* Whatever al-Ghazālī might have thought of that claim, al-Qaraḍāwī's work unleashed a virtual flood of books (some critical of al-Qaraḍāwī for his liberal views) devoted to distinguishing the *ḥalāl* from the *ḥarām* in daily life. Such works, including that of al-Qaraḍāwī, are now widely available in languages other than Arabic. Their contents derive, however, from the subsequently developed categories of classical Islamic law and, as such, they extend well beyond qur'ānic declarations of lawfulness and unlawfulness, to cover the full range of activities possible in contemporary life. See also LAW AND THE QUR'ĀN; ETHICS AND THE QUR'ĀN.

Joseph E. Lowry

Bibliography

Primary: Bayḍāwī, *Anwār;* al-Ghazālī, Abū Ḥāmid Muḥammad, *Iḥyā' 'ulūm al-dīn,* 5 vols., Cairo 1967, v, 2, 112-99 (Ger. trans. H. Bauer, Erlaubtes und verbotenes Gut, in *Islamische Ethik,* 4 vols., Halle/Saale 1916-40, iii; Fr. trans. R. Morelon, *Le livre du licite et de l'illicite,* Paris 1981, 1991[2] [rev. ed.]); Y. al-Qaraḍāwī, *al-Ḥalāl wa-l-ḥarām fī l-Islām,* Cairo 1960 (Eng. trans. K. El-Helbawy et al., *The lawful and the prohibited in Islam,* Indianapolis 198-); Rāzī, *al-Maḥṣūl fī uṣūl al-fiqh,* 2 vols., Beirut 1988; al-Shāfi'ī, Muḥammad b. Idrīs, *al-Risāla,* ed. A. Shākir, Cairo 1940; Ṭabarī, *Tafsīr,* ed. Shākir.
Secondary: M. Cooperson, *Classical Arabic biography,* Cambridge 2000; J. Henninger, Pureté et impureté, in H. Cazelles and A. Feuillet (eds.), *Supplément au Dictionnaire de la Bible,* Paris 1973, ix, cols. 460-70 (Arabic); T. Izutsu, *Concepts,* 237-41; S. Jackson, *Islamic law and the state,* Leiden 1996; Jeffery, *For. vocab.;* id., *Materials;* N. Kinberg, *A Lexicon of al-Farrā''s terminology in his Qur'ān commentary,* Leiden 1996; A. Rippin, Qur'ān 21:95. 'A ban is on any town,' in *JSS* 24 (1979), 43-53, repr. in id., *The Qur'ān and its interpretative tradition,* Aldershot 2001, article VII; E. Rowson, Shubha, in *EI*[2], ix, 492-3; J. Schacht, *An introduction to Islamic law,* Oxford 1965 (rev. ed.); C. Versteegh, *Arabic grammar and qur'ānic exegesis in early Islam,* Leiden 1993; Wansbrough, *QS;* B. Weiss, *The spirit of Islamic law,* Athens, GA 1998.

Laziness

see VIRTUES AND VICES, COMMANDING AND FORBIDDING

Leader

see KINGS AND RULERS; IMĀM

Leaf

see WRITING AND WRITING INSTRUMENTS; SCROLLS; TREES

Learning

see KNOWLEDGE AND LEARNING

Leather

see HIDES AND FLEECE; ANIMAL LIFE

Left Hand and Right Hand

The terminal part of each arm, often with connotations of evil and good, respectively (see GOOD AND EVIL; HANDS). The left hand *(shimāl,* pl. *shamā'il, mash'ama)* and the right hand *(yamīn,* pl. *aymān, maymana)* appear in the Qur'ān in two contexts: first, the *ḥisāb,* a record or statement of personal deeds to be given to every person on the day of judgment (*yawm al-dīn,* see LAST JUDGMENT; RECORD OF HUMAN ACTIONS); second, the placement of the resurrected (see RESURRECTION) before they are sent off to either paradise (q.v.) or hell (see HELL AND HELLFIRE). In this connection, the left hand or the left side is attested six times and the right hand or the right side fourteen times.

Those who refused to believe in the resurrection or persisted in their terrible sins (*al-ḥinth al-ʿaẓīm,* frequently explained as polytheism; see POLYTHEISM AND ATHEISM; SIN, MAJOR AND MINOR) will receive their record in their left hand (Q 56:41; 69:25) and will regret having relied on their wealth or power (*sulṭān,* Q 69:25-9). They are identified as *al-ḍāllūn al-mukadhdhibūn* (those who erred and denied Muḥammad's prophethood, Q 56:51; see ASTRAY; ERROR; OPPOSITION TO MUḤAMMAD). They will be punished (see REWARD AND PUNISHMENT) with burning winds (see AIR AND WIND) and boiling waters (see WATER) and will eat of a tree called Zaqqūm (Q 56:9, 41-56; see AGRICULTURE AND VEGETATION); they will be fettered with a chain seventy cubits long and will roast in hell (Q 56:92-4; 69:30-7; 84:10-25; 90:19-20). In contrast, those who followed their *imām* (q.v.; generally explained as prophets or holy books; see BOOK; PROPHETS AND PROPHETHOOD) and performed good deeds (q.v.) such as freeing a slave (see SLAVES AND SLAVERY), feeding an orphan (see ORPHANS) in famine (q.v.) or exhorting one another to show pity and compassion will be given their record (*kitāb*) in their right hand (Q 17:71; 90:12-8). Their reckoning will be easy (Q 84:7-9) and their light (q.v.) will run forward before them and by their right hands (Q 57:12; 66:8). Their abode will be paradise, there to be served by immortal boys while enjoying spreading shade, plentiful waters, abundant fruits and perfect virgins (Q 56:8, 27-40, 90-1; 69:19-24; see HOURIS). They include a group from among the pre-Muḥammadan believers (*al-sābiqūn*) and Muḥammad's followers (*al-ākhirūn,* cf. Muqātil, *Tafsīr,* iv, 219). They will ask one another about those who entered hell (*saqar,* Q 74:39-56; cf. 90:18 f.).

Exegetes (see EXEGESIS OF THE QURʾĀN: CLASSICAL AND MEDIEVAL) deal extensively with these topics, using traditions attributed to the Prophet, to his Companions (see COMPANIONS OF THE PROPHET) or even to *quṣṣāṣ* (preachers and tellers of legends; see ḤADĪTH AND THE QURʾĀN). They make a connection between *aṣḥāb al-mashʾama* (Q 56:9) or *aṣḥāb al-shimāl* (Q 56:41) with those who will be given their records (*kitāb*) in their left hand, and *aṣḥāb al-maymana* (Q 56:8) or *aṣḥāb al-yamīn* (Q 56:38, 90-1) with those who will be given their *kitāb* in their right hand. The term *al-mutalaqqiyāni* recorded in Q 50:17-8 is explained as referring to the two "recording angels" sitting (*qaʿīd*), one on the right of each human being, recording his good acts (*ḥasanāt*) and one on the left recording his sins (Ibn al-Jawzī, *Tabṣira,* ii, 254). These records form the *ṣaḥāʾif al-aʿmāl,* which will be presented during the final reckoning and judgment. Exegetes tried to elaborate and complete the qurʾānic picture of the various elements that constitute this special phase of the last judgment. Since the qurʾānic references to this reckoning are abundant but not always sequenced, there were many attempts to assign a chronological order to the different stages of this critical process. The most prevalent accounts assert that after the resurrection each person will be escorted by his two recording angels (Qurṭubī, *Tadhkira,* i, 295-6). All will be gathered in the courtyards (*ʿaraṣāt al-qiyāma*). Those who receive their *kitāb*s in their left hands or behind their backs (*warāʾa ẓahrihi,* Q 84:10; the explanation of receiving the book behind the back is that the right hands of these people will be fettered to their necks and their left hands will be turned to their backs, Ibn Kathīr, *Tafsīr,* viii, 378-9 ad Q 84:7-10) will regret that death was not their final step and that now they must be judged (see JUDGMENT). Their good deeds will be annulled and their bad deeds (see EVIL DEEDS) will be doubled in order to double their penalty (Qurṭubī, *Jāmi*ʿ, xix, 271-3 ad Q 84:7-10). Their reckoning *(ḥisāb)* will be discussed, that discussion being a sign of their imminent punishment. Those who receive their *kitāb*s in their right hands will undergo an "easy reckoning" (*ḥisāb yasīr,* Q 84:7) consisting merely of a simple *ʿarḍ,* God's review or inspection of the resurrected (Qurṭubī, *Tadhkira,* i, 382), and will rejoin their relatives in paradise. Al-Ḥasan al-Baṣrī (d. 110/728) speaks about three *ʿurūḍ,* the first and the second comprising elements of discussion *(jidāl)* and excuse *(maʿādhīr),* the third, the scattering of the sheets (*taṭāyur al-ṣuḥuf,* Ibn Kathīr, *al-Nihāya,* ii, 41). In some sources, these records *(kutub)* are connected with the *mawāzīn,* "balances" (recorded in Q 7:8, 9; 23:102, 103; 101:6, 8; see INSTRUMENTS; WEIGHTS AND MEASURES). The good deeds will tilt the balance and open the way to paradise. Those whose balance of good deeds is too light will be sent to hell (Schimmel, *Deciphering the signs,* 219-41).

There were attempts to interpret the qurʾānic verses dealing with *aṣḥāb al-yamīn* and *aṣḥāb al-shimāl* as references to specific persons or parties (see PARTIES AND FACTIONS). According to al-Zuhrī (d. 124/742), the first two brothers to receive their records will be the Companion Abū Salama b. ʿAbd al-Asad who will receive it in his right hand and the enemy of the Prophet, Sufyān b. ʿAbd al-Asad, who will receive it in his left hand (al-Nabīl, *Awāʾil,* 34, no. 82). Shīʿī sources (see SHĪʿISM AND THE QURʾĀN), citing a tradition attributed to the sixth imām Jaʿfar al-Ṣādiq (d. 148/765), report that Q 69:19 refers to ʿAlī b. Abī Ṭālib (q.v.) as the first to receive his *kitāb* in his right hand and that Q 69:25 refers to Muʿāwiya b. Abī Sufyān or *al-Shāmī laʿanahu llāh,* "the Syrian, may God curse him," who will receive his *kitāb* in his left hand (Qummī, *Tafsīr,* ii, 384; Majlisī, *Biḥār al-anwār,* viii, 518, l. 11-12). A report attributed to ʿAlī b. Abī Ṭālib attests that the *aṣḥāb al-yamīn* in Q 56:27 are *aṭfāl al-muslimīn,* "children of Muslims" (ʿAbd al-Razzāq, *Tafsīr,* ii, 270; Ṭabarī, *Tafsīr,* xxvii, 179). Qatāda (d. ca. 117/735) reportedly interpreted *"min aṣḥābi l-yamīn"* in the verse "'Peace be with you' from those on the right hand" (*fa-salāmun laka min aṣḥābi l-yamīn,* Q 56:91) as meaning "from God" *(min ʿindi llāhi)* or "from his angels" (cf. Ṭabarī, *Tafsīr,* xxvii, 213); but al-Qummī (fl. fourth/tenth cent.; *Tafsīr,* ii, 350) reports that the reference is to *aṣḥāb amīr al-muʾminīn,* meaning the adherents of ʿAlī, the "prince of the believers."

The question of *qadar,* "predestination," (see FREEDOM AND PREDESTINATION) which forms part of the pillars of belief (*arkān al-īmān,* see FAITH; BELIEF AND UNBELIEF) is addressed by most exegetes when they deal with the question of *aṣḥāb al-yamīn* or *aṣḥāb al-shimāl.* Traditions report that Muḥammad appeared one day with two lists, one in each hand: the one in his right hand containing the names of those who will enter paradise, and the other, in his left hand, containing the names of those destined for hell (Tirmidhī, *Ṣaḥīḥ,* no. 2067; Ibn Ḥanbal, *Musnad,* no. 6275). The records *(kutub)* will be distributed before they are examined and each group will be directed to their destiny (q.v.). Since one of the most beautiful names of God (*al-asmāʾ al-ḥusnā,* see GOD AND HIS ATTRIBUTES) is *al-ʿadl,* "the righteous," authors tried, each one according to his creed (see CREEDS) or sectarian affiliation, to harmonize the contradictory qurʾānic statements. This trend led to the belief that the last judgment will be a mere formality. Generally, with the exception of the Muʿtazila (see MUʿTAZILĪS) and the Qadariyya (the group which held the position of free will), authors discussing the problem of the last judgment dealt more with the definition of a believer or unbeliever than with the matter of deeds themselves (Rippin, *Muslims,* 68-82; Gimaret, *Théories,* 335-6 [for the Muʿtazilites]).

According to Q 39:67, on the day of resurrection, "the heavens (see HEAVEN AND SKY) shall be rolled up in his right hand." Traditions add that the earth (q.v.) shall be rolled up in God's left hand (Muslim, *Ṣaḥīḥ, Ṣifat al-qiyāma,* no. 4995; see APOCALYPSE). Generally, this is taken to refer to God's power (see POWER AND IMPOTENCE), especially by the Muʿtazila and the negators of anthropomorphism (q.v.), but some circles, like the Ḥanbalīs and particularly the Wahhābīs, interpret it literally. Such interpretation led to the belief that God has two hands but that both are right ones, since the left hand is an epithet of created beings, and not of the creator (see CREATION): *inna li-khāliqinā yadayn kiltāhumā yamīnān, lā yasāra li-khāliqinā idhi l-yasāru min ṣifati l-makhlūqīn* (Ibn Khuzayma, *al-Tawḥīd,* 66; Ibn Fūrak, *Mushkil al-ḥadīth,* 37-8; Blachère, *Introduction,* 216-21; Gimaret, *Dieu à l'image,* 202-4; Abdel Haleem, *Understanding the Qurʾān,* 107-22). Saʿīd b. Jubayr (d. 95/714) attributed to Ibn ʿAbbās a tradition stating that the letter *yāʾ* at the opening of Q 19 *(kāf, hāʾ, yāʾ, ʿayn* and *ṣād)* stands for *yamīn* which is one of the names of God (*Lisān al-ʿArab,* s.v. *y m n',* xiii, 459). According to a ḥadīth, the Kaʿba (q.v.) is considered to be the right hand of God since it is touched and kissed *(istilām)* during the pilgrimage (q.v.; *Lisān al-ʿArab,* op. cit.).

In many ancient cultures, the right side was considered better than the left side (*Gen* 48:13-20). It symbolized goodness and kindness, while the left represented evil, the sinister, the bad. In Latin, the term *sinistra* means both left and sinister. In the Bible, God's right hand represents his strong arm (*Exod* 15:15; *Isa* 62:8; *Ps* 118:15-6; 139:10). The Qurʾān itself (as discussed above) and later Islamic tradition attest to similar understandings of "left" *(shimāl)* and "right" *(yamīn)*. The *bayʿa,* "pledge of allegiance," must be performed with the right hand (see CONTRACTS AND ALLIANCES; OATHS); eating with the left is prohibited since this hand is used for cleansing after elimination and since Satan (see DEVIL) usually eats and drinks using his left hand (Muslim, *Ṣaḥīḥ,* no. 3763-6; see FOOD AND DRINK; RITUAL PURITY; LAWFUL AND UNLAWFUL). One should enter a mosque (q.v.) with the right leg and leave with left. During the prayer (q.v.), it is prohibited to expectorate in the direction of the *qibla* (q.v.) or the right side; while it is permitted toward the left side (ʿAbd al-Razzāq, *Muṣannaf,* i, 430-4). Until recently, it was customary in some Muslim countries to oblige left-handed children to use their right hand. This practice is based on the beliefs mentioned above and goes back at least to the first period of Islam: when Khālid b. al-Walīd received Abū Bakr's (q.v.) letter ordering him to leave Iraq (q.v.) for Syria (al-Shām) to support the Muslim forces there, his furious reaction was: "this [decision] was surely taken by the left-handed man," meaning ʿUmar b. al-Khaṭṭāb (q.v.; cf. Ṭabarī, *Taʾrīkh,* iii, 415). ʿUmar was, in fact, left-handed *(Lisān al-ʿArab,* iv, 565, *ʿ-s-r)*. Finally, it is worth mentioning that the Arabic root *y-s-r* means both "to be or become easy, prosperous," and "left, left side." In Q 87:8, *al-yusrā* is explained as paradise and in Q 92:10, *al-ʿusrā* is hell.

The terms *shimāl* and *yamīn* also represent north and south. In the archives of Mari, the Old Babylonian royal city on the banks of the middle Euphrates river, the west Semitic *yamīna,* "right," designates the cardinal point south, and *simʾal,* "left," indicates north. This use of south and north is deduced from the designation, known only from Mari, of certain tribes as *dumu.Meš-yamīna* and *dumu.Meš-simʾal,* 'sons of the right' and 'sons of the left' respectively (Malamat, *Mari and the early Israelite experience,* 33, 67-8; cf. id., *Mari and the Bible,* 299). The term *semol,* spelled *s-m-ʾ-l,* appears in Genesis 14:15 and is generally translated as "north" — the north representing calamity (*Jer* 1:14). In later Jewish sources, the Devil is called Samaʾel or Semiʾel (see SAMUEL). The Arabic name for Greater Syria is al-Shaʾm or al-Shaʾām. Arab lexicographers explain that this name is derived from *shuʾm,* "bad luck, misfortune" (Bashear, Yemen, 351-3). But, might one also suppose that Shaʾm is an Arabic derivation of the West Semitic Simʾal = Shimʾal, particularly in the light of the clear etymology of al-Yaman (Yemen), another ancient Arabic designation of a geographic area and a cardinal point?

Isaac Hasson

Bibliography
Primary: ʿAbd al-Razzāq, *Muṣannaf;* id., *Tafsīr,* ed. Muṣṭafā Muslim Muḥammad; al-Ghazālī, Abū Ḥāmid Muḥammad, *al-Durra al-fākhira fī kashf ʿulūm al-ākhira,* ed. M.ʿA. ʿAṭā, Beirut 1987, 20-1, 51-7, 72-9; Ibn Fūrak, Abū Bakr Muḥammad b. al-Ḥasan al-Anṣārī, *Kitāb Mushkil al-ḥadīth wa-bayānihi,* Beirut 1980; Ibn Ḥanbal, *Musnad;* Ibn al-Jawzī, *al-Tabṣira,* 2 vols., Beirut 1986, ii, 254; Ibn Kathīr, *al-Nihāya fī l-fitan wa-l-malāḥim,* ed. M.A. ʿAbd al-ʿAzīz, 2 vols., Cairo 1986; id., *Tafsīr,* ed. Ghunaym et al.; Ibn Khuzayma, Muḥammad b. Isḥāq al-Nīsābūrī, *Kitāb al-Tawḥīd wa-ithbāt ṣifāt al-rabb,* Beirut 1983; *Lisān al-ʿArab;* al-Majlisī, Muḥammad Bāqir b. Muḥammad, *Biḥār al-anwār,* lithographic ed., 25 vols.; Muslim, *Ṣaḥīḥ;* al-Nabīl, Aḥmad b. Abī ʿĀṣim, *Kitāb al-Awāʾil,* ed. M.S. Zaghlūl, Beirut 1987; Qummī, *Tafsīr,* ii, 384; Qurṭubī, *Jāmiʿ;* id., *al-Tadhkira fī aḥwāl al-mawtā wa-umūr al-ākhira,* ed. M. al-Bastawīsī, 2 vols., Medina 1997, i, 382-91; S. Quṭb, *Mashāhid al-qiyāma fī l-Qurʾān,* Beirut 1975; M.A. Ṣāliḥ, *al-Qiyāma. Mashāhiduhā wa-ʿiẓātuhā fī l-sunna al-nabawiyya,* 3 vols., Beirut 1994, iii, 171-4; M.M. al-Shaʿrāwī, *Mashāhid yawm al-qiyāma,* Cairo 2000, 110-20, 226-8; Ṭabarī, *Tafsīr,* ed. A.S. ʿAlī et al.; id., *Taʾrīkh,* ed. Ibrāhīm; Tirmidhī, *Ṣaḥīḥ.*
Secondary: M. Abdel Haleem, *Understanding the Qurʾān. Themes and style,* London 1999; K. Ahrens, *Muhammed als Religionsstifter,* Leipzig 1935; R. Arnaldez, *Mahomet,* Paris 1975, 110-22; S. Bashear, Yemen in early Islam, in *Arabica* 36 (1989), 351-3; Blachère, *Introduction;* P. Casanova, *Mohammed et la fin du monde,* Paris 1911; M. Gaudefroye-Demombynes, *Mahommet,* Paris 1969, 414-20; D. Gimaret, *Dieu à l'image de l'homme,* Paris 1997; id, *Théories de l'acte humain en théologie musulmane,* Paris 1980; J.A. MacCulloch, Hand, in *ERE,* vi, 492-9; A. Malamat, *Mari and the Bible,* Leiden 1998; id., *Mari and the early Israelite experience,* Oxford 1989; D.S. Margoliouth, Symbolism [Muslim], in *ERE,* xii, 145-6; A. Rippin, *Muslims. Their religious beliefs and practices,* New York 2001²; A. Schimmel, *Deciphering the signs of God,* New York 1994; J.I. Smith and Y. Haddad, *The Islamic understanding of death and resurrection,* Albany 1981, 76-97, 127-46; W.M. Watt, *Free will and predestination in early Islam,* London 1948, esp. 12-31.

Leg see ANATOMY; ANTHROPOMORPHISM

Legends see NARRATIVES; MYTHS AND LEGENDS IN THE QURʾĀN

Legion see RANKS AND ORDERS

Legislation see LAW AND THE QURʾĀN

Leper see ILLNESS AND HEALTH

Letters see MYSTERIOUS LETTERS; ARABIC SCRIPT

Liar see LIE

Lie

To deceive; anything which deceives. The polemical context of the qurʾānic revelation and the discursive nature of qurʾānic scripture make lying one of the most frequently mentioned sins in the Qurʾān (see SIN, MAJOR AND MINOR). Furthermore, the Qurʾān's oft-repeated references to itself as "the truth" (q.v.; *al-ḥaqq*) and the declaration that God created the entire world "with truth" (Q 46:3), make dishonesty a central characteristic of unbelief *(kufr)* and polytheism *(shirk),* such links sometimes being explicitly stated (Q 16:39; 29:17; see BELIEF AND UNBELIEF; POLYTHEISM AND ATHEISM; IDOLATRY AND IDOLATERS). Thus, the foremost liars in the Qurʾān are polytheists *(mushrikūn)* who make false claims about God and his prophets, among them the accusation that the prophets lie (see PROPHETS AND PROPHETHOOD). Both sides in this polemic (see POLEMIC AND POLEMICAL LANGUAGE) use the same terms: the most common being *kadhaba, iftarā* and *ifk*. In the mouths of unbelievers such falsehoods are regarded as among the most serious of sins. In the Qurʾān, various forms of *kadhaba* are attested eighty-two times, *iftarā* sixty times, and *ifk* in the sense of "lie" thirteen times. Other terms include *zūr,* attested four times, and a form of *kh-r-q* that is used once with the meaning to "falsely attribute" (offspring) to God (*kharaqū,* Q 6:100; see GOD AND HIS ATTRIBUTES; CHRISTIANS AND CHRISTIANITY; ANTHROPOMORPHISM).

The gravity of lying is seen in the repeated question "who is more wicked than one who invents falsehoods about God..." *(wa/[fa]-man aẓlamu mimman iftarā ʿalā llāhi kadhiban)*. This question is posed nine times in this form (Q 6:21, 93, 144; 7:37; 10:17; 11:18; 18:15; 29:68; 61:7), and twice with derivatives of *k-dh-b* (Q 6:157; 39:32). This is usually directed at polytheists but Q 61:7, following an excursus on those who rejected Jesus (q.v.), seems directed at Jews (see JEWS AND JUDAISM). Commentators such as al-Ṭabarī (d. 310/923), al-Zamakhsharī (d. 538/1144) and al-Rāzī (d. 606/1210) think that Jews and Christians may also be targets in other cases. These passages and others also show that lying in the sense of "freely inventing falsehoods" cannot in the qurʾānic context be wholly dissociated from "denying the truth" *(kadhdhaba)* as in "who is more wicked than one who invents falsehoods about God or *(aw)* denies the truth" (*aw-kadhdhaba bi-l-ḥaqq,* Q 29:68). Due to this, and to the fact that terms such as *kadhaba* and *kharaqa* may denote not only a false statement that the speaker knows to be false (and by which he means to deceive others), but also a false statement that the speaker thinks true, it is sometimes difficult to restrict the qurʾānic meaning of "lies" to "freely invented falsehoods"; for those who cling to what is simply false — or dress the truth with falsehood — (*bāṭil* in Q 2:42; cf. 29:68 and eleven other places) are also taken to task (see ERROR; ASTRAY). The hypocrites (*munāfiqūn,* see HYPOCRITES AND HYPOCRISY) are, in the case of Muḥammad's prophetic mission, the second most prominent liars after the polytheists. "God bears witness that the hypocrites are lying" (Q 63:1; see also Q 3:167 and 9:77; see WITNESSING AND TESTIFYING). Other notable liars include those who slander other people's wives (the scandal of ʿĀʾisha, Q 24:11-24; see ʿĀʾISHA BINT ABĪ BAKR; GOSSIP; WIVES OF THE PROPHET), Joseph's (q.v.) brothers and Potiphar's wife (Q 12:17, 23-8; see WOMEN AND THE QURʾĀN) and, of course, poets (Q 26:224-6; see POETRY AND POETS).

Daniel Beaumont

Bibliography
ʿAbd al-Bāqī; Rāzī, *Tafsīr,* Cairo 1352/1933, viii, 140-1; x, 123-6; xxvi, 278; xxviii, 2-3; xxix, 312-3; Ṭabarī, *Tafsīr,* ed. ʿAlī, iv, 5; vii, 105, 180-2; viii, 50-1; xiv, 77-8; xxvi, 2; Zamakhsharī, *Kashshāf,* Cairo 1387/1968, ii, 10-1, 34-5, 57; iii, 53, 190, 201, 293, 514-6.

Life

The vital force that distinguishes organic from inorganic matter. At the heart of the qurʾānic evocation of life are a paradox and two paradigms. The paradox arises from a dual attitude to, or sense of, "life" *(ḥayāt)*. On the one hand, life as an animating force in the body is perceived as utterly sacred. Humans are urged not to kill their children (q.v.) out of fear of being reduced to poverty (*imlāq*, Q 17:31; see POVERTY AND THE POOR). God promises that he will provide for both parent and child (see FAMILY; PARENTS) and warns that infanticide (q.v.) is a grievous sin (see SIN, MAJOR AND MINOR). The sanctity of life is stressed again a little later in the same sūra: "Nor take life *(al-nafs)* — which God has made sacred *(allatī ḥarrama Allāh)* — except for just cause" (*bi-l-ḥaqq*, Q 17:33; see BLOODSHED; MURDER; RETALIATION). Yūsuf ʿAlī's translation of *nafs* in Q 17:33 is closer to the corporeal sense intended than Arberry's which reads: "And slay not the soul *(al-nafs)* God has forbidden (q.v.), except by right *(bi-l-ḥaqq)*."

Life in the sense of living out one's corporeal existence is, however, paradoxically fraught with danger, illusion and deception. The Qurʾān exhibits an almost platonic rejection of the life of this world *(al-ḥayāt al-dunyā)*, characterizing it as nothing but "play and amusement" *(laʿib wa-lahw)* and contrasting it with the reward of the righteous in the hereafter (Q 6:32; see GOOD AND EVIL; REWARD AND PUNISHMENT). There is a virtual repetition of the same words in Q 57:20 where this leitmotiv of *al-ḥayāt al-dunyā* as *laʿib wa-lahw* is further amplified by its being powerfully designated as "goods and chattels of deception" *(matāʿ al-ghurūr)*. In the emphasis placed by the text on a physical world of transitory illusion and deception, and the explicit contrast in Q 6:32 of this world and the next, there are obvious echoes of the lament in Ecclesiastes 1:2-3.

The first paradigm flows directly from God's qurʾānic designation as "the living" (*al-ḥayy*, Q 2:255; 3:2; 20:111; 25:58; 40:65; see GOD AND HIS ATTRIBUTES): God is the central focus of life *(al-ḥayāt)* in the Qurʾān. From him all else that is alive takes its being; by him everything is created *ex nihilo* (see CREATION; COSMOLOGY). To use Ibn Sīnā's (d. 428/1037) famous phrase, the production of all other life means that God is "the necessitating force behind existence" (*wājib al-wujūd*, Goichon, *Lexique*, 417-8). The Throne Verse (see THRONE OF GOD), which enshrines this concept in the Qurʾān, is rightly accorded considerable prominence and respect in Islam:

God! There is no god but he, the living *(al-ḥayy)*, eternal *(al-qayyūm)*. No slumber can seize him, nor sleep (q.v.). His are all things in the heavens (see HEAVEN AND SKY) and on earth (q.v.). Who is there who can intercede (see INTERCESSION) in his presence except as he permits? He knows what [appears to his creatures as] before or behind them. Nor shall they compass aught of his knowledge except as he wills. His throne does extend over the heavens and the earth, and he feels no fatigue in preserving them both. For he is the most high, the supreme [in glory] (Q 2:255).

This Throne Verse is "one of the most famous and beloved of the verses of the Qurʾān, frequently recited as a protection against harm or evil" (Netton, *Popular dictionary*, 45; see POPULAR AND TALISMANIC USES OF THE QURʾĀN; EVERYDAY LIFE, THE QURʾĀN IN). It is a verse which proclaims God's life, his self-subsisting and eternal nature, his vigilance, his divine ownership of his creation, his omniscience, his divine will (see FREEDOM AND PREDESTINATION), his transcendence and unknowableness, his power, his glory (q.v.) and his unity. It thus encapsulates a lucid, thumbnail sketch of many of the most important divine attributes. Although they are articulated as separate epithets, "the living" *(al-ḥayy)* and "the eternal" *(al-qayyūm)* are logically to be identified as a unity according to the classical doctrine of the oneness of God (*tawḥīd,* see POLYTHEISM AND ATHEISM; ETERNITY). Commenting on this verse, Yūsuf ʿAlī (1872-1953) notes: "His Life is absolute Life, his Being is absolute Being, while others are contingent and evanescent..." (Yūsuf ʿAlī, *Holy Qurʾān,* 103, n. 297). For Islam and the Qurʾān, God is life and the creator and divine dispenser of life.

R. Arnaldez (Ḥayāt, 302) reminds us that "al-Zamakhsharī [d. 538/1144] states that *ḥayy,* in the technical language of the theologians, describes one who has knowledge and power" (see KNOWLEDGE AND LEARNING; POWER AND IMPOTENCE). This concentration of "life" and "power" is an ancient archetype of the divine as seen, for example, in the hieroglyphic portrayals of the deities in Egypt (q.v.; see Hornung, *Conceptions of God,* 199-200; but cf. 230-3). Further, such ancient archetypes portray an idea of "the creator's loving care" for his creation — rather than Aristotle's "unmoved" First Mover. In the Islamic paradigm, as well, the creator maintains (chosen) life by means both ordinary and extraordinary. Divine benefaction and sustenance *(rizq)* is mentioned frequently as are such acts of intervention as sending angels (see ANGEL) to fight on the side of Muḥammad at the battle of Badr (q.v.) in 2/624 (Q 3:123-5; 8:4, 9).

The verses in the Qurʾān which refer to life *(al-ḥayāt)* and to God as "the living" *(al-ḥayy),* were revealed in a particular historical milieu (see HISTORY AND THE QURʾĀN; CHRONOLOGY AND THE QURʾĀN). Despite such barbarities as the burial alive of newly born female infants (see Q 17:31; Yūsuf ʿAlī, *Holy Qurʾān,* 703 n. 2214), the pre-Islamic notion of Mecca (q.v.) as a sanctuary for visitors and as a sacred territory (*ḥaram,* see GEOGRAPHY) together with the concept of sacred months (q.v.; Shaban, *Islamic history,* 3; Q 2:194, 217), illustrate an environment in which there was some attempt at respect for, and preservation of, life. Later under the new qurʾānic dispensation, blood revenge (*thaʾr,* see BLOOD MONEY) would be replaced by just retaliation (*qiṣāṣ,* see Q 2:178-9; 17:33), thus inaugurating a new "respect for life" and, theoretically, further diminution of bloodshed and life lost.

God's fundamental generative power whereby he creates new life *ex nihilo* is a basic leitmotiv of the sacred text. It is clothed with a basic biology (Q 23:12-16; see BIOLOGY AS THE CREATION AND STAGES OF LIFE) in which the human body is portrayed as developing, dying (see DEATH AND THE DEAD) and then being brought to life again (lit. *tubʿathūna,* Q 23:16) on the day of judgment (*yawm al-qiyāma,* see LAST JUDGMENT). The image here is of new, eternal life being born, or reborn, out of the distress, fires, convulsions and terrors of that last day, with a greater fire (q.v.), that of hell, as the final reward of the wicked (Q 52:13-4; see HELL AND HELLFIRE). While eternal life will be born out of the cataclysm of the last day, humankind's diurnal present life *(al-ḥayāt al-dunyā)* is likened in the Qurʾān to rainwater (*māʾ,* see WATER; NATURE AS SIGNS; BLESSING). This is sent down by God from the skies to refresh the earth (see AGRICULTURE AND VEGETATION), assist in the production of food and provide an, albeit ephemeral, earthly paradise (q.v.) which God will cause to pass (Q 10:24; see FOOD AND DRINK; GARDEN). It is this temporary aspect of the results of the life-giving water which is stressed here, together with the transient dimension of human life. There is a vivid and obvious contrast that can be made between these images and the water imagery of the New Testament in which it is proclaimed "The water I give him will be a spring of water within him, that flows continually to bring him everlasting life" (John 4:14; see SCRIPTURE AND THE QURʾĀN).

The first paradigm mentioned above is that of God's creative gift of life and of the individual's grateful return of that life to God at the moment of death. This life has, ideally, been enriched by faith (q.v.) and good works (Q 2:277; 9:19-20; see GOOD DEEDS) if paradise is to be the final destination of the individual (see GRATITUDE AND INGRATITUDE; GIFT-GIVING). In the beginning, God creates the first man, Adam (see ADAM AND EVE), from clay (q.v.), breathes into him his spirit (q.v.) and displays him to the angels for their admiration and respect (Q 15:26-39). There is an archetypical "gifting" at the beginning of human time of new life to a new creation. And God does not forget his creation but guides, sustains and cures the previous life he has instituted (Q 26:78-80; see ASTRAY; ILLNESS AND HEALTH), sends the final revelation, that of the Qurʾān as the last and ultimate guidebook to paradise (Q 31:3; see REVELATION AND INSPIRATION). On the last day, he will raise the old life to a new one (Q 26:81; see RESURRECTION). According to this paradigm, God, the archetypical and only creator and controller of life, gives life twice, first at birth and then by ultimately raising his creation to a new form of existence (Q 56:60-2).

The second paradigm interwoven into, and to be extrapolated from, the fabric of the Qurʾān is that of life as a journey (q.v.) from terrestrial to celestial life. Man's life involves much exertion and a hard toiling (*kādiḥ*, see WORK) towards his lord (q.v.) but the final encounter is assured (Q 84:6) after a journey from "stage to stage" (*ṭabaqan ʿan ṭabaqin*, Q 84:19). As Yūsuf ʿAlī puts it in his comment on the latter verse: "Man travels and ascends stage by stage. In Q 67:3 the same word in the form *ṭibāqan* was used of the heavens, as if they were in layers one above another. Man's spiritual life may similarly be compared to an ascent from one heaven to another" (Yūsuf ʿAlī, *Holy Qurʾān*, 1711 n. 6047).

During the life journey the human is tested (Q 2:155; 3:186; 47:31; 57:25; see TRIAL) and perhaps the archetypical "questing and testing" encounter in the Qurʾān, one which graphically illustrates that in such testing God's ways are not human ways, is the famous encounter between Moses (q.v.; Mūsā) and al-Khiḍr (see KHAḌIR/KHIḌR). This occupies a substantial section of the eighteenth sūra, Sūrat al-Kahf ("The Cave," Q 18:60-82). The essential nature of a human's life journey (a journey palely adumbrated in this qurʾānic encounter between Moses and al-Khiḍr but with a different objective) is that it is always a return to God, for reward or punishment. The created return to their source, the creator (Q 6:60, 72; 10:45-6).

Life, then, in the Qurʾān has both a macro and a micro dimension, if it is viewed in terms of a journey *(riḥla)*. From the global or macro viewpoint, all living beings, originating in, and created by, God, are journeying *en masse* in multifarious form towards the final cataclysm of the last day, a day of rebirth as well as destruction: "One day the earth will be changed to a different earth, and so will be the heavens" (Q 14:48; see APOCALYPSE). From a micro perspective, each human life has an individual path to tread and an individual salvation (q.v.) to achieve: the wicked will be reborn to new life in eternal torment and the just and the righteous, who have followed "the straight path" (*al-ṣirāṭ al-*

mustaqīm, see PATH OR WAY) articulated so clearly and so often in the Qurʾān, will be reborn to eternal bliss. It is a return and a rebirth to a new life which will be accomplished in profound haste, almost as if both return and rebirth were long overdue, or the divine cosmic patience with humanity had suddenly exhausted itself: "On that day we shall leave them to surge *(yamūju)* like waves on one another: the trumpet will be blown, and we shall collect them all together (Q 18:99).... The day whereon they will issue from their sepulchres in sudden haste *(sirāʿan)* as if they were rushing *(yūfiḍūna)* to a goal-post [fixed for them]" (Q 70:43).

In conclusion, earthly life, the return and the eschaton are, for the Muslim, different aspects of a single, multi-dimensional, eschatological frame (see ESCHATOLOGY). This is, as it were, our ultimate paradigm and ultimate paradox. Real life, for Islam, of necessity involves death coupled with a realizable eschatology whose basis is eternal life:

All of human history, then, moves from the creation to the eschaton. Preceding the final judgement will come signs (both cosmic and moral) signaling the arrival of the Hour as well as the specific events of the resurrection and assessment. Within this overall structure is the individual cycle which specifies the events of creation, death and resurrection. Part of the fatalistic determinism of the pre-Islamic Arabs was their sense that each human life is for a fixed term or ajal. It is immutably set; on the appointed day one's life comes to an end. This idea of an ajal is repeated in the Qurʾān, both for individuals [Q 6:2; 7:34; 16:61; 20:129] and for nations [Q 10:49, 15:4-5]" (Smith and Haddad, *Islamic understanding,* 5).

This remains the fundamental Islamic paradigm for both medieval and modern Islamic theology (see THEOLOGY AND THE QURʾĀN), whatever the glosses of individual verses *(āyāt)* by contemporary exegesis (see EXEGESIS OF THE QURʾĀN: EARLY MODERN AND CONTEMPORARY). It is worth noting, however, that the medieval philosophers *(falāsifa)* often developed a different set of conceptions about the cycle of life, some of which appear difficult to reconcile with the basic theological positions of the Qurʾān (see Arnaldez, Ḥayāt, 303).

Ian Richard Netton

Bibliography
Primary: A. Yūsuf ʿAlī (trans.), *The holy Qurʾān. Text, translation, commentary,* Kuwait 1984; Arberry, 2 vols., London 1971; Ibn Sīnā, Abū ʿAlī al-Ḥusayn b. ʿAbdallāh, *Kitāb al-Ishārāt wa-l-tanbīhāt,* ed. S. Dunyā, 4 vols., Cairo 1957-67; R. Knox (trans.), *The holy Bible,* London 1960; Zamakhsharī, *Kashshāf.*
Secondary: R. Arnaldez, Ḥayāt, in *EI²*, iii, 302-3; N.J. Coulson, *A history of Islamic law,* Edinburgh 1964; A.-M. Goichon, *Lexique de la langue philosophique d'Ibn Sina,* Paris 1938; E. Hornung, *Conceptions of God in ancient Egypt. The one and the many,* trans. J. Baines, London 1983; J. Horovitz, *Jewish proper names and derivations in the Koran,* Hildesheim 1925, 54 (for *ḥayy* in the Qurʾān); I.R. Netton, *A popular dictionary of Islam,* London 1992; id., Theophany as paradox. Ibn al-ʿArabī's account of al-Khaḍir in his *Fuṣūṣ al-ḥikam,* in *Journal of the Muhyiddin Ibn ʿArabi Society* 11 (1992), 11-22; id., Towards a modern tafsīr of *Sūrat al-Kahf.* Structure and semiotics, in *Journal of qurʾanic studies* 2 (2000), 67-87; M.A. Shaban, *Islamic history A.D. 600-750 (A.H. 132). A new interpretation,* Cambridge 1971; M.A. Sharif, *Searching for solace. A biography of Abdullah Yusuf Ali, interpreter of the Qurʾān,* Kuala Lumpur 1994; J.I. Smith and Y.Y. Haddad, *The Islamic understanding of death and resurrection,* Albany 1981; W.M. Watt, *Companion to the Qurʾān,* London 1967.

Life after Death

see ESCHATOLOGY; RESURRECTION; PARADISE; HELL AND HELLFIRE; REWARD AND PUNISHMENT

Lifetime see DESTINY; FATE; LIFE; DEATH AND THE DEAD

Light

The emanation from a light-giving body: the essential condition for vision (see VISION AND BLINDNESS; SEEING AND HEARING) — the opposite of darkness (q.v.). The Qurʾān is rich in references to light, both in the literal sense of the word as well as in symbolic and metaphoric senses (see METAPHOR; SYMBOLIC IMAGERY). The most common word for light is *nūr*, although *ḍiyāʾ* also appears on three occasions (also *miṣbāḥ* and *sirāj;* see also LAMP and FIRE).

Light as *nūr* most frequently appears juxtaposed to darkness *(ẓulumāt)*. This is most common in the phrase "From the darkness into the light" *(mina l-ẓulumāti ilā l-nūri)* which appears at least seven times in the Qurʾān (Q 2:257; 5:16; 14:1, 5; 33:43; 57:9; 65:11). In this context, light functions both as that with which one can see clearly in a literal sense and also as a metaphoric source of guidance and illumination, wherein darkness is akin to ignorance (q.v.) and being led astray (q.v.). In the first sense, light versus darkness is compared to having sight versus being blind (e.g. Q 13:16: "Say: Is the blind equal with one who sees or is darkness equal with light?"; this verse is repeated almost verbatim in Q 35:19). Elsewhere the direct connection between light and seeing versus darkness and not seeing is clearly evoked: "God took away their light and left them in darkness so they could not see" (Q 2:17), and the evocative "Or like the darkness in a deep ocean surmounted by crashing waves with dark clouds above — darknesses, one on top of the other. If he puts out his hand he can hardly see it. Therefore for anyone for whom God did not make a light, there is no light" (Q 24:40).

In its sense as guidance, light is very closely related to the important issues of revelation and prophecy (see REVELATION AND INSPIRATION; PROPHETS AND PROPHETHOOD). The Torah (q.v.) and Gospel (q.v.; *injīl*) are referred to as "guidance and light" *(hudan wa-nūrun)* in Q 5:44 and Q 5:46. This is repeated for the Torah again in Q 6:91: "Say: Who sent down the book (q.v.) that Moses (q.v.; Mūsā) brought as light and guidance for humankind *(nūran wa-hudan lil-nās)?*" Elsewhere, the word *ḍiyāʾ* is used for the revelation sent to Moses: "Indeed we gave Moses and Aaron (q.v.; Hārūn) the criterion (q.v.; *al-furqān*) and a light *(ḍiyāʾan)* and a reminder for those who do right" (Q 21:48; see MEMORY).

Light is also used to indicate the revelation received by Muḥammad (see NAMES OF THE QURʾĀN): "So believe in God and his messenger (q.v.), and the light *(nūr)* that we sent down" (Q 64:8); "And thus we sent to you a spirit (q.v.; *rūḥ*) by our command. You did not know what the book was nor faith (q.v.), but we made it a light *(nūr)* with which we guide whom we wish of our servants" (Q 42:52); "O humankind! Indeed a proof (q.v.; *burhān*) has come to you from your lord (q.v.). And we sent down to you a manifest light *(nūran mubīnan)*" (Q 4:174). The majority of instances, however, appear to use "light" *(nūr)* as a reference to prophecy rather than qurʾānic revelation: "There has come to you from God a light and a clear [or manifest] book *(kitābun mubīnun)*" (Q 5:15); "It is those who believe in him, honor him, help him, and follow the light that is sent down with him — it is they who will prosper" (Q 7:157). In one instance, Muḥammad is referred to explicitly as a source of light: "And an inviter to God by his leave, and a light-giving lamp *(sirājan munīran)*" (Q 33:46; see NAMES OF THE PROPHET).

The word *mubīn,* normally translated as "clear" or "manifest," has a special significance in instances where "light" refers to revelation and prophecy, since in Arabic *mubīn* and the root *b-y-n* mean not only "clear" but also "readily apparent." Thus phrases such as *kitāb mubīn,* "clear book" (as in Q 5:15 mentioned above) or the common *āyāt bayyanāt,* "manifest signs (q.v.), clear verses (q.v.)," carry a connotation of being "lit up" and clearly visible, not just "clear" in the sense of "easily understood."

Three verses refer to the light *(nūr)* of God: "And the earth will shine with the light of its lord" (Q 39:22); two are almost identical in their phrasing: "They wish to extinguish the light of God with their mouths, but God will not allow but that he would perfect his light, even though the unbelievers detest it" (Q 9:32; also Q 61:8; see BELIEF AND UNBELIEF). Commentators on the Qur'ān (see EXEGESIS OF THE QUR'ĀN: CLASSICAL AND MEDIEVAL) have understood this variously to refer to the glory (q.v.) of God or to his message.

Light also refers to the sun (q.v.) and moon (q.v.) where moonlight is called *nūr* and sunlight *ḍiyā':* "He is the one who made the sun a light and the moon a light (*ja'ala l-shams ḍiyā'an wa-l-qamar nūran,* Q 10:5). Elsewhere, the moon is referred to as light *(nūr)* while the sun is called a lamp (*sirāj,* Q 71:16; cf. 25:61; 78:13).

The most important reference to light is in Q 24:35: "God is the light of the heavens and the earth. The parable of his light is as a niche *(mishkāt)* in which is a lamp; the lamp encased in glass; the glass as if it were a shining star lit from a blessed tree, an olive, neither of the east nor of the west, whose oil would burn bright even if no fire touched it. Light upon light, God guides to his light whom he wishes, and God puts forth parables for human beings, and God is knowing of all things." The sūra of the Qur'ān in which this verse occurs is named Sūrat al-Nūr, "The Light," and the verse is popularly known as the Light Verse *(āyat al-nūr).* It has enjoyed a special significance in mystical commentaries on the Qur'ān (see ṢŪFISM AND THE QUR'ĀN). Thus the early and influential Ṣūfī Sahl al-Tustarī (d. 283/898) sees this verse as a reference to the "light of Muḥammad" *(nūr Muḥammad),* which functions in its primordial sense as a veil to hide the inscrutable nature of God (Böwering, *Mystical,* 149-51). The Persian mystic Rūzbihān Baqlī al-Shīrāzī (d. 606/1209) took a particularly esoteric reading of this verse, speaking of a darkness of non-being *(ẓulmat al-'adam)* lying between the letters *kāf* and *nūn* of the word *kawn,* "existence," and untouched by the light of either letter (see ARABIC SCRIPT). *Kawn,* existence, is like an illuminated niche, lit up by the light of divine qualities (*ṣifāt;* see GOD AND HIS ATTRIBUTES). By looking at this niche we can see the light of the letters *kāf* and *nūn* of "existence" (Shīrāzī, *'Arā'is,* 81; cf. Bursawī, *Tafsīr,* vi, 152 f., for further discussion of this verse).

Light as an important religious concept became central to Ṣūfī practice and in the philosophy of virtually all Muslim neo-Platonists (see PHILOSOPHY AND THE QUR'ĀN). It also occupied a central place in the Persian Islamic philosophical tradition commonly referred to as the illumination *(ishrāqī)* school, whose most famous exponent, Shihāb al-Dīn Yaḥyā al-Suhrawardī, was executed for holding heretical beliefs in 587/1191 (see HERESY; LITERATURE AND THE QUR'ĀN).

Jamal J. Elias

Bibliography
Primary: S. Ateş, *İşārī tefsīr okulu,* Ankara 1974; al-Bursawī, Ismā'īl Ḥaqqī, *Tafsīr rūḥ al-bayān,* 10 vols., originally written in 1721, repr. n.d.; Rūzbihān Baqlī al-Shīrazī, *'Arā'is al-bayān fī ḥaqā'iq al-Qur'ān,* Cawnpore 1884.

Secondary: Böwering, *Mystical;* H. Corbin, *The man of light in Iranian Sufism,* Boulder 1978; U. Rubin, Pre-existence and light. Aspects of the concept of nūr Muḥammad, in *IOS* 5 (1975), 62-119; J. Walbridge, *The science of mystic lights. Quṭb al-Dīn Shīrāzī and the illuminationist tradition in Islamic philosophy,* Cambridge, MA 1992.

Lightning see WEATHER

Lion see ANIMAL LIFE

Lips see ANATOMY

Listen see HEARING AND DEAFNESS; SEEING AND HEARING

Literacy

The ability to read and, often, to write. Literacy (framed in contemporary Arabic by expressions such as *maʿrifat al-qirāʾa wa-l-kitāba, thaqāfa* and their derivatives) is in many cultures considered a primary requisite for learning and education. In Arabia at the beginning of the first/seventh century, however, oral transmission of knowledge, memorization and the spoken word had a long tradition and were highly appreciated among the tribes (see TRIBES AND CLANS; ORALITY AND WRITING IN ARABIA; MEMORY; SPEECH). Until that time, the use of writing and written matter — due also to the material conditions at that time — played a minor role (see MATERIAL CULTURE AND THE QURʾĀN). Apparently reflecting this situation, the Qurʾān seems to consider issues related to literacy of subordinate importance to those of its counterpart, illiteracy. Nevertheless, literacy is implied to a certain extent and acquires significance whenever mention is made of the holy book (q.v.; *al-kitāb, al-Qurʾān*), reading and teachings from holy scriptures *(kutub, ṣuḥuf),* knowledge and education in more general terms (see KNOWLEDGE AND LEARNING), or means of writing such as ink and pencil (see WRITING AND WRITING MATERIALS; INSTRUMENTS).

The qurʾānic statements concerning the theologically important question of whether the Arabian Prophet was literate or not remain ambiguous. In Q 25:5, for example, Muḥammad's opponents (see OPPOSITION TO MUḤAMMAD) discredit the Prophet by claiming that he was not receiving a divine revelation but was merely relying on "writings of the ancients *(asāṭīr al-awwalīn,* see GENERATIONS) which he has written down [or which he has had written down] *(iktatabahā)* and which were dictated to him *(tumlā ʿalayhi)* at dawn and in the early evening (q.v.; see also DAY, TIMES OF)." On the other hand, Q 29:48 addresses Muḥammad by stating "not before this [revelation] did you read/recite *(tatlū)* any book or inscribe it with your right hand, for then those who follow falsehood would have doubted." (For this question and for the possible meanings of *al-nabī al-ummī,* see Günther, Muḥammad, 7-12; see also UMMĪ; ILLITERACY.)

The five verses that are generally considered by Muslim tradition to comprise the first revelation to Muḥammad stress the written nature of religious knowledge:

Read/recite *(iqraʾ)* in the name of your lord who created. Created man of a blood-clot (see BLOOD AND BLOOD CLOT)! Read/recite [words of the holy scripture]! And your lord, the most generous, is the one [variant a:] who taught [the use of] the pen [variant b:] who taught by the pen. Taught man what he knew not [before]! (Q 96:1-5).

Although another tradition favors Q 74:1-5 as the first verses revealed, Q 96:1-5 nevertheless belongs to the very oldest parts of the *textus receptus* of the Qurʾān. This would mean that Islam, from its very beginning, in a remarkably impressive way prioritizes the gaining of (religious) knowledge, learning and education.

Q 96:4-5, "who taught by the pen, taught man what he knew not" *(alladhī ʿallama bi-l-qalami; ʿallama l-insāna mā lam yaʿlam)* seems, according to a translation variant, to make an allusion to the "art of writing" as being a divinely granted human ability. The prepositional expression *bi-l-qalami* is then not to be understood as instrumental ("with the help of the pen") but as a kind of second object ("the pen," like in Q 2:282, with its allusion to God's teaching writing; see GRAMMAR AND THE QURʾĀN). This understanding, "who taught writing with the pen" *(ʿallama al-khaṭṭa bi-l-qalami),* is reported to have been found in the ancient Qurʾān codex of ʿAbdallāh b. al-Zubayr, who was a member of the commission appointed by the third caliph, ʿUthmān (r. 23-35/644-56), to collect officially and publish the text of the Qurʾān (cf. Jeffery, *Materials,* 229; see COLLECTION OF THE QURʾĀN; CODICES OF THE QURʾĀN). It would indicate that God is the one who taught humankind the script "and other things" they did not know before *(maʿa ashyāʾa ghayri dhālika,* Ṭabarī, *Tafsīr,* xii, 646) by teaching them the use of the pen. This understanding is reflected in the Qurʾān translations by Yūsuf ʿAlī, "He who taught (the use of) the pen," Shakir, "Who taught (to write) with the pen," and Paret (see also Nöldeke, Review, 723; and Paret, *Kommentar,* 515).

It is also possible (as a second variant), however, to understand the phrase as a general reference to knowledge of the revelation (see REVELATION AND INSPIRATION), which has been handed down by God to humankind through holy scriptures (Buhl, *Das Leben,* 137-8; Bell, *Origin of Islam,* 93-4; id., *Qurʾān,* ii, 635; Paret, *Kommentar,* 515; the translations by Arberry, "Who taught by the pen," and Pickthall, "Who teacheth by the pen" are in this vein). Such an understanding would associate the content of these — God's teachings — with the "guarded tablet" *(al-lawḥ al-maḥfūẓ,* Q 85:22; see PRESERVED TABLET; HEAVENLY BOOK), on which the revelation is preserved in heaven in written form (see also Fück, Das Problem, 1). It would refer to the heavenly archetype of the Qurʾān, whose "pages [are] highly-honored, uplifted, purified by the hands of scribes *(safara)* noble, pious" (Q 80:13-5; see also 85:21-2; 56:77-80; 98:2-3; 74:52; for *safara* meaning "scribes," "reciters" or "angels," see Ṭabarī, *Tafsīr,* xii, 445-6; Qurṭubī, *Jāmiʿ,* xix, 216; for the Semitic context of *safara* that clearly indicates the meaning of "scribes," see Horovitz, *Proper names,* 229; furthermore Jeffery, *Qurʾān,* 13, 15; Paret, *Kommentar* 502).

On the other hand, this passage could refer more specifically to the holy scriptures (see also Q 2:151; 4:113; 6:91; 55:1-4), which had emerged from the heavenly "tablet" and which had been revealed to prophets before Muḥammad (such as *ṣuḥuf Ibrāhīm wa-Mūsā,* the "scrolls of Abraham [q.v.] and Moses [q.v.]," in Q 87:18-9; also 2:53; 46:12; see PROPHETS AND PROPHETHOOD). Jews and Christians had been reading these older scriptures *(yaqraʾūna l-kitāb,* Q 10:94), even though some among them had denied them when Muḥammad came to them (Q 2:101-2; see JEWS AND JUDAISM; CHRISTIANS AND CHRISTIANITY). (For the meaning of *kitāb* and *ahl al-kitāb* in the Qurʾān, see BOOK, PEOPLE OF THE BOOK, SCRIPTURE AND THE QURʾĀN; Augapfel, Das *kitāb,* also provides specific information; cf. Berg, Tabari's exegesis; Buhl, 'Die Schrift'; Künstlinger, Die Namen; Tisdall, 'The Book'.)

The term *talā,* "reading" and/or "reciting," occurs sixty-three times in the Qurʾān: the Children of Israel (q.v.) study the scripture *(tatlūna l-kitāb,* Q 2:44); Jews read in the Torah (q.v.; Q 3:93); Jews and Christian read/recite their scripture (*yatlūna l-kitāb,* Q 2:113), some of them at night (Q 3:113; see DAY AND NIGHT). Reading the scripture in an accurate manner means to believe in God or, believe in it (i.e. the Scripture; Q 2:121). Biblical narratives, which provide exemplary instruction for believers, are reported to have been read, and it is said that they be read/"re"-cited: such narratives include the story of Cain and Abel (q.v.; Q 5:27), Solomon (q.v.; Q 7:175), Noah (q.v.; Q 10:71), Abraham (Q 26:69), Moses and the Pharaoh (q.v.; Q 28:3). Q 18:83 indicates that Muḥammad (or possibly Moses) is even directed to read/recite something relating to *dhū l-qarnayn* (generally understood to be Alexander the Great, but possibly here referring to the devil [q.v.]; see ALEXANDER) when asked about him. But reading or reciting is not solely a human activity: satans read/re-cite *(tatlū)* something about Solomon (Q 2:102).

Most times, however, *talā* refers in general terms to reading the holy scriptures *(kitāb, ṣuḥuf),* reciting verses of the Qurʾān, or reading the Qurʾān (Q 2:44, 113; 129, 151, 252; 3:58, 101, 108, 164; 6:151; 8:2, 31; 10:15, 16, 61; 13:10; 17:107; 18:27; 19:58; 19:73; 22:72; 23:66, 105; 27:92; 28:45, 53; 28:59; 29:45, 51; 31:7; 33:34; 34:43; 37:3; 39:71; 45:6, 8, 25, 31; 46:7; 62:2; 65:11; 68:15 like 83:13; 98:2; see RECITATION OF THE QURʾĀN). *Talā ʿalā* indicates more emphatically that God establishes a rule for people, which they learn by reading/reciting the teachings of the holy book (Q 4:127; 5:1; 22:30; 23:72; see LAW AND THE QURʾĀN; BOUNDARIES AND PRECEPTS; LAWFUL AND UNLAWFUL; FORBIDDEN; PROHIBITED DEGREES). In Q 68:15 and Q 83:13, an unnamed unbeliever is mentioned who, "when our signs (q.v.) are read/re-cited to him," will say "[these are only] 'writings of the ancients'." That the expression *asāṭīr al-awwalīn,* which is relevant in this regard as well, refers to "writings" can be understood, for example, from Q 68:37, "Or do you have a book in which you study!" (For further references, see ILLITERACY; for *yasṭurūna* meaning *yakhuṭṭūna, yaktubūna,* see Ṭabarī, *Tafsīr,* xii, 177-8.)

Another important term, *qaraʾa,* also indicates both "reading" and "reciting." Only the verses of Q 96:1-3 start with the imperative, *iqraʾ,* to introduce God's command to the Prophet to "repeat" verses of the revelation (see also Paret, *Muhammed,* 47-8). This mode of introduction, "re-cite" or "read," seems to express in one word the primary motive for the entire proclamation of the Qurʾān and its programmatic character: Muḥammad was called upon to speak aloud a holy text. If *qaraʾa* means "reciting," however, it would not necessarily imply a writing or the ability to read as prerequisites. If it refers to "reading," Muslim commentators have noted that Muḥammad was inspired by a scripture in a divine language (see LANGUAGE, CONCEPT OF), which would not require any knowledge of reading or writing profane language. (For the idea that it was a "writing" from which Muḥammad was ordered to "read," see the famous biography of the Prophet by Ibn Isḥāq [d. ca. 150/767]; see Ibn Isḥāq, *Sīra,* i, 236, n. 5; Ibn Isḥāq-Guillaume, 106; see also, Schoeler, *Charakter,* 59-117; for the etymology and the meaning of the word "Qurʾān," see NAMES OF THE QURʾĀN, ARABIC LANGUAGE; ARABIC SCRIPT, SCRIPTURE AND THE QURʾĀN; RECITATION OF THE QURʾĀN.)

Q 7:145 confirms that God had "written" *(kataba)* for Moses "an admonition (see EXHORTATIONS) of every kind, and a distinguishing of everything," and he had done so "upon the tablets," which he had handed over to Moses on Mount Sinai (q.v.) so that he would command his people according to those laws (see COMMAND-

MENTS). Q 5:110 states that God had taught Jesus (q.v.) the "book *(kitāb),* the wisdom (q.v.), the Torah and the Gospel" (q.v.; see also Q 3:48-9). The Qurʾān is taught by God as well (Q 53:5; 55:1-2). It is then the duty of God's messengers (see MESSENGER) to "read" God's signs to the people *(yatlū ʿalayhim āyātihi)* and to "teach them the book and the wisdom, and [to] purify them" (Q 3:164; also Q 2:129, 151; 4:113; 62:2; 65:4).

A warning of certain writings is given in Q 2:78-9; there are books written by some Jews who do not "read" (or consciously "ignore") the holy scripture but fabricate by themselves writings different from the holy text as revealed (see FORGERY): "And there are some among them (i.e. the Jews) who are not reading the holy scripture *(ummiyyūn),* who do not know the book but know only fancies and mere conjectures. But woe to those who write the book with their hands and then say 'This is from God,' that they may sell it for a small price. So woe to them for what their hands have written...."

The books in which all the deeds of human beings are recorded until the day of judgment (see LAST JUDGMENT), and the idea that God "writes" *(kataba)* everything that people do, are mentioned many times (see RECORD OF HUMAN ACTIONS). For example, the Qurʾān warns that God "write[s] down what they (the people) send before and what they have left behind. [He has] taken account of everything in a clear register" (Q 36:12); his "messengers (i.e. the guardian angels) are writing down what you are devising" (Q 10:21; also 43:80); "everything that they have done is in the scrolls (of the former generations); and everything, great or small, is inscribed *(mustaṭar)*" (Q 54:52-3); God "writes down" *(wa-llāhu yaktubu)* everything that some people think up all night (or plot, *yubayyitūna*) "other than" what you [Muḥammad] say (Q 4:81; cf. also Paret, *Der Koran,* 68).

Sūra 68, entitled "The Pen," starts with the oath "[I swear] by the pen, and that which they inscribe" *(wa-l-qalami wa-mā yasṭurūna).* This verse, possibly the second oldest verse in the qurʾānic revelation (Ṭabarī, *Tafsīr,* xii, 645), lends itself to several explanations: it is understood to allude to (a) the art of writing or (b) the scripture of revelation or, again, to (c) the pen with which all the deeds and the fate of every person are recorded (Paret, *Kommentar,* 516). Medieval commentators draw special attention to the latter concept, i.e. that before heaven (see HEAVEN AND SKY), water (q.v.) and earth (q.v.), God created the pen which inscribes all happenings until the day of resurrection (q.v.; *awwālu mā khalaqa llāhu al-qalam*..., based on a prophetic saying; see e.g. Ṭabarī, *Tafsīr,* xii, 177-8). Incidentally, the idea of the many pens and seas of ink (*midād,* Q 18:109; cf. 31:27) also occurs in Jewish sources (cf. Strack/Billerbeck, *Kommentar,* ii, 587; Haeuptner, *Koranische Hinweise,* 99-100).

Writing as a way to fix juridical matters, however, is clearly favored in the Qurʾān. In Q 2:282-3, the need for people who are able to write, the importance of written documents, and the practices of writing and dictating become evident. Detailed instructions as to how to proceed are even given: "O believers, when you contract a debt (q.v.) one upon another for a stated term, then write it down! And let a writer *(kātib)* write it down between you justly. And let not any writer refuse to write it down, as God has taught him [i.e. the art of writing]. So let him write it down. And let the debtor dictate! [...] And if the debtor be a fool, or weak, or unable to dictate himself, then let his guardian (see GUARDIANSHIP) dictate justly... [...] And be not loath to write it down, whether it (i.e. the amount) be small or great...! That is more equitable in God's sight... But take witnesses whenever you are trafficking one with another! And let neither a scribe nor a witness suffer harm. [...] And if you are upon a journey, and you do not find a writer, then a pledge [?] in hand [should be required]" (cf. Ṭabarī, *Tafsīr,* iii, 117; Tyan, *Histoire,* i, 73; Schacht, *Origins,* 186; Nöldeke, *GQ,* i, 78-84; Buhl, *Das Leben,* 136-8; Khoury, *Koran,* iii, 249-54 for more detailed explanations and references).

Sebastian Günther

Bibliography
Primary: Ibn Isḥāq, *Sīra,* ed. Ṣaqqā et al.; Ibn Isḥāq-Guillaume; Qurṭubī, *Jāmi*ʿ, Cairo 1952-67; Ṭabarī, *Tafsīr,* 12 vols., Beirut 1992.
Secondary: Arberry; J. Augapfel, Das *kitāb* im Qurʾān, in *WZKM* 29 (1915), 384-92; Bell; id., *Origin of Islam in its Christian environment,* London 1926; H. Berg, Tabari's exegesis of the qurʾānic term *al-Kitāb,* in *Journal of the American Academy of Religion* 63 (1995), 761-74; F. Buhl, 'Die Schrift' und was damit zusammenhängt im Qurʾān, in C. Adler and A. Ember (eds.), *Oriental studies dedicated to Paul Haupt as director of the Oriental Seminary of the Johns Hopkins University,* Baltimore 1926, 364-73; id., *Das Leben Muhammeds,* trans. H.H. Schaeder, Leipzig 1930; J. Fück, Das Problem des Wissens im Qurʾān, in S. Günther (ed.), *Vorträge über den Islam. Aus dem Nachlaß hrsg. und um einen Anmerkungsteil ergänzt von S. Günther,* Halle (Saale) 1999, 1-31; S. Günther, Muḥammad, the illiterate Prophet. An Islamic creed in the Qurʾān and qurʾānic exegesis, in *Journal of qurʾanic studies* 4 (2002), 1-26; E. Haeuptner, *Koranische Hinweise auf die materielle Kultur der alten Araber,* Ph.D. diss., Tübingen 1966; J. Horovitz, *Jewish proper names and derivatives in the Koran,* Ohio 1925, repr. Hildesheim 1964; Jeffery, *Materials;* id., *The Qurʾān as scripture,* New York 1952; A.Th. Khoury, *Der Koran. Arabisch-Deutsch Übersetzung und wissenschaftlicher Kommentar,* Gütersloh 1991 f., vol. iii; D. Künstlinger, 'Kitāb' und 'ahlu l-Kitāb' im Ḳuran, in *RO* 4 (1926), 238-47; id., Die Namen der 'Gottes-Schriften' im Qurʾān, in *RO* 13 (1937), 72-84; M. Lecker, Zayd b. Thābit, 'a Jew with two sidelocks.' Judaism and literacy in pre-Islamic Medina (Yathrib), in *JNES* 56 (1997), 259-73; Nöldeke, *GQ,* esp. i, 14, 159-60; id., Review of J. Wellhausen, *Skizzen und Vorarbeiten.* Drittes Heft Reste arabischen Heidenthumes, in *ZDMG* 41 (1887), 707-26; Paret, *Kommentar;* id., *Koran;* id., *Mohammed und der Koran. Geschichte und Verkündigung des arabischen Propheten,* Stuttgart 1957; J. Schacht, *The origins of Muhammadan jurisprudence,* Oxford 1950; G. Schoeler, *Charakter und Authentic der muslimischen Überlieferung über das Leben Mohammeds,* Berlin 1996 (esp. chap. 2); Speyer, *Erzählungen;* H.L. Strack and P. Billerbeck, *Kommentar zum Neuen Testament aus Talmud und Midrasch,* 6 vols. in 7, Munich 1922-61, ii; W.St.C. Tisdall, 'The Book' of the 'People of the Book,' in *MW* 2 (1916), 164-70; É. Tyan, *Histoire de l'organisation judiciaire en pays d'Islam,* vol. i, Paris 1938; rev. ed., Leiden 1960².

Literary Structures of the Qurʾān

Rhetorical, grammatical and linguistic devices utilized in the conveyance of meaning. The message of the Qurʾān is couched in various literary structures, which are widely considered to be the most perfect example of the Arabic language (q.v.; see also LANGUAGE AND STYLE OF THE QURʾĀN). Arabic grammars were written based upon the qurʾānic language (see GRAMMAR AND THE QURʾĀN), and, by the general consensus of Muslim rhetoricians, the qurʾānic idiom is considered to be sublime. This article is concerned with these literary structures and how they produce meaning in the Qurʾān in an effective way.

Muslim doctrine holds that the Qurʾān is inimitable, its inimitability (q.v.) lying not only in its matchless literary style (see FORM AND STRUCTURE OF THE QURʾĀN) but also in its religious content. As such, the Qurʾān is considered the avowed miracle (see MIRACLES) of the prophet Muḥammad, testifying to the truth (q.v.) of his prophethood and the enduring veracity of his message (see PROPHETS AND PROPHETHOOD; MESSENGER). These doctrinal considerations frame classical Muslim considerations of the literary structures of the Qurʾān and their manner of generating religious meaning. It should be emphasized that these literary structures are not deemed mere otiose embellishments of the text of the Qur'ān but are rather the factors that produce its powerful effect in the specific forms presented. If the form of a qur'ānic text is changed in any way, however small or seemingly innocent, the meaning is modified, often significantly. Take, for example, *"iyyāka naʿbudu"* (Q 1:5). By syntactically placing the pronominal object *(iyyāka)* before the verb *(naʿbudu)*, rather than after it (as the pronominal suffix *-ka*), the meaning of the qur'ānic verse is specified to be "only you do we worship." This is significantly different from "we worship you" *(naʿbuduka)*, which declares worship of God but does not exclude the possibility of worshiping other deities as well (see POLYTHEISM AND ATHEISM). Syntax, therefore, is an important element of the literary structures of the Qur'ān, for it helps to determine the specific meaning of the text.

A further example will highlight another aspect of the quality of qur'ānic literary structures: *"wa-lakum fī l-qiṣāṣi ḥayātun"* (Q 2:179), which means "and in retaliation (q.v.), there is life for you." Muslim rhetoricians have compared this qur'ānic verse with the pre-Islamic Arabian proverb, *"al-qatlu anfā lil-qatli,"* which means "killing is more likely to preclude killing" (see PRE-ISLAMIC ARABIA AND THE QUR'ĀN; MURDER; BLOOD MONEY). Although the two statements are not exactly congruent, they both advocate the application of the death penalty in cases of murder, maintaining that such a punishment results in a safer society, as it both deters others and removes the murderer from the community (see COMMUNITY AND SOCIETY IN THE QUR'ĀN; CHASTISEMENT AND PUNISHMENT). Attention has been drawn to the sound of the words in these two statements; the phonemes of the pre-Islamic proverb are difficult to pronounce in succession, alternating — as they do — between the sounds of *a* and *q* at opposite ends of the laryngeal uttering process, interposed between the repetitive dental cluster *tl*, whereas the phonemes of the qur'ānic verse, in contrast, flow easily on one's tongue. Phonology, therefore, is another important element in literary structures, for it governs and ensures the acoustic and phonic fluidity of the qur'ānic text, helping it to achieve good reception and deliver its meaning effectively (see RECITATION OF THE QUR'ĀN).

As these examples demonstrate, the Arabic language forms the basis for the literary structures of the Qur'ān, and is the vehicle through which the intended meaning has been conveyed. The Qur'ān was revealed to the prophet Muḥammad in Arabic, as the text itself reiterates (e.g. Q 12:2; 20:113; 39:28; 41:3; 42:7; 43:3) and it is in Arabic that his contemporaries first heard the message, a message that affected both their hearts (see HEART) and minds (see INTELLECT). It is in Arabic that later generations of Muslim believers of all ethnic and linguistic backgrounds have continued to hear and recite the qur'ānic text, the text from which they have drawn guidance to shape their lives. To them a translation of the Qur'ān into any other language is not really the Qur'ān (lit. "recitation"; see ORALITY; ORALITY AND WRITING IN ARABIA), irrespective of its accuracy and faithfulness to the Arabic original. Furthermore, like other languages, Arabic has its own specific way of conveying meaning, which has been connected with particular cultural contexts; the Qur'ān's use of this idiom is notably unique and, for believers, miraculous. Muslims therefore celebrate this unique and inimitable Qur'ān, and aspire to retain the authentic association of language, culture and faith (q.v.) so central to their lives.

The qur'ānic text in the prophet Muḥammad's lifetime

According to tradition, the Qur'ān was revealed piecemeal to the prophet Muḥammad in about twenty-three years (between 610 and 632 C.E.). It was orally received and memorized (see MEMORY), and some qur'ānic passages were probably written down by his literate Companions (see COMPANIONS OF THE PROPHET) on flat stones, shoulder blades, palm leaves, parchment and other materials (see CODICES OF THE QUR'ĀN; LITERACY). Although qur'ānic passages of different lengths were revealed intermittently — frequently with specific reference or in response to particular circumstances and events — and were thus not necessarily intended or taken as continuing where the previously revealed text had left off (see OCCASIONS OF REVELATION; CHRONOLOGY AND THE QUR'ĀN), it was the prophet Muḥammad who — according to tradition — instructed the early believers as to the proper placement of these passages in the larger (and growing) oral text that would become the holy scripture of Islam. By the end of Muḥammad's life in 10/632, the Qur'ān had 114 sūras ranging from the shortest — with three verses (Q 103, 108, and 110) — to the longest, with 286 verses (Q 2). Muslim tradition says that Muḥammad designated the position of every verse but one (Q 4:176), since that verse was revealed just before his death. His Companions chose the place for this verse based upon its meaning, context, and style (see Draz, *Introduction*, 15, n. 3).

The qur'ānic text after the prophet Muḥammad's death

When the oral Qur'ān was later "collected" by the Prophet's Companions in "book" form in ca. 28/650, the 114 sūras were arranged largely according to size, and not according to the chronological order of revelation; the longer sūras were placed first and the shorter ones followed in a generally descending order of length. The notable exception to this arrangement is Q 1, Sūrat al-Fātiḥa ("The Opening"), which, although it has only seven verses, was placed at the beginning of the qur'ānic codex. According to Muslim tradition, copies of the Qur'ān have normally been disseminated in this form since its initial collection (one revisionist theory of the collection and compilation of the Qur'ān is provided by John Wansbrough, who, in his *Qur'ānic studies*, argues that the Qur'ān did not attain its current form until about the end of the second/eighth and beginning of the third/ninth century; see COLLECTION OF THE QUR'ĀN; MUṢḤAF).

One should keep in mind the originally oral character of the Qur'ān and the amount of time that elapsed before each of its sūras, especially the longer ones, were revealed in their entirety. Hence, it is necessary to look at the literary structures of the sūras (q.v.) to discover how each forms a unit, canonically constituting one chapter. Some pre-modern Muslim exegetes (see EXEGESIS OF THE QUR'ĀN: CLASSICAL AND MEDIEVAL) examined these structures, and offered theories of *naẓm* (lit. "order") highlighting the verbal organization of the sūra's wording with regard to its syntax and rhetorical figures of speech (see RHETORIC OF THE QUR'ĀN); others offered theories of *munāsaba* or *tanāsub* (lit. "relationship") about the linear relatedness of verses (q.v.) within the sūra, or even of one sūra and the next. But the treatment of the sūra as a unit was not really broached by Muslim scholars until the twentieth century, notably by Amīn Aḥsan Iṣlāḥī (1906-97) and Sayyid Quṭb (1906-66).

The sūra *as a unit*

In his *Tadabbur-i Qur'ān* (1967-80), Amīn Aḥsan Iṣlāḥī concentrates on the semantic and thematic content of the sūra as a coherent unit. He finds that, semantically, the sūras are linked in complementary pairs and that the Qurʾān contains seven groups of sūras, each with a block of Meccan sūras and a block of Medinan ones, which deal, respectively, with theoretical and practical aspects of the block's theme. Iṣlāḥī's concept is insightful, if a little too schematized, but it does not give literary structures their due place in generating and conveying the meaning of the qurʾānic sūras in his systematized scheme.

In his *Fī ẓilāl al-Qurʾān* (1952-9), Sayyid Quṭb focuses on the coherent unity of each sūra — mostly with regard to its semantic and thematic qualities — but he does identify structural characteristics related to its diction, syntax, imagery and phonology that reflect the intended meaning and mood of the sūra. He finds that each sūra has a core or central point, a theme that he calls its *miḥwar* (lit. its "axis"), around which it revolves. In his view, the sūra may have one topic *(mawḍūʿ)* tightly bound to its theme or it may have more topics so bound; the theme may sometimes be double-lined (as in long *sūra*s), but each line *(khaṭṭ)* of the theme is then strongly bound to the other. For example, Sayyid Quṭb believes that Q 2 has a double-lined theme whose two lines are strongly bound together. The first thematic line revolves around the hostile attitude of the Jews (see JEWS AND JUDAISM) to Islam in Medina (q.v.) and their friendly relations with the Arabian polytheists and hypocrites (see HYPOCRITES AND HYPOCRISY). The second thematic line revolves around the corresponding attitude of the Muslims in Medina and their growth as a believing community prepared to carry the responsibility of God's call after Jewish rejection. Both lines are complementary and tightly bound together throughout the sūra, which eventually ends as it began: by exhorting (see EXHORTATIONS) human beings to belief in God (see BELIEF AND UNBELIEF), his prophets, his scriptures (see BOOK; SCRIPTURE AND THE QURʾĀN) and the metaphysical unseen world (see HIDDEN AND THE HIDDEN). From beginning to end, the several topics of the sūra are related to this double-lined theme.

In all circumstances, Sayyid Quṭb believes each sūra has a special atmosphere *(jaww)* integrating its topic or topics harmoniously and a musical rhythm *(īqāʿ mūsīqī)* consonant with its topic or topics. He maintains that both *jaww* and *īqāʿ mūsīqī* strengthen the effective delivery of its intended meaning. The aesthetic effects of the Qurʾān's literary structures are discussed at some length by Sayyid Quṭb in his books *al-Taṣwīr al-fannī fī l-Qurʾān* (1945) and *Mashāhid al-qiyāma fī l-Qurʾān* (1947), where he gives a detailed view of the manner in which the structures generate the intended meaning and deliver it with verbal beauty and psychological power.

Some Western scholars, on the other hand, have criticized the Qurʾān because they perceived it as lacking in certain literary virtues. None other than T. Nöldeke stated "dass der gesunde Sprachsinn der Araber sie fast ganz davor beewahrt hat, die eigentlichen Selsamkeiten und Schwächen der Koransprache nachzuahmen" (Zur Sprache, 22; Fr. trans. "Le bon sens linguistique des Arabes les a presque entièrement préservés de l'imitation des étrangetés et faiblesses propres à la langue du Coran," in id., *Remarques critiques,* 34). Thomas Carlyle (cf. Arberrry, *Koran,* i, 12), no mean admirer of the prophet Muḥammad as a hero, thought of the Qurʾān as "toilsome reading" and considered it to be "a wearisome, confused jumble, crude, incondite." R.A. Nicholson (cf. Arberry, *Koran,* ii, 9) referred to European readers of the Qurʾān who held that "it is obscure, tiresome, uninteresting; a farrago of long-winded narratives and prosaic exhortations." W. Montgomery Watt (Watt-Bell, *Introduction,* 73) spoke of "disjointedness" as "a real characteristic of Qurʾānic style."

Yet Mohammed Marmaduke Pickthall, the first modern British Muslim to make an English translation of the Qurʾān (which he did not call "The Qurʾān," but pointedly entitled *The meaning of the glorious Koran* and subtitled "An explanatory translation") refers to the Qurʾān in his foreword as "that inimitable symphony, the very sounds of which move men to tears and ecstasy." Another Englishman, Arthur J. Arberry, who also translated the Qurʾān into English, offered his translation as only *The Koran interpreted* and devised "rhythmic patterns and sequence-groupings" in it to reflect certain aspects of its literary structures in Arabic. Although in his introduction Arberry admits (*Koran,* i, 24) that it is "a poor copy of the glittering splendour of the original," he later says that each "*sūra* will now be seen to be a unity within itself, and the Koran will be recognized as a simple revelation, self-consistent to the highest degree" (*Koran,* ii, 15-6). More recently, the works of Angelika Neuwirth have focused on the literary merit and integrity of whole sūras (cf. e.g. Neuwirth, Zur Struktur der Yūsuf-Sure; see also N. Robinson, *Discovering the Qurʾān*).

The study of the qurʾānic sūra as a unit with coherent unity is still in need of focused, philological elaboration in modern scholarship. With the possible exception of the German school of qurʾānic studies, the analytical tools and categories for such research, as well as the relevant technical methods and terminology, need to be developed and established, as has been achieved — however dissonantly — with the study of other scriptures and of other literary genres. Such a study will help better understand not only the sūra and its literary structures, but also — ultimately — the whole Qurʾān as a holy scripture with a singular message. The study of the macrostructure of the Qurʾān should build on the conclusions of studying its microstructures as manifested in the sūra and its individual, componential pericopes (see NARRATIVES; for an example of the contemporary German scholarship on the macro- and microstructures of the Qurʾān, see the *EQ* articles by Angelika Neuwirth, esp. SŪRAS; FORM AND STRUCTURE OF THE QURʾĀN; RHETORIC OF THE QURʾĀN).

The prose of the Qurʾān

As Arabic is the language of the Qurʾān, its use in a variety of literary forms should be closely examined. To be noted first and foremost is the fact that the qurʾānic text is written in prose. It is a very special kind of prose, to be sure, and it is unique in many ways; but it is definitely prose and not verse. Classical Arabic verse has regular meter and recurring rhyme as two of its basic features, which are partly responsible for its symmetry and harmony. These features are clear in the long tradition of the Arabic *qaṣīda,* the ode. The prose of the qurʾānic text, on the other hand, is not at all metrical; furthermore, its rhyme is neither regular nor constantly based on an identical rhyme-letter as in classical Arabic verse. It is often replaced by assonance, and, sometimes, completely ignored.

Muslim scholars have been reluctant to call the prose of the qurʾānic text *sajʿ,* "rhymed prose" (q.v.), possibly because this term is associated with the prose pronouncements of pagan priests and the prose utterances of fortune-tellers (see FORETELLING; DIVINATION) or soothsayers (q.v.) in pre-Islamic Arabia (see also POETRY AND POETS), as well as with the prose of later Arabic writings in Islamic history characterized by a degree of artificiality or mannerism. The term *sajʿ,* however, is not appropriate mainly because not all of the qurʾānic text is written in rhymed prose. Muslim scholars prefer to designate the prose of the qurʾānic text as one divided into *fawāṣil,* "rhetorical periods" (singular *fāṣila*). Each period in the text contains a semantic-grammatical unit forming an *āya,* "a verse," usually ending with rhyme or assonance echoing the rhyme or assonance of other verses in the proximate textual neighborhood. Sometimes, however, a rhetorical period ends without such rhyme or assonance.

An *āya* may be short and can consist of as few as one word (e.g. Q 69:1; 101:1) or even a couple of "mysterious letters" (q.v.) at the beginning of certain sūras (e.g. Q 20:1; 36:1). It may also be quite long and consist of as many as fifty words or more. When the *āyāt* are short, the effect of the rhymes or assonances in the text is powerful because, given their proximity to one another, they continue to ring in the immediate memory of the reader or listener and instill the meaning with persistence. When, however, the *āyāt* are long, the effect of the rhymes or assonances as such is less powerful on account of the distance between one and the next, thus possibly allowing for them to fade in the immediate memory; in these instances, however, their effect is usually reinforced through their inclusion within a brief rhyming phrase or clause tagged to the end of the *āya* as a coda, a device which can serve to remind the reader or listener of the preceding statement, pressing it home, and clinching the argument of the *āya.*

A few examples will suffice to demonstrate the nature of rhyme or assonance in both the short and long verses of the Qurʾān. Some examples of the short verses are as follows: 1. After the *basmala* (q.v.), Q 112 (in full) reads: (1) *qul huwa llāhu aḥad* (2) *Allāhu l-ṣamad* (3) *lam yalid wa-lam yūlad* (4) *wa-lam yakun lahu kufuwan aḥad.* Here the rhyme is *-ad.* To be noted is the fact that the final inflection of the rhyme-word is disregarded lest the rhyme be broken; otherwise, the final words would not rhyme and would read, respectively: *aḥadun, l-ṣamadu, yūlad,* and *aḥadun.* 2. Verses 9-11 of Q 93 read: (9) *fa-ammā l-yatīma fa-lā taqhar* (10) *wa-ammā l-sāʾila fa-lā tanhar* (11) *wa-ammā bi-niʿmati rabbika fa-ḥaddith.* Here the rhyme of verses 9 and 10 is *-ar* but it is ignored in verse 11. Examples of long verses are as follows: 1. Q 2:143 has forty-five words, ending with the coda *inna llāha bi-l-nāsi la-raʾūfun raḥīm,* the rhyme of which is *-īm,* echoing the majority of the other rhymes in the sūra, which consist of *-īm* and of the assonantal *-īn* and *-ūn.* There are, however, verses in this sūra that end in *-īr* (Q 2:148) or *-āb* (Q 2:165-6), or *-ār* (Q 2:167), as well as other consonantal endings, in which the rhyme or assonance of the majority of the verses of the sūra is ignored. 2. In the same sūra, verse Q 2:255 has fifty words and ends with the coda *wa-huwa l-ʿaliyyu l-ʿaẓīm.* The verse that follows, Q 2:256, which consists of twenty-four words, ends with the coda *wa-llāhu samīʿun ʿalīm.* Both verses rhyme in *-īm,* echoing most of the other rhymes and assonances in the sūra, and the coda in each reinforces and clinches the argument of the *āya.*

From the above, it can be observed that the verses of the qurʾānic text are of various lengths. In the longer sūras, the verses are usually long and in the shorter sūras they are usually short, but this is not an invariant rule. Even within a single sūra, the verses vary in length. Although they tend to be of a fairly similar length, they are not necessarily equal in length nor are they composed of parallel and corresponding syllables, as in metrical composition with prosodic feet, to produce the exact symmetry of versification. Nonetheless, the prose of the qurʾānic text has a certain rhythm to it, which varies from sūra to sūra and even within one sūra, particularly if it is a long one. This rhythm is not that of a fixed meter but that of a unique composition that allows the topic at hand to qualify it and modify its cadences, using verses of varying lengths, mostly with rhymes or assonances and sometimes without. The topic of the sūra may gradually unfold different aspects of its major theme, and the verses of the sūra may accordingly have a different rhyme-letter for each aspect, especially in sūras of some length; but, again, this is not an invariant rule.

In sum, the prose of the Qurʾān is not totally rhymed prose, nor is it totally unrhymed free prose. It is a unique blend of both, with an important contribution by assonance, couched in a variety of short and long verses dispensed in sūras of various lengths. The different patterns of rhymes, assonances and free endings in the verses, as well as the different lengths and rhythms of these verses and the varying lengths of the sūras themselves, are all literary structures related to the meaning offered. In the final analysis, they comprise an essential element of the effective delivery of the total message of the Qurʾān.

Phonology

From the Arabic text of the Qurʾān, it is obvious that sound plays a major role in the effect its words produce, an effect that a translation of the Qurʾān into other languages fails to preserve, despite the best efforts of the translators. Arthur J. Arberry made a genuine effort in his English translation of the Qurʾān "to devise rhythmic patterns and sequence-groupings in correspondence with what the Arabic presents." Despite his commendable effort, he admits that, in the end, his interpretation is a poor echo of the original, as noted above.

The sound of Arabic words in the Qurʾān is an important element of literary structure in producing a rhetorical medium that delivers the meaning effectively. This element functions at different levels. At the level of vocabulary, there is what rhetoricians would come to describe as the "eloquence of the single word" *(faṣāḥat al-mufrad):* the individual words in the Qurʾān consist of letters that flow harmoniously without tongue-twisting difficulties or ear-jarring sounds, each word agreeing with common usage and the morphological rules of Arabic. These later rhetoricians also noted the "eloquence of composition" *(faṣāḥat al-murakkab)* with regards to the wording of individual verses: the order of words is such that their phonemes flow with ease from one word to the next in pronunciation and are aurally perceived with a pleasant sensation. Meanwhile, the construction follows the rules of correct syntax, allowing variations that cater to the rhetorical intention and effectiveness of semantic delivery. At the level of passages consisting of shorter or longer sequences within a sūra, the verses of varying lengths are threaded together by rhymes and assonances, their rhythms varying according to their topics and modulated according to their moods in order to produce maximum effect. At the level of the whole Qurʾān, which consists of short, middle-sized and long sūras, the total message leaves a phonological and semantic impression that is considered absolutely sublime and that has often been said to go beyond the exquisite harmony of music; this is "that inimitable symphony" according to Marmaduke Pickthall. Muslim rhetoricians have called this unique composition of the Qurʾān *naẓm al-Qurʾān* (lit. "the order of the Qurʾān"), a reference to the beautiful fusion of its wording and meaning in accordance with principles of grammar, rhetoric, and phonology, briefly outlined above. Considering the Qurʾān's divine provenance to be a matter of faith and deeming its content transcendent and its composition unique, Muslim theologians have considered it to be the prophet Muḥammad's miracle and declared it to be beyond human ability to imitate. By the early part of the third/ninth century, they developed the doctrine of *iʿjāz al-Qurʾān,* literally, the Qurʾān's incapacitation (of humans and jinn [q.v.]), but technically denoting the miraculously inimitable character of the Qurʾān. According to the theologians, the doctrine that human beings and jinn are incapable of imitating the Qurʾān has been proven by their continuing inability to meet its clear challenge to them to do so (Q 10:38; 11:13; 17:88; see Boullata, Rhetorical interpretation, 149-57).

Transtextuality

As in music, repetition plays an essential role in any literary text of poetic effectiveness. In the Qurʾān, it takes the form of repeated rhythms, rhymes, assonances, refrains, patterns of structure and variations on the same theme. It is meant to inculcate the qurʾānic message with power while employing a sublime language that seizes the heart and mind — without being enthralling or entrancing in the pejorative, incantatory sense of enslaving comprehension, spiritual absorption, and meaningful reaction.

Transtextuality allows several kinds of repetition, whereby a usage with strong associations of meaning in one part of the Qurʾān is encountered in another part or in other parts of it with echoes of the earlier usage, either at the intratextual level of the same sūra or at the intertextual level of all the sūras. Two obvious examples of refrains may be used to demonstrate this repetition at the intratextual level. The refrains are repeated several times, with a stronger effect each time as the text builds to a climax. The first example is Q 55, a sūra consisting of seventy-eight short verses, of which thirty are a refrain asking the rhetorical question: "Which then of the favors (see GRACE; BLESSING) of your lord (q.v.) will you two deny?" The first instance of this refrain occurs after verse 12, and appears thereafter following every verse or two; after verse 44, the refrain alternates with every verse until the end of the sūra. The sūra enumerates the bounties of God to the two kinds of creatures: human beings and jinn (see CREATION). It mentions God's creation of humankind, the jinn, the orderly universe and the world (see COSMOLOGY) with its wonders, blessings, gifts, bounties, and benefits that are granted to all out of his mercy (q.v.). One of these blessings is God's teaching of the Qurʾān. On the day of judgment (see LAST JUDGMENT), all creatures will be rewarded or punished according to their deeds (see GOOD DEEDS; EVIL DEEDS; RECORD OF HUMAN ACTIONS). The sūra describes the physical features of the reward and punishment (q.v.), leaving no excuse for anyone to deny the prior favors of the lord, which are incrementally stressed throughout the sūra, culminating in the climax, with the thirty repetitions of the rhetorical question.

The other example of refrains recurring throughout a single sūra is found in Q 77, which consists of fifty short verses, ten of which are a refrain in the form of a threat: "Woe on that day to those who deny" (see LIE; GRATITUDE AND INGRATITUDE). The day in question is *yawm al-faṣl,* "the day of decision," on which the physical features of the world will collapse and all creatures will be brought before God for judgment (see APOCALYPSE). The sūra begins with a succession of enigmatic oaths (q.v.) assuring everyone that what has been promised will indeed occur. Then it proceeds to a frightening description of the universe as it collapses. Creatures are reminded that God had created them and the world's benefits for them. They are reminded that

God had destroyed the evil-doers of yore (see GENERATIONS) and will punish all sinners (see SIN, MAJOR AND MINOR), whose tricks will not avail against them nor protect them from the blazing flames (see FIRE; HELL AND HELLFIRE). Meanwhile, the righteous will dwell amid shades and fountains, eating fruits and consuming and drinking what they desire, in just reward for their pious lives (see GARDEN; PARADISE; FOOD AND DRINK; PIETY). God's favors and his promised punishment throughout the sūra are punctuated by the repeated threat of woe to those who, on that day of decision, deny the truth of God's power, but will not be permitted to speak and excuse themselves. The repeated threats serve to highlight the fearful punishment and, in contrast, the blissful joy of reward (see JOY AND MISERY; HOPE).

Repetitions in the form of refrains like these two examples do not occur elsewhere in the qurʾānic text. There are, however, other kinds of repetition in the form of words or turns of phrase that are too many to enumerate, which contribute to that specific quality of the qurʾānic style, giving it a particular tone. That which was called coda above, namely a maxim that comes at the end of a verse clinching its purport, is an example of such a repetition, a refrain that occurs in the Qurʾān at both the intratextual and the intertextual levels. An example of such a coda is *wa-huwa l-ʿazīzu l-ḥakīm,* "And he is the mighty, the wise" (Q 29:42). This also occurs without the definite article but usually with *Allāh* ("God") instead of the pronoun *huwa* ("he"), as in Q 5:38: *wa-llāhu ʿazīzun ḥakīm,* "And God is mighty, wise." This coda occurs about forty times in the Qurʾān. Variations — with a different attribute of God (see GOD AND HIS ATTRIBUTES) — also occur, such as Q 44:42: *innahu huwa l-ʿazīzu l-raḥīm,* "Verily, he is the mighty, the merciful," or Q 67:2: *wa-huwa l-ʿazīzu l-ghafūr,* "And he is the mighty, the forgiving" (see FORGIVENESS). Among the many other codas is the one found in Q 2:20: *inna llāha ʿalā kulli shayʾin qadīr,* "Verily, God is powerful over everything," which also occurs without *inna* ("verily") and begins with *wa* ("and"), as in Q 2:284: *wa-llāhu ʿalā kulli shayʾin qadīr,* "And God is powerful over everything." The pronoun *huwa* or *hu* may also be substituted for *Allāh,* as in Q 30:50 and Q 41:39, respectively. This coda occurs about thirty times in the Qurʾān.

Another form of repetition in the Qurʾān is the telling of punishment stories (q.v.), in each of which a messenger is sent by God to a certain people to teach them, to turn them away from their evil deeds and to warn (see WARNER) them against God's punishment if they do not heed. When they persist in their evil ways, God's punishment is visited upon them in a variety of terrible ways. Such is the story of the messenger Hūd (q.v.) sent to the Arabian pre-Islamic group of people called ʿĀd (q.v.). Likewise, it is the story of the messenger Ṣāliḥ (q.v.) sent to a certain people of ancient Arabia called Thamūd (q.v.). Some of the stories have biblical equivalents, such as the story of the messenger Shuʿayb (q.v.) sent to the people of Midian (q.v.) or the story of Noah (q.v.) and his people or of Lot (q.v.) and his people or some aspects of the story of the prophet Moses (q.v.) and Pharaoh (q.v.). Q 26 contains a group of these punishment stories, some of which are repeated with variations in Q 54, Q 7, Q 11, Q 51, and elsewhere. Not only is the pattern of events in these stories generally parallel, but the wording is often similar, sometimes even identical in certain parts of the story (see Welch, Formulaic features). The oral nature of the original qurʾānic message is very evident in these stories, repeated in a variety of similar ways to suit different audiences in the Prophet's lifetime. Their purpose, then and later, is to warn and threaten unbelievers, to convince them of the power of God and the certainty of his punishment, and to reassure those who believe in God and accept Muḥammad's message that he is truly God's messenger sent to the world as a warner and a bearer of good tidings (see GOOD NEWS) about a new religion and a new societal order. The rhetoric of thematic and verbal repetition in the stories inculcates this purpose strongly and helps instill the meaning effectively.

Imagery and figurative language

Metaphors (see METAPHOR) and other figures of speech abound in the Qurʾān. As in the scriptures of other world religions and in the literatures of all nations, figurative language is used to enhance the effect of what is said by making it beautiful, impressive, aesthetically striking, and semantically powerful. It persuades through literary devices that stir the imagination and appeal directly to the senses. On this count, the Qurʾān often offers dramatic uses of figurative language in its literary structures, as well as original and daring insights of unforgettable aesthetic and semantic effect.

There is much in the Qurʾān that continues to adhere to the literal usage of the Arabic language, that is, the use of words for what they have commonly been used to designate. Yet, as in other languages, there are some words whose figurative usage has become so common as to be accepted as normal literal usage. English words like leg, neck, and eye, which originally refer to parts of humans or animals, are no longer considered metaphorical when used in such expressions as "the leg of a table," "the neck of a bottle" and "the eye of a needle." In a similar manner, the Arabic word *sharīʿa,* which originally refers to a path leading to water sought for drinking, has come to refer metaphorically to religious law, as attested in Q 45:18 (see LAW AND THE QURʾĀN). This religious law is — if obeyed — the path leading to the quenching of spiritual thirst and the preservation of societal health and well-being, hence the connection of *sharīʿa* referring to Islamic law. Another similar qurʾānic use is the Arabic word *fatra,* which originally meant tepidity, but has been commonly used to mean interval of time between happenings; Q 5:19 reads: *qad jāʾakum rasūlunā yubayyinu lakum ʿalā fatratin min al-rusuli,* "Our messenger has come to you to make things clear to you after an interval between the messengers." Here *fatra* may also effectively be read — as originally intended in Arabic — to mean tepidity. The qurʾānic statement can then be understood as saying: "Our messenger has come to you to make things clear to you after the tepidity of [people's faith in earlier] messengers" (for further discussion, see Abu-Deeb, Studies in the *majāz*). Aside from these matters, however, the Qurʾān has an amazing abundance of fresh and vivid images and figures of speech in its literary structures, an abundance that has made a perceptive modern literary critic and exegete like Sayyid Quṭb argue that what he calls *taṣwīr fannī,* "artistic imagery," is indeed the preferred style of the Qurʾān (see Boullata, Sayyid Quṭb's literary appreciation). Classical rhetoricians and exegetes of the Qurʾān writing in Arabic, like al-Jurjānī (d. 471/1078) and al-Zamakhsharī (d. 538/1144), among others, have long drawn particular attention to this inherent quality of imagery in the qurʾānic style.

The primary instance to be noted is the fact that the Qurʾān speaks of God in anthropomorphic language (see ANTHROPOMORPHISM). Although it says of God *laysa ka-mithlihi shayʾun* (Q 42:11), "Nothing is like unto him," it speaks of the "hand of God" (e.g. Q 3:73; 5:64; 48:10) and sometimes speaks of "his hand" (e.g. Q 23:88;

36:83; see HAND[s]). Muslim theologians have long discussed such wording and often differ — each according to his theological school — about the explanation. But it appears evident that, linguistically, there is figurative speech here, the word hand metonymically referring to God's power (see POWER AND IMPOTENCE). The same applies to the "eye of God," as in *li-tuṣna'a 'alā 'aynī* (Q 20:39), i.e. "that you [Moses] may be formed before my eye," metonymically meaning under God's protection and according to his will (see EYES). In the same manner, the Qur'ān ascribes attributes to God, such as mercy (q.v.), knowledge (see KNOWLEDGE AND LEARNING), hearing (see HEARING AND DEAFNESS), sight (see VISION AND BLINDNESS; SEEING AND HEARING), speech (q.v.), love (see LOVE AND AFFECTION), justice (see JUSTICE AND INJUSTICE), power, generosity (q.v.), forgiveness, oneness, wisdom (q.v.), glory (q.v.), greatness and so on. God is also said to have sat on the throne (*thumma stawā 'alā l-'arsh*, Q 7:54; 10:3; 13:2; 25:59; 32:4; 57:4 and elsewhere), with the word "throne" taken to be a symbol (see SYMBOLIC IMAGERY) of his omnipotence and majesty (see THRONE OF GOD).

Likewise, the afterlife (see ESCHATOLOGY) is described in the Qur'ān in terms of physical pleasure in paradise and physical pain in hell, denoting, respectively, reward and punishment for deeds done on earth (q.v.) in this life, and fulfilling God's promise of reward and his threat of punishment elaborated in the Qur'ān. The material joys of paradise are concurrent with the spiritual satisfaction of being near God, experiencing eternal peace and bliss, and delighting in the beatitude of salvation (q.v.). The material sufferings of hell are concurrent with the spiritual affliction of being exiled from God's presence, the frustrating experience of eternal self-blame and regret, and the permanent agony of being condemned to the misery of damnation. Jewish and Christian literature have parallel details of the afterlife, but the qur'ānic image is, on the whole, *sui generis*. This image can be culled from different, scattered texts of various lengths in the Qur'ān, most of them found in the Meccan sūras. Each text concentrates on specific scenes from paradise or hell, or from both, usually presented in a contrastive way. Each text, with its different details, adds to the total picture of the afterlife. In his *Mashāhid al-qiyāma fī l-Qur'ān*, Sayyid Quṭb surveys 150 scenes taken from eighty sūras of the Qur'ān, sixty-three of them from the Meccan period and seventeen from the Medinan period.

Perhaps even more graphic is the qur'ānic image of the last day, the time when history comes to a climax: the universe is dismantled, the dead are resurrected (see DEATH AND THE DEAD; RESURRECTION), the last judgment occurs, and an eternity (q.v.) in paradise or hell begins for those consigned to either according to their deeds. What happens on this last day is described in ominous words such as in Q 82:1-5: "(1) When heaven is cleft asunder, (2) When the stars (*al-kawākib*, see PLANETS AND STARS) are dispersed, (3) When the seas are burst, (4) And when the tombs are laid open, (5) Each soul shall then know its former and latter deeds." Or, Q 81:1-14, "(1) When the sun is rolled up, (2) When the stars *(al-nujūm)* are darkened, (3) When the mountains are made to move, (4) When the ten-month pregnant she-camels are abandoned (see CAMEL), (5) When the wild beasts are herded together, (6) When the seas are made to seethe, (7) When the souls are united, (8) When the female infant buried alive (see CHILDREN; INFANTICIDE) is asked, (9) For what sin she was killed, (10) When the scrolls (q.v.) are spread out, (11) When heaven is stripped off, (12) When hell is set ablaze, (13) And when paradise is brought near, (14) Each soul shall then know what it has produced." Of grammatical note in these qurʾānic passages is the fact that the main verbs are used in the passive voice and without mention of the specific doer of the action, or that they occur in the seventh or eighth morphological verbal form, forms which usually denote passivity. This structure increases the perception of the passivity of the universe at the end of time as it obeys an omnipotent God who does not even need to be mentioned as the doer because he is known to be the only one with commensurate power and authority to act at that cosmic scale.

There are several other qurʾānic passages with such ominous, eschatological and cataclysmic scenes foreshadowing humans being brought to account on the last day, the day of resurrection and the day of judgment. The event is heralded by a terrible shout (*ṣayḥa,* Q 36:53), a thunderclap (*ṣākhkha,* Q 80:33), one blast of a trumpet (Q 69:13: *nufikha fī l-ṣūri nafkhatun wāḥida*) or two blasts (Q 39:68: *nufikha fī l-ṣūri [...] thumma nufikha fīhi ukhrā*), and other portents (as mentioned above). The Qurʾān often gives this day a special, alarming attribute such as *al-ḥāqqa* (Q 69:1) or *al-qāriʿa* (Q 101:1) or *yawm al-faṣl* (Q 77:13). In order to magnify the unknown and unexpected dread of the day, it immediately follows this attribute with a rhetorical question or double question, asked in awe-inspiring tones, as in Q 69:2-3, "What is *al-ḥāqqa?* And what shall make you know what *al-ḥāqqa* is?" or Q 101:2-3, "What is *al-qāriʿa?* And what shall make you know what *al-qāriʿa* is?" or Q 77:14, "And what shall make you know what *yawmu l-faṣl* is?" In a similar way, the Qurʾān gives hell other names, such as *saqar* (Q 74:26) or *al-ḥuṭama* (Q 104:4) and follows that name with a rhetorical question, asking as in Q 74:27, "And what shall make you know what *saqar* is?"; and Q 104:5, "And what shall make you know what *al-ḥuṭama* is?" A menacing description is then provided, with terrifying details.

Among the other qurʾānic names of hell are *al-jaḥīm* ("the hot place"), *al-saʿīr* ("the blaze"), *laẓā* ("flame"), and *al-nār* ("the fire"). These very names evoke the physical torment of the damned by fire and burning, hence the qurʾānic image of hell's inmates asking those in paradise for water but being denied it (Q 7:50). To drink, they are given boiling water like molten lead *(ka-l-muhli),* scalding their faces (Q 18:29), or they are given festering liquid pus *(māʾin ṣadīdin)* which they can hardly swallow (Q 14:16-7). They are given to eat from the *zaqqūm* tree, whose bitter fruits are like heads of devils (Q 37:62-5; see AGRICULTURE AND VEGETATION). They burn in hell but do not die or live, and they are not consumed; whenever their skins are seared, they are given fresh skins so that they may continue to be tormented (Q 4:56). Their torment reaches to their very souls and they wish they could ransom themselves with all their earthly possessions and they feel remorse within them on seeing their punishment (Q 10:54; see REPENTANCE AND PENANCE). They bite their hands in regret and wish they had chosen the messenger's way (Q 25:27). They wish they could return to the world and be believers (Q 26:102), and they cry for help to the lord to be let out in order to do righteous deeds, but they will not be helped, for they had been forewarned (Q 35:37).

In contrast, the eternal reward of the good and just people is a place of physical pleasure and spiritual bliss; it is *jannāt al-naʿīm* ("the gardens of delight") or *jannāt al-firdaws* ("the gardens of paradise") or simply *al-janna* ("the garden"). Through it, rivers flow (Q 5:119), rivers of unpolluted water, rivers of milk (q.v.) unchanging in flavor, rivers of delicious wine (q.v.), and rivers of clear honey (q.v.; Q 47:15). The inmates recline with their spouses on couches in pleasant shades, enjoying fruits and whatever they call for (Q 36:56-57). They are adorned with bracelets of gold (q.v.) and wear green garments of silk (q.v.) and brocade (Q 18:31). They are served by immortal youths carrying goblets, ewers, and cups filled from a pure spring (see SPRINGS AND FOUNTAINS); and they do not have headaches by drinking therefrom, nor are they intoxicated (see INTOXICANTS). They eat fruits and the flesh of fowls as they desire. They have fair wide-eyed maids who are like well-preserved pearls (see HOURIS). No vain or sinful talk do they hear, but rather greetings of peace (Q 56:17-26; see GOSSIP). They experience no fear (q.v.) or sorrow (Q 7:49) and they are happy forever (Q 11:108). Their faces are radiant, looking toward their lord (Q 75:22-3); for they are the *muqarrabūn*, "those brought near" (Q 56:11), in the gardens of delight.

Although these contrasting images can be filled out with further details from other qurʾānic passages on the afterlife, they suffice here to give an idea of the impressive imagery of the Qurʾān. They demonstrate some of the most striking aspects of the imaginative power of the Arabic language to paint large scenes. The literary structures of the Qurʾān, however, also use this imaginative power to paint small scenes. This usage is found in many of the Qurʾān's similes (q.v.), metaphors, and figures of speech of every kind. A few examples should give an idea of the wide-ranging qurʾānic employment of such figurative language. The following is one of the complex similes: The futility of praying to false gods who never respond (see IDOLS AND IMAGES) is likened to a man who stretches out his open palms to scoop water to his mouth but cannot bring any water to it (Q 13:14). One of the metaphors utilizes an oath, swearing by the personified morning as it begins: *wa-l-ṣubḥi idhā tanaffasa* (Q 81:18), meaning, "And by morning when it breathes." The vivid expressiveness comes not from the mere personification of morning, but from the ascription of breathing to the rise of day, denoting the resumption of life and movement after night's stillness. Another example of a metaphor appears when Zechariah (q.v.; Zakariyyā) describes his old age. In Q 19:4, he is reported as saying, "And my head is ablaze with hoary hair" *(wa-shtaʿala l-raʾsu shayban)*. The spread of white hair on his head with advancing age is portrayed as the spread of fire, which may first begin with one or two sparks then grows inexorably into a flame. The image is made more striking by its grammatical construction: the head itself is the subject of burning, not the hoary hair, which is added as an accusative of specification.

In conclusion, it can be said that the Qurʾān utilizes a wide variety of literary devices to convey its message. In its original Arabic idiom, the individual components of the text — sūras and *āyāt* — employ phonetic and thematic structures that assist the audience's efforts to recall the message of the text. Whereas scholars of Arabic are largely agreed that the Qurʾān represents the standard by which other literary productions in Arabic are measured, believing Muslims maintain that the Qurʾān is inimitable with respect to both content and style (see LITERATURE AND THE QURʾĀN). From a linguistic standpoint, moreover, an understanding of the harmony within and between the Qurʾān's literary structures will be further enhanced by continuing study of macro and micro units of the text.

Issa J. Boullata

Bibliography
Primary: al-ʿAskarī, Abū Hilāl al-Ḥasan b. ʿAbdallāh, *Kitāb al-Ṣināʿatayn. Al-kitāba wa-l-shiʿr,* ed. A.M. al-Bijāwi and M.A.F. Ibrāhīm, Cairo 1952; Bāqillānī, *Iʿjāz;* Jurjānī, *Asrār;* id., *Dalāʾil,* ed. M. ʿAbduh and M. al-Shanqīṭī, annotated by R. Riḍā, Cairo 1902; Rummānī et al., *Rasāʾil;* Suyūṭi, *Itqān;* id., *Tanāsuq;* Zamakhsharī, *Kashshāf,* Beirut 1947; Zarkashī, *Burhān,* Cairo 1957.
Secondary: K. Abu-Deeb, *al-Jurjānī's theory of poetic imagery,* Warminster 1979; id., Studies in the *majāz* and metaphorical language of the Qurʾān. Abū ʿUbayda and al-Sharīf al-Raḍī, in I.J. Boullata (ed.), *Literary structures of religious meaning in the Qurʾān,* Richmond 2000, 310-53; A.J. Arberry (trans.), *The Koran interpreted,* London 1964; A. Baumstark, Jüdischer und christlicher Gebetstypus im Koran, in *Der Islam* 16 (1927), 229-48; I.J. Boullata, Iʿjāz, in *ER,* vii, 87-8; id. (ed.), *Literary structures of religious meaning in the Qurʾān,* Richmond 2000; id., The rhetorical interpretation of the Qurʾān. Iʿjāz and related topics, in Rippin, *Approaches,* 139-57; id., Sayyid Quṭb's literary appreciation of the Qurʾān, in I.J. Boullata (ed.), *Literary structures of religious meaning in the Qurʾān,* Richmond 2000, 356-8; A.M. Draz, *Introduction to the Qurʾān,* London 2001; L. Gardet, Djahannam, in *EI²,* ii, 381-2; id., Djanna, in *EI²,* ii, 447-52; R. Geyer, Zur Strophic des Qurʾāns, in *Wiener Zeitschrift für die Kunde des Morgenlandes* 22 (1908), 265-86; Graham, *Beyond;* A.A. Iṣlāḥī, *Tadabbur-i Qurʾān,* 8 vols., Lahore 1967-80; Jeffery, *Materials;* M. Mir, *Coherence in the Qurʾān. A study of Iṣlāḥī's concept of* naẓm *in* Tadabbur-i Qurʾān, Indianapolis 1986; id., The *sūra* as a unity. A twentieth century development in Qurʾān exegesis, in Hawting and Shareef, *Approaches,* 211-24; F. Müller, *Untersuchungen zur Reimprosa im Koran,* Bonn 1969; A. Neuwirth, Images and metaphors in the introductory sections of the Makkan *sūras*, in Hawting and Shareef, *Approaches,* 3-36; id., Zur Struktur der Yūsuf-Sure, in W. Diem and S. Wild (eds.), *Studien aus Arabistik und Semitistik. Anton Spitaler zum siebzigsten Geburtstag von seinen Schulern überreicht,* Wiesbaden 1980, 123-52; Nöldeke, *GQ* (contains extensive discussion of the literary structures in the Qurʾān); id., *Remarques critiques sur le style et la syntaxe du Coran,* trans. G.-H. Bousquet, Paris 1953 (Fr. trans. of *Neue Beiträge*); id., Zur Sprache des Korans, in id., *Neue Beiträge zur semitischen Sprachwissenschaft,* Strassburg 1910, 1-30; M.M. Pickthall (trans.), *The meaning of the glorious Koran,* London 1930; New York 1968; S. Quṭb, *Mashāhid al-qiyāma fī l-Qurʾān,* Cairo 1947; repr. 1966, 1981; id., *al-Taṣwīr al-fannī fī l-Qurʾān,* Cairo 1945, repr. 1966; Cairo and Beirut 1987, repr. 1993; id., *Ẓilāl;* F. Rahman, Translating the Qurʾān, in *Religion and literature* 20 (1988), 23-30; G. Richter, *Der Sprachstil des Koran,* Leipzig 1940; Rippin, *Approaches;* N. Robinson, *Discovering the Qurʾān. A contemporary approach to a veiled text,* London 1996; M. Sells, *Approaching the Qurʾān. The early revelations,* Ashland 1999; id., A literary approach to the hymnic *sūra*s of the Qurʾān. Spirit, gender, and aural intertextuality, in I.J. Boullata (ed.), *Literary structures of religious meaning in the Qurʾān,* Richmond 2000, 3-25; id., Sound and meaning in *sūrat al-Qāriʿa,* in *Arabica* 40 (1993), 402-30; D. Stewart, *Sajʿ* in the Qurʾān. Prosody and structure, in *JAL* 21 (1990), 101-39; A.L. Tibawi, Is the Qurʾān translatable? Early Muslim opinion, in *MW* 52 (1962), 4-17; Wansbrough, *QS;* Watt-Bell, *Introduction;* A.T. Welch, Formulaic features of the punishment-stories, in I.J. Boullata (ed.), *Literary structures of religious meaning in the Qurʾān,* Richmond 2000, 77-116; Wild, *Text;* M. Worton and J. Still (eds.), *Intertextuality. Theories and practice,* Manchester 1990.

Literature and the Qurʾān

This article deals with two main topics: the Qurʾān as literature, which focuses on the literary aspects of the Qurʾān, and the Qurʾān in literature, which focuses on the use of the Qurʾān in various Islamic literatures: Arabic, Persian, Urdu, Punjabi, and Malay. For further and more comprehensive discussion of the utilization of the Qurʾān in various non-Arabic Islamic literatures, see the articles SOUTH ASIAN LITERATURE AND THE QURʾĀN; SOUTHEAST ASIAN LITERATURE AND THE QURʾĀN; TURKISH LITERATURE AND THE QURʾĀN; PERSIAN LITERATURE AND THE QURʾĀN; AFRICAN LITERATURE.

Qurʾān as literature

The literary study of the Qurʾān focuses on how the Qurʾān uses its form, i.e. its language, style, and structure (see LANGUAGE AND STYLE OF THE QURʾĀN; FORM AND STRUCTURE OF THE QURʾĀN) to convey its message or content, i.e. its worldview, values and norms (see ETHICS AND THE

QURʾĀN). The emphasis in such a study falls on the "how" rather than on the "what" of the qurʾānic presentation. The literary aspect of the Qurʾān has been, in one form or another, a subject of study since early times but generally the context of such treatment has been theological, confessional or didactic rather than literary (see THEOLOGY AND THE QURʾĀN). The starting point in most such works on this topic is the challenge that the Qurʾān issues to the disbelievers, namely, to produce a work like the Qurʾān if they doubt its divine origin (see INIMITABILITY; REVELATION AND INSPIRATION; BOOK; WORD OF GOD). This approach is illustrated by the works of Abū Bakr al-Bāqillānī (d. 403/1012) and ʿAbd al-Qāhir al-Jurjānī (d. 471/1078) — *Iʿjāz al-Qurʾān* and *Dalāʾil al-iʿjāz*, respectively. Both al-Bāqillānī and al-Jurjānī seek to show that, as the word of God, the Qurʾān is inimitable and, since it cannot be replicated by any human being, in whole or in part, it constitutes a miracle (q.v.). As such, it is a proof (q.v.) of the authenticity of Muḥammad's prophecy (see PROPHETS AND PROPHETHOOD) and, consequently, of the religion of Islam. Such works do not, in principle, attempt to isolate the literary aspect of the Qurʾān for independent consideration. In 1939, Sayyid Quṭb (d. 1966) wrote that while works on the rhetorical aspect *(balāgha)* of the Qurʾān do indeed exist (see RHETORIC OF THE QURʾĀN), no independent literary, i.e. artistic, study of the Qurʾān exists "to this day" (Quṭb, Taṣwīr, i, 206). In recent years, the literary aspect of the Qurʾān has received greater attention. A significant work in this connection is *Literary structures of religious meaning in the Qurʾān,* edited by Issa Boullata (see LITERARY STRUCTURES OF THE QURʾĀN). As Boullata (*Literary structures,* x) points out in his introduction, literary structures include such diverse elements as "diction, phonology, morphology, syntax [see GRAMMAR AND THE QURʾĀN], rhythm, rhetoric, composition and style, in addition to matters related to tone, voice, orality [q.v.], imagery, symbolism [see SYMBOLIC IMAGERY; METAPHOR], allegory, genre, point of view, intertextuality, intratextual resonance and other literary aspects — all of which are set within a historic epistemology and cultural ambiance." In combination with one another, these elements produce "the total meaning which it (the Qurʾān) contains and which many generations have tried to comprehend" (ibid.).

Historically, the atomistic style of exegesis (see EXEGESIS OF THE QURʾĀN: CLASSICAL AND MEDIEVAL), which has dominated in qurʾānic studies, has militated against the development of a proper literary approach to the Qurʾān. In the atomistic approach, individual verses (q.v.) and verse segments become the focus of study, with little literary significance attached to the larger units of composition. Little wonder that this approach laid the Qurʾān open to the charge of disjointedness: the reader gets a strong impression that the Qurʾān moves from one subject to another quickly and arbitrarily, and perhaps without following any organizing principle. And it is no surprise that few studies of narrative — of plot, dialogue, characterization — in the Qurʾān consequently exist, for the very concept of narrative presupposes the existence of sustained presentation, which an atomistic approach does not allow (see NARRATIVES; MYTHS AND LEGENDS IN THE QURʾĀN).

One can argue that the charge of disjointedness against the Qurʾān is overstated. First, it obviously does not apply to many of the shorter sūras (q.v.; for example, to sūras 80-114), to a number of medium-sized sūras, and to many passages and sections in larger sūras. In many places, an easily identifiable principle of composition is seen to impart unity to portions of the text, as in Q 56:7-44 and Q 37:72-148, where a brief opening statement in each case is followed by details. Second, a closer study of the Qurʾān can identify certain patterns of composition in it. Al-Zarkashī (d. 794/1391) has shown, for instance, that the Qurʾān follows certain rules of ordering with fair regularity. Thus, it nearly always mentions existence before nonexistence, the heavens (see HEAVEN AND SKY) before the earth (q.v.), place (see GEOGRAPHY; SPATIAL RELATIONS) before time (q.v.), darkness (q.v.) before light (q.v.) and night before day (see DAY AND NIGHT), hearing before sight (see SEEING AND HEARING), messenger (q.v.; *rasūl*) before prophet *(nabī)*, Jesus (q.v.) before Mary (q.v.), and the Meccan Emigrants before the Medinan Helpers (see EMIGRANTS AND HELPERS; see, for these and other details, Zarkashī, *Burhān*, iii, 233 f.). Rules are likewise respected in serial descriptions; Q 4:23-4, for example, lists, in order of increasingly distant relationships, the women a man is forbidden to marry (see PROHIBITED DEGREES). Third and most important, the Qurʾān, perhaps more than any other scripture, has a living context that is vital to understanding its message. This living context is comprised of the direct and immediate record of the life and struggle of Muḥammad (q.v.) and his followers in first/seventh-century Arabia (see PRE-ISLAMIC ARABIA AND THE QUR'ĀN), and, in many cases, includes, as background, unspoken assumptions, unstated questions and objections, unexpressed concerns, doubts, and reservations, knowledge of all of which was shared among the participants in a given situation (see OPPOSITION TO MUḤAMMAD; OCCASIONS OF REVELATION). Proper consideration of this living context shows that the Qurʾān possesses a high degree of coherence and continuity. It must also be noted that a number of modern scholars of the Qurʾān, Muslim and non-Muslim, have seen many patterns at work in the Qurʾān and have drawn attention to previously unnoticed compositional elements therein (see EXEGESIS OF THE QUR'ĀN: EARLY MODERN AND CONTEMPORARY; CONTEMPORARY CRITICAL PRACTICES AND THE QUR'ĀN).

Literary features

The Qurʾān has a rich repertoire of literary features, among the best known being rhymed prose (q.v.; *sajʿ*) and economy of expression, with its two subtypes of "ellipsis" *(ḥadhf)* and "terseness" *(ījāz)*. The rhythm of the Qurʾān is best appreciated when the Qurʾān is recited or chanted (see RECITATION OF THE QUR'ĀN). In the pages that follow, we will review selected literary features of the Qurʾān, to see how they are used to convey, enhance and set off its meaning-content.

Words. Individual words used in many places in the Qurʾān turn out, on closer examination, to have special significance in the contexts in which they occur. The prophet Jonah (q.v.), convinced that the people of Nineveh would never believe, decides to leave the city. The word used to describe his departure is *abaqa* (Q 37:140), a word which is typically used in Arabic for a runaway slave (see SLAVES AND SLAVERY). Jonah is no slave. But then he is indeed one — God's (see SERVANT). Being in the service of God, Jonah ought not to have decided on his own to quit prophesying but should have waited for God's command. The use of *abaqa* for Jonah, thus, transforms his departure from a simple physical act to one that is fraught with moral implications. Again, the city of Medina (q.v.), which is almost invariably so called in the Qurʾān, is designated by its pre-emigration name, Yathrib, only once, in Q 33:13. This is significant because in that verse the call "O people of Yathrib" is made by those who would desert the ranks of the Muslims at a time of crisis, hoping that Islam would soon be wiped out and that Medina would revert to its earlier pagan status and to its pre-Islamic name, Yathrib (see HYPOCRITES AND HYPOCRISY; POLYTHEISM AND ATHEISM; IDOLATRY AND IDOLATERS). The use of "Yathrib" in Q 33:13, thus, graphically portrays the mentality of a certain group of people at a crucial juncture in the early history of Islam.

Two words used for the same object or phenomenon in the Qur'ān each appear to have contextual relevance. *ʿAṣā*, the general word for a rod (q.v.), occurs when the referent is the staff of Moses (q.v.; as in Q 2:60 and 7:117). But the word for an old man's staff is *minsaʾa*, and it is a *minsaʾa* on which Solomon (q.v.) leans just before his death (Q 34:14), the word indicating, without any further help from the context, that Solomon died an old man. Similarly, Q 10:5 uses the word *ḍiyāʾ*, which denotes bright light and also heat, for sunlight, but the word *nūr*, which is more general, for moonlight (see SUN; MOON).

In a large number of cases, sets of two or more words acquire their full meaning only when they are seen in a dialectical relationship with each other (see PAIRS AND PAIRING). An obvious category of examples is that of the divine attributes, of which one example should suffice (see GOD AND HIS ATTRIBUTES). Many verses speak of God as being powerful *(ʿazīz)* and wise *(ḥakīm)*: since he is wise, he does not abuse his might; since he is mighty, his is not ineffectual wisdom (q.v.; see also POWER AND IMPOTENCE). A complementary relationship thus comes to exist between the attributes of *ʿazīz* and *ḥakīm*. On a higher level, the Qur'ān sometimes uses several words for one essential meaning — except that each word has a different nuance. A most interesting example occurs in Q 7:198. In describing expertly crafted idols (see IDOLS AND IMAGES) that look quite real, this verse employs three words for the verb "to see": *wa-tarāhum yanẓurūna ilayka wa-hum lā yubṣirūna* (see VISION AND BLINDNESS). A detailed analysis of the highly complex relationship between the three words — *raʾā*, *naẓara*, and *abṣara* — is not possible here, though a tentative English translation, "And you *notice* that they are *looking* at you, but they do not *see*," might suggest the degree of complexity.

In view of its concern with nuance, one can expect to find wordplay in the Qur'ān. Q 12:70 has an extended play on the word *saraqa*, "to steal" (see THEFT): Joseph's brothers are "accused" of stealing the king's cup (see CUPS AND VESSELS) but are, in fact, being accused of having "stolen" Joseph (q.v.) away from his father. In a similar manner, Q 2:61 plays on the word *miṣr*, which means both a "city" (q.v.) and "Egypt" (q.v.). Thus, Moses, unhappy at the wandering Israelites' (see CHILDREN OF ISRAEL; JEWS AND JUDAISM) demand for the good food to which they were accustomed in Egypt, says: "Go into some *miṣr* and you shall have what you have asked for!" As an indefinite noun, *miṣr* means "city," but as a diptote it is the name of the country, Egypt. The use of *miṣr* in the verse draws a contrast between the simple food eaten in the freedom of desert life and the more elegant food eaten in a state of servility in Egypt and, thus, the Israelites' demand is put in a political and moral context.

Imagery. Sayyid Quṭb (d. 1966) has argued that the distinctive literary feature of the Qur'ān is its ability to picture abstractions. A fine example is Q 24:35, the Light Verse, which states at the outset that God is the light of the heavens and the earth, then proceeds to give details of that light in terms of a similitude. Other examples of this phenomenon are found in the many passages that give graphic details of the cataclysmic last hour and have a truly epical quality (e.g. Q 39:67; 69:13-8; 82:1-4; see APOCALYPSE; LAST JUDGMENT). The frequent occurrence of similes, metaphors and parables in the Qurʾān gives evidence of the Qurʾān's tendency to create vivid imagery.

Although many of the qurʾānic similes are drawn from the everyday life of the Arabs (q.v.) and from the environment familiar to them, the contexts in which they appear radically change their function and quality. The Arabs had seen tree-stumps being blown around by a strong wind but they must have been struck by the description of the rebellious people of ʿĀd (q.v.) being destroyed by a fierce wind, their dead bodies drifting about "as if they were stumps of hollow date-palms" (Q 69:7; see also 54:20; see AIR AND WIND; PUNISHMENT STORIES). Q 54:7 depicts a scene of the last day, where human beings, raised from the dead (see DEATH AND THE DEAD) and in a state of confusion, are "as if they were locusts scattered all over" (cf. Q 101:4: "like moths scattered all around"). The mountains, which today seem immovable, will, on the last day, float around "like carded wool" (Q 101:5; see also 70:9). Q 29:41 says that those who rely on someone other than God rely on the spider's web — "the weakest of houses."

The metaphors of the Qurʾān, like its similes, use images that were familiar to the Arabs but acquire new significations in the Qurʾān. Q 2:187 calls husband and wife "garments" to each other, implying, on the one hand, that marriage protects one's chastity (q.v.), and, on the other, admonishing the marriage partners to remain faithful to each other (see MARRIAGE AND DIVORCE). And since the Arabs engaged in trade and commerce, several metaphors involving the notions of buying, selling, and giving a loan hark back to this context (e.g. Q 2:16, 141, 245; 9:111; 35:29; 57:11; see SELLING AND BUYING; DEBT; MARKETS).

Qurʾānic parables usually illustrate key ideas of the Qurʾān. There is a variety of such parables, which are often signaled by a phrase like "The parable of [such-and-such a person] is...." We may take as an example Q 2:17-8, which describes the attitude of those who refuse to accept the guidance they have been looking for when it is presented to them — ironically missing the opportunity for which they have been looking: "Their parable is that of a man who kindled a fire (q.v.); when it had lit up the surrounding area, God took away their light, leaving them in layers of darkness, unable to see as they are. Deaf (see HEARING AND DEAFNESS), dumb, blind — so they shall not return!" Q 2:264-5 makes the point that only acts of charity done to win God's pleasure will be rewarded in the hereafter (see ESCHATOLOGY; REWARD AND PUNISHMENT; GOOD DEEDS): condescension toward or harm of the recipient of a favor will wipe out a charitable act, just as the dust on a rock is wiped clean by rain, whereas charitable acts done in a true spirit of piety will grow, just as a garden on a height will grow and prosper even if it gets a drizzle.

Parallelism, chiasmus, and epanados. Various kinds of emphasis are produced through parallelism, which has an ABA'B' structure (as in Q 11:24: those who are blind and those who are deaf/those possessed of sight and those able to hear; see also Q 20:118-9; 28:73). Emphasis is also produced through chiasmus or reverse parallelism, which has an ABB'A' structure (as in Q 40:58: those who are blind and those who are sighted/those who believe [see BELIEF AND UNBELIEF] and do good deeds and those who do evil deeds [q.v.]). Some of these arrangements are quite elaborate and complex, as in Q 35:19-22, where parallel and chiastic structures interpenetrate. In the story of Joseph in the twelfth sūra, the plot is constructed on the principle of chiasmus; as Mustansir Mir (The qurʾānic story of Joseph) has shown, the first half of the sūra builds a series of tensions which are then resolved in reverse order in the second half. In *epanados,* one returns to the idea with which one started *(reditus ad propositum),* highlighting, on the one hand, the importance of the reiterated idea and, on the other hand, the interconnectedness of the materials enclosed between the two occurrences of the idea. Q 17:22-39, thus, begins and ends with the prohibition of setting up false deities; and Q 23:1-11 enumerates a number of qualities of the true believers — those who will "achieve success" — the passage underscoring the importance of the prayer (q.v.) ritual by referring to it at the beginning (Q 23:2) and toward the end (Q 23:9; cf. a similar emphasis on prayer in the large section of Q 2:163-238, where prayer is mentioned at the beginning, in Q 2:177 and at the end, in Q 2:238).

Other devices. We will briefly note several other devices used in the Qurʾān, giving one example of each and indicating the purpose it serves in its context. Q 2:51 accuses all of the Israelites of worshipping the calf (see CALF OF GOLD) when only some of them had done so. This substitution of the whole for a part *(synecdoche)* underscores the principle of collective responsibility. God sends down rain from the skies but Q 45:5 says that God sends down *rizq,* "sustenance": by substituting effect for cause *(metonymy),* the verse focuses our attention on the actual products of the rainwater we consume, eliciting from us a response of gratitude (see GRATITUDE AND INGRATITUDE; BLESSING; GRACE). Q 4:102 asks the embattled Muslims to "take their guard *(ḥidhr)* and their weapons *(asliḥa).*" The verb for "take," *akhadha,* applies literally to "weapons," but only metaphorically to "guard." The use of one verb in two senses *(syllepsis)* indicates that the best way to take one's guard in a situation of war (q.v.) is to have one's weapons ready. Q 9:62, using the singular pronoun for God and Muḥammad when one would expect the dual, deliberately violates grammar for effect *(enallage),* implying that, in order to please God, the believers must first please his messenger by obeying him, for to obey Muḥammad is to obey God (see OBEDIENCE). Q 21:89-90 says that God granted Zechariah's (q.v.) prayer for a son, even though Zechariah was very old and his wife was sterile: "We granted his prayer and gave him John (see JOHN THE BAPTIST), and we made his wife fertile for him." The sequence, one feels, should have been: We granted his prayer; we made his wife fertile for him; and [having done so] we gave him John. The reversal of the expected sequence *(hysteron proteron)* in the verse suggests immediacy: Zechariah's prayer was granted without any delay at all, so much so that the detail itself, "We made his wife fertile for him," was not allowed to intervene between the prayer and its acceptance. In many verses, a series of divine attributes is presented without the use of the conjunction "and" *(wa),* as in Q 59:23: "He, God, is the one other than whom there is no god: King, possessor of glory, [source of] peace, giver of security, protector, mighty, dominant, proud." Such an omission of the conjunction *(asyndeton)* serves to emphasize the unity or integrality of all the divine attributes and their simultaneous existence in the same deity — and, by thus negating division or distribution of the attributes among several deities, to reinforce the doctrine of monotheism. In Q 21:63, Abraham (q.v.), tongue in cheek, rejects the charge of demolishing the idols of the temple, imputing the act to the chief idol, whom he had spared, and suggesting that the temple custodians ask the broken idols about the matter. This affirmation through denial *(apophasis)* enables him to checkmate his opponents, for he means to drive home the point that a dumb piece of rock does not deserve to be deified.

Irony. Irony is created through a contrast between appearance and reality, for example, between a situation as it is or might develop and the situation as it appears to someone. In tempting Adam and Eve (q.v.) in the garden (q.v.) of Eden, Satan (see DEVIL) suggests to them that the fruit of the forbidden tree could transform them into angels but that God would not like them to become angels; hence the prohibition to eat of the tree (Q 7:20). But the angels have already bowed (see BOWING AND PROSTRATION) before man (Q 2:30-4) and acknowledged his supremacy, so that man's attempt to become an angel (q.v.) constitutes a descent, not an ascent, on his part (see FALL OF MAN). In the story of the People of the Garden (Q 68:17-33), the rich but niggardly owners of the orchard, upon seeing their orchard destroyed, think that they must have arrived at someone else's orchard, and so they exclaim, "We have lost our way!" (*innā la-ḍāllūna,* Q 68:26). But they do not realize that they have lost their way not in the literal sense but in the figurative — moral — sense. Upon realizing that it is their own orchard they have reached after all, they say that they are *maḥrūmūn* (Q 68:27), that is, deprived of the produce, not realizing that they have been deprived of God's blessings in this world and the next. The qurʾānic story of Joseph (Q 12), like the biblical, offers a dramatization of the thesis that God's purposes are inexorably fulfilled and irony is one of the principal means of establishing that thesis (see Mir, Irony in the Qurʾān).

Characterization and dialogue. Very few of the persons mentioned or referred to in the Qurʾān are actually named. In almost all cases, however, they are distinctive enough to be recognizable. The qurʾānic Moses is, of course, unmistakable, but so is the unnamed man who comes rushing in from the far end of the city to inform Moses of the Egyptians' plot to kill him (Q 28:20). The qurʾānic Joseph is easily recognizable but so is the unnamed Egyptian noblewoman who tries to seduce him (Q 12:23). A few points about characterization in the Qurʾān may be noted (comparisons with characterization in the Bible will be fruitful). First, there is very little physical description. This absence indicates that such detail is not a crucial element of character: people must not be judged on their appearance but on the strength of their deeds (cf. Q 49:13: "The noblest of you in the sight of God is the most pious one of you"; see PIETY). Second, the Qurʾān does not recount the day-to-day events and happenings in the lives of its characters, whom we encounter only at decisive moments when, through their speech or action, they reveal their true selves, or provide significant clues about their views, attitudes, and inclinations, and help us "place" them. Third, there are not only individual but also collective characters in the Qurʾān. In many places (e.g. in Q 11, "Hūd"), the Qurʾān speaks of small or large groups of people, even nations, as if they were a single personality speaking or acting in unison. Thus, in a dialogue, a prophet might be represented as addressing a number of courtiers or nobles who speak and act as if they were a single entity. The implication, of course, is that the view held in common, or the action done in concert, is more important than the individuality of the characters. Even in these cases, however, the group *qua* group is usually seen to have its distinctive identity. Thus, Joseph's brothers (in Q 12), the magicians of Pharaoh (q.v.; Q 7:113-26; 20:65-73; 26:41-51), and the People of the Garden (Q 68:17-32) have clearly identifiable personalities. Fourth, just as there are groups that look like individuals, so there are individuals who represent types. It is true that qurʾānic characters are, as a rule, presented within the general framework of the conflict between good and evil (q.v.), but they are not abstractions. Regardless of their moral alignment, most characters come across as men and women of flesh and blood and display traits that are very much human. And while many of the qurʾānic characters are either "good" or "bad," they can hardly be called flat — in the sense in which E.M. Forster famously used the term. Moses, quite obviously, is a multidimensional figure, as are Abraham, Joseph, the Queen of Sheba (see BILQĪS), and Pharaoh's magicians, who all undergo some kind of change and development with time. (On dialogue in the Qurʾān, see DIALOGUES.)

Taṣrīf *as a narrative principle. Taṣrīf,* a word used in the Qurʾān to denote the changing patterns of movement of the winds (Q 2:164; 45:5) and also the diverse modes of presentation of the qurʾānic message (*nuṣarrifu,* as in Q 6:65; and *ṣarrafnā,* in Q 17:41; 46:27), may be called a qurʾānic narrative principle. Typically, the Qurʾān does not present, for example, a story all in one place but breaks it up into several portions, relating different portions in different places, often with varying amounts and emphasis of detail, as they are needed and in accordance with the thematic exigencies of the sūras in which they occur. The Qurʾān does not tell a story for its own sake but in order to shed light on the theme under treatment in a particular sūra. In doing so, it eliminates chronology (see CHRONOLOGY AND THE QURʾĀN) as an organizing principle in narration, replacing it with the principle of thematic coherence, a principle that determines which portion of a story will be narrated in what place. In other words, the story told in a given sūra is likely to be sūra-specific. A number of Western writers — among them Angelika Neuwirth, Anthony Johns, Neal Robinson and Matthias Zahniser (see bibliography) — have attempted to see qurʾānic sūras as unities or as possessing thematic and structural coherence.

Repetition. The Qurʾān appears to be repetitive in respect of both thematic substance and formal expression. Muslim scholars who have dealt with this phenomenon have concluded that repetition in the Qurʾān, whether in form or substance, is usually quite significant and purposeful. At a basic level, repetition serves to put emphasis on a point, catching an overflow of meaning, as in Q 19:42-5, where Abraham, imploring his father to abandon the worship of idols, utters *yā abati* ("O my dear father!") no fewer than four times, the repetition indicating his deep love and concern for the salvation (q.v.) of his father. Sometimes, repetition is used to insure a cumulative impact, as when a series of verses or sentences, beginning with the same word or words create a crescendo effect, leading to a climactic point (e.g. Q 7:195; 52:30-43). One or more phrases repeated two or more times, say, at the beginning of a series of passages, may serve as a frame for presenting an argument or making a comment. Q 26:104-90 relates the stories of five prophets — Noah (q.v.), Hūd (q.v.), Ṣāliḥ (q.v.), Lot (q.v.) and Shuʿayb (q.v.) — and their nations. All five passages in this section have an almost identical beginning. The repetition in this passage may appear to be formulaic but in fact it highlights (here and in many similar passages, e.g. Q 7:59-102) several things: that the many prophets sent by God all preached the same essential message; that each of these prophets was a member of the nation he addressed, so that the people, who knew him to be truthful and thus had little reason to reject his message, opposed him out of sheer stubbornness (see LIE; TRUTH; INSOLENCE AND OBSTINACY); that although each prophet sought to rectify the evil peculiar to his nation, all of them began their preaching by calling their peoples to the correct faith (q.v.), which is the foundation of all good conduct; and that Muḥammad the prophet should not grieve at his rejection by the people of Mecca (q.v.), for just as God has punished the rebellious nations of those prophets, so he will punish the Meccans if they continue to oppose him. The formal identity of expression in the several parts of the passage thus conveys a complex set of meanings.

At times the Qurʾān employs refrain. A celebrated example occurs in Q 55, where the verse "Which of the blessings of God will you, then, deny?" occurs no fewer than thirty-one times. According to Amīn Aḥsan Iṣlāḥī (1906-97), this sūra was revealed in Mecca at a time when Muḥammad's opponents adamantly refused to accept the Qurʾān, defiantly asking for the punishment with which they were threatened in case they disbelieved. The sūra, accordingly, uses the refrain to force their attention. As Iṣlāḥī puts it: "This stylistic feature of repeatedly drawing someone's attention to something is, of course, used only when the addressee is either so stubborn that he is unwilling to accept what goes against his wishes, or so obtuse that he cannot be expected to see reason unless he is held by the scruff of his neck and forced to pay attention to every single thing" (Iṣlāḥī, *Tadabbur-i Qurʾān,* vii, 119). In other words, the refrain in Q 55 serves to bring into relief the particular mentality of the Meccan disbelievers at a certain stage of Muḥammad's ministry. Iṣlāḥī notes that Q 54 was revealed in a similar set of circumstances, and that it, too, has a refrain ("How were my punishment and my threat?" see id., *Tadabbur-i Qurʾān,* vii, 119).

The classical works on the Qurʾān are important aids to understanding the Qurʾān. Yet, from an artistic or literary point of view, they have certain limitations; the principal one being that, in these works, the literary study of the Qurʾān rarely achieves independence of theological considerations. In this respect, the study of the Qurʾān as literature in the modern sense of the term is in its beginning stages. Such study will definitely be helped by insights gleaned from the study of the Bible as literature, though the differences between the two scriptures will require that each be approached essentially on its own terms (see SCRIPTURE AND THE QURʾĀN). The field of the literary study of the Qurʾān holds considerable promise and is one in which cooperation between Muslim and Western scholars can be quite fruitful.

Qurʾān in literature

There is no doubt that the Qurʾān exerted a tremendous influence on various Islamic literatures, just as it did in other areas of artistic and intellectual activity in Islamic civilization. Its influence on Arabic literature in particular was, as expected, the earliest, but also the most intensive and enduring: Arabic, after all, was the language in which the Qurʾān was revealed. But as Islam moved beyond its initial area of dissemination, both in the first centuries of its expansion but also in subsequent periods of commercial, military and missionary activity, the Qurʾān interacted with numerous linguistic and literary cultures.

Qurʾān in Arabic literature

Although Arabic, as a language and a literary tradition, was quite well developed by the time of Muḥammad's prophetic activity, it was only after the emergence of Islam, with its founding scripture in Arabic, that the language reached its utmost capacity of expression, and the literature its highest point of complexity and sophistication. Indeed, it probably is no exaggeration to say that the Qurʾān was one of the most conspicuous forces in the making of classical and post-classical Arabic literature.

According to the Muslim scholars (both of the Qurʾān and of literature), the use of the Qurʾān in literature is to be clearly distinguished from the "imitation" of the Qurʾān, *muʿāraḍa,* deemed to be beyond the capability of human beings. Comparing the two phenomena, the literary scholar al-Thaʿālibī (d. 429/1039) has the following to say in the theoretical introduction to the earliest and most comprehensive book on the subject, his *al-Iqtibās min al-Qurʾān al-karīm* (Thaʿālibī, *Iqtibās,* i, 37-9; see also Gilliot, Un florilège coranique). He first dwells on the idea of the Qurʾān as God's most beautiful and majestic speech (q.v.) whose revelation sent shock waves among the eloquent Arabs of the time and made them admit humbly of its superiority, of their inability to produce anything like it, and hence of its being the Prophet's miracle — like Moses' rod and Jesus' ability to heal the sick and raise the dead. Understandably, he concludes, anyone who tried to imitate the Qurʾān after the spread of Islam failed; what people could do was "to borrow" from it (*iqtibās,* as in the book's title). Consequently, according to al-Thaʿālibī, whereas imitation of the Qurʾān was a breach of the distinctive status of the Qurʾān and the Prophet, unfeasible and foolish, borrowing from the Qurʾān protected the Qurʾān's and the Prophet's distinguished status, and was therefore both feasible and wise. It adorned the litterateurs' speech, beautified it, and made it more eloquent, elevated, and sublime. Thaʿālibī offers this as an explanation for the borrowing from the Qurʾān that was widely practiced by all involved in the various branches of literary expression, both oral and written, up until his own day.

Al-Thaʿālibī — writing in the late fourth/early eleventh century — was not only in favor of qurʾānic borrowing in literature but also completely oblivious to the issue of its legitimacy. Before him, only two religious scholars had expressed their aversion to it: al-Ḥasan al-Baṣrī (d. 110/728; see Qalqashandī, *Ṣubḥ,* i, 190) and al-Bāqillānī (d. 403/1012; see Zarkashī, *Burhān,* i, 483). Later, however (possibly as late as the eighth/fourteenth century), the question of the legitimacy of qurʾānic borrowing became a subject of discussion in the works of scholars of the Qurʾān, literature, and rhetoric (see Zarkashī, *Burhān,* i, 481-5; Suyūṭī, *Itqān,* i, 147-9; Qalqashandī, *Ṣubḥ,* i, 190-1; Macdonald/Bonebakker, Iḳtibās, 1092). Significantly, though, almost all of these scholars noted that, with the exception of the Mālikīs, the vast majority of the scholars found qurʾānic borrowing either permissible or commendable. While these authors themselves did not object to the *principle* of mixing the sacred (see SANCTITY AND THE SACRED) with the profane (q.v.), they examined and regulated its *suitability:* there were places where such usage could be considered befitting, and hence would be acceptable (e.g. in sermons, speeches, testaments); not unbefitting, and hence permissible (e.g. in love poetry, letters, stories); and unbefitting, and hence impermissible (e.g. in jest, vulgarity and profanity; and cf. Thaʿālibī, *Iqtibās,* chap. 16). In these judgments they seem to have been guided by matters of precedence and historical reality. For the scholars could not deny the numerous reports that the Prophet and some of his most venerable Companions (see COMPANIONS OF THE PROPHET) had used qurʾānic citations in their speech/ḥadīth (see ḤADĪTH AND THE QURʾĀN), as well as the fact that borrowing from the Qurʾān in literature was very widespread in the works of litterateurs, among them some of the most pious and strict religious scholars, such as al-Shāfiʿī (d. 204/820) and

ʿAbd al-Qāhir al-Baghdādī (d. 429/1037). All of this confirms — as is alluded to by al-Suyūṭī (d. 911/1505; *Itqān*, i, 147, l. 11-2) — that the theoretical discussion of the legitimacy of qurʾānic borrowing is a late phenomenon and that before that time the Qurʾān was used freely in literature.

What the scholars meant exactly by "borrowing" can be gleaned from the terms they used to describe this phenomenon. The first two terms which we encounter are rather peculiar and seemingly negative: they are *sariqa*, "theft or plagiarism" — as in the title of ʿAbdallāh b. Yaḥyā b. Kunāsa's (d. 207/822) now lost book, *al-Kumayt's [d. 126/744] thefts* [sariqāt] *from the Qurʾān* (Ibn al-Nadīm, 77/70-1/i, 155) — and *ikhtilās*, "theft or misappropriation" — as in al-Hamdānī's (d. 334/945) description of Bishr b. Abī Kubār al-Balawī's (d. after 202/817) Qurʾān-studded letters (Hamdānī, *Ṣifāt*, 86). The context of these terms, however, indicates that they meant something positive like "plucking" — a kind of stealthy, unexpected appropriation of qurʾānic materials which takes the readers/listeners (pleasantly) by surprise. After the fourth/tenth century, the terms for qurʾānic borrowing become more clearly neutral and more or less standardized: *intizāʿ*, "extraction," *taḍmīn*, "insertion" (a word taken over from the insertion of poetry or proverbs in prose), *iqtibās*, "borrowing," *ʿaqd* (used for the Qurʾān in poetry only), also *istishhād*, "citation," *talwīḥ/talmīḥ*, "allusion," *ishāra*, "reference," in addition to two more words which mean "extraction": *istinbāṭ* and *istikhrāj* (Tawḥīdī, *Baṣāʾir*, ii, 230; Thaʿālibī, *Iqtibās*, i, 193; Zarkashī, *Burhān*, 483; Qalqashandī, *Ṣubḥ*, i, 189, 194, 197, 199, 200; Suyūṭī, *Itqān*, i, 147; Jomaih, *The use of the Qurʾān*, 1-2). As understood by Muslim scholars, then, qurʾānic borrowing in literature occurs when litterateurs extract some material from the Qurʾān and insert it skillfully into their literary products in the form of citation, reference, or allusion.

The use of the Qurʾān in Arabic literature began as early as the lifetime of the Prophet, for we know that some of the new poet-converts to Islam, ʿAbdallāh b. Rawāḥa (d. 8/629), Kaʿb b. Zuhayr (d. 26/645), and Ḥassān b. Thābit (d. 54/674), used it extensively in their poetry (Khan, *Vom Einfluss des Qurʾāns*; see POETRY AND POETS). As the Islamic community expanded, this use grew conspicuously and was undertaken not only by Muslims but also by non-Muslims, like the Christian Umayyad poet al-Akhṭal (d. 90/709) and the Sabian ʿAbbāsid prose writer Abū Hilāl al-Ṣābī (d. 384/994). This was unavoidable for a number of reasons: the Qurʾān was not only a powerful religious guide and companion in ritual for the believers but also an equally powerful literary text for all of the residents of the Islamic realm, believers and non-believers alike. Its text and script (see ARABIC SCRIPT; ARABIC LANGUAGE; COLLECTION OF THE QURʾĀN; CODICES OF THE QURʾĀN) were standardized early enough to make it reasonably accessible even to non-native speakers of Arabic. From the earliest times, professional Qurʾān reciters roamed the empire, teaching and transmitting it (see TEACHING AND PREACHING THE QURʾĀN). Teachers in the informal schools made it a primary item in their curricula; scholars established disciplines of learning to investigate each aspect of it (see TRADITIONAL DISCIPLINES OF QURʾĀNIC STUDY); and the supremacy of Arabic as the language of state, society and civilization made it practically impossible to escape its impact. Indeed, before the end of the Umayyad period (132/750), the Qurʾān was identified by the chief secretary of the central chancery, ʿAbd al-Ḥamīd al-Kātib (d. 132/750), as the first item in the required list of studies needed by the state's secretaries (al-Qāḍī, The impact of the Qurʾān, 287), many of whom became leading figures of Arabic literature for centuries to come. This idea became rooted so deeply that it was repeated by scholars over and over again (see Qalqashandī, *Ṣubḥ*, i, 200-1). In the sixth/twelfth century a secretary to the Fāṭimids, Ibn al-Ṣayrafī (d. 542/1147), wrote an entire book entitled *Intizāʿāt al-Qurʾān al-ʿaẓīm* (as yet unpublished) in which he listed the qurʾānic verses that could be used by the state's secretaries in the presentation of a multitude of topics. On another level, the Qurʾān seemed to be the only — or at least, the principal — factor of stability in the early, turbulent decades of Islam, when factionalism was rampant, there were conflicts galore and the search for the "true" Islam was taken very seriously in all the sectors of the community. This made the Qurʾān an indispensable reference for all those groups and, with that, it became an organic part of their consciousness. In addition, the Qurʾān — in this crucial formative period — was frequently memorized (see MEMORY), even when its study was accompanied by a written text, as indeed it still is today. This gave it, from the early days of Islam, a prominent mental presence in the minds of the people living in Islamic lands and it could not but become part of the literature they produced.

The main areas in which the Qurʾān exerted noticeable influence on Arabic literature are diction and themes; other areas are related to the literary aspects of the Qurʾān, particularly oaths (q.v.), metaphors, imagery, motifs, and symbols. As far as diction is concerned, one could say that qurʾānic words, idioms, and expressions, especially "loaded" and formulaic phrases, appear in practically all genres of literature and in such abundance that it is simply impossible to compile a full record of them (see SLOGANS FROM THE QURʾĀN). For not only did the Qurʾān create an entirely new linguistic corpus to express its message, it also endowed old, pre-Islamic words with new meanings and it is these meanings that took root in the language and subsequently in the literature. Again, because in qurʾānic borrowing words can be taken out of their qurʾānic context, there are almost limitless contexts in which they may be used.

Qurʾānic themes also occur frequently in literature. Themes pertaining to God and his power/mercy (q.v.), to the Qurʾān with its many names (see NAMES OF THE QURʾĀN), to prophethood and the stories of various prophets and messengers, to the relation of God to humans and of humans to God with various aspects, to the human condition from the Fall onward, to the Islamic experience and early history beginning with the mission of Muḥammad, and to many aspects of morality, ethics, law (see LAW AND THE QURʾĀN), theology, cosmology (q.v.) and eschatology, are, among others, themes that many litterateurs used in their work. Such themes tended to occur in some genres more than others; one encounters them most frequently, for example, in elegies, self-praise, panegyric and its opposite, satire, and above all in ascetic, Ṣūfī and devotional literature (see ṢŪFISM AND THE QURʾĀN).

The use of the literary aspects of the Qurʾān is more difficult to categorize: it could occur anywhere, sometimes in the most unexpected places, as in a poem on wine-drinking — hardly a positive activity in Islam (Zubaidi, The impact, 328; see WINE; INTOXICANTS). Other examples collected by Zubaidi (The impact, 325, 326, 334) indicate that images in literature derived from the Qurʾān can be coined through similes and metaphors as well as qurʾānic motifs, like the motif of exile from heaven, as in al-Farazdaq's (d. 110/728) portrayal of himself after he had divorced his beloved wife: "She was my paradise (q.v.), from which I was exiled/Like Adam when he rebelled against his lord (q.v.; see also REBELLION)."

More frequently, qurʾānic characters with powerful symbolic values (like Joseph for beauty [q.v.], Abraham for faith, Pharaoh for persistence in disbelief, and so forth; see BELIEF AND UNBELIEF) are mentioned in literature to draw striking images of the ideas the litterateur wants to communicate. The most enduring of these symbolic characters is the devil, the arch-representative of disobedience and sin (see SIN, MAJOR AND MINOR), whose image is often portrayed vividly and in great detail in political and other literature, notably by ʿAbd al-Ḥamīd al-Kātib (see al-Qāḍī, The impact, 304-6).

Initially, the insertion of qurʾānic material in Arabic literature happened effortlessly and without any particular purpose in mind, as manifested by the poetry of the Prophet's contemporaries (mentioned above). With the passage of time — but still quite early — as the litterateurs became more aware of the Qurʾān's great potential, they drew upon it with both more consciousness and more sophistication. They began to use it out of piety, to beautify their literary products, to render them more witty, forceful and effective (particularly in sermons, speeches and political literature), or to make them more convincing to their audiences, especially when dealing with controversial issues that could benefit from divine sanction, like sectarian beliefs (see Jomaih, *The use of the Qurʾān,* loc. cit.). The letters of the second/eighth century prose writer Bishr al-Balawī (see below) are a shining example of the degree of sophistication and complexity that qurʾānic borrowing reached, as we find, for example, in a letter describing his delight at the addressee's promise to give him money, and then his despair when this promise was rescinded (al-Qāḍī, *Bishr ibn Abī Kubār,* 161):

> ... when I mentioned [my need to you], you brightened up like dawn, rejoicing as if at good news (cf. Q 80:38-9), and you promised "a fair promise" (Q 20:86). So I spent my pension on account of your brightening up, and I became liberal with my children on account of your rejoicing, and I borrowed from my friends on account of your promise. But when I came to you requesting fulfillment, you frowned and showed displeasure (cf. Q 74:22), then you turned away in pride (cf. Q 74:23). Now the money is gone, hope (q.v.) is cut off, and I have despaired of [attaining] my ambition "as the disbelievers have despaired of those who are in the graves" (Q 60:13).

The use of the Qurʾān for ideological purposes and for propaganda also occurred early due to historical circumstances and it still occurs today. Its use for social and political criticism resonates in many literary works and has lately become particularly conspicuous in modern Arabic literature, as in the politically scathing poems of the contemporary Egyptian poet Aḥmad Maṭar, where one reads, for example (*Lāfitāt,* 11):

> I read in the Qurʾān:
> "The power of Abū Lahab will perish." (Q 111:1)
> The submission media declared:
> "Silence is golden."
> [But] I loved my poverty . . . [So] I continued to recite:
> "And he will perish." (Q 111:1)
> "His wealth and gains will not exempt him." (Q 111:2)
> My throat was confiscated,
> For incivility.

And the Qur'ān was confiscated,
Because it spurred me to [incite] trouble.

The way in which qur'ānic materials were used in both poetry and prose varied greatly from one author to another and within the works of a single author, sometimes even within a single piece (see al-Qāḍī, The limitations). Not infrequently, qur'ānic words, expressions, parts of *āya*s and full *āya*s are cited verbatim; and sometimes more than one of these elements are juxtaposed in a literary text and linked together with some sort of a conjunction. More frequently than not, such qur'ānic citations are inserted in the text without an explicit introduction or antecedent statement indicating that the Qur'ān is being used. Explicit indication, however, does occur sometimes, and sentences like "as God, may he be exalted, said in his book" signal the author's departure from his words to those of the Qur'ān.

Since literal citation is costly for litterateurs, in that it forces them to make both syntactical and stylistic accommodations to their texts (the poets had to deal with the additional restrictions of meter and rhyme), the litterateurs, more often than not, tended to modify or rephrase qur'ānic materials before inserting them into their texts. This gave them greater freedom in their selection of qur'ānic materials, and kept their own stylistic preferences intact, all the while enabling them to achieve what they wanted from qur'ānic borrowing. In fact, modified borrowing could give their text greater force since, with the source of their borrowed segments obscured, they could easily appropriate those segments and, skillfully blending them into their own texts, convey the impression that the segments' words were their own. And, since modified borrowing in one instance did not bar literal citation in another, it became quite usual in the works of versatile writers to mix both ways, even within a single work.

The techniques used by authors to modify qur'ānic materials are numerous and can be studied on the level of syntax and style (see al-Qāḍī, *Bishr ibn Abī Kubār*, 99-109; id., The impact, 289-307). On the level of syntax, authors made changes in person (first to third, or second to third) and number (plural to singular, and vice versa). They used pronouns for qur'ānic nouns when they needed, and replaced the nouns with verbs from the same root. A qur'ānic definite noun could become indefinite, and a phrase in the imperative mood could be changed to the indicative if the syntax required such a modification. Changes of qur'ānic materials dictated by style are a little more complex and their detection requires familiarity not only with the qur'ānic text but also with the writer's style. If the writer tends to use parallelism in his work, he is likely to resort to amplification, where he would take, for example, a two-word qur'ānic expression, break it up, bring a synonym for each word, then add a conjunction in the middle, thereby ending with a pair of parallel expressions. To amplification also belongs a technique called analogy, where the writer takes a qur'ānic expression, adds to it one or more parallel expressions of his own, thereby amplifying the text analogically. Conversely, an author may also resort to reduction when brevity is the goal, as in invocations, for example. Of the techniques of reduction, one could mention coining. This consists of the creation of single-word terms that are summations of whole qur'ānic phrases. Another technique, grammatical translation, consists of taking one or more qur'ānic *āya*s of a particular mood (e.g. imperative) and then "translating" them into words (e.g. He ordered...), thereby causing the qur'ānic statements to be reduced. On a simpler level, a writer could, for stylistic purposes, use synonyms or antonyms for qurʾānic words, re-arrange words and expressions in the borrowed sentences, and consciously change the length of the borrowed or added segments so as to accord with the author's preferences in musical cadence.

Finally, the use of the Qurʾān in literature also took the form of allusion or reference, whereby a writer makes incidental mention of some qurʾānic material which is so well-known as to evoke clear and strong associations, like, for example, Abraham's fire (Q 21:68-71), Lot's wife (Q 66:10), Joseph's shirt (Q 12:18), Moses' rod (Q 2:60; 7:107, 117, 160; 26:32, 45, 63; 27:10; 28:31), Ṣāliḥ's she-camel (Q 7:73, 77; 11:64-5; 17:59; 26:155-7; 91:13-4), or the People of the Cave (*aṣḥāb al-kahf*, Q 18:9-26; see MEN OF THE CAVE). Since this technique requires minimal accommodation from the writer and at the same time allows him optimal benefit from the Qurʾān's presence in the text, it was used very frequently in literature, particularly in poetry.

The Qurʾān is used slightly differently in Arabic poetry than in Arabic prose. This is due to two differences between poetry and prose: genre and historical origin. With the exception of the relatively recent free verse, the generic restrictions of meter and rhyme in Arabic poetry limited qurʾānic borrowing quantitatively and qualitatively. In comparison with prose writers, who could introduce their borrowed materials by statements indicating their source (e.g. "as God, may he be exalted, said in his book..."), cite verbatim entire *āya*s no matter how long, and relate in detail entire qurʾānic narratives, poets had to limit the number of *āya*s on which they could draw, cut them short except in rare instances, depend heavily on various techniques of reformulation and give precedence to allusion and reference over citation and leisurely tracing. Consequently, while a prose piece could have most of its sentences drawn from qurʾānic materials, like many of the sermons of Ibn Nubāta (d. 374/984; see Canard, Ibn Nubāta), a poem comprised entirely of qurʾānic references is considered a noticeable aberration and could be judged flatly as "bad" (Thaʿālibī, *Iqtibās*, ii, 57).

Another factor in the greater latitude of Arabic prose in qurʾānic borrowing is that, at the rise of Islam, it had shallow roots in the pre-Islamic literary tradition — in contrast with poetry, which was deeply entrenched in that tradition: the highly stylized, complex, and sophisticated poetic form, the ode *(qaṣīda)*, had an extremely important social function as it reflected the Arabs' environment, activities, beliefs, and value system. Thus, when the Qurʾān became a part of the Arabs' new world, prose fell almost completely under its spell. Poetry resisted — despite the Qurʾān's hostile attitude towards pagan poets and poetry (see Q 26:224-6). This tension is particularly notable since the Qurʾān did not offer itself as a poetic work to replace the old poetic tradition but was rather an inimitable divine revelation (see Q 21:5; 37:36-7; 52:30-1; 69:40-1). As a result, the ode as a mono-rhymed, dual hemstitched form and segmented structure survived and remained, with variations, the basic form of poetic expression in Arabic literature until modern times, allowing the Qurʾān to influence its diction, themes, powerful images, motifs and symbols. Prose, on the other hand, allowed the Qurʾān to influence, in addition to the above, its very form and structure, style and rhythm, even to the point of creating new genres in it.

In the area of form, the Qurʾān generally influenced Arabic literary prose, contrary to poetry. Like each of the Qurʾān's sūras, a typical prose piece would begin with the Qurʾān-based formula "in the name of God, the merciful, the compassionate," called the *basmala* (q.v.); indeed, prose pieces lacking the *basmala* are considered *batrāʾ*, "clipped" or "docked," indicating imperfection. In epistolary prose — the most pervasive genre in Arabic literature until the modern period — in particular, this beginning is often followed, after naming the sender and the addressee, by another Qurʾān-based formula "I praise [before you] God other than whom there is no god," as attested from the first/seventh century in the papyri and elsewhere (see e.g. Becker, *Papyri*, 58, 62, 68, 92, 96, 100). Still another qurʾānic formula is found at the ends of most letters: "peace be upon you," or briefly "peace." In a way, perhaps not unlike qurʾānic sūras, Arabic prose displayed a great deal of formal variety within a recognizable unity. Genres as diverse as letters, treatises, testaments, sermons, invocations, and incantations exist, and works from each of these genres vary in length and complexity. Yet, each would be recognizable as a letter, treatise, testament, etc. Perhaps this is what explains a rather peculiar phenomenon in Arabic literary prose, namely that a piece of it — usually a short one — would be composed exclusively of one or more qurʾānic verses.

On the level of structure, prose pieces often betray specific qurʾānic influence in that they build upon a qurʾānic concept, phrase, or word and allow those elements to dictate their structure. One example is the letters or sermons which begin with the qurʾānic formula *al-ḥamdu li-llāh* (thanks/praise be to God) or, less frequently, the almost synonymous and equally qurʾānic *subḥāna llāh* (see GLORIFICATION OF GOD; LAUDATION). Such prose pieces tend to be cyclical in structure since each section (or cycle) begins with the same formula, followed by what God is being praised for (see ʿAbbās, *ʿAbd al-Ḥamīd*, 161-2; al-Qāḍī, The impact, 295-6). This kind of writing was developed in the early second/eighth century and was so distinct and potent that it was given the name *taḥmīd (te deum)* genre. Similarly, letters or testaments which begin with the qurʾānic concept *ūṣīka bi-taqwā llāh*, "I counsel you to fear God," tend to have a spiral structure, in the sense that they are composed of successive pieces of advice that end only when the author has completed his treatment of the virtues he wishes to advocate (see VIRTUES AND VICES, COMMANDING AND FORBIDDING). A third example consists of letters or proclamations that begin with qurʾānic concepts and phraseology to the effect that God chose Islam to be his religion. Such prose pieces normally have a carefully constructed three-part "sequential" structure, the first of which discusses pre-Muḥammadan human history, the second the mission of Muḥammad, while the third discusses the main topic of the piece.

Stylistically, the Qurʾān greatly influenced Arabic prose. It is conceivable that one of the most conspicuous features of Arabic prose, parallelism *(izdiwāj)*, i.e. repeating one meaning in two or more phrases, goes back to qurʾānic influence. More certainly, the fairly frequent tendency of prose writers to use antithetical pairing *(taḍādd)* has its origin in the style of the Qurʾān, where opposites are often juxtaposed (e.g. good/evil; believers/non-believers). Probably even rhymed prose *(sajʿ)*, whose use flourished in mid- and late medieval times but was never completely absent from prose in other periods, had its roots in the Qurʾān's style, too (see Heinrichs and Ben Abdesselem, Sadjʿ, 734-6). This matter is somewhat problematic since *sajʿ* was condemned by the Prophet. Because, however, this condemnation is linked to the utterances of the pre-Islamic pagan soothsayers (q.v.; *kuhhān*) and is thus deemed unsuitable for supplication (*duʿāʾ*; see Wensinck, *Concordance*, ii, 431), its use outside this sphere was taken, in varying degrees, to be acceptable. Such was especially the case as the Qurʾān, by example, rendered it implicitly permissible. All of the stylistic features that have been mentioned serve the musical cadence of sentences, an area in which the Qur'ān excelled, particularly at the ends of *āya*s. And here, again, Arabic prose followed in the footsteps of the Qur'ān, making musical cadence a stylistic value after which it constantly strives.

Finally, there are some genres of prose whose very existence would have been inconceivable had the Qur'ān not been their guiding light, in particular that of the sermon, which is almost entirely dependent on qur'ānic ideas, formulations and stories of ancient peoples (see GENERATIONS). On another level, there are two Arabic literary works whose foundational principle lies deep in the qur'ānic vision of the day of judgment and the fate of people in heaven or hell (see HELL AND HELLFIRE); without this vision they could not have been written. These are Ibn Shuhayd's (d. 393/1003) *al-Tawābiʿ wa-l-zawābiʿ* and al-Maʿarrī's (d. 449/1057) *Risālat al-ghufrān,* both of which consist of imaginary journeys undertaken by their respective authors to the afterworld where they encounter litterateurs and scholars and ask them about their salvation or about their condemnation to hellfire, in addition to discussing with them matters of art, language and literature. Al-Maʿarrī's other work, *al-Fuṣūl wa-l-ghāyāt,* must also be mentioned among the works whose *raison d'être* is the Qur'ān. This book, whose very title, "The book of paragraphs and endings composed as an analogy of the verses and sūras [of the Qur'ān]," speaks of its indebtedness to the Qur'ān, is an ascetical piety work devoted to the praise of God and the poet's expression of fear of him and hope in his forgiveness (q.v.). It is actually written as an imitation of the styles of the Qur'ān. Last but not least, no study of the Qur'ān in Arabic literature is complete without a pause at the Yemeni second/eighth-century prose writer mentioned above, Bishr b. Abī Kubār al-Balawī, who was "famous for stealing/appropriating the Qur'ān" (Hamdānī, *Ṣifat,* 86). Although only seventeen of his letters have survived, it is clear that the Qur'ān is the overpowering force behind them, driving them in diction, style, images, symbols, word-, phrase- and sentence-order, and in both their internal and external structures. Indeed the Qur'ān governs the totality of each letter in its artistic imagination and internal movements, as well as its details. Indeed, at the hands of al-Balawī, the use of the Qur'ān in literature became an art unto itself.

Qur'ān in Persian literature

The Muslim conquest of Persia in the first/seventh century led to the rise of a new literature, produced in Arabic by the converts to Islam. But the Pahlavi literary tradition continued to exist and prosper. The attempt of Firdawsī (d. 411/1020) to avoid the use of Arabic words in his *Shāhnāma,* a poetical recounting of Sasanian history down to the Muslim conquest of Iran, represents the will to assert the independence of the native literary tradition rather than the rejection of Arabic literature — with the Qur'ān at its center — as an alien tradition. Niẓāmī (d. 605/1209) in his romance *Haft paykar,* "Seven beauties," deals with a similar theme — the life-story of the Sasanian ruler Bahrām Gūr — but his work, though it draws heavily on that of Firdawsī, contains many references and allusions to the Qur'ān.

The Qur'ān influenced Persian literature in several ways. The qur'ānic literary feature of *sajʿ,* "rhymed prose," influenced not only the stylized prefaces and introductions that the authors wrote for their works but, in varying degrees, the general style of authors, as well. The literary genre known as "mirrors for princes" came to include a treatment of qur'ānic themes and characters. Since study and knowledge of the Qur'ān were an important part of classical Persian culture in the Islamic period and since this culture was shared between the secular and religious sectors of society, the ability, in conversation and writing, to cite appropriately from the Qur'ān and to recognize such citations came to be viewed as a mark of sound general education. Reference to the Qur'ān can be expected to occur in almost all genres of literature — and in almost any writer's work. Abū Naṣr Aḥmad b. Manṣūr Asadī (d. before 423/1041) invented the *munāẓara* ("debate") poem (see DEBATE AND DISPUTATION). In one such poem (Browne, *Literary history,* ii, 150-2), Night and Day each claim to be superior to the other, both presenting a series of arguments, many of them based on the Qur'ān. Night argues, for example, that it was at night that Muḥammad departed for his heavenly journey (Q 17:1) and that it is the Night of Power (q.v.; *laylat al-qadr*), that, in the Qur'ān, is deemed better than a thousand months (q.v.; Q 97:3). Day retorts that fasting (q.v.) is observed during the day (Q 2:187), that the Friday prayer (q.v.) is performed during the day (Q 62:9) and that resurrection (q.v.) will occur at daytime. ʿUmar al-Khayyām (d. before 530/1135) is not a particularly religious writer. Yet, in one of his quatrains (*Rubaiyyat,* 210, no. 379), he justifies wine-drinking by claiming to have found in the Qur'ān a "luminous verse" on wine *(bar-gird-i payāla āyatī rawshan ast),* and, in another (ibid., no. 381), compares the wine-cup to Noah's ark (q.v.), saying that it will save one from the storm of sorrow (*ṭūfān-i gham,* see JOY AND MISERY). To ʿUmar al-Khayyām is also attributed a satirical quatrain, quoted by Browne (*Literary history,* ii, 254), in which the apparently cryptic *bal hum* is, as Browne explains (ibid., n. 2), a reference to Q 7:179 (vs. 178 in Browne) and Q 25:46 (vs. 44 in Browne), a qur'ānic comment to the effect that a certain type of people are "like animals, or rather even more misguided."

It is, however, in Persian mystical poetry that the influence of the Qur'ān, in terms of both substance and language, is most evident. The *Manṭiq al-ṭayr* of Farīd al-Dīn ʿAṭṭār (513-627/1119-1230) takes its name from Q 27:16 and the birds of the story are guided in their search for their king, Simurgh, by the wise hoopoe — the bird mentioned in the same sūra (Q 27:20; ʿAṭṭār makes use of the unmistakable wordplay on the hoopoe's Arabic name, *hudhud,* and the qur'ānic concept of *hudā,* "guidance"). Saʿdī's *Majālis-i panjgāna,* "Five sessions," are studded with qur'ānic quotations. Ḥāfiẓ (d. 791 or 792/1389 or 1390), addressing himself, swears "by the Qur'ān you have preserved in your breast" to support his claim of having written exquisite poetry (*Dīwān,* 280). Indeed, his poetry contains not only easily identifiable qur'ānic phrases but also subtle allusions to qur'ānic events and characters. *Gar man ālūda dāmanam chi ʿajab/hama ʿālam gawāh-i ʿiṣmat-i ū'st,* "What is the wonder if my hem is soiled [i.e. if I am seen to be guilty] — the whole world bears witness to his/her innocence!" (ibid., 36) is a verse that is clear in itself but is also a powerful appropriation of a qur'ānic incident: in Q 12, the innocent Joseph is framed and Potiphar's wife, Joseph's would-be seducer, is allowed to go scot-free. The allusion enables Ḥāfiẓ to imbue his verse with the ironic overtones present in the qur'ānic narration of the incident.

But it is, perhaps, Jalāl al-Dīn Rūmī's poetry that offers the most remarkable instance of the influence of the Qur'ān on Persian literature. Nicholson's index *(fihrist)* of the qur'ānic verses that have been cited by Rūmī in his *Mathnawī* gives some idea of the Qur'ān's influence (*Mathnawī*, iv, 391-408). It is, however, not exhaustive, for Rūmī not only cites actual phrases and verses from the Qur'ān but also reworks them, gives a Persian rendition of them and makes subtle allusions to qur'ānic themes or characters. In the First Book *(daftar)* of the *Mathnawī* alone there are about two hundred explicit or implicit references to the Qur'ān, only a few of which we will note here. Emphasizing the need to surrender to God's will, Rūmī says: *ham-chu Ismāʿīl pīshash sar bi-nih,* "Lay down your head before [i.e. obey] God like Ishmael (q.v.)" (who willingly offered to be sacrificed by Abraham at God's behest; *Mathnawī,* i, 8; see Q 37:102-3). In one of the stories, the hare succeeds in ensnaring the mighty lion and then rushes off to inform the other animals: *sūi nakhchīran dawīd an shīr-gīr/ka'bshirū yā qawmu idh jā'a l-bashīr,* "That lion-catcher ran off to the animals, saying, 'Good news (q.v.) for you, my people, for one bearing good tidings has come'" (*Mathnawī,* i, 83). *Abshirū* is the greeting the people of heaven will receive (Q 41:30), whereas *idh jā'a l-bashīru* evokes Q 12:96, wherein a harbinger informs Jacob (q.v.) in Canaan of the safety and well-being of his son Joseph in Egypt. Stressing the importance of listening over speaking, Rūmī first says that hearing is the proper path to speech and then writes an Arabic couplet, the first hemistich of which (*udkhulū l-abyāta min abwābihā/wa-ṭlubū l-aghrāḍa fī asbābihā,* "Enter houses by the door, and seek goals using the means proper to them") is a slightly modified version of Q 2:189, a verse criticizing certain pre-Islamic pilgrimage (q.v.) practices. Again, immortality is to be sought only through self-loss in God: *kullu shay'in hālikun juz wajh-i ū/chūn na'ī dar wajh-i ū hastī majū,* "Everything is going to perish except his countenance; if you are not before his countenance, do not seek to have existence," a line clearly reliant on Q 28:88 (see FACE OF GOD). Rūmī keeps bringing his readers back to the Qur'ān, ensuring that their contact with the Qur'ān, whether on the level of thought or of language, is never broken. Not without reason did the poet ʿAbd al-Raḥmān Jāmī (d. 898-9/1492) call the *Mathnawī* the Qur'ān in Pahlavi.

Qur'ān in Urdu literature

Compared with Persian, Urdu is a young language, whose proper literary career did not start until the early eighteenth century. While it continued the historical legacy of the Perso-Arabic Islamic culture in India — it succeeded Persian as the court language of Mughal India — Urdu developed under certain peculiar circumstances. Unlike Persian, Urdu was strongly influenced in its formative phase by writings with a religious and moral orientation. In fact, the history of the development of Urdu as a language is closely linked with the history of Islamic reformism in India. Some of the figures in this broad reform movement whose writings contributed to the growth of Urdu as a literary language are the first translators of the Qur'ān into Urdu, Shāh Rafīʿ al-Dīn (1750-1818) and Shāh ʿAbd al-Qādir (1753-1813), who were sons of Shāh Walī Allāh al-Dihlawī (1703-73); Sayyid Aḥmad Khān (1837-98), the founder of the Aligarh Movement; Naẓīr Aḥmad (1831-1912), author of several edifying novels (one of these, *Tawbatu'n-naṣūh,* takes its title from Q 66:8); and Alṭāf Ḥusayn Ḥālī (1837-1914), author of the powerful poem *Rise and ebb of Islam.* The writings of these authors reflect their preoccupation with Islamic, including qur'ānic, themes and motifs. There are, of course, writers in whose works such themes and motifs receive a deliberately pronounced emphasis, as in the poetry of the eighteenth-century mystic Khwāja Mīr Dard (1721-1785), who is preoccupied with the transience of worldly existence and in the masterly prose of the twentieth-century reformist Abū l-Kalām Āzād, who frequently cites qur'ānic verses to support his arguments, inviting Muslims to base their thought and action on the Qur'ān.

References and allusions to the Qur'ān will, however, be encountered in all manner of Urdu literature. In Mīr Ḥasan's (d. 1786) *Siḥru l-bayān,* "The spellbinding story," one of the best known of the Urdu *mathnawīs*, the childless king is dissuaded from becoming a hermit by his courtiers who remind him of the qur'ānic injunction of *la taqnaṭū,* "Do not despair" (Q 39:53). In a *qaṣīda,* Sawdā showers praise on a ruler, saying that, compared with him, even Solomon would be dwarfed to an ant — an allusion to the story of Solomon and the ants in Q 27:18-9 (see ANIMAL LIFE). In a *ghazal,* Ibrāhīm Dhawq (1790-1854) says: "He who is not found to be a world-loving dog (q.v.) — the like of him will not be found among angels," which recalls Q 7:176. In another verse, he says that killing a tiger, lion or python is not as great a feat as is the killing of the *nafs-i ammāra* (the baser self that impels one to evil), to which allusion is made in Q 12:53. In his poetry, Ghālib (d. 1869) makes a number of allusions to the Qur'ān, most of them playful. In one place (*Dīwān,* 49), he says that one like him would have withstood the impact of the divine epiphany much better than Moses (according to Q 7:143, Moses fell down unconscious when, at his demand, God manifested himself on Mount Sinai; see SINAI), commenting wryly that a wine-drinker should be served only as much wine as he can take without losing his senses. He compares his dejection-filled heart to Joseph's dungeon — a reference to Q 12 (ibid., 9). One of his verses reads (ibid., 188): *waraq tamām hu'a awr madḥ bāqī hai/safīna chāhi'e is baḥr-i be-karān ke li'e,* "The sheet of paper is filled up, but there is still more praise to offer: a ship is needed to cross this boundless sea." This is a possible allusion to Q 31:27, according to which God could not be praised enough even if all the trees in the world were to become pens and all the seas were to become ink (see WRITING AND WRITING MATERIALS). In a few verses Ghālib cites portions of qur'ānic verses verbatim (e.g. ibid., 74, 214).

It is, however, Muḥammad Iqbāl's (d. 1938) poetry that bears the deepest imprint of the Qur'ān; this is true of Iqbāl's Persian as well as his Urdu poetry, but only the latter will be discussed here. Many of his verses appear to be adaptations of qur'ānic verses. For example, Iqbāl describes some of the qualities of a true Muslim in the following words (*Kulliyyāt,* 507): *ho halqah-i yārān to baresham ki taraḥ narm/razm-i ḥaq-o-bāṭil ho to fawlād hai mu'min,* "In the company of friends the believer is soft like silk (q.v.), but in the clash of truth and falsehood he is like steel." This instantly brings to mind Q 48:29. Alluding to Q 21:68-9, according to which Abraham was thrown into the fire by the king of his time (called Nimrod [q.v.] by tradition), Iqbāl points to the modern challenges to Islam, asking a question (ibid., 257): "Again there is a fire, there is Abraham's offspring, and Nimrod, too!/Is all of this meant to put someone to the test?" In a poem about Khiẓr (Ar. Khiḍr; the Islamic literary tradition gives this name to the man, referred to in Q 18:65, who was sent by God to initiate Moses into some of the mysteries of the divine administration of the universe; see KHAḌIR/KHIḌR), Iqbāl writes (*Kulliyyāt,* 256): *kashti-e miskīn-o jān-i pāk-o dīwār-i yatīm/*

ʿilm-i Mūsā bhī hai tere sāmne ḥayrat-firōsh, "The poor man's boat, the pure soul (q.v.), and the orphan's (see ORPHANS) wall! Even Moses' knowledge suffers from bewilderment before you." Here, the first hemistich, which consists of three two-word phrases, makes a compact reference to the three uncommon incidents which are narrated in Q 18:71-82, and which a surprised Moses witnessed in the company of Khiẓr. Iqbāl borrows or adapts from the Qurʾān a large number of terms and phrases, but these terms and phrases in his works are not, as they might have been in another writer's, embellishments, but are rather essential instruments of his thought. A full study of the impact of the Qurʾān on Iqbāl's poetry is yet to be made.

Qurʾān in Punjabi literature

Punjabi Ṣūfī literature shows definite signs of the influence of the Qurʾān. Addressing a wide but illiterate audience and using earthy language while drawing on scenes and events of daily life, Muslim mystics stress the need to worship God with a pure heart, live a simple, honest life, seek a wisdom higher than that found in dry books, shun empty ritualism (see RITUAL AND THE QURʾĀN), abandon pride, greed and hypocrisy, and remember death and the day of judgment. These are broad Islamic themes but, in many instances, they have a definite qurʾānic basis, as a study of the works of major Ṣūfī poets will show. In a poem, Bullhe Shāh (d. 1172/1758) wonders why people are quarreling over God when God is closer to them than their jugular vein, a clear reference to Q 50:16 (see ARTERY AND VEIN). In more than one place, Bullhe Shāh says that all one needs to study is *alif,* the first letter of the Arabic alphabet and the first letter of the divine name, *Allāh.* This is a simple but dramatic way of highlighting the centrality of the doctrine of God in the Qurʾān — *Allāh* being, incidentally, the noun with the highest frequency in the Qurʾān. Implying that advice and guidance will be lost on a confirmed sinner, Sulṭān Bāhū (d. 1103/1691) says that rain will not benefit a stony heart, which reminds one of Q 2:264; and, again, that a stone is better than a heart that is forgetful of God, an obvious reference to Q 2:74. Bābā Farīd (569-665/1173-1266) says that one who has been misled by Satan will not listen even if words of wisdom and good counsel were shouted at him — a statement that brings to mind Q 2:17 (possibly also Q 7:175 and 58:19). Shāh Ḥusayn's (d. 1002/1593) frequent references to the transient nature of the world and of worldly pleasures are qurʾānic in their spirit. In a number of instances, Punjabi Ṣūfī poets cite short phrases from the Qurʾān, either in the original Arabic or in translation. A careful reader of these poets, especially of Sulṭān Bāhū, cannot fail to note the influence of the Qurʾān — both at the level of theme and at the level of language — on this literature.

Qurʾān in Malay literature

Islam arrived in the Malay world in the fourteenth century C.E. but, notwithstanding the works of a writer like the mystic Ḥamza Fansūrī (sixteenth-seventeenth centuries), Malay language and literature cannot be said to have been influenced by Islam or the Qurʾān in the same way as were some of the other Muslim languages and literatures. Like Malay society, Malay literature emphasizes uniformity and conventionality and tends to view assertion of individualism or originality and expression of spontaneous feeling as wayward and disruptive (anonymity of authorship is typical of classical Malay literature). This emphasis limited the stock of literary themes and devices available to a writer, who was further limited by the social context of this literature. As essentially a palace literature, a literature of patronage, Malay writers depicted mostly the lives and exploits of rulers and aristocrats. The emphasis on conventionality also restricted the scope of foreign literary influence. Accordingly, classical Malay literature, even when it was influenced by Islam, largely retained its pre-Islamic thematic repertoire and structural framework. Thus, the well-known and predominant genre of prose romance called *ḥikāyat* continued to deal with the themes of the ancient Hindu epics. Even when heroes from Muslim history were introduced or substituted in stories, they were usually cast in the roles of familiar pre-Islamic figures, the *ḥikāyat* generally receiving only an Islamic varnishing. But instances of Islamic or qurʾānic influence on *ḥikāyat* literature do exist, as suggested by such titles as *Ḥikāyat Iblīs* and *Ḥikāyat nabī Yūsuf*, and — as clearly and significantly illustrated in the *Ḥikāyat mahārāja ʿAlī* — by the employment of qurʾānic terms, phrases and invocatory expressions (see EXHORTATIONS), by the treatment of such qurʾānic themes as God's ability to accomplish his purposes against all odds and the need for human beings to put their trust in God (see TRUST AND PATIENCE) and by the adaptive use of such qurʾānic stories as that of the prophet David (q.v.) and his wise son Solomon (Q 21:78-9) or that of Jesus' miraculous power to revive the dead (Q 3:49).

There is one other, and rather peculiar, way in which the Qurʾān influenced Malay literature. Classical Malay written literature, which no less than Malay oral literature was meant to be heard rather than read, acquired certain qualities associated with oral literature. Since Malay literature, in general, had to be chanted, the tradition of Qurʾān recitation, according to Sweeney (*Authors and audiences*, 32), gave a "definite Islamic flavor to the chant."

Wadad Kadi (al-Qāḍī) and
Mustansir Mir

Bibliography

Qurʾān as literature.
Primary: Bāqillānī, *Iʿjāz;* Ibn Qayyim al-Jawziyya, Muḥammad b. Abū Bakr, *al-Fawāʾid al-mushawwiqa ilā ʿulūm al-Qurʾān wa-ʿilm al-bayān*, Beirut n.d.; A.A. Iṣlāḥī, *Tadabbur-i Qurʾān*, 8 vols., Lahore 1967-80; Jurjānī, *Dalāʾil*, ed. M.M. Shākir, Cairo 1984; Zarkashī, *Burhān*, ed. M. Abū l-Faḍl Ibrāhīm.
Secondary: M. Abū Zahra, *al-Qurʾān. Al-muʿjiza l-kubrā*, Cairo [1390/1970]; I. Boullata (ed.), *Literary structures of religious meaning in the Qurʾān*, Richmond, Surrey 2000; A.H. Johns, The qurʾānic presentation of the Joseph story. Naturalistic or formulaic language? in Hawting and Shareef, *Approaches*, 37-70; M. Mir, The qurʾānic story of Joseph. Plot, themes, and characters, in *MW* 76 (1986), 1-15; A. Neuwirth, *Studien zur Komposition der mekkanischen Suren*, Berlin/New York 1981; S. Quṭb, al-Taṣwīr al-fannī fī l-Qurʾān, 2 parts, in *al-Muqtaṭaf* 93 (1939), 205-11; 313-8; N. Robinson, *Discovering the Qurʾān. A contemporary approach to a veiled text*, London 1996; M. Sells, Sound, spirit, and gender in *sūrat al-qadr*, in *JAOS* 111 (1991), 239-59; Watt-Bell, *Introduction;* M. Zahniser, Major transitions and thematic borders in two long *sūras*. *Al-baqara* and *al-nisāʾ*, in I. Boullata (ed.), *Literary structures of religious meaning in the Qurʾān*, Richmond, Surrey 2000, 26-55.
Qurʾān in literature.
Qurʾān in Arabic literature.
Primary: Balawī, see below, al-Qāḍī, *Bishr ibn Abī Kubār;* al-Hamdānī, Abū Muḥammad al-Ḥasan b. Aḥmad, *Ṣifat jazīrat al-ʿarab*, ed. M. al-Akwaʿ al-Ḥawālī, Riyadh 1974; Ibn al-Nadīm, *Fihrist;* Ibn al-Nadīm-Dodge; Ibn al-Ṣayrafī, Abū l-Qāsim ʿAlī b. Munjib, *Intizāʿāt al-Qurʾān al-ʿaẓīm* (ms.); al-Qalqashandī, Abū l-Abbās Aḥmad b. ʿAlī, *Ṣubḥ al-aʿshā fī ṣināʿat al-inshā*, offset edition of the first edition, 14 vols., Cairo n.d.; Suyūṭī, *Itqān;* id., *Rafʿ al-libās wa-kashf al-iltibās fī ḍarb al-mathal min al-Qurʾān wa-l-iqtibās*, ed. S.M. al-Laḥḥām, Beirut 1999 (no. 19 of *Rasāʾil al-Suyūṭī;* this work contains the positions of a number of classical authors, such as al-Ghazālī and al-Nawawī, as well as a discussion of the practices of the Companions); al-Tawḥīdī, Abū Ḥayyān ʿAlī b. Muḥammad, *al-Baṣāʾir wa-l-dhakhāʾir*, ed. W. al-Qāḍī, 10 vols., Beirut 1988; Thaʿālibī, *Iqtibās;* Zarkashī, *Burhān*, Cairo 1957.

Secondary: I. ʿAbbās, *ʿAbd al-Ḥamīd ibn Yaḥyā al-kātib wa-mā tabaqqā min rasāʾilihi wa-rasāʾil Sālim Abī l-ʿAlāʾ*, Amman 1988; C.H. Becker, *Papyri Scott-Reinhardt I*, Heidelberg 1906; M. Canard, Ibn Nubāta, in *EI²*, iii, 900; T. Fahd, W. Heinrichs and A. Ben Abdessalam, Sadjʿ, in *EI²*, viii, 732-9, esp. pp. 734-6; C. Gilliot, Un florilège coranique. Le *Iqtibās min al-Qurʾān* de Abū Manṣūr al-Ṯaʿālibī, in *Arabica* 47 (2000), 488-500; I. Jomaih, *The use of the Qurʾān in political argument. A study of early Islamic parties (35-86 A.H./656-705 A.D.)*, Ph.D. diss., Los Angeles 1988; M.R. Khan, *Vom Einfluss des Qurʾāns auf die arabische Dichtung*, Leipzig 1938; W. al-Qāḍī, *Bishr ibn Abī Kubār al-Balawī. Namūdhaj min al-nathr al-fannī al-mubakkir fī l-Yaman*, Beirut 1985; id., The impact of the Qurʾān on the epistolography of ʿAbd al-Ḥamīd, in Hawting and Shareef, *Approaches*, 285-313; id., The limitations of qurʾānic usage in early Arabic poetry. The example of a Khārijite poem, in W. Heinrichs and G. Schoeler (eds.), *Festschrift Ewald Wagner zum 65. Gerburtstag*, 2 vols., Beirut/Wiesbaden 1994, ii, 162-81; D.B. Macdonald/S.A. Bonebakker, Iḳtibās, in *EI²*, iii, 1092-3 (and see bibliography for additional sources on rhetoric); A. Maṭar, *Lāfitāt — 1*, London 1987; Wensinck, *Concordance;* A.M. Zubaidi, The impact of the Qurʾān and *ḥadīth* on medieval Arabic literature, in A.F.L. Beeston et al., *Arabic literature to the end of the Umayyad period*, Cambridge 1983, 322-43.
Qurʾān in Persian literature.
Primary: ʿAṭṭār, Farīd al-Dīn, *Manṭiqu ʾṭayr [Manṭiq al-ṭayr]*, Teheran [?] 1988; Ḥāfiẓ, *Dīwān of Ḥāfiẓ*, ed. M. Qazwīnī and Q. Ghanī, [USA] 1986; Jalāl al-Dīn Rūmī, *Mathnawī-maʿnawī*, ed. R. Nicholson, 4 vols., Teheran 1364; Saʿdi, *Kulliyyat-i nafis*, 4th printing, [Iran], 1364; Niẓāmī, *Haft paykar. A medieval Persian romance*, tran. J.S. Meisami, Oxford 1995; Umar al-Khayyām, *The Rubaiyyat of Omar Khayyam*, translated into English quatrains by Mehdi Nakosteen, with corresponding Persian quatrains in translator's calligraphy, Boulder, CO 1973.
Secondary: E.G.A. Browne, *Literary history of Persia*, 4 vols., Cambridge, UK 1902-21; Iranbooks reprint, 1997; J.T.P. de Bruijn, *Persian Sufi poetry. An introduction to the mystical use of classical Persian poems*, Richmond, Surrey 1997.
Qurʾān in Urdu literature.
Ghālib, *Dīwān-i Ghālib*, ed. Ḥāmī ʿAlī Khān, Lahore 1995; Harunuʾr-Rashid, *Urdu adab awr islam*, 2 vols., Lahore 1968-70; Muḥammad Iqbāl, *Kulliyyāt-i Iqbāl — Urdū*, Lahore 1973; D.J. Matthews, C. Shackle and Shahrukh Husain, *Urdu literature*, London 1985.
Qurʾān in Punjabi literature.
Maqbul Anvar Daʾudi (ed.), *Abyāt-i Bāhū*, Lahore n.d.; id. (ed.), *Bullhe Shāh kehnde nen*, Lahore [1987]; id. (ed.), *Kalām Bābā Farīd shakar ganj*, Lahore [1987]; id. (ed.), *Kīhyā Shāh Ḥusayn nen*, Lahore [1987]; M. Mir, Teachings of two Punjabi poets, in D.S. Lopez Jr. (ed.), *Indian religions in practice*, Princeton 1995, 518-29.
Qurʾān in Malay literature.
A. Bausani, *Notes on the structure of the classical Malay hikayat*, trans. (from It.) Lode Brakel, Melbourne 1979; A. Sweeney, *Authors and audiences in traditional Malay literature*, Berkeley 1980.

Liturgical Calendar see FESTIVALS AND COMMEMORATVE DAYS

Load or Burden

Something carried or borne, often with difficulty. The concept of load or burden appears in the Qurʾān approximately fifty times, in several forms, conveying a range of implications that can be classified as descriptive, metaphorical (see METAPHOR), and morally didactic.

As a term of physical description, variants of the radical *ḥ-m-l* frequently depict the load borne by animals such as cattle, donkeys and camels (Q 12:72; 16:7; 62:5; see CAMEL; ANIMAL LIFE); as the cargo aboard ships (q.v.; Q 23:22; 40:80) or related to natural elements such as clouds laden with rain (Q 51:2; see AIR AND WIND; NATURE AS SIGNS). It also applies, usually as the verbal noun *ḥaml*, to the bearing of children (q.v.; Q 7:189; 22:2; 65:6; see also BIOLOGY AS THE CREATION AND STAGES OF LIFE). Its usages, however, are not restricted to expressly material burdens, as, for example, angels (see ANGEL) are described as supporting the weight of the heavenly throne (Q 40:7; 69:17; see THRONE OF GOD).

As a metaphor, the Qurʾān may specify load or burden as a generalized onus, the significance of which depends on the surrounding context. It alludes to the burdens *(awzār)* of war (q.v.; Q 47:4) or it contrasts two men, one who follows the straight path (see PATH OR WAY) while the other is a burden *(kall)* upon his master (Q 16:76; see SLAVES AND SLAVERY; CLIENTS AND CLIENTAGE). The term *iṣr* which occurs more rarely, refers at one point to the load placed by God upon those who accept his covenant (q.v.; Q 3:81) and elsewhere to the load that the Prophet will lift as a yoke, to relieve those who heed his message (Q 7:157). Another passage mentions the earth (q.v.) "throwing out its burdens" *(athqāl,* Q 99:2), an apocalyptic image which al-Bayḍāwī (d. ca. 700/1301; *Anwār,* ad loc.) interprets as the tombs yielding up their dead (see DEATH AND THE DEAD; APOCALYPSE). Likewise, the Qurʾān speaks of God opening up the breast (see HEART) of Muḥammad and "removing your burden which was breaking your back" (Q 94:2-3) which appears to indicate the anxious and vulnerable circumstances Muḥammad experienced at the outset of his mission in Mecca (q.v.; see also OPPOSITION TO MUḤAMMAD).

Finally, load or burden arises in a number of similar phrases that reflect a key teaching of the Qurʾān regarding the fundamental responsibility of each individual for his or her own moral and religious growth and integrity (see ETHICS AND THE QURʾĀN). The line "no one who carries a burden bears the load of another" occurs with slight variation six times (Q 6:164; 17:15; 24:54; 35:18; 39:7; 53:38) and in every instance it is accompanied by allusions, direct or indirect, to the day of judgment (see LAST JUDGMENT). The *Jalālayn* consistently offer a succinct gloss for "burden" *(wāzira)* in commenting on these passages, equating it with *āthām* or *dhunūb,* meaning sins or faults (see SIN, MAJOR AND MINOR). Likewise, they and other commentators emphasize the reference to the accountability of each single individual before God in the acquisition of eternal reward or punishment (see EXEGESIS OF THE QURʾĀN: CLASSICAL AND MEDIEVAL; REWARD AND PUNISHMENT; ETERNITY).

One instructive variant on this theme recounts an incident when disbelievers called upon believers (see BELIEF AND UNBELIEF): "Follow our way; we shall carry the burden of your sins." In response, the Qurʾān not only refutes the fallacy of this presumption on the part of the disbelievers but adds that those who lead others astray (q.v.) by such claims "will carry their own loads and other loads besides their own" (Q 29:12-3). This passage offers a qualification of the statements that limit the moral responsibility of individuals to their own behavior by indicating that leading others astray by offering to bear their burdens, will reap a penalty of the sort that renders these deceivers an extra measure of culpability in much the fashion that they themselves had suggested.

Al-Ṭabarī (d. 310/923) notes that this doctrine of individual moral accountability echoes the Prophet's recognition of the consequences of personal freedom in moral terms (see FREEDOM AND PREDESTINATION), just as his statement with regard to belief was formulated in his famous final declaration: "You have your religion and I have my religion" (Q 109:6; see FAITH; RELIGIOUS PLURALISM AND THE QURʾĀN). A number of ḥadīths (see ḤADĪTH AND THE QURʾĀN) elaborate upon these verses with accounts of a surprise encounter after one's death at which each individual soul will be confronted by a set of vivid forms, one beautiful and the other repulsive, which will identify themselves as the good and evil deeds (q.v.) performed during that person's lifetime (see also GOOD DEEDS; GOOD AND EVIL; RECORD OF HUMAN ACTIONS).

More recent schools of interpretation,

such as those represented in the twentieth century by al-Mawdūdi and Rashīd Riḍā, reflecting upon these same verses, have emphasized a reformist agenda. They point out, for instance, that the logic of strictly individualized merit and retribution serves to refute many aspects of popular piety (see FESTIVALS AND COMMEMORATIVE DAYS). They have been especially critical of elaborate funerary and memorial rituals, including the establishment of *waqf* endowments in support of such tomb-centered practices as well as the cult of saints and prayerful appeals for their intercession (q.v.).

Patrick D. Gaffney

Bibliography
Primary: A. Ali, *al-Qurʾān. A commentary translation*, Princeton 1984; Bayḍāwī, *Anwār; Jalālayn;* A. al-Mawdūdi, *The meaning of the Qurʾān*, 16 vols., Lahore 1988; Rashīd Riḍā, *Manār;* Ṭabarī, *Tafsīr.*
Secondary: Baljon, *Modern;* K. Cragg, *The weight in the word*, Brighton 1999; J. Jomier, *Le commentaire coranique du Manār*, Paris 1954; Mir, *Dictionary;* F. Rahman, *Major themes of the Qurʾān*, Minneapolis 1980.

Loan see DEBTS; ECONOMICS; USURY

Locust see ANIMAL LIFE; PLAGUE

Lord

One who has power and authority. One of the most frequent nouns in the Qurʾān, "lord" generally refers to God but on a few occasions designates a human master. Three terms in the Qurʾān can be rendered into English as lord: *rabb, mawlā* and *walī*.

Rabb recurs 971 times in the Qurʾān, never as an isolated word with the definite article *(al-rabb)* but always as the first term in a genitive construct (i.e. the lord of the heavens and the earth), most often with a personal pronoun as suffix. *Rabb* conveys not only the meanings of lord and master but also of caregiver, provider, sustainer (cf. the Arabic verb *rabba*, "to be lord," and also "to bring up, to care for"). The word is used to express the universal lordship of God (cf. Q 4:1, the lord of all humankind *[al-nās]*) with special reference to his (but see GENDER for a discussion of the complexities of gender in Arabic grammar) creative act ("the lord of all the worlds/of the whole creation" [q.v.; *rabb al-ʿālamīn*], in forty-two instances); the lord of previous prophets ("the lord of Moses [q.v.] and Aaron [q.v.]," Q 7:122; 26:48; cf. 20:70; see PROPHETS AND PROPHETHOOD); as well as the special relationship between the lord and the believer ("God is my lord," Q 19:36, "and Noah [q.v.] called unto his lord," Q 11:45; see BELIEF AND UNBELIEF). When in the plural *(arbāb)*, the term indicates gods other than the one God and the opposition between the numerous gods and the one God is emphasized (Q 9:31: "they have taken their rabbis and their monks for their lords *[arbāb]* beside the God [*min dūni llāhi*, see JEWS AND JUDAISM; CHRISTIANS AND CHRISTIANITY; MONASTICISM AND MONKS]; and "... diverse lords... or the one God," Q 12:39; also Q 3:64; cf. Quṭb, *Ẓilāl*, 15; see POLYTHEISM AND ATHEISM).

The term *rabb* with reference to a human master is found in Sūrat Yūsuf ("Joseph," Q 12). In this lively and linguistically interesting narrative of Joseph's life (see NARRATIVES), the tension between loyalty to the human master and to the eternal lord is sustained by the consecutive use of the same term in both its meanings; Joseph (q.v.) says to the wife of his master (Potiphar): "Goodly has my master *(rabbī)* made my lodging" (Q 12:23), with the narrative continuing "and he [Joseph] would have succumbed had he not seen a proof of his lord's truth *(burhān rabbihi)*" (Q 12:24). The link is even more evident in Joseph's own words to the king's messenger: "Go back to your lord (*rabbika,* "the king") ... my lord *(rabbī)* [alone] has full knowledge of their [the women's] guile" (Q 12:50). *Rabb* as human master occurs again in Q 12 with reference to the Egyptian king in Q 12:41 and 42 (see PHARAOH).

The lordship and majesty of God over the whole creation are conveyed through expressions such as *rabb al-ʿālamīn,* as mentioned earlier, and also "the lord of the heavens (see HEAVEN AND SKY) and the earth (q.v.) and what is between them" (Q 26:24), "the lord of the east and the west and what is between them" (Q 26:28), "the lord of the seven heavens" (Q 23:86), and "the lord of the two easts and the two wests" (Q 55:17). Lordship expressed through creation implies not a once and for all action but a continuous process (Quṭb, *Ẓilāl,* 15-7): *rabb* is not only the originator but also that which preserves, manages and regulates this creation (Ibn al-ʿArabī, *Tafsīr,* 10).

In some instances the terms *rabb* and *Allāh* are found together so as to reiterate the identity and specificity of lordship and divinity: "My lord is God" (*rabbī Allāh,* Q 40:28), or "God is my lord" (Q 3:51; 19:36; 43:64), as well as "our lord is God" (Q 22:40; 46:13). Moreover, the use of *rabb* as lord could imply the correct relationship to be entertained between the creator and his creation, especially with the human being whose role as servant (q.v.; *ʿabd*) is to worship the creator (cf. Q 3:51; 89:28-9; cf. Abū Ḥayyān, *Baḥr,* 18; Qūnawī, *Iʿjāz,* 293). The majority of classical as well as modern exegetical *(tafsīr)* works (see EXEGESIS OF THE QURʾĀN: CLASSICAL AND MEDIEVAL; EXEGESIS OF THE QURʾĀN: EARLY MODERN AND CONTEMPORARY) provide explanations for the meanings of the term *rabb* in the Qurʾān. *Rabb* describes God as master, sustainer and owner of his creation (Ṭabarī, *Tafsīr,* i, 141-3; Ālūsī, *Rūḥ,* i, 77-8), as the incessant caretaker of the whole universe (Quṭb, *Ẓilāl,* 15, Rashīd Riḍā, *Tafsīr,* 36). *Rabb* indicates the lord of creation by virtue of the act of bringing the world into existence out of non-existence (Rāzī, *Tafsīr,* i, 233-4; see COSMOLOGY). Accordingly, being creator, God is the only one worthy of lordship (*rubūbiyya;* Bayḍāwī, *Anwār,* ii, 123; Ṭabāṭabāʾī, *Mīzān,* i, 29-30). Elaborating on this aspect, mystical exegesis (see ṢŪFISM AND THE QURʾĀN) identifies the term *rabb* with the level at which divine lordship, being related to the act of creation, can be known. Consequently, scholars such as Sahl al-Tustarī (d. 283/896), Ibn al-ʿArabī (d. 638/1240) and al-Qūnawī (d. 673/1274) distinguish the level of God as *rabb* (i.e. lord of creation) from that of God as *Allāh* which they consider to express divinity untouched by creation (Qūnawī, *Iʿjāz,* 296). Ṣūfīs such as Abū l-Ḥasan al-Nūrī (d. 295/907), or al-Muḥāsibī (d. 243/857) before him, express a similar concept by stressing the relation between *rabb* (master) and *marbūb* (subject) to indicate the first human cognitive stage of the majesty of God (see KNOWLEDGE AND LEARNING).

The modernist Egyptian scholar Maḥmūd Shaltūt, *shaykh* of al-Azhar during 1958-63, elaborates further on the lordship of God by linking it to three main aspects of divine providence. Firstly, God is the sole lord of the world through his physical creative providence, which not only caused the world to come into existence but also constantly preserves, nourishes and protects it. Secondly, God is lord as he provides humankind with the rational faculty which allows humans to identify the signs (q.v.) of God in the world and to distinguish good from evil (see GOOD AND EVIL). Thirdly, God is lord through revelation of the laws he communicated through inspiration to the prophets and which are preserved in the scriptures as constant reminders to the whole of humankind (see REVELATION AND INSPIRATION; SCRIPTURE AND THE QUR'ĀN; BOOK).

In his seminal and controversial work *The foreign vocabulary of the Qur'ān* (136-9), the scholar Arthur Jeffery believed the qur'ānic use of the term *rabb* with reference to God to be the result of a linguistic borrowing from Aramaic or Syriac and also that the use of *rabb* to indicate "human chieftains" but also pre-Islamic gods was already attested by pre-Islamic poetry and inscriptions (ibid., 137; see FOREIGN VOCABULARY). It should nevertheless be added that there is evidence of the use of *rabb* or *rabbanā* as a title to address the pre-Islamic *kāhin*, "priest/officiant of sacrifices" (Fahd, *Divination*, 107-8; see SOOTHSAYERS). In a 1958 article, the French Islamicist J. Chelhod, applying criteria similar to those used in biblical textual criticism, analyzed the frequency of occurrence of the terms *rabb* and *Allāh* for a tentative chronology of the qur'ānic sūras. Chelhod noted that while the use of the term *rabb* clearly decreases in the Medinan sūras, that of *Allāh* increases considerably from the third period of Meccan sūras onwards. Such observations led Chelhod to posit some hypotheses (summarized in Böwering, Chronology, 329-30), which importantly link qur'ānic language and style (see LANGUAGE AND STYLE OF THE QUR'ĀN) to the inner chronology of the Qur'ān (see CHRONOLOGY AND THE QUR'ĀN).

The Qur'ān also uses *mawlā*, "tutor, trustee, helper, ally," carrying the connotation of protector to signify divine lordship (Q 47:11: "God is the *mawlā* of the faithful, the unbelievers have no *mawlā*"; also Q 2:286; 3:150; 6:62; 8:40; 9:51; 22:78; 47:11; 66:2). In other instances, however, *mawlā* is clearly used in a non-religious non-divine sense to indicate a friend, an ally (Q 16:76; 19:5; 44:41). *Walī*, one of the ninety-nine divine names (see GOD AND HIS ATTRIBUTES), occurs in several instances as lord in the sense of protector, guardian (Q 2:257; 3:68; 4:45; 7:155; 13:11), but also of friend (Q 5:55; 6:14; 42:9; 45:19; see FRIENDS AND FRIENDSHIP). It is also used, often in the plural form *(awliyā')*, with reference to a human protector or friend (Q 3:28, 175; 4:89, 144; 5:51; etc.).

Simonetta Calderini

Bibliography
Primary: Abū Ḥayyān, *Baḥr*, 18; Ālūsī, *Rūḥ*, i, 77-8; Bayḍāwī, *Anwār*, i, 25-6; ii, 12; Ibn al-ʿArabī, *Tafsīr*, i, 10; al-Qūnawī, Ṣadr al-Dīn Muḥammad b. Isḥāq, *Kitāb Iʿjāz al-bayān fī ta'wīl umm al-Qur'ān*, ed. ʿA. ʿAṭā (in *al-Tafsīr al-ṣūfī lil-Qur'ān*), Cairo 1969, 289-307; Quṭb, *Ẓilāl*, i, 15-7; Rashīd Riḍā, *Manār*, 36; Rāzī, *Tafsīr*, i, 233-7; M. Shaltūt, *Tafsīr al-Qur'ān al-karīm (al-ajzā' al-ʿashara al-ūlā)*, Cairo 1982[9], 22-3, 363-4; Ṭabarī, *Tafsīr*, Cairo 1954, i, 141-3; Ṭabāṭabā'ī, *Mīzān*, trans. A. Rizvi, Tehran 1983, i, 29-30.
Secondary: G. Böwering, Chronology and the Qur'ān, in *EQ*, i, 316-35; S. Calderini, *Tafsīr* of *ʿālamīn* in *rabb al-ʿālamīn*, Qur'ān 1:2, in *BSOAS* 57 (1994), 52-8; J. Chelhod, Note sur l'emploi du mot *rabb* dans le Coran, in *Arabica* 5 (1958), 159-67; T. Fahd, *La divination arabe*, Paris 1987, 107-8; Jeffery, *For. vocab.*, 136-7; Mir, *Dictionary*, 177; Nwyia, *Exégèse*, 65 f.; A.J. Wensinck, Mawlā, in *EI²*, vi, 874; id. and T. Fahd, Rabb, in *EI²*, viii, 350.

Lot

The prophet sent to the people of Sodom as mentioned in both the Bible and the Qur'ān. In the latter, he is attested twenty-seven times. Among the qur'ānic stories of divine punishment (see PUNISHMENT STORIES; CHASTISEMENT AND PUNISHMENT), that of Lot (Lūṭ) and Sodom is second in terms of quantity to that of Noah (q.v.) and the flood. As in the Bible, it continues, in Q 11:69-83, 15:57-77, and Q 29:31-5, the story of the three angels (see ANGEL) who visited Abraham (q.v.), announcing the birth of Isaac (q.v.), and of Abraham's dispute with them on the fate of Sodom (*Gen* 18-9). More frequently it is an independent tale, the angels playing their part as Lot's guests: Q 7:80-4; 26:160-74; 27:54-8; 37:133-8; 54:33-7.

In many details, the story is the same as other qur'ānic tales of divine punishment: Lot was the brother *(akhū)* of his people (*qawm,* see BROTHER AND BROTHERHOOD), a messenger (q.v.; *mursal, rasūl*) who admonished his people to fear (q.v.) God; he demanded obedience (q.v.) and did not ask for remuneration. Like Noah, Hūd (q.v.), Ṣāliḥ (q.v.), Moses (q.v.) and other prophets (see PROPHETS AND PROPHETHOOD), he was accused of being a liar (cf. Q 3:184; see LIE). His people were addicted to homosexuality (q.v.), held up travelers (see HOSPITALITY AND COURTESY; HIGHWAY ROBBERY), and practiced wickedness in their councils (see GOOD AND EVIL; SIN, MAJOR AND MINOR). In vain Lot tried to convert them, offering them his daughters for marriage (see MARRIAGE AND DIVORCE). He showed hospitality to the angels, protecting them from the obtrusiveness of his people. The evildoers (see EVIL DEEDS) tried to enter his house by force but were deprived of their eyesight by divine interference (see VISION AND BLINDNESS). When the inhabitants threatened to expel Lot from the city, he prayed to God for help. The angels told Lot and his family to leave the city at night, forbidding them to turn back. Punishment came at sunrise. Rain fell on the evildoers, the city was turned upside down, and stones *(hijāra min sijjīl)* hailed from the sky. According to other versions, the punishment was a cry, a sandstorm *(ḥāṣib)* or a convulsion from the sky *(rijz min al-samā')*. Lot and his family were rescued but his wife remained in the city and died. She was punished because she had conspired with the sinners. Like Noah's wife, she is an example of unbelieving wives who betrayed their husbands (Q 66:10; see WOMEN AND THE QUR'ĀN).

In Muslim folklore the story has been developed extensively from biblical and extra-biblical Jewish and Christian tradition, much of which has been included in the exegetical tradition (*tafsīr,* see EXEGESIS OF THE QUR'ĀN: CLASSICAL AND MEDIEVAL). Lot's people lived in three cities, five cities according to some, of which Sodom was the capital. It was reduced to an ugly, evil smelling lake, which is obviously the Dead Sea. God made it "a sign for those who believe" (Q 15:77; see BELIEF AND UNBELIEF; SIGNS; GEOGRAPHY). The cities are called *al-Mu'tafikāt* because Gabriel (q.v.) tore them out of the earth, lifted them with his wing, turned them upside down, and crushed them on the ground, then stones were hurled on them. Lot's people, men and women alike, were the first of humankind to practice homosexuality. The men were married but had unnatural intercourse with their wives. Lot did not offer them his own daughters, for as a prophet he was the father of his community, the same as Muḥammad (whose wives have been called "mothers of the believers"; cf. Q 33:6; see WIVES OF THE PROPHET). In Arabic, homosexuality is *"lūṭiyya"* and unnatural intercourse of men with women is termed "minor *lūṭiyya*" (*lūṭiyya ṣughrā,* cf. Wensinck, *Concordance,* vi, 152; see SEX AND SEXUALITY). According to a ḥadīth (see ḤADĪTH AND THE QUR'ĀN), *lūṭiyya* is forbidden on pain of death for both partners. Homosexuals will be stoned as stones killed Lot's people (see STONING; BOUNDARIES AND PRECEPTS). Abū Ḥanīfa (d. 150/767) taught that the transgressors should be thrown from a height *(al-lā'iṭ yulqā min shāhiq)*, and then stoned.

Heribert Busse

Bibliography
Primary (in addition to the classical commentaries on Q 11:70-83; 15:57-76; 26:160-74): Kisāʾī, *Qiṣaṣ*, 145-50; Ṭabarī, *Taʾrīkh*, ed. de Goeje, i, 325-43, trans. W.M. Brinner, *The history of al-Ṭabarī. ii. Prophets and patriarchs*, Albany 1987, 111-25; Thaʿlabī, *Qiṣaṣ*, 90-4.
Secondary: B. Heller/G. Vajda, Lūṭ, in *EI²*, v, 832-3; H.Z. Hirschberg, Lot, in *Encyclopaedia Judaica*, ed. C. Roth, 16 vols., Jerusalem 1972, xi, 507-9; D. Künstlinger, Christliche Herkunft der kurānischen Loṭ-Legende, in *RO* 7 (1929-30), 281-95; D. Marshall, *God, Muhammad and the unbelievers*, Richmond, Surrey 1999; A. Rothkoff/M. Avi-Yonah, Sodom and Gomorrah, in *Encyclopaedia Judaica*, ed. C. Roth, 16 vols., Jerusalem 1972, xv, 70-2; Speyer, *Erzählungen*, 150-8; R. Tottoli, *Biblical prophets in the Qurʾān and Muslim literature*, Richmond 2002, 27-8 (trans. of *I profeti biblici nella tradizione islamica*, Brescia 1999, 50-2); Wensinck, *Concordance*.

Lote Tree

see AGRICULTURE AND VEGETATION; TREES; ASCENSION

Love and Affection

Feelings of personal attachment induced by kinship (q.v.) or sympathy. *Aḥabba* is the most used verb to express the idea of love. The lexical field of the concept "love" has other roots, however, such as *w-d-d*, among others. The verbal noun *ḥubb*, "love," is mentioned nine times in the Qurʾān. Love links humankind to God, human beings to one another and the individual to earthly life and its pleasures. As far as God's love is concerned, it focuses on persons but also on their qualities or their actions. In fact, the human being is often split between two contradictory attachments, one capable of leading to his damnation, the other to his salvation. And thus love is not dissociated from faith (q.v.) in the relationship with God or with humankind.

God takes the initiative in everything and his love anticipates that of human beings: "He will cause people to come whom he will love and who will love him" (Q 5:54). This divine love appears as a pure act of election (q.v.), especially in the case of a prophet (see PROPHETS AND PROPHETHOOD) such as Moses (q.v.): "And I have projected upon you a love *(maḥabba)* on my part" (Q 20:39). Nonetheless, people attract God's love to themselves by their works and especially by imitation of the Prophet, but there can be no pretension of loving God on their own initiative. It is said thus to the Prophet: "Say: if you truly love God, follow me, God will love you" (Q 3:31). To say that one is loved by God is, in the view of the Qurʾān, all the more unacceptable in that such a pretension is part and parcel of a certain confusion of the human and the divine (cf. Q 5:18, "The Jews and the Christians have said: We are the sons of God and his well-beloved ones" *[aḥibbāʾuhu]*, see JEWS AND JUDAISM; CHRISTIANS AND CHRISTIANITY).

The Qurʾān qualifies God as he who loves *(al-wadūd)*, a name which, in the two places it occurs (Q 85:14; cf. 11:90, where the definite article is not used), is linked to the attributes of mercy (q.v.) and forgiveness (q.v.). In the same way it is the "all-merciful" *(al-raḥmān)* who places in the hearts (see HEART) of the believers (see BELIEF AND UNBELIEF) love of or attachment to him *(wudd)* by way of response to their faith and their works (cf. Q 19:96). If the name *al-wadūd* gives the clearest expression to the reciprocity of love between God and humans, other divine names also suggest on God's part a form of affection comparable to that of humans: He is the good, the merciful (*al-barr al-raḥīm*, Q 52:28), just as people are good towards their parents (q.v.; cf. Q 19:14, 32; see also FAMILY). He shows compassion as does the Prophet towards the believers: "He has at heart that which you suffer, he has care for you, for the believers, compassionate *(ra'ūf)* and merciful" (Q 9:128). This same compassion *(ra'fa)* can be found in the disciples (see APOSTLE) of Jesus (q.v.), although it is not clear whether the sentiment is directed towards God or towards creatures. It is doubtlessly both, since the tender care shown to John (q.v.; Yaḥyā) by God *(ḥanānan min ladunnā)* manifests itself in his filial piety (cf. Q 19:13, 14).

Love, in the sense of affection and compassion, thus appears as a movement by God towards humans that is reciprocated, and then a movement by a human being towards his fellow creature. The verb *aḥabba/yuḥibbu* often, however, indicates another type of relationship. God is said to love or not to love such conduct. Love, and its opposite, establishes from then on a law defining human actions according to the extent to which they conform or fail to conform to the divine will (see LAW AND THE QUR'ĀN). God loves those who act for the best *(al-muḥsinūn*, five times; see GOOD DEEDS; GOOD AND EVIL) or the just *(al-muqsiṭūn*, three times; see JUSTICE AND INJUSTICE), in such a manner that whoever performs acts lovable to God attracts the divine love to himself: "those men who love to purify themselves and God loves those who purify themselves" (Q 9:108). On the other hand, God does not love qualities that clash with his nor does he love types of behavior contrary to his law, such as shown by the unjust *(al-ẓālimūn*, three times) or the transgressors *(al-mu'tadūn*, three times; see BOUNDARIES AND PRECEPTS), etc.

As we shall soon see, love or friendship between human beings is not fully recognized by the Qur'ān unless confirmed by faith. It is also worth noting that the term *ḥubb*, in the sense of human love, is only used once with an apparently negative connotation. In Q 12 (Sūrat Yūsuf, "Joseph"), love in all its various forms plays a complex role. Jacob's (q.v.) preference for Joseph (q.v.) and the jealousy (see ENVY) of the latter's brothers ("Joseph is more beloved *[aḥabbu]* of our father than are we," Q 12:8; see BROTHER AND BROTHERHOOD; BENJAMIN) are indirectly the cause of the love of the wife of al-'Azīz (see KINGS AND RULERS). But whether or not Joseph was sensitive to this, according to the divergent interpretations of the commentators (see EXEGESIS OF THE QUR'ĀN: CLASSICAL AND MEDIEVAL) on Q 12:24 (cf. De Prémare, Joseph, 63-5), the passionate type of love that grips the heart (cf. Q 12:30, *qad shaghafahā ḥubban*) is attributed only to women (see WOMEN AND THE QUR'ĀN). Tempted afresh, Joseph calls on divine protection against the wiles of women and states that he would prefer *(aḥabbu)* prison to his inclination for woman *(aṣbu ilayhinna*, Q 12:33-4). Even if subsequent tradition places (greater) value on the love between Joseph and Zulaykha, we have to recognize that it is the love of Jacob for his son that guides the story, from beginning to end. By way of contrast, the legitimate attraction felt by the daughter of Jethro (Shu'ayb [q.v.]) for Moses is only barely hinted at (cf. Q 28:25-6). This also applies to the Prophet's attraction for Zaynab (Q 33:4; see WIVES OF THE PROPHET), another instance which illustrates how little attention the Qur'ān devotes to the love of a man for a woman or that of a woman for a man. In Q 33 (Sūrat al-Aḥzāb, "The Clans"), despite an entire passage being devoted to the Prophet's spouses, marital love is only alluded to in the command given to the Prophet to ensure that his wives experience joy (see JOY AND MISERY) and satisfaction (cf. Q 33:51). Several verses recall that in the beginning man and woman were a unique entity which marriage implicitly aims to re-establish (see MARRIAGE AND DIVORCE). Developing this idea, however, one verse qualifies the love between spouses as one of those mysteries of creation (q.v.) which lead to knowledge of God (see KNOWLEDGE AND LEARNING): "Among his signs (q.v.) he has created for you, out of your very souls (see SOUL), spouses so that you may find rest in them and he has placed between you love *(mawadda)* and mercy. Surely there are in that signs for people who reflect" (Q 30:21). Seen from this vantage point, the happiness obtained by or for wives and by the descendants issuing from this happiness is expressed by a term (*qurrat aʿyun,* "the freshness of the eyes") that emphasizes its paradisiacal nature (compare Q 25:74 and 33:51 with Q 32:17; see PARADISE). As a whole, the passages in Q 2 (Sūrat al-Baqara, "The Cow") and Q 4 (Sūrat al-Nisāʾ, "Women") that relate to marriage deal with the relationships between spouses in terms that are too legal to suggest bonds of love or affection. The reciprocal attraction between the future spouses is simply suggested in connection with re-marriage or a proposal of marriage (Q 2:232, 235), or with reference to the equality to be observed between the spouses (Q 4:3, 129). As the commentators emphasize in their interpretation of these latter verses, equality cannot relate to love that man cannot control. A further qurʾānic image of spouses is found in Q 2:187, in which the pair are portrayed as garments for each other (see CLOTHING).

The passages giving strong expression to the love between God and humans or between spouses thus occur infrequently in the Qurʾān. The term *ḥubb* (and verbal derivatives of *ḥ-b-b* such as *aḥabba*) is used much more often for that which occupies the human heart first and foremost, passion and worldly goods: "and you devote to material goods a terrible love" (Q 89:20; see WEALTH). Humans are inevitably pushed to the desire for things and persons rather than to the things or persons themselves: "Embellished for people is the love of desires, the desire of women, of children, of massed quintals of gold (q.v.) and silver, thoroughbred horses, flocks and crops. That is the joy of the life here below, but being with God is an excellent return" (Q 3:14). The opposition between the love of things and the return to God is contained in an element of the qurʾānic discourse that places faith in opposition to other attitudes (such as hypocrisy or disbelief; see HYPOCRITES AND HYPOCRISY). Thus the love of God is opposed to the worst of sins (see SIN, MAJOR AND MINOR): "There are people who choose, outside of God, rivals whom they love as the love of God, but the believers have a stronger love for God (*ashaddu ḥubban lillāhi,* Q 2:165).

In the same way that human beings are naturally borne towards sensual desires, "it is God who has made you love *(ḥabbaba)* the faith and has embellished it in your hearts and has made you detest *(karraha)* impiety, prevarication (see LIE) and disobedience" (q.v.; Q 49:7). Humanity thus finds itself split between two incompatible loves: the one that leads to faith and conformity with the divine will, and the other, which brings one to the nether world (cf. Q 2:216; see HELL AND HELLFIRE). The close link between faith and love also conditions love between human beings. One can only truly love believers, since love for unbelievers separates one from God and attracts one towards this world: "You will not find people who believe in God and the last day (see LAST JUDGMENT) and who [also] show their friendship (*yuwāddūn,* see FRIENDS AND FRIENDSHIP) towards those opposed to God and to the one he has sent" (Q 58:22). Here friendship *(mawadda)* links up again with the concept of *walāya,* "friendship, alliance, attachment" (see CONTRACTS AND ALLIANCES). Adopting unbelievers as friends or allies *(walī,* pl. *awliyāʾ)* is equivalent to lining up on the side of the enemies (q.v.) of God (cf. Q 60:1). God alone can turn this hostility into friendship. But meanwhile one can show goodness and justice towards the unbelievers on condition that they show no hostility towards Islam (cf. Q 60:7-8). It is one of the duties incumbent on the one who calls on God to bring about the transformation of the enemy into a close friend (*walī ḥamīm,* cf. Q 41:34). In the same way, the relationships with the People of the Book (q.v.) are defined in terms of friendship and hostility. They cannot be adopted as *awliyāʾ* (cf. Q 5:51). A distinction is made, however, between the Jews and the Christians, "closer in friendship *(aqrabahum mawaddatan)* to the believers" (Q 5:82). True friendship thus rests on faith and a shared expectation of the world to come (see ESCHATOLOGY), so much so that on the day of the resurrection (q.v.) the unbelievers will find themselves without "a close friend" (*ṣadīq ḥamīm,* cf. Q 26:101; also Q 40:18; 70:10). It is in this kind of eschatological context that the Prophet appeals to love or friendship for one's relatives (*al-mawaddata fī l-qurbā,* Q 42:23). Al-Ṭabarī (d. 310/923; *Tafsīr,* xxv, 15-7) lists four different interpretations of this expression, while showing preference for the first: 1) the Qurayshites (see QURAYSH) are invited to love the Prophet because of his kinship with all the clans of his tribe; 2) the believers should love the close kin of the Prophet (see FAMILY OF THE PROPHET); 3) they must love God in approaching him through their works; 4) they should also love their own kin. From an historical point of view the first two interpretations could, respectively, correspond to the Meccan and Medinan phases of the revelation (see CHRONOLOGY AND THE QURʾĀN; OCCASIONS OF REVELATION; REVELATION AND INSPIRATION), while the second two minimize the importance of the love of the Prophet's family, the People of the House (q.v.; *ahl al-bayt*). Taken overall, these ancient commentaries show the many possible directions of love in the Qurʾān: love of God confirmed by works, love of the Prophet and his kin, love for one's own kin, which, in a sense, implies the whole body of believers, as is also said of the *walāya* (cf. Q 5:55; see COMMUNITY AND SOCIETY IN THE QURʾĀN). The presence of God, the source and finality of all things, gives direction to the entire discourse of the Qurʾān: love and friendship can only come from God and lead back to him. The loving relationship between man and woman is disregarded except on this condition. The ideal wives are called *qānitāt,* obedient and devoted, both to God and to their husbands (cf. Ṭabarī, *Tafsīr,* viii, 294, on the subject of Q 4:34). In the Qurʾān only the love and friendship of God extend beyond the limits of this world.

The few passages in the Qurʾān dealing with love have scarcely encouraged authors to extract from the Qurʾān the fundamentals of divine and human love. Traces of the affective side of love are found mainly in the sunna (q.v.; see also ḤADĪTH AND THE QURʾĀN). The Ṣūfīs themselves (see ṢŪFISM AND THE QURʾĀN), when quoting verses such as Q 2:165 or Q 5:54, are more likely to express their love for God in terms of the Arabic tradition, poetic and private. In his *Ḥaqāʾiq al-tafsīr,* al-Sulamī (d. 412/1021) is more preoccupied with bringing together the statements concerning love made by the spiritual masters than he is with commenting on Q 3:31. A commentator such as Fakhr al-Dīn al-Rāzī (d. 606/1210; *Tafsīr,* iv, 204-8) gives an outline of a theory of love based on Q 2:165. But Ibn al-ʿArabī (d. 638/1240) in his *al-Futūḥāt al-makkiyya* (ii, 327-32; Gloton, *Traité,* 69-92) has especially illuminated the foundations of the metaphysical doctrine of love found in the Qurʾān. Yet — unless the present writer is mistaken — it seems that no author has attempted a synthesis of all the passages in the Qurʾān dealing with love and its associated concepts.

Denis Gril

Bibliography
Primary: Ibn al-ʿArabī, Muḥyī l-Dīn, *al-Futūḥāt al-makkiyya*, Cairo 1911; Fr. trans. M. Gloton, *Ibn ʿArabī. Traité de l'amour*, Paris 1986; Rāzī, *Tafsīr;* Sulamī, *Ḥaqāʾiq al-tafsīr*, ms. *Fātiḥ* 261, ff. 27b-28b and *Ziyādāt* 25-6; Ṭabarī, *Tafsīr*, Beirut 1972; ed. Shākir, Cairo 1971[2].
Secondary: A.-L. de Prémare, *Joseph et Muhammad. Le chapitre 12 du Coran*, Aix-en-Provence 1989; id., Les rapports entre hommes et femmes dans quelques textes islamiques primitifs, in M. Bernos (ed.), *Sexualité et religions*, Paris 1989, 135-63.

Lowly see OPPRESSED ON EARTH, THE

Loyalty

Being true to anyone to whom one owes fidelity. The idea or concept of "loyalty" occurs discursively in the Qurʾān and is dispersed under a variety of rubrics. Even though there is no single term that specifically deals with the theme of "loyalty," it nevertheless features in the discussions and exegesis of a number of verses (see EXEGESIS OF THE QURʾĀN: CLASSICAL AND MEDIEVAL). The concept is most frequently encountered in relation to "pacts of mutual assistance" (*muwālā*, see CONTRACTS AND ALLIANCES; BREAKING TRUSTS AND CONTRACTS) and other formations of the Arabic root *w-l-y*, whose basic meaning is "friend/ally" (*walī*, see FRIENDS AND FRIENDSHIP). In an eschatological context (see ESCHATOLOGY), on the day of judgment (see LAST JUDGMENT), those who are consigned to hell (q.v.; see also REWARD AND PUNISHMENT) are said to have no "bosom" or "close" — i.e. "loyal" — friend (*ḥamīm*, e.g. Q 69:35; *ṣadīq*, Q 26:101) or intercessor (see INTERCESSION). The notions conveyed by terms like "friend," "close" and "ally" normally, however, occur as adjectives in the Qurʾān and are therefore not exact equivalents of the English noun, "loyalty."

Loyalty is not explicitly defined in the commentaries but it is frequently described and illustrated contextually. Two kinds of loyalty are discernable from various Qurʾān passages: (1) corporate loyalty that demands a commitment to the community of faith (q.v.; see also COMMUNITY AND SOCIETY IN THE QURʾĀN) and (2) individual loyalty displayed towards fellow Muslims as well as to non-Muslims, a phenomenon that is more ambiguous and complex (see ETHICS AND THE QURʾĀN). Corporate loyalty is framed by those passages of the Qurʾān that regulate the relationship between believers and unbelievers as well as those verses that define the covenantal relationship between the Muslim and God (see BELIEF AND UNBELIEF; COVENANT). The qurʾānic narrative unmistakably implies that inter-human conduct — irrespective of whether it occurs within the confessional community of Muslims or with outsiders — is largely contingent on the relationship between humans and God.

This theistic dimension casts its shadow on the themes of loyalty and friendship. Thus, the believers who fulfill God's will are clearly identified with God's cause and his people (see PATH OR WAY). Any partisanship and association with those who reject God's will shall have castigatory consequences depending on the extent to which such links are offensive to God and the cause of righteousness on earth. Showing affection or displaying dislike to any human being ought to be exclusively for the sake of God *(al-ḥubb lillāh wa-l-bughḍ lillāh)*, a phrase frequently cited by commentators as a saying attributed to the Prophet (see ḤADĪTH AND THE QURʾĀN). Thus, the God of the Qurʾān mediates the most intimate bonds of friendship, confidence, privacy and loyalty (see TRUST AND PATIENCE).

Explicit traces of Islam's founding history (see HISTORY AND THE QURʾĀN; OCCASIONS OF REVELATION) are evident in qurʾānic narratives (q.v.) and norms that structure the notions of friendship and loyalty. The qurʾānic narrative reflects the vagaries of the intense inter-communal relationships between believers on the one hand, and polytheists, Jews and Christians on the other, as the nascent community of believers became a sizeable political entity in Medina (q.v.; see also JEWS AND JUDAISM; CHRISTIANS AND CHRISTIANITY; POLYTHEISM AND ATHEISM). Initially, qurʾānic pronouncements meticulously regulate the political relationships, but the moralizing discourse that colors these identities gradually grows and intensifies (see POLITICS AND THE QURʾĀN; RELIGIOUS PLURALISM AND THE QURʾĀN).

Prior to the normative influence of Islam (q.v.) in Arabia, alliances customarily were based on grounds of kinship (q.v.; *nasab*) while military and political strength depended on one's choice of political friends or allies (*walī*, pl. *awliyāʾ*, see PRE-ISLAMIC ARABIA AND THE QURʾĀN). The increasing hostilities between the Muslims and their Meccan opponents, exacerbated by the support of the Medinan Jews for Muḥammad's enemies (q.v.) correlate directly with the Qurʾān's prohibition and restriction of corporate loyalty and mutual help pacts *(muwālā)* between Muslims and non-Muslims (see OPPOSITION TO MUḤAMMAD). Verses in seven different passages repeatedly stress the fact that believers ought not to take unbelievers as their allies (Q 3:28; 4:89, 139, 144; cf. 5:51, 57, 80-1).

In one instance even the People of the Book (q.v.; Jews and Christians in this case), towards whom the Qurʾān generally shows deference, are deplored as potential partners in alliance since they are alleged to have loyalties with each other and they are suspected of harboring vengeful enmity towards the Muslim community (Q 5:51). In fact, the rhetoric becomes so intense that the verse even goes on to assert that those Muslims who transgress this prohibition and form such alliances are deemed to "be part of them," namely one of the Jews or Christians, a severe rejection that equates the identity of the offender with the ideological "other." The Qurʾān specifically prohibits loyalty treaties with non-Muslim parties when the latter are favored "in preference to believers" (*min dūni l-muʾminīn*, Q 3:28). In other words, if alliances with non-believers turn out to harm the interests of fellow Muslims then they are outlawed as a matter of principle. Only expediency (*taqiyya*, see DISSIMULATION) permits the continuation of loyalty treaties with unbelievers, especially if breaking such treaties would pose a genuine threat to the welfare and safety of Muslims.

Nevertheless, the Qurʾān does permit Muslims to show kindness as well as to exhibit virtuous conduct and justice to those non-Muslims who are not engaged in active hostility towards them (Q 60:8-9). While this passage has general implications, and could easily be viewed as also sanctioning corporate loyalty across religious boundaries, many commentators only permit its interpretation as reference to individual and private loyalty. Again, such relationships are subject to the caveat that they do not harm the general welfare of Muslims. Q 58:22 also reinforces the theme of individual loyalty found in Q 60:8-9. It, however, forcefully plays off loyalties based on kinship against loyalties based on faith. Q 58:22 deems it unimaginable that one can show "love" (q.v.) to someone who is related by blood and kinship ties but who contests and disputes the divine message and prophecy (see PROPHETS AND PROPHETHOOD). The inference is clear: bonds of faith outweigh loyalties based on family and kinship ties. Even though he is said to have lied three times (cf. Gilliot, Trois mensonges), the prophet Abraham (q.v.; Ibrāhīm) is cast as the paragon of loyalty toward the divine as in Q 53:37. Abraham's willingness to fulfill *(waffā)* his commitments to God, including his readiness to sacrifice (q.v.) his son (cf. Q 37:99-111) and his disavowal of his father's idolatry (cf. Q 6:74-84; see IDOLATRY AND IDOLATERS), turns him into God's loyal friend (Q 4:125; see ḤANĪF). In Q 2:40 the Children of Israel (q.v.) are reminded of their duty to fulfill their part of the covenant *(wa-awfū bi-ʿahdī ūfi bi-ʿahdikum)* as a sign of loyalty to God. Fulfillment *(īfāʾ)* of promises, contracts and agreements are crucial supplements to the Qurʾān's covenant-based worldview (see OATHS). There is also an isomorphic relationship between secular and cosmological loyalties because it is presumed that one who has a sound creed (see CREEDS) would also be better equipped ethically to fulfill worldly commitments and contractual obligations.

Some pre-modern and modern exegetes (see EXEGESIS OF THE QURʾĀN: EARLY MODERN AND CONTEMPORARY) are confronted by two major interpretative questions with regard to the exegesis of loyalty. Firstly, controversy exists about whether Q 60:8-9, which permits relations with non-hostile unbelievers, is abrogated by the later revelation of Q 9:5 (known as the "verse of the sword"; see ABROGATION; FIGHTING). The latter abrogates all agreements and treaties that Muḥammad had with non-Muslim political entities and fosters an uncompromising hostility towards all unbelievers. Secondly, if Q 60:8-9 is not abrogated, then does it sanction the tolerance of personal and individual loyalty across religious boundaries as opposed to the prohibition of corporate loyalty of a political nature?

The Persian exegete al-Ṭabarī (d. 310/923) argues that Q 3:28 decisively prohibits believers from taking unbelievers *(kuffār)* as their "helpers *(aʿwān),* protectors *(anṣār)* and partisans *(ẓāhirīn).*" Taking non-Muslims as protectors in preference to believers, he adds, is tantamount to affirming their religion, thereby strengthening the false beliefs of the enemy against those of the Muslims (Ṭabarī, *Tafsīr,* iii, 228). Even though believers are admonished not to make pacts that favor unbelievers in "preference to fellow believers," most exegetes deem it acceptable to maintain strategic loyalties for the purpose of survival. In the view of a number of commentators, the struggle of belief against unbelief is a permanent one and thus there is an — albeit implicit — general rule that prohibits loyalty pacts. Therefore, al-Ṭabarī views the act of a Muslim displaying loyalty to non-Muslims to be an extremely displeasing and a hostile act against God, his Prophet and the believers at large. And any Muslim who shows loyalty to Jews and Christians, he goes on to say, has "declared war on the people of faith" (Ṭabarī, *Tafsīr,* vi, 276).

Interestingly, the Shīʿī exegete al-Ṭabarsī (d. ca. 552/1157; see SHĪʿISM AND THE QURʾĀN) understands the Qurʾān's prohibition against alliances and friendships with non-Muslims to be for reasons of power. Seeking alliances and loyalty pacts with non-Muslims is tantamount to seeking a position of invincibility with those whose faith is unacceptable to God. Such alliances undermine the believers' faith in God and affect God's estimation of their belief (Ṭabarsī, *Majmaʿ*, v, 261). The terms "Jews" and "Christians" generically represent all classes of unbelievers, towards whom hostility is obligatory and thus friendship and loyalty with them is, implicitly, outlawed (Ṭabarsī, *Majmaʿ*, vi, 119). Al-Ṭabarsī treats unbelief in an almost undifferentiated manner, because he maintains that all non-Muslims have "a single hand against the Muslims." He also believes that the summons to show virtuous and equitable treatment of non-Muslims in Q 60:8-9 was abrogated by the "verse of the sword." He concedes, though, that Q 60:8-9 allowed some Muslims during the Prophet's time to interact with their non-Muslim relatives who did not actively show hostility to Muslims. This specific verse permits loyalty affiliations with non-Muslims with whom Muslims have treaties, says al-Ṭabarsī, citing a general consensus that permits the demonstration of kindness to persons deemed to be subjects of the "territory of war" (q.v.; *dār al-ḥarb*).

The Andalusian exegete al-Qurṭubī (d. 671/1272) declares with unequivocal finality that unbelievers, Jews as well as those Muslims who espouse heretical tendencies (see HERESY), cannot be treated as friends and relied upon as loyal intimates (*Jāmiʿ*, iv, 178). He believes that Q 3:118 strictly forbade believers to take as loyal confidants *(biṭāna)* a person from another religion. "Every person," he adds, "who is contrary to your way of life *(madhhab)* and religion *(dīn),* [surely] there is no need for you to converse with him." He goes so far as to say that appointing "protected persons" *(ahl al-dhimma)* as agents in transactions or as clerks and secretaries in government is not permissible. In his jeremiad he rails against the "ignorant and stupid governors and princes" of his day who had ignored the Qurʾān's teachings on these matters (Qurṭubī, *Jāmiʿ*, iv, 179). Al-Qurṭubī's vehemence stems from the prohibition found in Q 5:51 that severs loyalty pacts *(muwālā)* with unbelievers, a command he claims will remain in force "till the day of judgment" (Qurṭubī, *Jāmiʿ*, vi, 217). He went so far as to disallow the employment of non-Muslims even in instances that might be beneficial to the religion of Islam (Qurṭubī, *Jāmiʿ*, v, 416). Al-Qurṭubī's antipathy for alliances and interactions with non-Muslims was most likely fuelled by the common perception among the Muslim religious classes of his day that the rulers of his native Andalusia had capitulated to Christian political influences and had endangered the suzerainty of Islam in the Iberian peninsula.

For the modern revivalist commentator Sayyid Quṭb (d. 1966), the verses examined above suggest the impossibility of inter-religious political co-existence. For him, the Qurʾān mandates the "total isolation" of Muslims from other ideological communities (Quṭb, *Ẓilāl*, ii, 907). Employing a qurʾānic idiom, Quṭb says that Muslims are the only group that can legitimately be called "the party of God" *(ḥizāb Allāh)* as a model for universal moral rectitude (see PARTIES AND FACTIONS). Among worldviews, he attributes this separatist understanding as unique to Islam, for it necessarily and inevitably anticipates an ideological confrontation with the anti-Islamic mores and norms of non-Muslim societies at large. This separatist imperative, in his view, makes it impossible for Muslims to give political loyalty to any other ideological group since doing so would be tantamount to apostasy (q.v.). Islam's tolerance for the People of the Book should not be confused with an endorsement of loyalty pacts. Quṭb argues that modern history — especially the history of colonialism, and the creation of the state of Israel that resulted in the dispossession and expulsion of the Palestinians from their native land — was achieved as a result of a hostile Christian and Jewish collusion. He saw this as conclusive proof that loyalty to such religious communities could be nothing but an anathema to Muslim sensibilities (Quṭb, *Ẓilāl,* ii, 907-17; id., *Maʿālim,* passim).

In his commentary on Q 60:8-9, Quṭb retreats from his earlier position, which was absolutely against loyalty pacts across religious boundaries. Here he concedes that God permits "mutual friendly relations" *(mawadda)* on an individual level towards those non-Muslims who do not show aggression towards Muslims. While reiterating the ban on loyalty pacts, he implicitly concedes that pacts may be possible with friendly non-Muslim entities (Quṭb, *Ẓilāl,* vi [xxviii], 3544). His rhetoric becomes conciliatory by arguing that Islam is a dogma *(ʿaqīda)* of love and it has no interest in conflict if there is no hostility directed at Muslims.

The Pakistani ideologue S. Abū Aʿlā Maudūdī (d. 1979) interprets the verses that deal with loyalty pacts in a functional manner. For him they serve as a reminder to Muslims not to become instruments in the service of enemies who, in the end, will undermine their existential interests. While Maudūdī's tone, unlike that of Quṭb, is subdued, he also argues that the Qurʾān prohibits friendship with hostile non-Muslims and taking them into confidence, while recommending kind and just treatment for those non-Muslims who do not demonstrate active enmity towards Muslims (Maudūdī, *Message,* ii, 19). Muḥammad Asad (d. 1992), the Austrian-born convert and Qurʾān commentator, states that the verses prohibiting loyalty pacts with non-Muslims cover both political and moral alliances. His interpretation is that those who deny the truth of the divine message are precluded from being real friends to believers in a corporate sense, while not ruling out friendship between individuals of different religions (Asad, *Message,* 252-3, n. 82). The Qurʾān, however, permits corporate loyalty pacts with those non-Muslims who are well disposed towards them (Asad, *Message,* 155, n. 73).

From this brief and select sample of exegetical materials it becomes apparent that the notion of loyalty is framed within the evolving narrative of the Qurʾān's discourses on the construction of the Muslim individual and corporate "self" in the mirror of the non-Muslim "other." Genuine loyalty can only occur among those who are ideologically of one's own kind, according to some Muslim exegetes. Most early commentators follow a strict chronological hermeneutic. One sees therefore an initial tolerance for loyalty based on kinship being gradually supplanted by a loyalty based on faith as the pax-Islamica grows in Arabia. Corporate inter-faith loyalty, in turn, can only occur under certain limited conditions, while there is some leeway for Muslims to maintain individual loyalties across the boundaries of faith. Theism and bonds of faith ultimately mediate loyalty. Loyalty to a fellow-believer reinforces one's belief in a common God which, in turn, creates a notion of community that transcends kinship and ethnicity.

Ebrahim Moosa

Bibliography

Primary: M. Asad, *The message of the Qurʾān,* Gibraltar 1980; S. Abū Aʿlā Maudūdī, *The meaning of the Qurʾān,* trans. M. Akbar, ed. A.A. Kamal, Lahore 1985; Qurṭubī, *Jāmiʿ;* S. Quṭb, *Maʿālim fī l-ṭarīq,* Cairo 1980; id., *Ẓilāl,* 30 vols. in 6, Beirut 1977³; Ṭabarī, *Tafsīr,* Cairo 1968³; Ṭabarsī, *Majmaʿ.*

Secondary: C. Gilliot, Les trois mensonges d'Abraham dans la tradition interprétante musulmane, in *IOS* 17 (1997), 37-87; J.D. McAuliffe, Christians in the Qurʾān and tafsīr, in J. Waardenburg (ed.), *Muslim perceptions of other religions. A historical survey*, New York 1999, 105-21 (esp. 110-12); R. Mottahedeh, *Loyalty and leadership in an early Islamic society*, Princeton 1980.

Luqmān

A personage whom the Qurʾān notes for his wisdom. Only Q 31, the sūra bearing his name, mentions this wise man, and it devotes eight of its thirty-four verses (Q 31:12-19) to Luqmān's wisdom (q.v.). At the time of Muḥammad, the Arabs may have known two Luqmāns: one, the son of ʿĀd (q.v.), renowned for intelligence, leadership, knowledge, eloquence and subtlety (Heller, Lukmān, 811; see KNOWLEDGE AND LEARNING); the other, Luqmān the Sage *(al-ḥakīm),* famous for his wise pronouncements and proverbs (see PRE-ISLAMIC ARABIA AND THE QURʾĀN). The latter — if these two are not in fact one — appears in Q 31.

Luqmān's identity, however, is by no means certain. Muslim interpreters (see EXEGESIS OF THE QURʾĀN: CLASSICAL AND MEDIEVAL) identify him as a Nubian, an Ethiopian or an Egyptian slave who worked as a carpenter or a shepherd. Some others place him among the Hebrews as the nephew of Job (q.v.), the son of Bāʿūrāʾ, son of Nāḥūr, son of Tāriḥ, the father of Abraham (q.v.; Ibrāhīm) who lived long enough to provide knowledge for David (q.v.; Dāʾūd) the king. The majority of interpreters agree that he was not a prophet and not an Arab (see PROPHETS AND PROPHETHOOD; ARABS). Orientalists (see POST-ENLIGHTENMENT ACADEMIC STUDY OF THE QURʾĀN) have associated Luqmān with such figures as Prometheus, Lucian and Solomon (q.v.). He is identified with the biblical Baalam (= Ibn Bāʿūrāʾ), partly because the Hebrew *bālaʿ* and the Arabic *laqima* both meaning "to swallow." The modern commentator al-Qāsimī (d. 1914; see EXEGESIS OF THE QURʾĀN: EARLY MODERN AND CONTEMPORARY) also mentions this connection. Because his admonition, "lower your voice; for the harshest of sounds... is the braying of the ass" (Q 31:19), finds a counterpart in the Syriac sayings of Aḥiqār, Luqmān has also been identified with that legendary sage (see SYRIAC AND THE QURʾĀN). Finally, the contemporary scholar Mahmud Muftic shows that the Luqmān of the Qurʾān can be identified with the Greek physician and Pythagorean philosopher Alcmaeon (571-497 B.C.E.), a position also assumed by some Orientalists. Their names are clearly similar and the extant fragments of Alcmaeon's writing exhibit a striking similarity to the teachings of Q 31. Muftic finds in this sūra a physicians' oath that he thinks is superior to the oath of Hippocrates (460-377 B.C.E.; cf. Muftic, Which oath?; see MEDICINE AND THE QURʾĀN).

Two themes occurring prominently in the Luqmān section of Q 31 provide coherence for the sūra: (1) the greatness of the one God (see GOD AND HIS ATTRIBUTES) and the necessity of worshipping him exclusively and (2) the importance of being good to parents (q.v.) within the limits of a higher allegiance to God. Luqmān models ideal parenthood, instructing his son in a life of gratitude and exclusive worship (q.v.) of God (Q 31:12, 13; see GRATITUDE AND INGRATITUDE; CHILDREN; FAMILY). The striking shift from Luqmān's voice to God's voice in verses 14 and 15 focuses the reader's attention on the commands in the verses: be good (see GOOD AND EVIL) to parents; show gratitude to God and to them; and obey them unless they require worship of something other than God (see OBEDIENCE). The sūra closes with a warning: neither parent nor child can help each other on the day of judgment (Q 31:33; see

LAST JUDGMENT; INTERCESSION). A final verse stresses the greatness of God (Q 31:34). Whatever his more specific identity may have been, Luqmān stands out in the Qurʾān as a wise parent, exhorting his son to grateful worship of God, grateful obedience to his parents, personal piety (q.v.) and communal responsibility (see COMMUNITY AND SOCIETY IN THE QURʾĀN).

A.H.M. Zahniser

Bibliography

I. Abyārī and ʿA. Marzūq, *al-Mawsūʿa al-qurʾāniyya,* 6 vols., Cairo 1969, vi, 516 f.; Council for Islamic Affairs of the United Arab Republic, *al-Muntakhab fī tafsīr al-Qurʾān al-karīm,* Cairo 1968; B. Heller/N.A. Stillman, Luḳmān, in *EI*², v, 811-3; Horovitz, *KU,* 132-6; M. Muftic, Which oath? Luqman's as given in the Qurʾān or Hippocrates's? in *The Islamic review and Arab affairs* 56 (1968), 6-8; M. Jalāl al-Dīn al-Qāsimī, *Tafsīr al-Qāsimī (Maḥāsin al-taʾwīl),* 17 vols., Cairo 1957, xiii, 4796.

Lust see VIRTUES AND VICES, COMMANDING AND FORBIDDING; DESIRE; SEX AND SEXUALITY

Lūṭ see LOT

M

Madness see INSANITY

Madyan see MIDIAN

Magians

Originally a term for the professional priesthood of the pre-Islamic religious institution in Iran, in qurʾānic usage it is presumably a term for all followers of that religion. The Arabic term translated as "Magians," *(al-majūs)* is attested once at Q 22:17, a late Medinan sūra (see CHRONOLOGY AND THE QURʾĀN), where the list Jews (see JEWS AND JUDAISM), Christians (see CHRISTIANS AND CHRISTIANITY) and Sabians (q.v.) attested in Q 2:62, now also includes them. The etymology and history of the term and the question whether the Magians are People of the Book (q.v.) are the two large issues raised by this single attestation.

The old Persian *maguš* as the title for a professional priestly tribe is well attested in surrounding languages, Akkadian, Armenian, Hebrew, Aramaic, Syriac, Greek, Sanskrit and presumably old Sinitic (see FOREIGN VOCABULARY). These religious professionals appear to have traveled far beyond Iranian held lands. Their religious aura seems to have been widely recognized but they also played administrative, military and commercial roles. In the Sasanian dynasty a wider array of titles were used within the priestly bureaucracy but the special status of the title in its middle Persian forms survived. The older term, however, also was widely circulated, presumably because of the prominent Christian mention of the Magi in the birth stories of Jesus. It likely passed into Arabic through Syriac (see SYRIAC AND THE QURʾĀN; ARABIC LANGAUGE). Early Muslim commentators do not limit the term to professional priests and describe the Magians as worshippers of the sun (q.v.), an interpretation also attested in Sanskrit sources. Later commentators recognize that fire (q.v.) is the stereotypical object of worship by the Magians. The fire-cult is the hallmark of the Magian tradition for later heresiographers and in Islamic literature, especially within the Persianate context (see PERSIAN LITERATURE AND THE QURʾĀN).

The enumeration of apparently six forms of religion in Q 22:17 has been the primary focus of commentary (see EXEGESIS OF THE QURʾĀN: CLASSICAL AND MEDIEVAL). The text lists believers, Jews, Sabians, Christians, Magians and those who associate something else with God (see POLYTHEISM AND ATHEISM; BELIEF AND UNBELIEF; GOD AND HIS ATTRIBUTES). Debate on this and other passages has focused on the status of the intermediate four traditions. Are they to be classed with the believers or the associators or are they in an intermediate position (see FAITH)? While some have argued that there is only one true and five false religions here mentioned, the bulk of the tradition either recognizes that at least some members of the four named traditions are to be classed with the believers or the traditions themselves are the so-called religions of the book in addition to Islam (q.v.; see also RELIGION; RELIGIOUS PLURALISM AND THE QURʾĀN). Whether the Magians were to be included among the People of the Book (q.v.) was debated since it appeared that the religion lacked a prophet (see PROPHETS AND PROPHETHOOD) and a scripture (see BOOK), and there was also significant theological controversy concerning their identity as monotheists and their doctrine of the creation (q.v.) and the power of evil (see GOOD AND EVIL; THEOLOGY AND THE QURʾĀN).

Apologists worked hard to counter these charges and to argue that they belonged in the category of religions of the book. The story of Alexander the Great's (q.v.) destruction of the original scripture became prominent and the attempts already made by the Sasanians to organize the remaining written tradition were consolidated. The legend of Zoroaster was remolded to present him along the lines of Islamic prophethood. In general, Islamic authorities have granted them partial status as a People of the Book (see LAW AND THE QURʾĀN). Interestingly, Muslim authorities have also recognized the affinity that exists between the Magian priest and the Islamic judge, exercising a political and juridical role that depended on the close cooperation of religious functionary and ruler, a Persian ideal that became central to Islamic notions of the state (see KINGS AND RULERS; POLITICS AND THE QURʾĀN).

William R. Darrow

Bibliography
J.C. Bürgel, Zoroastrians as viewed in medieval Islamic sources, in J. Waardenburg (ed.), *Muslim perceptions of other religions. A historical survey*, New York 1999, 202-12; Jeffrey, *For. vocab.*; V.H. Mair, Old Sinitic **myag*, old Persian *Maguš* and English "magician," in *Early China* 15 (1990), 27-47; McAuliffe, *Qurʾānic*; M.G. Morony, *Iraq after the Muslim conquest*, Princeton 1984; S. Shaked, Some Islamic reports concerning Zoroastrianism, in *JSAI* 17 (1994), 43-84.

Magic

The art which claims to produce effects by the assistance of supernatural beings or by a mastery of secret forces in nature. The contrast between the rational and the irrational, of supreme importance to the human being, even in the present day, suggests the question: "Is magic credible?" The Qurʾān replies in the affirmative, both when speaking about magic — describing its deeds and consequences — as well as by concluding with two apotropaic sūras, which are often regarded as protective talismans (see POPULAR AND TALISMANIC USES OF THE QURʾĀN), and thus confirmations of magic. To this could be added the various ḥadīths of the Prophet (see ḤADĪTH AND THE QURʾĀN) in which something like magic is spoken of (see DIVINATION; FORETELLING; GAMBLING), or enchanting magical acts that affect the Prophet himself are described. Despite this apparent credibility of magic, it should be understood that normative Islam does not conceive of or admit to the existence of powers other than those of God (see POWER AND IMPOTENCE), or to a belief that one can accept help from anyone or anything other than God (see

BELIEF AND UNBELIEF; POLYTHEISM AND ATHEISM). Magic, therefore, is depicted as a distorted appropriation of fideistic values, wrongly understood or poorly expressed by demons, as the Qurʾān itself states numerous times.

In this, the religion of the pre-Islamic Arabs, who made sacrifices to the gods and the forces of nature, and who trusted magic without, however, experiencing the necessity of believing in a future life (see FATE; DESTINY; SACRIFICE; PRE-ISLAMIC ARABIA AND THE QURʾĀN) is totally different from the religion of Islam. I would therefore assert that the hypothesis, put forward by various scholars (Chelhod, *Introduction;* id., *L'arabie du sud,* for example), that Islam might derive from religions present in pre-Islamic Arabia should be rejected (see AGE OF IGNORANCE; SOUTH ARABIA, RELIGION IN PRE-ISLAMIC).

The Arabic word used for magic, *siḥr (*from *s-ḥ-r),* can be understood in both a restrictive and an expansive sense. The word appears twenty-eight times in the Qurʾān (Q 2:102; 5:110; 6:7; 7:116; 10:76, 77, 81; 11:7; 20:57, 58, 63, 66, 71, 73; 21:3; 26:35, 49; 27:13; 28:36, 48; 34:43; 37:15; 43:30; 46:7; 52:15; 54:2; 61:6; 74:24). *Siḥr* literally means "enchantment" and etymologically the word seems to indicate that type of seduction which affects a hypnotized person. It can also mean a circumlocution of an exaggeratedly rhetorical nature (thus one speaks of beautiful words giving rise to enchantment). The great theologian Ibn al-ʿArabī (d. 638/1240) defined magic as something that passes *(ṣarf)* from its true nature *(ḥaqīqa)* or from its natural form *(ṣūra)* to something else, something that is unreal, or merely an appearance *(khayāl).*

From the root *s-ḥ-r* is derived the qurʾānic word for "witch" *(sāḥira* or *saḥḥāra;* masc. *saḥḥār);* the infinitive verbal form *saḥara* indicates "to bewitch, to fascinate"; the wizard or conjurer is termed *saḥḥār,* or *sāḥir* (some other Arabic terms for those who deal in magic, which do not occur in the Qurʾān, are *silʿāt,* "sorceress," and *quṭrubī,* "wizard"). The Persian *magu (*Gk. *magos)* was used by the Zoroastrian priests, and furnished the term *majūs* in Arabic, where it continued to indicate the Zoroastrian priests. It is in this same form that we find the word in the Qurʾān, used to specify the very same Zoroastrian priests (Q 22:17; see MAGIANS). To denote an astrologer, or fortune-teller, we have the word *kāhin,* from the triliteral root *k-h-n.* In pre-Islamic Arabia, the *kāhin* very closely resembled the figure of a priest (the term can be linked to the Hebrew *kōhēn,* which, for the most part, carries the meaning of "priest"). From the same root is derived the verbal noun *kahāna,* "premonition and prophecy," and *kahana,* "predicting the future" (Q 52:29: "Therefore, take heed *[fa-dhakkir]* because, by the grace of your lord, you are neither a fortune-teller *[kāhin]* nor possessed *[majnūn]*"; see LIE; INSANITY). But in pre-Islamic Arabia, it is very possible that the "prophetess" (or sibyl, *kāhina*) played the more important role, with her male counterpart, the *kāhin,* as *ʿarrāf* (deriving from *ʿirāfa:* having a knowledge of invisible things and future events), being relegated to the function of relocating lost or stolen objects (see GENDER; PATRIARCHY).

As they pronounced their oracles in rhymed prose (q.v.; *sajʿ*), the *kuhhān* were considered poets (*shāʿir,* pl. *shuʿarāʾ;* see POETRY AND POETS), with whom they were often confused in pre-Islamic Arabia. The verbal polemics among the Arab tribes of this period, occasioned by major feast days (see FESTIVALS AND COMMEMORATIVE DAYS), large markets (q.v.), or great pilgrimages (see PILGRIMAGE), were famous. Each of these tribes was guided by a judge (*ḥakam, ḥākim,* see JUDGMENT; JUSTICE AND INJUSTICE) who was often a poet fortune-teller. Such poets would praise the feats of war (q.v.), the power and the honor (q.v.) of the tribe (see TRIBES AND CLANS), countering the self-praise of his opponents. Such contests for precedence and glory *(mufākharāt, munāfarāt)* generated a large body of poetic literature which has been the subject of study and authentication.

Various *kuhhān* enter the legends surrounding Muḥammad, as for example the magician Saṭīḥ, who is said to have lived six centuries and, after having predicted the advent of Islam, died on the very same day in which the Prophet was born. The Qurʾān, which more than once alludes to the accusations that Muḥammad engaged in "magic," attests to the fact that the Prophet himself was called *sāḥir* and *masḥūr,* "bewitched," and even "poet" in the fortune-teller sense of the word (Q 10:2; 11:7; 21:2-3; 25:7-8; 34:43-7; 37:14-5; 38:4; 43:30-1; 46:7; 52:29-30; 54:2; 69:38-43; see OPPOSITION TO MUḤAMMAD; POLEMIC AND POLEMICAL LANGUAGE). Walīd b. Mughīra, one of the richest idol worshipers (see IDOLS AND IMAGES; IDOLATRY AND IDOLATERS) of Mecca (q.v.), was heard saying, upon hearing the Prophet: "In all this, I find only borrowed magic."

Despite the qurʾānic and Islamic denunciation, even renunciation, of magic, there are two main currents of "magic" in the Islamic world: that found in the Mediterranean region and that of central Asia. The first, based upon an ancient philosophical heritage, evinces the fruits of the indestructible Mesopotamian teachings of astrology, of numerology (q.v.), and talismanic arts (of which the Babylonians and the Chaldeans were perhaps the greatest inventors). Also evident here is an Egyptian influence (particularly in reference to Hermes Trismegistus, Ar. *Hirmis al-muthallath bi-l-ḥikma*), as well as the legacy of King Solomon (q.v.), the incontestable founding figure of great magicians. The second current gathers elements from Shamanism, Taoism and Hinduism, all of which are very rich in magicians, magical arts and magical texts. Whereas the Mediterranean culture gave rise to numerous theories and practices which penetrated European countries via various forms of translation (in particular that of alchemy, *al-kīmiyā*), the central Asiatic culture gave birth to great currents of mystic thought. This "mysticism" was studied by various Ṣūfī orders (see ṢŪFISM AND THE QURʾĀN), especially in some orders *(ṭuruq,* sing. *ṭarīqa)* of the Ḥurūfiyya, the Bektashiyya and the Miṣriyya, wherein it was adapted to the charisma of the particular order.

Let us now turn our attention to the last two sūras of the Qurʾān, Q 113 (Sūrat al-Falaq, "The Oncoming Dawn," or "The Crack"; *al-falaq* being the moment of separation between day and night) and Q 114 (Sūrat al-Nās, "Humankind"), which are known as the *muʿawwadhitān,* "the two seekers of refuge." Popular Muslim practice holds that by reciting them one is saved from curses through the search of a divine protector. According to the traditional Muslim chronology of revelation (see REVELATION AND INSPIRATION), they are, respectively, the twentieth and the twenty-first sūras (see CHRONOLOGY AND THE QURʾĀN). As they were revealed in Mecca (q.v.), they are considered to be among the most ancient. The "darkness" (q.v.; *ghāsiq*) mentioned in the third verse of Q 113 ("from the evil of darkness as it spreads") is, according to the commentators, not evil in itself but a favorable moment for the propagation of evil, of malicious deeds (see EVIL DEEDS), of criminal acts (see SIN, MAJOR AND MINOR), of the actions of demons and sorcerers (see GOOD AND EVIL; NIGHT AND DAY). This is linked to the belief that the influence of magic was more easily diffused during the night. The fourth verse of the same sūra ("and from the evil of the women who blow on knots") refers to the blowing upon knots made in the proper fashion (i.e. tied nine or eleven times), a magical practice much in use in Semitic circles, above all Canaanite, Mesopotamian, Egyptian and Hebrew, but also found in many tribes of central Asia. It was particularly popular in Jewish circles, despite its rigid prohibition in the Pentateuch (*Deut* 18:9-14; regarding this, one may turn to *Gen* 44:5; *Lev* 19:31; *Num* 22:7-11; *Ezek* 21:26-8, etc.; see JEWS AND JUDAISM). An allusion to this practice is found in the Sumerian *Maqlū (The Burnt Tablets),* where we read: "His knot is open, his witchcraft has been cancelled, and his spells now fill the desert." The blowing itself, the bad breath and the spit, are considered an enemy's curse. Along these lines, Babylonian writings define an "evil one" as "the one with an evil face, mouth, tongue, eye, lip, and saliva."

Well-known in Arabia long before the advent of Islam, these knots were used to tie good and evil forces in equal measure. As he left his house, an Arab would tie a knot around a branch of a hedge. If upon his return he discovered that the knot had been undone, he understood that his wife had betrayed him (see ADULTERY AND FORNICATION). A similar practice is followed today in the oases of the Sahara desert, where healers make eleven knots in a red or black woolen thread, reciting at each knot the appropriate invocations in a soft voice. They then wrap the thread around the head of anyone who wishes to be healed of eye discomfort.

Muslim tradition mentions a particular situation of this in relation to Muḥammad. A sorcerer had made eleven knots in a rope, reciting spell-like formulas in order to do harm to the Prophet, who then became ill. He returned to normal health only after having recited Q 113 and 114 eleven times. Q 113 relates above all to the evil spells used against one's physical state, against the healthy body, protecting it against that which could render turbid one's psyche, soul, and serenity (see ILLNESS AND HEALTH). It is believed to save one from the psychic disturbances inserted in human mortals by Satan (that occult persuader; see DEVIL), whether through demons (see JINN) or through other evil humans (see ENEMIES; for further discussion of the use of Q 113 and 114 as imprecations for deliverance from evil, see Graham, *Beyond,* 109).

The very first sūra of the Qurʾān, Sūrat al-Fātiḥa ("The Opening," see FĀTIḤA) is also considered a talisman of great potency. According to the traditional chronology, it is the fifth sūra revealed to the Prophet at Mecca (in the year 610 or 611). All of the letters of the Arabic alphabet (see ARABIC SCRIPT; ARABIC LANGUAGE) are contained therein, except seven *(f, j, sh, th, ẓ, kh, z)*. These seven letters came to be called "the missing letters of Sūrat al-Fātiḥa" (*sawāqiṭ al-fātiḥa,* cf. Mandel Khān, *L'alfabeto arabo,* 177). Those who fashion talismans consider these letters rich in magical virtue and thus often use them in their charms.

The three sūras mentioned above were, for many centuries, used as talismans, written on pieces of paper and carried on one's person or enclosed in a specially shaped case. These cases were often made of silver (q.v.) and had an oblong shape, frequently in hexagonal sections. From the ninth/fifteenth century onwards, the cases were often made from hard stone and no longer had an inner space to enclose writings, thereby becoming imitations of the original case. Nevertheless, these cases became, in themselves, a sort of luck charm, even when they no longer contained verses from the Qurʾān (see EPIGRAPHY AND THE QURʾĀN).

In addition to the above-mentioned verses, which are held to be the most effective, other verses, of an apotropaic nature, were used to ward off danger. For example, Q 21:80, a short verse known as "the tunic of arms," or "the iron-shirted tunic," was carried into battle by soldiers, in the hope of avoiding the enemy's blows. Soldiers also made use of Q 67:22, to guard against being bitten by a possibly rabid dog (q.v.) or other animal (see AMULETS for further discussion of the use of qurʾānic verses for protection from harm).

The Qurʾān itself contains teachings related to other magical valences. Q 41:16-7 speaks of days full of misfortune. For Muslims, the lucky days are Monday, Thursday, and Friday. A popular tradition of al-Ṭabarī (d. 310/923; *Tafsīr,* xxiv, 95) cites Tuesday as the day in which God created all that is detestable for humankind. For the Shīʿīs (see SHĪʿISM AND THE QURʾĀN) and for all who were drawn into their sphere, the last Wednesday of the month of Ṣafar (which is the second month of the Muslim calendar; see CALENDAR; MOON) was notoriously unlucky, and nicknamed "Black Wednesday." The months (q.v.) that were considered to be totally unlucky were — always in the Muslim calendar — the first month of the year, Muḥarram, and the second, Ṣafar. Islamic astrologers used Q 41:16-7 to support their belief that, according to the days of the week and the position of the stars (see PLANETS AND STARS), human beings experience lucky days and unfavorable days, as reported in full detail by Fakhr al-Dīn al-Rāzī (d. 606/1210; *Tafsīr,* xxvii, 113).

Two qurʾānic prophets have long been associated with the realm of magic and the esoteric: Moses (q.v.) and Solomon. Narratives about Moses (Mūsā) may be found, with variations and repetitions, in sūras 2, 5, 7, 10, 18, 20 and 28, in addition to brief mention in other passages. In Q 20:56-70, the Qurʾān touches upon his "magic contest," in which, with the help of God, he is victorious over the magicians of Pharaoh (q.v.). Q 18:60-82 is understood to allude to another magical episode involving Moses, which post-qurʾānic tradition describes as having taken place on a journey in search of the fountain "of eternal youth."

Q 2:101-2 and its reference to Solomon (Sulaymān) is of particular importance because it speaks of the probable origins of magic on the earth. This was due to Hārūt and Mārūt, hung by their feet in the well of the Temple of Astarte in Babylon. According to a Hebrew legend, also present in the pre-Islamic milieu, Hārūt and Mārūt were two angels, condemned by God to live upon earth because they had become infatuated with a woman (cf. Thaʿlabī, *Qiṣaṣ,* 43-7 for an Islamic version of this story; see HĀRŪT AND MĀRŪT for further [Islamic and pre-Islamic] details on these figures). In the Hebrew environment, this brings to mind the "sons of Elohim," who loved the daughters of man and the fallen angel, masters of magic.

Al-Bayḍāwī (d. ca. 716/1316-7), using his concise and terse style, dedicates an entire page of his commentary to Hārūt and Mārūt, while al-Zamakhsharī (d. 538/1144), in his *Kashshāf,* devotes a page and a half. Even longer sections are to be found in the commentaries of al-Ṭabarī and al-Rāzī (see EXEGESIS OF THE QURʾĀN: CLASSICAL AND MEDIEVAL). These commentators discuss another "magical" allusion in the Qurʾān, one found in Q 15:16-8; 37:6-10; 67:5 and 72:8-9: these passages recount how demons sometimes push forward towards the limits of a celestial judicial assembly, listen to what the angels and the blessed are saying, and then descend to earth to treacherously whisper what they have heard to magicians and sorcerers.

In the short verses of Q 27:17; 34:12-4; and 38:34-40, the Qurʾān speaks repeatedly of Solomon, and of the magical powers which God bestowed upon him, offering him the aid of jinn. Narratives such as these contributed to the legends found in later European sources, in which Solomon appears as a great magician, endowed with a supernatural power over demons, the forces of nature and animals (see ANIMAL LIFE). He perfectly understood all their languages (see Mandel Khān, *Salomone* [in addition to SOLOMON] for further discussion of the powers of this qurʾānic figure). According to such tales, he even wrote magic procedures in various books, which he then had buried under his throne (or inserted into its base) and these books would one day be re-discovered, at least in part, and spread about by ordinary magicians.

Ḥadīths also speak widely of magic. Abū Saʿīd al-Khudrī (cf. Bukhārī, *Ṣaḥīḥ,* 75:33) makes specific reference in a ḥadīth to the protective value of the recitation of the Fātiḥa used as an act of exorcism. Al-Aswād b. Zayd remarked that he questioned ʿĀʾisha (see ʿĀʾISHA BINT ABĪ BAKR) about the use of magic as a cure for poisonous animal bites and she answered: "The Prophet authorizes its use against every sort of poisonous animal" (Bukhārī, *Ṣaḥīḥ,* 76:37). Also, according to ʿĀʾisha, the Prophet was able to perform exorcisms while invoking God (Bukhārī, *Ṣaḥīḥ,* 76:38, 2). According to a Companion of Muḥammad, Abū Qatāda (see COMPANIONS OF THE PROPHET), the Prophet stated: "Our good dreams (see DREAMS AND SLEEP; FORETELLING) come from God, and the bad ones from the demonic. When one of you has a bad dream, breathe three times once you are awake, and recite the talismanic sūras that protect us from evil, and your dream will not cause you any harm" (Bukhārī, *Ṣaḥīḥ,* 76:39, 1). An evil eye launched against the Prophet was also described in detail by ʿĀʾisha (Bukhārī, *Ṣaḥīḥ,* 76:47).

On the basis of the magic accepted by the Qurʾān and ḥadīth, there arose a series of eminent Islamic scholars, essayists, and authors of treatises upon specialized subjects of magic, some of whom were magicians themselves. Many books were written about the topic from a sociological or a psychological point of view. More popular works were composed about how to construct talismans, lucky charms, or an evil eye to circulate among people, using either praiseworthy "white" magic *(al-ṭarīqa al-maḥmūda)* or blameworthy "black" magic *(al-ṭarīqa al-madhmūma)*. The following are only the principal figures from this myriad of authors: In the third/ninth century there were Abū ʿAbdallāh Jābir b. Ḥayyān, a Ṣūfī alchemist and magician known as Geber in Europe, and Dhū l-Nūn Abū l-Fayḍ al-Miṣrī (d. 246/861), a great Ṣūfī master. Later came Ibn al-Nadīm Muḥammad b. Isḥāq, author of the *Fihrist* (fl. fourth/tenth cent.), Abū Ḥāmid al-Ghazālī (d. 505/1111) one of the greatest Ṣūfī and Muslim theologians, and Abū l-Qāsim Maslama b. Aḥmad al-Majrīṭī (d. 398/1007), known in Europe as "pseudo Picatrix" (the "pseudo Hippocrates") who, along with Ibn Waḥshiyya (fl. prob. fourth/tenth cent.), was very well known in the occidental world, and from whose books "the secret alphabets" and the symbols used by alchemists were taken. In the sixth/twelfth century, one can count the famous theologian and exegete Fakhr al-Dīn al-Rāzī, whose studies are of exemplary balance, and Abū l-ʿAbbās al-Būnī (d. 622/1225), of whose works manuscripts abound (cf. Dietrich, al-Būnī). Of paramount importance is the first sociologist of Islam, the historian Ibn Khaldūn (d. 808/

1406), who in his writings dealt fully with magic and talismans. In the present day, both Yūsuf al-Hindī and Muḥammad al-Afghānistānī of Cairo have written much and gathered a large amount of information related to curses and evil spells as well as lucky charms.

Reading the texts of the many Muslims who busied themselves with magic, both of the authors cited here, and of many others, it becomes apparent that, in practice, the topic is subdivided into different fields: 1) the "science of letters," letters divided into the quadrants of fire, air, earth, and water (see COSMOLOGY; NATURE AS SIGNS); 2) the "mysterious letters" (q.v.) of the Qurʾān which open some sūras, and those "missing" in the first sūra; 3) the value of numbers; 4) the power of the ninety-nine exceptional and indescribable name-attributes of God (see GOD AND HIS ATTRIBUTES), in particular that of the secret name, the hundredth, to perform miracles; 5) the use of the names of demons in invocations related to black magic.

We also observe the construction and utilization of magical quadrants such as lucky charms for protection from the evil eye or as reinforcements in exorcisms. The culmination of this science is the production of lucky charms and talismans, for which the following are utilized: 1) texts from the Qurʾān; 2) the hand motif (*khamsa,* the five fingers), called "the hand of Fāṭima" in the West (for one example, see Figure x of EPIGRAPHY); 3) vegetative and related materials; 4) animal motifs; 5) hard, precious stones (see METALS AND MINERALS); and 6) tattooing.

Some scholars have seen a relation between knowledge of these values and those necessary for the spiritual evolution of the mystic of Islam, the Ṣūfī, who nears a greater comprehension of God by rising to the seven levels of spiritual evolution, symbolized by: 1) sound (see HEARING AND DEAFNESS); 2) light (q.v.); 3) number (geometry, construction, subdivision of luminosity; see MEASUREMENT; NUMBERS AND ENUMERATION); 4) a letter (the secret meanings of names, grammatical constructions; see GRAMMAR AND THE QURʾĀN); 5) word (*dhikr,* the recitation of the ninety-nine names of God, or the recitation of the Qurʾān [q.v.]); 6) symbol (see METAPHOR; SIMILE); 7) rhythm and symmetry.

One can note in summation that while the Qurʾān counters the human tendency to ascribe divinity, or divine attributes, to various supernatural beings, it does not deny the existence of such beings. Rather, while recognizing the human need to come to terms with the intangible — be it through dreams, fables or magic — the primary message of the Qurʾān is the affirmation of the submission of all of creation — visible and invisible — to the one God. See also SOOTHSAYERS.

Gabriel Mandel Khān

Bibliography
Primary: al-Afghānistānī, Yūsuf Muḥammad, *Kabīr kuttāb al-sirr,* Cairo 1918; Bukhārī, *Ṣaḥīḥ;* al-Būnī, *Kitāb Shams al-maʿārif,* Cairo 1946; al-Darayb, Aḥmad, *Fatḥ al-Malik al-Majīd,* Cairo 1905; Ibn Khaldūn, *al-Muqaddima,* Eng. trans. Bollinger Found., New York 1958; Fr. trans. Commission Internationale pour la Traduction des Chefs-d'Oeuvre, Beirut 1967; Rāzī, *Tafsīr;* al-Rudhuwī (Radhawī), Muḥammad, *al-Luʾluʾ al-manẓūm fī ʿulūm al-ṭalāsim,* Cairo 1926; al-Sharjī al-Yaman, Aḥmad b. ʿAbd al-Laṭīf, *Kitāb al-Fawāʾid,* Cairo 1903; Suyūṭī, Jalāl al-Dīn, *Kitāb al-Raḥma fī l-ṭibb,* Istanbul 1961; Ṭabarī, *Tafsīr;* Thaʿlabī, *Qiṣaṣ,* Beirut n.d.; al-Tilimsānī, Ibn al-Ḥājj, *Shumūs al-anwār wa-kunūz al-asrār,* Cairo 1904, Istanbul 1938; Zamakhsharī, *Kashshāf;* al-Zarqāwī, Aḥmad Mūsā, *Mafātīḥ al-ghayb,* Cairo 1909.
Secondary: B. Bambergen, *Fallen angels,* Philadelphia 1952; J. Chelhod, *L'arabie du sud. Histoire et civilisation,* 3 vols., Paris 1984-5; id., *Introduction à la sociologie de l'Islam. De l'animisme à l'universalisme,* Paris 1958; A. Dietrich, al-Būnī, in EI[2] Supplement, 156-7 [fasc. 3-4]; E. Doutté, *Magie et religion dans l'Afrique du Nord,* Paris 1984; Graham, *Beyond;*

G. Mandel Khān, *L'alfabeto arabo. Stili, varianti, adattamenti calligrafici,* Milan 2000; id., *La magia nell'Islām,* Milano 1997; id., *Salomone. Alla ricerca di un mito,* Milano 1977; S.H. Nasr, *An introduction to Islamic cosmological doctrines,* Cambridge, MA 1964; B. Violle, *Traité complet des carrées magiques,* 3 vols., Paris 1938; E. Westermarck, *Ritual and belief in Morocco,* Casablanca/Paris, 1926-31.

Magog see GOG AND MAGOG

Maidens see MODESTY; VIRTUE; SEX AND SEXUALITY; HOURIS

Maintenance and Upkeep

Preservation and repair of property, or, more commonly in the Qurʾān, the care for one's dependents. In Islamic law, *nafaqa* indicates the obligation to maintain one's dependents (see GUARDIANSHIP). The Qurʾān uses *nafaqa* of expenditures in general, even those against Islam at Q 8:36. It is enjoined by Q 2:215-6 for the benefit of parents (q.v.), relatives (see KINSHIP), orphans (q.v.), the poor (see POVERTY AND THE POOR) and wayfarers (see JOURNEY; similarly Q 17:26; 30:38). Repeated injunctions to do good to one's parents *(wa-bi-l-wālidayn iḥsānan)* have also been taken to require their maintenance (Q 4:36; 6:151; 17:23; 46:15). Q 2:240 calls for the maintenance of the widow (q.v.) for a year, apparently from the man's estate. Q 25:67 indicates that they do best whose expenditures are neither excessive nor stingy. In the context of divorce, finally, Q 65:6-7 enjoins husbands to allow their wives to live where they themselves do and not to be hard on them if they are pregnant (see MARRIAGE AND DIVORCE).

Later Islamic law (see LAW AND THE QURʾĀN) lays out the duty of maintenance in specific terms, which have the advantage of being more or less enforceable by temporal authority but necessarily lack the generous, free character of the qurʾānic injunctions. Jurisprudents agree that *zakāt* covers one's duty of maintenance toward non-relatives (see ALMSGIVING; COMMUNITY AND SOCIETY IN THE QURʾĀN). The duty of maintenance is laid especially on men but also, with reference to Q 2:233 and 65:7, on women toward their children (see WOMEN AND THE QURʾĀN; BIRTH). Maintenance specifically includes food (see FOOD AND DRINK), clothing (q.v.), shelter (see HOUSE, DOMESTIC AND DIVINE) and the provision of a servant (q.v.) if the beneficiary's social status requires it (see also SLAVES AND SLAVERY; SOCIAL RELATIONS). For men, it may also include *iʿfāf,* the provision of a licit sexual partner (see CONCUBINES; SEX AND SEXUALITY). Partly on the basis of Q 2:219, wives claim maintenance before parents or children, for they provide reciprocal favors. If a husband refuses to maintain his wife, she may ask the religious judge *(qāḍī)* to dissolve the marriage. Jurisprudents disagree over the relatives to whom one owes *nafaqa,* the Mālikīs going so far as to require maintenance of parents and children alone. See also WEALTH.

Christopher Melchert

Bibliography

Primary (in addition to juridical handbooks and other standard commentaries): Ṭabarī, *Tafsīr.*
Secondary: J. Burton, *The sources of Islamic law,* Edinburgh 1990 (esp. chap. 5, on the jurisprudents' reduction of the claims of widows); C. Gilliot, Le commentaire coranique de Hūd b. Muḥakkam/Muḥkim, in *Arabica* 44 (1997), 179-233 (esp. 214-6 for this problem for the Ibadites; see bibliography for further references for the topic in general, and also for standard commentaries and juridical handbooks); Y. Meron, *L'obligation alimentaire entre époux en droit musulman hanéfite,* Paris 1971; W. al-Zuḥaylī, *al-Fiqh al-islāmī wa-adillatuhu,* 11 vols., Beirut 1984, vii, 350-69.

Majesty see GOD AND HIS ATTRIBUTES

Majūs see MAGIANS

Male see GENDER

Malice see ENEMIES

Malikis (Mālikī) see LAW AND THE QUR᾿ĀN

Manāt see IDOLS AND IMAGES

Manna see MOSES; FOOD AND DRINK

Manners see HOSPITALITY AND COURTESY

Manslaughter see MURDER; BLOODSHED

Manual Labor

Literally "work with one's hands," it often carries the implication of strenuous physical exertion. Manual labor is not a topic explicitly addressed in the Qur᾿ān though the term "forced laborer" *(sukhrī)* is mentioned once and the Qur᾿ān describes some of the ancient prophets (see PROPHETS AND PROPHETHOOD) as having been able to achieve prominence by using forced and voluntary labor in great building projects (see ART AND ARCHITECTURE AND THE QUR᾿ĀN; ARCHAEOLOGY AND THE QUR᾿ĀN).

The Qur᾿ān states that it is God who "raises some to levels above others so that some of them compel others to work for them" (Q 43:32; see SOCIAL INTERACTIONS; SOCIAL RELATIONS; COMMUNITY AND SOCIETY IN THE QUR᾿ĀN). The point of this verse is not to justify forced labor. Rather, it is to deny that this kind of worldly power, although permitted by God, is an indication of God's favor (see BLESSING; GRACE; KINGS AND RULERS; POLITICS AND THE QUR᾿ĀN; POWER AND IMPOTENCE; AUTHORITY). Accompanying verses state that even though Muḥammad was not the most successful man in Mecca (q.v.) or Medina (q.v.), God nonetheless chose him as his prophet. In Q 43:32, "the mercy (q.v.) of your lord (q.v.) is better than what they amass," the last term is understood as a reference to wealth (q.v.) and worldly success.

The qur᾿ānic description of Solomon (q.v.) regally commanding labor from jinn (q.v.) and satans (Q 21:82; 34:12-3; see DEVIL), perhaps as a form of punishment (*ʿadhāb*, Q 34:14; see CHASTISEMENT AND PUNISHMENT), contrasts sharply with the humble image he and other prophets assume in early Islamic literature. Only Moses (q.v.) is explicitly stated in the Qur᾿ān to have done work requiring physical strength (Q 28:26). Nevertheless, the "stories of the prophets" *(qiṣaṣ al-anbiyā᾿)* relate that all the prophets practiced a trade. Books on economics (q.v.) also discuss the professions of the prophets: a work attributed to al-Shaybānī (d. 189/804) relates that Solomon wove baskets, Noah (q.v.) was a carpenter and Idrīs (q.v.) was a tailor (Shaybānī, *Kasb*, 76).

The significance of the attribution of humble labor to the prophets can perhaps best be discerned in the story that David (q.v.) — who is described in the Qur᾿ān only as having been "taught by God" how to forge iron (Q 21:80) and that God "made iron soft for him" (Q 34:10; see METALS AND MINERALS) — actually worked the iron with his own hands in order to support himself after having been criticized for "eating from the state treasury" (Shaybānī, *Kasb*, 77). This echoes the criticism leveled against the Umayyad caliphs for drawing from the state treasury for all their expenses, in contrast to the "rightly guided caliphs" who are said to have tried to support themselves (see CALIPH).

Similarly, a group of early Ṣūfīs (see ṢŪFISM AND THE QUR'ĀN) is criticized for refusing to earn a living, preferring to live on charity (see ALMSGIVING). The obligation to earn a living *(al-kasb, al-iktisāb)* is particularly advocated by scholars like Aḥmad b. Ḥanbal (d. 241/855) who criticize any dependence on the support of corrupt governments (see LAW AND THE QUR'ĀN). To avoid forbidden earnings it may be necessary to engage in manual labor, these scholars argue, using examples of the prophets and Companions (see COMPANIONS OF THE PROPHET) to support their position that there is nothing inherently dishonorable in manual labor (Mattson, *Believing slave,* 220). Indeed, argues al-Shaybānī (*Kasb,* 73), Muslims could not fulfill their ritual obligations (see RITUAL AND THE QUR'ĀN; RITUAL PURITY) if, among other things, some people did not make jars to carry water for ablution (see CLEANLINESS AND ABLUTION) and others did not weave clothes to cover the body for prayer (q.v.).

The issue of the honor (q.v.) or dishonor of manual labor is not prominent in the Qur'ān despite the great importance this issue assumes in the corpus of ḥadīth and early anti-Ṣūfī polemics (see ḤADĪTH AND THE QUR'ĀN). Similarly, the Qur'ān does not discuss the effect a woman's status will have on whether she is required to perform household chores, although this is an important legal issue in early Islam (Mattson, *Believing slave,* 192). The Qur'ān indicates that status differences based on family and tribal affiliation (see KINSHIP; TRIBES AND CLANS) were generally more important at the rise of Islam than considerations of profession. No doubt this can be attributed to the fact that the Ḥijāz at the rise of Islam was not as well developed as the urban centers of the Fertile Crescent, where sharp divisions of labor and hereditary professions were important aspects of society (see GEOGRAPHY; CITY; BEDOUIN; IRAQ; PRE-ISLAMIC ARABIA AND THE QUR'ĀN).

The issue of honor aside, early Muslim scholars admitted that it was generally difficult and tiring to earn a living. According to some commentators, one of the worst consequences of being removed from paradise (q.v.) for Adam (see ADAM AND EVE) was that he subsequently had to exhaust himself earning a living (Shaybānī, *Kasb,* 75). The Qur'ān indicates that one of the rewards of paradise will be freedom from having to engage in tiring work (*al-naṣab,* Q 35:35; see also MAINTENANCE AND UPKEEP).

Ingrid Mattson

Bibliography
Primary: Aḥmad b. Ḥanbal, *Kitāb al-Waraʿ,* n.p. 1921; al-Shaybānī, Muḥammad b. al-Ḥasan, *Kitāb al-Kasb,* ed. ʿA. Abū Ghudda, Aleppo 1997.
Secondary: I. Mattson, *A believing slave is better than an unbeliever. Status and community in early Islamic law and society,* Ph.D. diss., University of Chicago 1999; M. Shatzmiller, *Labour in the medieval Islamic world,* Leiden 1994.

Manuscripts of the Qur'ān

Within the handwritten heritage of the Islamic world (see ORTHOGRAPHY; ARABIC SCRIPT), the Qur'ān occupies by far the most conspicuous place — at least in terms of sheer volume. Until the present day, copyists, amateurs as well as professionals, have devoted much time and effort to transcribing the revealed text by hand. It is therefore no wonder that the topic "manuscripts of the Qur'ān" should cover a wide variety of cases: Qur'āns are found in one volume (*muṣḥaf,* q.v.) or sets *(rabʿa)* from two to sixty volumes but also as excerpts, usually connected with prayers (see PRAYER). In all these cases, the manuscripts take the form of a codex, that is a book made up of one or many quires obtained by folding together a varying number of sheets of parchment, paper or perhaps also papyrus. Qur'āns are also found on other materials, like wood or textile, and in other formats, rolls or sheets, for instance, both being used as talismans. The following article will focus solely on the manuscripts in codex form. It should, however, be noted that the study of these manuscripts is unevenly developed: some aspects like illumination (see ORNAMENTATION AND ILLUMINATION) or calligraphy (q.v.) have already been well investigated while others, e.g. the early written transmission of the text, still await comprehensive studies. The bulk of the material, manuscripts without illumination or in more ordinary hands of later periods, have not even been examined or catalogued in spite of their importance for the study of a wide range of subjects, from popular piety to the diffusion of the book in the Islamic lands.

Modern printed editions (see PRINTING OF THE QUR'ĀN) tend to reproduce the features of "classical" Qur'āns — including even the catchwords — which were prevalent during past centuries. Yet, before this "classical" form was attained, the qur'ānic manuscripts underwent many changes, at a rather rapid pace, during the first centuries of Islam. As a consequence, this article will devote a great deal of attention to the early period, since it witnessed many variations and reforms and paved the way for the modern qur'ānic codex.

Pre-'Uthmānic manuscripts

The first "manuscripts" are only known through the reports of early Muslim scholars. According to their sources, the text was initially written on shoulder blades from camels (for a later example, see Fig. III of FĀTIḤA), flat stones or pieces of leather during the Prophet's lifetime in order to preserve the revelations as they came (see OCCASIONS OF REVELATION). Even if the concept of "book" (q.v.; *kitāb*) was already familiar to the first Muslim community, there is no evidence that any codex with the text of the revelation was available before Muḥammad's death (see CODICES OF THE QUR'ĀN). Such a format is closed and therefore ill-adapted to a situation in which the Qur'ān was still receiving additions. The heterogeneous materials mentioned in the Muslim tradition suggest that these amounted to notes meant for private use, and hence quite different from a text which has been "published" in a sense close to the modern use.

Be that as it may, nothing from these early notes has been preserved — another argument supporting the idea that they were not considered manuscripts in the full sense of the word — and the later development of the qur'ānic codex left all these materials completely aside (see COLLECTION OF THE QURĀN). Shoulder blades with Qur'ān excerpts are known from later periods, but do not correspond to any attempt to have had the whole text recorded in that fashion. According to one Christian source, early Muslims did write the text of the Qur'ān on scrolls, in imitation of the Jewish Torah (q.v.; al-Kindī, *Risāla*). Here again, though, no material evidence has survived that would substantiate that claim; the parchment rolls with qur'ānic text published by S. Ory are *rotuli* and not *volumina* like the Torah.

Some time before the sixth/twelfth century, ancient copies of the Qur'ān gained the reputation of having been written by 'Uthmān (q.v.) or 'Alī (see 'ALĪ B. ABĪ ṬĀLIB) or other prominent figures of early Islam: in some cases, as in Cordoba, the text in question contained only a few pages, while in Damascus, an entire copy of such a Qur'ān was kept in the Great Mosque (al-Harawī, *Kitāb al-Ishārāt,* 15; Ṣ. al-Munajjid, *Études,* 45-60). Judging from the manuscripts that have survived, the attribution is often based on a note by a later hand but sometimes a colophon does seem to lend support to this claim. Ṣ. al-Munajjid has attempted to counter such claims, maintaining that the material involved is later, dating mainly from the third/ninth century (see for instance Topkapı Sarayı Museum, TKS A1, or Türk Islâm Eserleri Müzesi, TIEM 458 — both in Istanbul). Additionally, the above-mentioned colophons sometimes contain gross mistakes (in Istanbul, one example is found at the Topkapı Sarayı Museum, TKS Y 745: the copyist is supposed to be 'Alī b. Abū *[sic]* Ṭālib; his name is written at a right angle to the normal disposition of the text). Original expressions of worship developed around these relics: in Cordoba, two servants took the bound volume with the leaves from a treasury in the Great Mosque; a third man, carrying a candle, walked in front of them. They all went to the place where the imām (q.v.) stood for prayer in order to lay the volume on a Qur'ān stand (al-Maqqarī, *Nafḥ,* i, 360; see RITUAL AND THE QUR'ĀN). A. Grohmann has compiled a list of dated early qur'ānic manuscripts (Problem, 216 n. 17): the oldest dates from 94/712-3 but this Qur'ān has never been published and there is considerable doubt about it. Qur'ānic palimpsests have also been said to antedate the 'Uthmānic edition (Mingana and Lewis, *Leaves*).

The Ḥijāzī and Umayyad codices

The earliest Qur'ān manuscripts and fragments do not contradict the information provided by the Islamic sources about the "edition" of an official recension of the Qur'ān by the third caliph, 'Uthmān (r. 23-35/644-56). Attempts to assign codex fragments to an earlier period have not been conclusive: the palimpsests published by A. Mingana and A. Lewis are certainly among the earliest fragments preserved, but nothing indicates that they necessarily predate many others. The same also holds for the two palimpsests sold at an auction in 1992. The oldest text on both is written in the so-called "Ḥijāzī" script, a designation coined by M. Amari in the middle of the nineteenth century — he spoke of "écriture du Ḥidjāz" — on the basis of Ibn al-Nadīm's (d. ca. 385/995) description of the earliest Arabic scripts:

The first of the Arab scripts was the script of Makkah, the next of al-Madīnah, then of al-Baṣrah, and then of al-Kūfah. For the *alifs* of the scripts of Makkah and al-Madīnah there is a turning of the hand to the right and lengthening of the strokes, one form having a slight slant (trans. B. Dodge).

The study of the early Qur'ān manuscripts and fragments in the Paris collection enabled Amari to identify those fragments that demonstrated the various features noted by Ibn al-Nadīm. Unfortunately, his work has remained largely ignored, and research on these documents did not advance significantly until N. Abbott's contribution to the subject *(Rise of north Arabic script)*. The methodical publication in facsimile of these early Qur'āns was begun in 1998 (cf. Déroche and Noseda [eds.], *Sources de la transmission du texte coranique*).

The name of the script — Ḥijāzī — (like the designation "Kūfic") does not mean that these manuscripts were transcribed in the Ḥijāz. The bulk of the material presently known comes from three repositories of old qur'ānic codices, in Damascus, Fusṭāṭ and Ṣan'ā'. (The present locations of these codices also cannot be taken as a conclusive argument as to their origin, which remains for the moment uncertain.) On the other hand, the fact that the collection in Qayrawān does not contain such material only has the value of an argument *e silentio*. A preliminary survey shows that the script varies widely — as if the peculiarities of the individual hands were of little concern to the scribes, the patrons or the readers. This diversity might be ascribed to regional habits, but this does not satisfactorily explain why, in manuscripts written by more than one scribe from the same region, the hands of the various copyists are so different from one another that they can be recognized at first glance (e.g. Bibliothèque nationale de France, BNF Arabe 328a f. 28a and b [for f. 28a see Fig. I], or Dār al-Makhṭūṭāt, inv. no. 01-21.1). A common standard concerning the script had probably not yet developed, and it would thus be safer to speak of Ḥijāzī style, rather than Ḥijāzī script. For the sake of convenience, we shall use here the designation of Ḥijāzī codex.

The dating of this material relies mainly on paleographic arguments: slant and shape of the *alif*, elongation of the shafts, but also the similarities with the script of the earliest papyri as pointed out by M. Amari and later by A. Grohmann. So far, no direct evidence — for instance, a colophon — has been found. One could perhaps expect confirmation from a Carbon 14 analysis of the parchment, but, since the geographic provenience is not clear, such results could only be taken as an indication of its age. The dating to the second half of the first/seventh century can therefore only be tentative, and future research might throw light on the chronology of the Ḥijāzī codices. The defective writing of the *alif* (*qala* instead of *qāla* being the best known instance) adds weight, however, to the early dating of these manuscripts and fragments, some of which count the *basmala* (q.v.) as a verse (see Bibliothèque nationale de France, BNF Arabe 328a). With the exception of these peculiarities, most of the manuscripts currently known are very close to the canonical text. Some fragments of Ḥijāzī codices found in Ṣanʿāʾ are said to include some textual variants which were not recorded by later literature (see READINGS OF THE QURʾĀN), and to offer an order of the sūras differing from the arrangements of both the canonical text and the codices of Ibn Masʿūd and Ubayy (Puin, Observations, 111; see FORM AND STRUCTURE OF THE QURʾĀN).

In these Ḥijāzī codices [of Ṣanʿāʾ], the script is slender and regularly spread out on the page. The spaces between characters, regardless of whether the said character is part of a word or not, are always identical; as a consequence, words can be divided at the end of a line. Clusters of dots show the ends of verses but groups of five or ten verses do not seem initially to have been singled out. Vowels are not recorded and diacritical dots are used in varying degrees by the copyists; when two or more copied a text together, they do not appear to have agreed on common rules but dotted the letters according to their own habits (compare for instance Bibliothèque nationale de France, BNF Arabe 328a f. 7b and 38a). The number of lines varies from one page to another, even though the copyists used ruling. A blank space is left between sūras, but some of the fragments suggest that crude decorations in ink were already allowed (if they do not belong to a second stage of the Ḥijāzī codices). The sūra titles found on these manuscripts are often in red ink: they were added later. There are a few instances of division of the text into seven parts, with the indication within the written area itself — i.e. British Library, BL Or. 2165, where such division is indicated in green ink. This is in contrast to the later practice of adding the indications of the textual divisions in the margins (the indications that do not appear in the margins are also additions but the shortness of these marks makes it impossible to date them, and thus to assess how much time had elapsed between their addition and the copying of the qurʾānic text itself).

The material available to us shows that early Muslims made a choice which was to shape the history of the Qurʾān as a manuscript: they adopted for their own scriptures the kind of book which was common at that time, namely the codex, and started copying the text in long lines — whereas in other book traditions of the Middle East the texts were arranged in columns. Most of the Ḥijāzī codices are in the then usual vertical format, except a few, which are in the oblong format that was to become the rule for Qurʾān codices during the second/eighth century: as the script of these latter manuscripts is more regular than in other Ḥijāzī codices, it has been suggested that they belong to a later stage of development — perhaps the end of the first/seventh or the beginning of the second/eighth century.

All of the earliest qurʾānic manuscripts that have come down to us were written on parchment. The amount of text on the few fragments of papyrus published by A. Grohmann is too small to establish whether Qurʾān codices on papyrus existed side by side with parchment ones or not: these fragments could just as well have come from extracts. As is the case with the script, the way in which the parchment was used to produce quires varies greatly from one manuscript to another — inasmuch as enough folios remain to allow a reconstruction of the original quires.

The anticipated use of the various Ḥijāzī codices cannot be determined: the size of many of them would suggest a public use, in a mosque (q.v.) for instance. Judging by the evidence of a Paris manuscript (Bibliothèque nationale de France, BNF Arabe 328a; see Fig. 1), these codices seem to have been cared for over a long period of time: some places of this manuscript where the ink appears to have faded have been written over by a hand which can not be dated to earlier than the end of the third/ninth century.

By the end of the first/seventh or beginning of the second/eighth century, a new trend was changing the appearance of the qurʾānic codex. As far as can be determined by the best reconstruction of the chronology of the qurʾānic scripts, it was the Umayyad period that witnessed the emergence of a style in which the letter forms were more regular and the shafts more vertical. This may be linked with the reforms of ʿAbd al-Malik who decided that the chancery of the empire should use Arabic instead of Greek and Persian, thus promoting the use of the Arabic script. On the other hand, one consequence of these administrative decisions could have been the emergence of the concept of specifically qurʾānic scripts. The script of the papyri of the first/seventh century and that of the Ḥijāzī codices have similarities; this will no longer be the case in the following period, and the gap between qurʾānic and secular scripts will widen. Another argument for the dating of this style to the Umayyad period are sūra headbands of a Qurʾān found among the Damascus fragments (Türk Islâm Eserleri Müzesi, TIEM ŞE 321) which are clearly related to the decorative repertory of the mosaics on the Dome of the Rock (see AQṢĀ MOSQUE). Ornament is thus making its way into the qurʾānic manuscripts (the evidence that is available today indicates that this is the first instance of the use of gold in qurʾānic ornamentation). Other experimentations are documented in this group of manuscripts and fragments: in some of them, as was usual at that time, a blank line has been left between two sūras, but the place is highlighted by the use of colored inks (red and/or green) for the first lines of the beginning of the next sūra and sometimes also for the last lines of the preceding one. This is also when groups of ten verses begin to receive a special marker, in some cases only a letter with numerical value *(abjad)*. In one fragment (Bibliothèque nationale de France, BNF Arabe 330c), it is written in gold. Other attempts which can be attributed to this period or somewhat later are more puzzling: for example, calligrams with colored inks developing over the writing surface. The orthography itself was changing: it is far from homogeneous from one manuscript to another, and sometimes even changes within the same manuscript, but overall it does show an evolution towards the *scriptio plena*.

Another Qur'ān attributed to the Umayyad period is more difficult to evaluate: some fragments (Dār al-Makhṭūṭāt, inv. no. 20-33.1) are the only remnants of a large manuscript (51 × 47 cm), which originally contained about 520 folios. The impressive illuminations (particularly the two representations of a mosque) have no equivalent and the script foreshadows later developments; an elaborate frame surrounds the written area on the first folios of the text (for examples of these fragments, see Figs. 1 of FĀTIḤA and 1 of ORNAMENTATION AND ILLUMINATION).

The qur'ānic codex in early 'Abbāsid times

Our knowledge of the Qur'āns of the third/ninth century, which include a few dated manuscripts, is fairly developed. The earlier part of the 'Abbāsid period, however, remains somewhat unclear as the information about it is still very scarce. Here again, the dating of Qur'āns to the second/eighth century relies mainly on paleography. But, as compared with the evidence from the first/seventh century, we are on surer footing in this century, since more paleographic evidence has survived. The qur'ānic scripts of that period are traditionally known as "Kūfic," but "early 'Abbāsid scripts" would be more accurate; the linking of any of them with the town of Kūfa remaining unclear. As a whole, the scripts bear witness to the emergence of a body of highly skilled scribes and a complex set of rules concerning the use of the various styles. In the eighties of the twentieth century, a tentative typology was created in order to classify the material: it defines six groups of scripts (called A to F), subdivided into a varying number of styles (for instance B II or D IV; see Déroche, *Abbasid tradition*, 34-47; id., *Catalogue, I/1. Aux origines de la calligraphie coranique*, 37-45). The terminology and results of this typology have been used here in order to provide clarity to the following account.

A major development of this period is the introduction of a system for the notation of the vowels. These are indicated through the positioning of red dots with respect to the consonant: an "a" — *fatḥa* — above the letter, an "i" — *kasra* — below it or a "u" — *ḍamma* — after it; the indefinite case ending *(tanwīn)* is noted by a duplication of the dot. Although it was reportedly invented by Abū l-Aswad al-Du'alī (d. 69/688), this system does not seem to have been used before the end of the first/seventh century. Qur'āns from the Umayyad period have red dots: but are they contemporaneous with the script itself? Since the dots were necessarily an addition (neither the ink nor paint nor the writing implement were those used for the copy of the unadorned orthography, i.e. *rasm*), doubt always remains about the time that elapsed between the copying of the text and the addition of the dots. The system was later perfected with the addition of dots for the glottal stop — *hamza* — (green or yellow) and the consonantal duplicator — *shadda* — (yellow, orange or blue); sometimes their modern form is written with colored ink. The sign for the absence of a vowel — *sukūn* — is rarely indicated. Other signs were used in the Maghrib in order to note more accurately the pronunciation (see Nuruosmaniye Library 23, completed in Palermo in 372/982-3). This system remained dominant until the end of the fourth/tenth century and was apparently still used late into the tenth/sixteenth century for a Yemeni (?) Qur᾿ān. In the Maghrib, but also in qur᾿ānic manuscripts in Sūdānī script, the *hamza* was indicated by a dot until very recently (see Bibliothèque nationale de France, BNF Arabe 576, dated 1195/1781).

Early in the period under discussion here, some Qur᾿āns were still in the vertical format: the B I group of scripts could be typical for the early part of the second/eighth century (see Institute of Oriental Studies in St. Petersburg, IOS C 20 or Bibliothèque nationale de France, BNF Arabe 331) and bear witness to the transition from the Ḥijāzī codex — to which its somewhat slender script is probably related — to the early ʿAbbāsid one. Alongside this tradition, which was gradually fading out, another stouter kind of script (akin to that of Dār al-Makhṭūṭāt, inv. no. 20-33.1) came to be the qur᾿ānic script *par excellence*. It is commonly associated with the oblong format, although the change from the vertical format cannot have been motivated solely by script aesthetics. One reason for this shift — unrecorded in our sources, however — may have been a desire to give the Qur᾿ān a visual identity clearly different from that of the Torah (roll) or the Gospels (vertical codex; see GOSPEL). Another development which probably played a role in the horizontal lay-out of the Qur᾿ān, but about whose influence on this matter the sources are also silent, is the nearly contemporary controversy about writing down ḥadīth (see ḤADĪTH AND THE QUR᾿ĀN). During the period, the number of lines to the page became increasingly regular: this evolution may stem from a will to control the text more easily.

The earliest sūra titles contemporaneous with the copy of the text itself are found in manuscripts tentatively attributed to the second/eighth century, but such texts are not the rule. For, up until this time, the sūras were separated from each other by a blank space or by an ornament — ranging from very crude ones to highly sophisticated illuminations. The headband had not yet found its shape: some ornaments occupy irregularly the rectangular space of the line, others are already enclosed within an outer rectangular frame; the vignette also appears, sometimes at both ends of the headband (see Forschungs- und Landesbibliothek, FLB Ms. orient. A 462, ff. 6 b and 11 a). The origin of the vignette has been connected with the *tabula ansata* of classical Antiquity; but since the early sūra headbands are an-epigraphic and devoid of vignette, one wonders whether this explanation, borrowed from epigraphy (see EPIGRAPHY AND THE QUR᾿ĀN), can be applied to manuscripts. Coptic paragraph marks show that marginal devices were known to the copyists of the period. At any rate, the need for information led very soon to the introduction of the sūra titles into the Qur᾿āns. Depending on the manuscripts, these were noted either at the beginning or at the end of the sūra. In the former case, the sūra title is introduced by a formula including the word *fātiḥa* ("opening"), in the latter by *khātima* ("ending"; both can be developed in various ways and even combined). During the third/ninth century, it became the rule to indicate the title at the beginning of the sūra, without any introductory formula. The names given to some of the sūras vary from one manuscript to another. The number of verses is generally given next to the title and the ends of the verses are usually, but not always, indicated. Only rarely do ornamental verse end markers number the individual verses with *abjad* numerals (see NUMBERS AND ENUMERATION; NUMEROLOGY): most copies distinguish only groups of five and ten verses.

The most impressive achievement of the period is a group of giant Qurʾāns (Bibliothèque nationale de France, BNF Arabe 324 and Forschungs- und Landesbibliothek, FLB Ms. orient. A 462 contain fragments of one of them), dating probably from the second part of the second/eighth century (a Carbon 14 dating of one page suggested a date between 640 and 765 C.E.; the earlier date seems more in keeping with other data). They may have been inspired by earlier attempts, like the above-mentioned Dār al-Makhṭūṭāt, inv. no. 20-33.1. The manuscripts measure roughly 68 × 53 cm and have twelve lines of text per page — in one case, the figure is slightly more than double this amount: twenty-five lines on a single page. Reconstructions based on the state of the manuscripts indicate that they would have had more than 600 folios, each of them composed of the hide of one animal. In spite of their thickness, they seem to have been bound as single-volume Qurʾāns. These manuscripts were much larger than any earlier Qurʾān that has been preserved, and their production would have required an extraordinary financial investment. They were most probably ordered for mosques, but their size suggests that they would have served a purpose other than simply recitation or reading (see RECITATION OF THE QURʾĀN). We are told that ʿUmar b. al-Khaṭṭāb abhorred Qurʾāns in small script and was delighted when he saw large copies. In spite of the anachronism of this anecdote, it draws attention to the fact that large copies were favored by Muslims of the first centuries. Since congregational readings, such as that during the Friday prayer (q.v.), do not require such massive volumes, they may have served an apologetic or political function.

There is no clear evidence that multi-volume sets existed before the beginning of the third/ninth century, even if some of the earlier manuscripts contain marginal indications of divisions into sevenths, for instance. But from the third/ninth century on, both the manuscripts and the texts attached to them – mainly endowment documents *(waqfiyyāt)* — indicate that multi-volume sets were common. Some of the scripts, like D I, actually seem closely connected with this kind of Qurʾān, their size demanding a full text of such magnitude that it would have been impossible to bind all the folios as a single book. This led to the appearance of boxes *(tābūt, ṣundūq)* which could keep all the volumes of a set together. In the case of Amājūr's Qurʾān, the endowment document *(waqfiyya)* of 262/876 states that two boxes were needed to store the thirty *juzʾ* (Déroche, Qurʾān of Amāǧūr, 61). This manuscript had only three lines to the page — which means that the total number of folios was enormous. It seems that such multi-volume Qurʾāns were the solution needed for the production of manuscripts in this period that were, in the end, as large as the second/eighth century giant Qurʾāns described earlier. As a rule, wealthy patrons ordered them for mosques. Qurʾānic codices are also known to have been the property of individuals: a few are actually dated according to notes recording births or deaths in a family. These were usually single volumes written in smaller scripts like B II, for instance.

There is also a greater range of illumination to be found in Qurʾāns from the early ʿAbbāsid period, which may be, however, simply due to the fact that more material has been preserved than for the earlier period. Some Qur'āns have no decoration whatsoever, or minimal indication of titles and divisions in red, green or yellow, while others use gold for the same purpose. The most sophisticated manuscripts may have an opening page — without any text — that spans two folios (very few have more than two such pages), sūra headbands with a vignette in the margin and a variety of verse or group markers. The beginning of the text itself is sometimes set into a decorated frame. Some Qur'āns also have an illuminated double page at the end. Multi-volume sets offered as many opportunities as there were volumes in which to illuminate the beginning (and possibly the end) of each section of text (see the series of which Topkapı Sarayı Museum, TKS EH 16 is part). Gold is heavily used in illumination, but also for the copying of the text. In spite of earlier statements by Muslim scholars like Mālik b. Anas (d. 179/796) against the use of gold for that purpose, chrysography seems to have received wide acceptance. Even if the story reported by Ibn al-Nadīm (*Fihrist*, 9) that a Qur'ān in gold script was produced for 'Umar II were a forgery, a famous manuscript of 'Abbāsid times, the "Blue Qur'ān," is far from being the only instance of gold script used for copying the Qur'ān. Other refinements, like dyed parchment, were also in use: blue parchment has been mentioned, but yellow, pink and orange are also documented.

With the exception of a text by al-Jahshiyārī, who recorded an anecdote about silver binding in Umayyad times (*Kitāb al-Wuzarā'*, 26; Latz, *Das Buch*, 79), we have no information about the bindings of qur'ānic manuscripts until the third/ninth century. From that period onwards, various collections, but mainly that of Qayrawān, have bindings of a distinctive shape: they are indeed closer to boxes than to any kind of binding previously known. The boards are made of wood and are covered with leather, often decorated; in front of the three outer edges, a continuous strip of leather glued onto the lower board protects the Qur'ān. When the upper board is down and the book is closed, a leather thong fastened to the gutter side of the lower board can be tied over a metal peg projecting out of the edge of the upper board: the manuscript can thus be kept tightly closed. Bindings of non-qur'ānic manuscripts are almost unknown for this period, making comparison impossible; but it has been suggested that the bindings described here were specifically made for the Qur'āns.

A century of change

During the fourth/tenth century, the appearance of the qur'ānic codex is altered by various developments, some of which were already in evidence by the end of the third/ninth century. The first one involves the scripts: a new style, connected to scripts already in use in non-qur'ānic manuscripts and administrative documents, received increasing acceptance as a qur'ānic script, only to be superseded — slightly later — by *naskhī* and *naskhī*-related scripts.

This new style is the last script to have been in use in qur'ānic manuscripts all over the Islamic world. While variants appear in the execution, it basically relies on well-defined aesthetics and a clear repertoire of letterforms. The names given to the more refined versions of this script — Persian Kūfic, Oriental Kūfic — are somewhat misleading: the earlier name of "Kūfic *naskhī*" is a better descriptive since the basic shapes are closer to the so-called "cursives." The earliest Qur'ān in this script is a multi-volume set copied on parchment before 292/905, possibly in a Persian speaking area; in addition to the script, its vertical format foreshadows the changes of the next decades (Chester Beatty Library, CBL 1431). The new style was nevertheless also used in manuscripts with an oblong format, like the Qur'āns copied on parchment in Palermo in 372/982-3 (Nuruosmaniye Library 23; see Fig. II of ORNAMENTATION AND ILLUMINATION) or on paper in Iṣfahān in 383/993 (Türk Islâm Eserleri Müzesi, TIEM 453-6).

The calligraphic possibilities of the new style might explain why it remained in use for a considerable period of time. Whereas the last dated Qur'ān in early 'Abbāsid script from the central Islamic lands was — according to the current state of our knowledge — written in 362/972, the latest dated qur'ānic manuscript in the new style was finished in 620/1223 (Mashhad, Āsitān-i Quds 84). One cannot exclude the existence of later copies since it remained a favorite script among illuminators, and was used, for instance, in titles. A short excerpt of the Qur'ān was even written in a highly ornamental variant of the script as late as 909/1503 (Topkapı Sarayı Museum, TKS R. 18 in Istanbul).

A major evolution of the fourth/tenth century was the use of so-called cursives, commonly called *naskhī*, as qur'ānic scripts. The earliest dated example of a *naskhī*-related script for a Qur'ān originates from Upper Mesopotamia or northern Syria; it is dated to 387/997. Somewhat later in the same century, a parchment fragment in the oblong format with the last sūras in an unmistakably Maghribī hand bears a colophon stating that the copy was ended in Rajab 398/March-April 1008. This evidence indicates a growing trend towards making the qur'ānic codex more legible to the ordinary people, and towards closing the gap between the script of the qur'ānic codices and that which was used in daily matters, a gap which had opened during the second half of the first/end of the seventh, beginning of the eighth century, but was gradually disappearing. It also documents the emergence of a split between the eastern and western parts of the Islamic world represented by the Maghribī script, which would become the hallmark of the manuscript production in the Maghrib and in Muslim Spain. Interestingly enough, the earliest Maghribī fragments show a greater respect for the material aspects of the qur'ānic codex tradition, namely the oblong format and the parchment. Once again the transition to the "modern" scripts was by no means a quick one, as is witnessed by the production of Qur'āns in the 'new style' during a long period, albeit in decreasing numbers; further research will have to investigate the possible use in the Maghrib of early 'Abbāsid scripts after the end of the fourth/tenth century. Even if calligraphers of the early 'Abbāsid period skilled in very small script succeeded in reducing the number of pages and the size of the Qur'āns, early manuscripts in *naskhī* (for instance British Library, BL Add. 7214; see Fig. III) attained an even greater compactness, perhaps explaining the success of these last-named copies (which may also have been less expensive).

The development of grammar (see GRAMMAR AND THE QUR'ĀN) led to the invention of systems that were increasingly precise in order to note the correct pronunciation of the Qur'ān. The modern system of vowels was used on the Qur'ān of 292/905, but since the older system of red dots is also present on that manuscript, it is highly probable that the modern vowels are a later addition. The Palermo Qur'ān, on the other hand, is fully punctuated: vowels but also other orthoepic signs indicate the correct pronunciation. The modern system of vowels and orthoepics came into use during the fourth/tenth century. During this period, the modern signs for *shadda* and *sukūn*, both in color, were associated with the red-dot vocalization. Modern vowels and orthoepics were written in color by the copyist of the "Nurse's Qurʾān" in Qayrawān in 410/1019-20: the document recording his work states that he vocalized the manuscript. The same ʿUthmān b. Ḥusayn al-Warrāq completed a thirty-volume Qurʾān in 466/1073-4, probably in eastern Iran: he also recorded that he added vowels and orthoepics — in color — to the text (Mashhad, Āsitān-i Quds 4316). The famous "Qurʾān of Ibn al-Bawwāb" contrasts with this practice: vowels and orthoepics are written with the same ink as the rest of the text (Chester Beatty Library, CBL 1431, dated 391/1000-1); this is also the case in the manuscript of 387/997. The western Islamic world followed another path, as will be shown below.

The second major development of the period is the introduction of paper, which gradually replaced parchment — at least in the east. The earliest datable Qurʾān on paper was completed by the end of the first half of the fourth/tenth century, almost a century later than the earliest non-qurʾānic Arabic manuscript on paper. The increasing use of this material also altered the appearance of the qurʾānic codex. The third development, perhaps connected with the second, has to do with the format of the text: a return to a vertical format is seen in this period. Even if, as evidenced by the Iṣfahān Qurʾān, it was possible to produce paper Qurʾāns in the oblong format, the majority were now in the vertical format, thus suggesting that it was better adapted to the new material. All these changes did not go hand in hand, even if they seem somewhat interrelated, and they did not meet with general acceptance overnight. Their economic implications also need to be evaluated. Paper was less expensive than parchment, even if we do not know exactly how much cheaper it was. Should we assume that books became more affordable for a larger number of people, even though they remained a luxury, and that therefore their production pace had to increase? There were two ways in which the need for more manuscripts could be met: the first one being an increase in the copyist's speed, the second one an increase in the number of copyists. There is finally another question that arises: was the new style more legible for readers as well as faster for copyists, since it was easier to write?

The new vertical sizing also forced the qurʾānic manuscripts to adapt new formats for complete page illumination. It appears that this was not simply a matter of rotating the existing compositions by ninety degrees since the relationship between height and width had changed. Rather, this changed dimension of the illuminations is possibly the reason why compositions based either on a central circle or on the repetition of a small pattern in order to cover the surface became increasingly popular. Another evolution was the introduction of text into the illuminated opening pages: the earliest instances are not clearly dated (perhaps already at the end of the third/ninth century) but a few dated manuscripts of the fourth/tenth century include on the opening double page information about the number of sūras, verses, words and letters found in the Qurʾān.

Few manuscripts document the continued production of large Qurʾāns during this period. Multi-volume sets, however, remain quite common. The Iṣfahān Qurʾān had four volumes and The Nasser D. Khalili Collection of Islamic Art Qur 89, which is perhaps slightly later, had originally seven; many had thirty. All are of a comparatively small size, particularly those composed by division into thirtieths *(juzʾ)*. The "Nurse's Qurʾān" attests to the production of large-

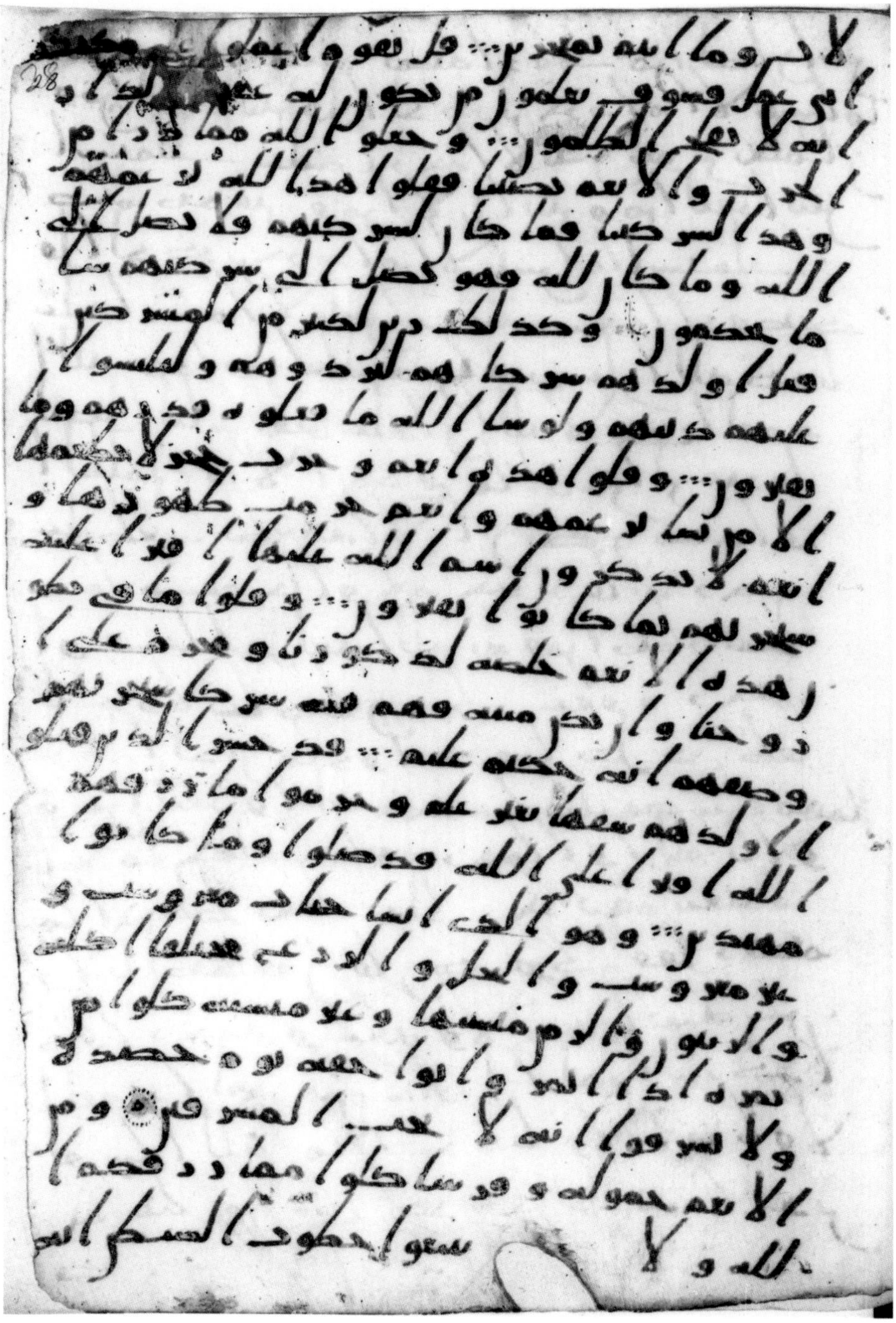

[I] Early Ḥijāzī qur'ānic codex (second half of the first/seventh century) on parchment containing Q 6:134-42. Courtesy of the Bibliothèque nationale de France, Paris (BNF Arabe 328, f. 28a).

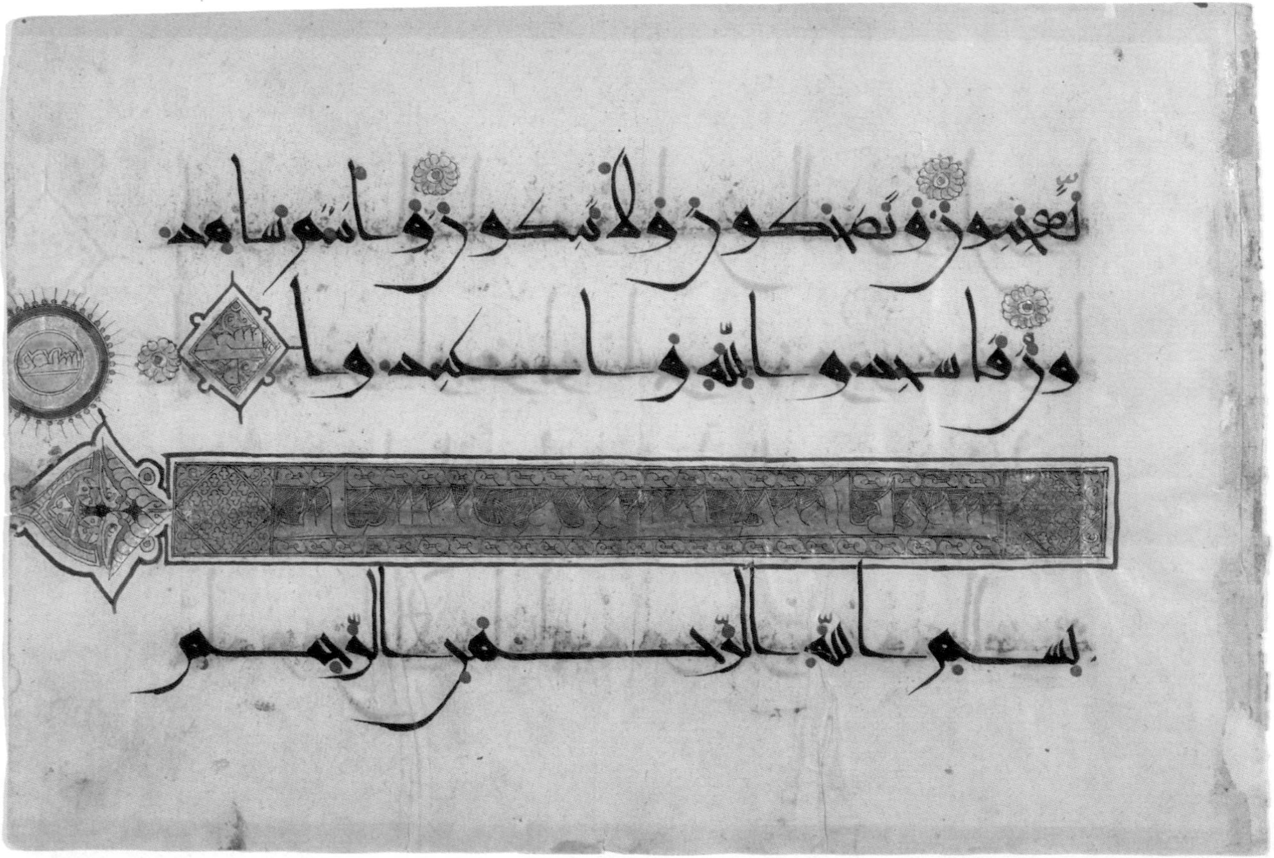

[II] Qur'ānic codex in New Style script (Iṣfahān, 383/993). Q 53:59-54:1 is shown here. Courtesy of The Nasser D. Khalili Collection of Islamic Art, London (KFQ 90r).

[III] Early qurʾānic manuscript in *naskh* script (dated 427/1036) exemplifying the degree of compactness such manuscripts attained. Q 16:31-72 is seen here. Courtesy of the British Library, London (BL Add. 7214, f. 32b).

[IV] Example of a qur'ānic manuscript in which the lines of script alternate in height and length (dated to 582/1186). Q 18:93-110 is shown here. Reproduced by kind permission of the Trustees of the Chester Beatty Library, Dublin (CBL 1438, f. 109a).

[v] Qur'ān manuscript from the western Islamic world (on parchment, dated 703/1304), with a marginal ornament indicating the daily readings for the month of Ramaḍān in the lower part of the margin. The text contains Q 26:220-27:20. Courtesy of the Bibliothèque nationale de France, Paris (BNF Arabe 385, f. 80a).

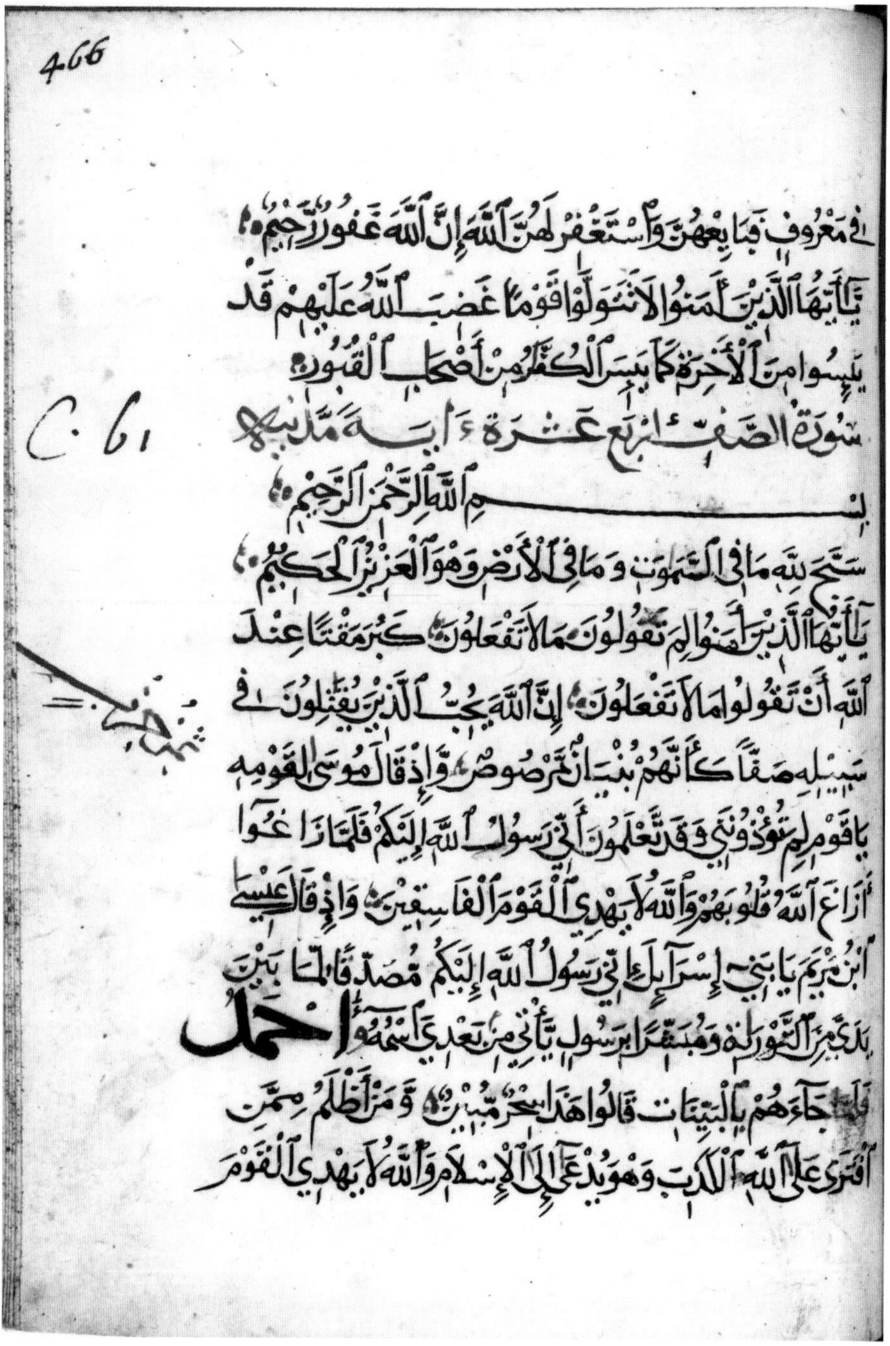

[vi] Example of a qur'ānic manuscript (dated 923/1517) in which "Aḥmad" of Q 61:6 appears in larger writing. Q 60:12 – 61:7 is shown here. Courtesy of the Bibliothèque nationale de France, Paris (BNF Arabe 413, p. 466).

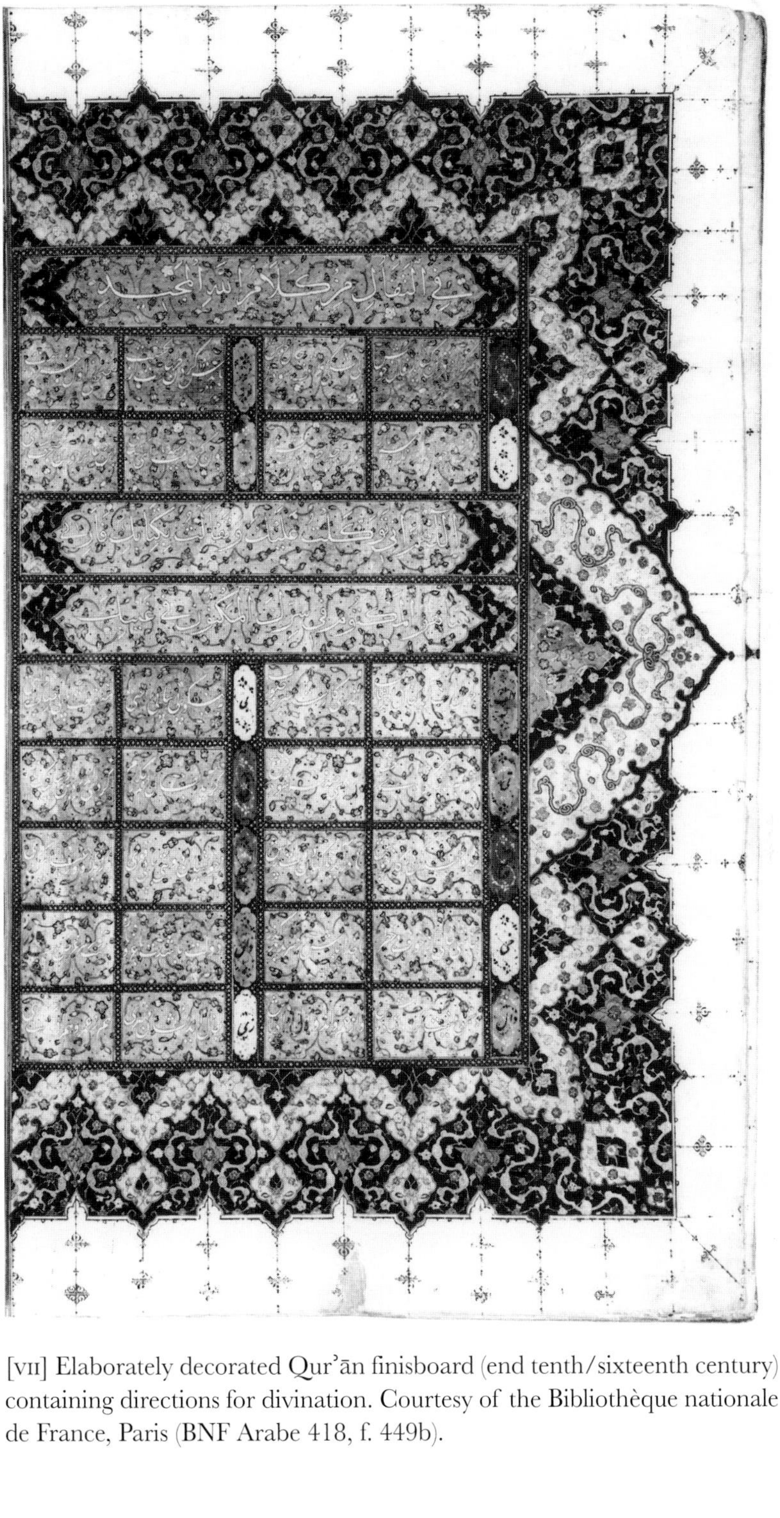

[vii] Elaborately decorated Qurʾān finisboard (end tenth/sixteenth century) containing directions for divination. Courtesy of the Bibliothèque nationale de France, Paris (BNF Arabe 418, f. 449b).

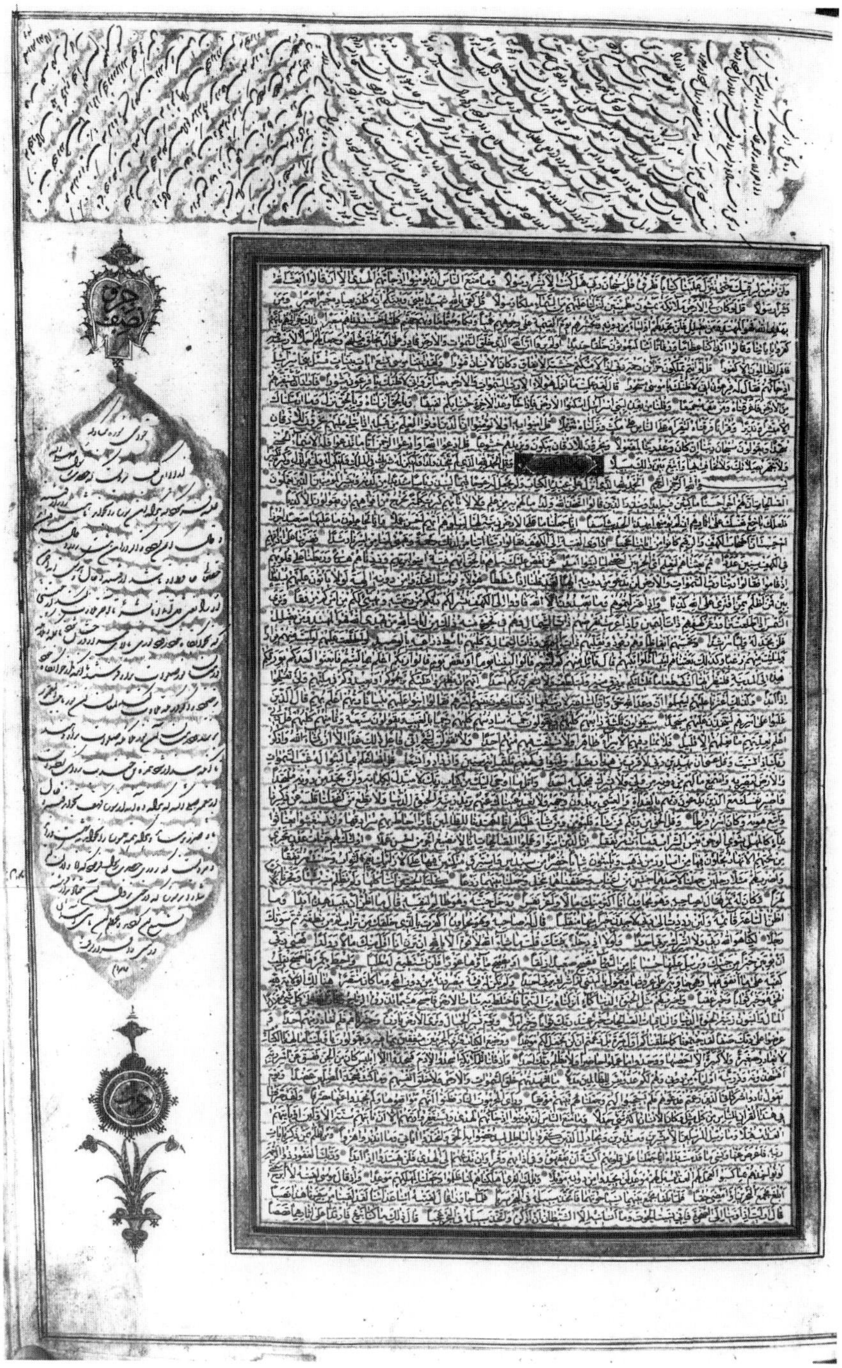

[VIII] Later Iranian Qur'ān manuscript (dated to 1126/1714) in a minute hand, in which an entire *juz'* (a thirtieth of the Qur'ān) appears on two facing pages (here, only one such page – containing a *ḥizb*, or a sixtieth of the Qur'ān – is shown). In the margin, there are accounts in Persian about Muḥammad's life and commentaries by the sixth imām, Jaʿfar al-Ṣādiq. Courtesy of the Bayerische Staatsbibliothek, Munich (BSB Cod. arabe 1118, f. 17v).

sized Qur᾿āns in the western part of the Islamic world. In 410/1019-20, the otherwise unknown scribe *(warrāq)*, ʿAlī b. Aḥmad, wrote the thirty *juz᾿* of this Qur᾿ān in Qayrawān; he was also responsible for its vowel signs, illumination and binding. 552 pages of this work have been preserved: they measure 45 × 29 cm and have only five lines of text on a page. The set was kept in a large wooden box that contains an inscription commemorating its being donated to a mosque by Fāṭima, the nurse of the Zirid ruler al-Muʿizz b. Bādīs.

Towards the modern qur᾿ānic codex

Over the following centuries and down to the present day, Qur᾿āns were written in a wide variety of the so-called "cursive" scripts, some of them — such as *nastaʿlīq* (see Topkapı Sarayı Museum, TKS HS 25, dated 945/1538-9) — used only in exceptional cases. A few styles were more frequently used for qur᾿ānic manuscripts than other documents. Even if copyists would also transcribe other texts with these styles, their designation as "qur᾿ānic" scripts retained its validity. In the central Islamic lands, the manuscripts of higher quality were most frequently written in the scripts which the literature about calligraphy calls *naskh (*also *naskhī), muḥaqqaq, rayḥānī (*also *rayḥān)* and *thuluth (*also *thulth).* Regional varieties of scripts emerged in other areas. In India, for instance, Biḥārī was in use during the late eighth/fourteenth and the ninth/fifteenth century. Classical styles could undergo regional modifications: the script typical of Chinese Qur᾿āns of the ninth/fifteenth century has been described as a peculiar form of *muḥaqqaq* deriving from earlier Persian models. The Biḥārī might in turn have been imitated on the eastern coast of Africa, where the influence of India is known to have been felt (The Nasser D. Khalili Collection of Islamic Art Qur 706, dated 1162/1749).

The particular script usually remains homogeneous from the beginning to the end of a manuscript — this also applies to copies with alternating lines in two or three different styles. In some cases, the word *Allāh* or even entire sentences are highlighted: they are either written in larger letters or in ink different from that of the text itself (see for example John Rylands University Library, UL 760-773). Other manuscripts are more puzzling: in some, only the names *Aḥmad* (Q 61:6) and *Muḥammad* (Q 48:29) are written in larger letters (see Bibliothèque nationale de France, BNF Arabe 413 [see Fig. VI], and The Metropolitan Museum of Art, MMA Rogers Fund 1940). Such features could be related to specific forms of religious behavior, which still need to be investigated.

Page setting was seen by copyists and patrons as a way of enhancing the appearance of the text. At the beginning of our period, the Qur᾿āns were apparently all written in long lines of identical height and length. Later, the copyists started playing with both elements, perhaps influenced by chancery traditions that are apparent in pilgrimage certificates from Saljūq times found in Damascus. An early example of this revised page setting is Chester Beatty Libray, CBL 1438, dated 582/1186 (see Fig. IV). In some Qur᾿āns in Biḥārī script, the copyists used two sizes of script side by side, the larger one for the first and last lines of each page, the smaller one for the rest of the text (Leiden University Library [Oriental Department], Or. 18320 dated 811/1408-9). Later manuscripts document the use of various colors of ink in order to achieve a more complex effect on the whole page. In Persianate areas, but also in Turkey, a complex grid, usually with three larger lines framing two groups of smaller script written in black ink became popular; the larger lines, in white, blue, red or gold, contrast sharply with the rest. This page setting is also known in Chinese Qurʾāns where the difference between the lines is somewhat subdued — in terms of size as well as of color, black being used throughout the page. From the eleventh/seventeenth century onwards, Indian qurʾānic manuscripts feature a page setting which looks like that found in Qurʾāns from Safavid Iran: the written surface, defined by a golden frame, is divided into identically-sized large bands in which the text is written, and which are separated from one another by smaller bands that could contain a translation. A second frame, close to the edge of the page and larger than the former one, marks off an area surrounding the text which may either be blank — with the exception of markers for the groups of verses or such indication — or contain a commentary to the Qurʾān.

It is obviously difficult to summarize here the "rules" of qurʾānic illumination: the material available is far too vast and offers many variations. The following, therefore, are only a few of what may be termed "general guidelines." One rule is strictly observed: the qurʾānic manuscript was never illustrated — to date, the only published example of an "illustrated" qurʾānic manuscript (Gottheil, Illustrated copy, 21-4) is a fake. Even if scholarly interest has been primarily focused on the works of master illuminators found on the most expensive manuscripts, one has to remember that many Qurʾāns received an ornament of some kind, even if it was only a rubricated frame for the beginning of the text. The concept of the double-page played a major role in qurʾānic manuscripts, especially in their illumination: the artists tried to balance the composition, overcoming the physical division of the two pages and giving it an overall unity. Whatever its quality may be, illumination held more or less the same role and place which had been progressively agreed upon during the first centuries. The function of the ornament is primarily to indicate the beginning or the end of a part of the text: it can be the beginning of the manuscript and, since these Qurʾāns have no title page, the ornament is meant to send a kind of signal or, with the help of qurʾānic quotations, to "name" the book. Q 56:77-80 is perfectly suited to this task: "That this is indeed a *Qurʾān* most honorable in a *book* (q.v.) well-guarded, which none shall touch but those who are clean." After the preliminary pages — one double-page or more of pure ornament, with or without writing — illumination occurs in various places: within the written surface are the divisions into verses or groups of verses but also the titles of the sūras. In the margins are indicators for the verse groupings (more developed than those already mentioned), for the various divisions of the text into equally-sized parts, or for the ritual prostrations (*sajda*, see BOWING AND PROSTRATION; RITUAL AND THE QURʾĀN), and the vignettes corresponding to the sūra headings. The beginning and the end of the text itself can also be highlighted by an illuminated frame: for the beginning of single-volume Qurʾāns, the main option is either to have the opening sūra, the Fātiḥa (q.v.), on a double page and the first verses of sūra 2 on the next one, or to have the Fātiḥa facing the beginning of sūra 2 on the same double page. In some early multi-volume Qurʾāns, the Fātiḥa is repeated at the beginning of each *juzʾ*. The last sūras may also be set within a frame; some Qurʾāns have additional illuminated pages with a prayer and/or a divination formula *(fāl-nāma)*. In some multi-volume qurʾānic manuscripts, a first-page illumination may provide the number of the volume within the series; the end of each volume may receive an ornament with Q 83:26.

The repertoire of ornamentation inherited from the previous period relied mainly on geometric and vegetal forms. Illuminations were geometrically structured until the end of the ninth/fifteenth century, when more fluid forms of ornament were introduced. These broad orientations were translated in various ways in the different parts of the Islamic world: this is reflected in the studies on qur᾿ānic illumination which usually present the material according to periods and regions. Such categorizations are often decisive in determining the provenance of a Qur᾿ān. One should nevertheless be aware that some areas have not yet been sufficiently investigated, or offer various difficulties. This, for instance, is the case of India, where the existence of many centers of Qur᾿ān-production with local orientations, as well as lasting ties with Afghanistan or Iran may have confused the researchers, often unable — at least for the moment — to distinguish Qur᾿āns copied in India from others imported from the north. For areas like China or Indonesia, the study of illumination is only beginning and, even if its features seem as a whole quite distinctive, it has to be remembered that some periods remain unexplored.

The early qur᾿ānic bindings that have been preserved were apparently meant to distinguish the Qur᾿ān from any other manuscripts. When this practice came to an end is not clear; bindings from the fifth/eleventh century indicate that Qur᾿āns of that time were bound in the same manner as other manuscripts, but solutions had to be found in order to identify easily the sacred book of Islam. According to authors like al-ʿAlmawī (d. 981/1573), the etiquette concerning book storage recommended that Qur᾿āns should be put on top of the pile. But this might have been insufficient (in medieval times, books were stored horizontally), hence the practice of using qur᾿ānic quotations in lieu of a title on the binding. The fore-edge flap was likely the primary place for such a quotation: stamping a text on bindings was not completely new, since some early bindings for Qur᾿āns already had inscriptions on their boards — usually eulogies like *al-mulk li-llāh* ("God's is the dominion") — and later bindings of multivolume sets bore the number of each volume on the fore-edge flap: the Qur᾿ān in ten volumes completed in Marrakesh by ʿUmar al-Murtaḍā in 654/1256 bears witness to this practice (see British Library, BL Or. 13192). Mamlūk bindings show early instances of the use of qur᾿ānic verses thereon (Museum für Islamische Kunst, SMPK I. 5622). The stamping of texts was facilitated by the development of the binders' techniques which led to the introduction of plates in the stamping process: on later bindings, it became customary to have Q 56:77 on the fore-edge flap; Q 6:115 is more unusual in this place. On the boards, there was room for more developed texts: around the field, a series of cartouches could contain qur᾿ānic verses (Q 2:255 or 56:77-80; both appear on Chester Beatty Library, CBL 1545) or ḥadīth (see Türk Islâm Eserleri Müzesi, TIEM 423). Quotations also occur on the inner side of the board: Q 2:255, the "Throne Verse (see THRONE OF GOD)," and Q 33:56 (see Bibliothèque nationale de France, BNF Arabe 418). The use of precious metals and stones was continued: very ancient examples do not seem to have survived, but Ottoman bindings are well-known (Topkapı Sarayı Museum, TKS Inv. 2/2121; see MATERIAL CULTURE AND THE QUR᾿ĀN).

Animal hides (mainly sheep and goats) were used as the raw material for parchment; the dimension of the final sheet was limited by the size of the species used. Paper technology allowed for the production of far larger sheets: the mobile form technique limited their size to what craftsmen were able to handle in and out of the paste vat, while the fixed form, although not as efficient as the former in production levels, could help in the manufacture of very large sheets of paper. On the other hand, pasting was opening possibilities unknown to parchment users. The development of very large Qur'āns benefited from these technical advances during the seventh/thirteenth and eighth/fourteenth centuries. Both single and multi-volume qur'ānic manuscripts are involved: the Ölcaytu Qur'ān in thirty *juz'* has five lines of text on pages reaching 72 × 50 cm, and the pages of the so-called Baysonghur Qur'ān measure 177 × 100 cm. The latter has been related to an anecdote recorded by Qāḍī Aḥmad, showing Tīmūr despising a miniature Qur'ān written by a calligrapher who, a few months later, came back with a Qur'ān so huge that it had to be carried on a cart. In Mamlūk Egypt, a number of very large single-volume Qur'āns — they usually measure about 100 cm high or more — were ordered for the mosques by wealthy patrons. The use of multi-volume qur'ānic manuscripts is also better documented: those produced for sultans or emirs were part of the stipulations of the documents of religious endowments *(waqfiyya)* they established in Cairo. The texts of these legal documents show that readers were appointed for daily recitation of the *juz'*; a keeper in charge of the manuscripts would also distribute them among the readers. Rashīd al-Dīn's provisions for his own tomb in Tabrīz included qur'ānic reading by three persons.

In the fourth/tenth century, some of the manuscripts begin to include "scientific information" about the text itself. Previously, such information had been limited to the sūra titles and possibly to their verse count. Now, on double page illuminations, global data about the text and its various components (sūras, verses, words, letters, and so on) are available. At the same time, concordances (in fact, methodical repertories of verse endings) often register an increasing wealth of information for each sūra: for example, the various verse counts and the relative position within the revelation. Together with the title, this information, which may also have been available in contemporary works of exegesis *(tafsīr),* found its way into qur'ānic manuscripts possibly during the fifth/eleventh century. As far as we know, Qur'āns with alternative readings (see READINGS OF THE QUR'ĀN) were produced during the sixth/twelfth century: The Nasser D. Khalili Collection of Islamic Art Qur 572 was provided in 582/1186 with abbreviations in red within the text and notes in the margins giving information about the correct recitation of the text and its variants. At the end of the manuscript, the qur'ānic text is followed by a series of short pamphlets on subjects like the recitation of the Qur'ān, the authorized readings (here, the Ten) as well as the differences in verse counts according to the various schools or the chronology of the revelations. This tradition of "scientific" Qur'āns, which were probably used for teaching purposes or as memoranda for scholars, was maintained over the centuries — as shown by the manuscript Bibliothèque nationale de France, BNF Arabe 448, dated 979/1572, which contains such information.

Qur'āns with interlinear translation were probably not meant for the same audience, although the situation is not always completely clear with respect to qur'ānic commentaries *(tafsīr),* which sometimes look like qur'ānic manuscripts. Assessing the date of the introduction of interlinear translations proves to be difficult: it is sometimes hard to be certain about the contemporaneousness of the qur'ānic text and translation — which latter is, *de facto,* an addition. In many — but not all — instances, the page layout is planned so as to leave room for the interlinear translation. Among the earliest dated manuscripts of this group are Mashhad, Āsitān-i Quds 464 (translation into Persian, dated 584/1188) and Türk Islâm Eserleri Müzesi, TIEM 73 (translation into eastern Turkish, dated 734/1333-4). Qurʾāns with marginal *tafsīr* can also be mentioned here: they were not necessarily meant for scholars, and they also often include an interlinear translation (usually below the line, rarely above it). Most seem to have been written in Iran and India after the tenth/sixteenth century, and the Persian commentary is written in the margins according to a carefully planned page layout. Qurʾānic manuscripts copied in India in Biḥārī script during the ninth/fifteenth century and provided with commentaries written in a more casual manner are among the early instances of the integration of such texts into qurʾānic manuscripts (see King Faisal Centre, Riyadh 2825). Commentaries added to a Qurʾān well after it had been written are clearly quite another case.

The manuscripts of the Qurʾān very often also contain other texts. As stated above, there are early examples of literature related to the correct reading of the text, as well as indications of its components (the number of sūras, verses, letters, etc.). Often at the end of the Qurʾān, there is the prayer that is recited upon the completion of the reading/reciting of the text. Its length and appearance vary: in luxury copies, it is written on a double page in gold letters, within an illuminated frame (see, for instance, Chester Beatty Library, CBL 1544 or Museum für Islamische Kunst, Inv. Nr. I. 42/68). Other prayers are also found in this position: in the manuscript at the Bibliothèque nationale de France, BNF Arabe 448, one of the earliest attributed to al-Ghazālī (d. 505/1111), the prayer is adapted for magical operations (see MAGIC); a second prayer, which aids in falling asleep, is also provided. Other texts are also related to the Qurʾān, like the various divination formulas *(fāl-nāma)* found in numerous manuscripts (see Bibliothèque nationale de France, BNF Arabe 418; see Fig. VII).

The qurʾānic codex in the western Islamic world and in west Africa

In the handwritten tradition of the Qurʾān, regional developments can be recognized but nowhere do they seem so pronounced as in the western Islamic world. The first qurʾānic codices in Maghribī script were written as early as the end of the fourth/tenth century, but further study of the Qayrawān collection might show that distinctive Maghribī features — i.e. script, decoration, but also techniques — were already present at an earlier stage. The earliest fragments are written on parchment, a material which remained in use until the eighth/fourteenth century. They are of the oblong format, although most Maghribī Qurʾāns are in a square format reminiscent of that used for a group of manuscripts of the second/eighth century. This square shape is found mainly in copies written on vellum, but small Qurʾāns of the thirteenth/nineteenth century written on paper still preserve this peculiar format (see The Nasser D. Khalili Collection of Islamic Art Qur 434). Nevertheless, when paper became the material commonly used for copies of the Qurʾān, the manuscripts as a whole changed to the vertical format.

The script has many varieties, a small hand commonly known as Andalusī being used for single-volume Qurʾāns; larger scripts are found in multi-volume manuscripts. For a long time, the vowels retained the red color which was the rule in early Qurʾāns; dots were still in use on the earliest Maghribī copies, but in the fifth/eleventh century the modern signs became the rule. For an extended period, dots were also used for the *hamza* (yellow; see Bibliothèque nationale de France, BNF Arabe 576, dated 1195/1781) and sometimes for the *waṣla* (green); other orthoepics, with their modern shape, are in blue (or sometimes in red).

Illuminations were produced over a long period of time according to patterns, some of which were already in use during the fourth/tenth century; in this respect, geometry played a major role with full page illuminations, and the inscriptions were only exceptionally integrated into the illuminated opening pages (see Istanbul University Library A 6754). Not infrequently, the text was followed by an illuminated page containing a prayer or a colophon written within a frame in a script very different from that of the qur'ānic text itself (see Bibliothèque nationale de France, BNF Arabe 385; see Fig. v). Gold and silver were also used in copying the text itself: Bibliothèque nationale, Smith-Lesouëf 217 contains a few folios of a delicate example of Maghribī chrysography, and a five-volume Qur'ān was written with silver ink on paper dyed purple (Bibliothèque nationale, BNF Arabe 389-392 are four such folios). The manufacture of dyed papers for qur'ānic manuscripts continued for some time, a fact to which some manuscripts on blue and green paper bear witness (see Bibliothèque Générale et Archives, BGA D 1304).

The large Qur'ān tradition was alive in the western Islamic world as shown by the above-mentioned "Nurse's Qur'ān" and by two volumes now in Istanbul (Türk Islâm Eserleri Müzesi, TIEM 359 and 360, 52 × 55 cm): their 994 remaining folios, with seven lines to the page (one line is roughly 6.5 cm high) and their richly illuminated sūra titles indicate that a colossal investment was needed to carry out this project.

Qur'ānic manuscripts in Sūdānī script are only known in recent times — from the second half of the eleventh/seventeenth century onwards. The Sūdānī is reminiscent of Maghribī scripts and is rather conservative. The vowels are often in red, the *hamza* being indicated by a yellow dot. Illuminations are usually geometrical and seem to rely only on colors — gold has so far not been reported. The beginning of the Qur'ān is often highlighted with a larger ornament in the shape of a frame; on top of it, outside the frame, there is sometimes the *basmala* (q.v.) and also the *taṣliya*. In other manuscripts, the ornament separates the first sūra from the second one. Other larger illuminations are usually found at the beginning of the second half of the Qur'ān (which in Sūdānī tradition is equivalent to Q 19:1), but also, in addition to that, at the beginning of the second and fourth quarters (see, for instance, Leeds University Library, Arabic ms. 301). Even if the divisions into seven and sixty parts *(ḥizb),* as well as the subdivisions of the latter into eight sections, are frequently indicated in the margins, in this handwritten tradition, the four parts are evidently of greater importance.

These qur'ānic manuscripts are also set apart by their traditional binding: the flap is oversized — its extremity almost reaching the back of the volume when it is closed — and terminates with a leather thong that can be rolled several times around the book in order to keep it closed. Moreover, in a number of cases the manuscript was provided with a leather pouch (in those instances in which it is missing, it may have been lost), which was intended as an external protection for the Qur'ān. These peculiarities may be related to another feature of Sūdānī manuscripts, namely the fact that they were written on bi-folios or even folios that were left loose; with neither quires nor sewing, a very protective binding was the only solution against the folios being lost or mixed up.

Later developments

With the exception of the *juz'* (thirtieth) and the *ḥizb* (sixtieth), some of the divisions of the text into parts of identical size fell into disuse and were only rarely indicated in the margins of single-volume Qur'āns. Sets of four or seven volumes became rarer, even if some examples could still be found: a seven-part Qur'ān was written in India by the end of the twelfth/eighteenth century (The Nasser D. Khalili Collection of Islamic Art Qur 70), while four-volume sets are known in the Maghrib during the same period (see Bibliothèque nationale de France, BNF Arabe 586 or 6989). In contrast, the *juz'* became more important for organizing the text, even in single-volume Qur'āns. As early as the beginning of the ninth/fifteenth century, a Qur'ān in Biḥārī script in one volume is distinguished by the use of developed illumination in the margins of each opening corresponding to the beginning of a *juz'* (Leiden University Library Or. 18320, dated 811/1408-9), a practice which became common in later Iranian deluxe Qur'āns (see Chester Beatty Library, CBL 1542 or Staatsbibliothek, SB 10450). In less expensive copies only the middle of the text is indicated in this way (Bibliothèque nationale, BNF Arabe 418 or Chester Beatty Library, CBL 1544). Qur'ān sets in thirty volumes are plentiful, ranging from the more modest to gorgeous ones, and can be found from the Maghrib to China. This evolution may possibly be connected to a wider practice of Qur'ān reading. Other elements point in the same direction: in Iran, and also in India, according to historical records, copyists used a minute script in order to fit each *juz'* to the space available on a double page; the reader wishing to read a section of the text each day, in order to complete the reading within one month, thus had the daily reading in a concise format (for instance Bayerische Staatsbibliothek, BSB Cod. arab. 1118; see Fig. VIII). There are even instances of Qur'āns in the so-called *ghubār* script written on two pages, each being divided into fifteen areas corresponding to the *juz'* (see Sotheby's sale L00502, 10 October 2000, lot 26).

The *juz'* was evidently important in the religious customs, but also proved to be an extraordinary tool for the more efficient copying of the sacred text. Early in the twelfth/eighteenth century, Ottoman copyists apparently reached an optimal calibration of the Qur'ān and found a way of matching the *juz'* with the kind of quire they were commonly using, namely the classical ten folios quire. It followed from this that the subdivisions of the *juz'* matched a definite amount of folios. The clever use of the possibilities of extension or contraction of the Arabic script even resulted in every page finishing with a verse ending: hence the name *āyāt ber-kenār* for these Qur'āns written with fifteen lines to the page in a small format, on ca. 300 folios (that is, thirty quires of ten folios). It was perhaps a step towards a more efficient production process — to some extent reminiscent of similar moves in late medieval Europe, when the printing press was threatening the traditional book production. Illumination also became standardized to some extent, with a double opening page containing sūra 1 and the beginning of sūra 2, gilded frame for the text, floral markers for the *juz'*, and so forth. This presentation was highly successful, and modern printed editions still follow this model.

This development is certainly behind the further elaboration of the qur'ānic text. It was probably noticed at about the same time that the same words/groups of words appeared in almost the same position on every opening. While keeping the text division previously described, some copyists succeeded in moving those words or groups so that they appeared on both pages of every opening on the same line and in a symmetrical position, highlighted in red ink. In the case of Q 26, whole verses were treated in this fashion. Attempts to trace this peculiar page layout back to specific milieus or to speculations on the qur'ānic text have so far been unsuccessful. Its diffusion was not restricted to the Ottoman empire (Türk Islâm Eserleri Müzesi, TIEM 469): it was also known in the Maghrib, where Ottoman influence was felt (National Library, NL 14.246, in Tunis).

Some manuscripts contain only selected parts of the Qur'ān. The excerpts are usually chosen because they may be recited during a prayer, but the choice is not always so simple to explain, as shown by a copy of Sūrat al-Fatḥ done in a highly sophisticated style (Topkapı Sarayı Museum, TKS R. 18, dated 909/1503). In the Ottoman empire, these small volumes were called *En'am,* since they usually begin with an extract from Q 6 (Sūrat al-An'ām), often following the Fātiḥa; the selection may vary but in many cases ends with the last sūras. Q 36 is also popular and is sometimes the first of the volume. In Iran and India, this sūra appears as the first in qur'ānic selections (followed by Q 48, 56, 67 and 78; see The Nasser D. Khalili Collection of Islamic Art Qur 280). Obviously, the choice was not restricted to these sūras, and a survey of this material would certainly give some insights into Muslim piety of later centuries — most of the manuscripts so far published seem to date from the tenth/sixteenth century or later.

Production and conservation

Matters of manuscript production are still largely ignored by scholars, as are the economic aspects. Is it lawful to sell or buy a Qur'ān? Is it permissible to copy the qur'ānic text for a fee? The debate about these issues arose at an early date and was quickly answered in the affirmative. Many anecdotes are told about the high prices commanded by copies written by famous calligraphers. But the cost of a more ordinary Qur'ān remains obscure, as does the importance of the diffusion of the qur'ānic manuscripts in the Islamic lands. For more recent times, a study of the archives and of what remains of the production may provide limited though very valuable answers, but it seems difficult to determine how much access the Muslims of the eleventh/seventeenth century, for instance, had to a copy of their sacred text. How much time was needed to copy a Qur'ān? Information found in the manuscripts themselves is scattered but could give more concrete data: according to the colophons of the *juz'* of an Egyptian Qur'ān dated 1175/1751, the copyist was writing a *juz'* in eight days (Bibliothèque nationale de France, BNF Arabe 515). Some Ottoman copyists indicate the number of Qur'āns they had so far transcribed.

The price of the manuscripts was high, and they were usually used over a long period of time. They were treated with reverence, and when they fell into decay special care had to be taken about their fate. Some scholars considered that the parchment or the paper could be reused for the preparation of the boards of a Qur'ān binding, while others insisted that the manuscript should be buried or burned. There are also instances of deposits, as in Qayrawān, Cairo or Damascus, which are close to the Jewish practice of the genizah.

Attempts have been made to relate the manuscripts to specific milieus (Whelan, Writing the word) or to correlate a change in the script with religious developments

(Tabbaa, The transformation), but the lack of comprehensive surveys of the material hampers such approaches. As a result, we still know too little about the role played by qur'ānic manuscripts within the Islamic world until a comparatively late period.

François Déroche

Bibliography

N. Abbott, Arabic paleography, in *Ars islamica* 8 (1941), 67-104; id., An Arabic-Persian wooden kur'anic manuscript from the Royal Library of Shah Husain Safawi I, 1105-35 H., in *Ars islamica* 5 (1938), 89-94; id., The contribution of Ibn Muklah to the North-Arabic script, in *American journal of Semitic languages and literatures* 56 (1939), 70-83; id., *The rise of the north Arabic script and its kur'anic development. With a full description of the Kur'an manuscripts in the Oriental Institute,* Chicago 1939; M. Amari, Bibliographie primitive du Coran, in G. Salvo Cosso (ed.), *Centenario della nascita di Michele Amari,* 2 vols., Palermo 1910, i, 1-22; M. Anastassiadou, Livres et "bibliothèques" dans les inventaires après décès de Salonique au XIXe siècle, in F. Hitzel (ed.), Livres et lecture dans le monde ottoman, in *REMMM* 87-8 (1999), 111-41; A.J. Arberry, *The Koran illuminated. A handlist of Korans in the Chester Beatty Library,* Dublin 1967; id., A Koran in 'Persian' kufic, in *Oriental College magazine* 40 (1964), 9-16; S. Aykoç, F. Çağman and N. Tapan, *The Anatolian civilisations III. Seljuk/Ottoman,* Istanbul 1983; M. Bayani, A. Contadini and T. Stanley, *The decorated word. Qur'āns of the 17th to 19th centuries,* London 1999; A.D.H. Bivar, The Arabic calligraphy of west Africa, in *African language review* 7 (1968), 3-15; id., A dated Koran from Bornu, in *Nigeria magazine* 65 (June 1960), 199-205; J.M. Bloom, The Blue Koran. An early Fatimid kufic manuscript from the Maghrib, in F. Déroche (ed.), *Les manuscrits du Moyen-Orient,* Istanbul/Paris 1989, 95-9; G. Bosch, J. Carswell and G. Petherbridge, *Islamic bindings and bookmaking,* Chicago 1981; H.-C. von Bothmer, Architekturbilder im Koran. Eine Prachthandschrift der Umayyadenzeit aus dem Yemen, in *Pantheon* 45 (1987), 4-20; id., Frühislamische Koran-Illuminationen, in *Kunst und Antiquitäten* 1 (1986), 22-33; id., Masterworks of Islamic book art. Koranic calligraphy and illumination in the manuscripts found in the Great Mosque in Sanaa, in W. Daum (ed.), *Yemen. 3000 years of art and civilization in Arabia Felix,* Innsbruck 1988, 178-81, 185-7; id., Ein seltenes Beispiel für die ornamentale Verwendung der Schrift in frühen Koranhandschriften. Die Fragmentgruppe Inv. Nr. 17-15.3 im 'Haus der Handschriften' in Sanaa, in H.-W. Stork, C. Gerhardt and A. Thomas (eds.), *Ars et Ecclesia. Festschrift für Franz J. Ronig zum 60. Geburtstag,* Trier 1989, 45-67; A. Brockett, Aspects of the physical transmission of the Qur'ān in 19th century Sudan. Script, decoration, binding and paper, in *Manuscripts of the Middle East* 2 (1987), 45-67; J. Burton, Muṣḥaf, in *EI*², vii, 668-9; K. Dachs et al., *Das Buch im Orient. Handschriften und kostbare Drucke aus zwei Jahrtausenden,* Wiesbaden 1982; Dār al-Āthār al-Islāmiyya, *Maṣāḥif Ṣan'ā',* Kuwait 1985; U. Derman, Hat, in *Sabanci Koleksiyonu,* Istanbul 1995, 12-179; id., Une sourate coranique calligraphiée au XVIe s. en caractères coufiques laqués, in F. Déroche (ed.), *Les manuscrits du Moyen-Orient,* Istanbul/Paris 1989, 113; F. Déroche, *The Abbasid tradition. Qur'āns of the 8th to the 10th centuries A.D.,* London 1992; id., A propos d'une série de manuscrits coraniques anciens, in F. Déroche (ed.), *Les manuscrits du Moyen-Orient,* Istanbul/Paris 1989, 101-11; id., *Catalogue des manuscrits arabes,* 2e partie, I/1. *Les manuscrits du Coran. Aux origines de la calligraphie coranique,* Paris 1983; id., *Catalogue des manuscrits arabes,* 2e partie, I/2. *Les manuscrits du Coran. Du Maghreb à l'Insulinde,* Paris 1985; id., Coran, couleur et calligraphie, in *I primi sessanta anni di scuola. Studi dedicati dagli amici a S. Noja Noseda nello 65° compleanno. 7 luglio 1996,* Lesa: Fondazione Ferni Noja Noseda (forthcoming); id., Les manuscrits arabes datés du IIIe/IXe siècle, in *REI* 55-7 (1987-9), 343-79; id., The Ottoman roots of a Tunisian calligrapher's 'tour de force', in Z. Yasa-Yaman (ed.), *Sanatta etkileşim/Interactions in art,* Ankara 2000, 106-9; id., Quelques reliures médiévales de provenance damascaine, in *REI* 54 (1986), 85-99; id., The Qur'ān of Amāǧūr, in *Manuscripts of the Middle East* 5 (1990-1), 59-66; id., Une reliure du Ve/XIe siècle, in *Nouvelles des manuscrits du Moyen Orient* 4 (1995), 2-8; F. Déroche and A. von Gladiss, *Buchkunst zur Ehre Allāhs. Der Prachtkoran im Museum für Islamische Kunst,* Berlin 1999; F. Déroche and S. Noja Noseda (eds.), *Sources de la transmission du texte coranique. I. Les manuscrits du style hiǧāzī. vol. i. Le manuscrit arabe 328 (a) de la Bibliothèque nationale de France,* Lesa 1998; *vol. ii. Le manuscrit or. 2165 (f. 1 a 61) de la British Library,* Lesa 2001 (both are with a CD-rom); A. Dessus Lamare, Le muṣḥaf de la mosquée de Cordoue et son mobilier mécanique, in *JA* 230 (1938), 551-75; U. Dreibholz, Some aspects of early Islamic bookbindings from the Great Mosque of Sana'a, Yemen, in F. Déroche and F. Richard (eds.), *Scribes et manuscrits du Moyen-Orient,* Paris 1997, 16-34; Y. Dutton, An early *muṣḥaf* according to the reading of Ibn ʿĀmir, in *Journal of qurʾanic studies* 3 (2001), 71-89 (on Paris BN Arabe 328a); id., Red dots, green dots, yellow dots and blue. Some reflections on the vocalization of early qurʾānic manuscripts. Part 1, in *Journal of qurʾanic studies* 1 (1999), 115-40; and Part 2, in *Journal of qurʾanic studies* 2 (2000), 1-24; J. Eckmann, *Middle Turkic glosses of the Rylands interlinear Koran translation*, Budapest 1976; A. Ersoy, *Türk tezhip sanatı*, Istanbul 1988; R. Ettinghausen, Manuscript illumination, in A.U. Pope and Ph. Ackerman (eds.), *A survey of Persian art from prehistoric times to the present*, 9 vols., London 1938, iii, 1937-74; M.A. Fikrat, *Fihrist-e nasakh-e khattī-ye Qorʾānhā-ye mutarjam-e ketābkhāne-ye markazī-ye āstān-e Qods-e Razavī [A catalogue of the manuscripts of the holy Qurʾān in translation]*, Mashhad 1985; A. Golčin Maʿani, *Rāhnomā-ye Gangīne-ye Qorʾān*, Mashhad 1969; R. Gottheil, An illustrated copy of the Koran, in *REI* 5 (1931), 21-4; B. Gray, The monumental Qurʾāns of the Il-khanid and Mamluk ateliers of the first quarter of the fourteenth century (eighth century H.), in *RSO* 59 (1985), 135-46; A. Grohmann, The problem of dating early Qurʾāns, in *Der Islam* 33 (1958), 213-31; *The holy Qurʾān in manuscript*, Jeddah 1991; al-Harawī, ʿAlī b. Abī b. Bakr, *Kitāb al-Ishārāt ilā maʿarifat al-ziyārāt*, ed. J. Sourdel-Thomine, Damascus 1953; Ibn al-Nadīm, *Fihrist*, ed. Tajaddud; Ibn al-Nadīm-Dodge; al-Jahshiyārī, Muḥammad b. ʿAbdūs, *Kitāb al-Wuzarāʾ wa-l-kuttāb*, ed. H. von Mzik, Leipzig 1926 (facsimile ed.); part. trans. J. Latz, *Das Buch der Wezire und Staatssekretäre von Ibn ʿAbdus al-Gahsiyari*, Walldorf, Hessen 1958; D. James, *After Timur. Qurʾāns of the 15th and 16th centuries*, London 1992; id., *Master scribes. Qurʾāns from the 11th to the 14th centuries*, London 1992; id., *Qurʾāns and bindings from the Chester Beatty Library. A facsimile exhibition*, London 1980; id., *Qurʾāns of the Mamlūks*, London 1988; Jeffery, *Materials;* al-Kindī, ʿAbd al-Masīḥ, *Risāla*, ed. A. Tien, London 1885; King Faisal Center for Research and Islamic Studies, *Arabic calligraphy in manuscripts/al-Khaṭṭ al-ʿarabī min khilāl al-makhṭūṭāt*, Riyadh 1986; J. Lemaistre (ed.), *Splendeur et majesté. Corans de la Bibliothèque nationale*, Paris 1987; G. Levi della Vida, *Frammenti coranici in carattere cufico nella Biblioteca Vaticana*, Vatican 1947; M. Lings, Andalusian Qorans, in *British Museum quarterly* 24 (1961-2), 94-6; id., *The qurʾānic art of calligraphy and illumination*, London 1976; id. and Y.H. Safadi, *The Qurʾān*, London 1976; H. Loebenstein, *Koranfragmente auf Pergament aus der Papyrussammlung der Österreichischen Nationalbibliothek*, 2 vols., Vienna 1982; al-Maqqarī, Aḥmad b. Muḥammad, *Nafḥ al-ṭīb*, 2 vols., Leiden 1855-61; G. Marçais and L. Poinssot, *Objets kairouanais, IXe au XIIIe siècle. Reliures, verreries, cuivres et bronzes, bijoux, fasc.* 1, Tunis/Paris 1948; A. Mingana and A.S. Lewis, *Leaves from three ancient Qurʾāns possibly pre-ʿOthmanic. With a list of their variants*, Cambridge 1914; B. Moritz, *Arabic palæography. A collection of Arabic texts from the first century of the hidjra till the year 1000*, Cairo/Leipzig 1905; Ṣ. al-Munajjid, *Dirāsāt fī taʾrīkh al-khaṭṭ al-ʿarabī mundhu bidāyatihi ilā nihāyat al-ʿaṣr al-umawī*, Beirut [1971]; Fr. *Études de palaeographie arabe*, Beirut 1972; Musée du Petit Palais (Paris, France), *De Carthage à Kairouan, 2000 ans d'art et d'histoire en Tunisie*, Paris 1983; N. Nebes (ed.), *Orientalische Buchkunst in Gotha*, Gotha 1997; Nöldeke, *GQ*, iii, 249-74; Y.A. Pétrosyan, *De Bagdad à Ispahan. Manuscrits islamiques de la Filiale de Saint-Pétersbourg de l'Institut d'études orientales, Académie des Sciences de Russie*, Paris 1994; G.-R. Puin, Methods of research on qurʾānic manuscripts. A few ideas, in Dār al-Āthār al-Islāmiyya, *Maṣāḥif Ṣanʿāʾ*, Kuwait 1985, 9-17; id., Observations on early Qurʾān manuscripts in Ṣanʿāʾ, in Wild, *Text*, 107-11; H. Rebhan and W. Riesterer, *Prachtkorane aus tausend Jahren. Handschriften aus dem Bestand der Bayerischen Staatsbibliothek München*, Munich 1998; E. Rezvan, The Qurʾān and its world: VI. Emergence of the canon. The struggle for uniformity, in *Manuscripta orientalia* 4 (1998), 13-54; id., Yet another "ʿUthmānic Qurʾān.' On the history of Manuscript E20 from the St. Petersburg Branch of the Institute of Oriental Studies, in *Manuscripta orientalia* 6 (2000), 49-68; P. Ricard, Reliures marocaines du XIIIe siècle. Notes sur des spécimens d'époque et de tradition almohades, in *Hespéris* 17 (1933), 109-27; D.S. Rice, *The unique Ibn al-Bawwāb manuscript in the Chester Beatty Library*, Dublin 1955; B. Robinson et al., *Islamic painting and the arts of the book*, London 1976; J.M. Rogers, *L'empire des sultans. L'art ottoman dans la collection de Nasser D. Khalili*, Geneva 1995; J. Sadan, Genizah and genizah-like practices in Islamic and Jewish traditions. Customs concerning the disposal of worn-out sacred books in the Middle Ages, according to an Ottoman source, in *BO* 43 (1986), 36-58; Y.H. Safadi, *Islamic calligraphy*, London 1978; B. Saint Laurent, The identification of a magnificent Koran manuscript, in F. Déroche (ed.), *Les manuscrits du Moyen-Orient*, Istanbul/Paris 1989, 115-24; A.N. Shebunin, The kūfic Qurʾān in the Khedivial library in Cairo, in *Zapisok Otdvlenia Imperatorskogo russkogo arkheologicheskogo obshchestva* 14 (1902), 105-7 (in Russian); id., The kūfic Qurʾān of the Public Imperial Library in Saint-Petersburg, in *Zapisok Otdvlenia Imperatorskogo russkogo arkheologicheskogo obshchestva* 6 (1891), 69-133 (in Russian); T. Stanley, *The Qurʾān and calligraphy. A selection of fine manuscript material*, London n.d.; A. Stoilova and Z. Ivanova, *The holy Qurʾān through the centuries. A catalogue of the exhibition of manuscripts and printed editions preserved in the SS Cyril and Methodius National Library,* Sofia 1995; Y. Tabbaa, The transformation of Arabic writing. Part I. Qurʾānic calligraphy, in *Ars orientalis* 21 (1991), 119-48; Z. Tanındı, 13-14. Yüzyılda yazılmış Kurʾanlarin Kanuni dönemde yenilenmesi, in *Topkapı Sarayı Müzesi* 1 (1986), 140-52; A. Welch and S.C. Welch, *Arts of the Islamic book. The collection of Prince Sadruddin Aga Khan,* Ithaca 1982; E. Whelan, Writing the word of God. I, in *Ars orientalis* 20 (1990), 113-47; J.-J. Witkam, Manuscripts & manuscripts. [6] Qurʾān fragments from Dawrān (Yemen), in *Manuscripts of the Middle East* 4 (1989), 154-74; E. Wright, An Indian Qurʾān and its 14th-century model, in *Oriental art* 42 (1996-7), 8-12.

Markets

Public places in which commercial transactions occur. The term *aswāq,* "markets," occurs in two places in the Qurʾān, but is used incidentally to indicate that the prophets were men who shared the same nature as those they were sent to teach: "What sort of a messenger is this who eats food and walks through the markets?" (Q 25:7); "And the messengers whom we sent before you all ate food and walked through the markets" (Q 25:20; see PROPHETS AND PROPHETHOOD; FOOD AND DRINK; MESSENGER; IMPECCABILITY). The Qurʾān makes no reference to any particular market (see CITY; GEOGRAPHY; PRE-ISLAMIC ARABIA AND THE QURʾĀN). This is despite the fact that there were some very large markets in Arabia both during the pre-Islamic period and during the time of the revelation of the Qurʾān (see REVELATION AND INSPIRATION) and with which Muḥammad would have been very familiar. Aside from the famous market of ʿUkāẓ near Mecca (q.v.) and that of Medina (q.v.), there was the market of al-Ḥajar which was the biggest and richest oasis on the peninsula, that of al-Ḥīra, the capital of the Lakhmids and a vital caravan city between Persia and Arabia, and Dūmat al-Jandal, an oasis town on the direct route between Medina and Damascus and one of the principal markets of northern Arabia. The birthplace of the Qurʾān was initially Mecca and its second home was Medina, both prosperous commercial centers (but cf. P. Crone, *Meccan trade,* 133-48). That the Qurʾān was initially addressed to people who were engaged in commercial activities is clearly reflected in its ideas and language (see LANGUAGE OF THE QURʾĀN; LITERARY STRUCTURES OF THE QURʾĀN; OCCASIONS OF REVELATION). Only a few examples out of many will be given here.

The commercial language of the Qurʾān is not only used in illustrative metaphors but also to express fundamental points of doctrine (see METAPHOR; THEOLOGY AND THE QURʾĀN). Thus, the last judgment (q.v.) is a reckoning or an accounting: "Then he that will be given his record *(kitāb)* in his right hand will say, 'Here, read my record' " (Q 69:19; see also Q 69:25); "Then he who is given his record in his right hand, soon will his account be taken by an easy reckoning" (*ḥisāb,* Q 84:7-8; see also Q 84:10 f.; see RECORD OF HUMAN ACTIONS; LEFT HAND AND RIGHT HAND). It is at this time that human actions will be weighed: "We shall set up scales of justice for the day of judgment" (Q 21:47; see WEIGHTS AND MEASURES; JUSTICE AND INJUSTICE); "Then he whose balance [of good deeds] will be found heavy, will be in a life of good pleasure and satisfaction" (*ʿīshatin rāḍiyatin,* Q 101:6-7; see also Q 7:8-9).

The Qurʾān often makes use of the concept of trade *(tijāra).* Occasionally the meaning is prosaic: "Let there be among you traffic and trade *(tijāra)* by mutual goodwill" (Q 4:29). But more usually the meaning is metaphorical: "There are those who have bartered guidance for error (q.v.); but their trade is profitless" (Q 2:16); "Those who rehearse the book (q.v.) of God, establish regular prayer (q.v.; *al-ṣalāt*) and send in charity (see ALMSGIVING) out of what we have provided for them, secretly and openly, hope for a trade that will never fail" (Q 35:29; see also Q 61:10). Similarly, the concepts of buying and selling are often used metaphorically, for example: "God has purchased from the believers their persons and their goods; for theirs in return is the garden (q.v.) of paradise" (q.v.; Q 9:111; see BELIEF AND UNBELIEF; FAITH; REWARD AND PUNISHMENT). Selling is used to express renouncing God's revelation: "Do not sell the covenant (q.v.) of God for a miserable price" (Q 16:95; see also Q 2:41; 3:77); "These are the people who buy the life (q.v.) of this world at the price of the hereafter" (Q 2:86; see ESCHATOLOGY); "Miserable is the price for which they have sold their souls" (Q 2:90; see also Q 2:175); "Those who purchase unbelief at the price of faith" (Q 3:177); "The signs (q.v.) of God have they sold for a miserable price" (Q 9:9).

In several places the Qur'ān stresses the need to give fair weight and measure: "My people, give just weight and measure" (Q 11:85); "Give weight with justice" (Q 55:9); "Woe to those that deal in fraud, those who when they have to receive by measure from people exact full measure, but when they have to give by measure or weigh for them, give less than is due" (Q 83:1-3; see also Q 6:152; 17:35).

Given Muḥammad's intimate concern with commercial affairs, it is perhaps not surprising that he is said to have been the first to appoint persons with jurisdiction over the markets (a post later to develop into that of the Islamic market inspector, the *muḥtasib*), who were to ensure the orderly and fair running of business transactions. He is reported to have employed Saʿīd b. Saʿīd b. al-ʿĀṣ as inspector of the market of Medina sometime after the conquest of Mecca (8/630; Ibn ʿAbd al-Barr, *Istīʿāb*, ii, 621). Samrāʾ bint Nuhayk al-Asadiyya, a contemporary of the Prophet, is mentioned as frequenting the market of Medina, asking people to behave well there (ibid., iv, 183). It is likewise reported that Muḥammad enjoined ʿAlī b. Abī Ṭālib (q.v.) to "order good and forbid evil" (*al-amr bi-l-maʿrūf wa-l-nahī ʿan al-munkar;* Sergeant, A Zaidi manual, 11-2; see GOOD AND EVIL) — a qur'ānic injunction which eventually became synonymous with the *muḥtasib*'s duties — and that ʿAlī used to go round the markets every morning like a *muḥtasib*, ordering the merchants to give fair measure. See also SELLING AND BUYING.

Ronald Paul Buckley

Bibliography
Primary: Ibn ʿAbd al-Barr al-Qurṭūbī, *al-Istīʿāb fī maʿrifat al-aṣḥāb*, Cairo n.d.
Secondary: S. al-Afghānī, *Aswāq al-ʿArab fī l-Jāhiliyya wa-l-Islām*, Damascus 1960, repr. Cairo 1993; Th. Bianquis and P. Guichard, Sūḳ. 1. In the traditional Arab world, in *EI²*, ix, 786-9; M. Cook, *Commanding right and forbidding wrong in Islamic thought*, New York 2000; P. Crone, *Meccan trade and the rise of Islam*, Princeton 1987; M.J. Kister, The market of the Prophet, in *JESHO* 8 (1965), 272-6; id., *Society and religion from Jahiliyya to Islam*, Aldershot 1990; id., *Studies in Jahiliyya and early Islam*, London 1980; A. Rippin, The commerce of eschatology, in S. Wild (ed.), *The Qurʾān as text*, Leiden 1996, 125-35; R.B. Sergeant, A Zaidi manual of Hisbah of the 3rd century (H), in id., *Studies in Islamic history and civilisation*, London 1981, vii, 1-34; C.C. Torrey, *The commercial-theological terms in the Koran*, Leiden 1892.

Marriage and Divorce

The social institution through which a man and a woman are joined in a social and legal dependence for the purpose of forming and maintaining a family (q.v.), and the regulated dissolution of such a union. Both marriage and divorce are legal issues extensively dealt with in the Qur'ān (see LAW AND THE QUR'ĀN). Marriage between a man and a woman is called *nikāḥ*. In most cases, the verb *nakaḥa*, "to marry," is used to denote men marrying women, but in one case, also women marrying men. Giving a woman away in marriage is *ankaḥa* when there is mention of a father or guardian (see GUARDIANSHIP), *zawwaja* when God is mentioned. The marriage partners are both called *zawj* (pl. *azwāj*), the husband also *baʿl* (pl. *buʿūla*). Divorce is called *ṭalāq;* the corresponding verb *ṭallaqa,* "to divorce," always occurs with men as the subject of the verb.

Marriage

Aims of marriage

(1) In the Qurʾān, marriage is, first of all, the favored institution for legitimate sexual intercourse between a man and woman (the secondary institution being concubinage; see CONCUBINES; SEX AND SEXUALITY). This is obvious from the different rules concerning marriage as well as behavior prescribed in dealing with the other sex (see SOCIAL INTERACTIONS), condemnation and punishment of illegal sexual intercourse (see ADULTERY AND FORNICATION) and the fact that even partnership between men and women in paradise (q.v.) is thought to have the form of marriage (e.g. Q 2:25; 44:54). Chastity (q.v.) is one of the cardinal virtues demanded of Muslims (see VIRTUES AND VICES, COMMANDING AND FORBIDDING). To marry is therefore desirable for every member of the community of believers, even for slaves (Q 24:32; see SLAVES AND SLAVERY). (2) Marriage is a means to strengthen the relationship between different individuals and groups of the community (see SOCIAL RELATIONS), and the prohibition of intermarriage is a means to prevent relationships between certain individuals and groups (Q 2:221; 4:24-5; 5:5; 24:3, 26; 60:10; see COMMUNITY AND SOCIETY IN THE QURʾĀN). (3) Marriage is seen as a necessary institution to secure the reproduction of the community and to guarantee the offspring an effective upbringing (Q 4:1; 7:189; 16:72; 17:24; see CHILDREN). (4) The marriage relationship is the most elementary form of society, the nucleus which is thought to guarantee for its individual members a harmonious life because of the physical and mental support which husband and wife give each other (Q 30:21). (5) Marriage serves as an institution to support or protect female members of the community who have lost the backing of their family, such as orphans (q.v.) and widows (Q 4:3, 127; see WIDOW; WOMEN AND THE QURʾĀN).

Marriage partners

There are rules concerning the choice of partners, largely formulated from the perspective of Muslim men (see PATRIARCHY; GENDER; FEMINISM AND THE QURʾĀN). Certain groups of people are forbidden (q.v.), others permitted, the criteria being religion, relationship, social status and moral behavior (see PROHIBITED DEGREES). Forbidden are: heathens (polytheists; Q 2:221; 60:10; see POLYTHEISM AND ATHEISM); close blood relatives (see BLOOD AND BLOOD CLOT; KINSHIP); the corresponding milk (q.v.) relatives (see FOSTERAGE); close in-laws; previous partners of ascendants or descendants; two sisters at the same time (Q 4:22, 23; see SISTER); and fornicators or adulterers (the latter may, however, intermarry or marry heathens; Q 24:3, 26). The fact that heathens (see IDOLATRY AND IDOLATERS; BELIEF AND UNBELIEF) and adulterers are prohibited as marriage partners for chaste Muslims carries the consequence that existing marriages must be terminated if one of the spouses falls into such a category (Q 60:10). Permitted are: Muslims, women of the People of the Book (q.v.), the parallel cousins from among the close relatives and slaves (even for freemen and freewomen) provided they are chaste (Q 2:221; 4:24-5; 5:5; 24:32; 33:50).

Furthermore, the number of partners is mentioned in the Qurʾān: Men may marry up to four women at the same time, provided they think they are able to treat them equally (Q 4:3; for the syntactic problems of the verse cf. Motzki, Muḥṣanāt, 207-10). In view of the doubts which Q 4:129 expresses about an individual's ability to really meet this condition, some have argued that monogamy seems to be preferred to polygamy. Contrary to what Muslim commentaries claim (see EXEGESIS OF THE QURʾĀN: CLASSICAL AND MEDIEVAL), polygamy does not seem to have been a prevalent social custom in pre-Islamic Mecca (q.v.) and Medina (q.v.; cf. Ṭabarī, *Tafsīr*, vii, 534 ad Q 4:3; Stern, *Marriage*, 62, 70; see PRE-ISLAMIC ARABIA AND THE QURʾĀN). Q 4:3's injunction to marry more than one woman at the same time appears to have been prompted by special historical circumstances in Medina: the unfair treatment of female wards by their guardians. The Prophet is granted special consideration concerning the number of wives he might take (see WIVES OF THE PROPHET): originally, there was no limit for him, but at a certain moment in his career in Medina, he was forbidden to marry again (Q 33:50, 52; see OCCASIONS OF REVELATION).

The contraction of marriage

The Qurʾān presupposes that a marriage is preceded by a marriage proposal, called *khiṭba* (Q 2:235), which the suitor has to make to the woman's guardian. The guardian of the woman draws up the marriage contract *(ʿuqdat al-nikāḥ)* on her behalf and must ensure that it is fulfilled (see CONTRACTS AND ALLIANCES; BREAKING TRUSTS AND CONTRACTS). He is, therefore, called "the one who has the marriage contract in his hand" (Q 2:237). Although mediated, the marriage is considered a legal agreement concluded between the man and the woman herself, called a *mīthāq ghalīẓ*, "firm bond," in Q 4:21. An important element of the marriage contract is the bridewealth (q.v.), which becomes the bride's property. In Muḥammad's time, the bridewealth was sometimes fixed at the betrothal, sometimes later (Q 2:236-7). The marriage is not definitely concluded until its consummation, through which all legal consequences become effective. A prerequisite of the consummation of marriage is that the partners have reached the marriageable age (Q 4:6), which most exegetes equate with the beginning of puberty (*ḥulum, ḥayāḍ;* cf. Motzki, Volwassen, 56-8).

The legal consequences of marriage

By the marriage contract, sexual intercourse between the partners becomes legitimate and both are entitled to inherit from each other (Q 4:12; for the shares, see INHERITANCE). Additionally, each marriage partner has certain obligations: The wife is obliged to grant her husband sexual intercourse whenever he wishes except during her menstruation (q.v.), the time of her obligatory fasting (q.v.) and during the pilgrimage (q.v.; *ḥajj*, Q 2:187, 197, 222-3), and she must accept her husband's authority (q.v.; Q 2:228; 4:34). The husband is liable to give to his wife the bridewealth due to her, which remains exclusively her own property (q.v.), and to provide clothes, food and lodging for her and their joint children (Q 2:233, 240; see MAINTENANCE AND UPKEEP). The financial gifts that the woman receives are the prime reason for her marital obligations mentioned above (Q 4:34; see also GIFT-GIVING).

A special feature or effect of marriage is that it makes a slave woman "chaste" *(muḥṣana),* meaning that by a marriage to a Muslim (free or slave), sexual intercourse with others becomes prohibited for her (Q 4:25). Slaves are thus not necessarily considered to be chaste because they are deemed to be the property of their owners who can use them sexually, be it as concubines or by forcing them into prostitution (Q 24:33). Marriage curbs such power of the owner (see Motzki, Muḥṣanāt, 199-201).

A few early exegetes tried to find evidence in Q 4:24 for a form of marriage called *nikāḥ al-mutʿa,* "marriage of enjoyment," which differs considerably from the regular marriage described throughout the Qurʾān in that it is limited in time and legal consequences, and shows peculiarities which makes it appear close to prostitution (see TEMPORARY MARRIAGE). That such a type of marriage is meant in Q 4:24 is improbable, however, in view of the rules of marriage propagated by the Qurʾān as a whole (cf. Motzki, Muḥṣanāt, 201, 212; the subject is fully treated in Gribetz, *Strange bedfellows* and S. Haeri, *Law of desire*).

Divorce

Aims of divorce

According to the Qurʾān, divorce is a means by which the man purposely brings his marriage to an end — in contrast to the end of marriage by the death of one of the spouses. As described by the Qurʾān, marriage is intended to be long lasting and unbounded in time. This is suggested by labeling it a "firm bond" between a man and a woman and by the rules concerning divorce. The relation between the spouses should ideally be determined by love (q.v.) and understanding *(mawadda wa-raḥma,* Q 30:21; cf. 2:228) and important decisions concerning both should be made with mutual approval and consultation (Q 2:233). When this harmony does not develop, however, or fades away in the course of time, the Qurʾān allows or even advises spouses to bring the marriage to an end (Q 2:231), thus giving both individuals a chance for a new and perhaps happier relationship. This does not mean, however, that every tiny difference of opinion between the spouses should be solved by divorce. The Qurʾān admonishes the husband to treat his wife with equality, even if he does not love her (Q 4:19, 129); to forgive her when she had opposed him so that he had to discipline her (Q 4:34; see DISOBEDIENCE; FORGIVENESS; CHASTISEMENT AND PUNISHMENT; INSOLENCE AND OBSTINACY); and to try first to come to an agreement other than divorce (Q 4:129). If the spouses are not able to settle their dispute themselves, then the community is asked to intervene and to appoint two arbiters, one from each of the spouses' families, in order to mediate a reconciliation between the spouses (Q 4:35). There are, moreover, other measures to avert hasty divorces: First, there are two waiting periods of three months prescribed by the Qurʾān before the divorce is final (see WAITING PERIOD). These periods of physical separation between the spouses give the man the chance to rethink his decision and allow him to annul the divorce. Secondly, a man who, in a fit of anger, takes an oath not to have any sexual intercourse with his wife, is allowed a four-month period to break this oath which otherwise leads automatically to divorce (Q 2:226).

Types of divorce

In the Qurʾān, four types of divorce can be distinguished: two direct forms of divorce, *ṭalāq* and *ṭalāq* by *iftidāʾ,* and two procedures resulting in divorce, *īlāʾ (*or *ẓihār)* and *liʿān.*

(1) *Ṭalāq* is the declaration made by the husband to divorce his wife; it becomes

final only after his wife has completed three menstrual periods (or months), provided that the husband has not withdrawn his divorce in the meantime. He has the right to declare and withdraw a *ṭalāq* only twice. The wife does not have the right to divorce her husband in this fashion. The principal reason for this lack of equality is the bridewealth that the man would have given to his wife at marriage and that becomes her property. A divorce costs the man not only his wife but also the investment he has made to marry her. If the wife had the power to divorce, she would have power over his property, including herself. The husband may renounce his privilege by giving his wife the choice between divorce and continuation of marriage (Q 33:28; the Prophet is asked to do that), but he alone can declare her divorced. A definitive divorce has to be made public by declaring it before two witnesses (Q 65:2; see WITNESSING AND TESTIFYING). (2) The connection between bridewealth and divorce shows how it is possible for an unhappily married woman to receive a divorce from a husband who is not prepared to let her go generously: bargaining for it. The Qurʾān (Q 2:229) suggests this possibility through the term *iftadat,* "to ransom herself." (3) Q 2:226-7 and Q 58:2-4 deal with the case in which a man "swears his wife off," which means that he makes an oath (see OATHS) not to have sexual intercourse with her anymore. Such an oath is effective (although the *ẓihār* oath is disapproved of in the Qurʾān) and, if it is not broken in the course of the following four months, i.e. if the man does not resume conjugal intercourse, leads to divorce. (4) When a husband accuses his wife of adultery without being able to prove it by producing four witnesses, he must swear to the truth of his accusation four times and then call God's curse (q.v.) upon himself in case he is lying (see LIE). His wife escapes punishment by the same procedure if she swears that he is lying (Q 24:6-9). Since marriages between Muslims and adulterers are prohibited and the relationship between the spouses is irretrievably ruined by such an accusation, divorce seems to be the only logical consequence.

Legal consequences of divorce

Two sorts of consequences can be distinguished: those resulting from the declaration of divorce and those of the finalized divorce. If a menstruating woman is declared divorced after the consummation of the marriage, she must observe a waiting time *(ʿidda)* of three menstrual periods. A woman who is not menstruating must wait for an interval of three (lunar) months. During this time she may not remarry. If the woman realizes during this interval that she is pregnant, she must inform her husband. For a pregnant woman the waiting time is prolonged until childbirth (Q 2:228; 33:49; 65:1, 4). During the waiting months, the woman has the right to stay in the house in which she is living and her husband must provide for her (Q 2:241; 65:1, 6).

After divorce has been finalized, the man cannot remarry his divorced wife until she has been married to another man (Q 2:230). The former husband has no further obligations towards the divorced woman, except if she has a baby. During the period of breast-feeding, which a mother is entitled to sustain until her child is two years old (see LACTATION), the former husband (or his heirs) must provide for the maintenance and clothes of the mother and child and pay her a wage for the breast-feeding (Q 2:233; 65:6). In the case of an unconsummated marriage, divorce obliges the man to compensate the divorced woman (if the bridewealth was not yet fixed) or to pay her half of the bridewealth (Q 2:236-7).

Conclusion

The impact of the qur'ānic ideas and rules concerning marriage and divorce can only be understood by viewing them within the context of Arabian society during the sixth century C.E. Before Islam, Arabs (q.v.) married and divorced according to unwritten rules of customary law (for a sociological theory explaining the peculiarities of the Arab marriage system see Motzki, Dann machte, 613-8). These rules, however, were only elementary and could vary according to region or tribe. Whether they were observed depended on the authority of the individuals and groups involved. In such a system the powerless (see POWER AND IMPOTENCE) ran the risk of becoming losers; women (especially orphans and widows) and slaves were particularly vulnerable. The qur'ānic rules of marriage and divorce represented an important change in many respects. They provided a fixed set of norms for all Muslims, backed by divine authority and enforced by the community. Customary practices which were inconsistent with these norms were prohibited. In this manner, legal certainty was enhanced. Additionally, powerless individuals, such as women and slaves, were more effectively protected and their situation was improved by the qur'ānic rules and suggestions (see BOUNDARIES AND PRECEPTS). The fact that the bridewealth was given to the bride instead of to her male relatives, together with the possibility of intermarriage between Muslim slaves and (poor) free people, must even be considered revolutionary innovations in the Arab society of the time.

Harald Motzki

Bibliography

Primary: Ṭabarī, *Tafsīr*, ed. Shākir; *Jalālayn*.
Secondary: A. Gribetz, *Strange bedfellows.* Mutʿat al-nisāʾ *and* mutʿat al-ḥajj. *A study based on Sunnī and Shīʿī sources of* tafsīr, ḥadīth *and* fiqh, Berlin 1994; S. Haeri, *Law of desire. Temporary marriage in Shi'i Iran,* Syracuse, NY 1989; S. Kohn, *Die Eheschließung im Koran,* London 1934; H. Motzki, Dann machte er daraus die beiden Geschlechter, das männliche und das weibliche... (Koran 75:39) — Die historischen Wurzeln der islamischen Geschlechterrollen, in J. Martin/ R. Zoepffel (ed.), *Aufgaben, Rollen und Räume von Frau und Mann,* Freiburg 1989, 607-41; id., Geschlechtsreife und Legitimation zur Zeugung im frühen Islam, in E.W. Müller (ed.), *Geschlechtsreife und Legitimation zur Zeugung,* Freiburg 1985, 479-550; id., Volwassen worden in de vroeg-islamitische periode. Maatschappelijke en juridische gevolgen, in *Sharqiyyāt* 6 (1994), 55-70; id., *Wal-muḥṣanātu mina n-nisāʾi illā mā malakat aimānukum* (Koran 4:24) und die koranische Sexualethik, in *Der Islam* 63 (1986), 192-218; G.H. Stern, *Marriage in early Islam,* London 1939.

Martyrs

Those who die (generally at the hands of others) for their faith. In a Sunnī Islamic context, martyrs are primarily those who fight unbelievers for the advancement of Islam, and sacrifice their lives for this (see FIGHTING; BELIEF AND UNBELIEF; SUICIDE). This represents a marked difference with the situation of the defensive martyrs of early Christianity, who voluntarily suffered death as the consequence of witnessing to and refusing to renounce their religion. Christian martyrs were killed by hostile authorities in a period when their religion had no prospect of earthly success, whereas the early Sunnī martyrs fell in battle during generally successful military campaigns (see EXPEDITIONS AND BATTLES; WAR; POLITICS AND THE QUR'ĀN). Shīʿī martyrdom has a coloring of its own (see SHĪʿISM AND THE QUR'ĀN). It was shaped by the case of the martyr *par excellence,* Ḥusayn b. ʿAlī (see FAMILY OF THE PROPHET; ʿALĪ

B. ABĪ ṬĀLIB; FĀṬIMA), who was killed at Karbalāʾ in a heroic, but predictably doomed battle against fellow Muslims (61/680). For Shīʿites, as for Christians, it is the spiritual victory in the face of a worldy defeat that matters. Moreover, they often emphasize the redemptive character of Ḥusayn's martyrdom, whereas the intercession (q.v.) of Sunnī martyrs plays but a marginal role.

Shahīd

The common Arabic word for martyr is *shahīd,* pl. *shuhadāʾ,* a term that abounds in Islamic literatures from tradition literature onwards (see ḤADĪTH AND THE QURʾĀN). *Shahīd* occurs frequently in the Qurʾān, but at first glance means only "witness" (see WITNESSING AND TESTIFYING; WITNESS TO FAITH) or "confessor." Under the influence of early Christian usage, however, traditionists and exegetes (see EXEGESIS OF THE QURʾĀN: CLASSICAL AND MEDIEVAL) occasionally did interpret the qurʾānic *shahīd* as "martyr." The Greek *martys* and Syriac *sāhdā* had similarly developed semantically from "witness" via "confessor, testifier to the faith" to "martyr" (Goldziher, *MS,* ii, 350-1; Wensinck, *Oriental doctrine,* 147, 155).

Q 3:140, "God may know who are the believers and choose *shuhadāʾ* from among you," is embedded in a war-context; it is therefore no wonder that al-Ṭabarī (d. 310/923) and the authorities he quotes (*Tafsīr,* nos. 7912-16) speak exclusively of martyrdom. Other verses give far less reason for such readings. Yet, in Q 4:69, "Those who obey (see OBEDIENCE) God and the messenger (q.v.) will be with those whom God has favored, prophets (see PROPHETS AND PROPHETHOOD), just men, *shuhadāʾ* and the righteous...," both al-Ṭabarī (*Tafsīr,* ed. Shākir, viii, 532) and Muqātil (d. 150/767; *Tafsīr,* iv, 243) interpret *shuhadāʾ* as those "killed in God's way" (see PATH OR WAY). In Q 57:19, "the pious and the *shuhadāʾ* in their lord's sight" are martyrs according to Muqātil (*Tafsīr,* iv, 243); al-Ṭabarī mentions "those who fell in battle or died in God's way" as one of the possible interpretations (*Tafsīr,* xxvii, 134). The comments on the *shahīd*-verses in early Sunnī exegetical works (sing. *tafsīr*) are generally meagre: the verses about those who were killed in battle generated much more exegesis.

The Qurʾān on those who fell in battle

Without using the term *shahīd,* the Qurʾān speaks in several Medinan sūras of those who fight for the cause of God ("in God's way," *fī sabīli llāhi;* see JIHĀD) and are killed. Whoever trades this life for the life to come concludes a profitable deal and is promised "a great reward" (Q 4:74; see ESCHATOLOGY; REWARD AND PUNISHMENT). God buys from the believers their lives and their wealth (q.v.) in return for paradise (q.v.; Q 9:111). "And were you to be killed or to die in the way of God, forgiveness (q.v.) and mercy (q.v.) from God are better than what they amass. And were you to die or to be killed, it is to God that you will be gathered" (Q 3:157-8). As a matter of fact, *all* Muslims will be gathered, but those killed in action are privileged. They are often believed to enter paradise directly after having been killed, by virtue of a verse like this one: 'Those who die in the way of God, he will not let their works be lost. He shall guide them and set their minds aright; and shall admit them into paradise, that he has made known to them" (Q 47:4-6; cf. 9:111). The martyrs are thus spared the torment in the grave, the "intermediate state" (see BARZAKH) and the last judgment (q.v.). They are not even dead (see DEATH AND THE DEAD): "And do not consider those who have been killed in the way of God as dead; they are alive with their lord, well-provided for" (Q 3:169; cf. 2:154).

Commentary and ḥadīth on those who fell in battle
In connection with the qurʾānic verses mentioned above, the state and whereabouts of the martyrs and their reward in the hereafter are discussed in the biographies of the Prophet (see SĪRA AND THE QURʾĀN), in commentaries on the Qurʾān (sing. *tafsīr,* see EXEGESIS OF THE QURʾĀN: CLASSICAL AND MEDIEVAL) and in tradition literature. In the early *tafsīr* works, the material is distributed throughout the discussions of a number of qurʾānic verses rather randomly, and in ḥadīth collections it is also scattered over many different places. Here, therefore, a thematic arrangement seems more appropriate than a verse-by-verse treatment. Some large clusters of relevant ḥadīth and *tafsīr* are to be found in Ṭabarī, *Tafsīr,* ad Q 2:154 (ed. Shākir, iii, 214-9); ad Q 3:169 (ed. Shākir, vii, 384-95); ad Q 47:4-6 (ed. Shākir, xxvi, 26 f.), and in ʿAbd al-Razzāq (d. 211/827), *Muṣannaf,* v, 263-6, no. 9553-62.

Historical martyrs
"Those who are killed in God's way" are said to be those fighters who fell at Uḥud (Ibn Isḥāq, *Sīra,* 604, 605; Eng. trans. Ibn Isḥāq-Guillaume, 400; ʿAbd al-Razzāq, *Tafsīr,* ad Q 47:4-6, no. 2873; Ṭabarī, *Tafsīr,* nos. 7913, 8205, 8214-15), or at Badr (q.v.; Muqātil, *Tafsīr,* ad Q 2:154, 47:4-6).

Among the Muslims fallen at Uḥud was the father of Jābir b. ʿAbdallāh. Muḥammad said to Jābir: "I will give you good news, Jābir. God has restored life *(aḥyāhu)* to your father who was killed at Uḥud…" (Ibn Isḥāq, *Sīra,* 605; Eng. trans. Ibn Isḥāq-Guillaume, 400; Ṭabarī, *Tafsīr,* no. 8214). The word *aḥyāhu* implies that he was brought back to life shortly after having been killed. ʿAbdallāh had asked the lord whether he could be sent back to the world to fight and be killed once more. In some traditions, this episode is presented as the "occasion for the revelation" (see OCCASIONS OF REVELATION) of Q 3:169 (Ibn Māja, *Sunan, muqaddima,* 13, 190; Tirmidhī, *Ṣaḥīḥ, tafsīr* ad Q 3, 18).

ʿAbdallāh was not the only person who wanted to go back to earth. According to the "birds-tradition" (see below) all martyrs so wish, and even the Prophet said he would like to be killed repeatedly in God's way (e.g. Bukhārī, *Ṣaḥīḥ, jihād,* 7; Ibn Ḥanbal, *Musnad,* ii, 231).

The prerogatives of martyrs
A prophetic tradition enumerates nine (or three, or six, or ten) prerogatives of a martyr. His sins (see SIN, MAJOR AND MINOR) will be forgiven with the first gush of blood (see BLOODSHED); he will be shown his abode in paradise; he will be dressed in the garment of belief; he will be married to the houris (q.v.); he will be protected against the torment of the grave; he will be safe from the great terror [i.e. the last judgment]; the crown of dignity, one ruby of which is better than this world, will be placed on his head (see METALS AND MINERALS); he will be married to seventy-two wives from among the houris; he will intercede for seventy of his relatives (Ibn Ḥanbal, *Musnad,* iv, 131, 200; ʿAbd al-Razzāq, *Muṣannaf,* 9559; Ibn Māja, *Sunan, jihād,* 16/2799; see KINSHIP).

The houris in paradise
During his ascension (q.v.), the Prophet saw in paradise an attractive "damsel with dark red lips." In response to his question, she told him that she was promised for Zayd b. Ḥāritha, his adoptive son (Ibn Isḥāq, *Sīra,* 270; Eng. trans. Ibn Isḥāq-Guillaume, 186). The text does not state that the woman was promised to Zayd because he was to be killed in battle, nor when he would obtain her. But in other texts the connection between martyrdom and the enjoyment of beautiful women in paradise is unmistakable. The above text

on the prerogatives of martyrs even mentions the houris twice. Another tradition promises only two women: "The blood of a martyr will hardly be dry on the earth, when his two spouses will already be rushing to meet him" (e.g. ʿAbd al-Razzāq, *Muṣannaf,* 9561; Ibn Māja, *Sunan, jihād,* 16/2798), but here it is clear that the martyrs will be united with them at the very moment of their death.

Do martyrs go to paradise immediately after death?

According to the last tradition, the martyrs are in paradise immediately after their death. Other texts support this belief. When the believers once admired a costly gown, the Prophet asked: "Do you admire this? By him in whose hand my life is, the napkins of Saʿd b. Muʿādh in paradise are better than this!" (Ibn Isḥāq, *Sīra,* 903; Eng. trans. Ibn Isḥāq-Guillaume, 608). Saʿd had died from a war injury and hence was a martyr, feasting in paradise.

More frequent, however, are comments that make a point of the martyrs abiding near paradise, but not *in* it. "They are with their lord, they are provided with the fruits of paradise and they feel its breeze, but they are not in it" (Ṭabarī, *Tafsīr,* no. 2317). Or they are "by the Bāriq river, at the gate of paradise, in a round green tent, their provision from paradise coming out to them morning and evening" (Ibn Isḥāq, *Sīra,* 605; Eng. trans. Ibn Isḥāq-Guillaume, 400; Ṭabarī, *Tafsīr,* nos. 2323, 8210; Ibn Ḥanbal, *Musnad,* i, 266; van Ess, *TG,* iv, 525, Eklund, *Life,* 39). The only privilege of the martyrs, says al-Ṭabarī, is that in their "intermediate state" *(barzakh)* they will be provided with food from paradise, which will be given to no other believer before the resurrection (q.v.; Ṭabarī, *Tafsīr,* ed. Shākir, iii, 216).

Although the Qurʾān clearly speaks of paradise as the abode of those who fell, it does not say when they will arrive there. The exegetes may have sensed a theological difficulty: how were their blood-stained, mutilated bodies to be physically restored at the end of times, together with all other human beings, if they were in paradise already?

The frequently quoted "birds-tradition" (van Ess, *TG,* iv, 523-5; Eklund, *Life,* 16-20, 67-8) seems to aim at a compromise: the souls of the martyrs are close to God and may well visit paradise, but they do not stay there permanently before they are rejoined with their bodies. The text occurs in too many variations to cite all of them here; for this tradition, see the reference to the larger ḥadīth and *tafsīr* clusters above. In a simple form it runs as follows: "The souls of the martyrs are in the shape of white birds that feed on the fruits of paradise" (ʿAbd al-Razzāq, *Muṣannaf,* 9553). The souls (see SOUL) can be "in the shape of birds," or "like birds with God," "turned into green birds" or be just "birds." Or they are "in birds"; "in the bellies *(jawf)* of birds"; "in the crops *(ḥawṣala)* of green birds," etc. These birds eat *(taʾkulu)* or obtain necessary sustenance (*taʿlaqu,* Abd al-Razzāq, *Muṣannaf,* 9557) from the fruits of paradise, or forage *(tasraḥu)* wherever they want in paradise. But often they are said to "nestle in (golden) lamps that are hung *(muʿallaqa)* under the throne of God (q.v.)," and the throne is not in paradise. (*Muʿallaqa* may be inspired by the word *taʿlaqu* in an earlier version.) In many places (e.g. ʿAbd al-Razzāq, *Muṣannaf,* 9554), the lord appears and asks whether they desire anything else. Of course they do not, but, like Jābir's father, they would wish to go back into their bodies to fight and be killed again. This wish is refused, but in some versions the martyrs are comforted with the promise that their relatives on earth will be informed about their present state, which then results in the revelation of Q 3:169-70. In two versions of the "birds-tradition," they live in paradise after all "... in the shape of green birds in paradise" (Ṭabarī, *Tafsīr,* no. 2322); and: "the souls of the martyrs are in round white tents in paradise, in each of which are two spouses" (Ṭabarī, *Tafsīr,* no. 2324; see MARRIAGE AND DIVORCE; TENTS AND TENT PEGS). Or they get to know each other in white birds that eat from the fruits of paradise; their dwellings are near the 'lote-tree of the boundary' (*sidrat al-muntahā,* cf. Q 53:14; see AGRICULTURE AND VEGETATION; TREES), wherever that may be (Ṭabarī, *Tafsīr,* nos. 2319, 8215).

Other traditions on martyrdom

Certain ḥadīth explain how martyrs should be buried, or what should be done about their debts (q.v.); but this is not the place to discuss such details which bear no relation to the Qurʾān (see Wensinck, *Handbook,* 146-8; Kohlberg, *Shahīd*).

In Sunnī Islam, martyrdom is connected with jihād. Since, after the expansionist first century of Islam, gradually, fewer and fewer battles against unbelievers were fought, there was less chance to take part in war, and hence to be killed in action. Therefore, and also to enable as many believers as possible to share in the blessing of martyrdom, the term *shahīd* was given a wider interpretation and was understood to encompass every sacrifice (q.v.) for God's cause, or any difficult act of whatever nature (see TRIAL). According to prophetic traditions, one could become a martyr by dying abroad, in an epidemic, in childbirth, by pleurisy or by drowning (q.v.), or by being killed in defence of one's family or one's property (q.v.; Kohlberg, *Shahīd*). And, last but not least, "the ink of the scholars is of more value than the blood of the martyrs" (Goldziher, *MS,* ii, 390; see WRITING AND WRITING MATERIALS).

Martyrdom in later times

In times and places where jihād was militarily revived, the idea of martyrdom was reactivated as well. During the Ottoman conquests in Europe, and during rebellions against European colonial powers, Muslim soldiers who fell in battle could rightly be called martyrs (see REBELLION). In writings about jihād, there was not always an interest in martyrdom. Ibn Taymiyya (661-728/1263-1328), for instance, a major source of inspiration for Islamists in our days, eagerly expands on jihād, but hardly ever refers to martyrdom.

The twentieth century saw the rise of militant Islamist groups, to whose concept of jihād the writings of Ibn Taymiyya contributed greatly (see EXEGESIS OF THE QURʾĀN: EARLY MODERN AND CONTEMPORARY). Perhaps the first modern Sunnī Muslim who explicitly preached martyrdom was the Egyptian Ḥasan al-Bannā (1906-49), the founder of the Muslim Brothers. In his *On jihād* he quotes the relevant qurʾānic verses and a host of traditions that extol the blessings of martyrdom, and ends his treatise with a sturdy, rhetorically impressive plea for it. Since he was murdered by the secret police, his followers had no difficulty in recognising him as a martyr. Martyrdom recurred as a topic in the publications of the Brothers, and the many who were executed by the Nasser regime in the fifties and sixties became martyrs themselves. Another famous Islamist martyr, who has had an enormous impact in militant circles, was the Egyptian Sayyid Quṭb. After years in prison, he was hanged in 1966. In his often reprinted Qurʾān commentary *Fī ẓilāl al-Qurʾān* he quotes the familiar traditions in reference to Q 2:154, but adds an almost lyrical passage on martyrdom (Quṭb, *Ẓilāl*, i, 199-202; cf. ibid., iv, 314).

Modern Iran

In traditional Shīʿism, there was no clear connection between jihād and martyrdom. Ḥusayn b. ʿAlī (d. 61/680) was venerated for his ostentatious suffering rather than for his military prowess. Since the last Shīʿī imām (q.v.) was believed to be 'hidden,' there was no one who could lawfully proclaim a religious war. From the 1960s onwards a new, activist and reformist type of jihād was propagated, combined with a tendency towards active martyrdom. Leading figures in this movement were the sociology professor ʿAlī Sharīʿatī, and the Ayatollahs Ṭāleqānī and Muṭahharī (Abedi and Legenhausen, *Jihād*). After the Islamic revolution in 1979, the fresh ideological fervor was stained by the bloody reality. During the war with Iraq in the 1980s, masses of soldiers and child-soldiers were encouraged to seek martyrdom as cannon fodder and in mine fields, the "key of paradise" hanging around their necks.

Lebanon and Palestine

From 1982 on, the Shīʿī, Iranian-guided faction Ḥizballāh (lit. "party of God") organized suicide squads in Lebanon against Israel and the United States, motivated by the certainty that they would die as martyrs. Present-day individual suicide bombers in Palestine are the spiritual heirs of the Muslim Brothers, but are also influenced by a centuries-old popular tradition of glorifying death on the battlefield (Jarrar, Martyrdom). Although Sunnī legal scholars do not agree on how far one can go in *seeking* martyrdom, suicides invariably have been motivated by qurʾānic verses and traditions, prophetic as well as non-prophetic *(akhbār)*, on the immediate reward for martyrs in paradise, with an emphasis on the heavenly brides. Traditions on martyrdom that slumbered for centuries have turned out to inspire modern militants, who only thirty years ago would still have fought under secular banners (see also OPPRESSION; OPPRESSED ON EARTH, THE).

Wim Raven

Bibliography

Primary: ʿAbd al-Razzāq, *Muṣannaf;* id., *Tafsīr,* ed. Qalʿajī; M. Abedi and G. Legenhausen (eds. and trans.), *Jihād and shahādat* [sic]. *Struggle and martyrdom in Islam. [Essays and addresses by] Ayatullāh Maḥmūd Ṭaleqāni, Ayatullāh Murtaḍā Muṭahhari, Dr. ʿAlī Sharīʿati,* Houston 1986; Ḥ. al-Bannā, *Majmūʿat rasāʾil al-imām al-shahīd Ḥasan al-Bannā,* Beirut 1984[3]; trans. and annot. Charles Wendell, *Five tracts of Ḥasan al-Bannā (1906-49). A selection from the* Majmūʿat rasāʾil al-imām al-shahīd Ḥasan al-Bannā, Berkeley 1978; Bukhārī, *Ṣaḥīḥ;* Ibn Ḥanbal, *Musnad;* Ibn Isḥāq, *Sīra;* Ibn Isḥāq-Guillaume; Ibn Māja, *Sunan;* Mujāhid, *Tafsīr,* ed. Suwartī; Muqātil, *Tafsīr;* Quṭb, *Ẓilāl,* Beirut 1971[7]; Suyūṭī, *Abwāb al-saʿāda fī asbāb al-shahāda.* ed. N. Khalaf, Cairo 1981; Ṭabarī, *Tafsīr,* ed. Shākir (for the ḥadīth citations and two statements by Ṭabarī himself); Cairo ed. 1323-9/1905-11 (for the volume and page citations); Tirmidhī, *Ṣaḥīḥ.*

Secondary: S. Aḥmad, *al-Imām al-shahīd fī l-tārīkh wa-l-īdiyulūjiyya,* Beirut 2000; M. Ayoub, *Redemptive suffering in Islam,* The Hague 1978; M.Q. al-Baghdādī, *al-Shahāda. Taʾṣīl l istiʾṣāl. Dirāsa mawḍūʿiyya muʿāṣira lil-naẓariyya l-istishāhdiyya fī l-manṣūr al-islāmī,* 4 vols., Beirut 1993; W. Björkman, Shahīd, in *EI*[1], vii, 259-61; O. Carré, *Mysticism and politics. A critical reading of* Fī Ẓilāl al-Qurʾān *by Sayyid Quṭb,* trans. C. Artigues, Leiden 2003, 1-20 (on Quṭb as a martyr), 330-2 (Quṭb on the martyrs in paradise); J. Damūnī, *al-Shahāda wa-l-shuhadāʾ. Aḥkam al-shahīd fī l-sharīʿa l-islāmiyya,* London 2000; R. Eklund, *Life between death and resurrection according to Islam,* Uppsala 1941; van Ess, *TG;* Goldziher, *MS,* ii, 387-90 (Ger.); ii, 350-4 (Eng. trans.); M. Jarrar, The martyrdom of passionate lovers. Holy war as a sacred wedding, in A. Neuwirth et al. (eds.), *Myths, historical archetypes and symbolic figures in Arabic literature. Towards a new hermeneutic approach,* Beirut 1999, 87-107; F. Khosrokhavar, *L'islamisme et la mort. Le martyre révolutionnaire en Iran,* Paris 1995; E. Kohlberg, *Medieval Muslim views on martyrdom,* Amsterdam 1997; id., Shahīd, in *EI*[2], ix, 203-7;

A. Naqvi, *The martyr of Karbala*, trans. S. Akhtar, Karachi 1984 (Eng. trans. of *Shahīd-i insāniyat*); Quṭb, *Ẓilāl. Selections. al-Shahāda wa-l-istishhād*, ed. ʿU. al-Ṭībī, Cairo 1994; ʿA. al-Ṣiddīq al-Ḥasanī (Ghumārī), *Itḥāf al-nubalāʾ bi-faḍl al-shahāda wa-anwāʿ al-shuhadāʾ*, Cairo 1970; N. Takrūrī, *al-ʿAmaliyyāt al-istishhādiyya fī l-mīzān al-fiqhī*, Damascus 1997; D. Talmon-Heller, Muslim martyrdom and quest for martyrdom in the crusading period, in *al-Masaq. Islam and the medieval Mediterranean* 14 (2002), 131-9; Wensinck, *Concordance*, s.v. *shahīd;* id., *Handbook*, s.v. 'Martyr(s)'; id., The oriental doctrine of the martyrs, in *Mededeelingen der Koninklijke Akademie van Wetenschappen te Amsterdam, Afdeeling Letterkunde* 53 (1921), Ser. A, No. 6, 147-74 (repr. in id., *Semietische studiën uit de nalatenschap van Prof. Dr. A.J. Wensinck*, Leiden 1941, 90-113).

Mārūt see HĀRŪT AND MĀRŪT

Marvels

Amazing, incredible matters and events. Besides the specific contents of qurʾānic verses employing the root *ʿ-j-b*, the *ʿajāʾib al-Qurʾān* ("marvels of the Qurʾān") came to refer to a vast genre of literature comprising travels (see JOURNEY; TRIPS AND VOYAGES), cosmography (see COSMOLOGY), biology (see BIOLOGY AS THE CREATION AND STAGES OF LIFE; SCIENCE AND THE QURʾĀN), and the supernatural (see MAGIC). Eight of the sixteen qurʾānic instances of this root in which it has this sense, are verbs (e.g. "Do you wonder?") and refer to surprise at God's actions; the rest are nouns, adjectives and adverbs. The words occur in some of the most influential passages of the Qurʾān: many announce God's sending of a warner (q.v.; e.g. Q 38:4); two concern Abraham (q.v.) and Sarah's reaction to the news of a new child (Q 11:72, 73; see GOOD NEWS); one refers to the Sleepers in the Cave (Q 18:9; see MEN OF THE CAVE); and another to Moses (q.v.), Khiḍr (see KHAḌIR/KHIḌR) and a fish (Q 18:63). But the *ʿajāʾib al-Qurʾān* do not refer to these narratives (q.v.) specifically; instead this genre came to signify God's creation (q.v.) and power (see POWER AND IMPOTENCE) as mentioned in the Qurʾān (see NATURE AS SIGNS), such as stars, planets (see PLANETS AND STARS), animals (see ANIMAL LIFE), seas, plants (see AGRICULTURE AND VEGETATION), rain, thunder, seasons (q.v.), eclipses, geography (q.v.), the human body, and so forth. All of creation, its entities and processes, was viewed as part of the 'signs' (q.v.) of God, demonstrating his existence, majesty and order for the world. Since the Qurʾān frequently calls upon the believers to pay attention to the signs, studying the features of creation, the marvels of the world, became one form of worship of and reverence for God.

Three of the most famous works of this genre are *ʿAjāʾib ʿulūm al-Qurʾān* ("The wonders of the sciences of the Qurʾān") by Ibn al-Jawzī (d. 597/1200), *Nukhbat al-dahr fī ʿajāʾib al-barr wa-l-baḥr* ("A cosmography of the wonders of the land and the sea") by Shams al-Dīn Muḥammad b. Abī Ṭālib al-Dimashqī (d. 727/1327) and *ʿAjāʾib al-makhlūkāt* ("The wonders of creation") by Zakariyyā b. Muḥammad al-Qazwīnī (d. 682/1283). Al-Qazwīnī distinguishes between *ʿajīb* (marvel, wonder) and *gharīb* (strange), in that the former impairs the human being in his ability to understand the cause of anything, especially the familiar (such as the sun [q.v.] rising), while *gharīb* consists of unusual things (such as earthquakes). Thus, by contemplating even the everyday occurrences of life — the growing of plants, the digestion of food, the flowing of the tides — the believer marvels at the real, has a sense of wonder and amazement, and is thereby led to an awareness of the transcendence of God. Contemplation of the unusual or strange occurrences which rupture the normal pattern of events *(naqḍ al-ʿādati)* can serve to enhance this sense of wonder at the creator's power even further. In an iterative fashion, recording such extra-qur'ānic marvels turned the believer's attention back to the unique and miraculous nature of the Qur'ān itself (see INIMITABILITY). Many writers, in order to expand their catalogues of wondrous things undertook great journeys (cf. e.g. the *Riḥla* of Ibn Baṭṭūṭa [d. 778/1377], entitled *Tuḥfat al-nazzār fī gharā'ib al-amṣār wa-'ajā'ib al-asfār*).

The *'ajā'ib al-Qur'ān* genre followed on an earlier group of writings known as *kutub al-'aẓama,* which aim at the glorification of God (q.v.; *ta'ẓīm Allāh*) through the study of the world. The best known is *Kitāb al-'aẓama* of Abū al-Shaykh al-Anṣārī of Iṣfahānī (d. 369/979), considered the model for al-Ghazālī's (d. 505/1111) *Kitāb al-Tafakkur,* part of the latter's *Iḥyā' 'ulūm al-dīn*. Mention should also be made of the works entitled *Kitāb al-'Aẓama* by al-Muḥāsibī (d. 243/857; this work, however, has not survived intact; see van Ess, *Die Gedankenwelt,* 163-7 for a Ger. trans. of a segment that has survived), by al-Sijistānī, and Burhān al-Dīn Ibrāhīm b. Muḥammad al-Ḥalabī al-Dimashqī (d. 956/1549).

See MIRACLES for discussion of the qur'ānic accounts of supernatural interventions in human affairs.

Alice C. Hunsberger

Bibliography

Primary: Abū l-Shaykh al-Anṣārī, *Kitāb al-'Aẓama,* ed. M. 'Ashur and M. al-S. Ibrāhīm, Cairo 1990; al-Ghazālī, Abū Ḥāmid Muḥammad, *Kitāb al-Ḥikma fī makhlūqāt Allāh,* Cairo 1903; Ibn al-Jawzī, *Funūn* (which addresses the "wondrous" nature of the Qur'ān itself); al-Qazwīnī, Zakariyyā b. Muḥammad, *'Ajā'ib al-makhlūqāt wa-gharā'ib al-mawjūdāt,* ed. F. Sa'd, Beirut 1977; Ger. trans. H. Ethé, *Die Wunder der Schöpfung,* Leipzig 1868, repr. Frankfurt 1994.
Secondary: M. Arkoun et al., *L'Étrange et le merveilleux dans l'Islam médiéval. Actes du colloque tenu au Collège de France (en mars 1974),* Paris 1978; id., Peut-on parler de merveilleux dans le Coran? in id., *Lectures,* 87-108; J. van Ess, *Die Gedankenwelt des Ḥarīṯ al-Muḥāsibī,* Bonn 1961; A.M. Heinen, Tafakkur and Muslim science, in *Journal of Turkish studies* 18 (1994), 103-10; M. Rodinson, La place du merveilleux et de l'étrange dans la conscience du monde musulman medieval, in M. Arkoun et al., *L'Étrange et le merveilleux dans l'Islam médiéval. Actes du colloque tenu au Collège de France (en mars 1974),* Paris 1978, 167-87.

Marwa

see ṢAFĀ AND MARWA

Mary

Mary (Ar. Maryam) the mother of Jesus (q.v.; 'Īsā) is the most prominent female figure in the Qur'ān and the only one identified by name (see WOMEN AND THE QUR'ĀN). Her story is related in three Meccan sūras (19, 21, 23) and four Medinan sūras (3, 4, 5, 66; see CHRONOLOGY AND THE QUR'ĀN), and the nineteenth sūra, Sūrat Maryam, is named for her. Overall, there are seventy verses that refer to her and she is named specifically in thirty-four of these (Smith and Haddad, Virgin Mary, 162). According to the qur'ānic accounts, signs of divine favor surrounded her from birth. As a young woman, she received the angels' (see ANGEL) message that God had chosen her and purified her, chosen her above the women of the worlds, followed by their annunciation of a child born from God's spirit (q.v.), a word from God (see WORD OF GOD) cast into Mary, whose name was Jesus son of Mary, the "anointed one" or Messiah, one of God's righteous prophets (see PROPHETS AND PROPHETHOOD). The qur'ānic revelation celebrates Mary as an example for the believers because of her chastity (q.v.), obedience (q.v.) and faith (q.v.); it also affirms God's oneness by emphasizing the created nature of Mary and of her son Jesus (see GOD AND HIS ATTRIBUTES; CREATION).

Mary, Zechariah, Jesus, and John

In sūras 3, 19 and 21, Mary's story is intertwined with that of her guardian, the prophet Zechariah (q.v.; Zakariyyā). In sūras 19 and 21, the accounts of Zechariah's prayer for a child in old age and the glad tidings of the birth of John (Yaḥyā; Q 19:2-15; 21:89-90; see JOHN THE BAPTIST; GOOD NEWS) directly precede the passages on Mary's sinless conception of the prophet Jesus (Q 19:16-35; 21:91; see SEX AND SEXUALITY). In sūra 3, however, Zechariah's story (Q 3:38-41) is inserted between the verses on Mary's birth and childhood (Q 3:33-7) and the angels' message to Mary of God's special grace (q.v.) upon her, followed by their annunciation of the birth and prophethood of Jesus (Q 3:42-51). The angels' words announcing the birth of John to Zechariah (Q 3:39) are almost identical with those on the birth of Jesus to Mary (Q 3:45); and Zechariah's (Q 3:40) and Mary's (Q 3:47) questioning of the message, and the divine, or angelic, affirmation of God's omnipotence to Zechariah (Q 3:40) and Mary (Q 3:47) also bear strong similarities. Furthermore, the wording of God's praise and blessing on John (Q 19:12-5) is almost identical with Jesus' words of blessing about himself, spoken in the cradle (Q 19:30-3; see FORM AND STRUCTURE OF THE QUR'ĀN).

This close association between the figures of Zechariah and Mary on the one hand and those of John and Jesus on the other establishes a special place for Mary in the qur'ānic context of prophetic history. Some medieval Muslim theologians (see THEOLOGY AND THE QUR'ĀN) — especially of the short-lived Ẓāhirī school, such as Ibn Ḥazm of Cordoba (d. 456/1064) — even assigned the rank of "prophethood" *(nubuwwa),* as opposed to "messengerhood," (*risāla,* see MESSENGER) to Mary and also the mothers of Isaac (q.v.) and Moses (q.v.) and the wife of Pharaoh (q.v.). They justified this classification on the grounds that these women received knowledge (see KNOWLEDGE AND LEARNING) from God through word or inspiration (Ibn Ḥazm, *Milal,* 119-21; see REVELATION AND INSPIRATION). Consensus-based Sunnī theology, however, strongly rejected this position as a heretical innovation (q.v.; *bid'a,* see also HERESY).

Mary's birth and service in the temple

The story of Mary's birth, early life in the temple, and divinely-decreed superior rank is related in sūra 3, revealed in Medina (q.v.). The qur'ānic verses affirm that Mary's special status began even before she was born. God privileged Adam (see ADAM AND EVE), Noah (q.v.), the family of Abraham (q.v.) and the family of 'Imrān (q.v.) with special status (Q 3:33). Before giving birth to Mary, her mother, the wife of 'Imrān, consecrated her unborn child to God's service (assuming that she was carrying a boy). Seeing that the baby was a girl, and knowing that service in the temple was a male prerogative, she was bewildered, since God had accepted the offering even though the child was female (see GENDER).

'Imrān's wife named her daughter Mary and invoked God's protection (q.v.) upon her and her offspring against Satan (Q 3:35-6; see DEVIL). God accepted Mary graciously and made her grow up in a goodly manner, placing her in the charge of Zechariah (Q 3:37). Whenever Zechariah would enter upon her in her prayer room, he found miraculous sustenance with which God had provided her (Q 3:37). According to authenticated tradition, it was because of her mother's prayer for God's protection that both Mary and her son Jesus escaped "the pricking of the devil" at birth, which happens to all other human beings and is the reason why babies cry when they are born (Ibn Kathīr, *Qiṣaṣ*, ii, 370-1, 461).

The exegetical literature (*tafsīr*, see EXEGESIS OF THE QUR'ĀN: CLASSICAL AND MEDIEVAL) and the genre of literature known as "tales of the prophets" *(qiṣaṣ al-anbiyā')* further relate that Mary grew up in the temple where she worshiped day and night until her unequalled piety (q.v.) and righteousness became known among the Israelites (Ṭabarī, *Tafsīr*, vi, 402-3; see CHILDREN OF ISRAEL; JEWS AND JUDAISM). She lived in the *miḥrāb*, a secluded cell or upstairs chamber; the door to this chamber was always locked and only Zechariah had the key. He would lock her into the room but, as noted above, whenever he visited her, he found wondrous provisions: winter fruit during summer time and summer fruit during winter time (Ṭabarī, *Tafsīr*, vi, 353-8; Kisā'ī, *Qiṣaṣ*, 328; Ibn Kathīr, *Qiṣaṣ*, ii, 373, 385; Baljon, *Koran interpretations*, 22, 65-6). Among the people who served with Mary in the temple, mention is made of Joseph, a carpenter, who is sometimes identified as Joseph son of Jacob and/or Mary's cousin on her mother's side (Ṭabarī, *Tafsīr*, xvi, 49-50; Rāzī, *Tafsīr*, xxi, 202; Ibn Kathīr, *Qiṣaṣ*, 388, 390).

Mary's rank and purification

Following four verses that tell of the tidings to Zechariah of John's birth (Q 3:38-41), the relevant verses of sūra 3 further pursue the theme of God's special favor on Mary: (1) in the words of the angels, "God has chosen you and purified you and chosen you above the women of the worlds" (Q 3:42); (2) their exhortation to be "devoutly obedient toward your lord (q.v.), prostrate yourself, and bow down with those who bow down" (Q 3:43; see BOWING AND PROSTRATION); and (3) an indication that the right to her guardianship was settled by the casting of lots among quarrelling contestants (Q 3:44; see GAMBLING).

Exegesis has interpreted the "first choosing" in Q 3:42 (i.e. the first item in this tripartite divine message to Mary) as God's acceptance of Mary for his service, providing her in the temple with sustenance that freed her from all labor (see MANUAL LABOR) and granting her the ability to hear the angels' words. The "second choosing" (i.e. the third item in this divine message) is said to have consisted in God's gift of Jesus without a father, the child's words in Mary's defense from the cradle, the status of Mary and Jesus as a sign or miracle (q.v.; *āya*, see also SIGNS) for the world and God's guidance of Mary (Zamakhsharī, *Kashshāf*, i, 277; Rāzī, *Tafsīr*, viii, 45-6; Bayḍāwī, *Anwār*, i, 155).

On the question of Mary's rank above the women of the worlds, the exegetical debate is remarkable both for its intensity and the lack of consensus. At stake is Mary's ranking among the qur'ānic women figures but also, and perhaps more importantly, in relation to the elite women of Islam, especially the Prophet's wives Khadīja (q.v.) and 'Ā'isha (see 'Ā'ISHA BINT ABĪ BAKR) and his daughter Fāṭima (q.v.). The problem is addressed by questioning whether Mary's preeminence is absolute (over all other women and for all times) or relative (over the women of her own time). The larger number of traditions recorded in *tafsīr* and *qiṣaṣ al-anbiyā'* literature establish, on the authority of the Prophet (see ḤADĪTH AND THE QUR'ĀN), that Mary and Fāṭima, Khadīja and Āsya (the Pharaoh's wife) are the best women of the world and also the ruling females in heaven (see HEAVEN AND SKY; KINGS AND RULERS); traditions on 'Ā'isha's inclusion in this group are fewer in number. While Āsya's and Mary's merit is established on the basis of Q 66:11-2, Khadīja's merit is seen in her great service to the Prophet's mission, and that of 'Ā'isha in her status as Muḥammad's most beloved wife (see WIVES OF THE

PROPHET) and a prominent authority on his legacy after his death (Ṭabarī, *Tafsīr,* vi, 393-400; Rāzī, *Tafsīr,* viii, 45-6; Ibn Kathīr, *Qiṣaṣ,* ii, 375-81; Rashīd Riḍā, *Manār,* iii, 300). According to some *qiṣaṣ al-anbiyāʾ* reports, Mary and Āsya, Khadīja and ʿĀʾisha share the privilege of being Muḥammad's wifely consorts in paradise (q.v.; Ibn Kathīr, *Qiṣaṣ,* ii, 375-83; see MARRIAGE AND DIVORCE).

This leaves the question of Mary's ranking in relation to the Prophet's daughter Fāṭima. In Muslim piety, especially Shīʿī piety (see SHĪʿISM AND THE QURʾĀN), the figures of Mary and Fāṭima are closely associated. Mary was one of four miraculous midwives who assisted Khadīja in Fāṭima's birth (McAuliffe, Chosen of all women, 26-7), Mary appeared to Fāṭima to console her during her last illness (Ayoub, *Redemptive suffering,* 50), both were visited by angels, and both received miraculous sustenance during childhood and the periods of isolation preceding the birth of their child, or children. Their association also involves attribution to both of a shared quality of purity (*ṭahāra,* see RITUAL PURITY), which meant freedom from menstruation (q.v.) and bleeding at childbirth (McAuliffe, Chosen of all women, 22-3; Ayoub, *Redemptive suffering,* 70-2, 75; see BIRTH; BIOLOGY AS THE CREATION AND STAGES OF LIFE), while their deepest tie lies in their joint image of mistress of sorrows (Ayoub, *Redemptive suffering,* 27, 30, 39, 48-50). Although according to the Qurʾān, Jesus was persecuted and rejected by his people but not slain, Shīʿī hagiography has recognized strong affinities between Jesus and Ḥusayn (Ayoub, *Redemptive suffering,* 35; see FAMILY OF THE PROPHET), as also between their holy mothers. In popular devotions (see FESTIVALS AND COMMEMORATIVE DAYS), Mary and Fāṭima, sacred figures of solace and hope (q.v.), are at times revered simultaneously (Smith and Haddad, Virgin Mary, 180-1). While some traditions — reported on the authority of the Prophet — award Mary and Fāṭima equal rank as the two reigning females in the celestial realm of the hereafter, most Shīʿī authorities rank Fāṭima above Mary; indeed, Fāṭima is sometimes referred to as *Maryam al-kubrā,* "Mary the Greater" (McAuliffe, Chosen of all women, 23-4, 26-7). In the Sunnī *tafsīr,* these notions are almost absent, while opinions are also largely divided on the exact meaning of Mary's purity *(ṭahāra)* or purification *(taṭhīr).*

Most interpreters rely on those traditions which establish that, in the physical sense, Mary was a woman like all others. She is said to have begun menstruating during the time of her service in the temple, from which Zechariah removed her to his wife's care until she had regained physical purity, and to have been ten, or thirteen, or fifteen years old at the time of the angelic annunciation of the birth of Jesus, by which time she had completed two menstrual cycles (Ṭabarī, *Tafsīr,* xvi, 45-6; Zamakhsharī, *Kashshāf,* iii, 7-8; Rāzī, *Tafsīr,* xxi, 196-201; Bayḍāwī, *Anwār,* i, 578-9; Kisāʾī, *Qiṣaṣ,* 328; Ibn Kathīr, *Qiṣaṣ,* ii, 385, 457). Traditions on the forty days of isolation that Mary is said to have observed after the delivery of her child "until she was healed of childbirth" further indicate to many interpreters that Jesus' birth was in its physical symptoms an ordinary event (Zamakhsharī, *Kashshāf,* iii, 11; Ibn Kathīr, *Qiṣaṣ,* ii, 393). Conversely, some interpreters have recorded traditions and/or their own scholarly opinions that Mary's purity included chastity as well as freedom from bleeding (Rāzī, *Tafsīr,* viii, 46; Bayḍāwī, *Anwār,* i, 155). According to the modernist Muḥammad ʿAbduh (d. 1905), it was this quality of purification that enabled Mary to serve in the temple while Fāṭima's equally miraculous freedom from the defilement of menstruation was the cause of her honorific title *al-zahrā'*, "the radiant, luminous" (Rashīd Riḍā, *Manār,* iii, 300). In classical as well as modern sources, however, such readings have remained marginal to the consensus-based doctrine that Mary's purity was "ethical," meaning that it concerned her character and soul (see ETHICS AND THE QUR'ĀN). While physically a woman like all others, she was free of all lowly character traits and exempted from all sin (see SIN, MAJOR AND MINOR). Sunnī exegesis thus came to define Mary's purity in terms of *'iṣma,* "sinlessness," the quality that Islamic dogma ascribes to God's prophets (see IMPECCABILITY). Nevertheless, to the scholars who interpreted her story, Mary's status remained *sui generis* because of the equally consensus-based Islamic doctrine that her physical nature was that of an ordinary woman (Ṭabarī, *Tafsīr,* vi, 400; Zamakhsharī, *Kashshāf,* i, 277; Rāzī, *Tafsīr,* viii, 46; Bayḍāwī, *Anwār,* i, 155; Ibn Kathīr, *Qiṣaṣ,* ii, 374; Rashīd Riḍā, *Manār,* iii, 300). In the medieval sources, some prominence was awarded to the link between Mary's purity and her mother's prayer to God to protect her daughter and her daughter's offspring against Satan (Q 3:36; cf. Ibn Kathīr, *Qiṣaṣ,* ii, 370-1, 461). A few modernist qur'ānic interpreters have questioned whether Mary's holiness, quite apart from all considerations of her physical purity, would not qualify her for inclusion among men in the full sense of their status in Islamic doctrine, liturgy and law (Smith and Haddad, Virgin Mary, 173, 179; see FEMINISM AND THE QUR'ĀN; EXEGESIS OF THE QUR'ĀN: EARLY MODERN AND CONTEMPORARY).

Concerning the matter of Jesus' conception without a human father, consensus among classical and modern scripturalist scholars has consistently maintained that Mary was a virgin *(batūl)* when she conceived her child from God's spirit. While the term 'virgin' *(batūl)* does not appear in the Qur'ān, the devout often use it in reference to Mary. In Sunnī and especially Shī'ī popular piety, the title is also applied to Fāṭima (Smith and Haddad, Virgin Mary, 179-80). Exegetical literature largely disregards the question of whether Mary's virginity prevailed after Jesus' birth. While Mary's purification "from the touch of men" implied perpetual virginity to some religious scholars (cf. Rāzī, *Tafsīr,* viii, 46), the matter was not fully discussed, and some modern interpreters appear to deny that Mary retained her virginity beyond Jesus' birth (cf. Bahī, *Sūrat Maryam,* 14). Even though, however, some nineteenth and twentieth century modernist Islamic scholars on the Indian subcontinent have rejected the notion of Mary's motherhood while a virgin (Baljon, *Koran interpretations,* 69-70; Parrinder, *Jesus,* 69 f.; Smith and Haddad, Virgin Mary, 175), mainstream Islamic consensus has upheld the tenet of the virgin birth of Jesus.

God's spirit (rūḥ) *and a word* (kalima) *from God: Mary and the birth of Jesus*

The earliest and longest account of the events surrounding the birth of Jesus is found in the sūra of Mary (Q 19:16-33), revealed in Mecca, which relates the annunciation, Jesus' birth, and Jesus' first words.

Mary had withdrawn from her family to an eastern place and was in seclusion. And we sent our spirit *(rūḥ)* to her, and it took the shape of a well-proportioned human. She said: "I take refuge with the Compassionate from you. [Go away] if you fear God." He said: "I am only your lord's messenger, that I give you a pure boy." She said: "How could I have a boy when no human has touched me and I am not an unchaste woman?" He said: "Thus. Your lord says: It is easy for me, and so that we make him a sign for the people and a mercy (q.v.) from us. It is a settled matter" (Q 19:17-21).

Mary conceived and retired to a remote place where the pains of childbirth drove her to the trunk of a palm tree (see DATE PALM). In her despair she cried out that she wished she had died before this and been forgotten, but then she heard a voice from below her instructing her to cease grieving, drink of the little brook that God had placed beneath her, eat of the fresh ripe dates of that tree, be joyful and abstain from speaking with anyone. When she then brought her baby to her people, they accused her of unchastity, but Jesus in the cradle announced himself to them as God's blessed prophet whom God had charged with prayer, almsgiving and filial piety toward his mother (Q 19:22-33).

In Q 21:91, also of the Meccan period, Mary is called "She who guarded her shame. Then we breathed (or blew) into her of our spirit *(rūḥ),* and we made her and her son a sign for the worlds," while in Q 23:50, also of the Meccan period, the son of Mary and his mother are likewise revealed to be a sign from God. The third passage about God's spirit in the context of Mary's motherhood is found in Q 66:11-2, dated to Medina, "And God has given an example to those who believe... [in] Mary the daughter of ʿImrān who protected her shame and we breathed (or blew) into it [or her] of our spirit *(rūḥ).* And she testified to the truth of her lord's words and his books and was of the devoutly obedient." According to Q 19:17, 21:91, and 66:12, Mary thus conceived Jesus from God's spirit.

In Q 4:171, Jesus is identified as "God's messenger *(rasūlu llāh),* his word that he cast into Mary and a spirit from him." Jesus was supported with the holy spirit (q.v.; *rūḥ al-qudus,* Q 2:87, 253; 5:110). The casting of God's spirit into Mary recalls the gift of God's spirit to Adam shaped from clay (q.v.; Q 15:29; 32:9; 38:72) while Jesus' support by means of the holy spirit recalls the strengthening of those in whose hearts (see HEART) faith is firmly established "with a spirit from himself" (Q 58:22). The Qurʾān speaks of the trusted spirit as the agent of God's revelation (Q 26:193; cf. 16:102). The spirit is mentioned together with, but separate from, the angels (Q 70:4; 78:38; 97:4) and as a gift conveyed by the angels to God's chosen servants (Q 16:2). In its role as conveyor of revelation, the spirit is identified as Gabriel (q.v.; Jibrīl, Q 2:97). In Mary's story, the spirit is the life-creating force of, or from, God. Qurʾānic commentary, however, has consistently differentiated between "our spirit sent to Mary in the form of a well-proportioned man" (Q 19:17) and "our spirit [of] which we breathed into Mary" (Q 21:91; 66:12), identifying the former with the angel Gabriel and the latter with the life substance with which God (directly) awakened Adam to life from clay, just as it (directly) awakened Jesus to life in Mary's womb (Rāzī, *Tafsīr,* xxi, 196, 200-1; xxii, 218; xxx, 50; Ṭanṭāwī, *Tafsīr,* 26, 30; Quṭb, *Ẓilāl,* iv, 2306).

The classical interpreters established that Gabriel was a means, or instrument, of God's creative power, whence they linked his agency with God's breathing, or blowing, of his spirit into Mary by developing the theme of Gabriel's blowing at Mary's garment or person (Ṭabarī, *Tafsīr,* xvi, 48; Zamakhsharī, *Kashshāf,* iii, 8; Rāzī, *Tafsīr,* xxi, 201; Bayḍāwī, *Anwār,* i, 578-9; Kisāʾī, *Qiṣaṣ,* 328; Ibn Kathīr, *Qiṣaṣ,* ii, 387-8). In contrast to the usual course of nature *(kharq al-ʿāda),* the divine breath caused Mary to conceive. While the physical aspect of how this occurred was of interest to some medieval rationalist exegetes like al-Rāzī (d. 606/1209; *Tafsīr,* viii, 50-2) and a few modernist interpreters like ʿAbduh and Rashīd Riḍā (d. 1935; *Manār,* iii, 308), most classical and modern interpreters have reckoned the physical manner of Mary's conception from the spirit a divine mystery beyond human understanding and, therefore, not of human concern (Bahī, *Sūrat Maryam,* 14; Quṭb, *Ẓilāl,* i, 396-7; iv, 2307).

A second angelic annunciation scene to Mary is related in Q 3:45-51, revealed in Medina, where it is preceded by the accounts of Zechariah's guardianship of Mary and Mary's special blessings in the temple, presented above. In Q 3:45, the angels announce to Mary that "God gives you glad tidings of a word *(kalima)* from him whose name is the Messiah *(al-masīḥ)* Jesus son of Mary, highly regarded in this world and in the hereafter (see ESCHATOLOGY), and one of those brought close [to God]." Similar to her words to the divine spirit/God's messenger in Q 19:20, Mary then questions her lord, "How shall I have a son when no man has touched me?" He said: "Thus. God creates what he wills. When he has decreed a matter he only says to it: 'Be!' and it is" (Q 3:47; see COSMOLOGY). The angels' glad tidings to Mary of a word *(kalima)* from God who is her son (Q 3:45) is reiterated in Q 4:171 which speaks of Jesus as "the Messiah Jesus son of Mary, God's messenger and his word that he cast into (or bestowed upon) Mary, and a spirit from him."

Qur'ānic exegesis has recorded different interpretations of the meaning of God's word *(kalima)* in the context of Jesus as a word from God (Q 3:45) and Jesus as his (i.e. God's) word which he cast into, or bestowed upon Mary (Q 4:171). The richest formulation of this theological debate is found in the *Tafsīr* (viii, 49-50) of the medieval rationalist theologian Fakhr al-Dīn al-Rāzī, whose arguments were at least partially based on older sources such as al-Ṭabarī's (d. 310/923) *Tafsīr* (vi, 411) but were also reiterated, with little change, by the nineteenth century modernist rationalist school of Muḥammad ʿAbduh (Rashīd Riḍā, *Manār,* iii, 304-5). To these exegetical authorities, the meaning of God's *kalima,* "word," in the context of Mary's conception of Jesus is multifaceted and in large part metaphorical (see METAPHOR). It connotes God's creative power and his (verbal) act of the creation of Jesus. But *kalima* also indicates the gospel (q.v.), the essence of Jesus' prophetic mission; elsewhere, Jesus himself is figuratively referred to as "God's word" by way of defining his mission, which is to clarify God's message anew and cleanse the record of past revelations from distortion (see FORGERY). Finally, *kalima,* the word, is said to be God's message to Mary *about* the birth of Jesus. To most modern and contemporary religious experts, however, who show little interest in the whole scholastic rationalist tradition, the theological problematic of Jesus as a word from God (Q 3:45) or (God's) word bestowed upon Mary (Q 4:171) is not an urgent concern, and they place it in the category of the Qur'ān's obscure *(mutashābih)* teachings, "a matter above human understanding and, therefore, none of man's concern" (e.g. Quṭb, *Ẓilāl,* i, 397; see AMBIGUOUS; DIFFICULT PASSAGES).

Membership in the created order

Both major accounts on the manner in which Mary conceived and bore her son Jesus (Q 19, Meccan, and Q 3, Medinan, quoted above) end with the affirmation of Jesus' full humanity. Speaking in the cradle, Jesus announces that

I am God's slave. He has given me the book (q.v.) and has made me a prophet. He has made me blessed wherever I be and has charged me with prayer (q.v.) and almsgiving (q.v.) as long as I live, and filial piety toward my mother. And he has not made me tyrannical and villainous (see OPPRESSION; ARROGANCE). And peace be upon me the day I was born and the day I die and the day I am resurrected alive (see RESURRECTION). Such is Jesus the son of Mary — to say the truth which they doubt. It is not for God to acquire (or to take to himself) any child. Praised be he (see GLORIFICATION OF GOD; LAUDATION)! When he decides a matter he only says to it: 'Be!' and it is (Q 19:30-5).

Jesus' apostleship, his prophetic career, and the special blessings from God which are outlined in greater detail in Q 3:48-58, at the end of the angels' annunciation to Mary of the birth of her son (Q 3:45-47), also conclude with the affirmation of his creaturedom: "Jesus is before God like Adam. He created him from dust then said to him: 'Be!' and he is" (Q 3:59). In the verses of Q 4:171-2 and Q 5:17, 72-3, 75-6, and 116-7, revealed in Medina, special emphasis is placed on Mary's and Jesus' full humanity, including refutation that they should form part of a "trinity" (q.v.).

In their interpretations, Muslim exegetes assert that the affirmation of God's oneness is the central issue and purpose of all the verses on Mary. Mary, God's handmaiden, and her son Jesus, God's slave and prophet, are not "gods" (Q 5:17, 72, 75-6, 116). The refutation of the notion of "three" (trinity) of Q 4:171 and Q 5:73 is the divinely-revealed correction of a blasphemous Christian association (see CHRISTIANS AND CHRISTIANITY) of Mary "the female consort" and Jesus "the son" with God, in a "family setting." The qur'ānic refutation of this blasphemy (q.v.) corresponds with the rejection of equally blasphemous pagan Arabian allegations that the angels were God's "daughters" whom God begat with the jinn (q.v.; in interpretation of Q 37:149-59; cf. 43:19-20) or that pagan deities were God's "daughters" (53:19-23; see SOUTH ARABIA, RELIGION IN PRE-ISLAMIC; POLYTHEISM AND ATHEISM; SATANIC VERSES).

Mary and Eve

In clarifying the nature of Jesus as fully human, the Qur'ān repeatedly likens Jesus to Adam because both are God's creations whom God brought to life by his divine word and decree. Ḥadīth has expanded this equation into a human tetragram where Mary parallels Adam, and Jesus parallels Eve. Just as Eve was created from Adam without a woman, so was Jesus created from Mary without a man (Ibn Kathīr, *Qiṣaṣ*, ii, 387). The Qur'ān-based Muslim doctrine that Adam's and Eve's disobedience (q.v.) was but a "slip" or "error" (q.v.), repented and forgiven (by the divine gift of prophethood; see REPENTANCE AND PENANCE; FORGIVENESS), has, however, precluded any other linkage between Eve and Mary in this context. It is only in some esoteric Ṣūfī (see ṢŪFISM AND THE QUR'ĀN) sources that the tetragram of Adam, Eve, Mary, and Jesus, placed into the context of God's self-revelation, has been said to signify God's forgiveness for the sin of Eve through Mary (Smith and Haddad, Virgin Mary, 182-3).

Barbara Freyer Stowasser

Bibliography
Primary: M. al-Bahī, *Tafsīr sūrat Maryam*, Cairo 1978; Bayḍāwī, *Anwār;* Ibn Ḥazm, *Milal*, 5 vols., Jeddah 1982; Ibn Kathīr, *Qiṣaṣ al-anbiyā'*, 2 vols., Cairo 1968; Kisā'ī, *Qiṣaṣ;* id., *The tales of the prophets of al-Kisa'i*, trans. W.M. Thackston, Boston 1978; Quṭb, *Ẓilāl*, 6 vols, Beirut 1982; Rashīd Riḍā, *Manār;* Rāzī, *Tafsīr*, 32 vols., Cairo 1934-62; Ṭabarī, *Tafsīr*, 16 vols., Cairo 1954-68; 32 vols., Beirut 1972; M. al-Sayyid Ṭanṭāwī, *al-Tafsīr al-wasīṭ lil-Qur'ān al-karīm.* Part xvi. *Tafsīr sūrat Maryam*, Cairo 1985; Zamakhsharī, *Kashshāf*, 4 vols., Cairo 1953.

Secondary: J.-M. Abd-el-Jalil, *Marie et l'Islam*, Paris 1950; M. Ayoub, *Redemptive suffering in Islam. A study of the devotional aspects of 'Ashura' in Twelver Shiism*, The Hague 1978; Baljon, *Modern;* J. Iskander, *Maria im Koran*, Augsburg 1999; J.D. McAuliffe, Chosen of all women. Mary and Fatima in qur'ānic exegesis, in *Islamochristiana* 7 (1981), 19-28; G. Parrinder, *Jesus in the Qur'ān*, London 1965; N. Robinson, *Christ in Islam and Christianity*, Albany 1991, esp. 156-66; J.I. Smith, and Y.Y. Haddad, The virgin Mary in Islamic tradition and commentary, in *MW* 79 (1989), 161-87; B.F. Stowasser, *Women in the Qur'ān, traditions, and interpretation*, New York 1994.

Maryam see MARY

Massacre see MURDER

Master see LORD; SCHOLAR

Material Culture and the Qur'ān

In view of the all-encompassing significance of the Qur'ān in the faith (q.v.) of the Muslim community it is to be expected that its influence would be manifested in many spheres of life (see EVERYDAY LIFE, QUR'ĀN IN). The holy book has had an impact not only through its cultic role but also as a venerated object and through its importance to other cultural practices. The Qur'ān's effect on material culture is an extension of the various functions it plays in devotional life and although some of these must have been prominent since the establishment of the faith in the seventh century, other uses have evolved over time and continue to be modified by the community's geographical expansion as well as by the broader development of its religious and visual culture.

Although one might assume that the Qur'ān had its greatest impact on the way of life of the Muslim community in the centuries that immediately followed its promulgation, evidence in the form of surviving manuscripts (see CODICES OF THE QUR'ĀN) and of qur'ānic citations on objects or architecture suggests that in fact the opposite is true — that the importance of the Qur'ān in both religious and material terms has grown more complex and elaborate over time and indeed continues to evolve today (see ART AND ARCHITECTURE AND THE QUR'ĀN; ARCHAEOLOGY AND THE QUR'ĀN; EPIGRAPHY AND THE QUR'ĀN). The reasons for its escalating importance are not always discernible but we hope that our exposition will spark further inquiry into this question. Despite the subject's obvious importance, the various ways in which the Qur'ān has affected the material culture of the broad expanse of the Muslim community has yet to receive sustained analytical consideration. The following essay should thus be considered a preliminary sketch on this topic rather than a definitive statement about it.

In order to provide an outline of the major phases and issues involved, this essay will have a general introduction followed by both chronological and thematic divisions. Its first phase will cover the period in which the evidence is the most fragmentary, from the rise of Islam in the seventh century C.E. until the fifth/eleventh century, and will concentrate on the regions of the new faith's birth and early expansion — the Middle East, north Africa and Spain. The second period, the twelfth through fifteenth centuries, witnessed an increasing impact of the Qur'ān on material culture as well as a broad extension of Islam into new regions. Because of its abundance and complexity, evidence from this and the succeeding period will be treated within geographical regions and according to dynastic divisions. Dynasties that straddle these broad periods will be discussed in the epoch of their greatest importance. The final section, devoted to developments from the sixteenth century to the present, will again be treated regionally. Special attention will be given to areas not well represented in earlier periods such as east and southeast Asia and sub-Saharan Africa.

Despite the broad chronological and geographical scope of this topic, certain aspects of the Qurʾān's connection with material culture are encountered in most regions, although their relative prominence probably fluctuated over time. In every region and period special care was given to the manufacture, use and preservation of individual copies of the Qurʾān (see MUṢḤAF) — be they manuscripts in codex, scroll or single-sheet format (see MANUSCRIPTS OF THE QURʾĀN) or, more recently, printed copies (see PRINTING OF THE QURʾĀN). Scholars have debated when and where the text first assumed the form it retains today and the scripts with which it was copied have been classified and analyzed (see ARABIC SCRIPT; ORTHOGRAPHY). Little attention has been given, however, to the importance of sectarian, regional or dynastic views for determining the various ways that the Qurʾān's text has been transcribed over the centuries nor has adequate attention been given to the question of whether a particular copy's physical features reveal the use for which it was intended. Many of the practices connected with the manufacture or preservation of Qurʾān copies are believed by modern scholars to have had a wider effect in stimulating the development of the book arts. It has often been suggested that there was a transfer of techniques or styles ranging from calligraphy (q.v.) to illumination (see ORNAMENTATION AND ILLUMINATION) and binding from the Qurʾān to other kinds of books but the possibility that Qurʾān manuscripts borrowed features from elsewhere has been little investigated.

It has often been noted that portions of the Qurʾān's text appear on certain kinds of portable objects and are inscribed on many architectural monuments but rarely has such an observation led to any sustained consideration of the reasons behind this use. Studies have explored the significance of the inscriptions belonging to specific buildings and a broader compilation of such texts accompanied by indices and interpretative essays published by E. Dodd and S. Khairullah has suggested that qurʾānic citations on religious architecture fulfill the communicative and symbolic role played by images in some other faiths (see ICONOCLASM). They acknowledge, however, that it is often difficult to provide a consistent explanation for the popularity or use of a specific sūra or verse in architecture (see SŪRAS; VERSES). R. Hillenbrand's evaluation of their findings has likewise concluded that in the case of mosques the selection and application of qurʾānic citations was often "surprisingly undirected."

The use of the Qurʾān's text on objects has been even less studied than its role in architecture. The reasons why portions of its text appear on some types of objects and not on others have not been clearly elucidated. Each quotation is not of equal importance; over time some usages became formulaic and probably were almost mechanical. Nevertheless, even the repeated use of a given text on a particular type of object or in a specific architectural context is potentially indicative of a deeper connection which links the object or structure in question to a facet of the Qurʾān's text or to its significance for religious practice and daily life.

Another virtually universal role of the Qurʾān is as a source of comfort and support for the individual believer in this life as well as in the next (see ESCHATOLOGY), although the history and development of such practices is often difficult to establish. The appearance of citations from the Qurʾān on tombstones or other funerary structures is often the earliest sign of the presence of Muslims in a given region. Its text is also inscribed on a range of objects that functioned as amulets (q.v.) or talismans (see POPULAR AND TALISMANIC USES OF THE QURʾĀN) intended to bring succor to an individual believer in daily life (see TRUST AND PATIENCE).

The formative period: seventh to eleventh centuries (first to fifth centuries hijrī)

The importance of the Qurʾān for the Umayyad period: 41-132/661-750

Most of the extant early Qurʾān copies derive from caches of manuscript pages, detached bindings and related religious materials that were discovered during the nineteenth and twentieth centuries in several mosques, including the Great Mosque of Qayrawān in Tunisia, the mosque of ʿAmr in Cairo, the Umayyad mosque in Damascus and the Great Mosque of Ṣanʿāʾ in the Yemen. The overwhelming majority of such Qurʾāns survive only in a very fragmentary state, indicating that these copies were probably discarded because they had sustained damage that made them unsuitable for further use. The rather disorderly manner in which these fragments were preserved also tends to underscore the conclusion that initially the recited Qurʾān was of greater liturgical significance than its written version (see ORALITY; ORALITY AND WRITING IN ARABIA; RECITATION OF THE QURʾĀN). Despite their wide geographic distribution, few of these Qurʾān fragments retain any documentation about their date and place of copying. Examination of these pages by a succession of scholars including B. Moritz, N. Abbott, A. Grohmann and F. Déroche has established that they derive from various early Qurʾān manuscripts but no consensus has emerged about either the date or geographical origin of these fragments. The initial hope that some might date to the seventh century has been largely, but not entirely, abandoned in favor of dates ranging from the eighth to tenth centuries.

The traditional recollection of the Muslim community that the Qurʾān's text was compiled in the mid-seventh century during the caliphate of ʿUthmān (q.v.; 23-35/644-656; see also COLLECTION OF THE QURʾĀN) cannot be confirmed through manuscript evidence, and claims that certain extant copies were written by him or even were splattered with his blood are probably legends. A study by E. Whelan has established that as early as the late seventh century the preparation of Qurʾān manuscripts was entrusted to specialists who were both skilled calligraphers and persons respected for their religious knowledge. Links can also be made between the manuscript tradition and early monumental epigraphy because both textual and visual evidence demonstrates that calligraphers trained to copy the Qurʾān were responsible for designing the mosaic inscriptions in monuments erected with the patronage of the Umayyad caliphs ʿAbd al-Malik b. Marwān (r. 64-86/684-705) and his son al-Walīd (r. 86-96/705-15).

The reign of ʿAbd al-Malik marks the moment when the Qurʾān's importance as a symbol of the power and legitimacy of the new Muslim polity was made manifest not only to the Muslims themselves but also to their non-Muslim subjects and to their adversaries, the Byzantines (q.v.). The reforms that ʿAbd al-Malik instituted — whereby Arabic became the primary language of administration and governance (see ARABIC LANGUAGE) — also gave citations from the Qurʾān a new level of public prominence. This transition, which reached its climax in 77/696-7 with the minting of new epigraphic gold coins, probably began five years earlier in 72/691-2 (see MONEY). During these five years the Qurʾān was used alongside texts or designs of Byzantine origin in various contexts. One of the first places in which the Qurʾān made its appearance is on the papyrus rolls produced in Egypt by the state-controlled factory. By 74/693-4 or 75/694-5, Arabic appeared alongside Greek in the *protokollon,* a text written on the first sheet in a papyrus roll. Both the Arabic text and its Greek translation consisted of phrases from different parts of the Qurʾān fused into a continuum. Usually the protocol text included phrases from Q 3:173; 6:163; 9:33, 61; 47:19; 61:1, 9 and most of Q 112. A key example of this transition between Byzantine traditions and the new Umayyad approach is the undated double-sided lead seal of ʿAbd al-Malik preserved in the Topkapı Sarayı, Istanbul and published by I. Artuk in 1952. In shape, structure and design it is modeled on the lead seals that Byzantine authorities affixed to important documents or various kinds of goods. In this case, the seal's obverse bears cartouches inscribed with the caliph's name and his titles (in Arabic) flanking a large letter "A" that, in turn, is framed by a pair of long-necked birds. The obverse's outer border bears short phrases reiterating key beliefs of the Muslim community from Q 6:163; 39:45; 48:29; and Q 49:19, a selection of texts similar to those used on ʿAbd al-Malik's reform coins (see NUMISMATICS) and his bilingual papyrus protocols. The border of the reverse carries a grapevine and its center combines a pair of lions with the name *Filasṭīn* (Palestine) in Arabic.

Qurʾānic phrases also appear on the gold dinars struck in Damascus and other cities after ʿAbd al-Malik's monetary reform in 77/696-7, and on silver dirhams struck from 79/698-9 onward (for an example of such coinage, see Fig. I of EPIGRAPHY). The caliph's use of the Qurʾān on coins elevated coinage to a position as signifier of sovereignty (q.v.) among Muslim rulers and led later dynasties to employ its text as a source for inscriptions appropriate to their own position and ambitions (see POLITICS AND THE QURʾĀN). Both the obverse and reverse of ʿAbd al-Malik's reformed coins have texts at their center and around their perimeter. The central text of the obverse consists of the three distinct citations that create the profession of the faith (Q 6:163; 39:45; 47:19; see WITNESS TO FAITH) and these texts overlap so that the last word of the first phrase also functions as the first word of the second phrase: "There is no God but *God; God* alone." The marginal text, composed of phrases from Q 48:29 and 9:33, establishes Muḥammad's prophetic mission. The central text of the coin's reverse carries Q 112:1-3 and reiterates a belief in God's unity, eternity (q.v.) and absolute singularity (see GOD AND HIS ATTRIBUTES; POLYTHEISM AND ATHEISM).

Monumental architecture

Extensive citation of qurʾānic passages on architectural monuments, one of the characteristics of structures built for Muslim patrons in many regions and periods, also begins with ʿAbd al-Malik. The earliest surviving example of this practice, the Dome of the Rock *(qubbat al-ṣakhrā)* in Jerusalem, bears a date (72/691-2) that probably documents the beginning of its construction. Those inscriptions with gold letters silhouetted against a dark blue ground were executed in glass mosaic or painted on embossed metal plaques. The outer face of the interior's octagonal ambulatory bears five distinct prayers each of which opens with qurʾānic citations affirming God's unity and eternity. Passages cited in one or more of these prayers include Q 6:112,163; 17:111; 39:45; 47:19; 57:2 or Q 64:1. The Prophet's role as divine messenger (q.v.) and intercessor (see INTERCESSION) is also reiterated using both Q 48:29

or Q 33:56 and extra-qurʾānic invocations. The mosaic inscriptions of the ambulatory's inner face augments these themes with praises of Jesus (q.v.), son of Mary (q.v.), and stresses his role as divine messenger, while also providing a refutation of Christian beliefs about the Trinity (q.v.; Q 4:171-2; 19:34-6; see CHRISTIANS AND CHRISTIANITY). Originally, inscribed metal plaques were probably situated at the building's four entrances but only two of them survive. The north door panel enunciates Muḥammad's missionary role and his links to earlier prophets (Q 2:136; 3:84 or Q 61:9; see PROPHETS AND PROPHETHOOD), whereas the eastern one stresses God's omnipotence and eschatological themes (Q 2:255; 6:12, 101, 112; 3:26; 7:156).

The style of the script used in the Dome of the Rock's inscription and the presence therein of diacritical signs link it to scribal practices used in preparing manuscript copies of the Qurʾān; it is likely, therefore, that its designer or designers were among those who specialized in that exacting task. A qurʾānic scribe is mentioned as the designer of a mosaic inscription of the Great Mosque of Medina erected under the patronage of al-Walīd b. ʿAbd al-Malik between 88-91/706-10. This mosque's *qibla* (q.v.) wall was inscribed with Q 93 and Q 114, sūras that stress eschatological themes. Literary descriptions of the Medina mosque suggest that other sections of the Qurʾān, and possibly its entire text, were inscribed over its doors, around its courtyard and within the sanctuary. Qurʾānic inscriptions executed in mosaic were also included in the Great Mosque of Damascus, another important commission of al-Walīd.

Evidence from the Umayyad period demonstrates the wide influence of actions taken by members of that dynasty in defining the contexts in which qurʾānic citations would appear for several centuries. In order to have such a lasting impact, their actions must also have been in consonance with the preferences of their co-religionists. The fact that qurʾānic excerpts appearing on their papyrus protocols, personal seals, coins and monumental architecture are closely related variants reiterating the core tenets of Islam suggests that the Umayyad leaders' primary concern was to affirm and disseminate those beliefs.

Excursus on the importance of the Qurʾān for individual Muslims

During the second/eighth through fourth/tenth centuries brief excerpts from the Qurʾān also played a role in the more personal spheres of life and appear on seals, seal rings, amulets and tombstones. A third/ninth or fourth/tenth century amulet case inscribed with Q 112 was excavated in eastern Iran at Nīshāpūr. Tombstones from Egypt, Syria and north Africa believed to date from the eighth and ninth centuries are inscribed with a variety of short qurʾānic phrases. The earliest Syrian tombstones carry a variant of the profession of faith *(shahāda)* that combines the phrases from Q 6:163 and Q 47:19 that affirm God's absolute unity, phrases also contained in many papyrus protocols. A Tunisian tombstone of 270/883 contains Q 3:185, "Every soul shall taste of death," a text that became one of the standard citations on funerary monuments but Q 37:61, "For the like of this, let the workers work," popular in Egypt in the first Islamic centuries, is little used in later periods (see DEATH AND THE DEAD). A number of early tombstones from Egypt and Syria employ phrases that stress reliance on or trust in God such as *"ḥasbiya llāhu"* (Q 9:129; 39:38) or its close variant *"ḥasbunā llāhu"* (Q 3:173; 9:59). These phrases were also engraved on ring-stones where they may have had a talismanic function. A small lead dish attributed to the second/

eighth or third/ninth century in the Nasser D. Khalili Collection of Islamic Art (MTW 621) that may have served a medical-magical purpose is impressed with figures of birds and animals as well as the *basmala* (q.v.) and *ḥasbiya llāh* (Q 9:129; 39:38).

Use of the Qurʾān between 132/750 and 494/1100

During the first centuries of ʿAbbāsid rule from 132/750 to ca. 494/1100, links between the Qurʾān and broader aspects of culture appear to have intensified; trends begun under the Umayyads continued without interruption but new approaches were also formulated. One of the continuing practices is the striking of coins with qurʾānic citations and another is the custom of inscribing the Qurʾān on architecture. Monuments from this period suggest that the selections used for the latter purpose could convey very specific messages reflecting particular facets of the local religious landscape, as well as aspects of dynastic policy. Rulers whose subjects included significant numbers of Christians appear to have been particularly enthusiastic about developing special modes of honoring and displaying the Qurʾān. These features are present in monuments erected under the sponsorship of not only the ʿAbbāsids, but also of their rivals — the Umayyad rulers of Spain and the Fāṭimids of Egypt and Syria.

The ʿAbbāsids and the Qurʾān

Stress placed by the ʿAbbāsids on their kinship (q.v.) with the Prophet, a relationship that was a key factor in the establishment of their dynastic legitimacy (see KINGS AND RULERS; CALIPH; IMĀM), led them naturally to a close association with the Qurʾān. In addition to the inclusion of the Qurʾān on coins and in monumental architecture, practices initiated under the Umayyads and shared by most later Islamic dynasties, the early ʿAbbāsid period also laid the foundation for new approaches that would, in subsequent centuries, expand this book's roles in material culture. From the late third/ninth century onward the ʿAbbāsids included a Qurʾān associated with ʿUthmān himself in their court regalia; it was carried in processions and used in ceremonies. This practice probably stimulated other rulers to include Qurʾāns of unusual sanctity in their own religious and courtly rituals.

The debate over whether the Qurʾān was created or eternal (see CREATEDNESS OF THE QURʾĀN), which occupied religious scholars during the third/ninth through fourth/tenth centuries, was contemporary with important developments in calligraphy that made manuscripts of its text more legible. Baghdād appears to have been the locus of experiments whereby the Qurʾān was transcribed with cursive scripts previously used for a variety of secular needs, a practice traditionally linked with the names of calligraphers associated with the ʿAbbāsid court including Ibn Muqla (272-328/885-940), Ismāʿīl b. Ḥammād al-Jawharī (d. ca. 392/1002), and ʿAlī b. Hilāl al-Sitrī known as Ibn al-Bawwāb (d. ca. 413/1022). ʿAbbāsid support for the ʿUthmānic recension of the Qurʾān as revised by Ibn Mujāhid (d. 324/936) helped to promulgate more standardized versions of its contents and generally to increase the prestige of manuscript copies, even as the use of paper made such books more widely available. The earliest surviving Qurʾān manuscripts written on paper date to the mid fourth/tenth century and from that date onward some copies include charts that document the number of words, letters and diacritical signs in the Qurʾān's text. Certain specimens are believed to come from Iran but similar volumes, including copies in Dublin and Istanbul (Chester Beatty Library, CBL MS 1431; Türk Islâm

Eserleri Müzesi, TIEM 449) linked to Ibn al-Bawwāb, were probably produced in Iraq (the opening page of the Ibn al-Bawwāb Qurʾān in the Chester Beatty Library can be seen in Fig. II of BASMALA). A Qurʾān in the Khalili Collection (Qur 572) dated to 582/1186 appears to have been made for a scholar specializing in qurʾānic studies. It has not only the usual tabulation of the text's contents but also a full critical apparatus, including the ten canonical reading variants (*qirāʾa,* see READINGS OF THE QURʾĀN) and their transmitters as well as other particulars on the text's pronunciation during recitation.

Widespread acceptance of the views enunciated by religious scholars that the Qurʾān was the eternal speech (q.v.) of God (see also WORD OF GOD) had important consequences for the text's roles in many spheres of life, including material culture. From the second/eighth to the fourth/tenth centuries the Qurʾān was the focus of study by commentators who analyzed both its exoteric and esoteric significance (see EXEGESIS OF THE QURʾĀN: CLASSICAL AND MEDIEVAL); practices that exploited the symbolic or magical power of the Qurʾān's text had a more profound impact on material culture than the more literal exoteric tradition (see ṢŪFISM AND THE QURʾĀN). The establishment of a finite and largely canonical text fostered new approaches that focused on the value of not only its constituent words but also on the mysterious letters (q.v.) placed at the beginning of many sūras. These and other key phrases or passages including the beautiful names of God *(al-asmāʾ al-ḥusnā)* were subjected to particular scrutiny.

Belief in the eternal nature of the Qurʾān also encouraged its use to safeguard persons and property through the development of a variety of magical-protective devices ranging from seals to rings, amulets and talismans, and these views were probably also instrumental in its citation on weapons, helmets, armor or other accoutrements of war (see INSTRUMENTS). Iraq had long been a center for the use of magical and protective rituals, but it was during the early ʿAbbāsid period that the Qurʾān appears to have usurped the role of other texts and materials in these procedures with the composition of treatises by the ʿAbbāsid caliph al-Maʾmūn (r. 198-218/813-33) and by Jamāl al-Dīn Yūsuf al-Kindī (d. 256/870). One technique that gained popularity was the conversion of the Qurʾān's words, or even of its individual letters, into numbers that could, in turn, be used to create diagrams and formulas (see NUMEROLOGY). Among the Shīʿa (see SHĪʿISM AND THE QURʾĀN), knowledge about how to create amulets and talismans from qurʾānic extracts was attributed to the imāms and in particular to Jaʿfar al-Ṣādiq (d. ca. 148/763). Although the intellectual foundations of these developments were laid in the early ʿAbbāsid period, most of the evidence about their implementation comes from later centuries.

The Umayyad rulers of Cordoba and the Qurʾān: 139-423/756-1031

The initial stages of the development of a distinctive approach to the copying and use of the Qurʾān in Spain probably coincided with the rule of the Umayyads at Cordoba, but the earliest surviving Qurʾān manuscript that can be firmly linked to this region dates to 382/1090. It is written on vellum in an angular script with rounded sub-linear components often described by modern authors as "Maghribī."

The Great Mosque of Cordoba, a structure erected in several phases between 169/785 and 483/1009, exemplifies the ways in which the rituals occurring in a religious structure could have a dynamic relationship with the qurʾānic texts inscribed upon it (see MOSQUE). Inscriptions commemorating the mosque's renovation by al-Ḥakam in 354/956 include citations from the Qurʾān and are clustered around the *miḥrāb* and in the bays flanking it to the left and right. Those on the dome in front of the *miḥrāb* (Q 2:38; 31:22) urge the believer to be steadfast in his faith and those in the adjacent bay and on the walls of the *miḥrāb* chamber itself (Q 22:77-8) remind the worshiper of a Muslim's obligations to pray and give alms (see PRAYER; ALMSGIVING). Texts inscribed on the *miḥrāb*'s outer frame (Q 2:286; 3:8; 5:101-2) urge the believer to be steadfast in his faith and those in the adjacent bay (i.e. Q 7:43; 40:65), through which the caliph or imām entered the building, emphasize God's omnipotence, singularity and the absence of a consort or progeny. The latter comments were seemingly aimed at the Cordoban ruler's Christian subjects or competitors.

This theme is elaborated upon in texts inscribed on the approach to the *miḥrāb* that refer to the Qurʾān and to its superiority over the scriptures of the Christians and the Jews (see JEWS AND JUDAISM; SCRIPTURE AND THE QURʾĀN), including Q 3:3, 7, 19; 35:31. The date at which these texts were inscribed on the building is uncertain, but their presence has been linked to the fact that the Cordoba mosque also owned an unusually large and venerable Qurʾān, a few unbound pages of which were believed not only to have been copied by the caliph ʿUthmān b. ʿAffān but even to carry traces of his blood. The date and circumstances of this manuscript's arrival in Spain are obscure, but it eventually became the focus of a ceremony that appears to emulate aspects of the Christian liturgy current in medieval Spain. At the beginning of the prayer service the carefully wrapped Qurʾān was removed from a chamber along the *qibla* wall and carried by two men in a candlelight procession to the mosque's *miḥrāb,* where it was placed on a special stand and its text was read to the assembled worshipers.

If this elaborate ceremonial use of a venerated Qurʾān began in Spain's Umayyad period, the book's presence may even help to explain unusual features of the Cordoba mosque's construction and embellishment, including the presence of qurʾānic passages affirming the holy book's superiority over those of rival faiths. In the mid sixth/twelfth century Cordoba's ʿUthmānic Qurʾān was transferred to the Great Mosque of Marrakesh at the request of the Almohad ruler ʿAbd al-Muʾmin (r. 524-58/1130-63), where it continued to be the focus of veneration.

Egypt: third/ninth to sixth/twelfth centuries
Monuments connected with ʿAbbāsid patronage followed Umayyad precedents in their programmatic citation of the Qurʾān in architecture, and one of the best examples is situated in Egypt. Although normally a measuring device would not be considered a religious structure, the portions of the Qurʾān inscribed on the Nilometer *(miqyās al-nīl)* at Fusṭāṭ, essentially a stone-lined pit linked to the Nile that measured the height of its flood, stress its links to God's beneficence and generosity (see BLESSING; GRACE). According to historical accounts, in 247/861 the ʿAbbāsid caliph al-Mutawakkil ordered the Nilometer, which was of Byzantine date, to be rebuilt, and he entrusted the task of providing it with appropriate citations from the Qurʾān to Abū l-Raddād, a muezzin *(muʾadhdhin)* and Qurʾān instructor attached to the mosque of ʿAmr in Fusṭāṭ. The latter claimed to have selected the texts and then to have carved them on marble panels, which were later integrated into the Nilometer's inner walls on two different levels. The lower set consists of four separate excerpts of equal length extolling

God's munificence in sending the rain that permits the vegetation to grow and sustains all life (Q 22:5, 62; 42:28; 50:9; see AGRICULTURE AND VEGETATION; WATER). The carved panels of these texts were set into the wall's four sides at the level that marked the height of the flood. As the level of the Nile rose, those panels were submerged, thereby linking their text with the example of God's bounty that they celebrated. A fifth text placed above the high-water mark enjoins man to offer gratitude for the rain that leads to the creation of rivers on which ships (q.v.) can sail to the sea (Q 14:32-3; see GRATITUDE AND INGRATITUDE).

The Fāṭimid dynasty of north Africa and Egypt (297-567/909-1171) both continued earlier practices such as inscribing the Qurʾān on their coins and devised new ways to use it in their celebrations and architectural monuments. A Qurʾān copy said to have been written by ʿAlī b. Abī Ṭālib (q.v.) that was housed in the mosque of ʿAmr was the focus of personal veneration by members of the dynasty. Carefully wrapped copies of the Qurʾān were also carried through Cairo and Fusṭāṭ during the processions that marked important holidays and festivals (see FESTIVALS AND COMMEMORATIVE DAYS).

The dynasty's claim to possess a special insight into the Qurʾān's significance by virtue of their kinship to the prophet Muḥammad raises the possibility that their use of the holy book could have reflected both esoteric interpretations of its text aimed at their supporters and exoteric ones intended for the general public. P. Sanders and others have suggested that the manner in which the Qurʾān is inscribed on the mosque of al-Ḥākim (completed ca. 401/1010) at Cairo reveals these dual goals. Texts on the building's exterior, notable for their legibility and visual prominence, include passages that remind Muslims of their religious duties (Q 9:18; 24:36-7). Although intelligible to the populace at large, these verses could also refer to the Ismāʿīlī mission. Those on the interior were probably intended primarily for perusal by supporters of the dynasty and may make indirect reference to the Fāṭimids and their religious role as guides for the community (Q 3:1-17; 6:1-7; 7:1-22; 8:1-13; 48:1-22). The same message was probably reinforced by a pair of white silk curtains embroidered in red with Q 62 and Q 63 that were suspended near the mosque's *miḥrāb* during the month of Ramaḍān (q.v.). Even the Fāṭimid placement on military banners of Q 61:13, a widely used verse about the divine source of victory (q.v.), may have had such a dual significance. Fāṭimid coins have the distinction of carrying two separate verses on their obverse, Q 9:33 and Q 5:55.

Iran: third/ninth to fifth/eleventh centuries

Qurʾānic inscriptions on Iranian architecture of the fourth/tenth and fifth/eleventh century generally reveal a building's intended function, but some ensembles are noteworthy for the way in which the selected texts can be linked to broader religious questions. One such structure is a domed square building in the city of Yazd now known as the "Twelve Imāms," erected in 429/1038 under the patronage of a local dynasty of Daylamī origin with Shīʿa leanings (the Kākūyids). This structure was probably intended to commemorate an event or person of religious importance. Its qurʾānic texts (Q 2:255, 163; 40:65) focus on God's omnipotence, uniqueness and omnipresence, and this has led S. Blair to suggest that it was intended to evoke the presence of the Twelfth Imām believed to be alive, yet in occultation.

Several sets of architectural inscriptions make reference to the beautiful names of God *(al-asmāʾ al-ḥusnā),* using either qurʾānic or extra-qurʾānic texts demonstrating the growing popularity of these epithets. Three fifth/eleventh century tombs, one at Safīd Buland in the Farghānā valley and two at Kharraqān in western Iran between Hamadān and Qazvīn, refer to them by using Q 59:21-4, but a fourth monument, the north dome of the Great Mosque of Iṣfahān, dated to 481/1088, includes an extra-qurʾānic litany enumerating thirty-two divine epithets.

The ways in which extracts from the Qurʾān can be used to establish the function and interpretation of monumental architecture is demonstrated by the foundation inscriptions of the two large domes belonging to the Great Mosque of Iṣfahān. The *qibla* dome erected for Sultan Malikshāh by Niẓām al-Mulk in 479/1086-7 carries the opening sections of Q 23 that remind the individual Muslim of his religious duties, a selection that underscores that ruler's role as supporter of the faith. The northern dome built by the latter's rival Tāj al-Mulk in 481/1088 is inscribed internally with texts that extol the benefits of night prayer (i.e. Q 3:97; 17:78-9; see DAY AND NIGHT) and enumerate the divine attributes *(al-asmāʾ al-ḥusnā)*. This combination suggests that this chamber was the site of nocturnal vigils during which the holy names were recited or recollected.

The paucity of objects that survive from early Islamic Iran makes it difficult to judge the degree to which the Qurʾān appeared on personal effects during the second/eighth to fifth/eleventh centuries. Some ceramic vessels produced in eastern Iran or Transoxiana during the third/ninth through fourth/tenth centuries have carefully executed Arabic inscriptions written in a hand that resembles that used in contemporary Qurʾān manuscripts. Most of their texts consist of maxims with a practical bent but some are ḥadīth and a recently published bowl in the Ṭāriq Rajab Museum dated to 300/912 is inscribed with Q 68:51-2 (see Fig. 1). The Khalili Collection contains a number of amulets that have been attributed to the third/ninth or fourth/tenth century, on which citations from the Qurʾān are juxtaposed with schematically drawn animals. Some are small pendants, tubes or pierced disks probably intended to be worn, but others are spoons or spindle whorls. The portions of the Qurʾān most often cited are Q 1:2; 8:46; 12:21; 21:87; 105; 109; 112; 118.

Twelfth to fifteenth centuries (sixth to ninth centuries hijrī)

If in the first Islamic centuries citations from the Qurʾān on buildings, objects and documents suggest that it was used as a resource for the self-definition of the Muslim community, from the sixth/twelfth to the ninth/fifteenth centuries greater stress was laid on the holy book as a sacred object and on the Qurʾān as a support for the devotional life of the community. Citations of the Qurʾān on buildings and objects have a more consistently interpretive or programmatic character than in earlier centuries and reflect a more focused linking of its text with a building's function or the setting in which an object was used. These centuries also coincided with the rise of institutional Ṣūfism and many prominent Qurʾān calligraphers were affiliated with such groups. Most Ṣūfīs, particularly those with a Sunnī orientation, made study and recitation of the Qurʾān a cornerstone of their devotional life. Ṣūfī communities often commanded a substantial popular following that included rulers and highly placed officials who, in turn, constructed residences for Ṣūfīs. These residences, known variously as *ribāṭ*s, *khānqāh*s and *zāwiya*s, were often provided with endowments that financed the recitation, study and copying of the Qurʾān. The faith and practices of Islam were also carried to new regions of Asia and Africa largely through an expansion of trade and cultural contacts, thereby expanding the geographical scope of the Qurʾān's impact.

In addition, the spread of Ṣūfism introduced a broad spectrum of the population to exoteric and esoteric interpretations of the Qurʾān that had previously been the concern of small clusters of scholars and ascetics (see ASCETICISM). The authors of commentaries and symbolic interpretations drew attention to passages that were both religiously charged and particularly eloquent, an emphasis that encouraged the repetition of those texts on buildings or objects. Inter-related concepts disseminated in this period held that God's reality is manifested in every letter, word, verse and chapter of the Qurʾān's text and that this essence could also be symbolically expressed in numbers. This view enunciated in the late fourth/tenth century by scholars including Ibn Baṭṭa (d. ca. 365/975) was popularized by Ibn al-ʿArabī (560-638/1165-1240) who focused particular attention on meanings and symbolic values of the attributes of God *(al-asmāʾ al-ḥusnā)* enumerated in Q 59:22-4 and extra-qurʾānic litanies.

These beliefs led to the creation of diagrams constructed with letters, words or their numerical equivalents that made a coded reference to key portions of the Qurʾān. The *Shams al-maʿārif* of Shihāb al-Dīn al-Būnī (d. 622/1225) was a popular compendium about the occult properties of the Qurʾān, the benefits to be derived from the use of the divine attributes *(al-asmāʾ al-ḥusnā)* and methods for arranging them in "magic squares." Although al-Būnī himself was born in north Africa and died in Cairo, the popularity of "magic squares" and other talismanic schemes was widespread and enduring.

Within the broad territorial expanse in which Islam was practiced and over the three centuries in question, it is possible to discern regional and dynastic divergences in the manner in which the Qurʾān interacted with material culture and in the degree to which it became a vehicle of personal piety or dynastic legitimization. The clearest distinctions are between the parts of the Muslim world that encouraged the development of new approaches to the study, transcription, decoration and use of the Qurʾān (Mesopotamia, Iran, the Levant, Anatolia, and Egypt) and those regions where the conservatism of the religious authorities appears to have slowed the pace of change (north Africa, Spain and the western Sudan). Special conditions also pertained in regions such as the Indian subcontinent, southeast Asia and China where Islam competed with well-established local faiths and their deeply ingrained cultural practices.

North Africa, Spain and the western Sudan

Manuscripts produced in north Africa and Spain during the sixth/twelfth to ninth/fifteenth centuries are notable for their conservatism. Their archaic features include transcription on parchment and a reliance on modes of decoration resembling those in Qurʾāns from earlier centuries. Simple unornamented sūra headings were used in north African manuscripts long after they had been replaced by more elaborate framed varieties in areas further east. The local preference for Qurʾāns in a square format that persisted into the ninth/fifteenth century may also have a religious foundation because it helped to distinguish them from other books in which a more vertical format was customary.

The persistence of archaic features in this region may be connected with the conservative views about the Qurʾān espoused by the Mālikiyya, followers of Mālik b. Anas (d. 179/796), some of whom believed that Qurʾān manuscripts should not only be unornamented but even devoid of punctuation or sūra headings. Some Mālikīs considered the introduction of manuscript copies into mosques an unacceptable innovation because the books could challenge the liturgical primacy of the spoken and remembered text (see MEMORY).

Despite these scruples, the Qurʾān continued to be integrated into various spheres of daily activity even in areas where Mālikī views prevailed. Legends and ceremonies surrounding the ʿUthmānic codex of Cordoba suggest that some Qurʾān manuscripts acquired a liturgical role even in a region where the views of Mālik's followers had great prestige. Although under the Almoravids (r. 454-541/1062-1147) Mālikī religious authorities relegated study of the Qurʾān to a secondary position behind that of Islamic law (*fiqh*, see LAW AND THE QURʾĀN), that dynasty did not abandon the practice of inscribing the Qurʾān on their coins. Their approach is evident in the coins struck by the Almoravid Yūsuf b. Tāshufīn (r. 453-500/1061-1106). The obverse carries the usual profession of faith as well as his titles, but the reverse has Q 3:85, in which Islam is proclaimed as the only faith acceptable in God's eyes, conveying a more sectarian message.

The Almoravids' competitors and successors, the Almohads (524-668/1130-1269), made the Qurʾān a focus of their devotional life and also used it as an instrument of dynastic legitimization. An indication of the Almohad enthusiasm for the Qurʾān is the battle flag of Abū Yaʿqūb Yūsuf II captured after his defeat at Las Navas de Tolosa in 609/1212 (see Fig. III). The inscription on it, Q 61:10-2, encourages Muslims to undertake wars for the sake of the faith (see WAR; FIGHTING; JIHĀD), in return for which God will forgive them their sins (see SIN, MAJOR AND MINOR; FORGIVENESS) and admit them to the paradisiacal gardens (see GARDENS; PARADISE; REWARD AND PUNISHMENT). The Almohad's reverence for the Qurʾān is also evident in their treatment of the ʿUthmānic codex belonging to the Great Mosque of Cordoba mentioned above. In the mid sixth/twelfth century it was transferred to the Great Mosque of Marrakesh at the request of ʿAbd al-Muʾmin (r. 524-58/1130-63). There, he and his successors devised new ways to honor and use the precious volume. It was stored in a special chamber along the *qibla* wall from which it emerged during the prayer service, as if by magic, supported on an "X" shaped stand or *kursī* that rested, in turn, on a metal track along which it moved into and out of the prayer hall. The mechanism on which the Qurʾān and its support moved resembled the one used to transport the nearby *minbar* from its special storage chamber to the prayer hall and back again. Even when not in use, this Qurʾān had a special status, for it was provided with a binding ornamented with precious materials, wrapped in magnificent textiles and stored in a specially constructed chamber. After the demise of the Almohad dynasty, this manuscript is said to have passed into the hands of later north African rulers including the Marīnid Abū Yaʿqūb Yūsuf (r. 685-706/1280-1307). At times of crisis, the Marīnids carried the ʿUthmānic Qurʾān into battle wrapped in precious textiles and protected by a leather shoulder bag. The more recent west African habit of producing unbound Qurʾān manuscripts and of storing them in leather bags may also have some distant connection with this practice and with the memory that the most venerable leaves of Cordoba's ʿUthmānic Qurʾān were unconstrained by a binding.

Islam's penetration into the western sub-Saharan zone between the sixth/twelfth and ninth/fifteenth centuries was facilitated by the positive attitude toward the faith adopted by a number of regional rulers, but the manner in which Islam was disseminated in sub-Saharan Africa also had important reverberations for that region's material culture. In Africa persons versed in the principles of Islam and the text of the Qurʾān spread their knowledge primarily through oral instruction; indeed some influential Muslim scholars are said to have arrived in the area without any books. The knowledge that they transmitted was written by their students on small individual writing boards and then committed to memory. The importance accorded to oral transmission in the region may help to explain why so few Qurʾān manuscripts from there are known before the eighteenth or nineteenth centuries.

Evidence from Naṣrid Spain suggests that ambivalence existed there towards a wider integration of the Qurʾān into daily life. The Naṣrids made extensive use of the extra-qurʾānic phrase *lā ghāliba illā llāh,* "Victory comes only from God." It was inscribed on their weapons, on the walls of their palaces at the Alhambra as well as on their personal seals and talismans — places in which other dynasties of the period such as the Mamlūks or Ottomans might have used the nearly synonymous qurʾānic expression *naṣr min Allāh,* "Victory comes from God" (Q 61:13). The walls of the Alhambra were, however, also inscribed with quotations from the Qurʾān and a small leather pouch that is among the surviving personal effects of Muḥammad II, the last Naṣrid ruler of Granada, may well have once contained a miniature Qurʾān. Small square Qurʾāns appear to have been quite popular in ninth/fifteenth century Spain, suggesting that the custom of wearing a manuscript on one's person was not restricted to the dynastic family.

The Qurʾān in the east

During the sixth/twelfth to ninth/fifteenth centuries in the Levant, Anatolia, Iraq and Iran, the rising importance of the Qurʾān as a religious artifact is signaled by both literary and material evidence. Its centrality to religious practice is also evident in the endowments given to *madrasa*s and *khānqāh*s that supported specialists in the discipline of Qurʾān recitation or scribes who prepared manuscript copies, both of whom often had students under their tutelage. Some of the most splendid Qurʾāns appear to have been copied for members of dynasties that ruled in Iran, Anatolia, Syria and Egypt ranging from the Saljūqs and Ayyūbids to the Mamlūks, Mongols, and Tīmūrids. Many of these were large and elaborately decorated multi-volume sets intended for deposit in the monuments constructed by their respective patrons, particularly their tombs. Important mausoleums were often provided with teams of Qurʾān reciters whose perpetual chanting was believed to benefit both the living and the dead.

The importance of Qurʾān manuscripts to funerary rites is underscored by the fact that ornamented and inscribed "X" shaped reading stands described in their inscriptions as *raḥl* or *kursī* were placed in the tombs of important political or religious figures in Iran and Anatolia. Several examples dated to the thirteenth or fourteenth century are known, including three from the Konya region of Turkey.

Syria and Egypt are associated with a branch of study that sought to harness the power of the Qurʾān to enhance the health and well-being of the believers. This impulse led to the composition of treatises on "prophetic medicine" (*al-ṭibb al-nabawī,* see MEDICINE AND THE QURʾĀN), in which references to the Qurʾān and ḥadīth (see ḤADĪTH AND THE QURʾĀN) were combined with practical advice on a variety of topics affecting health (see ILLNESS AND HEALTH).

Some of the most respected authors of texts on this topic were Syrians primarily remembered for their religious knowledge, such as Shams al-Dīn al-Dhahabī (d. 748/1345) or Ibn Qayyim al-Jawziyya (d. 751/1350). Their work was continued by the Egyptian scholar al-Suyūṭī (d. 911/1505). The praise lavished on bees in the Qurʾān (Q 16:68-9), where honey (q.v.) is extolled as a source of healing, gave this natural product particular prominence in such treatises. This positive attitude probably led, in turn, to the creation of beehive covers inscribed with religious formulas. Although the most popular texts on prophetic medicine *(al-ṭibb al-nabawī)* were composed in the eighth/fourteenth or ninth/fifteenth century in Syria and Egypt, the publications of inscribed beehive covers attribute them to thirteenth/nineteenth century Iran. Sweets based on honey also play a significant role in the celebration of religious holidays, particularly in north Africa.

This period and region was also hospitable to the development of quasi-magical methods for harnessing the Qurʾān's curative power to alleviate the afflictions of daily life. Metal bowls inscribed internally or externally with selections from the holy book along with other prayers provide a point of intersection between medical treatment and religio-magical practices (see Fig. II). The earliest dated examples bear the name of a Syrian ruler, Nūr al-Dīn Zanjī (r. 569-77/1174-81), and others are traditionally linked to the Ayyūbid ruler Ṣalāḥ al-Dīn (i.e. Saladin; r. 564-89/1169-93); both also financed the construction of hospitals, the former in Damascus and the latter in Cairo. The academic scholarship of medicine associated with such institutions derives from the humoral tradition of Late Antiquity but that scientific tradition appears to have coexisted with the more popular approach exemplified in the magical-medical bowls. Their popularity is demonstrated by the vast numbers which survive, as well as by the fact that they were produced over a wide area including Iran, India, China and Indonesia and as late as the thirteenth/nineteenth century. In later centuries, qurʾānic citations were often augmented by other invocations, such as prayers to the imāms and talismanic devices, particularly "magic squares."

Syria

Evidence about the veneration accorded to some Qurʾān manuscripts and the new ways in which its text was used comes from Syria. A study by J.M. Mouton of the ʿUthmānic Qurʾān that occupied a place of honor in the Umayyad mosque of Damascus between the late eleventh and late nineteenth centuries C.E. demonstrates the extent to which it had become an object endowed with numinous powers rather than a book to be read. It was housed in a special container near the mosque's *miḥrāb,* displayed at regular intervals to the congregation for their veneration, and in times of crisis carried in procession through the city's streets for protection against invading armies or other dangers. Mouton has suggested that the transfer of this venerated Qurʾān from Tiberias to Damascus in 492/1099 and the ways in which it was subsequently used were stimulated by the presence of crusaders in the Levant and the resultant Muslim-Christian conflicts. He also documents how the Būrid and Ayyūbid rulers of Damascus encouraged the manuscript's cult so as to strengthen public support for their own governments. Another of their goals was to shift to the ʿUthmānic codex the popular veneration accorded to a Qurʾān ascribed to the hand of ʿAlī b. Abī Ṭālib that had been deposited in the Damascus mosque during Fāṭimid rule.

The various roles played by the Qurʾān in the religious life of Ayyūbid Aleppo are documented in the inscriptions found on monuments erected in that city during the sixth/twelfth and seventh/thirteenth centuries and published by Y. Tabbaa. The al-Sulṭāniyya *madrasa* was founded by the local ruler al-Ẓāhir Ghāzī (r. 582-613/1186-1216), who is buried on its premises. In addition to legal scholars, this institution supported a Qurʾān reciter who was to instruct others in his craft; these activities were expected to provide a benediction to the sultan buried within its precincts. Another Aleppo monument, the *khānqāh-madrasa* al-Firdaws erected with the patronage of al-Ẓāhir's wife Ḍayfa Khātūn (d. 641/1243) contains programmatic inscriptions from the Qurʾān amplified by other texts that reveal the structure's intended functions. The foundation text opens with Q 43:68-72, which details the joys awaiting the faithful in paradise. A long poetic inscription engraved around the building's courtyard describes the ecstatic rituals of nightly prayers and qurʾānic recitations that will ensure a spiritual reward for the building's Ṣūfī residents, who may have followed the teachings of al-Suhrawardī al-Maqtūl (d. 587/1191). The complex's mosque has a *miḥrāb* inscribed with Q 38:17-22, a text that depicts David's (q.v.) penitence in his *miḥrāb* and the wisdom (q.v.) granted to him by God to adjudicate disputes. This text suggests that the building's Ṣūfī residents arbitrated disputes brought before them in that chamber.

ʿAbbāsid Iraq and affiliated regions

Developments in ʿAbbāsid Iraq continued to exert a formative influence on regions within the dynasty's cultural sphere that persisted even after the latter's extinction in 656/1258 at the hands of Mongol invaders. Paradoxically the ʿAbbāsids' end served to canonize Iraqi traditions and to make them a point of reference, even as new cultural and artistic centers developed in other regions including Iran, Syria, Egypt and Anatolia. Iraq was also important as a center for the rise of institutionalized Ṣūfism, and many prominent Qurʾān calligraphers were affiliated with such groups.

The Qurʾān's centrality to the culture of the late ʿAbbāsid period is evident in the fact that the era's most celebrated calligrapher, Yāqūt al-Mustaʿṣimī (d. ca. 697/1298), an official secretary *(kātib al-dīwān)* of the last ʿAbbāsid caliph, gained his fame not through the execution of his official duties but through the copying of the Qurʾān. Copies allegedly written by Yāqūt are preserved in various collections, and calligraphers are known to have emulated his style in Iran during the fourteenth through seventeenth centuries as well as in Ottoman Turkey. The proliferation of these "Yāqūt" Qurʾāns underscores the role played by the self-conscious emulation of famous models in the practice of calligraphy. Other prominent Iraqi scribes and illuminators of the late ʿAbbāsid period found employment in Egypt under the Mamlūks (648-923/1250-1517), a dynasty that placed special emphasis on preserving the religious legacy of the ʿAbbāsid caliphate and under which the veneration of the Qurʾān was given particular prominence.

D.L. James' study of seventh/thirteenth and eighth/fourteenth century Qurʾāns has demonstrated that lavishly ornamented manuscripts were often produced by teams of specialists, a circumstance which underscores the high level of skill involved in their manufacture. Although the practice of creating especially lavish manuscripts probably arose in late ʿAbbāsid Baghdād, a beautifully calligraphed and illuminated specimen manuscript produced for the Zanjid ruler of the northern Jazīra, Muḥammad b. Zanjī (r. 594-616/1197-1219), demonstrates that even minor rulers aspired to own manuscripts of the highest quality. The most impressive examples, however, were produced for the Īlkhānid Mongols, their close associates and successors, or for Mamlūk emirs and sultans in Syria and Egypt. A manuscript that may have been destined for the mausoleum of the Īl-Khān Ghazan, with its *muḥaqqaq* script and diacritics entirely in black, was copied by Aḥmad b. al-Suhrawardī, who was both a disciple of Yāqūt and a member of a famous family of Ṣūfīs from western Iran. There also are large-scale sets produced for the funerary complex of the Īlkhānid ruler Öljeytü (r. 703-16/1304-16) by three different teams of calligraphers and illuminators in Baghdād, Mawṣil and Hamadān.

The division of labor in the production of luxury Qur'āns probably both reflected and encouraged an increasing specialization and professionalization of book production. This phenomenon may be linked to another development that occurred within the ʿAbbāsid cultural zone — the transfer of decorative modes from elaborate copies of the Qur'ān to other texts. This process is particularly striking in Iran and Anatolia but can also be documented in Mamlūk Egypt. The parallels between qur'ānic and non-qur'ānic manuscripts seem to be most evident with texts that are religious in character. Examples of this phenomenon include a sixth/twelfth or seventh/thirteenth century copy of the *Duʿā' al-munājāt,* a book of prayers attributed to the Imām Zayn al-ʿĀbidīn, from Iraq or Iran (now in the collection of G.I. Shaker). This volume has opening illumination and calligraphy comparable to Qur'āns of the same period and region. Another case in point is provided by lavishly illuminated late seventh/thirteenth or early eighth/fourteenth century copies of the *Mathnavī al-Maʿnavī* of Jalāl al-Dīn Rūmī (now in Konya and Vienna), a text sometimes described as a "Persian Qur'ān." The Rūmī manuscripts possess elaborate gold-illuminated frontispieces and headings at the opening of each section of the text. The transfer of decorative modes associated with Qur'ān manuscripts to other texts continued during the ninth/fifteenth century, especially in the Indo-Iranian cultural sphere, until the two traditions of book production effectively merged.

Mamlūk Egypt

By any measure, veneration of the Qur'ān was central to both personal and public piety in Egypt under the Mamlūks. A number of the Mamlūk sultans or their high officials devoted substantial resources to the support of activities connected with the recitation, study or copying of the Qur'ān. This focus not only explains why the Mamlūks commissioned substantial numbers of large, lavishly produced Qur'āns but helps to explain why those manuscripts also had a broad impact on the portable arts and on the design and decoration of religious architecture. Enameled and gilded glass lamps from Mamlūk buildings inscribed with the Light Verse (Q 24:35) are the best-known examples of this interconnection, but other manifestations of this enthusiasm can be documented (for an example of a Mamlūk mosque lamp, see Fig. IV).

Baybars al-Jāshnikīr (r. 708-9/1309-10) gave evidence of his attachment to the Qur'ān during his career as emir and sultan. He made a substantial endowment to the al-Ḥākim mosque that included support for two instructors in the art of Qur'ān recitation, for a scribe to prepare Qur'ān copies and for twenty Qur'ān reciters. His mausoleum that overlooked one of Cairo's main streets was linked to a *khānqāh.* Daily recitation of the Qur'ān played an important role at both institutions. Qur'ān reciters attached to his mausoleum performed this task in a window embellished with a grill taken from the caliphal palace in Baghdād. It is fitting that the earliest surviving Mamlūk Qur'ān was prepared for him. Its seven volumes, now in the British Library, were extensively illuminated by three painters and copied in gold by a Baghdād-trained calligrapher who may also have designed the prominently placed qur'ānic inscription (Q 24:36-8) on the funerary complex's street facade.

Craftsmen linked to Iraq also produced chests to store Qur'āns of particular importance. One such chest, dated to 723/1322, made for the sultan al-Nāṣir Muḥammad and signed by one Aḥmad al-Mawṣilī, is now in the al-Azhar mosque. An undated box now in Berlin was made by a certain Muḥammad b. Sunqur al-Baghdādī. Both are square containers of metal-sheathed wood with inscriptions executed in silver inlay. Inscriptions on the Berlin box include Q 56:76-80, which both celebrates the Qur'ān's revelation (see REVELATION AND INSPIRATION) and stresses the need to protect the holy book from contamination (q.v.), a text widely used on either the binding or opening illumination of manuscripts from the ninth/fifteenth century onward. The presence of Q 59:22-4, which enumerates the divine attributes *(al-asmā' al-ḥusnā),* on the box's lid underscores the container's shrine-like character.

Further evidence of the Qur'ān's importance to the Mamlūks is provided by the funerary *madrasa* and *khānqāh* founded by Barqūq al-Yalbughawī in 788/1386. Its endowment provided for the training of Qur'ān reciters and the study of qur'ānic commentaries, as well as for professional Qur'ān reciters attached to both its *khānqāh* and mausoleum. The design of the panels of this building's doors and its domed portal reflect the designs used in qur'ānic binding and illumination, underscoring the practical and aesthetic connections that existed between architectural decoration and the book arts in fourteenth century Cairo. *Kursī*s, platform stands designed to support large-scale Qur'āns and to provide an elevated seat for a reader, were constructed for mosques, especially in Egypt, from the eighth/fourteenth century onward. The popularity of *kursī*s suggests that the liturgical use of large-scale Qur'āns increased in the Mamlūk period.

Yemen

Despite the fact that the Yemen was one of the first regions to embrace Islam, the role of the Qur'ān in its religious and cultural life has so far been but little explored. Mosques and *madrasa*s constructed with the patronage of two local dynasties, the Rasūlids (626-858/1228-1454) and the Ṭāhirids (858-923/1454-1517) provide the best evidence about local attitudes toward the Qur'ān. A recent study of the ʿAmariyya Madrasa in Rada illustrates the ways in which citations from the Qur'ān — augmented by short litanies painted over the mosque's doors and on its walls and domes — articulate that building's meaning and functions. The ensemble is notable for the way it links litanies about God's power and omnipotence (Q 3:15-8; 9:18) with descriptions of the rewards that await the faithful in paradise. This theme is reiterated over doors linking the sanctuary to lateral chambers that probably served as classrooms where students were instructed in the Qur'ān, ḥadīth and *fiqh.*

Iran and central Asia

Strong regional differences are evident within this zone. Its western portions were tightly linked to the traditions of late ʿAbbāsid Baghdād but in eastern Iran,

[1] Left half of a double-page frontispiece from a fragmentary copy of the Qurʾān (late first/early eighth century) found in the Great Mosque at Ṣanʿāʾ depicting two buildings with arcades and hanging lamps, commonly believed to depict mosques. Courtesy of Hans-Caspar Graf von Bothmer, University of Saarbrücken (Ṣanʿāʾ, Dār al-Makhṭūṭāt, inv. no. 20-33.1).

[II] Double-page with Q 23:43-61 from a parchment copy of the Qur'ān copied at Madīnat Ṣiqilliyya (i.e. Palermo) in 372/982-3. Courtesy of The Nasser D. Khalili Collection of Islamic Art, London (Qur 261, ff. 8b-9a).

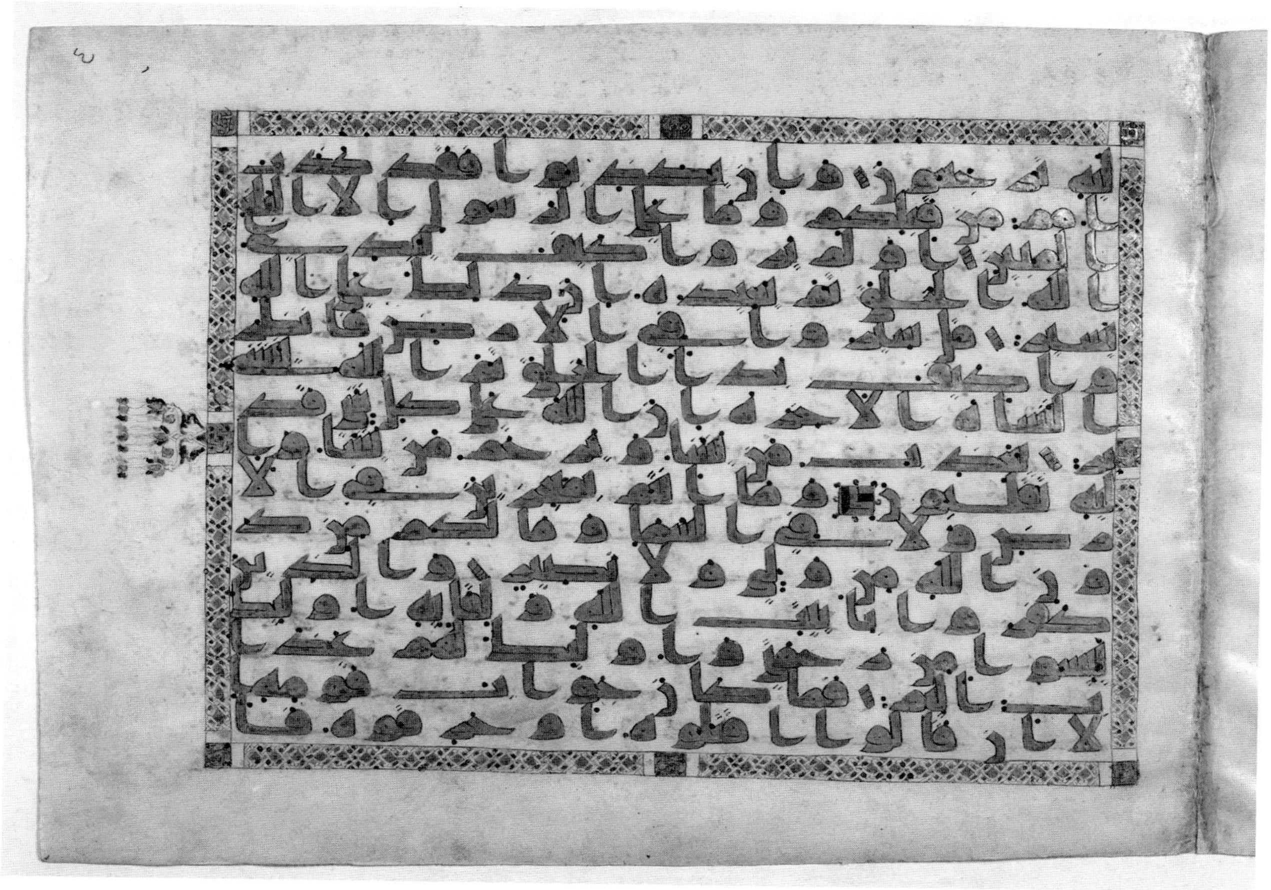

[III] Page with Q 29:16-21 from a unique copy of the Qur'ān transcribed in gold on parchment. Courtesy of The Nasser D. Khalili Collection of Islamic Art, London (KFQ 52, f. 4a).

[IV] Right-hand side of opening double-page with Q 1-2:6 from the copy of the Qur'ān transcribed by Ibn al-Bawwāb at Baghdād in 391/1000. Note the sūra titles in rectangular frames with palmettes extending into the outer margins. Reproduced by kind permission of the Trustees of the Chester Beatty Library, Dublin (CBL 1431, f. 9b).

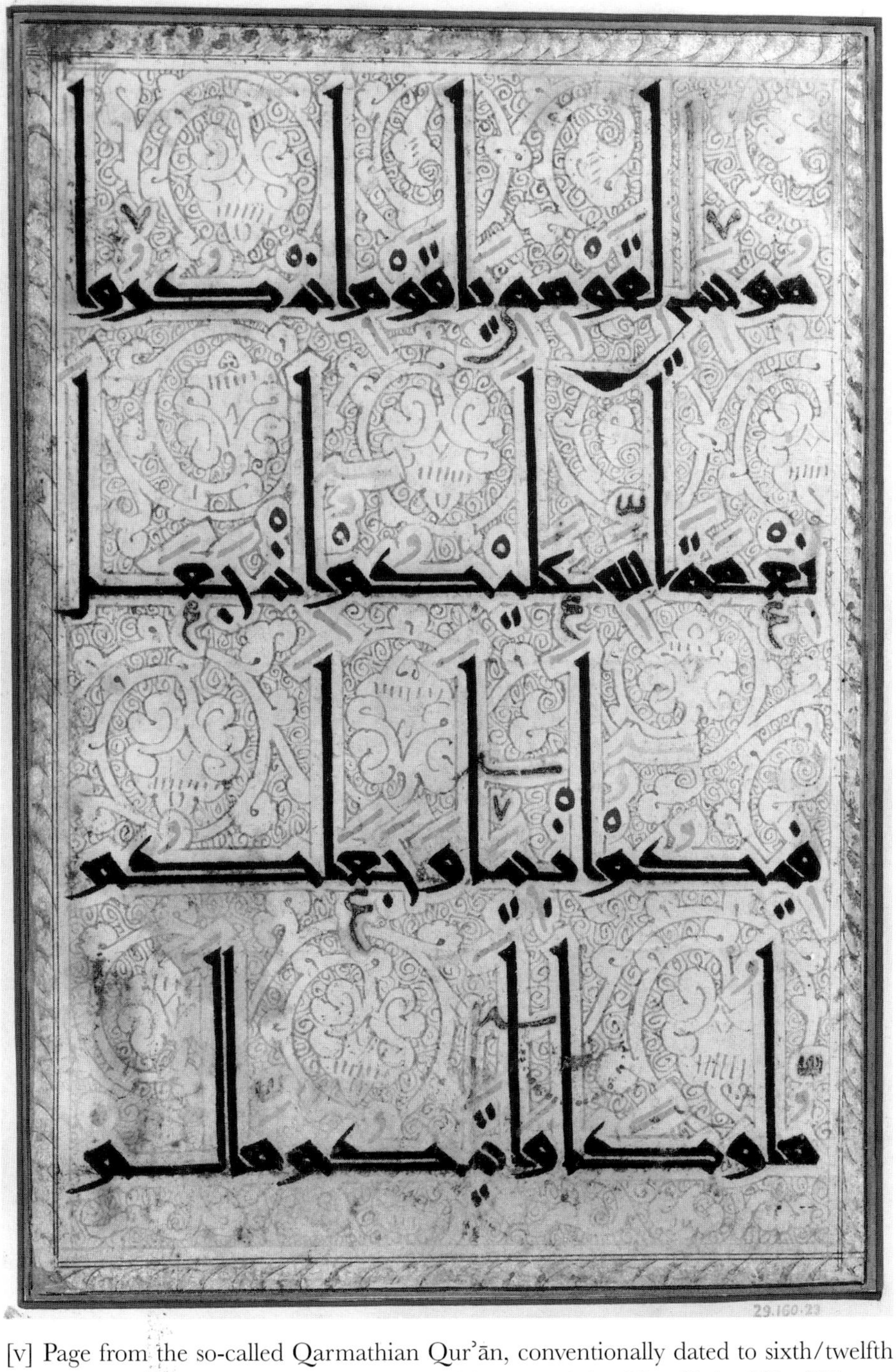

[v] Page from the so-called Qarmathian Qur'ān, conventionally dated to sixth/twelfth century Iran. Courtesy of the Metropolitan Museum of Art, New York. Gift of Horace Havemeyer, 1929 (29.160.23).

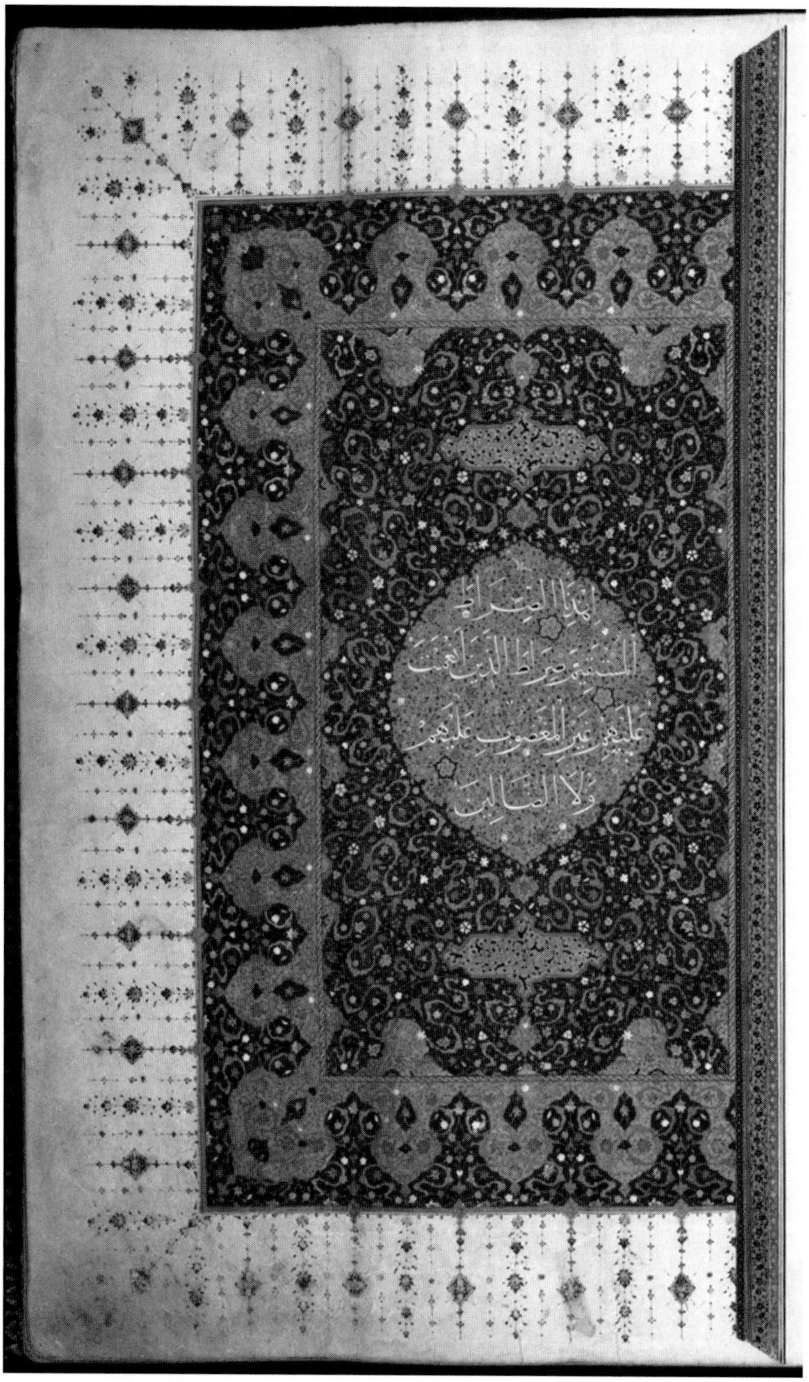

[VI A] Left-hand side of the opening double page with Q 1 from a copy of the Qur'ān transcribed by Rūzbihān Muḥammad at Shīrāz, ca. 965/1558. Reproduced by kind permission of the Trustees of the Chester Beatty Library, Dublin (CBL 1558, f. 3r).

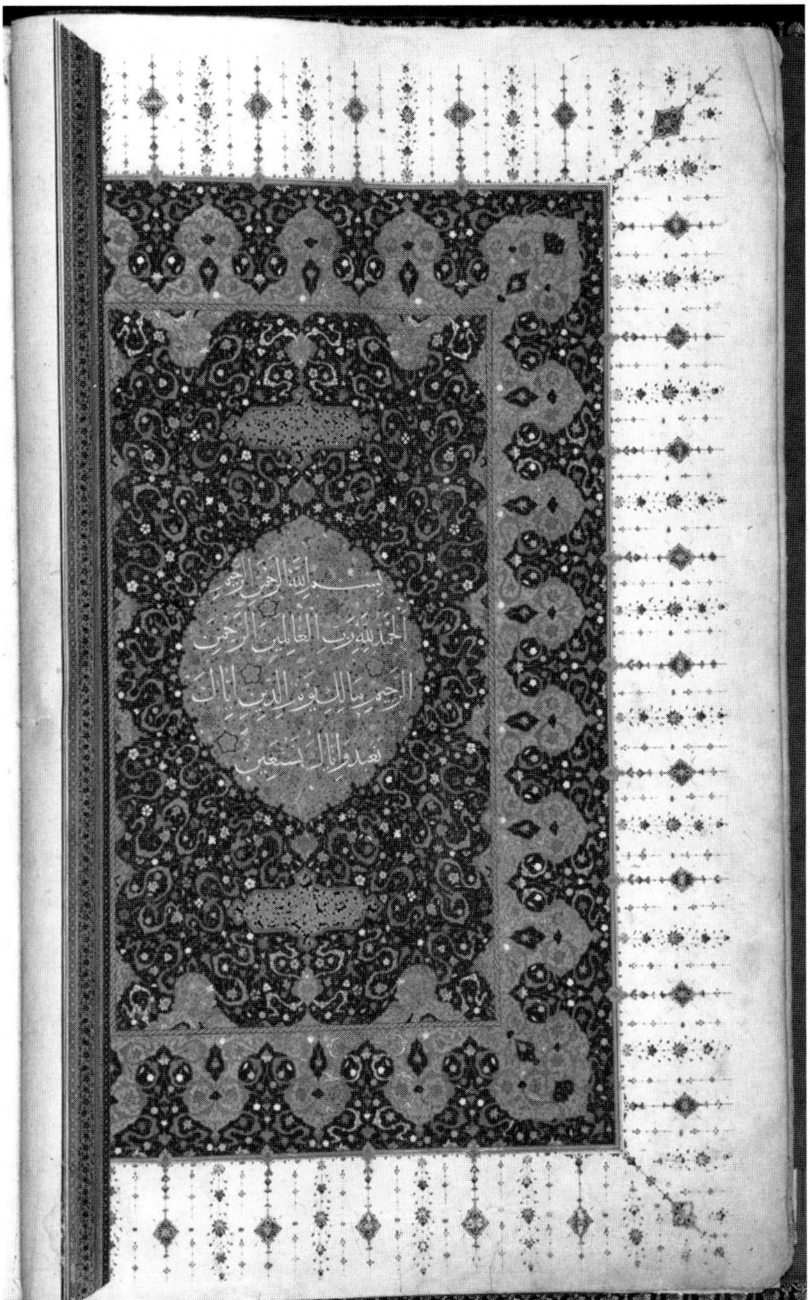

[VI B] Right-hand side of the opening double page with Q 1 from a copy of the Qurʾān transcribed by Rūzbihān Muḥammad at Shīrāz, ca. 965/1558. Reproduced by kind permission of the Trustees of the Chester Beatty Library, Dublin (CBL 1558, f. 2v).

[VII] Right side of a double-page frontispiece from the anonymous Baghdād Qur'ān illuminated by Muḥammad b. Aybak (early eighth/fourteenth century). Reproduced by kind permission of the Trustees of the Chester Beatty Library, Dublin (CBL Is 1614.2).

central Asia and Afghanistan an idiosyncratic and rather archaic approach lingered until the Mongol invasion. In Afghanistan a mannered and angular script sometimes called "eastern Kūfic" was used in Qurʾān manuscripts; the major facades of religious buildings were embellished with even more elaborate versions of this script. Monuments erected in Afghanistan by members of the Ghūrid dynasty (r. 401-612/1011-1215) were practically wrapped in a blanket of inscriptions, many of which are qurʾānic. The most spectacular example, a 213 foot high minaret on the Harī Rūdh at the Ghūrid capital of Fīrūzkūh/Jām carries the entire text of Q 19 in eight pairs of intertwined vertical inscription bands executed in cut-brick, as well as Q 61:13-4 and the name of its patron Muḥammad b. Sām (r. 558-99/1163-1203; see Fig. V of EPIGRAPHY). The Ghūrid habit of displaying substantial sections of the Qurʾān or other religious texts on building facades gave their architecture a didactic character that is also evident in monuments erected by their subordinates and successors, the Delhi sultans.

Calligraphers trained in ʿAbbāsid Baghdād and broadly associated with the legacy of Yāqūt became established in western Iran during the late seventh/thirteenth and eighth/fourteenth centuries and their skills were transferred to subsequent generations. The career of Yaḥyā b. Naṣr al-Jamālī al-Ṣūfī exemplifies the way in which personal piety, calligraphic skill and the support of important patrons all served to enhance the prestige of Qurʾān manuscripts. Yaḥyā, a practicing Ṣūfī, modeled his writing on that of Yāqūt and is traditionally linked to the latter's student Mubārak Shāh b. Quṭb of Tabrīz. Despite his illustrious pedigree, Yaḥyā's calligraphic legacy was perpetuated largely through his association with the ruler of Shīrāz Jamāl al-Dīn Abū Isḥāq Injū (r. 743-54/1343-53). Both Abū Isḥāq and his mother Tashī Khātūn demonstrated a personal devotion to the Qurʾān and in particular to its manuscripts. In 751/1351 Abū Isḥāq erected a special structure (known as *Bayt al-maṣāḥif*) in the courtyard of the principal mosque of Shīrāz to house his Qurʾān collection. Its Qurʾāns were intended for mosque use and, possibly, also for study and emulation by scribes. The repository's foundation inscription was designed by Yaḥyā al-Ṣūfī. Tashī Khātūn was particularly devoted to the tomb and cult of the ʿAlid Aḥmad b. Mūsā al-Riḍā, locally known as Shāh-i Chirāgh, and she provided his funerary complex with Qurʾān manuscripts and endowed it with funds to ensure the holy book's perpetual recitation. Several Qurʾān manuscripts signed by Yaḥyā al-Ṣūfī survive, including a set from 745-7/1344-6 given by Tashī Khātūn to the Shāh-i Chirāgh shrine.

The calligraphic traditions of ʿAbbāsid Iraq, particularly those linked to the transcription of the Qurʾān, continued to shape scribal practice in Shīrāz and the other book production centers of Iran and central Asia during the Tīmūrid era and beyond. Two of Tīmūr's grandsons, Ibrāhīm Sulṭān b. Shāh Rukh and Baysonghur b. Shāh Rukh, attained renown for their skill as Qurʾān calligraphers. Ibrāhīm Sulṭān's residence in Shīrāz appears to have encouraged his emulation of the tradition of Yaḥyā al-Ṣūfī (for an example of Ibrāhīm's penmanship, see Figs. IVA and B of FĀTIḤA), whereas Baysonghur designed large-scale qurʾānic inscriptions for architectural monuments including the shrine of Imām ʿAlī al-Riḍā in Mashhad.

The Tīmūrid period was also marked by experiments in producing Qurʾāns of unusual dimensions. A certain ʿUmar al-Aqṭaʿ is said to have presented two Qurʾāns to Tīmūr — one so small that it could be concealed under a ring-stone, and the other gargantuan. Tīmūr is said to have been unimpressed by the miniscule manuscript but delighted at the large one. Whatever the veracity of this account, other evidence demonstrates that both very large and very small manuscripts were produced during the ninth/fifteenth century. A white stone Qurʾān stand designed to hold a manuscript about two meters in height is situated at the center of the courtyard of the mosque of Bībī Khānum in Samarqand (see Fig. v of MOSQUE), and pages from a manuscript of similar scale often attributed to Tīmūr's grandson Baysonghur b. Shāh Rukh are preserved in several collections. Ninth/fifteenth century miniature manuscripts also survive.

South, southeast and east Asia

The eastward expansion of Islam from the sixth/twelfth to ninth/fifteenth centuries into the Indian subcontinent, as well as into China and the Indonesian archipelago, can be documented in historical sources, but it is often difficult to define the role played by the Qurʾān in the material culture of newly islamicized areas. This question is particularly perplexing for the Indian subcontinent, where colonies of Muslims were established along the coast of Sind as early as the second/eighth century and shortly thereafter in enclaves along India's western and eastern coasts. At present, however, monuments erected during the sixth/twelfth and seventh/thirteenth centuries by the Ghūrids or their representatives and successors, particularly the first Delhi sultans, provide the earliest tangible evidence for the role played by the Qurʾān in the region.

A series of buildings in Pakistan and India carry bold and even dramatic inscriptions from the Qurʾān or related ḥadīth in a manner reminiscent of monuments erected in Afghanistan with Ghūrid patronage. The best examples include the Ribāṭ of ʿAlī b. Karmak, dated ca. 572/1176 and situated near Multān, and mosques in Delhi and Jaunpur erected between the 580s/1190s and the early seventh/thirteenth century. A. Welch (Qurʾān and tomb) has suggested that qurʾānic inscriptions on the Great Mosque of Delhi, popularly known as Quwwat al-Islam, help to articulate that structure's meaning to both Muslims and non-believers. Its minaret, the Quṭb Manār, is inscribed with Q 48:6 and 2:256-8 which link God's omnipotence to the punishment awaiting hypocrites and idolators (see IDOLATRY AND IDOLATERS; HYPOCRITES AND HYPOCRISY). Within the mosque, however, the *qibla* facade with its freestanding arches is inscribed with texts that reiterate the basic tenets of the faith and remind Muslims of their religious obligations.

The extensive use of qurʾānic citations on mosques and tombs built by the first Delhi sultan, Iletmish, and his close associates may have grown out of the extensive use of texts in Ghūrid architecture, but the Indian examples are both more legible and more overtly didactic, suggesting that such mosques served as instructional aids to the faithful. The scanty physical evidence for the production of Qurʾān manuscripts in the Indian subcontinent during the sixth/twelfth to ninth/fifteenth centuries is often ascribed to the region's climatic conditions but other factors may also have inhibited the growth of scriptoria. Qurʾānic inscriptions and foundation texts on Indian monuments from the eighth/fourteenth and ninth/fifteenth centuries are executed in a mannered, even convoluted script known as *ṭughrāʾī* that has more in common with chancery scripts than with normal book hands, raising doubt about whether their designers also copied Qurʾān manuscripts.

East Asia

Although some of the coastal cities of China had substantial colonies of Muslims from the second/eighth century onward, their customs and beliefs had little impact on the remainder of the population. That situation changed with the advent of the Yuan dynasty (1279-1368 C.E.), when Muslims held positions of power and authority second only to that of the Mongols themselves. The dispersal of Muslim soldiers and administrators throughout Yuan territory introduced Islam into new regions. Most of the physical evidence connected with the practice of Islam in Yuan China is in the form of Qurʾān manuscripts or inscriptions on architecture. It comes from two areas, the Mongol capital Khanbaliq (later Beijing), and from the province of Yunnan. There were exceptions to the general characterization of the Ming period (1368-1644 C.E.) as a time when Chinese Muslims were forcibly sinicized: for example, in the early Ming period some Muslims continued to copy Qurʾāns and sponsor religious institutions.

The oldest known Qurʾān in China, dated to 718/1318 and connected with the Dongsi mosque in Khanbaliq/Beijing, remains unpublished. Two ninth/fifteenth century Chinese Qurʾāns are in the Khalili Collection. One, Qur 934, is dated to 804/1401 and was copied in Khanbaliq for that city's principle mosque known as the Mosque on Niu Jie (Ox Street); the other, Qur 960, was copied in 875/1471 at the *Dār al-Ḥadīth Madrasa* in *Madīnat Yunnan* (probably Yunnanfu, later Kunming). These two specimens suggest that Chinese Qurʾāns had distinctive features. They resemble the Qurʾāns of the late ʿAbbāsid period in that they were written in the *muḥaqqaq* script and divided into thirty volumes, but their illumination contains floral elements of local origin and the doublures of their bindings were cloth covered.

The blending of Chinese and imported features seen in these eighth/fourteenth and ninth/fifteenth century Qurʾāns has an architectural parallel in the best preserved of China's historic mosques, the Great Mosque of Xian, described by J.S. Cowen as "a mosque in the guise of a Buddhist temple." The wall framing its *miḥrāb* is inscribed with parts of the Qurʾān that reiterate the principles of the faith and remind the faithful of their religious obligations (Q 19:18-9; 48:2-4, 11-2) and are executed in a script related to that found in Chinese Qurʾāns. The earliest phase of the present structure can be traced to 796/1392. Historical sources also link it to the patronage of Cheng Ho (1371-1433? C.E.), the powerful Muslim eunuch who served the Yung-lo emperor (r. 1403-25) as chief admiral of the Ming fleet. He directed a series of voyages that sought to expand Ming influence and cultivate trade with both insular southeast Asia and regions to the west. Some of his expeditions reached the Arabian peninsula and the eastern coast of Africa. These connections affected material culture in both the Near East and China, but the evidence in hand for China concerns the local replication of Near Eastern metalwork in blue and white porcelain, a phenomenon unconnected to the Qurʾān.

Despite the prominence and wealth attained by Cheng Ho there is also evidence from the Ming period that Chinese Muslims adjusted their practices to conform to local traditions. A Bukhāran, Shams al-Dīn ʿUmar, known as Sayyid-i Ajall (1211-79 C.E.), one of the most important Muslims in Yuan service, became the governor of the Yunnan province and his descendants continued to be prominent there for several generations. Some of their tombs have been identified, but their inscriptions are in Chinese and make no reference to the Qurʾān.

Southeast Asia

The expansion of Islam to the regions of Malaysia and Indonesia was a gradual process accomplished largely through peaceful means. This situation is particularly striking in the islands that comprise Indonesia, where Islam was introduced through the actions of traders who brought to the region the traditions of their own homelands. These were often amalgamated to the prevailing local traditions already permeated with Hindu-Buddhist features. Among the earliest traders were Muslims from the Malabar and Coromandel regions of India, although it is uncertain whether they should be linked to the tombstones with Arabic inscriptions and occasional qurʾānic phrases dated to the fifth/eleventh-seventh/thirteenth centuries that have been discovered in coastal settlements along the Malay peninsula and in Sumatra.

Sixteenth to twentieth centuries (tenth to fourteenth centuries hijrī)

Many of the long established uses for the Qurʾān continued; its text was still inscribed on buildings and objects, although its citation on coins diminished — especially after Muslim countries adopted currencies modeled on those of Europe. Innovations of this period appear directed at the individual believer; manuscripts of the Qurʾān were more frequently provided with devotional aids such as commentaries, special prayers or supplementary instructions. Special anthologies were developed for personal use that contained only a few sūras or linked the Qurʾān with other religious texts. Another practice that gained strength in most regions was the use of amulets and talismans, in which extracts from the Qurʾān were combined with other symbols including "magic squares." Explanations given in a widely used magical compendium cited earlier, the *Shams al-maʿārif* of al-Būnī (d. 622/1225), had helped to popularize this practice, but further details and examples were provided by later treatises such as the *Shams al-āfāq* of ʿAbd al-Raḥmān al-Bisṭāmī composed in 827/1423 (see MAGIC). Such diagrams appear to have been used over a wider geographical region and employed in more diverse ways during the tenth/sixteenth to thirteenth/nineteenth centuries. These devices were produced in a bewildering variety of forms and made from a wide range of materials. They include cases to hold texts or diagrams, small metal plaques or engraved stones worn around the neck or tied to the arm, magical-medicinal bowls from which curative potions were drunk, and even garments covered with densely written words and symbols. The latter could either be worn or carried folded in a pouch. Some garments may even have been intended for funerary use. More recently, talismanic texts or diagrams were written on leather, cloth or paper or even printed for mass distribution. Some types of materials are primarily associated with specific regions, but the diversity of these devices and the paucity of publications about them make it difficult to separate amulets or talismans into clear groups or to postulate their historical development; in some areas their production continued well into the fourteenth/twentieth century.

In order to better explore these themes, as well as to delineate local developments, the Qurʾān's role in material culture from the tenth/sixteenth to fourteenth/

twentieth centuries will be treated in three geographical zones with subdivisions where appropriate: a central zone comprising the Ottoman empire, Iran, central Asia and the Indian subcontinent, another devoted to Africa and a third encompassing east and southeast Asia.

Central Islamic regions

In the Mediterranean region, largely dominated by the Ottoman empire, and within the Iranian cultural sphere, where Islam had been firmly entrenched for centuries, this period brought incremental rather than dramatic change. Qurʾānic scribes followed well-established calligraphic traditions but manuscripts exhibit greater diversity with respect to their size, shape and critical apparatus. Innovations of this period shared by both the Ottoman Mediterranean and the Indo-Persian cultural sphere were a fondness for manuscripts executed in a minute script, the extensive production of talismanic devices incorporating portions of the Qurʾān believed to have protective powers, and the Qurʾān's use for prognostication (see FORETELLING; DIVINATION). The text continues to be inscribed on architectural monuments, often in programmatic ensembles that also include relevant ḥadīth. Portions of the Qurʾān also appear on diverse objects including banners used by armies and Ṣūfīs alike, swords, helmets, body armor, tomb furnishings and clothing. Although these practices are known to some extent in most regions, their popularity and the date of their first appearance vary from one locality to another.

Calligraphers working in Iran appear to have enjoyed great prestige over a wide area. Their methods of transcribing the Qurʾān were often emulated; ownership seals and other evidence demonstrate that Iranian manuscripts were prized among the Ottomans and in India. Many tenth/sixteenth century Iranian Qurʾāns have a demonstrable continuity with the calligraphic practices of late ʿAbbāsid Iraq in their juxtaposition of different hands in the text's transcription, but they also acquired new features including prayers to be recited before and after consulting the holy text, and they frequently end with a *fāl-nāma*. The latter tabulates the good or bad fortune associated with each letter of the alphabet to aid in interpreting auguries derived from a random consultation of the Qurʾān, a process known as *istikhāra*.

Shīrāz scribes appear to have been the most prolific producers of Qurʾān manuscripts during the tenth/sixteenth century, but their copies rarely contain any indication of the patron for whom they were commissioned. The same scribes also produced a wide variety of literary manuscripts that can be almost as lavishly decorated as their Qurʾāns. The two sets of manuscripts have some common features; the insertion of a pair of illuminated pages at the Qurʾān's midpoint (Q 18:1) is paralleled in Shīrāz copies of Firdawsī's *Shāhnāma*. The routine inclusion of a *fāl-nāma* in tenth/sixteenth century Shīrāz Qurʾāns may have some connection with the widespread bibliomantic use of the *Dīvān* of Ḥāfiẓ, a local poet.

The largest and most opulent Shīrāz Qurʾān manuscripts have extensive illumination shimmering with gold, blue and other colors. One copy, Khalili Qur 729, dated to 959/1552, that may have belonged to the Safavids and later entered the Mughal imperial library, employs the contrast of blue and gold in its delicately executed floral illumination, throughout the Qurʾān's text and in the appended "concluding prayer" *(duʿā-i khātim)*. Just as the Qurʾān was often juxtaposed with selected ḥadīth in the inscriptions on Safavid religious architecture, panels containing ḥadīth frame both this manuscript's gilded covers and its opening pages.

A late thirteenth/nineteenth century Persian treatise in the Khalili Collection (Ms. 412) furnishes a more complete guide to qur'ānic bibliomancy than does the *fāl-nāma* commonly appended to the holy text. Detailed procedures for taking auguries are linked both to a technical manual on Qur'ān recitation and to a talismanic chart that invokes the names of the imāms and presents other kinds of devotional aids in tabular form. One chart links individual sūras of the Qur'ān with particular months of the year.

Iranian scribes also produced Qur'āns in which the text is compressed into a very small space. Qur'āns transcribed in this fashion took several different forms; some were miniature books of rectangular or polygonal, usually octagonal, format but in other cases the text was densely transcribed on a few pages of normal size, a single sheet of paper or a scroll. Usually their scribes used scripts known collectively as the *ghubār* (dust-mote) hands that are often said to have been developed for use with the pigeon-post but were probably also employed for the production of amulets worn or carried on the person. As amulet cases are known from the third/ninth or fourth/tenth century onward, the practice of making miniature Qur'āns is likely to antedate the earliest literary references to their production, which link them to the patronage of Tīmūr (r. 771-807/1370-1405). A miniature octagonal Qur'ān now in the Khalili Collection (Qur 371) is dated to the ninth/fifteenth century and a hexagonal one in the Chester Beatty Library (Ms. 1517) may be from ninth/fifteenth century Turkey, but most published examples are from the tenth/sixteenth century or later. Although, as was mentioned earlier, miniature Qur'āns were popular in Naṣrid Spain, their transcription in *ghubār* script is closely associated with Iran, whence this practice spread westward to the Ottoman empire and eastward to the Indian subcontinent.

Miniature octagonal Qur'āns produced in Ottoman Turkey are often described in publications as *sanjaq* (Battle-standard) Qur'āns, with the presumption that they were placed in metal cases and tied to military banners. The Ottomans also used scroll-format Qur'āns for this purpose, and a tenth/sixteenth century example in the Topkapi Sarayı Museum retains not only its octagonal cylindrical case but also the red cord by which it was once tied to a staff.

In Iran, miniature Qur'ān codices in octagonal format and their associated cases appear to have been mainly carried or worn by individuals for their personal protection; their cases were often designed to be tied to the upper arm as part of a *bāzū-band* (a bracelet for the upper arm). Some Iranian scribes demonstrated their virtuosity by using several sizes of *ghubār* script in a single volume. Those working in the city of Shīrāz appear to have produced miniature Qur'āns on a commercial basis during the tenth/sixteenth and eleventh/seventeenth centuries.

A miniature Qur'ān dated to 1085/1674-5 now on loan to the Kuwait National Museum (LNS 373 HS) was probably copied in India and has a bejeweled jade binding of Indian manufacture. This densely written rectangular manuscript was originally transcribed as a continuous text without illumination or internal divisions. Both were subsequently added, largely in the book's margins, as were prayers to be recited before and after consulting the manuscript, and a *fāl-nāma*.

The practice of wearing a miniature Qur'ān is also attested among the Tatar princes living within the Russian empire.

The collection of the Hermitage Museum, St. Petersburg, includes a small rectangular silver case inlaid with turquoise and lapis lazuli and dated to 1002/1593-4 that was made for Uraz Muḥammad, a ruler of the Kasimov Khānate. This case, designed to be attached to a belt, is inscribed with Q 2:255, a verse widely believed to have protective powers.

By the mid-eleventh/seventeenth century the focus of Qurʾān production and study in Iran had shifted from Shīrāz to Iṣfahān, where the last phase of the Safavid period coincided with a revival of religious studies. The leading qurʾānic calligrapher of the late eleventh/seventeenth and early twelfth/eighteenth century was Aḥmad Khān Nayrizī, active between the 1080s/1670s and the 1150s/1740s. He produced monumental inscriptions for architecture but was particularly renowned for his Qurʾāns that were copied in a clear, confident *naskh;* many of them were provided with an interlinear gloss in Persian. Although Persian interlinear translations of the Qurʾān were first introduced in the tenth century, they became more common in the late Safavid period as part of a campaign to diffuse knowledge of the Qurʾān among a wider spectrum of the population. Most often included was the translation/gloss of ʿAlī Riḍā Ardakānī composed in 1084/1694-5. Many Qurʾāns also had marginal commentaries attributed to the Shīʿī imāms. The calligraphy and presentation of Nayrizī's Qurʾāns were widely emulated during the twelfth/eighteenth and thirteenth/nineteenth centuries.

During the period from the tenth/sixteenth to thirteenth/nineteenth centuries Iran also witnessed an expanded popularity for amulets and talismans in which sūras believed to offer protection against a wide variety of misfortunes and illnesses were combined with prayers to the imāms, other texts and symbols. The most elaborate Iranian talismans are transcribed onto sheets of parchment, perhaps gazelle skin, and were apparently folded and carried in cases. One is dated to 1337/1919 and others are probably from the thirteenth/nineteenth century. Some feature "magic squares" with thousands of units based on the mysterious letters that open certain sūras, selected qurʾānic texts, the divine names *(al-asmāʾ al-ḥusnā)* and other prayers, or their numerical equivalents.

A few talismanic garments have also been attributed to Iran, but the protection provided by metal magical-medicinal bowls appears to have been more appreciated locally; inscribed bowls were probably exported eastward from Iran to south and east Asia, where local variants were produced. Metal plaques used as arm amulets and inscribed with a variety of brief qurʾānic citations were popular in eastern Iran during the thirteenth/nineteenth century. A variant type employing some Hebrew letters and known from Iraq may be linked to that region's folk traditions.

Arms and various accoutrements of war ranging from swords to helmets, body armor and military banners were inscribed with texts from the Qurʾān in both the Ottoman empire and the Indo-Iranian world, but this practice is especially well-documented among the Ottomans, where it was well underway by the early tenth/sixteenth century.

The Ottoman realm

This discussion will have two parts: the first devoted to the ninth/fifteenth through the eleventh/seventeenth centuries and the second focusing on the twelfth/eighteenth through the fourteenth/twentieth centuries. The wide territorial expanse of the Ottoman empire and that dynasty's extraordinary longevity (ca. 680-1342/1281-1924) ensured that there was no single

Ottoman approach to the veneration of the Qurʾān and that its uses evolved with time. The fissiparous tendencies of such a large-scale state were, however, counterbalanced by the development, in the course of the ninth/fifteenth and tenth/sixteenth centuries, of a strongly hierarchical and centralized bureaucratic and military structure that was often mirrored in cultural life. The religious or aesthetic preferences of the sultans were often widely emulated by their subordinates.

Fifteenth to seventeenth centuries (ninth to eleventh centuries *hijrī*)

The Ottoman sultans saw themselves as leaders of the Muslim world and their approach to the Qurʾān synthesized and elaborated upon features developed by their predecessors, especially the ʿAbbāsid caliphs and their successors, including the Īlkhānid Mongols and the Tīmūrids. The sultans Bāyezīd II (r. 886-918/1481-1512) and Süleymān (r. 926-74/1520-66) were particularly influential in establishing a distinctive Ottoman approach to the Qurʾān's transcription and veneration. The main calligraphic tradition that took root at the Ottoman court derived from Irano-Iraqi precedents, in particular the calligraphic modes associated with Yāqūt and his successors; it also focused particularly on the transcription of the Qurʾān and other religious texts. A preference for the six canonical scripts as they were codified in the late ʿAbbāsid period is evident in both manuscript copies of the Qurʾān and in citations from it rendered in stone-cut inscriptions placed over mosque portals, as well as in the inscriptions, whether painted or executed in glazed ceramics, that were widely applied to the walls, vaults and domes of religious buildings, particularly tombs and mosques. The Qurʾān even appears in some parts of the Topkapi Sarayı, such as in the ceramic tile revetments of the bedchamber of Murād III (r. 982-1003/1574-95).

Ottoman court calligraphers created monumental qurʾānic inscriptions, manuscripts of the holy book as well as more specialized devotional tracts containing only a few sūras or even a single one. The calligraphic lineage that predominated in Ottoman court manuscripts of the Qurʾān began with the son of a Suhrawardī shaykh from Bukhārā, Shaykh Ḥamd Allāh also known as Ibn al-Shaykh (d. 926/1520). He was closely associated with Sultan Bāyezīd II as a *şehzade* both during the latter's residence in Amasya and in Istanbul, after he ascended the throne. In addition to Qurʾān manuscripts copied in *naskh* script, Shaykh Ḥamd Allāh also designed monumental qurʾānic inscriptions and produced devotional manuals focusing on individual sūras including Q 6, 18, and 78 that were often combined with other religious texts. Another seminal calligrapher, Aḥmad Qarāḥiṣārī (d. 963/1556), active during the reign of Sultan Süleymān, was particularly renowned for his design of large-scale inscriptions for architectural use, a skill that was also cultivated by his pupil and adopted son Ḥasan Çelebi (d. 1002/1593).

The hierarchical structure of Ottoman patronage linked the size of a Qurʾān donated to a religious institution with the status of its donor, with the largest ones reserved for the sultans themselves. Aḥmad Qarāḥiṣārī began to copy the largest known Ottoman Qurʾān, which measures 62 by 43 cm, for Sultan Süleymān but it remained unfinished at the scribe's death in 963/1556. Documents about this manuscript published by Filiz Çağman demonstrate that between 992/1584 and 1005/1596 subsequent sultans devoted substantial sums to its completion. The Ottoman association of the largest Qurʾāns with royal patronage may spring from the above-mentioned enthusiasm of Tīmūr and his descendants for oversized Qurʾāns — a practice known to the Ottomans through literary sources as well as from actual manuscripts.

A religious anthology copied by Qarāḥiṣārī in 945/1547 (Türk Islâm Eserleri Müzesi, TIEM 1438) epitomizes the Ottoman use of calligraphy as the kinetic extension of devotional practice. It contains Q 6, the *Burda* of al-Buṣīrī, and assorted prayers and ḥadīth. This manuscript is also a virtuoso sampler, juxtaposing scripts with one another. Its opening pages contain invocations in three dramatic and distinct hands while the main body of the text is also transcribed in three different hands, large-scale *thulth*, medium-sized *naskh*, and fine *ghubār*. The manuscript uses a page scheme described by Ottoman sources as the "Yāqūt format," which juxtaposes a line in large-scale gold *thulth* at the top and bottom of the page with a densely written central panel in black *naskh* script.

The career of Ḥāfiẓ ʿUthmān Efendi (d. 1110/1698) exemplifies the varied skills required of Ottoman court calligraphers; he excelled both at composing monumental qurʾānic inscriptions and transcribing Qurʾān manuscripts. He also taught calligraphy at the court, where his students included Sultan Muṣṭafā II (r. 1106-15/1695-1703). Perhaps because of their varied responsibilities, court scribes were not always able to satisfy the needs of their patrons so that the latter sought manuscripts produced elsewhere; during the tenth/sixteenth century Qurʾāns from the Iranian city of Shīrāz appear to have been particularly popular in Turkey.

The 923/1517 conquest of the Mamlūk domains by the Ottomans generated a transfer of Syrian and Egyptian artisans to Istanbul; the new arrivals added a further dimension to the Turkish treatment of the Qurʾān. The Ottomans emulated the Mamlūk practice of protecting Qurʾān manuscripts of unusual sanctity with special chests; most of the surviving examples come from dynastic tombs. Ottoman Qurʾān chests often take the shape of miniature, domed buildings made from wood and embellished with inlays in contrasting colors or of different materials. They resemble architectural models and may have been designed, or even built, by court architects.

The most varied and extensive citations found on arms and various accoutrements of war occur on swords. The many traditions that were attached to the swords of the Prophet gave this weapon a special status among Muslims, although how that status was expressed in material terms varied from time to time and place to place. Literary traditions affirm that the ʿAbbāsids made use of swords believed to have belonged to the Prophet himself in their ceremonies and regalia, but few details about their physical appearance are known. A group of swords from the end of the Naṣrid period in Spain that survive in various Spanish collections have hilts inscribed with pious phrases, but these do not appear to have included qurʾānic citations. Some Mamlūk swords have inscribed blades but those texts are historical rather than qurʾānic.

An Ottoman sword dated to 914/1509 provides an example of the verses linked to weaponry. It is inscribed with the most frequently cited texts: Q 2:137, Q 61:3 (the Victory Verse) and Q 2:255 (the Throne Verse), reminders that God's support is sufficient against any adversary. More unusual is the evocation of the Men of the Cave (q.v.; *ahl al-kahf*, identified as the Seven Sleepers) and their dog (q.v.), Qiṭmīr. Their revival after a long sleep is viewed as a harbinger of the resurrection (q.v.). This assortment of texts contrasts with the simple, direct statement taken from Q 65:3, enjoining trust in God and confidence in his oversight, inscribed on the blade of a sword dated to 940/1533-34 that was made for Sultan Süleymān. Qurʾānic passages are also frequently inscribed on helmets and body armor. The most popular verses on both groups of objects are again Q 61:13 and 2:255; both appear on an iron helmet inlaid with silver (now in Vienna) that is said to have belonged to Soqollu Meḥmed, vizier to three sultans between 972/1565 and 987/1579.

The practice of inscribing the Qurʾān on garments occurred in several regions, but the earliest and best-documented examples were made for members of the Ottoman court ranging from the sultans to their sons or high-ranking officials between the late ninth/fifteenth and early eleventh/seventeenth centuries. One served as a shroud, some were worn under armor in battle, and still others with particularly elaborate calligraphy or ornamentation may have been worn on ceremonial occasions. The association of these garments with leading members of the Ottoman court is reflected in the elaboration of their design and the quality of their calligraphy. The range of Qurʾān citations that are inscribed upon them defies easy categorization and suggests that some were produced for individual use at a specific moment.

Eighteenth to twentieth centuries (twelfth to fourteenth centuries *hijrī*)

It is during this period that the Qurʾān's use for prognostication began to shape its transcription and visual presentation. The bibliomantic use of the Qurʾān — in which a person opens the book at random and then seeks guidance from its text — often focused on key words or phrases of particular import. Some twelfth/eighteenth and thirteenth/nineteenth century Ottoman manuscripts used a variety of techniques to draw the reader's attention to portions of the text that were of special significance, such as by writing them in a contrasting color such as red. This highlighting of key phrases was often accompanied by other enhancements of the text's appearance. Sometimes each page of the text was treated as a discrete physical unit by ensuring that all its verses were complete, an approach that required a careful modulation of the spaces between words. A Qurʾān in the Khalili Collection (Qur 10) dated to 1124/1712 exemplifies this approach.

A group of calligraphers connected to the city of Shumnu/Shumen in Bulgaria during the middle of the thirteenth/nineteenth century, including Seyyid Meḥmed Şükrü, specialized in the production of Qurʾāns that augmented the significance of some pages through an even more complex procedure. In this case each half of a pair of facing pages had a mirror image relationship to the other. This symmetry extended even to individual words or phrases of particular importance, such as the epithets of God, so that when the book was closed the key words on one page were in alignment with those on the opposite side.

Banners carried by the Ottoman armies or used on their naval vessels were also inscribed with citations from the Qurʾān, in addition to other texts and symbols. Most of the extant examples are of thirteenth/nineteenth century date but they are believed to replicate designs used in earlier centuries. The portions of the Qurʾān cited include Q 4:95-6, 61:13 and Q 112. Symbols used include a schematic representation of the sword of the prophet Muḥammad and then ʿAlī b. Abī Ṭālib *(dhū l-faqār)* and of the standard carried by Ayyūb al-Anṣārī. Members of Ottoman dervish orders also carried similar banners on their pilgrimage to Mecca (see Fig. VI).

The Indian subcontinent

The establishment of the Mughal dynasty (932-1274/1526-1858) inaugurated the most brilliant phase of Islamic culture in the subcontinent. Many of its characteristic features were developed during the fifty year reign of that dynasty's third ruler, Akbar (962-1014/1556-1605), but this general rule does not apply to the role of the Qurʾān in the region's religious and cultural life. Akbar's personal interest in religious syncretism that culminated in his proclamation of a new era and a new faith, the *Dīn-i Ilāhī*, also led him to relegate the Qurʾān to a secondary role. Despite his well-documented fascination with manuscripts, Akbar is not known to have commissioned a single Qurʾān — although he did own a parchment copy attributed to the caliph ʿUthmān. Among Akbar's acts in 992/1584 that signaled the promulgation of the *Dīn-i Ilāhī* was the removal of the profession of faith *(shahāda)* from Mughal coins, thereby creating a rupture with a religio-political tradition that stretched back to the Umayyads. The text used in its place, *Allāhu akbar jalla jalāluhu*, "God is great, splendid is his glory," is ambiguous, for it simultaneously makes reference to God and to Akbar. The same phrase is also inscribed on Akbar's cenotaph at Sikandra, along with citation of the ninety-nine names of God, a combination that once again could be interpreted in more than one fashion. These texts are amplified by Akbar's eulogy, in Persian prose, inscribed on the exterior portal of his tomb complex. His mausoleum was completed during the reign of his son and successor Jahāngīr (1014-37/1605-27), who continued many of his father's religious practices.

Radical though they might have been, Akbar's actions did not mean that in the Mughal empire the Qurʾān disappeared from the public arena, much less from the devotional practice of the individual Muslim. His views about the Qurʾān failed to diminish enthusiasm for its use in amulets and talismans including "magical-medicinal bowls." Although no such metal vessels from his reign appear to have survived, they must have existed. One inscribed with his name and the title of one of his high officials, the Khān-i Khānān, was replicated in over-glaze painted porcelain by Chinese artisans; examples are preserved in both Malaysian and European collections.

The most significant use of the Qurʾān among the Mughals is its role in funerary or commemorative structures. By the sixteenth century the tombs of saintly personages were firmly established as the emotional locus of popular piety and the most important event of the liturgical calendar was the commemoration of a saint's death that was believed to mark the moment they attained unity with God, a union described as an *ʿurs* (mystical wedding; see MARRIAGE AND DIVORCE; MONASTICISM AND MONKS). The metaphorical interpretation of the tomb as a gateway to heaven is evident in the qurʾānic inscriptions placed on their portals; in some instances tomb inscriptions also allude to the heavenly union of the deceased with God.

Although these practices were formulated in conjunction with the tombs of Ṣūfī saints, they were also applied in monuments supported with royal patronage. For example at Fatehpur Sikri, Akbar's palace city near Agra, constructed between 979/1571 and 994/1585, the *Boland Darwaza* or principal gateway to the mosque-shrine complex that houses the tomb of Shaykh Sālim Chishtī (d. 980/1572) is inscribed with Q 39:73-5, 41:30-1 and 41:53-4, texts that describe the welcome awaiting the faithful at the gates of paradise. The most extensive epigraphic program of this character on a Mughal monument is, however, that of the Tāj Maḥall, the funerary complex erected by Shāh Jahān for his wife, Arjumand Bānū Begum, known as Mumtāz Maḥall, following her death in 1040/1631, and in which he, too, was subsequently buried (for an example of this craftsmanship, see Fig. VIII of EPIGRAPHY).

Mughal sources describe the Tāj Maḥall as the *Rawẓa-i munavvara,* "The Illuminated Tomb," a name that reflects the building's white marble facing and that material's numinous associations. The black stone qurʾānic inscriptions inlaid on the two faces of its main (south) gate, the tomb chamber's external and internal facades and its cenotaphs convey the monument's significance and demonstrate how its architectural form and ornamentation were used to convey a message at once personal and religious that celebrates this tomb as the site of the paradisiacal *ʿurs* of Mumtāz Maḥall and Shāh Jahān.

Those inscriptions were designed, and probably selected by, a Persian-born calligrapher and religious scholar, ʿAbd al-Ḥaqq Shīrāz Amānat Khān. His scheme utilizes portions of the Qurʾān that describe the last days and the reception awaiting the believer in paradise; their placement evokes a litany recited in the course of a visit. An unusual aspect of his scheme is the fact that most of the sūras are cited in their entirety. The south face of its main gate is inscribed with Q 89, its northern side with Q 93, 94 and 95. The ensemble of texts inscribed on the tomb proper propels the visitor on a clockwise circumambulation of the exterior from south to west and on a counter-clockwise movement around the interior chamber from southeast to south. The exterior's four portals carry the majestic verses of Q 36 (known as *Yā Sīn*), widely recited to commemorate the dead; the doors within those portals are framed by Q 81, 82, 84, and 98 with their dramatic evocation of the world's end (see APOCALYPSE; LAST JUDGMENT). The tomb's interior chamber also has two levels of inscriptions. The upper one encircles the wall and concludes in the frame of the southeast niche; it contains Q 67 with its evocation of God's role as creator (see CREATION) and ultimate judge. The lower series consisting of Q 48 and 76, describing the eternal rewards awaiting the faithful, encircles the remaining niches and doorways from southeast to south. The south doorway, facing the cenotaphs, is surrounded by Q 39:53-4 describing God's compassion (see MERCY). The upper surface of Mumtāz Maḥall's cenotaph is inscribed with a prayer addressed to God recalling his promise of salvation (q.v.) that combines Q 41:30 and 40:7-8.

The reliance on the Qurʾān for the Tāj Maḥall's inscriptions demonstrates the degree to which Shāh Jahān (r. 1037-68/1628-57) had broken with the religious policies of his father and grandfather. Not surprisingly, he placed the profession of faith *(shahāda)* on his coins and sponsored more traditional forms of Islamic piety including Qurʾān recitations in his public audience chamber on the occasion of religious festivals. This trend was further augmented during the reign of his son Awrangzīb (1068-1118/1658-1707), who made the Qurʾān the foundation of his personal devotional life. A Qurʾān in the Khalili Collection (Qur 417) was copied in 1080/1669-70 by one of his daughters, Zīnat al-Nisāʾ, and probably illuminated by her Persian tutor, Muḥammad Saʿīd.

The revival of interest in the Qurʾān at the Mughal court was affected by the local religious climate, in particular by actions taken by members of the Naqshbandiyya Ṣūfī order. ʿAbd al-Bāqī Ḥaddād, an Iranian calligrapher active at Awrangzīb's court, is credited with introducing to India the practice of transcribing Qurʾāns within a small space. The cumulative effect of these trends encouraged a broader interest in the Qurʾān in the region during the later seventeenth and eighteenth centuries. Not only does the local production of its manuscripts increase but that text is used in a variety of physical contexts. These include the production of talismans and talismanic garments as well as the addition of religious texts to weapons, body armor and banners. These practices may well have reached India from Iran or even from the Ottoman empire, but they also acquired a local flavor. Indian talismanic garments normally contain the integral text of the Qurʾān instead of the combination of texts and symbols that predominate in Iran and Turkey. Many of the published Indian accoutrements of war were produced for local Deccani rulers during the twelfth/eighteenth century, and these often combine qurʾānic citations with Shīʿī litanies. The same combination of qurʾānic texts and Shīʿī prayers also appears on talismans that were produced in both Iran and India (for an example of this combination on an Iranian battle standard, see Fig. x of EPIGRAPHY).

East Asia

The reign of the Cheng-te emperor (1506-21 C.E.) exemplifies the manner in which Muslim eunuchs at the Ming court helped to integrate the Qurʾān into Chinese material culture. He is remembered for the way in which he delegated the administration of his empire to the eunuchs of the imperial household, many of whom were Muslim. It was through their control over palace workshops that some of the blue and white porcelain produced at the imperial kilns in Jingdezhen bear inscriptions in Persian and Arabic, including passages from the Qurʾān. Most of the objects follow Chinese traditions in form and function; those with the longest qurʾānic texts are vertical screens designed to be placed on a table, where they could have served in lieu of a *miḥrāb* for private devotions. One in the Percival David Foundation, London, is inscribed with Q 72:18-20 (see Fig. v). A fragment bearing a prayer in Arabic was recently excavated at the site of the Ming imperial kilns in Zushan.

Whether these goods for court use were linked to a broader production of inscribed objects or vessels intended for export to Muslim regions is not yet clear. A few other bowls from the Cheng-te reign preserved in Near Eastern collections and inscribed with Arabic texts may have been sent as gifts to Muslim rulers. The expanded production of bowls inscribed with qurʾānic passages occurs in the "Swatow porcelains" decorated in over-glaze enamels generally linked to the Wan-li reign (1573-1619 C.E.). Two series of magical-medicinal bowls now in Malaysian and European collections, one type directed at a Sunnī audience and another with Shīʿī prayers, are inscribed internally with selections from the Qurʾān as well as historical inscriptions that link their design to a high official at the court of the Mughal emperor Akbar. A third group focuses primarily on Q 2:256 and is non-sectarian. These three groups of bowls exhibit a broad range of quality, but in the best examples the accuracy of their inscriptions suggests that Muslims were involved in their production. The decoration of a fourth series of porcelain magical-medicinal bowls dating to the twelfth/eighteenth century combines a central "magic-square" with concentric rings of qurʾānic citations. The inscriptions on many of them appear to have been drawn rather than written, suggesting that artisans with no knowledge of Arabic were replicating a model supplied to them.

The question of how these vessels inscribed with the Qurʾān affected the material culture of China's Muslim population is uncertain. Any broader examination of the role of the Qurʾān in China must take account of the manner in which Islam absorbed features from the region's dominant cultural traditions, particularly Confucianism. This current is epitomized by the hesitant approach of Chinese Muslims toward the printing and translation of the Qurʾān (see TRANSLATIONS OF THE QURʾĀN). Although excerpts from the Qurʾān had been either paraphrased or transliterated into Chinese since at least the sixteenth century, the first integral translations were produced only in the fourteenth/twentieth century. The knowledge of the Qurʾān was, for most Chinese Muslims during these centuries, limited to passages memorized for devotional use under the tutelage of their *ākhūnd*s.

Malaysia and the Indonesian archipelago

The character of Muslim practice in this region has always blended local traditions with imported features, but the source of the latter has varied over time. During the tenth/sixteenth and eleventh/seventeenth centuries connections were strong with the Muslims of Gujarat in western India, who brought with them connections to various Ṣūfī orders; more recently, links to the Arabian peninsula have assumed a primary importance. Initially, acceptance of Islam appears to have caused only limited changes in the island's material culture, although this perception may be shaped by a climate that precludes the preservation of organic materials such as manuscripts. One topic that deserves further investigation is the way in which the importance of textiles in the region's local social and ceremonial life led to their use in religious observances. The Khalili Collection contains a *selendang,* a kind of shawl worn draped around the head or shoulders, which is covered with densely written Arabic inscriptions that include the widely used "Victory Verse" (Q 61:13; see Fig. VII).

Studies of the religious life of the region have demonstrated the popularity of short religio-magical tracts that have a qurʾānic foundation, but are independent compositions often written in vernacular languages and distributed to believers by local religious figures with mystical tendencies (see also SOUTHEAST ASIAN LITERATURE AND THE QURʾĀN). The twelfth/eighteenth and thirteenth/nineteenth century Qurʾāns from Malaysia or Indonesia are generally copied in a form of *naskh* and written on European paper. Their illumination contains luxuriant foliage embellished by finials that derives from local decorations in other media. A Qurʾān in the Shaker Collection may have been written primarily with a brush rather than a pen.

Africa

The religious and cultural traditions of Muslim Africa can be divided into three broad geographic zones. The first, which stretches along the Mediterranean from Egypt to Morocco, has been covered in earlier sections of this essay so here attention will be focused on sub-Saharan west Africa and on the continent's eastern portion, a region that includes the Sudan, Somalia and the eastern littoral as far as Mozambique, often called the "Swahili coast." These western and eastern regions differ in their approach to religious architecture, in their modes of transcribing the Qurʾān, and also in the manner in which the sacred text was integrated into the activities of daily life (see also AFRICAN LITERATURE). Many roles assumed by the Qurʾān in west Africa bear the impress of the religious and cultural traditions of north Africa, particularly Morocco, whereas customs along the Swahili coast often display a close affinity to the practices of south Arabia.

West Africa

It is often said that in Africa, Islam develops distinctive features in response to local traditions and rituals. One distinctive regional tradition, copying the Qurʾān on loose folios or even a collection of single sheets that are then stored and carried in a leather pouch, probably derives from north Africa, where texts from the seventh/thirteenth century mention the storage and transportation of Qurʾāns in leather bags. The earliest surviving west African manuscripts of this type appear to date from the eleventh/seventeenth century, and they continued to be produced into the thirteenth/nineteenth century. The script with which the text was transcribed in west Africa also is rooted in north African scribal practice.

Other west African approaches to the Qurʾān appear to derive from local needs and customs including a fondness for linking portions of its text with specific designs or images, creating an iconographic whole that can be used in conjunction with particular rituals. A good example of such a fusion are the talismans that combine a highly stylized image of Burāq, the Prophet's mount during his heavenly ascension (q.v.), not with Q 17:1 (where that event is described), but rather with the ever popular Q 2:255. In Sierra Leone these text-image hybrids were customarily affixed to the doorways of houses to protect the inhabitants against nefarious forces or evil spirits.

Three printed talismans purchased ca. 1970 C.E. at Mopti in Mali and published by G.C. Anawati (Trois talismans musulmans) offer a more elaborate fusion of text and image than this simple Burāq amulet, and were intended to provide protection against a wider variety of difficulties. One features a circular device, possibly symbolic of a cave, containing the names of the Seven Sleepers and their dog Qiṭmīr (mentioned in Q 18) that is framed by Q 2:255 and is accompanied by seven additional verses of particular potency (Q 9:51; 10:107; 11:6, 56; 29:60; 35:2; 39:39). A second, said to offer protection during voyages by ship, has the drawing of an oblong object, possibly a boat, and a "magic square" filled with the numerical equivalents of selected divine attributes *(al-asmāʾ al-ḥusnā)*. The accompanying qurʾānic citation links fragments taken from a number of verses and culminates in the mysterious letters prefaced to several sūras. The third talisman, intended for protection against the maladies of love, has a square of nine units divided by diagonal lines into a series of triangular compartments. This frame is composed with the words of Q 94, and the Prophet's name is inscribed at the intersections of four sets of lines (see NAMES OF THE PROPHET). A simpler version of this design, focusing only on the word *Allāh*, was used ca. 1980 C.E. in Ghana by the Imām of Techiman to decorate cloth for ceremonial use.

Copying and memorizing the Qurʾān was the foundation of education for the Muslims of both west and east Africa, a circumstance that helped to link the symbolic language of the two zones (see TEACHING AND PREACHING THE QURʾĀN). Even the materials used in that transfer of knowledge gained a power and prestige of their own. Children customarily copied the Qurʾān onto hand-held writing boards with pen and ink. After a given section of the text had been memorized, the board was washed to prepare it to receive the next installment; the resulting mixture of ink and water was prized for its curative and protective powers. Writing boards were also decorated with various abstract patterns and those designs were, in turn, transferred to other objects. Among the Hausa of Nigeria, persons skilled in qurʾānic calligraphy were often called upon to prepare patterns for embroideries and other decorations.

The writing board itself can even become a kind of symbolic replacement for the Qurʾān. Its distinctive outline of an upright rectangle with an arrow-shaped handle protruding from one narrow side appears in architectural decoration and on portable objects. The fusion between the Qurʾān's text and the manner in which it was transmitted is epitomized in an elaborately decorated writing board from Omdurman in the Republic of the Sudan (see Fig. VIII). Its central zone is inscribed with Q 97, which describes the Qurʾān's revelation on the Night of Power (q.v.), an event linked to 27 Ramaḍān and celebrated with considerable pomp in the region.

East Africa

Most of the east African objects in western collections are linked to the epic struggles centered in the present Republic of the Sudan between the British army and the Mahdiyya movement led by Muḥammad Aḥmad al-Mahdī (d. 1313/1895) and his successor Khalīfa ʿAbdullāhī (d. 1317/1899). Those objects coupled with contemporary descriptions and photographs demonstrate the varied ways in which the Qurʾān served to bolster the Mahdī and his army. They recited it as they went into battle, followed banners inscribed with its text, carried swords with qurʾānic inscriptions and wore armor festooned with qurʾānic phrases and other prayers inscribed on leather-covered amulets or written on miniature writing boards.

There are too few published east African Qurʾāns to support broad conclusions. One in the Khalili Collection, Qur 706, dated to 1162/1749, appears to have been made by a professional scribe for a religious scholar because it also contains supplementary texts about techniques of recitation, as well as selected ḥadīths and prayers. Its *naskh* script has some affinities with hands used in western India; the manuscript was once in Zanzibar. An example dated to 1296/1879 in the Safwat Collection appears to have been copied by its owner for his personal use in the region of Ḥelwān on the Egyptian-Sudanese border. Its *naskh* script resembles scholarly hands used in Egypt, but its boldly executed red and black illumination must spring from local traditions.

Priscilla P. Soucek

Bibliography

N. Abbott, *The rise of the north Arabic script and its kurʾanic development,* Chicago 1939; D. Alexander, *The arts of war arms and armour of the 7th to 19th centuries,* London 1992; R. Amador de los Rios, *Inscripciones árabes de Córdoba,* Madrid 1880; G. Anawati, Trois talismans musulmans en arabe provenant du Mali (marché de Mopti), in *AI* 11 (1972), 287-339; I. Artuk, Emevilerden Halife Abdülmelik bin Mervan adina kesilmiş eşsiz bir kurşun mühür, in *Belleten* 16 (1952), 21-5; E. Atil, *The age of Sultan Süleyman the Magnificent,* Washington, DC 1987; M. Bayani, A. Contandini, and T. Stanley, *The decorated word. Qurʾāns of the 17th to 19th centuries,* London 1999; W. Begley, Amanat Khān and the calligraphy on the Tāj Maḥal, in *Kunst des Orients* 12 (1978-9), 5-60; id., *Monumental Islamic calligraphy from India,* Villa Park, IL 1985; id. and Z. Dessai, *Tāj Maḥal. The illumined tomb,* Seattle 1989; A.D.H. Bivar, Arabic documents of northern Nigeria, in *BSOAS* 22 (1959), 324-49; S. Blair, The epigraphic program of the tomb of Uljaytu at Sultaniyya. Meaning in Mongol architecture, in *Islamic art* 2 (1987), 43-96; ead., *Monumental inscriptions from early Islamic Iran and Transoxiana,* Leiden 1992; Sh. Boaz, *Popular culture in medieval Cairo,* Cambridge 1993; H.C. von Bothmer, Architekturbilder im Koran. Eine Prachthandschrift der Umayyadenzeit aus dem Yemen, in *Pantheon* 45 (1987), 4-20; R. Bravmann, *African Islam,* Washington, DC 1983; F. Çağman and S. Aksoy, *Osmanli Sanatinda Hat,* Istanbul 1999; G. de Casparis and I.W. Mabbett, Religion and popular beliefs of south east Asia before ca. 1500. The beginnings of Islam, in N. Tarling (ed.), *The Cambridge history of southeast Asia. i. From early times to c. 1800,* Cambridge 1992, 330-3; J. Cowen, Dongdasi of Xian. A mosque in the guise of a Buddhist temple, in *Oriental art* 19 (1983), 134-47; L.-C. Damais, Études javanaises. I. Les tombes musulmanes datées de Tralaye, in *Bulletin de l'École Française de l'Extrême-Orient* 48

(1957), 353-415; P. Demonsablon, Notes sur deux vêtements talismaniques, in *Arabica* 33 (1986), 216-50; W. Denny, A group of silk Islamic banners, in *The Textile Museum journal* 4 (1974), 67-81; F. Déroche, *The Abbasid tradition,* Oxford 1992; id., Les Écritures coraniques anciennes. Bilan et perspectives, in *REI* 48 (1980), 207-24; A. Dessus La Mare, Le mushaf de la mosquée de Cordoue et son mobilier mécanique, in *JA* 230 (1938), 551-75; S. Digby, A Qur'ān from the east African coast, in *AARP: Art and archaeology research papers* 7 (1975), 49-55; E. Dodd, The image of the word. Notes on the religious iconography of Islam, in *Berytus* 18 (1969), 35-62; ead. and S. Khairullah, *The image of the word,* 2 vols., Beirut 1981; J. Dodds (ed.), *Al-Andalus. The art of Islamic Spain,* New York 1992; B.A. Donaldson, The Koran as magic, in *MW* 27 (1937), 254-66; E. Doutte, *Magie et religion dans l'Afrique du Nord,* Paris 1908; R. Elgood, *Islamic arms and armour,* London 1979; T. Fahd, *La divination arabe. Études religieuses, sociologiques et folkloriques sur le milieu natif de l'Islam,* Paris 1987; L. Fernandes, *The evolution of a Ṣūfī institution in Mamlūk Egypt. The khanqah,* Berlin 1988; M. Fierro, The treatises against innovations (kutub al-bida'), in *Der Islam* 69 (1992), 204-46; A. Fodor, A group of Iraqi arm amulets (Popular Islam in Mesopotamia), in *QSA* 5-6 (1987-8), 259-77; C. Gandy, Inscribed silver amulet boxes, in J. Allan (ed.), *Islamic art in the Ashmolean Museum [vol. x pt. 1 of Oxford studies in Islamic art],* Oxford 1995, 155-66; P. Gignoux and L. Kalus, Les formules des sceaux sasanides et islamiques. Continuité ou mutation, in *SIr* 11 (1982), 123-53; O. Grabar, *The great mosque of Isfahan,* New York 1990; id., *The shape of the holy,* Princeton 1996; A. Grohmann, *Arabische Paläographie I,* Vienna 1967; id., *From the world of Arabic papyri,* Cairo 1952; id., The problem of dating early Qur'āns, in *Der Islam* 33 (1958), 213-31; C. Hame and A. Epelboin, Trois vêtements talismaniques provenant du Sénégal, in *BEO* 44 (1992-3), 217-24; R. Hasson, *Early Islamic jewelry,* Jerusalem 1987; D. Heathcote, *The arts of the Hausa,* London 1976; R. Hillenbrand, Qur'ānic epigraphy in medieval Islamic architecture, in *REI* 54 (1986), 171-87; D.L. James, *The master scribes. Qur'āns of the 10th to 14th centuries,* London 1992; id., *Qur'āns and bindings from the Chester Beatty Library,* London 1980; id., *Qur'āns of the Mamlūks,* New York 1988; M. Jenkins and M. Keene, *Islamic jewelry in the Metropolitan Museum of Art,* New York 1982; L. Kalus, *Catalogue des cachets, bulles et talismans islamiques,* Paris 1981; id., *Catalogue of Islamic seals and talismans. The Ashmolean Museum, Oxford,* Oxford 1986; M. Keene with S. Kaoukji, *Treasury of the world. Jewelled arts of India in the age of the Mughals,* London 2001; R. Kriss and H. Kriss-Heinrich, *Volksglaube im Bereich des Islam,* 2 vols., Wiesbaden 1960-2; M. Lings, *The qur'ānic art of calligraphy and illumination,* New York 1987; D. Little, Religion under the Mamluks, in *MW* 73 (1983), 165-81; F. Maddison and E. Savage-Smith, *Science, tools and magic. Parts one and two,* Oxford 1997; K. Moaz and S. Ory, *Inscriptions arabes de Damas. Les stèles funéraires, I. Cimetière d'al-Bab al-Saghir,* Damascus 1977; J. Moline, The minaret of Ǧam (Afghanistan), in *Kunst des Orients* 9 (1973-4), 131-48; H. Motzki, The collection of the Qur'ān. A reconsideration of western views in light of recent methodological developments, in *Der Islam* 78 (2001), 1-34; J. Mouton, De quelques reliques conservées à Damas au moyen âge, in *AI* 27 (1993), 245-54; S. Ory, *Cimetières et inscriptions du Hawran et du Ǧabal al-Duruz,* Paris 1989; P. Pelliot, Les plus anciens monuments de l'écriture arabe en Chine, in *JA* n.s. (1913), 177-91; M.B. Piotrovsky et al., *Art of Islam. Heavenly art. Earthly beauty,* Amsterdam 1999; E. Quatremère, Mémoire sur le goût des livres chez les Orientaux, in *JA* n.s. (1838), 35-78; J.-T. Reinaud, *Monuments arabes, persans et turcs. Du cabinet de M. le Duc de Blacas et d'autres cabinets,* Paris 1828; D.S. Rice, *The unique Ibn al-Bawwab manuscript in the Chester Beatty Library,* Dublin 1955; A. Rippin, *Muslims, their religious beliefs and practices. i. The formative period,* New York 1990; C.F. Ritter, The role of calligraphy in the Islamic architecture of Iran, in *Oriental art* 22 (1976), 77-87; J.M. Rogers, *Empire of the sultans. Ottoman art from the collection of Nasser D. Khalili,* Geneva 1995; id. and R.M. Ward, *Süleyman the Magnificent,* London 1988; N. Safwat, *The art of the pen,* Oxford 1996; id., *Golden pages. Qur'āns and other manuscripts from the collection of Ghassen I. Shaker,* Oxford 2000; P. Sanders, *Ritual, politics, and the city in Fatimid Cairo,* Albany 1994; A. Schimmel, Calligraphy and Ṣūfism in Ottoman Turkey, in R. Lifchez (ed.), *The dervish lodge. Architecture, art and Ṣūfism in Ottoman Turkey,* Berkeley 1992, 242-52; ead., Some glimpses of the religious life in Egypt during the later Mamluk period, in *Islamic studies* 4 (1963), 353-91; ead., Translations and commentaries of the Qur'ān in Sindhi language, in *Oriens* 16 (1963), 224-43; J. Sourdel-Thomine, *Die Kunst des Islam,* Berlin 1973; Y. Tabbaa, The transformation of Arabic writing. Part I: Qur'ānic calligraphy, in *Ars orientalis* 21 (1991), 119-48; Part II: The public text, in *Ars orientalis* 24 (1994), 119-47; id., *The transformation of Islamic art during the Sunni revival,* London 2001; W. Thackston, The role of calligraphy, in M. Frishman and H.-U. Khan (eds.), *The mosque. History, architectural development and regional diversity,* London 1994, 43-54; A. Welch, Qur'ān and tomb. The religious epigraphs of two early sultanate tombs in Delhi, in F.M. Asher and G.S. Gai (eds.), *Indian epigraphy. Its bearing on the history of art,* New Delhi 1985, 256-67; M. Wenzel, *Ornament and amulet. Rings of the Islamic lands,* Oxford 1993; E. Whelan, Forgotten witness. Evidence for the early codification of the Qurʾān, in *JOAS* 118 (1998), 1-14; ead., Writing the word of God. Some early Qurʾān manuscripts and their milieus. Part I, in *Ars orientalis* 20 (1990), 113-47; Jin Yijiu, The Qurʾān in China, in *Contributions to Asian studies* 17 (1982), 95-101.

Mathānī see OFT-REPEATED

Maturity

Full physical and mental capacity. The notion of maturity *(ashudd, rushd)* has reference to a person who has attained complete natural development, who is fully grown and capable of assuming the responsible management of his or her own affairs.

Physical maturity

The common word indicating physical maturity is *ashudd,* from the root *sh-d-d* meaning "to strengthen." It occurs eight times in the Qurʾān, in every instance in conjunction with some form of the root *b-l-gh,* which in itself connotes "coming of age." The same root also yields words that signify eloquence in speech, thus suggesting a connection between maturity and the ability to express oneself forcefully and elegantly. An individual who has passed puberty and achieved majority is *bāligh.* In two instances, Q 6:152 and Q 17:34, a phrase with derivatives of these two roots has reference to guardianship (q.v.) over the property (q.v.) of orphans (q.v.). Guardians are commanded not to appropriate the wealth (q.v.) of orphans and to act with regard to it only in a proper ("the best") manner until the minor comes of age, at which time his property must be turned over to him, if he be found capable of managing it. The legal schools extended the same rule to the guardianship of a father over the property of his own children (q.v.; see also FAMILY; LAW AND THE QURʾĀN).

Exceptions to the absolute prohibition of a guardian's use of a ward's wealth are allowed, however, as in Q 4:6, where something like a wage for the guardian's efforts in overseeing the property of his ward seems to be permitted for those who do not enjoy great wealth of their own. Important is that the guardian should act always in the best interest of the ward and not waste the latter's resources recklessly or foolishly. There is a specific warning against speedily devouring a ward's wealth in order to utilize it all for the guardian's purposes before the ward comes of age and is entitled to his or her property.

The connection between maturity and the control of property is also made in the story of Moses' (q.v.) encounter with one of the servants of God to whom had been "granted mercy (q.v.) from us and to whom we had taught knowledge (see KNOWLEDGE AND LEARNING) from ourselves" (Q 18:65), a figure who is usually identified with Khiḍr (see KHAḌIR/KHIḌR). The explanation for Khiḍr's restoration of a broken-down wall in a city that had received him and Moses ungraciously lay in a treasure buried beneath the wall. The treasure belonged to two orphaned boys whom God intended should reach their maturity and thus be able to claim their treasure.

According to the legal schools, the indications of maturity are the physical developments that normally accompany puberty. In the case of boys they are the appearance of pubic hair and the occurrence of nocturnal emissions, while in girls they are the onset of menstruation (q.v.), the consummation of marriage and the fact of the woman's having lived with her husband for a period of time (see MARRIAGE AND DIVORCE). Pregnancy is also an evidence of maturity in girls.

There is disagreement among the legal schools about the age at which maturity is achieved if the usual physical signs are absent. The majority holds that age fifteen marks the passage to maturity. If the signs of puberty are present, some would allow the age to be pushed back as far as nine years but no farther. Abū Ḥanīfa (d. 150/767) allows a guardian to maintain custodianship of a ward's property until age twenty-five if the latter is deemed incompetent to manage it properly alone. In such a case the criterion for determining maturity is clearly not solely physical.

The age of maturity is made somewhat unclear by certain other considerations. For example, a child is considered to have achieved the power of discrimination by the age of seven, discrimination being certainly one of the aspects of maturity. Seven is the age at which boys must begin to fulfill the religious duties, such as prayer (q.v.), that are incumbent upon adult Muslims. In cases in which there is dispute between parents about the custodianship of a child who has reached seven years, the child is held to have sufficient powers of discrimination to be able to choose with which of the parents he will live. There is a similar ambiguity about maturity in connection with the age of marriage. Although betrothal may occur at any age through the action of a child's custodian, the consummation of a marriage is presumably an occurrence that marks the full development of an individual. Pregnancy is, therefore, an indication of maturity.

There are some matters for which maturity is a necessary condition. The disposition of one's self or one's property cannot be made until maturity is reached, the responsibility before that time falling upon the custodian or guardian of the immature person. Guardianship of a minor is, therefore, restricted to those who are of full age and free (see SLAVES AND SLAVERY). A *walī* or guardian who provides a marriage partner for a minor child must be a person of full age. Similarly it is only a person of full age who may adopt a child, though a woman must also have the consent of her husband to do so. Maturity is also a necessary but not a sufficient condition for one who wishes to enter into a contract (see CONTRACTS AND ALLIANCES). The primary requisite for a witness in a criminal case is that he should be a male Muslim of good character who has reached either puberty or the age of fifteen (see WITNESSING AND TESTIFYING; SIN, MAJOR AND MINOR). In general, as these examples show, maturity is a necessary condition of legal competence in the purview of Islamic law.

Mental maturity (rushd)

In the verses that deal with the management of the property of orphans, guardians are commanded to test the orphans before turning their property over to them (Q 4:6). The basis for delivering the property is "if you find in them *rushd*," i.e. sound judgment (q.v.) or mental competence for the handling of their own affairs (see INSANITY). The negative expression of the same point is made in Q 4:5 where the command is given "make not over your property… to the weak of understanding." Mental competence is also associated with attaining full age in the story of Joseph (q.v.) where it is said of him "and when he reached his maturity we gave him wisdom and judgment" (Q 12:22). Precisely the same is said of Moses (Q 28:14). Māwardī (d. 450/1058) and other classical exegetes (see EXEGESIS OF THE QURʾĀN: CLASSICAL AND MEDIEVAL) insist that mental maturity (glossed as *ʿāqil*) be a requirement for the caliphate (cf. al-Qāḍī, Term; see also CALIPH; IMĀM).

Spiritual maturity

A verse that enjoins loving treatment for one's parents (q.v.; Q 46:15; see also SOCIAL INTERACTIONS; KINSHIP), indicates that a true realization of God's goodness comes when one "attains maturity and reaches forty years of age." At that time a person begins to thank God for the blessing (q.v.) bestowed upon the parents and himself, to ask that he may do good that pleases God, to pray for the well-being of his offspring, and to affirm his submission to God (see GRATITUDE AND INGRATITUDE; GOOD AND EVIL). Full spiritual realization, thus, seems to come long after physical maturation.

Maturity as proof of God's creative power

In two verses of the Qurʾān (Q 22:5 and 40:67) the attainment of maturity is presented as an argument for God's sovereignty over the world as its creator (see CREATION; COSMOLOGY). He is described as the one who created people from dust, effected their development in the womb and brought them forth as babies so that they might achieve their maturity (see BIOLOGY AS THE CREATION AND STAGES OF LIFE). The creative process and its stages are offered as a proof (q.v.) against those who deny the resurrection (q.v.). The God who brought the human race into being can restore what has apparently been lost. In Q 40:68, immediately following the description of a human being's development through the stages of life, the point is driven home by the statement "He it is who gives life (q.v.) and causes death (see DEATH AND THE DEAD), so when he decrees a thing, he only says to it, 'Be,' and it is."

Charles J. Adams

Bibliography
Primary: Ibn Qayyim al-Jawziyya, *Tuḥfat al-mawdūd fī aḥkām al-mawlūd*, Bombay 1961.
Secondary: S.A. Adesanya, Marriage according to the local Islamic rites of southern Nigeria, in *Journal of Islamic and comparative law* 2 (1968), 26-44; O. Arabi, Contract stipulations (shurūṭ) in Islamic law. The Ottoman Majalla and Ibn Taymiyya, in *IJMES* 30 (1998), 29-50; R. Brunschvig, Considérations sociologiques sur le droit musulman ancien, in *SI* 3 (1954), 61-73; ed., Bāligh, in *EI²*, i, 993; M.T. El Imari, Rights of children, in *Journal of Islamic and comparative law* 8 (1978), 1-27; A. Giladi, *Children of Islam. Concepts of childhood in medieval Muslim society*, New York 1992, esp. 23 and 52; D.J. Hill, Comparative survey of Islamic law and the common law relating to the sale of goods, in *Journal of Islamic and comparative law* 2 (1968), 89-127; R. Levy, *The social structure of Islam*, Cambridge 1939², esp. 141 f.; W. al-Qāḍī, The term "khalīfa" in early exegetical literature, in *WI* 28 (1988), 392-411.

Maymūna

see WIVES OF THE PROPHET

Measurement

Finding the magnitude of a physical quantity such as length, area, volume, weight, and time. The full meaning of the term 'measurement' covers five constituent parts: (i) the quantity to be measured, (ii) the act of measuring, (iii) the measuring instrument (see INSTRUMENTS), (iv) the magnitude (measure) of the quantity measured, and (v) the unit of measurement. The present discussion touches upon each of the five components, with the understanding that the qurʾānic mention of any one of them would imply their totality, i.e. the actual performance of a complete measurement. It should be noted that the actual measurement of length, area, volume and weight is done on a material object or a substance. In the case of time, the measurement is of an event whose duration is to be calculated.

The usual Arabic equivalent of 'measurement' is *qiyās* (or *qays*, *qaws*) from the roots *q-y-s* and *q-w-s* (Lane, ii, 2577-8, 2574-5), but this noun and all other words that could be derived from these roots, except the word *qaws* ('bow'), are absent from the Qurʾān. There are some words, however, derived from the root *q-d-r* which are synonyms to those derived from the previous two roots *(q-y-s* or *q-w-s);* examples of these are: *qaddara,* corresponding to *qāsa,* 'to measure', and *miqdār,* corresponding to *miqyās,* 'a measure' (Jawharī, *Ṣiḥāḥ,* iii, 967). Such words from the root *q-d-r* are found in various verses and imply measurements of length, volume, weight and time. Beside these, there are other words connected with the different types of measurements and these are derived from various roots: *dh-r-ʿ, q-w-s, ṭ-w-l* and *ʿ-r-ḍ* for length; *m-s-ḥ* for area; *k-y-l* and *ṣ-w-ʿ* for volume; and *w-z-n, th-q-l* and *kh-f-f* for weight measurements.

Measurement of length

In the following qurʾānic passages we find words derived from the roots *q-d-r, dh-r-ʿ, q-w-s, ṭ-w-l* and *ʿ-r-ḍ.* Q 34:18 reads "We measured *(qaddarnā)* the [length of the] journey (q.v.) between them (i.e. the cities)," where the act of measuring is to be understood metaphorically (see METAPHOR). In Q 34:11, however, the verb is used in the literal sense: "measure *(qaddir)* the link [i.e. of armor; see DAVID]." Q 69:32 utilizes both *dharʿ* ('a measure of [length]') and *dhirāʿ* ('a cubit'): "a chain [i.e. of the inhabitants of hell; see HELL AND HELLFIRE; REWARD AND PUNISHMENT] whose measure is seventy cubits." *Qāb* ('a measure') and *qawsayn* ('two [Arabian] bows'; equivalent to two cubits; see *Tāj al-ʿarūs,* iv, 235) appear in Q 53:9: "He [Gabriel, q.v.] was (at a distance) whose measure is two bows or nearer" (see ASCENSION; VISIONS). As an expression, the length of 'two bows' commonly connotes a short distance.

Q 17:37 utilizes *ṭūl,* a term that ordinarily signifies length, to indicate "height": "You will never reach the mountains in height." The vast difference between the height of the mountains and human height is emphasized by this uncharacteristic use of *ṭūl.*

Finally, the notion of 'breadth' is indicated by the term *ʿarḍ:* "a paradise (q.v.) whose breadth is as the breadth of the heaven(s) and the earth" (Q 57:21; cf. 3:133; see HEAVEN AND SKY; EARTH). The word 'breadth' is used rather than 'length', as it is actually the ratio of breadth or width to the greater length of, for example, a rectangular figure, that convey an idea of great magnitude. This verse illustrates the vast expanse of paradise in breadth (and, of course, in length), whose dimensions are known to God alone, a theme taken up in ḥadīth literature, as well.

Measurement of area

There are three qurʾānic passages that include words derived from the root *m-s-ḥ,* a root which has the connotation of passing one's hand over an area, as also in ablutions (see CLEANLINESS AND ABLUTION) and anointing. The term for "area" *(misāḥa),* although derived from this root, eventually came to have a meaning independent of the actual act of wiping one's hands over a surface. "Wipe (with your wet hands) your heads and feet to the ankles… and wipe *(imsaḥū)* your faces and hands with it (i.e. clean soil or earth)" (Q 5:6). Q 4:43 also contains this second injunction. Q 38:33 reads as follows: "Then he began wiping (or stroking; *masḥan*) the shanks and necks (i.e. of the horses)." In these verses, the various forms of *m-s-ḥ* imply passing (one's hand) over a surface (e.g. face, neck). One can say that this action, on a larger scale, can be taken to resemble the surveying of a plot of land in order to obtain its area, but of course, in that case, an actual 'measurement' of certain quantities (e.g. length and breadth) is done, from which the precise area is calculated. By such extrapolation the Arabic term *massāḥ* corresponds to 'a surveyor' and *misāḥa* means 'area.' Yet, despite the presence of qurʾānic terminology related to the Arabic word for "area" *(misāḥa),* there is no Qurʾān reference to an actual measurement of area, whether in the real or metaphorical sense.

Measurement of volume

A number of qurʾānic verses containing words derived from the roots *k-y-l, q-d-r,* and *ṣ-w-ʿ* signify meanings associated with the measurement of volume. The words derived from the root *k-y-l* are: *kāla,* to measure the volume or to give a measure of volume (cf. Q 17:35; 83:3); *iktāla, yaktālu* (in the form *naktal*), to receive a measure of volume (Q 12:63; cf. 83:2); *kayl,* a measure of volume (Q 6:152; 7:85; 12:59-60, 63, 65, 88; 17:35; 26:181), together with the special measure, *kayl baʿīr,* camel's load (Q 12:65; see CAMEL; LOAD); and *mikyāl,* a measure of volume (Q 11:84, 85). This vocabulary specifically connotes an act of measurement and the use of a vehicle or vessel of measurement (see CUPS AND VESSELS). One example of such a vessel is a "cup" or "goblet." Q 12:72 speaks of the *ṣuwāʿ* or drinking cup, a word derived from the root *ṣ-w-ʿ.* (A related but non-qurʾānic term, *ṣāʿ,* signifies either a measuring vessel of a specific capacity or a unit of volume measurement.)

The words derived from the root *q-d-r* are *qaddara,* to measure the volume (Q 76:16) and *qadar,* a measure of volume (Q 13:17; 23:18; 43:11). The passages just cited vary in the degree of measurement specificity which they convey.

Measurement of weight

The words included in qurʾānic verses dealing with the measurement of weight are derived from the roots *w-z-n, th-q-l, kh-f-f* and *q-d-r.* Words derived from the root *w-z-n* include *wazana,* 'to weigh' (Q 83:3; cf. the imperative *zinū* in Q 17:35 and 26:182, and the verbal noun *wazn* at Q 7:8; 18:105; 55:9). In Q 7:8 and 18:105 the 'weighing' is that of the deeds of people at the day of judgment (see LAST JUDGMENT; GOOD DEEDS; EVIL DEEDS; RECORD OF HUMAN ACTIONS), and thus a metaphorical use, while in Q 55:9, the act of weighing is a real one. Another derivative of *w-z-n* is *mīzān (*pl. *mawāzīn),* which has three different meanings in the Qurʾān: firstly, it is used as a symbol of justice (Q 42:17; 55:7; 57:25; see JUSTICE AND INJUSTICE). Secondly, it means 'a weight' either literally as in Q 6:152; 7:85; 11:84-5; 55:9, or metaphorically, when speaking of those whose good deeds are heavy or light in comparison with their bad deeds (Q 7:8-9; 23:102-3; 101:6, 8). An expanded translation would be: "those whose weights on the scales or balances are heavy or light," in keeping with the figurative use of *mīzān* in the passages. Lastly, *mīzān* means the instrument for measuring weight, i.e. a balance or a scale used in the real sense (Q 55:8), or metaphorically, as in Q 21:47, "We set up the just balances for the resurrection (q.v.) day." In three successive verses in Q 55 (Sūrat al-Raḥmān; Q 55:7-9), the same word *(mīzān)* has the three meanings: 'justice,' 'a balance or a scale' and 'a weight', respectively. Fakhr al-Dīn al-Rāzī (d. 606/1210; *Tafsīr,* xxix, 91) gives also the alternative meanings: *mīzān* (a balance or a scale), *wazn* (weighing) and *mawzūn* (the weighed object). In Q 17:35 and 26:182, *qisṭās* (a synonym of *mīzān,* 'a balance') is used in the real sense.

The words derived from the root *th-q-l* are *thaqula,* 'to be heavy' (Q 7:8; 23:102; 101:6) and *mithqāl,* 'weight' (Q 4:40; 10:61; 21:47; 31:16; 34:3, 22; 99:7-8). From the root *kh-f-f* comes *khaffa,* 'to be light' (Q 7:9; 23:103; 101:8), while *q-d-r* yields *miqdār* (Q 13:8), *qadar* (Q 15:21; 42:27; 54:49) and *qadr* (Q 65:3); these last three all mean 'a measure' of weight but are often used metaphorically (see FATE; DESTINY; FREEDOM AND PREDESTINATION).

There are other words mentioned in the Qurʾān that represent certain weights. In Q 3:75, *qinṭār* (= 100 pounds) is used as a symbol for heavy weights, in contrast with the small weight of the *dīnār* (about 4 g; see MONEY). The *dirham* (pl. *darāhim*), which is equivalent to about 3 grams, is also attested (Q 12:20), although this verse actually refers to *dirhams* in its commercial connotation (see SELLING AND BUYING).

Measurement of time

Terminology for the measurement of intervals or duration of time is found in several qurʾānic verses. Four of these contain words derived from the root *q-d-r:* "God measures (or determines the measure of; *yuqaddiru*) the night and the day" (Q 73:20; see DAY AND NIGHT; DAY, TIMES OF); "a day whose measure *(miqdar)* is a thousand/fifty thousand years" (Q 32:5; 70:4; see DAYS OF GOD); "to a known measure (or term; *qadar*)" (Q 77:22). In four other verses (Q 3:30; 18:12; 57:16; 72:25), the Arabic word *amad* is used, corresponding to 'a term' or 'an interval of time' or 'a measure of time.' Among the verses just cited, in Q 32:5 and 70:4 the 'measure' or 'magnitude' of time is given; in Q 18:12, 73:20 and 77:22 it is known to God alone; while in Q 3:30, 57:16 and 72:25, it is described as a long measure of time.

One of the units of time measurement is the year *(sana)* mentioned in Q 32:5 and 70:4. The other is "a day" *(yawm),* mentioned in the same verses. One should, however, differentiate between the word 'day' *(nahār)* of Q 73:20 meaning 'daytime' or 'daylight' and the *yawm* used in Q 32:5 and 70:4, which denotes the sum of the durations of nighttime *(layl)* and daytime or daylight (*nahār,* see NOON; CALENDAR; PRAYER). The word *sāʿa* 'hour' is mentioned in 48 verses; and in 40 of these, it is used as an expression for the time of the beginning of the day of resurrection. In one verse (Q 9:117), it is described as the 'hour of hardship,' thus meaning an unspecified period of time. In the remaining 7 verses (Q 7:34; 10:45, 49; 16:61; 30:55; 34:30; 46:35), however, it can be taken to mean the unit of time (i.e. the hour); note the expression 'hour of daylight' (Q 10:45; 46:35).

Accuracy of measurement

A number of qurʾānic verses contain commands to perform measurements of volume and weight in an accurate manner by giving full (or complete) measurements. These will require the use of accurate measuring instruments (a balance or a scale with the correct counterweights and a vessel of the correct volume or capacity). Also there must be no manipulation of the measuring instruments that would result in 'giving short' *(yunqiṣ)* measurement of volume or weight, or 'giving less than due' *(yukhsir)* of the measured volume or weight (see CHEATING). Justice *(qisṭ)* is also to be observed when performing the measurements, and is achieved by giving or receiving no more and no less than due of the measured quantity. Such commands are the following: "Give full measurements of volume and weight" (*awfū l-kayla wa-l-mīzāna,* Q 7:85), "give full measurements of volume and weight with justice *(qisṭ)*" (Q 6:152; cf. 11:85), "perform your weighing with justice and do not give less weight than due" (Q 55:9), "do not give short measurements of volume and weight" (Q 11:84), and "give full measurement of volume, and be not of those who give less (volume) than due" (Q 26:181). As mentioned in the introductory section of this article and as also indicated by al-Ṭabarsī

(d. 518/1153; *Majma*ʿ) in his commentary on the verses Q 7:85 and 11:85, the words "volume" and "weight" mentioned above connote the substance (or object) whose volume or weight is to be measured. In the injunction to "weigh with the right (accurate) balance" (*al-qisṭās al-mustaqīm*, Q 17:35; 26:182), Fakhr al-Dīn al-Rāzī (*Tafsīr*, xx, 206) defines *al-qisṭās al-mustaqīm* as the well-leveled balance that does not tilt to either side. Finally, in Sūrat Yūsuf (Q 12, "Joseph"), there are two verses containing statements in accord with the command of giving full measurement of volume. In Q 12:59, Joseph (q.v.) tells his brothers (see BROTHER AND BROTHERHOOD): "Do you not see that I give full measurement of volume?" And in Q 12:88, his brothers say to him: "Give full measurement of volume to us."

While emphasis in the verses just cited is on the measurements of volume and weight, where these cover numerous commodities in everyday life, it is reasonable to assume that the other types of measurements (i.e. of length, area, and time) were expected to be performed accurately as well.

Measurement and Muslim society

Measurement of length, area, volume, weight, and time were implemented in the everyday life of traditional Muslim society. These measurements were required in such matters as commerce, selling and buying (e.g. food, drink, clothing [q.v.]; see also FOOD AND DRINK), housing, and land surveying. They are also required in observing the rules of the Islamic law (*sharīʿa*, see LAW AND THE QURʾĀN) connected with prayers *(ṣalāt)*, almsgiving (q.v.; *zakāt*), land taxation (*kharāj*, see TAXATION), and inheritance (q.v.; *irth*); all need some kind of measurement, using the appropriate measuring instruments and units (see, for example, Māwardī, *Aḥkām*). As an example, prayers require measurement of time and land taxation needs measurements of area, volume and weight.

In addition to the units mentioned in the Qurʾān *(dhirāʿ, ṣāʿ, qinṭār and sāʿa)*, a variety of other units, related to those mentioned above, have been used in different countries at different times. Example of these are *"qaṣaba"* for length, *jarīb* and *faddān* for area, *qisṭ* and *wasq* for volume, *ūqiyya* (ounce) and *raṭl* (pound) for weight (see Hinz, *Islamische Masse und Gewichte*), and *daqīqa* (minute) for time measurements.

An official 'Bureau of Standards' (*dār al-ʿiyār;* see Ibn Mammātī, *Qawānīn*, 333-4 and Maqrīzī, *Khiṭaṭ*, ii, 242-3) was established early on in Islamic polities in order to issue 'legal' standard glass coin weights and heavy weights and measuring vessels *(dīnār, dirham* and *fals* [coin weights]; *ūqiyya* and *raṭl* [weights]; and *qisṭ* [vessels], together with their fractions of 1/4 or 1/3 or 1/2; see Miles, *Early Arabic glass weights;* Balog, *Umayyad, ʿAbbasid and Tulunid glass weights;* and Morton, *Catalogue)*. These standards were used by the market inspector *(al-muḥtasib)* to check the accuracy of the weights of coins and of heavy weights as well as that of the capacities of measuring vessels in circulation in the market place (see ECONOMICS). The master standards were kept in the bureau.

In medieval societies, by the orders of the rulers (caliphs) or their representatives (see CALIPH; KINGS AND RULERS), certain words and pious legends were inscribed on volume and weight standards (Miles, *Early Arabic glass weights;* Balog, *Umayyad, ʿAbbasid and Tulunid glass weights;* Morton, *Catalogue*) in order to comply with the qurʾānic commands of giving full measurements of these quantities (see EPIGRAPHY AND THE QURʾĀN; MATERIAL CULTURE AND THE QURʾĀN; EVERYDAY LIFE, QURʾĀN IN). These include the word *"wāfī,"* meaning 'full capacity' or volume if inscribed on measuring vessels and 'full weight' when inscribed on weights. Others are pious legends such as the verse Q 26:181 (mentioned above) and the two statements: *"al-wafā' lillāh"* and *"amara Allāh bi-l-wafā',"* which, respectively, have the implicit meanings: "give full measurements of volume and weight as commanded by God" and "God commands [you] to give full measurements of volume and weight." See also WEIGHTS AND MEASURES; TIME; SPATIAL RELATIONS.

Said S. Said

Bibliography

Primary: Ibn Mammātī, As'ad, *Kitāb Qawānīn al-dawāwīn,* ed. 'A.S. 'Aṭiyya, Cairo 1943; al-Jawharī, Ismā'īl b. Ḥammād, *al-Ṣiḥāḥ. Tāj al-lugha wa-ṣiḥāḥ al-'arabiyya,* ed. A.A. 'Attār, 6 vols., Beirut 1984; al-Maqrīzī, Taqī l-Dīn, *Kitāb al-khiṭaṭ al-maqrīziyya* [known as *Kitāb al-mawā'iẓ wa-l-i'tibār fī dhikr al-khiṭaṭ wa-l-āthār*], 4 vols., Cairo 1906-8, ii; Māwardī, *al-Aḥkām al-sulṭāniyya wa-l-wilāyāt al-dīniyya,* ed. K.A. al-'Alamī, Beirut 1990; Rāzī, *Tafsīr;* Ṭabarsī, *Majma';* *Tāj al-'arūs,* Cairo 1306-7/1888.

Secondary: 'Abd al-Bāqī; A.A.M. 'Ali, *Measuring and weighing terms in the Qur'ān. Their meaning with reference to six English translations,* Ph.D. diss., Durham, UK 1998; P. Balog, *Umayyad, 'Abbasid and Tulunid glass weights and vessel stamps,* New York 1976; M. Fakhry, *The Qur'ān. A modern English version,* Reading 1997; W. Hinz, *Islamische Masse und Gewichte,* Leiden 1970; al-Jazā'irī, Abū Bakr Jābir, *Aysar al-tafāsīr li-kalām al-'Alī al-kabīr,* 2 vols, Medina 2002; H.E. Kassis, *A concordance of the Qur'ān,* Berkeley 1983; Lane, Cambridge 1984; G.C. Miles, *Early Arabic glass weights and measure stamps,* New York 1948, 51, 58, 63; A.H. Morton, *A catalogue of early Islamic glass stamps in the British Museum,* London 1985; Pickthall.

Mecca

The city (q.v.) in the Arabian peninsula that was the birthplace of Muḥammad, which, due to the presence of the Ka'ba (q.v.) therein, is revered as one of the "holy cities" in Islamic culture. A description of Mecca based strictly upon the Qur'ān could lead to the radical revision of a large number of stories from classical Arabic sources, which are most often of a mythical or legendary kind (see GEOGRAPHY; HISTORY AND THE QUR'ĀN). It can be argued that the historiographical elements provided by these sources with respect to Mecca, a city of great religious and political importance, should only be considered insofar as they are corroborated by the Qur'ān, in some shape or form. All elements which the Qur'ān ignores, such as the retrospective emphasis on the site at Mecca or its position as the "center of the universe" should be avoided because they refer to an intellectual framework that belongs to later stages in the evolution of the corpus of Islamic beliefs and representations.

Mecca is explicitly mentioned only twice, in two relatively late passages of the Qur'ān (Q 48:24 *[makka]* and Q 3:96, spelt *bakka;* see CHRONOLOGY AND THE QUR'ĀN). These may well be derivations from a more complete rendering of the name, which would be recognized in the *Macoraba* mentioned by Ptolemy. Several other passages make reference to the city or its surroundings, such as Q 14:37, "a valley without cultivation." It will be noted, too, that Medina (q.v.), another qur'ānic place of tremendous importance, is in a similar position, as it is named on only three occasions: Q 33:13 *(Yathrib),* Q 33:60 and Q 9:120. The presence of these place references in the text of the Qur'ān indicates that the tribal tradition reported in the ancient historical writing of the 'Abbāsid period can be cautiously taken as a general framework for analysis, particularly when this tradition is not distorted by a perspective of Islamic aggrandizement, such as an overestimation of the role of the family or clan of Muḥammad (see FAMILY OF THE PROPHET; PEOPLE OF THE HOUSE).

Initially it was only the tribe of Quraysh (q.v.; see also TRIBES AND CLANS) which lived in the city of Mecca, and of which Muḥammad was a member, that was the intended recipient of the Qurʾān's message. The very short sūra Q 106 (Sūrat Quraysh) sets out the fundamental elements of the dialogue between the *rabb*, the divine being (who will be given several names during the course of the revelation; see LORD; GOD AND HIS ATTRIBUTES), Muḥammad (most often represented as "you") and the tribe (referred to as "they" or "you," for example, "their assembly..." of Q 38:6, *al-malaʾu minhum*). This dialogue was to last for the entire period preceding the expulsion of Muḥammad, which would take place in 622 C.E. (the date according to post-qurʾānic tradition), and which is clearly indicated in Q 47:13: *qaryatuka allatī akhrajatka*, "your city, which has expelled you...." *Qarya* is the general term used in the Qurʾān for a "place of fixed abode" in contrast to the nomadic world (see NOMADS; BEDOUIN). In the Medinan period of the qurʾānic revelation (see REVELATION AND INSPIRATION), *umm al-qurā*, the "mother of the cities" (Q 42:7; 6:92), indicates Mecca, which Muḥammad has been given the task of converting. In numerous other passages, this term is applied to rebel cities (singular or plural), which have been punished by God, according to the Qurʾān (see PUNISHMENT STORIES; GENERATIONS). This is a warning and an example of the fate that is promised to the inhabitants of Mecca if they continue to reject the divine command addressed to them.

The Quraysh, who are named only once in the Qurʾān (Q 106:1), are immediately summoned to "worship" (q.v.; *ʿibāda*) the "lord" *(rabb)* of the "house" (*bayt*, see HOUSE, DOMESTIC AND DIVINE) from which we can conclude that this house was located in their city. Q 48:24, gives the precise location of this sacred place, which is situated "in the lower regions of Mecca" *(baṭn makka)*, that is in the lowest part of the town, into which the rainwater runs and wherein are located the famous wells of Zamzam (these are not, however, mentioned in the Qurʾān; see SPRINGS AND FOUNTAINS). The *bayt*, the Meccan "house" of the supernatural, is correctly identified as the Kaʿba. This is apparent from two late references, Q 5:95 and 5:97; the latter uses the specific expression *bayt* for it. The fact that it is shared with non-Muslims — thus showing that the cult surrounding it dates from an earlier time — can be read in Q 8:34-5, which criticizes the tribal ritual (see SOUTH ARABIA, RELIGION IN PRE-ISLAMIC). Those who do not render thanks to God, the *kāfirūn* or the idolaters *(mushrikūn)*, those who associate others with God (in other words, those who refuse to listen to the message conveyed by Muḥammad; see GRATITUDE AND INGRATITUDE; IDOLATRY AND IDOLATERS; POLYTHEISM AND ATHEISM), are not, however, formally excluded from the rituals connected to the Kaʿba until the very end of the Medinan period (Q 9:28). In any event, the word *bayt* does not indicate a temple, as one reads all too often, but a collection of sacred pre-Islamic stones, around which were made a series of "turns" *(ṭawāf)*, to which the Qurʾān alludes elsewhere (Q 22:29 and Q 2:158). The black stone, which would have been the principal sacred stone, is not mentioned in the Qurʾān.

The Meccan tribe, according to Q 106, ought therefore to give due recognition to the "lord of the house" for the protection (q.v.) he bestowed upon them: preserving them from famine (q.v.) and from fear (q.v.; *takhaṭṭuf*, i.e. from attacks on their town, cf. Q 28:57; 29:67), ensuring the success of their (commercial) voyages in winter and in spring *(ṣayf)*, the establishment of "alliances (with the tribes)" (*īlāf*, see CONTRACTS AND ALLIANCES) which he had allowed them to conclude (another mention of the protection of caravans afforded by the divinity is in connection with the Sabaean Yemenites, Q 34:18-9; see CARAVAN; YEMEN; SHEBA). Primitive worship undoubtedly included the sacrifice (q.v.) of large domesticated animals (*naḥr*, dromedaries; see CAMEL; CONSECRATION OF ANIMALS) at the actual site at Mecca, as another very early verse (Q 108:2) indicates (other later passages describe the sacrifices as taking place *intra muros*, within the walls, viz. Q 22:33; 5:95, 97). The place of sacrifice was to be found in the immediate vicinity of the "house," in all likelihood on the small hill of al-Marwa (see ṢAFĀ AND MARWA). Although the Qurʾān does not give an exact location, the fact is touched upon in Muslim tradition. The Qurʾān mentions the high hills of al-Ṣafā and al-Marwa as places which are "marked out" (*shaʿāʾir*, Q 2:158), indicating that they were designated places of ritual. This would have consisted of a *ṭawāf*, circumambulation, culminating finally in the sacrifice at al-Marwa.

The sacrifice at the close of the pilgrimage (q.v.) was transferred, however, to the valley of Minā during the lifetime of Muḥammad himself, in the ceremonies at the end of the year 10/632, which took place shortly before his death (see FAREWELL PILGRIMAGE). This move was a political decision — to bring together in a single trip two pilgrimages that had been hitherto separated, both in time and location, that is the pilgrimage of the people of Mecca and of other places in western Arabia and the pilgrimage of the surrounding nomads. Thus the "holy month" (in the singular; see MONTHS) is mentioned several times in the Qurʾān, when dealing with the rites of the Kaʿba (Q 2:196, 217); this may be a reference to the rites of spring of the seventh month (Rajab), which took place exclusively on the site of Mecca. On the other hand, it is the bedouin ritual (of autumn), *ʿarafāt*, which is clearly intended in Q 2:197-9. The nomads' religious calendar had three holy months when they were forbidden to mount their normal raiding parties (see FIGHTING; WAR): the eleventh and twelfth months of the current year and the first month of the following year. Q 9:2, 5, 36 mention four holy months, thus adding the holy period of those who lived in a settled location to the three successive months of the nomads. As for the seasonal separation of the "intercalary month" *(nasīʾ)*, clearly an anti-bedouin measure, this was proclaimed only at the very end of the Medinan period, when the Medinan tribal confederation had gained effective control of the entire region (Q 9:37).

The very early qurʾānic passages of Q 106 and Q 108 are typically local in nature. One cannot yet discern any biblical influence, not even monotheism (see SCRIPTURE AND THE QURʾĀN). The Meccans are simply told not to mistake their protector. The theme of Mecca as a secure city, benefiting from effective protection, is repeated throughout the Meccan period, using a terminology which is to recur constantly: *ḥaram āmin*, an inviolable and secure place (Q 28:57; 29:67; the "protected city," *al-balad al-amīn*, of Q 95:3 certainly refers to Mecca, as does the city "which [God] made inviolable," *ḥarramahā [al-rabb]*, of Q 27:91). The same theme recurs in the Medinan period with the settling in the Meccan valley of Abraham (q.v.) and his family, including his sons Ishmael (q.v.) and Isaac (q.v.), in Q 14:35-9. Furthermore, it is in accordance with this ban, which preserves the city of Mecca from any violence, that the Muslims from Medina (who had entered the city in 630 C.E. to take control of it, following an agreement with the leading ʿAbd Shams clan) are asked to restrain their passions as fighters and plunderers (Q 2:190-5; see BOOTY).

Interest in Mecca, which seemed to have

diminished during the first part of the exile of Muḥammad to Medina (see EMIGRATION), was rekindled in the light of several political and religious episodes. They were centered on the presence of the Meccan "house" as a focal point for the developing religion, and functioned as a pretext for reaching a political settlement with the tribe of Quraysh. First of all there was the matter of the *qibla* (q.v.), the correct direction to face while praying, reported in Q 2:142-51. The change of the *qibla* was the result of the break with the Jews of Medina (see JEWS AND JUDAISM). Although the previous direction for prayer was not definitely Jerusalem (q.v.) but more probably a picture of the mountain of Moses (q.v.) and the holy valley around it (Q 79:16, etc.; see SINAI), the new direction imposed by the Qurʾān was absolutely unambiguous. The formula *al-masjid al-ḥarām*, already seen in Q 17:1, refers to the site of the Kaʿba at Mecca. Repeated several times in the passage on the *qibla* (Q 2:144, 149, 150) it becomes a customary Medinan formula when referring to the Meccan ritual pilgrimage. It would perhaps be better in etymological terms, nevertheless, to translate *masjid* as signifying "place of prostration" (see BOWING AND PROSTRATION) rather than "mosque" (q.v.).

The second episode to advance Mecca is that which the Qurʾān calls *al-fatḥ*, both a divine "victory" (q.v.) and a divine "gift" (see GIFT-GIVING). It refers to an agreement reached in the year 628 C.E., called the pact of al-Ḥudaybiya in Muslim historiography. The relevant passages in the Qurʾān refer to a "vision" (*ruʾyā*, see VISIONS). This foretold that Muḥammad and his followers would make a pilgrimage to Mecca, even though the Meccans denied them access to the city (Q 48:27). The subsequent unfolding of events and the happy ending are described, which allow the simultaneous emergence of both a political compromise and the completion of the ritual pilgrimage and sacrifice on the site at Mecca *intra muros* (Q 48:10, 18, 24, 25). Other passages recall the episode *a posteriori* (Q 8:34; 5:2; 22:25, 27-9, 33). In Q 22:29, 33 there appears a previously unknown phrase, which describes the Kaʿba as *al-bayt al-ʿatīq*, the "ancient house."

The most remarkable new development with regard to Mecca during the Medinan period concerns the position and behavior ascribed to Abraham by the Qurʾān. First and foremost a biblical prophet, by the end of the Meccan period Abraham has become the leading exponent of monotheism in the face of the conflict against idols (see IDOLS AND IMAGES) in his father's land (Q 21:51-70). He is thus portrayed in Medinan passages of the Qurʾān as the founder of the Kaʿba, the first divine "house" on earth, and then as the originator of the Meccan ritual *intra muros* (cf. Q 2:125-8; 3:96-7; 22:26-8; it is later tradition which attributed the exterior rituals, which are of nomadic origin, to Abraham). The formula *maqām Ibrāhīm*, "the place which Abraham holds," of uncertain meaning, is mentioned twice (Q 2:125; 3:97). It is possible that, originally, it actually indicated the entire site of Mecca. Muslim tradition probably prescribed the precise limits of its meaning by a particular story, one which described a rock situated to the east of the Kaʿba in which there is a deep footprint of the patriarch, which was made when he built the divine "house" here.

Thus Abraham (and his family) became the first to "submit to God" *(muslim)*. The primordial religious "voice," called by Abraham *(millat ibrāhīm)*, and "hanifism" *(ḥanīfiyya)*, the religion of the "pure" (the meaning of *ḥanīf* [q.v.], first used in Q 3:67, is uncertain) are presented as directly producing the Islam of Muḥammad. Furthermore, according to Q 2:129, Abraham himself asks God to send a "messenger" (q.v.; *rasūl*) to the Meccans to provide them with revelation. This spectacular development results directly from the ideological break with the Jews of Medina, which had become irreparable. Ishmael became associated with the actions of his father at Mecca without being really assigned a precise role, nor is there any independent story about him in his own right. Later Muslim thought was to develop its portrayal of the role of Ishmael at Mecca considerably, in particular his dramatic arrival in the valley of Mecca with his mother Hagar. As for the sacrifice of Abraham mentioned in Q 37:107, the historiographical tradition and Muslim exegesis place it in the valley of Minā. Before Ishmael was brought into this, there was some doubt concerning the identity of the sacrificial victim. The Qur'ān, however, is devoid of these anecdotal developments (see NARRATIVES).

J. Chabbi

Bibliography

Chabbi, *Seigneur;* P. Crone, *Meccan trade and the rise of Islam,* Oxford 1987; W. Dostal, Mecca before the time of the Prophet. Attempt of [sic] an anthropological interpretation, in *Der Islam* 68 (1991), 193-231; M. Gaudefroy-Demombynes, *Le pèlerinage à la Mekke,* Paris 1923; G. Hawting, The origins of the Muslim sanctuary at Mecca, in G.H.A. Juynboll (ed.), *Studies on the first century of Islamic society,* Edwardsville 1982; Jeffery, *For. vocab.;* M.J. Kister, *Studies in jāhiliyya and early Islam,* London 1989; M. Lecker, *Jews and Arabs in pre- and early Islamic Arabia,* London 1998; A.L. de Premare, *Les fondements de l'Islam,* Paris 2002; C. Snouk Hurgronje, *Mecca,* The Hague 1888-9; W.M. Watt, Makka. I. The pre-Islamic and early Islamic periods, in *EI²*, vi, 144-7; id., *Muhammad at Mecca,* Oxford 1953; J. Wellhausen, *Reste Arabischen Heidentums,* Berlin 1887; F. Wüstenfeld, *Die Chroniken der Stadt Mekka,* Leipzig 1857-61.

Media and the Qur'ān

The Qur'ān has been embodied and circulated in an ever-expanding variety of media forms during the modern period. The material qualities of these different media technologies have had an impact both on the ways the revealed text has come to be used, and the structures of knowledge and authority (q.v.) that those usages serve to uphold. Any inquiry into these transformations must begin with the premise that media practices are not determined by the physical qualities of technological forms but, rather, are always structured by cultural processes. In the case of the Qur'ān, these processes include the standards of usage and interpretation that Muslims have attempted to apply to the shifting set of media environments they have encountered so as to sustain and enrich the traditions they have inherited. They also include the limits and uneven results of those attempts.

Historians of Islam have often been puzzled about why Muslim societies adopted printing technology so late in its development (see PRINTING OF THE QUR'ĀN), and especially about why Muslim scholars historically expressed reticence in regard to its use for the Qur'ān. Despite the fact that presses, operated by Christians and Jews, had become commonplace in the urban centers of the Ottoman Empire by the mid-sixteenth century, it was not until three centuries later that Muslims began to make extensive use of the technology; and even then, its application to the Qur'ān continued to provoke considerable opposition. This reluctance to adopt printing technology has often been taken as evidence either of an attempt by religious authorities to retain their monopoly over the dissemination of knowledge, or of a more general traditionalism or conservatism characteristic of Muslim societies — a resistance to the innovations of the modern world apparent in everything from dress styles to forms of government (see POLITICS AND THE QUR'ĀN). An entire generation of Orientalists came to see the Muslim response to print technology as an attempt to resist the forces of historical change by a society whose ability to shape its own history was beginning to wane in the face of expanding European power. The fact that the printing press provoked similar reactions and resistances in Europe at the time of its first appearance was often forgotten in such accounts, a historical amnesia no doubt indebted to the triumphalist account of Western historical progress.

Much of the earlier scholarship concerning the use of new media technologies for the reproduction and dissemination of the Qur'ān assumed the history of the Bible as normative, and viewed those instances where Muslim practice diverged from that norm as historical distortions requiring explanation. As a number of recent scholars have pointed out, however, the Qur'ān cannot easily be assimilated to the generic category of scripture, a category founded on biblical scholarship and thus of limited applicability to other religious traditions (see BOOK; SCRIPTURE AND THE QUR'ĀN). New media technologies have posed different problems for Muslim scholars than they have for their Christian counterparts, a difference owing to the distinct ways revelation has been conceptualized within the respective traditions (see REVELATION AND INSPIRATION). By exploring some of the concerns expressed by Muslims in regard to the use of diverse media forms for the reproduction and dissemination of the Qur'ān, we can perhaps gain further insight into the kind of historical object the Qur'ān has been for Muslims in the modern period.

Print

In order properly to frame the question of media and the Qur'ān, a few observations on the concept of revelation within the Islamic tradition will be useful. As an audition not heard by the ear but received (silently, as it were) by the heart (q.v.) of the prophet Muḥammed, the Qur'ān presupposes and demands an epistemology that defies and challenges ordinary ways of knowing. Insofar as the Islamic account of revelation combines and interconnects the ear, heart, voice, and text, any attempt to apprehend the Qur'ān through a single sensory modality will necessarily be inadequate (see ORALITY). For this reason, the Qur'ān always exceeds its specific textual embodiments. Within both scholarly and non-scholarly contexts, the written text has tended to remain subordinated to a complex of oral and recitational practices (see RECITATION OF THE QUR'ĀN), more an *aide mémoire* than the thing itself (see ORALITY AND WRITING IN ARABIA; ORTHOGRAPHY; ARABIC SCRIPT), whose primary locus is in the human heart. These practices, and the structures of discipline and authority that uphold them, ensure the Qur'ān's correct reproduction and reception, its proper embeddedness in hearts, in voices, as well as in written texts. Indeed, prior to the adoption of the printing press, even the production of manuscript copies generally required the vocalization of the text as an intermediary step along the process, understood as a necessary condition of its accurate reproduction in textual form (see MANUSCRIPTS OF THE QUR'ĀN). In fact, when the Egyptian standard edition of the Qur'ān was produced in the 1920s, the scholars entrusted to ensure its accuracy relied not on manuscript versions, but on the study of different traditions of recitation (cf. as-Said, *Recited Qurʾān;* Weiss; Modern phonographic collection; see also READINGS OF THE QURʾĀN). In short, the Qurʾān's various verbal and textual instances have always remained thoroughly interwoven and interdependent, the revealed word never reducible to a stable, self-sufficent object, such as a book (see WRITING AND WRITING MATERIALS). In light of this fact, Muslim concerns about the application of new media technologies to the Qurʾān did not simply reflect the privileging of the human voice within Islamic epistemologies, as some scholars have argued. Such technologies posed a broader challenge: namely, how can the practical and institutional conditions that ensure an ethical response to divine revelation be upheld across new and rapidly changing media environments?

Not surprisingly, one of the worries expressed by early modern scholars in regard to the printing press was that the mass dissemination of printed copies of the Qurʾān would lead to its circulation to locations where proper moral comportment was not upheld, as well as into the hands of nonbelievers (see BELIEF AND UNBELIEF) where the text would not be treated with the required respect and care. In its capacity to reproduce versions of the Qurʾān in vast, seemingly infinite quantities, the printing press threatened to unleash the sacred text from the structures of discipline and authority that governed its social existence and ensured its ethical reception. In addition, Muslims must have been rather horrified by the first highly flawed, and generally poor quality copies of the Qurʾān printed by Europeans. It is worth remembering here that, contrary to our usual assumptions, accuracy was not one of the qualities generally ascribed to the early printing presses in Europe. Indeed, the "stigma" of — i.e. the lower status accorded to — printed books earned them a reputation in some circles of the later Renaissance as being less faithful to the original than were those produced by hand in late-medieval and early modern *scriptoria*. For Muslims, the possibility of mistakes remained an ongoing concern as long as the structures of expertise, supervision, and authority, as well as the technological means, remained inchoate. Outright opposition to the printing press, however, became increasingly unsustainable by the early nineteenth century, as Muslim societies were gradually being reorganized in accord with Western social and political models. As a technology central to the exercise of power and the organization of political life within modern societies, the press came to be viewed as an instrument essential to any reform project. The fact that Christian missionaries made extensive use of the press in order to disseminate the Bible provided a further incentive for Muslim reformers to adopt printing technology. Thus, once Muslims saw that the benefits afforded by such mass duplication (in making the Qurʾān universally available) outweighed the dangers, Muslim presses begin to reproduce printed versions in large numbers. This occured in the mid-nineteenth century both in czarist Russia and British controlled India, and somewhat later in the century in different regions of the Middle East.

Phonograph

The phonograph raised a rather different set of questions for Muslims when it was first introduced into Islamic societies. Snouck Hurgronje provides an account from 1915 of an early appearance of the phonograph in Java, Indonesia. The first phonographs on the island were operated by itinerant performers who, for a fee, would set them up in public locations and demonstrate their use with records of both musical selections and recited verses of the Qur'ān. In the incident recounted by Hurgronje, one such demonstration was attended by a Javanese scholar, Sayyid Othman, who subsequently produced a *fatwā* on the permissibility of listening to phonographic records of the Qur'ān (see LAWFUL AND UNLAWFUL). His discussion of the issue is worth examining as it reveals a style of reasoning that reappears throughout the modern historical period in debates about the technological mediation of the Qur'ān. The *fatwā* begins with the assertion that it is acceptable for Muslims to attend demonstrations involving the phonographic reproduction of the Qur'ān as long as the conduct of those in attendance remains decent, and as long as the act of listening does not produce sensual excitement or lead to temptation. It is forbidden, however, to use the device in a place of amusement, or where non-Muslims are present, as the qur'ānic verses may "produce derision and mockery (q.v.)," and hence serve as an agent of unbelief (Hurgronje, Phonograph, 163). Up to this point, Sayyid Othman's argument bears considerable similarity to those put forth by much earlier scholars in regard to the printing press on the need to ensure that certain ethical norms be followed in the distribution and use of printed versions of the Qur'ān. The next part of the *fatwā*, however, responds to the question of whether one receives divine reward for listening to the Qur'ān reproduced phonographically, a question specific to phonic, but not print, technologies. Here, Sayyid Othman notes that, insofar as "the sounds of the Qur'ān are no longer produced by the organs of speech destined for each one of them... [and therefore] do not possess the peculiar, legally demanded, qualities," no divine reward will accrue to their listener (Hurgronje, Phonograph, 163). Here we see an attempt to define authoritatively the limits of phonographic technology for the reproduction of the Qur'ān, an attempt grounded in an (implicit) theory of mediation. In the passage from human voice to vinyl disk to mechanically reproduced sound, certain qualities essential to the recitation as an act of worship (q.v.) are lost. Admittedly, Sayyid Othman's opinion on this matter was not (and is not today) universally shared (Hurgronje mentions a dissenting view from a scholar in Singapore; Phonograph, 164-5). It is in the kind of questions the Javanese scholar asks, however, that we find the outline of an Islamic tradition of inquiry into questions of media technology, a tradition that has played a key role in defining the interpretive conventions and norms of use for new media forms in Muslim societies.

Radio

This tradition can be further elaborated by reference to an early disagreement over the use of the radio for broadcasting qur'ānic recitation. In the 1950s, a broadcasting system was established in Nigeria with the transmission of qur'ānic recitation included in the programming content. Concerned with the moral and legal probity of the practice, the then Emir of Kano sent out requests to scholars for *fatāwā* on whether such programming was permitted by the Islamic *sharīʿa* (see LAW AND THE QUR'ĀN). Among the *fatāwā* he received opposing the broadcasts, one by the Emir Ja'afaru Ishaq of Zaria argued that by inserting segments of recitation between non-religious programs on sports or news, the broadcasts violated the injunction stipulating that the Qur'ān must always be placed within contexts suitable to its divine and revered status. In other words, it is the structure of the medium itself (the serial ordering of radio programming) that elicits his concern, not the context of reception foregrounded by Sayyid Othman in regard to the phonograph. In another *fatwā*, a Senegalese Ṣūfī shaykh (see ṢŪFISM AND THE QUR'ĀN), Ibrahim Niass, countered this claim by emphasizing the self-contained and independent quality of each program on the radio, and thus the immunity of the recitation segment from the corruptions of the programs that preceded and followed it. In short, while the opinions of these scholars diverged sharply, their reasoning exhibits a shared set of concerns about the suitability of certain media contexts for the Qur'ān in light of the respect demanded by the revealed word. It is in this sense that these viewpoints — as well as those mentioned above in relation to print and phonographic technology — exemplify a shared tradition of reflection on the topic of media and the Qur'ān. And while today there are few Muslim scholars who oppose the broadcasting of qur'ānic recitation programs, and indeed, most argue that more air time should be given to such religious topics, it is not unusual to find requests for *fatāwā* on the ethical distinction between live and mediated auditions.

Cassettes and CDs

The dissemination of the Qur'ān via new media forms is not a process determined by scholarly debate alone. Popular media practices are also largely shaped by the ordinary users of those technologies. For example, one of the most popular media forms for the audition of qur'ānic recitation in recent years has been the cassette tape and, more recently, the CD ROM. Commecially produced recordings of famous reciters, such as ʿAbd al-Basīṭ ʿAbd al-Ṣamad (Egypt), Hajjah Maria Ulfah (Indonesia), and Mustafa Ozcan Gunesdogdu (Turkey), have become ubiquitous throughout Muslim societies. People listen to these tapes and CDs in all sorts of situations and locations, alone in their homes, in stores, cafes, and barbershops, as well as in taxis, buses, and other forms of public transportation (see EVERYDAY LIFE, QUR'ĀN IN). For some of those who listen to them, Qur'ān tapes represent an Islamic alternative to other kinds of commercialized popular entertainment. Indeed, as opposed to recordings of popular music, these tapes and CDs tend to bring with them some of the norms of sociability associated with the mosque (q.v.), such that when they are played in a public location, like a store or bus, they produce an environment wherein certain styles of speech and comportment become marked as inappropriate, and are likely to draw public censure from others present. A heated argument between customers at a café in Cairo or Fez, for example, may well elicit the comment, "Show some respect while the Qur'ān is being recited!" Practices such as these reflect popular sensibilities more than the pronouncements of scholars.

"Qur'ānic commodities"

The rendering of the Qur'ān in the form of popular media commodities, such as recitation tapes, raises several important and interesting issues. As a number of scholars have noted, the omnipresence of the Qur'ān, embedded in multiple artifacts and media technologies, has affected the sense of sacredness the text elicits, the sensibilities and emotions that constitute a human response to God's word. Insofar as the printed Qur'ān, *muṣḥaf* (q.v.; pl. *maṣāḥif*), recorded qur'ānic recitations, and a variety of objects bearing qur'ānic verses are produced, marketed and displayed in a manner similar to other commodities, they have become connected to forms of consumption and pleasure not previously integral to qur'ānic practices of interpretation (see EXEGESIS OF THE QUR'ĀN: EARLY MODERN AND CONTEMPORARY), memorization (see MEMORY), and recitation. For example, since Qur'ān tapes are often played at the same times and in the same locations as other popular entertainment media, recordings of qur'ānic recitation have come to function as a kind of background sound, one that signals the religious commitment of the store owner or taxi driver, but does not demand the sort of attention traditionally associated with practices of recitation. Moreover, in much of the Middle East and south Asia today, *maṣāḥif* are sold not only in bookstores, but also in shops that carry household goods, stationery, clocks, and other kinds of merchandise. The fact that the text is placed among a jumbled assortment of commercially available artifacts in a store suggests that the distinction the *muṣḥaf* may be accorded by those who purchase it (evident, for example, in the care with which it is displayed in the home) may not carry over to contexts of commercial display and sale. In other words, the kind of respect shown to the *muṣḥaf* may be increasingly context dependent, as consumers come to distinguish between commercial and religious contexts, as well as public and private ones (Starrett, Religious commodities, 158-60).

Beyond printed copies of the Qur'ān, qur'ānic verses now adorn a vast assortment of religious commodities, such as wall plaques, brass trays, posters, stickers, and greeting cards, as well as newspapers, magazines, calendars and other printed materials (see MATERIAL CULTURE AND THE QUR'ĀN). People commonly use these decorative items inscribed with verses to adorn the walls of their houses (see HOUSE, DOMESTIC AND DIVINE) or shops, or the windows and dashboards of their cars. Taxi drivers in the Middle East frequently carry a small *muṣḥaf* mounted on the dashboard. Indeed, the development of a market in what might be called "religious commodities" has driven the creation of ever-new qur'ānic artifacts over recent years. Computer games geared to help children memorize verses of the Qur'ān and learn about the lives of the prophets are now available in multiple languages (see COMPUTERS AND THE QUR'ĀN; NARRATIVES; PROPHETS AND PROPHETHOOD); phone services allow callers to hear a sūra (see SŪRAS) of their choosing for a small fee; video tapes of well-known Qur'ān reciters are easily found (though, for the time being, they remain far less popular than audio versions); key chains, amulets (q.v.), clocks, lighters, bumper stickers, all bearing qur'ānic inscriptions, abound (see POPULAR AND TALISMANIC USES OF THE QUR'ĀN).

In many countries where Muslims predominate, newspapers have adopted certain qur'ānic verses as mottos. Newspaper articles on practically any topic may begin with a segment of qur'ānic verse. In addition, it is now common for newspapers to dedicate considerable space to discussing the meaning and theological importance of particular verses (q.v.). Occurring in these very different practical contexts, these heterogeneous usages of qur'ānic language mediate distinct patterns of response from Muslims, as consumers, worshippers, or national citizens. In this regard, the sociologist Fariba Adelkhah notes that the feeling of mourning that Shī'ite Muslims (see SHĪ'ISM AND THE QUR'ĀN) have traditionally associated with the Qur'ān has been attenuated to a certain extent by the text's wide circulation and general ubiquity in contexts of everyday life (Adelkhah, *Being modern*, 108). Similarly, the prefacing of all forms of public oratory with either the *basmala* (q.v.) or other qur'ānic expressions has become so standardized since the Iranian revolution that it is now made the object of popular jokes. A popular example from contemporary Tehran goes as follows: when a farmer is now asked what he uses to fertilize his fields, he responds, "In the name of God, sh*t!"

It would be wrong, however, to conclude from these observations that the Qur'ān is simply being rendered another form of commodified popular entertainment. Despite the reproduction and dissemination of "qur'ānic commodities" within commercial domains, and the extensive recourse to qur'ānic citations within modern political and social life, we continue to find the establishment of certain normative standards of use informed by ideas of the respect and distinction owed to the divine word (see WORD OF GOD). Thus, while qur'ānic verses may be imprinted on many household items, they are usually not applied to those used in activities that would compromise their purity, such as cooking, eating, or cleaning. Likewise, as decorative objects, *maṣāḥif* and other popular religious artifacts bearing qur'ānic verses will usually be displayed in a manner that respects their high status and value, placed above other artifacts that may be hanging on a wall, for example, or set apart from surrounding objects of display. When mounted on the dashboard of a car, *maṣāḥif* are ordinarily placed in a central location, and enclosed in a protective box covered in velvet or some other attractive material.

This proliferation of such "qur'ānic commodities" has been met with a variety of responses from Muslim scholars and intellectuals: while for some it is seen as evidence of a renewed religiosity among Muslims, for others, including many of those religious scholars *('ulamā')* trained in traditional institutions (see TRADITIONAL DISCIPLINES OF QUR'ĀNIC STUDY; TEACHING AND PREACHING THE QUR'ĀN), it represents a kind of commercialization inappropriate for the Qur'ān. Differences of opinion aside, insofar as the ability of the *'ulamā'* to direct the course of development within Islamic societies has been gradually attenuated as these societies have adopted secular legal and political structures, the *'ulamā'* frequently find themselves having to adjust to these new conditions. In short, attempts by the scholarly community to direct the introduction of the new media technologies, to define their uses and epistemological and ethical limits, while not entirely without effect, are often severely limited by the marginalization of this community from social and political power.

Internet

Perhaps the impact of new media forms on the Qur'ān is nowhere more visible today than on the internet. The Qur'ān is available online through thousands of different websites. It can be found in both text and audio formats, as well as in numerous translations (see TRANSLATIONS OF THE QUR'ĀN). Insofar as the internet medium offers new techniques for accessing the Qur'ān and related materials, it makes possible new kinds of reading practices. For example, internet versions of the Qur'ān can be accessed and explored via keywords, subjects or themes, or personal names. Moreover, those accessing the Qur'ān online through one of the many websites that make it available will often find themselves at the nexus of a vast body of secondary sources of information (scholarly guides, commentaries, speeches, sermons, audio versions) on the particular verse or chapter they have chosen to read. Some of the translations of the Qur'ān found within this domain incorporate short glosses or commentaries within the text itself, thereby redefining the text's traditional boundaries. Given the novelty of these practices, many of the ethical, theological, and practical issues raised by such a "virtual Qur'ān" have received little scholarly attention. Not surprisingly, within the advice sections and chat rooms of Islamic websites it is not uncommon for visitors to raise such questions as: Must one approach a virtual Qur'ān in a state of ritual cleanliness (see CLEANLINESS AND ABLUTION; RITUAL PURITY)? If one moves sections of text around on the screen, is one commiting an offense to the divine word? It remains to be seen as to what kinds of norms will develop in relation to the use of the Qur'ān within the internet. What is clear, however, is that the technical and practical operations that this medium makes available will certainly generate new uses and interpretive possibilities for those who avail themselves of it. As has been the case with other media forms, the task for Muslims will be to ensure that the ethical and epistemological conditions essential to the ways the text positions itself within Islamic traditions are upheld.

Media, authority, knowledge

The availability of the Qur'ān in ever-new media forms has also influenced the sociology of religious knowledge in Muslim societies (see SOCIAL SCIENCES AND THE QUR'ĀN). As the anthropologist Dale Eickelman and others have noted, the mass reproduction and diffusion of the Qur'ān, together with the advent of universal modern literacy (q.v.), has enabled recent generations of Muslims to engage with the text in ways that had previously been available only to scholars (see SCHOLAR). Muslims increasingly study and interpret the text outside the institutions of religious knowledge that had previously secured the authority of particular readings. Moreover, individuals now bring forms of literacy acquired in secular public schools to their reading of the Qur'ān, an innovation that has lead to a proliferation of new interpretive and citational practices (see CONTEMPORARY CRITICAL PRACTICES AND THE QUR'ĀN; LITERATURE AND THE QUR'ĀN). One result of this has been what some scholars have labeled a "democratization" of religious knowledge, a transformation often compared to that associated with the advent of Protestant Christianity in Europe during the sixteenth century. This process is evident in the proliferation of sites of Islamic authority (e.g. Islamic research institutes, preaching organizations, popular Islamic media-intellectuals), in the multiplicity and heterogeneity of media forms involved in the production and circulation of Islamic knowledge, and in the relocation of scholarly arguments outside the traditional institutions of religious learning into a wider public arena. Such a shift was already evident in Egypt as early as the 1920s, in such practices as the publication of Muḥammed 'Abduh's *tafsīr* in the pages of the journal *al-Manār* (as collected and edited by his student, Rashīd Riḍā), one of the new popular Islamic media forms that emerged at the time and that was geared to a broad, non-specialist audience. Indeed, as mentioned above, it is now common to find theological debates taking place within media oriented toward a general public, in newspapers, popular magazines, or booklets sold inexpensively in bookstalls and on sidewalks (see THEOLOGY AND THE QUR'ĀN). In addition, many of the most influential Muslim thinkers and activists today have never received training within traditional centers of Islamic learning, but are instead essentially self-taught. As these examples suggest, the structures of Islamic authority have undergone considerable change as they have become increasingly dependent on the institutions and media practices of national and transnational public spheres.

Charles Hirschkind

Bibliography
F. Adelkhah, *Being modern in Iran*, London 1999; M. Albin, The book in the Islamic world. A selective bibliography, in G. Atiyeh (ed.), *The book in the Islamic world. The written word and communication in the Middle East*, Albany, NY 1995, 273-81; id., Early Arabic printing. A catalogue of attitudes, in *Manuscripts of the Middle East* 5 (1990-1, 1993), 114-22; id., An essay on early printing in the Islamic lands with special relation to Egypt, in *MIDEO* 18 (1998), 335-44; T. Asad, *The idea of an anthropology of Islam*, Washington, DC 1986; G. Atiyeh (ed.), *The book in the Islamic world. The written word and communication in the Middle East*, Albany, NY 1995; G. Beckerlegge (ed.), *From sacred text to internet*, Aldershot 2001; G. Bunt, *Virtually Islamic. Computer-mediated communication and cyber Islamic environments*, Cardiff 2000; F. Denny, Exegesis and recitation. Their development as classical forms of qur'ānic piety, in F.E. Reynolds and T.M. Ludwig (eds.), *Transitions and transformations in the history of religions*, Leiden 1980, 91-123; D. Eickelman, Mass higher education and the religious imagination in contemporary Arab societies, in *American ethnologist* 19 (1992), 643-55; id. and J. Anderson (eds.), *New media in the Muslim world. The emerging public sphere*, Bloomington 1999; ids., Print, Islam, and the prospects for civic pluralism. New religious writings and their audiences, in *JIS* 8 (1997), 43-62; M. Gaborieau, Traductions, impressions et usages du Coran dans le sous-continent indien (1786-1975), in *RHR* 218 (2001), 97-111; Graham, *Beyond;* S. Hurgronje, Islam and the phonograph, in *MW* 5 (1915), 159-65; Institut Kefahaman Islam, *Seminar on Islamic understanding for the mass media. 25-26 June 1993*, Kuala Lumpur 1993; B. Larkin, *Uncertain consequences. The social and religious life of Media in northern Nigeria*, unpub. Ph.D. diss., New York University 1998; R.C. Martin (ed.), *Approaches to Islam in religious studies*, Tucson 1985; B. Messick, *The calligraphic state. Textual domination and history in a Muslim society*, Berkeley 1993; Rābiṭat al-Jāmi'āt al-Islāmiyya, *Wasā'il al-ittiṣāl al-ḥadītha wa-atharuhā 'alā l-mujtama'āt al-islāmiyya (Modern means of communication and their impact on the Muslim societies). Buḥūth al-nadwa allatī 'aqadathā al-Munaẓẓama al-Islāmiyya lil-Tarbiya wa-l-'Ulūm wa-l-Thaqāfa... [Cairo 5-7 Jumādā al-Ūlā 1415/10-12 October 1994]*, Rabat 1996; Rashīd Riḍā, *Manār;* F. Robinson, Technology and religious change. Islam and the impact of print, in *Modern Asian studies* 27 (1993), 229-51; L. as-Said, *The recited Qur'ān*, Princeton 1975; M. Sells, *Approaching the Qur'ān. The early revelations*, Ashland, OR 1999 (including compact disc); G. Starrett, The political economy of religious commodities in Cairo, in *American anthropologist* 97 (1995), 51-68; B. Weiss, *Al-muṣḥaf al-murattal.* A modern phonographic collection *(jam')* of the Qur'ān, in *MW* 64 (1974), 134-40.

Medicine and the Qur'ān

There is very little in the Qur'ān that is strictly medical in content. The most direct reference is in Q 16:69, which states that the drink *(sharāb)* produced by bees, i.e. honey (q.v.), is "healing" *(shifā')* for people (see ILLNESS AND HEALTH). The word *shifā'*, "health," is further attested three times but in contexts where it is often understood in the meaning of remedy against ignorance (q.v.; *jahl*) of God and the revelation (see REVELATION AND INSPIRATION). The word illness *(maraḍ)* is attested thirteen times but in all these cases it refers to the heart (q.v.), and is traditionally interpreted to denote religious doubt and not any actual physical ailment. Sick people *(marīḍ*, pl. *marḍā)* are referred to in connection with religious duties and illness is in these cases presented as a valid excuse not to perform a particular duty. In addition to these direct references, there are in the Qur'ān injunctions that have been given a medical interpretation. Among these are the dietary instructions and the requirement to fast regularly (see FOOD AND DRINK; FASTING).

In the first/seventh century, Muslims became acquainted with Greek medical views and gradually the medicine of Hippocrates and Galen gained a position of authority. The Muslim physicians and medical theorists systematized it and elaborated on the Greek theory and the resulting synthesis is usually called Islamic or Graeco-Islamic medicine. It is not, however, in any way Islamic in character but is based solely on teachings of the Greek masters and their Muslim counterparts such as Ibn Sīnā (d. 428/1037) and al-Rāzī (d. 313/925). Despite its high status,

Graeco-Islamic medicine was not the only medical system applied to the treatment of illnesses; people resorted to a variety of alternative treatments based on home remedies and local curing traditions. One alternative approach was expressed in the so-called Prophet's medicine *(al-ṭibb al-nabawī),* which was developed by scholars of the religious sciences and was based on the Qurʾān and the sunna (q.v.) of the Prophet. The authors of the Prophet's medicine showed that medical principles could be found in the Qurʾān and that the medical views that the Prophet had expressed were not in contrast with the current medical theory. The authors did not deny the achievements of the physicians working within the established medicine of the period but often referred to a number of authorities in the field. What they wanted to achieve by developing the Prophet's medicine was a further improvement and elaboration that would give medicine a clearly Islamic character.

The development of the Prophet's medicine

From fairly early on, Muslims showed an interest in finding out what had been the Prophet's view on illnesses and how he had treated them. The major collections of the Prophet's sayings that were compiled in the third/ninth century (see ḤADĪTH AND THE QURʾĀN) include ḥadīths that have a medical content. Among them are the general injunctions to treat the sick but some of them also contain more specific instructions or advice. These sayings mainly reflect the contemporary medical views of the Arabs (q.v.) and either accept or reject the traditional cures, while some of them refer to the changes that Islam had brought to curing practices and even to the concept of illness. Sayings such as "The Qurʾān is the best medicine" and "Rise to pray, for prayer (q.v.) is a cure" introduced new religious therapies, whereas the saying "Do not curse fever; it removes sins like fire removes dross from iron" indicated that illnesses should not be seen as meaningless suffering but as an atonement (q.v.) and, as such, as something positive (Ibn Māja, *Sunan, Ṭibb,* nos. 3458, 3469, 3501). These ḥadīths were usually put together in special chapters, e.g. al-Bukhārī's (d. 256/870) *al-Ṣaḥīḥ* has a chapter on the sick *(Kitāb al-marḍā)* and a chapter on medicine *(Kitāb al-ṭibb).* In Ibn Māja's (d. 273/887) *Sunan,* all the medical ḥadīths are assembled in one chapter on medicine *(Kitāb al-ṭibb).*

These medical sayings aroused further interest among some scholars and they started to compile specialized collections, where only medical sayings were included. These collections formed the beginning of the literary genre known as the Prophet's medicine *(al-ṭibb al-nabawī).* The earliest surviving books entitled *al-Ṭibb al-nabawī* date from the fourth/tenth and fifth/eleventh centuries. The largest of them was compiled by Abū Nuʿaym al-Iṣfahānī (d. 430/1038) and it contained as many as 838 medical ḥadīths. He was able to expand the number of ḥadīths by including several variants of a ḥadīth as independent items; thus he had no less than twenty-six entries containing a variant of the saying "for every illness there is a cure." The interest for medical ḥadīths was not confined to Sunnī scholars but also Shīʿī scholars collected them (see SHĪʿISM AND THE QURʾĀN). They concentrated on the medical sayings of the imāms (see IMĀM) and usually titled their collections "Medicine of the imāms" *(Ṭibb al-aʾimma).* One of the earliest compilations was written by the brothers Abū ʿAttāb ʿAbdallāh and al-Ḥusayn b. Bisṭām b. Shāpūr and has been dated to the fourth/tenth century.

These early collections were mere compilations of medical ḥadīths and they did not contain any attempts to analyze the medical advice or opinions expressed in the sayings. The most interesting aspect of these collections was their arrangement: the ḥadīths were arranged in chapters by subject and the chapter division followed that of the contemporary standard medical books. The next stage of development occurred in the seventh/thirteenth century, when ʿAbd al-Laṭīf al-Baghdādī (d. 629/1231) took up in his "Forty medical traditions" *(al-Arbaʿīn al-ṭibbiyya)* some of the Prophet's sayings and commented on their medical content. Al-Baghdādī was not only a ḥadīth scholar but also a practicing doctor, well acquainted with the medical theories of the day. About a century later, another doctor, the oculist ʿAlāʾ al-Dīn al-Kaḥḥāl b. Ṭarkhān (d. 720/1320) commented upon a large number of medical sayings in his book "The prophet's rulings on the art of medicine" *(al-Aḥkām al-nabawiyya fī l-ṣināʿa al-ṭibbiyya)*. He also listed eighty-three simple drugs or foodstuffs that were mentioned in the ḥadīth material.

Al-Baghdādī and al-Kaḥḥāl b. Ṭarkhān proved that the Prophet's advice and instructions were acceptable in the light of contemporary medical theory. Their commentaries still concentrated on individual ḥadīths but formed a basis for further development, where the Prophet's medicine was presented in a systematic manner including both theoretical discussion and practical advice. This new stage is apparent in the texts of two eighth/fourteenth century scholars Muḥammad al-Dhahabī (d. 748/1348) and Ibn Qayyim al-Jawziyya (d. 751/1350), both entitled *al-Ṭibb al-nabawī*. In addition to presenting and analyzing ḥadīths dealing with particular cures or illnesses they tried to place these sayings in a wider medical framework and therefore took up issues related to medical theory, such as the elements, humors and general causes of illnesses. In this discussion they did not only refer to the Prophet's sayings but also quoted qurʾānic verses and interpreted them in order to support their argumentation.

Both al-Dhahabī and Ibn al-Qayyim were acquainted with the current Graeco-Islamic medicine and admitted its achievements, but they wanted to show that it was not necessary to refer to non-Islamic authorities such as Hippocrates or Galen. It was perfectly possible to create a medical practice that was based on Islam, on the guidance of the Prophet and the Qurʾān. The texts of the two authors differ from each other in their treatment of the subject. Al-Dhahabī's text forms a small medical handbook presenting the basic theoretical issues, albeit in a very concise manner. In the practical section of the book he chose to discuss some common illnesses and their cures, disregarding the fact that not all of them were mentioned in the ḥadīth material. Ibn al-Qayyim also presented the main theoretical issues but confined himself to discuss in detail only those illnesses of which the Prophet had spoken. He was very much concerned with the religious implications of the Graeco-Islamic medicine and discussed these matters much more thoroughly than al-Dhahabī, who showed a more unquestioning acceptance of the current medical theory. This makes Ibn al-Qayyim's text far more interesting and useful for an analysis of the special features of the Prophet's medicine. He attempted to solve the problematic issues in a manner that secured an adherence to the teachings of Islam but also made it possible to follow the guidelines of the accepted medical theory.

Anti-medical views

The development of the Prophet's medicine can be seen as a reaction to the anti-medical views present in the Muslim community. The early ascetics (see ASCETICISM) stressed complete reliance on

God alone *(tawakkul)* and the extreme forms of reliance prevented the ascetic from any form of action. The wider community of Muslims never accepted the most extreme practices but it seems that even people outside ascetic circles shared the idea that medication meant meddling with God's divine purpose (see FREEDOM AND PREDESTINATION). According to a tradition, Abū al-Dardā', one of the Companions of the Prophet (q.v.), had refused treatment: "A doctor with his medicine and medicaments cannot protect me against what God has foreordained for me" (Dhahabī, *Ṭibb,* 152). Some scholars of the religious sciences claimed that a person who resorted to medication acted against the qur'ānic injunction: "In God let the believers put all their trust" (Q 9:51; Reinert, *Die Lehre,* 207-13; see TRUST AND PATIENCE; BELIEF AND UNBELIEF). Other scholars refuted these arguments by referring to abundant ḥadīth material that attested the Prophet's approval of medicine. One of the most explicit sayings is: "Servants (see SERVANT) of God, use medicaments! God did not give an illness without giving it a cure" (Ibn Māja, *Sunan, Ṭibb,* no. 3436).

It may be that especially the earliest collections of medical ḥadīths were assembled in order to counter the anti-medical views. The numerous sayings showed that the Prophet had not only advised others to be treated but also that he himself had received medical treatment. The Muslim community accepted medication as the sunna of the Prophet and refused the view that medical treatment was an action indicating a weakness in belief. Quite the contrary, by resorting to medication an individual proved his reliance on God and belief in God, because he accepted the medicaments as God's gift (see GIFT-GIVING) and wisdom (q.v.; Ibn al-Qayyim, *Ṭibb,* 10).

Another issue that made medicine controversial was the theological problem of causality (see THEOLOGY AND THE QUR'ĀN). The speculative theologians, both Muʿtazilīs (q.v.) and Ashʿarīs, held the view that God directly created all events (see CREATION) and that the nexus between cause and effect was not real but only apparent. According to them, illnesses were accidents *(aʿrāḍ)* created by God and an individual remained ill as long as God continuously recreated the illness in him or as long as he did not order it to disappear (cf. Wolfson, Philosophy, 522-43). Medicaments were useless because they did not have any natural properties that would affect the illness. This attitude made some theologians reject medication and it was possibly the motive that led the Muʿtazilī scholar Muḥammad b. ʿAbdallāh al-Iskāfī (d. 240/854) to ignore his doctor's advice. Al-Iskāfī consulted a doctor, got a prescription but decided to take drugs that were considered to have an effect opposite to the prescribed ones. He did not, as he may have believed would happen, get well in spite of the wrong medication, but, instead, his condition deteriorated and he soon died (Rosenthal, *Defence,* 524).

The Ashʿarī scholars accepted the view that the perceived connection between a cause and an effect is not something that occurs independently but is each time created by God. It was God's custom *(ʿāda)* always to create a sequence in the same way and therefore a pattern emerged which looked like causality. Al-Ghazālī (d. 505/1111) illustrated the doctrine by explaining that when cotton was brought into contact with fire, it was not the fire that caused the cotton to burn. It was God who created the burning at the time when the cotton touched the fire. The fire did not have any natural ability to burn nor cotton the ability to be burned. The burning would not have taken place if

God had not created it (Wolfson, *Philosophy*, 544).

The practical consequences of this theory did not lead the Ashʿarīs to reject medicaments. Al-Ghazālī argued that medicaments could be used, because medication and recovery formed a sequence that was constantly created by God. Medicaments could be used but an individual should remember that the drugs did not have any inherent curing properties. It was actually God who created the recovery each time a drug was used (Ghazālī, *Iḥyā᾿*, iv, 250-1).

In contrast to the ascetics and speculative theologians, the traditionalist scholars did not have scruples in accepting medication. They supported their positive attitude by referring to ḥadīths that illustrated the Prophet's acceptance of medical treatment. They did not share the theoretical view that causality did not exist but maintained that, in a causal connection, God acted through intermediary causes. This meant that God had created intermediaries with effective qualities. These were means *(asbāb)* that God had intended people to use and benefit from. Among these were medicaments, which God had endowed with natural capacities that made them effective factors in curing illnesses (Perho, *Prophet's medicine*, 70-5).

The authors of the Prophet's medicine, according to whom medication was an effective way to combat illnesses, belonged to the traditionalist school. Ibn Qayyim al-Jawziyya referred to the fate of the people of ʿĀd (q.v.; Q 46:21-7) and stated that it was the wind (see AIR AND WIND) that destroyed them, i.e. God had used the wind as an intermediary of destruction and the capacity to destroy was in the wind's character (see PUNISHMENT STORIES). The Qur᾿ān could be seen to attest that God had placed in all created things qualities *(ṭabā᾿iʿ)* and capacities *(quwan)* that could influence other created things. God created medicaments and he had given them qualities and capacities that could be used to cure illnesses; the causal nexus between medication and cure was true and not only apparent (Ibn al-Qayyim, *Ṭibb*, 9, 130).

Further, Ibn al-Qayyim found the three purposes of medicine, i.e. the restoration of health, its preservation and the prevention of illness, all attested in the Qur᾿ān. He quoted the verse that allows a traveler to postpone his fasting (Q 2:184) and explained that if a traveler would add fasting to the hardships caused by travel conditions, he would endanger his health (see JOURNEY; TRIPS AND VOYAGES). The qur᾿ānic permission of postponement presented the medical principle of preserving health. The principle of restoring health was evident in Q 2:196 allowing a person who did not participate in the actual pilgrimage (q.v.) to compensate for it by fasting or giving alms (see ALMSGIVING). According to Ibn al-Qayyim, he could then shave his head like a pilgrim and the shaving was in his case good for his health, because it opened pores and allowed harmful substances to leave the body. Here Ibn al-Qayyim referred to the contemporary medical principle of releasing corrupt substances from the body in order to restore health. The third objective of medicine was to prevent illnesses from occurring and this principle Ibn al-Qayyim saw reflected in Q 4:43, where a sick person is advised to perform his ablutions (see CLEANLINESS AND ABLUTION) with sand instead of water (q.v.). According to Ibn al-Qayyim this provision was made to prevent the individual from exposing himself to water that may contain substances that could worsen his condition. This Ibn al-Qayyim saw as God's guidance for the prevention of illnesses (Ibn al-Qayyim, *Ṭibb*, 2-3).

Theory in the Prophet's medicine in the eighth/fourteenth century

According to the Graeco-Islamic theory, all things are composed of four elements: fire (q.v.), air, water and earth (q.v.). In humans, these elements are present in the form of four humors: yellow bile, blood, phlegm and black bile. In a healthy individual the humors are in balance, whereas an illness is seen as an imbalance that should be rectified either by a diet or actual medication. Life is maintained by the innate heat *(ḥarāra gharīziyya),* which is contained in the heart and nourished by spirits (Gk. *pneumata,* Ar. *arwāḥ*). There are three types of spirits: natural, animal and psychic spirits, which support the corresponding faculties that govern the various physiological processes in the body. Natural spirit originates in the liver, animal spirit in the heart and psychic spirit in the brain. The spirits and faculties reach the various organs through veins, arteries and nerves and maintain life in the organ and enable it to function (see ARTERY AND VEIN). For example, the psychic spirit and the psychic faculty are carried from the brain by nerves to the organs and enable humans to perceive and move.

This theory was not only known and appreciated by the medical profession but it seems that it received a wide recognition in society. One indication of this is the fact that even the scholars of religious learning, al-Dhahabī and Ibn Qayyim al-Jawziyya who formulated the theory of the Prophet's medicine, considered it a valid description of human physiology. In the Prophet's medicine, the Graeco-Islamic views of physiology were not usually discussed in very great detail but the theory was cursorily presented indicating that it was generally known and widely accepted.

In some cases, the authors referred to the Qur'ān and pointed out that certain aspects of the theory were, in fact, confirmed in the revelation. For example, in discussing fetal development al-Dhahabī accepted the Graeco-Islamic view that the fetus originated in a mixture of male and female semen (see BIOLOGY AS THE CREATION AND STAGES OF LIFE). In his opinion this was also attested in the Qur'ān and he quoted the verse "We created man of an extraction of clay (q.v.), then we set him, a drop *(nuṭfa),* in a receptacle secure" (Q 23:12-3). The traditional interpretation identified the word *nuṭfa,* "drop," as male sperm but al-Dhahabī ignored this and spoke of both male and female semen. He claimed that "from the fluid of the man are created the basic organs and from the fluid of the woman is created the flesh" (Dhahabī, *Ṭibb,* 215). By broadening the meaning of the word "drop" to include also female semen, al-Dhahabī was able to show that there was no contradiction between the accepted medical theory and the Qur'ān.

Ibn Qayyim al-Jawziyya took up the Graeco-Islamic idea of elements as the basic components of the human being and compared this view to the information given in the Qur'ān. He could find three of the four elements attested in the Qur'ān: water, earth and air (Ibn al-Qayyim, *Ṭibb,* 15). Water is mentioned in Q 25:54: "And it is he who created of water a mortal *(bashar).*" The element earth is referred to in a number of verses according to which God created man of dust *(turāb),* e.g. Q 18:37. A combination of water and earth is indicated when it is said that man was created from clay *(ṭīn),* e.g. Q 6:2. The presence of air is attested in Q 55:14: "He created man of a clay like potter's." This clay *(ṣalṣāl)* is dried clay and, therefore, its ingredients are not only earth and water but also the air that dried it.

Ibn al-Qayyim accepted that these three elements were present in man, but he rejected the fourth element, fire. The Qur'ān says explicitly that the devil (q.v.; Iblīs) was created from fire whereas humans were not (Q 7:12), therefore it was impossible that fire would be an element in them. The question, however, of the original four elements and their presence in human beings was a rather distant theoretical issue, whereas the humors and their characteristics had a more important role in practical medicine. Even though Ibn al-Qayyim did not accept the presence of fire in man, he did not doubt the existence of all the four humors. He also accepted that heat was an observable characteristic in the body, it was just not caused by fire. Therefore, in spite of his rejection of fire as an element, he accepted the correctness of the Graeco-Islamic humoral theory and approved of its use in the diagnosis and treatment of illnesses.

Causes of illnesses

The authors of the Prophet's medicine accepted that God as the creator was also the ultimate cause of all illnesses. They did not think that illnesses were God's punishment but that they were God's warning and guidance (see ASTRAY; CHASTISEMENT AND PUNISHMENT). The Prophet's saying: "The fever is a breath of hell (see HELL AND HELLFIRE)," indicated that God had created fever in order to warn people about the torments of hell. Illness could also be God's gift, a chance to atone for sins (see SIN, MAJOR AND MINOR) through patient suffering (q.v.) and this was attested by the Prophet's saying: "One day's fever corresponds to one year's atonement" (Ibn al-Qayyim, *Ṭibb*, 22-3). Incurable diseases were trials (see TRIAL) sent by God and if a person succumbed to them, his death was that of a martyr (q.v.; Ibn al-Qayyim, *Ṭibb*, 214; Dhahabī, *Ṭibb*, 189).

God created illnesses through intermediary causes and these were the physical causes that could be observed. Similarly, God also created the cure for an illness, but also this occurred through secondary causes, i.e. through the use of medicaments and therapies. Medicaments were means given by God for the benefit of the people. The Prophet's words "For every illness there is a cure. God did not give an illness without giving it a cure," were seen as an encouragement to study medicine, to determine the causes of illnesses and to search for methods of curing. The authors of the Prophet's medicine stressed that in this process of searching, the medical practitioners should also pay attention to the medical knowledge of the Prophet. The physicians should look for help in the spiritual cures that God had revealed to the Prophet and learn how reliance on God or turning to God in prayer could be used to cure illnesses of the soul (q.v.). But also the cures that the Prophet had recommended for physical illnesses should be studied, because God may have given him useful information concerning causes of illnesses, medicaments and curing methods (Ibn al-Qayyim, *Ṭibb*, 7; Dhahabī, *Ṭibb*, 52).

The authors of the Prophet's medicine accepted the Graeco-Islamic view that the physiological cause of an illness was an imbalance of the four humors. The imbalance was caused either by an abnormal increase of one of the humors or by corruption of the humors. These changes were again caused by external factors such as corrupted air, unsuitable diet, imbalance in rest and motion of the body, imbalance in the soul, too much or too little sleep, and abnormalities in excretion and retention of bodily fluids (Ibn al-Qayyim, *Ṭibb*, 4-5; Dhahabī, *Ṭibb*, 22). These six factors were the so-called six non-naturals of the Graeco-Islamic theory and their role in preserving health and correcting imbalances was decisive.

In addition to these causes, the authors of the Prophet's medicine also recognized witchcraft (*siḥr,* see MAGIC) and the evil eye (*ʿayn,* see EYES) as etiological factors. The major authorities of the Graeco-Islamic medicine did not usually recognize these factors but the religious scholars were convinced of their existence (see TRADITIONAL DISCIPLINES OF QURʾĀNIC STUDY). According to them, the existence of the evil eye was attested in the Qurʾān: "The unbelievers wellnigh strike you down with their glances" (Q 68:51; see SEEING AND HEARING; VISION AND BLINDNESS). The effect of the evil eye and witchcraft was based on the influence of spirits. The Graeco-Islamic theory taught that in the human body there were three types of spirits (Gk. *pneumata,* Ar. *arwāḥ*) that supported various physical functions. In the Prophet's medicine these spirits gained some new characteristics and powers: the spirits could be either good or evil (see GOOD AND EVIL; SPIRIT; JINN) and their effect could be projected onto other people. If a person's humors were badly imbalanced, the evil spirit could gain power over his soul. It could then further damage both the soul and body but it could also damage other persons because the affected individual could send the evil influence towards others and cause an illness in them.

Ibn al-Qayyim considered the evil eye to be an illness that its possessor could not control. The envy (q.v.) the person felt was the cause of the evil eye and he could not prevent the damage it caused. The only way to cure the disease was to eradicate the feeling of envy from the soul. When a believer accepted that God was the one who determined what each individual had or did not have, he would see the wrongness of being envious. He should follow the example of the Prophet, who said: "Whatever God wills. There is no might except in God." By strengthening his faith in God, a person could prevent the evil spirits from gaining power, because if a person allowed God to fill his heart, the evil influences of witchcraft and the evil eye would not affect him (Ibn al-Qayyim, *Ṭibb,* 98-101; 127-33).

Ibn al-Qayyim also ascribed some incurable illnesses, such as epilepsy and plague, at least partially to evil spirits. In this way he was able to explain why the Graeco-Islamic medicine provided only insufficient treatment. The evil spirits did not respond to ordinary medicaments and therefore the physicians were unable to cure the diseases the spirits caused. They were unaware of the merits of the religious cures, such as prayer, recitation of the Qurʾān (q.v.) and almsgiving. If the physicians accepted the guidance of the Prophet's medicine in this matter, they would learn the complete etiology of diseases and understand the benefits of religious cures. These cures strengthened the good spirits that also resided in people and the good spirits would then fight against the evil spirits and diminish their influence (Ibn al-Qayyim, *Ṭibb,* 30-1; 51-4).

The problem of contagion (ʿadwā)

The Graeco-Islamic medical theory recognized that certain illnesses were contagious, i.e. they could be transmitted from a sick person to a healthy one. According to the theory, epidemics, such as plague, began when people inhaled air that was corrupted by stagnant water, decaying cadavers or drought. The contagious disease caused the sick persons to discharge damaging vapors that corrupted the surrounding air and when a healthy person inhaled this air, it reached his spirit (Gk. *pneuma,* Ar. *rūḥ*) and corrupted it. The spirit got into the blood (see BLOOD AND BLOOD CLOT) and the body lost its temperamental balance, causing the person to develop the symptoms of the disease. All contagious diseases did not spread through miasma, corrupted air, but through touch or, as in the case of pink eye (ophthalmia, *ramad*), through eyes. A person suffering from ophthalmia did not corrupt the surrounding air but his sight rays *(shuʿāʿ baṣarī)* were corrupt and could damage a healthy eye (Qusṭā b. Lūqā, *Iʿdāʾ*, 24-6; Dols, *Black death*, 88-92).

The existence of contagious diseases was acknowledged in the medical literature, but the scholars of religious sciences did not find it easy to accept contagion. If it was God who caused illnesses, how could a sick person independently infect a healthy person? Especially speculative theologians who rejected causality found it impossible to accept contagion. But even the traditionalist scholars who recognized the reality of the causal nexus, linking cause and effect, encountered problems in the question of contagion. As usual, they studied the opinions of the Prophet but had to admit that the ḥadīth material did not provide a clear answer. The ḥadīths were contradictory, some stating that the Prophet had denied contagion: "There is no contagion *(ʿadwā)*, no augury, no owl, and no snake" (Bukhārī, *Ṣaḥīḥ*, *Ṭibb*, *bāb* 45; see FORETELLING; DIVINATION; SOOTHSAYING). This ḥadīth connected contagion to other pre-Islamic beliefs: reading omens (see PORTENTS) in birds' flight, believing that the dead could reside in owls, or thinking that stomach pain was caused by a gnawing snake (Ibn Ḥajar, *Fatḥ al-bārī*, x, 132, 165; Juynboll, *Authenticity*, 140 n. 5). The ḥadīths rejecting contagion were contradicted by others showing that the Prophet had recognized the contagious character of some diseases: "Do not take a sick one to a healthy one" (Bukhārī, *Ṣaḥīḥ*, *Ṭibb*, *bāb* 54).

The authors of the Prophet's medicine tended to accept the existence of contagion but they were aware of the ambiguous nature of the ḥadīth material. Al-Dhahabī presented both types of ḥadīths, those that recognized contagion and those that rejected it. He admitted that contagion did exist and was caused by miasma, corrupted air. A person could contract an illness by being in contact with people suffering from specific illnesses. He reminded people, however, that they should not fear contagion because God predestined all illnesses and epidemics. He seemed to connect an overt fear of catching a contagious illness to the pre-Islamic belief that some people were ill omened and therefore best avoided (see FATE; DESTINY). This kind of excessive fear was what the Prophet had meant when he said, "There is no contagion" (al-Dhahabī, *Ṭibb*, 167-8, 187).

Ibn Qayyim al-Jawziyya expressed his acceptance of contagion in a much more unequivocal manner. In his opinion, God had given some diseases an ability to be transmitted. These transmittable *(naqqāla)* illnesses spread from person to person through miasmatic air, as was explained in the current medical theory. To support his view, he quoted several ḥadīths that seemed to accept the existence of contagion. He admitted that many scholars considered it difficult to establish the Prophet's opinion on the question and saw the ḥadīths to be contradictory. Ibn al-Qayyim did not share this view but stated that the contradiction was only apparent and was based on the scholars' imperfect understanding of their content. He then gave a number of suggestions that would solve the conflict and maintained that the Prophet's basic view had been to recognize the transmittable character of some illnesses (Ibn al-Qayyim, *Ṭibb*, 116-21).

The term *naqqāla*, "transmittable," that Ibn al-Qayyim used to characterize contagious illnesses was carefully chosen. Ibn al-Qayyim used it to differentiate the medically defined contagion from the one about which the Prophet had said: "There is no contagion *(ʿadwā)*." When he limited the

Prophet's rejection to a particular pre-Islamic, non-medical belief in contagion, it was possible to accept the general medical views of transmissibility of illnesses. Like al-Dhahabī, also Ibn al-Qayyim stressed that even though contagion existed, people should not think it was the sole cause of illnesses. Contagion was a cause created by God and to deny its existence was to deny God's law, but to think that contagion alone caused an illness would be idolatry (*shirk*, see IDOLATRY AND IDOLATERS) because it would equate contagion with God. God had created the causal nexus between contagion and illness but he was able to remove the causality if he so desired. Everything that happened was ultimately subject to God's will; therefore an exaggerated fear of contagion indicated that a person believed more in contagion than in God and this could damage the soul and endanger salvation (q.v.; Ibn al-Qayyim, *Miftāḥ*, 269).

Interdependence of body and soul

The Graeco-Islamic medicine represented a holistic approach to health and illness, where both physical and emotional balance were seen as prerequisites of health. In order to maintain health, it was important that a person followed a life-style suitable to his or her temperament. Apart from suitable diet and physical activities, people should avoid excessive emotions because these could affect the balance of the body and lead to serious physical symptoms. Excessive emotions were seen as illnesses of the soul *(amrāḍ al-nafs)* and included emotions such as anger (q.v.), worry and passionate love (see LOVE AND AFFECTION). In order to cure a patient suffering from the symptoms caused by these emotions, the physicians had to realize that the patient's emotions were out of balance and treat both the emotional and physical balance of the patient.

Because the health of the soul and the health of the body were understood to be closely linked, the physicians not only prescribed suitable diets but also gave advice on proper ethical and moral behavior (see ETHICS AND THE QUR'ĀN; VIRTUES AND VICES, COMMANDING AND FORBIDDING). The purpose of these instructions was to prevent emotional disturbances. Muḥammad b. Zakariyyā al-Rāzī (d. 313/925) stated that in order to preserve emotional balance, a person should endeavor to live quietly without quarrelling with people, be just and honest, help others and feel sympathy towards them (Rāzī, *Ṭibb*, 91-2). The physicians' view on a balanced, good way of life was based on the teachings of philosophers and did not contain any religious references. The scholars of religious sciences did not usually approve of the physicians' general philosophical advice but wanted to define the best way of life in more religious terms. The Ḥanbalī scholar Ibn al-Jawzī (d. 597/1200) wrote a book that had the same title as al-Rāzī's book, namely *al-Ṭibb al-rūḥānī*, "Spiritual medicine." The choice of title indicated that he wanted to counter the physician's advice by his own. Ibn al-Jawzī agreed that emotional balance was a crucial factor in health and his advice on preserving that balance was in many ways close to that of al-Rāzī. The significant difference was his choice of vocabulary that gave the advice a religious content. He recommended that people should defeat their passions and avoid what God has forbidden (q.v.), treat others with fairness (see JUSTICE AND INJUSTICE) and help them with advice when needed. The body should be among people but the soul *(qalb)* should be with God (Ibn al-Jawzī, *Ṭibb*, 66-7).

The authors of the Prophet's medicine shared the Graeco-Islamic holism and warned against the dangers of uncontrolled emotions. Al-Dhahabī pointed out that anger heated the body and dried it, whereas worry and grief could cause fever. He found that also the Qurʾān advised people to avoid excessive emotions: "Do not exult; God loves not those that exult" (Q 28:76; see BOAST; ARROGANCE) and "A garden (q.v.) whose breadth is as the heavens and earth, prepared for the godfearing who… restrain their rage" (Q 3:133-4). According to al-Dhahabī, the Prophet had been exemplary in his avoidance of excessive emotions and he illustrated this by quoting ḥadīths in which the Prophet had shown restraint or advised Muslims to do so (Dhahabī, *Ṭibb*, 45-7).

Ibn Qayyim al-Jawziyya also stressed the interdependence of body and soul. Following the current medical views, Ibn al-Qayyim advised against emotional imbalance and recognized the physical damages caused by excessive emotions — emaciation, fevers, in severe cases even death. His main concern, however, was not to restore the emotional balance in order to cure the physical symptoms but, instead, he considered the physical suffering a transitory matter that could be endured. The more serious danger that the illnesses of the soul entailed was the danger they posed to the individual's salvation and eternal life (see ETERNITY).

Ibn al-Qayyim based his view about the seriousness of these diseases on the fact that they were mentioned in the Qurʾān as something leading to sin and loss of faith (q.v.). The diseases of the soul *(nafs)* were the diseases of the heart *(qalb)* referred to in the Qurʾān. These illnesses could be divided into two groups: disease of doubt *(shakk)* and disease of lust *(shahwa)*. The disease of uncertainty (q.v.) and doubt was referred to in the verse: "What, is there sickness in their hearts, or are they in doubt, or do they fear that God may be unjust towards them and his messenger (q.v.)? Nay, but those — they are the evildoers" (Q 24:50; see EVIL DEEDS). It is also attested in two other verses, namely Q 2:10 and Q 74:31. The disease of lust was mentioned in the verse: "Wives of the Prophet (q.v.), you are not as other women. If you are godfearing, be not abject in your speech, so that he in whose heart is sickness may be lustful; but speak honorable *(maʿrūf)* words" (Q 33:32). The diseases of the heart were specified to include the excessive emotions that the Graeco-Islamic medicine categorized as illnesses, namely passionate love, worry and grief (Ibn al-Qayyim, *Ṭibb*, 2).

The dangers of excessive emotions

According to Ibn al-Qayyim, indulging in excessive emotions endangered the salvation of an individual because the emotions were a sign that the person did not really trust in God. Al-Rāzī, the physician, pointed out that it was foolish to grieve for losses because everything in the world perishes (Rāzī, *Ṭibb*, 67-8). In Ibn al-Qayyim's opinion excessive grief was not only folly but also an act of disobedience (q.v.). He reminded his readers that everything that God had created was God's property (q.v.) and whatever humans possessed (see WEALTH; POSSESSION) was only lent to him by God. Inasmuch as God possessed everything, a person did not have the right to consider anything his or her own and instead of grieving for a loss, should accept it as the will of God and remain patient. This he saw recommended in the Qurʾān: "Who, when they are visited by an affliction, say, 'Surely we belong to God, and to him we return'; upon those rest blessings (see BLESSING) and mercy (q.v.) from their lord (q.v.), and those — they are the truly guided" (Q 2:156-7). Despair (q.v.) could lead a believer to think that God was unjust and he could end in losing his faith. In this way succumbing to temporal grief would lead to eternal punishment, whereas patience in adversity would assure eternal happiness in paradise (q.v.; Ibn al-Qayyim, *Ṭibb*, 147-57; see also REWARD AND PUNISHMENT).

The Graeco-Islamic medical theory considered passionate love *(ʿishq)* an imbalance of the soul, which then damaged the physical functions of the body. In the most serious cases it could weaken the innate heat and cause death. The Prophet's medicine also recognized the physical effects of passionate love but more attention was paid to the spiritual damage the illness caused. Ibn al-Qayyim warned that an unchecked passion could develop into idolatry *(shirk)* if the lover was so obsessed with the desire of his beloved that his love for God was replaced by his passion for the beloved. The passionate desire for a created being would expel from his heart the love for his creator and this would mean that he had abandoned Islam. The physicians were concerned with the physical effects of the illness and the danger it posed to the patient's survival. For Ibn al-Qayyim, it was more important that the patient realized the threat the excessive emotion posed to the eternal life of his soul. The purpose of the recommended therapies was to make the patient see that he had to regain emotional balance in order to save his soul (Ibn al-Qayyim, *Ṭibb*, 207-8, 212-3).

Medicaments and other curing methods

According to the medical theory, illnesses were the results of humoral imbalance and curing meant reestablishment of the balance. Changing the patient's diet often did this, but if this was not sufficient, drugs were administered. The purpose of the drug therapy was to counter the corrupted humor and evacuate it from the body. The drugs were chosen in accordance with the allopathic principle, i.e. the drug used had a quality that was opposite to that of the disease. If a disease was deemed to be hot, a drug that was temperamentally cold should counter it. The basic drugs were simple, consisting of only one herb, fruit or other foodstuffs or minerals but the physicians could also prescribe compound drugs consisting of a large number of ingredients.

The authors of the Prophet's medicine accepted the allopathic principle and in their lists of simple drugs and foodstuffs they recorded the temperament of the substance and listed the complaints against which it could be used. Their descriptions of these qualities tallied well with the standard medical opinions and they obviously based them on information given in Graeco-Islamic medical books. For the most part, their lists consisted of drugs mentioned in the ḥadīths or the Qurʾān (see METALS AND MINERALS; AGRICULTURE AND VEGETATION) but also other, generally known drugs were included. The ḥadīths the authors quoted in their lists of drugs were rarely medical in content and it seems to have been sufficient that a medical item was mentioned by the Prophet: "The believer, who recites the Qurʾān, is like a lemon: pleasant to taste and pleasant to smell" (Ibn al-Qayyim, *Ṭibb*, 218; Dhahabī, *Ṭibb*, 52). Even though the content of the ḥadīth did not point to any medical use of the item mentioned, it proved that the Prophet had not rejected its use. The same applied to verses of the Qurʾān, e.g. the verse referring to the pomegranate as one of the benefits bestowed by God (Q 55:68) was quoted in connection with presentations of the fruit's medical properties (Ibn al-Qayyim, *Ṭibb*, 243; Dhahabī, *Ṭibb*, 89).

The authors of the Prophet's medicine also accepted the use of compound drugs, even though the ḥadīths showed that the Prophet had favored simple drugs. They based their acceptance on the Graeco-Islamic medical view that the patient's habits and circumstances should be taken into account when determining a suitable treatment. Ibn al-Qayyim pointed out that the Muslims of the early community (see COMMUNITY AND SOCIETY IN THE QURʾĀN) had led a simple life and followed a simple diet. Therefore, also their humoral imbalances could be treated with simple drugs. In contrast, city (q.v.) dwellers were used to a more complex diet and, consequently, their illnesses were also more complex. If a physician deemed that simple drugs were not sufficient to treat an illness, he should, in that case, prescribe compound drugs (Ibn al-Qayyim, *Ṭibb*, 5-6, 57; Dhahabī, *Ṭibb*, 50, 143).

Apart from drugs, the Graeco-Islamic medicine further recognized cupping, venesection and cautery as efficient methods of curing. Cupping and venesection were used to evacuate corrupted humors, whereas cautery — burning with hot iron — was used to treat pains, tumors and bleeding wounds. All these methods were also accepted in the Prophet's medicine, although the ḥadīth material gave, once again, conflicting evidence of the Prophet's opinion regarding venesection and cautery. Limiting the applicability of those ḥadīths that rejected venesection and cautery solved the problem. Ibn al-Qayyim stated, referring to the authority of physicians, that venesection should not be used in hot climates — as in the Ḥijāz — or during hot seasons. The Prophet's rejection of venesection meant that it should not be used in circumstances that might harm the patient (Ibn al-Qayyim, *Ṭibb*, 41-2). Similarly, traditions rejecting cautery did not make the method forbidden but limited its use to medically accepted purposes. What the Prophet had rejected were the superstitious beliefs that some people had regarding the method (Ibn al-Qayyim, *Ṭibb*, 50; Dhahabī, *Ṭibb*, 182-3).

The Graeco-Islamic medicine accepted the use of wine (q.v.) in the treatment of illnesses because it was considered to have a high nutritious value. The scholars of Islamic law held wine to be forbidden basing their view on Q 5:90-1 (see INTOXICANTS) and therefore the authors of the Prophet's medicine could not accept its medical use. They did, however, admit that wine had beneficial qualities and had proved to be able to cure some illnesses. They rejected wine because God had forbidden it and to use something God had forbidden would damage the believer's soul and endanger his salvation. Taking up the interdependence of body and soul, Ibn al-Qayyim added that it was important to choose a curing method and medication that the patient could accept and trust. If a physician prescribed a drug that his patient knew to be a substance God had forbidden, the patient could not believe in its curative powers and, as a result, the medicine would not cure him. The anxiety caused by disobedience to God's commands could actually make the patient's condition worse (Ibn al-Qayyim, *Ṭibb*, 123-4; Dhahabī, *Ṭibb*, 75-6; see COMMANDMENTS; BOUNDARIES AND PRECEPTS).

Divine medicaments

A special feature of the Prophet's medicine was its promotion of curing practices that had been recommended by the Prophet or could be found in the Qurʾān. The authors called them divine medicament *(adwiya ilāhiyya)* or the Prophet's medicaments *(adwiya nabawiyya)* and they were prayer *(ṣalāt)*, patience *(ṣabr)*, fasting *(ṣawm)*, jihād (q.v.), the Qurʾān itself and incantations *(ruqan*, sing. *ruqya)*. These medicaments could be used to cure physical disorders and their efficiency as cures was based on their spiritual and physical influence. For example, the ritual prayer was seen both as a physical exercise, where the performer moved his joints and relaxed his inner organs, and as a religious act that directed the performer's thoughts towards the hereafter (see ESCHATOLOGY), away from pain, strengthening his soul and faculties (Dhahabī, *Ṭibb*, 201; Ibn al-Qayyim, *Ṭibb*, 164).

The use of the Qur'ān as a medicament was based on Q 17:82: "And we send down, of the Qur'ān, that which is a healing and a mercy to the believers." According to Ibn al-Qayyim and al-Dhahabī, the Qur'ān was the perfect cure for all diseases, both those of the body and those of the soul. The book could be used as a curing object by bringing it into contact with the diseased part of the body, either by placing it on the painful spot or, in the case of eye diseases, letting the eye gaze at the Qur'ān (Ibn al-Qayyim, *Ṭibb*, 272; Dhahabī, *Ṭibb*, 202). In explaining the efficiency of the Qur'ān as medicament, Ibn al-Qayyim again referred to the patient's need to believe in the cure; as in the use of any other medicament, in the use of the Qur'ān it was also required that the patient believed firmly in the benefits of the cure. Only in that case could the disease be defeated (Ibn al-Qayyim, *Ṭibb*, 272).

The verses (q.v.) of the Qur'ān could also be used as cures. The authors instructed that a verse could be written in ink, either on a paper or directly on the inside of a vessel and then the text was dissolved in water. The patient then drank the water as a medicine. It was also possible simply to recite a verse or recite it over water, which was then drunk by the patient or was sprinkled over him. Some verses had specific uses — Q 6:98, for instance, could be used against toothache, Q 12:111 and Q 46:35 in cases of difficult birth (q.v.), and Q 11:44 against nosebleed. The authors indicated that the verses should be written in this way only to cure actual illnesses and should not be used as protective amulets (q.v.; Dhahabī, *Ṭibb*, 197-9; Ibn al-Qayyim, *Ṭibb*, 277-8; see also PROTECTION).

Written cures did not necessarily have to consist of qur'ānic verses; other texts were also permissible. Al-Dhahabī stressed that these texts should be seen as supplications to God and, therefore, they should be texts with meaning and should not contain anything non-Islamic (Dhahabī, *Ṭibb*, 165). Ibn al-Qayyim and al-Dhahabī rejected the use of protective amulets that were very popular in the contemporary society. Magic was taken seriously and scholars like Ibn Khaldūn (d. 808/1406) considered the art of talismans and letter magic as sciences (Ibn Khaldūn, *Muqaddima*, iii, 156-227; see MYSTERIOUS LETTERS; NUMEROLOGY; POPULAR AND TALISMANIC USES OF THE QUR'ĀN). Physicians used charms as a part of their therapy and the magic squares or geometric symbols they used were based on ancient magical traditions. Ibn al-Qayyim and al-Dhahabī advised against relying on this type of charm and, instead, guided people to base their incantations on qur'ānic verses or simple devotional texts.

The later development of the Prophet's medicine

The books of Ibn Qayyim al-Jawziyya and al-Dhahabī presented the Prophet's medicine in a systematic manner combining the ḥadīths and current medical theory. The authors did not want to reject the established Graeco-Islamic medicine but they wanted to add an Islamic dimension to current medical practices. In the authors' opinion, the Graeco-Islamic medicine would benefit from the inclusion of the special knowledge that God had given to his Prophet. The divine medicaments — prayer, fasting, incantations, etc. — were treatments that the physicians should study and adopt. The authors did not uncritically promote everything that the Prophet had recommended but reviewed the instructions in the light of Graeco-Islamic theory and then either accepted the Prophet's guidance or rejected it as having been applicable only in the environmental conditions of the Ḥijāz in the Prophet's time.

Ibn al-Qayyim's and al-Dhahabī's books influenced some of the later authors of the genre. The Ḥanbalī scholar Jalāl al-Dīn Yūsuf b. Muḥammad al-Surramarrī (d. 776/1374) wrote "The book on curing pains in the medicine of the people of Islam" *(Kitāb Shifāʾ al-ālām fī ṭibb ahl al-Islām)* and followed in the arrangement of his material the model set by al-Dhahabī. The Ḥanafī scholar Ibn Ṭūlūn al-Dimashqī (d. 953/1546) quoted both al-Dhahabī and Ibn al-Qayyim extensively in his book "The thirst-quenching spring of the Prophet's medicine" *(al-Manhal al-rawī fī l-ṭibb al-nabawī)*. He arranged his material in accordance with *al-Mūjaz* written by Ibn al-Nafīs (d. 687/1288), one of the major scholars of Graeco-Islamic medicine in the later period.

The Shāfiʿī scholar Jalāl al-Dīn al-Suyūṭī (d. 911/1505) compiled medical ḥadīths in his work "The correct method and the thirst-quenching spring of the Prophet's medicine" *(al-Manhaj al-sawī wa-l-manhal al-rawī fī l-ṭibb al-nabawī)*. He continued the tradition set by the early collections and simply assembled ḥadīths under headings taken from medical books, leaving them unglossed. He did not discuss the ḥadīths nor did he present any details of the medical theory. There is, however, some indication that he may have studied the works of the earlier authors of the Prophet's medicine, even though he did not refer to them in his book on medical ḥadīths. In the commentary on the Qurʾān, *Tafsīr al-Jalālayn,* which al-Suyūṭī completed, he commented on the verse "He was created of gushing water" (Q 86:6) and stated that the water *(māʾ)* issued from both the man and the woman *(dhī indifāq min al-rajul wa-l-marʾa)*. This interpretation was not traditional (cf. Ṭabarī, *Tafsīr,* ad loc.) but indicates that al-Suyūṭī was aware of the medical views on this issue. His commentary reflects very closely the idea of male and female semen expressed by al-Dhahabī in his book *al-Ṭibb al-nabawī.*

The influence of the Prophet's medicine on practicing physicians and the treatments they recommended is difficult to determine. The Prophet's medicine seems to have remained a genre adopted by the religious scholars, whereas the standard medical literature of the period from the eighth/fourteenth to the eleventh/sixteenth centuries was dominated by Graeco-Islamic medicine. There are, however, some texts written by physicians indicating that the Prophet's medicine was indeed used and its recommendations applied. One of these was written by Mahdī b. ʿAlī al-Ṣanawbarī (or al-Ṣubunrī) al-Yamanī (d. 815/1412) and it was titled "The book on mercy in medicine and wisdom" *(Kitāb al-Raḥma fī l-ṭibb wa-l-ḥikma)*. Another was written by Ibrāhīm b. ʿAbd al-Raḥmān al-Azraqī (d. after 890/1485) with the title "The book on the benefits of medicine and wisdom made accessible" *(Kitāb Tashīl al-manāfiʿ fī l-ṭibb wa-l-ḥikam)*. Nothing much is known of the authors but they seem to have been physicians practicing in Yemen. Their texts are usually classified as belonging to the Prophet's medicine, even though references to Graeco-Islamic authorities abound. Al-Azraqī actually listed standard Graeco-Islamic medical books as his major sources and the only book on the Prophet's medicine he quoted was Ibn al-Jawzī's *al-Luqaṭ*.

Al-Azraqī's book contains very few references to the Prophet or to the Qurʾān and the treatments recommended by the Prophet are only listed as one of the alternatives. There is no attempt to discuss any of the religious issues taken up by earlier authors of the Prophet's medicine. The same applies to al-Ṣanawbarī's book and, although he quoted more ḥadīths than al-Azraqī, he was not concerned with the theological implications of the medical theories. Al-Ṣanawbarī supported the medical view of the four elements and, in contrast to Ibn al-Qayyim, did not reject the status of fire as one of the elements, but actually claimed that the Prophet had accepted it: "God created man from four things, from water, clay, fire, and wind. If the water dominates, the person is a scholar (q.v.) or noble. If the clay dominates, he sheds blood (see BLOODSHED), is evil and insolvent in this world and the hereafter. If the fire dominates, he is oppressive or tyrannical (see OPPRESSION). If the wind dominates, he is a liar (see LIE)" (Ṣanawbarī, *Raḥma,* 3-4). Al-Ṣanawbarī did not give any reference to the source of the ḥadīth and it cannot be found in the major collections (cf. Wensinck, *Concordance,* s.v. *khalaqa*). Al-Ṣanawbarī obviously felt the need to provide the ḥadīth to prove his point, but he did not further discuss the issue.

In the eleventh/sixteenth century, Dā'ūd al-Anṭākī (d. 1008/1599) wrote a medical handbook, "Memorandum for those who understand" *(Tadhkirat ūlī l-albāb),* which represents the views of the Graeco-Islamic school. In the book, he stressed the importance of medicine and claimed it to be the most important of the sciences, one that enjoys a position more noble than the religious sciences (see SCIENCE AND THE QUR'ĀN). He supported this by quoting ʿAlī b. Abī Ṭālib's (q.v.) words: "Knowledge is of two types; the knowledge of religions and the knowledge of bodies" (see KNOWLEDGE AND LEARNING). According to al-Anṭākī, ʿAlī had added: "and the knowledge of bodies has precedence over knowledge of religions" (Anṭākī, *Tadhkira,* i, 11).

Otherwise, al-Anṭākī's references to ḥadīths are rare and quotations from the Qur'ān non-existent. Interestingly, the only chapter with a larger number of ḥadīths is that on plague *(ṭāʿūn).* The plague was endemic in the Middle East and the death toll was high each time an epidemic broke out. In addition to countering the plight medically, society also responded by stressing observance of religious duties and encouraging recitations of the Qur'ān and the ḥadīths (cf. Dols, *Black death*). This must have made those sayings of the Prophet that dealt with plague very well known, and thus al-Anṭākī included them in his handbook. He not only quoted them but also discussed their meaning. His opinions did not present anything controversial but followed the mainstream views (Anṭākī, *Tadhkira,* iii, 217-9).

Al-Azraqī, al-Ṣanawbarī and al-Anṭākī presented talismanic cures alongside allopathic herbal or dietetic treatments. Al-Anṭākī devoted a separate chapter to talismans and gave instructions on how to prepare them and explained the meanings of the symbols. Al-Azraqī and al-Ṣanawbarī included talismans in the presentation of cures for various diseases. They also provided instruction on how to write them, but they did not discuss their meaning or underlying systems. When compared to the written texts that Ibn al-Qayyim and al-Dhahabī recommended for curing some illnesses, the talismans of the three physicians look very different. They do not generally consist of qur'ānic verses or known prayers but contain symbols, numbers and letters reflecting a magical tradition older than Islam. Al-Ṣanawbarī did occasionally recommend the use of qur'ānic verses as well, but a verse alone did not usually suffice. For example, as one of the cures of small-pox *(judarī)* he recommends that part of the verse Q 2:243 be read over seven grains of barley — over each grain three times. The last quoted word "die" is repeated twice followed by an incantation (Ṣanawbarī, *Raḥma,* 100).

The medical books of these three authors reflect the contemporary medical practices that sought to ease the sufferings of the sick by diets, medicaments, religious cures, and talismans. The books are concise handbooks that do not dwell very much on the theoretical aspects of medicine but offer practical advice. There was an obvious need for such books, as al-Azraqī himself stated: "When I saw that [today] there are very few people who concern themselves with medicine but those who seek help from it are many, and this art being buried under the great and common need for it on the part of the people, it appeared to deserve special devotion since no human being can avoid it.... This, then motivated me to collect certain materials concerning this art" (Azraqī, *Tashīl,* 2-3; Eng. trans., Rahman, *Health,* 45). The interest in illnesses and their cures remained strong and when printing was introduced the books of al-Ṣanawbarī and al-Anṭākī became popular reference works for home remedies (cf. Gallagher, *Medicine and power,* 26-7; Gallagher accepts the mistaken ascription of *Kitāb al-Raḥma* to al-Suyūṭī).

Contemporary development

When the Europeans gave up the humoral theory as the basis of human physiology in the nineteenth century C.E., its support in the Islamic world started to wane as well. The strong European presence in the Middle East enabled the elites to become acquainted with the scientific progress made in Europe, and they increasingly resorted to the services of European physicians. The local practitioners continued to treat the masses of the population, among whom the traditional medicine still retained its status. In the areas that were colonized by the Europeans, the situation started to change rapidly because the colonial masters supported Western medicine as the only legitimate practice and considered all other forms to be charlatanry or quackery. The medical education was standardized to follow Western models and gradually the humoral theory fell into oblivion. The Graeco-Islamic medicine and the Prophet's medicine survived as folkloric ideas and influenced home remedies and dietary customs (Gallagher, *Medicine and power,* 83-96).

In the Indian subcontinent the Graeco-Islamic medicine — which was there called Unani medicine, i.e. Greek medicine — resurfaced in the twentieth century C.E. and in the independent states of India and Pakistan it has, with the help of government-funded research, become a competitive and serious alternative to Western medicine. Also elsewhere in the Islamic world, the recent years have shown an increasing interest in the holistic approach that the Graeco-Islamic medicine provides. It is seen as an alternative to the symptom-centered Western medicine and its dietary and herbal therapies are gaining support among people who have seen that the expensive Western chemical drugs are not necessarily more effective in combating illnesses.

The Prophet's medicine has also benefited from the growing interest in alternative medical practices. The medical sayings of the Prophet have not been forgotten but form a part of the popular medical wisdom that offers simple household remedies for common ailments. In addition, old treatises of the Prophet's medicine have been reprinted. Currently, one of the most readily available texts is Ibn Qayyim al-Jawziyya's *al-Ṭibb al-nabawī.* In some cases, the editors not only printed the treatise, but also supplied footnotes that explain the eighth/fourteenth century medical concepts to the modern readers and provide modern medical views on the illnesses and treatments discussed in the text.

There are also contemporary books on

the Prophet's medicine but usually they do not promote the humoral concepts presented in the older text. Instead, they interpret the ḥadīths in the light of modern medical knowledge. This is due to the background of the authors who are typically physicians trained in Western medicine. In their way, they are doing the same as their early predecessors did: namely, trying to combine the Prophet's medical guidance with contemporary medical theory. Some of these books can be seen as apologies intended to prove the superior knowledge of the Prophet also in medicine. Book titles such as "The inimitability of the Prophet's medicine" *(I'jāz al-ṭibb al-nabawī)* indicate this approach.

There are, however, contemporary books that have more ambitious goals. One of the most substantial of these is *al-Ṭibb al-nabawī* written by Maḥmūd Nāẓim al-Nasīmī (d. 1986). Maḥmūd al-Nasīmī was a physician well acquainted with the modern developments of medicine. In his book, he takes up contemporary issues, such as birth control (q.v.) and organ transplants, and discusses thoroughly the ethical and religious implications of the practices. In his argumentation, he regularly refers to the Qur'ān, ḥadīths and Islamic legal literature (see LAW AND THE QUR'ĀN). After presenting various arguments on a particular medical issue, he proceeds to give a ruling, which he himself calls a *fatwā*, a term that belongs to Islamic jurisprudence *(fiqh)*. His method is apparent in his discussion of smoking. He first analyzes the opinions of the jurists who gave their rulings in the eleventh/seventeenth century when the use of tobacco spread to the Middle East. He concludes that the scholars considered smoking as forbidden *(ḥarām)* or abominable *(makrūh)* on the basis that it was addictive, it smelled bad and was expensive. Al-Nasīmī continues by giving a detailed account of the health risks that modern medical opinion connects with smoking, also taking up aspects such as second-hand smoke and the effects of smoking on the fetus. His ruling is that the extensive health risks make smoking forbidden *(ḥarām)* or at least abominable *(makrūh)*. He supports this ruling by quoting the qur'ānic injunction against suicide (q.v.; Q 4:29). He also quotes a ḥadīth according to which all those who eat poison on purpose will suffer eternally in hell (Nasīmī, *Ṭibb*, i, 343-73).

Al-Nasīmī clearly wanted to formulate an Islamic opinion on various medical issues and practices that have ethical implications. Some may see the Prophet's medicine as an alternative holistic approach to illnesses, in line with the Graeco-Islamic or Unani medicine. But al-Nasīmī is a representative of a viewpoint that does not want to revive the Prophet's medicine as an independent, special medical system based on humoral principles but rather wants to use it as a tool to formulate an Islamic medical approach. In this, he is following in the footsteps of Ibn Qayyim al-Jawziyya and Muḥammad al-Dhahabī, who wanted to situate their contemporary medical practices within an Islamic framework. The modern authors have the same ambition of extending the applicability of Islamic norms to medicine and assuring that modern medicine does not exceed the bounds of what is considered ethically sound.

Irmeli Perho

Bibliography

Primary: Abū Nu'aym Aḥmad b. 'Alī al-Iṣfahānī, *al-Ṭibb al-nabawī*, ms. 65 Ṭ n/4538 al-Ẓāhiriyya, Damascus; al-Anṭākī, Dā'ūd b. 'Umar al-Ḍarīr, *Tadhkirat ūlī l-albāb*, 2 vols., Cairo 1282/1866 (see C. Gilliot, Textes arabes anciens édités en Égypte au cours des années 1992 à 1994, in *MIDEO* 22 [1995], 271-412, esp. 390-1 for other editions of this work); al-Azraqī, Ibrāhīm b. 'Abd al-Raḥmān, *Kitāb Tashīl al-manāfi' fī l-ṭibb wa-l-ḥikam*, Cairo 1313/1895; al-Baghdādī, 'Abd al-

Laṭīf b. Yūsuf, *al-Arbaʿīn al-ṭibbiyya,* ms. Khizānat al-Kānūniyya, Tangier; Bukhārī, *Ṣaḥīḥ,* Leiden 1908; al-Dhahabī, Shams al-Dīn Muḥammad b. Aḥmad, *al-Ṭibb al-nabawī,* ed. al-Sayyid al-Jumaylī, Cairo n.d.; al-Ghazālī, Abū Ḥāmid Muḥammad, *Iḥyāʾ ʿulūm al-dīn,* 4 vols., Cairo 1916; Ibn Ḥajar, *Fatḥ al-bārī,* Cairo 1313/1895, x; Ibn al-Jawzī, *Luqaṭ manāfiʿ fī l-ṭibb,* ms. We 1180, Staatsbibliothek Berlin; id., *al-Ṭibb al-rūḥānī,* ed. M. al-Saʿīd b. Basyūnī Zaghlūl, Cairo 1986; Ibn Khaldūn-Rosenthal; Ibn Māja; Ibn Qayyim al-Jawziyya, *Miftāḥ dār al-saʿāda,* Cairo 1945; id., *al-Ṭibb al-nabawī,* ed. ʿA. ʿAbd al-Khāliq et al., Cairo 1957; Ibn Ṭūlūn al-Dimashqī, *al-Manhal al-rawī fī l-ṭibb al-nabawī,* ed. ʿA. Bayk, Hyderabad 1987; Ibnā Shāpūr, Abū ʿAttāb ʿAbdallāh and al-Ḥusayn b. Bisṭām, *Islamic medical wisdom. The ṭibb al-aʾimma,* trans. B. Ispahany, ed. A.J. Newman, London 1991; *Jalālayn;* al-Jumaylī, al-Sayyid, *Iʿjāz al-ṭibb al-nabawī,* Beirut 1985[2] (rev. ed.); al-Kaḥḥāl b. Ṭarkhān, *al-Aḥkām al-nabawiyya fī l-ṣināʿa al-ṭibbiyya,* ed. ʿA. Hāshim Ḥāfiẓ, Cairo 1955; al-Nasīmī, Maḥmūd Nāẓim, *al-Ṭibb al-nabawī wa-l-ʿilm al-ḥādith,* 3 vols., Beirut 1984, 1987[2]; Qusṭā b. Lūqā, *Kitāb al-iʿdāʾ. Abhandlung über die Ansteckung,* ed. and trans. H. Fähndrich, Stuttgart 1987; al-Rāzī, Abū Bakr Muḥammad b. Zakariyyā, *al-Ṭibb al-rūḥānī,* in P. Kraus (ed.), *Rasāʾil falsafiyya (Opera philosophica),* Cairo 1939, 1-96; al-Ṣanawbarī, Mahdī b. ʿAlī, *Kitāb al-Raḥma fī l-ṭibb wa-l-ḥikma,* Cairo 1313/1895; al-Surramarrī, Abū l-Muẓaffar Yūsuf b. Muḥammad, *Kitāb Shifāʾ al-ālām fī ṭibb ahl al-islām,* ms. 3584 Fatih, Istanbul; Suyūṭī, *al-Manhaj al-sawī wa-l-manhal al-rawī fī l-ṭibb al-nabawī,* ms. 168, Ẓāhiriyya, Damascus; Ṭabarī, *Tafsīr,* Beirut 1992.
Secondary: M. Dols, *The black death in the Middle East,* Princeton 1977; N.E. Gallagher, *Medicine and power in Tunisia. 1780-1900,* Cambridge 1983; G.H.A. Juynboll, *The authenticity of the Tradition literature. Discussions in modern Egypt,* Leiden 1969; R. Nabielek, Biologische Kenntnisse und Überlieferungen im Mittelalter (4.-15. Jh.), in I. Jahn (ed.), *Geschichte der Biologie. Theorien, Methoden, Institutionen, Kurzbiographien,* Jena 1998, 113-5 (for the Qurʾān and medicine); I. Perho, *The Prophet's medicine. A creation of the Muslim traditionalist scholars,* Helsinki 1995; F. Rahman, *Health and medicine in the Islamic tradition. Change and identity,* New York 1987; B. Reinert, *Die Lehre vom Tawakkul in der klassischen Sufik,* Berlin 1968; F. Rosenthal, The defence of medicine in the medieval Muslim world, in *Bulletin of the history of medicine* 43 (1978), 519-32; M. Ullmann, *Die Medizin im Islam,* Leiden 1970; trans. J. Watt, *Islamic medicine,* Edinburgh 1978; Wensinck, *Concordance;* H.A. Wolfson, *The philosophy of kalām,* Cambridge, MA 1976.

Medina

One of the primary settlements of the Ḥijāz in Muḥammad's time, to which he emigrated (see EMIGRATION) from Mecca (q.v.), and where he died. The town of Medina is mentioned in the Qurʾān only in passing (see below). If based solely on the qurʾānic data, therefore, any entry concerning Medina would be unduly short because our knowledge of pre- and early Islamic Medina derives almost entirely from other, and usually much later, source material. On the other hand, Medina is the setting for much of the qurʾānic message, and the later period of Muḥammad's prophetic career as well as the beginnings of Islam are unlikely to be understood without a proper knowledge of the town, its settings and its inhabitants.

Medina, one of the major settlements of the Ḥijāz and some 350 km to the north of Mecca, was in pre-Islamic times commonly called "Yathrib" (the *Iathrippa* of the Greek geographers). As such, the town is named in Q 33:13 where the Medinan Muslims are addressed as "people of Yathrib" *(ahl yathrib)*. This name is also present in pre-Islamic poetry and in the so-called "Constitution of Medina," and it remained current in later Arabic poetry as well (see PRE-ISLAMIC ARABIA AND THE QURʾĀN; POETRY AND POETS). The term *al-madīna,* which means simply "the town" in Arabic, appears as the designation for Yathrib in Q 9:101, 120, 63:8 and quite possibly in Q 33:60; in other instances, however, the noun *al-madīna* (pl. *al-madāʾin)* is not used as a proper name but refers to other cities (e.g. Q 7:123; 12:30; 15:67, etc.; see CITY). The origin of the name "Medina" for the settlement of Yathrib is uncertain, though it seems more likely that it derives from the Aramaic term for town/city/settlement *(madītā)* than that it is an abbreviated form of the Arabic epithet "the town of the

Prophet" *(madīnat al-nabī),* as later Islamic tradition has it. The town was also given many honorific epithets, which were reckoned as names as well. The most prominent among these is *al-ṭayba,* "the perfumed" or also "the healthy." In the modern age, the name of Medina is commonly extended to *al-madīna al-munawwara,* "Medina the illuminated," whereas in former centuries one often spoke of *al-madīna al-sharīfa,* "the noble city" (or also "Medina the noble").

Early Islamic Medina

As stated above, there is next to no information about the town, its history and topography in the Qurʾān itself. Any account of Medina in pre- and early Islamic times must therefore be based on later literary sources. The earliest local history, now lost but amply cited in later works, was written by Ibn Zabāla (d. ca. 200/815). Although these sources provide a wealth of material, we encounter here the general predicament of early Islamic history, namely that the historicity of this information proves very hard to establish and evaluate (see HISTORY AND THE QURʾĀN). Much of what we can say about pre- and early Islamic Medina is thus hypothetical. Although some studies of recent years, especially those by M.J. Kister and M. Lecker, make thorough use of the material available, their results — as valuable as they are for the details that they offer — must, on the whole, be seen as conjectural; topographical and genealogical features can be reconstructed more easily than strictly historical events and developments. Of little help so far have been archaeological records of Medina and its surroundings, mainly because there is little opportunity for fieldwork focused on pre- and early Islamic history in the Ḥijāz (see ART AND ARCHITECTURE AND THE QURʾĀN; ARCHAEOLOGY AND THE QURʾĀN).

At the time of the Prophet, the Medinans were essentially living off of their agricultural production (see AGRICULTURE AND VEGETATION), and local dates (see DATE PALM) were among the most cherished products. The hot climate, however, is described as unhealthy and the vast lava-fields outside the town diminished the size of the arable land. Although a number of markets (q.v.) existed there, Medina cannot be regarded as a town of commerce like, for example, Mecca. The settlement itself was a loose grouping of living quarters or zones, interspersed with groupings of palm groves and fields, with the individual living quarters often fortified by strongholds *(āṭām).* Medina extended over a large area (of several square miles) and thus covered a wider — but less densely populated — area than does the modern town; no city walls are known from before the fourth/tenth century.

The population of pre-Islamic Medina consisted of pagan Arab and Jewish clans (see JEWS AND JUDAISM; TRIBES AND CLANS), with only a marginal presence of other monotheists (see SOUTH ARABIA, RELIGION IN PRE-ISLAMIC; POLYTHEISM AND ATHEISM; IDOLATRY AND IDOLATERS). It is not known with certainty whether the Jews had come from Palestine or whether they were Arab proselytes. Some smaller Arab tribes do, however, appear to have been either affiliated with Jewish tribes, or converts to Judaism, and the sources report cases of Arab-Jewish marriages (see MARRIAGE AND DIVORCE). Furthermore, the literary heritage of the Medinan Jews, Arabic poetry, indicates that they were an integral part of the local culture (see ARABIC LANGUAGE). The intricate and still partly obscure history of the Medinan Jews has been much researched especially as they were a constant and dominant factor in pre- and early Islamic Medinan society (for further discussion, see NAḌĪR, BANŪ AL-; OPPOSITION TO MUḤAMMAD; QURAYẒA). The two Arab super-clans known as Aws and Khazraj constituted the most important pagan faction in Medina. These groups had emigrated in pre-Islamic times from Yemen to Medina, where they eventually overcame the previously dominant Jewish faction. The result was a sort of unstable stalemate that lasted until the Prophet's arrival in Medina (see POLITICS AND THE QURʾĀN). The Arab clans, in any case, were also engaged in inner conflicts that often resulted in feuds and mutual bloodshed (q.v.).

This much can be said on the basis of the source material, yet much else remains in the dark. For example, scattered notices are encountered in later writings about the ties of the Medinan Jews with Sasanid Persia and Yemen (q.v.). Yet it is impossible to detail what these ties might have looked like and what influence they could have exerted. It seems clear, though, that Medina (and central Arabia in general) was not cut off from the centers of post-Hellenistic culture. Such contact is surmised from the commercial ties (see SELLING AND BUYING; CARAVAN) of the Ḥijāz with Syria (q.v.) and the pervasive presence of monotheistic ideas throughout the area in pre-Islamic times. Moreover, it is difficult to imagine that the Medinan Jews and other monotheists would not have had any contact with their coreligionists elsewhere, although substantial information is lacking in that regard.

When the Prophet came to Medina in 622 C.E., the town was divided between the various pagan and Jewish clans. According to Islamic tradition, Muḥammad was invited by deputies of the Aws and Khazraj to settle in Medina and to act as an arbiter of internal affairs. Once Muḥammad arrived in Medina, most members of the Aws and Khazraj became Muslims and were henceforth known as the Prophet's "Helpers" *(al-anṣār)* although some continued to oppose him in secret (see EMIGRANTS AND HELPERS). Muḥammad settled first at Qubāʾ, at the southern fringe of Medina, and there he also erected the first mosque (q.v.) of Islam. Although the Prophet enjoyed the support of the Arab clans he avoided becoming too closely affiliated with them and tried to remain aloof from their societal bonds (see COMMUNITY AND SOCIETY IN THE QURʾĀN). Rather, he tended to rely upon his fellow Emigrants *(al-muhājirūn),* which brought about misgivings between the Medinan Helpers and the Meccan Emigrants and resulted in a tension between both groups that was not resolved until much later in Islamic history.

The decade following the Prophet's move from Mecca to Medina is commonly dubbed "the Medinan period" (see CHRONOLOGY AND THE QURʾĀN). According to the accounts in the classical sources, the outline of events during that time is fairly well known and there is no need to repeat it here (see Watt, *Muhammad at Medina*). It is important, however, to note that Muḥammad first adopted a conciliatory policy among the Arab clans and towards the Jews (as is shown by the so-called "Constitution of Medina"), yet after growing troubles in Medina and the overt enmity of the Meccans he switched to a more resolute attitude that made him send raids and engage in greater battles, in Medina itself (against the Jews) as well as in its surroundings (e.g. against the Meccans at Badr [q.v.] and Uḥud; see EXPEDITIONS AND BATTLES). The outcome of the Prophet's determination was, especially after the capture of Mecca and the defeat of the Medinan Jews, the formation of the first Islamic community. In the view of many modern Muslims, this Medinan period saw the creation — and at the same time the apogee — of the true Islamic state, whose exemplary character is seen as the model for all future Islamic societies.

For Islam as a religion, Medina was the place where almost all decisive elements of the Islamic creed (see CREEDS; FAITH) took definite shape. The longer Medinan sūras of the Qurʾān have been deeply influential in the formation of Muslim life. Many details of ritual (e.g. fasting [q.v.] and the direction of prayer; see QIBLA; RITUAL AND THE QURʾĀN) were introduced during Muḥammad's Medinan years, and his discussions with the Medinan Jews on theological matters helped to formulate and clarify his message (see THEOLOGY AND THE QURʾĀN). The Prophet's presence in Medina also conferred, in the eyes of later Muslims, a unique sacredness on the town, and the later legal authority Mālik b. Anas (d. 179/796) would not mount a donkey in the town because he would not allow its hooves to trample upon the soil that contained the Prophet's sepulchre.

Medina in later Islamic history

After the death of Muḥammad in Medina the town did not immediately lose its political importance. Nonetheless, events soon turned the attention of the Muslims away from the Ḥijāz. Shortly after Muḥammad's death, ʿAlī (see ʿALĪ B. ABĪ ṬĀLIB) had shifted the center of governance to Kūfa and, after some twenty years of caliphal presence in Medina (see CALIPH), the Umayyads moved the capital of the Islamic polity to Syria. Politically, Medina was thus cast at the margins of Islamic history, where it has remained ever since. One major revolt against Umayyad caliphal power in the first century was launched in Medina in 63/683 but it was crushed and Medina was looted. In the following century, we hear of Shīʿī uprisings which were likewise subdued (see SHĪʿISM AND THE QURʾĀN). Until modern times, the only events of a political nature were short-lived conflicts between the governors of Medina, the emirs of Mecca, and other local potentates during the Ayyūbid and Mamlūk periods. The local powers, however, were always weak and the region largely depended upon the Yemenite Rasūlids and the Mamlūk sultans, before it became part of the Ottoman empire and, finally, of the Wahhābī kingdom (see WAHHĀBĪS).

In contrast to the insignificance of Medina as a center of power, the town has always, albeit in varying degrees, remained a center of both scholarship and devotion. As a locus of devotion, Medina is second only to Mecca. In fact, the sepulchre of the Prophet in Medina — the Muslim "holy tomb" *par excellence* — has led some Muslim scholars to prefer Medina over Mecca because "the spot of the Prophet's tomb is nobler than the Kaʿba (q.v.) and the Throne of God (q.v.)" (al-Samhūdī, *Wafāʾ*, i, 28). "The visitation of the Prophet" *(ziyārat al-nabī)*, i.e. the visitation of his sepulchre, grew over the centuries into an almost obligatory sequel to the pilgrimage to Mecca (see VISITING; FESTIVALS AND COMMEMORATIVE DAYS). The resurgence of Sunnism in the central Islamic lands from the sixth/twelfth century onwards, together with the newly defined role of the Prophet as intercessor (see INTERCESSION), further bolstered the importance of Medina. In addition, the Medinan Baqīʿ cemetery, arguably the most significant single burial area in Islam (largely destroyed by the Wahhābīs in modern times), has been an important site of visitation for both Sunnīs and Shīʿīs.

As a center of scholarship and intellectual activities, Medina remained over the centuries a place of learning. In the second Islamic century, Medina hosted a range of important jurisprudents (e.g. Rabīʿat al-

Ra'y; Mālik b. Anas, eponym of the "Medinan" tradition of law; see LAW AND THE QUR'ĀN), *sīra* scholars (e.g. Mūsā b. ʿUqba; Ibn Isḥāq; see SĪRA AND THE QUR'ĀN), and traditionists (e.g. al-Zuhrī; Hishām b. ʿUrwa; see ḤADĪTH AND THE QUR'ĀN). From the fourth to the seventh Islamic centuries, Medina proved to be the most significant link for the transmission of knowledge from the eastern part of the Islamic world to the western (al-Andalus). From the early Mamlūk period onwards, the town finally developed into an important center of scholarship and mysticism. Many secular rulers and pious persons endowed a number of sites of learning and other facilities in Medina. In the later Mamlūk age and during the Ottoman period, Medina seriously rivaled Cairo and Damascus as a place of learning; the distance of Medina from the centers of political power seems to have favored this development. Among the most famous scholars who were active in Medina are Ibn Farḥūn (d. 799/1397), al-Sakhāwī (d. 902/1497), al-Samhūdī (d. 911/1506) and Ibrāhīm al-Kūrānī (d. 1101/1690). Finally, the importance of Medina for Islamic culture and devotion in general gave rise to the Arabic poetical genre of "praising Medina" or "longing for Medina" *(al-tashawwuq ilā l-madīna)*. This interesting genre, which is closely connected to poetry in praise of the Prophet, has been little studied and appreciated by modern scholarship.

Marco Schöller

Bibliography

(Pre- and early Islamic Medina is discussed in most of the better-known writings dealing with the Prophet's life; the same holds true for early legal compendia [of the *siyar* type], Qur'ān commentaries, and ḥadīth anthologies. For the later ages, there is much material in history books, geographical and biographical dictionaries, and travel literature, e.g. by Ibn Jubayr and Ibn Baṭṭūṭa. Most modern biographies of Muḥammad and general monographs about early Islam also contain accounts of pre- and early Islamic Medina. The best sources for our knowledge of Medina in general derive, however, from Arabic town histories.)

Primary: Ibn al-Najjār, *al-Durra al-thamīna fī tārīkh al-Madīna,* Beirut n.d.; Iṣfahānī, *Aghānī* (an important source of notices about pre-Islamic Medina); al-Jamāl al-Maṭarī, *Tārīkh al-Madīna al-sharīfa,* Riyadh 1997; al-Marjānī al-Makkī, *Bahjat al-nufūs wa-l-asrār fī tārīkh dār hijrat al-nabī al-mukhtār,* 2 vols., Riyadh 1998; Qays b. al-Khatīm, *Der Dīwān des Ḳais ibn al-Khaṭīm,* ed. Th. Kowalski, Leipzig 1914 (a collection of pre-Islamic poets that is an important source of material on pre-Islamic Medina); al-Sakhāwī, *al-Tuḥfa al-laṭīfa fī tārīkh al-Madīna al-sharīfa,* 2 vols., Beirut 1414/1993 (a biographical dictionary of persons connected to Medina; a very important source); al-Samhūdī, *Wafā' al-wafā bi-akhbār dār al-muṣṭafā,* 4 vols. in 3, 1374/1955 (and repr.; partly trans. by J. Wellhausen, *Geschichte der Stadt Medina,* Göttingen 1860; this is the most copious of the town histories in Arabic, and the one upon which most modern scholarship depends); ʿUmar b. Shabba, *Akhbār al-Madīna (Kitāb tārīkh al-Madīna),* 2 vols., Beirut 1996 (diverse editions of this Arabic town history abound).

Secondary: ʿA. al-Anṣārī, *Āthār al-Madīna al-munawwara,* Medina 1953, repr. 1958²; id. (ed.), *Studies in the history of Arabia. i. Sources for the history of Arabia,* Riyadh 1979; B. Finster, Arabien in der Spätantike, in Deutsches Archäologisches Institut, *Archäologischer Anzeiger,* Berlin 1996, 287-319; ʿA. al-Kaʿkī, *The pictorial collection of the most peculiar places in Almadinah Almonawarah (al-Majmūʿa al-muṣawwara li-ashhar maʿālim al-Madīna al-munawwara,* Arabic/English), 3 vols., Medina 1999 (this is a mine of information, and the many hundreds of images and maps make these volumes a basic source of visual reference for any non-Muslim who today is barred from Medina); M. Kister, *Society and religion from Jāhiliyya to Islam,* Aldershot 1990; id., *Studies in Jāhiliyya and early Islam,* London 1980; H. Laoust, *L'Arabie occidentale avant l'Hégire,* Beirut 1928; M. Lecker, *Jews and Arabs in pre- and early Islamic Arabia,* Aldershot 1998; id., Muḥammad at Medina. A geographical approach, in *JSAI* 6 (1985), 29-62; id., *Muslims, Jews and pagans. Studies on early Islamic Medina,* Leiden 1995; Kh. Muṣṭafā, *Historical sites of Madina* (150 *ṣūratan min al-Madīna al-munawwara,* Arabic/English), Cairo 1997 (an illustrated volume); B. Najafi, *Madine-ye shenāsi* [in Persian], vol. i, Cologne n.d. (an illustrated work); W.M. Watt, *Early Islam. Collected articles,* Edinburgh 1990; id., *Muhammad at Medina,* Oxford 1962; A.J. Wensinck, *Muḥammad and the Jews of Medina,* trans. W.H. Behn, Berlin 1982².

Memory

The power, function or act of reproducing and identifying what has been learned or experienced; the faculty of remembering. The Qurʾān presents memory not as a faculty or storehouse but as a primary mode of divine-human interaction. The primary qurʾānic words related to memory are based upon the radical *dh-k-r: dhikr, dhakara, dhikrā, tadhkira,* and *tatadhakkara;* depending on context, the primary sense of remembrance, reminder, contemplation, taking heed, or recitation (see RECITATION OF THE QURʾĀN) is meant by these Arabic words. The believer is enjoined to remember and the object of remembrance varies widely and includes, for example, God, the lord (q.v.), the name of God (see GOD AND HIS ATTRIBUTES), the final day (see ESCHATOLOGY; LAST JUDGMENT), God's bounty or grace (q.v.; *niʿma,* see also BLESSING), compassion (*raḥma,* see MERCY), sacrifice (q.v.; Q 22:36), the stories of the prophets (see PROPHETS AND PROPHETHOOD), and the signs (q.v.; *āyāt*). Remembrance is a central human obligation, yet it is also an expansive concept, one that partially overlaps with other obligations and promises. Qurʾānic injunctions to remember are linked to injunctions to perform the ritual prayer (q.v.; *ṣalāt*), the *zakāt* (see ALMSGIVING) and the pilgrimage (q.v.; *ḥajj,* Q 2:198), to recount the stories of the prophets and the praises of God (see LAUDATION; GLORIFICATION OF GOD); to aspire to God and the last day (Q 33:21), to fear God (Q 7:205; see PIETY; FEAR), to be grateful (see GRATITUDE AND INGRATITUDE), to be patient in suffering (q.v.; Q 38:17; see also TRUST AND PATIENCE), to heed God's warnings (see WARNING), to take heart in God's promises, to be in a state of awe or trembling of the heart (q.v.; Q 8:2; 22:35) and to keep the faith (q.v.; Q 33:41). The Qurʾān commonly enjoins the hearer to remember and to remind others of the figures of earlier prophetic cycles.

Remembrance is at the center of a web of metonymy attaching it to a range of concepts, each of which is a partial extension of *dhikr* even as *dhikr* serves as an extension or instantiation of the pair concept. In the case of remembrance and revelation (see REVELATION AND INSPIRATION), for example, the message of the Qurʾān is continually called a *dhikr* or *dhikrā* and the Qurʾān is given the epithet "that which contains or embodies remembrance" (*dhī l-dhikri,* Q 38:1). The Qurʾān is both the occasion or catalyst for *dhikr* as well as what should be recalled, the object of *dhikr*. It is the object of *dhikr* in another sense as well, the object of reminder that can be meditative (one mentions or recalls *dhikr* for oneself) or social (proclamation or recitation as a reminder for others). In the case of the prophets, remembrance opens onto a series of temporal and semantic frames: God has made the Qurʾān easy to remember (Q 54:17-40); the Qurʾān enjoins the believer directly to remember the prophets; the Qurʾān itself which tells their story is a reminder; the believer is commanded to remind others of the Qurʾān and its stories; and the prophets themselves should serve as a reminder, even as their stories depict them reminding their peoples or urging them to remember. Each new act of remembrance is an enactment of the acts of remembrance that occurred with previous revelations, all of which are drawn up into the Qurʾān as articulations in a collapsing telescope. The People of the Book (q.v.) are called *ahl al-dhikr* (Q 16:43; 21:7). The qurʾānic revelation is nothing but a "reminder to all beings" (Q 38:87; 81:27).

Dhikr overlaps with other central qurʾānic concepts in equally robust fashion. The injunction to "be patient and remember" (cf. Q 38:17-8) links patience and *dhikr* in a manner that can suggest that one will result in the other, that they are aspects of a single act, or that they are two distinct acts. The same injunction goes on to make a dyad of the remembrance of a prophet (in this case the prophets David [q.v.] and Job [q.v.]) and the patience modeled by the prophet as an example to those who remember him.

The mutual implication of *dhikr* with the qur'ānic obligations is also shown in the case of prayer, for which it is both occasion and catalyst: "When you have carried out the prayer, remember God standing and sitting and on your side" (Q 4:103). Yet the postures of the body can also become, more generally, the moment of *dhikr:* another verse employs the same formula ("standing, sitting, and on your side") in a context unconnected to ritual prayer (Q 3:191). *Dhikr* should not only be embodied through its connection to the physical positions and postures, but it is also closely tied to the act of articulating the praises of God, *tasbīḥ,* as an expression of frequency: "And remember your lord often and recount his praises by evening (q.v.) and by the break of day" (Q 3:41; see DAWN) or morning (q.v.) and afternoon (q.v.; Q 7:205; 76:25), even as the times of day (see DAY, TIMES OF) are clearly then reinforced by the prayer as a form of *dhikr*. Remembrance also serves as a link among obligatory rituals (blessings over sacrifice, *ṣalāt,* and *zakāt,* see RITUAL AND THE QUR'ĀN) as well as a link among those practices and divine-human and human-human relational obligations such as the injunction to have a heart that trembles at the mention of God (Q 22:35; see ETHICS AND THE QUR'ĀN; COMMUNITY AND SOCIETY IN THE QUR'ĀN).

The Qur'ān commonly states that it is only those with a spiritually discerning intellect (q.v.; *ūlū l-albāb*) who heed and dwell upon the signs *(tatadhakkara)* and allow those signs to serve as a reminder, to instigate the act of remembrance (e.g. Q 3:190-1). The signs are commonly the creation (q.v.) of the heavens and earth (q.v.; see also HEAVENS AND SKY), the alternation of day and night (q.v.), and polarities of odd and even, male and female (see GENDER; PAIRS AND PAIRING), or verses (q.v.) of the Qur'ān. Yet neither the signs by themselves nor the ability to heed them can guarantee a successful act of remembrance. As with all human activity, God's will serves as a cause or at least a primary condition: "They do not remember except by the will of God" (Q 74:56; see FREEDOM AND PREDESTINATION). Another injunction, "Remember God when you forget" (Q 18:24), sharpens the paradox of "remembering to remember" that would be explored in depth by theologians such as al-Muḥāsibī (d. 243/857). Remembrance also forms a dyad with awe (Q 8:2), gratefulness (cf. Q 5:110), faith ("You who keep the faith and remember God often," Q 33:41), and hope (q.v.; "And seek the grace of your lord and remember God that you might prosper," Q 62:10).

Dhikr is a key factor in forgiveness (q.v.), promised for those who, "when they have committed a shameful act or oppressed themselves, remember God" (Q 3:135), even as prohibited acts (wine [q.v.], gambling [q.v.]; see FORBIDDEN) prevent a believer from remembering. Whoever turns away after being reminded of his lord will suffer great pain (Q 72:17). To those who remember God, God also promises reciprocity: "Remember me. I will remember you" (Q 2:152). Remembrance is at the heart of the covenant (q.v.) between God and the human being: "Children of Israel (q.v.), remember my bounty to you and keep faith with my covenant" (Q 2:40). The qur'ānic concept of *dhikr* interacted throughout Islamic civilization with the poetic notion, especially the remembrance of the beloved in love poetry (see LOVE AND AFFECTION). In Ṣūfism (see ṢŪFISM AND THE QURʾĀN) both concepts were merged into ritual practice, with the meditative use of the *dhikr,* that is a meditative utterance, most often a qurʾānic quote, the *tahlīl* (*lā ilāha illa llāh,* "there is no god but God"), or a divine name or names, repeated aloud or silently. The ritual use of *dhikr* was matched by a developed theological understanding of it.

Michael A. Sells

Bibliography
Primary: al-Muḥāsibī, Abū ʿAbdallāh al-Ḥārith, *Kitāb al-Riʿāya li-ḥuqūq Allāh,* ed. ʿA.A. ʿAṭā, Beirut 1986; Nawawī, *Riyāḍ al-ṣāliḥīn,* trans. M.Z. Khan, *Gardens of the righteous,* London 1975; Qurṭubī, *Jāmiʿ;* Qushayrī, *al-Risāla al-qushayriyya,* trans. B.R. von Schlegell, *Principles of Sufism,* Berkeley 1992, 206-14.
Secondary: ʿAbd al-Bāqī; H. Kassis, *A concordance of the Qurʾān,* Berkeley 1983.

Men of the Cave

Name given to the protagonists of a long qurʾānic passage containing a version of the story of the seven sleepers of Ephesus. The Qurʾān states that the Men of the Cave *(aṣḥāb al-kahf)* and of al-Raqīm (see below) were among God's signs, and says they were youths who took refuge in a cave (q.v.) and invoked God's mercy (q.v.; Q 18:9-10). God made them and their dog (q.v.) fall into a deep sleep (q.v.) for many years and then woke them from their slumber. The Qurʾān explains that they were pious youths fleeing from the idolatry (see IDOLATRY AND IDOLATERS) of their people and that they found refuge in a cave (Q 18:11-7). When the youths awoke they were under the impression that only a day or so had passed, and decided that one of them should take some coins and go to buy food in the town. God used them to demonstrate to the inhabitants of the town that there is no doubt concerning the hour (see APOCALYPSE; LAST JUDGMENT; ESCHATOLOGY). The inhabitants of the town argued about building a place of worship dedicated to the youths (Q 18:18-21). The final part of this passage recounts the arguments among the people about how many youths were in the cave: people will insist variously that, in addition to the dog, there were three or five or seven people (see NUMBERS AND ENUMERATION). Muslims are instructed not to dispute these questions with anybody since only God really knows how many of them were there and the length of time that they spent asleep in the cave which, it is stated, was a total of 309 years (Q 18:22-6). The sūra containing this episode (Q 18) is entitled Sūrat al-Kahf ("The Cave").

Later traditions (see ḤADĪTH AND THE QURʾĀN; EXEGESIS OF THE QURʾĀN: CLASSICAL AND MEDIEVAL) added particulars that elaborated upon the qurʾānic contents. According to Wahb b. Munabbih (d. ca. 112/730), the youths adopted their faith from a Christian apostle (see CHRISTIANS AND CHRISTIANITY) and found refuge in a cave while they were fleeing from their king who regarded them as having caused his son's death (ʿAbd al-Razzāq, *Tafsīr,* i, 397-8). Other accounts state that the youths were believers in God, sons of notables of their town or even princes. Upon the Roman emperor Decius' entrance into their town — usually referred to as Ephesus or Tarsus — they and their dog escaped into a cave to avoid both the idolatry of their fellow citizens and the emperor's persecution. The emperor, instead of capturing them in the cave, had the entrance walled up, erecting on the spot a tablet in which their story was told. This tablet was made of lead or stone and put into a box of copper and, according to some traditions, was prepared by two believers belonging to the house of Decius. God caused the youths and their dog to fall asleep in the cave and 309 years later, the Roman emperor Theodosius, exasperated by Christian disputes about the resurrection (q.v.), asked for a clear sign from God. It thus happened that a shepherd reopened the entrance of the cave and at that moment God raised them up. One of the youths was sent to buy food in the town and he wandered dazed and confused since he was convinced that he had only been asleep for one day (Thaʿlabī, *Qiṣaṣ*, 380-4). When the inhabitants of the town saw his coins they immediately suspected that he had found a treasure but later discovered the truth when the youth took them to the cave and they were able to read the inscription on the tablet.

Other exegetical reports attempt to elucidate some of the more controversial qurʾānic passages. Several solutions are proposed for the mysterious name al-Raqīm (Q 18:9): it was the name of the valley, of the town, of the dog or, even better, of the one or two tablets bearing the names and story of the Men of the Cave (cf. Māwardī, *Nukat*, iii, 286-7). The youths are usually numbered as seven but some traditions state that there were more. The various estimates of their number mentioned in the Qurʾān are attributed in the exegetical tradition to differing Christian opinions about the matter. The reports — as is common in qurʾānic exegesis *(tafsīr)* — also include full descriptions and the names of all the characters of the story, i.e. the dog, the town, the month and even the cave. The great popularity of this qurʾānic story is also attested by the numerous and varied localizations of the cave and by the sanctuaries relating to the Men of the Cave all over the Muslim world as is attested in geographical literature (Kandler, *Die Bedeutung*, 82-98; Hernández Juberías, *La península imaginaria*, 137-61).

Roberto Tottoli

Bibliography

Primary: ʿAbd al-Razzāq, *Tafsīr*, i, 397-401; Abū l-Layth al-Samarqandī, *Tafsīr*, ii, 289-96; Bukhārī, *Ṣaḥīḥ*, 8 vols., Beirut 1992, iv, 502-3 no. 3465; Ibn al-Jawzī, *al-Tabṣira*, Beirut 1970, i, 366-70; id., *Zād*, 9 vols., v, 107-31; Ibn Kathīr, *Bidāya*, ii, 113-7; id., *Tafsīr*, 4 vols., Beirut n.d., iii, 119-31; Khāzin, *Lubāb*, iv, 197-208; al-Majlisī, Muḥammad Bāqir, *Biḥār al-anwār*, 111 vols., Beirut 1983, xiv, 407-37; al-Maqdisī, Muṭahhar b. Ṭāhir, *al-Badʾ wa-l-taʾrīkh*, ed. C. Huart, 6 vols., Paris 1899-1919, iii, 128-30; Māwardī, *Nukat*, iii, 286-300; Muqātil, *Tafsīr*, ii, 574-82; Rāzī, *Tafsīr*, xxi, 69-97; Suyūṭī, *Durr*, 8 vols., Cairo 1983, v, 362-79; Ṭabarī, *Tafsīr*, Cairo 1968, xv, 197-233; id., *Taʾrīkh*, ed. de Goeje, i, 775-82; Thaʿlabī, *Qiṣaṣ*, 370-86.

Secondary: Gimaret, *Jubbāʾī*, 573-6; R. Gramlich, Faḫr al-Dīn ar-Rāzīs Kommentar zu Sure 18, 9-12, in *Asiatische Studien/Etudes Asiatiques* 33 (1979), 99-152; J. Hernández Juberías, *La península imaginaria. Mitos y leyendas sobre al-Andalus*, Madrid 1996, 121-61; Horovitz, *KU*, 95, 98-9; H. Kandler, *Die Bedeutung der Siebenschläfer (Aṣḥāb al-kahf) im Islam*, Bochum 1994; L. Massignon, Les "sept dormants" apocalypse de l'Islam, in *Analecta bollandiana* 68 (1950), 245-60; G.D. Newby, *The making of the last prophet*, Columbia, SC 1989, 212-23; R. Paret, Aṣḥāb al-kahf, in *EI²*, i, 691; N.N. Roberts, A parable of blessing. The significance and message of the qurʾānic account of the Companions of the Cave, in *MW* 83 (1993), 295-317.

Menstruation

The monthly flow of blood from the uterus. Menstruation is explicitly mentioned by the Qurʾān in two contexts: ritual purity (q.v.) and the law of marriage and divorce (q.v.). In the context of ritual purity, menstruation is one of a fairly broad set of bodily functions (also mentioned within the text of the Qurʾān are excretion and sexual activity, Q 4:43; 5:6; see SEX AND

SEXUALITY) requiring ablutions in order to restore the state of *ṭahāra* required for prayer (q.v.) and other rituals (see RITUAL AND THE QURʾĀN; CLEANLINESS AND ABLUTION). Menstruation is categorized in Islamic law as a cause of major impurity analogous to that entailed by sexual intercourse (see LAW AND THE QURʾĀN). In the context of marital law, the menstrual period provides evidence that a widowed or divorced woman is not pregnant by her previous husband and provides the unit of measurement for the waiting period (q.v.), or *ʿidda,* that must expire before she may contract another marriage.

Despite the complexity of Islamic law relating to menstrual purity, the Qurʾān touches on the subject only once. "They ask you about menstruation *(al-maḥīḍ),*" states Q 2:222, "say, it is an *adhan.* Remain aloof from menstruating women and do not approach them until they become pure again; when they have purified themselves, go to them as God has instructed you. Indeed, God loves those who repent (see REPENTANCE AND PENANCE) and those who purify themselves." The word *adhan,* derived from a root meaning "to cause harm to," is semantically very open; it has been translated with English words as diverse as "hurt," "pollution," "strain" and "nuisance." The word is used nine times in the Qurʾān, to refer to inconveniences and incapacities as diverse as ailments of the scalp (Q 2:196), rain during (outdoor) prayer (Q 4:102) and scornful patronage directed towards the objects of charity (Q 2:262, 263, 264; see ALMSGIVING; PATH OR WAY). In verse Q 2:222 both the nature of the harm involved and the identity of the person suffering it are unspecified.

Many exegetes interpret it in terms of the "dirtiness," smelliness and general offensiveness of menstrual blood; this is the dominant opinion in medieval commentaries, particularly those based closely on transmission from early Muslim authorities (see EXEGESIS OF THE QURʾĀN: CLASSICAL AND MEDIEVAL). Others, particularly modern interpreters, focus on the indisposition of, or possible harm to, the menstruating woman herself (see EXEGESIS OF THE QURʾĀN: EARLY MODERN AND CONTEMPORARY). This harm is often understood in medical terms (see MEDICINE AND THE QURʾĀN). Thus, the Egyptian modernist Muḥammad Rashīd Riḍā (d. 1935; *Manār,* ii, 359) writes that "[even] if the man escapes from… harm the woman can scarcely escape it, because intercourse disturbs her reproductive organs for something that they are neither ready nor prepared to do, because they are occupied with another natural function, which is the expulsion *(ifrāz)* of the… blood." Similarly, the Shīʿī (see SHĪʿISM AND THE QURʾĀN) commentator Muḥammad al-Sabzawārī (d. ca. 1297/1880; *Jadīd,* i, 266) writes, "Menstruation's being a 'harm' . may be from the point of view of the woman's state, because she experiences weakness and is overcome with lassitude when the bleeding occurs and suffers a great deal of hardship and discomfort.… It may possibly also be from the point of view of [the menstrual blood's] being ill-smelling and substantively impure *(najis);* the man may be repelled by it, and the woman may [thus] be harmed, even if [only] psychologically.…" In contrast, the Egyptian revivalist Sayyid Quṭb (d. 1966; *Ẓilāl,* ii, 241-2) understands the prohibition of marital intercourse during menstruation in terms of the *fiṭra,* the fundamental human constitution. Only in the period of purity (when the woman is not menstruating) can intercourse achieve both the natural desire for physical pleasure and the fundamental aim *(ghāya fiṭriyya)* of sexual intercourse, which is the continuation of the species (see BIOLOGY AS THE CREATION AND STAGES OF LIFE). Finally, some commentators also note that the word *adhan* is used elsewhere in the Qurʾān specifically to refer to minor and insignificant hardships (cf. Q 3:111), thus minimizing the harm or offense associated with menstruation.

The main legal issue in the interpretation of Q 2:222 is the degree of avoidance implied by the verse's injunction to "remain aloof from" *(iʿtazilū)* menstruating women. Although the most obvious literal reading of the verse itself would suggest complete separation from menstruants, the tradition of occasions of revelation (q.v.; *asbāb al-nuzūl*) suggests a much more limited form of avoidance. According to this tradition, the verse was sent down in response to the questions of Companions of the Prophet (q.v.) who observed that the Jews (or, in other versions, the pagan Arabs [q.v.] or the Zoroastrians; see JEWS AND JUDAISM; PEOPLE OF THE BOOK; PRE-ISLAMIC ARABIA AND THE QURʾĀN) would not share food with a menstruating woman or remain in the same house with her. When the verse was revealed, the Prophet clarified it by saying, "Do anything but have sexual intercourse [with them]." Hearing of this, the Jews exclaim, "This man does not want to leave a single thing in which he does not contradict *(khālafa)* us!" (In some versions, the questioners then wonder if they can have sexual intercourse during menstruation, which the Prophet emphatically forbids.) This narrative frame reverses the initial impact of the verse itself, from an injunction to avoid menstruating women to an injunction to limit their exclusion. (Many commentators suggest that the word *maḥīḍ* should be read as a noun of place, and that the verse should actually be understood to enjoin avoidance of the place of menstruation, i.e. the genital area, rather than of the menstruating woman herself.) The avoidance of sexual intercourse, but not of commensality or other physical contact, is often seen to manifest the moderate "middle path" of the Islamic dispensation (cf. Q 2:143), striking a balance between the Christians (who allowed intercourse with menstruating women; see CHRISTIANS AND CHRISTIANITY) and, variously, Jews, Zoroastrians and pagans (who shunned them altogether; see POLYTHEISM AND ATHEISM; SOCIAL INTERACTIONS; SOCIAL RELATIONS).
See also CONTAMINATION.

Marion Holmes Katz

Bibliography
Primary: Mawlana Abul Kalam Azad, *The tarjumān al-Qurʾān*, ed. and trans. Syed Abdul Latif, 2 vols., Bombay 1962-7, ii; Ibn Abī Zayd al-Qayrawānī, *La Risâla. Ou, Epître sur les éléments du dogme et de la loi de l'Islâm selon le rite mâlikite*, ed. and Fr. trans. L. Bercher, Alger 1945 (s.v. "menstrues" in Index, p. 358); Qurṭubī, *Jāmiʿ*, 20 vols., Cairo 1967; Quṭb, *Ẓilāl*; 6 vols., Beirut 1973-4; Rashīd Riḍā, *Manār*; M. al-Sabzawārī, *al-Jadīd fī tafsīr al-Qurʾān al-majīd*, Beirut 1402-6/1982-5; al-Shīrāzī, Abū Isḥāq, *Kitâb et-tanbîh. Ou, Le livre de l'admonition touchant la loi musulmane selon le rite de l'Imâm ech-Chafé'î*, Fr. trans. G.-H. Bousquet, 4 vols., Alger 1949, i, 23-4 ("Le rituel"); Suyūṭī, *Durr*, 4 vols., Beirut 1403/1983; Ṭabarī, *Tafsīr*, 30 vols., Cairo 1373/1954.
Secondary: A. Yusuf Ali, *The holy Qurʾān*, Indianapolis 1992; T.B. Irving (al-Hajj Taʿlim ʿAli), *The Qurʾān. The first American version*, Brattleboro, VT 1985; M.H. Katz, *Body of text. The emergence of the Sunnī law of ritual purity*, Albany, NY 2002; id., *Purified companions. The development of the Islamic law of ritual purity*, Ph.D. diss., Chicago 1997.

Merchandise see SELLING AND BUYING

Mercy

Forbearance from inflicting harmful punishment on an adversary or offender; disposition to exercise compassion or forgiveness. The term "mercy" *(raḥma)*, with its cognates and synonyms, is omnipresent in the Qurʾān; and derivatives of the triliteral root *gh-f-r* which carry many of the same connotations are also attested throughout the Qurʾān. Muḥammad, for example, is characterized as a merciful man (Q 9:128) and believers are exhorted to show mercy and kindness in their daily lives (as at Q 7:199; 17:23-4; 42:43; 64:14; 90:17). "Compassion and mercy" are singled out as admirable characteristics of the followers of Jesus (q.v.; Q 57:27; see also CHRISTIANS AND CHRISTIANITY). Muslims are "strenuous with infidels, but merciful among themselves" (Q 48:29; see BELIEF AND UNBELIEF; POLYTHEISM AND ATHEISM; JIHĀD).

Mercy as an attribute of God

Overwhelmingly, though, the Qurʾān focuses upon mercy as an attribute of God (see GOD AND HIS ATTRIBUTES). He is *ahl al-maghfira*, "the source [or owner] of forgiveness" (Q 74:56), "who forgives sin and accepts repentance" (Q 40:3), "merciful and loving" (Q 11:90), "the most merciful of those who show mercy" (Q 7:151; 12:64; 21:83; compare Q 7:155; 23:109, 118). In fact, humans are exhorted to be merciful precisely because they hope for mercy from him (see Q 24:22). With the exception of the ninth sūra, every chapter opens with an invocation of God as "the merciful, the compassionate" *(al-raḥmān al-raḥīm)* and that phrase occurs, along with variant statements of the same concept, dozens of times within the text itself. Commentators early and late (see EXEGESIS OF THE QURʾĀN: CLASSICAL AND MEDIEVAL; EXEGESIS OF THE QURʾĀN: EARLY MODERN AND CONTEMPORARY) have sought to understand the distinction between *raḥmān* and *raḥīm*, both of which are derived from *r-ḥ-m*, the same Arabic root from which *raḥma* comes. Classical commentators frequently argued that *raḥmān* is stronger, more inclusive, than *raḥīm* (see, for example, the discussions at Ṭabarī, *Tafsīr*, i, 42-3 and Ibn Kathīr, *Tafsīr*, i, 17-21, where various authorities are cited to the effect that the mercy associated with the former applies to all creatures, whereas the latter is bestowed only upon believers, or that, while both operate in this world, only the former extends into the world to come). Modern orientalist exegesis tends rather to view the two terms as paronomastic repetition, sometimes translating them together as "all-merciful" (thus, for example, Paret, *Kommentar*, 11.)

In fact, as attested upwards of forty times (as at Q 17:110), "the Merciful" *(al-raḥmān)* serves as an alternate name for God. Sūra 55 is titled "The Merciful" and the great classical commentator al-Ṭabarī (d. 310/923) maintained that, unlike *al-raḥīm*, the title *al-raḥmān* belongs uniquely to God and cannot legitimately be given to any creature. *"Al-raḥmān,"* declared the early ascetic and traditionist al-Ḥasan al-Baṣrī (d. 110/728; see ḤADĪTH AND THE QURʾĀN), "is a forbidden name" (see Ṭabarī, *Tafsīr*, i, 45-6; compare Nöldeke, *GQ*, i, 112-3, 121; Q 40 [Sūrat al-Muʾmin], "The Believer," is sometimes known as Sūrat Ghāfir ["Forgiving One"], from *ghāfir*, another attribute of God with connotations of mercy or forgiveness, found in Q 40:3). As the uniquely merciful, God wants to make things easy, not difficult, for humans (see Q 2:185). "Both his hands are outstretched" (Q 5:64; compare Q 110:3). Accordingly, he makes allowance for their weaknesses and for the constraints under which they live (Q 2:263; 4:25, 43, 98-9; 5:3, 6, 45; 6:145; 9:91-2; 16:106, 115; 20:73; 24:33; 58:12; 73:20), is indulgent with human frailties like ignorance (q.v.; Q 4:17; 16:119; 33:5) and is patient with their sins (Q 22:48; 24:14, 20; see SIN, MAJOR AND MINOR). Indeed, were God to punish humans according to what they deserve, none would remain alive (Q 16:61; 35:45; see CHASTISEMENT AND PUNISHMENT; PUNISHMENT STORIES;

REWARD AND PUNISHMENT). His provision of material blessings (see BLESSING; GRACE) such as rain, the seasons (q.v.), the winds (see AIR AND WIND), the alternating of night and day (see DAY AND NIGHT), the oceans, and the celestial bodies (see PLANETS AND STARS), is emblematic of his kindness and mercy toward humankind (see, for example, Q 2:22, 29, 164, 243; 14:32-4; 16:2-8; 17:66; 22:65; 25:47-8; 27:63; 28:73; 30:46, 50; 42:28, 32-4; compare Ṭabarī, *Tafsīr,* i, 43; see NATURE AS SIGNS; COSMOLOGY; WATER). Even more importantly, divine revelation (see REVELATION AND INSPIRATION) is a mercy from God (as at Q 2:121-2; 6:153, 157; 7:63; 11:118-9; 17:86-7; 18:65; 36:5-6) and it is by his mercy that the righteous are not led astray (q.v.; Q 4:113; 12:53). It is also through his mercy that they are delivered from destruction at the hands of the wicked or from the consequences of their own errors (for various examples, see Q 2:37, 47, 63-4; 7:72; 11:43, 47, 58, 66, 94; 20:121-2; 54:34-5; see ERROR).

But God's mercy is not bestowed indiscriminately (see JUSTICE AND INJUSTICE). Revelation is not given to everybody. Not everyone is saved (see SALVATION). He recompenses all people according to their works (Q 11:111; 14:51; see GOOD DEEDS; EVIL DEEDS; RECORD OF HUMAN ACTIONS). Whereas the righteous merit his forgiveness, the wicked earn his wrath (see ANGER). At the final judgment (see LAST JUDGMENT), people will "see their works, so that whoever does an atom's weight (see WEIGHTS AND MEASURES) of good will see it and whoever does an atom's weight of evil will see it" (Q 99:6-8; compare Q 3:115). The wicked will confess their sins but will nonetheless be consigned to the flames of hell (Q 67:11; see HELL AND HELLFIRE). "God will show them their works, and they will sigh regretfully, yet they will not escape the inferno" (Q 2:167). There, their punishment "shall not be lightened nor shall they be helped" (Q 2:86). No individual will be wronged; God is not unjust (Q 3:25). But, for believers, his verdict will be more than just. For he accepts repentance (see, for example, Q 4:16; 24:5; 42:25; cf. 2:192; 9:102-4; 27:11; 39:53-4; see REPENTANCE AND PENANCE), and the Qurʾān exhorts humankind to seek his mercy (see, for example, Q 2:199; 4:106; 17:24; 27:46; 47:19; 71:10) as earlier prophets (see PROPHETS AND PROPHETHOOD) and others have done (e.g. Noah [q.v.], at Q 11:47; 71:28; Moses [q.v.], at Q 7:151, 155; David [q.v.], at Q 38:24; Solomon [q.v.], at Q 38:35; cf. 27:19). Even the angels (see ANGEL) of the divine court implore forgiveness for the righteous faithful (see Q 42:5). Believers should strive, even vie, to gain his mercy (Q 57:21). To receive it is far greater than to amass material treasure (Q 3:157; 6:16; 43:32). "God will pardon the worst of their deeds, and reward them for the best of what they have done" (Q 39:35). "We shall accept from them the best of what they have done and overlook their misdeeds" (Q 46:16). Whoever repents, believes, does good works, and follows right guidance will be forgiven (Q 20:82; compare, for example, Q 7:204; 8:2-4; 39:9). God will give believers "a double portion of his mercy" (Q 57:28) and overcompensate their good deeds (Q 4:40; 6:160; 10:26; 64:17). But he will not accept deathbed repentance (Q 4:18; 6:158; 23:63-7, 99-101; 38:3; 40:84-5; 44:10-14). Nor does he admit human or angelic intercession (q.v.; Q 2:123; 3:192; 4:109, 123; 10:27; 39:54; 44:41-2), except by his own appointment (Q 10:3; 19:87; 43:86; 53:26; 63:5-6; believers are sometimes expressly forbidden to pray for the unrighteous; see, for example, Q 9:84, 113-4). No soul can bear the burden of any other soul (Q 17:15; 39:7) and, on the day of judgment, family and other human relationships will count for nothing (Q 23:101; 35:18; 66:10; 70:8-15).

Several passages affirming God's disposition to forgive simultaneously stress the swiftness and severity of his punishments. "Tell my servants that I am the forgiving, the merciful one, and that my punishment is the painful punishment" (Q 15:49-50; compare Q 5:98; 6:147, 165; 7:167; 13:6; also Q 3:4, 11; 5:2; 17:57). And, in fact, the eminent traditionist and exegete Ibn ʿAbbās (d. ca. 68/688) maintained that the very meaning of God's title *al-raḥmān al-raḥīm* is that he "is gentle with those to whom he wishes to exercise mercy, and distant and severe with those whom he wishes to treat with rigor" (cited in Ṭabarī, *Tafsīr,* i, 44). For God does not love the unbelieving and unrighteous (Q 2:276; 3:32, 57, 140; 4:107); indeed, he is their "enemy" (Q 2:98; see ENEMIES). "Who despairs of the mercy of his lord except those who have gone astray?" (Q 15:56; see DESPAIR). And, though God may forgive anything else (even apostasy [q.v.]; see Q 3:85-91, 106; 4:137), he will not show mercy to those who persist in the worship of any god but himself (Q 4:48, 116; see IDOLS AND IMAGES; IDOLATRY AND IDOLATERS). Moreover, the Qurʾān's portrayal of God as merciful is further complicated by its insistence upon predestination (see, for example, Q 15:4-5; 16:35; 18:57-8; 26:200; 81:27-9; see FATE; FREEDOM AND PREDESTINATION) and upon his role in fostering a disposition to evil among the wicked (as at Q 2:7, 10, 15; see GOOD AND EVIL; DESTINY). The Qurʾān emphasizes God's sovereign freedom to bestow or withhold his mercy and to favor wherever he will (e.g. at Q 2:105; 4:48-9; 6:83-8;10:107; 33:17; and many other places). See also FORGIVENESS.

Daniel C. Peterson

Bibliography
Primary: Ibn Kathīr, *Tafsīr,* Aleppo 1980; Ṭabarī, *Tafsīr,* Beirut 1978.
Secondary: J. Jomier, Le nom divin "al-Raḥmān" dans le Coran, in *Mélanges Louis Massignon,* 3 vols., Damascus 1957, ii, 361-81 (Eng. trans. "The divine name 'al-Raḥmān' in the Qurʾān," in A. Rippin (ed.), *The Qurʾān. Style and content,* Aldershot 2001, 197-212); Nöldeke, *GQ;* Paret, *Kommentar.*

Merriment see LAUGHTER; JOY AND MISERY

Messenger

One who comes bringing information. The main word for messenger in the Qurʾān is *rasūl,* denoting "one sent with a message," which occurs 236 times and its plural, *rusul,* ninety-five times. *Mursal (*pl. *mursalūn),* the passive participle of a verb from the same root letters, and which also means "one sent with a message," occurs thirty-six times. Both *rasūl* and *mursal* usually refer to a human agent whom God sends to guide a people by communicating to them in a language they understand (Q 14:4; see LANGUAGE, CONCEPT OF; ARABIC LANGUAGE; REVELATION AND INSPIRATION). The central message of these messengers is to shun false gods (see POLYTHEISM AND ATHEISM; IDOLATRY AND IDOLATERS; IDOLS AND IMAGES), the powers of evil (see GOOD AND EVIL; DEVIL) and injustice (see JUSTICE AND INJUSTICE), and to worship (q.v.) the one true God (Q 16:36; see BELIEF AND UNBELIEF). Muḥammad, through whom God revealed the Qurʾān and through whom God guides all humankind, represents the model and final *rasūl* of God (Q 33:21, 40).

Arabia before and at the time of Muḥammad (see PRE-ISLAMIC ARABIA AND THE QURʾĀN) was acquainted with the term *rasūl.* Al-Hamdānī (d. ca. 334/945) cites traditions about south Arabian tomb inscriptions that identify Hūd (q.v.) and

Shuʿayb (q.v.) but also Ḥanẓala b. Ṣafwān as messengers of God (see ARCHAELOGY AND THE QURʾĀN). One of the inscriptions even designates Ḥārith b. ʿAmr the *rasūl* of the *rasūl Allāh,* Shuʿayb (Hamdānī, *al-Iklīl,* 134, 136, 139, 142). Musaylima (q.v.) — another Arabian prophet — referred to himself as "the messenger of Allāh" in a letter to Muḥammad (Ṭabarī, *Taʾrīkh,* i, 1749).

While the Qurʾān states that it has not narrated the stories of all the messengers sent by God (Q 40:78; see NARRATIVES), it identifies — among a long line of prophets preceding Muḥammad (see PROPHETS AND PROPHETHOOD) — some as messengers *(rusul)* by name: in the biblical tradition, Noah (q.v.; Nūḥ), Lot (q.v.; Lūṭ), Ishmael (q.v.; Ismāʿīl), Moses (q.v.; Mūsā) and Jesus (q.v.; ʿĪsā); Shuʿayb, messenger to his people the Midianites (see MIDIAN); and the Arabians Hūd and Ṣāliḥ (q.v.), sent to their respective tribes, ʿĀd (q.v.) and Thamūd (q.v.). In Q 37:123 and 139 respectively, Elijah (q.v.; Ilyās) and Jonah (q.v.; Yūnus) are included as among the *mursalūn.* Although whether the Qurʾān reveals a clear distinction between the roles of prophets and messengers is disputed, generally speaking, prophets are found exclusively among the People of the Book (q.v.), that is in the biblical tradition (see SCRIPTURE AND THE QURʾĀN), and messengers are depicted as closely connected with a people/community (*qawm, ahl, umma,* see COMMUNITY AND SOCIETY IN THE QURʾĀN). The non-biblical messengers, Hūd, Ṣāliḥ, and Shuʿayb are sent to specific communities but are never referred to as prophets. Al-Bayḍāwī (d. ca. 716/1316-7; *Anwār,* ad Q 22:52) distinguishes prophets who bring no divine law *(sharīʿa)* from messengers who bring divine law (see LAW AND THE QURʾĀN) and a holy book (q.v.). But no clear qurʾānic evidence supports this distinction. The Qurʾān designates neither Abraham (q.v.; Q 87:19; 53:36-37) nor David (q.v.; Q 17:55; 4:163) specifically as messengers, yet they are both connected with scriptures. The Qurʾān designates Moses, Jesus and Muḥammad as both prophets (Q 6:83-9; 3:68) and messengers (Q 7:104; 3:49; 3:144). Ibn Kathīr (d. 774/1373; *Tafsīr,* ad Q 4:163) says reports differ but one well-known tradition enumerates 124,000 prophets, among them 313 messengers.

Several sūras of the Qurʾān contain a series of stories of similar structure featuring all or most of a set of seven messengers (see FORM AND STRUCTURE OF THE QURʾĀN): Noah, Hūd, Ṣāliḥ, Lot, Shuʿayb, Abraham (Ibrāhīm), and Moses. The fact that among these messengers the Qurʾān fails to designate only Abraham as a *rasūl* may suggest his status as a messenger is assumed. Q 26:10-191 contains all seven narratives; and an incomplete set of these narratives occurs in Q 7:59-93; 11:25-123; 37:75-148; 54:9-42. In most of these, the messenger declares a message; his people reject him; God rescues him along with his faithful followers; and some calamity punishes those who reject the message (see PUNISHMENT STORIES). These accounts support the notion that messengers are distinguished from prophets by their association with a people/community. This structure coincides closely with the experience of Muḥammad, providing him comfort, reassuring his supporters and warning his opponents (see OPPOSITION TO MUḤAMMAD). In Q 26, for example, each separate account ends with this reassuring refrain, "Surely in this there is a sign; yet most of them do not believe. Your lord is the mighty one, the merciful" (e.g. Q 26:67-8).

While the calls of the messengers and any personal struggles they may have had are left out of the qurʾānic stories, their nature and role are strikingly consistent and may be fairly summarized as follows. These merely human agents (Q 16:43; 25:20) come to announce (see GOOD NEWS) and warn (Q 18:56; see WARNING) and must be obeyed (Q 4:64; see OBEDIENCE). Although some messengers are higher in rank than others (Q 2:253), the faithful believe in all of them and do not distinguish among them (Q 2:136; 4:150-2). Just as every city (q.v.) has a "warner" (*nadhīr,* Q 35:24; cf. 26:208) and a guide (cf. Q 13:7) and every people will have a "witness" (*shahīd,* see WITNESSING AND TESTIFYING) on the day of judgment (Q 16:84, 89; 4:41; see LAST JUDGMENT), so every people will have received a messenger (Q 10:47; 28:59) to proclaim the oneness of God and warn against idolatry and injustice (Q 16:36; 17:15). Messengers proclaim God's word in their own people's language (Q 14:4) and only perform miracles (q.v.) with God's permission (Q 40:78). The coming of a messenger precipitates a crisis in which some reject and others accept the challenge to believe in and obey God and his messenger. Unbelievers consistently mock them (Q 15:11; see MOCKERY) and accuse them of falsehood (Q 2:87; 23:44; see LIE). All messengers are affected by Satan (Q 22:52) and, if repentant, can be forgiven (cf. Q 27:10-12; see REPENTANCE AND PENANCE; FORGIVENESS). Like prophets (Q 2:61, 91; 3:21, 112, 181; 4:155), messengers may even be killed (Q 2:87; 5:70; see MURDER). But they will be avenged (Q 30:47). Messengers are so closely linked with the divine that obedience to them amounts to obedience to God (Q 4:80). References to messengers before Muḥammad occur almost always among Meccan verses (see CHRONOLOGY AND THE QURʾĀN) — the exceptions being references to Moses and Jesus (Q 61:5-6).

The Qurʾān terms some messengers *ūlū l-ʿazmi,* "gifted with determination," but these are not named (Q 46:35). Post-qurʾānic interpretation considers *ūlū l-ʿazmi* to mean exalted messengers. The angels are also called *mursalūn* (Q 15:57; 51:31) and *rusul* (Q 10:21; cf. 42:51). Royal messengers are designated by both terms (Q 12:50; 27:35). The feminine plural of *mursal, mursalāt,* possibly designates winds in Q 77:1 (see AIR AND WIND). The Qurʾān never uses *rasūl* to designate disciples of Jesus (Q 3:52-3; 61:14; 5:111). It calls them *ḥawāriyyūn,* "apostles" (see APOSTLE). These helpers and followers of Jesus profess to be *muslim* (Q 3:52; 5:111) and ask him to bring down a table from heaven to strengthen their faith (Q 5:112-3).

Muḥammad is called "the messenger of God" (Q 7:158; 48:29). God sends him to a people never previously visited by a messenger (cf. Q 28:46; 32:3). Like other messengers, he must "rise and warn," communicating the proper social and ritual responses to God's oneness (Q 74:2). Muḥammad's mission extends to all creatures (*lil-ʿālamīn,* Q 21:107), he being both "the messenger of God" and the "seal of the prophets" (Q 33:40). The phrase "God and his messenger" occurs at least eighty-five times, all but one (Q 72:23) in Medinan passages (Q 7:158 being a Medinan verse). The phrase links obedience and disobedience (q.v.) to God with obedience and disobedience to Muḥammad twenty-eight times — all in Medinan passages, e.g. Q 5:92. No such linkage exists in passages where Muḥammad is referred to as a prophet *(nabī).*

A.H. Mathias Zahniser

Bibliography

Primary: Bayḍāwī, *Anwār;* al-Hamdānī, al-Ḥasan b. Aḥmad, *al-Iklīl. al-Juzʾ al-thāmin,* ed. N.A. Faris, Princeton 1940 (Eng. trans., N.A. Faris, *The antiquities of South Yemen,* Princeton 1938); Ibn Kathīr, *Tafsīr,* Cairo 1971; Ṭabarī, *Taʾrīkh,* ed. de Goeje.

Secondary: H. Askari, The qurʾānic conception of apostleship, in D. Cohn-Sherbok (ed.), *Islam in a world of diverse faiths,* New York 1991, 88-103; W.A. Bijlefeld, A prophet and more than a prophet? Some observations on the qur'ānic use of the terms "prophet" and "apostle," in *MW* 59 (1969), 1-28 (fundamental); T. Fahd, Nubuwwa, in *EI²*, viii, 93-7; D. Marshall, *God, Muhammad and the unbelievers*, Richmond, Surrey 1999; F. Rahman, *Major themes of the Qur'ān*, Minneapolis 1980, 80-105; A. Welch, al-Ḳur'ān, in *EI²*, v, 400-29 (esp. 423-4); A.J. Wensinck, Muhammed und die Propheten, in *AO* 2 (1924), 168-98 (Eng. trans. Muḥammad and the prophets, in U. Rubin [ed.], *The life of Muḥammad*, Aldershot 1998, 319-43); id., Rasūl, in *EI²*, viii, 454-5; G. Widengren, Muḥammad, the apostle of God, and his ascension (King and Saviour V), in *Uppsala Universitets Arsskrift* 1 (1955), 7-24.

Messiah see JESUS

Metals and Minerals

Substances that have luster, are opaque and may be fused, and chemical elements or compounds occurring naturally as a product of inorganic processes. The Qur'ān does not utilize the generic term for both metal and ore *(ma'din)*, but references the two most widespread metals in common use on the planet: iron *(ḥadīd)*, which is mentioned six times, and copper, *(nuḥās)* mentioned once, as well as molten copper *(qiṭr)*, mentioned twice. Iron, which gives its name to Q 57 (Sūrat al-Ḥadīd) and which God sent down to earth, possesses great strength and is very useful to humankind (Q 57:25); it comes in the shape of lumps (Q 18:96); truncheons are made from it (Q 22:21) and God made it malleable for David (q.v.; Q 34:10). Copper will be hurled at the guilty on the day of judgment (Q 55:35; see LAST JUDGMENT); Dhū l-Qarnayn (see ALEXANDER) poured molten copper on a dam between two mountains (Q 18:96) and God had this metal flow from a spring (see SPRINGS AND FOUNTAINS) for Solomon (q.v.; Q 34:12). The exact nature of the molten metal called *muhl*, which appears three times — in connection with the sky (Q 70:8), the tree of Zaqqūm (Q 44:45; see TREES) and the potion for wrongdoers in hell (Q 18:29; see HELL AND HELLFIRE; REWARD AND PUNISHMENT; FOOD AND DRINK) — is unknown. As to precious metals, gold (q.v.; *dhahab*) is attested seven times in the Qur'ān, and silver *(fiḍḍa)* six times; they are twice used in conjunction. Gold is mentioned as being hoarded (Q 3:14; 9:34), and as a material from which bracelets (Q 18:31; 22:23; 35:33; 43:53) and dishes (Q 43:71) are made. The Qur'ān notes that silver, too, is hoarded together with gold, and that vases, flasks and bracelets are made (Q 76:15, 16, 21) from it (see CUPS AND VESSELS; INSTRUMENTS).

The mineral mentioned most frequently in the Qur'ān is stone (q.v.; *ḥajar*, pl. *ḥijāra*), spoken of twelve times. Moses (q.v.) hit the stone with his stick (see ROD) and twelve springs gushed out (Q 2:60; 7:160; see SPRINGS AND FOUNTAINS); stones will feed the fire of hell (Q 2:24; 66:6); although stones are hard, some may split and others may break up (Q 2:74); there are also stones that God sends from heaven (Q 8:32; 11:82; 15:74; 17:50; see HEAVEN AND SKY), as well as those that Abraham's (q.v.) messengers (see MESSENGER) throw at the guilty and those that flights of birds throw on enemies (q.v.; Q 51:33; 105:4; see ABRAHA). The second mineral named in the Qur'ān is clay (q.v.; *ṭīn*), mentioned ten times in connection with the creation (q.v.) of humans by God. Two other mentions are in relation to the building of a tower by Pharaoh (q.v.; Q 28:38) and to the stones that Abraham's messengers throw (Q 51:33). There are two kinds of clay: clinking clay *(ṣalṣāl)* such as pottery (Q 55:14), extracted from malleable mud (*min ḥama'in masnūnin*, Q 15:26, 28, 33), and hard clay named *sijjīl (*from the Latin *sigillum* or from the Aramaic *sgyl)*, with which some of the stones thrown from heaven are made (Q 11:82; 15:74; 105:4).

Concerning precious minerals, the Qurʾān knows but three: ruby *(yāqūt),* coral (q.v.; *marjān*) and pearls *(luʾluʾ),* which are compared to the ephebes and the houris (q.v.) of paradise (q.v.; Q 52:24; 55:58; 76:19); coral and pearls come from the seas (Q 55:22) and pearls will be used for adorning the believers (see BELIEF AND UNBELIEF) in paradise (Q 22:23; 35:33).

Gérard Troupeau

Bibliography
Primary: ʿAbd al-Bāqī; Ibyārī, *Mawsūʿa;* Jawālīqī, *Muʿarrab; Lisān al-ʿArab;* al-Rāghib al-Iṣfahānī, *Mufradāt; Tāj al-ʿarūs.*
Secondary: E. Ashtor, Maʿdin, in *EI²*, v, 963-7; F.C. de Blois, Sidjill, in *EI²*, ix, 538; A. Dietrich, Nuḥās, in *EI²*, viii, 111-2; A.S. Ehrenkreutz, Dhahab, in *EI²*, ii, 214; id., Fiḍḍa, in *EI²*, ii, 883; Jeffery, *For. vocab.*; J. Ruska, Ḥadīd, in *EI²*, iii, 22; G. Troupeau, Le premier traité arabe de minéralogie, in *AI* 32 (1998), 219-38; M. Ullmann, *Die Natur- und Geheimwissenschaften im Islam,* Leiden 1972; V. Vacca, Sidjdjīl, in *EI²*, ix, 538.

Metaphor

Literary device that conveys semantic equation without a linking participle such as "like" or "as." Metaphor *(istiʿāra)* is the subject of much discussion and classification in the science of Arabic rhetoric (cf. Bonebakker, Istiʿāra); this article will of necessity confine itself to major classifications and to uses that relate to how religious scholars (see EXEGESIS OF THE QURʾĀN: CLASSICAL AND MEDIEVAL) have sought to understand metaphor's appearance and use in the Qurʾān.

Definition

Metaphor is an example of figurative language *(majāz)* as opposed to "literal" or "true" expression (*ḥaqīqa,* cf. Reinert, De Bruijn and Stewart-Robinson, Ma<u>dj</u>āz). Within the realm of figurative language, metaphor, like its close associate, simile (*tashbīh, tamthīl,* see SIMILES), refers to joining or linking two or more concepts for purposes of comparison or semantic equation. Arab rhetoricians detail numerous subcategories for both metaphor and simile; nonetheless, their basic distinction between the two resembles that found in the Western rhetorical tradition. In both, simile achieves comparison by means of a linking particle that suggests similarity: "as, like," etc. (e.g. "in battle, this man fights like a lion"). Metaphor, however, denotes semantic equation; its semantic overlap or "borrowing" *(istiʿāra)* is direct and does not rely on linking particles (e.g. "in battle, this man is a lion").

As in most rhetorical traditions, Muslim scholars and critics debated the merits and limits of metaphor. They agreed that to the extent that metaphors link or equate concepts not commonly associated, they may create images of striking semantic impact and aesthetic force. One can, however, push metaphors too far. Far-fetched metaphors, when they are unbelievable or ridiculous, distort or dilute meaning. The pre-modern Arabic poetic tradition contains much discussion of the semantic and artistic appropriateness of metaphors that poets created, especially those of the "new school" (cf. Khalafallah, Badīʿ; see POETRY AND POETS). Representatives of this school, such as Abū Tammām (d. 231/845) and al-Buḥturī (d. ca. 284/897), became famous for formulating rhetorically embellished metaphors and other forms of figurative language that were considered either brilliantly daring or shockingly outrageous by their various admirers and opponents. Critics, however, also recognized that continuous use usually lessens the aesthetic force of metaphors so that they become trite: the above-mentioned "he is a lion in battle" is an example of such an over-used metaphor.

Between these two poles of the far-fetched and the hackneyed falls the metaphor whose appearance measurably enriches, perhaps almost imperceptibly, the aesthetic power, eloquence, and grace of a text: "And, out of kindness, lower to [your parents] the wing of humility" (Q 17:24). The appearance of this third class of metaphor in the Qurʾān is for Muslim scholars one of the text's proofs of inimitability (q.v.; *iʿjāz*, cf. Von Grunebaum, Iʿdjāz; Baqillānī, *Iʿjāz*, 69-112; Jurjānī, *Dalāʾil*, 66-73, 262 f.). As al-Jurjānī states, "Speech does not deserve the term eloquent unless meaning precedes expression, and expression meaning" (Jurjānī, *Dalāʾil*, 267). This is what a good metaphor does.

Al-Suyūṭī (d. 911/1505) mentions several definitions of metaphor in his *Itqān*. He settles on the following: "The essence of metaphor is when a word is borrowed from something for which it is known and applied to something for which it is not known." In other words, metaphor occurs when a concept is borrowed from its customary semantic domain and applied to a semantic domain in which it is not usually employed. For example, in the qurʾānic verse cited above, "wing" is "borrowed" from its usual determination as the limb of a bird that enables it to fly and then applied to prescribe one aspect of children's respect for their parents. The power of this metaphor is enhanced by its denotation that, as a sign of humility, the respectful child "lowers his wing," a symbol of independence. "The purpose of metaphor," al-Suyūṭī (*Itqān*, ii, 780-1) continues, "is to reveal an aspect that is hidden, to emphasize something that is not sufficiently clear, to exaggerate, or to achieve the joining or overlap (of concepts)."

Use and interpretation

The Qurʾān is replete with metaphors. It is useful to distinguish, however, between two types. On the one hand, there are metaphors whose import is mainly stylistic and figurative — such as "wing of humility" or "the morning (q.v.), when it takes breath" (Q 81:18; see AIR AND WIND) — and which may be taken as examples of the *iʿjāz* or inimitable style of the Qurʾān. On the other hand, there are expressions that may or may not be deemed as metaphorical, depending on the theological stance or persuasion of the commentator. Prominent examples of this second category are qurʾānic expressions attributing physical attributes or mental or emotional operations to God (see ANTHROPOMORPHISM). Such metaphors became the subject of much theological controversy between the Muʿtazila and their opponents (see Gimaret, Muʿtazila; see also MUʿTAZILĪS). Examples are the Qurʾān's attribution to God of such physical attributes as "face" (q.v.), "hand" (q.v.) or "thigh"; such emotional states as "mercy" (q.v.) or "wrath" (see ANGER); or qurʾānic representations of God's agency or acts by means of physical description (God's creation of Adam, or his descent to his throne, for example; see THRONE OF GOD; CREATION; ADAM AND EVE). At issue here is the question of whether such attributions were "metaphorical" or "real." On the one hand, there was the theological position of the Muʿtazila, who held that God transcended physical representation; hence, references in the Qurʾān to divine possession of physical attributes or human emotions were "metaphorical" (Gimaret, Muʿtazila, 788-9). Other theological schools, such as the Ḥanbalīs and the Ẓāhirīs, however, believed that literal meanings in the Qurʾān should be upheld as true. The position that the Ashʿarīs developed was intermediate; they held that one should take the literal meaning of the Qurʾān "without asking how" (*bi-lā kayf*). Of particular interest for the topic of metaphor is that this provides a case study of how even deciding what is literal and what is metaphorical may easily develop into a matter of heated theological controversy, especially when the literal truth of a religious text is a principle of faith (q.v.; see also THEOLOGY AND THE QUR'ĀN).

At times, theological controversies are less often unequivocally resolved than made moot through prolonged discussion. Passions burn brightly for a time but their flames eventually ebb, in the same way, perhaps, that metaphors too often used become banal. Hence, by the time of al-Suyūṭī, the Qur'ān's reference to God's possessing physical attributes, such as a face or hand, is categorized as an example of the ambiguous (q.v.) or multivalent verses in the Qur'ān rather than a topic for elaborate theological discussion (Suyūṭī, *Itqān*, i, 639-70). In this context, he specifically cites Q 3:7:

He it is who sent down the book (q.v.) to you. In it are verses (q.v.), decisive — they are the mother of the book — and others multivalent. As for those in whose hearts (see HEART) is deviancy, they follow that which is multivalent in it, desiring dissension, and desiring its interpretation. Yet no one knows its interpretation except God, and those who are firmly rooted in knowledge (see KNOWLEDGE AND LEARNING) say, "We have faith in it, for it is all from our lord (q.v.)." Yet none remember except those who are possessed of prudent minds (see MEMORY; INTELLECT).

In his discussion of the clear and decisive *(muḥkam)* and multivalent or ambiguous *(mutashābih)* verses, al-Suyūṭī adopts an exegetical stance that by his time had become standard among mainstream Sunnī commentators. This approach holds, in essence, that however one may define certain verses or parts of the Qur'ān as ambiguous, one should understand their meaning in the context of the verses that are perceived of as clear and decisive (see Ayoub, *Qur'ān*, ii, 20-46). An instance of this approach as applied to metaphor lies in the verse itself, where the meaning of the phrase "mother of the book" is defined by the term *muḥkam*. In other words, it does not refer to a literal "mother" but rather to "clear and decisive meaning." Interestingly, this exegetical approach is to a large extent a mirror image of al-Suyūṭī's definition of metaphor cited above: "The essence of metaphor is when a word is borrowed from something for which it is known and applied to something for which it is not known." Instead of moving from the known to the unknown, as one does to create a metaphor, the traditionalist commentator determines the semantic intent of an ambiguous phrase, such as appearances of metaphorical usage, through reference to known clear and unequivocal expressions that envelop an otherwise too open semantic field. The goal here is to restrict interpretation that may transgress the boundaries of accepted faith.

If traditionalist commentators restrict the limits of interpreting metaphor through reliance on non-figurative verses of the Qur'ān, the Islamic philosophers did the same by relying on rational interpretation (see PHILOSOPHY AND THE QUR'ĀN). Typical of this approach is Ibn Rushd (Averroes, d. 595/1198) in his work *Faṣl al-maqāl*, "The decisive treatise." Similar to the approaches of Ibn Sīnā (Avicenna, d. 428/1037) and al-Fārābī (d. 339/950) and following an hermeneutical tradition that can be traced back to Plato and the Stoics, Ibn Rushd distinguishes among classes of human intellectual ability and their resultant capacity to "assent" to the truth value of a text. For him, "demonstration," i.e. reliance on syllogistic argument, is the clear path to truth (q.v.). Nonetheless, he recognizes that relatively few individuals have the intellectual capacity to master philosophy and thus employ demonstration effectively. Religion, however, must be accessible to all. Hence metaphors and other rhetorical devices (see RHETORIC OF THE QURʾĀN) are a necessary component of a religious text such as the Qurʾān so that it may convince all types of people to believe in its message. As Ibn Rushd (*Faṣl*, 46, also 30-1; Eng. trans. 59, 49) states:

God has been gracious to those of his servants who have no access to demonstration, on account of their natures, habits, and lack of facilities for education. He has coined for them images and likeness of these things, and summoned them to assent to those images that come about through the indications common to all men, that is, dialectical and rhetorical indications.

The presence in the Qurʾān of such rhetorical devices as metaphors is thus for philosophers a necessary communicative tool. Their eloquence and beauty are doubtless proof of the holy text's inimitability, but they are also intrinsic to its natural functionality: they are needed to promote assent and to inspire belief among the general populace.

A third exegetical stance toward metaphors in the Qurʾān also became prominent. This approach did not seek to delimit the interpretation of metaphors, but rather to better understand their import through elaboration or meditation. Prominent examples of this trend are the mystics (see ṢŪFISM AND THE QURʾĀN), yet many groups (Ismāʿīlīs, *ḥurūfīs*, etc.) whose vision of Islam encompasses an esoteric dimension have also embraced it. A well-known mainstream example of this trend is al-Ghazālī (d. 505/1111). For him, the symbolic language of the Qurʾān was an object of profound reflection, a pathway that enabled believers to bridge the physical world of human activity to the spiritual realm of divine truth. An example of his approach is his treatise *Mishkāt al-anwār,* "The niche for lights." This work is based mainly on Q 24:35, the Light Verse:

God is the light (q.v.) of the heavens and the earth; the likeness of his light is as a niche wherein is a lamp (q.v.) — the lamp is in a glass, the glass as it were a glittering star — kindled from a blessed tree, an olive that is neither of the east nor of the west whose oil wellnigh would shine, even if no fire touched it; light upon light; God guides to his light whom he will. God strikes similitudes for humans, and God has knowledge of everything.

Typical of al-Ghazālī's method is his discussion of the metaphor: "God is the light of the heavens and the earth." Al-Ghazālī proceeds to distinguish among three levels in regard to the meaning of light. The first is that of physical phenomenon whereby the human eye sees the earth by means of the light of the sun. The second is the mental plane, whose eye is the faculty of intelligence as illuminated by the light of the truth found in the Qurʾān itself. Finally, there is the spiritual dimension, where gnostic intuition is illuminated by the rays of the light of the divine presence. For al-Ghazālī , a mature believer is someone who attains perception of each of these levels of knowledge (Ghazālī, *Mishkāt al-anwār,* 41-64; Eng. trans. 79-121; see MATURITY).

It is clear that the theological or hermeneutical issues that the presence of metaphors in the Qurʾān may provoke can be just as significant as their rhetorical or aesthetic effects — as important as these latter are. This suggests the pertinence of the idea that much of how one understands a text depends on the exegetical approach or theological stance that one brings to its study. See also LANGUAGE AND STYLE OF THE QURʾĀN; LITERARY STRUCTURES; SYMBOLIC IMAGERY.

Peter Heath

Bibliography

Primary: Baqillānī, *Iʿjāz;* al-Ghazālī, Abū Ḥāmid, *Mishkāt al-anwār,* ed. A. al-ʿAfīfī, Cairo 1973; trans. W.H.T. Gairdner, *al-Ghazzali's Miskat al-anwar,* London 1924; Ibn Rushd, Abū l-Walīd, *al-Faṣl al-maqāl fī mā bayna l-ḥikma wa-l-sharīʿa min al-ittiṣāl,* ed. M. ʿImāra, Cairo 1972; trans. G.F. Hourani, *Averroes on the harmony of religion and philosophy,* London 1961; Jurjānī, *Asrār;* id., *Dalāʾil,* ed. M.M. Shākir; Suyūṭī, *Itqān.*

Secondary: M. Ajami, *The neckveins of winter. The controversy over natural and artificial poetry in medieval Arabic literary criticism,* Leiden 1984; M.M. Ayoub, *The Qurʾān and its interpreters. ii. The House of Imran,* Albany 1992; S.A. Bonebakker, Istiʿāra, in *EI²,* iv, 248-52; J. Fück, Review of T. Sabbagh, *La métaphore dans le Coran,* in *ZDMG* 98 (1944), 410-4; H. Gätje, *The Qurʾān and its exegesis. Selected texts with classical and modern Muslim interpretations,* trans. and ed. A. Welch, Oxford 1996; D. Gimaret, Muʿtazila, in *EI²,* vii, 783-93; G.E. von Grunebaum, Iʿdjāz, in *EI²,* iii, 1018-20; M. Khalafallah, Badīʿ, in *EI²,* i, 857-8; T. Lohmann, Die Gleichnisreden Muhammeds im Koran, in *Mitteilungen des Instituts für Orientforschung* (Berlin) 12 (1966), 75-118; 416-69; B. Reinert, J.T.P. de Bruijn and J. Stewart-Robinson, Madjāz, in *EI²,* v, 1025-8; T. Sabbagh, *La métaphore dans le Coran,* Paris 1943; S. Sacks (ed.), *On metaphor,* Chicago 1978; F. Sherif, *A guide to the contents of the Qurʾān,* Reading, England 1995, esp. 54-8, 64-6; S.P. Stetkevych, *Abu Tammām and the poetics of the ʿAbbāsid age,* Leiden 1991; J. Wansbrough, *Majāz al-Qurʾān.* Periphrastic exegesis, in *BSOAS* 33 (1970), 247-66.

Meteor see PLANETS AND STARS

Michael

An angelic being, Michael (Ar. Mīkāl; also Mīkaʾīl; Mīkāʾil; Mīkaʾil) is mentioned by name only once in the Qurʾān (Mīkāl, Q 2:98) in a verse affirming belief in God's angels (including Gabriel; see ANGEL; GABRIEL) and apostles (see MESSENGER) as a requirement of faith (q.v.) for the community of believers (*muʾminīn,* see BELIEF AND UNBELIEF; COMMUNITY AND SOCIETY IN THE QURʾĀN). The role of Michael, however, is elaborated in ḥadīth and qurʾānic interpretation (see ḤADĪTH AND THE QURʾĀN; EXEGESIS OF THE QURʾĀN: CLASSICAL AND MEDIEVAL). This angel, whose ontological status seems to be (along with Gabriel) higher than that of other angels, appears in several types of literature in the Islamic world: the traditional histories of Muḥammad and the prophets (see SĪRA AND THE QURʾĀN; PROPHETS AND PROPHETHOOD) as well as cosmological, mystical and eschatological literature (see COSMOLOGY; ESCHATOLOGY; ṢŪFISM AND THE QURʾĀN).

Many versions of Muḥammad's night journey *(al-isrāʾ)* and ascension (q.v.) to the throne (*al-miʿrāj,* see THRONE OF GOD), based on Q 17:1, describe Michael and Gabriel as appearing to Muḥammad, preparing him for his journey. Al-Ṭabarī's (d. 310/923) narrative has Gabriel asking Michael to bring a basin of water from Zamzam so that Gabriel can purify the Prophet's heart (q.v.; *Tafsīr,* ad Q 17:1). Gabriel cuts open the Prophet's chest, washes his heart three times with the three (successive) basins of water brought by Michael, removing all malice and inserting the qualities of gentleness, knowledge (see KNOWLEDGE AND LEARNING), faith, certitude and submission. This sūra serves as a basis for the Islamic belief in the Prophet's protection from sin (see IMPECCABILITY). Michael also figures in versions of the "tales of the prophets" *(qiṣaṣ al-anbiyāʾ)* literature. In a story clearly meant as a teaching on the virtue of trust in God alone (*tawakkul,* see TRUST AND PATIENCE; FEAR; PIETY), Abraham (q.v.) refuses the aid of all the archangels, including Michael, who visited him when he was cast into the fire (q.v.) by Nimrod (q.v.). Michael is also credited with giving aid to the faithful Muslims during the battle of Badr (q.v.).

The medieval cosmographer al-Qazwīnī (d. 682/1283) uses Qurʾān, ḥadīth and later anecdotes to describe fourteen kinds of angels (*ʿAjāʾib al-makhlūqāt* in Damīrī, *Ḥayāt,* i, 94-107). According to al-Qazwīnī, Michael is charged with providing nourishment for bodies (see FOOD AND DRINK) and knowledge for souls (see SOUL). He stands at the "swelling sea" (Q 52:6) in the seventh heaven (see HEAVEN AND SKY) and, if he were to open his mouth, the heaven would fit within it like a mustard seed in the ocean. Al-Qazwīnī also quotes a ḥadīth in which Muḥammad declares that "every prophet has two viziers from the inhabitants of heaven and two from the inhabitants of earth; my two from heaven are Gabriel and Michael."

Saʿīd al-Dīn Farghānī (d. ca. 700/1300) expands on Ibn ʿArabī's (d. 638/1240) discussion of angels in the *Futūḥāt al-makkiyya,* connecting the archangels to four fundamental attributes of God: life (q.v.), knowledge, will and power (see Murata, Angels; see also GOD AND HIS ATTRIBUTES; POWER AND IMPOTENCE). Michael manifests will, having been placed in charge of distributing the formal and supra-formal sustenance upon which continued existence depends. This sustenance includes spiritual food, such as knowledge and understanding, imaginary food, such as position and honor, and sensory food, such as the bounties (see BLESSING; GRACE) of the earth (q.v.).

Eschatological literature includes Michael in a number of narratives. The *Kitāb Aḥwāl al-qiyāma* describes God commanding the stages of the final annihilation of the created order (see CREATION; APOCALYPSE), affirming the qurʾānic assertion that all will perish but the face of God (q.v.; Q 28:88; 55:26-7); among the last to perish is Michael (along with the angel of death, Isrāfīl; see DEATH AND THE DEAD; for references to the *Kitāb Aḥwāl al-qiyāma,* see Smith and Haddad, *Islamic understanding,* 71, 81). Some narratives have Michael and Gabriel operating the balance, the *mīzān,* the principle of justice, upon which the good and bad deeds of individuals will be weighed (see GOOD DEEDS; EVIL DEEDS; JUSTICE AND INJUSTICE; WEIGHTS AND MEASURES; INSTRUMENTS). Although mentioned only once in the Qurʾān, Michael's pairing with Gabriel provided the basis for his (exalted) status in later literature.

Gisela Webb

Bibliography
Primary: al-Farghānī, Muḥammad b. Aḥmad, *Muntahā l-madārik,* 2 vols., Cairo 1876, i, 51-2, 67-71; Ibn al-ʿArabī, Muḥyī l-Dīn, *Fuṣūṣ al-ḥikam,* ed. A. ʿAfīfī, Beirut 1966, 50-1; id., *al-Futūḥāt al-makkiya,* 4 vols., Beirut 1968, ii, 61; Kisāʾī, *Qiṣaṣ; Kitāb Aḥwāl al-qiyāma,* Ger. trans. M. Wolff, *Muhammedanische Eschatologie,* Leipzig 1872 (The *Kitāb* is an adaptation of Imām ʿAbd al-Raḥīm b. Aḥmad al-Qāḍī's [prob. 11th cent.] *Daqāʾiq al-akhbār fī dhikr al-janna wa-l-nār* [Eng. trans. ʿĀ. ʿAbd al-Raḥmān, *The Islamic book of the dead,* Norwich, UK 1977]); al-Qazwīnī, Zakariyyā, *ʿAjāʾib al-makhlūqāt,* in Damīrī, *Ḥayāt,* Cairo 1954, i, 94-107; Suyūṭī, *al-Ḥabāʾik fī akhbār al-malāʾik,* ed. M. ʿĀshūr, Cairo 1990, 29-30; Ṭabarī, *Tafsīr.*
Secondary: C. Glasse, *The concise encyclopedia of Islam,* San Francisco 1989; Horovitz, *KU,* 243; S. Murata, Angels, in S.H. Nasr (ed.), *Islamic spirituality. Foundations,* New York 1987, 324-44; J. Smith and Y. Haddad, *The Islamic understanding of death and resurrection,* Albany 1981; A.J. Wensinck, Mīkāl, in *EI²,* vii, 25.

Midian

The name of a geographic locale and of a people mentioned in the Qurʾān. In post-qurʾānic Islamic tradition and in the Hebrew Bible, Midian (Ar. Madyan) is also the name of one of Abraham's (q.v.) sons through Keturah (cf. *Gen* 25:2), the eponymous ancestor of the Midianites. The origin of the name is unknown. Mendenhall *(Studies)* notes that the Hebrew *midyān* (from the root *mady-*) is non-Semitic and may be a cognate to the later term, *māday,* from which Medes is derived. In the Septuagint, the word is found as Madian or Madiam. The biblical Midianites were linguistically and culturally an Arab people associated with camel (q.v.) nomadism, caravan (q.v.) trading and shepherding (see NOMADS; BEDOUIN; ARABS). Most Midianite names mentioned in the Hebrew Bible occur also in pre-Islamic Arabic inscriptions (see EPIGRAPHY AND THE QURʾĀN; PRE-ISLAMIC ARABIA AND THE QURʾĀN), with the Midianite priest and father-in-law of Moses (q.v.), *Yitro* (Eng. Jethro), also rendered as *Yeter* (orig. Ar. *Yatru?; Exod* 3:1; 4:18; 18:1, 2, 5, 6, 12, etc.), retaining the old Arabic nominative case ending which is rare in Hebrew names (cf. the Ar. *Geshem/Gashmu* in *Neh* 2:19; 6:1, 2, 6). Archaeological evidence in the northern Ḥijāz east of ʿAqaba (see GEOGRAPHY) seems to confirm biblical portrayals of Midian/Madyan as an important political entity that emerged in that vicinity during the thirteenth century B.C.E. Midian successfully projected its political and military power over Israelites, Moabites and other peoples in areas corresponding to today's Jordan, Israel and Palestine. The name is attested in Greek and Latin sources and turns up well into the period of Islam's emergence in the seventh century C.E., although the powerful Midianite polity may have died out as early as the tenth century B.C.E. Later biblical references seem to be geographical or genealogical in nature rather than political.

Arab geographers generally locate Midian in the northern Ḥijāz west of Tabūk, although a variant tradition associates it with Kafr Manda near Tiberias, close to where the Druze (q.v.) today locate the grave of their major prophet, Shuʿayb (q.v.).

In the Qurʾān, the people of Midian are one of the ancient but no longer existing peoples *(al-umam al-khāliya),* destroyed because they refused to listen to the warnings of their divinely-sent prophets (see PROPHETS AND PROPHETHOOD; PUNISHMENT STORIES; WARNING). The Qurʾān echoes the biblical portrayal of Midianite trading in its criticism of their dishonesty in commercial transactions (Q 7:85; 11:84; possibly also Q 11:95; see ECONOMICS; WEIGHTS AND MEASURES). The name Madyan, which occurs in the Qurʾān ten times, refers either to a geographical place to which Moses fled (Q 20:40; 28:22-3) or to a people or folk to whom the prophet Shuʿayb was sent (Q 7:85-93; 9:70; 11:84-95; 22:44; 29:36-7). The former set of references parallels the biblical Midian of Exodus while the latter most likely reflects indigenous pre-Islamic Arabian tradition (see MYTHS AND LEGENDS IN THE QURʾĀN). The two separate trajectories of traditional lore are joined in the Qurʾān because of their common reference to Midian. That connection became embellished in the later exegetical tradition where the prophet Shuʿayb becomes Moses' father-in-law (Ṭabarī, *Taʾrīkh,* i, 443; id., *History,* iii, 30-1; Thaʿlabī, *Qiṣaṣ,* 145, 154; Kisāʾī, *Qiṣaṣ,* 191, 207-8), and the Midianites are the people whom King Saul (q.v.) was commanded to proscribe (Ṭabarī, *Taʾrīkh,* i, 561; id., *History,* iii, 141-2; cf. 1 *Sam* 15), etc.

The qurʾānic Midianites are also closely connected with the "people of the tanglewood" (or "thicket," *aṣḥāb al-ayka,* Q 15:78-9; 38:13; 50:14; see PEOPLE OF THE THICKET). Shuʿayb is sent to both (Q 26:176-89) and both also exhibit dishonest trading practices. Beeston (The 'Men') suggests that both qurʾānic designations refer to the same group, who are designated either by their ethnic or kinship (q.v.) identity as Midianites or by their religious association with the vegetation deity, *dhū l-sharā*

(Greek Dusares) as the "people of the tanglewood." The latter association must of course be much later than the probable historical dating for the strong Midianite polity of the early Iron Age. Thus the long-lived legend of the ancient Midianites may have been conflated with the great Nabatean civilization that flourished and then died out in the general vicinity a millennium later.

Reuven Firestone

Bibliography
Primary: Kisāʾī, *Qiṣaṣ;* Ṭabarī, *The history of al-Ṭabarī. iii. The children of Israel,* trans. W.M. Brinner, Albany 1991, 30-1; id., *Tafsīr,* Beirut 1984; id., *Taʾrīkh,* ed. De Goeje; Thaʿlabī, *Qiṣaṣ,* Beirut n.d.; Yāqūt, *Buldān,* Beirut 1990, v, 92.
Secondary: A.F.L. Beeston, The 'Men of the Tanglewood' in the Qurʾān, in *JSS* 13 (1968), 253-5; C.E. Bosworth, The qurʾānic prophet Shuʿayb and Ibn Taimiyya's epistle concerning him, in *Muséon* 87 (1974), 425-40; J. Horovitz, *Jewish proper names and derivatives in the Koran,* Hildesheim 1925, 9-10; id., *KU,* 93-4 *(aṣḥāb al-ayka);* G. Mendenhall, *Studies in the history of Arabia,* Riyadh 1984, 137-45; P. Parr, Contacts between northwest Arabia and Jordan in the Late Bronze and Iron Ages, in H. Hadidi (ed.), *Studies in the history and archaeology of Jordan,* Amman 1982-, i, 127-33; A. Sprenger, *Die alte Geographie Arabiens,* Bern 1875, 150, 294-5 n. 1.

Miḥrab

see QIBLA; ART AND ARCHITECTURE AND THE QURʾĀN; MOSQUE

Milk

Fluid secreted from the mammary glands of female mammals for the nourishment of their young. The two verses in which the Arabic word for milk, *laban,* occurs are Q 16:66 and 47:15. They have distinct contextual references, though they share the sense of belonging to the signs (q.v.) of God's bounty (see BLESSING) toward humankind and of being a reward for believers' acknowledgment of the divine economy (see BELIEF AND UNBELIEF; REWARD AND PUNISHMENT). The first verse refers to terrestrial existence. "In cattle (see ANIMAL LIFE) too you have a worthy lesson. We give you to drink of that which is in their bellies… pure milk, pleasant for those who drink it" (see FOOD AND DRINK). The second verse is one of the many descriptions of the afterlife (see ESCHATOLOGY). "The likeness of paradise (q.v.) which the righteous have been promised. There shall flow in it rivers of purest water (q.v.), and rivers of milk forever fresh; rivers of wine (q.v.; see also INTOXICANTS) delectable to those who drink it and rivers of clearest honey" (q.v.). The famous ḥadīth scholar and historian al-Dhahabī (d. 748/1348) noted in his work on prophetic medicine (see MEDICINE AND THE QURʾĀN) that the best fresh milk is human milk drunk directly from the breast (see LACTATION; WET-NURSING). He further observed that all milk in time loses its freshness and becomes sour; hence God described the milk of paradise as "forever fresh."

In traditions reported by Abū Dāwūd (d. 275/889) and al-Tirmidhī (d. ca. 270/883-4) from Ibn ʿAbbās (d. 68/686-8), the Prophet said that whomever God has given milk should bless God saying, "'May he give us more,' for I know of no food or drink to replace it." Another story, found in the six so-called canonical collections of traditions (see ḤADĪTH AND THE QURʾĀN) from the Companion Anas (d. 91-3/710-12; see COMPANIONS OF THE PROPHET), recalls some people suffering from a stomach disorder for which the Prophet recommended they drink the milk and urine of she-camels, a remedy that cured their ailment (see ILLNESS AND HEALTH). The same remedy is found unattributed in the early compendium by Ibn Ḥabīb (d. 238/853) of medical folklore and Galenic data and likely belongs to traditional Arab practice (see PRE-ISLAMIC ARABIA AND THE QUR'ĀN). Of the various kinds of milk available, sheep, goat, donkey, buffalo, camel, and cow's milk appear especially favored next to that of the human breast. Ibn Ḥabīb also preserves a statement he attributes to the Prophet in which the milk of cows is described as a marvel, their butter as a remedy and their meat as a medicine. In a tradition related by al-Nasāʾī (d. 303/915) from Ibn Masʿūd (d. 32/652-3), the Prophet said, "God did not bring down any disease without also creating a remedy for it; so drink the milk of cows, for they feed off all kinds of plants." This implied that there were different milks for different ailments to which Ibn Ḥabīb added the detail that owing to this characteristic of cow's milk, it was a cure for every ailment except senility and old age *(haram)*.

The only cautionary note concerning milk in general is found in a tradition preserved by al-Bukhārī (c. 256/870) and Muslim (d. ca. 261/875) from Ibn ʿAbbās that the fat of milk was bad for anyone with a fever or headache owing to the swiftness with which the milk is turned into bile. It is possible that this reflects the traditional notion, expressed by al-Ḥārith b. Kalada (d. 13/634-5), that milk is good for pains so long as it is drunk with the fat removed *(laban makhīḍ)*. Finally, an interesting "ethnographic" item has been passed down by Abū Hurayra (d. ca. 58/678) — found in both al-Bukhārī and Muslim — concerning women of the Children of Israel (q.v.; Banū Isrāʾīl) who lost their fear of mice because the tiny rodent was believed to drink goat's milk but would not touch camel's milk, and Jews neither ate camel (q.v.) meat nor drank its milk (see JEWS AND JUDAISM; FORBIDDEN; LAWFUL AND UNLAWFUL).

David Waines

Bibliography
Primary: al-Dhahabī, Shams al-Dīn Muḥammad, *al-Ṭibb al-nabawī*, Cairo n.d.; Ibn Ḥabīb, ʿAbd al-Malik, *Mukhtaṣar fī l-ṭibb (Compendio de medicina)*, ed. and trans. C. Alvarez de Morales and F. Girón Irueste, Madrid 1992; M. Marín and D. Waines (eds.), *Kanz al-fawāʾid fī tanwīʿ al-mawāʾid*, Beirut/Stuttgart 1993.
Secondary: I. Perho, *The Prophet's medicine. A creation of the Muslim traditionalist scholars*, Helsinki 1995.

Miracles

Supernatural intervention in the life of human beings. When defined as such, miracles are present in the Qurʾān in a threefold sense: in sacred history, in connection with Muḥammad himself and in relation to revelation. Although an almost indispensable attribute of prophecy, Muḥammad was not thought to have been granted any miracles in the traditional sense as they were not, *ipso facto*, sufficient to convince unbelievers (see PROOF; BELIEF AND UNBELIEF). In the Qurʾān, the concept of miracle takes on a cosmological and eschatological dimension (see COSMOLOGY; ESCHATOLOGY), and the supreme miracle is finally identified with the Qurʾān itself: divine speech in human language (see WORD OF GOD). The threefold sense of the miracle corresponds to the three meanings of the word *āya* (pl. *āyāt)*, a qurʾānic term which indicates the "verses" (q.v.) of the book (q.v.), as well as the "miracle" of it and the "signs" (q.v.), particularly those of creation (q.v.). The term *āya* is often followed or replaced by its nominalized qualifier, *bayyina* (pl. *bayyināt*), i.e. "a clear sign," a designation which underlines the relation between miracles and the Qurʾān, which is itself qualified by *bayān*, ("clear, evident speech"). At times the sense of astonishment and wonder which the concept of "miracle" evokes may be rediscovered in the term *ʿajab*, a word used with regard to the attitude of humans, positive or negative, when faced with the supernatural or revelation (see REVELATION AND INSPIRATION; MARVELS).

Miracles in sacred history

There are few biblical or Arab prophets (see PROPHETS AND PROPHETHOOD) in whose stories (see NARRATIVES) miracles do not play a part. Adam (see ADAM AND EVE) had no one to convince and was not favored by a single miracle, nor did he perform any. This shows that, first and foremost, the miracle is intended, if not to convince, then at least to confute unbelievers who deny the truthfulness of a given prophet (see LIE). The oven *(tannūr)* out of which the water burst and announced the flood is an appropriate sign for Noah (q.v.; Q 11:40; 23:27). Hūd (q.v.), the prophet of the ʿĀd (q.v.), had no particular sign, thus prefiguring Muḥammad. To his people who rebuked him for not producing a miracle *(bayyina)* he answered: "Are you surprised that a message *(dhikr)* has come to you from your lord (q.v.), through a man of your own people, to warn you?" (Q 7:69; see WARNER). In contrast, the mission of Ṣāliḥ (q.v.) was confirmed by a she-camel with its young appearing miraculously from a mountain. By cutting the she-camel's hamstrings, the prophet's opponents brought forth their punishment (Q 7:73; 11:64; 54:27-9; 91:11-5; see PUNISHMENT STORIES; CHASTISEMENT AND PUNISHMENT). For these three peoples, divine punishment arrived in the form of a sudden, natural catastrophe.

The story of Abraham (q.v.) is marked by several miracles. God commands the blazing fire (q.v.) into which he was thrown to become "coolness and a means of safety" (Q 21:69). A sacrificial animal is sent to replace his son who was about to be killed (Q 37:107; see SACRIFICE; CONSECRATION OF ANIMALS). In some of the prophet narratives, it is worth noting that the miraculous apparition may simultaneously bring life and death (Q 11:69-73; 15:51-6; 37:112): angels (see ANGEL) announce the birth of Isaac (q.v.) at the same time as the punishment of Lot's (q.v.) people. God's insistence on the total destruction of the city by a cry, a shower of rocks or a complete upending emphasizes dramatically the miracle of divine protection afforded to Lot and his family (Q 11:81; 54:37). The list of peoples annihilated is rounded off by the "Companions of the Wood" *(aṣḥāb al-ayka,* see PEOPLE OF THE THICKET), identified as the Midianites (see MIDIAN) and destroyed either by a cry or by an earthquake, although their prophet Shuʿayb (q.v.) was still not favored with a particular miracle (cf. Q 7:88; 11:84, 94; 15:83; 29:36).

Moses (q.v.), the most frequently mentioned prophet in the Qurʾān, is one with a twofold mission, to both Pharaoh (q.v.) and the Children of Israel (q.v.). He is also accompanied by the greatest number of miraculous events of all of the qurʾānic prophets. Rescued from the waters, spared from the massacre of the male infants and restored to his mother as a result of divine protection (q.v.; Q 20:37-41; 28:7-13), God speaks to him from the "bush." It is then that he receives the two signs of his mission: the staff (see ROD), which becomes a serpent when it is cast down before the magicians but regains its normal shape when held again, and his hand, which is white, but not infected by leprosy. These signs were intended to persuade Pharaoh to allow the Children of Israel to leave Egypt (q.v.). Only the magicians (see MAGIC) are convinced by the miracle of the staff, which devours their own staffs when transformed into snakes (Q 7:115-26; 20:65-76; 26:38-51). This story shows the difference, despite appearances, between miracles and magic, between divine intervention and human manipulation. Only the eyes of faith (q.v.), however, can see this difference. This story also shows the soteriological function of the miracle: when they behold this, the magicians become believers and prefer the world to come, declaring that they are ready to face the earthly punishment of Pharaoh. There is also a clear parallel with the qur'ānic term for its revelations — the *āyāt* — considered as magic by the Quraysh (q.v.). Pharaoh deals with magical portents (Q 27:12), the signs called *āyāt bayyināt* (Q 17:101) or *āyāt mufaṣṣalāt*, all of which are expressions that could be applied to the revelations that Muḥammad receives (cf. Q 11:1; 41:3, etc.).

Among the "nine" signs of Moses there are five plagues of Egypt (rather than the biblical ten). They are qualified as *mubṣira* or *baṣā'ir* because they should awaken inner meditation in those for whom they are destined, the audience and readers of the story. The confrontation between Moses and Pharaoh is brought to a close by the destruction wrought in the crossing of the Red Sea (e.g. Q 20:77-8; 26:60-8), an episode often recounted in the tales of peoples who have been destroyed. The miracles with which the Children of Israel are favored in the Sinai (q.v.) desert are both a testimony to their being a chosen people (see ELECTION) and an adverting to the perils of straying (see ASTRAY; ERROR): the manna (see FOOD AND DRINK) and the quails, the protective cloud (see SECHINA), the twelve springs (see SPRINGS AND FOUNTAINS) which Moses makes gush forth when he strikes the rock with his staff (Q 2:57; 7:160; 20:80). Should we consider as miraculous the revelation of God on the mountain, a vision which terrified Moses (Q 7:143), the "resurrection" of the Children of Israel, struck down because they demanded to see God (Q 2:55), the mountain rising in front of them at the time of the covenant (q.v.; Q 2:63, 93; 4:154) or the tablets given to Moses on Mount Sinai (Q 7:145; see COMMANDMENTS)? In all these instances, the miracle is always closely related to eschatology and revelation.

Miracle and revelation are also clearly distinguished from their opposites, as in the episode of the golden calf (see CALF OF GOLD), where both occur simultaneously. The personage that the Qur'ān calls al-Sāmirī brings the statue to life by throwing onto it a handful of earth which has been touched by the shoe of Gabriel's (q.v.) horse. This individual thus possesses certain knowledge (see KNOWLEDGE AND LEARNING) of the life-giving power of something bearing the mark of the spirit (q.v.; see also HOLY SPIRIT). By appropriating for himself miraculous power, however, contrary to the will of God and without the knowledge of the prophet, he merely works an "anti-miracle" and leads men astray (Q 20:87-8, 96). Likewise the case of Korah (q.v.; Qārūn), who claims to owe his wealth "to a knowledge" he possesses, of which he boasts (see BOAST). In the end he is swallowed up by the earth, just as Pharaoh is swallowed up by the waves (Q 28:76-81).

The story of the cow which Moses commands the Children of Israel to sacrifice so that a murder (q.v.) victim, touched by a part of the animal, may come back to life to identify his murderer, is clearly meant as a symbol of resurrection (q.v.). It should be understood to have an inner meaning, as it shows the hardening of hearts (see HEART), a theme that is touched upon immediately afterwards (Q 2:67-74). The fish which comes back to life "at the meeting of the two seas" (see BARZAKH) leaps from the basket and "makes its way back into the sea in an amazing manner *('ajab)*" in order to show Moses and his servant that they have reached the place where they must stop, clearly assumes a similar meaning (Q 18:63). It may be observed that the term *'ajab* is spoken not by the prophet, but by his young servant. In the remainder of the story, the mysterious servant, traditionally called al-Khaḍir (see KHAḌIR/KHIḌR), whose disciple Moses becomes at one point, does not perform any miracles as such; Moses does not need them. By his presence at events, he merely points out to Moses the knowledge that God has given him as a gift. Here the miracle is quite simply the knowledge given to certain men, inspired directly by God, linking the miraculous directly to revelation (Q 18:62-82).

In Q 2 (Sūrat al-Baqara, "The Cow"), the Qurʾān again retells a biblical story (see SCRIPTURE AND THE QURʾĀN), with the accession of Saul (q.v.; Ṭālūt) to the throne confirmed by a miraculous sign: the return of the ark (q.v.) of the covenant, carried by angels (Q 2:248). His successors, David (q.v.) and Solomon (q.v.), are also granted miraculous powers: the former is given expertise with iron (see METALS AND MINERALS) and the mountains glorify God (see GLORIFICATION OF GOD; LAUDATION) with him; the demons (see DEVIL), jinn (q.v.) and winds (see AIR AND WIND) obey the latter (Q 34:10-3; 38:36-9) and he is taught the "language of the birds" (Q 27:16; see ANIMAL LIFE). Endowed with these powers by virtue of their position, both David and Solomon are tested in the exercise of their kingship by supernatural intervention (see KINGS AND RULERS). Two angels appear before David in his private chamber as litigants to remind him of his sin with regard to his general, and a "body" is placed on Solomon's throne to remind him that he is only king by divine delegation (Q 38:21-4, 34). Solomon does likewise with the Queen of Sheba (see BILQĪS) by having her throne moved. It is not Solomon himself who carries out this miraculous deed, but one of his companions, traditionally named as Āṣaf b. Barakhyā. Endowed with a "certain knowledge of the book," he is more powerful than the jinn. In this story, the miracle is not performed by the prophet, who simply thanks God, but by a man acting on his authority (q.v.) and in accordance with revelation (Q 27:40). Theologians and Ṣūfīs were later to find in this story the model for the miracles of the saints as a continuation of those of the prophets (see ṢŪFISM AND THE QURʾĀN).

The Qurʾān also mentions the miraculous cure of Job (Q 38:42-4) as well as the incident in which Jonah, having been swallowed by the whale, is cast up on land where there is the plant (*yaqṭīn*, a squash or something similar) with which God covers him to protect him from the sun (Q 37:139-46). In these two instances, the miracles of the cure and the protection are examples of the grace reserved for those who have been chosen after being put to the test (see TRIAL).

As was the case with Isaac (q.v.), the births of the last two prophets of the Children of Israel, John (see JOHN THE BAPTIST) and Jesus (q.v.), are announced, respectively, to Zechariah (q.v.) and Mary (q.v.) by angels (Q 3:39 and Q 3:45-6) or directly by God and the spirit (Q 19:7, 17-21). At the time of the birth of Jesus, Mary, who miraculously receives sustenance in Zechariah's chapel in the temple (Q 3:37), has to shake the trunk of a withered palm tree to have fresh dates fall from it, while underneath runs a stream (according to one meaning of *sarī*, Q 19:24-5). Jesus speaks from the cradle (Q 19:29-30) and, as the human manifestation of the creative power of the word *(kun)*, is constantly performing miracles. He proclaims to his people: "I bring you a sign/miracle on behalf of your lord; I will make for you a bird from clay with God's permission *(bi-idhni llāh)*, I will cure the blind and the leper, I will resurrect the dead (see DEATH AND THE DEAD) and I will tell you what you eat and what you store in your homes. This will be a sign for you if you are believers" (Q 3:49; also Q 5:110). This passage, while stressing the specific calling of Jesus, also defines the conditions and the limits of the miracle: the prophet does not act on his own accord, and the miracle is only useful to someone who believes; likewise, the verses of the book are only understood by those who recognize the truth (q.v.) that is in them. The cognitive purpose of the miracle is made clear in the story of the food from heaven (*māʾida*, see TABLE), which Jesus asks God to send down at the request of the apostles (see APOSTLE). He answers their request by praying that this may be a commemoration (*ʿīd*) and a sign (*āya*), but he first of all questions their faith. The disciples justify themselves by saying that they wanted peace of mind (Q 5:113-4). Jesus leaves this world as miraculously as he entered it because he is taken up by God (Q 4:158).

Abraham does likewise. When he has asked God to let him see the resurrection of the dead, the response is: "Don't you believe?" Next he is commanded to sacrifice four birds, cut them up and scatter them. When he summons them, the birds are made whole again and restored to life (Q 2:260). Here, the miracle involves contemplation of the mystery; it has the sole function of elevating the intellect (q.v.) to a different plane of understanding, bringing the peace, that is, of heartfelt certainty.

Neither the distinction between the miracles of the prophets and those of the saints, nor the respective terms used to describe them (*muʿjizāt, karāmāt*) are from the Qurʾān. Among non-prophetic miracles, the Qurʾān mentions some *āyāt* (Q 18:9, 17) with regard to the Men of the Cave (q.v.). Likewise, the man who wonders about resurrection and whom God makes die and then resurrects one hundred years later is identified variously as Ezra (q.v.; ʿUzayr), as al-Khaḍir, or as someone who does not believe in resurrection (Q 2:259). The miracle is an exemplum and is convincing when God wishes it to be.

Prophetic and saintly miracles in extra-qurʾānic literature

Theological treatises ascribe a general pattern of development to prophetic miracles, as evidence of prophecy and in order to distinguish them from the miracles of the saints (*karāmāt*). For Ashʿarī and Ṣūfī writers (see THEOLOGY AND THE QURʾĀN), the stories in the Qurʾān about individuals who are not prophets, such as Mary, the Men of the Cave, al-Khaḍir or Āṣaf b. Barakhyā, serve as proof of the existence of miracles by the saints. ʿAbd al-Qāhir al-Baghdādī (d. 429/1037) describes how miracles are an indispensable part of prophecy and sets out the miracles of the main prophets in the Qurʾān up to Muḥammad (cf. his *Uṣūl al-dīn*, 169-85). In his work on the distinction between prophetic and saintly miracles (*Kitāb al-Bayān ʿan al-farq bayna l-muʿjizāt wa-l-karāmāt wa-l-ḥiyal wa-l-kahāna wa-l-siḥr wa-l-nāranjāt*), al-Bāqillānī (d. 403/1013) discusses theological controversies on the subject in an abstract manner, without recounting the stories of the miracles. The same applies to al-Juwaynī (d. 478/1085) who, on the subject of prophecy, devotes several passages to prophetic miracles, without giving a single example from the Qurʾān (cf. *al-Irshād*, 178-205 [Ar. text], Fr. trans. 266-305). This is also the case with Qāḍī ʿAbd al-Jabbār (d. 415/1025; cf. *al-Mughnī*, vol. xv *al-Tanabbuʾāt wa-l-muʿjizāt*).

Theologians are, however, inclined to follow the Qurʾān by linking the question of miracles (*muʿjizāt*) with the insuperable nature of the text of the Qurʾān (*iʿjāz*), the main proof of its divine origin (cf. Antes, *Prophetenwunder*, 21-8; Gimaret, *La doctrine d'al-Ashʿarī*, 459-66). In his general study of Islamic dogma, Hermann Stieglecker sets out the positions of Sunnī theologians regarding miracles and then devotes a long passage to the prophetic figures of Islam. His description of Muḥammad's life is followed by an extensive discussion of the miraculous nature of the Qurʾān and the subject of its inimitability (q.v.; *iʿjāz;* cf. *Die Glaubenslehren des Islams,* 161-9, 189-338, 372-408, and under the index entries Wunder, Wundercharakter des Qurʾān). Richard Grämlich does likewise in his study of the miracles of the saints. His presentation makes clear, in particular, the twofold aspects of divine power and divine favor in miracles and the distinction made by Ṣūfīs and theologians between *muʿjizāt* and *karāmāt.* He also discusses miracles in the Qurʾān that are not prophetic (cf. *Die Wunder der Freunde Gottes,* 16-81; on the miracles in the Qurʾān as models for the miracles of the saints, see D. Gril, Les fondements scripturaires).

Supernatural intervention in sacred history thus occurs in many forms. The miracle shows either divine omnipotence (see POWER AND IMPOTENCE) — with its fate of punishment and destruction, whether of peoples or individuals — or (divine) favor, bestowed above all on the prophets or others who have been chosen. Angels, the messengers (see MESSENGER) of the unseen (see HIDDEN AND THE HIDDEN), are often its heralds or its vehicle. The favor (see GRACE; BLESSING) is often portrayed as sustenance (q.v.) or protection (q.v.). The miraculous powers which the prophets or their followers receive may only be exercised with divine permission. Once this is granted, nothing can prevent their effectiveness; it is this, among other things, which sets them apart from magic. The miracles of resurrection, demonstrations of favor and omnipotence are intended to enable perception of divine action and to make a proclamation of the advent of the world to come. The miracle shares this eschatological function with revelation. The prophetology and cosmological teaching undergirding these stories in the Qurʾān demonstrates to us the small role of the miracle that it permitted to its very first auditor, Muḥammad himself.

The Prophet and miracles

While the attitude of earlier prophets, especially their endurance when put to the test is constantly recalled to Muḥammad as a model to follow and a source of comfort, the miracles which served to confirm and authenticate their missions are denied him. In more than one passage of the Qurʾān we find him vainly asking God for a sign to convince his people: "If you could wish for a passage opening into the ground or a ladder up to the sky in order to give them a sign! If God had wanted to he would have gathered them all on guidance. Therefore do not be among those who are ignorant" (Q 6:36; see IGNORANCE). Elsewhere are listed miracles sought by the Prophet: the simple descent (from heaven) of a book or an angel (Q 6:7-8), the outpouring of a spring or a stream in a garden, a downpour from the skies, a house full of treasure, and his being transported to heaven (Q 17:90-3). This last request appears in the sūra that begins with a reference to the journey by night (see ASCENSION). This shows that "the greatest signs" that the Prophet must contemplate during the course of his ascension are intended for him rather than for the unbelievers. The Qurʾān thus explains the relative pointlessness of miracles: since God has not given faith to the unbeliever, he is incapable of belief (see FREEDOM AND PREDESTINATION). Furthermore the refusal of divine signs and the coming of angels risks provoking divine punishment (e.g. Q 25:20-2). Like others before him, Muḥammad is accused of untruthfulness and magic (Q 54:2; 74:24, etc.) and his people challenge him to bring about the punishment that he proclaims. Confronted by such accusations, he is reminded of the pointlessness of miracles. Instead of this he must assert his own human nature (see IMPECCABILITY) and repudiate all miraculous power (e.g. Q 6:50), but proclaim instead the revealed character of his inspiration and actions. This abolition of miracles is only an apparent contradiction of the prophetic models set forth as examples for him. The humanity and the weakness of other prophets, especially at the time of the miracles, receive great emphasis: the fear of Abraham during the visit of the angels (Q 51:28) or the fear of Moses confronting the magicians (Q 20:67). Jesus, as we have seen, only performed miracles with divine sanction (Q 3:49, 79; 13:38).

Nonetheless, the miracle is not completely absent from references to the life of the Prophet and his Companions (see COMPANIONS OF THE PROPHET). Angels intervene to help believers at Badr (q.v.) and Ḥunayn (q.v.; Q 3:124-6; 8:9-13; 9:25-6). Although the Qurʾān does describe a magical action of the Prophet (*ramā,* i.e. his throwing of stones in the face of the enemy at Badr, thus, according to tradition, causing the defeat of the Quraysh), it immediately denies the efficacy of this act, just as it lays bare the actions of the believers: "You have not killed them; it is God who has killed them, you did not advance, when you advanced; God advanced (*ramā*)..." (Q 8:17). For the majority of religious commentators (see EXEGESIS OF THE QURʾĀN: CLASSICAL AND MEDIEVAL), the splitting of the moon (q.v.) mentioned at the beginning of Q 54 (Sūrat al-Qamar, "The Moon") is indeed a miracle received by the Prophet to convince the Quraysh: "The hour is approaching and the moon is split asunder. But if they see a sign, they turn away or say: transient magic!" (Q 54:1-2). These verses, as we can see, lay particular stress upon the meaning of the sign and the charge of magic, and thus upon the pointlessness of the miracle for the unbelievers. Muḥammad does not perform miracles himself: this makes the divine act appear all the more striking, and indicates that the signification of the miracles of earlier prophets may be rediscovered in the revealed book and its verses and signs.

Miracles and revelation

At the same time as miracles are refused to the Prophet, the gauntlet is thrown down to jinn and men to produce a similar book or even ten sūras (Q 17:88; 11:12-3); elsewhere, the challenge is to produce a single sūra (Q 2:23; 10:38; see PROVOCATION). These passages have led theologians to say that the miracles of the Prophet are characterized by challenge *(taḥaddin),* and to elaborate the doctrine of the inimitable nature of the Qurʾān *(iʿjāz).* As a miracle is a display of omnipotence as well as of divine favor and mystery, the Qurʾān calls upon the Prophet and his followers to recognize its "miraculous" nature from the evidence of its signs and verses: "But it [the Qurʾān] provides clear signs *(āyāt bayyināt)* in the breasts of those who have received knowledge. Only the unjust dispute our signs; they say, why are [miraculous] signs not sent down to him by his lord. Answer, the signs are close to *(ʿinda)* God and I am only one who gives a clear warning" (Q 29:49-50; see also Q 6:109). On the one hand, the Qurʾān contains all the signs and nothing has been omitted from it (cf. Q 6:37-8; 18:54); on the other, the signs are close to *(ʿinda)* God, as well as "in the breasts." The miracle of the Qurʾān is therefore of the interior kind. The miracle, however, is also in creation, since it reveals in its many signs, which the Qurʾān has enumerated in a great number of verses, the action and unity of God. In more than one passage, the response to a request for a miracle by the Prophet is a call to contemplate the signs of creation (e.g. Q 10:20 f.; 13:7 f.; see NATURE AS SIGNS). These signs are often symbols of resurrection just as the miracle foreshadows the world beyond, whether via the annihilation of the unjust or by the contemplation of the other world, where the extraordinary is ordinary (see REWARD AND PUNISHMENT). In addition to this traditional view of the miracle of the Qurʾān, it should also be noted that one trend in modern qurʾānic exegesis is the examination of the Qurʾān for predictions of the scientific discoveries of recent times — the so-called *tafsīr ʿilmī*. For more on this topic, see EXEGESIS OF THE QURʾĀN: EARLY MODERN AND CONTEMPORARY; SCIENCE AND THE QURʾĀN.

But for the person who knows how to read the world, the ordinary signs of earthly life reveal the spiritual realm, just as the multiplication of a grain seven hundredfold foretells the reward of almsgivers (see ALMSGIVING) in the next world (Q 2:261). This is why the Qurʾān is astonished at the astonishment of men who have difficulty believing that a divine reminder should be given to them via a human intermediary. Thus prophecy and revelation are indeed "the miracle" in the true meaning of the word (Q 7:63, 69; 10:2; cf. 38:4-5; 50:2). Jinn describe the Qurʾān as "marvelous" *(ʿajab)* to indicate the difference between their inspiration and that of prophecy. In the same way, unbelievers marvel at resurrection while it constantly takes place before their eyes (Q 13:5). Granted or denied, the miracle is indeed at the center of qurʾānic discourse, of the prophetology, of the cosmology and of the eschatology of the sacred text.

Denis Gril

Bibliography

Primary (General histories, the "stories of the prophets" literature and the majority of commentaries on the verses cited above contain details of the miracles in the Qurʾān and the individuals associated with them. The following is only a partial list of these works.): ʿAbd al-Jabbār, *al-Mughnī*. xv. *al-Tanabbuʾāt wa-l-muʿjizāt*, ed. M. al-Khuḍayrī and M. Qāsim, Cairo 1965; al-Baghdādī, ʿAbd al-Qāhir, *Uṣūl al-dīn*, Istanbul 1928, 169-85; Bāqillānī, *Kitāb al-Bayān ʿan al-farq bayna l-muʿjizāt wa-l-karāmāt wa-l-ḥiyal wa-l-kihāna wa-l-siḥr wa-l-nāranjāt*, ed. R.J. McCarthy, Beirut 1958; Ibn Kathīr, *Bidāya;* al-Juwaynī, ʿAbd al-Malik, *al-Irshād*, ed. and Fr. trans. J.-D. Luciani, Paris 1938; Ṭabarī, *Taʾrīkh;* Thaʿlabī, *Qiṣaṣ;* ed. M.A. Jād al-Mawlā, *Qiṣaṣ al-Qurʾān*, Beirut 1985 (a modern edition of this work).

Secondary: T. Andrae, *Die person Muhammeds in lehre und glauben seiner gemeinde*, Stockholm 1918, 23-91 (the legend of the Prophet), 92-123 (the miracles of the Prophet in theology); P. Antes, *Prophetenwunder in der Asʿarīya bis al-Ghazālī*, Freiburg 1970, 21-8; Abū ʿAbd al-Raḥmān, M. ʿAṭiyya, *al-Muʿjizāt wa-l-ḥujaj al-bayyināt fī l-radd ʿalā munkirihā*, Beirut 1995 (modern Muslim discussion); D. Gimaret, *La doctrine d'al-Ashʿarī*, Paris 1990, 459-66; Richard Grämlich, *Die Wunder der Freunde Gottes*, Wiesbaden 1987, 16-81; D. Gril, Les fondements scripturaires du miracle en islam, in D. Aigle (ed.), *Miracle et karāma. Hagiographies médiévales comparées*, Turnhout 2000, 237-49; M.ʿA. Khafājī, *al-Qurʾān muʿjizat al-ʿuṣūr*, Cairo 1988 (an example of modern Muslim scholarship on the miraculous nature of the Qurʾān); Saʿīd Nūrsī, *Dhū l-fiqār fī l-muʿjizāt al-qurʾāniyya wa-l-muʿjizāt al-aḥmadiyya*, Beirut 1974 (modern Muslim discussion); M.M. al-Shaʿrāwī, *Muʿjizat al-Qurʾān*, Cairo 1978 (another example of the array of modern Muslim scholarship on this topic); B.A. Siddiqi, *Modern trends in tafsir literature. Miracles*, Lahore 1988 (modern Muslim interpretation of miracles in the Qurʾān); H. Stieglecker, *Die Glaubenslehren des Islams*, Vienna 1962, 161-9, 189-338, 372-408, and under the index entries Wunder, Wundercharakter des Qurʾān.

Mischief see CORRUPTION

Misery see JOY AND MISERY

Misguidance see FREEDOM AND PREDESTINATION; ASTRAY; ERROR; GUIDANCE

Mission see PROPHETS AND PROPHETHOOD

Mīthāq see COVENANT

Mockery

Insulting or contemptuous action or speech. Mockery *(h-z-ʾ, s-kh-r)* figures regularly in the Qurʾān. The nouns and verb forms derived from *h-z-ʾ* appear forty-three times, those derived from *s-kh-r* fifteen times. Both are used synonymously as is attested by Q 6:10 and Q 21:41. Mockery in the Qurʾān usually expresses disbelief (see BELIEF AND UNBELIEF) in God and is thus closely linked with the subject of disbelieving laughter (q.v.). It does so in a more or less formulaic way and in a manner that underlines the assumed universality of Muḥammad's prophetic experience: God's prophets are derided (*wa-mā yaʾtīhim min rasūlin illā kānū bihi yastahziʾūna*, "No messenger [q.v.] came to them whom they did not mock"; Q 15:11; also Q 36:30; 43:7; see PROPHETS AND PROPHETHOOD). The formula *ittakhadha huzuwan*, "He took in mockery," typically describes God's signs (q.v.) and his messengers as being the objects of mockery (e.g. Q 2:231; 18:56, 106; 21:36; 25:41; 31:6; 43:35; 45:9). In Q 5:57-8, it is the believers' religion (q.v.) and prayer (q.v.) that become the objects of mockery and playful joking *(huzuwan wa-laʿiban)*. Only once do the unbelievers suspect their prophet Moses (q.v.) of mocking them (Q 2:67) — as if their roles were reversed.

The Qurʾān counters such ridicule with threats of past and future revenge (see VENGEANCE): God will punish the mockers with hell (see HELL AND HELLFIRE) at the last judgment (q.v.) and — lest this should not impress the unbelievers — has already done so before in specific cases (see PUNISHMENT STORIES; REWARD AND PUNISHMENT). The most common formula for this is the strangely suggestive phrase *wa-ḥāqa bihim mā kānū bihi yastahziʾūna*, "They shall be/were encompassed by that at which they mocked" (future: Q 11:8; 39:49; 45:33; past: Q 16:34; 40:83; 46:26). A variant substitutes *wa-ḥāqa bihim mā…* with *fa-sawfa yatīhim anbāʾu mā…* "News (q.v.) shall reach them of that…" (Q 6:5; cf. 26:6), with *kadhdhabū bi-l-ḥaqq*, "They denied the truth (q.v.)," as the preceding misdemeanor (see LIE). The complete argument runs thus: "Messengers indeed were mocked *(h-z-ʾ)* before you. Then those that scoffed at them *(s-kh-r)* were encompassed by that at which they mocked *(h-z-ʾ)*" (Q 6:10; 21:41). The idea of retaliation (q.v.) is best expressed in instances of exact reversal: God will mock the mocking hypocrites (see HYPOCRITES AND HYPOCRISY) and whoever ridicules the believers (Q 2:15; 9:79). A prophet like Noah (q.v.) can say the same: "If you scoff at us we shall surely scoff at you as you scoff now!" (Q 11:38) — God's punishment is imminent. As for the mocking hypocrites, their excuse — "We were only chatting and joking *(l-ʿ-b)*" — will not be accepted (Q 9:64-6). The qurʾānic discourse does not allow for anything beyond truth and its denial; the realm of play, fiction and joking remained ontologically incomprehensible and morally suspect in relation to these narrow premises.

There are three explicit orders regarding mockery, all of them prohibitive. The first warns the believers against befriending those who ridicule their religion and their call for prayer (Q 5:57-8); believers must not stay when their companions start to mock God's signs (Q 4:140 with a probable reference back to Q 5:57-8). The provision is, of course, a variant of the universal wisdom to avoid bad company. The simple "Do not take God's signs/verses (q.v.) in mockery" of Q 2:231 seems more loaded when interpreted in its context. This passage falls, in fact, in the middle of the rules of divorce and remarriage (see MARRIAGE AND DIVORCE). This might well mean that they are not to apply God's rules in jest, thus pointing to an unspoken fear: that a body of rules accommodating whims invites men to treat divorce as a joke and thus abuse God's revelation (see REVELATION AND INSPIRATION). Q 49:11, finally, forbids all believers, male and female, to ridicule each other as the person mocked at may be better than his or her mocker. The prohibition is uttered in a series of rules against anything likely to split the Muslim community (see COMMUNITY AND SOCIETY IN THE QUR'ĀN; COMMANDMENTS; BOUNDARIES AND PRECEPTS). They jointly constitute a call for peace and harmony among the believers who are idealized as brothers (Ammann, *Vorbild und Vernunft*, 35-7; see BROTHER AND BROTHERHOOD). Further occurrences of *h-z-'* and *s-kh-r* are to be found in Q 2:212; 9:79; 13:32; 15:95; 23:110; 30:10; 37:12-4; 38:63; 39:56.

Ludwig Ammann

Bibliography (in addition to classical *tafsīr* on the verses noted above, see LAUGHTER for further bibliographic suggestions): L. Ammann, *Vorbild und Vernunft. Die Regelung von Lachen und Scherzen im mittelalterlichen Islam*, Hildesheim 1993; ʿA. al-Ḥ. Ḥifnī, *Uslūb al-sukhriyya fī l-Qur'ān al-karīm*, Cairo 1978; S.Ḥ. Qārūn, Review of ʿA. Ḥifnī's *Uslūb al-sukhriyya fī l-Qur'ān al-karīm*, in *Majallat al-Azhar* 51/5 (June 1979), 1231-4.

Moderation

The action or an act of moderating, i.e. to abate the excessiveness of an act, to render less violent, intense, rigorous, extreme or burdensome. This concept appears in various contexts in the Qur'ān. For instance, Q 17:33 calls for the self-restriction of those who have been given the right to avenge the death of one's kin (see BLOOD MONEY; VENGEANCE; RETALIATION), and Q 17:110 advises neither to utter the prayer (q.v.) aloud nor in a silent voice "and to seek a way between that" (cf. Q 49:3; 7:205).

The moderation of God's punishment (see CHASTISEMENT AND PUNISHMENT; REWARD AND PUNISHMENT) is expressed eleven times in the Qur'ān by the adjective *ḥalīm*, forbearing or clement (see GOD AND HIS ATTRIBUTES; MERCY). Q 2:225 and 235 conclude that God is "forgiving and forbearing" *(ghafūrun ḥalīmun)*, since he does not judge the fulfillment of the believers' oaths (q.v.) and their promises by what they have expressed unintentionally (see BREAKING TRUSTS AND CONTRACTS). Al-Zamakhsharī (d. 538/1144) explains God's forbearance *(ḥilm)* as suspension of punishment *(lā yuʿāliju bi-l-ʿuqūba)* and mildness from tyranny (*ḥalīm ʿan al-jā'ir*, see OPPRESSION; KINGS AND RULERS), a fact that itself is part of God's promise to mankind (*Kashshāf*, i, 394, 473, 510). *Ḥalīm* also appears as an attribute of three outstanding humans. Abraham (q.v.; Ibrāhīm, Q 9:114, 11:75), the son he is about to offer (Q 37:101), and — in an ironic allegation used by his adversaries — the prophet Shuʿayb (q.v.; Q 11:87) are considered *ḥalīm*, "patient, not rushing to take revenge if wronged" (*Jalālayn*, ad Q 11:75). These passages together with evidence from pre-Islamic poetry (see PRE-ISLAMIC ARABIA AND THE QUR'ĀN; POETRY AND POETS) led Goldziher to conclude that *ḥilm* in the sense of calmness, moderation, and resistance to the vengeful ways of pre-Islamic tribal society is a central virtue in Islam (see VIRTUES AND VICES, COMMANDING AND FORBIDDING; COMMUNITY AND SOCIETY IN THE QUR'ĀN; ETHICS AND THE QUR'ĀN). He assumed that *ḥilm* and not knowledge *(ʿilm)*, should be considered the opposite of the pre-Islamic 'Age of Ignorance' (q.v.;

jāhiliyya, see also IGNORANCE), understood by Goldziher as the passionate "era of barbarity" (*MS,* i, 221 f.).

Moderation as a principle of human action expressed in the roots *q-ṣ-d* and *w-s-ṭ* appears in six verses. The value judgment on this principle is ambiguous. In Q 31:19, Luqmān (q.v.) calls on his son to be moderate in his walk and to lower his voice because God loves no one who is pompous and boastful (Q 31:18; see BOAST; ARROGANCE). The invitation is expressed through the imperative of the verb *qaṣada* that originally means "to direct oneself towards something" and the verse could have been understood as a demand "to straighten one's walk" (on this and the connection to the Aramaic Aḥiqār texts, cf. Horovitz, *KU,* 136). The derived meaning of "following the middle course" is more directly expressed through the eighth form of this verb. Q 5:66 mentions a "moderate community" *(ummatun muqtaṣidatun)* among the People of the Book (q.v.) who have not engaged in the trespassing of their peers (see BOUNDARIES AND PRECEPTS). In Q 35:32 a moderate part is also considered among the chosen group of God's servants. Its place is between those who wrong themselves and some who outdo each other in good deeds (q.v.). Q 31:32 connects a moderate attitude with negative associations. Those who are *muqtaṣid* seem to lack commitment in their belief. Q 68:28 and Q 2:143 express, however, the positive connotations of a "middle position" *(awsaṭ* and *wasaṭ).* This is most explicit in the latter verse where the believers are described as a "community in the middle" *(ummatan wasaṭan)* because they serve both as witnesses against the people *(shuhadāʾ ʿalā l-nās)* and they accept the Prophet as a witness for themselves (see WITNESSING AND TESTIFYING).

The exegetical literature connects the two concepts of a well-balanced middle with that of a mediator. It refers to the usage among the Arabs (q.v.) and translates the word *wasaṭ* in Q 2:143 as *khiyār,* "choice, option." There is little explanation for what this means. Al-Ṭabarī (d. 310/923; *Tafsīr,* iii, 142), for instance, starts at a different point and argues that *wasaṭ* stands for the middle of two extremes and describes the moderation of the Muslim believers: "They are neither exaggerators *(ahl al-ghuluww)* in respect to religion, (...) nor those who reduce something *(ahl al-taqṣīr).*" Al-Ṭabarī interprets *wasaṭ* therefore as *ʿadl,* "equity," and concludes that this is what *khiyār* means. The identification of *wasaṭ* with *ʿadl,* "justice," already appears in the ḥadīth (Tirmidhī, *Ṣaḥīḥ, tafsīr al-Qurʾān,* 3, 8; see ḤADĪTH AND THE QURʾĀN) and is later supported by various arguments (Rāzī, *Tafsīr,* iv, 108 f.). The same interpretation is also applied to *muqtaṣid* (Bayḍāwī, *Anwār,* i, 266 f.). For Sayyid Quṭb (d. 1966; *Ẓilāl,* i, 130 f.), the *ummatan wasaṭan* of Q 2:143 expresses the central place of the Muslim community among humankind. The Muslim community is endowed with *ʿadl,* understood as equitable justice *(qisṭ)* and demonstrates it towards humankind (see JUSTICE AND INJUSTICE). The moderation of one's commitment, however, was, following Q 31:32 and 35:32, seldom regarded as an exemplary behavior and al-Ghazālī's (d. 505/1111) book *al-Iqtiṣād fī l-iʿtiqād,* for instance, does not argue for a moderation of one's convictions but refers to the moderate depth of instruction in the Muslim creed (see CREEDS) within this book.

Frank Griffel

Bibliography

Primary: Bayḍāwī, *Anwār,* i, 88 f., 166 f.; ii, 114, 153; al-Ghazālī, Abū Ḥāmid Muḥammad, *al-Iqtiṣād fī l-iʿtiqād,* ed. H. Atay and I.A. Çubukçu, Ankara 1962, 215; Ibn Ḥanbal, *Musnad,* iii, 32; *Jalālayn;* Quṭb, *Ẓilāl,* i, 130 f.; ii, 940 f.; v, 2790;

Rāzī, *Tafsīr,* iv, 108 f.; xii, 47; xxv, 150, 162; xxvi, 24; Ṭabarī, *Tafsīr,* iii, 141 f.; x, 465 f.; ed. Beirut 1994, vi, 130, 137 f.; Tirmidhī, *Ṣaḥīḥ,* v, 190 f.; Zamakhsharī, *Kashshāf,* ed. Beirut 1366/1947, i, 317, 641; iii, 234, 237.
Secondary: G.-H. Bousquet, Études islamologiques d'Ignaz Goldziher. Traduction analytique (III), in *Arabica* 7 (1960), 237-273, 246-9; A. Dietrich, Review of E. Tyan, *Institutions du droit public musulmane,* in *Oriens* 8 (1955), 163 f., 164; R.M. Frank, *Al-Ghazālī and the Ashʿarite school,* London 1994, 71; Goldziher, *MS,* i, 220-2; J.R. Harris et al., *The story of Aḥikar,* Cambridge 1913, lxxvi; Horovitz, *KU,* 136; Izutsu, *Concepts,* 28-35; Paret, *Kommentar,* 35, 125 f., 395, 485; Ch. Pellat, Concept of ḥilm in Islamic ethics, in *Bulletin of the Institute of Islamic Studies* (Aligarh) 6 and 7 (1962-3), 1-12; id., Ḥilm, in *EI²,* iii, 390-2.

Modesty

Evincing decorum in one's actions and dress. The Qurʾān enjoins Muslims to observe modesty in their clothing and honesty in their behavior. It is said in Q 7:26 "We have sent down raiment (see CLOTHING) to hide your nakedness (see NUDITY) and splendid garments, but the raiment of piety (q.v.) is the best." Instead of specifying or requiring any particular form of clothing or covering for Muslims (see VEIL), the Qurʾān sets forth fairly broad statements of principle regarding modesty. Q 24:31 states "Tell the believing women... not to display their adornment except that part of it which appears outwardly" (see WOMEN AND THE QURʾĀN; BELIEF AND UNBELIEF). Q 24:30 reads "Tell the male believers to avert their eyesight..." and Q 33:59, "O Prophet, tell your wives and daughters and the women of the Muslims to let down over them a part of their outer garments; it is more suitable *(dhālika adnā)* that they will thus be recognized and not molested" (see WIVES OF THE PROPHET; FAMILY OF THE PROPHET). The term *hawn* means modesty or humility in Q 25:63: "The servants of [God], most gracious are those who walk in the earth in humility, and when the ignorant (see IGNORANCE) address them, they say "Peace!" (see ARROGANCE). *Istaḥā* means "in a bashful way" in Q 28:25: "Afterwards one of the [damsels] came back to him, walking bashfully *(ʿalā stiḥyāʾin)...*" In the absence of qurʾānic specification, it is the responsibility of divergent schools of law (see LAW AND THE QURʾĀN) to define the way such principles should be interpreted and executed on the basis of textual indicators, analogy, or other methods of legal reasoning such as *istiḥsān* and *istiṣlāh* (see EXEGESIS OF THE QURʾĀN: CLASSICAL AND MEDIEVAL; TRADITIONAL DISCIPLINES OF QURʾĀNIC STUDY).

The Qurʾān teaches extreme simplicity with regard to dress. At the time of the Prophet, the basic articles of clothing for both male and female consisted of an undergarment, a body shirt, a long dress, gown, or tunic, and an outer garment such as a mantle coat or wrap, footgear consisting of shoes or sandals, and a head covering. As underwear would interfere with the circulation of air, it is said that originally none was worn, a practice that may have been common before the coming of Islam. The *izār* (undergarment) and the *sirwāl* (under-drawers) were worn, however, at the time of the Prophet. We may consider undergarments as one of the accommodations to the new moral sensibilities since they were an effective mark of modesty (see ETHICS AND THE QURʾĀN; PRE-ISLAMIC ARABIA AND THE QURʾĀN).

A central concept in Sunnī law concerning dress is the *ʿawra*. The *ʿawra* is that part of the human body that is to be covered in ordinary public settings. The term is perhaps best translated as "the modesty zone," meaning that part of the body the covering of which is required for purposes of public modesty or decency. Since indecent exposure is one of the factors that, according to most jurists, invalidate a prayer (q.v.), it was necessary for the Muslim jurists to clarify the concept of indecent exposure. It is in this connection that they go to great lengths to explain what constitutes the *ʿawra*. Generally speaking, the *ʿawra* that must be covered in the ritual prayer is identical with the *ʿawra* that must be covered in ordinary public settings, although a few authors draw a distinction between an "*ʿawra* in prayer" and an "*ʿawra* outside of prayer." In addition to those sections of the law books that deal with ritual prayer, the subject of dress emerges in discussions of *naẓar*, "looking," which are found in the "Book of marriage" in the Shāfiʿī, Mālikī, and Ḥanbalī schools (see MARRIAGE AND DIVORCE; CHASTITY; ABSTINENCE; ADULTERY AND FORNICATION). Within Ḥanafī law books, however, the subject of *naẓar* is placed variously under "Book of preference" *(kitāb al-istiḥsān),* "Book of abominations" (*kitāb al-karāhiya,* see SIN, MAJOR AND MINOR) or "Book of forbidding and permitting" (*kitāb al-ḥaẓr wa-l-ibāḥa,* see LAWFUL AND UNLAWFUL; FORBIDDEN). Under these headings are placed the discussions of what parts of the body may be seen and what parts may not be seen.

As a whole, the Ḥanafī, Shāfiʿī and Mālikī schools all agree that the entire body of a free woman is her *ʿawra* except her face and palms. The Ḥanbalī school is the only school that regards the palms of a free woman as part of her *ʿawra*. The four schools also agree that the area between the navel and the knees is the *ʿawra* of a man. Most Shāfiʿīs and all Mālikīs and Ḥanbalīs exclude the navel and the knees from a man's *ʿawra,* while the Ḥanafī jurists agree that the navel is not part of the *ʿawra* but the knee is. The Ḥanafīs generally regard the *ʿawra* of the slave woman the same as the *ʿawra* of the man, although some regard a slave woman's bosom *(ṣadr)* as part of the "*ʿawra* in prayer," not as part of the "*ʿawra* outside prayer" (see SLAVES AND SLAVERY).

According to the Mālikīs and Ḥanbalīs, a man is allowed to look at and touch the entire body of a child who is not yet seven years old (see CHILDREN; MATURITY). According to the Shāfiʿīs, a man is allowed to look at the whole body of free female children except what is between the navel and knees. The Ḥanbalīs hold that a man is allowed to look at the head, face, neck, hands, shanks and feet of free female minors under the age of nine. The Ḥanafīs say that there is no rule of *ʿawra* for a little child's body since there is no fear of temptation in the looking and touching.

The voice of a woman is sometimes considered part of the *ʿawra*. Concerning the voice of a free adult female stranger (see STRANGERS AND FOREIGNERS), there are different opinions among the Ḥanafī jurists. In the opinion of al-Ḥaskāfī (d. 1088/1677), the voice of a woman is not *ʿawra*. The opposing view is expressed in the succinct phrase, "The melody of the woman is *ʿawra*" *(naghmat al-marʾa ʿawra).* Ibn ʿĀbidīn (d. 1258/1842) says that it is recorded in *al-Kāfī,* authored by al-Marwazī al-Ḥākim al-Shahīd (d. 334/945): "Do not follow (a woman) in public, because her voice is *ʿawra*" (Ibn ʿĀbidīn, *Ḥāshīya,* 406). One of the conditions that allow women to visit a mosque (q.v.) is that women are forbidden to raise their voice during the prayer. For the Prophet said: "Glorification of God (q.v.) is for men, tapping the hands is for women" *(al-tasbīḥ lil-rijāl wa-l-taṣfīq lil-nisāʾ).* If the imām (q.v.) has to be warned of an error, men should say *subḥān Allāh,* "God be glorified," but women should only tap their hands. See also SEX AND SEXUALITY.

Shiu-Sian Angel Hsu

Bibliography
Primary: Abū Dāwūd; Ibn ʿĀbidīn, Muḥammad Amīn b. ʿUmar, *Ḥāshīyat radd al-mukhtār. Kitāb al-Ṣalāt,* 8 vols., Cairo 1966², vi, 336-430.

Secondary: Shiu-Sian Angel Hsu, *Dress in Islam. Looking and touching,* Ph.D. diss., U. of Utah 1994; P. Storm, *Functions of dress. Tool of culture and the individual,* Englewood Cliffs, NJ 1987, 243-7.

Monasticism and Monks

From well before the rise of Islam, and then well into the later Middle Ages, monasticism was a distinctive feature of Christian life, both in the milieu in which Islam was born (see CHRISTIANS AND CHRISTIANITY; SOUTH ARABIA, RELIGION IN PRE-ISLAMIC), and in the Christian communities subsequently integrated into the world of Islam. Accordingly, from the perspective of its relationship to Islam, one must consider the phenomenon of Christian monasticism under three headings. In the first place, there is its presence in the Arabic-speaking communities before and up to the time of Muḥammad (see ARABS; ARABIC LANGUAGE). Then, there are the passages in the Qurʾān that mention "monks" (three times) and "monasticism" (once). Finally, "monks" and "monasticism" are discussed in the Islamic texts that both interpret the Qurʾān and set the boundaries of Islamic life in later times.

Already by the fifth Christian century monks and their monasteries were plentiful on the borders of Arabia. From the deserts of the Sinai (q.v.) peninsula northward into Syria/Palestine (see SYRIA), eastward along the edge of the Syrian desert into Mesopotamia and southward into Iraq (q.v.), monastic communities flourished. Monastic institutions were at the heart of Christian church-life in nearby Egypt (q.v.) and Ethiopia (see ABYSSINIA). In a number of places, such as the monastery of St. Euthymius in the Judean desert, the monks actively fostered the growth and development of Christianity among the neighboring Arab tribes, who then had the monastery as the center of their religious life. Similarly, the shrines of St. Simeon the Stylite at Dayr Samʿān/Telanissos and of St. Sergius at Ruṣāfa/Sergiopolis in Syria regularly attracted large numbers of Arab tribesmen among their frequent visitors. On the borders between the territories of the Byzantine Romans and the Arab tribes of Arabia proper, the Ghassānid tribal federation, allies of the Byzantines (q.v.), presided over a widely distributed population of monks and monasteries to an extent that a closer examination of texts and archeological data are only lately revealing (see ARCHAEOLOGY AND THE QURʾĀN). Similarly, on the northeastern frontier between the territories controlled by the Persian Sasanids and the tribesmen of Arabia, in the territories of the Lakhmid allies of the Persians, centered near the city of Ḥīra in lower Mesopotamia, monastic communities flourished. Natively Arabic-speaking monks seem to have made up a large part of these monastic populations, usually with a Syriac theological and liturgical heritage (see SYRIAC AND THE QURʾĀN); Arab pastoralists regularly sojourned among the Syriac-speaking Arameans of the area.

From these monastic centers on the near periphery of Arabia, in the fifth and sixth centuries monks and monasticism penetrated into Arabia proper. Remains of their establishments have been uncovered along the southern coasts of Arabia as well as in cities in the interior such as Najrān (q.v.). A few Syriac texts speak of the activities of monks in Arabia, and a number of pre-Islamic and early Islamic Arabic texts similarly record their presence. Poets, for example, in the classical *qaṣīda*s sometimes mention the lights burning in the cells of monks in the dark of night (cf. Cheikho, *Le christianisme*). More helpfully, the biographical traditions concerned with Muḥammad's early years mention several encounters between monks and the young prophet-to-be, most famously his encounter with the monk Baḥīra, who reportedly recognized the sign of prophecy on his body (see PROPHETS AND PROPHETHOOD). A monk Fīmiyyūn is also named in the *sīra* (see SĪRA AND THE QURʾĀN) in connection with the establishment of Christianity in Najrān (see Ibn Isḥāq, *Sīra,* i, 31). And the early Persian Companion of Muḥammad (see COMPANIONS OF THE PROPHET), Salmān, is said to have come to the profession of Islam due to his earlier association with monks, one of whom had premonitions about the coming of Muḥammad and Islam (see Ibn Isḥāq, *Sīra,* i, 217-8). These and other mentions and allusions in Arabic texts to monks and monasticism in the world in which Islam was born testify to their common presence among the Christians known to Muḥammad and the Qurʾān. They do not suggest a wide and well-established monastic presence in the Ḥijāz and its environs, in the heart of Arabia. But by Muḥammad's day monks and monasticism were certainly known to be an integral feature of Christian life, and monks may well have been prominent among the Christians actually known to Muḥammad.

In the Qurʾān, "monks" *(ruhbān)* are mentioned three times (Q 5:82; 9:31, 34) and "monasticism" *(rahbāniyya)* once (Q 57:27). In general, one may say that the Qurʾān's attitude to monks mirrors its ambivalent attitude towards Christians at large. On the one hand, the Qurʾān says that the reason Muslims will find those claiming to be Christians "closest in affection to the believers" is that "there are among them priests *(qissīsīn)* and monks, and they are not arrogant" (Q 5:82; see ARROGANCE). On the other hand, the Qurʾān also says that Jews (see JEWS AND JUDAISM) and Christians respectively "take their rabbis *(aḥbār)* and monks as lords (*arbāb,* see LORD) besides God" (Q 9:31). And the text goes on to say, "many of the rabbis and monks devour the wealth (q.v.) of the people unjustly and turn [others] from the way of God" (Q 9:34; see PATH OR WAY). While in the many translations and interpretations of the Qurʾān into western languages there are a number of variations in rendering the technical terms in these passages, usually due to lexical or exegetical considerations, the sense of the judgments about the monks remains the same in all of them.

In one passage the Qurʾān addresses the institution of monasticism itself but there is significant disagreement among commentators and translators, both medieval and modern (see EXEGESIS OF THE QURʾĀN: CLASSICAL AND MEDIEVAL; EXEGESIS OF THE QURʾĀN: EARLY MODERN AND CONTEMPORARY), Muslim and non-Muslim, about what the text actually says (cf. Beck, Das christliche Mönchtum). In one understanding, the text speaks of the followers of Jesus (q.v.), of whom God says, "We put into the hearts (see HEART) of those who followed him mercy (q.v.), compassion, and monasticism; they innovated/renovated/invented it; we prescribed for them only to please God, but they did not exercise a proper compliance. So we provided their reward for those of them who believed; many of them are sinful" (Q 57:27; see REWARD AND PUNISHMENT; SIN, MAJOR AND MINOR). On this reading monasticism is understood to be something initially instituted by God; subsequently Jesus' followers re-invented it and introduced innovations into it. Alternatively, most Muslim interpreters have understood the verse to say, "We put into the hearts of those who followed him mercy and compassion. Monasticism they invented — only to seek to please God. We did not prescribe it for them. And they did not exercise a proper compliance. So we provided their reward for those of them who believed; many of them are sinful." On this reading monasticism is understood to be a human innovation totally, not something mandated by God. Most interpreters favor some form of the second reading, regarding the first one to be the product of a faulty grammatical construction on the part of those who would accept it (see esp. Ṭabarī, *Tafsīr;* Zamakhsharī, *Kashshāf,* ad Q 57:27; cf. Gimaret, *Jubbāʾī,* 787; see GRAMMAR AND THE QURʾĀN). Nevertheless, some earlier Muslim exegetes and some modern scholars have in fact entertained the theoretical possibility of some form of the first reading (cf. McAuliffe, *Qurʾānic,* 260-84).

Traditionally, Muslim scholars have considered monasticism to be an instance of the Christians' putting religious burdens on people beyond what God has mandated and then not being able to support them. By way of contrast, the prophetic tradition (*ḥadīth,* see ḤADĪTH AND THE QURʾĀN) according to which, "There is no monasticism in Islam," gradually gained currency among Muslims. While many scholars have questioned the authenticity of this tradition, it is nevertheless widely reported and accepted. Similarly, another controversial prophetic tradition says, "The monasticism of this community is jihād (q.v.)." These traditions seem to have come into prominence in the context of debates among Muslim scholars in the early centuries about the legitimacy of Ṣūfism (cf. Massignon, *Essay,* 99; see ṢŪFISM AND THE QURʾĀN). Muslim scholars have also been careful to point out that the disapproval of monasticism should not be mistaken for a disapproval of the hermit's way of life (see ASCETICISM), or the practice of a religious retreat, including sexual abstinence (q.v.), undertaken for a time for legitimate religious reasons. Rather, what is rejected in monasticism, according to many scholars, is the commitment to lifelong celibacy that the Christian institution entails. Celibacy is seen by some commentators to be the innovation introduced by Christians into what Muslims could consider to be an otherwise acceptable, even divinely instituted, monasticism.

After the rise of Islam and the consolidation of the territories of the Christian, ecclesiastical provinces of Alexandria, Antioch and Jerusalem under Muslim rule, Christian monks writing in Syriac, Greek and Arabic were the first to call attention to the doctrinal and moral challenges of Islam to Christians (see ETHICS AND THE QURʾĀN; THEOLOGY AND THE QURʾĀN). Monks were also the first Christians to adopt Arabic as an ecclesiastical language, to write theology in Arabic and to translate the Christian Bible and other classical Christian texts into Arabic. In the agreements drawn up to govern the relationships between Muslims and Christians in early Islamic times, monks were often exempted from the payment of the poll tax (q.v.; *jizya*), and often the authority of the Prophet himself was claimed for this dispensation. Monasteries were often considered to be privileged places by Muslims and Christians alike, where help could be sought and interreligious conversations could take place. Some of them claimed to have patents offering them special protection. Contrariwise monks and monasteries were sometimes targets of anti-Christian attacks. In Arabic secular literature from the early period a genre of poetic writing often called *diyāriyyāt,* or "monastic poems," developed that celebrated monasteries as places of revelry. See also CHURCH; INFORMANTS.

Sidney H. Griffith

Bibliography

Primary: Gimaret, *Jubbāʾī,* 787 (for an early Muʿtazilī reading of Q 57:27); Ibn Isḥāq, *Sīra,* ed. M.M. ʿAbd al-Ḥamīd, 4 vols., Cairo 1937;

W. Nassau Lees, *The Qoran. With the commentary of the Imam Aboo al-Qasim Mahmood bin ʿOmar al-Zamakhshari, entitled "The Kashshāf ʿan haqāʾiq al-tanzīl,"* 2 vols., Calcutta 1856, ii, 1453-4; al-Shābushtī, Abū l-Ḥasan ʿAlī b. Muḥammad, *Kitāb al-Diyārāt,* ed. J. ʿAwwād, Baghdad 1966; Ṭabarī, *Tafsīr,* 30 vols., Cairo 1903, xxvii, 123-5. Secondary: T. Andrae, *Les origines de l'Islam et le Christianisme,* Paris 1955; E. Beck, Das christliche Mönchtum im Koran, in K. Tallqvist (ed.), *Studia orientalia,* vol. xiii, Helsinki 1946, 3-29; Y. Calvet, Monuments paléo-chrétiens à Koweit et dans la région du Golfe, in R. Lavenant, *Symposium syriacum VII* [*Orientalia christiana analecta* 256], Rome 1998, 671-85; L. Cheikho, *Le christianisme et la littérature chrétienne en Arabie avant l'Islam,* Beirut 1912 and 1919-23; E. Key Fowden, *The barbarian plain. Saint Sergius between Rome and Iran,* Berkeley 1999; S.H. Griffith, *Arabic Christianity in the monasteries of ninth-century Palestine,* Aldershot, Hampshire 1992; id., From Aramaic to Arabic. The languages of the monasteries of Palestine in the Byzantine and early Islamic periods, *Dumbarton Oaks papers* 51 (1997), 11-31; L. Massignon, *Essay on the origins of the technical language of Islamic mysticism,* trans. B. Clark, Notre Dame, IN 1997; McAuliffe, *Qurʾānic;* I. Shahīd, *Byzantium and the Arabs in the sixth century,* vol. 2, part 1, Washington 2002; R. Tardy, *Najrān. Chrétiens d'Arabie avant l'Islam,* Beirut 1999; J. Spencer Trimingham, *Christianity among the Arabs in pre-Islamic times,* London 1979; G. Troupeau, Les couvents chrétiens dans la littérature arabe musulmane, in *La nouvelle revue de Caire* 1 (1975), 265-79; M.S. al-Ṭurayḥī, *al-Diyārāt wa-l-amkina l-naṣrāniyya fī l-Kūfa wa-ḍawāḥīhā,* Beirut 1981; J. Wensinck, Rahbāniyya, in *EI²*, viii, 396-7; id., Rāhib, in *EI²*, viii, 397.

Money

Measure of value or medium of exchange. Money as such is barely attested in the Qurʾān. A small number of terms refer to coins of indistinct weight and fineness. Some other words denote vague units of weight (see WEIGHTS AND MEASURES) or have no monetary significance, though they often appear as monetary terms in later classical Arabic (see ARABIC LANGUAGE). Words or phrases identifying definite units of value are absent.

The phrase *darāhim maʿdūda,* "a counted number of silver coins," in Q 12 (Sūrat Yūsuf, "Joseph"; Q 12:20) indicates silver coins of no particular weight and fineness. Al-Zamakhsharī (d. 538/1144; *Kashshāf,* ad loc.) emphasizes here that the term *darāhim* means "not gold (q.v.) coins" *(ay lā danānīr).* Most early commentators speculate on the number of coins implied, suggesting numbers from twenty to forty. The verse agrees generally with the Hebrew Bible where Joseph (q.v.) is sold for twenty shekels (see SCRIPTURE AND THE QURʾĀN). The qurʾānic reference, however, is anachronistic since it refers specifically to coins and not standard weights of silver. Modern scholarship places the historical figure of Joseph in the early second millenium B.C.E., long before the invention of coinage in the seventh century B.C.E.

The term *wariq,* sometimes read *warq,* in Q 18:19 also refers generally to silver coins. It may derive from the thin silver drahms of the Sasanians, particularly the later Sasanians. These coins resemble leaves, familiar from the cognate *waraq.* Wahb b. Munabbih (d. ca. 114/732) equates it with *darāhim* (Ṭabarī, *Tafsīr,* viii, 197). Ikrima (d. 105/723-4), Ibn Isḥāq (d. ca. 150/767) and ʿAbdallāh b. ʿUbayd b. ʿUmayr use it in a lengthy exegetical story to mean coins plainly identifying the king who struck them (Ṭabarī, *Tafsīr,* viii, 197-203).

Other terms mark only standard weights or vague units of weight. The sole attestation of *dīnār* appears as a fraction of *qinṭār* (Q 3:75). Since the term derives from the Roman *denarius* and Byzantine *dinarion,* it may refer to a weight of gold. The reference differs somewhat from later classical Arabic where *dīnār* refers variously to a denomination of Muslim gold coins, a standard unit of weight corresponding to the weight of this denomination or a gold coin of any standard.

Mithqāl refers to the abstract concept of weight or a vague but very light unit of weight. It appears in a number of verses as an indication of a very small weight — glossed variously as of an ant, or an atom or a mite (*mithqāl dharratin,* Q 4:40; 10:61; 34:3, 22; 99:7, 8) — or, specifically, as the weight of a mustard seed (*mithqāl ḥabbatin min khardalin,* Q 21:47; 31:16; see SCIENCE AND THE QURʾĀN; NATURE AS SIGNS). In contrast, the term later usually identifies a standard weight corresponding to the weight of Sasanian drahms or Muslim dinars, slightly more than four grams, or to Sasanian drahms themselves.

No other terms in the Qurʾān shed any light on the existence or use of money. The term *ʿayn* occurs without any monetary sense though in later Arabic it often signifies gold, gold coins or ready cash. References to gold *(dhahab)* and silver *(fiḍḍa)* usually appear in connection with bracelets, vessels and platters (see INSTRUMENTS; CUPS AND VESSELS; FURNITURE AND FURNISHINGS; MATERIAL CULTURE AND THE QURʾĀN; METALS AND MINERALS).

The language of the Qurʾān reflects generally the monetary situation of the Ḥijāz of the early seventh century C.E. (see GEOGRAPHY; HISTORY AND THE QURʾĀN). Coinage circulated in small quantities from the neighboring lands of Syria and Iran but played a very minor role in its commerce (see CARAVAN; SELLING AND BUYING). It was only loosely tied, if at all, to any system of weights and measures. See also NUMISMATICS; EPIGRAPHY AND THE QURʾĀN.

Stuart D. Sears

Bibliography
Primary: Abū ʿUbayd al-Qāsim b. Sallām, *Kitāb al-Amwāl,* ed. M.Kh. Hiras, Cairo 1981; al-Balādhurī, Abū l-Ḥasan Aḥmad b. Yaḥyā, *Futūḥ al-buldān,* ed. Ṣ. al-Munajjid, Cairo 1957; al-Maqrīzī, Aḥmad b. ʿAlī, *Shudhūr al-ʿuqūd fī dhikr al-nuqūd,* ed. M.ʿA. ʿUthmān, Cairo 1990; Mujāhid, *Tafsīr;* Muqātil, *Tafsīr;* Sufyān al-Thawrī, *Tafsīr;* Ṭabarī, *Tafsīr,* 12 vols., Beirut 1992; Zamakhsharī, *Kashshāf.*
Secondary: G.C. Miles, Dīnār, in *EI²,* ii, 297-9; id., Dirham, in *EI²,* ii, 319-20; H. Sauvaire, Matériaux pour servir à l'histoire de la numismatique et de la métrologie musulmanes, traduits ou récueillis et mis en ordre, in *JA* 14 (1879), 499-533; 15 (1880), 228-77, 421-78; 18 (1881), 459-516; 19 (1882), 23-77, 97-163, 281-327 (abr. trans. S. Lane-Poole, The Arabian historians on Mohammadan numismatics, in *Numismatic chronicle third series* 4 [1884], 66-96).

Monks see MONASTICISM AND MONKS

Monotheism see GOD AND HIS ATTRIBUTES; POLYTHEISM AND ATHEISM

Months

The portions into which the year is divided, each one corresponding approximately to the length of a complete revolution of the moon (q.v.). As with many qurʾānic notions, it is extremely difficult, if not impossible, to isolate the original meaning of the word "month" from its later exegetical elaboration (see EXEGESIS OF THE QURʾĀN: CLASSICAL AND MEDIEVAL). Despite efforts to identify this original meaning either contextually or by reference to parallel passages, the influences and stereotypes of this rich exegetical tradition impinge heavily upon attempts to understand this qurʾānic word. The only way to avoid these influences and stereotypes is to become a "clean slate" and to approach this term without any prior knowledge of the developed exegetical tradition, an epistemological stance that is difficult or impossible to achieve.

The term "month" *shahr* (pl. *shuhūr* and *ashhur)* occurs twenty-one times in the text of the Qurʾān: four times in what are generally believed to be "Meccan" sūras and seventeen times in the ones which are usually associated with the "Medinan" period of Muḥammad's life (cf. Amir-Ali, The "month"; see CHRONOLOGY AND THE QUR'ĀN). In the four Meccan sūras only the singular grammatical form is used, although in two instances it refers to more than one month. In the sūras from the Medinan period it appears in the singular, dual and two different forms of the plural. Perhaps the earliest sūra to mention the term is Q 97:3, which deals with the famous night of revelation or of the divine determination (*laylat al-qadr*, see NIGHT OF POWER). In Q 46:15, the singular form appears in the phrase "thirty months." Finally, in a rather obscure passage from Q 34:12, God gives Solomon (q.v.; Sulaymān) power over the winds (see AIR AND WIND), which "made a month's journey in the morning and a month's journey in the evening." In the sūras from the Medinan period the word "month" is usually associated with various religious rites (e.g. the slaughter of sacrificial animals and the minor and greater pilgrimages, that is the *ʿumra* and the *ḥajj*; see PILGRIMAGE; CONSECRATION OF ANIMALS; SACRIFICE) as well with the fast (see FASTING) of Ramaḍān (q.v.). In such contexts, it is often qualified by the epithet "sacred" or "holy" (*al-shahr al-ḥarām*, e.g. Q 2:194, 217; 5:2, 97).

It is often argued that some of these passages, namely Q 5:2 and 97, refer to an ancient religious festival and pilgrimage which the pagan tribes of Arabia celebrated in Rajab (Wellhausen, *Reste*, 98-101; see PRE-ISLAMIC ARABIA AND THE QUR'ĀN; SOUTH ARABIA, RELIGION IN PRE-ISLAMIC). Originally observed in spring, Rajab was the month of the *ʿumra* pilgrimage, during which pre-Islamic Arabs (q.v.) abstained from warfare (see WAR) and brought sacrificial animals to the Meccan sanctuary (ibid., 94; Kister, Rajab, 191-2; see GEOGRAPHY; MECCA; SACRED PRECINCTS). Whether the festival of Rajab also involved a period of obligatory fasting remains unclear. The special place, however, of this month in Muslim popular piety, which appears to be a carryover from the pagan Arabian past (see AGE OF IGNORANCE), is richly attested by Muslim literature and ethnographic evidence from various areas of the Muslim world (Kister, Rajab, 191-2). At the same time, Q 9:5 mentions several sacred months (*al-ashhur al-ḥurum*, cf. Q 2:197); furthermore, Q 2:197 specifies that the *ḥajj* should take place "in months well known." These statements caused some confusion among Muslim interpreters who could not understand why the plural form (and not the dual or the singular) was used in these passages. Those who held that two Arabian "sacred" months are implied, namely Rajab, which initially was the season of the lesser pilgrimage (*ʿumra*) and Dhū l-Ḥijja, which was the month of the *ḥajj* proper, were unable to explain why the dual form of the word *shahr* was not used here. Others, such as al-Ṭabarī (d. 310/923) and Ibn Kathīr (d. 774/1373), considered the plural form to be a reference to the months that immediately precede Dhū l-Ḥijja, namely Shawwāl and Dhū l-Qaʿda, all of which formed a triad of holy months (Ṭabarī, *Tafsīr*, ii, 541; cf. Ali, *Holy Qurʾān*, 79, n. 217). This explanation is tenuous. While the sacredness of Dhū l-Qaʿda is abundantly attested by both the pre-Islamic and early Islamic traditions, Shawwāl did not play any special role in either. Nor was it protected by the taboo against violence which was associated with the four sacred months mentioned in Q 9:36 (see MURDER; FIGHTING; BLOODSHED). Most Muslim commentators agreed that the passage in question refers to Dhū l-Qaʿda, Dhū l-Ḥijja, al-Muḥarram and perhaps also to Rajab.

A number of Western scholars accepted this explanation (see POST-ENLIGHTENMENT ACADEMIC STUDY OF THE QUR'ĀN). They provided different reasons, however, for the sacredness of these months. J. Wellhausen (*Reste,* 88) argued that before Islam most of Dhū l-Qaʿda was occupied by annual festivities and fairs at ʿUkāẓ and Majanna, whereas the first two weeks of Dhū l-Ḥijja were dedicated to the annual fairs and pilgrimage rites at Dhū l-Majāz, ʿArafa, and Minā. As for al-Muḥarram, in Wellhausen's view, it was the first month of the ancient Arabian calendar (q.v.), which was originally celebrated in autumn with the annual *ḥajj*. He also argued that Rajab was its spring counterpart, corresponding to the Jewish Passover (ibid., 98-9; see JEWS AND JUDAISM). Over the centuries, both months gradually moved from their original places due to the inability of pre-Islamic Arabs to keep proper record of time (q.v.). Thus, by the time of Muḥammad's life Rajab was celebrated in autumn, while the *ḥajj* now took place in spring. According to Wellhausen, the month of the *ḥajj* eventually turned into three consecutive months due to local differences in time-reckoning as well as the desire on the part of the Quraysh (q.v.) to accommodate all prospective pilgrims from across Arabia. Interesting as this explanation is, it seems rather far-fetched and fails to account for the fact that al-Muḥarram is a relatively late name of the month of Ṣafar I (see e.g. *Lisān al-ʿArab,* iv, 463), which together with Ṣafar II and the other "paired" months of the Arab calendar formed what Wellhausen described as the "Wintersemester" (ibid., 97). Unless it can be determined when and why Ṣafar I became a sacred month, it is difficult to accept Wellhausen's thesis without serious reservations (see SANCTITY AND THE SACRED).

Q 9:36 is also significant in that it stipulates twelve as the proper number of the months of the year, which it describes as being part of "the right" or "true" religion (q.v.). Furthermore, the verse that follows (Q 9:37) contains what some scholars regard as the prohibition to "postpone" or "transfer" *(nasīʾ)* the sacred month from its usual place. The exact meaning of this passage and especially of the term *nasīʾ* mentioned here still eludes both Muslim and Western researchers. A. Moberg (An-Nasīʾ) suggested a compelling solution to this problem. In elaborating on the Muslim exegetical tradition Moberg argued that the verse in question refers to the intercalation of an additional month every two or three years by the pre-Islamic Arabs who strove to keep their lunar calendar in line with the seasonal one. According to Moberg, this practice was necessitated by the particularity of the lunar calendar, whose months total an average of about 354 days per year as opposed to the 365 days of its solar/seasonal counterpart. The difference of approximately eleven days per year was made up by the intercalation, which, according to some Muslim authors, was entrusted to certain members of the Banū Kināna tribe (see TRIBES AND CLANS). As a result, pre-Islamic Arabs found themselves living by a combined lunar-solar calendar, which facilitated their trade with the agricultural populations of the Fertile Crescent and Mesopotamia (see IRAQ; CARAVAN), who, quite naturally, relied on a seasonal calendar (Paret, *Mohammed,* 19-20; Beeston, *Epigraphic,* 18-9).

In consequence of the intercalation, the Arab tribes faced the problem of how to deal with three successive sacred months, which had been traditionally associated with the *ḥajj*, namely Dhū l-Qaʿda, Dhū l-Ḥijja, and al-Muḥarram. Since the intercalary month was inserted after the last month of the year (i.e. Dhū l-Ḥijja), they could treat it as profane and thus engage in raids and warfare against their neighbors (see EXPEDITIONS AND BATTLES). Alternatively, they could declare it sacred and hence observe "God's peace," as required by Arabian custom. In the former case, the succession of three holy months would be interrupted and the original sacred month would be separated from its two predecessors by an intervening profane month. In the latter case, however, the original sacred month (Dhū l-Qaʿda) would lose its sacred status and that would be transferred *(nasaʾa)* to the intercalated month.

That neither solution was satisfactory for the fledgling Muslim community is attested by Q 9:37, which, according to the tradition, was revealed during the last year of the Prophet's life. Whether the practice condemned by Q 9:37 involved actual manipulation of the calendar in the form of intercalation or was simply the realignment of sacred and profane months within a year is a moot point (see e.g. Effendi, Mémoire; Fück, Zur an-nasīʾ; Plessner, Review). Later, F.C. de Blois (Taʾrīkh) suggested that a prototype of this practice can be found in an early Sabaean inscription (see ARCHAEOLOGY AND THE QURʾĀN). There, a Sabaean community asks God's forgiveness for deferring certain ritual activities until a later date. If we accept the traditional dating of Q 9:37, which places it in the tenth year after the emigration (q.v.; *hijra*) of the Prophet from Mecca to Medina (q.v.), i.e. shortly before the Prophet's death, it can be argued that the prohibition of the *nasīʾ* was occasioned by the desire on the part of the Muslim community and its leader to dissociate themselves from the practices of their pagan neighbors and to reassert themselves as a totally new religious community (see ISLAM). This line of argument could further suggest that it also marked the rupture with the Judaic tradition, whose adherents practiced intercalation to keep their religious holidays within the same season. Seen from this perspective, the prohibition of intercalation may fall into the same category as the relocation of the fast of the ʿĀshūra to Ramaḍān or the change of the direction of the prayer from Jerusalem (q.v.) to the Meccan sanctuary (see KAʿBA; QIBLA). In other words, it may constitute either conscious or unconscious assertion of a separate identity by the new religious community and its leader.

A review of qurʾānic passages that contain the word "month" reveals that it is often linked to the lunar calendar. Thus, in Q 2:185, the word *shahr* seems to denote the new moon that signals the beginning of a new calendar month. This usage is richly attested by Arab lexicographers who trace the etymology of the word to the root *sh-h-r,* "to be apparent," or "to manifest one/itself" (*Lisān al-ʿArab,* iv, 431-3; cf. Ṭabarī, *Tafsīr,* i, 552). This meaning is further confirmed by epigraphic evidence from south Arabia, where *sh-h-r* was "a synonym for the first day of the calendar-month" (Beeston, *Epigraphic,* 8; see EPIGRAPHY AND THE QURʾĀN; ARABIC SCRIPT). In many verses, the new moon is expressly described as the measurement of time *par excellence*. A typical example is Q 2:189: "They will question you concerning the new moons *(al-ahilla)*. Say: 'They are appointed times for the people, and the pilgrimage.'" This and other similar verses indicate that the beginning of the month or of the year must be established by an actual observation of the new moon (Q 10:5; cf. 71:16). According to Ibn ʿAbbās (d. 69/688), the meaning of this verse is that "by means of it (i.e. the new moon) [the people] determine the affairs of their religion, the waiting periods of their wives, the time of their pilgrimage and the due dates for their debts" (Ṭabarī, *Tafsīr,* i, 580; see DEBT; WAITING PERIOD; MARRIAGE AND DIVORCE). This commentary conveniently demarcates the spheres of human activities that are to be regulated by lunation. In another exegetical statement "the affairs of their religion" are specified as "the periods of fasting and of breaking the fast." They are to be determined by the "observation of [the moon's] waning and waxing" (ibid., 581; cf. Ibn Kathīr, *Tafsīr*, i, 503).

Q 10:5 and 36:39 give us an insight into how pre-Islamic Arabs and the first Muslims reckoned their time. These verses refer to the system of twenty-eight lunar mansions *(manāzil)*, i.e. stars, groups of stars or spots on the sky in which the moon "is located on each successive night of the sidereal (not the synodic) month" (de Blois, Taʾrīkh, 260; see STARS AND PLANETS). Whereas later Muslim astronomers abandoned this system in favor of more precise astronomical calculations, it has survived until today and lies at the foundation of agricultural calendars in many Arab countries and their neighboring areas.

One consequence of the qurʾānic injunction to use the moon for keeping time is the practice of watching for the new crescent to determine the beginning and the end of Ramaḍān. Of all Muslim schools of law (see LAW AND THE QURʾĀN) and sects (see THEOLOGY AND THE QURʾĀN) only the Ismāʿīlīs (see SHĪʿISM AND THE QURʾĀN) rely on mathematics to calculate the length of their months (see SCIENCE AND THE QURʾĀN; MEASUREMENT). All other Muslim communities insist that the beginning and end of the new month, especially of Ramaḍān, be determined by the sighting of the new crescent. The importance of Ramaḍān for the Muslim ritual is attested by the fact that it is the only month of the calendar that is explicitly mentioned in the Qurʾān (Q 2:185; see FESTIVALS AND COMMEMORATIVE DAYS; RITUAL AND THE QURʾĀN). Commentators add that, apart from its sacred status as the month of fasting, the holiness of Ramaḍān springs from its being the month of revelation (*inzāl al-Qurʾān*, see REVELATION AND INSPIRATION). The night in which, according to the tradition, the whole of the Qurʾān was revealed to Muḥammad falls on 27 Ramaḍān. Commentators consider it especially propitious, since Q 97:3 describes this night *(laylat al-qadr)* as being "better than a thousand months."

Another important religious activity associated with a calendar month is the pilgrimage *(ḥajj)*, which takes place during the month of Dhū l-Ḥijja. This month is second in the previously-discussed triad of sacred months, which were respected by many Arab tribes before Islam. According to commentators, their sacred functions are evident from their names. Dhū l-Qaʿda is interpreted as the period of "sitting still," when the warlike bedouins (see BEDOUIN) of Arabia stayed in their tents and abstained from raiding and fighting their neighbors (Ṭabarī, *Tafsīr*, ii, 589). The name of Dhū l-Ḥijja is indicative of its function as the month of pilgrimage, although the actual ritual activities are limited to four days, i.e. seventh — tenth, but in practice continue until the thirteenth. The name of al-Muḥarram ("the sacred" or "protected") speaks for itself (see PROTECTION; FORBIDDEN). It is the month of peace, whose sanctity is assured by God himself. Likewise, the name of Rajab also connotes the idea of veneration and reverence (Lane, iii, 1033 and *Lisān al-ʿArab*, i, 411). Its special status is further accentuated by its numerous honorific epithets, such as "the deaf" *(al-aṣamm)*, because no rattling of swords or other weapons was heard during it, or "the one that pours forth [divine mercy]" (*al-aṣabb*, see PIETY; MERCY). Before Islam, it was celebrated by the sacrifice of the first-born of the flock — a practice that was abolished by the Prophet in a special ḥadīth. Despite this prohibition, many Muslims hold Rajab in high regard and mark it by fasting on certain days and by slaughtering sacrificial animals (Kister, Rajab; see SLAUGHTER).

Finally, a substantial body of traditions exalts the eighth month of the Muslim calendar, Shaʿbān, which many consider to be a month of voluntary fasting. The night of the fifteenth of Shaʿbān is regarded as the holiest time of the whole month. A number of ḥadīths recommend that one should spend it in "vigil prayer and supplication, and the morrow in fasting" (Kister, Shaʿbān, 23-4; see BOWING AND PROSTRATION; VIGILS). Furthermore, some commentators identify it with the "blessed night" *(layla mubāraka)* of Q 44:3, which is considered to be the night of the remission of all sins (see SIN, MAJOR AND MINOR; FORGIVENESS). Hence its popular name, "the night of acquittance" *(laylat al-barāʾa)*. Some Muslims mark it with special prayers and supplications in the hope of obtaining divine rewards that are promised "to those who exert themselves in devotion during this night" (ibid., 27). At the same time, many commentators rejected this tradition, arguing that *laylat al-barāʾa* was the night of revelation and thus is identical with *laylat al-qadr* of Q 97:1. Although the Qurʾān itself is silent about the special status of the months just discussed, except for Ramaḍān, their importance is thrown into sharp relief in the famous ḥadīth that quotes the Prophet as saying "Rajab is the month of God, Shaʿbān is my month, and Ramaḍān is the month of my community" (ibid., 37).

Alexander Knysh

Bibliography

Primary: A.Y. Ali, *The holy Qurʾān. Text, translation and commentary*, repr. Elmherst, N.Y. 1987; Ibn Kathīr, *Tafsīr*, ed. S. al-Salāma, 8 vols., Riyadh 1997; *Lisān al-ʿArab;* Ṭabarī, *Tafsīr*, ed. Ṣ.ʿA. al-Khālidī and I.M. al-ʿAlī, 7 vols., Damascus 1997.

Secondary: H. Amir-Ali, The "month" in the Qurʾān, in *IC* 51 (1977), 21-30; A.F.L. Beeston, *Epigraphic south Arabian calendars and dating*, London 1956; F.C. de Blois, Taʾrīkh, in *EI²*, x, 257-64; M. Effendi, Mémoire sur le calendrier arabe avant l'islamisme, in *JA* 11 (1858), 109-92; J. Fück, Zur an-nasīʾ, in *OLZ* 36 (1933), 280-3; M.J. Kister, "Rajab is the month of God..." A study in the persistence of an early tradition, in *IOS* 1 (1971), 191-223; id., "Shaʿbān is my month." A study of an early tradition, in J. Blau et al. (eds.), *Studia orientalia memoriae D.H. Baneth dedicata*, Jerusalem 1979, 15-37; Lane; E. Littman, Über die Ehrennamen und Neubenennungen der islamische Monate, in *Der Islam* 8 (1918), 228-36; A. Moberg, An-Nasīʾ *in der islamischen Tradition*, Lund 1931; Paret, *Kommentar;* id., *Mohammed und der Koran. Geschichte und Verkündigung des arabischen Propheten*, Stuttgart 1957; M. Plessner, Review of A. Moberg, An-Nasīʾ *in der islamischen Tradition*, in *Der Islam* 21 (1933), 226-8; J. Wellhausen, *Reste arabischen Heidentum*, Berlin 1927.

Moon

The satellite of the earth, which takes a little less than one solar-calendar month to complete its revolution. In the Qurʾān, the general Arabic term for moon *(qamar)* occurs twenty-seven times, usually paired with the sun (q.v.; *shams*). Sūra 54 is entitled "The Moon" (Sūrat al-Qamar), in reference to the moon seeming to split in two at the time the Meccans began to persecute the Muslims (see MECCA; OPPOSITION TO MUḤAMMAD). The new or crescent moon *(hilāl)* appears only once (in its plural form, *ahilla*, Q 2:189), and neither the term for the full moon *(badr)* nor that for the night when no moon is visible (i.e. *sirār*) is mentioned.

The moon has a multi-faceted role in Islamic culture: its phases define the Muslim (*hijrī*, see EMIGRATION) calendar (q.v.) of twelve months (q.v.); the sighting of the new moon during Ramaḍān (q.v.) begins the fasting (q.v.) month; the moon's positioning in the sky can be used to mark time (q.v.); lunar symbols abound in Islamic mysticism and esoterica; and the lunar eclipse has theological significance (see THEOLOGY AND THE QURʾĀN; ṢŪFISM AND THE QURʾĀN). There is a rich vocabulary in classical Arabic for the moon and the days of the lunar month (Ibn Sīda, *Mukhaṣṣaṣ*, ix, 26-32). Every three nights of the lunar month were grouped together under a special name. In Arabic poetry, the moon, especially the crescent moon, figures prominently (Tīfāshī, *Surūr al-nafs*, 65-80). As an important Islamic symbol, the crescent moon dates back to the Umayyad period and is currently used on the flags of many Muslim countries (see EPIGRAPHY AND THE QURʾĀN).

The qurʾānic allusions to the moon are varied. It appears in a dream (see DREAMS AND SLEEP) of Joseph (q.v.; Q 12:4), as well as in the story of Abraham's (q.v.) conversion (Q 6:77; see IDOLATRY AND IDOLATERS; ḤANĪF). It is the object of oaths (q.v.; e.g. Q 74:32; see FORM AND STRUCTURE OF THE QURʾĀN). As one of the signs (q.v.) of God's beneficence to humankind (e.g. Q 14:33; see GRACE; BLESSING; COSMOLOGY; NATURE AS SIGNS), the moon, too, prostrates to God (Q 22:18; see CREATION; BOWING AND PROSTRATION; GLORIFICATION OF GOD). God placed the moon in the heavens (see HEAVEN AND SKY) as an aid to humans: while it functions as a light (q.v.; Q 71:16), its primary use is to mark time (cf. Q 2:189; 6:96; see DAY AND NIGHT; DAY, TIMES OF).

Of the twelve lunar months, only Ramaḍān is mentioned by name in the Qurʾān (Q 2:185). In pre-Islamic Arabia an intercalary month *(nasīʾ)* was added to bring the shorter lunar calendar of 354 days into alignment with the seasons (q.v.), but this was expressly forbidden in the Qurʾān (Q 9:37) and in statements of Muḥammad (see PRE-ISLAMIC ARABIA AND THE QURʾĀN). The rationale ordinarily given for this ban is that holy months, such as Ramaḍān, could then be confused with ordinary months. Each month began with the first sighting of the crescent moon, resulting in elaborate rules in legal texts for determining the beginning of the fasting month (see LAW AND THE QURʾĀN). By the ninth century, al-Khwārizmī compiled a table showing lunar crescent visibility for the latitude of Baghdād. Despite such astronomical models for predicting the lunar crescent, religious law stipulated that the new moon be physically seen by a male Muslim of good standing.

An alternative lunar calendar was provided by charting the nightly progression of the moon vis-à-vis the stars for a full lunation, a period of about twenty-seven and one-third days. This system of twenty-eight lunar stations *(manāzil al-qamar)* is elaborated in Islamic astronomical and astrological texts, but is not specifically mentioned in the Qurʾān. Another pre-Islamic calendar plotted months by noting the number of days after the crescent moon until the moon conjoined with the Pleiades *(thurayyā)*. While commentators often associate Sūrat al-Najm ("The Star," Q 53), with the Pleiades, there is no specific mention of this conjunction calendar in the Qurʾān or ḥadīth (see ḤADĪTH AND THE QURʾĀN).

Although Muḥammad condemned the use of stars for prediction (see FORETELLING; DIVINATION; PLANETS AND STARS) — an interdiction against the so-called *anwāʾ*, which Arab scholars linked to the lunar stations — and worship of the sun or moon is forbidden in the Qurʾān (Q 41:37; see IDOLS AND IMAGES; SOUTH ARABIA, RELIGION IN PRE-ISLAMIC), the moon has a variety of symbolic associations in Islamic esoterica and mysticism. As one of the seven "planets" *(al-kawākib al-sayyāra)*, the moon figures prominently in astrology, especially when it enters zodiacal houses and lunar stations. The moon was considered cold and wet in the humoral system and was generally linked in esoteric lore with the lungs in the body, the faculty of intelligence (see INTELLECT; KNOWLEDGE AND LEARNING), salty food, saffron, camphor (q.v.), white sandalwood incense, silver and chrysolite. The waxing and waning of the moon were believed to influence the growth of plants and animal hair, milk and egg production, the movements of animals and even the flavor of meat (Qazwīnī, *ʿAjāʾib*, 48-52). Religious mystics used the moon as a symbolic metaphor for the prophet Muḥammad. Some of the divine names of God (see GOD AND HIS ATTRIBUTES), e.g. "the knowing" *(al-ʿalīm)* and "the creator" *(al-khāliq)*, are particularly associated with the moon. There is a single reference in the Qurʾān (Q 75:8) to the moon being eclipsed *(khasafa)* on the day of judgment (*yawm al-qiyāma*, see LAST JUDGMENT; APOCALYPSE). Legal texts record a special prayer for both lunar and solar eclipses. In Arab folklore there was much speculation about the meaning of an eclipse, including a widespread story that a fish had swallowed the moon.

Daniel Martin Varisco

Bibliography
Primary: al-Bīrūnī, Abū l-Rayḥān Muḥammad b. Aḥmad, *al-Āthār al-bāqiya ʿan al-qurūn al-khāliya*, Eng. trans. *The chronology of ancient nations*, London 1879, 70-81; Ibn Sīda, Abū l-Ḥasan ʿAlī b. Ismāʿīl, *al-Mukhaṣṣaṣ*, 17 vols. in 5, Beirut 1965; al-Qazwīnī, Abū Yaḥyā Zakariyyā b. Muḥammad, *ʿAjāʾib al-makhlūqāt*, Beirut 1981; al-Tīfāshī, Abū l-Abbās Aḥmad b. Yūsuf, *Surūr al-nafs bi-madārik al-ḥawās al-khams*, Beirut 1980.
Secondary: D. King, Science in the service of religion. The case of Islam, in *Impact of science on society* 159 (1990), 245-62; P. Kunitzsch, Manāzil, in *EI²*, vi, 374-6; D. Pingree and M. Rodinson, al-Ḳamar, in *EI²*, iv, 517-9; M. Rodinson, La lune chez les Arabes et dans l'Islam, in *Sources orientales. v. La lune. Mythes et rites*, Paris 1962, 153-214; J. Schacht and R. Ettinghausen, Hilāl, in *EI²*, iii, 379-85; D. Varisco, Islamic folk astronomy, in H. Selin (ed.), *Astronomy across cultures. The history of non-western astronomy*, Dordrecht 2000, 615-50; id., The magical significance of the lunar stations in the 13th century Yemeni *Kitāb al-Tabṣira fī ʿilm al-nujūm* of al-Malik al-Ashraf, in *QSA* 13 (1995), 19-40.

Morality see ETHICS AND THE QURʾĀN

Morning

The early part of the day (see DAY AND NIGHT). Morning as a part of the day is mentioned on several occasions in the Qurʾān. Three sūras are named after particular times or phenomena of the morning: Sūrat al-Fajr ("Dawn," Q 89), Sūrat al-Ḍuḥā ("Forenoon," Q 93) and Sūrat al-Falaq ("Daybreak," Q 113). In English, as in other Indo-European languages, uncertainty exists as to which time span the term "morning" actually covers. In these languages, morning is often interpreted as denoting "the first part of the day, until noon (q.v.)," "from sunrise (see DAWN) to noon," or also "the time from midnight to noon." The word that is frequently used in Modern Standard Arabic as an equivalent of the English "morning" is *ṣabāḥ*. Words that are derived from the Arabic root *ṣ-b-ḥ* form, however, only one part of a larger number of words that are used in the Qurʾān to describe the morning time.

Terminology

In the Qurʾān, morning or parts of it are described by a number of lexical expressions: the Arabic *bukra* (Q 19:11, 62; 25:5; 33:42; 48:9; 54:38; 76:25) and *ibkār* (Q 3:41; 40:55) designate the early morning, or the first part of the day, between the time of the prayer (q.v.) of the daybreak and sunrise (Lane, s.v. *bukra*). The term *ḍuḥā* (Q 7:98; 20:59; 93:1; 79:29, 46; 91:1; 93:1) describes the early part of the forenoon, after sunrise: according to some, this is when the sun (q.v.) is yet low, according to others, when the sun is somewhat high (Lane, s.v. *ḍuḥā*) or up to the moment when the sun has traversed the diurnal arc (Pellat, Layl and nahār). According to al-

Hamadhānī (d. 319/932; *Alfāẓ*, 287), *ḍuḥā* follows *al-ghadāt*. The term *fajr* (Q 2:187; 17:78; 24:58; 89:1; 97:5) is often rendered as "daybreak," "dawn," or "the light of morning" (Lane, s.v. *fajr*). The term *falaq*, "daybreak, the bright gleam of dawn," is derived from the Arabic root *f-l-q*, "to split, cleave." It occurs in one passage of the Qurʾān (Q 113:1) in the phrase *rabb al-falaq*, "lord (q.v.) of the daybreak." Words derived from the root *gh-d-w* like *ghadāt* and *ghuduww* (Q 6:52; 18:28; also Q 7:205; 13:15; 40:46) again denote the first part of the day, the period between the time of the prayer of daybreak and sunrise. Before the terms that describe the times of prayer were standardized, for some time after Muḥammad's death *ghadāt* was sometimes used as an alternative term to describe the morning prayer, which later became commonly described as *ṣalāt al-fajr* (cf. Wensinck, Mīḳāt). The words *saḥar* (Q 54:34) and *asḥār* (Q 3:17; 51:18) are related to the Semitic **šaḥr* which, in various forms, is used to denote "dawn" in a number of Semitic languages (Mustafa, Morgenanbruch, 113). The Arabic word *ṣubḥ* is commonly rendered as "daybreak, dawn, or forenoon," counted from sunrise to noon or, according to some, from midnight to noon or from the beginning of the latter half of the night to the time when the sun declines from the meridian (Lane, s.v. *ṣubḥ*). *Ṣubḥ* (Q 11:81; 74:34; 81:18; 100:3) and other words derived from the root *ṣ-b-ḥ* (*ṣabāḥ*, Q 37:177; *iṣbāḥ*, Q 6:96) occur in a number of qurʾānic phrases describing the morning time. Verbal forms of the root *ṣ-b-ḥ*, like *ṣabbaḥa* (Q 54:38), *aṣbaḥa* (e.g. Q 29:37) or *muṣbiḥīna* (Q 15:83) are rendered as "to enter upon the time of morning" or "morning prayer" (Q 30:17). They also have the sense of "to come to be in the morning," as in Q 67:30 (Lane, s.v. *aṣbaḥa*).

On the other hand, several metaphorical expressions (see METAPHOR) are used to describe the morning as, for example: by the night when it journeys on (*wa-l-layli idhā yasrī*, Q 89:4; see OATHS); at the declining of the stars (*idbār al-nujūm*, Q 52:49); the rising of the sun (*ṭulūʿ al-shams*, Q 50:39); the first part of the day (*wajh al-nahār*, Q 3:72); after sunrise until midday, or at sunrise (*ishrāq*, Q 38:18); at sunrise (*mushriqīna*, i.e. entering upon the time of sunrise; Q 15:73; cf. Q 26:60). The word *tasraḥūna*, to pasture in the morning (Q 16:6), may also be interpreted as a metaphorical description of the morning time.

Morning as a part of the day

Ancient oriental systems of belief describe the morning as the time at which humankind is transferred from the realm of darkness (q.v.), chaos and death (see DEATH AND THE DEAD) to the realm of light (q.v.), life (q.v.) and justice (Görg and Lang, *Lexikon*, ii, 46; Gurney, *Hethiter*, 150; see JUSTICE AND INJUSTICE). In the Hebrew Bible (*Ps* 46:6), morning is the time when God supports the believers (see BELIEF AND UNBELIEF). In the Qurʾān, morning marks the end of the dark night, as in Q 97:5 where the dawn (*fajr*) heralds the end of the Night of Power (q.v.; *laylat al-qadr*). For the Arabs (q.v.) in pre-Islamic times, however, the morning was not necessarily the beginning of the full or official day (Fischer, "Tag und Nacht," 749, 756; see also DAY, TIMES OF).

In the qurʾānic narrative, morning is the time of rest (Q 18:62; *ghadāʾ*, the morning meal, signifies a period of rest after a long journey) or of important activity, e.g. when Muḥammad leaves his household to prepare for a battle against the unbelievers (see BELIEF AND UNBELIEF; EXPEDITIONS AND BATTLES) in the morning (Q 3:121). As in the Bible (e.g. *Ps* 104:23), morning is represented in the Qurʾān as the time when daily work, e.g. harvesting the garden (q.v.), begins (Q 68:21-5). In the same pericope, however, morning is the time of chastisement (see CHASTISEMENT AND PUNISHMENT), when the fruit that the unbelievers intend to gather have been taken away by God overnight to send them a sign of his power (see POWER AND IMPOTENCE) and a warning (q.v.; Q 68:26-33). There are other episodes that identify morning as the time in which God inflicts or threatens to inflict evil upon the unbelievers (Q 7:98; 37:177; see PUNISHMENT STORIES; GOOD AND EVIL). In Q 54:38, Q 11:81 and Q 15:73, morning is denoted as the time of chastisement of the people of Lot (q.v.) who had previously disputed the warnings of God. The punishment of the tribe of Thamūd (q.v.), who had ignored God's message that was brought to them by Ṣāliḥ (q.v.), also comes in the morning (Q 7:78; 11:67). This pattern is repeated in the passages on the punishment of the Madyan (q.v.; Q 29:37; see MIDIAN) and the people of al-Ḥijr (Q 15:80; see ḤIJR). The consequence of the punishment of the people of Lot will become visible in the morning (Q 15:66) and Q 46:25 also determines morning as the time when the results of the punishment of the tribe of ʿĀd (q.v.) become manifest. At the same time, morning is the time of mercy (q.v.) when the folk of Lot are exempted from the punishment brought upon them (Q 54:34). The regular return of the sun after night is attributed to God as one of his marvelous creations (Q 79:29; see CREATION; SIGNS; MARVELS; BLESSING). He is mentioned as the one who splits the sky into dawn (*fāliq al-iṣbāḥ*, Q 6:96) and the epithet "lord of the daybreak" (*rabb al-falaq*, Q 113:1) is used in the same sense.

Morning as a metaphor

In Q 79:46 the term *ḍuḥā* stands for a short period of time stating that those who are called up from their graves to final judgment (see LAST JUDGMENT) will feel that only an evening (q.v.) or its forenoon, i.e. a much shorter period of time (q.v.) than in reality, will have passed since they had been buried. Another occurrence of morning as a measure of time may be found in Q 34:12 where the giant morning stride of Solomon (q.v.) equals a month's journey (q.v.). *Ghadāt (ghuduww)* in combination with *ʿashī, aṣīl*, or *āṣāl* (evening) denotes the constancy of religious service or of another activity or phenomenon (Q 6:52; 18:28; 7:205; 13:15; 24:36; Hamadhānī, *Alfāẓ*, 291). The terms *bukra* and *ibkār, ishrāq* (or *mushriqīna*) and *ṣubḥ* (or *muṣbiḥīna*) also occur in conjunction with words denoting evening to suggest constancy of a particular activity. In Q 16:6, bringing the cattle home in the evening and driving it to pasture in the morning *(tasraḥūna)* again stands for a recurrent activity that illustrates the beauty of God's creation. In Q 3:72, morning, i.e. the beginning of the day *(wajh al-nahār)*, and evening *(ākhirahu)* denote two different times in which the Jewish people (see JEWS AND JUDAISM) shall act in a different manner, namely believe and disbelieve in the holy scripture. In some passages (e.g. Q 28:18), morning appears as a narrative means of indicating the beginning of a new episode of a particular story (see LITERARY STRUCTURES OF THE QURʾĀN). This usage of morning is known also from the Bible (Görg and Lang, *Lexikon*, 846).

Divine service, religious and everyday life

Morning is mentioned as one of the times of the day at which prayer (*ṣalāt al-fajr*, e.g. Q 24:58) and glorification of God (q.v.; *tasbīḥ*, e.g. Q 30:17; 33:41; 38:18; 48:9) must be performed. Q 51:18 promises paradise (q.v.) to those who asked God for forgiveness (q.v.) during the morning prayer (see

Ṭabarī, *Tafsīr,* v, 227 [ad Q 2:238] for an exposition on the advantages of the morning prayer). Q 17:78 calls upon the believers to recite the Qurʾān in the morning (see RECITATION OF THE QURʾĀN). Commentators of the Qurʾān state that during this recital of the Qurʾān the angels (see ANGEL) are present (Sawār, *Qurʾān,* 74). Q 7:205 demands that believers shall remember God in the morning.

Morning marks the beginning of the ritual practice of fasting (q.v.) during the month of Ramaḍān (q.v.). In Q 2:187 the believers are instructed to resume fasting when a white thread is clearly distinguishable from a black one at dawn. In several cases, morning is part of formulaic evocations (Q 74:34; 81:18; 89:1; 91:1; 93:1). This again may be understood as a reference to the creative powers of God.

Lutz Wiederhold

Bibliography
Primary: ʿAbd-al-Bāqī; E.E. Calverly, *Worship in Islam,* Madras 1925, Lahore 1957² (Eng. trans. of al-Ghazālī's *Iḥyāʾ;* see esp. p. 187 for a discussion of the dawn prayer); al-Hamadhānī, ʿAbd al-Raḥmān b. ʿĪsā, *Kitāb al-Alfāẓ al-kitābiyya,* ed. L. Cheikho, Beirut 1885, 287-8 *(sāʿāt al-nahār),* 290-1 *(intihāʾ al-layl wa-wurūd al-ṣubḥ),* 291 *(fiʾl al-shayʾ ṣabāḥan wa-masāʾan);* M. Sawār (ed.), *al-Qurʾān al-karīm bi-l-rasm al-ʿuthmānī wa bi-hāmishihi Tafsīr al-Jalālayn,* Beirut n.d.; Ṭabarī, *Tafsīr,* ed. Shākir.
Secondary: C.C. Berg, Ṣawm, in *EI¹,* vii, 192-9; A. Fischer, "Tag und Nacht" im Arabischen und die semitische Tagesberechnung, in *Abhandlungen der Philosophisch-Historischen Klasse der Königlichen Sächsischen Gesellschaft der Wissenschaften* 27 (1909), 741-57; M. Görg and B. Lang (eds.), *Neues Bibel-Lexikon,* 3 vols. to date, Zürich 1988-, ii, 846 (Morgen); S. Günther, Tag und Tageszeiten im Qurʾān, in W. Beltz and S. Günther (eds.), *Erlesenes. Sonderheft der Halleschen Beiträge zur Orientwissenschaft anläßlich des 19. Kongresses der Union Européenne d'Arabisants et Islamisants,* Halle, Saale 1998, 46-67; O.R. Gurney, *Die Hethiter,* Dresden 1969; A.H. Mustafa, Morgenanbruch in den nordwestsemitischen Sprachen, in *Hallesche Beiträge zur Orientwissenschaft* 13/14 (1990), 113-6; Ch. Pellat, Layl and nahār, in *EI²,* v, 707-10; M. Plessner, Ramaḍān, in *EI¹,* vi, 1111; I.M. Ta-Shma, Day and night, in C. Roth (ed.), *Encyclopaedia judaica,* 16 vols., Jerusalem 1972-, v, 1374-6; A.J. Wensinck, Mīḳāt, in *EI¹,* v, 492-3.

Moses

The most prominent pre-Islamic prophet in the Qurʾān and in extra-qurʾānic Islamic tradition (see PROPHETS AND PROPHETHOOD). Moses' name (Mūsā) is attested 136 times in the Qurʾān, in passages of varying length and narrative complexity. The qurʾānic narratives dealing with Moses and the allusions to him far exceed those relating to other figures of the Islamic history of salvation (q.v.), including Abraham (q.v.). The references to Moses are spread throughout the Qurʾān, with mentions already in the Meccan sūras. Most narratives (q.v.) about Moses, however, date from the Medinan period of revelation (see CHRONOLOGY AND THE QURʾĀN), when Muḥammad came in close contact with Jews (see JEWS AND JUDAISM).

The topics in the qurʾānic account of Moses go back to biblical and post-biblical narratives. The details in the Qurʾān and in early Islamic exegesis testify to the great influence of Jewish Haggada on Muḥammad and early Islam (see SCRIPTURE AND THE QURʾĀN). This does not mean, however, that the qurʾānic Moses fully corresponds to the Moses of Jewish tradition. The Qurʾān has its own point of view and its own interpretation of the older narrative material. The essential feature of the allusions to the past is a typological interpretation of the earlier narratives, by which the biography of Moses is seen in the light of the biography of Muḥammad (q.v.). The Qurʾān reminds its audience of Moses' deeds and the events connected with him, associating these deeds and events with the circumstances in Muḥammad's life (see OCCASIONS OF REVELATION; REVELATION AND INSPIRATION). There are two major themes that emerge in the story of Moses: God as creator (see CREATION) and lord (q.v.; *rabb*), and a typological pattern that draws parallels to Muḥammad. As in all of the qur'ānic stories of the prophets, emphasis is placed upon Moses' monotheism (see POLYTHEISM AND ATHEISM) and his role as a divine messenger (q.v.): he has to endure accusations of lying (see LIE), as well as oppression (q.v.) and hostility at the hands of the unbelievers (see BELIEF AND UNBELIEF) and evildoers (see EVIL DEEDS) to whom he is sent until he and his followers are rescued and his enemies (q.v.) destroyed by God (see PUNISHMENT STORIES). In the qur'ānic purview, such details of the story of Moses prefigure Muḥammad's biography (see SĪRA AND THE QUR'ĀN). Although in most cases the qur'ānic verses address Muḥammad directly, their contents are to serve as a reminder to the Qur'ān's audience, as the conclusion to a long passage relating the story of Moses demonstrates: "Thus do we recount to you some of the stories of the past. And we have caused to come to you from us a reminder" (Q 20:99; see MEMORY).

Moses' infancy

The Qur'ān tells of Moses' infancy, when God suggests to Moses' mother that she leave him in a box *(tābūt)* in the sea. She does this, and the sea throws it upon the shore, where the family of Pharaoh (q.v.) finds him. The wife of Pharaoh (and not, as in the Bible, his daughter) protects the child. Moses is therefore brought up among the people of Pharaoh as a child and remains for years among them (Q 26:18). Moses' sister follows the child and watches Moses from afar, without Pharaoh's people being aware. Since Moses refuses the milk (q.v.) of the nurses (see LACTATION; WET NURSING), his sister says to the people of Pharaoh: "Shall I show you a household who will rear him for you and show good will to him?" (Q 28:12). In this way, she directs the people of Pharaoh to his natural mother, who suckles him. God restores Moses to his mother, that she might be comforted and might know that the promise of God is true (Q 20:37-40; 28:7-14; see TRUST AND PATIENCE).

Moses' killing of the Egyptian

Moses' break with the polytheistic background of his childhood comes about when he reaches maturity (q.v.) and is given jurisdiction and knowledge (Q 28:14; cf. 26:21; see KNOWLEDGE AND LEARNING): "He entered the city at a time when its people were not paying attention, and in it he found two men fighting, one belonging to his faction and the other to his enemies. The one who belonged to his faction called him to help against the one who belonged to his enemies, so Moses struck him and finished him. He said: 'This is the work of Satan *(hādhā min ʿamali l-shayṭāni)*. He is clearly an enemy who leads astray (q.v.; *muḍill*)'" (Q 28:15). God forgives Moses (Q 28:16). When early theology (see THEOLOGY AND THE QUR'ĀN) discussed the origin of sin *(maʿṣiya,* see SIN, MAJOR AND MINOR), the Qadariyya-Muʿtazila quoted Q 28:15 as evidence that "leading astray" *(iḍlāl)* is not from God (Ritter, Studien, 72; see ERROR; MUʿTAZILĪS; FREEDOM AND PREDESTINATION; JUSTICE AND INJUSTICE). This verse provides a starting point for the Muslim discussion of causality (Ṭabarī, *Tafsīr,* ad loc.; Rāzī, *Tafsīr,* xxiv, 201; see also DEVIL). Moses' break with Pharaoh and his people is cemented (cf. Q 26:19). Pharaoh's council *(al-mala')* — Moses' later opposition — take counsel against him, to kill him (Q 28:20) and he goes forth from Egypt (q.v.) afraid (Q 28:21).

Moses' flight to Midian
On his flight from Egypt Moses comes to Midian (q.v.; Madyan; Q 28:22-8). There he helps two women, the daughters of an old man *(shaykh kabīr),* to water their flocks. Their father says to Moses: "I wish to marry you to one of these two daughters of mine, on condition that you hire yourself to me for eight years, and if you do complete ten, that is of your own will…" (Q 28:27). Although the Qur'ān does not mention the name of the old man who hired Moses, commentators (see EXEGESIS OF THE QUR'ĀN: CLASSICAL AND MEDIEVAL) identify him as Yathrā (Jethro; cf. *Exod* 3:1; 4:18; 18:1 f.) or the qur'ānic prophet Shu'ayb (q.v.; Ṭabarī, *Tafsīr,* ad loc.; Rāzī, *Tafsīr,* xxiv, 206 f.).

Moses' election and mission to Pharaoh
When Moses fulfills his term, he goes out with his household. In the holy valley of Ṭuwā (q.v.) he receives a divine message and mission: "He perceived on the side of the mount a fire (q.v.)…" (Q 28:29). "When he came to it he was addressed: 'O Moses, I am your lord. Take off your sandals, for you are in the holy valley Ṭuwā. I have chosen you, so listen to what is inspired. I am God. There is no God but I. Serve me and establish the prayer for my remembrance…" (Q 20:11-17; cf. Q 28:30; 79:16). Commentators explain that Moses' sandals were made from the skin of the carcass of an ass, i.e. one that was not slaughtered; therefore, Moses was ordered to take them off (Ṭabarī, *Tafsīr,* ad loc.). The order Moses received, when he came to the fire and was called "from the tree" *(shajara,* Q 28:30), marks the beginning of Moses' prophetic mission. He is sent with two proofs *(burhānān)* to Pharaoh and his council of nobles *(mala'),* namely the sign *(āya)* of his staff (see ROD) that was transformed into a serpent and the sign of his hand that became white (Q 20:17-23; 28:31-2; see PROOF; SIGNS; MIRACLES). God orders Moses to tell Pharaoh: "Go to Pharaoh! He has rebelled (see REBELLION; ARROGANCE). And say: Do you have any desire to purify yourself, and that I should guide you to your lord in fear (q.v.)?" (Q 79:17-9). Moses' brother Aaron (q.v.) is sent to Pharaoh together with Moses; in this mission, they are given authority (q.v.; *sulṭān,* Q 23:45; 28:35; cf. 4:153; 11:96). Al-Ṭabarī (d. 310/923; *Tafsīr,* ad loc.) explains Moses' authority *(sulṭān)* as the signs *(āyāt)* and evidences *(bayyināt)* that God gave him.

Moses' signs and evidences
The signs *(āyāt)* and evidences *(bayyināt)* of Moses' prophethood are significant elements of the typological schema of the qur'ānic story about him (Q 2:92; 7:103, 105; 11:96; 14:5; 17:101; 23:45; 28:36; 29:39; 40:23; 43:46-7): as al-Ṭabarī (*Tafsīr,* ad loc.) explains, these are an argument *(ḥujja)* of Moses' truthfulness *(ṣidq)* and prophethood *(nubuwwa).* Pharaoh and the nobility *(al-mala')* of his people *(qawm,* Q 7:127) — a type of council or assembly — reject, however, these signs and proofs: "Then… we sent Moses with our signs *(bi-āyātinā)* to Pharaoh and his council of nobles *(mala'ihi)…*" (Q 7:103; cf. Q 11:97; 23:46; 28:32; 43:46). "Moses said: O Pharaoh, I am a messenger from the lord of the worlds… I came to you with an evidence *(bayyina)* from your lord, so send forth with me the Children of Israel (q.v.). [Pharaoh] said: If you came with a sign, bring it, if you are one of those who speak the truth. So [Moses] threw his staff, and lo, it was a serpent manifest. And he drew forth his hand, and lo, it was white to the onlookers.

The nobility of Pharaoh's people *(al-malaʾ min qawmi firʿawn)* said: 'Surely this is a knowing magician...'" (Q 7:104-9; cf. 26:30-5; see MAGIC). There are nine signs that Moses brings to Pharaoh and his people (Q 17:101; 27:12). According to early commentators, these are: flood, locusts, vermin, frogs, blood, Moses' staff, Moses' hand, destruction, and the sea (Ṭabarī, *Tafsīr,* ad loc.).

The underlying narrative of these qurʾānic passages is the biblical account of Moses' and Aaron's encounter with Pharaoh, the miracles they perform, the calamities they bring down upon Egypt and Israel's exodus from Egypt. The qurʾānic version of this narrative is, however, remodeled in accordance with its typological interpretation of the story of Moses. Moses' signs and proofs correspond to Muḥammad's signs and proofs. Pharaoh's council of nobles corresponds to the leading clan representatives *(malaʾ)* of Mecca (q.v.; see also TRIBES AND CLANS), Muḥammad's opposition (Q 38:6; see COMMUNITY AND SOCIETY IN THE QURʾĀN; OPPOSITION TO MUḤAMMAD), above all the leader of the Banū ʿAbd Shams, Abū Sufyān, and the leader of the Banū Makhzūm, Abū Jahl, both archenemies of Muḥammad.

Moses' patience

After Moses shows his signs and evidences, whereupon the defeated magicians of Pharaoh are cast down, prostrate themselves and proclaim their faith in God and Moses' and Aaron's message (Q 7:113-26), the nobility of Pharaoh's people *(al-malaʾu min qawmi firʿawni)* say to Pharaoh: "'Will you leave Moses and his people to cause corruption (q.v.) in the land, so that he may forsake you and your gods?' He said: 'We shall kill their sons, and keep their females alive, and over them be victors.' Then Moses said to his people: 'Seek help in God and endure patiently *(wa-ṣbirū)*! The earth belongs to God, he makes whomsoever he wants of his servants inherit it, and the end result *(al-ʿāqiba)* is to those who are piously in fear of God.... It may be that your lord will destroy *(an yuhlika)* your enemy...'" (Q 7:127-9; cf. Q 2:49; 14:6). Patience *(ṣabr)* is another keyword of the typological pattern. Before Moses and his people are rescued and their enemies defeated, they have to be patient. This corresponds to Muḥammad's biography. According to Islamic exegesis and historiography Muḥammad and his followers in the Meccan period had to endure the hostility of the Meccan "nobles" *(malaʾ)* patiently. When they had to migrate to Medina (q.v.; see also EMIGRATION), they were allowed to fight against the Meccan Quraysh (q.v.), Muḥammad's own clan, and were victorious over them by the help of God (see also EXPEDITIONS AND BATTLES; VICTORY). According to the early Qurʾān commentators, the turning point was the revelation of Q 22:39-41: "Permission is given to those who fight because they have been wronged, God is well able to give them victory. Those who have been driven out of their houses without right only because they said God is our lord..." Early commentary maintains that this was the first revelation to allow armed fighting (q.v.; *qitāl*) and war (q.v.; *ḥarb*) against unbelievers (Ṭabarī, *Tafsīr,* ad loc.; see also JIHĀD). Until these verses (q.v.) were revealed, Muḥammad "had simply been ordered to call men to God and to patient endurance *(ṣabr)* against insult... The Quraysh had persecuted his followers, seducing some from their religion, and exiling others from their country..." (Ibn Isḥāq, *Sīra,* i, 467; Ibn Isḥāq-Guillaume, 212).

Patience (*ṣabr,* Q 14:5-6) is combined with thankfulness (*shukr,* see GRATITUDE AND INGRATITUDE): "We sent Moses with our signs *(āyāt)*: 'Bring your people from the darkness (q.v.) to the light (q.v.), and remind them of the days of God (q.v.; *ayyām Allāh*).' Therein are signs for everyone who is patient and thankful *(ṣabbār shakūr).*" Commentators explain that people have to be patient when they are tested (*ubtuliya,* see TRIAL), and thankful when God bestows favor (*niʿma,* see GRACE; BLESSING) upon them (Ṭabarī, *Tafsīr,* ad loc.). Moses and his people, therefore, were obliged to be patient before their rescue, and to be thankful after they were rescued by God's favor.

Moses' deliverance and Pharaoh's destruction

The qurʾānic story of Moses reaches its peak at the rescue, or deliverance (q.v.; *najāt*), of him and his people and the punishment (see CHASTISEMENT AND PUNISHMENT) and destruction *(halāk)* of Pharaoh and his army *(jund)* by drowning (q.v.): "So we took vengeance (q.v.) on them and drowned them in the sea, for having counted our signs false, and having been neglectful of them. And we caused the people who had been oppressed (see OPPRESSED ON EARTH, THE) to inherit the east and the west of the land on which we had bestowed blessing. The good word of your lord was fulfilled upon the Children of Israel for their patience. And we destroyed what Pharaoh and his people had been constructing and embellishing" (Q 7:136-7). Pharaoh's council of nobles *(malaʾ),* who "thought themselves great" were also destroyed: "They accused them [i.e. Moses and Aaron] of lying, and were among those who were destroyed" (Q 23:45-8). While God drowned Pharaoh and his army, he rescued Moses and his followers who had passed through the sea: "When we divided the sea for you and delivered you and drowned the people of Pharaoh before your eyes" (Q 2:50; cf. Q 7:138; 8:54; 10:90; 17:103; 26:52-68; 43:55; 44:23-4). Q 44:23-31 (cf. Q 26:52) tells the history of Moses' departure from Egypt. God told Moses: "Set out by night with my servants. You are going to be followed. And leave the sea gaping wide. They are an army *(jund)* to be drowned." Q 26:63-6 (cf. also Q 20:77-8) is more detailed with regard to Moses' dividing the sea: "We inspired Moses: 'Strike the sea with your staff, and it separated *(infalaqa)*.' Each part became like a mighty cliff. We brought thither the others. We delivered Moses and those with him, all of them. Then we drowned the others." The drowning of Pharaoh and his people is a *topos* for God's helping the believers to triumph, giving them power and bringing about the defeat and destruction of the unbelievers, especially the unbelieving sovereign (see KINGS AND RULERS). ʿAbbāsid propaganda used this *topos* against the Umayyads. In the year 132/750, when the last Umayyad caliph (q.v.) Marwān b. Muḥammad was defeated at the river Zāb, the pontoon bridge was cut. Al-Ṭabarī (*Taʾrīkh,* iii, 41; Eng. trans. J.A. Williams, *History,* xxvii, 164 f.) reports: "More were drowned that day than were slain in battle." The victorious ʿAbbāsid, ʿAbdallāh b. ʿAlī, then recited Q 2:50 and someone else recited verses reviling Marwān: " now the oppressor is the oppressed… a Pharaoh in persecution…."

Besides Pharaoh the Qurʾān mentions two other enemies of Moses who were also destroyed, Korah (q.v.; Qārūn) and Hāmān (q.v.; Q 29:39-40).

God speaks to Moses and Moses wants to see God

After the deliverance of Moses and the Children of Israel and their departure from Egypt, God "appointed for Moses forty nights" (Q 2:51); in the meantime Aaron replaced Moses among his people (Q 7:142). "When Moses came to our appointment, and his lord spoke to him *(kallamahu rabbuhu),* he said: 'My lord, show me [yourself] that I may gaze upon you.'

He replied: 'You will not see me. But gaze upon the mountain, and, if it stands still in its place, then you will see me.'" When God revealed himself to the mountain, he sent the mountain crashing down, and Moses fell down senseless. When he recovered, he said: "Glory unto you (see GLORIFICATION OF GOD; LAUDATION)! I turn to you repentant (see REPENTANCE AND PENANCE), and I am the first of the believers" (Q 7:143).

While early commentators explained these verses by reference to earlier biblical and extra-biblical narratives (Ṭabarī, *Tafsīr*, ad loc.), theologians raised the following questions: How did God speak with Moses, and what does God's speaking *(kalām)* mean (see WORD OF GOD; SPEECH)? Did God speak only to Moses, or also to others? Does Moses' request for seeing God with his eyes *(ruʾya)* mean that it is possible to see God (see SEEING AND HEARING; ANTHROPOMORPHISM)? Why did Moses ask God to see him with his eyes (q.v.) though he undoubtedly knew that it is impossible to see God in this world (*dunyā*, see FACE OF GOD; ESCHATOLOGY)? Is the ability to see God *(ruʾya)* only impossible in this world, or is it also impossible on the day of resurrection (q.v.) and in the hereafter? They discussed also whether Moses' request to see God was a sin *(dhanb)*, since Moses returned repentant *(tāba)* from it (Rāzī, *Tafsīr*, xiv, 186 f.). After Moses' "returning" *(tawba)* from his request to see God, God says to Moses: "I have chosen you above humankind by my message and by my speaking *(bi-kalāmī)*. So hold what I have given you and be thankful. And we wrote for him, upon the tablets *(alwāḥ)*, a lesson to be drawn from all things... then [told him]: 'Hold it fast, and command your people, to take the best of it...'" (Q 7:144-5; see PRESERVED TABLET; COMMANDMENTS). Q 4:164 also reports God's speaking to Moses: "and to Moses God spoke directly *(kallama... taklīman)*" (cf. Q 7:144). Therefore commentators hold that God's speaking to him is a special favor that distinguishes Moses from all other prophets (Rāzī, *Tafsīr*, xii, 87). At the time that God spoke to Moses, the Children of Israel constructed the calf of gold (q.v.) and worshiped it (Q 7:148-9; 20:85-91). "When Moses returned to his people, angry and sad... he cast down the tablets *(al-alwāḥ)*... (Q 7:150; cf. 20:86). "When Moses' anger (q.v.) calmed down, he took up the tablets..." (Q 7:154).

Moses' kitāb *and* furqān

Q 2:53 speaks of the "book" (q.v.) or "scripture" (*kitāb*, cf. Q 2:87; 6:154) of Moses: "When we gave Moses the scripture and the criterion (q.v.; *al-furqān*), in the hope that you might be guided" (cf. Q 2:87; 6:154; 11:17, 110; 17:2; 19:51; 21:48; 23:49; 25:35; 28:43; 32:23; 41:45; 46:12). Some early commentators gloss *kitāb* and *furqān*, explaining *furqān* as the separation *(farq)* and distinction *(faṣl)* between true *(ḥaqq)* and false *(bāṭil);* with this gloss, they interpret *furqān* in the sense of "criterion." This exegesis is al-Ṭabarī's and Fakhr al-Dīn al-Rāzī's (d. 606/1212) starting point for a more complex interpretation. Al-Ṭabarī explains the *kitāb* as the *tawrāt* (see TORAH), which "we wrote for him *(katabnā lahu)* upon the tablets *(al-alwāḥ)*" (Q 7:145), given to Moses by God. This scripture *(kitāb)* is the *furqān*, in so far as God "separated" *(faraqa)* true from false by this scripture. Furthermore, the Torah *(tawrāt)*, in so far as it is "separation" *(furqān)* of true and false is guidance (*hudā*, cf. Q 7:154: "the tablets, and in their inscription there is guidance") for those who follow what is contained theirein (Ṭabarī, *Tafsīr*, ad loc.). Al-Rāzī (*Tafsīr*, iii, 73) explains the "separation" *(furqān)* of true and false as part of the *tawrāt*, namely as the "roots *(uṣūl)* and branches *(furūʿ)* of religion *(dīn)*." Other early commentators explain *furqān* according to the qurʾānic typology. They liken

Q 2:53 with Q 8:41: "and what we sent down to our servant on the day of the *furqān,* the day the two parties met." "The day of the *furqān*" is explained as an allusion to "the day of Badr," i.e. the day of the battle of Badr (q.v.) where God "separated" *(faraqa)* true and false: i.e. with Muḥammad on one side and the Meccan polytheists on the other. God separated "the two parties" by saving and rescuing Muḥammad and giving victory *(naṣr)* to him and defeat to the Meccan polytheists (see PARTIES AND FACTIONS). On this basis commentators draw a parallel to the *furqān* given to Moses: just as God "separated" Muḥammad and the polytheists, so he "separated" Moses and Pharaoh, proceeding in the case of the former as he had with the latter (Ṭabarī, *Tafsīr,* ad loc.). The victory *(naṣr)* distinguishes between the one who speaks the truth *(ṣādiq)* and the one who lies (*kādhib,* Rāzī, *Tafsīr,* iii, 73).

Moses' guidance

The contrasting concepts of guidance *(hudā)* on the one hand and leading astray *(iḍlāl)* on the other are also associated with a qurʾānic typology. Since at "the day of Badr" one of Muḥammad's archenemies, Abū Jahl, led the Meccan polytheists, Muḥammad is paralleled to Moses. Abū Jahl, moreover, reminds one of Pharaoh, "who led his people astray *(aḍalla),* and did not guide *(mā hadā)*" (Q 20:79). Moses' scripture, on the other hand, was light *(nūr)* and guidance *(hudā)* for the people *(al-nās),* namely his people (*qawm,* e.g. Q 2:67; i.e. the Banū Isrāʾīl, cf. Q 6:91; 17:2; 23:49; 28:37; 40:53-4). In Q 2:47 and Q 2:49 the people of Pharaoh are contrasted to the people of Moses. While Moses is the type who brings God's guidance to his people, his enemy Pharaoh is the anti-type, who leads his people astray *(iḍlāl).* As Q 11:98 states: "He shall precede his people on the day of resurrection" (see LAST JUDGMENT). In early theology Pharaoh's leading astray is also used as a paradigm: since guidance *(hudā)* comes from God (e.g. Q 2:38; 92:12-13) the question arose as to whether leading astray *(iḍlāl)* also comes from God. The early Qadariyya-Muʿtazila held that "guidance is from God and leading astray is from man." In one of the oldest documents of early theology, the Pharaoh of the qurʾānic story of Moses is the example for the "leading astray of man" (Ritter, Studien, 71; Schwarz, Letter, 23).

The pages of Moses

Q 87:18-9 mentions the "first" or "former pages" *(al-ṣuḥuf al-ūlā)* of Moses: "Verily this is in the first pages, the pages of Abraham and Moses" (cf. Q 20:133; see also ORALITY AND WRITING IN ARABIA). Some commentators identify that which "is in the first pages" with the preceding verses, Q 87:14-7: "Prospered has he who purifies himself (see CLEANLINESS AND ABLUTION), makes mention of the name of his lord and prays (see PRAYER). No, you prefer the world *(dunyā),* but the hereafter is better and more lasting." The exegesis of other commentators follows a more restricted method of interpretation, namely that Q 87:18-9 refers only to the immediately preceding verse, i.e. Q 87:17: "But the hereafter is better and more lasting." Commentators also explain the "pages of Moses" *(ṣuḥuf Mūsā)* as part of those "former pages," namely the pages of all other former prophets. None of these interpretations, however, necessitates a difference between "the pages of Moses" and the "book of Moses" *(kitāb Mūsā)* or the Torah (*tawrāt,* Ṭabarī, *Tafsīr,* ad loc.; Rāzī, *Tafsīr,* xxxi, 135-6).

Moses and the servant of God whom God had taught of his knowledge

Q 18:60-82 refers to a journey in which Moses, accompanied by a boy *(fatā),* searches for "the meeting place of the two seas" (see BARRIER): "When they reached the meeting place of the two seas they forgot their fish and it took its way in the sea freely" (*saraban,* Q 18:61). When Moses noticed that they forgot the fish, he said: "This is what we have been seeking." On their way back to the place whence they had come they found "one of our servants (*ʿabd min ʿibādinā),* upon whom we had bestowed mercy (q.v.; *raḥma*) and taught knowledge" (*ʿilm,* Q 18:64-5). The narrative commentary combines the story of the fish with the *topos* of Moses boasting of knowledge. When Moses was preaching, someone asked: "Who of the people knows best?" Moses replied: "I do," not attributing knowledge to God. Therefore God tells him that there is a servant of God at "the meeting place of the two seas" (Q 18:60), who knows more than Moses. When Moses asks how to find him, God replies: "Take a fish and put it in a basket. When you miss it, he will be there" (Ṭabarī, *Tafsīr,* ad loc.; id., *Taʾrīkh,* i, 417; Brinner, *History,* iii, 6). When Moses finds the servant of God whom God had taught of his knowledge, Moses says to him: "'May I follow you, so that you may teach me the right conduct which you have been taught?' He says: 'Lo! You cannot bear with me'... 'If you go with me, do not ask me anything until I myself mention it to you" (Q 18:66-70). Then the Qurʾān reports the story of the three deeds of the unnamed servant of God. Moses is not able to suffer the deeds to occur without interpretation, since he lacks the knowledge to understand (Q 18:71-82). Commentary and tradition (*ḥadīth,* see ḤADĪTH AND THE QURʾĀN) identify Moses' boy companion *(fatā)* with Yashūʿ b. Nūn, the biblical Joshua, Moses' servant (*Exod* 24:13; *Num* 11:28). The servant *(ʿabd)* of God who was endowed with knowledge is identified as al-Khiḍr, "the green man, the green" (see KHAḌIR/KHIḌR). His knowledge, which was superior to that of Moses, raised the question of their relationship. Muslim scholars discussed the type of knowledge he had and whether or not he was a prophet (Rāzī, *Tafsīr,* xxi, 126 f.; Brinner, *History,* iii, 1 n. 1; Franke, *Begegnung,* 70 f.; 306-14).

Cornelia Schöck

Bibliography
Primary: Ibn Isḥāq, *Sīra,* ed. M. al-Saqqā; Ibn Isḥāq-Guillaume; Rāzī, *Tafsīr;* H. Ritter (ed.), Studien zur Geschichte der islamischen Frömmigkeit, i, in *ZDMG* 21 (1933), 1-83 (includes the so-called *Risāla ilā ʿAbd al-Malik,* ascribed to al-Ḥasan al-Baṣrī); Ṭabarī, *Tafsīr;* id., *Taʾrīkh,* ed. Shākir; Eng. trans. W.M. Brinner, *The history of al-Ṭabarī. iii. The Children of Israel,* New York 1991; J.A. Williams, *The history of al-Ṭabarī, xxvii. The ʿAbbāsid revolution,* New York 1985.
Secondary: M. Causse, Théologie de rupture et théologie de la communauté. Étude sur la vocation prophétique de Moïse d'après le Coran, in *Revue d'histoire et de philosophie religieuses* 44 (1964), 60-82; Eng. trans. The theology of separation and the theology of community. A study of the prophetic career of Moses according to the Qurʾān, in A. Rippin (ed.), *The Qurʾān. Style and contents,* Aldershot 2001, 37-60; P. Franke, *Begegnung mit Khidr. Quellenstudien zum Imaginären im traditionellen Islam,* Stuttgart 2000; I. Friedlaender, *Die Chadirlegende und der Alexanderroman,* Leipzig 1913; Y. Moubarac, Moïse dans le Coran, in H. Cazelles et al., *Moïse. L'homme de l'alliance,* Paris 1955, 373-91; M. Schwarz, The letter of al-Ḥasan al-Baṣrī, in *Oriens* 20 (1967), 15-30; H. Schwarzbaum, *Biblical and extra-biblical legends in Islamic folk-literature,* Walldorf 1982; Speyer, *Erzählungen;* R. Tottoli, Il bastone di Mosè mutato in serpente nell'esegesi e nelle tradizioni islamiche, in *AIUON* 51 (1991), 225-43; 383-94; id., Il Faraone nelle tradizioni islamiche. Alcune note in margine alla questione della sua conversione, in *QSA* 14 (1996), 19-30; id., La moderna esegesi islamica ed il rifiuto delle *isrāʾīliyyāt.* Le leggende sul bastone di Mosè mutato in serpente, in *Annali di Ca' Foscari. Rivista della Facoltà di Lingue e Letterature Straniere dell'Università di Venezia* 29 (1990), 25-35; id., *Vita di Mosè secondo le tradizioni islamiche,* Palermo 1992; B. Wheeler, *Moses in the Quran and Islamic exegesis,* London 2002.

Mosque

A Muslim place of prayer (q.v.). The English word "mosque" derives, via the French *mosquée,* the Old French *mousquaie,* the Old Italian *moschea* and *moscheta,* and the Old Spanish *mezquita,* from the Arabic word *masjid,* meaning a place of prostration (*sajda,* see BOWING AND PROSTRATION) before God. The word *masjid* (and its plural *masājid*) appears twenty-seven times in the Qurʾān, fifteen times in the phrase *al-masjid al-ḥarām,* "the holy mosque," where it presumably refers to the sanctuary surrounding the Kaʿba (q.v.) in Mecca (q.v.). The word *masjid* is used once in the phrase *al-masjid al-aqṣā,* "the furthest mosque" (Q 17:1). In Muḥammad's lifetime this probably referred to a place of prayer in heaven (see ASCENSION), although later commentators have universally understood this phrase to refer generally to the sanctuary of Jerusalem (q.v.) and specifically to the mosque erected at the south end of the Temple Mount. Other uses of the word *masjid* in the Qurʾān indicate that it could be applied to any place where God was worshipped, whether in Islamic or pre-Islamic times, as, for example, the tomb of the Seven Sleepers mentioned in Q 18:21 (see MEN OF THE CAVE). Later authors agreed that the concept of the *masjid* was not specific to Islam; the historian al-Ṭabarī (d. 310/923) mentions that King David (q.v.), for example, had a *masjid* (Pedersen, Masdjid). The word *muṣallā,* referring specifically to a place for *ṣalāt,* or prayer, appears only once in the Qurʾān (Q 2:125), where God made the *maqām Ibrāhīm,* "station of Abraham," in Mecca "a place of prayer" (see ABRAHAM). Whereas any place where ritual worship (q.v.) is performed would technically be a *muṣallā,* the word has taken on a special meaning in Islam as a large undifferentiated space, usually outside the city, where the extraordinary *ṣalāt*s are performed (see RITUAL AND THE QURʾĀN). These include the festival prayers (see FESTIVALS AND COMMEMORATIVE DAYS) marking the end of the holy month of Ramaḍān (q.v.) and the tenth day of Dhū l-Ḥijja, when animals are also slaughtered (see SLAUGHTER; CONSECRATION OF ANIMALS) in commemoration of Abraham's (Ibrāhīm's) sacrifice (q.v.), as well as the extraordinary prayers for rain. In later times, particularly in Persian-speaking lands, the festival *muṣallā* is normally known by the Persian name *ʿīd-gah,* "festival place." The word *muṣallā* has also taken on a secondary meaning in some regions of the Muslim world as "the covered part of a mosque." *Jāmiʿ,* a third word commonly applied in later times to congregational mosques, does not appear in that form in the Qurʾān but derives from the later usage *masjid al-jāmiʿ,* "congregational mosque," which itself was also transformed into such phrases as the Persian *masjid-i jumʿa,* "Friday mosque" and the Urdu *jamaʿ masjid,* "congregational mosque." In modern usage, the word *masjid* (Turkish *mescit*) is sometimes used to refer to a small mosque for daily prayer, while the word *jāmiʿ* (Turkish *cami;* Ottoman *cāmiʿ*) is understood to refer to a congregational mosque for communal worship on Friday (see FRIDAY PRAYER).

The Qurʾān gives absolutely no indication of what, if any, form a *masjid* should take, and perfectly valid worship may be performed after ablution (see CLEANLINESS AND ABLUTION) virtually anywhere, using only the most minimal markings on the ground or a mat or rug. When Muslims gather in groups for communal worship, they line up in rows facing the *qibla* (q.v.), or direction of prayer, and repeat a series of prayers and, following the imām (q.v.) or prayer leader, perform a series of prostrations. Starting from these modest beginnings, over the centuries Muslims have built praying-places of great power and beauty that count among the finest examples of world architecture (see ART AND ARCHITECTURE AND THE QURʾĀN). This article will discuss the history and development of such structures and their constituent elements as they evolved over the centuries.

Early history and constituent parts

It is generally accepted by both Muslim and non-Muslims alike that the simple house erected by the prophet Muḥammad after he emigrated from Mecca to Medina (q.v.) in 622 (see EMIGRATION) played a key role in the evolution of the mosque. According to later accounts, this building was a roughly-square building with mud-brick walls approximately 100 cubits (ca. fifty meters) to a side. Several doors led to the interior, which comprised an open court with several small rooms along the eastern wall in which the Prophet and his wives lived (see WIVES OF THE PROPHET). Porticoes supported on palm-trunks and thatched with palm fronds running along the north and south walls provided shade for the activities of Muḥammad, his family and his Companions (see FAMILY OF THE PROPHET; PEOPLE OF THE HOUSE; COMPANIONS OF THE PROPHET). Until Muḥammad broke with the Jews (see JEWS AND JUDAISM) in Rajab or Shaʿbān 2/December 623-January 624 and the *qibla,* or direction of prayer, was changed from Jerusalem to Mecca (Q 2:136), the northern portico, known as the *mughaṭṭa,* or "covered area," was used for prayer and the southern portico, known as the *ṣuffa,* "row (of columns)," was used for accommodating Muḥammad's dependents and guests, who were known as the *ahl al-ṣuffa* (see HOSPITALITY AND COURTESY; COMMUNITY AND SOCIETY IN THE QURʾĀN). After the *qibla* was shifted to Mecca, these arrangements were reversed, with the larger covered area on the south and the smaller one on the north. Following this precedent in later times, the mosque might provide temporary lodging for travelers and scholars (Grabar, *Formation,* 105-38; Hillenbrand, *Islamic architecture,* 30-128).

On Fridays, the Prophet would lead noon (q.v.) congregational worship in the court, his position marked by his lance *(ʿanaza)* thrust in the ground. He would address the community of believers from a raised seat, or pulpit, made from tamarisk wood, which was moved into position as needed. Although the *minbar* is not mentioned in the Qurʾān, the Prophet's seat was derived from the pre-Islamic judges' seat and symbol of authority (Becker, Die Kanzel). The *minbar* is the only common feature of the later mosque to have been used by the Prophet. The earliest *minbars* had only two or three steps, but the earliest example to survive is a teakwood specimen with many steps from the ninth century in the Great Mosque of Qayrawān, now in Tunisia.

Following Muḥammad's death in 632, he was buried under the floor of one of the living rooms to the side of the court. The Prophet had disapproved of any monumental commemoration of the dead (see DEATH AND THE DEAD) but his grave was eventually surrounded by a low screen and covered with a dome as the building was expanded. Although the grave became the focus of popular veneration, it was never allowed to become a focus of prayer (see INTERCESSION). In later times, bodies were not buried under mosques but tombs of important individuals were sometimes erected adjacent to them. In other cases, when the tomb of a particularly holy figure in some cemetery became the focus of popular veneration, a mosque might eventually be built to accommodate worship there.

Muḥammad's immediate successors, the caliphs (see CALIPH), continued to use the house-mosque in Medina and it was expanded to accommodate the increased numbers of believers. As a result of the rapid expansion of the faith throughout Arabia and into Iraq (q.v.), Syria (q.v.) and Egypt (q.v.), believers resident in these regions needed places for communal worship. In some regions, such as Syria, existing churches (see CHURCH) provided sufficient and suitable space, and they were either appropriated or divided between the Christians and Muslims. In other regions, such as Egypt or Iraq, where suitable buildings were lacking in the required places, new structures were erected. In Jerusalem, according to the European pilgrim Arculf, the Muslims had erected a massive but rather crude structure at the southern end of the Temple Mount (see AQṢĀ MOSQUE) by ca. 50/670 (Creswell, *Muslim architecture;* id., *A short account*). According to much later accounts, the first mosque in Egypt was built at Fusṭāṭ; it was a small structure measuring 50 × 30 cubits (25 × 15 meters) with a very low roof supported on multiple columns or piers. In Iraq, where the new towns of Kūfa and Baṣra were founded in 19/640, the first mosques were marked out by a ditch or low wall and orientated towards Mecca. The Mecca-facing, or *qibla,* part of the mosque might be covered with a palm-thatch roof supported on multiple columns or piers to provide shade. As Muslim power was consolidated in the following decades, these makeshift and temporary structures were rebuilt with more durable materials, but the many-columned ("hypostyle") system of supports was maintained.

The second and fourth caliphs, ʿUmar (q.v.) and ʿAlī (see ʿALĪ B. ABĪ ṬĀLIB), were murdered in mosques and the third, ʿUthmān (q.v.), was murdered while reading the Qurʾān, so it was thought necessary to provide some sort of protection for the ruler when he attended the mosque. This screened enclosure, which allowed the ruler to be seen but not approached, was known as the *maqṣūra*. The eighth/fourteenth-century historian Ibn Khaldūn ascribed the introduction of the *maqṣūra* to the first Umayyad caliph Muʿāwiya (r. 41-60/661-80) or to one of his successors, Marwān I (r. 64-5/684-5), but the sources are in some disagreement about the date. The first examples were made either of brick or wood, and the oldest to survive is the magnificent wooden example from the fifth/eleventh century also in the Great Mosque of Qayrawān. In later centuries, when the Islamic rulers participated with less frequency in Friday worship, the *maqṣūra* came to serve less of its original practical function, although it and the area immediately around the *miḥrāb* and *minbar* remained the focus of the mosque's interior decoration. The Ottoman sultans later introduced a royal loge, *hünkar mahfil,* into their mosques. Unlike the centrally-placed *maqṣūra,* the Ottoman loge was placed to the side of the mosque and in some instances, such as the Selīmiye mosque (Selīm II, r. 974-82/1566-74) in Edirne, raised on the second floor (see Fig. VIII).

With the establishment of the Marwānid branch of the Umayyad family and the shift of the capital from Arabia to Syria, the caliphs ʿAbd al-Malik (r. 65-86/685-705) and al-Walīd (r. 86-96/705-15) embarked on an ambitious program of construction in the major cities of the realm. The "sacred mosque" *(al-masjid al-ḥarām)* in Mecca and the Prophet's mosque in Medina, which had already been enlarged several times to accommodate larger numbers of Muslims, were completely rebuilt, as was the mosque of Damascus, which the Muslims had heretofore shared with the Christians of that city. The Umayyad mosque of Medina is known only through later texts (Sauvaget, *Mosquée omeyyade*) but the Damascus mosque, despite a disastrous fire in the late nineteenth century, survives largely intact. Built within the walls of a Roman temple enclosure, the Damascus mosque was one of the most ambitious architectural projects of the time. Like the Dome of the

Rock in Jerusalem, the mosque used the forms and motifs of late antique architecture, such as basilical halls with columns, arches, gables, domes, mosaics and marble revetments, to create a new Islamic architecture. On the south, slightly less than half the enclosed space was covered as a prayer hall; the rest was left open as a courtyard.

The most notable feature of the Damascus as well as the Medina mosque was the introduction of the *miḥrāb*, a semicircular niche in the center of the *qibla* wall (Whelan, Origins). Although the origins and meaning of the *miḥrāb* remain a matter of intense speculation, the form seems to have had a commemorative function, to judge from a slightly earlier silver *dirham* decorated with a niche enclosing an upright that has been interpreted as the Prophet's spear (Miles, Mihrab and ʿAnazah). In any event, the *miḥrāb* immediately became a distinguishing feature of virtually all mosques (Papadopoulo, *Le mihrab*) and the *minbar* was, from an early date, placed to the right of the *miḥrāb*.

At Damascus, the area immediately in front of and beside the *miḥrāb*, which presumably comprised the caliph's *maqṣūra*, was architecturally emphasized by a massive gabled bay and dome (see Fig. 1). Comparable but more modest forms were used to emphasize the *miḥrāb* area at Medina. The interior walls of the Damascus and Medina mosques were decorated with mosaics and inscriptions (see EPIGRAPHY AND THE QURʾĀN); the surviving mosaics at Damascus show a riparian landscape with houses and pavilions which perhaps depicts paradise (q.v.) as it is described in the Qurʾān, but few, if any, other mosques had such specific decoration.

The disposition of some mosques, such as those in Aleppo, Diyār Bakr and Ḥarrān, may have been based more or less closely on the example of the Damascus mosque, but the Umayyads do not seem to have established a standard mosque type. Rather, the Umayyad idea of a mosque appears to have comprised a rather flexible association of constituent parts, which should include (in decreasing order of importance): orientation towards Mecca, a *miḥrāb* in the *qibla* wall, open and covered spaces, arcades surrounding the courtyard, domes or raised roofs in the area near the *miḥrāb*, and a *maqṣūra*. Some or all of these features can be seen in smaller mosques of the Umayyad period, such as at Qaṣr al-Ḥayr al-Sharqī, Jabal Says, etc.

The ʿAbbāsids, who seized power from the Umayyads in 132/749, appear to have had no doctrinal objection to the mosque as it had evolved under Umayyad patronage — although the ʿAbbāsids did claim that the Umayyads' excessive elevation of the *minbar* was wrong. The ʿAbbāsids consequently ordered *minbar*s reduced in size but as the Qayrawān *minbar* (mid-third/ninth century) still has many steps, the order seems not to have been effective. Literary sources indicate that the ʿAbbāsids established mosques in the second half of the second/eighth century at Baghdād, their new capital in Iraq, as well as in other cities. None has survived intact, but they do not appear to have deviated from the Umayyad norm in any significant way. By the early third/ninth century, however, many ʿAbbāsid mosques began to have a single tower located next to the entrance in the wall opposite the *miḥrāb*.

These towers are traditionally understood to have been places from which the call to prayer *(adhān)* was given by the muezzin *(muʾadhdhin)* but there is no evidence to suggest that these towers were erected for this purpose (Bloom, *Minaret*). In early Islamic times, the first call to prayer was normally given from the doorway or the roof of the mosque; Shīʿīs in particular continued to follow this practice (see SHĪʿISM AND THE QURʾĀN). Under the later Umayyads, several mosques had a small structure on the roof, known epigraphically as *miʾdhana* (place for the *adhān*), which was presumably meant to protect the muezzin from the elements. Only the mosque of Medina had four towers in Umayyad times, and these do not seem to have been used for the call to prayer. If, in later times, towers were often used for the call to prayer, the tower seems to have been introduced into the mosque simply to indicate its presence from afar. Such an interpretation would coincide with the most common Arabic name for these towers, which is *manāra,* "a place or thing that gives light" (cf. Hebrew *menorah*), whence (via the Turkish *minare*) the English word "minaret."

Like the mosque itself, there was no particular shape the minaret needed to take: the square and battered third/ninth-century tower of the Great Mosque of Qayrawān was modeled on a nearby Roman lighthouse (see Fig. II), while the contemporary towers attached to the mosques of al-Mutawakkil and Abū Dulaf at Sāmarrāʾ in Iraq are helicoidal spirals, a form invented by ʿAbbāsid builders. In Syria, square stone towers became common, while in Iran, cylindrical and polygonal towers of astonishing height showed off the talents of Iranian builders, particularly in the eleventh and twelfth centuries.

As ablution *(wuḍūʾ)* is required before ritual worship, many mosques are known to have been provided with facilities for washing, although few such installations have survived the centuries. The ninth/fifteenth-century Egyptian historian al-Maqrīzī (d. 845/1442) preserved a description of the late third/ninth-century ablution pavilion in the courtyard of Ibn Ṭūlūn's mosque in Cairo (which was, incidentally, surmounted by a place for the muezzins). A magnificently-decorated sixth/twelfth-century ablution pavilion has been preserved from the original Almoravid mosque of Marrakesh, although the mosque itself has not survived (Meunié and Terrasse, *Nouvelles recherches;* see Fig. III).

Other elements of mosque furniture include the *dikka,* a platform sometimes found in congregational mosques (for one example, see Fig. VI). They are used on Fridays by muezzins giving the third call to prayer before the *ṣalāt* in the mosque, as well as by "repeaters" *(muballigh)* to enable the entire congregation to hear in the pre-loudspeaker age. Reading-stands *(kursī)* held the large manuscripts of the Qurʾān that were often presented to mosques as pious gifts; some also provided a seat for the reader. Most *kursī*s were made of wood, elaborately carved and inlaid with colored woods and bone or ivory, but other materials were used. Perhaps the largest is the stone reading stand in the courtyard of the mosque of Bībī Khānum in Samarqand (see Fig. V). It is thought that it was made to hold the enormous manuscript of the Qurʾān whose pages measure over 1 × 2 meters, of which several leaves survive. From an early date, lamps (see LAMP) and candlesticks were installed in mosques to provide light (q.v.) at night. Some were made of metal elaborately decorated with piercing and inlaying (Behrens-Abouseif, *Metal lamps*), while others, particularly in the Mamlūk period, were made of glass enameled with intricate inscriptions and designs (Wiet, *Lampes et bouteilles;* for one example of the latter, see Fig. IV of MATERIAL CULTURE AND THE QURʾĀN). Some enameled glass Mamlūk lamps were inscribed with the Light Verse (Q 24:35), a particularly felicitous choice. Mats or carpets often covered the floors of mosques to prevent the worshiper from getting dusty. The Prophet is said to have initiated the custom of praying on a carpet, although some Muslims reject this practice as a later innovation.

Types of mosques

During the first centuries of Islam, Muslims carried the flexible idea of the hypostyle mosque from its homeland in Syria and Iraq throughout the Muslim world. Before ca. 400/1000, hypostyle or "Arab-type" mosques were erected everywhere from Spain and Morocco in the west to Iran and central Asia in the east. While all share general features of planning and orientation, Muslim patrons and builders were sufficiently flexible to accommodate local traditions of construction and decoration. Thus, the mosque of Cordoba in Spain, begun by Umayyad emigrants from Syria in the late second/eighth century, used a distinctive two-tiered system of supports and mixed construction of recycled stone and brick to support tile-covered gabled roofs. The third/ninth-century builders of the mosque at Qayrawān continued local Tunisian traditions of fine ashlar construction, using recycled antique stone columns and capitals to support a flat timber roof. In most of Iran, brick, whether sun-dried or fired, became the major material of construction for supports and coverings; the scarcity of wood had led Iranian builders in previous centuries to develop ingenious techniques for covering large spaces with brick vaults. In some areas of Iran and Anatolia, on the other hand, where timber continued to be available after the Muslims first settled the region in the late fifth/eleventh century, builders developed a timber-framed hypostyle mosque. Two examples are the small village mosque at Abyāna (Iran; before 1103 C.E.) or the Eşrefoğlu mosque at Beyşehir (696/1296), although this structure, like many other Anatolian mosques, is enclosed in stone walls. In the Maghrib the hypostyle type of mosque became typical, and its popularity excluded virtually all other types.

The inherent flexibility and adaptability of the hypostyle mosque made it so popular in such a wide variety of situations over such a long period that the name "Arab-type" mosque, which is sometimes used, is patently unsuitable. The plan, with some variation, is found for example in an early mosque in west Africa (e.g. the eighth/fourteenth-century Djingere-Ber mosque at Timbuktu) as well as a modern one in the same region (the Great Mosque of Mopti built in 1935). It is also found in east Africa (e.g. the Great Mosque, Kilwa Kisawāni; begun in the sixth/twelfth century), India (the Quwwat al-Islam mosque, Delhi; begun 592/1196), China (e.g. Yangzhou mosque, Jiangsu Province; begun 673/1275[?]) and southeast Asia (e.g. Masjid Agung, Demak; founded 881/1477); and modern architects continue to exploit its structural possibilities, as in the Mosque of the King (Marbella; 1981) or the King ʿAbd al-ʿAzīz mosque (Casablanca; 1983; Frishman and Khan, *The mosque*).

Most mosques surviving from the early centuries of Islam are large structures intended for congregational worship, but several smaller mosques also survive from the second/eighth century and later. Found in such cities as Toledo (Spain), Qayrawān and Sūsa (Tunisia), Fusṭāṭ (Egypt), Termez (Uzbekistan), and Balkh (Afghanistan) as well as in rural areas of Arabia and central Asia, this type of mosque is characterized by nine square units arranged in a 3 × 3 grid, with four columns or piers supporting the roof. The germ of the type is found in the Umayyad mosques of Khān al-Zabīb, Umm al-Walīd and Qaṣr al-Ḥallābāt. The widespread popularity of this "nine-bay" plan suggests that it, like the hypostyle mosque, was diffused from some central source (King, Nine bay).

The hypostyle mosque, whether large or small, may have been the most common type in early Islamic times, but literary evidence suggests that other types of struc-

[I] Courtyard of the Umayyad mosque of Damascus (85-96/705-15, with later additions) showing the axial transept and dome in front of the *miḥrab*. Photograph courtesy of Jonathan M. Bloom.

[II] Great Mosque of Qayrawān (mid third/ninth century) showing the three-storied minaret. Photograph courtesy of Jonathan M. Bloom.

[III] Ablution pavilion (known as the Qubbat al-Ibāḍiyyīn) from the destroyed Almoravid congregational mosque (Marrakesh, sixth/twelfth century). Photograph courtesy of Jonathan M. Bloom.

[IV] Congregational mosque of Iṣfahān (sixth/twelfth century and later) showing courtyard with two (of four) *īwāns*. Photograph courtesy of Sheila S. Blair.

[v] Stone reading stand for a monumental copy of the Qur'ān at the mosque of Bībī Khānum, Samarqand (801-6/1399-1404). Photograph courtesy of Sheila S. Blair.

[VI] Funerary mosque-*madrasa* of Sultan Ḥasan showing prayer hall with *dikka* (the platform on which the *muballigh* might stand) in foreground and *miḥrab* and *minbar* in background (Cairo, begun 756/1356). Photograph courtesy of Jonathan M. Bloom.

[VII] Interior of the prayer hall of the Atala mosque (Jaunpur, 810/1408). Photograph courtesy of Jonathan M. Bloom.

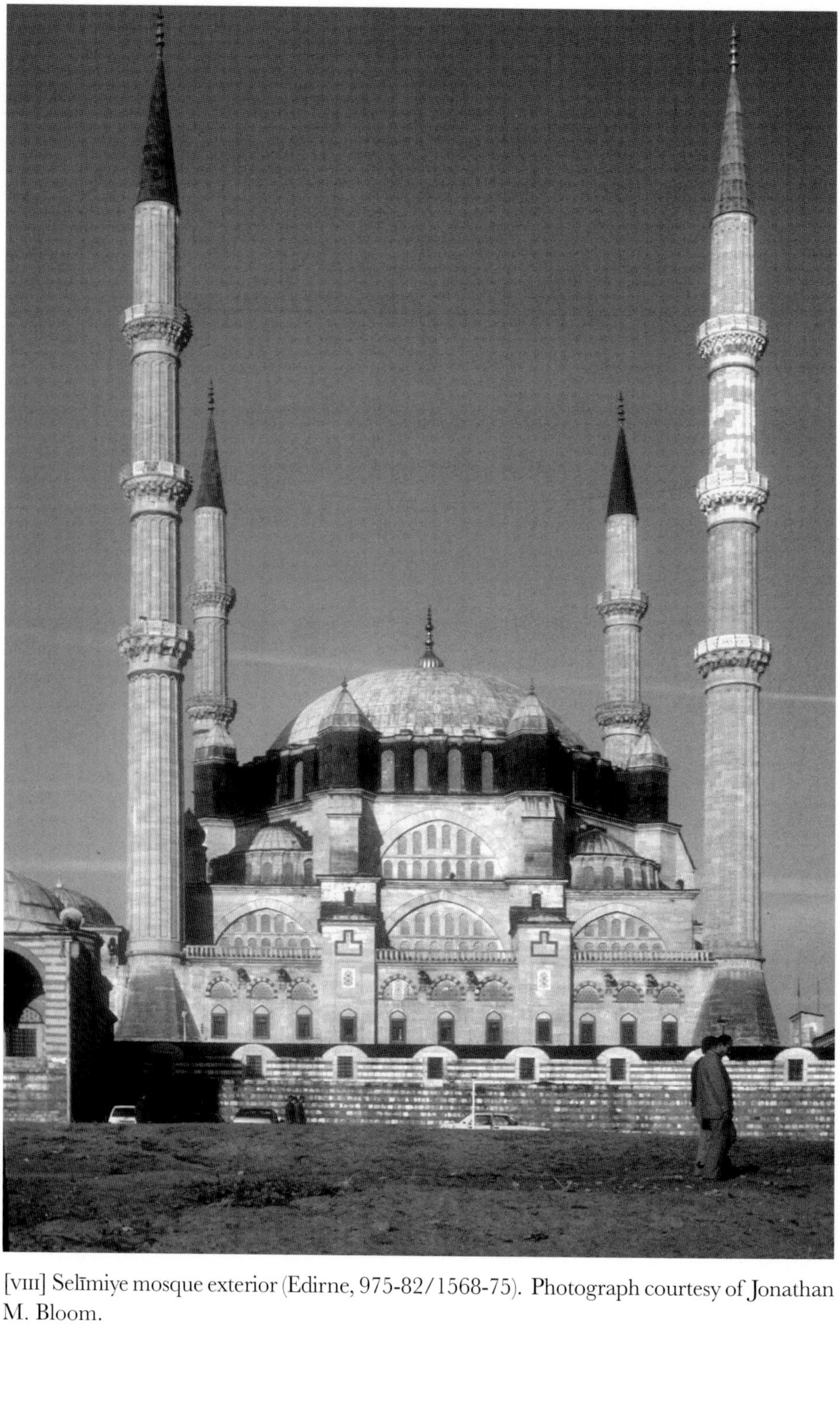

[VIII] Selīmiye mosque exterior (Edirne, 975-82/1568-75). Photograph courtesy of Jonathan M. Bloom.

tures were also used where available. In Iran, where free-standing domed chambers and vaulted halls had been essential elements of the architectural vocabulary in pre-Islamic times, it is possible that pre-existing domes and *īwān*s (a barrel-vaulted hall open at one end) would have been adapted for use as mosques, much as how, in Syria, basilicas had been transformed into mosques. The crucial archaeological evidence for this transformation is lacking, however, perhaps because many of these structures were built of mud-brick, and fell into dust once abandoned. The undated domed mosques at Yazd-i Khwāst and Qurva may be recycled older buildings. The prayer hall of the Iranian mosque at Nayrīz (perhaps begun 363/973) is a large single *īwān* which has a *miḥrāb* at one end and is open to the courtyard at the other.

In the late fifth/eleventh century, however, the Saljūq rulers of Iran, who made their capital at Iṣfahān, transformed the third/ninth-century hypostyle mosque of that city by removing many of the columns in the area immediately in front of the *miḥrāb* and inserting a huge freestanding brick dome in their place. The building of the Iṣfahān dome in 479-80/1086-7 by the powerful vizier Niẓām al-Mulk during the reign of Malik-shāh has been shown to have been directly inspired by Malik-shāh's restoration of the *maqṣūra* dome in the Damascus mosque, which had been destroyed by fire a few years before (Blair, Surveyor). While the idea of the great dome may have been inspired by the precedent of Damascus, the form this new dome took was dependent on earlier buildings in central Iran, such as the freestanding domed tomb in Yazd known as the Twelve Imāms (429/1038). Indeed, the Iṣfahān dome was initially freestanding within the hypostyle hall, but such a structure was both structurally unstable and visually awkward, so a massive *īwān* was soon erected in front of it. This *īwān* physically and visually linked the courtyard to the *maqṣūra* dome, and the flanking hypostyle halls were connected to the new parts. The *īwān*'s court facade was embellished by a high rectangular frame, known as a *pīshṭāq*, which was, perhaps at a later date, flanked by slender towers. By the early sixth/twelfth century, three other *īwān*s had been erected at the midpoints of the three other sides of the court, so that the mosque had taken on an entirely new aspect. In place of the hypostyle halls surrounding the spacious courtyard, there was now a massive arched *īwān* in each of its four sides; that on the *qibla* side terminated in a huge dome over the *miḥrāb*.

The prestige of the mosque in Iṣfahān (see Fig. IV), which was the Saljūq capital, coupled with the inherent flexibility of the four-*īwān* plan, which had been used for centuries on a much smaller scale in residential and palatine architecture, led builders throughout the Saljūq realm to copy the developments at Iṣfahān. Older hypostyle mosques were transformed by the addition of a dome and one or more *īwān*s (e.g. Ardistān), and new mosques were built from scratch using the new plan (e.g. Zawāra). Indeed, by the eighth/fourteenth century, the four-*īwān* mosque had become *the* Iranian mosque type, and such plans were used in various scales from the modest (Varamīn, 722/1322 and later) to the mammoth (Tīmūr's mosque of Bībī Khānum in Samarqand, 802-3/1399), where even the lateral *īwān*s were domed. The four-*īwān* type continued to be the most popular in later periods in Iran and central Asia, as for example in the Kalān mosque (920/1514) in Bukhārā or the Masjid-i Imām (formerly Masjid-i Shāh) erected by the Safavid Shāh ʿAbbās between 1021/1612 and 1040/1630 in Iṣfahān.

As Iranian cultural norms were prevalent in most of the eastern Islamic lands in the period after ca. 650/1250, the Iranian combination of an *īwān* leading to a dome over the *miḥrāb*, or even the four-*īwān* type plan, was widely disseminated, although, like the hypostyle mosque before it, its features were often creatively reinterpreted, as at the Ūlū Cāmiʿ (621/1224) at Malaṭya in southeast Anatolia, where the courtyard is very small, and the mosque of Baybars I (665/1266) in Cairo, where the *īwān* is a sort of hypostyle hall and the dome was built of wood.

The Iranian type of four-*īwān* mosque was used on the Indian subcontinent, as for example at Thatta (1054/1644), but the essential features of the plan were more commonly adapted to create a new Indian type of mosque more suited to the climate. Like earlier Hindu temples, this type of mosque is often raised on a high plinth. It comprises a vast walled court with minarets set at the exterior corners and massive portals on the main and lateral axes. On the exterior, these are approached by flights of steps and are topped with small minaret-like towers and open pavilions. Within the court, which often has no surrounding arcade, the prayer hall occupies most but not all of the *qibla* wall's width. Projecting into the court, the fairly shallow prayer hall comprises a central *īwān*-like portal leading to a dome chamber over the *miḥrāb* and *minbar*. This *īwān* and dome unit is usually flanked by smaller versions of it, other domed bays and towers linked together behind a screen-like facade. An early example is found at the Atala mosque at Jaunpur (810/1408; see Fig. VII); a later one is the Badshahi mosque at Lahore (1084/1673), said to be the largest mosque in the subcontinent.

Another distinctive type of mosque, characterized by a single large dome, developed in Anatolia, particularly under the Ottomans (r. 1281-1924 C.E.). After the region was opened for Muslim settlement following the Battle of Manzikert in 463/1071, the first mosques erected, such as the ʿAlāʾ al-Dīn mosque in Konya (550-617/1155-1220), were hypostyle structures. Perhaps in response to the severe Anatolian winter climate, these mosques had no courtyard, or only a vestigial one. Most early Anatolian mosques were, therefore, closed halls resting on a multitude of columns, sometimes fronted by courtyards akin to the forecourts of some Byzantine churches. Indigenous Byzantine experience with building domed and vaulted churches in stone, combined with the knowledge of Iranian traditions of building brick vaults and domes brought by the Saljūqs, undoubtedly encouraged local builders to experiment with the covering of mosques with domes and vaults; the subsequent history of the mosque in Anatolia, particularly under the Ottomans, is dominated by the desire to create a unified prayer space under a domical covering.

Scholars have debated the origins of the mature type of Turkish domed mosque. Some see its origins in the simple, single domed mosque preceded by a portico, such as the Mosque of Ḥacī Özbek at Iznīk (734/1333), while others see it in the more complex organization of domed and vaulted elements characteristic of the Bursa-type or *zāwiya* (Turk. *zaviyelī*) mosque usually associated with a dervish cloister, in which a domed central space precedes a vaulted or domed *īwān*-like prayer hall and is flanked by corresponding *īwān*-like spaces to the left and right which could be used for teaching, etc. (see ṢŪFISM AND THE QURʾĀN). Other vaulted or domed chambers in the corners, often furnished with fireplaces, could be used for lodging itinerant dervishes. This completely covered mosque type, well suited to the harsh Anatolian climate, is exemplified by the Yeşil Cāmiʿ (815-22/1412-19) at Bursa.

In the ninth/fifteenth and tenth/sixteenth centuries the Ottoman sultans sponsored a series of immense domed congregational mosques which combined various trends, including the single domed space (as at Iznīk), the completely covered space (as at Bursa), the large dome before the *miḥrāb* (as in Iranian mosques) and the open arcaded forecourt (as in the Great Mosque of Damascus or Byzantine churches). These buildings were the centerpieces of large religious and charitable foundations. The earliest examples, such as the Üç Şerefeli mosque in Edirne (841-51/1437-47), have vast central domes with low subsidiary spaces, but the best known examples represent creative responses to the models of Byzantine architecture, primarily the great church of Hagia Sophia in Istanbul, which had been founded by the emperor Constantine in the fourth century C.E. and rebuilt in the sixth century by the emperor Justinian. Immediately after the conquest of Constantinople in 857/1453 by the Ottoman emperor Meḥmed II the church was converted into the city's first congregational mosque by the addition of a *miḥrāb*, *minbar* and minarets. The Süleymāniye mosque in Istanbul (964/1557), the masterpiece of Ottoman architecture by the great architect Sinān, for example, follows the model of Hagia Sophia by using an immense central dome buttressed at either end by semi-domes. The many windows create a highly centralized space, which contrasts with the strongly directional space of the prototype. Unlike many mosques of earlier times, in which the exterior facade was often neglected in favor of a focus on the interior or courtyard, the exteriors of the imperial Ottoman mosques were clearly meant to be monumental, presenting cascades of domes and semi-domes punctuated by slender minarets. The central mass is often enveloped in the domes of the adjacent religious and charitable foundations, which frequently included the tomb of the founder.

The power and prestige of the Ottoman empire in the Balkans, north Africa and the Near East encouraged the construction of similar if somewhat simpler mosques (and complexes) in the capital cities of the Ottoman empire. Sometimes these structures incorporated local architectural motifs and techniques, such as the striped masonry used in the Sulaymāniyya complex at Damascus, completed in 962/1554-55, or the ogee windows of the tenth/sixteenth-century mosque of Sinān Pasha in Cairo. In the nineteenth and twentieth centuries C.E., the Ottoman type of domed mosque has been adapted throughout the world and has become one of the most popular designs for new mosques. These can range from banal copies of Sinān's masterpieces in reinforced concrete to inventive reinterpretations in modern materials, such as Vedat Dalakoy's State Mosque (1970-86) in Islamabad, Pakistan, or Skidmore, Owings and Merrill's Islamic Cultural Center (1987-91) in New York (Holod & Khan, *Contemporary mosque*).

Distinct types of mosques have also developed in other areas of the Islamic world. In Indonesia, for example, the Java-type mosque is set in a courtyard surrounded by a stone wall. It has a veranda on the front, and is characterized by a square plan, raised foundations, tapering roof two to five stories high, and a projecting *miḥrāb*. In China, many mosques, particularly those built under the Ming emperors, are reminiscent of indigenous Chinese temples. Other distinct styles have also evolved in east and west Africa.

Decoration of mosques

Virtually all media of Islamic art are represented in the decoration of mosques, with the one proviso that Islam forbids the representation of animate beings (i.e. humans and animals) in such situations where they might be taken as objects of devotion, as in mosques. Thus, one rarely, if ever, finds pictorial or sculptural representations in mosques, whose main decoration has consisted of inscriptions, often from the text of the Qur'ān, and vegetal and geometric designs. In the early period, the interior decoration of major Umayyad mosques, such as those in Mecca, Medina, Jerusalem and Damascus, adapted the techniques and many of the motifs of Byzantium, so colored and gold glass mosaic was popular. In later times, carved and molded plaster, carved and painted wood, glazed ceramic tile and marble paneling were commonly used media of decoration.

In many times and places, the interior of the mosque has been more important than the exterior, and the decoration has been concentrated largely on the inside. This may have resulted from the idea that the mosque is centered around the courtyard, and consequently the building is planned and intended to be seen from the courtyard outwards. The result is that exteriors were neglected, often irregular, and hardly distinguished from the surrounding urban fabric. At first, doorways were simple affairs with no great decoration, but eventually they became places of some importance, perhaps following the lead of the portals to the "sacred mosque" *(al-masjid al-ḥarām)* in Mecca, which were monumentalized at an early date, and eventually projected from the mosque wall itself. The earliest fancy portal to survive is the Bāb al-Wuzarā', "Vizier's Gate" (241/855-6) at the Great Mosque of Cordoba, in which the doorway has been embellished with inscriptions and carving (Brisch, Zum *Bāb al-Wuzarā'*). Congregational mosques of the Fāṭimid period emphasize the doorways, probably because of the Fāṭimid aversion to building minarets. The triple-arched portal of the Great Mosque at Mahdiyya (308/921), the first Fāṭimid mosque in Tunisia, is modeled on a late antique triumphal arch (Bloom, The origins). Archaeologists working in Iṣfahān in the 1930s discovered a large portal in baked brick and carved plaster. On the basis of its style, it has been identified as the portal of the Jurjir mosque built by the Būyid vizier Ibn ʿAbbād in the third quarter of the fourth/tenth century (Blair, *Monumental inscriptions*, 52-3).

Qur'ānic inscriptions in mosques were usually prepared as coherent programs of decoration, although few complete programs have survived and the meaning is usually inferred from surviving fragments. The mosaic inscriptions in the Great Mosque of Damascus, for example, are known to have focused on eschatological texts about the day of judgment (sūras 78 and 79 of the Qur'ān; Finster, Die Mosaiken; see ESCHATOLOGY; LAST JUDGMENT; APOCALYPSE), while the stucco inscriptions carved in the walls of the mosque of al-Azhar in Cairo (founded 363/972) used verses such as Q 21:101-7 to describe the paradise that awaited the true believers (see BELIEF AND UNBELIEF). Other decorative programs seem to have been somewhat less selective: medieval sources assert that the carved wooden friezes running under the ceiling of the mosque of Ibn Ṭūlūn in Cairo (265/879) repeated the whole text of the Qur'ān, and the inscriptions in the mosque of al-Ḥākim, also in Cairo, contain the opening verses of many different chapters (Bloom, Mosque of al-Hakim).

Nevertheless, specific qur'ānic verses were inscribed in appropriate situations. The most common qur'ānic text used for inscriptions in mosques is Q 9:18, which states that God's mosques should be reserved for good Muslims who believe in God, pray, pay alms (see ALMSGIVING), and worship God alone (Dodd and Khairallah, *The image;* Blair, Mosque inscriptions). The text, one of the few in the Qurʾān to actually mention mosques and what should be done within them, quickly became popular in congregational mosques. Other qurʾānic citations commonly found in mosques include the Throne Verse (Q 2:255; see THRONE OF GOD), which extolls God's majesty and is often used around domes, the Light Verse (Q 24:35-8), which describes God as the light (q.v.) of the heavens (see HEAVEN AND SKY) and the earth (q.v.), and Sūrat al-Fatḥ ("Victory," Q 48; see VICTORY). Although the Light Verse is often associated, because of a mistranslation, with the common motif of a lamp in a niche, certain verses were often associated with specific parts of mosques. *Miḥrāb*s often contained verses Q 17:78-9, which mention prayer and vigil (see VIGILS).

Qurʾānic verses were also selected to give a particular inscription a specific ideological position. An inscription once on the exterior of the mosque of al-Ḥākim (380-405/990-1013) quotes Q 28:5, which uses the word *aʾimma,* the plural of *imām,* the title by which the Fāṭimid rulers styled themselves. Similarly, an inscription on one of the same mosque's towers cites Q 11:73, containing the phrase *ahl al-bayt* ("people of the house"), which the Fāṭimids interpreted as a direct reference to themselves as the descendants of the Prophet (Bloom, Mosque of al-Hakim). Similarly, the portal of the Jurjir mosque in Iṣfahān (ca. 350/960) is inscribed with Q 3:18, in which the use of the word *qisṭ* may have been chosen to advertise the building's function as a Muʿtazilite foundation (Blair, The octagonal pavilion; see MUʿTAZILĪS). As sectarian struggles increased over the course of the fourth/tenth and fifth/eleventh centuries, such pointed uses of qurʾānic inscriptions only increased, but in later times verses with more general application came to be expressed in monumental tiled and painted inscriptions.

Jonathan M. Bloom

Bibliography
C.H. Becker, Die Kanzel im Kultus des Alten Islam, in C. Bezold (ed.), *Orientalische Studien Theodor Nöldeke zum siebzigsten Geburtstag (2. März 1906) gewidmet von Freunden und Schülern,* 2 vols., Gieszen 1906, i, 331-51; D. Behrens-Abouseif, *Mamluk and post-Mamluk metal lamps,* Cairo 1995; S. Blair, *The monumental inscriptions from early Islamic Iran and Transoxiana,* Leiden 1992; id., Mosque inscriptions, in Eric M. Meyers (ed.), *The Oxford encyclopedia of archaeology in the Near East,* 5 vols., New York 1997, iv, 58-60; id., The octagonal pavilion at Natanz. A reexamination of early Islamic architecture in Iran, in *Muqarnas* 1 (1983), 69-94; id., Surveyor versus epigrapher, in *Muqarnas* 8 (1991), 66-73; J.M. Bloom, *Minaret. Symbol of Islam,* Oxford 1989; id., The mosque of al-Hakim in Cairo, in *Muqarnas* 1 (1983), 15-36; id., The origins of Fatimid art, in *Muqarnas* 3 (1985), 20-38; K. Brisch, Zum *Bāb al-Wuzarāʾ* (Puerta de San Esteban) der Hauptmoschee von Córdoba, in *Studies in Islamic art and architecture in honour of professor K.A.C. Creswell,* Cairo 1965, 30-4; K.A.C. Creswell, *Early Muslim architecture. Volume I,* Oxford 1969²; id., *A short account of early Muslim architecture. Revised and enlarged by James W. Allan,* Aldershot 1989; E.C. Dodd and Sh. Khairallah, *The image of the word. A study of qurʾānic verses in Islamic architecture,* Beirut 1981; B. Finster, Die Mosaiken der Umayyadenmoschee, in *Kunst des Orients* 7 (1970), 83-141; F.B. Flood, *The great mosque of Damascus. Studies in the making of an Umayyad visual culture,* Leiden 2001; M. Frishman and H. Khan, *The mosque. History, architectural development and regional diversity,* London 1994; O. Grabar, *The formation of Islamic art,* New Haven 1973; R. Hillenbrand, *Islamic architecture. Form, function and meaning,* Edinburgh 1994; R. Holod and H. Khan, *The contemporary mosque. Architects, clients and designs since the 1950s,* New York 1997; G.R.D. King, The nine bay domed mosque in Islam, in *Madrider Mitteilungen* 30 (1989), 332-90; J. Meunié and H. Terrasse, *Nouvelles recherches archéologiques à Marrakech,* Paris 1957; G.C. Miles, Mihrab and ʿanazah. A study in early Islamic iconography, in G.C. Miles (ed.), *Archaeologia orientalia in memoriam Ernst Herzfeld,* Locust Valley, NY 1952, 156-71; A. Papadopoulo, *Le mihrab dans l'architecture et la religion musulmanes.*

Actes du Colloque International tenu à Paris en Mai 1980 publiés et pourvus d'une étude d'introduction générale, Leiden 1988; J. Pedersen, Masdjid, in EI², vi, 644-77; J. Sauvaget, *La mosquée Omeyyade de Médine. Étude sur les origines architecturales de la mosquée et de la basilique,* Paris 1947; E. Whelan, The origins of the *mihrab mujawwaf.* A reinterpretation, in IJMES 18 (1986), 205-23; G. Wiet, *Lampes et bouteilles en verre émaillé. Catalogue générale du Musée Arabe du Caire,* Cairo 1912.

Mosque of the Dissension

Scene (and symbol) of opposition to Muḥammad in Medina (q.v.) in 9/630, to which allusion is made in Q 9:107: "And those who have taken a mosque (q.v.) in opposition (*ḍirāran,* see OPPOSITION TO MUḤAMMAD) and unbelief (see BELIEF AND UNBELIEF), and to divide the believers, and as a place of ambush for those who fought God and his messenger (q.v.) aforetime, will swear 'We desire nothing but good'; and God testifies they are truly liars (see LIE)." This obscure incident took place in Qubāʾ, in upper (i.e. southern) Medina (see Lecker, *Muslims,* map. 2), sometime after Rajab 9/October 630 (the date of the expedition of Tabūk; see EXPEDITIONS AND BATTLES). The mosque (q.v.) to which the passage alludes has various designations: "mosque of the dissension" or "mosque of the opposition" (*masjid al-ḍirār;* less commonly, "mosque of division" or "mosque of hypocrisy" *[masjid al-shiqāq/al-nifāq];* see HYPOCRITES AND HYPOCRISY; CORRUPTION; PARTIES AND FACTIONS).

Although the accounts of the incident agree about the outline of the events, they do reveal some significant differences. The essential outline of events is as follows: well after Muḥammad's emigration (q.v.) from Mecca (q.v.), a group of "dissenters" established a mosque in lower Medina, rivaling a mosque already in place. As Muḥammad became more firmly established in Medina, the political leadership of lower Medina came under his control. Sometime after the erection of the mosque, but still within the Prophet's lifetime, and as the political opposition to Muḥammad decreased, the "mosque of the dissension" burnt to the ground.

Despite the qurʾānic assertion that the builders of the "mosque of dissension" erred, the report transmitted by Saʿd b. Jubayr (d. 93/714), is sympathetic to these builders: "The [clan of] ʿAmr b. ʿAwf built a mosque and their nephews, the [clan of] Ghanm b. ʿAwf [in some versions: the so-and-so; ʿUmar b. Shabba, *Taʾrīkh,* i, 53], envied them. They said: 'We, too, built a mosque and invited the messenger of God to lead our prayer (q.v.) in it as he did in the mosque of our companions. Perhaps Abū ʿĀmir will pass by and lead our prayer in it'. When the Prophet was about to set out to go to them, he had a revelation [prohibiting him to go]" (Balādhurī, *Ansāb,* i, 282; trans. Lecker, *Muslims,* 76-7). In the context of this report, it is noteworthy that Saʿīd b. Jubayr adopts an anti-Khazrajī position in the dispute between the tribe of Aws (specifically the ʿAmr b. ʿAwf) and the tribe of Khazraj (see TRIBES AND CLANS) over the identification of another mosque, that founded upon piety (q.v.; Q 9:108). From the account of ʿUrwa b. al-Zubayr (d. bet. 91/711 and 101/720), it could be inferred that the mosque of "dissension" was built before the battle of Badr (q.v.), that is, several years before its destruction in the year 9/630 (Balādhurī, *Ansāb,* i, 283; ʿUmar b. Shabba, *Taʾrīkh,* 54-5; Lecker, *Muslims,* 81-5). According to yet a third account, ascribed to Ibn ʿAbbās (d. 68/687-8), this mosque was built by order of the great opponent of Muḥammad, Abū ʿĀmir (the "monk"), as a "hostile stronghold" for a Byzantine expedition force (Ṭabarī, *Tafsīr,* xiv, 270, no. 17187; Lecker, *Muslims,* 85-7; see BYZANTINES).

The account of the exegete Muqātil b.

Sulaymān (d. 150/767), while agreeing with the outline of the accounts found in the other versions, adds a number of details to their testimony (Muqātil, *Tafsīr,* ii, 195-8; trans. Lecker, *Muslims,* 87-91). It reinforces the idea that we have here a case of local competition between two mosques in Qubāʾ (Sprenger, *Moḥammad,* iii, 34 n. 1 speaks of "Concurrenz-Bethaus") and that the twelve "hypocrites" *(munāfiqūn)* built this mosque in an attempt to harm the mosque of Qubāʾ (Lecker, *Muslims,* 95). Most of these "hypocrites" belonged to an ʿAmr b. ʿAwf clan (Ibn Isḥāq, *Sīra,* 356-9; Ibn Isḥāq-Guillaume, 243-4; Lecker, *Muslims,* 101 f.; for the list of the names of these individuals, see Ibn Isḥāq, *Sīra,* 907; Ibn Isḥāq-Guillaume, 609-10; they are also found in Ṭabarī, *Tafsīr,* xiv, 468-9, no. 17186; Muqātil, *Tafsīr,* ad loc.; Thaʿlabī, *Tafsīr,* ii, f. 161v, l. 20-3; ed. Ibn ʿĀshūr, 92v, l. 16-9).

The event of the mosque of the dissension is important because it reveals that in 9/630 many of the "Muslims" in Qubāʾ — i.e. those who had "submitted" (either by accepting Islam or by coming under the political leadership of Muḥammad) — were still opposed to the authority (q.v.) of Muḥammad as a prophet or as a leader (see POLITICS AND THE QURʾĀN). Members of the most important families of the ʿAmr b. ʿAwf (the tribe of Abū ʿĀmir) or perhaps others entertained the hope that their exiled military and spiritual leader Abū ʿĀmir might return (Lecker, *Muslims,* 145; see also MUSAYLIMA). This mosque was not only a gathering place for the supporters of this noteworthy man (termed "the sinner" by Muḥammad) but was also a symbol of their tribe's autonomy from Muḥammad's territorial base in lower Medina (the *sāfila*). Muḥammad, acting with resolution (he let this mosque burn), humiliated them and reduced the prestige of the most influential men of Qubāʾ (Lecker, *Muslims,* 146). Ironically, Mujammiʿ b. Jāriya, one of the twelve "builders" and the imām (q.v.) of this mosque, became the imām of the Qubāʾ mosque and the apologetic literature attests that the second caliph (q.v.), ʿUmar, forgave and rehabilitated him (Thaʿlabī, *Tafsīr,* ii, f. 162r, l. 9-18; ed. Ibn ʿĀshūr, 93v; Ibn Isḥāq, *Sīra,* 358; Ibn Isḥāq-Guillaume, 244; Lecker, *Muslims,* 152-3).

Claude Gilliot

Bibliography

Primary: ʿAbd al-Jabbār, *Tathbīt dalāʾil al-nubuwwa,* ed. ʿA. ʿUthmān, 2 vols., Beirut 1966, ii, 474-5 (see Lecker, *Muslims,* 145 n. 239); ʿAbd al-Razzāq, *Tafsīr,* ed. Qalʿajī, i, 254; ed. ʿAbduh, ii, 165-6; Baghawī, *Tafsīr,* ed. Kh. ʿA. al-ʿAkk and M. Sawār, 4 vols., Beirut 1992³, ii, 326-7 (abridged version of al-Thaʿlabī's Qurʾān commentary, *al-Kashf wa-l-bayān*); al-Balādhurī, Aḥmad b. Yaḥyā b. Jābir, *Ansāb al-ashrāf,* ed. M. Ḥamīd Allāh, Cairo 1959, 282-3; al-Bayhaqī, Abū Bakr Aḥmad b. al-Ḥusayn, *Dalāʾil al-nubuwwa,* ed. ʿA. Qalʿajī, 7 vols., Beirut 1985, v, 256-64; Ibn Isḥāq, *Sīra,* ed. Wüstenfeld, 906-7; ed. M. al-Saqqā, ii, 529-31; Ibn Isḥāq-Guillaume, 609-10; Muqātil, *Tafsīr,* ii, 195-8 (trans. in Lecker, *Muslims,* 87-91); al-Nuwayrī, Abū l-Abbās Aḥmad b. ʿAbd al-Wahhāb, *Nihāyat al-arab fī funūn al-adab,* 33 vols. to date, Cairo 1923-98, xvi, 427-8; Qurṭubī, *Jāmiʿ,* viii, 252-8; Rāzī, *Tafsīr,* xvi, 192-5; al-Ṣāliḥī al-Shāmī, Abū ʿAlī Muḥammad b. Yūsuf, *Subul al-hudā wa-l-irshād fī sīrat khayr al-ʿibād [*or *al-Sīra al-shāmiyya],* ed. ʿĀ.A. ʿAbd al-Mawjūd and ʿA.M. Muʿawwaḍ, 12 vols., Beirut 1993, v, 470 f.; ed. F.M. Shaltūt and ʿA. al-Azbāwī, 12 vols. to date, Cairo 1983-, v, 675 f.; Suyūṭī, *Durr,* iii, 276-9; Ṭabarī, *Taʾrīkh,* ed. de Goeje et al., i, 1703-5; trans. I.K. Poonawala, *The history of al-Ṭabarī,* ix, Albany 1990, 59-61; id., *Tafsīr,* ed. Shākir, xiv, 468-75; Thaʿlabī, *al-Kashf wa-l-bayān ʿan tafsīr al-Qurʾān,* ms. Istanbul, Ahmet III, II, f. 161v, l. 6-162v; ed. Abū Muḥammad Ibn ʿĀshūr, 10 vols., Beirut 2002; ʿUmar b. Shabba, *Taʾrīkh al-Madīna,* ed. F. Shaltūt, 4 vols., i, 52-7; Wāḥidī, *Wasīṭ,* ii, 524; Wāqidī, *Maghāzī,* iii, 1045-6; Zurqānī, *Sharḥ,* iv, 98-100.

Secondary: Buhl, *Das Leben,* 329 (who, however, incorrectly identifies the builders of the Mosque of Dissension as members of the Khazraj); L. Caetani, *Annali dell'Islam,* 10 vols. in 12, Milan 1905-26, i, 443 f.; J. Gagnier, *La vie de Mahomet,* Amsterdam 1748, 163-6 (where the "Ganamites," i.e. Ghanm b. ʿAwf, are considered to be Christians); M. Gaudefroy-Demombynes, *Mahomet,* Paris 1969, 186-8; M. Gil, The creed of Banū ʿĀmir, in *IOS* 12 (1992), 9-57, esp. 40; id., The Medinan opposition to the Prophet, in *JSAI* 10 (1987), 65-96, esp. 71-6; H. Grimme, *Mohammed. I. Das Leben nach den Quellen,* Münster 1892, 152; M. Lecker, *Muslims, Jews and pagans. Studies on early Islamic Medina,* Leiden 1995, 74-146, 150-3; W. Muir, *Life of Mahomet,* 4 vols., London 1861, repr. Osnabrück 1988, iv, 198-200; Nöldeke, *GQ,* i, 244-5; M. Rodinson, *Mahomet,* Paris 1968², 313-5; A. Sprenger, *Das Leben und die Lehre des Moḥammad,* 3 vols., Berlin 1869², iii, 33-4, 434; G. Weil, *Mohammed der Prophet. Sein Leben und seine Lehre,* Stuttgart 1843, 267-73.

Moth see ANIMAL LIFE

Mother see PARENTS; FAMILY

Mother of the Book see BOOK

Mount Ararat see ARARAT

Mount Sinai see SINAI; MOSES

Mountains see NATURE AS SIGNS; GEOGRAPHY; COSMOLOGY

Mourning see BURIAL; DEATH AND THE DEAD; WEEPING

Mouth see ANATOMY

Mud see CLAY

Muḥammad

The Muslim Prophet to whom God's revelation was "sent down" (*nuzzila,* Q 47:2; see PROPHETS AND PROPHETHOOD; REVELATION AND INSPIRATION). On three occasions the name is followed by the title "messenger" (q.v.; *rasūl*), i.e. God's messenger (Q 3:144; 33:40; 48:29).

Names and appellations

When, however, the Qurʾān addresses the Prophet directly in the second person, he is not referred to as "Muḥammad," but is called by various appellations that indicate his relation to God. Here, apart from *rasūl,* the title most frequently used is *al-nabī,* "prophet" (Q 8:64; 66:8, etc.). The appellation "servant" (q.v.; *ʿabd*) of God is also used most probably with reference to the Prophet (Q 17:1; 25:1; 39:36; 72:19). Other epithets allude to the purposes of his mission, the most frequent being *bashīr,* "announcer," and *nadhīr,* "warner" (q.v.; e.g. Q 2:119, etc.), as well as *mudhakkir,* "reminder" (Q 88:21). In Q 33:45-6, a series of titles is provided: *shāhid,* "witness" (see WITNESSING AND TESTIFYING), *mubashshir,* "bearer of good tidings" (see GOOD NEWS), *nadhīr, dāʿī,* "one who calls [unto God]" (see INVITATION), and *sirāj munīr,* "light-giving lamp" (see LIGHT; LAMP).

More particular designations are derived from his state at the time of the address (see OCCASIONS OF REVELATION). Thus the Qurʾān addresses him as *al-muzzammil,* "the enwrapped" (Q 73:1) and *al-muddaththir,* "the shrouded" (Q 74:1) when prompting him to rise and accomplish his mission. This pair of appellations probably symbolizes withdrawal and reluctance. See also NAMES OF THE PROPHET.

Revelation

The revelation of the divine message, which the qurʾānic Prophet is supposed to deliver, is described in a variety of terms depicting the content as well as the process of revelation. What is revealed to the Prophet is most frequently called *qurʾān* (e.g. Q 6:19; 20:2, etc.), which the Prophet is supposed to "recite" (*li-taqraʾahu,* Q 17:106; *an atluwa,* Q 27:92; see ORALITY; RECITATION OF THE QURʾĀN), or "chant" (*rattil,* Q 73:4). But the latter command may also be understood in a different sense (Paret, *Mohammed,* 492). The Qurʾān is not only recited by the Prophet but is also being recited to him during revelation (Q 75:18; cf. Q 87:6).

The revelation received by the Prophet is most frequently described as a *kitāb,* a "book" (q.v.; Q 4:105; 5:48, etc.). It is recited to him during revelation (Q 28:2-3) and he, in turn, is supposed to recite it (Q 18:27; 29:45). The plural, *kutub* ("books"), also appears as something recited *(yatlū)* by the Prophet, and as contained in purified pages (*ṣuḥuf muṭahhara,* Q 98:2-3; see WRITING AND WRITING MATERIALS). In this case the "books" are probably separate units of revelation.

Indeed, the Qurʾān refers more than once to separate units of revelation. The name most frequently used for them is *āyāt,* "signs" [q.v.; of God], which form part of the *kitāb* (Q 10:1, etc.; see also VERSES). They also stand for something that is revealed to him (Q 2:99), or recited *(natlūhā)* to him (Q 2:252; 3:108; 45:6; cf. 3:58), and the Prophet, for his part, is also expected to recite *(yatlū)* them to his audience (see Q 2:129, 151; 3:164; 28:45; 62:2; 65:11).

Another unit, which the Prophet is expected to recite, is *nabaʾ* (pl. *anbāʾ*), "report, tidings" (see NEWS). This term usually signifies stories about past generations (q.v.), mainly of biblical origin (see NARRATIVES). For example, the Prophet is instructed to recite *(utlu)* the *nabaʾ* of the two sons of Adam (Q 5:27; see ADAM AND EVE; CAIN AND ABEL), the *nabaʾ* of Noah (q.v.; Q 10:71) and of Abraham (q.v.; Q 26:69). Again, such stories are also recited to the Prophet upon being revealed to him, as is the case with the *nabaʾ* of Moses (q.v.; Q 28:3). These units are also being "related" *(naquṣṣu)* to him upon being revealed (Q 7:101; 11:100, 120; 18:13; 20:99). They are also referred to as *anbāʾ al-ghayb:* "stories of the unseen" (see HIDDEN AND THE HIDDEN), because the Prophet did not witness them in person (Q 3:44 of Mary [q.v.]; Q 11:49 of Noah; Q 12:102 of Joseph [q.v.]).

Stories of past generations recited by the Prophet may also be described as *dhikr,* as with the story of Dhū l-Qarnayn (Q 18:83; see ALEXANDER). This form is the infinitive of *dhakara,* to "mention," or to "remind," so that *dhikr* is an "allusion" to a story (see MEMORY). Nevertheless, the same term is also the name of the entire revelation (Q 16:44, etc.), probably because it alludes quite frequently to stories of past generations. In fact, the injunction *udhkur fī l-kitāb,* "mention in the book," is frequently used in passages prompting the qurʾānic Prophet to recount stories about previous prophets (Q 19:16, 41, etc.).

The primary stage of revelation that precedes public recitation of texts is represented by the verb *awḥā,* which is frequently used in the Qurʾān to describe the act of communicating divine texts to the Prophet. The *kitāb* is communicated to him in this way (Q 35:31), as well as the Qurʾān (Q 12:3) and the stories of the unseen (*anbāʾ al-ghayb,* cf. Q 3:44; 11:49; 12:102). That the verb *awḥā* describes the initial stage of revelation is indicated in several passages in which the Prophet is expected to recite what has been revealed *(awḥaynā; ūḥiya)* to him (Q 13:30; 18:27; 29:45), which means that an intimate process of revelation has preceded actual recitation. Instructions as to how revelation should be received are given to the Prophet in Q 20:114, where he is advised not to "hasten" *(lā taʿjal)* with the Qurʾān before the completion of revelation *(waḥy).* More specific directions are given in Q 75:16-9 where he is instructed not to move his tongue with (revelation) to hasten it, and wait with its recitation till it is recited to him (in full).

The revelations received as *waḥy* by the

Prophet originate in a person, an angel (q.v.), described as "terrible in power," who stood on the "higher horizon" and then drew nearer and nearer (Q 53:4-10). Elsewhere he is described as "having power, with the lord of the throne (see THRONE OF GOD) secure, obeyed moreover trusty," and the Prophet "saw him" *(raʾāhu)* in the clear horizon (Q 81:20-1, 23). The heart (q.v.; *al-fuʾād)* of the Prophet once "saw" *(raʾā)* this mighty person near a (celestial?) lote-tree called *sidrat al-muntahā* (Q 53:11-8; see AGRICULTURE AND VEGETATION).

The most prevalent verbs, however, which describe the imparting of texts to the Prophet are various derivatives of *n-z-l*, "to come down." For example, in Q 17:106 the Prophet is expected to recite the Qurʾān that was sent down successively *(nazzalnāhu)* to him. What was sent down to him this way is called in one instance *furqān* (Q 25:1; see NAMES OF THE QURʾĀN), which is also the name of what was given to Moses (Q 2:53). The process of sending down ends at the Prophet's heart *(ʿalā qalbika),* and is carried out by an intermediary called Jibrīl, the angel Gabriel (q.v.; Q 2:97), or *al-rūḥ al-amīn,* "the faithful spirit" (Q 26:193-4); elsewhere he is called *rūḥ al-qudus,* "the holy spirit" (Q 16:102; see HOLY SPIRIT).

The beginning of the process of sending down revelation seems to be indicated in Q 44:2-3 where it is stated that the *kitāb* was sent down during a "blessed night." Elsewhere this night is called *laylat al-qadr* (Q 97:1; see NIGHT OF POWER), and in yet another passage, the sending down of the Qurʾān is said to have taken place in the month of Ramaḍān (q.v.; Q 2:185). The sending down of the *kitāb* is praised as a grand manifestation of God's bounty (see BLESSING) to the Prophet, which has provided him with knowledge (see KNOWLEDGE AND LEARNING) that he did not have before (Q 4:113; 42:52). The Prophet himself has not asked for this favor (Q 28:86), and had it not been for God's mercy (q.v.), he might have withdrawn the revelation altogether (Q 17:86-7). God's benevolence, however, which emanates from the revelation of the book, also envelops the believers (see BELIEF AND UNBELIEF). The Prophet is expected to teach them the book, thus providing them with knowledge that they do not have yet (Q 2:151; 3:164; 62:2). The book is also the means by which the Prophet is expected to decide in matters on which the believers are disagreed (see JUDGMENT) and guide them to the right path (Q 16:64, 89; see PATH OR WAY; ASTRAY). Therefore the sending down of the book indicates God's compassion *(raḥma)* unto them (Q 16:89), as does also the sending of the Prophet himself as a messenger to all beings (Q 21:107).

Aims of the mission

The mission of the qurʾānic Prophet has a dominant apocalyptic aspect, as his role is to warn the unbelievers of their eschatological punishment (see APOCALYPSE; ESCHATOLOGY; REWARD AND PUNISHMENT). This aspect comes out in passages describing the aims of revelation. Thus in Q 38:70, the essence of what is revealed *(yūḥā)* to the Prophet is focused on his mission as a warner *(nadhīr)*. In Q 6:19, the Prophet says that the Qurʾān was revealed *(ūḥiya)* to him so that he "may warn you thereby," and in Q 21:45, he says that he warns only by the *waḥy*. Likewise, the book *(al-kitāb)* is said to have been sent down so that the Prophet may warn by it (Q 6:92; 7:2, etc.). What he is expected to warn of is the hour (e.g. Q 79:42-5, etc.), or the day of judgment (see LAST JUDGMENT) that the Qurʾān calls by various names (e.g. Q 14:44; 19:39; 40:18, etc.). Some passages do not explicitly refer to the eschatological future and focus instead on examples from the history of some extinct communities (see

HISTORY AND THE QURʾĀN; GEOGRAPHY). Here the Prophet is requested to warn his contemporaries of the calamity that befell the peoples of ʿĀd (q.v.) and Thamūd (q.v.; e.g. Q 41:13-6, etc.).

Other passages in which the Prophet is addressed directly bring out the monotheistic message in his mission. He is demanded to proclaim *(iqraʾ)* the name of his lord (q.v.; Q 96:1), or praise *(sabbiḥ)* his name (Q 56:96; 69:52; 87:1; see LAUDATION; GLORIFICATION OF GOD) or declare *(udhkur)* it (Q 73:8; 76:25). In other passages he is instructed not to worship idols apart from God (Q 17:22, 39; 26:213; 28:88), and not to be one of the *mushrikūn,* i.e. those who associate other deities with God (Q 12:108; 28:87, etc.; see IDOLS AND IMAGES; IDOLATRY AND IDOLATERS; POLYTHEISM AND ATHEISM).

Scope of the mission

The scope of the mission of the qurʾānic Prophet changes between universal and local. The latter comes out in passages in which the Prophet is supposed to warn his own people *(qawm)* in his own language *(bi-lisānika),* namely Arabic, thus making his message easy to understand (Q 19:97; see also Q 44:58). The local scope of the Prophet's mission is further evident in the statement that every messenger was sent to address his people *(qawm)* by their own language (Q 14:4). The same is implied in the idea that the Prophet has been sent to a *qawm* to which a warner was never sent before (Q 28:46; 32:3; 36:6; see also Q 34:44). His audience is even smaller in a passage commanding him to warn his closest clan (*ʿashīra,* Q 26:214). In another passage he is said to have been sent to a community *(umma)* that has been preceded by other nations (Q 13:30), which seems to mean that his audience is Arabian, and is different from previous nations (Jews and Christians). Moreover, in Q 62:2 he is presented as a messenger belonging to the *ummiyyūn,* i.e. the gentiles, to whom he has been sent to teach the book and the wisdom (q.v.). This corresponds to further passages in which he is presented as one of his own audience *(minkum, min anfusikum;* see Q 2:151; 9:128, etc.). Above all, he is said to have received an Arabic Qurʾān so that he may warn Umm al-Qurā (Q 42:7; see also Q 6:92, 90:1-2), which is probably Mecca (q.v.), and those who dwell around it. God himself, whom the Prophet is commanded to worship, is described as local, namely, "the lord of this town which he has made sacred" (Q 27:91). This again may be a reference to Mecca.

On the other hand, other passages, of a clear universal orientation, imply that the Prophet has been sent as a messenger, or to warn and bear good tidings, to all humankind *(lil-nās),* or all beings *(lil-ʿālamīn)* or human beings *(bashar),* without confining the audience to a specific group (Q 4:79; 7:158; 21:107; 25:1; 34:28; 74:36). When a specific group is nevertheless indicated, it is the People of the Book (q.v.), to whom the Prophet has come in order to warn and display many things that they have been concealing of the book (Q 5:15). He has come to them after an interval *(fatra)* between the messengers (Q 5:19), and is expected to judge them according to the book that has been revealed to him (Q 5:42-3, 48, 49; see also Q 4:65, 105). This is based on the idea that the Qurʾān can clarify for the Children of Israel (q.v.) most of the matters they dispute (Q 27:76). Apart from human beings, the Qurʾān also affects the demons *(jinn),* who listen to its recitation and become believers (Q 46:29-31; 72:1-2).

The faith of the qurʾānic Prophet

The qurʾānic Prophet was the first of his people to become a Muslim, one who has deserted *shirk* (i.e. the worship of deities other than God, considered as his "associates"). This is stated in Q 6:14: "Say: 'Shall I take to myself as protector other than God, the originator of the heavens (see HEAVEN AND SKY) and of the earth (q.v.; see also CREATION), he who feeds and is not fed?' Say: 'I have been commanded to be the first of them that became a Muslim *(aslama)*.' Be you not of the associators *(lā takūnanna mina l-mushrikīna)*." The battle against *shirk* that underlies the Prophet's monotheistic thrust also emerges in Q 6:162-3: "Say: 'My prayer (q.v.), my ritual sacrifice (q.v.), my living, my dying — all belongs to God, the lord of all being. He has no associate *(sharīk)*. Thus have I been commanded and I am the first of those who have become Muslims.'" The abandonment of *shirk* means the purification *(ikhlāṣ)* of one's faith (q.v.); it is this that has made the Prophet a Muslim: "Say: I have been commanded to serve God, purifying my religion (q.v.) for him, and I have been commanded to be the first of those who have become Muslims" (Q 39:11-2).

The qurʾānic Prophet and previous prophets

Although the Prophet is the first Muslim among his people, previous prophets are also described as fighting against *shirk* and are hence designated as Muslims. This is the case with Noah who is one of "those who became Muslims" (Q 10:72), while Moses is the "first of those who became believers" (Q 7:143). This reveals the notion that the Prophet is a link in a chain of prophets sent to previous communities. In fact, he is the final link, as indicated in the title *khātam al-nabiyyīn,* "seal of the prophets," by which the Qurʾān designates Muḥammad (Q 33:40). Muḥammad, so the Qurʾān states, is only a messenger following other messengers who passed away before him (Q 3:144). In this respect he is like any other messenger in that chain, for example, Jesus (q.v.), about whom it is also stated that other messengers passed away before him (Q 5:75). As a link in a successive chain, the Prophet appears in the list of prophets with whom God made a covenant (q.v.; Q 33:7) and here, apart from the Prophet himself, the other prophets mentioned are Noah, Abraham, Moses and Jesus.

The affinity between the Prophet and the previous ones comes out in the idea that all of them experienced the same process of revelation. This is stated in Q 4:163: "We have revealed to you *(awḥaynā ilayka)* as we revealed to Noah and to the prophets after him, and [as] we revealed to Abraham, Ishmael (q.v.), Isaac (q.v.), Jacob (q.v.), and the tribes (see ISRAEL), Jesus and Job (q.v.), Jonah (q.v.) and Aaron (q.v.) and Solomon (q.v.) and we gave psalms (q.v.) to David (q.v.)...." The book that was revealed to the Prophet is not unique to him either, as other prophets were also sent with "the book" that was designed to guide them and resolve their disputes (Q 2:213). The goals of revelation are also common to all prophets, including the Prophet. He was sent to give warning as well as good tidings *(bashshir)* to the believers (e.g. Q 2:25, etc.), and the same is applicable to the previous messengers who were also sent to warn the evildoers and bear good tidings to the righteous (Q 6:48, etc.; see GOOD DEEDS; EVIL DEEDS; GOOD AND EVIL). The model of the previous prophets is continued in the career of the Prophet, and this comes out most clearly in what is known as the "punishment stories" (q.v.; for which see e.g. Watt-Bell, *Introduction,* 127 f.). They describe the events in the lives of prophets such as Ṣāliḥ (q.v.) in terms identical to those used for the experience of the Prophet (ibid., 133-4). In one case (Q 73:15), the parallelism is explicitly drawn, where it is stated that God sent the Prophet in the same manner as a messenger (i.e. Moses) was sent to warn Pharaoh (q.v.).

As a result of the affinity between the Prophet and the other prophets, the religion revealed to all of them is one and the same (Q 42:13). Hence the Qurʾān urges the Muslims to believe in all that was sent down to each one of the prophets and not make division among any of them (Q 2:136, 285; 3:84). It follows that the message of the book that was revealed to the Prophet is essentially the same as that of the books revealed to previous messengers. Therefore, the Qurʾān asserts several times that the book that was sent down to the Prophet "confirms *(muṣaddiq)* what was before it" (Q 35:31; cf. 3:3; 5:48; 6:92). In one case, the Arabian provenance of the Prophet's book is declared (Q 46:12; see ARABS; ARABIC LANGUAGE) and here the Qurʾān points out a specific book that has preceded the Arabian one, namely, the book of Moses (see also Q 46:30). In the same way, Jesus is said to have confirmed the Torah (q.v.) that had been revealed before him (Q 3:50; 5:46; 61:6).

The messianic position of the qurʾānic Prophet

In some passages, however, the Prophet occupies a distinguished position among the prophets, and the covenant God makes with them revolves exclusively around his own person, which thus acquires a messianic position. To begin with, in Q 3:81 God establishes a covenant with the prophets to the effect that when a messenger comes and confirms the book that is with them, they should believe in him and support him. This seems to mean that all prophets, as well as their respective peoples, must join the Prophet whenever he appears. Moreover, the description of the qurʾānic messenger is said to have been written in the scriptures of the Jews and the Christians (see SCRIPTURE AND THE QURʾĀN; CORRUPTION; FORGERY), namely, the Torah and the Gospel (q.v.), where he is described as *al-nabī al-ummī,* "the gentile prophet" (cf. Rubin, *The eye,* 23-30; see UMMĪ; ILLITERACY), and God's mercy is promised to those among them who follow him (Q 7:157-8). A more specific name of the qurʾānic messenger as described in the scriptures of the previous prophets is Aḥmad, about whom Jesus brings to the Children of Israel the good tidings (Q 61:6). Taken together, these passages build up a messianic image of the Prophet behind whom humankind is supposed to unite as one community of believers (see COMMUNITY AND SOCIETY IN THE QURʾĀN).

The religion of Abraham

The universal link of the Prophet, which is based on the identity of the message he shares with the prophets of the Children of Israel, or the People of the Book, is absent from other passages that establish a direct connection between the Prophet and Abraham. Thus in Q 3:68 it is declared "those standing closest to Abraham are those who followed him and this Prophet, and those who believe." The qurʾānic Prophet is explicitly instructed to follow what is called the "religion" *(milla)* of Abraham, and such passages surely exclude the religion of the Jewish and Christian prophets from the scope of the Prophet's faith (see JEWS AND JUDAISM; CHRISTIANS AND CHRISTIANITY). Abraham himself is declared to have preceded the revelation of the Torah and the Gospel (Q 3:65), and to have been neither Jewish nor Christian, but a *ḥanīf* (q.v.), a Muslim and not a *mushrik,* "associator" (Q 3:67). As the latter designation stands mainly for Arabian polytheists (see SOUTH ARABIA, RELIGION IN PRE-ISLAMIC), following the religion of Abraham means dissociation not only from the Jewish and Christian religious legacy but also from the Arabian one. The Prophet is explicitly demanded to follow the religion of Abraham in Q 16:123, while the rest of the believers are ordered to do the same in Q 3:95. In

Q 2:135 the believers who adhere to the religion of Abraham are thus refraining from becoming Jews or Christians. In another passage the Prophet is merely instructed to become a *ḥanīf* and here the demand is designed to prevent the Prophet from being a *mushrik* (Q 10:105). Although Abraham's name is not explicitly mentioned, the demand again is probably to follow Abraham's model. The same applies to Q 30:30 where the Prophet is urged to become a *ḥanīf* and adhere to the religion which is God's "original creation" *(fiṭra),* upon which he created humankind. The relation between the idea of the "original" religion and Abraham is clear from other passages describing Abraham's natural monotheism (Q 6:79).

The particularistic trend of the passages which create a direct connection between Abraham and the Prophet again seems to confine the scope of the message of the Prophet to the Arabian sphere, because Abraham himself, when linked to the Prophet, features in a clearly local context. This is the case in Q 2:127-9, where Abraham and Ishmael "raise up" the foundations of the house (the Kaʿba [q.v.]), and then Abraham prays to God to send from among his descendants a prophet who will teach them the book and the wisdom.

The qurʾānic Prophet between God and man

As a messenger of God, the Prophet is a chosen person, because God "chooses *(yaṣṭafī)* messengers of the angels and of humankind" (Q 22:75). The Qurʾān is therefore described as the "speech (q.v.) of a noble messenger" (Q 69:40). As God's chosen messenger, the Prophet is the recipient not only of his revelation but also of his infinite supervision, compassion and protection (q.v.). This is noted in passages such as that in which God is said to have never forsaken the Prophet (Q 93:3), and to have exalted his fame (Q 94:4), or raised him up to a laudable position (*maqām maḥmūd,* Q 17:79). God's compassion towards the Prophet comes out in the statement that God himself, as well as the angels, pray for the Prophet's peace (Q 33:56). For his part, the Prophet is instructed to ask for God's pardon (Q 4:106; 47:19; see FORGIVENESS), and is in fact granted complete forgiveness for all sins (Q 48:2; see SIN, MAJOR AND MINOR). God's guidance is also secured for the Prophet (Q 93:7), as well as his benefaction. God thus has improved the socio-economic status of the Prophet (Q 93:6, 8), and gave him "abundance" (*al-kawthar,* Q 108:1), as well as the "oft repeated" (q.v.; *mathānī*) and the great Qurʾān (Q 15:87). God has also alleviated from him the burden of fears and anxieties (Q 94:1-3). God's guidance is also manifest in the ritual sphere (see RITUAL AND THE QURʾĀN), and it is he who instructs the Prophet on when to pray (e.g. Q 20:130; 40:55; 50:39-40), and on what the direction of prayer (*qibla* [q.v.]) should be (Q 2:144). The fact that the Prophet has become the first Muslim among his community is the result of God's ritual guidance. The Prophet is ordered to say (Q 6:162-3): "My prayer, my ritual sacrifice, my living, my dying — all belongs to God, the lord of all being. No associate has he, so I have been instructed, and I am the first of those who have become Muslims" (cf. Q 6:14).

The qurʾānic Prophet and the believers

God's mercy on the Prophet is extended to the community that is supposed to follow the Prophet and support him, and it is God who has consolidated the believers behind the Prophet. The Prophet could not have achieved this alone (Q 8:63). God's mercy for the Prophet generates the Prophet's mercy for the believers, or as stated in

Q 3:159: "It was by God's mercy that you were gentle to them...." In the subsequent part of the same passage, God advises his messenger to pardon the believers and ask forgiveness for them, and to consult them in his affairs. Accordingly, the Prophet is described as "a messenger from among yourselves; your suffering (q.v.) is grievous to him, and he is anxious for you, gentle and compassionate to the believers" (Q 9:128). Forgiveness of sins, which emanates from the Prophet's presence, is particularly emphasized. Thus in Q 4:64 it is stated: "... If, when they wronged themselves, they had come to you and prayed for God's forgiveness, and the messenger had prayed for forgiveness for them, they would have found God forgiving, compassionate" (see GOD AND HIS ATTRIBUTES). The Prophet's mercifulness towards the believers is also manifest in his function as a "witness" *(shahīd)* for his community (Q 2:143; 22:78). This seems to be an eschatological role, as is indicated in passages describing the last judgment in which the Prophet is a witness for his community while the other communities have their own witnesses, their prophets (cf. Q 4:41; 16:89; see also Q 16:84; 28:75). His role as a *shahīd* probably means that he gives evidence as to the identity of both the righteous among his people, and of the evildoers. For their part, the believers are expected to take the Prophet as their model *(uswa)* in their devotion to God and in hoping for his reward at the last judgment (Q 33:21). Their love for God is the reason why they must follow the Prophet, which is the only way to gain God's love and mercy in return (Q 3:31; see LOVE AND AFFECTION). From this affinity between God and his messenger follows the need to obey them both (Q 3:32; 4:59), because to obey the Prophet means obeying God (Q 4:80; see OBEDIENCE). Similarly, pledging allegiance *(bayʿa)* to the Prophet means pledging allegiance to God (Q 48:10) and God is indeed pleased with those who pledge allegiance to his Prophet (Q 48:18; see CONTRACTS AND ALLIANCES). Women, too, pledge allegiance to him and when they do they must follow strict religious and moral codes and obey him (Q 60:12; see ETHICS AND THE QURʾĀN; VIRTUES AND VICES, COMMANDING AND FORBIDDING; WOMEN AND THE QURʾĀN). Apart from obedience, the believers are expected to be more loyal to their Prophet than to their own selves (Q 33:6), and treat him with due respect (see LOYALTY). This means that when they are in his presence they cannot withdraw without first asking his leave (Q 24:62-3), and they are not permitted to raise their voices above his (Q 49:1-5, 7; see SOCIAL INTERACTIONS). As the believers' model of devotion, the Prophet is also the source of their law, which he gives to them through a revelation (see LAW AND THE QURʾĀN). Thus in Q 6:151-3 he is commanded to tell them: "Come, I will recite what your lord has forbidden (q.v.) you...." This is followed by a list of legal and moral regulations (see BOUNDARIES AND PRECEPTS).

The Qurʾān does not only deal with the duty to obey the Prophet but also with his own individual status among the believers. This is apparent mainly in verses defining his share in the spoils of war as compared with the shares of the rest of the believers (see BOOTY). In Q 59:7 the spoils belong to God and his messenger, as well as to his kinsmen (see FAMILY OF THE PROPHET; PEOPLE OF THE HOUSE) and needy Muslims (see POVERTY AND THE POOR), and the Prophet is given complete authority to distribute the booty: "Whatever the messenger gives you, take; whatever he forbids you, give up." Similarly, in Q 8:1 it is stated that the spoils *(anfāl)* belong to God and the messenger. In Q 8:41, however, only one-fifth of the booty belongs to the Prophet and the needy, and the rest is distributed among the participating warriors.

Reference is also made to the status of the Prophet's wives among the believers (see WIVES OF THE PROPHET). They are proclaimed as equal in status to the mothers of the believers, which means that they cannot become wives to the believers after the Prophet (Q 33:6). Special moral obligations are prescribed to them as wives of the Prophet, and their conduct must be immaculate. If they wish to remain his wives and not be divorced (see MARRIAGE AND DIVORCE), they must undertake not to behave indecently, remain in their homes, not display their finery, as was the custom in the first Age of Ignorance (q.v.; *jāhiliyya*) and they have to pray and give alms (see ALMSGIVING) and obey God and his messenger. God will reward them twice over for all this (Q 33:28-34). Instructions to the believers as to how to behave in the Prophet's household are also specified. The believers should not call uninvited, nor linger after meals. They have to ask his wives for any object they want only while standing behind a curtain (Q 33:53; see VEIL; BARRIER). Nevertheless, allusion is made also to some obscure domestic problems that the Prophet had with two of his wives (Q 66:1-5), as well as to a group of persons who "came with the slander *(ifk)*" (Q 24:11 f.; see GOSSIP). The nature of the slander is not disclosed in the Qurʾān, but Muslim tradition associates it with ʿĀʾisha (see ʿĀʾISHA BINT ABĪ BAKR). In contrast to the qurʾānic proclamation that the Prophet's wives are the mothers of the believers, the Qurʾān declares that Muḥammad is not the father of any of the believers (Q 33:40), meaning that he can marry their women after them. This statement is made in connection with the affair of Zayd (b. Ḥāritha), Muḥammad's adopted son, the only contemporary of Muḥammad — apart from the Prophet himself — who is mentioned by his proper name in the Qurʾān. It is stated that after Zayd accomplished what he would of his wife, God gave her in marriage to the Prophet, and the Qurʾān asserts that it is lawful for the believers to marry the wives of their adopted sons (Q 33:37; see LAWFUL AND UNLAWFUL).

The qurʾānic Prophet and the unbelievers

The relationship between the Prophet and the unbelievers occupies the bulk of the qurʾānic passages dealing with his prophetic mission, and many aspects of the negative reaction of the unbelievers to his message are described (see OPPOSITION TO MUḤAMMAD). Their disbelief is depicted in some chapters as a refusal to listen to him. In one passage the unbelievers say: "Our hearts are veiled from what you call us to, and there is heaviness in our ears (see HEARING AND DEAFNESS), and between us and you there is a veil" (Q 41:5). In another instance they almost strike him down with their glances when they hear him preach (Q 68:51). Scornful reactions are also typical when the Prophet reproaches them for worshipping deities other than God (Q 21:36; 25:41-2; see MOCKERY). The Qurʾān emphasizes the unbelievers' stubbornness (see INSOLENCE AND OBSTINACY) when stating that even if God sent the Prophet "a book on parchment which they can touch with their hands," they would still not believe in him (Q 6:7).

Disbelief is often focused on a specific article of the faith preached by the Prophet, namely resurrection (q.v.) and the last judgment, which the unbelievers usually reject as an impossible process (Q 17:49, 98; 21:38, etc.). The unbelievers also make specific demands as a condition for their belief in the qurʾānic Prophet. In

Q 10:15 they ask him to change the contents of his revelations and make them more agreeable, and in Q 2:120 (see also Q 2:135) the Jews and the Christians ask him to follow their religion. The disbelief of the Jews, or the People of the Book, is especially condemned. They have rejected the Prophet despite the fact that the book revealed to him confirms their own scriptures. They are accused of deliberately ignoring the injunctions of their own book [i.e. to believe in the Prophet] (Q 2:89, 91, 101; see also Q 4:47).

Active persecution by the unbelievers is also addressed in the Qurʾān, particularly their threat to expel *(akhraja)* the Prophet from his homeland (Q 17:76). In Q 8:30 this is one of a series of other options contemplated, such as confining him or even killing him. In Q 9:13 the scheme to expel the messenger is coupled with the violation of oaths taken by the unbelievers, two offences that justify waging war on them (see BREAKING TRUSTS AND CONTRACTS). The threat of expulsion recurs in stories about previous prophets (Q 14:13) such as Shuʿayb (q.v.; Q 7:88) and Lot (q.v.; Q 7:82; 26:167; 27:56), where it again forms a major component of persecution. Expulsion, however, is not merely a threat but is also an accomplished fact that emerges in the reference to "your city which has expelled you" (Q 47:13). The Prophet and the believers suffer expulsion from the homeland, as indicated in Q 60:1. Here, "expelling the messenger and you [i.e. the believers]" features as one of the offences of the unbelievers, and in Q 2:217 those expelled are the inhabitants of the sacred mosque (q.v.; see also SACRED PRECINCTS). Expelling them and denying them free access to the sacred mosque are denounced as offences worse than fighting (q.v.) during the forbidden months (q.v.). The believers who have been expelled are ordered to kill their foes "wherever you come upon them and expel them from where they have expelled you..." (Q 2:191), which again makes expulsion a cause for war (q.v.). The same offence of forced expulsion is also a reason for the believers to dissociate from unbelievers guilty of this offense, or of assisting others in it (Q 60:9).

Not only does the Qurʾān refer to the existence of disbelief but it also reveals the various reasons for it, which stem from different sources. In one case its origin is fear; the unbelievers say that if they follow the Prophet they will be snatched from their land (Q 28:57). Those who speak here are probably the people of Mecca, to whom God immediately answers that he has established for them a "secure sanctuary *(ḥaraman āminan),* into which are brought the fruits of everything" (Q 28:57; cf. Q 8:26; 29:67). The message of the Prophet stands here in clear contrast to the Arabian values on which the security of the people of Mecca rested. The disbelief of the contemporaries of the Prophet is often coupled with doubts as to the authenticity of his message, i.e. whether he truly is the messenger of God. These doubts originate with presumed faults in his personality and message. The personal accusations against the Prophet are often based on the claim that he is but human, and God does not usually send humans as his messengers, only angels (Q 17:94; 21:3). The Jews also held this point against him (Q 6:91), and similar reservations were also held about previous prophets by their contemporaries (e.g. Q 11:27, Noah; Q 26:154, Ṣāliḥ; Q 26:186, Shuʿayb). Even as a human being the social status of the Prophet is not elevated enough to be a prophet (see SOCIAL RELATIONS). This claim by the unbelievers is indicated in Q 43:31: "They say: 'Why was this Qurʾān not sent down to some distinguished *(ʿaẓīm)* man of the two cities?'"

As a result of the notion that a messenger of God must be an angel, the demand is often raised by the unbelievers that the Prophet produce signs from heaven, i.e. miracles (see MIRACLE). He is asked either to produce an unspecified sign *(āya)* himself (Q 7:203), or have one sent down to him from God (Q 13:7, 27). In Q 11:12 he is requested to have a treasure sent down to him, or an angel escorting him (see also Q 6:8-9; 25:7-8). A prolonged series of specific signs is required in Q 17:90-3: that a stream be made to gush forth (see SPRINGS AND FOUNTAINS); that he produce a garden (q.v.) of palms and vines with rivers flowing through it; that he make heaven fall; bring God and the angels as a surety; produce a house of gold (q.v.) ornamentation; go up to heaven and bring down a book that can be read. The People of the Book (Q 4:153) also ask for a real book from heaven, and the Jews expect to see a sacrifice that will be devoured by fire (q.v.; as a sign of its acceptance by God; Q 3:183).

Failing to produce proofs of his divine person, the Prophet is accused of being a sorcerer (Q 10:2; 11:7, etc.; see MAGIC) and a poet possessed by jinn (q.v.; *majnūn,* Q 37:36; 44:14; see also INSANITY; POETRY AND POETS). His prophetic message, too, is not accepted as divine, and is rejected as a "hotchpotch of dreams" (Q 21:5; see DREAMS AND SLEEP). The unbelievers usually mention such faults when refusing to abandon the worship of their deities (Q 37:36). His messages are often rejected as forged (Q 11:35; 46:8) or plagiarized (see FORGERY). In the latter case, his sermons are denounced as "fairy-tales of the ancients" that have been dictated to him (Q 25:4-6; see also Q 6:25-6, etc.), or have been learnt from a human master (Q 74:25; see also Q 44:14), whose origin is said to be non-Arab (Q 16:103; see INFORMANTS; see also Ahrens, *Muhammed,* 42-4). They too, so the unbelievers claim, can do the same (Q 8:31). His message, however, is also denounced as being an innovation previously unheard of in other religions (Q 38:7), one which deviates from the forefathers' religion (Q 34:43). The criticism in this respect is mainly directed against the clear dissimilarity between the structure of the Prophet's sermons and those of previous prophets. Thus in Q 28:48 the unbelievers wonder why the Prophet has not received a revelation like that of Moses, and in Q 25:32 they ask why the Qurʾān was not revealed to the Prophet all at once.

Divine protection

A large space is allotted in the Qurʾān to God's defense of the Prophet against the various aspects of rejection, providing the main basis on which rests the status of the Prophet as a messenger of God. In general, the Qurʾān asserts the absurdity of disbelief by stressing that it arose in spite of the unbelievers' original desire for guidance. Thus in Q 35:42 the unbelievers swear that if a warner came to them they would be more rightly guided than any other nation, and in Q 6:157 they swear that if a divine book was revealed to them they would be more rightly guided than any other nation (see also Q 37:167-70). God sets out to legitimize the authority of his messenger as an exclusive source of guidance, and for this a variety of arguments are set forth in defense of the authenticity of his message. In response to attacks on the mental integrity of the Prophet, God addresses the unbelievers saying: "Your comrade is not astray, neither does he err (see ERROR), nor does he speak out of caprice" (Q 53:2-3). In calling him "your comrade" *(ṣāḥibukum),* the Prophet is made one of their own kind, whose integrity must be well-known to them. In this manner God also addresses the unbelievers in Q 34:46, telling them that "no madness *(jinna)* is in your comrade" (cf. Q 7:184), and again in Q 81:22: "Your comrade is not possessed *(majnūn).*"

The origin of the Prophet's integrity and mental fitness is God's mercy *(niʿma)* which prevents him from being a *kāhin,* "soothsayer," or possessed (Q 52:29), and indeed God repeatedly asserts that he is neither a *kāhin,* nor a poet or possessed (Q 68:2; 69:40-2, etc.). To this context seems also to belong the frequent qurʾānic insistence that the Prophet is not expecting a reward or a wage *(ajr)* for his messages (e.g. Q 25:57; 34:47; 38:86), which means that he is delivering the word of God and not his own. A more straightforward statement about the authenticity of his revelation is repeated in numerous passages asserting that the Prophet was sent "with the truth" *(bi-l-ḥaqq;* cf. Q 2:119, 252; 4:170; 9:33; 35:24, etc.; see TRUTH), and that God and the angels bear witness to the truth of his message (Q 4:166; 13:43, etc.). The fact that the Qurʾān confirms the previous scriptures, and mainly the stories about earlier prophets, is also invoked in support of its authenticity (Q 12:110-1). Similarly, when the Prophet is himself beset by doubts as to the genuine nature of what has been revealed to him, he is advised to consult those who are well versed in previous scriptures — and thus know that the Qurʾān and those scriptures are alike (Q 10:94).

The Qurʾān also answers more specific aspects of the doubts raised by the unbelievers as to the authenticity of the Prophet's message. To the charge of plagiarism God responds by pointing to the Arabic language of the Qurʾān, which excludes the possibility of a non-Arab master teaching the Prophet, as insinuated by his opponents (Q 16:103). The Arabic language renders the Qurʾān clear to the audience (Q 12:2; 41:3) who would not have accepted a non-Arabic revelation that could not have been understood (Q 26:195, 198-9; 41:44). Perhaps the assertion that the Prophet did not read any book before the revelation of the Qurʾān or write it down (Q 29:48) is also designed to refute the charge of plagiarism. The human nature of the Prophet, which is held against him by his opponents, is admitted by God himself, who orders his messenger to say that he is merely a human being who (nevertheless) receives revelations (Q 18:110; 41:6; see also IMPECCABILITY). God stresses that the mortality of the Prophet does not prevent him from being a messenger of God, and to prove this, God tells his Prophet to remind the unbelievers that other prophets were mortals too. Thus God advises his Prophet to say that Moses received revelations as a human being (Q 6:91), and that messengers to older communities were also merely humans (*rijāl,* Q 12:109, etc.). The same argument is followed when the Qurʾān asserts that the Prophet is not an innovation among other messengers (Q 46:9). Moreover, a messenger of God always remains mortal, and he is not permitted to have other people worship him as a god (Q 3:79). While the human nature of the Prophet is acknowledged, however, the divinity of his message is emphasized. To prove this, God advises the Prophet to challenge the unbelievers who claim that the Qurʾān is forged to produce one or ten chapters (*sūras*) similar to the qurʾānic ones, if they can (Q 10:38; 11:13), or a story *(ḥadīth)* like it (Q 52:33-4; see INIMITABILITY; PROVOCATION). Due to the Qurʾān's divinity the human qurʾānic Prophet has no control over its contents, nor of the time of its revelation. This point is made when people demand that he change his message into a more agreeable one, to which he is prompted to say: "It is not for me to alter it of my own accord; I follow nothing except what is revealed to me... Had God willed it, I would not have recited it to you... I have been living among you a lifetime before it..." (Q 10:15-6).

The constant human nature of the

Prophet prevents him from complying with the demands for miracles, and when this demand is made, God commands his messenger to say that the unseen *(ghayb)* belongs to God alone (Q 10:20). This seems to mean that he is but a mortal messenger who cannot perform supernatural acts of his own volition. Only God has the power to produce signs, as the Qurʾān itself states elsewhere (Q 6:37, etc.), and it is for him to decide whom he wishes to guide (Q 13:27). Previous prophets are put in the same situation when commanded to produce signs, and they too answer that they are but mortals and that they can only produce miracles with God's permission (Q 14:10-11). Besides, the Qurʾān says that the unbelievers had a chance to draw a lesson from previous scriptures which they know (and not wait for fresh signs; cf. Q 20:133). The same reply, namely, that the Prophet has no knowledge of the unseen, is given when demands are made for signs of the approaching hour, i.e. the end of the world, about which the Qurʾān warns quite often (Q 7:187-8; 72:25-7). The demand to produce signs sent by God may take the form of a request to bring down from heaven a written text *(kitāb)* that humankind can read (see above). To this the Prophet is again directed to say: "I am but a mortal, a messenger" (Q 17:93). Elsewhere he is advised to say that he is not an angel, which also seems to be in response to the request for signs (Q 6:50; cf. Q 11:31, Noah). Nevertheless, the Prophet himself does get a chance to see God's signs, as stated in Q 17:1: "Glory be to him who carried his servant by night from the sacred mosque to the further mosque which we have blessed all around, that we might show him some of our signs...."

Apart from defending his authenticity in the eyes of the unbelievers, God directly helps the Prophet himself, which is designed to encourage him and offer him various kinds of comfort and moral support (see CONSOLATION). To begin with, comfort is offered through the statement that God exempts the Prophet from responsibility for the unbelievers, saying that his mission is only to deliver the message (Q 5:99), and that he is not supposed to be the guardian of the unbelievers (Q 6:107; 10:108; 17:54, etc.). God himself undertakes the responsibility for them (Q 42:6). To emphasize this point God says that the Prophet cannot guide the dead (see DEATH AND THE DEAD), the blind (see VISION AND BLINDNESS) and the deaf (Q 27:80-1; 30:52-3; 35:22), neither can he force them (to repent; Q 50:45; see TOLERANCE AND COMPULSION; REPENTANCE AND PENANCE). To comfort the Prophet and encourage him, God tells him that he is aware of the distress that the words of the unbelievers have caused him (Q 15:97), and advises him not to let his soul be wasted in regrets for the unbelievers (Q 35:8). Although the Prophet tends to consume himself with anguish over their disbelief (Q 18:6; 26:3), God tells him not to let the unbelievers torment him by what they do or say (Q 3:176; 5:41; 10:65; 15:88; 16:127; 27:70). God states that the Qurʾān has not been revealed to him to make him miserable (Q 20:2), nor to disquiet his heart (Q 7:2). In a series of passages God encourages the Prophet to bear patiently *(iṣbir)* the hardships and adhere to his prophetic mission (see TRUST AND PATIENCE). For example, in Q 10:109 he is urged to endure his sufferings patiently and to follow what is being revealed to him (cf. Q 43:43). In Q 20:130 he is told to bear patiently what the unbelievers say, and continue proclaiming the lord's praise day and night (see also Q 52:48-9, etc.). In other passages God demands that the Prophet patiently endure his sufferings along with those who call to their lord in the morning (q.v.) and evening (q.v.), and not yield to the temptations of worldly pleasures

(Q 18:28; cf. Q 20:131). When urging his Prophet to endure the hardships, the example of previous prophets is often adduced. Thus, in Q 46:35 he is entreated to be as patient as other prophets previously were, and in Q 38:17 he is told to exercise patience with what is being said to him and remember David the man of might. Conversely, he is told to be patient and avoid bad examples such as that of the "man of the whale" (Yūnus, i.e. Jonah; Q 68:48-50).

The example of previous messengers plays a central role in the encouragement of the Prophet (Q 11:120; cf. Q 23:44; 51:52-4). They too, God says, were rejected as liars by their respective peoples (Q 3:184; 6:33-4; 35:4; 41:43), and when they were almost overtaken by despair (q.v.), God rescued them, and the unbelievers suffered his retribution (Q 12:110; 38:14). Likewise, previous messengers were mocked (Q 6:10; 13:32; 21:41) and had enemies (q.v.), but God was their savior (Q 25:31). As for the signs demanded from him by the unbelievers, God says that such signs would be useless just as they were useless to previous prophets who were commanded to produce them (Q 2:118; 21:5-6). The Prophet can, of course, try and seek out a hole in the ground or a ladder in heaven if he were distressed because the unbelievers have turned away from him, but in the end it is God alone who can turn them into believers (Q 6:35).

In many passages God advises the Prophet how to remain on his own path when under pressure from different quarters. In some cases the Prophet is simply advised to part company with the unbelievers to avoid open confrontation. Thus in Q 73:10 God tells him to "forsake them *(wa-uhjurhum)* graciously," and in Q 43:89 he is told to turn away from them *(iṣfaḥ ʿanhum),* and the same is suggested to him in other passages (Q 51:54, *tawallā ʿanhum;* Q 15:94; 32:30, *aʿriḍ;* Q 15:3; 43:83, *dharhum*). In some instances God prompts him to tell the unbelievers that his own religion will remain different from the one they follow, as for example in Q 10:104: "I do not worship those you worship apart from God" (see RELIGIOUS PLURALISM AND THE QURʾĀN). Similarly, in Q 10:41 God says: "If they say that you lie, tell them: 'I have my work and you have your work. You have nothing to do with what I do, and I have nothing to do with what you do'" (see also Q 26:216). The same quietist policy is suggested to the Prophet in passages advising him to rely on God and await his final judgment. Thus in Q 22:68-9 God tells him: "And if they should dispute with you, say: 'God knows very well what you are doing, God shall judge between you on the day of resurrection....'" Elsewhere he is advised to say, when the people turn their backs on him: "God is sufficient for me, there is no God but he, in him I have put my trust" (Q 9:129; cf. Q 27:79; 33:48). Similarly, he is advised to debate with the unbelievers in a gentle and a refined manner (Q 16:125; 23:96; see DEBATE AND DISPUTATION).

When the unbelievers demand of the Prophet that he abandon his religion and follow them instead, God again advises him on how to stay firm. In one particular instance the Prophet and his followers are challenged to become Jews and Christians, in which case, staying firm means following the religion of Abraham (Q 2:135). In more general terms, the unbelievers would like to see the Prophet following their "evil inclinations" *(ahwāʾ),* and here God encourages him not to follow their *ahwāʾ* and adhere to his own *sharīʿa* (Q 45:18; 5:48-9; see also Q 42:15). In more explicit terms, God demands that he "not obey" the unbelievers and the *munāfiqūn,* "hypocrites" (see HYPOCRITES AND HYPOCRISY), and only follow what is being revealed to him (Q 33:1-2).

A unique case is Q 17:73-5 in which the unbelievers come near to tempting the Prophet away from that which has been revealed to him, inciting him to forge a more agreeable revelation, following which they will take him as their friend (see FRIENDS AND FRIENDSHIP). It is only thanks to God's intervention that he remains firm, and the Qurʾān asserts that if he had inclined to them God would have punished him severely. A similar situation of a distorted revelation is described in Q 22:52 with reference to previous prophets: Each one of them was subjected to the temptation of Satan who cast words of his own into their recitation. The Qurʾān, however, asserts that God annuls what Satan casts and confirms his own signs.

In other passages God's protection of his messenger is more active which implies a more militant clash between the Prophet and the unbelievers. To begin with, in Q 5:67 God grants him immunity from the people to help him deliver his message safely. When the unbelievers expel the Prophet, God sends him his sechina (q.v.; *sakīnatahu*) and supports him with unseen legions. This event occurs when the Prophet and a companion of his are hiding in a cave (q.v.) and he reassures his friend that God is with them (Q 9:40). To help the Prophet endure his expulsion, God promises him in a special vision *(ruʾyā)* that he and the believers will enter the sacred mosque and there perform the rituals (Q 48:27). A similar promise is perhaps made in Q 28:85: "He who imposed the Qurʾān on you will surely restore you to a place which will be home." In direct military clashes with the unbelievers, God actually fights for him (Q 8:17), and grants him victory (q.v.; *fatḥ*, Q 48:1). God's protection and aid emanate from his mercy and bountifulness towards the Prophet, which avert all attempts at injuring him (Q 4:113), and as a result of this God has rid him of those who mock him (Q 15:95), and promises to rid him of those who do not believe (Q 2:137). His foes are explicitly warned about God's wrath, as in Q 17:76, where those who plot to expel him from the land are warned of a swift destruction. Likewise, God took vengeance on the foes of previous prophets (Q 30:47). Fighting angels inflict God's wrath on the Prophet's foes, smiting them above the necks (Q 8:12-13). The angel Gabriel (q.v.) too is his protector, alongside the righteous among the believers and the other angels (Q 66:4). But God's retribution usually awaits the foes in hell (see HELL AND HELLFIRE). The fate of hell awaits those who assault the Prophet during prayer (Q 96:9-19), and those who make a breach with him (Q 4:115; 59:4; cf. Q 47:32). In response to such opposition, the Qurʾān sets clear limits to God's mercy as emanating from the Prophet, and explicitly excludes the unbelievers from it. Thus in Q 9:113 it is stated that "It is not for the Prophet and the believers to ask pardon for the associators, even though they may be near kinsmen (see KINSHIP), after that it has become clear to them that they will be the inhabitants of hell." For his part, the Prophet is commanded to wage holy war on the unbelievers, as stated in Q 9:73 and in Q 66:9: "O Prophet, struggle *(jāhid)* against the infidels and the hypocrites and be harsh with them; their refuge is hell — an evil homecoming" (see also Q 25:52; see JIHĀD). God's help to the Prophet also encompasses the entire community of believers, and his help is therefore described in several passages as being extended to them collectively. Thus in Q 8:26 God says: "Remember when you were few and abased in the land (see OPPRESSED ON EARTH, THE), and were fearful that the people would snatch you away; but he gave you refuge and assisted you with his help, and provided you with the good things, for which you might be haply thankful." Divine help is usually given to the believers on the battlefield, as seems to be the case in Q 3:13: "There has already been a sign for you in the two companies which encountered each other, one company fighting in the way of God and another unbelieving; they saw them twice the like of them, as the eye sees, but God assists with his help whom he will...." A specific designation of the place in which God helped the believers is provided in Q 3:123: "God helped you at Badr (q.v.) when you were abject...."

The Qurʾān and Muḥammad's sīra

The Qurʾān contains numerous allusions to events in the Prophet's life without placing them in a concrete context. Apart from issues already mentioned above there are many more allusions to incidents and experiences, most of which gain their context outside of the Qurʾān, in the realm of the *sīra*, i.e. Muḥammad's biography. Here the qurʾānic allusions to the Prophet's life and prophetic experience reappear as embedded in a clear chronological sequence of events. It is impossible to survey here all the qurʾānic allusions that are found in the *sīra;* only some of them will be highlighted.

One of the earliest *sīra* compilations in which a massive presence of qurʾānic allusions exists is by Ibn Isḥāq, whose *sīra* of Muḥammad is available in several recensions, the most famous of which is Ibn Hishām's (d. 218/833). Here the general narrative framework — which is retained in every other biography of Muḥammad — is as follows: The life of the Prophet is divided into two major phases, Meccan and Medinan, which corresponds to the traditional division of the Qurʾān into Meccan and Medinan periods. The Meccan period spans from Muḥammad's birth until his emigration (q.v.) to Medina (q.v.). The episodes covering this phase describe his birth and his early years in Mecca, his first revelation, the beginning of his public preaching, his persecution by his fellow Quraysh tribesmen, and his emigration to Medina. The Medinan period consists of episodes describing his arrival there, the consolidation of his relations with the local Arab tribes, his struggle against the local Jews, and primarily his campaigns and battles *(maghāzī)* against Mecca (see EXPEDITIONS AND BATTLES). These clashes culminated in the fall of Mecca, and in the eventual spread of Islam throughout Arabia. This sequence of events has a well-established chronological framework: The Meccan period begins with what is known as the "Year of the Elephant," in which, according to most traditions, Muḥammad is said to have been born (with reference to sūra 105, "The Elephant"; see ABRAHA). His first revelation is said to have occurred when he was forty, his emigration is dated to ten years later (622 C.E.), and the fall of Mecca is dated to 8/630, while Muḥammad's death is said to have taken place in 11/632.

The Meccan period

For the Meccan period the *sīra* uses qurʾānic passages that have been embedded in traditions describing Muḥammad's first revelation, first admonitions, and especially his persecution by the unbelievers (for details see Rubin, *Eye*, 103-66). For the first revelation the most prevalent passage that has been selected is Q 96:1-5: "Recite in the name of your lord who created...." For the subsequent event of the temporary lapse of revelation, Q 93:3 was chosen: "Your lord has not forsaken you nor does he hate [you]." For his first public sermon, Q 26:214 was adduced: "And warn your nearest relations...." Several qurʾānic passages appear in *sīra* descriptions of Muḥammad's persecution by the Meccans, e.g. sūra 111 in which Abū Lahab is cursed and promised punishment in hell. Abū Lahab is the designation of an uncle of Muḥammad and in the *sīra* he leads a strong opposition against the Prophet for which this chapter is said to have been revealed as divine retribution. Other passages that appear in the context of persecution describe the exchange of accusations between the Prophet and his opponents (e.g. Q 41:3-4; 13:31; 25:7-8; 17:90-3; 16:103). One of them, Q 38:4-8, is embedded in traditions describing the role of Abū Ṭālib, another of the Prophet's uncles, in helping his nephew confront the unbelievers. The passage about the Prophet and his companion in the cave (Q 9:40) appears in the descriptions of Muḥammad's journey *(hijra)* from Mecca to Medina, the companion being Abū Bakr (see COMPANIONS OF THE PROPHET).

The Medinan period

The Medinan period revolves around Muḥammad's campaigns against the Meccans as well as against the Jews, and in some cases the links between them and the Qurʾān are obvious, because the names of some campaigns are explicitly mentioned in scripture. This applies to Badr (2/624), which is mentioned in a passage describing angels assisting the fighting believers (Q 3:123-8), and to Ḥunayn (q.v.; 8/630). The latter location is mentioned in a passage again describing how the sechina as well as unseen legions (of angels) help the fighting believers (Q 9:25-6). In other cases the link is only revealed through the traditions (see ḤADĪTH AND THE QURʾĀN), while in the Qurʾān explicit links are missing. Thus there are additional passages linked in traditions to Badr, mainly Q 8:1-19 in which the division of spoils is discussed, and the help of angels smiting the unbelievers is described yet again. The connection with other campaigns is revealed through traditions only. Passages that are linked to the battle of Uḥud (3/625), for example, are Q 3:121-2, in which the Prophet lodges the believers in their ditches for the battle, and "two parties" of the believers are about to lose heart. The praise of martyrs (q.v.; *shuhadāʾ*), whom the Qurʾān describes as "living with their lord" and rejoicing in his bounty (cf. Q 3:169-71) is also linked to the believers who fell at Uḥud. The expulsion of the Jewish tribe of al-Naḍīr (see NAḌĪR, BANŪ AL-) from Medina is reported with reference to Q 59:1-3 which describes the expulsion of the unbelieving People of the Book from their habitations. They thought that their fortresses would defend them but God defeated them in the end. A link to the Battle of the Ditch (see PEOPLE OF THE DITCH) and the subsequent campaign against the Jewish tribe of Qurayẓa (q.v.; 5/626-7) is found in traditions about Q 33:9-27. Here the Qurʾān describes hosts of confederates *(aḥzāb)* coming against the believers whom God defeats by means of winds (see AIR AND WIND) and unseen legions (of angels).

Special reference is made to the role of the hypocrites *(munāfiqūn)* in spreading doubts among the Medinan believers, "people of Yathrib," and in inducing them to retreat. The faithful believers who have remained firm are praised, and the passage concludes with the defeat of the People of the Book who supported the confederates. They are brought down from their fortresses and the believers slay some of them and take others as captives. God bequeaths their lands and possessions to the believers. To the Jews of Qurayẓa are also linked the verses of Q 8:55-8 in which those who have broken their compact with the Prophet are severely criticized. The affair of al-Ḥudaybiya (6/628) and the subsequent campaign against the Jews of Khaybar are linked to the bulk of sūra 48. In it the believers pledge allegiance to the Prophet "under the tree," and God rewards them with a swift victory and many spoils.

Among the remaining qurʾānic allusions in the *sīra,* sūra 9 may also be mentioned. It is connected to events that took place during Muḥammad's campaign to Tabūk (9/630) as well as during Abū Bakr's pilgrimage (q.v.) to Mecca (9/631). Problems with opposing groups within Medina (led by Abū ʿĀmir and others) are also connected to this sūra, mainly to Q 9:107 in which reference is made to "those who have taken a mosque in opposition and unbelief, and to divide the believers..." (see MOSQUE OF THE DISSENSION). The final stages of his career, when most of the pagan Arabs became Muslims and delegations came from all over Arabia to pledge allegiance to the Prophet in Medina, are connected to Q 110 (Sūrat al-Naṣr, "Succor"). In it (Q 110:2) the Prophet sees "men entering God's religion in throngs." Muḥammad's farewell sermon which he delivered during his last pilgrimage to Mecca (10/632; see FAREWELL PILGRIMAGE), a few months before his death, has also many qurʾānic links, e.g. Q 5:3: "Today I have perfected your religion for you, and I have completed my blessing of you and I have approved Islam for your religion."

The chronology of revelation

The link between the Qurʾān and the life of Muḥammad as established in the *sīra* has provided the Qurʾān with a concrete context of revelation, or *asbāb al-nuzūl,* as this came to be known among Muslim Qurʾān exegetes. Since the mid-19th century C.E., scholars investigating the history of the Qurʾān have followed the *sīra* framework which the Qurʾān has acquired, and developed the traditional *asbāb al-nuzūl* into an elaborate chronology of revelation (see CHRONOLOGY AND THE QURʾĀN). They divided the qurʾānic passages not only into Meccan and Medinan periods, but also into "early Meccan," "late Meccan," and so on. Not all of the scholars have shown the same degree of dependence on Islamic tradition and some, like Bell, gave more weight to textual considerations of style and form (see FORM AND STRUCTURE OF THE QURʾĀN; LANGUAGE AND STYLE OF THE QURʾĀN). All of them, however, have treated the Qurʾān as the prophetic creation of the historical Muḥammad, and as a key to the study of his own spiritual development. The relationship between the qurʾānic text and the historical Muḥammad is, however, far from clear. Some, like John Wansbrough, have not even accepted the Arabian provenance of the Qurʾān. Above all, it should especially be borne in mind that the *sīra* and the *asbāb al-nuzūl* traditions are all part of ḥadīth material, the historical authenticity of which has been shown to be very problematic. A reconstructed chronology of revelation based on this material must therefore be taken with the utmost caution.

Uri Rubin

Bibliography

Primary (The following is a list of only the most noted of the qurʾānic commentaries and biographies of Muḥammad. The commentaries should be consulted for their commentary on the relevant qurʾānic passages cited in the article. See Jones, Maghāzī and Kister, Sīra for further details on the primary sources.): al-Balādhurī, Aḥmad b. Yaḥyā, *Ansāb al-ashrāf,* 2 vols., Jerusalem 1936-8 (incomplete ed.), facs. repr. Baghdad 1964 [?]; Ibn Isḥāq, *Sīra;* Ibn Kathīr, *Tafsīr;* Ibn Saʿd, *Ṭabaqāt;* Ṭabarī, *Tafsīr;* id., *Taʾrīkh.*
Secondary: K. Ahrens, *Muhammed als Religionsstifter,* Leipzig 1935; T. Andræ, *Die Person Muhammeds in Lehre und Glauben seiner Gemeinde,* Uppsala 1917 (see 23-91 for a discussion of the "legend" of the Prophet; 92-123 for the "miracles" of Muḥammad); Eng. trans. Th. Menzel, *Mohammed, the man and his faith,* London 1936; R. Bell, Mohammed's call, in *MW* 24 (1934), 13-9; id., Muhammad and previous messengers, in *MW* 24 (1934), 330-40; id., Muhammad's pilgrimage proclamation, in *JRAS* (1937), 233-44; id., Muhammad's visions, in *MW* 24 (1934),

145-54; H. Birkeland, *The legend of the opening of Muhammed's breast,* Oslo 1955; id., *Lord;* R. Blachère, *Le problème de Mahomet,* Paris 1952; Buhl, *Das Leben;* id., Fasste Muḥammed seine Verkündigung als eine universelle, auch für Nichtaraber bestimmte Religion auf? in *Islamica* 2 (1926-7), 135-49; L. Caetani, *Annali dell'Islam,* vols. i-ii, Milan 1905-7; M. Cook, *Muhammad,* Oxford 1983; F. Gabrieli, *Mahomet,* Paris 1965; M. Gaudefroy-Demombynes, *Mahomet,* Paris 1957; C.L. Geddes, *An analytical guide to the bibliographies on Islam, Muḥammad, and the Qur'ān,* Denver 1973; A. Geiger, *Was hat Mohammed aus dem Judentum aufgenommen?* Leipzig 1902 (repr.); trans. F.M. Young, *Judaism and Islam,* New York 1970 (re-published by Moshe Pearlman); C. Gilliot, Les 'informateurs' juifs et chrétiens de Muḥammad. Reprise d'un problème traité par Aloys Sprenger et Theodor Nöldeke, in *JSAI* 22 (1998), 84-126; id., Muḥammad, le Coran et les 'contraintes de l'histoire,' in Wild, *Text,* 3-26; H. Grimme, *Mohammed,* 2 vols., Munster 1892-; M. Hamidullah, *Le prophète de l'Islam,* 2 vols., Paris 1959; M.Ḥ. Haykal, *Ḥayāt Muḥammad,* Cairo 1963 (eighth repr.); J. Horovitz, Zur Muḥammad legende, in *Der Islam* 5 (1914), 41-53; Eng. trans., The growth of the Mohammed legend, in *MW* 10 (1920), 58; J.M.B. Jones, The maghāzī literature, in A.F.L. Beeston et al. (eds.), *Arabic literature to the end of the Umayyad period,* Cambridge 1983, 344-51 (for details on the primary literature); M.J. Kister, The sīra literature, in A.F.L. Beeston et al. (eds.), *Arabic literature to the end of the Umayyad period,* Cambridge 1983, 352-67 (for details on the primary literature); H. Lammens, L'âge de Mahomet et la chronologie de la *Sīra,* in *JA* [tenth series] 17 (1911), 209-50; Lecker, *Muslims;* H. Motzki (ed.), *The biography of Muḥammad. The issue of the sources,* Leiden 2000; W. Muir, *The life of Mohammad from original sources,* ed. T.H. Weir, Edinburgh 1912; R. Paret, Der Koran als Geschichtsquelle, in *Der Islam* 37 (1961), 24-42; id., *Mohammed und der Koran,* Stuttgart 1957; F.E. Peters, *Muhammad and the origins of Islam,* Albany 1994; H. Reckendorf, *Mohammed und die Seinen,* Leipzig 1907; M. Rodinson, *Mohammed,* trans. Anne Carter, New York 1971; U. Rubin, *The eye of the beholder. The life of Muḥammad as viewed by the early Muslims,* Princeton 1995; id. (ed.), *The life of Muḥammad (The formation of the classical Islamic world: Vol. 4),* Aldershot 1998 (full bibliography); id., Pre-existence and light. Aspects of the concept of Nūr Muḥammad, in *IOS* 5 (1975), 62-119; id., The shrouded messenger. On the interpretation of *al-muzzammil* and *al-mudaththir,* in *JSAI* 16 (1993), 96-107; A. Schimmel, *And Muhammad is his messenger. The veneration of the Prophet in Islamic piety,* Chapel Hill 1985; Sprenger, *Mohammed;* Wansbrough, *QS;* id., *The sectarian milieu. Content and composition of Islamic salvation history,* Oxford 1978; W.M. Watt, *Muhammad at Mecca,* Oxford 1953; id., *Muhammad at Medina,* Oxford 1956; id., *Muhammad's Mecca. History in the Qur'ān,* Edinburgh 1988; Watt-Bell, *Introduction;* A.T. Welch, Muhammad's understanding of himself. The koranic data, in R.G. Hovannisian and S. Vryonis (eds.), *Islam's understanding of itself. Eighth Giorgio Levi Della Vida Biennial Conference,* California 1983, 15-52; S. Wild, 'We have sent down to thee the book with truth…'. Spatial and temporal implications of the qur'ānic concepts of *nuzūl, tanzīl* and *inzāl,* in Wild, *Text,* 137-56; M. Zwettler, A mantic manifesto. The sūra of 'The Poets' and the qur'ānic foundations of prophetic authority, in J.L. Kugel (ed.), *Poetry and prophecy. The beginnings of literary tradition,* Ithaca 1990, 75-231.

Muḥkamāt wa-Mutashābihāt

see AMBIGUOUS; EXEGESIS OF THE QUR'ĀN: CLASSICAL AND MEDIEVAL; VERSES

Mule

see ANIMAL LIFE

Mu'minīn

see BELIEF AND UNBELIEF

Murder

The unlawful killing of a human being with malicious forethought. The Qur'ān uses the verb *qatala* to denote "kill" as well as "murder." In the latter sense it is used to describe both infanticide (q.v.), as in Q 6:140: "Lost are they who slay their children (q.v.) out of folly and ignorance (q.v.)," and the intentional killing of another without legal right, such as in Q 5:32: "Whosoever kills another — unless for murder or highway robbery (*fasād fī l-arḍ,* see THEFT; CORRUPTION) — it is as though he has killed the entirety of humanity." The penalty for the latter is the death of the murderer at the option of the victim's next of kin, as in Q 17:33: "Nor take life — which God has made sacred — except for just cause. And if anyone is murdered, we have given his heir authority [to demand *qiṣāṣ* or to forgive]." If they choose not to exercise this right, they are entitled to compensation, *diya,* as in Q 2:178, "If any remission is by the deceased's heir [lit. "brother"; see INHERITANCE], then reasonable demands are granted and generous compensation is his due" (see BLOODSHED; BLOOD MONEY; KINSHIP; BOUNDARIES AND PRECEPTS).

According to the Qurʾān, intentional murder is second only to associating other deities with God in terms of its sinfulness (see SIN, MAJOR AND MINOR; IDOLATRY AND IDOLATERS). Indeed, it is the only sin other than polytheism (see POLYTHEISM AND ATHEISM) for which the Qurʾān explicitly threatens eternal damnation (see ETERNITY; ESCHATOLOGY), at least in cases where the victim is a believer in God, as in Q 4:93, "Whosever intentionally kills a believer is punished in hell (see HELL AND HELLFIRE), to dwell therein forever, with the anger of God and his curse (q.v.); and God prepares for him an awful punishment" (see REWARD AND PUNISHMENT). The best reading of the Qurʾān, however, would also extend this threat to include the intentional murder of any person, simply by virtue of the victim's humanity. This non-sectarian reading of the absolute immorality of murder (see ETHICS AND THE QURʾĀN) is based on the general language of Q 5:32, which states in full: "Whosoever kills another — unless for murder or highway robbery *(fasād fī l-arḍ)* — it is as though he has killed the whole of humanity. And, whosoever saves a life (q.v.), it is as though he has saved the whole of humanity."

This verse appears at the end of the story of Cain and Abel (q.v.), and the Qurʾān describes this rule as having been decreed for the Children of Israel (q.v.). None of the commentators (see EXEGESIS OF THE QURʾĀN: CLASSICAL AND MEDIEVAL), however, suggest it is limited to that group but, instead, assume that its significance also extends to Muslims. One report attributed to al-Ḥasan al-Baṣrī (d. 110/728) explains this extension as follows: "Why should the blood of Jews (see JEWS AND JUDAISM) be more precious to God than our blood?" (Ṭabarī, *Tafsīr,* x, 239, ad Q 5:32). According to the Qurʾān, Cain killed Abel because he was jealous when his sacrifice to God was rejected but Abel's was not. When Cain resolved to kill Abel and informed him of that intention, Abel appears in the Qurʾān to accept calmly his brother's decision, announcing that he would rather die than kill his own brother unlawfully (see LAWFUL AND UNLAWFUL; BROTHER AND BROTHERHOOD). Indeed, Abel's apparent willingness to submit to his brother's plan gave pause to interpreters of the Qurʾān who argued that Abel must have defended himself. Accordingly, they agreed that he only meant that he would not kill his brother in self-defense for fear of killing him unlawfully. Alternatively, some argued that self-defense might not have been allowed at that time.

The classical commentators do not give an explicit answer about the relationship of Q 4:93, where the threat of eternal punishment for murder is expressly associated with the murder of a believer (see BELIEF AND UNBELIEF; COMMUNITY AND SOCIETY IN THE QURʾĀN), to the more general language of Q 5:32, except by explaining how it is possible to equate the murder of one person with the murder of all humankind. Indeed, this latter problem occupies most of the attention of the commentators. Al-Ṭabarī (d. 310/923; *Tafsīr,* ad Q 5:32) reports several different opinions on the meaning of this seemingly problematic analogy, beginning with an opinion attributed to Ibn ʿAbbās (d. 69/688). According to this report, *nafs,* "person," as used in Q 5:32, does not mean a generic person, but rather connotes either a prophet (see

PROPHETS AND PROPHETHOOD) or a religious leader (imām, q.v.). Most opinions al-Ṭabarī reports, however, suggest that the analogy is conceptual, viz. the sin of intentional murder should be deemed as monstrous as killing the whole of humanity. Al-Ṭabarī accepts this position mainly on the corroborating evidence of Q 4:93, which conclusively establishes the monstrosity of even one intentional murder. Al-Rāzī (d. 606/1209; *Tafsīr*, ad Q 5:32) further develops this argument, saying that the analogy has three plausible interpretations. The first is that humans should deem the intentional killing of even one of them as heinous as killing all of them; the second is that humans should act just as urgently to prevent the murder of one person as they would to prevent the murder of their species; and the third is that someone who is prepared to kill another intentionally for worldly gain, is prepared to kill again, and thus represents a threat to all humanity.

The question unanswered by al-Rāzī and al-Ṭabarī, however, is why the sin of murdering one person is morally comparable to killing all humanity. Al-Zamakhsharī (d. 538/1144; *Kashshāf*, ad Q 5:32) tries to explain why this is so. He argues that all human beings share certain common attributes, namely dignity *(karāma)* and a personal right to life *(ḥurma)*. An intentional murder does more than kill a single life; it also destroys a being whom God has honored and to whom God has granted this right to bodily integrity, thereby insulting something that God has honored. Thus, the relevant aspect of the analogy comes from the spiritual dignity humans enjoy as God's privileged act of creation (q.v.). Intentional murder, then, is not simply a despicable act for a fleeting gain; it is also a direct assault on God's creative plan (see also COSMOLOGY).

This last notion, while only implied by al-Zamakhsharī, is made explicit by al-Ṭabāṭabāʾī (d. 1982). He argues that humanity, although characterized by plurality, is united by a common essence that each member of the group enjoys. It is this trait of humanity that God wants to preserve throughout time. Intentional murder is then a direct interference with God's plan to preserve the human race (see also WAR; JIHĀD; HOSTAGES; DEATH AND THE DEAD).

Mohammad Fadel

Bibliography
Primary: Rāzī, *Tafsīr;* Ṭabarī, *Tafsīr*, ed. Shākir; Ṭabāṭabāʾī, *Mīzān;* Zamakhsharī, *Kashshāf.*
Secondary: N. ʿAbd al-Ḥāmid, *Jināyat al-qatl al-ʿamd fī l-sharīʿa al-islāmiyya wa-l-qānūn al-waḍʿī*, Baghdad 1975; Y. Ḥasan, *al-Arkān al-māddiyya wa-l-sharʿiyya li-jarīmat al-qatl al-ʿamd wa-ajziyatuhā al-muqarrara fī l-fiqh al-islāmī*, 2 vols., Amman 1982; M. Zayīd, *Dīwān al-qiṣaṣ. Al-qatl al-ʿamd wa-l-khaṭāʾ. Iṣābat al-ʿamd wa-l-khaṭāʾ, diyat al-nafs wa-l-aʿdāʾ, diyat al-janīn, al-qaṣama*, Cairo 1983.

Mūsā see MOSES

Musaylima

Musaylima b. Thumāma b. Kabīr b. Ḥabīb b. al-Ḥārith b. ʿAbd al-Ḥārith, a leader of the Banū Ḥanīfa and rival of the Prophet. Muslim sources derisively nickname him "Musaylima the liar" (*al-kadhdhāb*, see LIE). Musaylima is a diminutive form of Maslama; this can be deduced from a verse of ʿUmāra b. ʿUkayl (Mubarrad, *Kāmil*, iii, 26).

The basis of the rivalry between Muḥammad and Musaylima was the latter's claim to prophethood (see PROPHETS AND PROPHETHOOD). Musaylima made his people believe that he was receiving revelation from God the Merciful (*al-Raḥmān*, see GOD AND HIS ATTRIBUTES) through the angel Gabriel (q.v.). It is essential to stress that

Musaylima never denied the prophethood of Muḥammad; he rather claimed that he was destined to share this mission with him. In all their encounters, Muḥammad categorically rejected the quest of Musaylima to share his mission or be appointed Muḥammad's successor after his death (see CALIPH; POLITICS AND THE QURʾĀN; COMMUNITY AND SOCIETY IN THE QURʾĀN). The letters exchanged between them bear clear evidence of their contrasting attitudes. Musaylima wrote to Muḥammad using the title "Messenger (q.v.) of Allāh" and claimed that God bestowed on him partnership in prophethood *(fa-innī qad ushriktu fī l-amri maʿaka)*. "Half of the earth (q.v.) was given to Quraysh (q.v.) and the other half was allotted to us (i.e. to Banū Ḥanīfa), but Quraysh are people who exceed their bounds." In his response, the Prophet addresses Musaylima as "the liar," asserts that the earth (in its entirety) belongs to God who gives it "as heritage to whomever he pleases of his servants" (Bayhaqī, *Maḥāsin,* i, 49; see GEOGRAPHY; COSMOLOGY).

Early traditions (see ḤADĪTH AND THE QURʾĀN) may help establish the period of Musaylima's activity and his connections with Mecca (q.v.). According to reliable sources, he married Kayyisa bint al-Ḥārith of the Meccan aristocratic clan of ʿAbd Shams (see TRIBES AND CLANS). Musaylima was her second husband. The Prophet met Musaylima in Medina (q.v.) several times (it is reported that when Musaylima arrived in Medina for the first time accompanied by a unit of Banū Ḥanīfa warriors, he stayed in Kayyisa's grove). In reference to the impertinent demands of Musaylima, Muḥammad refused to give him "even a splinter of a palm branch" which he held in his hand. At a later meeting with a delegation of Banū Ḥanīfa, the members of the delegation decided to embrace Islam, but changed their minds after returning to Yamāma, and aligned themselves with Musaylima instead. Musaylima was held in high esteem: his companions called him "the merciful one of Yamāma" *(raḥmān al-Yamāma)*. Also, as befitted the usual manner in which holy persons, soothsayers (q.v.) and prophets appeared, he was veiled and disguised. There are many common features and methods in the prophetic careers of Musaylima and Muḥammad. Like Muḥammad, Musaylima claimed to be the recipient of divine revelation (see REVELATION AND INSPIRATION). Further, he claimed to heal the sick (see ILLNESS AND HEALTH) and work miracles (see MIRACLE). Naturally enough, Muslim tradition describes his claims to such powers as totally baseless.

In Yamāma, Musaylima succeeded in gaining the support of many tribal groups who came under his control after the death of Hawdha, the former chief of the area in the service of Persia. In the last years before the Prophet's death, he attempted to establish a social order based on an alliance (see CONTRACTS AND ALLIANCES) between the people of Yamāma and tribal groups which moved to Yamāma and settled there. Musaylima erected a safe area *(ḥaram)* in which certain places inhabited by his allies *(qurā al-aḥālif)* were included. According to Muslim sources, the *ḥaram* was managed in a corrupt way and the Banū Usayyid, who served as its guardians mistreated other groups. When these groups complained, Musaylima did not redress the injustice. Instead, he read to them "the answer he got from heaven," meaning a verse from his Qurʾān: "(I swear) by the darkness of the night and by the black wolf, the Usayyid did not violate [the sanctity] of the *ḥaram*" (see SANCTITY AND THE SACRED; JUSTICE AND INJUSTICE). When the Usayyid continued their transgressions, another verse was released: "[I swear] by the dark night and by the softly treading lion, the Usayyid cut neither fresh nor dry."

The death of the prophet Muḥammad raised the hopes of the community of Musaylima. In one of the speeches said to have been delivered in that period and which was directed to the Banū Ḥanīfa, Musaylima stressed the qualities of his people and his land in comparison with Quraysh and Mecca: "What made Quraysh more deserving of prophethood than yourselves? They are not greater in number than you; your land is wider than their land. Gabriel (Jibrīl) descends from heaven like he used to descend to Muḥammad." Musaylima claimed that the revelation transmitted to Muḥammad had ceased with his death and henceforth it would be transmitted to him alone. The feeling that he was now the sole prophet is expressed in a verse attributed to Musaylima:

O you, woman, take the tambourine and play,
and disseminate the virtues of this prophet!
Passed away the prophet of Banū Hāshim,
and rose up the prophet of Banū Yaʿrub
(Ibn Kathīr, *Bidāya,* vi, 341).

Musaylima's adherents grew in number and prestige. The situation in Yamāma inspired a feeling of security and peace (q.v.). This feeling was, however, shaken by the unexpected arrival of a former soothsayer (see DIVINATION; FORETELLING), who claimed that she had been granted revelations from heaven. Her name was Sajāḥ bt. al-Ḥārith. She was a Christian of the tribe of Tamīm but lived among the Christian Arabs of Taghlib (see CHRISTIANS AND CHRISTIANITY; ARABS). According to some sources, the forces led by Sajāḥ intended to attack the troops of Abū Bakr under the command of Khālid b. al-Walīd who set out to crush the apostasy (q.v.; *ridda*) of the tribes after the Prophet's death. In her forces were warriors from her people and others who joined them. After some skirmishes, she decided to fight Musaylima and conquer Yamāma. Musaylima invited her to meet him in order to negotiate a peaceful solution. He recognized Sajāḥ as his partner in prophethood and declared that the land allotted by God to Quraysh would be transferred to Sajāḥ and her people. The other half would belong to Musaylima. Moreover, Musaylima granted Sajāḥ the crops Yamāma had produced that year and promised her the crops of the next year. Sajāḥ returned to the Jazīra after a few days. (Some reports maintain that Musaylima married Sajāḥ, but differ as to whether she remained with him until his death, or if he cast her off soon after their marriage; cf. Vacca, Sadjāḥ.)

Abū Bakr became aware of the rising authority of Musaylima and decided to send Khālid b. al-Walīd at the head of the Muslim army to fight Musaylima and his forces. He wrote a letter to Khālid b. al-Walīd, stressing the power of the Banū Ḥanīfa and their courage. The bravery of Banū Ḥanīfa is said to have been mentioned in Q 48:16. On his way to fight Musaylima, Khālid b. al-Walīd informed his army of Abū Bakr's letter concerning Banū Ḥanīfa. In the clashes with the Banū Ḥanīfa, a division of the army that came from those Medinans who had assisted Muḥammad in his emigration (q.v.) from Mecca (the Anṣār, see EMIGRANTS AND HELPERS) attacked Yamāma and fought bravely together with the Meccans who had fled with Muḥammad (the Muhājirūn). They were summoned to help out in dangerous situations in the bloody battle of ʿAqrabāʾ. At the outset, the Banū Ḥanīfa succeeded in repulsing the bedouin (q.v.) attacks. The solution of Khālid was to put the bedouin fighters of the army behind the lines of the well motivated and steadfast warriors of the Emigrants (Muhājirūn) and Helpers (Anṣār). Cases of exemplary bravery on the part of these groups are recorded in the sources. Eventually, Waḥshī killed Musaylima with his javelin in a place dubbed in the Muslim sources as "the Garden of Death." According to some far-fetched traditions, Musaylima was 140 or 150 years old when he died in 11/632.

The intense loyalty of Musaylima's followers can be gauged from the various stories that have been passed down. A woman who heard about his death exclaimed, "Alas, prince of the believers!" *(wā amīr al-mu'minīnāh)*. A wounded warrior of the Banū Ḥanīfa, in his agony, asked a Muslim warrior to kill him in order to put him out of his misery. Upon hearing of Musaylima's death, he remarked: "A prophet whom his people caused to perish" *(nabiyyun ḍayya'ahu qawmuhu)*. The Muslim warrior, enraged by these words, gave him the *coup de grâce*.

The belief in the prophethood of Musaylima survived among his believers in the first decades of Islam. His adherents used to gather in the mosque of the Banū Ḥanīfa in Kūfa and the call *lā ilāha illā llāh wa-Musaylima rasūlu llāh* was heard from the minaret. 'Abdallāh b. Mas'ūd ordered the detention of the followers of Musaylima. Some repented and were released. Those who clung to their faith were executed.

M.J. Kister

Bibliography
Primary: al-Balādhurī, Aḥmad b. Yaḥyā b. Jābir, *Futūḥ al-buldān*, ed. 'A. Anīs al-Ṭabbā' and 'U. Anīs al-Tabbā', Beirut 1958, 119-20; al-Bayhaqī, Abū Bakr Aḥmad b. al-Ḥusayn, *Dalā'il al-nubuwwa*, ed. 'A. al-Qal'ajī, 7 vols., Beirut 1985, iv, 79; v, 330; al-Bayhaqī, Ibrāhīm b. Muḥammad, *al-Maḥāsin wa-l-masāwi'*, ed. M. Abū l-Faḍl Ibrāhīm, 2 vols., Cairo 1961, i, 49; al-Diyārbakrī, Ḥusayn b. Muḥammad, *Ta'rīkh al-khamīs*, 2 vols. in 1, Cairo 1283, repr. Beirut, ii, 157; Ibn 'Abd al-Barr al-Namarī, *al-Durar fī ikhtiṣār al-maghāzī wa-l-siyar*, ed. Sh. Ḍayf, Cairo 1966, 270; Ibn Ḥubaysh, 'Abd al-Raḥmān b. Muḥammad, *al-Ghazawāt*, ed. S. Zakkār, Beirut 1992; Ibn Sa'd, *Ṭabaqāt*, Beirut 1957, v, 550; al-Kalā'ī, Abū l-Rabī' Sulaymān b. Mūsā, *al-Iktifā' fī maghāzī rasūl Allāh wa-l-thalāta al-khulafā'*, ed. M. 'Abd al-Wāḥid, 2 vols., Cairo 1970, ii, 435; al-Kalbī, Hishām b. Muḥammad b. al-Sā'ib, *Jamharat al-nasab*, ed. N. Ḥasan, Beirut 1986, 543; al-Maqrīzī, Taqī l-Dīn Abū l-'Abbās Aḥmad b. 'Alī, *Imtā' al-asmā'*, ed. M.M. Shākir, Cairo 1941, 508-9; ed. M.A. al-Nāmisī, 15 vols., Beirut 1999, ii, 100-1; Muqātil, *Tafsīr*, ii, 555; al-Nuwayrī, Aḥmad b. 'Abd al-Wahhāb, *Nihāyat al-arab fī funūn al-adab*, 31 vols., Cairo 1964-92, xix (1975; ed. M. Ibrāhīm), 85-7; Suhaylī, *al-Rawḍ al-unuf*, ed. 'A. al-Wakīl, 7 vols., Cairo 1969, iv, 38-9; Ṭabarī, *Ta'rīkh*, ed. Cairo, iii, 276-300; al-Wāqidī, *Kitāb al-Ridda*, ed. M. Ḥamīdullah, Paris 1989, index.
Secondary: V.V. Barthold, Musaylima, in id., *Sočineniya*, 10 vols., Moscow 1963-73, vi, 549-74; D. Eickelmann, Musaylima. An approach to the social anthropology of seventh century Arabia, in *JESHO* 10 (1967), 17-52; V. Vacca, Sadjāḥ, in *EI*², viii, 738-9; W.M. Watt, Musaylima, in *EI*², vii, 664-5.

Muṣḥaf

A non-qur'ānic term (pl. *maṣāḥif*) denoting the written corpus of the Qur'ān; in both classical and modern contexts this term creates a theological distinction between the individual's copy of the Qur'ān and the hypostatized notion of God's speech (q.v.; see also HEAVENLY BOOK; PRESERVED TABLET; WORD OF GOD; BOOK). The term stems from the same root as the word *ṣuḥuf*, "pages, books," which the Qur'ān sometimes uses for documents of superhuman origin (for lexicographical details see Burton, Muṣḥaf, 668-9; see also INSTRUMENTS; WRITING AND WRITING MATERIALS). Several issues are connected with the written corpus of the Qur'ān: its origin; the history and art of writing down the Qur'ān (see COLLECTION OF THE QUR'ĀN; CODICES OF THE QUR'ĀN; CALLIGRAPHY; ARABIC SCRIPT; ART AND ARCHITECTURE AND THE

QUR'ĀN; ORNAMENTATION AND ILLUMINATION); its orthography (q.v.) and reading signs; and the etiquette of using the *muṣḥaf* (see MANUSCRIPTS OF THE QUR'ĀN; EVERYDAY LIFE, QUR'ĀN IN; RITUAL AND THE QUR'ĀN). The following will treat only the first issue; for the other aspects see the respective entries (see also TEXTUAL HISTORY OF THE QUR'ĀN).

The question of how the written corpus of the Qur'ān came into being is disputed among Muslim and Western scholars (see POST-ENLIGHTENMENT ACADEMIC STUDY OF THE QUR'ĀN). The dispute results from a difference in opinion concerning the reliability of the sources that can be used to answer the question (see CONTEMPORARY CRITICAL PRACTICES AND THE QUR'ĀN). No text or partial text of the Qur'ān can be reliably dated to the lifetime of Muḥammad: to date, there is no textual evidence that the Prophet himself or scribes whom he may have used penned any of the oldest surviving qur'ānic manuscripts (see ILLITERACY). Early manuscripts of the Qur'ān are rare and their dating is controversial (see CHRONOLOGY AND THE QUR'ĀN). The text itself does not contain clear indications as to its compiler. The view that the written corpus of the Qur'ān is a reliable collection of revelations received by Muḥammad is, therefore, essentially based on the Islamic tradition (see INIMITABILITY; REVELATION AND INSPIRATION; EXEGESIS OF THE QUR'ĀN: CLASSICAL AND MEDIEVAL). Many Western scholars doubt the reliability of this tradition, at least as far as the first Islamic century is concerned (see INFORMANTS). Nevertheless, most of them accept the gist of the reports on the collection and edition of the Qur'ān as historically true.

According to current Muslim opinion, the written corpus of the Qur'ān as it exists now — and as it is also attested in manuscripts dating at least from the third/ninth century, possibly even from earlier times — came into being as follows: When the Prophet died, there was no complete and definitive collection of the revelations that had been authorized by him. More or less extensive pieces of qur'ānic revelation had been committed to memory by his followers (see ORALITY; MEMORY); and several individuals had written some of the revelation down on various materials. Shortly after his death, the first collection of these written and memorized records of the revelation was made by order of the first caliph (q.v.), Abū Bakr (r. 11-13/632-4) and it was written on leaves *(ṣuḥuf)*. The reason given for this collection and compilation was the death of several Companions (see COMPANIONS OF THE PROPHET). These men, who were famous for their knowledge of the Qur'ān, had died during the wars of apostasy (q.v.; *ridda*) and people were afraid that with further deaths parts of the Qur'ān might become lost. Abū Bakr gave Zayd b. Thābit, a former scribe of the Prophet, the task of collecting all of the Qur'ān that was available. When Abū Bakr died, the leaves on which Zayd had written the Qur'ān passed to the caliph's successor, 'Umar (r. 13-23/634-44); and, after his death, to his daughter, Ḥafṣa (q.v.), who was also one of the widows of Muḥammad (see WIVES OF THE PROPHET). Some twenty years after Abū Bakr's collection, during the caliphate of 'Uthmān (r. 23-35/644-56), dissension between followers of other collections of the Qur'ān induced the caliph to issue an official collection of the Qur'ān, to deposit a copy in the most important administrative centers of the empire and to suppress other existing collections. This canonical version was again edited by the Medinan Zayd b. Thābit, helped by three men from Quraysh (q.v.), on the basis of the collection he had already made at Abū Bakr's request, and which Ḥafṣa put at the disposal of the committee. This caliphal edition of the Qurʾān, *al-muṣḥaf al-ʿuthmānī*, quickly achieved universal acceptance, becoming the *textus receptus* among Muslims. Such, in summary, is the traditionally accepted Muslim view of the origin of the written corpus of the Qurʾān. It is based on two reports that are transmitted in a large number of sources. Alternative accounts, which are also found in Islamic sources (see Schwally, Sammlung, 15-8, 50-4; Burton, *Collection*, 120-8; 138-59), found no permanent recognition.

Some Western scholars have challenged the Muslim view about the history of the *muṣḥaf*. F. Schwally rejected the historicity of the first collection, that made at the behest of Abū Bakr. Others considered the Islamic narrative on this double collection completely fictitious and provide various suggestions for the date of origin of the written corpus: the time of the caliph ʿAbd al-Malik (r. 65-86/685-705, Casanova, *Muḥammad;* Mingana, Transmission of the Ḳurʾān; Crone and Cook, *Hagarism*), or the third/ninth century (J. Wansbrough, *QS*), or the time of the Prophet himself (Burton, *Collection*). According to most of these scholars, the traditional reports concerning the collection and edition of the Qurʾān were fabricated during the third/ninth century. A recent study (Motzki, Collection) shows, however, that the two traditions upon which the current Muslim understanding of the history of the *muṣḥaf* is based have Ibn Shihāb al-Zuhrī (d. 124/742) as an undeniable common link (see ḤADĪTH AND THE QURʾĀN), and both were already in circulation by the first quarter of the second/eighth century. The content of these traditions probably goes back to the last decades of the first/seventh century. Accordingly, an official written corpus must have already existed in the second half of the first/seventh century. This suggests that the time of ʿUthmān may indeed be a reasonable date of origin for the *textus receptus* of the Qurʾān, a conclusion that is corroborated by several reports about ʿUthmān, which seem to be independent of each other. Yet, what the early dating of these traditions means for the reliability of the details they report still needs to be investigated.

The above-mentioned traditions suggest that before the official edition of the Qurʾān was promulgated, several written compilations of codices of the Qurʾān existed, which were made or owned by different Companions. Although they became obsolete after the emergence of the official version and allegedly were suppressed, there are reports of scholars who, as late as the fourth/tenth century, claim to have seen manuscripts based on Companion codices (Ibn al-Nadīm, *Fihrist*, 29). Variants of these *maṣāḥif* from the *textus receptus* were collected and discussed as early as the beginning of the second/eighth century (see Motzki, *Origins*, 110-11), a practice continued in subsequent centuries (see READINGS OF THE QURʾĀN). The reliability of the alleged variants is difficult to ascertain. According to Burton (*Collection*, 211) they are fictitious and contribute nothing to the understanding of the history of the written corpus. In view of the early date of some reports concerning the Companion codices, however, the issue requires further study.

According to Islamic tradition and as evidenced in the earliest extant manuscripts of the Qurʾān, the first copies of the *muṣḥaf* were devoid of diacritical points, vowel signs, markers to indicate the end of the verses and of the sūras (q.v.), and the names of the sūras (see RECITATION OF THE QURʾĀN; FORM AND STRUCTURE OF THE QURʾĀN; ARABIC LANGUAGE; ARABIC SCRIPT). Although these devices to make the reading of a text unambiguous (see AMBIGUOUS; DIFFICULT PASSAGES) and to facilitate its use developed only in the course of the first Islamic centuries (see

GRAMMAR AND THE QURʾĀN), the question of the permissibility of adding diacritical points *(naqaṭa)* and vowels *(shakala)* to the *muṣḥaf* was already being discussed by scholars during the first half of the second/eighth century (see Ibn Wahb, *Jāmiʿ*, 26).

Harald Motzki

Bibliography
Primary: Abū ʿUbayd, *Faḍāʾil*, 152-6; Bukhārī, *Ṣaḥīḥ*, 61:3; 66:2, 3; 65:9, 20; 93:37; Ibn Abī Dāwūd, *Kitāb al-Maṣāḥif*, ed. A. Jeffery, Leiden 1937; Ibn Ḥajar, *Fatḥ al-bārī bi-sharḥ Ṣaḥīḥ al-Bukhārī*, eds. ʿA. b. ʿA. Ibn Bāz and M.F. ʿAbd al-Bāqī, 16 vols., Beirut 1989; Ibn al-Nadīm, *Fihrist;* Ibn Wahb, *al-Jāmiʿ. Die Koranwissenschaften*, ed. M. Muranyi, Wiesbaden 1992; Suyūṭī, *Itqān*, i, 126-41; 154-60 (for further sources see Motzki, Collection); ʿUmar b. Shabba, *Taʾrīkh al-Madīna al-munawwara*, ed. F.M. Shaltūt, 4 vols., Jeddah n.d., 991-1017.
Secondary: Burton, *Collection;* id., Muṣḥaf, in *EI²*, vii, 668-9; P. Casanova, *Muḥammad et la fin du monde*, Paris 1911; P. Crone and M. Cook, *Hagarism. The making of the Islamic world*, Cambridge 1977, esp. 3-9; Gh.Q. Ḥamad, *Rasm al-muṣḥaf*, Baghdad 1982; A. Jones, The Qurʾān — II, in Beeston, *CHAL*, i, 235-9; A. Mingana, The transmission of the Ḳurān, in *Journal of the Manchester Egyptian and Oriental Society* 5 (1915-6), 25-47; H. Motzki, *The origins of Islamic jurisprudence. Meccan fiqh before the classical schools*, Leiden 2002; id., The collection of the Qurʾān. A reconsideration of western views in light of recent methodological developments, in *Der Islam* 78 (2001), 1-34; F. Schwally, Die Sammlung des Qorāns, in Nöldeke, *GQ*, ii, 1-121; Wansbrough, *QS;* A.T. Welch, al-Ḳurʾān, in *EI²*, v, 404-9.

Mushrikūn
see BELIEF AND UNBELIEF; POLYTHEISM AND ATHEISM

Music
see RECITATION OF THE QURʾĀN; RECITERS OF THE QURʾĀN

Muslim
see ISLAM

Mutawātir
see TEXTUAL CRITICISM OF THE QURʾĀN

Muʿtazila

A religious movement in early Islam, the Muʿtazila became the dominant theological school in the third/ninth and fourth/tenth century (see THEOLOGY AND THE QURʾĀN). The movement was allegedly founded by Wāṣil b. ʿAṭāʾ (d. 131/728-9) who was towards the end of his life joined by ʿAmr b. ʿUbayd (d. 143/760 or 144/761), a prominent disciple of al-Ḥasan al-Baṣrī (d. 110/728). Most issues related to the incubation phase of the movement as well as the original meaning of the term Muʿtazila — which has the sense of "those who dissociate themselves, who keep themselves apart" — remain enigmatic. Later sources offer a number of different explanations, sometimes blatantly tendentious. It was apparently Abū l-Hudhayl (d. ca. 227/841) who first defined the five principles of the Muʿtazila — the principle of God's unity (*tawḥīd*, see GOD AND HIS ATTRIBUTES), of God's justice (*ʿadl*, see JUSTICE AND INJUSTICE), of the promise and the threat (*al-waʿd wa-l-waʿīd*, see REWARD AND PUNISHMENT), of the intermediate state of the Muslim sinner (*al-manzila bayn al-manzilatayn*, see SIN, MAJOR AND MINOR) and the principle of enjoining what is good and forbidding what is evil (*al-amr bi-l-maʿrūf wa-l-nahy ʿan al-munkar*, see GOOD AND EVIL; VIRTUES AND VICES, COMMANDING AND FORBIDDING) — as indispensable to Muʿtazilī identity. Later authors differentiate between two periods of Muʿtazilism following the incubation phase. In the early phase (ca. 200-35/815-50), when Muʿtazilism was at the height of its political influence and public prestige, the representatives of the movement displayed great diversity on the doctrinal level. In the second, scholastic phase Muʿtazilī thought was systematized. Coherent theological frameworks were formulated by Abū l-Qāsim al-Kaʿbī al-Balkhī (d. 319/913), who was identified with Baghdād, and by Abū ʿAlī al-Jubbāʾī (d. 303/915), who was identified with Baṣra; the latter was followed by his son Abū Hāshim (d. 321/933), the founder of the so-called Bahshamiyya or Bahāshima. The last innovative school within Muʿtazilism originated with Abū l-Ḥusayn al-Baṣrī (d. 436/1044), who developed independent theological views that set him apart from the school of Abū Hāshim. Despite much criticism by the Bahshamiyya and later heresiographers that he introduced philosophy (see PHILOSOPHY AND THE QURʾĀN) under the cover of theology, Abū l-Ḥusayn's views were successful to the extent that his school established itself side by side with the Bahshamiyya. In some areas the Muʿtazila persisted until the Mongol invasion at the beginning of the seventh/thirteenth century. Muʿtazilism was also adopted by the Zaydiyya and the Twelver Shīʿa (see SHĪʿISM AND THE QURʾĀN) and determined their respective theological outlooks for centuries to come.

The nature of the Qurʾān

Because of their uncompromising interpretation of God's unity *(tawḥīd)* as expressed in Q 27:26, Q 112, etc., the Muʿtazilīs were strictly opposed to the admission of anything co-eternal with God (see ETERNITY). This applied first and foremost to God's essential attributes, which must be identical with him and not different eternal attributes or entitative determinants. This also applied in their view to the Qurʾān — the speech of God (*kalām Allāh,* see WORD OF GOD; SPEECH) — that cannot possibly be co-eternal with God but was necessarily created in time (see CREATEDNESS OF THE QURʾĀN). Thus they accused those denying that the Qurʾān had been created of asserting its eternity and of destroying God's unity by claiming that something was co-eternal with him. Among the standard Muʿtazilī arguments was Q 2:106, which was also the qurʾānic basis for the doctrine of abrogation (q.v.). The centrality of this doctrine for the Muʿtazilīs can be seen from the numerous titles of works on *khalq al-Qurʾān* listed by Ibn al-Nadīm (fl. fourth/tenth cent.) in the section of his *Fihrist* devoted to the Muʿtazila (Ibn al-Nadīm-Dodge, i, 388-9, 391, 393, 395, 396-7, 401, 412, 414-6, 418, 425, 429-30). It was basically this insistence of the Muʿtazilīs — on the createdness of the Qurʾān, in the sense of its temporality, and their accusation that the opponents, in fact, held to the eternity of the Qurʾān — which provoked the traditionists to combine their denial of the createdness of the Qurʾān with the affirmation of its eternity or pre-existence. This line of argumentation was first formulated by Aḥmad b. Ḥanbal (d. 241/855). In the pre-*miḥna* period (see INQUISITION), by contrast, the conflict over the nature of the Qurʾān was not concerned with the question of its temporality versus its eternity. Rather, the discussion was whether God speaks in a literal sense, i.e. whether the Qurʾān is the speech of God, as the upholders of an anthropomorphic concept of God held (see ANTHROPOMORPHISM), or whether God does not speak in a literal sense but rather creates the sound of speech which can be heard, as was the view attributed to Jahm b. Ṣafwān (d. 128/745). Both positions implied the temporality of the Qurʾān. Another discussion on the nature of the Qurʾān in the pre-*miḥna* phase associated with Abū Ḥanīfa (d. 150/767) and Imām Jaʿfar al-Ṣādiq (d. 148/765) revolved around the issue of whether the Qurʾān, in accordance with the commonly accepted dogma that everything besides God is created, is also created (see CREATION). Whereas Imām al-Ṣādiq reportedly rejected this conclusion, arguing that the

Qurʾān is neither creator nor created, but rather the speech of God, Abū Ḥanīfa apparently accepted the argument and held that the Qurʾān indeed is created. Again, those who denied the createdness of the Qurʾān in this second discussion refrained from combining their view with the notion of the uncreatedness or even eternity of the Qurʾān. It was therefore only after the *miḥna* and as an immediate result of the Muʿtazilī argumentation on this issue that the conflict turned on the question of the createdness of the Qurʾān, in the sense of its temporality, versus its uncreatedness in the sense of its eternity. A further difference to the pre-*miḥna* period was that, unlike the Jahmiyya, the Muʿtazilīs did not deny that God really speaks, and they affirmed that the Qurʾān is indeed the speech of God. The difference between human and divine speech is that God, because of his omnipotence (see POWER AND IMPOTENCE), does not need instruments when he produces speech. It was only Muʿammar (d. 215/830) among the Muʿtazilīs who deviated from this view. According to him, God does not actually speak nor does he have actual speech. He also maintained that the Qurʾān is brought forth *(muḥdath)* — not truly created — by the substratum in which it inheres. For the Qurʾān is an accident and God does not create accidents.

The majority of the Muʿtazilīs, like almost all theological schools, considered the Qurʾān as the principal miracle confirming Muḥammad's prophethood (see PROPHETS AND PROPHETHOOD; MIRACLE). The proof of its miraculous character was human inability to match the Qurʾān despite the challenge to do so (e.g. Q 10:38; 11:13; 52:33-4; also Q 2:23-4; 17:88; see INIMITABILITY). They differed among themselves, however, on the question of why those who were challenged were unable to match it. While some Muʿtazilīs maintained that the miraculous inimitability of the Qurʾān arises from its intrinsic quality, others denied this and argued that it is due to God's preventing humankind from matching it. The latter position was known as the doctrine of prevention *(ṣarfa)*. The view that God deprived the people of the power to match the Qurʾān is usually ascribed to Abū Isḥāq al-Naẓẓām (d. around 221/836), who was apparently the first to consider the Qurʾān a miracle. Another early representative of the *ṣarfa* doctrine was al-Jāḥiẓ (d. 255/869), who also composed a book on the choice and arrangement of words in the Qurʾān *(Kitāb fī l-iḥtijāj li-naẓm al-Qurʾān)*, as did Ibn al-Ikhshīd (d. 326/937; *Kitāb Naẓm al-Qurʾān*, see FORM AND STRUCTURE OF THE QURʾĀN; LITERARY STRUCTURES OF THE QURʾĀN; LANGUAGE AND STYLE OF THE QURʾĀN). Al-Jāḥiẓ' contemporary ʿAbbād b. Sulaymān (d. ca. 250/864) and the latter's teacher Hishām al-Fuwaṭī (d. ca. 218/832) are reported to have still denied that the Qurʾān is to be considered as a miracle proving Muḥammad's prophetic mission, although both subscribed to the doctrine of *ṣarfa* (van Ess, *TG*, iv, 7, 41, 609). The *ṣarfa*-doctrine was held by most of the representatives of the school of Baghdād. The majority of the later Baṣran Muʿtazilīs rejected the doctrine of prevention, arguing that the inimitability of the Qurʾān was based on the rhetorical uniqueness of the book (q.v.) and the excellence of its style (see RHETORIC OF THE QURʾĀN). ʿAbd al-Jabbār (d. 415/1025), for example, who devotes an entire volume of his *Mughnī* to the issue of *iʿjāz*, explains the miraculous inimitability of the Qurʾān with its intrinsic stylistic excellence and its eloquence *(faṣāḥa)* and argues against the doctrine of prevention. The earliest Muʿtazilī treatises on the issue of the miraculous inimitability of the Qurʾān were composed as early as the second half of the second/eighth century by two students of al-

Jubbāʾī: Muḥammad ʿUmar al-Bāhilī (d. 300/913) wrote a treatise entitled *Kitāb Iʿjāz al-Qurʾān;* and Muḥammad b. Zayd al-Wāsiṭī (d. 306/918) wrote *Kitāb Iʿjāz al-Qurʾān fī naẓmihi wa-taʾlīfihi.* Neither of these is preserved. The earliest extant independent Muʿtazilī treatise on this issue carrying the word *iʿjāz* in its title was written by ʿAlī b. ʿĪsā al-Rummānī (d. 384/994; *al-Nukat fī iʿjāz al-Qurʾān,* in Rummānī et al., *Rasāʾil*).

Qurʾānic exegesis

Among the extant Muʿtazilī commentaries on the Qurʾān, al-Zamakhsharī's (d. 538/1144) *al-Kashshāf ʿan ḥaqāʾiq al-tanzīl* is the most renowned. Its popularity was grounded in its mostly philological character; by contrast, it rarely provides theological argumentation, although al-Zamakhsharī was familiar with the last two school traditions within Muʿtazilism, the followers of Abū Hāshim al-Jubbāʾī and those of Abū l-Ḥusayn al-Baṣrī. Most of the earlier Muʿtazilī commentaries, which were apparently much more representative of the Muʿtazilī tendency, are lost. In some cases, only titles of works are preserved; for other commentaries, substantial portions are preserved in the writings of later authors. According to Ibn al-Nadīm, Ḍirār b. ʿAmr (d. 180/796?) composed two exegetical works, a commentary *(tafsīr)* and an interpretation *(taʾwīl)* of the Qurʾān (Ibn al-Nadīm-Dodge, i, 416-7). It is not clear whether these two titles refer to two different works or to one and the same, nor whether the(se) work(s) constituted complete Qurʾān commentaries or only dealt with selected passages. Among the Muʿtazilīs of the early third/ninth century, Ibn al-Nadīm reports that Bishr b. al-Muʿtamir (d. 210/825-6) composed a *Kitāb Taʾwīl mutashābih al-Qurʾān,* and Jaʿfar b. Ḥarb (d. 236/850) authored a *Kitāb Mutashābih al-Qurʾān,* both of which are lost (Ibn al-Nadīm-Dodge, i, 80, 391, 411). The latter-mentioned work was consulted by the Muʿtazilī Ibn al-Khallāl when he composed his *Radd ʿalā l-jabriyya al-qadariyya fī mā taʿallaqū bihi min mutashābih al-Qurʾān al-karīm* during the fourth/tenth century (van Ess, *TG,* vi, 288, no. 3). Ibn al-Nadīm further reports that Abū l-Hudhayl composed a book on *Mutashābih al-Qurʾān* (Ibn al-Nadīm-Dodge, i, 80; cf. also van Ess, *TG,* iii, 265 f.; v, 367-9, no. 55), traces of which are apparently preserved in ʿAbd al-Jabbār's *Mutashābih al-Qurʾān,* in al-Faḍl b. al-Ḥasan al-Ṭabarsī's (d. 548/1153) *Majmaʿ al-bayān fī tafsīr al-Qurʾān* and Muḥammad b. al-Ḥusayn al-Sharīf al-Raḍī's (d. 406/1015) *Ḥaqāʾiq al-taʾwīl.* Abū l-Hudhayl apparently defined in this work the criteria that need to be applied in Qurʾān exegesis. On the issue of how knowledge can be gained from the Qurʾān, he addressed the question whether passages of the Qurʾān that are formulated in a general manner may be restricted to a particular group of people. The issue was raised by the Murjiʾīs, who denied that qurʾānic verses that speak about the fate of the unbelievers (see BELIEF AND UNBELIEF) and the eternal punishment in hell (see HELL AND HELLFIRE) in a general manner are to be applied to Muslims also. As a Muʿtazilī, Abū l-Hudhayl believed in eternal punishment for grave sinners and therefore argued that general qurʾānic statements are to be understood in a general manner as long as there is no indication to the contrary. Abū ʿAlī al-Jubbāʾī later on adopted and further elaborated Abū l-Hudhayl's view, whereas his son Abū Hāshim took the opposite view. During the second quarter of the third/ninth century, Qāsim b. Khalīl al-Dimashqī (al-Dimishqī), who, according to al-Kaʿbī, was a student of Abū l-Hudhayl, wrote a commentary of which no traces are preserved (Ibn al-Nadīm-Dodge, i, 393;

van Ess, *TG*, iv, 236-7). Extensive systematic commentaries on the Qurʾān were composed by Abū Bakr al-Aṣamm (d. 201/816), Abū ʿAlī al-Jubbāʾī (d. 303/915), Abū l-Qāsim al-Kaʿbī al-Balkhī (d. 319/931) and by Abū Muslim Muḥammad b. Baḥr al-Iṣfahānī (d. 322/934; cf. Ibn al-Nadīm-Dodge, i, 76), whose *Jāmiʿ al-taʾwīl li-muḥkam al-tanzīl (*or *Jāmiʿ ʿilm al-Qurʾān)* is reported to have consisted of 14 or 20 volumes, or even more (Sezgin, *GAS*, i, 42-3; Kohlberg, *Medieval Muslim*, 203-4, no. 231). Although, again, none of these *tafsīr* works is preserved, ample quotations from them survive in the extant works of later authors, such as *al-Tafsīr al-kabīr* of Fakhr al-Dīn al-Rāzī (d. 606/1210), the Imāmī exegetical works of Abū Jaʿfar al-Ṭūsī (d. 459/1067; *al-Tibyān fī tafsīr al-Qurʾān*) and of al-Ṭabrisī *(Majmaʿ al-bayān)* and, most importantly, al-Ḥākim al-Jushamī's (d. 494/1101) *al-Tahdhīb*. Al-Aṣamm apparently dealt in his commentary on the Qurʾān with historical and philological issues as well as with doctrinal matters (van Ess, *TG*, ii, 403-7; v, 198-202 [texts nos. 15-21]). The work was consulted by Abū ʿAlī al-Jubbāʾī and fragments of it are preserved in Abū Manṣūr al-Māturīdī's (d. 333/944) *Taʾwīlāt ahl al-sunna*, in Aḥmad b. Muḥammad al-Thaʿlabī's (d. 427/1035-6) *al-Kashf wa-l-bayān fī tafsīr al-Qurʾān* and particularly in *al-Tahdhīb fī l-tafsīr* of al-Ḥākim al-Jushamī (d. 484/1091); the latter usually gives al-Aṣamm's view together with those of Abū ʿAlī al-Jubbāʾī and Abū Muslim al-Iṣfahānī. Al-Aṣamm's commentary is also often quoted by Abū l-Futūḥ al-Rāzī (first half sixth/twelfth century), by his contemporary al-Ṭabarsī and later on by Fakhr al-Dīn al-Rāzī, although it may be assumed that those later authors received al-Aṣamm's commentary through intermediary sources. No mention of al-Aṣamm's *Tafsīr* is to be found, by contrast, in al-Ṭabarī's (d. 310/923) *Jāmiʿ al-bayān ʿan taʾwīl āy al-Qurʾān*, although the possibility that the latter was familiar with the work cannot be excluded, nor is there any mention of his commentary in ʿAbd al-Jabbār's *Kitāb Mutashābih al-Qurʾān* or in Abū Jaʿfar al-Ṭūsī's *al-Tibyān*. To judge from the preserved fragments, al-Aṣamm endeavored to develop a comprehensive qurʾānic theology, dealt with the issue of abrogation, and formulated an original view on the distinction of clear *(muḥkamāt)* and ambiguous (q.v.) verses *(mutashābihāt)*, both of which can be grasped rationally; the only difference is that in the latter case deeper reflection is called for. Quotations from the multi-volume commentary of al-Kaʿbī are preserved in the *Amālī* of al-Sharīf al-Murtaḍā (d. 436/1044) and possibly in the *Kitāb al-Tawḥīd* of al-Māturīdī (d. 333/944). In particular, later commentaries preserve ample quotations and paraphrases of Abū ʿAlī al-Jubbāʾī's exegesis; this is especially true of *al-Tibyān* of Abū Jaʿfar al-Ṭūsī and *Majmaʿ al-bayān* of Abū ʿAlī al-Ṭabrisī among the Imāmīs, of *al-Tafsīr al-kabīr* of Fakhr al-Dīn al-Rāzī and, most significantly, of *al-Tahdhīb fī l-tafsīr* of the Muʿtazilī, later Zaydī, scholar al-Ḥākim al-Jushamī, which still awaits critical editing. On the basis of this material, Daniel Gimaret *(Jubbāʾī)* and Rosalind W. Gwynne *(The "Tafsir")* have tried to reconstruct Abū ʿAlī's commentary. Against the exegeses of Abū ʿAlī al-Jubbāʾī and Abū l-Qāsim al-Kaʿbī, Abū l-Ḥasan al-Ashʿarī (d. 324/935) wrote his *Tafsīr al-Qurʾān wa-l-radd ʿalā man khālafa l-bayān min ahl al-ifk wa-l-buhtān wa-naqd mā ḥarrafahu l-Jubbāʾī wa-l-Balkhī fī taʾlīfihimā* (Sezgin, *GAS*, i, 604 no. 10), of which only the introduction *(muqaddima)* and fragments are preserved.

Of the apparently very large commentary, *al-Jāmiʿ fī ʿilm (*or *tafsīr) al-Qurʾān*, of ʿAlī b. ʿĪsā al-Rummānī (d. 384/994), a follower of the school of Ibn Ikhshīd, who himself had abridged the commentary of al-Ṭabarī (Ibn al-Nadīm-Dodge, i, 76), only a small portion is extant in manuscript (Sezgin, *GAS*, viii, 112-3). It was highly regarded by later authors and has been used extensively by al-Ṭūsī in his *Tibyān*, the latter being, according to Daniel Gimaret, "un plagiat pur et simple de celui de ʿAlī b. ʿĪsā ar-Rummānī" (Gimaret, *Jubbāʾī*, 23). A contemporary of al-Rummānī, Abū ʿAlī al-Fārisī (d. 377/987), composed a work entitled *Kitāb al-Tatabbuʿ li-kalām Abī ʿAlī al-Jubbāʾī fī l-tafsīr*, which is lost (Sezgin, *GAS*, viii, 110). Also lost is a work of Aḥmad b. Muḥammad al-Khallāl al-Baṣrī (alive in 377/987) entitled *Mutashābih al-Qurʾān*, excerpts of which are preserved in writings of Ibn Ṭāwūs (d. 664/1266) (Kohlberg, *Medieval Muslim*, 292-3, no. 457). Various exegetical works authored by representatives of the Bahshamiyya, notably of ʿAbd al-Jabbār, are extant; to these belong his *Tanzīh al-Qurʾān ʿan al-maṭāʿin*, which was published twice before the discovery of its author's *summa theologica* during the 1950s in Yemen (Cairo 1326, 1329) and his *Mutashābih al-Qurʾān* which is concerned with the ambiguous verses, i.e., those that apparently convey meanings incongruent with Muʿtazilī positions. By contrast, ʿAbd al-Jabbār's most extensive commentary, apparently entitled *al-Muḥīṭ*, seems to be lost. The most significant Muʿtazilī work of exegesis after ʿAbd al-Jabbār was *al-Tahdhīb fī l-tafsīr* of al-Ḥākim al-Jushamī, a student of Abū Ḥāmid Aḥmad b. Muḥammad b. Isḥāq al-Najjār (d. 433/1041), who in turn was a student of ʿAbd al-Jabbār.

Sabine Schmidtke

Bibliography
Primary: ʿAbd al-Jabbār, *al-Mughnī fī abwāb al-tawḥīd wa-l-ʿadl*, vol. vii, *Khalq al-Qurʾān*, ed. I. al-Ibyārī, Cairo 1380/1961; vol. xvi, *Iʿjāz al-Qurʾān*, ed. A. al-Khūlī, Cairo 1380/1960; id., *Mutashābih;* Gimaret, *Jubbāʾī;* Ibn al-Nadīm-Dodge; Rummānī et al., *Rasāʾil*.
Secondary: M. Bernard, La méthode d'exégèse coranique de ʿAbd al-Ǧabbār à travers son Mutašābih, in *Mélanges de l'Univeristé St.-Joseph* 50 (1989), 87-100; I.J. Boullata, The rhetorical interpretation of the Qurʾān. Iʿjāz and related topics, in Rippin, *Approaches*, 139-57; J. Bouman, *Le conflict autour du Coran et la solution d'al-Bāqillānī*, Amsterdam 1959; id., The doctrine of ʿAbd al-Djabbār on the Qurʾān as the created word of Allāh, in Th.P. van Baaren (ed.), *Verbum. Essays on some aspects of the religious function of words, dedicated to Hendrik Willem Obbink*, Utrecht 1964, 67-86; J. van Ess, Muʿtazilah, in *ER*, x, 220-9; id., *TG;* Goldziher, *Richtungen*, 99 f.; R. Ward Gwynne, *The "Tafsir" of Abu ʿAli al-Jubbaʾi. First steps toward a reconstruction, with texts, translations, biographical introduction and analytical essay*, Ph.D. diss., U. Washington 1982; M.S. al-Juwaynī, *Manhaj al-Zamakhsharī fī tafsīr al-Qurʾān*, Cairo 1968; E. Kohlberg, *A medieval Muslim scholar at work. Ibn Ṭāwūs and his library*, Leiden 1992; W. Madelung, Imāmism and Muʿtazilite theology, in T. Fahd (ed.), *Le Shīʿisme imamite*, Paris 1970, 13-30; id., The origins of the controversy concerning the creation of the Koran, in J.M. Barral (ed.), *Orientalia hispanica sive studia F.M. Pareja*, vol. i/1, Leiden 1974, 504-25; ʿA.ʿA. Makram, Tafsīr al-Kashshāf li-l-Zamakhsharī, in *al-Fikr al-islāmī* 1/4 ([Beirut] 1970), 73 f.; R.C. Martin, *A Muʿtazilite treatise on prophethood and miracles being probably the* Bāb ʿalā l-nubuwwah *from the* Ziyādāt al-sharḥ *by Abū Rashīd al-Nīsābūrī*, Ph.D. diss., New York 1975; id., The role of the Basrah Muʿtazilah in formulating the doctrine of the apologetic miracle, in *JNES* 39 (1980), 175-89; U. Rudolph, *Al-Māturīdī und die sunnitische Theologie in Samarkand*, Leiden 1997; Sezgin, *GAS;* M. Siddiqi, Some aspects of the Muʿtazilī interpretation of the Qurʾān, in *Islamic studies* 2 (1963), 95-120; W.M. Watt, Early discussions about the Qurʾān, in *MW* 40 (1950), 27-40, 96-105; B.G. Weiss, Medieval Muslim discussions of the origin of language, in *ZDMG* 124 (1974), 33-41.

Mysterious Letters

The alphabetic characters of the Arabic language (q.v.) that appear in non-verbal combinations at the beginning of certain sūras (q.v.) of the Qurʾān, just after the *basmala* (q.v.). The gift of "letters" came to the Arabian peninsula by way of a slow evolution of orthographies (see ARABIC SCRIPT; CALLIGRAPHY; ORALITY AND WRITING IN ARABIA). While the whole story is quite complex, the cursive consonantal alphabet of twenty-eight letters in which the Qurʾān was recorded was derived from a form of the Nabatean script, which in turn had descended from Syriac/Aramaic forms (see SYRIAC AND THE QURʾĀN). It ultimately sprang from the same common ancestor whose innovation around 1500 B.C.E. gave rise to the Hebrew alphabet and the south Arabian alphabets that first recorded the exploits of the kings of Sabaʾ (see SHEBA) and Ḥadramawt (see PRE-ISLAMIC ARABIA AND THE QURʾĀN; KINGS AND RULERS). Indeed, with the exception of the far-eastern symbols and syllabaries still in use in China and Japan, every language on the earth is written today with forms that are related in some way to this alphabetic family.

One could hardly say too much regarding the impact of the Qurʾān culturally and literarily on the Arab peoples (see ARABS; LANGUAGE AND STYLE OF THE QURʾĀN). The Qurʾān is considered the epitome of the Arabic language, and the works of the classical grammarians and exegetes (see EXEGESIS OF THE QURʾĀN: CLASSICAL AND MEDIEVAL) who examined the inimitability (q.v.; *iʿjāz*) of the Qurʾān laid the groundwork for the rules of Arabic grammar (see GRAMMAR AND THE QURʾĀN). Eventually the Qurʾān was credited with a stabilization of speech (q.v.) and orthography (q.v.) that enabled increased expression, and a consequent advancement of learning (see KNOWLEDGE AND LEARNING). But it must be remembered that a substantial portion of the works of the early grammarians was devoted to attempting to explain those qurʾānic passages that fall outside of the purview of the normative "rules" of Arabic grammar. At an even more basic level, qurʾānic orthography is itself archaic (cf. Nöldeke, *GQ*, iii, 26 f.), and, in fact, can *not* be said to have become "standard." One mystery in the Qurʾān that endures is the existence of seemingly inexplicable combinations of letters that appear at the beginning of twenty-nine of the sūras. They are referred to as "the isolated/disconnected letters" *(al-ḥurūf al-muqaṭṭaʿa)* or "the opening letters" *(ḥurūf al-fawātiḥ)*. These "mystery letters" themselves and the sūras they precede are given here for reference: *alr,* Q 10, 11, 12, 14, 15; *alm,* Q 2, 3, 29, 30, 31, 32; *almr,* Q 13; *almṣ,* Q 7; *ḥm,* Q 40, 41, 43, 44, 45, 46; *ḥmʿsq,* Q 42; *ṣ,* Q 38; *ṭs,* Q 27; *ṭsm,* Q 26, 28; *ṭh,* Q 20; *q,* Q 50; *khyʿṣ,* Q 19; *n,* Q 68; *ys,* Q 36.

Before presenting contemporary and traditional explanations of these letters, mention must be made of the orthography of the mysterious letters in the context of the Arabic script, particularly that of the seventh century. There are eighteen Arabic graphemes *(alif, bāʾ, jīm, dāl, rāʾ, sīn, ṣād, ṭāʾ, ʿayn, fāʾ, qāf, kāf, lām, mīm, nūn, hāʾ, wāw, yāʾ),* fifteen in the non-final position (identical *bāʾ/nūn/yāʾ* and *fāʾ/qāf*), expressing a total of twenty-eight sounds (for further details, see ARABIC SCRIPT). In the earliest Arabic script, there were no dots to indicate the difference between letters that were represented by the same grapheme, but had different sounds: a *bāʾ* ("b") and a *tāʾ* ("t"), without the presence of, respectively, the single dot below or the double dots above the hooked form of the letter, become indistinguishable. The fourteen letters that compose the mysterious letters represent every consonantal form in Arabic as exemplified in this early script (in which *wāw, fāʾ* and *qāf* were the same grapheme, as were *dāl, dhāl* and *kāf*). Thus, the mysterious letters comprise — comprehensively — the graphemes of the Arabic script of the seventh century: the five that represent only one letter *(alif, lām, mīm, nūn, hāʾ),* as well as the other nine *(yāʾ, ḥāʾ, rāʾ, sīn, ṣād, ṭāʾ, ʿayn, qāf, kāf)*. It is not unreasonable to assume, therefore, that these mysterious letters were intended to represent the Arabic alphabet (see Welch, al-Ḳurʾān, 414), shedding new light on passages such as Q 16:103, which state that the revelation of the Qurʾān is "clear Arabic tongue/speech" *(lisānun ʿarabiyyūn mubīnun)*. But this theory does little to explain the reason for the placement of the letters at the head of their respective sūras (see also UNITY OF THE TEXT OF THE QURʾĀN). While Muslim scholars have developed a variety of explanations for these letters, a number of Western scholars have also set themselves the task of explaining both the meaning of the letters themselves, as well as the reason for their placement at the beginnings of these particular sūras.

Traditional explanations

To the faithful Muslim, these letters are part of the divine revelation of the Qurʾān itself (see REVELATION AND INSPIRATION). In the recitation of the Qurʾān (q.v.), these "openers" or "beginnings" of the sūras *(fawātiḥ al-suwar; awāʾil al-suwar)* are recited as letters of the alphabet (i.e. Q 2:1 is read *"alif lām mīm"*). A variety of explanations for the letters has been proffered in the classical commentaries: these letters are the names of the sūras or markers for the separation of the sūras, names of God or abbreviations of his names (i.e. *alr* standing for *al-raḥmān, alm* for *al-raḥīm* or *Allāh laṭīf majīd* ["God, gentle, glorious], etc.; cf. Welch, al-Ḳurʾān, 412; Robinson, Discovering, 320 n. 10; see GOD AND HIS ATTRIBUTES), oaths (q.v.) by which God proclaimed. Traditional sources also suggest that the letters are mystical signs with symbolic meaning (see ṢŪFISM AND THE QURʾĀN) based upon the numerical values assigned to the letters (see NUMBERS AND ENUMERATION; NUMEROLOGY), or, alternatively, suggest that the letters were a means of attracting the attention of the Prophet or his audience (cf. Suyūṭī, *Itqān*, iii, 21-30).

One theory that has gained interest and adherents among Muslims in more recent times concerns the claimed existence of multiple patterns of the number "nineteen" hidden in the text of the Qurʾān (cf. Khalifa, *Quran*). This is said to be an experientially provable sign of the inimitability of the Qurʾān, the inexpressible and unrepeatable quality of the Qurʾān's style. Some of these findings, while interesting, seem somewhat contrived, e.g. the assertion that "nineteen" can be found in the mysterious letters because twenty-nine sūras (by one calculation) in the Qurʾān begin with them, fourteen different letters from the alphabet are used (again, depending on whether one counts the single letters *ṣād, qāf* and *nūn* which occur before three sūras) and there are fourteen different combinations of these disconnected letters in the beginning of the sūras. The sum of these numbers is fifty-seven ($29 + 14 + 14 = 57$). Fifty-seven is a multiple of nineteen ($3 \times 19 = 57$).

Although, as can be seen from the preceding paragraphs, Qurʾān commentators have put forth many explanations for these mysterious letters (one of the most popular and enduring — although lacking any consensus — being that these mysterious letters are contractions of words or phrases; see Watt-Bell, *Introduction*, 64), most classical and contemporary Muslim scholars maintain that the full signification of these letters is known only to God (Welch, al-Ḳurʾān, 412).

Contemporary theories in western scholarship

Non-Muslim theories have varied widely, but tend to fall in two categories: abbreviationist and redactional. (Other recent, but less tenable, proposals include the theories that they are mystical symbols used as battle cries, or that they are mnemonic devices which summarize the contents of the sūras; Robinson, *Discovering,* 320 n. 10; Watt-Bell, *Introduction,* 64). Proponents of abbreviationist positions have tended to view the mysterious letters as independent of the original qurʾānic text. In this category may be listed Hans Bauer (Anordnung), who proposed that the letters stood for various catchwords, and Eduard Goosens, who has argued that the letters are contractions of earlier, now defunct, titles of the sūras. James Bellamy (Mysterious letters) proposed an abbreviation theory that is less arbitrary than the others: following the suggestions of classical qurʾānic commentators that the majority of the mysterious letters are abbreviations for *al-raḥmān* and/or *al-raḥīm,* Bellamy posits that most of the mysterious letters stand for these names of God in the *basmala* and that all of the other mysterious letters (with some emendations, which he elaborates upon in a later article; see his Proposed emendations, 572-3) are abbreviations for the *basmala*. In his view, these abbreviations were introduced (in the Meccan period, by the Prophet's scribes) at the beginning of 29 sūras instead of the *basmala,* and that later scribes did not understand the abbreviation and inserted the *basmala* in addition to the mysterious letters. Welch (al-Ḳurʾān, 413), however, argues that Bellamy's theory is not entirely consistent with the textual evidence concerning the chronology of the Qurʾān which would suggest that the letters are more likely from the Medinan period (see CHRONOLOGY AND THE QURʾĀN), and does not explain the relationship of the letters to their immediate contexts (i.e. why are they placed at these twenty nine sūras, and not others?).

The other category of theories, the redactional, examines the mysterious letters as a means for ordering the qurʾānic text (see FORM AND STRUCTURE OF THE QURʾĀN), and tends to see these opening letters as part of the original corpus (see MUṢḤAF). Although, as mentioned above, Bauer (Anordnung) believed the letters to be abbreviations of catchwords, he provided statistical support for the theory that the letters influenced the final arrangement of the Qurʾān (cf. Welch, 413-4 for a discussion of Loth and Schwally's contribution to the development of this theory). Bell saw both the mysterious letters and the *basmala* as part of the original corpus, albeit revised: he argued that they were early Medinan revisions adapting the sūras for inclusion in the written scripture (Welch, al-Ḳurʾān, 414; Watt-Bell, *Introduction,* 63-4, 138, 143). The current form of this redactional theory centers on the observation that the qurʾānic sūras are not strictly arranged from longest to shortest, even with the exclusion of the opening sūra (Sūrat al-Fātiḥa; see FĀTIḤA) and the two concluding sūras. It has been proposed that exceptions were made to the "decreasing-length" ordering for groups of sūras beginning with the same mysterious letters. In a recent study, however, Neal Robinson (*Discovering,* 260-70) has clearly demonstrated some problems with this theory: 1) there are some exceptions to the "decreasing-length" rule that cannot be accounted for even by the intervening sūras that begin with the mysterious letters and 2) not all the sūras that begin with the same letters are arranged together. While not entirely discounting the value of the sūra length and the presence of the letters in ordering the sūras, Robinson suggests that other factors (such as the repetition of key words or phrases in consecutive sūras) were taken into account by the redactors of the qurʾānic corpus.

But proponents of this theory have not only attempted to explain the discrepancies of the "decreasing-length" ordering of the sūras. They have also tried to explain what the individual letters stand for. In his ground-breaking study, Theodor Nöldeke (*GQ*, 215 f.) argued that the letters were abbreviations standing for the names of people whom Zayd b. Thābit had consulted for the readings of the sūras (see READINGS OF THE QURʾĀN; RECITERS OF THE QURʾĀN). He later believed that they were merely mystical and meaningless symbols attempting to imitate the heavenly book (q.v.; see also BOOK) the Prophet would have beheld (for further discussion of this change in Nöldeke's thinking, which was effected by Loth's argument of a Jewish Kabbalistic influence on Muḥammad in the late Meccan and early Medinan periods, see Welch, al-Ḳurʾān, 412; see also JEWS AND JUDAISM). Hartwig Hirschfeld expanded on Nöldeke's initial theory and attempted to identify the sources themselves, suggesting that the letters stood for the following individuals: *m* = Mughīra; *ṣ* = Ḥafṣa; *r[z]* = al-Zubayr; *k* = Abū Bakr; *h* = Abū Hurayra; *n* = ʿUthmān; *ṭ* = Ṭalḥa; *s* = Saʿd (b. Abī Waqqāṣ]; *ḥ* = Ḥudhayfa; *ʿ* = ʿUmar/ʿAlī/Ibn ʿAbbās/ʿĀʾisha; *q* = al-Qāsim b. Rabīʿa. The principal weakness of the Nöldeke/Hirschfeld theory, as with all the theories put forth on the issue, is that it does not — indeed, cannot — prove its case. The ability to produce identifications of the letters, whether they are names or whole words, does not prove that the identifications are correct. The catalogue of various identifications stands as a tribute to the imagination of the researchers rather than as a secure solution.

My own work on this issue has surfaced a previously undetected and potentially important detail about the mysterious letters. I observed that the patterns themselves produce a set ranking within the letters. Comparing the eleven different multiple-letter combinations in which thirteen different letters appear reveals that the order of the letters is not random or arbitrary. One would not expect this to happen if the letters stood for sentences or words; such a system would not have been likely able to prevent violations in a ranking. Thus, for example, the *mīm* never appears before the *sīn,* which in turn never appears before the *ʿayn;* the *lām* never appears before the *alif,* etc. (for a more detailed discussion of this "ranking" of the letters, see Massey, New investigation, 498-9). For this observation to hold true, however, some explanation is needed in the matter of Q 42, which begins with the pattern *ḥmʿsq*. At first glance, it seems that this violates the order (insofar as the *mīm* appears before the *sīn*). But the verse divisions have generally separated this cluster into *ḥm* and then *ʿsq*. In this case there are actually two separate patterns here. Another possibility is that, given the location of the sūra in the middle of six other sūras with the *ḥm* pattern, the *ḥm* has been added later by analogy.

Quite significantly, the set ranking I have observed goes well beyond the statistical possibility of a random production. Calculating the odds for such patterns if only two letters are used shows that there are about even odds of a random selection succeeding in having an inviolate pattern (156 possible patterns with seventy-eight [1/2] of them not violating any given pattern). When the pattern length is extended to three, however, the chance of randomness quickly diminishes (1716 possible patterns with only 286 of them [1/6] not violating any given pattern). In the case of the mysterious letters there are four cases of two letter patterns, four cases of three, four cases of four and one case of five. In this particular case, statistical analysis argues strongly against randomness. If the letters are not random, one can rule out the possibility that they are words or sentences. While such structures would have semantic intentionality, they would not prevent the violation of an ordered list of letters. Also ruled out is the theory that the letters are nothing other than the imitation of celestial characters or nonsense letters. This observation, I would argue, lends strong support to the Nöldeke/Hirschfeld theory. If the letters are an ordered list, the best candidate for referents is the names of people who, for some reason, are being ranked by the person who has put down the letters.

The letters, then, constitute a form of critical textual apparatus (see TEXTUAL CRITICISM OF THE QURʾĀN). According to reliable accounts from the early history of Islam, when Zayd b. Thābit, at the order of ʿUthmān (q.v.), compiled the Qurʾān (see MUṢḤAF; COLLECTION OF THE QURʾĀN; CODIFICATION OF THE QURʾĀN;), he used several sources. For those sūras that had either more than one source (or perhaps whose reading is supported by more than one source over and against other variant readings which he chose to reject), he acknowledged those sources by listing one-letter abbreviations of them, in his own perceived rank of importance and reliability. He was never inconsistent in his own ranking of the sources, hence the order we can now find among the mysterious letters was produced. Whether or not Hirschfeld has correctly identified the letters with the names for which they stand can simply never be known. He has astutely produced parallels for the letters from strong candidates of the period, but he may or may not be right. The names may all be scribes who never showed up in the tradition or any early literature. But the discovery of the ranking of these letters tips the scales in the direction of an ordered list of names. If this is a catalogue of sources the ʿUthmānic Qurʾān has carefully built into it an early attempt to assure the readers of the credibility of the text from which they were reading. It is possible, as some have suggested, that the letters that appear alone *(ṣād, qāf, nūn)* may not have the same purpose as the collections themselves. *Nūn* in particular has the story of Jonah (q.v.) and the great fish *(nūn)* as a cogent explanation of this letter.

Conclusion

Adequate explanation both for the meaning of the "mysterious letters" and why they occur before the 29 sūras in which they appear has yet to appear. Although a number of reasonable theories of the significance of these mysterious collections of letters has been proposed — abbreviations for the *basmala,* or for some of the divine names, or for various individuals (possibly reciters of the Qurʾān) — none is definitive. The inconsistencies with the observation that they appear largely before sūras that interfere with the "decreasing sūra-length" organization of the Qurʾān have yet to be explained satisfactorily. Finally, further study is needed about the fact that they represent, comprehensively, the graphemes of the earliest Arabic script.

Keith Massey

Bibliography

Primary: Suyūṭī, *Itqān.*
Secondary: H. Bauer, Über die Anordnung der Suren und über die geheimisvollen Buchstaben im Qoran, in ZDMG 75 (1921), 1-20; J. Bellamy, The mysterious letters of the Koran. Old abbreviations of the *basmalah,* in JAOS 93 (1973), 267-85; id., Some proposed emendations to the text of the Koran, in JAOS 113 (1993), 562-73; E. Goosens, Ursprung und Beduetung der koranischen Siglen, in *Der Islam* 13 (1923), 191-226; H. Hirschfeld, *New researches into the composition of the Qoran,* London 1902; A. Jeffery, The mystic letters of the Koran, in MW 14 (1924), 247-60; A. Jones, The mystical letters of the Qurʾān, in SI 16 (1962), 5-11; R. Khalifa, *Qurʾān. The final testament,* Fremont, CA 1992; K. Massey, Mystery letters of the Qurʾān, in *Arabica* 43 (1996), 497-501; Nöldeke, GQ; N. Robinson, *Discovering the Qurʾān. A contemporary approach to a*

veiled text, London 1996; Watt-Bell, *Introduction;* A. Welch, al-Ḳurʾān. 4d. The mysterious letters, in *EI*², v, 412-4.

Myths and Legends in the Qurʾān

Myths are narratives that serve to explain and describe the experienced world by laying bare its archetypal patterns (see COSMOLOGY); they are often staged in a cosmic or supernatural framework so as to manifest binding truths, to generate meaning and provide guidance. Legends, raising no such universal claim, may be understood as narratives of pious imagination celebrating an exemplary figure.

Are there myths and legends in the Qurʾān? Even today, this is a controversial question, since the term "myth," in particular, is sometimes thought to be irreconcilable with the concept of revelation (see REVELATION AND INSPIRATION). The reasons for such hyper-sensitivity are historical; to quote Jaroslav Stetkevych (*Golden bough,* ix):

> Within the premises of (the) Arabian stance — begun with the Qurʾān's instant, and almost total, doctrinal impact — Arabic cultural history with all its anthropological constructs, was supposed to have begun and thereafter forever to unfold in the clarity of broad daylight, as it were. All "falsehood" and all "truth" were forever absolutely differentiated into some timeless pre-revelation (the age of the Jāhilīyah) that was followed by an equally timeless revelation (the Qurʾān), that is, into that which exists not and that which exists: *al-bāṭil* and *al-ḥaqq*.

The two terms, myth/legend and revelation, once taken as indicators of different degrees of truth (q.v.), emanating from sources of unequal credibility, become mutually exclusive: Myths under such a perspective cannot be easily accepted as powerful expressions of significant human experience deemed worthy of transmittal to later generations because of their archetypal evidence and universal validity, but are, rather, suspected of representing deviance and willful ignorance *(jāhiliyya)*. Their re-use as a prop for scriptural events — a common practice in Christian iconography — occurred, although to a lesser degree, in the later haggadic elaboration of qurʾānic narrations (see EXEGESIS OF THE QURʾĀN: CLASSICAL AND MEDIEVAL). Events related in the Qurʾān itself, are, however, considered "true" and sufficient to represent the past (see HISTORY AND THE QURʾĀN). Non-qurʾānic pre-Islamic narratives are held to be devoid of meaning, as they were superseded by the only meaningful revelation (see SOUTH ARABIA, RELIGION IN PRE-ISLAMIC).

But the concepts of "myths and legends" cover not only ancient "pagan" narrative but have been redirected as terms to denote narratives informed with a particular hermeneutic code. It is their intrinsic ability to recall archetypal patterns of interaction that invites the listener to identify with or find guidance through particular figures. "Myth" and "legend," understood as hermeneutically distinguished genres of narrative, are to be found in all kinds of literature, irrespective of their profane or sacred character (see LITERATURE AND THE QURʾĀN). As diverse studies in the Hebrew Bible and the New Testament alike have shown (Alter and Kermode, *Literary guide;* Alter, *Biblical narrative;* Frye, *The great code*), mythic and legendary narratives figure amply in the two older monotheistic scriptures. The dynamics of their immanent mythopoiesis provides narrative texts with significant subtexts adding surplus meaning to the plot, thus proving not only effective with pre-revelation audiences, but also particularly fit to serve the aims of revelation itself.

Although this article focuses on the Qurʾān, it will be necessary to survey particular aspects of the problematic in the broader framework of scripture in general (see LITERARY STRUCTURES OF THE QURʾĀN). Not only does the Qurʾān typologically represent a manifestation of monotheistic scripture and thus partake in the hermeneutical characteristics of a sacred canon, the Qurʾān also displays, even more perspicuously than the two other scriptures, the process of the emergence of a scripture. If this is true, a comparison between the treatment of myth(s) and legends in the Qurʾān on the one hand, and in the two other monotheistic scriptures on the other, promises to throw important light on the particular developments of the Qurʾān. Subsequently, an attempt at a typology of myths and legends in the Qurʾān will be undertaken through consideration of a selection of significant cases. Since the qurʾānic narrative is often inconsistent, i.e. sophisticated structures appearing alongside fragmented panels of mythic images, it is important to discuss not only complete narrative units but also overall mythical visions looming under dispersed single elements. As against the positive evidence of mythopoiesis in the Qurʾān, the anti-mythic tendencies, which likewise exist, will also be considered.

Scripture and myth

Scripture as a medium of the demythification of the world

Myth, in the narrow sense of a narrative about personified or demonized supernatural powers working in individual or collective human life, is of course incompatible with the scriptural concept of one exclusive divine agent in nature and history. In fact, scripture as such has been credited as the medium of demythification *par excellence*. It has been noted of the three monotheistic religions that their scriptures do not, in the way mythic thinking does, refer back to an archaic sacred order, anchored in a primordial beginning that needs to be restored, but refer to events that themselves are part of an extended continuous nexus of happenings. This is particularly true for Christianity and Islam, two religions that are based on events that are understandable only in view of what preceded: neither initiates traditions but rather presupposes them. It is noticeable that in both religions human history receives a new evaluation through the central event that necessarily judges the preceding era to be of inferior quality and that promises to have an imprint on all further history. The basic structure of past, present and future thus cannot be viewed in a symmetrical way since the theological evaluations are unequal (Zirker, *Christentum*, see TIME).

The fact that scripture dissolves premonotheistic, iterative or circular patterns of memory (q.v.), that it tends to "historicize" memory, becomes most evident from its re-interpretation of the myth-imprinted "pagan" world submitted to ever repeating cyclical processes of seasonal change (see FATE; DESTINY; GENERATIONS; GEOGRAPHY). In contrast, the scriptural worldview reflects the process of an evolution in linear time. Monotheistic scripture marginalizes cosmic experience, the impact of the powers of nature as manifest in the seasonal cycle, in favor of historical experience, presenting decisive communal events as unique manifestations of divine power (see POWER AND IMPOTENCE; FREEDOM AND PREDESTINATION). Scripturally institutionalized feasts (see FESTIVALS AND COMMEMORATIVE DAYS) thus no longer serve to mark the yearly changes of seasons (q.v.) but commemorate outstanding events worked by the divine agent in the community in the past. Scriptural demythification thereby touches a realm of human life that is vital for the coherence of a society: i.e. rituals and feasts (see RITUAL AND THE QURʾĀN). Once having placed a taboo upon viewing spirits and demons (see JINN; DEVIL) as potent agents in the drama of the seasonal cycles, scripture has to provide etiological substitutes to give meaning to the feasts as well as to inspire the effervescence and the perception of renewal that make up the festal atmosphere (Assmann, Fest). This reconstruction has been, in the Islamic context, carried out in a particularly rigorous way. Whereas the two other monotheistic religions kept the time frame of older seasonal feasts and co-opted their essential symbols, enriching and reshaping them according to the new salvation-historical meaning of the individual feast — thus preserving a mythic subtext to be reclaimed whenever desired, Islamic festivals have fared differently. Though strikingly conservative in terms of ritual procedure, i.e. continuing many of the ancient pre-Islamic ritual performances clearly informed by the symbolism of changing seasons (Wellhausen, *Reste*), Islam has strictly dissociated them from their ancient Arabian precedents through a new calendar (q.v.) which bears no relation to the seasonal cycle, thus dismissing any mythic association emanating from that source (Neuwirth, Three religious feasts). Moreover, the Islamic rites were given new meanings commemorating historical events crucial to the community's identity, or were reinterpreted as mere acts of worship (q.v.) divinely imposed through the words of earlier prophets (see PROPHETS AND PROPHETHOOD).

But myth is not exclusively about supernatural powers working in nature (see MIRACLE); it is also about extraordinary human figures, excelling in strength, courage (q.v.), shrewdness, endurance and other heroic faculties. In the Hebrew Bible not a few characters of heroic standing have survived scripturalization, i.e. integration into a vision dominated by divine will: they appear to act autonomously rather than being directed by a divine force behind them. Although not consistently designated as heroic but responding to diverse challenges of human acting and suffering, and never totally severed from divine will or providence, major biblical figures, primarily Moses (q.v.) and David (q.v.), and to a lesser degree also Abraham (q.v.), Jacob (q.v.), Joseph (q.v.) and Solomon (q.v.) as well as more episodic figures like Samson, Ehud and Judith have retained a heroic image. As against that, few heroic figures would be found in the Qurʾān. Not only are the protagonists of narratives from the ancient Arabian lore absent, but also most of the biblical figures that do play a role in the Qurʾān are not represented as heroes either. Their appearance has been changed: as they do not receive a consistent portrayal, nor are their stories continuously followed over a span of time long enough to display character development, but are, rather, presented episodically in very diverse contexts, these figures are not developed enough to impress as heroes (see the discussion of Solomon and David below). Others, like the Arabian Hūd (q.v.), Ṣāliḥ (q.v.) and Shuʿayb (q.v.), do not act autonomously but remain throughout performants of the divine will, so that their actions seem to lack momentum, making it difficult for the reader to associate them with those key figures contained "in kindred structures and symbolic systems that range from Gilgamesh and the Hebrew Bible to Homer and Vergil" (Stetkevych, *Golden bough*, ix). Still, in the Qurʾān some figures do acquire heroic dimensions such as Noah (q.v.; Nūḥ), Abraham (Ibrāhīm), Joseph

(Yūsuf) and, most especially, Moses (Mūsā).

Qurʾānic scripture and story-telling

Scriptural demythification, which is particularly strong in the Qurʾān, also touches upon another vital need: the transmission of knowledge, particularly the practice of story-telling. Qurʾānic narrative has hitherto usually been considered as a continuum. Its continuous treatment of prophetic episodes with similar, sometimes identical, messages led scholars to the conclusion that there is something like "the qurʾānic narrative," attesting a cyclical concept of revelation (Paret, Geschichtsbild). Although Horovitz, in his groundbreaking study on qurʾānic narrative, strictly committed himself to Nöldeke's periodization, scholars after him have ordinarily failed to acknowledge, or even rejected, any substantial development in the qurʾānic representation of prophets and messengers (see MESSENGER) except in terms of increasing detail. In general the Qurʾān has been judged to evidence no serious interest in history. Fred Donner (*Narratives of origin*, 84) states:

> The purpose of stories in the Qurʾān, then, is profoundly different from their purpose in the Old Testament; the latter uses stories to explain particular chapters in Israel's history, the former to illustrate — again and again — how the true Believer acts in certain situations. In line with this purpose, qurʾānic characters are portrayed as moral paradigms, emblematic of all who are good or evil.... [The Qurʾān] is simply not concerned with history in the sense of development and change, either of the prophets or peoples before Muḥammad, or of Muḥammad himself, because in the qurʾānic view the identity of the community to which Muḥammād was sent is not historically determined, but morally determined.

This view, which relies on a macro-structural reading of the Qurʾān, not surprisingly conforms with the image of the Qurʾān that became dominant in Islam itself after the official canonization of the corpus by ʿUthmān b. ʿAffān (see COLLECTION OF THE QURʾĀN; CODICES OF THE QURʾĀN; ʿUTHMĀN): the Qurʾān was no longer perceived as a communicational process but as the time-transcending divine word (see WORD OF GOD) transmitted by the prophet Muḥammad, the final figure in a series of impeccable (see IMPECCABILITY) superhuman messengers bearing an identical message. This a-historical perception has recently been adopted by a number of modern scholars, inspired by postmodern methodological approaches no longer concerned with philological-historical problems (see CONTEMPORARY CRITICAL PRACTICES AND THE QURʾĀN; POST-ENLIGHTENMENT ACADEMIC STUDY OF THE QURʾĀN). To view the Qurʾān in such a "holistic" way — in accordance with its later Islamic reading — is, however, only one possible way of reading it, since the a-historical image of the Qurʾān covers another, more complex, layer of understanding that can be laid bare only through an acute micro-structural reading (see FORM AND STRUCTURE OF THE QURʾĀN).

To do justice to qurʾānic narrative, one has to look for earlier narrative traditions familiar to the community that may have influenced the qurʾānic narrative style (see LANGUAGE AND STYLE OF THE QURʾĀN; ORALITY AND WRITING IN ARABIA; NARRATIVES; SCRIPTURE AND THE QURʾĀN). Given the fact that the early sūras (q.v.) display a linguistic and stylistic character very close to the enunciations of pre-Islamic soothsayers (q.v.; *kāhin*, pl. *kahana*) whereas later sūras come close to monotheistic liturgies with pericopes of scriptural readings in their central part (for further discussion, see FORM AND STRUCTURE OF THE QURʾĀN), one arrives at the conclusion that qurʾānic narratives partake in diverse discourses and thus constitute at least two distinct groups: texts that still mirror the principle of a highly emphatic, succinct and sometimes enigmatic presentation current in *sajʿ al-kahana* (see RHYMED PROSE) on the one hand, and texts more inclined towards a lively episodic presentation displaying sophisticated narrative strategies, on the other. The former genre is more formalized and thus limited in its narrative range, relying strongly on repetition, parallelism and anaphors, etc.; the latter is flexible, tending towards detail and diversity. Whereas the former drives home one particular message, there are far more complex intentions behind the second.

Due to the new qurʾānic worldview, which staged past and present events as part of the drama of a series of divine interventions in human interactions, the orally transmitted scenarios of Arabian memory (see ORALITY; ARABS), whose protagonists were committed to worldly, often heroic, aims were widely marginalized — if not dismissed as a whole — or re-interpreted to fit the new paradigm. In the words of Stetkevych (*Golden bough,* 10):

The knowledge of the communal Arabian past and its inheritors' creative and re-creative self-knowledge within it were definitely not furthered by the concrete, a-historical and anti-mythical doctrinal stance that relegated mythic materials to anecdotal and "catechistic" functions.... The problem with a number of (these) nuclei of myth was that in their survival in the new code, that is, through their co-optation by the Qurʾān (and the subsequent dogmatizing tradition), they were put to the service of a rhetoric that was almost inimical to "narrative" itself — this despite the qurʾānic claim that there they are being told in the best of narrative ways. That is, in the Qurʾān, narrative and indeed everything else is subordinated to the overarching rhetoric of salvation [q.v.] and damnation.... [see REWARD AND PUNISHMENT] Rarely do we sense in the Qurʾān a self-sufficient and self-justifying joy in storytelling, indeed, rarely, if at all, does the Qurʾān allow for the formation of "themes" in the literary terminological understanding, that is, of descriptive (of imagist) units that possess their own formal and thematic circumscription and "sufficiency" and are not intruded upon by a stylistically disruptive rhetoric. Rather than themes in the literary sense, the Qurʾān, therefore, knows primarily rhetorically subordinated motifs.

What Stetkevych has labeled "rhetorics" is, however, deeply rooted in the qurʾānic message as such and thus from a different perspective should be viewed as complementary. It is true that qurʾānic storytelling does not express an authorial stance such as is that which Alter finds realizable in biblical narrating (*Biblical narrative,* 184):

Perhaps the most distinctive feature of the role played by the narrator in the biblical tales is the way in which omniscience and inobtrusiveness are combined.... In the Bible... the narrator's work is almost all récit, straight narration of actions and speech, and only exceptionally and very briefly discourse, disquisition on and around the narrated facts and their implications. The assurance of comprehensive knowledge is thus implicit in the narratives, but it is shared with the reader only intermittently and at that quite partially. In this way, the very mode of narration conveys a double sense of a total coherent knowledge available to God (and by implication, to His surrogate, the anonymous authoritative narrator) and the necessary incompleteness of human knowledge, for which much about character, motive, and moral status will remain shrouded in ambiguity.

As against the meticulous shaping of personages and the sophisticated coding and de-coding of their motives, which characterize biblical narrative, qur'ānic narrating pursues complex "para-narrative" aims. Narratives, at least insofar as they are unfolded to some extent and recall plots already known from biblical literature, are presented as excerpts or messages from the book (q.v.; *al-kitāb*), which is clearly taken to be a corpus of literature apart from the rest of the known stories that are currently available through oral tradition. This remoteness of "*kitāb*-generated" narrative certainly has a strong bearing on the style of the stories presented as *kitāb* readings. It forces on them a distinct linguistic code that, on the one hand, confers on the diction a highly stylized form (rhymed prose resulting in somewhat forced syntactic structures; see GRAMMAR AND THE QUR'ĀN), serving to distinguish it from profane narrative. On the other hand, it implants these narratives with the new message of the imminent eschatological catastrophe (see ESCHATOLOGY; CATASTROPHE), which brings the narrative close to an exhortative appeal (see EXHORTATIONS) or, later, a sermon. It is exactly the discursive elements so marginal in biblical narrative that matter primarily in the qur'ānic narrative: the explicit presentation of the moral or theological implications for the community that can be deduced from the narrated facts or speeches (see ETHICS AND THE QUR'ĀN; THEOLOGY AND THE QUR'ĀN). To fulfill this purpose, a stylistic device unknown to the Bible has been created to accommodate the particular moral or theological deductions from the qur'ānic discourse, the clausula (see Neuwirth, *Studien*). This stylistic device consists in a particular closure of the long verses of late Meccan and Medinan times (see CHRONOLOGY AND THE QUR'ĀN): the last sentence of a verse does not partake in the main strand of communication, but presents a comment on its contents indicating divine approval or disregard of the fact reported, e.g. "Truly you are of the faulty" (*innaki kunti min al-khāṭi'īn*, Q 12:29; see SIN, MAJOR AND MINOR; VIRTUES AND VICES, COMMANDING AND FORBIDDING). It may also refer to one of God's attributes (see GOD AND HIS ATTRIBUTES), e.g. "Truly he is the hearer, the seer" (*innahu huwa l-samīʿu l-baṣīr*, Q 17:1; see SEEING AND HEARING), which, in the later stages of qur'ānic development, have become parameters of ideal human behavior. This comment is clad in a widely formalized shape and is thus easily identifiable.

Qur'ān and history

How does the Qur'ān view prior history? Keeping the canonical process in mind, we have to ask the question on two different levels, distinguishing between two subsequent paradigms. The Qur'ān, in the beginning of its development, encodes history in the discourse of the *umam khāliya*, the accounts about the dispatchment of messengers to previous communities who called their people to worship and obey one God but who failed to convert their communities (see OBEDIENCE; PUNISHMENT STORIES). Here, the Qur'ān "pans over a landscape where time is less a chronology than a continuum" (Khalidi, *Arabic historical thought*, 8). The scenarios are mostly, though not exclusively, Arabian (see PRE-ISLAMIC ARABIA AND THE QUR'ĀN). The early qur'ānic messenger stories have replaced a previously existing culture-specific, coherent pre-Islamic Arabian myth. In Stetkevych's words (*Golden bough*, 3):

Arabia and the Arabia-nurtured and Arabic-speaking world [see ARABIC LANGUAGE] has most stubbornly denied itself the acknowledgment of a "mythological conditioning." An earnestness, and even somberness, of rigorous theological dogma came to reign with an almost puzzling... march through more than a millennium of history. It succeeded from the first qur'ānic moment in almost suppressing or banishing into unusually reclusive layers of subconsciousness that part of the counter-dogmatic Arabian cultural "self" which, under conditions of a less stable doctrinal rigor, would have had the strength to lead that culture to its remythologizing, or to an awareness of its "mythological conditioning." In this respect even more inhibiting than the suppressions and condemnations that came forth from the doctrinal apparatus which had formed itself around the newly-arrived Arabian sacred text and which soon succeeded in forming its own cultural code was the co-optation by that new code of much of the most centrally autochthony-determining materials of the old code.

The significance of the stories about the Arabian messengers lies in their endurance (*ṣabr*) and obedience in calling humans to accept divine guidance: every community should have been warned through a revelation in order to be spared temporary or eschatological punishment (see TRUST AND PATIENCE; WARNER). It is noteworthy that the qur'ānic virtue is no mere endurance, but

presupposes triumph. It is an outlasting of evil, rather than its transmuting. Its task is to outstay all opposition so that the good of prophecy is not overcome by the enmity of unbelief [see BELIEF AND UNBELIEF]. Its endurance keeps the cause from capitulation, so that it may anticipate the victory other factors will achieve. It is not, broadly, a suffering which in itself and of itself makes the fabric of the triumph that is to be. This calls for other forces whose opportunity tenacity ensures (Cragg, *Event*, 158).

It is sober, pragmatic thinking and acting, *ḥilm*, self-denying dedication to the divine message, *islām*, that is portrayed here — the reversal of *jahl*, heroic unrestraint (see ISLAM; FAITH; IGNORANCE). In fact, *jahl* in the Qur'ān itself was to become the label of the pre-Islamic epoch that was termed *jāhiliyya* (see AGE OF IGNORANCE).

Thus *jahl/jāhilīya* had to have been a singularly important concept (or state) in archaic Bedouinity [see BEDOUINS] to have deserved such a stupendous "transfer" into its new terminological prominence — and into its paradoxical semiotic self-denial. We must, therefore, entertain the strong notion that its denial by the new Arabia that emerged with Islam also meant Arabia's denial of myth as its cultural, autochthony-defining ingredient. For myth, all myth, is hardly conceivable without the presence of *jahl* somewhere near its very core. This *jahl*, however, also in its archaic Arabic understanding, is above all that kind of heroism that also contains its own tragic flaw (Stetkevych, *Golden bough*, 10).

The predicament of the ancient messengers whose message is rejected is shared by the Prophet himself (see OPPOSITION TO MUḤAMMAD). The contents of revelation in the *umam khāliya* discourse (i.e. the stories of earlier nations destroyed because of their unbelief) thus does not have a history; the bearers of the revelation and their addressees do not form a chain of succession.

History and revelation repeat each other following the same pattern.

This discourse has, however, to be differentiated from a grand narrative that emerges at a later stage in the Qurʾān. What is usually upheld to apply to the Qurʾān as such: the renunciation of a chronological frame for the events of pre-qurʾānic history, the repetitiveness of the qurʾānic narrative — "events are arranged in clusters, repetitive in form" (Khalidi, *Arab historical thought,* 8) — as a sign of the insistence of an identical message, the total disregard for mythic primacy, etc., on closer gaze, does not hold true except for the first paradigm. Here, "the whole history is present at once to God." But the situation successively changes substantially when a new paradigm is adopted, switching the focus from the deserted sites of the real homeland to the orbit of the messengers of the People of the Book (q.v.; *ahl al-kitāb*), the prophets *(anbiyāʾ),* whose discourse as intermediaries between God and man is much more sophisticated. Overtly, they form a prophetical succession and their activities taken together not only constitute a scenario of historical episodes, but, more and more, betray a tendency to chronology. Their communications and actions prove rich in experiences and fit to exert a mythopoeic impact on the self-understanding of the emerging community itself; indeed, these activities not seldom provide the matrix for the prophet's and his community's behavior in certain situations of crisis, and more often the matrix of their understanding of their own predicament (Neuwirth, Erzählen). It is no longer the projection of present experience onto the image of the past that was representative for the earlier discourse, but the converse: experiences of the past provide a model for the understanding of the present. The entrance of the qurʾānic community into the orbit of those earlier societies endowed with a scripture is presented as an event of seismic proportions: "If we sent down this Qurʾān upon a mountain, you would see it humbled, shattered by the fear of God" (Q 59:21; Khalidi, *Arab historical thought,* 7). This degree of self-confidence would not have been feasible in the earlier stages; it marks a caesura in arranging history that should not be ignored.

The wide canvas from Adam [see ADAM AND EVE] to Jesus [q.v.] depicts for Muḥammad's people the meaning and destiny of their own cause. Biblical material, in independent shape, is rehearsed in lively corroboration of qurʾānic authority. All prophecy accumulates towards it, so that revelation may culminate. Other Scriptures are mentors, not masters. It is the ruling theme of prophecy as crisis which they consistently serve. The patriarchal retrospect witnesses to a continuity of truth and multiplies the signs by which the Meccan/Medinan situation must be read both in conflict and prosperity (Cragg, *Event,* 171).

Consequently, it is little surprising to find a particular hermeneutic trait familiar from the Hebrew Bible (see TORAH) and especially the Gospels (q.v.) prominent again in qurʾānic narrative: typology (Busse, Herrschertypen). "Types" are exemplary representations in scripture of still more momentous events or more significant figures yet to come. Thus the divine trials (see TRIAL) of the past are to be considered "types" of the last judgment (q.v.) that will supersede everything preceding it, the dispatch of earlier prophets in a way "prefigures" Muḥammad's activities. This device is crucial for the qurʾānic image of history:

It is this historical review of the past in the present which gives to the Qurʾān and Islam the characteristic quality of *Jihād* [q.v.], or struggle, in the deepest and non-technical sense of that term. The very sequence of the prophets is a sequence of law and claim, of insubordination and nemesis. The logic within it is the unremitting necessity of struggle and the necessary sinews of strength. To bring a divine message is to incur a human enmity and so, in turn, to enter a trial of stamina and resolve, of the will and the means to outstay the opposition.... In this logic, suffering is present as a preliminary to its redress. It is that which has to be endured before it can be terminated. It bears the odds until they can be evened and reversed. The successful eventuality is held open by the refusal to be denied it, and this demands persistence and non-compromise.... Existence is poised, so to speak, between prophecy and eschatology, in that the prophetic address to humanity must have, in token and in fact, that writ of success which eschatology brings to final authenticity in the last judgment. The utter unambiguity of the eschatological must belong suitably and surely with the interim evidence of prophetic standing in time and in power (Cragg, *Event,* 171-2).

Reflexions of myth and mythopoiesis in the Qurʾān

Virtual myths of history

In the following an attempt will be undertaken to classify myths and legends in the Qurʾān as to their cultural contexts. (Myths and legends are not taken to be mutually exclusive: viewing the stories about earlier prophets as legends does not preclude taking note of their mythical elements.) A historical classification following the biblical succession of "scripturalized myths" does not appear too promising in view of the non-historical disposition of the Qurʾān and the absence of the notion of a linear historical process leading up to the present of the listeners. The "atomism of time" that underlies the qurʾānic vision of history, "which is typological in nature and focused on the history of the prophets," has been noted (for more, see Böwering, Chronology, 319 f.). The myth of man's first transgression, the story of Adam (*Gen* 1:3), in the Qurʾān does not serve to initiate history as an unpredictable and ambiguous process of divine-human interaction, but rather constitutes one exemplary episode of the "anthropological constant" of human vulnerability to being seduced. Except for the expulsion from the garden, however, this does not bear grave consequences for the fate of humankind (see FALL OF MAN). The myth, which is introduced at a rather late stage of qurʾānic development and is presented in diverse contexts, serves to demonstrate changing insights into the nature of evil: it is less a myth of beginning than a debate about evil (see GOOD AND EVIL). The account will therefore be treated in its typological context (see "Transgressions" below).

Noah

Similarly, the biblically prominent myth of the renewal of the world after the flood (*Gen* 6:5-8) in the Qurʾān does not appear in its mythical-historical setting as the closure of a period of immediate divine interventions into creation (q.v.) as a whole. This story is related (or alluded to) within the two discourses of the destroyed peoples *(umam khāliya)* and of the prophets *(anbiyāʾ)*. First conveyed as the initial account of a chain of punishment legends in Q 54:9-17 (followed by stories about ʿĀd [q.v.], Thamūd [q.v.], Lot [q.v.], and the people of Pharaoh [q.v.; Firʿawn]) and, subsequently as a story filling a complete sūra, Q 71 (Sūrat Nūḥ, "Noah"; Q 71:1-28), the legend of Noah is introduced in isolation from a particular salvation-historical beginning, although the event is obviously imagined as preceding all the other stories in time. It is shaped after the pattern of the punishment stories that emerge during the first Meccan period. Accordingly, both the flood and the ark (q.v.) are devoid of mythical dimensions, being reduced to mere instruments of individual punishment and salvation respectively. The story continues to be remembered through the entire Meccan period, not only in extended lists of punishment stories (Q 7:69; 11:89; 14:9; 38:12; 50:12; 51:46), but also in narrative form. In Q 37:75-9 it is followed by a story about Abraham's confronting his unbelieving community and other episodes of the history of the Children of Israel (q.v.; Banū Isrāʾīl); in Q 26:105-22 it is followed by stories about ʿĀd, Thamūd, the people of Lot, the "People of the Thicket" (q.v.; *aṣḥāb al-ayka*), always presenting Noah as a member of his people (*akh,* Q 26:106) who tries to convert them. None of these reports, however, dwell on the mythical dimension of the story as the first major caesura in history.

Noah receives new momentum after the change of paradigm and the new orientation to the *kitāb* tradition of the Children of Israel. The viewing of the prophets as a chain of succession within the orbit of scripture gives each one an individual significance. This change is reflected in a particularly extensive version of Noah's story in Q 11:25-49, followed by kindred stories of ʿĀd and others. Here, both the preparation of the ark *(fulk)* and the selection of the animal species are mentioned (see ANIMAL LIFE). The cosmic dimension of the flood is alluded to, the final blessing on Noah sounding as if the event was meant as a caesura in salvation history (an echo of this version appears in Q 10:71-4). At this later stage of the canonical process, when the world of the book has replaced the scenario around the sanctuary of Mecca (q.v.), Noah ascends from his stance as a mere warner *(rasūl)* to become a prophet *(nabī)* in the line of Adam — (Noah) — Abraham — Jesus. In this context, the longevity (Noah remained among his people 950 years; Q 29:14) and genealogical relations in general occasionally gain momentum: thus the Children of Israel are presented as the "seed of those whom we carried with Noah" *(dhurriyyata man ḥamalnā maʿa nūḥ,* Q 17:3; cf. 19:58). In still later, Medinan sūras, like Q 33:7, when the Prophet himself has entered the rank of the prophets *(anbiyāʾ)* and prophets are viewed as partners in a covenant (q.v.), Noah appears here as the first: *(wa-idh akhadhnā mina l-nabiyyna mīthāqahum wa-minka wa-min nūḥ)*. A structuring of prophetical history is in the making and it is this period of time into which Q 19:58 fits: "These are those whom God blessed from the prophets from the seed of Adam and of those we carried with Noah [on the ark]" *(ūlāʾika lladhīna anʿama llāhu ʿalayhim min al-nabiyyīna min dhurriyyati ādama wa-mimman ḥamalnā maʿa nūḥ...)*. This development reaches its climax in Q 3:33: "Truly God preferred Adam and Noah and the family of Abraham and the family of ʿImrān above all the creatures" *(inna llāha ṣṭafā ādama wa-nūḥan wa-āla ibrāhīma wa-āla ʿimrāna ʿalā l-ʿālamīna)*. Accordingly, the divine commandments (q.v.) have been transmitted through that line of succession: Q 42:13, "He ordained for you the religion (q.v.) that he commended to Noah and which we inspire in you" *(sharaʿa lakum mina l-dīni mā waṣṣā bihi nūḥan wa-lladhī awḥaynā ilayka)*.

Still, Noah remains part of two traditions, that of an episodic warner (in Medinan sūras; Q 9:70; 22:42) — one of many — whose people *(qawm)* vanishes and who thus would have no spiritual survival and that of a prophet *(nabī)* whose reception is secured through his participation in a succession of prophets who belong to the scriptural, i.e. biblical, tradition. What is most striking in the

Noah-legend is the lack, or at least the fading appearance, of the essentially mythical characteristics of the story. Thus, the catastrophic uniqueness of the event, the vehemence of the divine wrath (see ANGER) inducing the creator to annihilate humankind, the universality of the catastrophe, are nowhere expressed. The historical dimension, the total renewal after the drowning (q.v.) of humankind is not dramatized, the divine re-acceptance of humankind being only partial (Q 11:48; to say nothing of the conclusion of a new covenant between God and man). Not surprisingly, the age before the diluvium is not marked as it is in the Bible and in later Islamic historiography (al-Azmeh, *Ibn Khaldun*) by particular physical anomalies, such as the existence of fabulous creatures and miraculous qualities in humans, thus appearing as an epoch which does not yet partake of the historical period proper, but demands a new, a second beginning. In the Qurʾān the flood has no such function.

David and Solomon — virtual cultural heroes?

Nor does the "Solomonic mythic florilegium" (see DAVID; SOLOMON), which in the Qurʾān reflects post-biblical rather than biblical knowledge, constitute a consistent story. It focuses on the two heroes' power over the animal and spirit world, as well as natural phenomena: David is lord of the birds (Q 38:17-9), he commands the mountains (Q 38:18; 34:10); Solomon understands the language of the birds (Q 27:16) and of the ants (Q 27:18-9), he commands the wind (Q 21:81; 34:12; 38:36; see AIR AND WIND), and is in control over the demons *(shayāṭīn)* and jinn (Q 21:82). At the same time, both are in the rank of prophets *(anbiyāʾ)*, a merit that in David's case is underlined by his receiving the psalms (q.v.; *zubur*, Q 17:55), his competent judgment (q.v.; Q 38:21-6; cf. *2 Sam* 2:1-15) and his just government (see JUSTICE AND INJUSTICE; AUTHORITY), which qualifies him to be called a *khalīfa* on earth (Q 38:26; see CALIPH). In Solomon's case this rank is evidenced by his being granted command over nature and demons. Yet, both remain symbolic figures (see SYMBOLIC IMAGERY), Solomon's essential fame being due to his miraculous relationship with animals and demons with particular supernatural faculties — a privilege that, however, does not distract him from his devotion to the one God. His faithfulness is particularly manifest in the episode with the Queen of Sheba (see BILQĪS). When her throne is transferred to his palace by the *ʿifrīt* (q.v.), he understands the miraculous act not as his personal triumph but as a trial *(fitna)* to prove his gratefulness (Q 27:40; see GRATITUDE AND INGRATITUDE). His aesthetically stunning palace *(ṣarḥ)* with fittings so fine that they produce a "trompe d'oeil" — the Queen takes the brilliant floor to be a water pool — becomes the reason for the conversion of the Queen to the worship of the one God, thus constituting an "antitype" to the building erected by Pharaoh (also *ṣarḥ*) with the blasphemous intent to have a view on the God of Moses (see BLASPHEMY). There are some hints at the conception of both figures as innovators: David is instructed to make coats of mail (Q 21:80; 34:10-11), and Solomon is knowledgeable about a source of metal (Q 34:12); yet their story is hardly apt to serve as an etiology for the human attainment of control over material resources and individual technical inventions; nor do the related facts mark initial achievements sufficient to portray the protagonists as cultural heroes.

Moses' exodus *(isrāʾ)*

The only qurʾānic narrative that could be viewed as a myth of history is the report of the exodus of Moses, which, in Jewish tradition, signifies the deliverance of the Israelites from slavery; for the Muslim community, this exodus becomes a prototype for the believers' taking refuge from oppressive unbelieving rulers (see OPPRESSION; OPPRESSED ON EARTH, THE). The event of the exodus *(isrā')* has certainly effected a strong influence on the Prophet's own experience of his emigration (q.v.; *hijra*); moreover, before that event, it served as a pattern of finding spiritual relief *(isrā')* in a situation of social suppression in Mecca that had become unbearable to the believers (Neuwirth, Remote temple). Still, the story is not reflected through a full-fledged narrative but is only briefly evoked (i.e. Q 20:77; 26:15-7; 37:115-6). It does not, moreover, represent the decisive turn in the history of Moses' people. It is worth noting that in the qur'ānic story of Moses, the exodus is rivaled by another solution for the oppressed Children of Israel since the salvation of Moses' people is also portrayed in terms of a typological reprise of the flood story (Busse, Herrschertypen, 75). Thus, the invitation to Noah and his family to settle after the flood (Q 23:29) finds its analogy in Q 17:104, where the Children of Israel are given (cf. also Q 7:137; 26:59) the land of Egypt (q.v.) with all its gardens (see GARDEN), springs (see SPRINGS AND FOUNTAINS), fields and treasures (Q 26:57-8; 44:25-8; see BLESSING; GRACE; WEALTH). It is perhaps not the change of real place (as in the exodus) that matters. In the qur'ānic view the promised land may be anywhere that it is possible for the believers to live uncompromised — whether the place is purged of unbelievers through a divine trial, or whether the unbelievers have no further access to the believers after the latter have found refuge by an emigration *(hijra)*. Indeed, an "exodus," an *isrā'*, may even be performed spiritually, as shown in the example of the Prophet's night journey (see ASCENSION) — his nocturnal translation to the Jerusalem (q.v.) temple (Q 17:1; see AQṢĀ MOSQUE).

Power and violence

Local history inscribed with God's terror: *al-umam al-khāliya*

There appears to be one single — though variegated — archetypal paradigm in the Qur'ān that has retained its cathartic power throughout the development of the corpus: the story of the annihilated nations, *al-umam al-khāliya* (see PUNISHMENT STORIES). This archetypal topic, which in the Qur'ān has taken the place of the biblical myth of the destruction of the Babylonian tower, is about human hubris resulting in a divine retaliation that annihilates the community and destroys their ambitious project of self-sufficient existence. In the Qur'ān it is not one event but a cycle of similar happenings that demonstrates this pattern. Repeatedly, ancient communities have waxed proud in view of their social success, their wealth, sometimes their luxuriously built residences, their security and fame (see PRIDE; ARROGANCE). Being reminded by a divine messenger (see SHUʿAYB, ṢĀLIḤ, HŪD) of God's claim to worship and thanksgiving they defy and mock the warning (see MOCKERY). They are then overtaken by God's punishment and destroyed. The enigma of the still visible ruins and the vague memory of formerly flourishing communities in the broader neighborhood of the listeners have thus been given an explanation: Not unfavorable social conditions (as presupposed for the deserted living spaces recalled in the amatory introduction of the pre-Islamic *qaṣīda*) or changes in the area's balance of power, but a dramatic divine intervention, an outburst of divine wrath, caused the disappearance of the once glorious cities (see CITY). The two most expressively presented concepts in these punishment stories are human hubris on the one hand, unfolded in "quotations" of the unbelievers' words of rejection, and divine wrath on the other, manifest in the rapidity, the suddenness of destruction often initiated by a divine sign, a seismic scream, or brought about by a vehement storm, an earthquake and the like.

Horovitz (*KU*), who first examined the punishment stories, classified them as "legends." They deserve, however, to be considered as archetypes: human hubris, entailing blasphemy, leads to divine retaliation. What is missing from the stories is the expression of a fatal human intent to rival God — as is characteristic of the biblical tower-builders. The qurʾānic city-dwellers do not seek a confrontation with God: not being monotheistic believers they treat the divine warning rather indifferently, reacting (if at all) with arrogance and annoyance. The qurʾānic narrative, thus, as far as the contest between the peoples and their messengers is concerned, remains largely devoid of dramatic effects. The ever-recurrent typological pattern is overwhelming; it is due to an interpretation of history informed by the experience of the Prophet and his community (see OCCASIONS OF REVELATION): "Just as the qurʾānic emphasis on the atomism of time had frozen the flux of time into that of reiterated instants of God's action, so its typology of history had collapsed the rich variety of past events into a regularly recurring pattern" (see Böwering, Chronology, 319). This certain loss in terms of quantitative knowledge of historical facts may be viewed, however, as a gain in expressiveness in the process of conveying the message. It is God's role that retains highly dramatic traits; the divine figure appears sometimes strikingly close to that of a mythic agent: "And their [i.e. the Thamūd's] lord doomed them for their sin and razed [their dwellings]" (*fa-damdama ʿalayhim rabbuhum bi-dhanbihim fa-sawwāhā*, Q 91:14), "and your lord poured on them the disaster" (*fa-ṣabba ʿalayhim rabbuka sawṭa ʿadhāb*, Q 89:13). This highly metaphoric speech (see METAPHOR) is made possible by the linguistic medium of *sajʿ*, which would be ill-suited to accommodate complex narratives. One has to keep in mind that the historical and temporal scope of the Qurʾān cannot be viewed in isolation from the Qurʾān's rhetorical tradition, whose *kāhin*-speech models are undeniable (see RHETORIC OF THE QURʾĀN). *Kāhin* speech is shrouded in mystery; rather than revealing facts, it encodes them. Since the situation in antiquity is typologically close to that of the believing group around the Prophet, the vacuum is filled with rejoinders from their experience. Thus the current situation acquires surplus meaning by being underscored with an archetypal dimension whose pattern even appears inscribed into the landscape of the broader homeland.

Although the stories about the flood, on the one hand, and the destruction of Sodom and Gomorrah (see LOT) and the punishment of Pharaoh, on the other, are not geographically associated with the Arabian peninsula (belonging, rather, to the cycle of biblical stories situated in the Holy Land or its surroundings, a cycle which at a later stage of the qurʾānic development becomes dissociated from the punishment stories), they reveal in the early sūras the pattern of the Arabian retaliation (q.v.) legends. In summary, one may note that the punishment stories provide a pattern for the initial lack of success experienced by the Prophet and his community in Mecca. Worldly values held by the unbelieving elites and an endangered and isolated stance on the part of the messenger, make up the ever-repeated pattern without generating a linear relation between them (for a reconstruction of the pre-Islamic myth wrought about the ancient people of Thamūd, see Stetkevych, *Golden bough*).

Trangressions of boundaries

The first act of disobedience as a double etiology: Man's exile from paradise, Satan's representation of evil

An explicit divine interdiction was violated by the first man, Adam, and his unnamed wife: despite a divine injunction not to approach a particular tree in paradise (q.v.), they both tasted the forbidden (q.v.) fruit (see AGRICULTURE AND VEGETATION). Through this act they became aware of their nakedness (see NUDITY). Shocked by this new awareness that is felt as shameful exposure, they feel the need to cover themselves (see MODESTY). Soon afterwards, they are called on by God to render account for their transgression (see BOUNDARIES AND PRECEPTS). Instead of being cursed and condemned to hard work and painful childbearing as in the biblical precedent, they are treated rather gently. They are sent "down" from paradise *(ihbiṭū)* to settle on earth (q.v.) — not, however, to their fatal detriment, since this punishment is immediately followed by a new offer of divine guidance (Neuwirth, Negotiating justice; see also ASTRAY). Nor is the news of their mortality, which is disclosed to them together with the news of their exile (Q 20:117), momentous since it is alleviated by the simultaneous assurance of their ultimate resurrection (q.v.).

It is true that the story serves *inter alia* to explain the existence of humankind on earth; this is not, however, in any striking contrast to their sojourn in paradise since, in the qurʾānic understanding, their terrestrial habitat is decent if not luxurious. More often, the story is adduced to demonstrate the dangerous nature of Satan — his obsequiousness exposing man's nakedness (Q 7:27), his insincerity in promising benefits he will not deliver (Q 7:22). Satan, who from the beginning of the qurʾānic reception of the story (Q 20) is instrumental in the couple's transgression, is only in the last report (Q 7) ultimately to blame. It is obviously not the etiological dimension that caused the story to be repeatedly presented in the Qurʾān, since a few virtual etiologies (which, in the biblical report support the significance of the narrative as a cultural myth) remain undeveloped in the Qurʾān, such as the fact of the first couple's achieving a mature perception of themselves, their learning about their sexuality (see SEX AND SEXUALITY) and their inventing the custom of clothing (q.v.). The telos of the story, rather, points to theodicy. It is true, the first couple were not substantially blamed and punished for their disobedience (q.v.), yet the pattern of "transgression followed by rendering account" — a particularly effective archetype — has been established as the primordial pattern of human-divine interaction (see RECORD OF HUMAN ACTIONS). In the qurʾānic understanding the regret of the perpetrator saves him from a hard punishment (see REPENTANCE AND PENANCE).

Satan, under the name of Iblīs, was viewed in the beginning as the tester, the agent of legitimate challenge to humans. He was delegated to perform this task during a debate with God that arose after he had shown his defiance of blind obedience (q.v.), refusing to bow down before a being — namely Adam (Q 15:33) — other than his divine lord (q.v.). Indeed, the transition of created beings from submissive creatures to autonomous agents in the interaction with the Divine, belonging to Adam in biblical tradition, in the Qurʾān is Iblīs' achievement whose tragic consequences he takes upon himself. It is only through his work that the elect community, who is not liable to fall victim to his seduction, becomes distinguishable from the unbelievers. Whereas God himself in the first debate scene agreed to the project proposed by Iblīs (Q 15:41), in the further development of the community Iblīs' image — once his persona has merged with that of Satan *(al-shayṭān)* — darkens considerably: in the end he appears as the enemy of humans, the personification of evil *par excellence*. He and his escorts will therefore be annihilated in hellfire so as to re-establish justice at the end of times (see HELL AND HELLFIRE). Iblīs is, however, rehabilitated in later Islamic tradition. Although the qur'ānic account of creation does not culminate in human acquisition of knowledge (see KNOWLEDGE AND LEARNING) as a fruit picked from the forbidden tree at Iblīs' instigation, still Iblīs is raised — in the profane tradition — to the rank of the seducer, the permanent agent of provocation through whom a substantial broadening of horizons of experience becomes possible. He enjoys an equally unique position in at least one branch of Ṣūfī tradition (see ṢŪFISM AND THE QUR'ĀN) that has strongly influenced literature, where Iblīs is acknowledged as the sole figure possessing knowledge about the true will of God. His ongoing influence — not only as an ambivalent, but as a tragic figure as well — continues to manifest itself in diverse forms (Awn, *Satan's tragedy;* Shaikh, *Der Teufel*).

The elect space: From Mecca to Jerusalem

The mythical notion of a space that excels over all other space is traceable in the Qur'ān, though it is widely modified to suit the framework of a religion of revelation. While there is a strong notion of Mecca's excellence in the early sūras (Q 90:1; 95:3; 105; 106), the focus during the Meccan era switches to Jerusalem, which first enjoys the unique rank of being the point of orientation in the prayer (q.v.) of the early Muslim worshippers (see QIBLA). Although the Qur'ān itself does not explicitly mention Jerusalem by name, the adoption of the rite to pray towards it clearly presupposes its high rank in the community. The night journey *(isrā')* of the Prophet in a miraculous way transferred him temporarily to the "remote temple" (Q 17:1, *al-masjid al-aqṣā*), the destination of the prayers of the community. During the later Meccan activities of the Prophet, Jerusalem with its temple becomes the prototype of a holy city. In Medina (q.v.) it served as the model for the perception of a religious center, after which the new Islamic holy city was shaped. Mecca, which takes over as the space of origin for Islam, is thus not only a place from which the Islamic ritual originated, but also — in analogy to Jerusalem (cf. *Isa* 2:3: For out of Zion shall go forth the Torah and the word of the Lord from Jerusalem) — the birthplace of Islamic verbal worship, as indicated in Q 2:129: "Our lord! And raise up among them a messenger from them who will recite to them your signs and teach them the book and the wisdom and enrich them. Truly you are the mighty, the wise" *(rabbanā wa-b'ath fīhim rasūlan minhum yatlū 'alayhim āyātika wa-yu'allimuhumu l-kitāba wa-l-ḥikmata wa-yuzakkīhim innaka anta l-'azīzu l-ḥakīm;* see Neuwirth, Spiritual meaning). As the place at which all Muslim prayers converge, Mecca is the center of the earth, the *omphalos mundi*.

Love and sexuality

Joseph and Zulaykha

The myth of the woman who, through her seduction of the man, brought mischief into the world does not exist in the Qur'ān (see GENDER; WOMEN AND THE QUR'ĀN). Eve was not instrumental in Adams's transgression and is thus not considered responsible for Adam's predicament. Still the notion of a devious behavior innate in women is confirmed in the Qur'ān, labeled *kayd al-nisāʾ*, which is explicitly and *par excellence* attributed to the unnamed wife of Potiphar, the Egyptian official in whose house Joseph (q.v.) was lodged. Although she does not succeed in seducing Joseph and leading him astray from his way as a chosen one of God (see ELECTION), she does exercise some power over him. Being sexually attracted to her and thus distracted from his exclusive devotion to God, he finds the strength to resist her only through divine intervention (Q 12:24). Still, she is not categorically derogated in the Qurʾān; rather, unlike the situation in the biblical story, she is given the opportunity to repent and acknowledge her moral failure. This opens the way for her post-qurʾānic rehabilitation and elevation to the rank of Joseph's beloved and, later, wife. It is worth noting that though her behavior in the Qurʾān appears to be an attempted act of *zinā* (see ADULTERY AND FORNICATION), she is not actually accused of such a transgression of the limits set to female freedom (see BOUNDARIES AND PRECEPTS). In view of her positive image in the Qurʾān, it is not surprising that she could be accepted in Ṣūfism as a female icon.

The virgin mother: Mary

A reverse projection of the seductress is the virgin mother, Mary (q.v.; Maryam). She, again viewed from the outward appearance of her fate, manifests a case of transgression of the limits of female freedom, although is herself innocent. Having borne a child outside of marriage, she is rescued from the wrath of her relatives by a miracle: her baby son is endowed with the power of speech (q.v.) and speaks on her behalf. He presents himself as God's elect, a rank also enjoyed by John (Yaḥyā; see JOHN THE BAPTIST), the son of Zechariah (q.v.; Zakariyyā), whose birth was likewise accompanied by miraculous circumstances. Mary is the only female figure in the Qurʾān presented by name; she also has the privilege of being personally addressed by God's word through an angelic messenger (see WORD OF GOD; HOLY SPIRIT; GABRIEL). In the Qurʾān, Mary is not presented as a suffering woman as she is in Christianity (see CHRISTIANS AND CHRISTIANITY) since she does not have to see her son suffer (see SUFFERING; CRUCIFIXION). In Islam the prototype of the suffering woman is, in later tradition, embodied in Fāṭima (q.v.), the daughter of the Prophet. Thus, the role that, according to Christian understanding, Mary plays in the eschatological realm is, in Islam, taken over by Fāṭima, although with a marked difference:

> Only Mary has a necessary role in the scheme of redemption. Fatima plays a more active role at the End of Days than does Mary, but there is no suggestion in Islam that redemption would be impossible without her. According to the (Shiʿite) Islamic view of redemption as the fulfillment of human life through suffering, Fatima, as the greatest sufferer on earth, will enjoy the greatest rewards on the day of resurrection (Sered, Rachel, Mary, Fatima, 136).

Paradisiacal distributions of the genders

What is not stressed in the narratives is, however, presupposed in the qurʾānic worldview: it is male dominance that "informs life on earth and life in heaven.... While the Qurʾān assures women of faith that they will go to heaven [Q 4:124; 16:97] it offers them no insight as to what their place in heaven will be" (Combs-Schilling, *Sacred performances*, 61). Paradisiacal space — this has been lamented over and over by Muslim feminists (see FEMINISM AND THE QURʾĀN) — seems to be equipped solely for the believer of the male sex. It is true that the depictions of paradise, which appear in the early sūras and portray banquet scenes with the believers being served by beautiful youths and enjoying the company of (or being married to) beautiful young girls, labeled *ḥūr ʿīn* (see HOURIS) for the striking beauty of their eyes, reflect a purely male imagination of ultimate happiness (Q 55:56-8; 44:54). These descriptions of the qurʾānic *janna* (lit. "garden") have been discussed in detail by Horovitz *(Koranische Paradies),* who suggests that they reflect magnifications of festal banquets familiar in the circles of tribal elites and well-known to the listeners of the Qurʾān from their representation in ancient Arabic poetry. They may thus be understood as static tableaux of both natural and sensual consummation and spiritual bliss. Andrew Rippin (Commerce of eschatology, 134), in contrast, has viewed these images as a "fundamental appreciation of ideal human nature as the monotheistic tradition conceives it."

The images of the garden have been interpreted by anthropologists, — who view them through their exegetical amplifications — however, primarily under the aspect of sexual satisfaction:

With the *ḥūrī,* sexual satisfaction is never ending, and not marred by fear as it is on earth. Men have nothing to fear from the *ḥūrīs,* for they have no personalities, no individual desires, no chance for roaming; the Qurʾān guarantees their virginity, that they will not have been touched by man nor jinn when the believing male enters them, and they will be permanently attached to the man to whom they are given (Combs-Schilling, *Sacred performances,* 95).

Whereas earlier sūras insist on these projections into the eternal sphere of earthly bliss understood on the basis of male experience, later texts modified the image. Their explicit mentioning of female participation in paradisiacal recompense (Q 43:70-3) reflects a new understanding of earthly and heavenly life on the side of the listeners. Meanwhile, a community had been established, where women — not least in the Prophet's own household (see WIVES OF THE PROPHET; FAMILY OF THE PROPHET) — played vital roles. The issue of transcendent happiness was no longer taken as part of a symbolic realm, but debated in its details and fleshed out to form a reference text for the believers. The "impressionist," somewhat enigmatic and highly symbolic text of the old *janna*-descriptions was transformed into a reference text where, ritually and legally, in terms of justice and morals, everything should be spelled out unambiguously.

It may be helpful for understanding the contextuality and historical conditions for the qurʾānic descriptions of *janna,* to remember that the Prophet himself may have had a more complex and positive appreciation of women.

Early Islam exhibits much the same trajectory in the definition of the female as does early Christianity… Islam has its ʿAʾisha [see ʿĀʾISHA BINT ABĪ BAKR] just as Christianity has its Mary Magdalene. Both are highly charged sexual and sensual females — the one suspected of adultery in the desert, the other confirmed of prostitution — and yet each is valued as somehow intrinsically pure and good in the eyes of the founder of the faith, Muhammad or Jesus. It seems plausible that these founders did not dichotomize sexuality and spirituality in the ways that their followers did, and in fact found them persuasively combined in these women. Yet their esteem for that combination was not to endure. Neither ʿAʾisha nor Mary Magdalene became the dominant image of the proper female in the respective cultural traditions that arose out of the two faiths. Muslims on the whole find blasphemous the notion that it might have been good for ʿAʾisha… to have become a public model for other women, while Christians on the whole find blasphemous the notion that Jesus might have exchanged sexual tenderness with Mary Magdalene.... Yet it could be argued that the founders of the two faiths were broader in their understanding of the possible combinations of faith, womanhood, and sexuality than the majority of their followers, and that they made that acceptance clear — Muhammad by dying in ʿĀʾisha's arms and Jesus by first appearing after his crucifixion to Mary Magdalene, whom he authorized to go and tell the male disciples the earthshaking news that he still lived. These events are recorded in the hallowed texts. Yet the dominant cultural perspectives that have developed in the contexts of these faiths for the most part leave by the wayside these two women as embodiments of proper womanhood and instead concentrate the collectivity's attention and definitions on immaculate conception and virginal mothers (Combs-Schilling, *Sacred performances*, 91-2).

Fates of the hero

There are a few figures in the Qurʾān who acquire heroic dimensions, the most prominent being Abraham, Joseph, Moses (see for his appearance in Q 18, Jung, Four archetypes), and Jesus (see Bauschke, *Jesus*). Their stories are not devoid of archetypal traits as the following selected examples may illustrate.

Abraham, destroyer of idols

Abraham is the protagonist of a most diversified narrative reported in several qurʾānic texts (Q 6:74-84; 19:41-50; 21:51-73; 26:69-86; 29:16-27; 37:83-98; 43:26-7; 60:4). The earliest achievement in his career is the smashing of the idols (see IDOLS AND IMAGES), i.e. the destruction of the old order, thus making a new order possible. The incident, which is not biblical but midrashic, portrays him as a cultural hero. A debate with an unbelieving ruler usually identified with Nimrod (q.v.; Q 2:258-60) and the destruction of the idols of his father (Q 6:74-84; 19:41-50; 21:57-8; 26:16-27; 37:93; see IDOLATRY AND IDOLATERS), which is followed by his being sentenced to be burnt alive — a fate from which he is saved by God (Q 21:68-9; 29:24; 37:97-8), leads to his expulsion from his homeland. Abraham performs a *hijra*, a secession from his father and his homeland to encounter God in a new land where he will raise his family (Q 19:48-9; 21:71; 29:26). Though a number of further encounters with God are recalled in the Qurʾān (his intimate relationship with the divine lord earns him the title of a friend of God, *khalīl Allāh;* see FRIENDS AND FRIENDSHIP), it is his early identification as a monotheist (*ḥanīf*, q.v.) in a pagan world, that elevates him to his unique rank, in the Qurʾān and later in Islam, as the founder of monotheistic worship. With his emigration he sets an example for the believer who, when living under persecutors of religion, chooses emigration. He becomes the prototype of the prophet Muḥammad and, as such, rightly figures prominently in the text of the Muslim ritual prayer.

Abraham and sacrifice

The subverted approach to the problem of succession: not by the son's replacing the father, but the father's preparedness to annihilate his son is reflected in the Qurʾān in the episode of Abraham's sacrifice (q.v.) of his son (Q 37:102-13). Unlike the biblical case, in the Qurʾān the son voluntarily sacrifices himself (Q 37:102) but the father is spared the enactment of the sacrifice through divine intervention. The story, which is the central etiology of the Islamic pilgrimage (q.v.; *ḥajj*), a ceremony believed to have been initiated by Abraham, has been interpreted by anthropologists in terms of a corroboration of patriarchy (q.v.).

The Ibrāhīm myth powerfully undergirds the rightful domination of father over son, of senior men over junior men, of all males over females and children — of patriarchy. Ibrāhīm (Islam's archetypal father) submitted to God's demand even to the point of trying to kill his own son, and the son, because he was faithful and loyal (Islam's archetypal son) actively cooperated with the father's attempt at his own sacrifice; the son knowingly submitted to what was to be his death at this father's hands.... Islam's myth both transcends and reinforces patrilineality, the inheritance [q.v.] of goods and position through the male line. Transcendence comes because, as told in the Qurʾān, the prophet Ibrāhīm had to deny his own father in order to remain faithful to the one God (Ibrāhīm's father rejected monotheism and forced the fissure between father and son). Yet the Qurʾān also reinforces patrilineality by portraying the ultimate sacrifice that God demands of humans as the sacrifice of the most precious tie on earth... the fundamental patrilineal connection. The myth of sacrifice ennobles that bond over all others. So at the same time that the Qurʾān underlines the limits of patrilineal affiliation (Muslims must deny it if it threatens the faith), it reinforces patrilineality, for it was the father in connection with the son that made for connection to the divine and won for father and son — and by extension also humanity — long life on earth and eternal life thereafter. According to tradition, Ibrāhīm and his son walked away from the place of sacrifice and went on to establish some of the holiest places in Islam (Combs-Schilling, *Sacred performances*, 57 f.).

Moses — prophet and leader of his people
The closeness of the Islamic Prophet to Moses is attested already in early sūras. Q 52 and Q 95 start with an oath (see OATHS) by Mount Sinai (q.v.) and the sanctuary of Mecca, the scene of Muḥammad's own activity. Moses is evoked in Meccan sūras more than 120 times, more often than any other biblical figure. This is not surprising since Moses is the Israelite prophet *par excellence*. To him God had spoken with an intimacy unrivaled by any other messenger. He had been granted the Torah and, by leading the exodus out of Egypt, had shaped the destiny of the Israelites in most significant ways. It is worth noting that Moses is portrayed first as a messenger sent to an unbelieving ruler, Pharaoh. But unlike the rest of the early warners, he is uniquely equipped for his task: he was called by God at a sacred place (*al-wādi l-muqaddas ṭūwan*, Q 20:12; cf. 79:16) where he was allowed to hear the voice of God himself — a point elaborated in later reports (Q 20:13; see ANTHROPOMORPHISM) — and was ordered to perform (and endorse) the ritual prayer (q.v.; *aqimi l-ṣalāta*, Q 20:14). It is this particular authorization and his subsequent delivery from fear (q.v.) and anxiety (*ishraḥ lī ṣadrī*, Q 20:25) that give him the strength to speak out in front of Pharaoh, the stubborn denier of the oneness of God (see INSOLENCE AND OBSTINACY). Moses is thus a prefiguration of the Prophet himself, who also was granted an intimate encounter with God, experiencing a vision — according to one interpretation — of God himself seated on his throne (Q 53:6-7: *dhū mirratin fa-stawā wa-huwa bi-l-ufuqi l-aʿlā;* see VISIONS; THRONE OF GOD), a supernatural experience which, like Moses', was staged in a particularly exalted place, near "the garden of promise" (*jannat al-maʾwā*, Q 53:15). Like Moses, Muḥammad

experienced a widening of the breast (Q 94:1: *a-lam nashraḥ laka ṣadraka*) during the early phase of his prophetic activity.

Later portrayals of Moses complement his fate before his divine call to prophethood without embellishing his ambivalent personality: while still in Egypt, he unintentionally killed a person, and is thus obliged to hide. It is on his way back from his refuge in Midian (q.v.) that he receives the divine call. The emphasis remains on his debates with the powerful ruler, Pharaoh, whom he is unable to convince, and who prevails over the messenger. Not unlike other stubborn unbelievers, Pharaoh is punished in this world and awaits punishment in the next. As in previous retaliation legends, in this case, too, the believers are saved, with a miraculous passage through the sea. The exodus *(isrāʾ),* which typologically resembles the *hijra,* is, however, not compared to that latter event. Moreover, it serves as a prototype for the Prophet's and the Meccan believers' spiritual exodus (Q 17:1) out of their local situation of distress; i.e. by imagining the Holy Land and orienting themselves in their prayers towards Jerusalem. Moses' role as a leader and lawgiver of his people is often evoked but rarely presented (see LAW AND THE QURʾĀN) — his trial of the culprits of the blasphemous veneration of the golden calf (Q 2:51-4; 20:87 f.; see CALF OF GOLD) is the only example of his practicing the ethical injunction to command the good and forbid the wrong (*al-amr bi-l-maʿrūf wa-l-nahy ʿan al-munkar,* see VIRTUES AND VICES, COMMANDING AND FORBIDDING).

Moses has also left traces in Islamic ritual, since his receiving the tablets of the law on Mount Sinai became significant for the Islamic festal calendar, with Ramaḍān (q.v.) having its prototype in the Mosaic Day of Atonement (see FASTING; ATONEMENT).

In the Medinan Sūrat al-Baqara ("The Cow"; Q 2), the sūra that contains the promulgation of the fast of Ramaḍān (Q 2:187-90), one of the main themes carries the motifs of the Moses story connected with the Day of Atonement. "Moses' stay on Mount Sinai, the sin of the golden calf, God's forgiveness [q.v.] and bestowal of the book... are repeated in sūra 2 with much emphasis" (cf. Goitein, Ramaḍān, 190). There is also a hint as to the time of the implementation of the Mosaic rule of fasting: the mention of the bestowal of the revelation together with that of *al-furqān* (lit. "decision, redemption, liberation") in Q 2:185 (*bayyinātin mina l-hudā wa-l-furqāni;* cf. Q 44:1-4; see CRITERION) — recalls the text commemorating the battle of Badr (q.v.; Q 8:41: *wa-mā anzalnā ʿalā ʿabdinā yawma l-furqāni yawma ltaqā l-jamʿān,* "what we revealed to our servant on the day of discernment, the day the two groups met"). In this latter context, *furqān* connotes a decisive, liberating victory over threatening enemies. It is both experiences — as K. Wagtendonk *(Fasting)* has concluded — the decisive military victory of the Muslim community and the bestowal of the book upon them, that have given rise to the institution of the month of fasting in Islam. This is very much in accordance with the case of Moses (Q 2:53: *wa-idh ātaynā mūsā l-kitāba wa-l-furqāna,* "when we gave Moses the book and the criterion"), the central figure of the founding legend of Jewish fasting on the Day of Atonement, who likewise brought his people a twofold blessing, political liberation and divine revelation (see POLITICS AND THE QURʾĀN).

Angelika Neuwirth

Bibliography

R. Alter, *The art of biblical narrative,* New York 1981; id. and F. Kermode (eds.), *The literary guide to the Bible,* Cambridge, MA 1987; J. Assmann,

Der zweidimensionale Mensch. Das Fest als Medium des kollektiven Gedächtnisses, in id. (ed.), *Das Fest und das Heilige, Religiöse Kontrapunkte zur Alltagswelt. Studien zum Verstehen fremder Religionen,* Gütersloh 1991, 13-30; P.J. Awn, *Satan's tragedy and redemption. Iblis in Sufi psychology,* Leiden 1983; A. al-Azmeh, *Ibn Khaldun in modern scholarship. A study in Orientalism,* London 1981; M. Bauschke, *Jesus im Koran,* Köln 2001; G. Böwering, Chronology and the Qur'ān, in *EQ,* i, 316-35; H. Busse, Herrschertypen im Koran, in U. Haarmann and P. Bachmann (eds.), *Die Islamische Welt zwischen Mittelaltr and Neuzeit. Festschrift für Hans Robert Roemer zum 65. Geburtstag,* Beirut/Wiesbaden 1979, 56-80; id., *Die theologischen Beziehungen des Islam zu Judentum und Christentum. Grundlagen des Dialogs im Koran und die gegewärtige Situation,* Darmstadt 1988; M.E. Combs-Schilling, *Sacred performances. Islam, sexuality, and sacrifice,* New York 1989; K. Cragg, *The event of the Qur'ān. Islam in its scripture,* Oxford 1971; F. Donner, *Narratives of Islamic origins. The beginning of Islamic historical writing,* Princeton 1998; N. Frye, *The great code. The Bible and literature,* San Diego 1983; J.B. Gabel, Ch.B. Wheeler and A.D. York, *The Bible as literature. An introduction,* Oxford 2000; C. Gilliot, Abraham eut-il un regard peccamineux? in E. Chaumont et al. (eds.), *Mélanges Gimaret. Autour du regard,* Leuven 2003, 33-51; id., Les trois mensonges d'Abraham dans la tradition interprétante musulmane. Repères sur la naissance et le développement de l'exégèse en Islam, in *IOS* 17 (1997), 37-87; F. Goitein, Zur Enstehung des Ramadans, in *Der Islam* 18 (1929), 189-95; I. Goldziher, *Der Mythos bei den Hebräern und seine geschichtliche Entwicklung,* Leipzig 1879, repr. Leipzig 1987 (for the problem of myths in general); J. Horovitz, *Das Koranische Paradies. Scripta universitatis atque bibliothecae hierosolymitanarum. Orientalia et Judaica Volumen I. Curavit collegium eruditorum,* Jerusalem 1923; id., *KU;* C.J. Jung, Four archetypes. Mother/rebirth/spirit/trickster, in *The collected works of C.J. Jung,* vol. ix, part 1, trans. R.F.C. Hull, Princeton 1970 (1959), 69-81; T. Khalidi, *Arabic historical thought in the classical period,* Cambridge 1995; S. Lowin, *The making of a forefather,* Ph.D. diss., U. Chicago 2001; D. Marshall, *God, Muhammad and the unbelievers,* Richmond, Surrey 1999; A. Neuwirth, Erzählen als kanonischer Prozeß. Die Mose-Erzählung im Wandel der koranischen Geschichte, in U. Rebstock et al. (eds.), *Islamstudien ohne Ende* (forthcoming); id., From the sacred mosque to the remote temple. *Sūrat al-isrā'* between text and commentary, in J. McAuliffe, B. Walfish and J. Goering (eds.), *With reverence for the word,* Oxford 2003, 376-407; id., Negotiating justice. A pre-canonical reading of the qur'ānic creation accounts, in *Journal of qur'anic studies* 1 (1999), 25-41; 2 (2000), 1-18; id., The spiritual meaning of Jerusalem in Islam, in N. Rosovsky (ed.), *City of the great king. Jerusalem from David to the present,* Harvard 1996, 93-116, 483-95; id., *Studien;* id., Three religious feasts between texts of violence and liturgies of reconciliation, in Th. Scheffler (ed.), *Religion between violence and reconciliation,* Beirut 2002, 49-82; R. Paret, Das Geschichtsbild Mohammeds, in *Welt als Geschichte* 11 (1951), 214-24; A. Rippin, The commerce of eschatology, in Wild, *Text,* 125-36; id., Muhammad in the Qur'ān. Reading scripture in the 21st century, in H. Motzki (ed.), *The biography of Muhammad. The issue of the sources,* Leiden 2000, 298-310; S. Sered, Rachel, Mary, and Fatima, in *Cultural anthropology* 6 (1991), 131-46; Kh. Shaikh, *Der Teufel in der modernen arabischen Literatur. Die Rezeption eines europäischen Motivs in der arabischen Belletristik, Dramatik und Poesie des 19. und 20. Jahrhunderts,* Berlin 1986; Speyer, *Erzählungen;* J. Stetkevych, *The golden bough. Studies in Arabian myth,* Bloomington 1996; R. Tottoli, *I profeti biblici nella tradizione islamica,* Brescia 1999; K. Wagtendonk, *Fasting in the Koran,* Leiden 1968; J. Wellhausen, *Reste altarabischen Heidentums,* Berlin 1897, repr. 1927, 1961; H. Zirker, *Christentum und Islam. Theologische Verwandtschaft und Konkurrenz,* Düsseldorf 1989.

N

Nabī see PROPHETS AND PROPHETHOOD; MUḤAMMAD

Nadhīr see WARNER

Naḍīr (Banū al-)

One of several Jewish clans of Medina (q.v.) in pre- and early Islamic times (see JEWS AND JUDAISM; TRIBES AND CLANS; PRE-ISLAMIC ARABIA AND THE QUR'ĀN). In the Islamic tradition, they are usually considered part of the triad of important Medinan Jewish clans that also includes the Banū Qaynuqā' (see QAYNUQĀ') and the Banū Qurayẓa, though often only the Naḍīr and the Qurayẓa (q.v.) are mentioned. The latter two were sometimes called *al-kāhinān,* "the two priest clans" and Arabic sources provide an Arabicized "Israelite" genealogy of the Naḍīr reaching back to Aaron (q.v.; Hārūn).

The actual origin of the Naḍīr is obscure, as is the derivation of their name. A number of persons belonging to them are known by name from the Arabic sources and some of these play an important role in Muḥammad's Medinan period (see CHRONOLOGY AND THE QUR'ĀN). Among the latter are the poet Ka'b b. al-Ashraf, who mocked (see MOCKERY) the Prophet and was then assassinated in a nocturnal raid to Khaybar (see EXPEDITIONS AND BATTLES); Sallām b. Abī l-Ḥuqayq, likewise assassinated in Khaybar; and Ḥuyayy b. Akhṭab, the father of Ṣafīya, who eventually was one of Muḥammad's wives (see WIVES OF THE PROPHET). The Naḍīr, we are told, supported the Meccan allies against the Muslims, e.g. by sheltering Abū Sufyān and inciting the Meccans (as well as other Jewish clans) to oppose the Prophet (see OPPOSITION TO MUḤAMMAD).

The story of the Naḍīr and the exact chronology of events cannot, from today's perspective, be reconstructed with certainty. The most common version is as follows: After growing tensions, Ka'b b. al-Ashraf was killed in 3/625. Then, after the battle of Uḥud (q.v.), the Naḍīr attempted to assassinate Muḥammad by having a rock fall upon him. The plot failed but the Muslims laid siege to their quarter in late 3 or 4/625. After about two weeks and possibly without any serious fighting (q.v.), the Naḍīr capitulated; they had lost their spirit when Muḥammad ordered their palms (see DATE PALM) to be destroyed, reference to which is found in Q 59:5, according to

Muslim exegetes (see EXEGESIS OF THE QURʾĀN: CLASSICAL AND MEDIEVAL). The Naḍīr agreed to leave Medina for Khaybar on the condition that they carry away their movable belongings but surrender their lands and dwellings. When the Muslims conquered Khaybar in 7/628, the Naḍīr were expelled again and this time left for Syria (q.v.). In Khaybar, Ṣafīya was taken captive; the Prophet freed her, she converted to Islam and was married to him.

This "orthodox" account of the conflict with the Naḍīr is, if studied in detail, not without serious drawbacks. Other sources report diverse motives for the siege (e.g. the Naḍīr breaking a treaty with the Muslims), and the sequence of events remains confused; even the second expulsion of the Naḍīr from Khaybar is questionable. The actions of prominent members of the Naḍīr cannot be fully individualized, and some later descendants of the Naḍīr whose existence is ascertained for the first Islamic centuries remain completely obscure.

Although the Naḍīr are not named in the Qurʾān, a number of passages are often said to refer to them or to one of their members, e.g. Q 2:84 f., 178, 256; 4:51, 60; 5:11, 42. Q 59:2-15 is, however, by far the most important passage. These verses relate, according to the majority of sources, to the siege and expulsion of the Naḍīr. Although these verses do mention some details of what is reported in the "orthodox" version (e.g. the destruction of the palm trees), the bulk of this passage deals with the partition of the booty (q.v.) among the Muslims (Q 59:6-10). In any case, the general vagueness of Q 59:2-15 also supports those existing reports that differ from the "orthodox" version of what, exactly, happened to the Naḍīr and why. It seems significant that some early exegetes did claim — due to the use, in Q 59:2, of the ambiguous term *al-ḥashr*, which might mean a grouping together of people (such as for a siege or for an expulsion) or the congregation of humankind on the last day (see LAST JUDGMENT) — that these verses do not refer to a historical event at all, but rather to the fate of the Jews at the end of time (see ESCHATOLOGY; APOCALYPSE).

Marco Schöller

Bibliography
Primary (additional information may be gleaned from works on the so-called "occasions of revelation" [q.v.], but also from Qurʾān commentaries on the verses mentioned above, particularly Q 59:2 f.; legal compendia, especially the "war chapters" that deal with siege and expulsion, the partition of booty and the destruction of trees; ḥadīth collections; dictionaries [s.v. *n-ḍ-r*] and geographical writings): Ibn Isḥāq, *Sīra;* al-Samhūdī, *Wafāʾ al-wafā bi-akhbār dār al-muṣṭafā,* 4 vols. in 3, 1374/1955 (and repr.; partly trans. by J. Wellhausen, *Geschichte der Stadt Medina,* Göttingen 1860; this work is of paramount importance for the pre-Islamic period and topographical details); Wāqidī, *Maghāzī.*
Secondary: R. Bell, Sūrat al-Ḥashr. A study of its composition, in *MW* 38 (1948), 29-42; J. Horovitz, Biblische Nachwirkungen in der *Sīra,* in *Der Islam* 12 (1992), 184-9; M.J. Kister, Notes on the papyrus text about Muḥammad's campaign against the Banū al-Naḍīr, in *Archiv Orientální* 32 (1964), 233-6; M. Lecker, Did Muḥammad conclude treaties with the Jewish tribes Naḍīr, Qurayẓa and Qaynuqāʿ? in *IOS* 17 (1997), 29-36; id., *Jews and Arabs in pre- and early Islamic Arabia,* Aldershot 1998; H. Motzki (ed.), *The biography of Muḥammad. The issue of the sources,* Leiden 2000; U. Rubin, The assassination of Kaʿb b. al-Ashraf, in *Oriens* 32 (1990), 65-71; M. Schöller, *Exegetisches Denken und Prophetenbiographie. Eine quellenkritische Analyse der Sīra-Überlieferung zu Muḥammads Konflikt mit den Juden,* Wiesbaden 1998; id., Die Palmen *(līna)* der Banū n-Naḍīr und die Interpretation von Koran 59:5, in *ZDMG* 146 (1996), 317-80; id., In welchem Jahr wurden die Banū l-Naḍīr aus Medina vertrieben? in *Der Islam* 73 (1996), 1-39; A.J. Wensinck, *Muḥammad and the Jews of Medina,* trans. W.H. Behn, Berlin 1982[2].

Nafs

see SOUL; SPIRIT; LIFE; ANATOMY

Najrān

A major Arab urban center of pre-Islamic south Arabia, not attested by name in the Qurʾān, but probably alluded to in Q 34:18 and 85:10. The dominant group of the city was the tribe of Balḥārith, the chief clan of whom was Banū ʿAbd al-Madān (see TRIBES AND CLANS; ARABS; PRE-ISLAMIC ARABIA AND THE QURʾĀN). Najrān was both an agricultural and an industrial center producing cereals, fruits, vegetables, leather and textiles (see HIDES AND FLEECE; HUNTING AND FISHING; CITY; AGRICULTURE AND VEGETATION). It was also a caravan (q.v.) city, at which the celebrated spice route bifurcated, running through Yamāma into Mesopotamia and through the Ḥijāz into Syria (q.v.; Bilād al-Shām; see also GEOGRAPHY). But the flourishing caravan city became involved in religion — Judaism, Christianity, and Islam — which changed the course of its life and history (see JEWS AND JUDAISM; CHRISTIANS AND CHRISTIANITY).

Christianity reached it in the fifth century, and soon Najrān became an episcopal see and the main center of Christianity — predominantly Monophysite — in the Arabian peninsula. Around 520 C.E., Yūsuf, the Judaizing king of Ḥimyarite south Arabia (see YEMEN; SOUTH ARABIA, RELIGION IN PRE-ISLAMIC), persecuted the Christians of the region and some four hundred Najrānites were killed, both men and women, including their chief, al-Ḥārith/Arethas. Shortly thereafter, the Ethiopians (see ABYSSINIA) restored Christianity and this ushered in the golden period of Najrān as an Arabian martyropolis, "the city of martyrs," and the holy city of the Arabs for one hundred years. A great martyrion was built, Kaʿbat Najrān, which became a pilgrimage center for the Christian Arabs. The cult of relics was given an impetus, and martyria were constructed both in south Arabia and in Syria (Bilād al-Shām) among the Monophysite Ghassānids, relatives of the Balḥārith of Najrān. Its martyrs were canonized by the universal Church, which celebrates their feast on the 24th of October.

The rise of Islam in the seventh century profoundly affected the fortunes of Najrān. The two phases of its encounter with Islam, first the dialogue and then the confrontation, represent the earliest chapter in the history of Muslim-Christian relations. The first friendly encounter is reflected in the figure of Quss, said to have been the bishop of Najrān. It is not altogether incredible that he was such and that Muḥammad did indeed hear him preach at ʿUkāẓ. Najrān is implied in a qurʾānic verse (Q 34:18) either as one of the "blessed cities" or those "clearly visible" while a tradition attributed to Muḥammad (see ḤADĪTH AND THE QURʾĀN) considers it one of the protected, guarded cities. An echo of the martyrdom in Najrān may possibly be audible in a qurʾānic verse, Q 85:10 (and not in the allusion to the People of the Ditch [q.v.] of Q 85:4-9, as is often thought).

The Muslim conquest of south Arabia put Islam and Najrān on a collision course. A delegation reached the prophet Muḥammad from Najrān in Medina (q.v.) in 10/630. The objurgation (*mubāhala*, see CURSE; OATHS) was averted when the delegation withdrew from the contest, and Muḥammad concluded a treaty with them. In this treaty, the Najrānites were assured of their freedom of worship (q.v.) but they had to pay an annual tribute (see TAXATION; CONTRACTS AND ALLIANCES; RELIGIOUS PLURALISM AND THE QURʾĀN). This treaty was the first of its kind between the nascent Muslim state and a Christian one, the city-state of Najrān. Soon, during the caliphate of ʿUmar, the Najrānites were ordered to vacate their city, which they did, settling in Iraq (q.v.) in al-Najrāniyya, a locale not far from Kūfa.

Christianity, however, did not entirely vanish from Najrān but lingered into early Islamic times. Part of Balḥārith apparently remained and did not emigrate. In due course, Christian Najrān did vanish and became a toponym denoting a heap of ruins, called Ukhdūd (q.v.), while another Najrān, Muslim Najrān, arose to the north-west of Ukhdūd, and whose Arabs still call themselves Balḥārith; today, both lie in the district of ʿAsīr in Saudi Arabia.

Irfan A. Shahid

Bibliography
Primary: M. Ḥamīdullāh, *Majmūʿat al-wathāʾiq al-siyāsiyya,* Beirut 1985, 165-99; Ibn al-Mujāwir, Yūsuf b. Yaʿqūb, *Tārīkh al-mustabṣir,* ed. O. Løfgren, 2 vols., Leiden 1954, ii, 208-17; A. Moberg (ed. and trans.), *The Book of the Ḥimyarites,* Lund 1924; I. Shahīd, *The martyrs of Najrān,* Leuven 1971; Yāqūt, *Buldān,* Beirut 1957, v, 266-71 (esp. 269).
Secondary: J. Beaucamp, F. Briquel-Chatonnet and C. Robin, La persécution des chrétins de Nagrān et la chronologie himyarite, in *ARAM* 11-12 (1999-2000), 15-83; H. Lammens, Le califat de Yazid I, in *MFOB* (1912), v, 648-88; L. Massignon, *Opera minora,* 3 vols., Paris 1963, i, 550-72; Sezgin, *GAS,* ii, 180-1; I. Shahīd, Byzantium in south Arabia, in *Dumbarton Oaks papers* 33 (1979), 23-94.

Nakedness see NUDITY

Names of God see GOD AND HIS ATTRIBUTES

Names of the Prophet

The proper personal name as well as the titles and other additional names Muḥammad (q.v.) has claimed, or by which Muslims have recognized him.

The personal name of the Prophet

According to the rules of Arabic nomenclature, the full personal name of Islam's founder was Abū l-Qāsim Muḥammad b. ʿAbdallāh al-Hāshimī al-Qurashī. The *kunya* Abū l-Qāsim recalls that he was the father of a boy called al-Qāsim, who died at an early age. Some ḥadīths (see ḤADĪTH AND THE QURʾĀN) sought to limit the use of this *kunya,* after the time of Muḥammad (Déclais, La *kunya*). The name Muḥammad, "worthy of praise," had been used before Islam, albeit rarely (recently some western scholars have interpreted the belabored attempts to find attestations of "Muḥammad" in the Age of Ignorance [q.v.; *jāhiliyya*] as evidence that Muḥammad was not, in fact, the Prophet's given name). Ibn Saʿd collected several pious traditions, according to which five people (including an *usquf,* bishop) had been given this name before Islam. Their parents hoped that each would be the awaited prophet (see PROPHETS AND PROPHETHOOD). For his part, al-Qāḍī ʿIyāḍ (d. 544/1149) indicates that there were others who were called Muḥammad (*al-Shifāʾ,* 230) when he states: "God prevented those with this name from claiming to be prophets or others declaring them to be so or some cause manifesting itself in them which might make anyone consider the merits of their case." ʿAbdallāh is the name traditionally ascribed to Muḥammad's father. The other names indicate that he belonged to the Hāshim clan of the Quraysh (q.v.) tribe (see TRIBES AND CLANS; FAMILY OF THE PROPHET).

The Qurʾān mentions the name Muḥammad four times (Q 3:144; 33:40; 47:2; 48:29). In another verse (Q 61:6) the name appears as Aḥmad and its meaning is disputed. In this verse, Jesus (q.v.) states: "I announce a messenger (q.v.) who will come after me, whose name will be Aḥmad." The majority of commentators have regarded it as a proper name but it may be simply a superlative adjective: "whose name will be most deserving of praise" (a reference to the meaning of Muḥammad). In the reading of Ubayy b. Kaʿb, this verse is rather different: "I announce a prophet whose community (see COMMUNITY AND SOCIETY IN THE QURʾĀN) will be the final one and by whom God will put the final seal on prophets and messengers" (Paret, *Kommentar,* 476). Be that as it may, Aḥmad has become a proper name among Muslims. The expressions *al-rasūl,* "the messenger" (Q 2:143; 3:32, 86, etc.), and *al-nabī,* "the Prophet" (Q 3:68; 5:81, etc.), indicate his mission and serve as actual proper names in the same way as "Christ" is used to describe Jesus of Nazareth by Christians (see CHRISTIANS AND CHRISTIANITY).

The names and titles of the Prophet in the ḥadīth collections

Mālik b. Anas (d. 179/796) concluded his *Muwaṭṭaʾ* with a section entitled "Chapter on the Names of the Prophet," which contains the following single ḥadīth of Jubayr b. Muṭʿim: "The Prophet said: 'I have five names. I am Muḥammad; I am Aḥmad; I am al-Māḥī, because through me God abolishes unbelief; I am al-Ḥāshir because men will be gathered behind me (at the end of time); I am al-ʿĀqib ("the last").'" Al-Bukhārī (d. 256/870; *Ṣaḥīḥ, Kitāb al-Manāqib*) has a section entitled "The Names of the Prophet." He quotes Q 33:40, 48:29 and Q 61:6, cites the above-mentioned ḥadīth of Jubayr and adds the following ḥadīth of Abū Hurayra (d. ca. 58/678): "The messenger of God has said: 'Do you not admire how God has turned away from me the insult and the curse of the Quraysh? They insult a *mudhammam,* they curse a *mudhammam,* whereas I am a *muḥammad.*'" He ends with a parable upon "the seal of the prophets" and a ḥadīth on the Prophet's *kunya.* Muslim *(Ṣaḥīḥ, Kitāb al-Faḍāʾil)* has the same heading, under which he quotes the ḥadīth of Jubayr and the following one by Abū Mūsā al-Ashʿarī: "The messenger of God told us some of the names he had. He said 'I am Muḥammad and Aḥmad and al-Muqaffī (the one who comes after the others; cf. Q 2:87; 5:46; 57:27) and al-Ḥāshir and the Prophet of repentance (see REPENTANCE AND PENANCE) and the Prophet of mercy (q.v.).'" The *Musnad* of Ibn Ḥanbal quotes the same ḥadīths in the sections dedicated to Jubayr (iv, 80-4), to Abū Hurayra (ii, 244), to Abū Mūsā (iv, 404, with the variant "Prophet of battles" [see EXPEDITIONS AND BATTLES] instead of "Prophet of mercy"), and to Ḥudhayfa b. al-Yamān (v, 405). In the same way, he recounts from ʿAwf b. Mālik (vi, 25) how the Prophet proclaimed his titles before a Jewish assembly that refused to recognize him (see JEWS AND JUDAISM): "By God, I am al-Ḥāshir, I am al-ʿĀqib, I am the chosen Prophet *(al-nabī al-muṣṭafā)* whether you believe it or not!"

These lists have become a traditional, canonical set of information, as can be shown by Ibn Saʿd (*Ṭabaqāt,* i, 104), Ibn Ḥazm al-Andalusī (*Jawāmiʿ,* 19) or again by al-Ghazālī (d. 505/1111; *Iḥyāʾ, K. al-ʿĀdāt, ādāb al-maʿīsha wa-akhlāq al-nubuwwa*). Strictly speaking, these names are actually titles that define Muḥammad's mission. Their occurrence in collections of ḥadīth serves a dual purpose. Faced with the Arabs (q.v.) of Medina (q.v.) and the earlier religions (see SOUTH ARABIA, RELIGION IN PRE-ISLAMIC), it is an affirmation that the Prophet of Islam was entrusted with a definitive and universal mission. And it perhaps also seeks to restrain the enthusiasm of the devout by restricting the names of the Prophet to ten or fewer.

Devotional litanies

In the *Musnad* of Ibn Ḥanbal, the ḥadīth of Abū Mūsā is introduced thus: "The messenger of God told us his names. We have retained some of them but not others." This is an implicit admission that the Prophet had more names that are not known to us. There is nothing to prevent the faithful from seeking to find them once more and reciting them in certain instances, as in devotion. This is why lists appeared of what are called *al-asmāʾ al-sharīfa,* "the noble names," some comprising ninety-nine names, i.e. the same number as "the beautiful names" of God (see GOD AND HIS ATTRIBUTES), some with fewer, some with many more (cf. Epalza, Los nombros; Schimmel, *And Muḥammad,* 105-22). One example of the popular devotion that centered around the names of the Prophet (often taking the form of "litanies") is evidenced by the 201 names of Muḥammad contained in the list compiled by Imām al-Juzūlī (d. 869/1465; an Ar. version, with commentary, is found in al-Sharnūbī's *Sharḥ;* for an Eng. rendition of a similar list, see Ebied and Young, List; Rudvin, Supplementary note).

This phenomenon occurred at the same time as the establishment of the feast of the birth of the Prophet (*mawlid nabawī,* see FESTIVALS AND COMMEMORATIVE DAYS) in the seventh/thirteenth century; on this occasion, in fact, the faithful recited panegyrics in praise of the Prophet, in particular, the well-known *Burda,* "The Prophet's mantle," of the poet al-Buṣīrī (609-93/1213-95). Curiously, it was in this same period that devotion to the name of Jesus was becoming widespread in Christendom, particularly under the influence of St. Bernard (Noye, Jésus, 1115-20).

Certain scholars, such as al-Ghazālī (cf. Epalza, Los nombros, 152 n. 13, citing the thesis of F.M. Pareja, *Mahoma en el Islam,* Rome 1946, 67-8), criticized those who gave the Prophet names other than those that had been given him by his family and opposed the veneration of the names of the Prophet, a practice that, to them, seemed to involve a dangerous confusion with devotion to the names of God. Others, seeing these additional names as an established traditional collection, sought to understand and explain it. Thus al-Qāḍī ʿIyāḍ, an important figure in Andalusian Mālikī literature (see LAW AND THE QURʾĀN), dedicates eighteen pages of his popular work *al-Shifāʾ bi-taʿrīf ḥuqūq al-muṣṭafā,* "The healing through recognizing the rights of the chosen one," to the names of the Prophet (al-Qāḍī ʿIyāḍ, *Shifāʾ,* i, 228-46). In an initial chapter, he lists them as follows: Firstly, those laid down in the ḥadīths of Jubayr, Naqqāsh, Abū Mūsā and Makkī (who talks of "ten names," including Ṭā-Hā and Yā-Sīn, the initial letters of Q 20 and Q 36, respectively; it may be noted here that an exegetical trend existed wherein names of the Prophet were derived from the so-called "mysterious letters" [q.v.]). Secondly, there are those designations found in the Qurʾān itself, such as: *shāhid,* "witness" (see WITNESSING AND TESTIFYING); *mubashshir,* "bearer of glad tidings" (see GOOD NEWS); *nadhīr,* "warner" (q.v.); *dāʿī ilā llāh,* "caller to God" (see INVITATION); *sirājan munīran,* "shining lamp" (Q 33:46; see LAMP; LIGHT); or *al-ʿurwa al-wuthqā,* "the firmest handle" (Q 2:256); *al-nabī al-ummī,* "the Prophet coming from a pagan milieu" (Q 7:157-8; see ILLITERACY; LITERACY; UMMĪ; POLYTHEISM AND ATHEISM), etc.; or "in the earlier books of God, in the books (see BOOK) of the prophets, in the ḥadīths of his messenger, in the general practice of his community," as *al-muṣṭafā,* "the chosen one"; *al-ḥabīb,* "the beloved" (see LOVE AND AFFECTION); *sayyid waladi ādam,* "the lord (q.v.) of the sons of Adam" (see ADAM AND EVE), etc. Next, there are the names of supposed biblical origin, such as *al-mutawakkil,* "he who trusts" (see TRUST AND PATIENCE); *al-mukhtār,* "the chosen one";

muqīm al-sunna, "he who re-establishes the sunna (q.v.)"; *al-muqaddas,* "the holy one"; *rūḥ al-qudus,* "the spirit of holiness" and *rūḥ al-ḥaqq,* "the spirit of truth," "which is the meaning of Paraclete in the Gospel" (al-Qāḍī ʿIyāḍ, *al-Shifāʾ;* see HOLY SPIRIT; SPIRIT; TRUTH; GOSPEL). Finally, there are some names taken from earlier books, such as *mādh mādh,* which means *ṭayyib ṭayyib,* "twice good," the result of a midrashic interpretation of the Hebrew *ṭōv me ʾōd,* "very good," of Genesis 1:31. Other names are taken from Syriac (see SYRIAC AND THE QURʾĀN; SCRIPTURE AND THE QURʾĀN), such as *munḥaminnā,* "the comforter"; and from the Torah (q.v.), such as *uḥīd,* meaning "the man with the rod of fire" (cf. the Syriac *aḥīd kul,* "pankrator," and *Ps* 2:9; *Rev* 19:15) and taken to be an allusion to the "flexible sword" of Muḥammad. Al-Qāḍī ʿIyāḍ concludes: "In these books, there are many indications, titles and signs regarding him and, God willing, we will be satisfied with those we have mentioned."

The following chapter of al-Qāḍī ʿIyāḍ's book concerns "the honor (q.v.) which God has heaped upon the Prophet, by granting him some of his [i.e. God's] beautiful names and bestowing upon him some of his attributes." Indeed, if some prophets had one or two names in common with God, Muḥammad may be reckoned to have had some thirty. Al-Qāḍī ʿIyāḍ lists these and shows how the Qurʾān allows them to be attributed to the Prophet; *nūr,* "light," from Q 5:15 is but one example. Sometimes the justification comes from both the Qurʾān and the Bible: thus it is with *ʿaẓīm,* "great," from Q 68:4 and Genesis 21:18 (wherein, referencing Ishmael [q.v.], God says he "will make of him a great nation"). Sometimes, however, the explanation for a particular designation is taken from the Bible in spite of an explicit qurʾānic denial of the attribute to the Prophet; thus, although Q 50:45 states that Muḥammad is not *jabbār,* "a powerful hero, tyrant," he may be given this name because of Psalm 45:4, which invites the royal hero (*gibbōr* in Hebrew) to draw his sword and impose his law (see KINGS AND RULERS; OPPRESSION). The author concludes by warning against any danger of anthropomorphism (q.v.): "just as the being of God is unlike that of other beings, so his attributes do not resemble those of his creatures (see CREATION)."

Esoteric meditations

The faithful can express their devotion to the beloved by reciting a litany of his names and qualities. They may also focus their meditation on one or two of the names and draw from them knowledge (see KNOWLEDGE AND LEARNING) hidden from the eyes of the profane (q.v.). Here, we will make do with a few references to a field which is *ipso facto* without limit.

The direct relationship between God and the name of Muḥammad should be stressed. Ḥassān b. Thābit, "the poet of the Prophet," is thought to have composed the following verse: "[God] has shared his name with him to heap honor upon him, because the master of the throne (see THRONE OF GOD) is *maḥmūd* and he is *muḥammad*" (al-Qāḍī ʿIyāḍ, *Shifāʾ,* i, 237). The authors of stories concerning the Prophet were certain that the name of the Prophet was written upon the divine throne itself. Many have been pleased to note the proximity of the names Allāh and Muḥammad in the words of the *shahāda* (see WITNESS TO FAITH). Consequently, it became acceptable to apply the usual process of esoteric interpretation to the name of the Prophet. Several exegetes (see EXEGESIS OF THE QURʾĀN: CLASSICAL AND MEDIEVAL; ṢŪFISM AND THE QURʾĀN) noted that the four consonants of his name resulted from the following four words *Majd,* "glory" (q.v.), *raḤma,* "mercy," *Mulk,* "royalty," and

Dawām, "perpetuity" (see ETERNITY). The very shape of these Arabic letters *(m-ḥ-m-d),* when written together, call to mind the silhouette of a prostrate human being (see BOWING AND PROSTRATION), forming the model upon which Adam was created (Ḥallāj, *Ṭawāsīn*). This opinion was developed at length by Ibn al-ʿArabī (d. 638/1240; *La profession,* 114-27), who also advises: "This chapter, which we have devoted to the composition of the letters of the name of the chosen one, is not known by the doctors of religious law and escapes their knowledge, except if God wishes it." Furthermore, the resources of Arabic calligraphy (q.v.) have been used to illustrate the name of Muḥammad in a wide array of styles (see also ARABIC SCRIPT). Still others have based their poems and meditations upon a ḥadīth *qudsī* in which God speaks thus: *anā aḥmad bi-lā mīm,* "I am Aḥmad without the letter *mīm,*" or, put in another way: "I am *aḥad* [the one and only]," says God. *Aḥmad* is therefore the messenger who is a guide towards the one and only God (cf. Schimmel, *And Muḥammad,* 257-9). To be sure, these considerations go beyond the qurʾānic text itself. Nevertheless, they demonstrate how Islam turned its prophet into a quasi-supernatural personality.

Jean-Louis Déclais

Bibliography

Primary: Bukhārī, *Ṣaḥīḥ, Kitāb al-Manāqib,* 17; al-Ḥallāj, al-Ḥusayn b. Manṣūr, *Kitāb al-Ṭawāsīn,* Baghdad 1962; Ibn al-ʿArabī, Muḥyī l-Dīn, *La profession de foi,* trans. R. Deladrière, Paris 1985, 114-27; Ibn Ḥanbal, *Musnad,* ii, 244; iv, 80-4, 404; v, 405; vi, 25; Ibn Ḥazm, ʿAlī b. Aḥmad b. Saʿīd, *Jawāmiʿ al-sīra al-nabawiyya,* Beirut 1982, 19; Ibn Saʿd, *Ṭabaqāt,* ed. I. ʿAbbās, i, 104-7; ʿIyāḍ b. Mūsā al-Qāḍī, *al-Shifāʾ bi-taʿrīf ḥuqūq al-muṣṭafā,* 2 vols., Cairo n.d., i, 228-46; Mālik, *Muwaṭṭaʾ, Kitāb al-Faḍāʾil;* al-Maqrīzī, Tāqī l-Dīn, *Imtāʿ al-asmāʾ bi-mā li-rasūl Allāh min al-anbāʾ wa-l-amwāl wa-l-ḥafada wa-l-matāʿ,* ed. M. al-Namīsī, 15 vols., Beirut 1999, i, 5 (provides a succinct list of the names of the Prophet); Y. al-Nabhānī, *al-Anwār al-muḥammadiyya min al-mawāhib al-laduniyya,* Cairo 1895, 135-44 (an extensive list of the appellations of Muḥammad); al-Sharnūbī, ʿAbd al-Majīd, *Sharḥ dalāʾil al-khayrāt wa-shawāriq al-anwār fī l-dhikr ʿalā l-nabī al-mukhtār,* Cairo 1994, 9-13 (an edition of Imām al-Juzūlī's list of the appellations of the Prophet, with commentary). Secondary: T. Andrae, *Die Person Muhammeds in Lehre und Glaube seiner Gemeinde,* Uppsala 1917, 272-6; J.-L. Déclais, La *kunya* du Prophète et le partage du butin. Un midrash sur Josué? in *Arabica* 46 (1999), 176-92; R.Y. Ebied and M.J.L. Young, A list of the appellations of the prophet Muḥammad, in *MW* 66 (1976), 259-62 (this list uses the list of 201 appellations found in ms. Leeds Arabic MS 12, ff 75v-78r); M. de Epalza, Los nombros del Profeta et la teologia musulmana, in *Miscela ea comillar* 33 (1975), no. 63, 149-203; A. Fischer, *Muḥammad und Aḥmad. Die Namen des arabischen Propheten,* Leipzig 1932; I. Noye, Jésus, nom de, in *Dictionnaire de spiritualité,* Paris 1974, viii, 1109-26; U. Rubin, *The eye of the beholder. The life of Muḥammad as viewed by the early Muslims,* Princeton 1995, 39-45; A. Rudvin, A supplementary note to 'A list of the appellations of the prophet Muḥammad,' in *MW* 68 (1978), 57-60; A. Schimmel, *And Muhammad is his messenger. The veneration of the Prophet in Islamic piety,* Chapel Hill 1985, 105-22, 257-9.

Names of the Qurʾān

The Qurʾān calls itself by a variety of names, which throw light on the various aspects under which it presents itself. A study of the names of the Qurʾān thus becomes part of the exercise in understanding the qurʾānic phenomenon. Scholars number differently the names the Qurʾān uses for itself. According to al-Ṭabarī (d. 310/923), the divine revelation (*tanzīl,* see REVELATION AND INSPIRATION) has four names: *qurʾān, furqān, kitāb,* and *dhikr.* Al-Ṭabarī hastens to add that, in the Arabic language (q.v.), each of these four names has "a meaning and an aspect" quite distinct from the meanings and aspects of the other three — implying that the distinction is retained in the Qurʾān.

To these four names, al-Suyūṭī (d. 911/1505) adds *tanzīl,* which, in fact, occurs in the opening part of al-Ṭabarī's statement just quoted. Al-Zarkashī (d. 794/1392; *Burhān,* i, 272-82) quotes Abū l-Maʿālī ʿUzayzī as saying that the Qurʾān has fifty-five names (al-Zarkashī and, following him, al-Suyūṭī [*Itqān,* i, 50-2], give brief explanations of many of these); he quotes another writer as saying that the Qurʾān has more than ninety names. The difference in the numbering is due to the fact that some writers consider only the best-known names (and so may count only a few substantives as names) while others also regard as names the many adjectives or phrases that are descriptive of the Qurʾān.

It is probably best to take a moderate view of the matter. The figure of ninety odd names seems too large and the figure of four or five too small. It is true that certain names of the Qurʾān are very well-known and come to mind immediately but their meanings are explained, illustrated, and qualified in a significant way by at least a small number of other words and phrases, which, too, may properly be termed names of the Qurʾān. All such designations will be so treated in this article. After examining the five names that make up al-Suyūṭī's principal list, we will look at a number of less well-known names, focusing, in both categories, on substantives. Next we will consider adjectives that are used, whether attributively or predicatively, to describe the Qurʾān.

Qurʾān

A proper name *(ʿalam)* of the Islamic scripture, the word *qurʾān* is originally a *maṣdar* (verbal noun), and is used in this sense in Q 75:17, 18: "It is our responsibility to collect it and recite it *(qurʾānahu);* so, follow its recitation *(qurʾānahu)* when we recite it." It is sometimes used as an indefinite and sometimes as a definite noun, and may refer to a part (Q 72:1) or the whole (Q 6:19) of the scripture; in several places, qualifying adjectives meaning "noble" (*karīm,* Q 56:77; *majīd,* Q 85:21; *ʿajab,* "marvelous," Q 72:1) are used. It has, however, also been suggested that *qurʾān* was not always understood to be a proper name for the Muslim holy book, and that it has its origins in the Syriac *qeryānā* (see Jeffery, *For. vocab.,* 233; see also FOREIGN VOCABULARY; INFORMANTS).

The triliteral Arabic root letters that form the word *qurʾān (q-r-ʾ)* have the sense of "to collect." The Qurʾān, literally "recitation" or "reading," is so called because, in reading or reciting it, one joins — or collects — a number of letters and words, reciting or reading them in sequence (see RECITATION OF THE QURʾĀN; ORALITY). The meaning of "collection" has led scholars to see thematic and structural significance in the scripture (see FORM AND STRUCTURE OF THE QURʾĀN). According to some theologians, the name Qurʾān draws attention to the fact that the scripture contains ("collects" in itself) the essence of all the revealed books (see BOOK) — or rather the essence of all knowledge (see KNOWLEDGE AND LEARNING; in al-Rāghib's words: *li-kawnihi jāmiʿan li-thamarati kutubihi bal li-jamʿihi thamarata jamīʿi l-ʿulūmi*). Supporting evidence for this idea is found within the scripture, according to which the Qurʾān offers an elucidation (*tafṣīl,* Q 12:111) or exposition (*tibyān,* Q 16:89) of all things. Referring to the same meaning of "collection," others have argued that the Qurʾān is a well-structured discourse in that its verses (q.v.), passages, and sūras (q.v.) are well-knit or well-composed — or "collected" — rather than disconnected or "uncollected" (see LITERARY STRUCTURES OF THE QURʾĀN). This view, they maintain, must constitute one of the assumptions in reading and interpreting the Qurʾān, and, furthermore, that one's study of the

Qur'ān must be guided by the principles that underlie the composition or structure of the Qur'ān.

The Qur'ān is an Arabic *(ʿarabī)* Qur'ān (Q 12:2) — for Arabic was the language of the people to whom Muḥammad was sent as a prophet and to whom the Qur'ān was first addressed (see PROPHETS AND PROPHETHOOD): "We never sent a prophet except in the language of his nation, that he may make [matters] plain for them" (Q 14:4). Every prophet, therefore, speaks and presents his message in the language of his people. But according to the classical commentators verses like Q 12:2 do not necessarily suggest that the Qur'ān was addressed to the Arabs (q.v.) only, for the thrust of such verses is that the Arabs, since they were being addressed in their own language and so understood the Qur'ān without any difficulty, had no excuse for not accepting its message. Wordplay may also be involved in calling the Qur'ān Arabic. The root of the word *ʿarabī* has the meaning of clarity and lucidity — a meaning that is indicated in Q 16:103, where this word is contrasted with *aʿjamī*, "non-Arabic," which in this context has connotations of lack of clarity or lucidity (but for another conception of the linguistic milieu of the Qur'ān and the first qur'ānic audience, see LANGUAGE AND STYLE OF THE QUR'ĀN).

An interesting use of the word Qur'ān occurs in Q 15:91, where it seems to have been used for the Jewish scriptures — "those who tore the Qur'ān to shreds," a reference, according to the commentators, to the Jews' (see JEWS AND JUDAISM) violations of the commandments of the Torah (q.v.; cf. the ḥadīth, cited by al-Suyūṭī, in which the Prophet called the Psalms [q.v.; *zabūr*] of David [q.v.], *qur'ān*). *Qur'ān,* in this larger, generic sense of "scripture" would be analogous to the word *islām* (q.v.) in its generic or perennial sense (cf. Q 3:19; also Q 2:133, and other verses, where several prophets before Muḥammad are called *muslimūn*).

Furqān

Furqān, a word of non-Arabic origin, means "that which sets apart or distinguishes," and is usually translated as "distinction" or "criterion" (for an Aramaic derivation meaning "deliverance, redemption," see Jeffery, *For. vocab.,* 225-9). In Q 8:41, the word designates the battle of Badr (q.v.; in the year 624 C.E.), because it clearly marked off the party of truth (q.v.) from the party of falsehood (see LIE). In Q 21:48 it is used for the Torah (also Q 2:53, the *wāw* between *al-kitāb* and *al-furqān* being exegetical), and in Q 25:1 (also Q 2:185), for the Qur'ān. According to Amīn Aḥsan Iṣlāḥī (1906-97; *Tadabbur-i Qur'ān,* i, 169, ad Q 2:53), the revealed scriptures are called *furqān* in four senses: first, they offer a detailed account of the divine commandments (q.v.) and injunctions; second, they distinguish between truth and falsehood, and between the lawful and the unlawful (see LAWFUL AND UNLAWFUL); third, they are absolutely clear as to their intent and purpose; fourth, they afford human beings the wisdom (q.v.) that enables them to go through life with a full understanding of the distinction between good and evil (q.v.), and between right and wrong.

The two words so far discussed, *qur'ān* and *furqān,* are regarded by al-Ālūsī (d. 1270/1854; *Rūḥ,* i, 10) as the two most fundamental names of the Qur'ān: all other names are reducible to these two. According to al-Ālūsī, these two names are often taken by Ṣūfīs (see ṢŪFISM AND THE QUR'ĀN) to represent, respectively, knowledge in a compact form and knowledge in a detailed form: *qur'ān* stands for "esoteric knowledge of divine origin that is summative in character and is a compendium of all the truths" *(al-ʿilm al-ladunnī l-ijmālī l-jāmiʿ lil-ḥaqāʾiq kullihā),* whereas *furqān* is "detailed knowledge that serves to set truth apart from falsehood" *(al-ʿilm al-tafṣīlī l-fāriq bayn al-ḥaqq wa-l-bāṭil)* — and the Islamic scripture contains both types of knowledge. With this distinction between *qurʾān* and *furqān* in mind, he cites Ibn al-ʿArabī (d. 638/1240) as saying that while *qurʾān* includes *furqān,* the opposite is not true, for the whole *(qurʾān)* may be said to contain parts *(furqān),* but the parts may not be said to contain the whole. This may serve to show why, in al-Ālūsī's view, *qurʾān* and *furqān* are the most fundamental of all the names of the Qurʾān.

Kitāb

The word *kitāb,* as used in the Qurʾān, has several meanings, many of which become constituent elements of the meaning of the name *kitāb* as used of the Qurʾān. These meanings are: revealed scripture (Q 2:44); authoritative document (Q 37:157); the Preserved Tablet (q.v.) that is in the heavens (see HEAVEN AND SKY) and that contains a record of everything that has happened or will happen (cf. Q 6:59); deed-scroll (Q 69:19, 25; see RECORD OF HUMAN ACTIONS); divine decree (Q 8:68); legal injunction (Q 98:3); and epistle or written message (Q 27:28). As a book that has been revealed (for example, Q 14:1, *kitābun anzalnāhu ilayka,* "a book that we have sent down to you [Muḥammad]"), the Qurʾān is an authoritative message from God, containing as it does a series of prescriptive laws. In many verses, the word *kitāb* is used for pre-qurʾānic scriptures — as, for example, in Q 2:87 (Torah) and Q 19:30 (Gospel; see GOSPELS). The designation of the Qurʾān as *kitāb* thus makes it part of a larger tradition of revealed scriptures.

By calling itself a book — *kitāb* (Q 2:2 and elsewhere) — the Qurʾān makes a break with the oral tradition of Arabia (see ORALITY AND WRITING IN ARABIA). In contradistinction to the Jews and Christians (see CHRISTIANS AND CHRISTIANITY), who possessed scriptures and so were called *ahl al-kitāb,* "People of the Book" (q.v.; e.g. Q 3:65; see LITERACY), the idolatrous Arabs (see POLYTHEISM AND ATHEISM; SOUTH ARABIA, RELIGION IN PRE-ISLAMIC), who did not have a scripture, were called *ummiyyūn,* "unlettered ones" (see UMMĪ; ILLITERACY). While *ummiyyūn* was an identifying title of these Arabs, and, as such, was value-neutral, in certain religious contexts it did connote — and the Arabs themselves understood it to connote — inferiority of status, the People of the Book being viewed as enjoying, by virtue of their possession of scriptures, an elevated status. This explains why, for example, toward the end of the Meccan period of Muḥammad's ministry (see CHRONOLOGY AND THE QURʾĀN), the Quraysh (q.v.) sought to enlist Jewish and Christian "scriptural" support in their attempt to upstage Muḥammad by challenging qurʾānic pronouncements about biblical history and personages (see SCRIPTURE AND THE QURʾĀN; NARRATIVES; MYTHS AND LEGENDS IN THE QURʾĀN) — a fact that forms part of the background of such sūras as Q 18 (Sūrat al-Kahf, "The Cave"; see MEN OF THE CAVE) and Q 19 (Sūrat Maryam, "Mary" [q.v.]). With the advent of the Qurʾān — or rather the Qurʾān as *kitāb* — therefore, the Arabs came to possess a scripture similar to the Jewish and Christian scriptures, and were raised to the level of the Jews and Christians.

More important, the name *kitāb* highlights the function of scripture as law, for that which is written down is deemed to have at least three distinctive qualities (see LAW AND THE QURʾĀN). The first of these is clarity: a piece of writing is supposed to be free from ambiguity (cf. the word "graphic"; see ORTHOGRAPHY). The second is objectivity: a document, having an independent existence, serves as a check against subjective and arbitrary interpretation of the law — a function that, for example, the Twelve Tables were meant to perform in Rome during the early Republic when the plebeians agitated against patrician excesses. The use of *kitāb* in Q 68:37, "Do you have a book in which you read?" *(am lakum kitābun fīhi tadrusūn)* has this meaning of objectivity. The third is definitiveness: the written word has always enjoyed a putative authoritative status. As *kitāb,* then, scripture becomes a reliable source of knowledge and wisdom (Q 2:159; 35:40; in Q 10:1 and elsewhere, the Qur᾽ān is called *al-kitāb al-ḥakīm,* "the wise book"), a book that deserves to become one's object of study and reflection (Q 38:29; see TEACHING AND PREACHING THE QUR᾽ĀN), and an adjudicator of matters (Q 2:213; cf. 4:105). Q 46:30 parallels the Qur᾽ān — "a book that has been revealed after Moses (q.v.)" — with the Torah, highlighting the status of the Qur᾽ān as the law.

By calling itself *kitāb,* then, the Qur᾽ān claims to be a source of authority (q.v.). This explains the use of the plural *kutub* in the sense of "laws" in Q 98:3. Incidentally, when Muslim jurisprudents discuss the sources of Islamic law, they often use the word *al-kitāb* to designate the first source, the Qur᾽ān, probably because of the legal connotations of that word.

But the Qur᾽ān calls itself not just a book, but "the book" (*al-kitāb,* cf. the early Christian designation *ta Biblia,* literally "the books," for the scriptures). This serves to emphasize the status of the Qur᾽ān as an indispensable source of knowledge and guidance (see ASTRAY). *Al-kitāb,* in Q 2:2 for example, may also signify that the Qur᾽ān, being the final revelation from God, supersedes all other previous scriptures and that now it alone has the status of being the book.

In Q 39:23, the Qur᾽ān is described as *kitāban mutashābihan mathāniya. Mutashābih,* literally "resembling," implies that the contents of the Qur᾽ān are similar to, and concordant with, one another. In other words, the Qur᾽ān is marked by consistency, and, in spite of its considerable diversity of theme and variation of style, it possesses organic unity. As for *mathānī,* it is usually interpreted as "oft-repeated (q.v.) ones," which would be a reference to the fact that the Qur᾽ān frequently repeats its contents in order to fix these firmly in the minds of its listeners or readers.

Q 41:41 calls the Qur᾽ān *kitābun ʿazīzun,* "a mighty book." The Arabic word *ʿazīz,* usually translated "mighty," connotes unassailability. The Qur᾽ān is a book that — as the very next verse explains — is secure against any incursions of falsehood: "Falsehood does not encroach upon it from the front or from behind" *(lā yaʾtīhi l-bāṭilu min bayni yadayhi wa-lā min khalfihi).*

In a sense, the name *kitāb* is a complement of the name *qurʾān.* As ʿAbdallāh Drāz says *(Nabaʾ,* 13*), qurʾān* and *kitāb* together represent the fact that the Islamic scripture is both recited and written, and, furthermore, that the scripture can be properly recited and written only when it is preserved in both *ṣudūr,* "human breasts," and *suṭūr,* "documentary form" — which in turn means that memory (q.v.) and document shall reinforce each other in the project of preserving the integrity of the divine word. And, Drāz concludes, this is exactly how the universal Muslim community fulfilled its mission or responsibility in this regard (for more on *kitāb,* see Jeffery, *Qurʾān* and, more recently, Madigan, *Self-image*).

Dhikr

Literally "remembrance," *dhikr* is used of the Qur᾽ān in several places, for example in Q 38:8, which reports an objection raised by certain opponents of Muḥammad (see

OPPOSITION TO MUḤAMMAD): "Has the remembrance been sent down upon him [Muḥammad] from among all of us?" *(a-unzila ʿalayhi l-dhikru min bayninā);* the words *dhikrā* and *tadhkira* (as in Q 6:90 and Q 69:48, respectively) are also used. In Q 43:44, where the Qurʾān is called "a *dhikr* for you and your people" *(dhikrun laka wa-li-qawmika), dhikr* acquires the additional meaning of exaltation and honor. The Qurʾān is called "the wise remembrance" (Q 3:58), "a blessed remembrance" (Q 21:50), and "a remembrance for the entire world" (Q 68:52). Not only is the Qurʾān itself a remembrance, the act of taking remembrance by it, too, has been made easy (Q 54:17, 22, 32, 40), so that no one might claim that the Qurʾān remained a closed book.

Dhikr is of two main types: verbal, *dhikr bi-l-lisān,* literally, "remembering by means of the tongue," and mental, *dhikr bi-l-qalb,* literally "remembering by means of the heart (q.v.)." Both are mentioned in the Qurʾān — for example, the first in Q 68:51: *lammā samiʿū l-dhikra,* "when they hear the remembrance," and the second in Q 3:135: *dhakarū llāha fa-staghfarū li-dhunūbihim,* "They remember God, and then they seek forgiveness (q.v.) for their sins (see SIN, MAJOR AND MINOR)." In a verse like Q 38:1: "By the Qurʾān, one of remembrance" *(wa-l-qurʾāni dhī l-dhikri),* the two meanings are combined. To call the Qurʾān *dhikr,* therefore, is to say that the text of the Qurʾān ought to be recited by the tongue and its teachings kept in mind. Thus both the development of the Islamic art of qurʾānic recitation and the popularity of the Muslim practice of memorizing the text of the Qurʾān may be seen as the unfolding, in history, of the idea of the Qurʾān as *dhikr.*

Furthermore, *dhikr* as a name of the Qurʾān signifies that the scripture reminds human beings of certain truths of which, at some level, they are already aware. This implies that the message of the scripture is not alien to human nature (what the Qurʾān calls *fiṭra* in Q 30:30), or that the truths introduced by the scripture are not inconsistent with the truths of which human beings have an instinctive understanding. In turning to the Qurʾān and accepting its message, therefore, human beings will only be responding to the call of their *fiṭra.* Thus, the sending down of scripture by God does not constitute an imposition on human beings, but rather is to be understood and appreciated as valuable help in giving direction to human life.

Tanzīl

Tanzīl (Q 26:192 and elsewhere) is usually translated "revelation" but, strictly, the word denotes sending something down in portions or installments, as opposed to sending it down all at once. Q 25:32 quotes an objection of the opponents of the Qurʾān: "Why was the Qurʾān not sent down *(nuzzila)* upon him [Muḥammad] all at once?" In light of this objection, the name *tanzīl* acquires some significance, for the Qurʾān does address the objection. To begin with, Q 17:106 contains, besides the word *tanzīl,* the phrase "And a Qurʾān which we have divided into parts, so that you may recite it to people at intervals" *(wa-qurʾānan faraqnāhu li-taqraʾahu ʿalā l-nāsi ʿalā mukthin).* Q 16:102 may be taken to explain the wisdom behind *tanzīl.* According to this verse, *tanzīl* may have a threefold significance: first, it strengthens the believers by offering repeated and variegated expositions of the qurʾānic message; second, it provides for the believers, that is, the first-generation Muslims, guidance on matters and issues as they arise during their struggle to establish Islam in Arabia; and third, it reassures them by informing them that, like other believing nations in the past, they, too, will eventually meet with success in this world and in the next (see also Q 16:89; see ESCHATOLOGY; REWARD AND PUNISHMENT).

Additional designations

The Qurʾān uses a number of other names for itself, and these, too, have formed the basis for extended exegetical and theological reflection:

Kalām Allāh, "The word/speech of God" (Q 9:6; 48:15). This name is also used for the Torah (Q 2:75). Divine revelation is called *kalām Allāh* in order to distinguish it from the speech of humans, jinn (q.v.), and angels (see ANGEL). The essence of the word *kalām* is *lafẓ,* "word," and this, according to some scholars, is proof that the revelation a prophet receives from God takes verbal form. Historically, it is this name — *kalām Allāh* — which gave rise to the theological issue of the createdness of the Qurʾān (q.v.) leading Muslim theologians to distinguish between various meanings of the word *kalām* as applied to divine revelation.

Waḥy, usually translated "revelation," literally means "quick intimation" *(ishāra sarīʿa)* — which intimation, as al-Rāghib al-Iṣfahānī (fl. early fifth/eleventh cent.; *Mufradāt,* s.v. *w-ḥ-y*) explains, may take the form of word, sound, or gesture ("intimation" would seem to be a better word than Bell's [Watt-Bell, *Introduction,* 21] "suggestion," the connotations of which are somewhat different from those of the Arabic word). As a technical term, *waḥy* carries special importance because it is used in the Qurʾān both for the process and for the content of revelation (the same might be claimed for *tanzīl,* but the use of *waḥy* in the Qurʾān is more nuanced). The dual nature of *waḥy* can be seen in a verse like Q 53:4, "This is but a revelation that is being revealed" *(in huwa illā waḥyun yūḥā).* Q 42:51 identifies four ways in which God speaks to a human being *(an yukallimahu llāhu),* two of them involving *waḥy,* namely: God speaking to a person *waḥyan,* and a messenger (q.v.; that is, an angel) conveying *(yūḥī)* to a person whatever is willed by God. Q 2:97, which mentions Gabriel (q.v.) as the one who brought the Qurʾān to Muḥammad, would seem to establish the second of those two ways as the one in which Muḥammad received the scripture. Thus, *waḥy* as a name of the Qurʾān specifies the mode in which revelation was conveyed to Muḥammad. But the important point is that *waḥy* is identified in Q 42:51 with the speech, *kalām,* of God. Since *kalām,* as we have already noted, is verbal in character, the name would seem to lend support to the verbal conception of revelation. Furthermore, since *waḥy* is quick intimation, it is implied that a prophet's reception of revelation from an angel is virtually immediate — with the attendant implication that a prophet's revelation is unadulterated or uncompromised either by his own thought or imagination or by the intervention of any demonic power (see DEVIL; this last idea would in turn refute the objection, made by Muḥammad's opponents that, like the soothsayers [q.v.] of Arabia, he received revelation through the medium of jinn).

Hudā, "guidance" (Q 27:77). The Qurʾān is so called because it guides to the right path, clearly distinguishing it from the wrong path. The name implies that the choice to accept the *hudā* rests with human beings, the Qurʾān simply pointing the way (e.g. Q 76:3). For similar reasons, the Qurʾān is called *mawʿiẓa,* "advice, admonition" (Q 10:57; see EXHORTATIONS; WARNING).

Nūr, "light" (q.v.; Q 4:174). The Qurʾān brings human beings forth from darkness (q.v.) and ignorance (q.v.) and sets them on the well-lit path of guidance (Q 5:15-6). The phrase actually used in Q 4:174 is *nūran mubīnan,* "clear light," which implies that the light of the scripture is both unmistakable and easily accessible.

Baṣāʾir, "insights" (Q 7:203). The Qurʾān is a treasury of special insights, which, to interpret the Arabic word literally, help the listener or reader to "see" the truth (see SEEING AND HEARING; VISION AND BLINDNESS).

Ḥikma, "wisdom" (Q 17:39). The Qurʾān both contains and teaches wisdom. In Q 54:5 it is called *ḥikma bāligha,* "consummate wisdom," because it contains divine wisdom, which is the highest form of wisdom.

Raḥma, "mercy" (q.v.; Q 27:77). God, the creator of all, is the guide of all (Q 7:54: *a-lā lahu l-khalqu wa-l-amr,* "Behold, to him belong creation and command"). But guiding humanity, or furnishing it with a code of conduct, is a manifestation of the mercy of God. It is on account of his mercifulness that God has decided to save human beings by showing them the right course of action (see SALVATION). In Q 17:86-7, cessation of revelation is equated with denial or withholding of mercy.

Bashīr, "giver of good tidings" and *nadhīr,* "warner" (Q 41:4; see GOOD NEWS; WARNING). The Qurʾān promises reward to those who accept its message and threatens with punishment those who reject that message.

Rūḥ, "spirit" (q.v.; Q 42:52). The scripture is a life-giving force, and those who live by it will have true life (cf. *Deut* 8:3: "One does not live by bread alone, but by every word that comes from the mouth of the lord").

Aḥsan al-ḥadīth, "the finest discourse" (Q 39:23; see INIMITABILITY). The Qurʾān excels, both in point of beauty of style and in point of wisdom of content, any other discourse. In Q 12:3, the qurʾānic story of Joseph (q.v.) is called *aḥsan al-qaṣaṣ,* "the finest story."

Shifāʾ, "cure, remedy" (Q 10:57; 17:82; see ILLNESS AND HEALTH). The Qurʾān treats the maladies of the heart and the soul (q.v.), purging people's inner selves of ignoble traits.

Muhaymin, "supervisor, protector" (Q 5:48). The Qurʾān "watches over" the other scriptures in the sense that, on the one hand, it contains the essence of their teachings and completes those teachings, and, on the other hand, provides the yardstick by which the authenticity and validity of those scriptures may be judged (see *muṣaddiq,* below).

Ḥabl Allāh, "the cord of God" (Q 3:103). The word *ḥabl,* "rope, cord," is an Arabic metaphor (q.v.) for covenant (q.v.). The Qurʾān is God's *ḥabl* because it at once constitutes and explains the terms of the covenant that God makes with humanity. The salvation of human beings, therefore, depends on their fulfillment of the covenant with God.

Balāgh, "communication" (Q 14:52). The Qurʾān, according to this verse, is *balāghun lil-nās,* "a communication for people." The name implies, first, that the Qurʾān has been communicated to humanity fully and accurately — in the very form in which it was sent down by God — and, second, that human beings, once they receive it are responsible for deciding what their relationship to it shall be.

Finally, a number of adjectival names are used to describe the Qurʾān in various contexts. A brief review of some of them follows (some of them were noted in the discussion above, but will be dealt with here from a more general point of view).

Mubīn, which can mean both "clear (in itself)" and "that which clarifies," implies (as in Q 12:1 and Q 36:69) that the language of the Qurʾān, being standard Arabic, is neither convoluted nor ambiguous (q.v.), and, consequently, generously yields its true meaning to those who come to it on its terms (Q 5:15-6). The use of the word implies that those who are being addressed by means of it — the first addressees, that is — cannot reject it on the grounds that they are unable to understand it (see DIFFICULT PASSAGES).

Karīm, "noble" (Q 56:77). The Qurʾān is "noble" because it comes from a noble source, and, being noble, it deserves to be treated with reverence. The same may be said of *majīd,* "glorious, illustrious" (Q 85:21) and *ʿalī,* "exalted" (Q 43:4). In Q 80:13-4, the Qurʾān is called *ṣuḥuf,* "sheets/scriptures," that are *mukarrama,* "honored," *marfūʿa,* "exalted," and *muṭahhara,* "made pure."

Mubārak, "blessed" (Q 21:50; 38:29). The scripture is a source of blessings (Ar. *barakāt*) which, following Q 7:96, "blessings of the heaven and the earth" *(barakātin min al-samāʾi wa-l-arḍi),* can be interpreted as material as well as spiritual; compare with Q 5:66, which says that had the People of the Book upheld the Torah and the Gospel, "they would have eaten from above [their heads] and from under their feet," that is, they would have enjoyed material prosperity (see BLESSING; GRACE; WEALTH).

Ḥakīm, "wise" (Q 41:42). The word is used in the Qurʾān for both God and the scripture. This means that the Qurʾān, being the word of God (q.v.), reflects the attributes of the one who sent it down; both the word and its speaker are full of wisdom (see GOD AND HIS ATTRIBUTES). *Ḥakīm* also has the connotations of "solidity, firmness, decisiveness," and suggests that the Qurʾān is free from such weaknesses as vagueness, ambiguity, and doubt (q.v.; cf. *qawl faṣl,* "decisive word," in Q 86:13), and also that it has been made secure against any "interference" such as textual corruption (see FORGERY; CORRUPTION; COLLECTION OF THE QURʾĀN; TEXTUAL CRITICISM OF THE QURʾĀN).

Qayyim, "right, straight" (Q 18:2). This word is contrasted in the verse with *ʿiwaj,* "crooked, aberrant" (cf. Q 18:1). *Qayyim* (like *al-qayyūm,* which is used in Q 2:255 as an attribute of God) is one who or that which sustains not only himself or itself but also someone or something else. Al-Rāghib al-Iṣfahānī explains the word thus: "well-established [in its own right] and setting in order people's affairs as they pertain to this world and the next" *(thābit muqawwim li-umūr maʿāshihim wa-maʿādihim, Mufradāt,* ad loc.). Being *qayyim,* then, the Qurʾān both represents the straight course and ensures that those who follow it will stay on that course.

Muṣaddiq. The Qurʾān is "a *muṣaddiq* of that which precedes it" *(muṣaddiqan li-mā bayna yadayhi),* namely, the previous scriptures (Q 2:97). The Arabic word can mean "that which confirms (something else) to be true and correct," and this is the general interpretation of the word when it occurs in such a context. This, however, is not very convincing since the Qurʾān's confirmation of the previous scriptures would leave the matter of its own authenticity hanging in the balance — a thought that ill suits the contexts in which the Qurʾān is called a *muṣaddiq* of the earlier scriptures. A more plausible interpretation, one offered by Amīn Aḥsan Iṣlāḥī (*Tadabbur-i Qurʾān,* ad loc.), is that *muṣaddiq* in these contexts means "that which actualizes." In other words, the Qurʾān represents the materialization of the prophecies that were made in the early scriptures. The first meaning, "to confirm (something else)," would still be valid, but will have to be restated: the Qurʾān confirms those contents or parts of the early scriptures that agree with the Qurʾān's own outlook. In either case, the name *muṣaddiq* establishes an important connection between the Qurʾān and the earlier scriptures.

Conclusion

The foregoing makes it plain that a study of the names of the Qurʾān should be of considerable interest to a student of the Islamic scripture. The pre-Islamic Arabian practice of assigning many names to a being, entity, or phenomenon might explain, in part, why the Qurʾān, too, uses so many names for itself (see PRE-ISLAMIC ARABIA AND THE QURʾĀN). But the practice, whether by the pre-Islamic poets (see POETRY AND POETS) or by the Qurʾān, was not indulged in for its own sake; rather, it was aimed at elucidating, from as many angles as possible, the nature and attributes of the thing in question. With the Qurʾān, however, the practice is raised to a higher level: the many different names of the Qurʾān not only represent so many facets of the Islamic scripture, but they also make up, when seen in relation to each other, a coherent and meaningful statement in their own right, shedding light on the ethos, orientation, and function of the scripture. We will conclude by offering a few observations.

First, an analytical look at the names (both substantives and adjectives) of the Qurʾān will indicate that they underscore different aspects of the Islamic scripture. For example, some names *(kalām Allāh, waḥy)* speak to the origin of the Qurʾān, maintaining that it comes from God — and that it is not, therefore, the product of the Prophet's mind or the concoction of a soothsayer (see OCCASIONS OF REVELATION). Others *(bayān, mubīn, ʿarabī)* claim linguistic purity and excellence for the Qurʾān (see LANGUAGE, CONCEPT OF), implying that the Qurʾān presents its meaning with the utmost clarity, such that it cannot be rejected or disregarded on the grounds of incomprehensibility or ambiguity. Still others *(hudā, ḥikma)* draw attention to the function and purpose of the Qurʾān: this is a book that guides to the right path and furnishes the wisdom that is needed to lead a successful life. Some names *(kitāb, kalām Allāh),* since they are used of other scriptures as well, stress that the Qurʾān is part of the series of divine dispensations that have come from God to prophets (e.g. Q 4:163 says that God gave Muḥammad *waḥy* in the same way in which he gave *waḥy* to Noah [q.v.] and other prophets). Other names *(muhaymin, muṣaddiq)* point to the distinction of the Qurʾān among the scriptures. The name *kitāb* endows the Qurʾān with authenticity, while the name *dhikr* stresses the consonance of the qurʾānic teaching with human nature.

Second, most of the names of the Qurʾān will be found to occur throughout the period of Muḥammad's revelation, which lasted for about twenty-two years. Take, for example, the five names discussed in the beginning. While some of them occur more frequently than others, all of them occur in both Meccan and Medinan sūras, an indication that the manifold conception of the Qurʾān had started taking shape quite early.

Third, it appears that the listener or reader of the Qurʾān is meant to keep in mind the interrelation of the names. This becomes clear from the fact that the names are frequently used in conjunction with, or in close proximity to, one another. We have already noted that substantive names are frequently qualified by adjectival ones. A few additional examples may be noted. *Tanzīl al-kitāb (*where *tanzīl* is a *maṣdar)* occurs more than once. *Mawʿiẓa, shifāʾ, hudā,* and *raḥma* occur together in Q 10:57. Q 17:106 may contain a possible wordplay — *wa-qurʾānan faraqnāhu,* "and a Qurʾān that we have given in detail" — where *faraqnā,* from the same root as *furqān,* implies that the Qurʾān-as-collection is identical with the Qurʾān-as-distinction (see above).

Mustansir Mir

Bibliography
Primary: Ālūsī, *Rūḥ,* 30 vols. in 15, Beirut 1926; Iṣlāḥī, Amīn Aḥsan, *Tadabbur-i Qurʾān,* 6 vols., Lahore 1967-80; Mawdūdī, Abū l-Aʿlā, *Tafhīm al-Qurʾān,* 6 vols., Lahore 1949-72; al-Rāghib al-Iṣfahānī, *Mufradāt,* Riyadh 1997; Suyūṭī, *Itqān,* 4 vols., Riyadh 1996; Ṭabarī, *Tafsīr,* ed. Būlāq, 30 vols., repr. Beirut 1987; Zarkashī, *Burhān,* Cairo 1957.
Secondary: ʿA. Drāz, *al-Nabaʾ al-ʿaẓīm,* Kuwait 1970; Jeffery, *For. vocab.;* id., *The Qurʾān as scripture,* New York 1952; D. Madigan, *The Qurʾān's self-image. Writing and authority in Islam's scripture,* Princeton 2001; Mir, *Dictionary;* Watt-Bell, *Introduction.*

Nāmūs

Term found in early Muslim traditions on the Prophet's life (*sīra,* see SĪRA AND THE QURʾĀN), but not explicitly mentioned in the Qurʾān. Its original meaning was "the revealed law." The word was later interpreted as a designation for the angel Gabriel (q.v.; Jibrīl).

In an early Arabic translation of a gospel fragment, the Greek expression *en tō nomō autōn* (*John* 15:25), which means "the law of the Jews," i.e. the Torah (q.v.), is rendered as *fī l-nāmūs* (Ibn Isḥāq, *Sīra,* 150). This rendering is based on a Palestinian Syriac translation of the gospel (q.v.; Guillaume, Version, 292; see SYRIAC AND THE QURʾĀN).

In the *sīra* traditions the word *al-nāmūs* occurs most prominently in the Khadīja — Waraqa story, of which several versions were transmitted and which is part of the reports about Muḥammad's call to prophecy (see PROPHETS AND PROPHETHOOD; INFORMANTS). Waraqa, a cousin of Muḥammad's first wife Khadīja (q.v.), is said to have become a Christian (see CHRISTIANS AND CHRISTIANITY), to have studied with Jewish and Christian scholars (see SCHOLAR; JEWS AND JUDAISM) and to have translated some texts of the gospels into Arabic (the rarer variant "Hebrew" seems to be a transmission error) and to have written them down. After having been informed about Muḥammad's revelations, Waraqa, in one of the versions, says: "This is the *nāmūs* which was sent down upon Moses" (q.v.; *hādhā l-nāmūs alladhī unzila ʿalā mūsā;* ʿAbd al-Razzāq, *Muṣannaf,* v, 323; Bukhārī, *Ṣaḥīḥ,* i, 4-5; Muslim, *Ṣaḥīḥ,* i, 142). This immediately suggests that, in this case as well, *al-nāmūs* is adopted from the corresponding Syriac word meaning "the revealed law" for, according to the Bible and the Qurʾān, this is what Moses and Muḥammad received.

Recent studies have shown that the famous version of the story of Muḥammad's call to prophecy, at least its essential elements, most probably goes back to the Meccan storyteller *(qāṣṣ)* ʿUbayd b. ʿUmayr (d. 68/687-8; Schoeler, *Charakter und Authentie,* 59-117; Juynboll, Early Islamic society, 160-71). This version was already a combination of different reports and narrative motifs, which must have circulated independently at that time or even earlier (see ORALITY AND WRITING IN ARABIA). This assumption is corroborated by versions of the story which do not contain the vision of an angel (q.v.), and which seem to be independent of the narration that goes back to ʿUbayd b. ʿUmayr. In one of these versions, Waraqa says: "This is a *nāmūs* like the *nāmūs* of Moses" (*fa-hādhā nāmūs mithla nāmūs mūsā;* Ibn Saʿd, *Ṭabaqāt,* i, 195; Ibn Ḥanbal, *Musnad,* i, 312). The reference to the *nāmūs* of Moses seems, therefore, to belong to the original kernel of the story and must have meant God's law revealed to Moses.

The Syriac word put into the mouth of an Arab Christian suggests that the original Muslim narrator of the story, who lived in the first half of the first/seventh century but cannot be identified any further, was acquainted with the Christian expression. This does not hold for later transmitters and, in the course of time, the interpretation of the term changed. The fact that the Khadīja-Waraqa story came to be prefaced with narrations about visions of the angel Gabriel, contributed greatly to the development of the idea that *al-nāmūs* referred to this angel. This became, for Muslim scholars, the common understanding of the term *al-nāmūs* in the Khadīja-Waraqa story.

The change of meaning left both Muslim and Western scholars with a problem. Neither in the Qurʾān nor in the biblical book of Exodus is it said that Moses received his revelations through an angel. Muslim scholars solved the problem by generalizing Muḥammad's experience of revelation (cf. Q 2:97), claiming it for all prophets (see REVELATION AND INSPIRATION). Furthermore, Muslim scholars asserted that *al-nāmūs* is a word "applied to Gabriel by the people of the book" (Lane, 2854; see PEOPLE OF THE BOOK). Some Western scholars presumed that the idea of the *nāmūs* as an angelic being who came to Moses and other prophets had a Christian origin: in their purview, this interpretation resulted from a confusion of the terms *nomos* and *prophetēs*, which were used in conjunction in eastern Christian liturgical formulas (Baumstark, Das Problem, 565-6), and which were also closely related to one another in the Gnostic literature of Palestinian origin (Andrae, *Der Ursprung*, 204). The development of the meaning described above, however, makes such speculations superfluous. In later Muslim philosophical literature, the term *al-nāmūs* is used with the meaning of "the divine law" (Plessner, Nāmūs, 954-5; see LAW AND THE QURʾĀN).

Harald Motzki

Bibliography

Primary: ʿAbd al-Razzāq, *Muṣannaf;* Bukhārī, *Ṣaḥīḥ;* Ibn Ḥanbal, *Musnad,* 6 vols. Beirut 1969; Ibn Isḥāq, *Sīra,* ed. Wüstenfeld; Ibn Saʿd, *Ṭabaqāt,* ed. I. ʿAbbās; Muslim, *Ṣaḥīḥ*.

Secondary: T. Andrae, *Der Ursprung des Islams und das Christentum,* Uppsala 1926; A. Baumstark, Das Problem eines vorislamischen christlichen-kirchlichen Schrifttums in arabischer Sprache, in *Islamica* 4 (1931), 562-75; R. Bell, Mohammed's call, in *MW* 24 (1934), 13-9; H.L. Fleischer, [note on Nöldeke's translation of *al-nāmūs*] in *ZDMG* 12 (1858), 701-2; C. Gilliot, Les "informateurs" juifs et chrétiens de Muḥammad, in *JSAI* 22 (1998), 84-126 (esp. 99-104); A. Guillaume, The version of the gospels used in Medina circa 700 A.D., in *Al-Andalus* 15 (1952), 289-96; A. Hebbo, *Die Fremdwörter in der arabischen Prophetenbiographie des Ibn Hischām (gest. 218/834),* Frankfurt 1984, 349-50; G.H.A. Juynboll, Early Islamic society as reflected in its use of *isnāds,* in *Muséon* 107 (1994), 151-94; Th. Nöldeke, Hatte Muḥammad christliche Lehrer? in *ZDMG* 12 (1858), 699-708; M. Plessner, Nāmūs, in *EI²*, vii, 953-5; U. Rubin, *The eye of the beholder. The life of Muḥammad as viewed by the early Muslims. A textual analysis,* Princeton 1995, 103-12; G. Schoeler, *Charakter und Authentie der muslimischen Überlieferung über das Leben Mohammeds,* Berlin 1996; A. Sprenger, Über den Ursprung und die Bedeutung des arabischen Wortes Nāmūs, in *ZDMG* 13 (1859), 690-701; W.M. Watt, *Muhammad at Mecca,* Oxford 1953, 50-2.

Narratives

Stories of individuals and communities of the past, of varying length, many of which appear in numerous renditions throughout the qurʾānic text, but are found predominantly in the Meccan sūras of the Qurʾān (see CHRONOLOGY AND THE QURʾĀN). Although the Qurʾān does relate the tales of prophets (see PROPHETS AND PROPHETHOOD) and other notable persons, tales that presumably were already familiar to the first auditors of the Qurʾān (see ORALITY AND WRITING IN ARABIA; SOUTH ARABIA, RELIGION IN PRE-ISLAMIC), the stories that are characterized as "narratives" contain certain requisite structural features (Q 21, Sūrat al-Anbiyāʾ, takes its name — "The

Prophets" — from the fact that it is comprised of tales of various prophets, many of which fall within the parameters of this literary genre; see FORM AND STRUCTURE OF THE QUR'ĀN). The proportion of the narratives in the Qur'ān is very large: 1453 verses (Sherif, *Guide,* 46), or about a quarter of their total number (ca. 6000; Abū ʿAmr al-Dānī, in Suyūṭī, *Itqān,* i, 232). They consist of accounts concerning prophets or so-called prophets, messengers (25 of them fall into these two categories; Suyūṭī, *Itqān,* chap. 69, iii, 67; see MESSENGER), sages, historical, historico-mythical or mythical celebrities of ancient times (see MYTHS AND LEGENDS IN THE QUR'ĀN; HISTORY AND THE QUR'ĀN). Before discussing the narratives themselves, an overview of the Arabic terminology for "narratives," as well as an outline of the qur'ānic passages that are termed as such, is in order.

The semantic field of narratives in the Qur'ān

The following list is an overview of the most important Arabic words used within the semantic field of "narratives" in its broadest sense: *qiṣṣa* or *qaṣaṣ* (story, narrative); *sīra* (lit. "way of acting," it is also used for "battles," "story," or "biography"; see SĪRA AND THE QUR'ĀN); *ḥadīth* (denotes primarily a saying or an account of an action of the Prophet, and, secondarily, of his Companions [see COMPANIONS OF THE PROPHET], but also means "narrative," "speech," etc.; see ḤADĪTH AND THE QUR'ĀN); *ḥikāya* (the verb from which it derives means "to relate," thus, "narrative," "story"); *samar* (literary entertainment, mostly at night); *khurāfa* (incredible tale, legend); *usṭūra* (history without foundation, legend; in present usage, sometimes also myth); *riwāya* (the verb means to recite, transmit a story, a poem; thus, a transmission or version; nowadays, a novel); *nādira* (short, witty, subtle and amusing anecdote); *khabar* (information, statement, narrative, piece of history); *mathal* (parable); *maqāma* (appears in the 4th/11th cent.; assembly, Fr. "séance"; for further discussion of these terms, see Abdel-Meguid, Survey).

Qiṣṣa does not appear in the Qur'ān. *Qaṣaṣ,* which lends itself to the name of a sūra (Q 28, Sūrat al-Qaṣaṣ, "The Story"), is used with a sense relevant to the present discussion four times (three of which contain permutations of the corresponding verb): at Q 3:62, "This is the true story" (concerning Jesus [q.v.]); Q 7:176, "So relate the story" (order given to Muḥammad; this "story" is glossed as both "the Qur'ān" [Muqātil, *Tafsīr,* ii, 75] and "the recitation" [Dāmaghānī, *Wujūh,* ii, 159]; see RECITATION OF THE QUR'ĀN); Q 12:3: "We will relate to you the fairest of stories" (i.e. the tale of Joseph [q.v.]; here, Qatāda (d. 118/736) notes that *"qaṣaṣ"* means: "From the past books *[min al-kutub al-māḍiya]* and the ancient decrees of God about the nations *[wa umūr Allāh al-sālifa fī l-umam]*"; Ṭabarī, *Tafsīr,* ed. Shākir, xv, 551-2, no. 18772; Ibn Abī l-Zamanīn, *Tafsīr,* ii, 315); Q 28:25. The verb *qaṣṣa* (to tell a story, to relate; see above) is attested, among other places, at Q 11:100: "the cities whose tidings *(anbā')* we relate *(naquṣṣu)* to you (see CITY; PUNISHMENT STORIES)"; Q 11:120: "We relate to you tidings *(anbā')* of the messengers"; Q 18:13 (where it is used with *naba'*); Q 20:99 (with *anbā'*); Q 40:78; Q 4:164; Q 7:7. It is used in the third person singular imperfect at Q 6:57 (subject: God himself) and at Q 27:76 (subject: the Qur'ān). In Q 16:118, the verb is in the perfect, and the subject is God (here, Blachère offers the following translation: "ce que Nous t'avons énuméré").

Ḥadīth, pl. *aḥādīth,* also occurs in the Qur'ān with the meanings of talk, saying, discourse, story, tale (Q 31:6; 12:6; 23:44, etc.; Hirschberg, "Gottes-Schriften,"

79-80; Horovitz, *KU*, 7). *Usṭūra* is mentioned 9 times, but only in the plural *(asāṭīr)*, and always in the construct *asāṭīr al-awwalīn* (Q 6:25; 8:31; 16:24; 23:83; 25:5; 27:68; 46:17; 68:15; 83:13), usually translated as "tales/fairy tales of the ancients" (see GENERATIONS). But if we consider Q 25:5, where the opponents of Muḥammad (see OPPOSITION TO MUḤAMMAD) say "*asāṭīr* of the ancients that he has written down, so that they are recited to him at dawn and in the evening," the word could be also understood as "writings" or "scriptures" (see BOOK). Probably derived from Syriac (see SYRIAC AND THE QURʾĀN; FOREIGN VOCABULARY), it is found also in the Sabean *sṭr* (lit. inscription). The Qurʾān uses also the verb *saṭara* in the meaning of "to write" (cf. Q 17:58; 33:6), as did the ancient poets (Nöldeke, *GQ*, i, 15-7; Horovitz, *KU*, 69-70; Hebbo, *Fremdwörter*, 30-1; see POETS AND POETRY). Al-Naḍr b. al-Ḥārith (see INFORMANTS), who was in close contact with the Christians of al-Ḥīra (see CHRISTIANS AND CHRISTIANITY), is reported to have said: "Muhammad cannot tell a better story than I and his talk is only of old fables which he has copied as I have" (Ibn Isḥāq, *Sīra*, 235, Eng. trans. Ibn Isḥāq-Guillaume, 162). *Khabar* (pl. *akhbār*) occurs 5 times in the Qurʾān with the meaning of "news, information, tidings of" (Q 27:7; 28:29; 9:94; 47:31; 99:4).

Although not one of the more common Arabic words for "narratives," to this list we should also add *nabaʾ* (pl. *anbāʾ*; story, information, or tiding, and which appears in Q 5:27; 6:34; 7:175; 9:70; 10:71; 14:9; 26:69; 27:22; 28:3; 38:21; 64:5; 68:2, etc.).

Distribution of the narratives in the Qurʾān

A single story is the focus of some sūras: Q 105 ("The Elephant," which alludes to the story of Abraha [q.v.]; for a discussion of this sūra, see Neuwirth, *Studien*, 36, 234; Marshall, *God*, 40-2; Blachère, no. 41. For all the references to Blachère below, note that Blachère, nos. 1-48 correspond to the first Meccan period, 49-70 to the second, 71-92 to the third, and 93-116 to the Medinan; see CHRONOLOGY AND THE QURʾĀN.); Q 71 ("Noah"; Blachère, no. 53; Marshall, *God*, 90-3), in which there is an "arabization" of the pantheon of the opponents of Noah (q.v.): "Do not leave your gods, and do not leave Wadd or Suwāʿ..." (Q 71:23; Paret, Geschichtsquelle, 36-7; Fahd, *Panthéon*, 132-4, 154-6, 182-97, on the "five noachic idols"; see IDOLS AND IMAGES; IDOLATRY AND IDOLATERS; POLYTHEISM AND ATHEISM); Q 12 ("Joseph"; Blachère, no. 79), the longest narrative of the Qurʾān (see de Prémare, *Joseph et Muhammad*), but this, contrary to Q 105 and 71, ends with peroration (Horovitz, *KU*, 1); Q 28 ("The Story"; Blachère, no. 81) tells of Moses (q.v.), Aaron (q.v.) and Hāmān (q.v.; Q 28:2-46), adding an account on Korah (q.v.; Q 28:76-82; cf. Q 40:24; 29:39; ʿAbbās, *Qaṣaṣ*, 416-9), probably because it was omitted in the preceding section on Moses (Bell, *Commentary*, ii, 53), which reads like a summary of Numbers 16. Some exegetes see a connection in the ordering and the themes of Q 26:18-9 and Q 27:7 (both on Moses), and Q 28:2-46, viewing this latter section as a commentary on the two earlier passages (Suyūṭī, *Tanāsuq*, 108).

Some narrative pieces, which, although in the redaction of the Qurʾān we possess (see COLLECTION OF THE QURʾĀN; CODICES OF THE QURʾĀN), have been integrated into sūras containing non-narrative materials, can be isolated from their position in the sūra and appear to be originally independent units: Q 89:6-14 (Blachère no. 42; Marshall, *God*, 46-7), which discusses ʿĀd (q.v.), Iram (q.v.) of the pillars, Thamūd (q.v.) and Pharaoh (q.v.; on Iram see Horovitz, *KU*, 89-90). This segment has the same formulaic introduction as Q 105 ("Have you not seen how your lord did with..."). In

Q 38:67-88 (Blachère, no. 61), on Adam (see ADAM AND EVE), the angels (see ANGEL) and Iblīs (q.v.), the unity of the passage can be seen not only from the common subject, but from the rhymes in *īm, īn, ūn, ūm* (Nöldeke, *GQ*, i, 131; see RHYMED PROSE), and from introductory and conclusive formulas that both contain the word "tiding" *(naba')*. Q 14:1-21 ("Abraham"; Blachère, no. 78) can be isolated as a unity, although its limits are not as clear as in the preceding examples. The same thing could be said of Q 40:23-56 (Blachère, no. 80), on the incredulity of Pharaoh, because the following passage, Q 40:57-85, with rhyme in *īn* and *ūn*, has no relation to it (Nöldeke, *GQ*, i, 153; Horovitz, *KU*, 2).

In addition to these whole or partly closed narrative pieces we find other passages that are composed entirely of several stories, or which are built around a core of stories. Q 20 "Ṭā Hā," also called "the son of Moses"; Biqāʿī, *Maṣāʿid*, ii, 267; Kandil, Surennamen, 51; Blachère, no. 57) contains two stories, on Moses (Q 20:9-99) and Adam (Q 20:115-28), but it should be added that Q 20:1-113 appears as a textual unity, whose introduction is Q 20:1-8, the eschatological conclusion (see ESCHATOLOGY) being contained in Q 20:100-13. Q 20:115-35 seems to be an addition, as suggested by the content of Q 20:114: "So exalted be God, the true king...."

On the other hand, we also have a set of stories in Q 54:9-42 (Blachère, no. 50): Noah (Q 54:9-17), the people of ʿĀd (Q 54:18-22), Thamūd (Q 54:23-32), Lot (q.v.; Q 54:33-40) and Pharaoh (Q 54:41-2). But Q 54:1-8 and Q 54:43-55 are in an inner relationship, which is the eschatological theme ("The hour has drawn nigh," Q 54:1; "The Hour" is another name for this sūra, now called "The Moon" [Sūrat al-Qamar]). This is why some exegetes (see EXEGESIS OF THE QURʾĀN: CLASSICAL AND MEDIEVAL) say that Q 54 is related to the end of the preceding sūra, Q 53:57: "The imminent is imminent" (Rāzī, *Tafsīr*, xxix, 28), or that it develops and elucidates the end of the same sūra (Biqāʿī, *Naẓm*, vii, 339, ad Q 54:1; id., *Maṣāʿid al-naẓar*, iii, 39-40). In the same way, Q 26:10-189 (Blachère, no. 58; Marshall, *God*, 93-7) has a set of seven stories, to which Q 26:1-9 is the preamble, and Q 26:190-227 the conclusion: Moses (Q 26:10-68), Abraham (q.v.; Q 26:69-104), Noah (Q 26:105-22), Hūd (q.v.) and the people of ʿĀd (Q 26:123-40), Ṣāliḥ (q.v.) and Thamūd (Q 26:141-59), Lot (Q 26:160-75) and the People of the Thicket (q.v.; Q 26:176-89). See also Q 15:26-48 (Blachère, no. 59), on Adam and Iblīs, with a brief description of hell (see HELL AND HELLFIRE) and paradise (q.v.); Q 15:49-60, about Abraham: "Tell my servants (Q 15:49)... And tell them of the guests of Abraham" (Q 15:51); Q 15:61-75, on Lot; Q 15:76-9, on the People of the Thicket; and Q 15:80-4, on Ḥijr (q.v.; Horovitz, *KU*, 2).

In Q 19 ("Mary"; Blachère, no. 60), the two parts: Q 19:2-74 (composed only of stories) and Q 19:75-98, were probably not together initially, as seen from the difference in the rhyme scheme. In the narrative part (Q 19:2-63), we find some of the earliest qurʾānic mentions of New Testament figures: Mary (q.v.; in Q 19:28, Mary is called "the sister of Aaron"; later, at Q 3:35 and 66:12, she is likewise considered the daughter of ʿImrān [q.v.]; Horovitz, *Jewish proper names*, 10), Zechariah (q.v.), John the Baptist (q.v.) and Jesus (Q 19:2-40; Nöldeke, *GQ*, i, 130), followed by accounts of Abraham (Q 19:41-50), Moses, Ishmael (q.v.) and Idrīs (q.v.; Q 19:51-8). Q 38 ("Ṣād," also named "The Son of David"; Ibn al-Jawzī, *Zād*, vii, 3; Kandil, Surennamen, 51; Blachère, no. 61), one of whose narrative passages is discussed above, is constructed similarly: introduction (Q 38:1-11); stories: Q 38:12-6 (destroyed nations), Q 38:17-28

(David [q.v.]), Q 38:29-40 (Solomon [q.v.]), Q 38:41-4 (Job [q.v.]), Q 38:45-9 (mention of Abraham, Isaac [q.v.], Jacob [q.v.; in five qur'ānic verses he is seen as the son of Abraham, and not his grand-son; cf. Q 21:72; 29:27; 6:84], Ishmael, Elisha [q.v.], Dhū l-Kifl [q.v.]); and, finally, a conclusion on the believers and unbelievers in the afterlife (Q 38:50-66; Horovitz, *KU,* 2-3; for the rest of the sūra [Q 36:67-88], see above).

The construction of Q 18 ("The Cave" or "People of the Cave"; Blachère, no. 70) does not use the same mode of closure: introduction (Q 18:1-8), stories (Q 18:9-98), conclusion on the fate of the unbelievers and believers (Q 18:99-110). The stories are of: the Seven Sleepers (Q 18:9-26; see MEN OF THE CAVE), the master of the garden (Q 18:32-44; cf. Isaiah 5, the Song of the Vineyard; Luke 12:16-21; Hirschfeld, *New researches,* 87-8; Sabbagh, *Métaphore,* 217-18, §385, 265; Lohmann, Gleichnisreden, 88-96; cf. Q 68:17-33, "the masters of the garden"; Andrae, *Mohammed, sein Leben,* 70; id., *Mahomet,* 85 [Fr. trans.]; ʿAbbās, *Qaṣaṣ,* 419-23), Moses and the servant of God (Q 18:60-82), Dhū l-Qarnayn (lit. "the possessor of the two horns"; Q 18:83-98, with an evocation of the tale of Gog and Magog [q.v.]; Horovitz, *KU,* 150; see ALEXANDER). As we see here, Q 18:27-31 and Q 18:45-50 interrupt the set of stories. Q 27 ("The Ant," or the sūra of Solomon; Blachère, no. 69; Suyūṭī, *Itqān,* chap. 17, i, 194; Kandil, Surennamen, 51) also varies from the pattern. After the introduction (Q 27:1-6) we do find narrative sections: Moses (Q 27:7-14), David, Solomon, the hoopoe (see ANIMAL LIFE), the Queen of Sheba (Q 27:15-44, Lassner, *Demonizing;* Gilliot, La reine de Saba', légende ou réalité?; Norris, Elements, 256-7; see BILQĪS), Thamūd (Q 27:45-53), Lot (Q 27:54-8). But the rest of the sūra (Q 27:59-93) cannot be seen as the conclusion of the preceding stories; it is too long for that, and it has a hymnic, a polemical (see POLEMIC AND POLEMICAL LANGUAGE) and an eschatological content.

On the other hand, the major part of Q 11 ("Hūd"; Blachère, no. 77; Marshall, *God,* 97-105) deals with stories (Q 11:25-100), and is followed by eschatological reflections related to them (Q 11:101-17). The introduction (Q 11:1-24), however, appears not to have a close internal relationship to these two parts. The narrative sections are: Noah (Q 11:25-49), Hūd (Q 11:50-60), Ṣāliḥ (Q 11:61-8), Abraham (Q 11:69-83), Shuʿayb (q.v.; Wansbrough, *QS,* 21-5, 28-9) and the Midianites (Q 11:84-95; see MIDIAN) and Moses (Q 11:96-8). Q 29 (Blachère, no. 83) has various accounts: on Noah (Q 29:14-5), Abraham and Lot (Q 29:16-35), Midian, Shuʿayb, ʿĀd, Thamūd, Korah and Pharaoh, Hāmān and Moses (Q 29:36-40; Horovitz, *KU,* 23). In Q 7 (Sūrat al-Aʿrāf, "The Battlements"; Blachère, no. 89; Marshall, *God,* 106-14; see PEOPLE OF THE HEIGHTS) the narrative sections are predominant: Iblīs, Adam and his wife (Q 7:11-25; Hirschberg, Sündenfall, 33-6), Noah, Hūd, Ṣāliḥ, Lot and Shuʿayb, and the destroyed cities (Q 7:59-102), Moses, the magicians (see MAGIC) and the five scourges of Egypt (q.v.; Q 7:133), etc. (Q 7:103-62), the transgressors of the Sabbath (q.v.) transformed into monkeys (Q 7:163-8; Speyer, *Erzählungen,* 313-4, 340-1; see JEWS AND JUDAISM), reminder of the signs (q.v.) of God towards humankind (Q 7:169-74), reminder of the tidings *(naba')* of God (Q 7:175-6); but neither the long interruption in the text (Q 7:26-58), nor the end of this sūra (Q 7:177-206) are in an inner relation with these narratives. And in the introduction, we find only a brief allusion to them, in Q 7:4: "How many a city we have destroyed" (see Q 7:1-10; cf. Suyūṭī, *Tanāsuq,* 87, in which the relation between Q 6:6, "how we destroyed before them many a generation," and the beginning of Q 7 is stressed; see Horovitz, *KU*, 3). Q 2 (Blachère, no. 93) also contains several stories or legends: Adam (Q 2:30-9), Moses (Q 2:49-70; Marshall, *God,* 126-7; the name of the sūra "The Cow" is taken from Q 2:68 f.; cf. Numbers 1-10); Saul (q.v.), David (q.v.) and Goliath (q.v.; Q 2:243-52; Horovitz, *KU,* 106, 123; Jād al-Mawlā, *Qiṣaṣ,* 174-89).

Even if narrative sections do not comprise the major part of the entire text of other sūras, they do constitute an important part of some: Q 51:24-46 (on Abraham and his guests, Moses and Pharaoh, ʿĀd, Thamūd and Noah; Blachère, no. 49; Marshall, *God,* 48-9); Q 37 (Blachère, no. 52), on Noah (Q 37:75-80), Abraham and Isaac (Q 37:83-113), Moses and Aaron (Q 37:114-22), Elijah (Q 37:123-30), Lot (Q 37:133-8), Jonah (q.v.; Q 37:139-48); Q 44 (Blachère, no. 55), on Pharaoh (Q 44:17-33); Q 21 ("The Prophets"; Blachère, no. 67), on Moses and Abraham (Q 21:48-73), Lot, Noah, David, Solomon, Job, Jonah, Zechariah, John, with mention of Ishmael, Idrīs, Dhū l-Kifl, and allusion, without their names, to Mary and Jesus (Q 44:74-91; Horovitz, *KU,* 3); Q 36 (Blachère, no. 62), the parable/story of the inhabitants of the ungodly city who did not listen to the words of the three apostles (Q 36:13-29; often related to tales about disciples of Jesus at Antioch [see APOSTLE]; Ṭabarī, *Taʾrīkh,* i, 789-93; id., *History,* iv, 167-70; Masʿūdī, *Murūj/Prairies*, §127-8, 722; in particular, the figure of Ḥabīb the Carpenter, perhaps to be identified with Agabus, is often connected to this story; Vajda, Ḥabīb al-Nadjdjār; Grimme, *Mohammed,* ii, 97; Ahrens, *Mohammed,* 143-4; Bell, *Commentary,* ii, 138-9; Horovitz, *KU,* 19-20; Fück, Zum Problem, 74; Blachère, 250, n. 12: "Parabole des citadins impies"; Norris, Elements, 255-6); Q 34:10-9 ("Sheba"; Blachère, no. 87), on David, Solomon and al-ʿArim (q.v.; the last named possibly refers to the breaching of the dam of Mārib; Bell, *Commentary,* ii, 116); Q 6:74-83, on Abraham and his father Āzar (q.v.; Horovitz, *KU,* 85-6; Blachère, no. 91); Q 5 ("The Table"; Blachère, no. 116), on the two sons of Adam (Q 5:27-32; Cain and Abel [q.v.] are not named; cf. *Gen* 4:3-16), Jesus and the "table" (q.v.; *māʾida,* probably an Ethiopic derivative; Jeffery, *For. vocab.*, 255-6), etc. (Q 5:110-6, the "table" from which the sūra takes its name is often understood as a reference to the Eucharist; Norris, Elements, 255).

In other sūras the narrative sections are reduced to a few verses. This is the case in Q 69:4-12 (Blachère, no. 24), which references Thamūd, ʿĀd, Pharaoh, the subverted cities *(al-muʾtafikāt),* and the ark (q.v.; of Noah). Q 17 ("The Night Journey," also called "The Sons of Israel"; Blachère, no. 74; see ASCENSION) mentions Adam, the angels and Iblīs (Q 17:61-5), Moses and Pharaoh (Q 17:101-4). Some sūras have only allusive verses: Q 85 (Blachère, no. 43), to "the People of the Ditch" (q.v.; *aṣḥāb al-ukhdūd,* Q 85:1-7, this could be an allusion to the persecution of the Christians of Najrān [q.v.] by the Jew Dhū Nuwās; Muqātil, *Tafsīr,* iv, 647-8; this interpretation, and others, are seen in: Ṭabarī, *Tafsīr,* xxx, ed. ʿAlī, 131-5; Bell, *Commentary,* ii, 517-8; Horovitz, *KU,* 92-3), Pharaoh and Thamūd (Q 85:17-20; Marshall, *God,* 44-5); Q 53:50-4 (Blachère, no. 30; Marshall, *God,* 47), to ʿĀd, Thamūd, Noah, the subverted city *(al-muʾtafika);* Q 44:37 (Blachère, no. 55), to the people of Tubbaʿ (q.v.; Horovitz, *KU,* 102-3; for the longer narrative section of this sūra, see above). Finally, it should be noted here that the pericope of Sūra Luqmān (Q 31; see LUQMĀN) which deals with that legendary hero (Q 31:12-19; Blachère no. 84) pertains more to the genre of wisdom-literature than to that of narratives (Horovitz, *KU,* 132-6).

Still other verses contain a mere enumeration: Noah, the People of the Well/Ditch (*aṣḥāb al-rass*, see PEOPLE OF THE DITCH), Thamūd, ʿĀd, Pharaoh, Lot, the People of the Thicket and the people of Tubbaʿ (Q 50:12-4; Blachère, no. 56); Noah, ʿĀd, Pharaoh (in Q 38:12 Pharaoh is termed "he of the tent-pegs" [see TENTS AND TENT PEGS]; cf. Q 89:10; Muqātil [*Tafsīr*, iii, 638] describes some form of punishment supposedly practiced by him; Bell [*Commentary*, ii, 537] suggests boundary-posts or a form of punishment; Speyer [*Erzählungen*, 283] sees in it an allusion to the construction of the Tower of Babel attributed to Nimrod [q.v.]; Horovitz [*KU*, 130] thinks this eponym refers to constructions undertaken during his reign; see Q 28:38; Norris, Elements, 249), Thamūd and Lot (Q 38:12-4; Blachère, no. 42; see the discussion of the longer narrative section of this sūra above); the destruction of ʿĀd, Thamūd, the People of the Ditch, and other generations (Q 25:38; Blachère, no. 68); the people of Noah, of Abraham, of Lot, of Midian (Horovitz, *KU*, 138) and Moses, ʿĀd and Thamūd (Q 22:42-5; Blachère, no. 109; Marshall, *God*, 119-24); Abraham, Isaac, Jacob, Noah, David, Solomon, Job, Joseph, Moses, Aaron, Zechariah, John the Baptist, Jesus, Elijah, Ishmael, Elisha, Jonah, Lot (Q 6:83-7; Blachère, no. 91); see also Q 4:163-5 (Blachère, no. 102); Q 9:70 (Blachère, no. 115). The Qurʾān's transition from long narrative passages to such mere enumerations of narrative motifs is represented by passages which are very formulaic and concise, elliptical versions of stories, such as Q 21:74-91 (see above; Horovitz, *KU*, 3).

The reader of the Qurʾān is struck by the fact that the narratives and particularly the punishment stories occupy less space in the Medinan sūras than in the Meccan (Horovitz, *KU*, 25-7). In the Medinan period only a few brief narratives or set phrases (e.g. Q 2:246-51, where Muḥammad's new situation as a military leader is mirrored in the lives of Saul and David; Marshall, *God*, 162; Q 5:20-6, etc.), often in reference to punishment stories, "constitute the rather meagre narrative clothing of the believer-unbeliever relationship in Medina" (Marshall, *God*, 161). One explanation for why there is this difference in the pre- and post-emigration (*hijra*, see EMIGRATION) material could be the changed religious situation; yet another may be that Muḥammad's authority was better accepted in Medina (Marshall, *God*, 163), and that he therefore had to turn his attention to the legal matters involved in organizing a city: i.e. visions figured more prominently in the first stage of his mission, whereas practical matters absorbed much of the later part.

Categorization of the narratives

In a well known tradition, Muḥammad was taught to recite the Qurʾān according to seven *aḥruf* (pl. of *ḥarf*, edge, letter, word, aspect, etc.; Ṭabarī, *Tafsīr*, ed. Shākir, i, 43, no. 40; 50, no. 47; id., *Commentary*, i, 21 [Eng. trans.]; see READINGS OF THE QURʾĀN). This has been most commonly interpreted as dialects (q.v.), readings, etc. But, there are other understandings of "*ḥarf*," which seem to be a summary of the essential genres contained in the Qurʾān: "The Qurʾān was sent down according to seven *ḥarf*s: command and prohibition (see COMMANDMENTS; FORBIDDEN), encouragement of good and discouragement of evil (see GOOD AND EVIL), dialectic [a better rendition of *jadal* is controversy; see DEBATE AND DISPUTATION], narrative, and parable *(qaṣaṣ wa-mathal)*" (Ṭabarī, *Tafsīr*, i, 58-70; id., *Commentary*, i, 29; Gilliot, Les sept "lectures," 20-1; in other versions, "narrative" *[qaṣaṣ]* is replaced by "ambiguous" *[mutashābih]*; see AMBIGUOUS). Yet other interpretations understand the seven *ḥarf*s to be: "[...] Permitted and prohibited, command and prohibition, relation *(khabar)* of what was before them and will be after them, the exposition of parables" (Abū ʿUbayd, *Gharīb al-ḥadīth,* iii, 160). This seems to be a primitive attempt to classify the essential genres contained in the Qurʾān. In some versions, where "narrative" is replaced by "ambiguous," the question arises as to whether or not the narratives were "ambiguous" (Suyūṭī [*Itqān,* chap. 43, iii, 4] takes qurʾānic legal passages [see LAW AND THE QURʾĀN], as well as "promise and threat," or eschatological discussions, to be "well established," *muḥkam;* narratives and parables are termed "ambiguous," *mutashābih;* ʿAbd Rabbih [*Buḥūth,* 57] writes that narratives do not pertain to *mutashābih,* but he does not provide any further explanation), that is, in need of an interpretation. In this context the contrasting pair *muḥkam/mutashābih* (lit. clear/ambiguous) refers to the difference between legal proscriptions and prescriptions that must be obeyed, and the narrative materials, which are a matter of warning (see WARNER) and inquiry, or "the object of belief but not of conduct" (Abū ʿUbayd, *Nāsikh,* 3-4, according to Ibn ʿAbbās; Wansbrough, *QS,* 150-1). Be that as it may, the narratives appeared very early as one of the major components of the Qurʾān.

As for a classification of the narrative materials, we can distinguish between the stories of the prophets and messengers, the punishment stories (Watt-Bell, *Introduction,* 127-35; Welch, Formulaic features of the punishment-stories), which include large portions of the preceding category, and the other stories (see above under *Distribution of the narratives in the Qurʾān*).

Formulaic features in the narratives

It is well known that a wide variety of formulaic elements occur throughout the Qurʾān (see LANGUAGE AND STYLE OF THE QURʾĀN; GRAMMAR AND THE QURʾĀN). This is in keeping with its basically oral nature (see ORALITY), but perhaps is also a consequence of its reshaping. Such formulaic elements include introductory statements, refrains (e.g. "O which of your lord's bounties will the two of you deny?" in Q 55; see EXHORTATIONS), and repeated rhyme phrases, etc. (Nöldeke, *GQ,* i, 29-30; Wansbrough, *QS,* 25-7; Crapon de Crapona, *Coran,* 215 f.; Neuwirth, *Studien,* 175-8). The accounts of the Qurʾān also contain formulaic features, which are, in the words of Welch (Formulaic features, 77), "repeated elements that convey added force to passages that are already powerful in their warnings" to those who reject the supposed "messengers" of God.

The great deeds of God in history, in creation (q.v.) and in the universe (see COSMOLOGY) are his signs *(āyāt).* This is the reason why we find so many transitions in the Qurʾān from descriptions of creation to narrative sections, as is the case in the Psalms (*Ps* 68, 105, 106, etc.), with which the Qurʾān shares so many features, stylistic forms, and themes in common (Paret, Geschichtsquelle, 38; indeed, these similarities have led some scholars to speak of "Semitic" rhetorical structures; Meynet et al., *Rhétorique sémitique;* Cuypers, Structures rhétoriques dans le Coran, 109, 191-3; id., Structures rhétoriques des sourates 105 à 114, 192-3). This creation-narrative transition results in a peculiar type of ellipsis, in which short words (like *idh* [usually translated as "when"] and *wa-idh* ["and when"]) introduce something new in the development of the text, indicating that "something happened/will happen." *Wa-idh* is the most frequent sign of this type of transition: Q 2:30, 34; 18:16, 50, 60; etc. Almost always this formula introduces legends or legendary features (Nöldeke, *Neue Beiträge,* 17; Horovitz, *KU,* 4). *Idh* occurs only rarely in this function: Q 12:4; 27:7. These words are followed by the perfect, often of verbs expressing a mode of speaking *(qāla, nādā),* a fact which shows that, for the Qurʾān, it is not so much the events that are important, as the rendering of the words (Horovitz, ibid.; see SPEECH). The following are examples of other transitions:

One formula appears twice in the early period: "Have you not seen how your lord did with…" (Q 105:1; 19:6; also in Q 25:45, but here it is related to a natural phenomenon). A shorter (Medinan) formula: "Have you not regarded" (*a-lam tara ilā,* Q 2:243, 246, 258) is used in narrative sections, whereas a slight variation *(a-lam tara anna)* is frequent in hymnic descriptions (Horovitz, *KU,* 4-5).

The interrogative expression, "Have you received the story…" (*Hal atāka ḥadīth,* Q 85:17; 20:9; 51:24; 79:15; also in other contexts, such as the eschatological one of Q 88:1) is close to "Are there not come to you the tidings…" (*a-lam yaʾtikum nabaʾ,* Q 64:5; 14:9). A recurrent formula in the punishment stories is: "[So and So] cried lies" (*kadhdhabat,* Q 91:11; 69:4; 54:9, 18:23, 33; 26:105, 123, 141, 160; 38:12; 40:5; 50:12; see LIE).

Other formulas have as a common feature God speaking in the first person plural, as "Surely we have sent" *(laqad arsalnā),* "We have sent" *(innā arsalnā),* or "when we sent" (*idh arsalnā,* cf. e.g. Q 73:15; 71:1; 36:14; 23:23; 27:45; 2:151 ["as also we have sent," *kamā arsalnā*]); "we gave" *(wa-laqad ataynā)* or "we gave him" *(ataynāhu),* with an object (science, judgment [q.v.], wisdom, etc.; cf. Q 21:48, 51, 74, 79; 27:15; 31:12; 34:10); "we will recite to you something of the tidings of…" (*natlū ʿalayka min nabāʾi,* Q 28:3). See above for "we relate" (*naquṣṣu;* Horovitz, *KU,* 5).

"To recite" *(talā)* and " to inform" *(nabbaʾa,* see above under *nabaʾ),* however, are used mostly in the imperative: Q 26:69; 10:71; 7:175; 5:27. This is also the case for "to mention/remember" *(dhakara):* "and mention in the book" (Q 19:16, 41, 51, 54, 56); "and remember our servant" (Q 38:17, 41, 45); "and make mention of/remember" (Q 38:48; 46:21; Horovitz, ibid.). Another imperative is "Propose to them the parable/example of…" (*wa-ḍrib lahum mathalan,* Q 18:32; 36:13; cf. 16:112; 66:10, in which the subject is God, but neither of which is an imperative; Horovitz, ibid.). For the formulas particular to the punishment stories, see Horovitz, *KU,* 6 and Welch, Formulaic features.

It should be noted also that special formulas occur at the ends of legends in some sūras: "Now we have made the Qurʾān easy for remembrance" *(wa-laqad yassarnā l-qurʾāna lil-dhikri);* "Is there any who will remember" (*fa-hal min mudhakkir,* Q 54:17; cf. Q 54:22, 32, 40; or only with the end of this formula, Q 54:51); "Surely in that is a sign, yet most of them are not believers" (Q 26:8, 67, 103, 121, 139, 158, 174, 190). These *loci* belong to the broader genre of "sign-passages," an expression of R. Bell (Watt-Bell, *Introduction,* 123-7; Wansbrough, *QS,* 5-6).

Main characteristics of the narratives, their literary and theological effect

Most of these narratives present mythical characters of stereotyped figures. Their repetition throughout the Qurʾān, above all in the Meccan sūras, in long, middle-sized and short sections, or allusive passages, had and still has an effect on the listener or reader. Their binary oppositional form, peculiar to the myths, puts the listener/reader in a state of ethical or theological decision or choice concerning his or her own status (Gilliot, De l'impossible censure du récit légendaire; see ETHICS

AND THE QUR'ĀN; THEOLOGY AND THE QUR'ĀN). Some of these binary oppositions are: good vs. evil; staying on the right path *(hudā)* vs. straying from it (*ḍalāl*, see ERROR; ASTRAY); believers vs. unbelievers; submission *(islām)* to God vs. "rebellion" (q.v.; see also DISOBEDIENCE; CORRUPTION); hero vs. anti-hero; "messenger" or "prophet" (or king; see KINGS AND RULERS) vs. Pharaoh or "tyrant" (Gilliot, Récit, mythe et histoire, 280-3; see OPPRESSION; POLITICS AND THE QUR'ĀN); good cities vs. subverted or destroyed cities (see PAIRS AND PAIRING). Muslim exegetes, with the help of extra-qur'ānic traditions, use these passages to establish a real typology of submission to God and rebellion against him, adding many other narratives or details, so that the allusive text of the Qur'ān might be "completed" (Gilliot, Mythe, récit, histoire du salut, 241), and, above all, so that these narratives — particularly the accounts about the prophets and messengers — may appear as a *preparatio prophetica*, i.e. a preparation and anticipation of the character and deeds of the prophet Muḥammad (Gilliot, Récit, mythe et histoire, 278-9). It is therefore no wonder, given the importance of the narratives in the Qur'ān, that the tales/stories of the prophets became a genre in its own right in Arabic Islamic literature, which had its beginnings towards the end of the first/sixth century (Khoury, *Légendes prophétiques*). These traditions, like those contained in the qur'ānic commentaries (there is much overlap between the accounts found in these two literary genres), are borrowed from the Jewish, Christian, Arabic, Hellenistic, Persian, etc., lore of the Middle East, but they are chosen, reinterpreted and adapted according to the *Weltanschauung* of Muḥammad, the Qur'ān and Islam (q.v.).

But the Qur'ān itself, whose narrative passages evince a familiarity with the aforementioned lore of the Middle East (leading some to the conclusion that Muḥammad, his informants and Companions probably, in several cases, had Aramaic books and oral traditions at their disposal; Luxenberg, *Die syro-aramäische Lesart*, passim) already manifests this same process. These accounts, however, most of which are not long (that of Q 12, on Joseph, is the longest one), have been established according to a new situation, a new representation of God, the universe, creation, prophets, and humankind: "In speaking of the Biblical prophets, Muḥammad more than once fashioned his narrative on the contemporary situation in Mekka and Yathrib" (Rezvan, Qur'ān, 41b, with examples). The characters presented in these stories are anticipations of Muḥammad, particularly the character of Abraham, who appears as a "Muḥammadan Abraham" or "a biblical Muḥammad" (Fück, Zum Problem, 77, probably referring to Snouck Hurgronje, *Het Mekkaansche Feest*, 23-30 [Fr. trans. in id., *Selected works*, 186-93]; C.H. Snouck Hurgronje, La légende qorânique d'Abraham). One could even say that in the narratives on the prophets, Muḥammad "substitutes his person to that of the ancient prophets" (Ahrens, *Muhammed*, 139; Nöldeke, *GQ*, i, 119-20). With the psychological and theological evolution of Muḥammad, the individuality of the different messengers becomes more and more indistinct, and the similarities with the Arabian prophet greater (see Q 6:84-90, with a mere list: Isaac, Jacob, Job, Joseph, Moses, Aaron, Noah, David, Solomon, Zechariah, John, Jesus, Elijah, Ishmael, Elisha, Jonah, Lot, but this time without the "Arab prophets," Hūd, Ṣāliḥ, Shu'ayb; Blachère, no. 91). At the same time, their adversaries express the peculiarities of the contemporary opponents of Muḥammad (R. Paret, Geschichtsquelle, 36). This treatment of the prophets in the Qur'ān has led at least one scholar to speak of the "monoprophetism" of the Qurʾān and of Islam (A.-L. de Prémare, L'islam comme monoprophétisme), meaning that all the prophets are seen as Muḥammad saw himself in his conception of prophecy and in his life (cf. the allegation that the Arabian prophet had been foretold in the Hebrew and Christian scriptures in Q 7:157; Wansbrough, *QS*, 63-5). This is the consequence of Muḥammad's claim of finality, or completion (Ger. *Totalitätsanspruch;* Beck, Monotheistische Religion, 68), with respect to the preceding religions. These prophet narratives can therefore be considered one of the most important vehicles of qurʾānic and Islamic theology and ethics.

The narratives of the Qurʾān have, until the present day, continued to be very popular in Islam. Those on the prophets are especially so: they are presented in special books (even for children), together with the post-qurʾānic traditions about the prophets. Even if a number of contemporary Muslim scholars try to "purify" (censure) the Islamic exegetical literature of such "Judaica" (Abū Shahaba, *al-Isrāʾīliyyāt;* Rabīʿ, *al-Isrāʾīliyyāt fī Tafsīr al-Ṭabarī*), these "fairy tales" continue to be prized as narrative entertainment ("the pleasure of the text") and for the religious and ethical messages they convey. In fact, the passages described as narrative consist "not so much of narrative as of *exempla*" (Wansbrough, *QS*, 18), a remark which corresponds to the "fragmentary character of Muslim scripture" (ibid.; see SCRIPTURE AND THE QURʾĀN).

Today, debate occasionally arises among Muslim scholars concerning the literary qualification of qurʾānic narratives. All, or nearly all, are agreed upon the "inimitable" qualities of the Qurʾān, both in content and in style (Muṣṭafā, *al-Iʿjāz;* ʿAbd Rabbih, *Buḥūth*, 141-90; see INIMITABILITY). But some have insisted that the purpose of the narrative passages is not primarily "historical," but, rather, that the Qurʾān utilized the "narrative art" to convey its theological, social and ethical message (see CONTEMPORARY CRITICAL PRACTICES AND THE QURʾĀN; EXEGESIS OF THE QURʾĀN: EARLY MODERN AND CONTEMPORARY). For instance, M.A. Khalaf Allāh (born in 1916) wrote a thesis on the qurʾānic narratives, which he submitted in 1947 to the Fuʾād 1st University (now Cairo University), in Cairo. Under pressure from scholars of al-Azhar, it was refused. But the text was reworked by its author and published as a book in 1951 (Khalaf Allāh, *al-Fann al-qaṣaṣī;* Jomier, Quelques positions). The book takes a psychological approach towards the narratives (see also Naqra, *Sikūlūjiyyat al-qiṣṣa*), looking at the relations of Muḥammad and other prophets with their societies (see COMMUNITY AND SOCIETY IN THE QURʾĀN). It is also an apologetic work. Some suspected him (Khaṭīb, *al-Qaṣaṣ al-qurʾānī*, 275-348, where even the symbolism is rejected; ʿAbd Rabbih, *Buḥūth*, 215-61) of doubting, or bringing into question, the "historicity" of the qurʾānic accounts. While the work of Khalaf Allāh would not be a locus of controversy in European or North American universities, the standard insights of form criticism remain unacceptable in most Muslim institutions of higher learning. To apply the term 'myths' to the qurʾānic narratives, to speak of myths in the sense that historians of religion use the term in defining the generative and foundational elements of religion, is anathema in such institutions.

Claude Gilliot

Bibliography
Primary: Abū ʿUbayd, *Gharīb al-ḥadīth*, ed. M. ʿAbd al-Muʿīd Khān, 4 vols., Hyderabad 1964-7; Biqāʿī, *Maṣāʿid al-naẓar lil-ishrāf ʿalā*

maqāṣid al-suwar, ed. ʿAbd al-Samīʿ M.A. Ḥasanayn, 3 vols., Riyadh 1987; id., *Naẓm,* ed. ʿAbd al-Razzāq Ghālib al-Mahdī, 8 vols., Beirut 1995; Dāmaghānī, *Wujūh,* ed. Muḥammad Ḥasan Abū l-ʿAzm al-Zafītī, 2 vols., Cairo 1992-5; Ibn Abī l-Zamanīn, Muḥammad b. ʿAbd Allāh b. ʿĪsā al-Murrī al-Andalusī al-Ilbīrī, *Tafsīr,* ed. Abū ʿAbdallāh Ḥusayn b. ʿUkāsha and M.b. Muṣṭafā al-Kanz, 5 vols., Cairo 2002; Ibn Isḥāq, *Sīra,* ed. Wüstenfeld; Ibn al-Jawzī, *Zād;* Masʿūdī, *Murūj,* ed. Ch. Pellat, 7 vols., Beirut 1966-79; Fr. trans. C. Pellat, *Les Prairies d'or,* 5 vols., Paris 1962-97; Rāzī, *Tafsīr,* ed. M. Muḥyī l-Dīn ʿAbd al-Ḥamīd, ʿA.I. al-Ṣāwī et al., 32 vols., Cairo 1933-62; Ṭabarī, *The Commentary on the Qurʾān,* trans. J. Cooper, Oxford 1987, i; id., *Tafsīr;* id., *Taʾrīkh,* ed. M.J. de Goeje et al.

Secondary: Th. Abāẓa, *al-Sard al-qaṣaṣī fī l-Qurʾān al-karīm,* Cairo 1976?; F.Ḥ. ʿAbbās, *al-Qaṣaṣ al-qurʾānī, īḥāʾuhu wa nafaḥātuhu,* Amman 1985, 1992[2]; Abdel-Meguid (Abdel-Aziz), A survey of the terms used in Arabic for 'narrative' and 'story', in *IQ* 1 (1954), 195-204; S.ʿA ʿAbd Rabbih, *Buḥūth fī qiṣaṣ al-Qurʾān,* Beirut 1972; K. Ahrens, *Mohammed als Religionsstifter,* Leipzig 1935; T. Andrae, *Mohammed, sein Leben und sein Glaube,* Göttingen 1932; Fr. trans. Jean Gaudefroy-Demombynes, *Mahomet. Sa vie et sa doctrine,* Paris 1945; Eng. trans. Theophil Menzel, *Mohammed, the man and his faith,* London 1936; Anon., *ʿUlūm al-Qurʾān ʿinda l-mufassirīn,* 3 vols., Qum 1996, iii, 385-401 (narratives in the Qurʾān and the mystery of their repetition), 403-83 *(judaica);* M. Bayūmī, *Qiṣaṣ al-Qurʾān,* al-Mansūra 1999; E. Beck, Monotheistische Religion und Religionen im Koran, in *Kairos* 2 (1959), 68-77; Bell, *Commentary;* W.A. Bijlefeld, Controversies around the qurʾanic Ibrāhīm narrative and its "orientalist" interpretations, in *MW* 72 (1982), 81-94; Blachère; I.J. Boullata (ed.), *Literary structures of religious meaning in the Qurʾān,* Richmond, Surrey 2000; P. Crapon de Crapona, *Le Coran. Aux sources de la parole oraculaire. Structures rythmiques des sourates mecquoises,* Paris 1981; M. Cuypers, Structures rhétoriques dans le Coran. Une analyse structurelle de la sourate "Joseph" et de quelques sourates brèves, in *MIDEO* 22 (1995), 107-95; id., Structures rhétoriques des sourates 105 à 114, in *MIDEO* 23 (1997), 157-96; J. Fück, Zum Problem der koranischen Erzählungen (review of D. Sidersky, *Les origines des légendes musulmanes dans le Coran et dans les vies des prophètes,* Paris 1933), in *OLZ* 37 (1934), cols. 73-77; C. Gilliot, De l'impossible censure du récit légendaire. *Adab* et *tafsīr*. Deux voies pour édifier l'ethos de l'*homo islamicus,* in *IOS* 19 (1999), 49-96; id., Mythe, récit, histoire du salut dans le Commentaire coranique de Tabari, in *JA* 282 (1994), 237-70; id., Récit, mythe et histoire chez Tabari. Une vision mythique de l'histoire universelle, in *MIDEO* 21 (1993), 277-89; id., La reine de Sabaʾ. Légende ou réalité ? in *Yémen, au pays de la reine de Sabaʾ. Exposition présentée à l'Institut du Monde Arabe du 25 octobre 1997 au 28 février 1998,* Paris 1997, 64-6; H. Grimme, *Mohammed.* i. *Das Leben nach den Quellen,* and ii. *Einleitung in den Koran. System der koranischen Theologie,* Münster 1892-5; A. Hebbo, *Die Fremdwörter in der arabischen Prophetenbiographie des Ibn Hischām,* Frankfurt-am-Main 1984; J.W. Hirschberg, Die Namen der "Gottes-Schriften" im Qurʾān, in *RO* 13 (1937), 72-84; id., Der Sündenfall in der altarabischen Poesie, in *RO* 9 (1933), 22-36; H. Hirschfeld, *New researches into the composition and exegesis of the Qoran,* London 1902; Horovitz, *KU;* M.A. Jād al-Mawlā et al., *Qiṣaṣ al-Qurʾān,* Cairo 1969; A.H. Johns, The qurʾānic representation of the Joseph story. Naturalistic or formulaic language? in Hawting and Shareef, *Approaches,* 37-70; J. Jomier, Quelques positions actuelles de l'exégèse coranique en Égypte, in *MIDEO* 1 (1954), 39-72; A. Jones, Narrative technique in the Qurʾān and in early poetry, in *JAL* 25 (1994), 185-91; L. Kandil, Die Surennamen in der offiziellen Kairiner Ausgabe und ihre Varianten, in *Der Islam* 69 (1992), 44-60; M.A. Khalaf Allāh, *al-Fann al-qaṣaṣī fī l-Qurʾān al-karīm* (with a study by Kh. ʿAbd al-Karīm), London/Beirut 1951, 1999[4]; ʿA. al-Khaṭīb, *al-Qaṣaṣ al-qurʾānī fī manṭūqihi wa mafhūmihi. Maʿa dirāsa taṭbīqiyya li-qiṣṣatay Ādam wa-Yūsuf,* Cairo 1974, repr. Beirut n.d.; R.G. Khoury, *Les légendes prophétiques dans l'Islam,* Wiesbaden 1978; J. Lassner, *Demonizing the Queen of Sheba,* Chicago 1993; Th. Lohmann, Die Gleichnisreden Muhammeds im Koran, in *Mitteilungen des Instituts für Orientforschung* (Berlin) 12 (1966), 75-118; 416-469; Ch. Luxenberg, *Die syro-aramäische Lesart des Koran. Ein Beitrag zur Entschlüsselung der Koransprache,* Berlin 2000; discussed by C. Gilliot in Langue et Coran. Une lecture syro-araméenne du Coran, in *Arabica* 2003; D. Marshall, *God, Muhammad and the unbelievers,* Richmond, Surrey 1999; R.C. Martin, Structural analysis and the Qurʾān. Newer approaches to the study of Islamic texts, in *Journal of the American Academy of Religion* 47/4 Thematic Issue: *Studies in Qurʾān and tafsir* (December 1980), 619-34; R. Meynet et al., *Rhétorique sémitique,* Paris 1998; M.S.Ḥ. Muṣṭafā, *al-Iʿjāz al-lughawī fī l-qiṣṣa al-qurʾāniyya,* Alexandria 1981; T. Naqra, *Sikūlūjiyyat al-qiṣṣa fī l-Qurʾān,* Tunis 1987; Neuwirth, *Studien;* Nöldeke, *GQ;* id., *Neue Beiträge zur semitischen Sprachwissenschaft,* Strasbourg 1910; H.T. Norris, *Qiṣaṣ* elements in the Qurʾān, in Beeston, *CHAL,* i, 246-59; R. Paret, Der Koran als Geschichtsquelle, in

Der Islam 37 (1961), 24-42; A.-L. de Prémare, L'islam comme monoprophétisme, in A. Laurent (ed.), *Vivre avec l'islam? Réflexions chrétiennes sur la religion de Mahomet,* Versailles 1997, 150-62; id., *Joseph et Muhammad. Le chapitre 12 du Coran,* Aix-en-Provence 1989; Ā.M. ʿA. Rabīʿ, *al-Isrāʾīliyyāt fī Tafsīr al-Ṭabarī,* Cairo 2001; E.A. Rezvan, The Qurʾān and its world: IV, in *Manuscripta orientalia* 3/4 (1997), 35-44; T. Sabbagh, *La métaphore dans le Coran,* Paris 1943; F. Sherif, *A guide to the contents of the Qurʾān,* London 1985; M. Sister, Metaphern und Vergleiche im Koran, in *Mitteilungen des Seminars für Orientalische Sprachen zu Berlin,* 2. Abt. *Westasiatische Studien* 34 (1931), 103-54; C.H. Snouck Hurgronje, La légende qorânique d'Abraham et la politique religieuse du prophète Mohammed. Traduit par G.-H. Bousquet, in *Revue africaine* 95 (1951), 273-88; id., *Het Mekkaansche Feest,* Leiden 1880 (repr. in *Verspreide geschriften,* Bonn und Leipzig 1923-7, i, 1-124; G.-H. Bousquet and J. Schacht [eds.], *Selected works of C. Snouck Hurgronje,* Leiden 1957, 171-213); Speyer, *Erzählungen;* G. Vajda, Ḥabīb al-Nadjdjār, in *EI*², iii, 12-3; Wansbrough, *QS;* Watt-Bell, *Introduction;* A.T. Welch, Formulaic features of the punishment-stories, in I.J. Boullata (ed.), *Literary structures of religious meaning in the Qurʾān,* Richmond, Surrey 2000, 77-116.

Nāsikh wa-Mansūkh see ABROGATION

Nasr see IDOLS AND IMAGES

Nation see COMMUNITY AND SOCIETY IN THE QURʾĀN; POLITICS AND THE QURʾĀN

Nature as Signs

Creation, i.e. natural phenomena, as indications of God's existence and power. In Islamic belief the Qurʾān is God's final message *(risāla)* conveyed by God's last messenger (q.v.; *rasūl*) and Prophet (*nabī,* see PROPHETS AND PROPHETHOOD), Muḥammad, to all humankind. Not only is it a final, yet primary, message but it is also a lucid and enlightening message, a *Qurʾān mubīn* (Q 15:1; see NAMES OF THE QURʾĀN) which distinguishes the good from the bad (*qawl faṣl,* Q 86:13), and which was revealed in the Arabic language (q.v.; Q 12:2). Elaborating some general semiotic principles, Roman Jakobson (Language in relation) insists that all messages are composed of signs. The Qurʾān has no problems with this idea and, indeed, over and over again, articulates a fundamental semiotics of its own: it does not have the sophistication of the complex theories offered by a C.S. Peirce (1839-1914; *Collected papers*) or an Umberto Eco *(Theory of semiotics)* but in scope and breadth it has every claim to being their equal: God proclaims, for example, that he will show humankind his signs (q.v.; lit. *āyātinā*) on the furthest horizons as well as deep within themselves (Q 41:53). People, such as the prophet Joseph (q.v.; Yūsuf) and his brothers (see BROTHER AND BROTHERHOOD), can be signs for those who seek, or enquire after [the truth] (*al-sāʾilīn,* Q 12:7). The very heavens (see HEAVEN AND SKY) and earth (q.v.) are alive with the signs of God:

> Behold! In the creation (q.v.) of the heavens and the earth; in the alternation of the night and the day (see DAY AND NIGHT); in the sailing of the ships (q.v.) through the ocean for the profit of mankind; in the rain which God sends down from the skies, thereby giving life to an earth that is dead (see AGRICULTURE AND VEGETATION); in the beasts of all kinds that he scatters through the earth (see ANIMAL LIFE); in the change of the winds (see AIR AND WIND), and the clouds which they trail like their slaves between the sky and the earth; — (Here) indeed are signs for a people that are wise (*la-āyātin li-qawmin yaʿqilūna,* Q 2:164; see also Q 3:190).

It is clear from this brief quotation that natural phenomena comprise a large portion of the divine signs and it is with these that this article will deal. According to the Qurʾān, nature itself praises God (Q 24:41;

see PRAISE; LAUDATION; GLORIFICATION OF GOD).

We will examine firstly the classical Empedoclean elements of fire (q.v.), air, water (q.v.) and earth and then move from terrestrial phenomena, in terms of the semiotics of the flora and fauna of the Qurʾān, to an appraisal of the celestial phenomena, before concluding with a survey of the semiotics of nature in qurʾānic eschatology (q.v.).

The Empedoclean elements: The semiotic substratum

The pre-Socratic philosopher Empedocles (d. ca. 433 B.C.E.) held that the phenomenal world derived from the four key elements of fire, air, water and earth which would combine in varying proportions to produce all that we see around us. While the Qurʾān adheres to no such tidy theory, it is nonetheless clear that the four elements figure largely in a variety of forms and, importantly, denote or signify numerous salutary messages for the believers.

Fire

While fire is clearly a sign, reminder or memento *(tadhkira)* of God's providence to humankind (cf. Q 56:73), being in A. Yusuf Ali's words "an emblem of man's earliest civilisation" and standing "as a symbol of physical comfort and convenience to man [see BLESSING; GRACE], of the source of spiritual light [q.v.], and also of the warning to Evil [see GOOD AND EVIL] about its destruction" (Yusuf Ali, *Holy Qurʾān,* 1492, n. 5255), there can be little doubt that, for the majority of Muslims, fire *(al-nār),* primarily represents — indeed is! — hellfire (see HELL AND HELLFIRE; REWARD AND PUNISHMENT): and in harmony with his destined domain, Iblīs (see DEVIL) himself was created from fire. The wicked and the unbelievers (*kāfirūn,* see BELIEF AND UNBELIEF) are destined for hellfire where they will burn in appalling torment (see e.g. Q 40:70-2). Islamic eschatology, as Smith and Haddad *(Islamic understanding)* show, developed a vision of seven layers of *al-nār* with "each descending one an abode of increased torment." Thus "the purgatorial fire *(jahannam)*" will be reserved for grievously sinful Muslims (see SIN, MAJOR AND MINOR) while "the blazing fire *(saʿīr)*" will be for the Sabians (q.v.). Fire in the Qurʾān, then, in addition to being a gift (see GIFT-GIVING), may also signal pain, torment and loss. The latter, perhaps, constitute its primary signification.

Importantly, however, fire in the Qurʾān signifies presence, both divine and human (cf. Yusuf Ali, *Holy Qurʾān,* 791, n. 2541). For the prophet Moses (q.v.; Mūsā) the burning bush was a sign of God's presence and majesty (Q 20:10-12; see SECHINA). Immediate acknowledgement of that sacred presence was required in the divine command that Moses should remove his shoes (Q 20:12; compare *Exod* 3:1-5). God's voice "blazed forth" in the middle of nature itself, epitomized by that fire.

Finally, fire, paradoxically, signifies both danger and security in the Qurʾān: danger, because the giant-king Nimrod (q.v.) attempts to burn the prophet Abraham (q.v.; Ibrāhīm) to death in a fire (cf. Q 21:68-9, compare Daniel 3:16-50); security, because God commands the fire to be cool and to become a place of peace and safety *(salāman)* for Abraham.

Air

The standard Arabic word for "air, atmosphere, wind, weather, climate," is *al-hawāʾ* (pl. *ahwiya, ahwāʾ;* cf. Gk. *aēr).* It is in its synonyms, however, and especially in words for wind like *rīḥ* (pl. *riyāḥ)* which imply air, that we may best seek and survey this second Empedoclean element in the text of the Qurʾān. Wind is a sign of divine providence and bounty and, as A. Yusuf Ali puts it (*Holy Qurʾān,* 1663, n. 5864), the winds "are powerful factors in the government of the physical world… [and] point to the power and goodness of God" (see POWER AND IMPOTENCE; MERCY). The winds are both subject at all times to his will (cf. Q 42:33) and powerful implements of that will: they drive the rain-bearing clouds, reviving dead lands with a fruitful harvest in a manner akin to the forthcoming day of resurrection (q.v.; Q 7:57, see also Q 15:22; 30:48, 51). Q 77 is entitled Sūrat al-Mursalāt, which means literally "those who have been sent." Watt (*Companion,* 289) notes that the oath (see OATHS) that comprises Q 77:1-5 ("By the emissaries [winds] in succession, by the raging hurricanes") has been variously interpreted. It is possible that the first three verses are a reference to rain clouds while the fourth and fifth describe destroying winds. But he is aware that all the verses may be interpreted as referring to angels (see ANGEL). If the reference in Q 77:5 ("those who bring down a reminder") is indeed to the broadcasting of a reminder or message (*dhikr,* see MEMORY) by the winds, then A. Yusuf Ali's (ibid.) comment has some merit: "They literally carry sound, and therefore Messages, and metaphorically they are instrumental in making God's Revelation accessible to hearers." Fanciful or not, it is clear from the above that the air, in the form of the winds, serves as a major vehicle of God's power and bounty, and implies a less fearsome aspect of his natural creation than the terrible *nār.*

Water

Just as God has absolute power over the winds (cf. Q 42:33) so too he is lord of water: if he wished he could make it immediately undrinkable by rendering it bitter or salty *(ujāj an)* (Q 56:70; see also Q 11:7; see THRONE OF GOD). In a phrase that might variously have won the approval of both Empedocles and Darwin (although, of course, the Qurʾān does not teach evolution; see BIOLOGY AS THE CREATION AND STAGES OF LIFE), God states in the Qurʾān: "And we have made everything which lives out of water" (*wa-jaʿalnā min al-māʾ kulla shayʾin ḥayyin,* Q 21:30; see also Q 24:45). People themselves are essentially a creation by God from, or out of, water (Q 25:54). Water, then, participates in a fundamental qurʾānic semiotics of divine creation.

Abdel Haleem *(Understanding)* reminds us that there are more than sixty references to water in the Qurʾān, more than fifty to rivers and more than forty to sea. The sacred text itself insists that in the rain (lit.: "in what God sends down from the heavens in the way of water") "are signs for a people who understand" (*āyātin li-qawmin yaʿqilūna,* Q 2:164). The signs involve God's power and providence and may be divided semiotically into three major images and three simple signs, which build on these images: all together they constitute a kind of unstated covenant (q.v.) between God and man. It is not formally articulated in the style, for example, that the covenant is formulated in Genesis 15:18-21 and 22:15-8 between Yahweh and Abraham, but in its own way it is just as powerful.

Firstly, terrestrial life itself *(al-ḥayāt)* is likened to the rain that has a transitory effect on the parched earth: new plant life springs up but ultimately the earth absorbs the rainwater leaving only a more lasting aridity (Q 18:45). In the following verse, the Qurʾān points or signifies its own moral: money and heirs will pass but the merit derived from good deeds (q.v.) will endure in the sight of God (Q 18:46).

Secondly, water is a symbol and sign of life itself, terrestrially, but also, by extension, a sign of the divine life of God who has power over it. The Qurʾān asks what would happen if, one day, someone awoke to find that his water had vanished. Who could replace that flowing water? (Q 67:30; see also Yusuf Ali, *Holy Qurʾān,* 1583, n. 5591). There are interesting analogies to be drawn here (but not pressed overmuch) with John 4:13-4, where we read of the encounter by the well of Jesus (q.v.) and the Samaritan woman to whom God promises water that will quench every thirst and flow continually.

Our third major qurʾānic image, particularly apposite in its linkage of divine message and water, is that of the sea *(al-baḥr)* transformed into ink *(midādan)* and its never being sufficient to write out the words of God (lit. *kalimāt rabbī*) even if replenished with another sea of ink like it (Q 18:109; see WORD OF GOD; WRITING AND WRITING MATERIALS; INSTRUMENTS).

Building particularly on the last image of water as transformed into the inky vehicle for the divine message, we may now note that the Qurʾān tells us that God provides two kinds of water for the benefit of humankind: sweet fresh water and salt sea water (see Q 25:53; 35:12; see BARZAKH; BARRIER). Water is a divine gift to man (cf. Q 23:18-9; 50:9-11; 80:25). This is our first "simple sign," water as a sign of divine bounty.

Just as with water, humans are free to accept or reject the message of God, for there should classically be no compulsion in religion (cf. Q 10:99, see also *lā ikrāha fī l-dīn:* Q 2:256; see TOLERANCE AND COMPULSION; RELIGIOUS PLURALISM AND THE QURʾĀN). In which case, pursuing our metaphorical (but, nonetheless qurʾānic; see METAPHOR) identification of water as an inky vehicle for the divine message, that water may "become" our second and third "simple signs": it may be a sign of divine reward or a sign of divine punishment. The righteous will drink from the bounteous rivers *(anhār)* of paradise (q.v.; cf. Q 47:15); the wicked will drink boiling water *(ḥamīm)* in hell and resemble thirsty camels (see camel) whose thirst cannot be slaked *(al-hīm)* in their anguish (Q 56:54-5; see FOOD AND DRINK).

The covenant which may be deduced or extrapolated from all these watery images, real and metaphorical, is a very simple one; its spirit infuses the whole Qurʾān: God tells the believers that, if they show gratitude (see GRATITUDE AND INGRATITUDE) for the multifarious examples of his terrestrial bounty (an example of which is water), by doing good deeds, then they will assuredly receive a full reward in paradise. Ingratitude or contempt for that same bounty equals disbelief *(kufr)* and will plunge the ingrate into the fires of hell.

Earth

The Qurʾān refers much more to "the earth" *(al-arḍ),* i.e. this terrestrial world, by comparison with the heavens or skies *(al-samāwāt),* than earth *qua* earth in the stark, elemental Empedoclean sense. Thus there are references to the creation of the heavens and the earth (Q 2:164; 3:190) and that creation is indeed one of the signs *(āyāt)* of God, a semiotic indicator to those with real insight of God's majesty and power. The earth is full of God's signs (Q 51:20) and God is the lord of the heavens and the earth (*al-samāʾ wa-l-arḍ,* Q 51:23). That spacious earth (Q 29:56; also Q 15:19), provisioned by God (Q 77:27) as a gift to man (see Q 78:6-16) to be managed by man (Q 67:15), will one day be changed out of all recognition, at the end of time on the last day (Q 14:48; see LAST JUDGMENT; APOCALYPSE). On that terrible day of resurrection even the most hidden deeds (see EVIL DEEDS), which have been performed on the earth, will be made known (see Q 99:1-8; also Yusuf Ali, *Holy Qurʾān,* 1771, n. 6238; see RECORD OF HUMAN ACTIONS).

Much closer to the Empedoclean sense of earth *qua* earth, as opposed to *the* earth, is the Arabic word *ṭīn* meaning "clay" (q.v.) or "soil." In that great primal act of disobedience (q.v.), pride (q.v.) and rebellion (q.v.), Iblīs refuses to bow down before God's new creation, Adam (see ADAM AND EVE; BOWING AND PROSTRATION), as a mark of respect, proclaiming: *anā khayrun minhu: khalaqtanī min nārin wa-khalaqtahu min ṭīnin,* "I am better than he is: You created me from fire and you created him from clay" (Q 7:12; see also Q 2:34; 17:61; 38:71-6).

In addition to *ṭīn,* the Qurʾān also uses other Arabic words for the same event, which are closer to the Empedoclean elemental sense than *arḍ:* "Behold! your lord said to the angels: 'I am about to create man, from sounding clay, from mud molded into shape'" (*min ṣalṣālin min ḥamaʾin masnūnin,* Q 15:28; see also Q 15:33).

Terrestrial phenomena: The semiotics of the flora and fauna of the Qurʾān

Moving now from the four classical, simple Empedoclean elements of antiquity, fire, air, water and earth, out of which all natural phenomena were believed to be composed, we find that the Qurʾān is rich in the names of the more complex or compound natural structures or phenomena like trees (q.v.) and animals. These will be adumbrated here: several signify God's bounty to the earth, which he himself has created.

The Qurʾān mentions and symbolically utilizes a variety of trees (see SYMBOLIC IMAGERY). Some like the mysterious lote or lotus tree, *sidrat al-muntahā,* which grows in paradise, signify gardens (see GARDEN) and blessedness, especially when shorn of their thorns (Q 53:14; see also Q 56:28). A. Yusuf Ali (*Holy Qurʾān,* 1444, n. 5093) succinctly comments on the symbolism of this tree: "The wild Lote is thorny; under cultivation it yields good fruit and shade, and is symbolic of heavenly bliss.... The symbolism here is that the farthest Lote-Tree marked the bounds of heavenly knowledge as revealed to men (see KNOWLEDGE AND LEARNING), beyond which neither angels nor men could pass."

The lote tree, however, has a terrestrial as well as a celestial dimension. Besides being a sign of eternal life in paradise (see ETERNITY), it could also be a product and sign of terrestrial destruction and decay (see PUNISHMENT STORIES). The collapse of the Maʾrib dam in the sixth century C.E. in Sabaʾ (immortalized in the Qurʾān under the rubric of *sayl al-ʿarim,* "the flood of the dam," but recorded even before the revelation of the Qurʾān in the epigraphic south Arabian inscriptions, see CIH 541 in Conti Rossini, *Chrestomathia,* 73, 1.43; see also CIH 540 in ibid., 71, 1.6; see SHEBA; AL-ʿARIM; PRE-ISLAMIC ARABIA AND THE QURʾĀN) left in its wake, according to the Qurʾān, only two gardens "Producing bitter fruit and tamarisks, and some few (stunted) lote-trees" (Q 34:16; see GEOGRAPHY; EPIGRAPHY AND THE QURʾĀN).

Other trees of paradise named in the Qurʾān are the *ṭalḥ:* it is not entirely clear what kind of trees these are here but they are mentioned after the thornless lote trees (Q 56:29) and signify yet more examples of the joys and beauties of the plant life in the paradisiacal garden. A. Yusuf Ali (*Holy Qurʾān,* 1487, n. 5238) hazards that they may be a species of acacia tree and Arberry *(Koran)* has no hesitation in actually translating the word as acacias (Lane and Penrice, *Dictionary,* define *ṭalḥ* as a collective noun meaning a kind of acacia *[acacia gummifera]* but also as a banana tree). Both the thornless lote trees and these acacias are part of the furniture of paradise and, it hardly needs to be stressed here, the most common word for the latter in the Qurʾān has a particular semiotic significance in terms of visual beauty (q.v.): it is *al-janna,* the garden, a constant motif in qurʾānic eschatology. Thus we are told that it is in "gardens of ease [happiness or bliss]" *(jannāt al-naʿīm)* that the above-named trees will be found (Q 56:12).

All nature, then, is deployed in the qurʾānic imagery of paradise to indicate a state of bliss to which the believer should aspire and towards which that person should work with sound belief and good deeds (see FAITH; JOY AND MISERY). The celestial paradise is made credible by reference to terrestrial natural images with which the recipients of the qurʾānic message are already familiar.

Of course, not all the trees mentioned in the Qurʾān signify blessedness. The text offers us a short simile in which an "evil word" *(kalima khabītha)* is said to resemble an "evil tree" (*shajara khabītha,* Q 14:26; see GOSSIP). Perhaps the most famous of the "evil trees" mentioned in the Qurʾān is the tree of Zaqqūm (q.v.), "the cursed tree" (*al-shajara al-malʿūna,* Q 17:60; see also Q 37:62-6; 44:43-6; 56:52). This tree, which is "bitter" and "pungent" (see Yusuf Ali, *Holy Qurʾān,* 711, n. 2250), represents all that is unpleasant in the way of plant life. Netton has defined it (*Popular dictionary,* 264) as follows:

> Bitter smelling and fearsome tree in the pit of Hell with flowers which resemble demonic heads. The stomachs of sinners obliged to eat from this tree in Hell will be badly burned.... The Zaqqūm tree with its bitter fruit and foul smell was not only associated with the infernal regions of Hell but also with Arabia.

Again, then, a powerful semiotic (and olfactory!; see SMELLING) link is made between actual and perceptible terrestrial phenomena on the one hand, and threatened potential phenomena that may be encountered in another life, on the other.

Turning now from the semiotics of the principal flora of the Qurʾān to the fauna, we note firstly that there are two general statements made about animals in the Qurʾān. The first of these is that the creeping animals *(dābba)* and flying birds are all said to form "communities" *(umam)* like humankind (Q 6:38; see COMMUNITY AND SOCIETY IN THE QURʾĀN). The extensive intertextual weight borne in Islam by such a word as *umma* needs no underscoring. Suffice it to say that here the word signifies *inter alia* a divine ordering or harmony of creation "in groups" where mutual cooperation *(taʿāwun)* and generosity are expected. The semiotic antitheses of these virtues are numerous and include "self-centeredness," "individuality," "isolation," and the selfishness and greed born of such attitudes and lifestyles: the Qurʾān (e.g. Q 89:17-20) condemned them all (see also ETHICS AND THE QURʾĀN).

Here the parable of the two men in Q 18 (Sūrat al-Kahf, "The Cave"; Q 18:32-44) is instructive. The proud, selfish arrogant man, who has two well-endowed gardens that are eventually ruined, is in sharp contrast to his humbler neighbor whom he clearly despises. But in his fall from material wealth (q.v.) the proud man equates his selfish attitudes with polytheism itself (Q 18:42; see POLYTHEISM AND ATHEISM). In this parable, then, the Qurʾān signals in the most lucid way that selfishness and greed lead to ruin and that divine protection (q.v.) is to be had in the *umma* whose characteristics are generosity, mutual respect and cooperation. The two gardens in the parable, of course, are twin images or signs of God's gift of paradise to humankind. But that gift has to be earned even though, in the parable, it is "given" almost gratuitously. From the point of view of the semiotics of nature in the Qurʾān and its ubiquitous didactic aspect, it is instructive to note that the parable of the two men in Q 18 follows on immediately from a vivid description of the paradisiacal garden (lit. "the gardens of Eden," *jannāt ʿadnin,* Q 18:31), couched in the most physical — indeed natural — terms. The semiotic lesson is clear: Nature is an image of the garden of paradise itself. Nature misused, abused or taken for granted, signals contempt for the divine creator who will assuredly punish such attitudes and actions.

It comes as no surprise then, to learn that those who reject the signs of God, which are clearly present in the whole of nature (cf. Q 41:53), are specifically regarded as deaf *(ṣumm)* and dumb *(bukm)* and living in darkness (q.v.; Q 6:39; see vision and blindness; hearing and deafness).

The second major general statement about animals in the Qurʾān is that they have been created for the service of humankind whether they be cattle *(anʿām),* horses *(khayl),* mules *(bighāl)* or donkeys *(ḥamīr,* Q 16:5-8). The cattle provide warmth and food and foster a sense of beauty as they are driven backwards and forwards to pasture. The equines are for both riding and ornament *(zīna).* The semiotics of these verses are abundantly clear and need little further emphasis: as with the "good" trees and plants, the animal kingdom as it flourishes on earth is a sign of God's bounty to humankind and it is designed for the latter's use (see also HIDES AND FLEECE; HUNTING AND FISHING). The ethic which pertains is very similar to that in Genesis 1:26-8 in which man is placed in command of all the wildlife on earth.

There are numerous references to animals, birds and insects in the Qurʾān; some give their names to whole sūras: e.g. Q 2, "The Cow" (Sūrat al-Baqara); Q 6, "The Cattle" (Sūrat al-Anʿām); Q 16, "The Bee" (Sūrat al-Naḥl); Q 27, "The Ant" (Sūrat al-Naml); Q 29, "The Spider" (Sūrat al-ʿAnkabūt); and Q 105, "The Elephant" (Sūrat al-Fīl). Elsewhere, there are references to camels (e.g. Q 7:73), birds (e.g. Q 67:19) and the small creeping animal *(dābba)* which gnawed through the staff of the prophet Solomon (q.v.; Sulaymān) after the latter's death (Q 34:14) and which is variously translated as "worm of the earth" (A. Yusuf Ali), and "the Beast of the Earth" (Arberry). All of these signify, to one degree or another, God's creative presence, power and majesty. Perhaps, however, the most dramatic and starkest of all the animals mentioned in the Qurʾān, in terms of any identification with sign, is the "she-camel" *(nāqa)* in Q 7:73-84. The prophet Ṣāliḥ (q.v.) is sent to the Arabian tribe of Thamūd (q.v.). Ṣāliḥ orders the tribe to worship the one true God and identifies, as a sign of the covenant God makes with them through him, a she-camel. This is to be left unharmed and permitted to graze at leisure. But Ṣāliḥ's message is rejected, the she-camel is hamstrung and the tribe of Thamūd, in turn, is hit by an earthquake. The she-camel, originally a sign of true belief, covenant, blessing and good order becomes a symbol of divine vengeance and destruction. Thus good signs in the Qurʾān can, Janus-like, turn into symbols of doom.

Celestial phenomena: The semiotics of the heavenly spheres

Q 41:53 proclaims that God's signs are visible in nature and elsewhere, in the furthest lands of the earth *(fī l-āfāqi),* and nowhere is this more evident or ubiquitous than in the qurʾānic contrast between light and darkness (see PAIRS AND PAIRING). Light is a clear sign of God's transcendence, as in the famous and poetic Light Verse, Q 24:35: "God is the light *(nūr)* of the heavens and the earth. The parable of his light is as if there were a niche and within it a lamp (q.v.): the lamp enclosed in glass: the glass as it were a brilliant star...."

God is the creator of both light and darkness (Q 6:1) but the latter, as with many other world religions, can be a sign of evil and isolation from God. Those who reject God's signs are characterized, not only as being deaf and dumb, but as being "in darkness" (*fī l-ẓulumāt*, Q 6:39). The very alternation of day and night is a set of two signs: a reminder of God's presence, a divinely appointed calendar (q.v.). And if the "sign of the day" *(āyat al-nahār)* is designed for sight or enlightenment (Q 17:12), then, by analogy, the purpose of the "sign of the night" *(āyat al-layl)* is abundantly clear.

As with some of the fauna mentioned in the Qurʾān which we have surveyed, the natural phenomena of the heavens give their names to a number of different sūras in the Qurʾān: for example, we note Q 53, "The Star" (Sūrat al-Najm; see PLANETS AND STARS); Q 54, "The Moon" (q.v.; Sūrat al-Qamar); Q 85, "The Constellations" or "The Signs of the Zodiac" (Sūrat al-Burūj); Q 89, "The Dawn" (q.v.; Sūrat al-Fajr); Q 91, "The Sun" (q.v.; Sūrat al-Shams); and Q 113, "Daybreak" or "The Dawn" (Sūrat al-Falaq; see DAY, TIMES OF).

It is interesting that some of these natural celestial phenomena whose names figure above as sūra titles, also feature as oaths in the sacred text (see LANGUAGE AND STYLE OF THE QURʾĀN; LITERARY STRUCTURES OF THE QURʾĀN). For example: "By the star when it goes down" (Q 53:1); "By the break of day" (Q 89:1); "By the sun and his (glorious) splendor, by the moon as she follows him" (Q 91:1-2). All of celestial nature thus constitutes a body of powerful signs, witnessing to God's creative power and bounty to humankind. As such, the above are powerful oaths indeed. In Q 113 refuge is sought with "the lord of the dawn" from, *inter alia*, "the evil of dusk at nightfall as it spreads" (*sharri ghāsiqin idhā waqaba*, Q 113:3). Here is that vivid contrast again between light as a sign of God and goodness, and darkness as a symbol of evil.

Conclusion: The semiotics of nature in qurʾānic eschatology

On the last day we are told in the Qurʾān that the heaven will be split and the stars put out while the mountains are scattered (Q 77:8-10), and that the sun will become dark, the stars will be dispersed and fall, the mountains will disappear and the seas will boil and be poured forth (Q 81:1-14; 82:1-5). All these cataclysmic signs will be the most lucid natural evidence that an Islamic *parousía* is nigh. Not only that but they will signal in the most terrible way the dawn of real self-knowledge for each individual (Q 82:5).

The semiotics of nature in the Qurʾān may be condensed into a simple fundamental truth: Nature is a body of created signs that reveal God's bounty, mercy and creative goodness to humankind. But the beauty with which God has endowed the earth is also a test: "That which is on earth we have made but as a glittering show for the earth *(zīnatan lahā)*, in order that we may test them — as to which of them are best in conduct" (Q 18:7; see TRIAL).

Nature itself, then, shares in the general qurʾānic predilection for "questing and testing" (see especially Q 18, Sūrat al-Kahf; see also Netton, Towards a modern *tafsīr*). Nature can be a prime semiotic feature in the lesser testing of humankind on earth (see Q 18:7 above); its eschatological destruction will inaugurate the greater test of the last judgment.

Ian Richard Netton

Bibliography

M. Abdel Haleem, *Understanding the Qurʾān. Themes and style*, London 1999, 29-41; A. Yusuf Ali (trans.), *The Holy Qurʾān. Text, translation, commentary*, Kuwait 1984; A.A. Ambros, Geotaltung und Funktion der Biosphäre im Koran, in *ZDMG* 140 (1990), 290-325; A.J. Arberry, *The Koran interpreted*, 2 vols., London 1971; *CIH* = *Corpus Inscriptionum Semiticarum IV, Inscriptiones Sabaeas et Himiariticas, Continens,* vols. 1-3, 1889-1927; CIH 541 and CIH 540 are reprinted in C. Conti Rossini (ed.), *Chrestomathia arabica meridionalis epigraphica,* Rome 1931, 71-6; U. Eco, *Theory of semiotics,* Bloomington 1976; M. Farooqi, *Plants of the Qur'ān,* Lucknow 1989; C. Gilliot, Parcours exégétiques. De Ṭabarī à Rāzī (sourate 55), in *Études arabes. Analyses/Théorie* 1 (1983), 67-116 (but see only 92, 101-6 for the signs in nature seen within the hierarchical ordinance of the universe); W.A. Graham, "The winds to herald his mercy" and other "signs for those of certain faith." Nature as token of God's sovereignty and grace in the Qur'ān, in S.H. Lee, W. Proudfoot and A. Blackwell (eds.), *Faithful imagining. Essays in honor of Richard R. Niebuhr,* Atlanta 1995, 19-38; W.K.C. Guthrie, *The Greek philosophers from Thales to Aristotle,* London 1967; ʿA. al-ʿIzzī, *al-Muʿjam al-ṭabīʿī lil-Qur'ān al-karīm,* Beirut 2001; R. Jakobson, Language in relation to other communication systems, in id., *Selected writings,* vol. 2, The Hague 1971, 697-708; Lane; M. Naʿāl, *al-Muʿjam al-mufassar li-alfāẓ al-nabāt al-wārida fī l-Qur'ān al-karīm,* Jedda 1993 (on plants); I.R. Netton, *A popular dictionary of Islam,* London 1992, 264; id., Towards a modern *tafsīr* of *sūrat al-kahf.* Structure and semiotics, in *Journal of qur'anic studies* 2 (2000), 67-87; C.S. Peirce *Collected papers,* ed. Ch. Hartshorne, P. Weiss and A.W. Burks, 8 vols., Cambridge, MA 1931-58; Penrice, *Dictionary;* J.I. Smith and Y.Y. Haddad, *The Islamic understanding of death and resurrection,* Albany 1981; ʿU. Ṭībī, *Qiṣaṣ al-ṭayr wa-l-ḥayawān fī l-kitāb wa-l-sunna,* Beirut 1999 (on birds and animals); H. Toelle, *Le Coran revisité. Le feu, l'eau, l'air et la terre,* Damascus 1999; W.M. Watt, *Companion to the Qur'ān,* London 1967; H. Wehr, *A dictionary of modern written Arabic,* Wiesbaden 1979.

Neck see ANATOMY

Necklace see ʿĀʾISHA BINT ABĪ BAKR

Needle see INSTRUMENTS

Neighbor see HOSPITALITY AND COURTESY

News

Report of [recent] events. News in the Qurʾān centers around words derived from the root *n-b-ʾ,* especially the verb *nabbaʾa/yunabbiʾu,* meaning "to inform," which occurs forty-nine times, its synonym *anbaʾa/yunbiʾu,* occurring four times, and the noun *nabaʾ,* meaning "a piece of news," which, with its plural *(anbāʾ),* appears twenty-nine times. There is also a single appearance of *istanbaʾa/yastanbiʾu,* meaning "to ask for news" (Q 10:53). A completely different root, *kh-b-r,* provides seven occurrences of nouns meaning "news" or "information," *khubr, khabar,* and the plural of the latter, *akhbār.*

Qurʾānic references to news cover a considerable number of different meanings. Perhaps the most prevalent is the "great news" (*al-nabaʾ al-ʿaẓīm,* Q 78:2; cf. Q 3:15; 10:53; 34:7; 38:67, 88) of the coming day of judgment (see LAST JUDGMENT), one of the main bases of the prophet Muḥammad's teaching (see ESCHATOLOGY). This includes the frequently reiterated idea that God will inform all at the judgment of that which they used to do (Q 5:48, etc., often repeated; see RECORD OF HUMAN ACTIONS) and what they did not do (Q 75:13). In particular, God admonishes Jews (Q 62:8; see JEWS AND JUDAISM), Christians (Q 5:14; see CHRISTIANS AND CHRISTIANITY), hypocrites (Q 9:94, etc.; see HYPOCRITES AND HYPOCRISY) and unbelievers (Q 6:5; 26:6; see BELIEF AND UNBELIEF) that they will be informed at the judgment of their former actions. Furthermore, the prophet Muḥammad is particularly singled out as the bearer of various kinds of news. Thus, he informs his hearers about God and the afterlife (Q 3:15; 10:53; 15:49; 18:103). Muḥammad also imparts information from the unseen (see HIDDEN AND THE HIDDEN) concerning the fate of earlier peoples and their prophets (Q 5:60; 6:34; 7:101; 11:100, 120; 22:72; see GENERATIONS; PUNISHMENT STORIES; PROPHETS AND PROPHETHOOD), specifically giving stories or details about Adam (Q 5:27; see ADAM AND EVE; CAIN AND ABEL), Noah (q.v.; Q 10:71; 11:49), Abraham (q.v.; Q 15:51; 26:69), Joseph (q.v.)

and his brothers (Q 12:102; see BENJAMIN; BROTHER AND BROTHERHOOD), Moses (q.v.; Q 7:103; 20:99; 28:3), David (q.v.; Q 38:21), Dhū al-Qarnayn (Q 18:91; see ALEXANDER), Mary (q.v.; Q 3:44) and the Seven Sleepers of Ephesus (Q 18:13; see MEN OF THE CAVE). Such information is described as "news of the unseen" *(anbā᾽ al-ghayb),* indicating that God has miraculously transmitted it to the Prophet (Q 3:44; 11:49; 12:102; see KNOWLEDGE AND LEARNING). Indeed, as if to emphasize this point, God reminds the Prophet that he was not an eyewitness to these ancient events but God is providing him with precise information about them (Q 3:44; 12:102). On the other hand, some news about past peoples should be common knowledge, for it has been given before (Q 9:70; 14:9). Perhaps even closer to the common notion of prophecy as extra-sensory perception and precognition is Muḥammad's divinely conveyed knowledge about certain contemporary matters (Q 9:64, 94; 26:221; 66:3; see FORETELLING; DIVINATION). That various earlier prophets are also described as having such miraculous knowledge reinforces the concept of prophethood in general (Q 2:33; 3:49; 12:15, 36-7, 45; 18:68, 78). The ability of the prophets to give news of the unseen is contrasted with the inability of the angels (Q 2:31; see ANGEL) and the unbelievers (Q 6:143) to do the same.

Beside the more frequent qur᾽ānic usage of news to indicate divinely inspired information, the concept also refers occasionally to ordinary reports (Q 27:7, 22; 28:29; 33:20; 47:31; 49:6; 66:3). These include the interesting qur᾽ānic admonition to investigate ordinary news before acting on it, lest one make a regrettable mistake by a rush to judgment (Q 49:6). Associated with this concept is the idea that every piece of news has a final resting place (Q 6:67), which could be read as implying that a specific truth underlies every action, suggesting a positive view of reality. An equally positive view explains the verse as meaning that every piece of news about the afterlife will eventually be fully realized and fulfilled. See also GOOD NEWS.

Khalid Yahya Blankinship

Bibliography
Primary: Muqātil, *Tafsīr;* Qurṭubī, *Jāmi῾;* Ṭabarī, *Tafsīr.*
Secondary: D.B. MacDonald/L. Gardet, Ghayb, in *EI²*, ii, 1025-6; Watt-Bell, *Introduction;* A.J. Wensinck, Khabar, in *EI²*, iv, 895; id., Waḥy, in *EI¹*, iv, 1091-3.

Niche see LIGHT

Night see DAY AND NIGHT; DAY, TIMES OF

Night Journey see ASCENSION

Night of Power

The night during Ramaḍān (q.v.) when, according to classical exegesis, the Qur᾽ān was sent down. The phrase "Night of Power" *(laylat al-qadr)* appears in Q 97:1, and lends itself to the name of the sūra (Sūrat al-Qadr). Its Meccan or Medinan origin is in dispute, although it is usually associated with the early Meccan period (see CHRONOLOGY AND THE QUR᾽ĀN). This night is described as a night better than a thousand months (q.v.) in which angels (see ANGEL) and the spirit (q.v.; *rūḥ,* i.e. Gabriel [q.v.], other high angels, etc., cf. Rāzī, *Tafsīr,* xxxiii, 32) descend by leave of their lord from every command (*amr,* cf. Q 16:2), and there is said to be a peace that lasts until the break of dawn. The "blessed" night during which God sent down the Qur᾽ān (Q 44:3; cf. 2:185; see REVELATION AND INSPIRATION; BOOK) is believed to be the night of *qadr* (Ṭabarī, *Tafsīr,* xxv, 64).

Commentators have understood *qadr* as either power or empowerment *(qudra)*, or divine determination *(qadar)* or fate (q.v.; Sells, Sound, 255 and n. 50; see also DESTINY; FREEDOM AND PREDESTINATION).

Muslim commentators (see EXEGESIS OF THE QURʾĀN: CLASSICAL AND MEDIEVAL), following Ibn ʿAbbās (d. 68/686-8), have suggested that the Qurʾān was sent down from the Preserved Tablet (q.v.; cf. Q 85:21-2; see also HEAVENLY BOOK) to the lowest heaven (see HEAVEN AND SKY) on this night and then revealed by Gabriel to Muḥammad over a period of twenty or twenty-three years (Ṭabarī, *Tafsīr,* xxx, 166; cf. Ibn Isḥāq-Guillaume, 111-2); or, following al-Shaʿbī (d. ca. 103/721), that this night was the occasion of the first revelation (Ṭabarsī, *Majmaʿ,* ix, 516-21; Rāzī, *Tafsīr,* xxxiii, 27-8; cf. Ṭabarī, *Tafsīr,* xxx, 166); or, as noted by Sells (Sound, 244-5; cf. Burckhardt, *Introduction,* 43-4), following ʿĀʾisha (see ʿĀʾISHA BINT ABĪ BAKR) and ʿAbdallāh b. ʿUmar (d. 73/693), that the Qurʾān would have been revealed to Muḥammad not verbally but in an experience in which the words were inchoate (see ORALITY; FORM AND STRUCTURE OF THE QURʾĀN). Wagtendonk, Wensinck and Lohmann discuss its possible role as a new year's festival in pre-Islamic times. Bell (*Commentary,* ii, 563-4) alludes to the Christian feast of the eve of the Nativity (see CHRISTIANS AND CHRISTIANITY). Plessner, following Goïtein (Zur Entstehung, 189 f.), discusses its parallel with the Jewish holiday of the Day of Atonement (ʿĀshūrāʾ, see FASTING; JEWS AND JUDAISM). For al-Ṭabarī (d. 310/923; *Tafsīr,* xxv, 64), Ramaḍān was a propitious period for revelations (other religious traditions; see FESTIVALS AND COMMEMORATIVE DAYS).

Classical interpreters debated over which night constitutes the night of *qadr* but most believed, following Ibn ʿUmar, that it could fall on several odd-numbered nights in the last ten days of Ramaḍān (Bukhārī, *Ṣaḥīḥ,* 381-2; Muslim, *Ṣaḥīḥ,* ii, 822-4); moreover, following ʿĀʾishā and Abū Saʿīd al-Khudrī (d. 74/693), it is associated with the Prophet's retreats to the mosque (q.v.) for vigils (q.v.; *iʿtikāf*) during the last ten days of Ramaḍān (Muslim, *Ṣaḥīḥ,* 824, 828; Tirmidhī, *Ṣaḥīḥ,* v, 158-9). Due to uncertainty over the exact night, retreats to the mosque where vigils are held take place on several or all of these nights.

Present-day Shīʿī tradition celebrates this night along with the death of ʿAlī (the 19th, he is wounded; the 21st, he dies; the 23rd, the night of *qadr* proper; see SHĪʿISM AND THE QURʾĀN). In popular tradition, this night is associated with a number of wonders (found in ḥadīths; see ḤADĪTH AND THE QURʾĀN; MARVELS; MIRACLE): forgiveness (q.v.) of one's sins (see SIN, MAJOR AND MINOR), prostration of everything on earth (see BOWING AND PROSTRATION), determining every person's destiny for the upcoming year, direct entry into paradise (q.v.) for whoever dies on this night (see DEATH AND THE DEAD), granting of wishes (see WISH AND DESIRE), or, following al-Shaʿbī (d. 100/718-9), angels greeting every pious (see PIETY) human being (cf. Bousquet, Iʿtikāf; Qurṭubī, *Jāmiʿ,* xxviii, 134).

Roxanne D. Marcotte

Bibliography
Primary: Bukhārī, *Ṣaḥīḥ,* Riyadh 1998, 381-2; Ibn Isḥāq-Guillaume; Muslim, *Ṣaḥīḥ,* ii, 822-9; Qurṭubī, *Jāmiʿ,* Cairo 1962, xxviii, 130-8; Rāzī, *Tafsīr,* Cairo n.d., xxxii, 27-37; Ṭabarī, *Tafsīr,* Beirut 1987, xxx, 166-8; Ṭabarsī, *Majmaʿ,* Beirut 1953, ix, 516-21; Tirmidhī, *Ṣaḥīḥ,* Beirut n.d., v, 152-61.
Secondary: I.A. Aḥmad, The dawn sky on lailat-ul-qadr, in *Archaeoastronomy* 11 (1989-93), 97-100; A. Alves, *A Noite do destino. Laylat al-qadr,* Lisbon 1993; Bell, *Commentary;* G.H. Bousquet, Iʿtikāf, in

EI[2] (Fr. ed.), iv, 292; T. Burckhardt, *An introduction to Sufi doctrines*, trans. D. Matheson, Lahore 1959; S.D. Goïtein, Ramadan, the Muslim month of fasting, in id., *Studies in Islamic history and institutions*, Leiden 1966, 90-110; id., Zur Entstehung des Ramaḍāns, in *Der Islam* 18 (1929), 189-95; N. Hanif, Revelation, in N.K. Singh and A.R. Agwan (eds.), *Encyclopaedia of the holy Qur'ān*, 5 vols., Delhi 2000, iv, 1229-37 (esp. 1232-3); T. Lohmann, Die Nacht al-Qadr. Übersetzung und Erklärung von Sure 97, in *Mitteilungen des Instituts für Orientforschung* 15 (1969), 275-85; S.P. Manzoor, From the Night of Power to the Dawn of Peace, in *Afkar inquiry* 3 (1986), 28-33; M. Plessner, Ramaḍān, in *EI*[2] (Fr. ed.), viii, 417-8; M. Sells, Sound, spirit, and gender in *sūrat al-qadr*, in *JAOS* 111/2 (1991), 239-59; K. Wagtendonk, *Fasting in the Koran*, Leiden 1968; A.J. Wensinck, *Arabic new year and the Feast of Tabernacles*, Amsterdam 1925.

Nightmare see DREAMS AND SLEEP

Nimrod

Abraham's antagonist. Nimrod was, as is told in the Bible, the first potentate on earth. His empire included Babel and the surrounding countries (*Gen* 10:8-12). According to Islamic tradition, Abraham (q.v.) was his contemporary. Although Nimrod (Ar. Namrūd) is not named in the Qur'ān, he is, according to the exegetical literature (*tafsīr*, see EXEGESIS OF THE QUR'ĀN: CLASSICAL AND MEDIEVAL), the qur'ānic tyrant who pretends to be able to give life (q.v.) and death (see DEATH AND THE DEAD), a claim which Abraham successfully refutes (Q 2:258). Nimrod is also said to have been the one who tried to burn Abraham in a furnace, from which he was saved by God's command: "O fire (q.v.)! Be cool!" (Q 21:67-9).

In Islamic tradition, as expounded in exegetical *(tafsīr)* and "stories of the prophets" *(qiṣaṣ al-anbiyā')* literature, the story of Nimrod and Abraham is richly adorned with elements taken from extra-biblical Jewish and Christian sources (see JEWS AND JUDAISM; CHRISTIANS AND CHRISTIANITY; SCRIPTURE AND THE QUR'ĀN). It resembles the story of Pharaoh (q.v.) and Moses (q.v.) as told in the Qur'ān. Like Pharaoh, Nimrod ordered all children who were still nursing (see LACTATION) to be killed when he was informed — either in a dream (see DREAMS AND SLEEP) or by the astrologers — that a child was going to be born who would contest his claim to be God. He distributed food to his subjects, dismissing, however, without supply those who refused to confess his deity. Abraham's dispute as told in Q 2:258 allegedly occurred when he appeared before the king to obtain his family's ration. Naturally, he went away empty-handed, but miraculously brought home excellent food. According to another version the dispute took place when Abraham was summoned because he had destroyed the idols.

The building of the tower of Babel has also been ascribed to Nimrod; he wanted to see Abraham's God, a parallel to Pharaoh's high palace built for the same purpose (Q 28:38). Nimrod's tower was destroyed by a heavy storm: "God took their structures from their foundations" (Q 16:26). As a result, human language was confused. Another version says that Nimrod erected a high building to look down on Abraham in the furnace. The high building sometimes is said to be the pyramids. In fact, the names Pharaoh and Nimrod are exchangeable. Nimrod even went so far as trying to kill Abraham's God: He rose to the sky in a chest lifted by eagles and fancied that he had killed God when the arrow he had shot returned smeared with blood. His death was as painful as that of Titus the conqueror of Jerusalem as told in the Talmud (*Gittin* 56b): a gnat penetrated into his brain, tormenting him for four hundred years, the same length of time he had ruled as an ungodly king. See also NARRATIVES; MYTHS AND LEGENDS IN THE QURʾĀN.

Heribert Busse

Bibliography
Primary: Kisāʾī, *Qiṣaṣ* 121-45; Ṭabarī, *The history of al-Ṭabarī. ii. Prophets and patriarchs,* trans. W.M. Brinner, New York 1987, 105-15; id., *Taʾrīkh,* ed. de Goeje, i, 319-30; Thaʿlabī, *Qiṣaṣ,* 64, 66-8.
Secondary: B. Heller, Namrūd, in *EI²*, vii, 952-3; H.Z. Hirschberg, Nimrod, in C. Roth (ed.), *Encyclopaedia judaica,* 16 vols., Jerusalem 1972-, xii, 1166-7; H. Schützinger, *Ursprung und Entwicklunsgeschichte der arabischen Abraham-Nimrod Legende,* Bonn 1961; H. Schwarzbaum, *Biblical and extrabiblical legends in Islamic folk-literature,* Walldorf-Hessen 1989; R. Tottoli, *I profeti biblici nella tradizione islamica,* Brescia 1999, 49 n. 25, 172 n. 12, 198; Eng. trans. *Biblical prophets in the Qurʾān and Muslim literature,* Richmond 2002, 55 n. 26, 159 n. 12, 167.

Noah

One of the major prophets of Islam, Noah (Ar. Nūḥ, Heb. Nōaḥ) is an equally important figure in Judaism and Christianity (see SCRIPTURE AND THE QURʾĀN), where, however, he is not considered a prophet (see PROPHETS AND PROPHETHOOD). His biblical story, probably reflecting ancient Near Eastern precedents, occurs in Genesis 6-10 and in later Jewish texts. In the Qurʾān and in later Islamic tradition he is numbered among the prophets of warning (see WARNER), along with the Arabian prophets Hūd (q.v.) and Ṣāliḥ (q.v.), as well as the biblical Lot (q.v.; Lūṭ), Jethro (Shuʿayb, q.v.) and Moses (q.v.; Mūsā), conveying God's threats of punishment to their sinful peoples (cf. Q 9:70; 22:42; 25:37-8; 26:105; see PUNISHMENT STORIES; NARRATIVES).

Noah is attested in twenty-six sūras in the Qurʾān; Q 3:33 links him with Adam (see ADAM AND EVE), the descendants of Abraham (q.v.) and of Amram (ʿImrān, q.v.), the father of Moses and Aaron (q.v.). The contents of Q 71, which bears his name, consist primarily of Noah's recounting to God how he continually urged his people to repent (see REPENTANCE AND PENANCE) their sins (see SIN, MAJOR AND MINOR) while both warning them of the consequences of God's punishment and conveying to them God's promise of reward if they repented (see REWARD AND PUNISHMENT). The people did not accept his warnings and instead urged him to worship their pagan gods (see POLYTHEISM AND ATHEISM). This account ends with their being drowned in the deluge, being cast into the fire (q.v.) and Noah's asking God not to leave any unbelievers in the land; a similar account occurs in Q 23:23-30. Some stories in the Qurʾān stress the vilification and mistreatment Noah suffered as his people's response to his warnings of divine punishment for their misdeeds. Here he is viewed as the prototype of the prophet Muḥammad, suffering the same hatred and threats of physical harm that the Prophet was later to experience from his Meccan compatriots (see OPPOSITION TO MUḤAMMAD). This is mentioned clearly in Q 14:9; 22:42; 51:41-6; 54:18, 23, which link Noah with the earlier prophets Hūd and Ṣāliḥ, reassuring Muḥammad by telling him that they, too, had been denied, vilified and mistreated by their people. Some elements of the qurʾānic account seem to parallel certain Jewish post-biblical midrashic embellishments of the Bible story, in which Noah appears as a prophet and admonisher: his people laugh at his building the ark, and the unbelievers of his family are punished with hot water (*Tal. Sanhedrin* 108a-b; *Gen Rabba,* xxix-xxxvi). This last element in the story is reflected in qurʾānic and later Islamic texts, where the deluge *(ṭūfān)* sent by God begins with the *tannūr* (oven, cauldron, furnace or kiln) gushing forth with boiling water (Q 11:40; 23:27). Again, unlike the biblical account, Q 11:44 relates that after the deluge, the ark came to rest on the mountain al-Jūdī (see JŪDĪ) instead of the biblical "mountains of Ararat" (q.v.; *Gen* 8:4).

Later writers

Islamic Qurʾān exegetes, ḥadīth scholars and the authors of the literary genre of "tales of the prophets" *(qiṣaṣ al-anbiyāʾ)* expand and embellish the stories found in the Qurʾān and others found in the Bible (see EXEGESIS OF THE QURʾĀN: CLASSICAL AND MEDIEVAL; ḤADĪTH AND THE QURʾĀN). Using a variety of approaches, they base their work on the early biographers of Muḥammad, who tell of the many prophets before Muḥammad who were sent to their own peoples, beginning from creation (q.v.). A number of these biographical works, such as that of Ibn Saʿd (d. 230/845; *Ṭabaqāt*), which is based on earlier sources such as Ibn Isḥāq (d. ca. 150/767) and Ibn Hishām (d. 213/828 or 219/833), contain "tales" of various prophets. Ibn Saʿd tells of Noah's genealogy from Adam down to his father Lamech (Lamak), saying that because there was no one in those eras who prohibited forbidden (q.v.) acts, God made that Noah's task. Noah had preached to his people for 120 years without success and was commanded by God to build the ark when he was 600 years old. Differing from several other accounts, Noah had four sons (not the biblical three), the fourth being Canaan (Kanʿān), also called Yām by the Arabs, whereas in the Bible, Canaan is a son of Ham. Based on Q 11:43, some tales relate that Canaan refused to enter the ark, claiming that he could save himself from the deluge by climbing to the top of the highest mountain, but perished in the ever-rising water. We also learn that Noah's wife was one of the unbelieving people as was the wife of Lot. Both had married righteous men to whom they were unfaithful (Q 66:10), so when Noah asked God to have mercy on Canaan, God refused, saying that, as the offspring of his wife's deception, he was not his kindred (cf. Q 11:46).

In his *Ṣaḥīḥ,* al-Bukhārī (d. 256/870) relates that when Noah's people appear before God on the day of judgment (see LAST JUDGMENT) and are asked whether he had conveyed God's message to them, they would say that he had not, although Noah had previously told God that he had done so. When God asks him who would act as his witness regarding this matter, Noah answers that Muḥammad and his people would bear witness for him (see WITNESSING AND TESTIFYING). Noah came out of the ark on the tenth of Muḥarram, the ʿĀshūrāʾ, which therefore became a day of fasting (q.v.) for both humans and animals who had been in the ark for six months. Noah's wife is named Amzūra by al-Ṭabarī (d. 310/923) and joins Noah in the ark. But the later writer al-Bayḍāwī (d. ca. 685/1286) calls her Wāliya and, although in Q 66:10 she is simply referred to as a nonbeliever, here (and in some other accounts), she is left behind or drowned because she had said that Noah was *majnūn* ("insane"; see INSANITY) when he spoke to his people. For many scholars, the tales claiming that Noah's wife, otherwise said to have come out of the ark with him, was left behind or was drowned, raise the issue of how many humans were actually saved from the deluge. These numbers vary from seven, excluding her — Noah, his three sons and their wives — to eight, with her. In another version, however, the total number of those saved was eighty, including the pious children of Adam's son Seth.

The historian and Qurʾān exegete al-Ṭabarī, in his *Taʾrīkh,* tried to coordinate biblical figures like Noah with the semi-mythical early Persian rulers (see MYTHS

AND LEGENDS IN THE QURʾĀN). He states that "some people" claim that Noah lived during the reign of the evil king Bīwarasb, also known as al-Ḍaḥḥāk. Though he admits that the Persians did not know the story of the deluge, al-Ṭabarī, in the story of the Iranian king Afarīdūn, says that he mentions him only because "some people" say that he was Noah; he later claims that Afarīdūn's story resembled that of Noah. Al-Ṭabarī also tells of Noah's long life, saying that for 950 years he had called the people to God but whenever one generation passed away, the next one followed in unbelief. He also recounts that the oven from which the boiling water poured forth had belonged to Eve and came into Noah's possession, either in India, according to one tradition, or in Kūfa in Iraq, according to another tradition transmitted by al-Ṭabarī. We also read in this work the biblical story of the raven and the dove sent forth by Noah, which is not found in the Qurʾān.

Al-Ṭabarī's works served as a significant source for the important later *qiṣaṣ* work *ʿArāʾis al-majālis* of al-Thaʿlabī (d. 427/1036), much expanded with additional and different tales, most of them about many more prophets, including others from non-qurʾānic sources. We are told that Noah planted teak trees that he cut down to use for building the ark after they had grown for forty years. Al-Thaʿlabī relates that during those years Noah ceased calling the people to God and that God made the women barren so no children were born during that time. God told Noah to build the ark with "its head like the head of a cock, its middle like the belly of a bird, and its tail inclining like the tail of a bird." The tales of al-Kisāʾī (dates unknown) include the story of Noah in a style that may seem to reflect folk literature. He writes of an evil king, a great-grandson of Enoch, son of Cain (see CAIN AND ABEL), who ruled the land where Noah lived and "was a mighty tyrant and the first to drink wine (q.v.), gamble (see GAMBLING), sit on thrones (see KINGS AND RULERS), commission work in iron, brass and lead (see METALS AND MINERALS), and to adopt clothing spun with gold (q.v.)." He and his people worshipped idols (see IDOLS AND IMAGES), the names of which resemble some of the pagan gods mentioned in the Qurʾān. This caused Noah to withdraw to the wilderness until God had Gabriel (q.v.) send Noah as a prophet to his people. In his *Qiṣaṣ*, the Andalusian al-Ṭarafī (d. 454/1062), in a chapter on Noah's story, relates that, although Q 29:14 says that Noah lived for "a thousand years minus fifty," earlier writers are quoted as maintaining that was only his age at the time of the deluge, saying variously that he actually lived to be 1550 or 1650 years old. Al-Ṭarafī also relates many conversations between Noah and God.

In some *qiṣaṣ* tales, the sinful people of Noah's time, rejecting the divine warnings that he relays, are said to have descended from the union of the offspring of Cain with those of Seth. Thereupon God commanded Noah to build the ark (*fulk*, lit. "boat"), in order to save himself and other believers from the deluge with which God would punish the rest of humankind. In some versions of this tale, Noah built the ark unaided (using the wood of trees he himself had planted many years earlier), while in others he was helped by his sons. He was mocked (see MOCKERY) and attacked by the people of his town, who refused to believe his dire predictions of doom; like his wife, some of them even called him *majnūn* (Q 54:9). The *qiṣaṣ* literature gives us the dimensions, form and arrangements of the vessel. In al-Kisāʾī's version of one such tale, we are told that Jesus (q.v.), at the urging of the apostles (see APOSTLE), called upon Shem (Sām), the long-dead son of Noah, to rise from his grave and provide Jesus with information about the ark. We learn that its lowest level was for the animals, its second level for the humans, and the upper one for birds. The ants were the first creatures to enter the ark and the donkey the last, slowed down because Iblīs, the devil (q.v.), was holding on to his tail. Another unwanted figure who was saved from destruction was the giant Og (ʿŪj), son of ʿAnaq (Heb. for "giant"), who was too tall for the water to reach his head. The idea of his height is probably based on the biblical mention of Og being one of the last of the Rephaim, a people of giants (*Deut* 33:11, et al.).

Al-Kisāʾī states that the name Nūḥ means "he wailed (for his people)" from the verb *nāḥa*, whereas Jewish tradition derives it from the Hebrew *niḥam*, "he gave comfort." After the deluge the peoples of the earth became divided among Noah's three sons: Sām's descendants were the Arabs (q.v.), Persians and the Byzantines (q.v.; Rūm), the "good" nations; Yāfith (Japheth) was the ancestor of the Turks, Slavs and Gog and Magog (q.v.), possessing no good qualities. Because Ham (Ḥām) disobeyed the prohibition of intercourse while on the ark and had slept with his wife, his children were born black and all the black peoples of the earth are their descendants. In another version, blackness resulted from Noah's cursing Ham upon learning that, unlike his brothers, Ham had laughed when he saw his sleeping father's nakedness. The *Musnad* of Aḥmad b. Ḥanbal (d. 241/855) quotes the Prophet relating the testament of Noah to his sons, for example, forbidding idolatry (*shirk*, see IDOLATRY AND IDOLATERS) and pride (q.v.; *kibr*).

In Christian theology, Noah symbolizes the just man, providing an example of faith and submission to God, and becoming a prefiguration of Jesus. Elements of the story of Noah, the deluge, the ark and the dove are all incorporated into Christian symbolism. In Judaism Noah occupies a middle stage between Adam and Abraham, as a righteous and blameless man who walked with God and was saved from the flood to become the progenitor of a new human race. God's covenant with Noah (*Gen* 9:8-17) was expanded by the rabbis into the Noachide commandments, incumbent upon all humanity.

William M. Brinner

Bibliography
Primary: Ibn Ḥanbal, *Musnad*, Cairo 1313/1895, ii, 169-70; ed. A.M. Shākir/Ḥ.ʿA. Ḥātim et al., 20 vols., Cairo 1995, vi, 154-7, no. 6583; Kisāʾī, *Qiṣaṣ*, 85-102; trans. W. Thackston, *The tales of the prophets of al-Kisāʾī*, Boston 1978, 91-109; Ṭabarī, *The history of al-Ṭabarī. i. From the creation to the flood*, trans. F. Rosenthal, Albany 1989, 347-8; 354-71; *ii. Prophets and patriarchs*, trans. W.M. Brinner, Albany 1987, 10-23; id., *Taʾrīkh*, ed. De Goeje, i, 174-201; al-Ṭarafī, Abū ʿAbdallāh Muḥammad, *Storie dei profeti*, Genova 1997; trans. R. Tottoli, *Storia di Noe*, 59-71; Thaʿlabī, *Lives of the prophets*, trans. and annot. W.M. Brinner, Leiden 2002, 92-104 (trans. of *ʿArāʾis al-Majālis*).
Secondary: G. Canova, The prophet Noah in Islamic tradition, in K. Dévényi and T. Iványi (eds.), *Essays in honour of Alexander Fodor on his sixtieth birthday* [in *The Arabist* (Budapest) 23 (2001)], 1-20; A. Geiger, *Was hat Mohamed aus dem Judenthume aufgenommen?* Leipzig 1902 (rev. ed.), 104-11; Grünbaum, *Beiträge*, 79-89; B. Heller, Nūḥ, in *EI²*, viii, 108-9; H. Schwarzbaum, *Biblical and extra-biblical legends in Islamic folk-literature*, Walldorf-Hessen 1982 (see Index); D. Sidersky, *Les origines des légendes Musulmanes*, Paris 1933, 26-8 (Noe); Speyer, *Erzählungen*, 84-115; R. Tottoli, *I profeti biblici nella tradizione islamica*, Brescia 1999 (many references, esp. 18-22, 39-43; full bibliography); Eng. trans. *Biblical prophets in the Qurʾān and Muslim literature*, Richmond 2002, 5-9, 21-3; D. Young, Noa, in *Encyclopaedia Judaica*, ed. C. Roth, 16 vols., Jerusalem 1972, xii, 1191-8.

Nomads

Peoples who make and remake their settlements in a variety of places, often depending upon climactic conditions. Nomads *(aʿrāb)* are the non-urban population of the Arabian peninsula, attested ten times in the Qurʾān.

Oasis-town and countryside

By the time of the Prophet, the Near Eastern social trichotomy of peasants, townspeople and nomads had developed into the dichotomy of nomads and urbanites in northern and central Arabia (see CITY; PRE-ISLAMIC ARABIA AND THE QURʾĀN). This was the result of the "bedouinization of Arabia," a social process which had set in with the emergence, since the first half of the first millennium B.C.E., of the bedouin (q.v.) — belligerent tribes led by a tribal aristocracy that practiced large-scale camel herding (see CAMEL). The bedouin dominated large territories due to their enhanced mobility, and brought small-stock breeders and farmers into submission. They cooperated with the oasis towns in long-distance trade. Sedentary tribes like the Hudhayl (see TRIBES AND CLANS) adopted the social organization, attitudes, values, literary forms and the inter-tribal language of this literature from the bedouin (thus creating what became known as the *Dīwān Hudhayl*). The trade goods exported from Mecca to Syria were basically the products of Mecca's nomadic environment: leather, textiles and livestock (Q 16:5-7; 16-80; see HIDES AND FLEECE). Q 16:80 still presupposes the archaic, round tent made of leather *(ṭirāf, qubba),* attested as early as the seventh century B.C.E. (i.e. on the reliefs of Ashurbanibipal), instead of the now common rectangular black tent made of goat-hair *(bayt al-shaʿr),* already mentioned in the Bible in connection with north Arabian tribes of the fifth through third centuries B.C.E. (*Song of songs*, 1:5).

The qurʾānic attitude towards the nomads

The tribes in the vicinity of Medina (q.v.) are blamed for insufficient zeal to fight in the Prophet's wars (Q 9:90, 120; 48:11, 16; see EXPEDITIONS AND BATTLES; JIHĀD). Their orthodoxy is doubtful: "The nomads *(al-aʿrāb)* are the worst in unbelief (see BELIEF AND UNBELIEF) and hypocrisy (see HYPOCRITES AND HYPOCRISY)..." (see Q 9:97-101). These nomads say that they believe, but the Prophet is told to say to them "You do not believe, but you [only] say 'We submitted'; For faith (q.v.) has not entered into your hearts" (49:14; see HEART). The conflict which surfaced here is one between attitudes that are fundamentally irreconcilable: the Prophet demands submission to his faith and allegiance to his politics once and for all (see POLITICS AND THE QURʾĀN) while the nomads are accustomed to a political system in which allegiances, intra-tribal as well as inter-tribal, are open to constant renegotiation (see CONTRACTS AND ALLIANCES; BREAKING TRUSTS AND CONTRACTS). The Prophet acts as leader of a theocratic state-to-be, in which citizenship of a totally egalitarian nature is acquired by conversion, i.e. an individual act. In the nomads' world, kinship (q.v.) and the collective decision of the clan or tribe are the highest authorities — whereas all freeborn males of a single tribe may regard themselves as equals, they might not hold other tribesmen (not to speak of peasants) in similar esteem (see COMMUNITY AND SOCIETY IN THE QURʾĀN). Muḥammad himself was an urbanite; the sphere of the nomads represents the spatial and social opposite of the town (Q 33:20). None of the prophets (see PROPHETS AND PROPHETHOOD) whom he cites as his predecessors was sent to nomads; their destinations were always oases and towns (see PUNISHMENT STORIES; NARRATIVES). Although he claims that the Qurʾān is revealed in clear Arabic (Q 12:2; 13:37, etc.; see ARABIC LANGUAGE; REVELATION AND INSPIRATION), its orthography (q.v.) is not that of the literary language of the nomads (the language of classical Arabic poetry; see POETRY AND POETS). It is written down, rather, in the *koiné* of the west Arabian caravan (q.v.) towns (see ORALITY AND WRITING IN ARABIA). The term *ʿarab*, which never ceased to denote "nomad," had acquired the status of an ethnonym used by the Arabs themselves, as seen in the 328 C.E. funeral inscription of Imruʾ al-Qays from al-Namāra (*RCEA* I); hence the ambiguity in the term *ʿarabī* and the irony contained in its application to the language of the Qurʾān. See also ARABS.

Ernst Axel Knauf

Bibliography
W. Caskel, *Die Bedeutung der Beduinen in der Geschichte der Araber*, Köln 1953; P. Crone, *Meccan trade and the rise of Islam*, Oxford 1987; W. Diem, Untersuchungen zur frühen Geschichte der arabischen Orthographie, in *Orientalia* 48 (1979), 207-57; 49 (1980), 67-106; 50 (1981), 322-83; 52 (1983), 357-404; E. Haeuptner, *Koranische Hinweise auf die materielle Kultur der alten Araber*, Ph.D. diss., Tübingen 1966; E.A. Knauf, *Ismael. Untersuchungen zur Geschichte Palästinas und Nordarabiens im 1. Jahrtausend v. Chr.*, Wiesbaden 1989²; *RCEA*; J.M. Wagstaff, *The evolution of Middle Eastern landscapes*, London 1985.

Noon

The middle of the day. In the Qurʾān, the Arabic word *ẓuhr* does not designate solely a time of day (see DAY, TIMES OF). Reference to derivatives of *ẓ-h-r* is only made in the particular context of the noon observance of the ritual prayer (q.v.; *ṣalāt*) and the time prior to which it must not start; according to some interpretations, the "middle prayer" (*al-ṣalāt al-wusṭā*, Q 2:238) also alludes to noontime. Beyond the legal aspects of the noon prayer, however, discussion of the term involves issues of time and punctuality. It is in this respect that the institution is particularly significant as its point of reference is the sun (q.v.) at its zenith. The connection between noon prayer and the concept of time in general is clearly evidenced, among other indications, by the feminine form of verbs or adjectives associated with it, caused by the omission of the feminine noun, "prayer" (e.g. *wa-lammā kānat il-ẓuhr*; Ṭabarī, *Tafsīr*, ii, 98).

Noontime, like other prayer times, serves as the temporal anchor for various events, which go beyond the scope of this article. Suffice it to mention the rather interesting connection between noon and death (see DEATH AND THE DEAD), such as that of al-Maʾmūn (Ibn Kathīr, *Bidāya*, x, 280), to funerals (Baghdādī, *Taʾrīkh Baghdādī*, ix, 468), or to obituaries (Ibn al-Khaṭīb, *Wafāyāt*, i, 362). Noon served Gabriel (q.v.) more than once as the time in which he appeared to the Prophet: once when the direction of the prayer was changed (Ibn Ḥibbān, *Thiqāt*, i, 151; see QIBLA), another in the context of Qurayẓa (q.v.; ibid., i, 274). It was the time for many battles in history, such as the one waged against Abū Jahl (Ibn Kathīr, *Bidāya*, iii, 336), that against Quraysh (q.v.; ibid., iv, 14), and the battles of the first *fitna* (Qalqashandī, *Maʾāthir*, i, 95), among others (see EXPEDITIONS AND BATTLES; FIGHTING).

Segments of time connected with noon and the noon prayer often serve to indicate a definite time or period (Shāfiʿī, *Aḥkām*, i, 260) as well as its shortness or brevity (Abū Nuʿaym, *Ḥilya*, ix, 142). Whereas for the polytheists (see POLYTHEISM AND ATHEISM) the day of judgment (see LAST JUDGMENT) will continue for fifty thousand years, for the believer it will only last as long as the time between noon and evening (q.v.) prayer (Shawkānī, *Tafsīr*, v, 289).

Noon prayer

The origin of the name of the noon prayer is explained as derived from "the heat of the sun" *(ẓahīra)*, "the time most suitable (lit. apparent) for prayer" *(aẓharu awqāt al-ṣalāt),* or "the first prayer ever made public (lit. apparent) and prayed" (*awwalu ṣalāt uẓhirat wa-ṣulliyat, Lisān al-ʿArab,* iv, 527). This prayer was also called *ṣalātu l-hajīri,* "midday heat," by the Prophet (*Lisān al-ʿArab,* v, 254). Historically speaking, the noon prayer is not one of the first in Islam but rather followed the night, dawn (q.v.) and evening prayers (Q 30:17-8; 50:39-40; 76:25-6; see DAY AND NIGHT). It was not in existence at the time of Solomon (q.v.; Qurṭubī, *Jāmiʿ,* xv, 195), but, according to some, it was the first to be made by Muḥammad (Suyūṭī, *Durr,* vii, 136) with Gabriel, immediately following the night journey (*isrāʾ,* Ālūsī, *Rūḥ,* xv, 6; see ASCENSION), or, according to another version, was given in the morning of that day (Ibn Kathīr, *Bidāya,* iii, 118).

The noon prayer is the one most valued *(aʿjab)* by the Prophet, as he used to spend the most prolonged period of time in performance of it (Qurṭubī, *Jāmiʿ,* ii, 224). For Muslims, on the other hand, it is the hardest *(ashaqqu ʿalā l-muslimīna),* perhaps because the Prophet used to conduct it at the hottest time of the day (*hājira,* Suyūṭī, *Durr,* i, 720); the hypocrites, by contrast, find the dawn and night prayers the hardest (Bukhārī, *Ṣaḥīḥ,* i, 73; see HYPOCRITES AND HYPOCRISY). It was so important for ʿUmar that he ordered the man responsible for the pilgrimage (q.v.) to open all ceremonies with it (Ibn Saʿd, *Ṭabaqāt,* v, 364). Its primary value, however, is not accepted by everyone: for example, al-Bukhārī (d. 256/870; *Ṣaḥīḥ,* i, 72-5), who dedicates a paragraph to the issue of the "virtues of" each of the other prayers, fails to do so with regard to the noon prayer.

Composition

The noon prayer consists of four *rakʿa*s (see BOWING AND PROSTRATION), the first two of which the Prophet used to prolong (Ibn Taymiyya, *Iqtidāʾ,* i, 102). Jurists prohibit the addition of a fifth *rakʿa* or the repetition of the prayer except in extraordinary circumstances (id., *Majmūʿ,* xxiii, 260). On the other hand, it is reported that in certain cases the Prophet himself would be content with two *rakʿa*s only (id., *Kutub,* xxiv, 190), or that sometimes he would have four *rakʿa*s before the prayer itself (Qurṭubī, *Jāmiʿ,* ii, 224) and two following it (Ghazālī, *Asrār,* 296). The noon prayer is therefore one of three that could be shortened (Shāfiʿī, *Aḥkām,* 179). Sometimes the Prophet would recite in its course Q 84:1 *(idhā l-samāʾu nshaqqat)* or Q 87:1 *(sabbiḥi sma rabbika l-aʿlā).*

Time of prayer

Noon prayer must not be made before its earliest mandated time (Ibn Taymiyya, *Minhāj,* vi, 202) and perhaps the fear of breaking this prohibition made ʿUmar establish the ruling that this prayer be performed when an object's shadow is one foot long (id., *Iqtidāʾ,* iv, 196). As a general rule the Prophet used to make it at noon (*bi-l-hājira,* Muslim, *Ṣaḥīḥ,* i, 446) but its temporal boundaries were set by Gabriel. The angel, on two consecutive days, prayed it with the Prophet: the first time was at the earliest possible moment, i.e. when the sun moves from the zenith and casts a shadow of a given object as thin as a shoelace (Ibn Taymiyya, *ʿUmda,* iv, 150), when the sun had just declined *(dalaka)* from the center (Ṭabarī, *Tafsīr,* xv, 137), or disappeared from the "belly" of the sky (*zālat ʿan baṭni l-samāʾ,* Shāfiʿī, *Aḥkām,* iii, 248). A much more forgiving phrasing for this earliest permissible moment for the performance of the prayer is given by al-Ghazālī (d. 505/1111; *Asrār,* 299): when the movement of the sun is apprehended by the senses. On the next day, Gabriel set the latest time permissible as the time at which the shadow of the object equals its length (Ibn Taymiyya, *ʿUmda,* iv, 150), the time that is defined by the evening prayer (Shāfiʿī, *Aḥkām,* iii, 253). Once this moment has passed and the noon prayer has not been prayed, it is considered a sin (*fisq,* see SIN, MAJOR AND MINOR) and, being equivalent to the sins of adultery (see ADULTERY AND FORNICATION) or theft (q.v.), bars the believer from entering heaven (Ibn Taymiyya, *Kutub,* vi, 427; see REWARD AND PUNISHMENT; CHASTISEMENT AND PUNISHMENT). Some lawyers set the final period for the noon prayer as the setting of the sun (Qurṭubī, *Jāmiʿ,* viii, 75). These parameters are not all that rigid as far as the season of the year is concerned: in summer the required length of shadow is three to five feet, whereas in winter it is seven (*Lisān al-ʿArab,* xii, 470). This is also true for the weather: in winter, due to clouds, one may set the prayer time earlier *(taʿjīl)* than the above decree (Ibn Taymiyya, *Iqtidāʾ,* i, 133). On the other hand, some advocated the permissibility of postponing the noon prayer until after sunset because of the heat (Bukhārī, *Ṣaḥīḥ,* i, 198).

Relation to other prayers

Many identify the noon prayer as the "middle prayer" referred to in the Qurʾān, because it is "in the middle of the day" (Ibn Kathīr, *Bidāya,* i, 292). It is sometimes counted along with the afternoon prayer *(al-ʿaṣr)* as belonging to the evening (*al-ʿishāʾ,* Rāzī, *Mukhtār,* i, 183), without conceding the separate identity of each prayer: joining the noon prayer to that of the afternoon is judged to be a breach, and is typical of the Shīʿīs and the Rawāfiḍ (Ibn Taymiyya, *Minhāj,* v, 175; see SHĪʿISM AND THE QURʾĀN). In rare cases it is allowed, as when the Prophet himself did so at ʿArafāt (q.v.; id., *Jawāb,* vi, 372). The Friday prayer (q.v.) is made around noon time, and is sometimes referred to as "the abridged noon (prayer)" (*al-ẓuhr al-maqṣūra,* id., *Majmūʿ,* xxiv, 190) but in spite of this similarity, different rules apply to each (id., *Kutub,* xxiv, 190), e.g. the rules of the call to prayer (*adhān,* id., *ʿUmda,* iv, 98).

Action

Like other prayers, the noon prayer pardons sins that were committed during the time between the dawn prayer and its performance (Ibn Kathīr, *Bidāya,* ii, 463). It is also a reference point to phenomena and actions that are not necessarily of a religious nature. Often the structure of such an indication is "the Prophet prayed the noon-prayer then..." (Ibn Qāniʿ, *Muʿjam,* i, 249), or the time at which the subject arrived at a given place is given in relation to the time of the noon prayer (Ibn Qayyim al-Jawziyya, *Zād,* ii, 233; see JOURNEY; TRIPS AND VOYAGES).

Ilai Alon

Bibliography

Abū Nuʿaym, Aḥmad b. ʿAbdallāh al-Iṣfahānī, *Ḥilyat al-awliyāʾ,* Beirut 1984; Ālūsī, *Rūḥ;* Baghdādī, *Taʾrīkh Baghdād;* Bukhārī, *Ṣaḥīḥ,* ed. M. al-Bannā, Beirut 1986; al-Ghazālī, Abū Ḥāmid, *Asrār al-ṣalāt,* ed. M.M. ʿAlī, Cairo n.d.; Ibn Ḥibbān, Abū Ḥātim Muḥammad, *al-Thiqāt,* ed. A. Aḥmad, 9 vols., Beirut 1975; Ibn Kathīr, *Bidāya;* Ibn al-Khaṭīb, Aḥmad b. Ḥasan, *al-Wafayāt,* ed. ʿĀ. Nuwayhid, Beirut 1978; Ibn Qāniʿ ʿAbd al-Bāqī, *Muʿjam al-ṣaḥāba,* ed. Ṣ. al-Miṣrātī, 3 vols., Medina 1997; Ibn Qayyim al-Jawziyya, *Zād al-maʿād,* ed. Sh. and ʿA. al-Arnāʾūṭ, 5 vols., Beirut 1979, 1986[2]; Ibn Saʿd, *Ṭabaqāt,* ed. Z.M. Manṣūr, Medina 1987; Ibn Taymiyya, *Iqtidāʾ al-ṣirāṭ al-mustaqīm mukhālafāt aṣḥāb al-jaḥīm,* ed. ʿI.F. al-Ḥarastānī, Beirut 1993; id., *al-Jawāb al-ṣaḥīḥ li-man baddala dīn al-masīḥ,* ed. Nāṣir et al., 7 vols., Riyadh 1993, 1999[2]; id., *Kutub wa-rasāʾil wa-fatāwā Ibn Taymiyya fī l-ʿaqīda,* ed. ʿA.M.Q. al-Najdī, n.p. n.d.; id., *Majmūʿ al-fatāwā,* n.p. n.d.; id., *Minhāj al-sunna al-nabawiyya,* ed. M.R. Sālim, 9 vols., Riyadh 1985; id., *Sharḥ al-ʿumda fī l-fiqh,* ed. S.Ṣ. al-ʿAṭīshān, 3 vols.,

Riyadh 1992; *Lisān al-ʿArab;* Muslim, *Ṣaḥīḥ;* al-Qalqashandī, Abū l-ʿAbbās Aḥmad b. ʿAbdallāh, *Maʾāthir al-ināfa fī maʿālim al-khilāfa,* ed. ʿA.A. Farrāj, Kuwait 1985; Qurṭubī, *Jāmiʿ;* al-Rāzī, Muḥammad b. Abī Bakr, *Mukhtār al-ṣiḥāḥ,* ed. M. Khātir, Beirut 1995; Shāfiʿī, *Aḥkām;* Shawkānī, *Tafsīr;* Suyūṭī, *Durr;* Ṭabarī, *Tafsīr,* Beirut 1984.

Nose see ANATOMY

Nudity

The state of being devoid of clothing (q.v.). In general, the Qurʾān enjoins modesty (q.v.) and evokes nudity only negatively. Q 24:30-1 insists upon physical modesty for both men and women, while the narrative of Adam and his spouse in Q 7:19-27 (see NARRATIVES; ADAM AND EVE) associates nudity with the first human act of disobedience (q.v.).

As in the Hebrew Bible, the first couple's nudity is made manifest — the specific manner is disputed by the exegetes — after they partake of the fruit of the forbidden tree. Q 7:22 states, "So by deceit he [i.e. Satan; see DEVIL] brought about their fall (see FALL OF MAN): when they tasted of the tree, their *sawʾāt* became apparent to them, and they began to sew together the leaves of the garden over their bodies. And their lord called unto them: 'Did I not forbid you that tree, and tell you that Satan was an avowed enemy (see ENEMIES) unto you?' " The word *sawʾāt* is derived from the Arabic root meaning "to be bad, evil," and is sometimes interpreted to mean that Adam and Eve realized their error (q.v.) or "saw the evil of their [ways]." Following this interpretation, some English translations render the word as "shame" or "evil intentions." More concretely, the word *sawʾāt* is understood to refer to the genitals (*farj,* *ʿawra,* see SEX AND SEXUALITY). Certainly the idea of physical nakedness is implied by the qurʾānic text, in which the couple's reaction to the sudden manifestation of their *sawʾāt* is the fashioning of garments. For some exegetes, the word denotes the physical genitals while retaining connotations of moral negativity (see ETHICS AND THE QURʾĀN). Thus, the medieval Andalusian exegete al-Qurṭubī (d. 671/1272; *Jāmiʿ,* vii, 181) states that the private parts bear the names *sawʾa* and *ʿawra* because people find it unpleasant to display them *(li-anna iẓhārahu yasūʾu ṣāḥibahu).* Jurists derived from this verse the legal principle (see LAW AND THE QURʾĀN) that it is undesirable *(qabīḥ)* to expose one's genitals, and that in the absence of any other suitable material it is incumbent on one to fashion clothing of leaves.

Exactly how Adam and Eve's nakedness "became apparent" is not specified in the Qurʾān; a widely-reported tradition attributed to the Prophet's Companion Ibn ʿAbbās (d. 68/686-8; see COMPANIONS OF THE PROPHET) states that in the garden (q.v.) they were covered with a coating that then receded from their bodies and remained only on the tips of their fingers and toes, forming the nails. The "nakedness" of Adam and his spouse is not merely a physical but a moral denudation; the passage continues by evoking God's mercy (q.v.) in providing clothing and adornment for humankind, and concludes by stating "the garment of consciousness of God *(libās al-taqwā)* is best" (Q 7:26; see PIETY; KNOWLEDGE AND LEARNING).

The words *sawʾa* and *ʿawra* are used elsewhere in the Qurʾān to refer, not to nudity *per se,* but to other states of exposure, vulnerability and intimacy. In Q 5:31, God sends a raven to show Cain how to cover the shamefully exposed body *(sawʾa)* of his murdered brother (see CAIN AND ABEL). In Q 33:13, unwilling warriors make the excuse that their houses are exposed to attack (*inna buyūtanā ʿawra,* see FIGHTING); and

Q 24:58 refers to three times of the day (see DAY, TIMES OF) when it is customary to withdraw into privacy (as well as, according to many commentators, to undress) as *ʿawrāt*.

Marion Holmes Katz

Bibliography
Qurṭubī, *Jāmiʿ*, 20 vols., Cairo 1967; Suyūṭī, *Durr*, 8 vols., Beirut 1983; Ṭabarī, *Tafsīr*, ed. ʿAlī.

Nūḥ see NOAH

Numbers and Enumeration

Words representing amounts and the designation of the number of objects. The Qurʾān makes full use of a range of Arabic words denoting numbers and counting. In doing so, it employs the number words both in terms of literal counting and of representative images and symbols (see SYMBOLIC IMAGERY), many with an ancient heritage. Words are employed for each of the cardinal unit numbers and occasional higher numbers, including 10, 11, 12, 19, 20, 30, 40, 50, 60, 70, 99, 100, 200, 300, 1,000, 2,000, 3,000, 5,000, 50,000, and 100,000. The number words "one" and "two," although numerically indicated through grammar in Arabic (along with the generic plural, of course), are used both for emphasis and counting purposes. Of the ordinal numbers, 2nd, 3rd, 4th, 5th, 6th and 8th appear in the text. Fractions also figure significantly, primarily because of their legal usage in matters of inheritance (q.v.) as dealt with in Q 4; 1/2, 1/3, 2/3, 1/4, 1/5, 1/6, 1/8, and 1/10 are all employed.

In terms of mathematical concepts, the Qurʾān makes use of addition, subtraction, multiplication, division and ratios. "Addition" is conveyed by words related to *zāda*, which is, however, often best understood simply as "increase." In a passage such as Q 18:25, "And they tarried in the cave (q.v.) three hundred years, and they added nine more," specific addition of numbers is suggested. A sense of subtraction is found in the word "less" as expressed through the use of the word *illā* as in Q 29:14, "We sent Noah (q.v.) to his people, and he tarried among them a thousand years less fifty." Mathematical multiplication may be conveyed by *kaththara* in Q 7:86, "You were few and he multiplied you," and by *yadhraʾu* in Q 42:11, "He has appointed for you, of yourselves, pairs, and pairs also of the cattle, therein multiplying you," although both of those may be taken in the sense of "reproduce" rather than mathematical multiplying. Doubling things specifically uses *ḍāʿafa* (and *ḍiʿf* for "a double") but this is also often taken with a more generic sense of "multiply" as in Q 64:17, "If you lend God a good loan (see CONTRACTS AND ALLIANCES; DEBT), he will multiply it for you." Division in the sense of separating things into parts is conveyed via words related to *qasama*, as in Q 54:28, "And tell them that the water is to be divided between them, each drink for each in turn." A sense of ratios emerges in passages having to do with odds in battle (see VICTORY; FIGHTING; WAR) such as Q 8:66, "If there be a hundred of you, patient men, they will overcome two hundred; if there be of you, a thousand, they will overcome two thousand by the leave of God." Note may also be taken of the idea of "odd," *watr*, and "even," *shafʿ*, employed in Q 89:3, although these terms appear outside a mathematical context. "Pairs," *mathnā*, is an elaboration of "two" and is used in counting sequences, for example, in Q 4:3, "Marry such women (see MARRIAGE AND DIVORCE; WOMEN AND THE QURʾĀN) as seem good to you, in pairs, triples or quadruples" (also see Q 35:1 for the wings on angels; see ANGEL).

Counting itself — that is, doing mathematical reckoning — is quite frequently conveyed through *ʿadda,* "to number," and its derivatives, e.g. Q 9:36, "the number of months (q.v.) with God is twelve," and Q 19:84, "We are only numbering them for a number" in reference to the unbelievers (see BELIEF AND UNBELIEF). The root is also used in the sense of an indefinite number (i.e. "many") of items (Q 10:5, "the number of years"). The root *aḥṣā* is also used in a similar manner as in Q 36:12, "Everything we have numbered in a clear register." The use of both roots *(ʿ-d-d* and *ḥ-ṣ-w)* in Q 19:94 should be noted, "He has indeed counted *(aḥṣā)* them and he has numbered *(ʿadda)* them," in reference to all those in "the heavens (see HEAVEN AND SKY) and the earth (q.v.)." Another word, *ḥasiba,* and its derivatives convey a more general sense of "calling to account" with God as the reckoner.

On several occasions things are enumerated in the Qurʾān, simply for the purposes of counting, as in the debate regarding how many sleepers there were in the cave (Q 18:22; see MEN OF THE CAVE) or the presence of God being counted as one extra in groups who conspire secretly (Q 58:7).

The Qurʾān's vocabulary of numbers includes senses derived from the widespread Near Eastern symbolic value of numbers which undoubtedly permeated pre-Islamic culture as well as having been fully incorporated within the biblical tradition (see PRE-ISLAMIC ARABIA AND THE QURʾĀN; SCRIPTURE AND THE QURʾĀN). The social values, however, conveyed through number symbolism in the Qurʾān are less obvious than in other ranges of symbolism (e.g. as found in colors [q.v.]). For example, the symbolism of "seven" days in a week does not seem to convey a great deal about the social values of seventh century Arabia when it is employed in the Qurʾān. Rather, it speaks more significantly of the ancient heritage of such symbols whose actual social value has perhaps been lost but which provide a structuring to human experience nevertheless (see COMMUNITY AND SOCIETY IN THE QURʾĀN).

"Three" *(thalātha)* is a number of plurality, perhaps reflected in the fact that "two" can be indicated through the grammatical dual in Arabic whereas a separate word must be used for "three" (see GRAMMAR AND THE QURʾĀN; ARABIC LANGUAGE). Duality — whether expressed by the grammatical ending or by the word *ithnān* — is natural and perfect, whereas "three" indicates a collection of things (in common with the units up to ten), as is suggested by the use of the plural noun in grammatical construct case following the number word when enumerating things. The natural and perfect nature of "two" is reflected by the use of duality in the case of the animals going into Noah's ark (Q 11:40, "Embark on it two of every kind"; see ANIMAL LIFE) and in the description of creation (q.v.; Q 13:3, "And of every fruit he placed there two kinds"; see AGRICULTURE AND VEGETATION). There is also the qurʾānic injunction to have two male witnesses for contracts (although note one man and two women; Q 2:282; see WITNESSING AND TESTIFYING; CONTRACTS AND ALLIANCES). Duality is, at the same time, opposed to oneness — whether expressed in the word *wāḥid* or *aḥad* — quite clearly: "Take not to you two gods. He is only one God" (Q 16:51; see GOD AND HIS ATTRIBUTES). "Three," on the other hand, may be a number of pain and grief (see JOY AND MISERY; SUFFERING), especially as opposed to unity. Q 77:30 speaks of the punishment of the judgment day (see ESCHATOLOGY; REWARD AND PUNISHMENT; LAST JUDGMENT) in saying, "Depart to a triple-massing shadow," the three-ness of this shadow being an emphasis on its awfulness (see DARKNESS). "Three veils" encircle the child in the womb according to Q 39:6 (see BIRTH). Fasting (q.v.) for three days overcomes legal problems (Q 2:196; 5:89). The people of Ṣāliḥ (q.v.) can enjoy their homes for three days before punishment comes (Q 11:65; see PUNISHMENT STORIES). And, of course, the idea of worshipping three gods is firmly condemned (Q 4:171; see CHRISTIANS AND CHRISTIANITY; POLYTHEISM AND ATHEISM).

Attention has been drawn in scholarship to the symbolism of "four," *arbaʿ*, and its multiples in Arab historical narratives and the resultant lack of precision in associated historical details. The grounding of those symbols is to be found in the Qurʾān. The role of "forty" is especially prominent but this is founded upon the widespread symbol of "four" as representing "perfection, completion and culmination." "Forty" becomes a major chronological unit, building upon the formative one of Muḥammad as forty years old when he began to receive revelation (see REVELATION AND INSPIRATION), an age likely selected as reflective of Q 46:15 and its association of the age of forty with maturity (q.v.) and religious wisdom (q.v.). Of "four" and "forty," it has been suggested that they are "the numbers which determine or express the extent to which certain deeds arouse divine approbation or ire or simply demonstrate the hand of God at work in the world" (Conrad, Abraha, 231). The qurʾānic material, however, adds an extra level of specification to the symbol of "four," and, in doing so, stays within Near Eastern patterns. "Four" is the number of perfection, completion and culmination, specifically of the "material order," as reflected in ideas of the four elements of existence, the four directions of the compass, the four corners of the earth (q.v.), the four phases of the moon (q.v.), the four seasons (q.v.), and so on. "Four" in the Qurʾān is the number used in the context of legal requirements (see LAW AND THE QURʾĀN), certainly reflecting ideas of the wholeness and perfection of material culture but defining that material culture primarily in legal terms, as is appropriate to the Islamic social world (see MATERIAL CULTURE AND THE QURʾĀN). A man may marry up to four wives (Q 4:3); four witnesses are required to the accusation of adultery (Q 4:15; see ADULTERY AND FORNICATION); if there are not four witnesses, then an oath uttered four times suffices (Q 24:4-9, with, note, the fifth oath to say that he is not a liar; see LIE; OATHS); there are four months that are sacred (Q 9:2, 36).

"Four" related to a period of time has legal status as well: four months of abstention from one's wife for divorce (Q 2:226; see ABSTINENCE) and widows (see WIDOW) are to wait four months plus ten days before remarrying (Q 2:234) — the perfection of the number "ten" being added to the legal number "four." No other number used in the Qurʾān predominates in its legal application in the way that "four" does. "Four" as the symbol of legality continues in later Islam with the four schools of law and the four righteous caliphs (see CALIPH). Certainly, other instances of the use of "four" do not have a specific legal overtone: creation is separated out into two days plus four, and in the latter four, God "ordained therein its diverse sustenance" (Q 41:10) — that is, the creation of the material world.

"Five," *khamsa*, on the other hand, is half a group — that is, half of "ten" — and despite its later significance in Islam in the ideas of the "five" daily prayers (see PRAYER), the "five" ritual pillars, and the five "pillars" of the creed (see CREEDS; FAITH), it is not used in the Qurʾān with any such reference. The enumeration of rituals is not supported through a symbolic use of the number in the Qurʾān. "Five" is used in expressions of large numbers (5000 swooping angels in Q 3:125; one day is 50,000 years in Q 70:4; see DAYS OF GOD), and overall the number simply appears to convey a significantly large quantity.

The number "six," *sitta,* relates only to the number of days of creation in the Qurʾān; this is significant in that "six" is sometimes spoken of as a number symbolic of "incompleteness" because it is one less than the heavenly number of "seven." The Qurʾān does not use "six" apart from the creation story, and it speaks of those six days without giving any importance to the seventh day that follows it which, in the biblical tradition, completes the process. "Six" seems to have lost its symbolic value in the Qurʾān and is entirely subsidiary to Near Eastern creation traditions. It is also polemically charged — that is, it is used with an emphasis on the rejection of the day of rest, as in Q 50:38 and its "And no weariness touched us," along with the insistence upon creation being associated with God being on his throne (see THRONE OF GOD; SABBATH).

"Seven," *sabʿa,* like "three," is a prominent number of plurality but it clearly has a symbolic value deeply imbedded in the notion of the seven stars or planets from ancient Babylonian times (see PLANETS AND STARS). Virtually all the uses of "seven" in the Qurʾān relate to cosmography in one way or another (see COSMOLOGY). The seven heavens or firmaments (Q 17:44), seven gates to hell (Q 15:44; see HELL AND HELLFIRE), seven oceans (Q 31:27), and the motif of seven in the story of Joseph (q.v.) and the interpretation of the dreams (Q 12:43-8) all reflect this (see DREAMS AND SLEEP). "Seven" is the number of the supra-mundane world.

Such values continue in later Muslim tradition. Ibn ʿAbbās, while still a youth, is reported to have said to ʿUmar (see COMPANIONS OF THE PROPHET; ḤADĪTH AND THE QURʾĀN):

God is odd in number and he likes odd numbers. Days of the universe turn around seven, he created our sustenance out of seven, he created man out of seven, above us he created seven skies, below us he created seven layers of the earth, he gave us the seven oft-repeated (q.v.; *mathānī*), he forbade marriage with seven relatives in scripture (see PROHIBITED DEGREES), and he divided the legacy into seven parts, he confined the numbers of bows of our bodies [in prayer] to seven (see BOWING AND PROSTRATION), the messenger of God walked around the Kaʿba (q.v.) seven times and between al-Ṣafā and al-Marwa (see ṢAFĀ AND MARWA) seven times, he threw seven stones [at Minā], and the night of glory (see NIGHT OF POWER) is one of the last seven nights of Ramaḍān (q.v.; Suyūṭī, *Itqān,* iv, 206-7).

"Seven" used in the form of "seventy" is generally interpreted simply as "a large number" (see Conrad, Seven, 46; and references including Ibn Khaldūn who says that "seventy" is used by the Bedouin [q.v.] to mean "many").

"Eight," *thamāniya,* is used five times, plus once as "the eighth" in a counting sequence (Q 18:22), once as "an eighth" in matters of inheritance (Q 4:12) and once as "eighty" for the number of lashes for bearing false witness (Q 24:4). There appears to be no unifying symbolic value in the qurʾānic use of "eight."

"Nine," *tisʿa,* being one less than "ten" is used with the sense of one remaining to be added or to bring completion. Moses (q.v.) received nine clear signs before Pharaoh (q.v.; Q 17:101; 27:12); nine people did corruption (q.v.) in the city of Thamūd (q.v.) and conspired against the tenth person who was Ṣāliḥ. Also note the use of "ninety-nine" in Q 38:23, the only time a combination of tens and units that equals more than the number nineteen is used in the Qurʾān; again, it is counted as one less than a hundred, suggesting that something is lacking, just as in the relationship between "nine" and "ten".

Arabic uses a decimal numeration system, as reflected in digits that are multiples of ten and the existence of separate words for one hundred and one thousand. "Ten," *ʿashr,* as a basic number of counting, seems a reasonable extrapolation from the physiological fact that humans have ten fingers upon which to count. The Qurʾān uses "ten" to reflect this, in that it is the number of counting and of transaction (see SELLING AND BUYING), and of dealing with gifts (see GIFT-GIVING) and with people. "Ten" carries a good value. One good deed brings ten like it (Q 6:160; see GOOD DEEDS); feeding ten people expiates an oath (Q 5:89); the bringing of ten sūras like the Qurʾān is the challenge put forth (Q 11:13; see INIMITABILITY; PROVOCATION); ten is three plus seven for the days of a fast in lieu of an offering on the pilgrimage (q.v.) both major and minor (Q 2:196, *ḥajj* and *ʿumra*).

From eleven through nineteen, the singular noun is used following the counting number in Arabic. There is a sense of a "heap" here, a plurality of things becoming one undifferentiated group when eleven is reached. Eleven itself is used only once in the Qurʾān, in the eleven stars that bow down to Joseph (Q 12:4). "Twelve," on the other hand, is used five times, in reference to fountains (Q 2:60; 7:160; see SPRINGS AND FOUNTAINS), chieftains (Q 5:12), tribes (Q 7:160) and months (Q 9:36). It certainly conveys a sense of completion and perfection, suggesting that "twelve" is not always meant literally but sometimes signifies that a full complement is found in the group being counted. Most interesting is the assertion that God declares there to be twelve months. The resultant sense of a divine legitimatization for such an aspect of human culture is striking.

"Nineteen" is famous because of its use in expressing the number of angels in Q 74:30 and may be understood as the sum of "seven" and "twelve," two numbers of ancient symbolic value. While some have suggested that the number "nineteen" has been used merely for rhyme purposes in the verse (see LANGUAGE AND STYLE OF THE QURʾĀN; RHYMED PROSE), the usage of this number drew attention early in Islam, and traditions emerged regarding, for example, the use of nineteen letters within the *basmala* (q.v.; also see Wensinck, *Handbook,* 12a, for the traditions on "nineteen" as the number of words in the call to prayer, *adhān*). The number continues to fascinate, especially because of the recent work of the late Rashid Khalifa in the United States and his attempt to prove the miraculous character of the Qurʾān via the numerical significance of "nineteen" (see MYSTERIOUS LETTERS). The Internet has become the current forum for the discussion of his ideas through his mosque community in Tucson, Arizona, called the United Submitters International (see www.submission.org). As is common with such attempted numerical proofs, the results are based upon both the characteristics of numbers themselves and statistical analysis of dubious validity (see Gardner, *The new age,* 170-4: i.e. the "demonic" 666, etc.).

The Qurʾān, not unexpectedly, uses the symbolic language of the Near Eastern monotheist culture. The Arabic of the seventh century participates fully in those kinds of symbolic representations, although the values which they convey (for example, the auspiciousness of "seven" as reflected in its cosmographical usages in the very ancient world) are deeply embedded and not necessarily explicitly stated. The Qur'ān also uses these symbols with its own particular emphases, as in the legal character of the number "four" within the context of material culture. See also NUMEROLOGY.

Andrew Rippin

Bibliography
Primary: Suyūṭī, *Itqān*.
Secondary: A. al-Baqarī, *Dirāsāt naḥwiyya fī l-Qur'ān,* Alexandria 1982 (a grammatical study on numbers in the Qur'ān); L.I. Conrad, Abraha and Muḥammad. Some observations apropos of chronology and literary *topoi* in the early Arabic historical tradition, in *BSOAS* 50 (1987), 225-40 (on the number 40); id., Seven and the *tasbī'*. On the implications of numerical symbolism for the study of medieval Islamic history, in *JESHO* 31 (1988), 42-73; M.S. Dāwūdī, *Mu'jam al-arqām fī l-Qur'ān al-karīm,* Cairo 1986; M. Gardner, *The new age. Notes of a fringe watcher,* Buffalo 1988; U. Hartmann-Schmitz, *Die Zahl Sieben im sunnitischen Islam. Studien anhand von Koran und Ḥadīt,* Frankfurt 1989; F. Rosenthal, Nineteen, in *Analecta biblica* 12 (1959), 304-18, repr. in his *Muslim intellectual and social history. A collection of essays,* Aldershot 1990, article 1; A. Schimmel, *The mystery of numbers,* Oxford 1993 (important overview of the symbolism of numbers with an extensive bibliography); J.B. Segal, Numerals in the Old Testament, in *JSS* 10 (1965), 2-20 (good source of comparative material).

Numerology

Study of the occult signification of numbers. Number symbolism is built into the Arabic alphabet since each letter in the Old Semitic *abjad* ordering had a numerical equivalent (see Table 1 below; see ARABIC SCRIPT). Muslims practiced gematria in divination (q.v.) and healing (see MEDICINE AND THE QUR'ĀN) as well as in qur'ānic exegesis (see EXEGESIS OF THE QUR'ĀN: CLASSICAL AND MEDIEVAL). In Islamic cosmology (q.v.) the alphabet numbers were linked to stars and planets (see PLANETS AND STARS), the four humors, names of God (see GOD AND HIS ATTRIBUTES), angels (see ANGEL), demons (see DEVIL) and a large variety of esoteric phenomena. The first nine numbers were aligned in a magic square, known as *budūḥ* or Geber's Square, which added up to 15 in all directions:

4	9	2
3	5	7
8	1	6

Originally from ancient China, Arab scholars attributed this square to Adam (see ADAM AND EVE) and commonly wrote it on amulets (q.v.) as a protection against evil spirits and misfortune. Magic squares were also constructed for names, such as one that adds up to 66, the numerical sum of the letters in "Allāh."

In qur'ānic interpretation Muslim scholars noted that half, or fourteen, of the letters of the Arabic alphabet appeared at the beginning of sūras (see MYSTERIOUS LETTERS). These were called *ẓāhir,* "visible," or *nūr,* "light"; the remaining letters were *bāṭin,* "hidden," or *ẓulma,* "dark." Some Ṣūfīs (see ṢŪFISM AND THE QUR'ĀN) interpreted the fact that b (= 2) was both the first letter in the Qur'ān (from *bismillāh,* see BASMALA) and in the Hebrew Bible *(b'reshit)* as an allusion to the created world (see CREATION). The repetition of certain numbers in the Qur'ān held special interest. For example, seven was the number of creations (Q 78:12), heavens (Q 23:86; see HEAVEN AND SKY), lands (Q 65:12; see EARTH), seas (Q 31:27), gates (Q 15:44), cows and years in Joseph's (q.v.) vision (Q 12:46, 47; see VISIONS; DREAMS AND SLEEP) as well as the number of verses in the opening sūra of the Qurʾān, the Fātiḥa (q.v.), and words in the *shahāda* (see WITNESS TO FAITH). The seven letters that do not appear in the Fātiḥa were thought to be magically powerful (see MAGIC). Seven was also the number of days in a week, geographical zones, planets, stages of man (see BIOLOGY AS THE CREATION AND STAGES OF LIFE) and much more in Islamic belief and practice.

The Brethren of Purity *(ikhwān al-ṣafāʾ)* of fourth/tenth century Baṣra applied Pythagorean and Neoplatonic number theory in order to better understand the principle of unity at the center of Islamic belief. In their view, God relates to the world as one relates to other numbers. Of special interest was the perfect number (equal to the sum of its parts) 28, because it represents the letters in the Arabic alphabet, the lunar stations (see MOON), and vertebra in the backbone. This was also the sum of the top row and right column of the *budūḥ* (see above). See also NUMBERS AND ENUMERATION.

Daniel Martin Varisco

Table 1
The numerical value of Arabic letters in the *abjad* ordering of the letter values

ʾ	1	fire (q.v.; hot and dry)	s	60	air (hot and wet)
b	2	earth (cold and dry)	ʿ	70	water (cold and wet)
j	3	air (hot and wet)	f	80	fire (hot and dry)
d	4	water (q.v.; cold and wet)	ṣ	90	earth (cold and dry)
h	5	fire (hot and dry)	q	100	air (hot and wet)
w	6	earth (cold and dry)	r	200	water (cold and wet)
z	7	air (hot and wet)	sh	300	fire (hot and dry)
ḥ	8	water (cold and wet)	t	400	earth (cold and dry)
ṭ	9	fire (hot and dry)	th	500	air (hot and wet)
y	10	earth (cold and dry)	kh	600	water (cold and wet)
k	20	air (hot and wet)	dh	700	fire (hot and dry)
l	30	water (cold and wet)	ḍ	800	earth (cold and dry)
m	40	fire (hot and dry)	ẓ	900	air (hot and wet)
n	50	earth (cold and dry)	gh	1000	water (cold and wet)

Bibliography
Primary: al-Būnī, Abū l-Abbās Aḥmad b. ʿAlī, *Shams al-maʿārif,* Cairo n.d.; Ibn Khaldūn-Rosenthal, iii, 171-9; Ikhwān al-ṣafāʾ, *Rasāʾil Ikhwān al-ṣafāʾ,* 4 vols., Beirut 1957; Suyūṭī, *ʿĀlam al-arwāḥ,* Cairo n.d.
Secondary: L.I. Conrad, Seven and the *tasbīʿ*. On the implications of numerical symbolism for the study of medieval Islamic history, in *JESHO* 31 (1988), 42-73; K. Critchlow, *Islamic patterns,* New York 1976; E. Doutté, *Magie et religion dans l'Afrique du Nord,* Alger 1909; T. Fahd, Djafr, in *EI²,* ii, 375-7; id., Ḥurūf (ʿilm al-), in *EI²,* iii, 595-6; M. Lagarde, *La magie arabe,* Rome 1981; D.B. Macdonald, Budūḥ, in *EI²* (supp.), 153-4; S.H. Nasr, *An introduction to Islamic cosmological doctrines,* Boulder 1978; A.I. Sabra, ʿIlm al-ḥisāb, in *EI²,* iii, 1138-41; A. Schimmel, *The mystery of numbers,* Oxford 1993; H.A. Winckler, *Siegel und Charaktere in der muhammadanischen Zauberei,* Berlin 1930.

Numismatics

The subdiscipline of history that deals with coins as historical evidence. For Islamic coins, the use of qurʾānic inscriptions is an indicator of the issuing authority's religious belief and political loyalties (see POLITICS AND THE QURʾĀN).

Muslims in the Ḥijāz had used Roman and Persian coins, so it was natural, when they had conquered a large part of the Roman empire and the entire Sasanian empire of Iran, to allow similar coins to be minted in Egypt (q.v.), Syria (q.v.), and Iran. Only in Iran were Arabic inscriptions added under the early caliphs (see CALIPH). These were limited to simple brief religious statements added to the Persian images and inscriptions of the prototypes. The earliest, and most common, was *bism Allāh* ("in the name of God"; see BASMALA), and there are a variety of others (Gaube, *Arabosasanidische Numismatik*, plates 2-4), all merely slogans, in many cases used only by one governor, such as *bism Allāh rabbī* (on the coins of Ziyād b. Abī Sufyān, r. 47-55/668-75) or *bism Allāh al-ʿazīz* (on the coins of a certain ʿAbd al-ʿAzīz, 65/685-6).

Qurʾānic inscriptions do not appear until after ʿAbd al-Malik's conquest of the eastern caliphate in 72/691 (Crone and Cook, *Hagarism;* Whelan, Forgotten witness). In the same *hijrī* year, 72 (see CALENDAR; EMIGRATION), the mint of his capital Damascus began producing gold coins of Roman type and silver Persian-type coins with the *shahāda,* the Islamic creed (see WITNESS TO FAITH; CREEDS), which is not recorded before this date. The same formula appears among the inscriptions of the Dome of the Rock, built in 72/691, and on most Persian-type coins of the eastern caliphate beginning in 72 and 73 A.H. The *shahāda* does not appear as such in the Qurʾān, but it is composed of elements drawn from the Qurʾān: "There is no god but God" (*lā ilāha illā llāhu,* Q 37:35, and 47:19); "he alone" (*waḥdahu* applied to God, Q 7:70 and three other places); "He has no associate" (*lā sharīka lahu,* Q 6:163); and "Muḥammad is the messenger (q.v.) of God" (*Muḥammadun rasūlu llāhi,* Q 48:29). This formula, "There is no god but God alone, none is like unto him, Muḥammad is the messenger of God," remained a standard inscription on most Islamic coins for centuries, at least until the fall of the ʿAbbāsid caliphate in the seventh/thirteenth century, and thereafter, usually abbreviated to the first and last elements, into the twentieth century in some countries. In numismatic publications it is often called the *kalima,* perhaps an Anglo-Indian terminology.

The first two-thirds of the *shahāda* form the central obverse inscription of the first Islamic coins (without images, bearing only Arabic inscriptions), which were gold dinars minted in Damascus in 77/697, and silver dirhams beginning two years later (see MONEY; Fig. I of EPIGRAPHY). The central reverse inscription was Q 112:1-4, nearly the entire text of Sūrat al-Ikhlāṣ: "God is one, God is the eternal (see ETERNITY); he does not beget and he was not begotten, and there is nothing like him." The middle phrase suggests that the intended audience for this statement were the Christians, those of Rome and also those whom the Muslims ruled (see CHRISTIANS AND CHRISTIANITY; BYZANTINES). This inscription was standard only for the duration of the Umayyad caliphate, until 132/750, but it was used occasionally later, as late as the fifth/eleventh century; it would be interesting to examine the varied circumstances in which it was revived. These central inscriptions were arranged in horizontal lines on both faces. One of the two circular inscriptions that surrounded the central lines was another qurʾānic verse, "Muḥammad is the messenger of God, who sent him with guidance and the religion of truth to make it supreme over every religion, even if the polytheists detest it" (see POLYTHEISM AND ATHEISM). The first phrase, which completes the *shahāda,* is Q 48:29, while the rest is Q 9:33 or the identical Q 61:9. Here again, the statement is directed to the non-Muslims within and outside the caliphate. This sentence also became a standard part of the inscriptions on all coins until the fall of the caliphate, and for a long time thereafter in Egypt and some other countries. The other outer circular inscription stated that the coin was struck in the name of God, and continued with the *hijrī* date in words, as well as the name of the issuing mint on silver dirhams. With this latter exception, coin inscriptions at the beginning were exclusively religious, justifying the term "Islamic" which was applied to them in medieval and modern times.

These were the main standard inscriptions of the Sunnī caliphates. Early rebels against them added two more qurʾānic inscriptions. The Khārijīs (q.v.), in the rebellions of the 70s/690s and again in those at the end of the Umayyad era, added the statement *lā ḥukm illā lillāh,* "There is no judgment (q.v.) but God's," which is not literally qurʾānic but parallels *ini l-ḥukm illā lillāh* found in three places in the Qurʾān (Q 6:57; 12:40, 67), as well as many other references to God's judgment. The partisans of the rule of the Prophet's family (see FAMILY OF THE PROPHET; PEOPLE OF THE HOUSE; SHĪʿISM AND THE QURʾĀN) used another verse, Q 42:23, "Say: I do not ask of you for it any recompense except love of kin (see KINSHIP)," which appears on the coinage of ʿAbdallāh b. Muʿāwiya (r. 129/746-7) who claimed the caliphate for himself and that of Abū Muslim (d. 137/755) who fought for the ʿAbbāsids (Wurtzel, Coinage), as well as on ninth-century coins of the Zaydī imāms (see IMĀM).

With the victory of the ʿAbbāsid family, the central caliphal mint was transferred to Iraq, and the central reverse inscription of the Umayyads was replaced by the conclusion of the *shahāda,* "Muḥammad is the messenger of God," words which now appeared twice on the coins. This remained the standard central reverse inscription of most Islamic coins. The other inscriptions stayed the same, until, in 145/763, al-Mahdī, the governor of Khurāsān and the future caliph, was the first person allowed to put his name on dirhams (in an executive formula that replaced the normal reverse center inscription). Within a few years, it had become quite common for various individuals to be named on silver and then on gold coins, but the caliph al-Maʾmūn (r. 196-218/811-33) put a stop to this, restoring the completely anonymous, purely religious, inscriptions of the beginning of the ʿAbbāsid caliphate, and otherwise standardizing the coinage, making gold and silver coins alike in arrangement and epigraphy at all mints throughout the caliphate (see EPIGRAPHY AND THE QURʾĀN). He also made two additions to the former inscriptions, both of which remained standard for the duration of the ʿAbbāsid caliphate. In 193/809, when his father died leaving him as governor of the eastern caliphate on behalf of his brother the caliph, the single word *lillāh* was added to all coins issued in his realm in the space above the reverse inscriptions. This word, or rather prepositional phrase, has a clear meaning, either "for God" or "belonging to God," but its significance is not obvious. Does it apply to the coin or to the caliph who authorizes it? Whatever its import, it was probably put on the coins as an indication of al-Maʾmūn's piety in contrast to his brother al-Amīn (r. 193-8/809-13), whom he ultimately defeated in civil war. This victory was celebrated by the addition of another qurʾānic inscription, Q 30:4-5, "God commands *(lillāhi l-amru),* in the past and in the future; and on that day the believers will rejoice in God's victory (q.v.)," placed on the obverse of all coins as a second outer circular inscription (El-Hibri, Coinage reform). Al-Muʿtaṣim (r. 218-27/833-42), al-Maʾmūn's successor, retained all these standard inscriptions, but with one important addition: his own caliphal title, *al-Muʿtaṣim bi-llāh,* placed below *Muḥammad rasūl Allāh* on the reverse. His successors followed the same practice, and sometimes added other names: their son and anticipated successor most commonly, but also, with increasing frequency, the names of certain distinguished *wazīr*s, powerful generals, and autonomous provincial governors. Legally, the powerful Sunnī dynasts of the fourth/tenth century onwards were in the latter category. Although they were named on the coins and controlled their minting, they always named the caliph as overlord and included all the elements mentioned above on their coinage: the "Victory Verse" around the outer edge of the obverse, with "struck in the name of God" followed by the denomination, mint city, and date as the inner circular inscription; the first part of the *shahāda* as the central element of the obverse, sometimes abbreviated; on the reverse, *lillāh* above "Muḥammad is the messenger of God," with the "prophetic mission" verse (Q 9:33 or the identical Q 61:9) around the edge.

Rebels against the caliphate, and Islamic dynasties outside the ʿAbbāsid caliphate, often used different inscriptions to proclaim their ideology and differentiate themselves from the Sunnī ʿAbbāsids. The pro-ʿAlid Abū l-Sarāyā exhorted his troops on dirhams of Kūfa (199/814-15) with the verse "Indeed, God loves those who fight in his path in ranks, as though they were a building well-compacted" (Q 61:4; see FIGHTING; PATH OR WAY). In place of the usual outer circular inscriptions ʿAlī b. Muḥammad, the *ṣāḥib al-Zanj,* used the beginning of Q 9:111: "God has purchased from the believers their persons and their goods, in return for paradise (q.v.) if they fight in the path of God," a stirring call to arms; and on the reverse, "And those who fail to judge according to God's revelation, they are the unbelievers" (*kāfirūn,* cf. Q 5:47; see BELIEF AND UNBELIEF), justifying his war against the Muslims around him (Miles, Ninth century hoard, 71-4, 131-3). The Zaydī imāms in Daylam and Ṭabaristān used several qurʾānic verses at one time or another, including Q 42:23, the so-called "kinfolk verse," mentioned above; Q 22:39, "Permission [to make war (q.v.) is given] to those who are oppressed, and surely God is able to give them victory" (*wa-inna llāha ʿalā naṣrihim la-qadīrun,* see OPPRESSION; OPPRESSED ON EARTH, THE); the end of Q 33:33, "God only wants to remove pollution from you, O people of the house, and to purify you thoroughly"; and Q 17:81, "Say, the truth (q.v.) is come and falsehood has vanished, for falsehood indeed is bound to perish" (Miles, al-Mahdi al-Ḥaqq; Stern, Coins, 211-19). This latter verse was widely employed, being found on some of the coins of the Idrīsids in eighth century Morocco (Eustache, *Corpus*) and on many coins of Yemen, having been introduced there in 297/910 by the Zaydī imām al-Hādī ilā l-Ḥaqq (Bikhazi, Coins).

Outside the ʿAbbāsid caliphate, the Fāṭimids proclaimed their descent through the addition of *ʿAlī walī Allāh* after *Muḥammad rasūl Allāh,* and through various other references to ʿAlī b. Abī Ṭālib (q.v.) and Fāṭima (q.v.), but did not employ any new qurʾānic verses. As heirs of the Aghlabids, who followed ʿAbbāsid practice in effect when they became autonomous, the Fāṭimids took no notice of al-Maʾmūn's innovations but employed all the standard inscriptions of early ʿAbbāsid coinage (Lane-Poole, *Catalogue,* iv, 275) plus ʿAlid additions. In

Spain, the Umayyad emirs retained the inscriptions of caliphal Umayyad dirhams to the letter, and when they declared themselves caliphs, merely substituted their names and titles for the former Umayyad reverse, Q 112:1-4. The first new qurʾānic inscription in the Maghrib was introduced by the Almoravids whose standard obverse marginal inscription was Q 3:85, "And whoever desires a faith (q.v.) other than Islam, it will not be accepted from him, and in the end he will be among those who perish." Subsequently a great many different qurʾānic verses and references were used by the Almohads and their successors; Hazard (*Numismatic history,* 36-40) lists 61 different verses and phrases used in north Africa, which are keyed back to the issues on which they appear on pages 365-71. In fourteenth-century Spain, the Naṣrids of Granada, facing extinction by the Christians, used the verse "Say: O God, master of dominion, you give dominion to whom you wish and strip dominion from whom you wish, and you exalt whom you wish and humble whom you wish — in your hand is all good" (Q 3:26).

After the fall of the ʿAbbāsid caliphate, the Īlkhāns and their successors, although their coinages were very diverse, introduced a few exceptional inscriptions which were used briefly under Ölceytü and Abū Saʿīd. Ölceytü's coinage (between 703-9/1304-10) bore two qurʾānic verses not used elsewhere on coins, the long first half of Q 48:29, and most of Q 24:55, as well as phrases indicating his new Sunnī allegiance, whereas before he had designated ʿAlī as *walī Allāh* and named the twelve imāms. Abū Saʿīd, on his issue of 718-21/1319-22, used the end of Q 2:137, "God will suffice you against them, for he is the all-hearing, the all-knowing" (see SEEING AND HEARING; GOD AND HIS ATTRIBUTES), forming the words into an arch resembling a *miḥrāb* (see MOSQUE) enclosing the abbreviated *shahāda* (Lane-Poole, *Catalogue,* vi, lvi-lvii, 46, 62).

The use of long qurʾānic quotations went out of style in the early modern era. The Ottomans scarcely ever employed religious inscriptions on their coinage. The Shāhs of Iran at most used the *shahāda* with the addition of *ʿAlī walī Allāh* and the twelve imāms; the Mughals did the same, without the Shīʿī additions. More often, both empires filled the coin faces with Persian verses and long titulature. In Yemen, coins issued by the Zaydī imāms continued to bear ʿAbd al-Malik's *shahāda* past the middle of the twentieth century.

Michael L. Bates

Bibliography

R.J. Bikhazi, Coins of al-Yaman. 132-569 A.H., in *al-Abhath* 23 (1970), 1-127; O. Codrington, *A manual of Musalman numismatics* (*Asiatic Society monographs* 7), London 1904, 20-39 (the only work to provide a list of religious expressions on all Islamic coins, with many qurʾānic passages cited by chapter and verse and translated, but there is no indication of where, when, and by whom each expression was used; no one else has attempted a complete listing); P. Crone and M. Cook, *Hagarism. The making of the Islamic world,* Cambridge 1977; T. El-Hibri, Coinage reform under the ʿAbbāsid caliph al-Maʾmūn, in *JESHO* 36 (1993), 58-83; D. Eustache, *Corpus des dirhams idrīsites et contemporains. Collection de la Banque du Maroc et autres collections mondiales, publiques et privées,* Rabat 1970-1; H. Gaube, *Arabosasanidische Numismatik. Handbücher der mittelasiatischen Numismatik, II,* Braunschweig 1973; H.W. Hazard, *The numismatic history of late medieval north Africa,* New York 1952; S. Lane-Poole, *Catalogue of oriental coins in the British Museum,* 10 vols., London 1875-90 (the only full catalogue of a major museum collection of Islamic coins; each volume has indices of religious inscriptions, including qurʾānic verses, that refer back to specific coins); G.C. Miles, al-Mahdi al-Ḥaqq, Amīr al-Muʾminīn, in *Revue numismatique* 7 (1965), 329-41; id., A ninth century hoard of dirhems found at Susa, in *Mémoires de la Mission Archéologique en Iran,* XXXVII. *Mission de Susiane. Numismatique susienne. Monnaies trouvées à Suse de*

1946 à 1956, Paris 1960, 67-145; S.M. Stern, The coins of Āmul, in *Numismatic chronicle* 7/7 (1967), 205-78; E. Whelan, Forgotten witness. Evidence for the early codification of the Qur'ān, in *JAOS* 118 (1998), 1-14; C. Wurtzel, The coinage of the revolutionaries in the late Umayyad period, in *American Numismatic Society museum notes* 23 (1978), 161-99.

Nūn, Dhū al- see JONAH

Nurse see FOSTERAGE; WET-NURSING

O

Oaths

Solemn assertions or promises. In English the word "oath" has various related senses. One usually involves using the name of God, or of some other revered or dreaded being, object or place, in order to give force and solemnity to an utterance (an assertion, promise, denial, curse, etc.). Oaths of this type, where a statement includes a phrase such as "by God," "by the stars when they set," "by this land," etc., are common in the Qurʾān. Many such oaths occur in sūras traditionally regarded as having been among the earliest to be revealed, and their compressed grammar and unusual vocabulary pose difficulties of comprehension (see GRAMMAR AND THE QURʾĀN; LANGUAGE AND STYLE OF THE QURʾĀN). Understood as communications of God himself, there are nevertheless examples (e.g. Q 4:65; 16:63) where they are made "by God" *(tallāhi)* or "by your lord" (q.v.; *wa-rabbika*). The fact that God uses oaths in the Qurʾān is taken to be among the proofs of its inimitability (q.v.; cf. Suyūṭī, *Muʿtarak*, i, 449-55).

The interpretation of oaths to natural phenomena, such as stars (see NATURE AS SIGNS; PLANETS AND STARS), which occur in early sūras (see CHRONOLOGY AND THE QURʾĀN), has posed problems for exegetes (see EXEGESIS OF THE QURʾĀN: CLASSICAL AND MEDIEVAL; see also Kandil, Schwüre; Neuwirth, Images). Muqātil (d. 150/767) explains the oath of Q 53:1 ("by the star when it sets") as referring to the time that elapsed between revelations; the Qurʾān itself is therefore called *"najm"* (*Tafsīr*, iv, 159; cf. Ibn Qayyim al-Jawziyya, *Tibyān*, 161; al-Farrāʾ, *Maʿānī*, iii, 94). Later exegetes, such as al-Suyūṭī (d. 911/1505; *Itqān*, iv, 53-9), explain these oaths as following the custom of the Arabs (q.v.): as the Qurʾān was revealed in the language of the Arabs, it adopted their formulaic expressions (see ARABIC LANGUAGE; LANGUAGE, CONCEPT OF). The problematic is further complicated when the style of these formulaic expressions is examined: for, stylistically, these oaths have been understood to be akin to the rhymed prose (q.v.) of the pre-Islamic soothsayers (q.v.; see Ibn al-Naqīb, *Muqaddima*, 238-9; cf. Nöldeke, *GQ*, i, 60, 75; Wellhausen, *Reste arabischen Heidentums*, 135; see also POETRY AND POETS), yet the Qurʾān denies that Muḥammad is a soothsayer.

Finally, sometimes these oaths appear in the reported speech of, for example, Abraham (q.v.; Q 21:57: "By God, I shall set snares for your idols"; see IDOLS AND

IMAGES) or the sons of Jacob (q.v.) in Egypt (q.v.; Q 12:73: "By God, you know that we did not come to commit evil in the land…").

A second type of oath is typically a statement or promise guaranteed by calling upon a revered being or object as a witness, usually made to another person or party, often in a formal legal or quasi-legal context (see WITNESSING AND TESTIFYING; LAW AND THE QUR'ĀN). It is common to distinguish between an oath in this sense and a vow, a promise to do or avoid something, which may be made directly to God or some other being and may be made privately and internally. Inasmuch as the words of a vow, however, tend to follow fixed formulae, may involve other human beings, and may invoke the name of the being to whom it is being offered, the distinction between an oath and a vow is not always clear. There are some cases in the Qur'ān — and outside it — where derivatives of the root *y-m-n* (usually understood in connection with oaths) may be equally understood as referring to vows (see the discussion of *al-laghw fī aymānikum* below).

Vocabulary and types of oaths

The most common words indicating swearing and oaths in the Qur'ān are derivatives of the roots *y-m-n*, *ḥ-l-f*, and *q-s-m*. They seem to be used interchangeably and often jointly in expressions such as "oaths which you have sworn" (*aymānikum idhā ḥalaftum*, e.g. Q 5:89) or "they swear a solemn oath by God" (*aqsamū bi-llāhi jahda aymānihim*, e.g. Q 6:109). The root *q-s-m*, which is associated with the notion of dividing and apportioning, as well as with swearing and oath taking, is used both in connection with the oath as a forceful statement (Q 56:75-6: "I swear *[fa-lā uqsimu]* by the setting of the stars and that indeed is a mighty oath *[qasam]*, if only you knew"), and with it in relation to legal matters (Q 5:106-7 recommends that when making a will two just men should be chosen as witnesses and asked to swear — *yuqsimān* — that they will not act corruptly). The references in Q 2:67-71 to the cow which God commanded the people of Moses (q.v.) to slaughter are sometimes explained by exegetes in connection with the group oath known in Islamic law as the *qasāma*, which is not attested by name in the Qur'ān.

On the other hand, *nadhara* and *nadhr*, understood more in connection with vows, occur independently and on some occasions clearly refer to the promising of a pious act to God: in Q 19:26 Mary (q.v.; Maryam) says, "I have sworn/vowed a fast *(nadhartu … ṣawman)* to God" (see FASTING); in Q 3:35 ʿImrān's (q.v.) wife, pregnant with Mary, says to God, "I have sworn/vowed *(nadhartu)* to you what is in my womb as a consecrated offering."

The *bayʿa* (giving allegiance or entering a contract of clientage) may also be understood as a form of oath (see CONTRACTS AND ALLIANCES). The noun *bayʿa* itself does not occur in the Qur'ān but there are a number of cases where the third form of the verb is used, and Q 48:10 makes it clear that it involves a ritual acceptance of God's representative as one's patron (see CLIENTS AND CLIENTAGE): "Those who offer allegiance to you *(yubāyiʿūnaka)* do so to God. God's hand (q.v.) is over theirs [an allusion to the hand clasp involved in such contracts]. Whoever betrays his oath *(man nakatha)* only betrays himself but whoever fulfils what he has contracted to God *(awfā bimā ʿāhada ʿalayhu llāha)*, he will grant him a tremendous reward."

Two other procedures mentioned in the Qur'ān are related to swearing oaths and making vows. They involve a man renouncing sexual relations with a woman or women who would normally be available to him. Q 2:226-7 says that those who swear or vow not to have relations with their wives *(lilladhīna yu'lūna min nisā'ihim)* should wait for four months. If they revert *(fā'ū)* [i.e. resume relations?], God is forgiving and merciful; if they decide on divorce, he is all-hearing and all-knowing" (see MARRIAGE AND DIVORCE; ABSTINENCE; CHASTITY). Outside the Qur'ān the word *īlā'* is used with reference to a vow of (temporary) abstention from a certain woman or women. If the abstention lasts longer than four months, the man must either divorce the woman or resume relations with her (see SEX AND SEXUALITY). The vow is made invoking one of the names of God (see GOD AND HIS ATTRIBUTES) and is subject to an act of atonement *(kaffāra)* if broken. Some commentators say explicitly that *yu'lūna* means *yaḥlifūna*.

Q 33:4 and Q 58:2-3 refer unfavorably to the practice whereby a man makes a wife sexually unavailable to him by *ẓihār* — a noun which does not occur in the Qur'ān, but is implied in the use of the related verb form in such phrases as *azwājakumu llā'ī tuẓāhirūna minhunna* (Q 33:4) and *alladhīna yuẓāhirūna minkum min nisā'ihim* (Q 58:2). Commentators explain that this practice involved the man putting the woman in the category of those prohibited to him for sexual relations (see PROHIBITED DEGREES) by saying to her, "You are to me as the back *(ẓahr)* of my mother," where "back" has a sexual connotation. Although this is not strictly an oath or vow, it does involve the use of a ritual formula and is subject to acts of atonement (listed in Q 58:3-4) which are more severe than those laid down in Q 5:89 for the breaking of (other?) types of oath.

Vocabulary used in connection with the breaking of oaths includes *n-k-th* (explained as metaphorical use [see METAPHOR] of its literal association with unraveling or untwisting the fibers of a garment or a wooden toothpick, *siwāk*) and *n-q-ḍ*. *Ḥ-n-th*, which is used outside the Qur'ān often as a technical term in connection with breaking or incurring liability for oaths (see BREAKING TRUSTS AND CONTRACTS), but also more generally in the sense of "sin" (see SIN, MAJOR AND MINOR), occurs twice: in the story of Job (q.v.; Q 38:44) we are told that God ordered him *lā taḥnath*, which some commentators understand as "do not break your oath," while in Q 56:46 persisting in *al-ḥinth al-'aẓīm* is mentioned as the sin of those consigned to hell (see HELL AND HELLFIRE).

The opponents' oaths

Many references concern the oaths that the opponents (*mushrikūn, munāfiqūn* [see BELIEF AND UNBELIEF; POLYTHEISM AND ATHEISM; IDOLATRY AND IDOLATERS], "People of the Book" [q.v.], and others; see also OPPOSITION TO MUḤAMMAD) make, falsely, insincerely, or for worldly gain. "[The *munāfiqūn*] would come to you swearing by God that that they only wanted benificence and reconciliation *(iḥsānan wa-tawfīqan)*" (Q 4:62); "on the day when God will raise them all together they will swear to him as they swear to you… but they are liars" (Q 58:18; see RESURRECTION; LIE); "the *mushrikūn* swear by God one of their strongest oaths that they will believe if a sign (see SIGNS) comes to them. Say: The signs are with God alone…" (Q 6:109). "Those who barter God's covenant (q.v.) and their oaths for a small price" (Q 3:77) is often associated with the Jews (see JEWS AND JUDAISM) and sometimes understood to refer to the swearing of a false oath *(yamīn fājira)* in order to obtain property illegitimately. Satan (see DEVIL) is reported to have sworn to Adam and Eve (q.v.; *qāsamahumā*) that he was a good adviser to them (Q 7:21).

Q 68:10 refers to the unidentified opponents as *ḥallāf mahīn*, "despicable swearer of oaths." Subsequently (Q 68:17-33), their fate is compared to that of the unspecified "owners of the garden" (q.v.; *aṣḥāb al-janna*) who swore *(aqsamū)* to harvest it on the next morning. They failed, however, to make *istithnā'* — understood to mean that they omitted to say *in shā'a llāh*, "God willing," after swearing. While they slept, an affliction sent by God befell the garden, and when they came to harvest the fruit they found that there was none left. Mutual recriminations and recognition of guilt followed. The parable has been read as a warning against pride (q.v.) or complacency (Speyer, *Erzählungen*, 426).

In two passages (Q 58:16 and 63:2) the hypocrites *(munāfiqūn)* are accused of making their oaths a *junna*, "shield, armor," and turning others from the way of God (see PATH OR WAY). These are interpreted as referring to the oaths or the *ḥilf* which the hypocrites of Medina (q.v.) had made with the Muslims, claiming that they were believers, in order to deflect the Muslims from the way of God, i.e. from the putting into practice of God's commands regarding the People of the Book and the unbelievers, to which they should really have been subject.

There are other allusions — especially in Q 9 — to agreements guaranteed by oath between the qur'ānic community and its opponents (see COMMUNITY AND SOCIETY IN THE QUR'ĀN), although here too the emphasis is on the possibility or likelihood that the opponents will break them. Q 9:12-3: If the *mushrikūn* with whom you have made an agreement "undo their oaths after their agreement *(in nakathū aymānahum min ba'di 'ahdihim)* and attack your religion, fight the imāms (see IMĀM) of *kufr*. They have no oaths *(innahum lā aymāna lahum)*.... Will you not fight a people who have undone their oaths...." Traditional commentators associate the first twenty-nine verses of Q 9 with the period following the conquest of Mecca (q.v.), when agreements previously made between the Prophet and non-Muslims in Arabia were ended — after a period of four months' grace — and non-Muslims were barred from the Meccan sanctuary (see KA'BA; POLITICS AND THE QUR'ĀN).

The binding and loosing of oaths

There are so many such references to the opponents swearing oaths (often "by God") that the qur'ānic texts must reflect a society in which the swearing of oaths was a stock feature of speech (see PRE-ISLAMIC ARABIA AND THE QUR'ĀN). Q 2:224, "Do not make God an *'urḍa* to your oaths..." (see further below), and Q 5:89, "preserve *(wa-ḥfaẓū)* your oaths," are sometimes interpreted as injunctions against prolixity in the making of oaths. As in other societies where oath taking is an important part of everyday life, tension must have existed between, on the one hand, the idea that oaths were solemn undertakings which, once entered into, had to be kept and, on the other, an awareness that it was often impossible to keep an oath. In the latter case some way out had to be found. Various qur'ānic passages, taken together, seem to illustrate this tension.

The verses which stress most strongly the need to honor oaths are probably Q 5:89 (where *wa-ḥfaẓū* is more usually understood as "keep" in the sense of "fulfil") and Q 16:91-2, 94. The latter repeat an injunction to fulfil the covenant of God *('ahd Allāh)* when it has been entered into *(idhā 'āhadtum)* and not to break oaths *(lā tanquḍū l-aymāna)* after they have been affirmed. Breaking them is then likened to a woman who ruins her thread by untwisting *(n-k-th)* it, thus weakening it. A possible motive for breaking them is suggested by the phrase, "[Do not] take your oaths as a deception *(dakhalan)* between yourselves, one party *(ummatun)* being more numerous than another" *(tattakhidhūna aymānakum dakhalan baynakum an takūna ummatun hiya arbā min ummatin)*. Q 16:94 then echoes the first part of that last phrase, "Do not take your oaths as a *dakhal* between you."

Dakhal is generally glossed by words meaning "trick" or "deceit," and a tribal practice of the Age of Ignorance (q.v.; *jāhiliyya*) is suggested as the reason why the oaths in question were sometimes broken: one of the contracting parties (a tribe or other social group) was induced to abandon the other by the appearance of a third party which was bigger and stronger (*arbā* is understood as meaning "more numerous"). Nevertheless, the passage is understood to contain a general principle: al-Ṭabarī, (d. 310/923; *Tafsīr*, xiv, 163-9), while not ruling out that there may have been an occasion of revelation (see OCCASIONS OF REVELATION) about which it is impossible to be certain, nevertheless considers the ruling contained therein to be generally applicable *(wa-inna l-āya kānat qad nazalat li-sabab min al-asbāb wa-yakūna l-ḥukm bihā ʿāmman fī kull mā kāna bi-maʿnā al-sabab alladhī nazalat fīhi)*.

Q 2:225 and 5:89, while they reassure us that God will not hold us responsible for *al-laghw* ("slips," but see below) in our oaths, nevertheless stress that he will hold us responsible "for what your hearts (see HEART) have acquired" (Q 2:225) or "for that which you have contracted oaths" (Q 5:89).

Nevertheless, both of those verses recognize the possibility of *al-laghw* in an oath: God will not hold us liable for *al-laghw* in our oaths *(lā yuʾākhidhukumu llāhu bi-l-laghwi fī aymānikum)*. The commentators disagree on the precise meaning of *al-laghw fī l-aymāni* but they agree that it refers to oaths which, because of the mental or physical state of the one swearing — for example he may be angry, making a joke, or involved in bargaining — or because the words used are inappropriate, are not binding.

Other than appealing to the circumstances in which it had been made, the other obvious way out of an oath which had been sworn but which could not be kept is the *kaffāra* (see ATONEMENT), various forms of which are set out in Q 5:89. Commentators and jurists differ regarding whether a *kaffāra* is necessary in the case of *al-laghw fī l-aymān*.

Oaths (or vows) of abstention, made for ascetic or other reasons (see ASCETICISM), may have been a particular problem. The reference to *al-laghw* in Q 5:89 follows the previous verse's command to "eat of what God has given you as lawful and good" (see LAWFUL AND UNLAWFUL; FOOD AND DRINK), while that in Q 2:225 follows the injunction, "Do not make God an *ʿurḍa* to your oaths." This latter verse raises questions of interpretation. It is often understood to mean that if there is the possibility of performing a good deed (see GOOD DEEDS), you should not avoid doing so on the grounds that you have sworn something which you would have to violate in order to perform the good. If you have sworn such an oath, then you should violate it and make an act of atonement. Another interpretation cites the example of someone who declares that something God has made permissible is forbidden (q.v.) to him. This procedure of *taḥrīm al-ḥalāl* is also sometimes mentioned in discussions of the meaning of *al-laghw*.

The Prophet himself is understood as having sworn such an oath. Q 66:1 reads, "O Prophet, why do you declare forbidden what God has made lawful for you, seeking the pleasure of your wives (see WIVES OF THE PROPHET)...?" The following verse then goes on to say that God has made incumbent upon you (plural) the expiation (?) of your oaths *(taḥillat aymānikum)*. Commentators explain these verses as references to an incident in which the Prophet undertook to avoid something which was not contrary to God's law. Many versions talk of his expressing his determination to avoid sexual relations with a slave girl out of deference to one or two of his wives. Others refer to a certain drink or to honey (q.v.). God then made clear that it was not right that he should declare *ḥarām* what God had made *ḥalāl*.

Although Q 66:1 has a singular vocative addressed to the Prophet while Q 66:2 is understood as addressed to the Muslims in general, the reports about the Prophet's "declaring forbidden" tend to agree that it involved an oath. Whether the *taḥrīm* was in itself an oath, or whether it was made together with an oath, many reports refer to the Prophet's "swearing" *(ḥ-l-f* and *y-m-n)* and to his having to make a *kaffāra*. Some, interpreting the *taḥrīm* as a renunciation of sexual relations, use the noun *īlā'* and the verb *ālā*.

Questions concerning oaths and vows occupy considerable space in the classical works of Islamic law, and the qur'ānic materials are taken into account in the discussions. Typically oaths and vows are discussed under the heading *kitāb al-aymān wa-l-nudhūr* although *īlā'* and *ẓihār* are usually discussed mainly in the sections on divorce *(kitāb al-ṭalāq)*. For discussion of taking oaths *on* the Qur'ān, see EVERYDAY LIFE, QUR'ĀN IN; POPULAR AND TALISMANIC USES OF THE QUR'ĀN; RITUAL AND THE QUR'ĀN.

G.R. Hawting

Bibliography
Primary: Farrā', *Ma'ānī;* Ibn al-Naqīb, *Muqaddima;* Ibn Qayyim al-Jawziyya, *Tibyān,* Cairo n.d. [198-?] (for a discussion of the oaths that begin various sūras); Muqātil, *Tafsīr;* Qurṭubī, *Jāmi';* Shawkānī, *Tafsīr;* Suyūṭī, *Itqān,* ed. Ibrāhīm, Cairo 1974² (who follows Ibn al-Qayyim); id., *Mu'tarak al-aqrān fī i'jāz al-Qur'ān,* ed. 'A.M. al-Bajāwī, 3 vols., Cairo 1969-72; Ṭabarī, *Tafsīr,* ed. Sa'īd.
Secondary: R. Brunschvig, Voeu ou serment? Droit comparé du Judaïsme et de l'Islam, in G. Nahon and C. Touati (eds.), *Hommage à Georges Vajda,* Louvain 1980, 125-34; N. Calder, *Ḥinth, birr, taḥannuth.* An enquiry into the Arabic vocabulary of vows, in *BSOAS* 51 (1988), 213-39; P. Crone, Jāhilī and Jewish law. The *qasāma,* in *JSAI* 4 (1984), 153-201; 'A. al-Farāhī, *Im'ān fī aqsām al-Qur'ān,* Damascus 1994 (on the oaths in the Qur'ān); W. Gottschalk, *Das Gelübde nach älterer arabischer Auffassung,* Berlin 1919; G. Hawting, An ascetic vow and an unseemly oath? *Īlā'* and *ẓihār* in Muslim law, in *BSOAS* 57 (1994), 113-25; L. Kandil, Schwüre in den mekkanischen Suren, in Wild, *Text,* 41-58 (on the oaths in the Qur'ān); M.R.L. Lehmann, Biblical oaths, in *Zeitschrift für Alttestamentliche Wissenschaft* 81 (1969), 744-92; A. Neuwirth, Der Horizont der Offenbarung. Zur Relevanz der einleitenden Schwurserien für die Suren der frühmekkanischen Zeit, in *Gottes ist der Orient, Gottes ist de Okzident. Festschrift für A. Falaturi,* Cologne 1990; id., Images and metaphors in the introductory sections of the Makkan *sūras,* in Hawting and Shareef, *Approaches,* 3-36; Nöldeke, *GQ;* J. Pedersen, *Der Eid bei den Semiten,* Strassburg 1914; id., Nadhr, in *EI²,* vii, 846-7; id./Y. Linant de Bellefonds, Ḳasam, in *EI²,* iv, 687-90; S. Rosenblatt, The relations between Jewish and Muslim law concerning oaths and vows, in *Proceedings of the American Academy for Jewish Research* 7 (1935-6), 229-43; G.R. Smith, Oaths in the Qur'ān, in *Semitics* 1 (1970), 126-56; J. Wellhausen, *Reste arabischen Heidentums,* Leipzig 1927.

Obedience

Act or fact of complying with the demands of one in authority (q.v.). The idea of obedience, with its concomitant concepts of legitimate authority and power to command, occurs with considerable frequency in the Qur'ān. Though several different Arabic expressions convey the idea of obedience, derivatives of the root *ṭ-w-'*, especially the verb *aṭā'a/yuṭī'u,* predominate, as exemplified in the longest sustained passage on obedience (Q 24:47-56). While *aṭāʿa/yuṭīʿu* normally means, "to obey," it sometimes bears the less insistent meaning of "to heed" (Q 3:168). The verb *ittabaʿa/yattabiʿu* carries the meaning "to obey" (as perhaps in Q 3:31, 53) with even less frequency, as it normally means "to follow," often in a negative sense. Verbs of the root *s-l-m,* especially *sallama/yusallimu* and *aslama/yuslimu,* give the meaning "to submit" but these connote a relatively passive initial act of submission and usually lack the element of putting obedience into active practice found in the verb *aṭāʿa/yuṭīʿu,* the sense of which they only occasionally approach (as perhaps in Q 3:20; 4:65).

Obedience demanded in the Qurʾān is primarily to God and the prophet Muḥammad (eleven occurrences together of *aṭāʿa/yuṭīʿu* in the imperative). Only one verse (Q 4:59) adds obedience to "those having authority among you," who are best explained as appointees of the Prophet representing his authority in his absence, although other explanations have been offered (see CALIPH; KINGS AND RULERS; IMĀM). Obedience to God and his Prophet means unquestioning submission to God's commands mediated through the Prophet (Q 4:65; 33:36). It is, however, somewhat tempered by the instruction to the Prophet to consult with his followers before deciding on an action (Q 3:159; cf. Q 4:83; 42:38).

Several other types of obedience also appear in the Qurʾān. Obedient wives (see MARRIAGE AND DIVORCE) are said to deserve kind treatment (Q 4:34) and the Prophet's wives (see WIVES OF THE PROPHET) in particular are told to obey God and his Prophet (Q 33:33), while two verses imply that children (q.v.) should obey their parents in all cases except where the latter oppose them in religion (Q 29:8; 31:15; see FAMILY; KINSHIP). Conversely, the Qurʾān warns the Muslims not to obey devils (Q 6:121; see DEVIL), unbelievers (Q 3:149; see BELIEF AND UNBELIEF), some People of the Book (q.v.; Q 3:100) and counsels the Prophet not to heed those who try to prevent worship (q.v.; Q 96:19), various stripes of unbelievers (Q 13:37; 18:28; 25:52; 68:8, 10), hypocrites (Q 33:1, 48; see HYPOCRITES AND HYPOCRISY), sinners (Q 76:24; see SIN, MAJOR AND MINOR), and most people (Q 6:116). The Muslims are also warned not to try to get the Prophet to obey their wishes (Q 49:7).

Thus, the Qurʾān provides a rather simple doctrine of obedience, giving a chain of command from God to the Prophet to the Muslims, in which no contradiction or immediate difficulty is visible. Nevertheless, there clearly seems to be a development of the doctrine when the relevant verses are placed in their probable historical context (see CHRONOLOGY AND THE QURʾĀN) according to the Prophet's biography (see SĪRA AND THE QURʾĀN) and the alleged dates and occasions of revelation (q.v.). First, most of the commands to the Prophet not to heed unbelievers fall in passages attributed to the Meccan period. This suggests that the situation of Islam was not yet securely established, so that intrusive outside influences were to be feared and that such reminders were needed to avoid the temptation of taking an easier path of compromise. Also, no calls to obey the prophet Muḥammad personally occur in Meccan passages of the Qurʾān at all, perhaps because the Prophet's authority was already accepted by his small following on a firsthand basis. In verses attributed to the Meccan period, only certain of the former prophets command their followers to be obedient to them personally (see PROPHETS AND PROPHETHOOD). These prophets include Noah (q.v.; Nūḥ), Hūd (q.v.), Ṣāliḥ (q.v.), Lot (q.v.; Lūṭ), Shuʿayb (q.v.), Aaron (q.v.; Hārūn) and Jesus (q.v.; ʿĪsā; cf. Q 20:90; 26:108, 110, 126, 131, 144, 150, 163, 179; 43:

57, 63; 71:3). If a need to obey Muḥammad is discoverable in such verses, it is only by implication, for no connection is made explicit there.

Rather, all of the direct calls for obedience to God and his Prophet come from passages considered Medinan, starting in 1/622 but mostly dating from 4/626 and later. When Muḥammad moved from leading a small religious group trying to establish itself at Mecca (q.v.) to actually founding a polity and eventually a sovereign city-state at Medina (q.v.), obedience to him personally grew in importance as a theme (see POLITICS AND THE QUR'ĀN). As the Muslims became more numerous and started to be drawn from more diverse ethnic groups than the Quraysh (q.v.) alone, the need for personal obedience to the leader became more obvious (see COMMUNITY AND SOCIETY IN THE QUR'ĀN). This was especially the case when fighting (q.v.) was prescribed by qur'ānic revelation (traditionally first in Q 22:39-40), requiring obedience to military commands. The command to fight was revealed either just before the second oath of al-ʿAqaba in 621 C.E. (see OATHS; CONTRACTS AND ALLIANCES) or right after the emigration (q.v.; *hijra*) in 1/622 (see also WAR; EXPEDITIONS AND BATTLES; JIHĀD).

Thereafter, the various oaths of allegiance *(bayʿa* or *mubāyaʿa)* mentioned in the *sīra* and the ḥadīth (see ḤADĪTH AND THE QUR'ĀN) constitute important milestones in the institutionalization of obedience to the Prophet in his lifetime. The few chronological indications in these sources usually connect such oaths with the two oaths of al-ʿAqaba in 620-1 C.E. and the oath of al-Ḥudaybiya in 6/628. Only the latter, however, has a clear chronological connection with qur'ānic verses — namely Q 48:10 and 48:18, wherein the allusions to a formal oath of allegiance clearly refer to al-Ḥudaybiya and are one of the best-established chronological indications in the Qur'ān. Other allusions to formal oaths of allegiance in Q 60:12 and Q 9:111 are later, attributable to 8/629 and 9/630 respectively. The covenant (q.v.; *mīthāq*) of Q 5:7, involving a promise of "We hear and obey," must likewise refer to a contractual obligation of obedience by the believers but the verse most likely postdates al-Ḥudaybiya. Cognate verses, however, containing the phrase "We hear and obey" (Q 2:285; 24:51; cf. Q 64:16) may be earlier in date. Whatever the details, one sees a formalization of vows of obedience in the form of a personal oath of allegiance to the Prophet as the Medinan polity grew. On the other hand, long, late passages such as Q 9:38-57 and Q 9:81-106 suggest the continuing difficulty that the Prophet had in enforcing compliance.

Later exegesis (see EXEGESIS OF THE QUR'ĀN: CLASSICAL AND MEDIEVAL; EXEGESIS OF THE QUR'ĀN: EARLY MODERN AND CONTEMPORARY) mostly equates obedience to God and the Prophet with obedience to the Qur'ān and the sunna (q.v.) of the Prophet. Passages most often quoted in support of this include Q 4:58-69, 5:44-50 and 33:36 as well as many ḥadīths. Pro-government interpretations are rare, as exegetes eventually do not consider Muslim polities legitimate successors of the Prophet, whatever the pretensions of the regimes themselves may have been. See also DISOBEDIENCE.

Khalid Yahya Blankinship

Bibliography

Primary: Bukhārī, *Ṣaḥīḥ*, Cairo 1958, iv, 60-2 *(Kitāb al-jihād); ix, 78-9 (Kitāb al-aḥkām);* 91-2; 96-8; 99; Ibn Isḥāq, *Sīra*, Cairo 1955, i, 431-4, 438-49, 454-68, 501-4; ii, 315-6, 320-1; Ibn Isḥāq-Guillaume, 197-213, 231-3, 503-4; Muqātil, *Tafsīr;* Muslim, *Ṣaḥīḥ (Muslim bi-sharḥ al-Nawawī)*, 18 vols., Cairo n.d., xii, 222-30 *(Kitāb al-imāma);* 236-41; xiii, 2-11; Qurṭubī, *Jāmiʿ*; Ṭabarī, *Tafsīr;* id., *Taʾrīkh*, ed. De Goeje, i, 1213, 1541-2.

Secondary: K. Blankinship, Imārah, khilāfah, and imāmah. The succession to the prophet Muḥammad, in L. Clarke (ed.), *Shīʿite heritage. Essays on classical and modern traditions,* Binghamton 2001, 19-43; H. Dabashi, *Authority in Islam,* New Brunswick 1989, esp. 47-70 (Weberian analysis); D. Gimaret, Ṭāʿa, in *EI²*, x, 1-2; E. Landau-Tasseron, Features of the pre-conquest Muslim army in the time of Muhammad, in A. Cameron (ed.), *The Byzantine and early Islamic Near East,* Princeton 1995, iii, 316-24, 334-6 (Command structure); E. Tyan, Bayʿa, in *EI²*, i, 1113-4; W. Watt, al-ʿAḳaba, in *EI²*, i, 314-5; id., al-Ḥudaybiya, in *EI²*, iii, 539; id., *Muhammad at Mecca,* Oxford 1953, 141-9; id., *Muhammad at Medina,* Oxford 1956, 11-2, 50-1, 221-38.

Obscenity see CURSE

Obstinacy see INSOLENCE AND OBSTINACY

Occasions of Revelation

Reports, transmitted generally from the Companions of Muḥammad (see COMPANIONS OF THE PROPHET), detailing the cause, time and place of the revelation of a portion (usually a verse; see VERSES) of the Qurʾān. Underlying the material transmitted as "occasions of revelation" *(asbāb al-nuzūl)* are certain understandings about the process of qurʾānic revelation (see REVELATION AND INSPIRATION). The Qurʾān is understood to have been revealed piece by piece over the period of some twenty-two years of Muḥammad's preaching career. Muslim exegetes (see EXEGESIS OF THE QURʾĀN: CLASSICAL AND MEDIEVAL) have thus approached the Qurʾān through the framework of the life of Muḥammad, for example speaking of it as having different characteristics during the time Muḥammad was in Medina (q.v.) as compared to when he was in Mecca (q.v.). They also maintained that pieces of it were revealed in response to, or as reflections of, certain situations in the life of Muḥammad. Both the structure and the contents of the Qurʾān provided evidence to them of these conceptions (see LANGUAGE AND STYLE OF THE QURʾĀN; FORM AND STRUCTURE OF THE QURʾĀN). The apparent conflict between these ideas and the normative Muslim notion that the Qurʾān is the eternal word of God (q.v.; see also ETERNITY) seems to have occasionally surfaced; it is found both as a motif of argument between those who professed the Qurʾān's eternality and those who supported the opposing doctrine of the Qurʾān as the created word of God (see CREATEDNESS OF THE QURʾĀN) and as a topos of inter-religious polemic. Ultimately, however, any conflict was resolved by the dogmatic assertion that there is no conflict and that God always acts in the best interests of his creation (q.v.). For example, the fifth/eleventh century author of *Kitāb al-mabānī li-naẓm al-maʿānī* (40) simply states that the Qurʾān was revealed according to the needs of the situation but that the arrangement of the text as it stands today mirrors that found in the eternal "heavenly tablet" (on the author of this text, see Gilliot, Sciences coraniques, 57-60; see PRESERVED TABLET; BOOK; HEAVENLY BOOK).

Working on the basis that the text was revealed in certain circumstances, it was apparent to the exegetes, then, that the correct interpretation of a given verse could depend upon knowing those circumstances. This led to the identification and compilation of exegetical reports which talked about the revelation of a given verse; knowledge of those reports was asserted to be the key to all interpretation (although such claims are central to each and every approach to qurʾānic exegesis). Historically, it is not certain how the compilation of the *asbāb al-nuzūl* occurred. The reports may have originated within the context of the life story of Muḥammad (see SĪRA AND THE QURʾĀN); they may have been found among the stock of material used by the popular preachers in early Islam (see TEACHING AND PREACHING THE QURʾĀN); they may have been a part of the documentation used by legal scholars to understand how a qurʾānic law was to be applied (see LAW AND THE QURʾĀN); or they may have been a form of exegesis in and by themselves.

Fundamentally, as the material has been discussed and collected by Muslim exegetes, the *sabab* is differentiated by its literary character. A *sabab* is a report in which something or someone is characterized as having been involved in some way in the life of Muḥammad. The report will describe an event or situation and will state, "then the verse was revealed" *(fa-nazalat al-āya),* connecting a particular qurʾānic text to the situation. A typical example is as follows:

"They are asking you about wine [q.v.] and *maysir* [a type of gambling, q.v.]. Say: in them both is great sin [see SIN, MAJOR AND MINOR] and uses for the people, but their sin is greater than their use." This verse [Q 2:219] was revealed about ʿUmar b. al-Khaṭṭāb and Muʿādh b. Jabl and a group from the Anṣār ["Helpers"; see EMIGRANTS AND HELPERS] who came to the Prophet and said, "Give us a ruling about wine and *maysir* for the two of them are destroyers of the intellect [q.v.] and plunderers of property [q.v.]." So God revealed this verse (Wāḥidī, *Asbāb,* 64-5).

Such reports were an integral part of all exegesis, although in the early centuries the material was not separated out in any way — neither by technical terminology nor by literary form. The book of Abū l-Ḥasan ʿAlī b. Aḥmad al-Wāḥidī al-Nīsābūrī (d. 468/1075), *Kitāb Asbāb nuzūl al-Qurʾān,* collected together as many reports as the author could find, listing material relevant to sections of eighty-five sūras of the Qurʾān. This work is both the most famous of the genre devoted to gathering such material, and also one of the earliest (it is, at the very least, the work which firmly established the genre). Al-Wāḥidī's work may be seen as emerging at the time of the rise of traditionalism within Islamic learning in general, a period in which the authority of tradition, rather than reason, was judged to be supreme (thus making sense of al-Wāḥidī's explicit and polemical claim that the *asbāb* are the key to exegesis).

Several other works exist from the centuries after al-Wāḥidī which attempt either to gather more material or to refine the criteria used for collection. Among the works are those of al-ʿIrāqī (d. 567/1171), who attempts to distinguish the occasions of revelation from the stories of the prophets (*qiṣaṣ al-anbiyāʾ,* see PROPHETS AND PROPHETHOOD), two genres which al-Wāḥidī often conflates; al-Jaʿbarī (d. 732/1333), whose work provides an edited version of al-Wāḥidī's text; Ibn Ḥajar (d. 852/1449), who provides a compendium of reports from classical *tafsīr* sources; al-Suyūṭī (d. 911/1505), who both supplements al-Wāḥidī's sources (and thus has material on sections of 102 sūras) and eliminates reports he considers inappropriate; and al-Ujhūrī (d. 1190/1776), whose work gathers together material from various of the "sciences" *(ʿulūm)* of the Qurʾān including the "occasions of revelation" (see TRADITIONAL DISCIPLINES OF QURʾĀNIC STUDY). Other anonymous or unidentified works exist in the manuscript libraries of the world and a few modern works have been published, but overall the inventory of texts devoted to the topic is fairly slim as compared to such other exegetical genres as abrogation (q.v.), *al-nāsikh wa-l-mansūkh.*

Within general exegetical texts, the *asbāb al-nuzūl* reports are usually integrated and not distinguished from other material. When they are cited, they perform a number of exegetical functions. Central to these functions is the reports' capacity to embed lexical glosses, resolve literary figures, support variant readings (see READINGS OF THE QUR'ĀN), provide narrative expansion (see NARRATIVES) and clarify contextual definition for narrative and legal purposes.

Lexical glosses are easily incorporated in a story such that the wording of a qur'ānic verse is restated:

They said, "Oh Prophet of God, is charity given secretly better or charity given openly [see ALMSGIVING]?" So God revealed the verse [Q 2:271], "If you expose charity, it is still good. If you hide them and give them to the poor, that is better for you and will act as an atonement [q.v.] for you from your bad deeds" (Wāḥidī, *Asbāb*, 82; see EVIL DEEDS).

Here the qur'ānic *abdā (tubdū)*, "expose," is glossed as *ʿalāniya*, "give openly," and *akhfā (tukhfū)*, "hide," as *sirr*, "secretly." In other contexts, this type of glossing facilitates the restatement in literal language of the meaning of a qur'ānic metaphor (q.v.) or the provision of a word left out by ellipsis. Different reports can also be cited in order to support different readings of the text.

Narrative expansion seems to reflect the needs of the qur'ānic storyteller and his audience. Many of the *asbāb al-nuzūl* reports answer the questions of curious people who will ask, "Who was it who said that?" or "Why did somebody do that?"

ʿAlī [see ʿALĪ B. ABĪ ṬĀLIB] had only four dirhams. He gave away one of the dirhams at night, one at day, one secretly and one publicly. The Prophet said to him, "What has made you do this?" He said, "I did it so that I would be worthy of God who has made a promise to me." The Prophet said to him, "Now that is yours." So God revealed the verse [Q 2:274], "Those who give their possessions at night and at day, secretly and in public, they will have their reward with their lord" (Wāḥidī, *Asbāb*, 86; see REWARD AND PUNISHMENT).

Such a report clarifies who it was who did the action with those specific characteristics (why are only these four types of giving specified, it may have been wondered). Noticeable in this particular instance are the possibilities for ideological argumentation on the basis of the *asbāb al-nuzūl* reports. For example, this story would support the Shīʿīs (see SHĪʿISM AND THE QUR'ĀN) and their claims about ʿAlī.

While reports may well have additional implications in the legal realm, the impetus and relevance of the reports seem to lie primarily elsewhere. For example, when the Qur'ān proclaims in Q 2:189, "It is not piety to enter houses from their rear," it is difficult for the curious listener not to wonder just who it was who would have done such a thing (it was the pagan Arabs, although the circumstances under which they would have done so have varying interpretations; see PRE-ISLAMIC ARABIA AND THE QUR'ĀN). Likewise, when the Qur'ān states in Q 2:116, "They say, 'God has taken a son; glory be to him!'" a *sabab* can answer the question of who "they" were who said such a thing (it was the Jews of Medina and the Christians of Najrān [q.v.], according to Wāḥidī, *Asbāb*, 36; see JEWS AND JUDAISM; CHRISTIANS AND CHRISTIANITY).

Delimitation of the context of a given verse can in itself serve a number of functions. Sometimes, it is necessary to be able to assert the limits to a qur'ānic pericope in order to avoid misinterpretation of the following verses. In that sense, the *asbāb* function as indicating paragraphs within the otherwise unpunctuated text. This can prevent interpretations that could have serious legal implications. One such example may be seen in Q 2:114-5. The first verse deals with the destruction of mosques (in some *asbāb* reports this is specified as the Christians destroying the temple in Jerusalem [q.v.], Wāḥidī, *Asbāb,* 33; see MOSQUE); verse 115 then goes on to say "To God belongs the east and the west; wherever you turn, the face of God (q.v.) is there." There are some interpreters, then, who suggest that these two verses go together; that is, Q 2:115 refers to situations in which a mosque has been destroyed and thus the *qibla* (q.v.) cannot be determined (Qurṭubī, *Jāmiʿ,* ii, 83). A great majority of reports, however, separate the context of the two verses and, for the latter, speak of a situation in which some people at the time of Muḥammad were traveling (either with or without the Prophet; the story varies; see JOURNEY; TRIPS AND VOYAGES) and they stopped for prayer (q.v.). Because it was cloudy, dark or foggy they could not determine the *qibla.* Everyone prayed in the direction that they thought best but in the morning the error became clear. Then this verse was revealed. While this situation may be thought to follow the same principle as that of the destroyed mosque in Q 2:114, the report makes it clear that the ruling of verse 115 is not limited by the specific situation of verse 114 and has more general applicability (see Suyūṭī, *Lubāb,* 26-7, for one example). As is characteristic of the *asbāb al-nuzūl* literature, however, another series of reports is found which provides a radically different situation for the revelation of Q 2:115, separating it even further from verse 114. These reports all relate to the permission given to perform the supererogatory prayer while riding a camel regardless of the direction being faced (see Wāḥidī, *Asbāb,* 35, for one example).

Overall, but perhaps best understood as their primary function, the *asbāb al-nuzūl* reports serve to "historicize" the Qurʾān; they ground the text firmly in the life of Muḥammad and make an otherwise context-vague text very much a part of the seventh century Ḥijāz (see HISTORY AND THE QURʾĀN; CHRONOLOGY AND THE QURʾĀN). Regardless of what the report might say in terms of the details, this specificity always underlies the story, regardless of how trivial or how complex it may be. Muslim exegetes express this sense by pointing out the way in which the material demonstrates that the Qurʾān really is revelation: the *sabab* is the proof of God's concern for his creation. Al-Suyūṭī (*Itqān,* i, 83) explains this by saying that the *sabab* is the "rope" — that being one of the root senses of the word *sabab* itself — by which human contemplation of the Qurʾān may ascend to the highest levels even while dealing with the mundane aspects of the text.

Andrew Rippin

Bibliography
Primary: [Anon.], *Kitāb al-mabānī li-naẓm al-maʿānī,* Cairo 1954; Ibn Ḥajar al-ʿAsqalānī, Shihāb al-Dīn Aḥmad b. ʿAlī, *al-ʿUjāb fī bayān al-asbāb,* Dammam 1997; Ibn Isḥāq, *Sīra,* Cairo 1955; al-ʿIrāqī, Muḥammad b. Asʿad, *Asbāb al-nuzūl wa-l-qiṣaṣ al-furqāniyya,* Dublin, Chester Beatty manuscript 5199; al-Jaʿbarī, Burhān al-Dīn Ibrāhīm b. ʿUmar, *Mukhtaṣar asbāb al-nuzūl,* Cairo, Dār al-Kutub manuscript *majāmiʿ* 221; Qurṭubī, *Jāmiʿ,* Cairo 1935-36; Suyūṭī, *Itqān,* ed. Ibrāhīm, Cairo 1974², i, 107-26 [Chap. 9] (for the occasions of revelation); id., *Lubāb al-nuqūl fī asbāb al-nuzūl,* Cairo 1962 (many other prints exist); al-Ujhūrī, ʿAṭīyatallāh b. ʿAṭīya al-Burhānī, *Irshād al-raḥmān li-asbāb al-nuzūl wa-l-naskh wa-l-mutashābih wa-tajwīd al-Qurʾān,* Cairo, Dār al-Kutub manuscript *tafsīr* 42; Wāḥidī, *Asbāb;* Zarkashī, *Burhān,* Cairo 1957.
Secondary: C. Gilliot, Les sciences coraniques chez les Karrāmites du Khorasan. Le *Livre des fondations,* in *JA* 288 (2000), 15-81; Nöldeke, *GQ,* ii, 182-4; A. Rippin, The exegetical genre *asbāb al-nuzūl.* A bibliographical and terminological survey, in *BSOAS* 48 (1985), 1-15; id., The function

of *asbāb al-nuzūl* in qurʾānic exegesis, in BSOAS 51 (1988), 1-20; id., Al-Zarkashī and al-Suyūṭī on the "occasion of revelation" material, in IC 59 (1985), 243-58; repr. as The function of the occasion of revelation material, in M. Taher (ed.), *Studies in Qurʾān*, New Delhi 1997; U. Rubin, *The eye of the beholder. The life of Muḥammad as viewed by the early Muslims. A textual analysis*, Princeton 1995, chap. 14; S. al-Ṣāliḥ, *Mabāḥith fī ʿulūm al-Qurʾān*, Beirut 1979[11], 117-297 (the length of this chapter indicates the importance of this field for contemporary Muslim scholars); S. Syamsuddin, Bint al-Shāṭiʾ on *asbāb al-nuzūl*, in IQ 42 (1998), 5-23; Wansbrough, QS, 141-2, 177-85; id., *The sectarian milieu. Content and composition of Islamic salvation history*, Oxford 1978, chap. 1.

Ocean see WATER

Odors and Smells

Aromas — both pleasant and unpleasant — detected with the olfactory sense. In contrast to the many references to the senses of hearing and sight (see SEEING AND HEARING), smell is rarely mentioned in the Qurʾān. Two words from the root *r-w-ḥ* are used in this respect: *rīḥ* and *rayḥān*. The former appears nearly always with the meaning of "wind" (see AIR AND WIND), but on one occasion (Q 12:94) it is said that Joseph's (q.v.) father (see JACOB) perceives his son's scent *(rīḥ)* in the shirt brought to him by his brothers (see BROTHER AND BROTHERHOOD). As for the latter word, it occurs in Q 55:12, in the context of a description of God's creation (q.v.): "Fruits, and palm-trees (see DATE PALM) with sheaths, and grain in the blade (see GRASSES), and fragrant herbs *(rayḥān)*" (Q 55:11-2; see AGRICULTURE AND VEGETATION). The sweet odor which characterizes herbs such as basil-royal, common sweet basil or ocimum basilicum (see Lane, s.v. *rayḥān*) is considered here as one of God's gifts to humankind (see BLESSING). Herbal fragrances are, however, absent from the abundant references to heavenly gardens (see GARDEN), where other and more precious odors can be found.

Although the Qurʾān does not mention general Arabic terms for perfumes, such as *ṭīb* or *ʿiṭr*, it does mention that, in paradise (q.v.), "the pious shall drink of a cup (see CUPS AND VESSELS) whose mixture is camphor" (q.v.; Q 76:5) and "they are given to drink of a wine (q.v.) sealed whose seal is musk" (Q 83:25-6; see INTOXICANTS). In the ḥadīth literature (see ḤADĪTH AND THE QURʾĀN), camphor, which is distilled from the camphor tree, is repeatedly referred to in the context of funeral ceremonies (see DEATH AND THE DEAD). In the biographical texts about Zaynab, the daughter of the Prophet (see FAMILY OF THE PROPHET; PEOPLE OF THE HOUSE), Muḥammad, upon her death, is depicted as having ordered Zaynab's corpse washed. In these accounts, the body was afterwards perfumed with camphor (cf. Bukhārī, *Ṣaḥīḥ*, i, 316-7). In Islamic culture, musk, a perfume derived from animal products, has been traditionally considered as the best and most expensive of all perfumes; in the ḥadīth literature, it is used to perfume the Prophet's head. The ḥadīth literature also describes the sand of the rivers in paradise (see WATER OF PARADISE) as being made of musk. Both camphor and musk, which were not known in classical antiquity, are of east Asian origins. Shortly before the advent of Islam they are documented in the Sasanid empire and in Byzantium (see BYZANTINES). Musk was mentioned in pre-Islamic Arabic poetry (see PRE-ISLAMIC ARABIA AND THE QURʾĀN; POETRY AND POETS), as is attested in the poems by Imruʾ al-Qays. The presence of musk in the Qurʾān was to give this perfume a heightened status among other fragrances, enhancing its aromatic qualities with an added religious prestige. Musk and camphor were also used for pharmaceutical recipes and, in the luxurious and cosmopolitan kitchen of the ʿAbbāsid caliphs, for cookery (see MEDICINE AND THE QURʾĀN; FOOD AND DRINK).

On a more common level of consumption, good smell *(al-rīḥ al-ṭayyib)* could be obtained through other and less expensive perfumes. There was a general appreciation of the well-being that is derived from good smells and odors. Well-known traditions speak of the love of the Prophet for three things in this world: prayer (q.v.), women (see WOMEN AND THE QURʾĀN) and perfume. According to ʿĀʾisha (see ʿĀʾISHA BINT ABĪ BAKR), the Prophet was preceded by his scent and his favorite perfumes were musk and amber. Perfuming the body was, according to the ḥadīth, a part of bodily hygiene (see CLEANLINESS AND ABLUTION), which includes bathing, the use of a toothbrush, hair care, etc. While perfumes were accepted for both women and men, many traditions discourage the former from using them both within and outside the home, except when it is for the pleasure of their husbands.

Manuela Marín

Bibliography
I. Abū Ḥudhayfa, *Tarwīḥ al-arīb fī ādāb wa-aḥkām wa-anwāʿ al-ṭīb,* Tanta 1990; Bukhārī, *Ṣaḥīḥ,* ed. Krehl; P. Crone, *Meccan trade and the rise of Islam,* Princeton 1987; A. Dietrich, Kāfūr, in *EI*², iv, 417-8; id., Misk, in *EI*², vii, 142-3; M.I.H. Farooqi, *Plants of the Qurʾān,* Lucknow 1992, 86-95 (camphor), 143-5 (herbs); G.J. van Gelder, Four perfumes of Arabia. A translation of al-Suyūṭī's *al-Maqāma al-miskiyya,* in *Res orientales* 11 (1998), 203-211; F. Sanagustin, Parfums et pharmacologie en Orient médiéval. Savoirs et représentations, in *Res orientales* 11 (1998), 189-202.

Offspring see FAMILY; GENERATIONS

Oft-Repeated

One of the names of the Qurʾān (q.v.) or of parts of it. The Arabic form *mathānī* is the plural of *mathnā* or *mathnāt,* and is a derivative of the root *th-n-y,* which signifies repetition, duplication. In Q 39:23, the form *mathānī* occurs within the following description of the Qurʾān: "God has sent down the fairest discourse as a book (q.v.), similar in its oft-repeated *(mutashābihan mathāniya),* whereat shiver the skins of those who fear (q.v.) their lord (q.v.)...."

The most prevalent explanation is that the scripture has been called *mathānī* because its various themes — religious duties, laws and regulations (i.e. Ṭabarī, *Tafsīr,* i, 103; see LAW AND THE QURʾĀN; BOUNDARIES AND PRECEPTS), stories of previous prophets (i.e. Suyūṭī, *Itqān,* i, 184; see PROPHETS AND PROPHETHOOD; NARRATIVES), allusions to the reward awaiting the righteous in paradise (q.v.) and of the punishment of the sinners in hell (see HELL AND HELLFIRE; REWARD AND PUNISHMENT; SIN, MAJOR AND MINOR) — are repeated *(yuthannā)* throughout its chapters. Less frequently encountered explanations are that the Qurʾān is recited repeatedly and the audience never finds it boring (see RECITATION OF THE QURʾĀN). Another explanation takes *mathānī* as denoting the praise *(thanāʾ)* of God that is reiterated in the Qurʾān (see GLORIFICATION OF GOD; LAUDATION).

The term *mathānī* does not, however, always denote the entire Qurʾān: it is also explained as standing only for certain parts of scripture. This meaning is seen in the explanation that the term stands for the suffixes of the verses (Māwardī, *Nukat,* v, 123), which would be an allusion to the repetitive rhymed form of the verses (q.v.; see also LANGUAGE AND STYLE OF THE QURʾĀN; FORM AND STRUCTURE OF THE QURʾĀN).

More prevalent is the identification of the term with qur'ānic chapters or groups of chapters. This is the case in traditions stating that *mathānī* are the sūras (q.v.) that come next *(thanā)* in terms of length to the sūras containing at least a hundred verses. Twenty to twenty-six sūras are included in this group.

The perception of the term *mathānī* as standing for some chapters of the Qur'ān underlies also the interpretations of Q 15:87, in which God says to the qur'ānic Prophet: "We have given you seven of the *mathānī* and the glorious Qur'ān." Muslim exegetes (see EXEGESIS OF THE QUR'ĀN: CLASSICAL AND MEDIEVAL) have offered a variety of interpretations for the "seven of the *mathānī*," most of which hold that seven *mathānī* out of the entire Qur'ān are meant. The closing phrase, "and the glorious Qur'ān," is explained as denoting the rest of the Qur'ān that has been given to the qur'ānic Prophet in addition to the seven *mathānī*.

The seven *mathānī* are defined in two major ways. First, the seven longest chapters of the Qur'ān. Muslim exegetes explain that they were named *mathānī* because of their repetitive treatment of various subjects, such as legal matters, stories, parables and admonitions (see WARNING). The second definition is the seven verses of the opening chapter (Q 1, Sūrat al-Fātiḥa; see FĀTIḤA) of the Qur'ān. Muslim exegetes explain that the verses of the Fātiḥa have been called *mathānī* because they are repeated *(tuthannā)* daily in every prayer (q.v.; cf. Ṭabarī, *Tafsīr*, i, 103). A different explanation is that the Fātiḥa was called *mathānī* because God gave it exclusively *(istathnāhā)* to the qur'ānic Prophet, and withheld it from all other prophets (see PROPHETS AND PROPHETHOOD). Yet another interpretation is that this sūra has been divided into two *(ithnān)* parts, one containing the praise of God and the other, the entreaty of his servants. Another explanation is that some words and phrases are repeated in it, etc. An interpretation appearing only in relatively late commentaries identifies the seven *mathānī* with the seven *ḥawāmīm*, i.e. the sūras opening with the letters *ḥā'* and *mīm* (see MYSTERIOUS LETTERS).

There is also an interpretation that places the seven *mathānī* outside the scope of the Qur'ān, and is included in a tradition of Ja'far al-Ṣādiq (d. 148/765), the sixth Shī'ī imām (q.v.; see also SHĪ'ISM AND THE QUR'ĀN). He reportedly said that the seven *mathānī* are seven exclusive virtues *(karāmāt)* by which God has honored his Prophet: (1) righteousness, (2) prophethood, (3) mercy (q.v.), (4) compassion, (5) love (see LOVE AND AFFECTION), (6) friendship (see FRIENDS AND FRIENDSHIP), (7) sechina (q.v.; Māwardī, *Nukat*, iii, 171). Other Shī'ī traditions identify the seven *mathānī* with seven Shī'ī imāms ('Ayyāshī, *Tafsīr*, ii, 269-70).

Nevertheless, some exegetes held that the "seven of the *mathānī*" and the "glorious Qur'ān" are identical, being merely different designations of the one and the same object that was given to the qur'ānic Prophet. The clause "and the glorious Qur'ān" was explained as providing additional praise to the object described as "seven of the *mathānī*." From the syntactical point of view it was explained as a shortened or condensed form signifying: "... and [they, i.e. the seven *mathānī*, are] the glorious Qur'ān."

The object designated as "the seven *mathānī*" and as "the glorious Qur'ān" is explained in a variety of ways. Some exegetes identify it again with the Fātiḥa, in which case "the glorious Qur'ān" features as a name of this particular chapter, the seven verses of which constitute the seven *mathānī*. Yet other traditions say that the object named "the seven *mathānī*" and "the glorious Qurʾān" is actually the entire Qurʾān. In this case the seven *mathānī* are taken as signifying seven repetitive aspects of the Qurʾān's contents: (1) commands (see COMMANDMENTS), (2) prohibitions (see FORBIDDEN), (3) good tidings (see GOOD NEWS), (4) warnings (see WARNER), (5) parables (q.v.), (6) divine mercy, (7) stories of past generations (q.v.).

In accordance with the notion that the seven *mathānī* are the entire Qurʾān, some exegetes say that their number denotes the seven *asbāʿ*, i.e. the seven parts into which the Qurʾān is divided, or its seven volumes.

Uri Rubin

Bibliography
Primary (in addition to other classical commentaries on Q 15:87): ʿAyyāshī, *Tafsīr*, ed. Hāshim al-Rasūlī al-Maḥallātī, 2 vols., Beirut 1991; Māwardī, *Nukat*; Ṭabarī, *Tafsīr*, ed. Shākir; Suyūṭī, *Itqān*, ed. Ibrāhīm, Cairo 1974²; Zarkashī, *Burhān*.
Secondary: Horovitz, *KU*, 26-8; Jeffery, *For. vocab.*, 257-8; Paret, *Kommentar*, 279; U. Rubin, Exegesis and ḥadīth. The case of the seven mathānī, in Hawting and Shareef, *Approaches*, 141-56; Watt-Bell, *Introduction*, 134-5.

Old Age

see YOUTH AND OLD AGE; BIOLOGY AS THE CREATION AND STAGES OF LIFE

Olives

see AGRICULTURE AND VEGETATION

Omens

see PORTENTS; DIVINATION; FORETELLING

Omnipotence

see POWER AND IMPOTENCE

Opponent

see ENEMIES

Opposition to Muḥammad

Resistance to the political and religious authority (q.v.) of Muḥammad. The Qurʾān is very much a document that shows the struggle of a new faith (q.v.) coming into existence, and the career of Muḥammad is very much the story of a man who eventually defeated all odds when shaping the first community of believers (see COMMUNITY AND SOCIETY IN THE QURʾĀN). Additionally, the qurʾānic concept of prophecy (see PROPHETS AND PROPHETHOOD) is profoundly marked by the experience of opposition (see Q 25:31; 40:5). The fact of being opposed both theologically and politically (see POLITICS AND THE QURʾĀN; THEOLOGY AND THE QURʾĀN) has marked Islam from its beginnings, and the successful effort to overcome opposition was an important factor in its development which led to a self-confident religion of great appeal to possible converts.

Theological opposition was leveled against the tenets of the new faith as preached by the Prophet; political opposition was directed first against the social and economic consequences of nascent Islam in Muḥammad's hometown (see MECCA), then against the claim to hegemony of the quickly expanding Muslim community in Medina (q.v.). The most serious theological opposition came from Jews (see JEWS AND JUDAISM), while the Meccan pagans were hardly able, as far as we know, to counter Muḥammad's monotheistic vision (see below; see POLYTHEISM AND ATHEISM; SOUTH ARABIA, RELIGION IN PRE-ISLAMIC). The Christians (see CHRISTIANS AND CHRISTIANITY), who are generally portrayed in a more favorable light in the Islamic sources, appear less eager to enter into discussions with the Prophet (see DEBATE AND DISPUTATION) and are more frequently reported as having been persuaded by the new message. Active political and military opposition against Muḥammad and his followers was primarily the work of the Meccans (see EXPEDITIONS AND BATTLES; FIGHTING); the Jewish tribes in Medina and Khaybar opposed the Prophet without resorting to open aggression (although not a few sources tend to stress that the Jews either provoked the Muslims or took active measures against them). Even Muḥammad's own family (see FAMILY OF THE PROPHET) were guilty of opposing him (cf. Q 111:1-5, and commentaries on this sūra).

Muḥammad, who acted both as prophet and founder of a new religion and as a political and military leader of his supporters, was, naturally, the main target of the opponents of early Islam, no matter how their hostile intentions were defined. With the concerns of faith and the duties of the believers inextricably linked in his person, opposing the Prophet meant opposing God, or, put differently: "Whosoever obeys the messenger, thereby obeys God" (Q 4:80; see also Q 4:152; 58:5; 59:7). As a result of the opposition that arose against his person, Muḥammad suffered, during his years in Mecca, from humiliation, derision (see MOCKERY) and from being treated either like a madman (see INSANITY) or an outcast. Some people would even fling pebbles at him while he was praying and others kicked stones at him so that he had to run away with bleeding feet. During the Medinan period (see CHRONOLOGY AND THE QURʾĀN), he had to survive various attempts at his life, be it the poison of a Jewish woman or the drawn sword of a bedouin (q.v.; it is nevertheless difficult, as a perusal of the relevant sources shows, to link the specific events as reported in Islamic tradition and *sīra* literature with the rather vague qurʾānic allusions to such attempts: Q 5:11; 8:30, 71; 16:127; 48:20; see SĪRA AND THE QURʾĀN).

Muḥammad's reaction against his opponents varied in time and according to the possibilities within his reach. In the Meccan period, he was satisfied — due to the lack of effective means and a large group of followers — to merely censure the activities of his opponents and to turn his back on them in patience and to leave their punishment to God (see TRUST AND PATIENCE; PUNISHMENT STORIES). This attitude becomes obvious from numerous qurʾānic verses that are traditionally reckoned to belong to Meccan sūras (e.g. Q 6:66-70; 10:108; 13:43; 15:89-99; 16:125-8, etc.). Also, the so-called "punishment stories" (*Straflegenden;* see the list in Watt-Bell, *Introduction,* 132) were to provide the Prophet with fitting examples of what had happened in earlier times and in analogous situations. Once in Medina, however, and with military means at his disposal, the Prophet did not limit himself anymore to simply accusing and warning (q.v.) his opponents, but called his followers to actively fight for the cause of Islam (Q 2:190-3, 216; 3:146; 4:75 f., 84, 89 f.; 8:39, 65; 9:13 f., 29, 123; 47:4; 61:4) and was himself ordered to be the first in line (Q 9:73; see JIHĀD). The cause of Islam was thus no longer the cause of God alone, and Muḥammad exhorted the members of his community: "O believers! Fight the unbelievers who are in your vicinity and let them find you ruthless! And know that God supports the godfearing" (Q 9:123; see BELIEF AND UNBELIEF) — a sentiment very much in contrast to Muḥammad's passive stance during his former stay in Mecca. The transfer of power from God's hands into those of humans, that is, the switch from relying on eschatological punishment to settling matters in this world, seems complete (see ESCHATOLOGY).

As mentioned above, the two main groups of opponents during the career of Muḥammad were the Meccan pagans and the Jews. Both were eventually subdued by more or less violent means (see below). The Christians — much fewer in number than the Arabian Jews — never posed the same threat to the Prophet's community, and the encounter with the Christian population in northern Arabia (see PRE-ISLAMIC ARABIA AND THE QURʾĀN) and southern Syria (q.v.) in the last years of Muḥammad's lifetime generally did not lead to bellicose events; any conflicts were settled peacefully, e.g. by contracts (see CONTRACTS AND ALLIANCES). The same may be said of the bedouin tribes of the Ḥijāz (*al-aʿrāb*, see ARABS), who often opposed the Prophet's efforts to rally them to his cause (e.g. Q 48:11, 16) and thus, for a long time, were not an integral part of the nascent Islamic community (see Q 9:97-9). Also, tensions among the inhabitants of Medina had led to the formation of an, as it were, intra-Islamic group of opponents (a considerable part of whom were Jewish converts) known as "the hypocrites" (*al-munāfiqūn*, see HYPOCRITES AND HYPOCRISY; MOSQUE OF THE DISSENSION). Even though they feature prominently in the Medinan sūras (e.g. Q 59:11 f.; 63:1-8, but also 9:74, 106), their role can only be reconstructed from the extant sources with difficulty; nevertheless, their influence on the course of events in Medina as well as their potentially detrimental activities do not appear very threatening, at least when compared to those of the Meccans and the Jews.

The Meccan pagans

From the beginning of his prophetic mission, Muḥammad had to cope with the fierce opposition of many of his Meccan compatriots. Curiously, the qurʾānic data suggest that their opposition was primarily directed against elements of monotheist belief (Q 6:25), such as the resuscitation of the dead (see RESURRECTION), the day of judgment (see LAST JUDGMENT) or the denial of the existence of Arabian deities. In Islamic tradition, however, the pagans hardly figure as opponents on religious grounds. The few pagan "priests" (*kuhhān*, see SOOTHSAYERS) who appear in *sīra* literature and related genres are not depicted as Muḥammad's opponents but rather foretell or announce his prophethood. The Meccan leaders, on the other hand, are shown as being driven by the interest to preserve the status quo of the Meccan hierarchy, as well as by economic considerations (in order to save their sources of income which depended on pagan festivities); this is in accordance with the Qurʾān, which often censures their material greed (e.g. Q 89:17-20; 104:1-3; see WEALTH; MARKETS; SELLING AND BUYING; CARAVAN). When speaking, however, about the Meccan period as represented in the Qurʾān, W.M. Watt rightly observes: "There are virtually no factual details about the persons who accepted Islam, and only a modicum of general information about the opponents. Most of this last is about the verbal arguments between these and Muḥammad" (Watt, *Mecca*, 81).

What the Qurʾān does, in fact, convey is the sense of oppression Muḥammad must have felt in Mecca, coupled with an inability to counteract such adversities and even a fear of giving in to the pagans (Q 17:73 f.; see SATANIC VERSES). Over the years, Muḥammad's followers grew in number; with this, the opposition of the Meccans became less restrained. Some Muslims resorted to leaving their hometown and went into exile in Ethiopia (see ABYSSINIA). The Prophet himself first tried to gain a foothold in nearby Ṭāʾif but, when this had failed, he reached an agreement with the people of Medina at ʿAqaba. Thus the emigration (q.v.) of the Prophet to Medina was, initially, the outcome of the Meccans' opposition (Q 47:13). Many of his followers accompanied Muḥammad, and the Qurʾān alludes in a number of verses not only to the general hardships endured by the early Muslims (Q 2:155, 3:120, 3:186, 60:2), but also to the painful experience of losing one's home and possessions: "And those that emigrated in God's cause (see PATH OR WAY) after they were wronged, we shall surely lodge them in this world in a goodly lodging; and the wage of the world to come is greater, did they but know" (Q 16:41; see also Q 4:100 f., 16:110, 22:39, 60:8 f.).

The Medinan period brought about the change from putting up with pagan opposition to striking back. Muslims and Meccans met each other in various skirmishes and bigger clashes, several of which are described at length in the Qurʾān, although even among the "orthodox" non-qurʾānic sources, there is no complete unanimity — with the exception of Q 3:123 (battle of Badr), Q 33:20-5 (War of the Ditch; see PEOPLE OF THE DITCH; EXPEDITIONS AND BATTLES) and Q 9:25 f. (battle of Ḥunayn [q.v.]) — as to which verses refer to which event. The early *tafsīr* works in particular, e.g. those by Mujāhid (d. 104/722) and Muqātil (d. 150/767), often yield accounts different from the later accepted versions. Up to the decisive treaty of al-Ḥudaybiya, traditionally associated with Q 48 (Sūrat al-Fatḥ, "Victory"), however, the Meccan opposition had gradually lost much of its force, and the Muslim conquest of Mecca largely put an end to the Meccan opposition (Q 110, Sūrat al-Naṣr, "Succor").

The Arabian Jews

Muḥammad encountered the opposition of Jews while still living in Mecca, although non-verbal conflict broke out only when he was in Medina. Aside from the pagans, Muḥammad appealed particularly to the Jews (Q 2:40-8), despite knowing that their aversion was the greatest: "That because God has sent down the book (q.v.) with the truth; and those that differ regarding the book, are showing strong enmity [?]" (Q 2:176; cf. Paret, *Mohammad,* 28; see PEOPLE OF THE BOOK). And although the Qurʾān repeatedly stresses that putting in doubt elements of faith and resorting to dispute is merely a general human trait (Q 18:54; 22:3, 8), the Jews — both in the Qurʾān and the Islamic tradition — are portrayed as having been the most tenacious antagonists of Muḥammad (although the Christians, too, had a share in that; cf. Q 2:139; 3:65). In *sīra* literature, already in the pivotal account by Ibn Isḥāq (d. 150/767), we normally find one or more lengthy chapters that deal with Muḥammad's theological discussions with the Jews, together with indications of which qurʾānic verses were either the subject or the result of those disputes; such discussions, both with Jews and other opponents, are reflected variously in the Qurʾān, in particular in the verses which start with the phrase "They question you about…" (e.g. Q 2:217, 219; 5:4; 7:187; 17:85; 18:83, etc.). Inevitably, the Prophet is depicted as defeating the arguments of his opponents, who then take to cheating (q.v.) or will not argue on the accurate record of their revealed scriptures (Q 2:75; see also 2:89-91, 101; see FORGERY).

In Medina, when Muḥammad distanced himself from pagan opposition, the Jewish opposition soon became a major preoccupation. After initial and intense follow-ups to the disputes in Mecca, between the years 2/624 and 5/627 the Muslim community got rid of the three major Jewish tribes: they expelled the Jewish Banū Qaynuqāʿ and Banū l-Naḍīr from Medina, while the Banū Qurayẓa were killed and enslaved (see NAḌĪR, BANŪ AL-; QAYNUQĀʿ;

QURAYẒA). The qurʾānic verses traditionally associated with these events by the Muslim scholars are Q 33:26 f. and Q 59:1-15. Moreover, during the same period some leaders of the Jewish opposition, notably Kaʿb b. al-Ashraf, were assassinated either in Medina or Khaybar; the latter town was conquered in 7/628. In the sources it remains unclear, however, whether at that point there were no Jews left in the Ḥijāz or whether some Jewish settlements (e.g. Fadak) persisted.

Finally, it must be remarked that a reconstruction of the events relating to the opposition to Muḥammad and their relevant chronology relies heavily on the information provided in the vast Islamic tradition, as well as on the commonly accepted chronology of qurʾānic verses. Many studies in recent years have shown that the historical value of this tradition cannot always be trusted (see COLLECTION OF THE QURʾĀN; ḤADĪTH AND THE QURʾĀN; POST-ENLIGHTENMENT ACADEMIC STUDY OF THE QURʾĀN). On the other hand, by no means should Islamic tradition be considered irrelevant, as it might be utilized either in tracing the ideological differences within early Islam or in unearthing accounts which do not fit the "canonical" Islamic view (as developed from the late second/eighth century onwards); it could thus deepen or change our future understanding of early Islamic history.

Marco Schöller

Bibliography

Primary (see also other works in the genres of *sīra* literature, "occasions of revelation" [q.v.; *asbāb al-nuzūl*] and the "proofs of prophethood" [*dalāʾil* or *aʿlām al-nubuwwa*], as well as ḥadīth anthologies and the Qurʾān commentaries on the verses mentioned in the article): al-Bayhaqī, Abū Bakr Aḥmad b. al-Ḥusayn, *Dalāʾil al-nubuwwa wa-maʿrifat aḥwāl ṣāḥib al-sharīʿa*, ed. ʿA. Qalʿajī, 7 vols., Beirut 1988; Wāḥidī, *Asbāb*.

Secondary: J. Bouman, *Der Koran und die Juden. Die Geschichte einer Tragödie*, Darmstadt 1990; Buhl, *Das Leben;* Chabbi, *Seigneur;* M. Cook, *Muhammad*, Oxford 1983; F. Donner, Muḥammad's political consolidation in Arabia up to the conquest of Mecca, in *MW* 69 (1979), 229-47; M. Gil, The Medinan opposition to the Prophet, in *JSAI* 10 (1987), 65-96; C. Gilliot, Imaginaire social et *maghāzī*. Le "succès décisif" de la Mecque, in *JA* 275 (1987), 45-64; M. Kister, *Society and religion from Jāhiliyya to Islam*, Aldershot 1990; id., *Studies in Jāhiliyya and early Islam*, London 1980; M. Lecker, *Jews and Arabs in pre- and early Islamic Arabia*, Aldershot 1998; id., *Muslims, Jews and pagans. Studies on early Islamic Medina*, Leiden 1995; H. Motzki (ed.), *The biography of Muḥammad. The issue of the sources*, Leiden 2000; R. Paret, *Mohammed und der Koran*, Stuttgart 1980[5] (rev. ed.); H. Rahman, The conflicts between the Prophet and the opposition in Madina, in *Der Islam* 62 (1985), 260-97; U. Rubin, Abū Lahab and *sūra* CXI, in *BSOAS* 42 (1979), 13-28; id., The assassination of Kaʿb b. al-Ashraf, in *Oriens* 32 (1990), 65-71; id., *Between Bible and Qurʾān. The Children of Israel and the Islamic self-image*, Princeton 1999; id., *The eye of the beholder. The life of Muḥammad as viewed by the early Muslims. A textual analysis*, Princeton 1995; id. (ed.), *The life of Muḥammad*, Aldershot 1998; id., Muḥammad's curse of Muḍar and the blockade of Mecca, in *JESHO* 31 (1989), 249-64; M. Schöller, *Exegetisches Denken und Prophetenbiographie. Eine quellenkritische Analyse der Sīra-Überlieferung zu Muḥammads Konflikt mit den Juden*, Wiesbaden 1998; J. Wansbrough, *The sectarian milieu. Content and composition of Islamic salvation history*, Oxford 1978; W.M. Watt, *Early Islam. Collected articles*, Edinburgh 1990; id., *Muḥammad's Mecca. History in the Qurʾān*, Edinburgh 1988; Watt-Bell, *Introduction;* A.J. Wensinck, *Muḥammad and the Jews of Medina*, trans. W.H. Behn, Berlin 1982[2]; id., Muhammed und die Propheten, in *AO* 2 (1924), 168-98.

Oppressed on Earth, The

Those with no political or other power; the downtrodden. Several verses of the Qurʾān refer to those who are "weak" (*ḍaʿīf*, pl. *ḍuʿafāʾ*, and other derivatives of *ḍ-ʿ-f;* Q 2:266, 282; 4:9; 9:91; 11:91; 14:21; 40:47) or those who are "deemed or made weak" (*mustaḍʿaf*, pl. *mustaḍʿafūn*, as well as the tenth verbal form of *ḍ-ʿ-f;* Q 4:75, 97-8;

7:75; 8:26; 28:4-5; 34:31-3). R.B. Serjeant (The *ḍaʿīf,* 33) has argued that the qurʾānic term *ḍaʿīf* does not simply mean "weak," but rather usually refers to "persons without the capacity to fight for and defend themselves" (see FIGHTING; OPPRESSION). By extension, it refers to the peasants and shepherds (see POVERTY AND THE POOR), to women (see WOMEN AND THE QURʾĀN) and children (q.v.), to clients (see CLIENTS AND CLIENTAGE) and slaves (see SLAVES AND SLAVERY), and to all those who do not bear arms and are dependent on others for their protection. The term *mustaḍʿaf* often has connotations similar or identical to those of the *ḍaʿīf* (ibid., 36) but especially those of degradation and debasement and often also of persecution. Q 28:4-6 describes Pharaoh's (q.v.) persecution when "he had exalted himself in the land and had divided its inhabitants into sects (*shiyaʿan,* see SHĪʿA), abasing *(yastaḍʿifu)* one party of them, slaughtering their sons and sparing their women, for he was of the workers of corruption (q.v.). Yet we desired to be gracious to those that were abased in the land, and to make them leaders (*aʾimmatan,* see KINGS AND RULERS; IMĀM), and make them the inheritors, and to establish them in the land." A tradition in al-Ṭabarī (d. 310/923; *Taʾrīkh,* i, 1563 f.; also Serjeant, The *ḍaʿīf,* 34 f.) characterizes the earliest followers of Muḥammad as "the weak *(al-ḍuʿafāʾ),* the poor, the young, and women." In Q 8:26, in what is often understood by the exegetes to refer to the condition of the earliest Muslims in Mecca (q.v.) before the migration (see EMIGRATION) to Medina (q.v.), God reminds the believers of God's favor on them at a time "when you were few and abased in the land *(mustaḍʿafūna fī l-arḍ)*... he gave you refuge and confirmed you with his help." In Q 4:75, the believers are reproached for not fighting "in the way of God (see PATH OR WAY), and for the men, women, and children who, being abased, say, 'Our lord, bring us forth from this city (q.v.) whose people are evildoers *(ẓālim).*"

Those who are thus abased or oppressed are expected to migrate from the land where they have been persecuted. To have the ability to migrate from such a land and yet not do so is enough to imperil one's salvation (q.v.), as the Qurʾān's strong admonition of those who falsely claim the status of the *mustaḍʿafūn* makes clear (Q 4:97-9). This admonition refers, according to many exegetes (see EXEGESIS OF THE QURʾĀN, CLASSICAL AND MEDIEVAL), to those people in Mecca who had converted to Islam but had not migrated to Medina even though they had the ability to do so. Many of them were forced to participate in the battle of Badr (q.v.) on the side of the Meccans and against the Muslims of Medina (Ṭabarī, *Tafsīr,* ix, 100-12). The status of those killed while fighting on the side of the unbelievers, or those who died while still in Mecca was held by many exegetes to be the same as that of the unbelievers themselves, even though they claimed to have been coerced (cf. ibid., ix, 102 [no. 10259], 104 f. [no. 10263]; see BELIEF AND UNBELIEF; HYPOCRITES AND HYPOCRISY). Those, however, who were entirely lacking in any means to migrate — and who were, therefore, genuinely powerless — were excused. The famous scholar and Qurʾān exegete Ibn ʿAbbās (d. 67-8/686-8) claimed, together with his mother, to be among such *mustaḍʿafūn* in Mecca (Ṭabarī, *Tafsīr,* ix, 106 f.), though the exegetes found it more difficult to extend the same justification to his father, al-ʿAbbās — the uncle of the Prophet (see FAMILY OF THE PROPHET) and the progenitor of the ʿAbbāsid dynasty — who had fought on the side of the pagan Meccans under what he reportedly claimed were circumstances of coercion (cf. ibid., ix, 106, no. 10265).

The *mustaḍʿafūn* in the Qurʾān include believers as well as unbelievers. Though their status as *mustaḍʿafūn* is defined by their dependence on others and/or by their lowly and persecuted condition in society, the Qurʾān pointedly notes that each individual bears sole responsibility for his or her moral conduct and is to be held accountable for it (see ETHICS AND THE QURʾĀN; FREEDOM AND PREDESTINATION; on children as *mustaḍʿafūn* in the sense of not bearing such responsibility, however, cf. van Ess, *TG*, i, 277). To argue, like those of the *ḍuʿafāʾ/mustaḍʿafūn* who are consigned to hell (see HELL AND HELLFIRE), that they had merely followed their leaders in error (q.v.) would be as futile as to call upon the latter for any help on or after the day of judgment (cf. Q 14:21; 34:31-3; 40:47-8; see LAST JUDGMENT; INTERCESSION).

Many modern Muslims have seen in God's promise to establish the *mustaḍʿafūn* on earth, and to make them its leaders, a qurʾānic sanction for revolutionary activism (see REBELLION). Franz Fanon's *The wretched of the earth* was translated by ʿAlī Sharīʿatī in the early 1960s as *Mostaḍzʿafīn-i zamīn,* thus contributing to the social revolutionary connotations of this qurʾānic term, which now came to be understood as "the oppressed" and the disinherited in the sense, primarily, of being economically exploited (see ECONOMICS). Ayatollah Khomeini's speeches before and immediately after the Iranian revolution of 1979 were laced with references to the *mustaḍʿafūn* in this sense, and he often spoke of them as the main supporters of the revolution and thus as the people deserving to be its principal beneficiaries. A "Mustaḍʿafūn Foundation" *(bunyād-i mustaḍʿafīn)* was established in 1979 (as the successor to the powerful Pahlavī Foundation) to appropriate the properties belonging to those associated with the overthrown regime and to redistribute them among the poor; and the *mustaḍʿafūn* were prominent among those mobilized for participation in the Iran-Iraq war (1980-88). E. Abrahamian (*Khomeinism,* 52) has argued, however, that after the revolution, Khomeini came to moderate considerably his earlier rhetoric about a class struggle between the oppressed and their wealthy exploiters, and spoke increasingly of the need for harmonious ties between the middle and the lower classes; the term *mustaḍʿafūn* now "became — like the term sans culottes in the French Revolution — a political label for the new regime's supporters and included wealthy bazaar merchants."

In the context of the struggle against apartheid in South Africa, qurʾānic references to the *mustaḍʿafūn* became the basis of an Islamic variant of "liberation theology," with the prophet Muḥammad and indeed all the other prophets being seen as having struggled on behalf of the oppressed and the exploited. Where earlier understandings of the qurʾānic references to the *mustaḍʿafūn* seem to suggest that people would be judged in the hereafter on the basis of their conduct (see RECORD OF HUMAN ACTIONS; ESCHATOLOGY), and irrespective of their social standing in the world, certain contemporary religious intellectuals in South Africa have argued that the solidarity of the oppressed transcends differences of faith, and that the Qurʾān comes down on the side of the *mustaḍʿafūn* even when they are not believers (Esack, *Qurʾān, liberation and pluralism,* 98-103 and passim; see also POLITICS AND THE QURʾĀN).

Muhammad Qasim Zaman

Bibliography

Primary: Dāmaghānī, *Wujūh,* ii, 32-3 (see esp. p. 33, ad Q 4:97: *kunnā mustaḍʿafīn fī l-arḍ = maqhūrīn*); Ṭabarī, *Tafsīr,* ed. Shākir; id., *Taʾrīkh.*
Secondary: Arberry; E. Abrahamian, *The Iranian*

mojahedin, New Haven 1989; id., *Khomeinism. Essays on the Islamic republic,* Berkeley 1993; F. Esack, *Qurʾān, liberation and pluralism. An Islamic perspective of interreligious solidarity against oppression,* Oxford 1997; E. Moosa, The *sufahāʾ* in the Qurʾān. A problem in semiosis, in *Der Islam* 75 (1998), 1-27; A. Rippin, Ibn ʿAbbās's *al-lughāt fī l-Qurʾān,* in BSOAS 44 (1981), 15-25; R.B. Serjeant, The *ḍaʿīf* and the *mustaḍʿaf* and the status accorded to them in the Qurʾān, in JIS 7 (1987), 32-47; repr. in id., *Customary and sharīʿah law in Arabian society,* Hampshire (Variorum) 1991; Wensinck, *Concordance,* s.v. *d-ʿ-f.*

Oppression

Unjust or cruel exercise of authority or power. There is no single word in the Qurʾān that perfectly translates the term "oppression." An array of words, such as *baghy* (attested seven times), *qahr* (ten times), *ṭughyān* (nine times; cf. Izutsu, *Structure,* 140-2), *ʿudwān* (seven times; cf. Izutsu, *Structure,* 161-4), *istiḍʿāf* (five times) and the most frequently attested, *ẓulm* (ca. twenty times; cf. Izutsu, *Structure,* 152-61), all share an essential semantic aspect of this concept: i.e. exceeding the appropriate limits of behavior in dealing with others, while violating their essential human rights. The qurʾānic portrayal of the behavior of Pharaoh (q.v.) and his people, *al-malaʾ,* conveys perfectly the image of the oppressive ruler and the oppressive class on the one hand, and the oppressed subjects on the other. Similar models are conveyed in all the qurʾānic stories of the prophets and their peoples (see NARRATIVES; PROPHETS AND PROPHETHOOD), such as those of the people of ʿĀd (q.v.) and Thamūd (q.v.), of Noah (q.v.), Lot (q.v.), Abraham (q.v.) and Jesus (q.v.), where people are categorized as either *mustakbirūn* (lit. "proud, arrogant"; see ARROGANCE; PRIDE; cf. Izutsu, *Structure,* 131-44 for a discussion of the various aspects of haughtiness) or *mustaḍʿafūn* ("downtrodden"; cf. Q 7:75, 137, 150; 14:21; 28:4; 34:31-3; 40:47; and others; see OPPRESSED ON EARTH, THE). The former always deny God's revelation (see REVELATION AND INSPIRATION) and persecute the prophets and their followers, who are the *mustaḍʿafūn.* This is also the case of the prophet Muḥammad with the people of Mecca (q.v.; Q 8:26; cf. 4:75; see OPPOSITION TO MUḤAMMAD). In all such cases, the earth (q.v.) will be inherited by the oppressed, God promises (Q 28:5).

But Pharaoh exceeded even the limits of denying the divine message and persecuting Moses (q.v.) and his followers when he claimed divinity and the exercise of divine authority on earth. His image in the Qurʾān is that of the tyrannical ruler par excellence (Q 79:17; cf. 22:24, 34), who causes corruption (q.v.; Q 28:5), misleads his people (Q 20:79; see ASTRAY; ERROR) claims to be god (Q 29:40; 28:38) and demands the absolute submission and unquestioned obedience (q.v.) of the people (cf. Q 40:29). His actions cause the division of the people into the following groups (*shiyaʿ,* sing. *shīʿa,* Q 28:4; see SHĪʿA): on the one hand are the aristocrats *(al-malaʾ),* who are the privileged and ostentatious *(al-mutrafūn)* and, accordingly, the arrogant oppressors *(al-mustakbirūn);* on the other are the *mustaḍʿafūn* or the oppressed, those who have lost power, been marginalized, despised and persecuted. It is understandable, then, why the Qurʾān uses the same word to denote God's attribute (see GOD AND HIS ATTRIBUTES) of supreme power (*al-qāhir,* see POWER AND IMPOTENCE) and to refer to Pharaoh's oppressiveness. When Pharaoh responds to the conviction of his *malaʾ* that he must act against the people of Moses, the Qurʾān states: "Their male children will we slay; [only] their females will we save alive; and we have over them irresistible power" (*qāhirūn,* Q 7:127). The connotation of *qahr* in this specific context is very close to "oppression." This qurʾānic passage, therefore, lends itself to an argument that *qāhr* may most closely denote the concept "oppression." The verbal form *taqhar* is used by the Qurʾān in the context of advising the prophet Muḥammad and, as a matter of fact, all Muslims, not to mistreat orphans (q.v.; Q 93:9). When related to humans, the nominal form *qāhir* refers, then, to someone claiming to be God (who alone is *al-qāhir* and *al-qahhār*) who performs massive mistreatment, i.e. oppression against others. In modern times, the categorization of the enemy — be it America or Ṣaddām Ḥusayn, or the apartheid political regime of South Africa — as the "oppressor" came to be a very effective ideological weapon in sacralized struggle (see JIHĀD).

N. Abu Zayd

Bibliography
Primary: Ṭabarī, *Tafsīr,* 30 vols., Cairo 1388/1968.
Secondary: F. Esack, *Qurʾān, liberation and pluralism. An Islamic perspective of interreligious solidarity against oppression,* Oxford 1997 (repr. 1998); S.M. Gieling, *The sacralization of war in the Islamic Republic of Iran,* Ph.D. diss., Nijmegen 1998; Izutsu, *Concepts;* id., *The structure of the ethical terms in the Koran,* Tokyo 1959; F. Rahman, *Major themes of the Qurʾān,* Chicago 1980.

Oral Transmission

see READINGS OF THE QURʾĀN; ORALITY; ORALITY AND WRITING IN ARABIA; COLLECTION OF THE QURʾĀN

Orality

The quality of spoken, as opposed to written, communication. The Arabic Qurʾān emerged against the backdrop of a long history of oral poetic composition and recitation (see POETRY AND POETS; ORALITY AND WRITING IN ARABIA). It is a composite text consisting of oral recitations born in an oral culture of great refinement and long tradition. It is hard to over-emphasize the importance of oral poetry among the northern Arab tribal nomads (q.v.) of the pre-Islamic world (see PRE-ISLAMIC ARABIA AND THE QURʾĀN; ARABS; BEDOUIN). Their major art form was the spoken word of poetry, and in particular their three-part ode, or *qaṣīda.* The recitative chanting of their poetry was their music and the highest expression of their eloquence. Every tribe had a poet who could compose and recite verses in praise of it or in denigration of its opponents. Perfection of oral poetic composition and recitation was something much admired and much desired. It was in this oral poetic milieu that the qurʾānic recitations arose and became a new standard of oral literary and religious excellence and beauty (el Tayib, Pre-Islamic poetry; Zwettler, *Oral tradition,* 3-88; see RECITATION OF THE QURʾĀN).

Although the Qurʾān has had a rich and central role in the history of Muslim piety and faith as "sacred book," it has always been preeminently an oral, not a written text — as strikingly so as any of the world's great religious scriptures except the Vedas. In the history of Islamic piety and practice, the role of the written scriptural text has always been secondary to the dominant tradition of oral transmission and aural presence of the recited text. The qurʾānic revelation (see REVELATION AND INSPIRATION) recognized by Islamic tradition as the first given to Muḥammad, Q 96, begins: "Recite *(iqraʾ)* in the name of your lord (q.v.) who created." This signals clearly that the revelations were from the outset meant to be oral repetitions of the revealed word of God himself (see WORD OF GOD; SPEECH). The Prophet is quoted in one ḥadīth (see ḤADĪTH AND THE QURʾĀN) as saying, "Embellish the recitation *(al-qurʾān)* with your voices, for the beautiful voice increases the beauty of the Qurʾān" (al-Dārimī, *Sunan*, 23.33.14; cf. 13). This underscores the centrality of the oral and aesthetic dimensions of the Qurʾān in Muslim tradition. As Stanley Lane Poole put it, "from first to last the Koran is essentially a book to be heard, not read" (Zwemer, Translations, 82; although note that this judgment is anachronistic, in that there was no "book" of the Qurʾān until long after the early revelations to be recited were proclaimed by the Prophet; see MUṢḤAF; COLLECTION OF THE QURʾĀN; CODICES OF THE QURʾĀN; BOOK; MANUSCRIPTS OF THE QURʾĀN). In Muslim tradition, the highly developed system of rules for proper recitation *(tajwīd)* "is believed to be the codification of the sound of the revelation as it was revealed to the Prophet.... Thus the sound itself has a divine source and significance, and, according to Muslim tradition, is significant to the meaning" (Nelson, *Art*, 14). The only way to understand the Qurʾān and its place in Muslim history and contemporary life is to grasp the centrality of its role as oral text *par excellence*.

There can be little argument that the scripture *(al-kitāb)* of Muslims has been functionally a "spoken book" — the divine "word" itself, the very discourse of God *ipsissima vox*, given to Muḥammad as "an Arabic recitation" (*qurʾān ʿarabiyy;* cf. i.e. Q 12:2; 20:113; see ARABIC LANGUAGE). This has lent immense importance to the Arabic text of the Qurʾān, its verbatim memorization, and its artful and reverent recitation — so much so that the rejection of recitation of any translation of the Qurʾān (above all in the daily worship rituals, or *ṣalāt*, see PRAYER; RITUAL AND THE QURʾĀN; TRANSLATIONS OF THE QURʾĀN) has been almost total in Islamic societies.

Theologically, the Qurʾān as "word of God" in Islam compares not to the Bible in the Christian tradition (see SCRIPTURE AND THE QURʾĀN) but to the person of the Christ as the *logos tou theou*, the divine Word (Söderblom, *Einführung*, 117; cf. Graham, *Beyond*, 217 n. 3; Kermani, *Gott*, 465 n. 195; see CREATEDNESS OF THE QURʾĀN): the closest comparable Muslim practice to the Eucharist would consequently be either the ubiquitous practice among Muslims of oral recitation of the Qurʾān or that of learning the text by heart, *ḥifẓ al-Qurʾān* (Smith, Some similarities, 52, 56-7; see MEMORY). One of the most respected religious titles a Muslim can bear is that of *ḥāfiẓ(a)*, one who knows the entire Qurʾān by heart. Qurʾān recitation and memorization have always been central to deep spirituality as well as to everyday life in Muslim societies: "The discipline of qurʾānic memorization is an integral part of learning to be human and Muslim" (Eickelman, *Knowledge*, 63; see EVERYDAY LIFE, QURʾĀN IN).

Historically, the original meaning of the very word *qurʾān* testifies to this fundamental orality of the text from its inception: the qurʾānic revelations were oral texts meant to be rehearsed and recited, first by Muḥammad (as witness the more than 300 occurrences of *Qul!*, "Say! [oh Muḥammad]," before particular passages of the sacred text), then by the faithful to whom Muḥammad was to recite them. They were explicitly not revealed as "a writing on parchment" (Q 6:7; see WRITING AND WRITING MATERIALS). The word *qurʾān* is a verbal noun form derived from the root *q-r-ʾ*, "to recite, read aloud," and hence the proper translation of *al-qurʾān* is "the Reciting" or "the Recitation" (Graham, Earliest meaning). The Arabic word *qurʾān* is not attested prior to the Qurʾān itself and it was likely derived from, or influenced by, the Syriac cognate word *qeryānā*, "lection, reading," used by Syriac-speaking Christian communities (see CHRISTIANS AND CHRISTIANITY) both for the oral liturgical reading from scripture *(lectio, anagnosis)* and for the scripture passage that is read aloud *(lectio, periochė, anagnøsma)* in divine service (Bowman, *Holy scriptures;* A. Neuwirth and K. Neuwirth, *Sūrat al-fātiḥa;* cf. Graham, *Beyond,* 209 n. 36; see FOREIGN VOCABULARY; NAMES OF THE QURʾĀN). Both the Muslim and Christian usages have parallels also in the rabbinic use of the Hebrew cognates *qerīʾā* and *miqrāʾ* to denote the act of scripture reading and the pericope read aloud, respectively (J. Horovitz, Qurʾān, 67; Nöldeke, *GQ,* i, 32; Graham, *Beyond,* 209 n. 37). In the qurʾānic text itself, there are a number of uses of the word *qurʾān* that can best be taken as verbal-noun *(maṣdar)* usages: e.g. "the dawn (q.v.) recitation" in Q 17:78 and "...Ours it is to collect and to recite it *(qurʾānuhu),* and when we recite it, follow the recitation of it *(qurʾānahu)*" (Q 75:17-8). These readings are bolstered in the ḥadīth at various points, such as when Muḥammad speaks well of whoever "is constantly mindful of God during [his] reciting" (*qurʾān,* Ibn Ḥanbal, *Musnad,* iv, 159). Other examples: when Muḥammad explains to a companion who witnessed a horse trying to bolt during his night recitation, "That was the divine presence (*sakīna,* see SECHINA) that descended with the reciting" (*al-qurʾān,* Bukhārī, *Ṣaḥīḥ,* 66.11), and the report that Muḥammad "raised his voice in the recitation *(qurʾān)* in his prayer" (*ṣalāt,* Muslim, *Ṣaḥīḥ,* 4.145; cf. 4.149, 154; 6.232-37).

These examples of the early understanding of *qurʾān* as a verbal noun remind us of the strong historical basis for the ongoing orality of the Qurʾān in Muslim usage down the centuries to the present moment. This orality has always been a striking element in both Muslim religious practice and even in quotidian life in Islamic societies, where the use of qurʾānic formulae has been a permeating reality of everyday speech, even down to small repeated phrases that have passed into everyday usage (see SLOGANS FROM THE QURʾĀN). One thinks of the *basmala* (q.v.) and Fātiḥa (q.v.), or the many qurʾānic phrases such as *mā shāʾa llāhu* (Q 18:39) or *al-ḥamdu lillāhi* (Q 1:2; see LAUDATION) as only the most evident (for examples of such usages, see Piamenta, *Islam in everyday speech,* 10, 73, 75, 86-7; Jomier, La place du Coran). The five-times-daily ritual of prayer *(ṣalāt)* is the most obvious place to look for daily recitation of the Qurʾān, since without some qurʾānic recitation the *ṣalāt* is legally invalid (see LAWFUL AND UNLAWFUL). But well beyond penetration of qurʾānic phrases into everyday speech and the formal demands of the rites of daily worship, the recited word of scripture has always been prominent in Muslim communities. Recitation of the Qurʾān is woven into the very fabric of life in Muslim communities. A ḥadīth has Muḥammad say, "the most excellent form of worship (q.v.; *ʿibāda*) among my people is reciting the Qurʾān" (Ghazālī, *Iḥyāʾ,* 1.8.1). Qurʾān recitation has been a, if not the, major form of entertainment in Muslim societies, and it has for centuries been raised to an art form (see Nelson, *Art;* Kermani, chap. 3). Qurʾān memorization, recitation, and study have formed the core of Muslim education at all times and around the world in Islamic societies (see TEACHING AND PREACHING THE QURʾĀN). Centuries ago, Ibn Khaldūn (d. 784/1382; *Muqaddima,* iii, 260; Ibn Khaldūn-Rosenthal, iii, 300; cf. Graham, *Beyond,* 215 n. 35) noted that "teaching the Qurʾān to children is one of the marks of the religion that Muslims profess and practice in all their cities," and a still older ḥadīth text claims that "knowledge shall not perish so long as the Qurʾān is recited" (Dārimī, *Sunan,* 1.18.8; see KNOWLEDGE AND LEARNING).

In sum, the oral presence of the Qurʾān is a constant source of inspiration to Muslims in all walks of life. Al-Ghazālī

(d. 505/1111; *Iḥyā'*, 1.8.1) put it well: "Much repetition cannot make it [the Qur'ān] seem old and worn to those who recite it." The importance and power of the oral qur'ānic word are captured in the hyperbolic and metaphorical, but still acute, observation of the modern Iranian scholar, Muḥammad Taqī Sharī'aṭī-Mazīnānī, about the aural impact of the recited text: "The Qur'ān was a light [q.v.] that extended through the opening of the ears into the soul; it transformed this soul and as a consequence of that, the world" (as cited in Kermani, *Gott ist Schön*, 44). See also LANGUAGE AND STYLE OF THE QUR'ĀN.

William A. Graham

Bibliography
Primary: Bukhārī, *Ṣaḥīḥ;* Dārimī, *Sunan;* al-Ghazālī, Abū Ḥāmid Muḥammad, *Iḥyā' 'ulūm al-dīn*, 5 vols., Beirut n.d.; Ibn Ḥanbal, *Musnad;* Ibn Khaldūn, 'Abd al-Raḥmān, *al-Muqaddima*, ed. M. Quatremère, 3 vols., Paris 1858; Eng. trans. Ibn Khaldūn-Rosenthal; Muslim, *Ṣaḥīḥ*.
Secondary: J. Bowman, Holy scriptures, lectionaries and Qur'ān, in A.H. Johns (ed.), *International Congress for the Study of the Qur'ān. Australian National University, Canberra, 8-13 May, 1980*, Canberra 1981, 29-37; D. Eickelman, *Knowledge and power in Morocco. The education of a twentieth-century noble*, Princeton 1985; Graham, *Beyond;* id., The earliest meaning of *qur'ān*, in *WI* 23 (1984), 361-77; J. Horovitz, Qur'ān, in *Der Islam* 13 (1923), 66-9; J. Jomier, La place du Coran dans la vie quotidienne en Égypte, in *IBLA* 15 (1952), 131-65; N. Kermani, *Gott ist Schön. Das ästhetische Erleben des Koran*, Munich 1999; K. Nelson, *The art of reciting the Qur'ān*, Austin, TX 1985; A. Neuwirth und K. Neuwirth, Sūrat al-Fātiḥa — "Eröffnung" des Text-Corpus Koran oder "Introitus" der Gebetsliturgie? in W. Gross, H. Irsigler and T. Seidl (eds.), *Text Methode und Grammatik. Wolfgang Richter zum 65. Geburtstag*, St. Ottilien 1991, 331-57; Nöldeke, *GQ;* M. Piamenta, *Islam in everyday speech*, Leiden 1979; W.C. Smith, Some similarities and differences between Christianity and Islam, in J. Kritzeck and R.B. Winder (eds.), *The world of Islam. Studies in honour of Philip K. Hitti*, London 1959, 47-59; N. Söderblom, *Einführung in die Religionsgeschichte*, Leipzig 1920; A. el Tayib, Pre-Islamic poetry, in A.F.L. Beeston et al. (eds.), *Arabic literature to the end of the Umayyad period*, Cambridge 1983; S. Zwemer, Translations of the Koran, in id., *Studies in popular Islam*, London 1939, 81-99; M. Zwettler, *The oral tradition of classical Arabic poetry*, Columbus, OH 1978.

Orality and Writing in Arabia

Transmission of knowledge through the spoken and written word. In pre-Islamic Arabia, culture was largely transmitted orally, with writing being used for practical matters of daily life (i.e. trade; see SELLING AND BUYING) — although there was an awareness of Jewish and Christian scriptures (see SCRIPTURE AND THE QUR'ĀN; PRE-ISLAMIC ARABIA AND THE QUR'ĀN). Apart from a couple of inscriptions and some defectively written graffiti, no primary sources exist for pre-Islamic Arabic writing (see EPIGRAPHY AND THE QUR'ĀN; ARCHAEOLOGY AND THE QUR'ĀN). Oral sources, by their very nature, are transient. We are thus left to glean what we can about orality (q.v.) and writing/script from secondary Arabic sources that were committed to writing long after Arabic script (q.v.) was fully developed. It may be said, however, that the interplay of orality and writing in this milieu shows up most clearly in the Qur'ān itself (see LANGUAGE AND STYLE OF THE QUR'ĀN; FORM AND STRUCTURE OF THE QUR'ĀN).

Orally-transmitted attestations of writing and scripture in pre-Islamic Arabia

There were four kinds of oral literature in pre-Islamic Arabia: those of the poet (*shā'ir*, see POETRY AND POETS), the soothsayer (*kāhin*, see SOOTHSAYERS), the orator (*khaṭīb*) and the story-teller (*qāṣṣ*). The advent of Islam was very unfavorable to *kāhin* material and to pre-Islamic *khaṭīb* material, and the little that has survived has nothing to tell us about writing, a subject to which neither the *kāhin* nor the *khaṭīb* was likely to have referred in the first instance.

Poetry

We are more fortunate in what we can draw together from the surviving corpus of pre-Islamic poetry. It contains a fair number of references to writing, usually based on the convention by which the traces of an almost effaced, long deserted campsite are compared to written material. Both epigraphic and documentary writing are mentioned. Very rarely does the same poem refer to both. Thus the *Muʿallaqa* of Labīd has: "the stones there contain writings " (*ḍamina l-wuḥiyya silāmuhā*, l. 2) and "writings whose texts have been renewed by their pens" (*zuburun tujiddu mutūnahā aqlāmuhā*, l. 8).

The majority of references must be assumed to refer to a script for Arabic writing, though its form is uncertain; but there are some passages that might possibly refer, explicitly or implicitly, to south Arabian forms of writing. This possibility can be seen in a passage from Labīd's *Qaṣīda nūniyya:*

... ka-annahā
zuburun yurajjiʿuhā walīdu yamāni
mutaʿawwidun laḥinun yuʿīdu bi-kaffihi
qalaman ʿalā ʿusubin dhabulna wa-bāni
... as though they were
writings over which the Yemeni lad moved back and forth
in his accustomed way, clever, his hand moving
a pen over dried palm-fronds or over pieces of a *ben*-tree

Not only does *walīdu yamāni* point to the south, the terms *zubur,* "writings," and *ʿusub,* "palm-fronds," would appear to have south Arabian origins (see WRITING AND WRITING MATERIALS).

The corpus of poetry contains a fair number of references to Jews and Christians (see JEWS AND JUDAISM; CHRISTIANS AND CHRSTIANITY) but references to their scriptures are difficult to find. There are some references to the Christian anchorites (see ASCETICISM; MONASTICISM AND MONKS) using lights for their devotions at night (and, by implication, reading), as in the *Muʿallaqa* of Imruʾ al-Qays (lines 39 and 72). Once, however, Imruʾ al-Qays has part of a line referring specifically to Christian writings: "like a line of writing in the books of monks" *(ka-khaṭṭi zabūrin fī maṣāḥifi ruhbāni);* and al-Aswad b. Yaʿfur refers to Jewish written material: "the letters of two Jews from Taymāʾ or the people of Madyan [see MIDIAN] on/their parchments which they recite with accomplishment" *(suṭūru yahūdiyyayni fī muhraqayhimā/mujīdayni min Taymāʾa aw ahli Madyan).*

The accepted view is that these references to writing were part of poetic convention and that the bedouin (q.v.) tribesmen themselves were little concerned with writing, and there seems to be no reason to doubt this. That the illiterate poet Ṭarafa should liken his camel's cheek to "Syrian parchment" seems typical of the convention (see LITERACY; ILLITERACY). Nor does there seem to be an exception in the case of the poet — or two poets — known as al-Muraqqish (probably meaning "the one who puts black on white"). The name is thought not to derive from him acting as a scribe but to be a soubriquet that stems from part of a line that runs: "the traces resemble what a pen has inscribed on the back of the /parchment" *(wa-l-rusūmu ka-ma * raqqasha fī ẓahri l-adīmi qalam).*

Stories

Moving on from the evidence of poetry to the story-tellers' material, very little is to be found in the background stories that accompany most of the surviving poems or in the legends of the "days of the Arabs" *(ayyām al-ʿarab)*. Even then, the stories that have come down to us are at best problematical, as they were susceptible to recasting and accretion down to ʿAbbāsid times; and some of them, such as the placing of copies of the *muʿallaqāt* on the Kaʿba (q.v.), appear to be total fiction. Nevertheless, it is interesting to note two points from the famous story of the poets al-Mutalammis and Ṭarafa preserved in the *Kitāb al-aghānī* of Abū l-Faraj al-Iṣfahānī, in which they are portrayed as being sent off by the ruler of al-Ḥīra to the governor of al-Baḥrayn, each with a note telling the governor to execute the bearer of the note. In one way, the story hinges on the illiteracy of the two poets; in another, there is the assumption that literates who did not already know the contents of a message would be able to read it.

Extent of literacy in pre-Islamic Arabia

Overall, the background material seems to indicate that there was a certain amount of literacy in the settlements (see CITY), particularly the key centers of al-Ḥīra, Medina (q.v.) and Mecca (q.v.). This is plausible, though any direct evidence from the period is lacking. There is, for example, nothing to link Labīd's Yemeni youth with any particular place. It is not unreasonable, however, to suggest that his main concern was with documents and that the most likely place where documents would be produced was a settlement. But even if most of those employed in writing lived in settlements it is unlikely that they were numerous. It is also reasonable to assume that writing in Arabic script was for practical purposes, with other languages and scripts being used for religious purposes. Culturally this would have mattered little in pre-Islamic times, for the same sources make it clear that cultural material (that of the poets, soothsayers, orators and story-tellers) was orally transmitted.

There are other problems about the role of writing among the Arabs in the early seventh century C.E. to which we have no clear answer. One must accept the generalization that the crucial function of a script, whether alphabetic or not, is to convey a version of the spoken word in a form that can be recognized and understood by a person with knowledge of that script and of the language that it encodes. It is not clear, however, how this applied in early Arabic documents. Any document that has come down to us through traditional sources is now written in a fairly high register, and with no obvious colloquial features (see DIALECTS; GRAMMAR AND THE QURʾĀN). This may not be far from the mark; but, as is usual in Arabic sources, there is a total failure to pay any attention to the gradations of register between the four literary forms: *shāʿir* — *kāhin* — *khaṭīb* — *qaṣṣ*. Nor is there any sign of dialect. This simply does not tally with what we find in papyri, in which colloquialisms, a sign of dialect, are to be found from the earliest surviving documents onwards.

The traditional view is that Arabic script was defective until roughly the end of the seventh century C.E. This is certainly true of graffiti, but that is hardly germane to the discussion. The graffiti and the traditional view might also incline us to the view that the script functioned largely at an *aide-mémoire* level. Again it would appear that we are being pointed in the wrong direction. Labīd's vignette about the Yemeni youth and the story of al-Mutalammis and Ṭarafa seem to point to a fairly extensive use of writing, whether or not the script was fully formed.

Earliest literary evidence from the Islamic period

It is against this background that we should consider the implications of the surviving papyri and in particular of the earliest extant Islamic document, a papyrus from upper Egypt, now preserved in the Austrian State National Library and known as PERF 558 (for more on this papyrus, see Gruendler, *Development*, 157; Jones, Dotting). It has texts in both Arabic and Greek, and each bears a date: in Arabic "the month Jumādā I of the year 22" and in Greek "the thirtieth day of the month of Pharmouthi of the Indiction year 1" (25 April 643).

This invaluable dating is not the only important thing about PERF 558. The script is more advanced than we might expect if we accept the traditional accounts of the development of Arabic script (q.v.). The Arabic text is written in a clear cursive hand; and it contains a fair sprinkling of dots. There are dotted forms of six letters (*jīm, khāʾ, dhāl, zāy, shīn* and *nūn*, all of which are also to be found without dots); there are some long vowels (*ā, ī*, and *ū* are all to be found, though medial *ā* is most frequently omitted); and there are some examples of *alif maqṣūra*.

The script of PERF 558 is rightly characterized by Beatrice Gruendler (*Development*, 135) as being a "fairly developed script." She adds "the first cursive impulse must therefore be expected several decades earlier." This also seems a fair judgment. A period of several decades, however, dating back from 643 C.E. takes us back into the pre-*hijra* period (see EMIGRATION). We are thus forced to conclude that the traditional accounts of the development of Arabic writing, and of the diacritics in particular, i.e. that in the seventh century the Arabic script functioned at a primarily *aide-mémoire* level, must be wrong so far as a cursive form of Arabic is concerned.

There is another scrap of evidence that we might reasonably consider as providing some corroboration of this view. There is a hemistich in Labīd's *qaṣīda mīmiyya* beginning *ʿafā l-rasmu am lā* that runs: "There is a trace of Asmāʾ that has become dotted like a sheet of writing" *(li-Asmāʾa rasmun ka-l-ṣaḥāfati aʿjamā)*. It is true that Labīd lived for almost forty years in the Islamic period, but his language and thought are very traditional and again take us back to the earlier part of the seventh century C.E.

A full use of the script is also indicated by some material found in the literature on the Prophet's biography (*sīra*, see SĪRA AND THE QURʾĀN). There are no cogent reasons, for example, to reject the authenticity of the treaty documents now known as the Constitution of Medina, or to believe that these were not committed to writing at the time that they were drawn up. Equally, writing plays a crucial role in the story about the expedition to Nakhla in Rajab of 2 A.H., in which the sealed orders were issued to the leader of the Muslim raiding party.

Finally the Qurʾān shows itself to be strongly in favor of the use of writing for practical purposes. The key passages are a very lengthy one, Q 2:282-3, concerning the recording of debts (q.v.) and other transactions, and the much shorter Q 24:33, about writing documents. It would seem that these stipulations about the writing of documents are possible because there was a pre-Islamic *sunna* of writing for practical purposes, and, on the evidence of the papyri, writing was a tradition of accomplished scribes.

The writing of the Qurʾān (see ORTHOGRAPHY; MANUSCRIPTS OF THE QURʾĀN) is another matter, for its original mode of delivery was oral (see RECITATION OF THE QURʾĀN). Thus any written version is a secondary form, as the text depicts in a narrative (see NARRATIVES) about Moses (q.v.; Q 6:91). Given, however, that there was knowledge of copies of Jewish and Christian scriptures, the psychological pressure for the nascent Islamic community to have written copies of its own scripture must have been irresistible (see CODICES OF THE QURʾĀN; COLLECTION OF THE QURʾĀN). Tradition has it firmly that at least some of the Qurʾān was committed to writing during Muḥammad's lifetime, although there is no agreement about when the copying started or how much of it was copied during his lifetime — though most references are linked to the final years of his residence in Medina. This writing is said to have been done by a small group of scribes, known as the "scribes of the revelation" *(kuttāb al-waḥy)*. The authenticity of this material is disputed but even if it is rejected, it is likely to echo something of what happened.

This takes us back again to the form of writing used. It has always been thought that the development of the Kūfic form of Arabic script — without any diacritical dots — was a concomitant of the Qurʾān's being committed to writing. That may be so, but it would then point to a two-track evolution of Arabic script in the seventh century C.E.: Kūfic basically as a form of *aide-mémoire* to go with the oral text, while a more cursive form, which used dots at the whim of the writer, was employed for more practical documents.

Orality, writing and the Qurʾān

There is a remarkable contrast between the scanty gleanings set out above — i.e. the degree of literacy in the Arabia of Muḥammad's day, the function and nature of the Arabic script, and the evidence for the writing down of the Qurʾān during Muḥammad's lifetime (including the script in which it would have been recorded) — and what we find attested in the Qurʾān itself. First, the appurtenances of writing, though not frequently mentioned, are pretty well represented in the qurʾānic vocabulary: *qalam, raqq, qirṭās, sijill, lawḥ, ṣuḥuf, zubur, midād,* etc. Unfortunately there is nothing about the script beyond the odd phrase such as *kitāb masṭūr* (Q 52:2) and *kitāb marqūm* (Q 83:9, 20), which do not add to our overall knowledge.

The riches about writing, however, lie with the single root *k-t-b,* which is a key item in qurʾānic vocabulary. There are over fifty examples of the verb *kataba,* which are fairly evenly split between the concrete "to write" and the abstract "to prescribe." This is overshadowed, however, by the use of *kitāb,* which is the tenth most common noun in the text, with over 250 occurrences.

There are no real surprises about the meanings of *kitāb,* though perhaps they have a greater range than most of the central items of qurʾānic vocabulary. In over 200 of the occurrences it means what is normally translated as "scripture," with most of the rest meaning "document," "record" or "decree," with a couple examples each of "letter" and "fixed time" rounding off the meanings. Usage and context show, however, that when *kitāb* means "scripture" it is hardly ever concrete in sense.

There is, for example, the fact that *qurʾān,* "recitation," and *kitāb,* "scripture," are to some extent interchangeable. The most striking instance is the phrasing of Q 15:1, "These are the signs of the scripture and of a clear recitation" *(tilka āyātu l-kitābi wa-qurʾānin mubīn),* and Q 27:1, "These are the revelations of the recitation and a clear scripture" *(tilka āyātu l-qurʾāni wa-kitābin mubīnin)*.

Also Q 46:29 has "Who listened to the recitation" *(yastamiʿūna l-qurʾāna),* while the following verse has "We have heard a scripture" (*innā samiʿnā kitāban,* Q 46:30). There are also a number of verses which refer to the "scripture" being recited (see Q 2:44, 113, 121; 17:93; 29:51; also Q 29:48 quoted below).

There are, however, other passages that show that the essential relationship between the two words is more complex, with *kitāb* apparently referring to a heavenly exemplar and *qurʾān* to an earthly recitation (see HEAVENLY BOOK; PRESERVED TABLET). Thus in Q 41:3 we find "A scripture whose signs are expounded as a recitation in Arabic" *(kitābun fuṣṣilat āyātuhu qur'ānan 'arabiyyan),* and in Q 43:2-3, "By the clear scripture — we have made it a recitation in Arabic" (*wa-l-kitābi l-mubīni innā ja'alnāhu qur'ānan 'arabiyyan;* see also NAMES OF THE QUR'ĀN).

On the basis of these and similar passages, particularly with the phrase *kitāb mubīn* (Q 12:1; 26:2, etc.; cf. 5:19; 13:1), one can make a good case for arguing that "divine message" would give a clearer indication of the meaning of *kitāb* than "scripture" does. God does not transmit the divine message to his messengers in writing. The use of the verb *awḥā,* "suggest, inspire," is perhaps the clearest indication of that.

That the committing of the divine message to a written form is a secondary stage after the revelation is indicated most clearly by Q 6:91, "Say, 'Who sent down the scripture which Moses brought as a light (q.v.) and a guidance to the people? You put it on parchments, revealing them, but concealing much'" *(qul man anzala l-kitāba lladhī jā'a bihi mūsā nūran wa-hudan lil-nāsi; taj'alūnahu qarāṭīsa, tubdūnahā wa-tukhfūna kathīran).*

In one passage, Q 29:48, a verse denying that Muḥammad had had a revelation before the Qur'ān, writing may be seen as having the same standing as recitation: "You did not recite any scripture before this nor did you write it with your right hand" (*wa-mā kunta tatlū min qablihi min kitābin wa-lā takhuṭṭuhu bi-yamīnika;* see OPPOSITION TO MUḤAMMAD; UMMĪ; LEFT HAND AND RIGHT HAND). The Prophet is never, however, given the command to "write," though from time to time he is told to "recite," and frequently, of course, the instruction is "say."

Nevertheless, the importance of written scripture is acknowledged in such early passages as Q 52:2-3: "By a scripture inscribed on unrolled parchment" *(wa-kitābin masṭūrin fī raqqin manshūrin)* and Q 87:18-9: "This is in the ancient scrolls (q.v.), the scrolls of Abraham (q.v.) and Moses" *(inna hādhā la-fī l-ṣuḥufi l-ūlā ṣuḥufi Ibrāhīma wa-Mūsā).*

It is several times acknowledged that the People of the Book (q.v.), as the Jews and Christians are generally known, have written versions of the scripture, and what they do with them is commented on very adversely in Q 2:79 (see POLEMIC AND POLEMICAL LANGUAGE; CORRUPTION; FORGERY).

In the end, none of the passages containing the root *k-t-b* can be said directly to encourage the writing of the divine message, but there is one verse, Q 25:5, that indicates that the Meccans linked writing to the revelation, in a pejorative way: "They say, 'Fables of the ancients that he has had written down; and they are dictated to him morning and evening'" (*qālū asāṭīru l-awwalīna ktatabahā fa-hiya tumlā 'alayhi bukratan wa-aṣīlan;* see INFORMANTS). It is not fanciful to think that this priority of the oral over the written would have influenced early believers in one direction, while a very natural desire to have written copies would have pulled them in the opposite way.

On the other hand, the Qur'ān is strongly in favor of the use of writing for practical purposes. The key passage is a very lengthy one, Q 2:282-3, concerning the recording of debts and other transactions, which contains no less than eight places in which a form of *kataba* is used and one of *amalla,* "to dictate." One should also note the much shorter Q 24:33: "Such of those whom your right hands possess who seek the document, write it for them if you know some good in them" *(wa-lladhīna yabtaghūna l-kitāba mimmā malakat aymānukum fa-kātibūhum in ʿalimtum fī-him khayran)*. The meaning of "the document" in this verse is disputed, but however it is interpreted it is clear that writing is stipulated for a practical purpose, and this is precisely the same thrust that we see in Q 2:282-3.

Conclusion

Although the Qurʾān reflects a prejudice for an oral — as opposed to a written — preservation of scripture, papyri from the early Islamic period show a highly developed script. This evidence, together with material found in the *sīra* — and even the Qurʾān itself — lend support to a theory of a pre-Islamic development of Arabic script with diacritics. These two trends (oral preservation of culture, but the utilization of writing in mundane matters) indicate a two-fold development of the Arabic script: one (Kūfic, mentioned above) that served as a memory aid in the preservation of orally-transmitted culture and scripture, and a more differentiated one used in the transactions of daily life.

Alan Jones

Bibliography

Primary: I. ʿAbbās (ed.), *Sharḥ dīwān Labīd*, Kuwait 1962; Abū l-Farrāj al-Iṣfahānī, *Kitāb al-aghānī*, Cairo 1927-; A. Jones, *Early Arabic poetry*, vol. 2, Reading 1996, 52-86 and 164-202 (for the *Muʿallaqa*s of Imruʾ al-Qays and Labīd, respectively).

Secondary: N. Abbot, *The rise of the north Arabic script and its kurʾānic development*, Chicago 1939; B. Gruendler, *The development of the Arabic scripts*, Atlanta, GA 1993; R. Hoyland, *Arabia and the Arabs from the Bronze Age to the coming of Islam*, London 2001, chapter 8; A. Jones, The dotting of a script and the dating of an era, in *IC* 72 (1998), 95-103; id., The Qurʾān in the light of earlier Arabic prose, in id., *University Lectures in Islamic Studies*, London 1997, i, 67-83; id., The word made visible. Arabic script and the committing of the Qurʾān to writing, in *Essays in honor of Donald Richards*, Leiden 2003; F. Krenkow, The use of writing for the preservation of ancient Arabic poetry, in T.W. Arnold and R.A. Nicholson (eds.), *A volume of oriental studies presented to Edward G. Browne*, Cambridge 1922, 261-8; M. Maraqten, Writing material in pre-Islamic Arabia, in *JSS* 43 (1998), 292-303.

Original Sin see FALL OF MAN

Ornamentation and Illumination

From early times written copies of the qurʾānic text were embellished with various kinds of ornament that served to divide the text into manageable units, enhance readability, and enliven the visual qualities of the page and the book. Like the Torah of the Jews but unlike the Bible of the Christians, the Qurʾān was never illustrated with pictures, but rather embellished only with non-figural, nonrepresentational decoration. In contrast to the study of western manuscripts, where the term *illumination* encompasses both figural and non-figural decoration, scholars of Islamic art usually make a careful distinction between *illuminated* manuscripts, which were decorated only with non-representational geometric and vegetal designs, and *illustrated*, i.e. pictorial ones (see ICONOCLASM).

General considerations

Charting the origins and development of qurʾānic illumination is difficult since early manuscripts (i.e. those produced before the end of the third/ninth century) were never signed or dated (see MANUSCRIPTS OF THE QURʾĀN). Later manuscripts, in contrast, were often signed and dated by the calligrapher and sometimes even by the illuminator(s). In addition, otherwise-undated manuscripts can sometimes be dated by later inscriptions, such as endowment records *(waqfiyya)* or other external evidence. One of the benchmarks for dating early manuscripts in the so-called Kūfic, or angular, script, for example, is the multi-volume Qurʾān manuscript endowed by Amājūr, governor of Damascus for the ʿAbbāsids, in 262/876 to a mosque in Tyre (Déroche, Qurʾān of Amāğūr; see CALLIGRAPHY; ARABIC SCRIPT).

While it is unquestionably true that the general picture over the course of the centuries reveals a development from plain to ornately embellished manuscripts, it is often simplistically — but wrongly — assumed that the earliest copies of the text were always plain and that later examples carried increased amounts of ornament. This assumption is easily disproved by the discovery of at least one palimpsest, that is a reused parchment page, in Ṣanʿāʾ (Dār al-Makhṭūṭāt, MS 00-27.1), in which an unornamented version of the qurʾānic text in Kūfic script replaced an earlier one in a similar script embellished with ornamental headings. A cursory examination of the nearly 40,000 fragments from 1,000 early parchment manuscripts of the Qurʾān accidentally discovered in 1972 in the ceiling of the Great Mosque of Ṣanʿāʾ indicated that just one-eighth of them were illuminated (von Bothmer, Meisterwerke Islamischer Buchkunst).

In the fourth/tenth century, paper gradually began to replace parchment as the main medium for Qurʾān manuscripts, spreading from the east, where it was first used, to the west, where parchment remained the preferred support well into the seventh/thirteenth century. Coincident with this change of material was a shift in format from horizontal ("landscape") to vertical ("portrait"), as well as an increase in the amount and variety of the illumination, which was undoubtedly easier and therefore cheaper to execute on the new medium. The reverence universally accorded to the Qurʾān meant that calligraphers and illuminators used the finest materials for their work, and many Qurʾān manuscripts made in later centuries contain superb illumination, reckoning them among the finest works of art ever produced in the Islamic lands. Western scholars, accustomed to paying more attention to images than words or nonrepresentational decoration, however, have often neglected the study of qurʾānic illumination and decoration, and it is only in recent years that scholars, both Muslim and non-Muslim, have begun to address the subject with the care it deserves. Such careful study may help to localize and date particular manuscripts as well as to reveal how manuscripts of the Qurʾān were actually read and used.

Ornament was used in manuscripts of the Qurʾān to separate individual verses *(āyāt),* groups of verses, chapters (*sūras*) and divisions such as sevenths and thirtieths which allowed the text to be read over the course of a week or a month. As these divisions, as well as the titles of the sūras (see SŪRA), were not considered to be part of the revealed text, they were almost always differentiated in some way, whether by size, script, color, or illumination. Ornament was also used to frame and enclose the full text or individual volumes of it with decorative frontispieces and finispieces. In addition, volumes were protected by bindings of leather and pasteboard which themselves could be ornamented with tooling, stamping, gilding, and other fancy techniques. In later copies of the Qurʾān, similar or complementary designs were used on the pages and the binding, but as few, if any, early manuscripts of the Qurʾān have survived attached to their original bindings, it is still impossible to discuss the relationships between the decoration of text and binding in the early period.

Given these problems of establishing the chronology of early Qurʾān manuscripts, the following article is arranged typologically according to the size of the division marked by the ornament. It does not consider the variously colored dots found in early manuscripts of the Qurʾān; although they may appear decorative, they were used to indicate vocalization of the text (Dutton, Red dots [parts I and II]). This discussion moves from smallest to largest, beginning with markers used to separate verses (q.v.) and culminating in full and double pages of illumination with and without text. Within each section, examples are generally presented chronologically. A final section investigates the growing division of labor that accompanied the increased decoration of the qurʾānic text. For a discussion of the modern printed Qurʾān, however, see PRINTING OF THE QURʾĀN.

Verse markers and marginal ornaments

The division of the qurʾānic text into 114 sūras with approximately 6200 verses is very old and the subject of occasional disagreement, principally on the placing of divisions between the verses, not on the contents of the text or the order of the verses themselves (see CODICES OF THE QURʾĀN), which is generally thought to have been established during the reign of the caliph ʿUthmān (q.v.; r. 644-56; see also COLLECTION OF THE QURʾĀN). Division into verses is marked by the occurrence of rhyme or assonance (see RHYMED PROSE; FORM AND STRUCTURE OF THE QURʾĀN; LANGUAGE AND STYLE OF THE QURʾĀN); differences occur because of variants in reading (see READINGS OF THE QURʾĀN) and decisions about whether or not a particular rhyme marks the end of a verse. Another divergence occurs over whether or not the *basmala* (q.v.) is counted as a verse. The publication of the standard Egyptian edition of the Qurʾān in 1924 under the aegis of al-Azhar has provided a standard numbering system that is used by many scholars today. The divisions found in medieval manuscripts, therefore, do not necessarily correspond to those used at the present time, and it is possible that a close study of the variations of the verse markings used in different copies might help to establish localizations and chronologies for particular groups of manuscripts.

As calligraphers writing in the early Kūfic scripts did not generally differentiate between the internal spaces between the unconnected letters of a single word and the spaces between different words, let alone between sentences, division between verses might be indicated by something as simple as a series of diagonal slashes made by the calligrapher after writing the last word of a verse or by a gold circle or pyramid of three or six circles added by the calligrapher or someone else after the entire page had been copied. The celebrated calligrapher Ibn al-Bawwāb (d. 413/1022) discreetly marked the end of verses with three small dots in the copy of the Qurʾān he penned in the rounded *naskh* script in 391/1000-1, but did not otherwise interrupt the flow of his writing (Rice, *Unique Ibn al-Bawwāb manuscript*). Several centuries later, the Baghdādī calligrapher Yāqūt al-Mustaʿṣimī (fl. seventh/thirteenth cent.) typically used gold rosettes punctuated with blue dots to separate individual verses, and this style was later adopted by many calligraphers in Mamlūk Egypt, Ottoman Turkey, and elsewhere. Sometimes calligraphers left spaces for these verse markers; sometimes they wrote the text in an unbroken line, returning to add the verse markers above the line of script. A gold marker, whether a single rosette or a pyramid of circles, eventually became the standard indicator of the end of an individual verse.

To make it easier for a reader to locate a particular verse, especially in the longer chapters with hundreds of verses, calligraphers normally marked groups of five and ten verses. The standard marker for five verses was a teardrop shape, derived from the Arabic letter *hāʾ*, the alphanumeric *(abjad)* symbol for "five" (see NUMEROLOGY). As the alphanumeric symbol for "ten" — the letter *yāʾ* — would have been visually inappropriate, the standard marker for ten verses was a circle, often inscribed with the appropriate alphanumeric symbol for the decade (e.g. *sīn* for sixty). Since the alphanumeric system used in the Islamic west differed slightly from that used in the central and eastern lands, the way these systems count tens of verses can be an important means to distinguish manuscripts produced in the different regions. For example, the famous "Blue Qurʾān," written in gold on blue-dyed parchment, was once routinely attributed to ʿAbbāsid Merv and Persia. The manuscript, however, uses the western system of alphanumeric counting, where sixty is indicated by the letter *ṣād*, making an attribution to Qayrawān in Tunisia or elsewhere in the Maghrib much more likely (Bloom, Al-Maʾmun's Blue Koran).

To further facilitate finding one's place in the text, illuminators normally placed larger markers for groups of five and ten verses in the outer margin of the page at a place corresponding to where the group of verses ended in the text. Sometimes these markers repeat the teardrop or circular shape of the ornament found in the text; sometimes they stand in place of it. The teardrop shape is typically inscribed with the word *khams* (five), whereas the circular motif corresponding to the decades is normally inscribed with the number spelled out (e.g. *sittīn*, "sixty"). Sūras with many short verses, typically those revealed earlier in Mecca (q.v.), can require as many as six or seven marginal devices on a single page, thereby leading the illuminator to fill the outer margin with an alternation of oval and circular decorative motifs (e.g. Afarvand, *Gulchīnī*, 50).

Calligraphers and illuminators also came to use the outer margins to display other kinds of information, such as places in the text when bowing of the head *(rukūʿ)* or prostration *(sajda)* is indicated (see BOWING AND PROSTRATION; RECITATION OF THE QURʾĀN). Marginal notations were also employed to indicate division of the text into thirtieths *(juzʾ/ajzāʾ*; Pers. *sīpāra)*, sevenths *(subʿ/asbāʿ)* and sixtieths *(ḥizb/aḥzāb)*, which facilitated reading over the course of a month or a week. Such marginal notations do not appear in the earliest manuscripts of the Qurʾān, but became increasingly common from the fourth/tenth century onwards. For example, a manuscript of the Qurʾān made at Palermo in 372/982-3 has marginal ornaments outlined in black ink with red or green paint showing divisions into thirtieths, tenths, ninths, sevenths, and fifths (see Fig. II). The *sajda*s are similar in form, but are written in gold; and the sixtieths are indicated by a circle containing the word *ḥizb* written in gold between two vegetal motifs against a red-hatched ground (Déroche, *Abbasid tradition*, no. 81). One fifth/eleventh-century scholar considered *sajda*-markings irreverent additions to the holy text, a clear indication that they had become common by his time (Rice, *Unique Ibn al-Bawwāb manuscript*, 17 n. 1).

Another use for the margin was to allow the calligrapher to correct mistakes he had made in transcription. For example, when copying folio 137b of his Qurʾān manuscript, Ibn al-Bawwāb inadvertently left out the hundredth verse of sūra 17. When he discovered his mistake, he corrected the omission by adding the missing verse in a rectangular *tabula ansata* in the margin. To